J. H. COLTON'S

Maps, Charts, Guide-Books,

AND

GEOGRAPHICAL AND STATISTICAL WORKS.

Office, No. 86 Cedar Street, New York.

THE general accuracy and exactness of the works published from this long-established house, has been fully appreciated by the learned and intelligent of all parts of the world; and it is with pleasure that the publisher can refer to this fact, in soliciting a continuance of the public favor. It has ever been his care to procure the earliest and most reliable information, on all topics connected with the peculiar branch in which he is engaged, and being assisted in the several departments of his business by competent co-laborators, he has been enabled to invest his publications with that authenticity which has gained for him the confidence and approbation of all persons interested in geographical inquiries. His efforts, in the same direction, are unremitted, and by frequent revisions and the issue of new works, the public may rely upon receiving, in an authentic form, every new geographical and statistical fact at the earliest period. The following works from his Catalogue for 1852 (which may be had on application), are worthy of special notice:—

Mounted Maps.

WORLD, on Mercator's projection, engraved on steel and highly embellished, in *three* sizes, viz.: 80 by 60 inches; 44 by 36 inches; and 28 by 22 inches.

WORLD, in hemispheres, for the use of schools and churches, each hemisphere *six feet* in diameter.

NORTH AMERICA, SOUTH AMERICA, EUROPE, ASIA, AFRICA, } in *two* series; the size of one being 58 by 44 inches, and of the other 32 by 25 inches.

NORTH AND SOUTH AMERICA, 32 by 25 inches.

WEST INDIES, 32 by 25 inches.

UNITED STATES, &c., engraved on steel, in *two* sizes, viz.: 62 by 55 inches, and 45 by 36 inches.

MEXICO, 42 by 32 inches.

NEW YORK, in townships, 60 by 50 inches.

INDIANA, in sections, of *two* sizes, viz.: 66 by 48 inches, and 43 by 32 inches.

ILLINOIS, in sections, 43 by 32 inches.

MICHIGAN, in sections, 35 by 25 inches.

TOWNSHIP MAPS, of the States severally, a UNIFORM SERIES, size of each 32 by 29 inches, now in progress, and of which the following are completed—

MAINE, N. HAMP.,	OHIO,
VERMONT, CONN.,	WISCONSIN,
MASS., RHODE IS.,	MISSOURI,
NEW YORK,	IOWA,
VIRG., MD., DEL.,	&c., &c.

NEW ENGLAND, in townships, on steel and embellished, 64 by 56 inches.

SOUTHERN STATES, size, 80 by 60 inches (in progress).

WESTERN STATES, in townships, 30 by 26 inches.

Also, mounted Maps of PALESTINE, in *two* sizes, viz.: 80 by 62 inches, and 43 by 32 inches; EGYPT, ARABIA PETRÆA, &c., 32 by 25 inches; and a great variety of local Maps. Also, the STREAM OF TIME, an historical chart; PORTRAITS OF THE PRESIDENTS, &c.

Guide Books, &c.

Guide-Book through the United States, Canada, &c., with a large Map.
Route-Book through the United States, Canada, &c., with a large Map.
Guide-Book through New England and the Middle States, with a new Map.
Western Tourist and Emigrant's Guide, with a township Map.
Overland Guide to California and Oregon, by Horn, with a Map.
Isthmus of Panama Guide, with *three* Maps, by Dr. E. L. Autenrieth.
Western Portraiture, with a Township Map, by D. S. Curtiss.

Travelling Maps in Portable Form.

UNITED STATES, in several sizes.
NEW YORK, in two sizes.
MAINE, NEW BRUNSWICK, &c.
NEW HAMPSHIRE and VERMONT.
MASS., RHODE ISLAND, CONNECTICUT.
VIRGINIA, DELAWARE and MARYLAND.
WESTERN STATES, viz.: Ohio, Ind., &c.
OHIO, MICHIGAN, WISCONSIN.
ILLINOIS, IOWA, INDIANA.
NORTH and SOUTH CAROLINA.
MISSOURI, TEXAS, GEORGIA.
NEW YORK VICINITY, LONG ISLAND.

N. B.—All of the above Maps are complete in regard of railroads, canals, &c., up to the date which appears in the title, and in all respects are much more correct and detailed than any others hitherto published.

Besides his own publications, J. H. C. has constantly on hand an assortment of American and foreign Atlases, Maps, and other geographical works.

CRITICAL NOTICES.

"I have looked over the work with a good deal of interest. It appears to me to be a very useful publication. It brings down the geographical and statistical information of the various countries of the world to a much later period than any other work that has come under my observation, and will not only be useful to the student, but to every man desirous of obtaining the latest and most authentic information."

MILLARD FILLMORE, *Vice Pres. of U. S*

"The work appears to me a very excellent one, and a very valuable contribution to American literature."

CHARLES ANTHON, *LL.D.*

"I have examined it sufficiently to perceive that it contains an immense amount of interesting and useful information."

ROBERT C. WINTHROP, *M. C.*

"It deserves a place in that indispensable department of every private, and especially of every school library—the department of books of reference."

HENRY BARNARD, *Sup. Com. Schools in Conn.*

"I have been fully satisfied with the fullness and extent of the information its ample pages present in answer to every inquiry—embracing topography, physical geography, climate, products, mineral resources, commerce, and history."

S. W. SETON, *Agt. Pub. Sch. Soc. N. Y.*

"It appears to me to contain a more full and accurate exhibition of the world, in its geographical, commercial, and statistical aspects, than any work with which I am acquainted."

REV. R. R. GURLEY, *Chaplain U. S. Senate.*

"As a book of reference it is of great value, and contains more in the same space than any work of a similar character I have yet seen. * * * * I have great pleasure in recommending this book to all persons who desire to possess a work of reference touching the great interests of all nations."

ABBOTT LAWRENCE, *U. S. Minister to England.*

"The work, as a whole, may be said to constitute a library within itself. There is no point, scarcely, in art, science, literature, economy, or history, at all appropriate to the subjects treated upon, which, on reference to the work, will not be found fully elucidated; and the aim of the author seems to have been to condense into as small a space as possible the entire circle of human knowledge."

HUNT'S MERCHANTS' MAGAZINE.

"No work of a similar character, or on so magnificent a scale, has been issued from the American press since the volumes of the veteran Morse. * * * * The author has omitted nothing that could at all add to the perfection of his work."

DEMOCRATIC REVIEW.

"We feel asssured that the learned compiler of these volumes has spared no investigation and care to exhibit the world as it now is, and we can very confidently recommend the result of his labors. Such a work was especially needed."

NATIONAL INTELLIGENCER.

"It is written in a style at once easy, perspicuous, and energetic."

INDEPENDENT, N. Y.

"We feel satisfied that the greatest labor and pains-taking must have been expended, to have brought together such an amount of valuable information."

NEW YORK JOURNAL OF COMMERCE.

"Editors and politicians, especially, have great use for such a work. They have constant occasion to appeal to just such satistics as these volumes embody, to illustrate and enforce their arguments or explode the sophistries of dogmatists."

NATIONAL ERA.

"The 'Book of the World,' embodying as it does a vast and varied amount of information, drawn from all available authentic sources, possesses great intrinsic value, and must prove useful to all classes of American readers."

TEXAS WESLEYAN BANNER

THE

BOOK OF THE WORLD:

BEING AN ACCOUNT OF ALL

REPUBLICS, EMPIRES, KINGDOMS, AND NATIONS,

IN REFERENCE TO THEIR

GEOGRAPHY, STATISTICS, COMMERCE, &c.

TOGETHER WITH A

BRIEF HISTORICAL OUTLINE

OF THEIR

RISE, PROGRESS, AND PRESENT CONDITION,

ETC. ETC. ETC.

BY

RICHARD S. FISHER, M.D.

THIRD EDITION, CORRECTED BY THE CENSUS RETURNS OF 1851-2.

IN TWO VOLUMES.

VOL. I.

ILLUSTRATED WITH MAPS AND CHARTS.

LONDON: IMPORTED BY SAMPSON LOW, SON, AND CO.

British and American Publishers and Booksellers,

47, LUDGATE HILL.

1853.

PUBLISHER'S ADVERTISEMENT.

THE volumes herewith presented to the public, are intended to supply a standard of general reference, and a source to which the merchant and scholar may look for the most recent and best authenticated account of the world, in its several parts. The compiler has drawn information largely from the publications of late travellers and writers; much, also, has been derived from correspondence with the Ministers and Consuls of foreign nations, resident in this country.

With regard to that portion of the work relating to the United States, resort has been had to the State surveys, the periodical censuses, the official reports of the bureaux at Washington, and the returns of the several State Governments; while much new information has been collected at great cost and trouble. Every resource, indeed, has been taxed for authentic materials; and it is believed that the work will be found essentially complete in all its parts, geographical, statistical and social.

New-York, May 1st, 1849.

SECOND EDITION.

IN this edition will be found such additions and alterations as the progress of events to the end of the year 1849 has rendered necessary; and a thorough revision of the whole work has been made by the author. A copious Index has also been added. With these improvements, the publisher believes these volumes to be perfect in every particular, and, as such, he with confidence presents them to the world.

New-York, February 1st, 1850.

NEW EDITION.

In this edition will be found many and essential improvements. The American portion of the work has been entirely re-written, and the results of the recent census incorporated, with notices of all changes in the Constitutions of States, the latest statistics respecting education, churches, banks and other interests, and all the discoveries and developments of resources in the countries severally described. It is, in fact, a new work, and in every respect is applicable to the condition of the world at the present day.

New York, July 1, 1852.

TABLE OF CONTENTS.—Vol. I.

THE WORLD.

The Earth, the world we inhabit, forms one of the primary planets, which, at various distances, revolve round the sun as a centre, and receive from that resplendent source the blessings of light and warmth. It is a globular or orange-shaped mass of matter, and consists of an indefinite aggregation of earthy, metallic and other substances, chemically and mechanically combined. Vast as the earth appears to the external senses of man, its greatness is only acknowledged by the inferiority of our perceptions. Science has demonstrated the earth to be one of the least among the worlds which traverse the infinity of space, and which are linked together by the force of attraction into a splendid universe. It is only one-fourth the diameter of Uranus, and an eleventh the diameter of Jupiter, and forms therefore a comparatively small portion of the planetary system, and with reference to the stars, only a speck in the vastness of creation.

The earth, according to the calculations of astronomers, is 7,902 miles in mean diameter, and measures about 25,000 miles in circumference. But the diameter, or thickness, is greater at the middle or equatorial line, than in a contrary direction. The cause of this may be here adverted to. The diurnal motion of the earth on its axis, or imaginary poles, causes a greater velocity at the middle than at the extremities of the mass, and the earth, originally in a soft or fused state, has been then bulged out all around. The extent of this bulging is twenty-six miles on the whole thickness, or thirteen miles from the centre to the surface: thus, the globe has a spherical form, and is consequently twenty-six miles greater from one side to another at the equator than betwixt the poles. Such is the nice adjustment of the diurnal motion of the earth on its axis, that, if it were but a little accelerated, the sea would rise and fly off, and if the velocity were somewhat further increased, the whole mass of earth and water would be dispersed in fragments, or, in other words, destroyed: such, indeed, is the perfect balance of all its parts, that to add to, or abstract from, would destroy the whole fabric.

The world, as far as has been ascertained, is a solid mass or body, and consists of two kinds of matter, viz: land and water; the land is composed of rocks, metallic ores, mineral and vegetable soils, and a variety of other substances, to describe which is the province of the geologist; the water, as is well known, is a chemical combination of two gases and the most pervading of all other kinds of matter: as a general mass, it holds in solution various salines; but the water, when pure as it falls from the clouds, is fresh; the one is the water of the sea, while the other is peculiar to lakes and rivers. The greater portion of the earth consists of solid land, but an extensive area of it is covered by a superstratum of water; and therefore, to appearance, the ocean forms the principal portion of the globe. It is so, however, only in appearance, notwithstanding its imposing extent, the water being merely a superficial covering to the subjacent land.

The disposition of land and water is quite irregular, and the relative situation and dimensions of each is constantly shifting. The ocean daily encroaches on the land, while the land in other places is left dry, and becomes elevated above the level of the water. Thus, the external aspect of the globe is ever changing; and it may be safely averred, that there has been, in the course of ages, a thorough alteration over the whole terrestrial surface—that no part of the earth retains its primitive shape, or resembles that form which it originally possessed

The superficial area of the world has been calculated to contain 198,943,750 square miles, of which scarcely one-third is dry land; the remaining two-thirds being covered with water. The land is composed principally of two large masses or tracts: one of which is subdivided into the continents of Europe, Asia and Africa; the other into those of North and South America. All detached masses of land are called islands, and these taken together, are computed to contain as much land as the continent of Europe. Australasia may be considered as forming a third grand division. In reference to the map of the world, Europe, Asia, Africa, and Australasia, with their islands, are distinguished as lying in the eastern hemisphere, or half; while North and South America, with the West Indies and other islands, are comprehended in the western hemisphere. The waters which encompass these extensive tracts of land have various local names; but the two principal expanses are the Atlantic and Pacific Oceans: the first lying between the eastern shores of America and the continents of Europe and Africa, and the other between the western coast of America and the eastern margin of Asia. The extensive oceans which surround the polar regions, are called the Arctic or North Sea, and the Antarctic or South Sea: the everlasting ice which here presents a barrier to the intrepid explorer, frustrates the inquiries of man, and denies to him all knowledge respecting the character of these impenetrable regions. Great diversity of opinion prevails with respect to the depth of the ocean. By numerous investigations, it does not appear that the depth is much more than two or three miles—generally it is a great deal less; and it might be argued, that notwithstanding the large surface of the ocean, the body of its waters can only be considered as lying like lakes in the hollows of the land; for the earth, as already noticed, is near 8,000 miles in diameter, and to that large mass of dense matter the sea bears no proportion to its depth. While the surface of the land exhibits a great variety of mountain ranges, hills, vallies and plains, so also is the bottom of the sea varied in its configuration, abounding in sand-banks, hills, rocks and reefs; and the islands which rear their heads above the surface, are only the tops of the highest hills and mountains in the sea.

In accord with the beautiful harmony of design manifested throughout creation, the earth, with its ocean, its atmosphere, its rivers and its varying climates, forms an appropriate field for animal and vegetable existence. The power, the wisdom and goodness of God is imprinted in everything. The manner in which animals and plants are distributed in situations and circumstances exactly adapted to their character, is a matter of deeply interesting observation. Nature—by which, as a phrase of convenience, we denote the great Creating and Disposing Power—has appropriated very few forms of animal or vegetable life to be localized in any portion of the world approaching to its entire terrestrial surface. Most of them are calculated for certain climates, requiring for preserving their existence certain combinations of circumstances, and accordingly are to be found only in such localities as are possessed of those essentials requisite to the well-being of the individual. Thus, different animals and vegetables are distributed in regions or zones around the globe, or at certain elevations, with a direct reference, in all cases, to the temperature and other physical conditions of the locality. In Europe, and nearly all other temperate climates, we find the horse, the cow, the cat, the dog, the crow, the sparrow, the house-fly, and other creatures with which we are familiar, because the nature of these animals is suited to climates of moderate temperature. In the warm and dry regions of Asia and Africa, other forms of animal life prevail—as the lion, tiger, and camel—the latter being suited to traverse wide, sandy deserts, and to endure privations of water for a greater length of time than any other beast of burden. America has the condor, the Washington eagle, the llama and other great birds and beasts of prey peculiar to itself; and in Australasia, remarkable formations and peculiarities in animals distinguish them from those of all other countries: there the quadruped races are furnished with pouches for their young and move forward by leaping—peculiarities suitable to the locality in which they are designed to live. Man, alone, can accommodate himself to all vicissitudes, and change his scene of action with impunity. It appears from the researches of geologists, that the distribution of animal and vegetable forms, has, in the lapse of ages, undergone variations conformable to alterations of condition in soil, climate and other circumstances. The swallow, on the approach of winter, migrates to a more congenial clime; so it is with all living creatures: in consonance with the physical changes of a locality, life must either be pliant enough to accommodate itself to those changes, or migrate to more congenial regions, or become extinct. Races of animals have thus disappeared from the surface of the earth, while insular tracts of land, which have risen from the deep, have become clothed with vegetation, and are now the appropriate theatre of existence to various other kinds of animals. The dispersing power of winds and currents, not to speak of the active interference of man, is supposed to be capable of accounting for the distribution of many plants and animals; but it is clear that without the ever vigilant superintendence of the All-wise, the earth, taken in its whole extent, could not exhibit those remarkable forms of animal and vegetable life which are so nicely suited to the localities in which they are placed.

It has been found impossible, from the limited knowledge we have of the world as a unity, to ascertain with any degree of precision the relative extent of land and water on the earth's surface. Different inquirers have adduced proximate results, differing widely, indeed, but sufficiently accurate for all practicable purposes. The following are the estimates of Hassel and La Voisne:

ACCORDING TO HASSEL.	*Square Miles.*	ACCORDING TO LA VOISNE.	*Square Miles.*
Water surface	146,321,340	Water surface	157,328,135
Land surface	50,554,960	Land surface	41,648,651
	196,876.300		198,976,786

The distribution of the land among the grand divisions of the earth, has been as variously estimated by different inquirers; their results are embodied in the annexed table:

EXTENT OF LAND IN SQUARE MILES.

Weimar Almanac.		Balbi.	Hassel.	Grabery.	La Voisne.	Morse.
America	13,542,400	14,730,000	16,063,600	15,707,120	12,302,037	14,417,000
Europe	3,807,195	3,700,000	3,256,659	3,220,704	2,942,166	3,667,146
Africa	11,647,428	11,254,000	11,270,725	11,063,347	10,357,510	10,900,000
sia	17,805,146	16,045,000	16,282,808	15,301,736	12,144,738	15,700,000
eanica	3,347,840	4,105,000	3,681,168	4,655,520	3,902,200	4,000,000
Total	50,150,009	49,834,000	50,554,960	49,978,427	41,648,651	48,684,146

The population of the world is even more a subject of mystery, than the relative extents of land, and the distribution thereof. At the conclusion of this volume we will give a summary of the most recent censuses and estimates; but in the meantime present the following, as worthy attention :

Wiemar.		Balbi.	Hassel.	Grabery.	Volney.	Malte-Brun.
America	43,800,120	39,000,000	30,483.500	24,000,000	20,000,000	40,000,000
Europe	232,200,646	227,700,000	179,808.000	180,000,000	142,000,000	190,000,000
Africa	101,313,478	60,000,000	102,412,000	99,000,000	30,000,000	70,000,000
Asia	654,610,049	390,000,000	392,575,500	366,000,000	240,000,000	340,000,000
Oceanica	1,473,955	20,300,000	2,000,000	17,000,000	5,000,000	20,000,000
Total	1,033,398,251	737,000,000	707,279,000	686,000,000	437,000,000	660,000,000

Exclusive of the numerous national peculiarities among the inhabitants of the earth and the deviations produced by intermixtures, the human family has certain radical differences in physical conformation, which indicate to the physiologist the necessity of reducing them to a primary classification. Blumenbach, whose authority is undisputed, founds a system on the form and shape of the skull, in which he ascertains five essential conformations, and upon this basis has divided mankind into five classes or families, which he names the Caucasian, the Mongolian, the Ethiopian, the American, and the Malayasian.

In the *Caucasian* the head is of the most symmetrical shape, almost round; the forehead of moderate extent; the cheeks rather narrow, without any projection, but having a direction downwards from the malar process to the frontal bone; the alveolar edge well-rounded, and the front teeth of both jaws perpendicular. The face is oval, the features moderately prominent, the forehead arched, nose narrow and slightly arched, the mouth small, with the lips slightly curved out, and the chin round and full. The Caucasians are of all complexions, but the white seems to be the prevailing color; hence they are called the white race. In this class are comprised the inhabitants of Europe, with their descendants in America, and those of Western Asia and Northern Africa. Their hair, whether Melanic or Xanthous, is always long and lank, and never woolly, like that of negroes.

The *Mongolian class* has the head almost square; the cheek bones projecting, the nose flat and nostrils narrow, the arches of the eyebrows scarcely perceptible, and the chin slightly prominent. The face is broad and flat. The complexion is generally olive or sallow; and none of this class are known to be fair complexioned. The iris of the eyes is black; their hair black, straight, and strong, but seldom curled or in great abundance. They have little or no beard. This family inhabits Central and Eastern Asia; and perhaps the Fins and Laplanders of Europe, and the Esquimaux and other tribes in Arctic America may belong to this class The color is influenced somewhat by climate, and the degree of heat to which the body is exposed.

The *Ethiopic or Black race*, have the head narrow, and the forehead convex and vaulted; the cheek bones projecting, the nostrils wide, the jaws long, the skull generally thick and heavy. The lips, particularly the upper one, are very thick, the jaws prominent, and the chin retracted The skin of this class, and the iris, are deep black; the hair black and woolly. These characteristics are very uniform. The Ethiopic races inhabit Central and Southern Africa, Australia, and some of the Oceanic islands.

The *American family* approaches the Mongolian. This is fully described in another place.

The *Malays* have the top of the head slightly narrowed, the forehead a little arched, the cheek bones not prominent; the upper jaws a little pushed forward, and the prominence of the parietal bones strongly marked. The face is less narrowed than that of the negro, somewhat advancing in the lower part, when seen in profile; the features are more prominent, the nose full, broad and thick towards the point, or what is called a *bottle nose;* the skin is tawny; the hair black, soft, curled, and abundant. In this class are comprised all the natives of the islands in the Pacific Ocean: (excepting those already mentioned as belonging to the Ethiopic class;) likewise the dominant nations of the Indian Archipelago.

Such is Blumenbach's classification, which has been very generally adopted. Some naturalists, among whom is Cuvier, reduce the classes to *three*, considering the Malay to be only a sub-variety of the Caucasian, and the American as a variety of the Mongolian. Others carry the number to *eleven* or *fifteen* classes, and not without reason; for all the tribes comprised under each of Blumenbach's five classes, so far from having exactly the same characteristics, really differ in some cases from each other as much as the class under which they are ranged differs from the other classes. All classification, indeed, must be arbitrary; but this branch of science is only in its infancy, and the little progress that has been made in its study, leaves a wide field for the inquiring naturalist.

The following table exhibits Hassel's enumeration of the various families of mankind. Though differing materially from his estimate of the world's population, and the statistics of the present day, it will be found useful:

1.—*The Caucasian Races.*

Caucasians, Georgians, &c.	1,118,000
Arabians, Moors, Jews, Abyssinians, Berbers, Armenians, &c.	54,523,000
Hindoos, Persians, Affghans, Kurds, &c.	143,353,000
Tartar Nations:—Turks, Turcomans, Usbecks, Kirguses, &c.	17,095,000
Greeks,	4,834,000
Arnauts,	530,000
Sclavonic Nations:—Russians, Croatians, Poles, Lithuanians, &c.	68,255,000
Teutonic Nations:—Germans, English, Swedes, Dutch, Danes, &c.	60,604,000
Latin Nations:—French, Italian, Spanish, Walloons, Wallachians, &c.	75,829,000
Celts, Caledonians, Low Bretons, Basques, &c.	10,489,000
Total	436,625,000

2.—*Mongolian Races.*

Mongol Nations:—Thibetans, &c.	35,842,000
Chinese,	* 256,200,000
Burmans, Siamese, Anamese, &c.	33,850,000
Japanese,	41,100,000
Mantchoos,	19,320,000
Fins, Laplanders, Esquimaux, &c.	3,000,000
Total,	389,310,000

* Estimated generally at 360,000,000.

3.—*Malayasian Race.*

Malays, inhabiting Malay, Sumatra, Java, &c.	32,000,000

4.—*Ethiopian Race.*

Negroes of Africa,	62,983,300
Caffres,	5,200,000
Hottentots,	500,000
Papuans, Negroes of Australia, &c.	950,000
Total,	69,633,300

5.—*American Races.*

North America,	5,130,000
Caribbean Families of Guayana, West India Isles, &c.	17,000
South America,	5,140,000
Esquimaux, &c. (see Mongols.)	
Total,	10,287,000
Grand Total of World,	937,855,300

The number of languages in which the several nations communicate their ideas is unknown; but, as far as ascertained, there are—

In America,	1,214
In Europe,	545
In Asia and Oceanica,	991
In Africa,	276
Total of Languages and Dialects,	3,026

The various religions professed in the world are, according to Malte-Brun:

Christians:		
Catholics,	116,000,000	
Greek Church,	70,000,000	
Protestants,	42,000,000—	228,000,000
Jews,		4,000,000
Mahomedans,		103,000,000
Brahmins,		60,000,000
Shamans, (Grand Llama,)		50,000,000
Buddhists,		100,000,000
Fetichists,		100,000,000
Total,		645,000,000

Hassel computes them as follows: Pagans, 561,820,000; Christians, 252,565,000; Mahomedans, 120,000,000; and Jews, 3,930,000. Total, 938,415,000. From these it will be seen, that as yet three-fourths the world is shrouded in paganism and idolatry.

With these few general observations, as introductory to the subject upon which it is the purport of this work to relate, we will proceed at once to describe the world in its severalties: first giving a general survey of the physical and political condition of the grand divisions, and then more minutely describing each empire, kingdom, state, &c., separately.

AMERICA.

THE name of "AMERICA" has been applied to that vast continent, or rather to the two continents connected by the Isthmus of Darien, and the adjacent islands, discovered by Columbus and other adventurers, in the last decade of the 15th century, and which have been progressively explored and settled by European nations, to the present period. The existence of these masses of land were, in all probability, unknown to the ancients, whose "ultima thule" never extended further west than the Canaries. Some passages, however, in both Greek and Latin writers, have been supposed to refer to a knowledge of the actual position of these lands; but it is equally probable that an excited imagination has alone been able to draw an inference of this sort into the question of discovery.

There is some probability that the pseudo-historical accounts of the discoveries of the Northmen in the 9th and subsequent centuries, are not altogether fictitious. It is on record that these adventurous navigators, who had, for a long time anterior to these periods, been in the habit of visiting Iceland, discovered, and even planted colonies, and gave names to several districts on the Atlantic coast; and, indeed, it is said, and with some show of truth, that relics of fortifications and works of art, attributed to them, are at this day in existence in the neighborhood of Martha's Vineyard, and Bristol, in Rhode-Island, and are frequently visited by the curious antiquarian. Disease, war, and other calamities, however, swept away these colonies, and all remembrance of their existence was buried in the oblivion of the "dark ages" which succeeded, and overshadowed the intellect of the Christian world. A few ancient Icelandic MSS. alone, which have been lately discovered, tell the brief story of the rise and fall of these primitive settlements.

It has been asserted, indeed, that Columbus was acquainted with these discoveries; and, in order to rob that great man of the honor of having given to the world a new continent, his enemies have ruthlessly striven to maintain the assertion. It is improbable, however, that he should have profited by any lights he might have derived from Norwegian or Icelandic sources, in maturing his theory of a counterpoising mass of land in the west. His own statement of his ideas are a sufficient guarantee that enlightened philosophy alone indicated to him the probability of a continent in the antipodes; and to him alone are we indebted for all the prosperity, happiness and wealth, which his consummate ability and great labors have opened to the embrace of the world.

This vast double continent forms one of the grand divisions of the world in which we live, and is geographically placed between the meridians of 35° and 170° of west longitude, and between the latitudes of 72° north and 56° south. Its greatest length, from Point Beechy, on the Arctic Sea, by a curve line drawn along the Rocky Mountains and the Cordilleras of the Andes to the extremity of Cape Horn, is about 10,875 miles. The greatest breadth of North America, from Cape St. Louis on the 51st parallel to the Pacific Ocean, is about 3,250 miles; and of South America.

from San Roque in Brazil, to Cape Blanco in Peru, about 3,200 miles The narrowest portion is the Isthmus of Darien, which connects the two continents, and at one place, opposite Mandingo Bay, prevents the mingling of the waters of the Pacific Ocean with those of the Caribbean Sea, by a breadth of only 18 miles. The area of America, including the West India Islands, has been variously computed; the best authorities, with whom there is a general acquiescence, state it at about 15,000,000 square miles. This approximate estimate is corroborated by Balbi and Malte-Brun; and the "Encyclopædia Britannica" gives it as follows:

	Square Miles.
North America	7,400,000
West Indian Islands	150,000
South America	6,500,000
Greenland, and the Islands connected with it, north of Hudson's Straits	900,000
Total	14,950,000

In this estimate Greenland, and the islands in the Arctic Sea, are set down at 900,000 square miles; the extent of these, however, has never been ascertained, nor can a conjecture on this point lay claim to any degree of accuracy.

The whole of America is surrounded by the expanse of ocean. On the north, however, the outline of the coast has not been entirely determined; but the discoveries lately made by British explorers, leave no doubt of there being a water communication the whole extent. The Atlantic forms the eastern and south-eastern boundaries; while the western and south-western are washed by the waters of the Pacific. The sea to the north has been termed the Arctic Ocean, and that to the south, on which the extreme of South America rests, has received the name of the Antarctic Ocean.

The gigantic scale on which these continents are formed, is their distinguishing feature. The mountains, which traverse it from north to south, are the broadest, and except the Himalaya Mountains in Asia, the most elevated in the world. In South America they attain the altitude of 25,000 feet above the level of the sea. The Amazon and the Missouri rivers are the longest and most capacious; and the lakes in North America, covering thousands of square miles, are unequalled in extent. The vast plains, which spread over two-thirds of these regions, can be likened only to the broad ocean in solitude and grandeur. The cataracts, the bays and gulfs, in vastness, majesty and beauty, surpass all preconception. Every physical object exhibits a magnificence of proportions unknown in other parts of the world. The animal and vegetable kingdoms present the most extraordinary developments, and the most wonderful forms; and the mineral resources of America have been the means of enriching the whole earth with the precious and useful metals.

In considering the several portions of these continents, a separate account will be given of each, and a section will be allotted to a description of the islands forming the West Indies or Columbian Archipelago. The several nations, &c., will be treated of in as near a geographical order as convenient.

A

GENERAL DESCRIPTION OF

NORTH AMERICA.

North America, comprising a vast extent of country, lies between the parallels of 72° and 10° north latitude, and between the meridians of 29° and 170° west longitude from Greenwich. Its greatest length is about 4,000 miles, and its greatest breadth along the 51st parallel is 3,250 miles. The narrowest portion of the continent is the Isthmus of Darien or Panama, which connects North and South America, the breadth of which at one place, opposite Mandingo Bay, is little more than 18 miles. The estimated area of North America is 7,400,000 square miles; in these dimensions are not included Greenland or the Arctic Islands, of which, indeed, the extent is not known.

North America is bounded by the Arctic Ocean on the north; by the Atlantic Ocean and Gulf of Mexico on the east; by the Gulf of Mexico on the south and south-east, and by the Pacific Ocean on the west. There are many islands off the coasts, which belong either to the several native governments or are appropriated as colonies by Europeans.

The superficies of North America presents six distinct physical regions; distinguished by peculiar topographical features:

First.—The narrow region which separates the Gulf of Mexico and the Caribbean Sea from the Pacific Ocean, traversed through its whole length of 2,500 miles by ranges of mountains, which leave a narrow tract of low land along the sea coasts, while in certain portions of the interior they form elevated table lands.

Second.—The maritime region, between the Pacific Ocean on the west and the ridge of mountains, which extends from Cape San Lucas in California, northward to the peninsula of Alaska.

Third.—The elevated region, which forms a sort of table land between the maritime or coast chain above-mentioned on the west, and the Rocky Mountains on the east. In its southern portion it presents the arid salt plains of the Californian desert; between 40° and 45° north latitude it comprises a fertile region, with a mild and humid atmosphere; but, beyond the last mentioned parallel, it is barren and inhospitable.

Fourth.—The great central vallies of the Missouri and Mississippi, extending from the Rocky Mountains on the west, to the Alleghany or Appalachian Mountains on the east, and from the Gulf of Mexico northward to 45° or 50° north latitude. Between these parallels runs in a waving line the watershed, which divides the basins of the St. Lawrence and the Mississippi from those of the streams that flow to Hudson's Bay and the Arctic

Ocean. On the east this region is rich and well-wooded, in the middle it is divided into prairie and woodland, and extremely fertile; towards the west it is dry, sandy, and almost a desert.

Fifth.—The eastern declivities of the Alleghany Mountains, and the maritime region, extending to the shores of the Atlantic. This is a region of natural forests, and of mixed but rather indifferent soil, requiring cultivation to make it productive.

And *Sixth.*—The great northern plain beyond the 50th parallel, four-fifths of which are a bleak and desolate waste, overspread with innumerable lakes, and resembling Siberia in the physical character of its surface and the rigor of its climate.

The MOUNTAINS OF NORTH AMERICA form several distinct ridges, the principal of which stretch in the direction of north and south. It has been generally supposed that the Isthmus of Panama is traversed by a mountain range, connecting the Andes of South America with the mountains of Mexico; but this is not the case. At the eastern extremity of the isthmus, between the mouth of the Rio Atrato and the Bay of San Miguel, a level plain extends from one sea to the other, apparently not many yards above the level of either Here, then, the mountains of North America commence.

The ELEVATIONS WITHIN THE ISTHMUS are very few, and the highest point of the road which crosses the ridge between Panama and the mouth of the river Chagres, has been found to be only 633 feet above the level of the Pacific Ocean. From that point to the table land of La Puebla, 1,400 miles north, no certain information has been obtained respecting the mountains. The most considerable elevations are on the south-west side; and there are no less than *twenty-two* volcanoes within that space. From Puebla to Durango, the Mexican mountains spread out to form a table land or elevated plain, from 5,000 to 9,000 feet above the level of the sea, and from 100 to 300 miles in breadth. Across this plain, in 19° north latitude, are *five* volcanoes in a line, east and west. Two of these on the eastern side of the continent, with a group of four or five other cones between Xalapa and Cordova, have an elevation of more than 17,000 feet, and are the only mountains in Mexico that exceed the line of perpetual snows, which is here about 15,000 feet above the level of the ocean. Jorullo, the lowest of the five volcanoes, rose suddenly from the midst of a plain, in September, 1759; it is 1,600 feet above its base, and is surrounded by a number of smaller cones, or burning masses, within a compass of four square miles, which have been heaved up in the form of a dome. Near the tropic the Mexican Cordillera divides into three branches, one of which runs parallel to the eastern coast, at a distance of 30 or 40 leagues, and terminates in New-Leon; another, proceeding in a north-western direction, sinks gradually as it approaches the Gulf of California, in the state of Sonora; the third, or central chain, passes through Durango and New Mexico, separates the sources of the Rio Gila and the Rio Grande or Bravo del Norte, rising to an elevation of 4,000 feet.

The ROCKY MOUNTAINS now commence, and from this point extend northward, gradually becoming lower, till at last their elevation hardly exceeds 2,000 feet. They also divide in their northern portion into *fourteen* or *fifteen* ridges, separated by narrow vallies, which altogether occupy a breadth of about 200 miles, and skirt the Arctic Sea at a short distance. Many of the summits of the Rocky Mountains rise above the snow line, and their elevation, where they were crossed by Lewis & Clarke, and also further south, has been estimated at 10,000 and 12,000 feet. A shorter route from the valley of the Mississippi to the west coast has since been found, in the direction of the River Nebraska, (41° north latitude,) where an opening in the chain, called the South Pass, presents a passage so easy of access, that a wagon drawn by horses might travel through it.

From the southern point of California, a lower chain, the MARITIME RANGE, skirts the coast, as far as the volcano of Mount St. Elias, 60° north latitude; and between this chain and the Rocky Mountains several intermediate ridges occur, the whole forming, apparently, an elevated plateau, from 200 to 800 miles in breadth.

The ALLEGHANY or APPALACHIAN MOUNTAINS, which form the eastern boundary of the great central valley, consists of three, four, and, in some places, five parallel chains, extending from south-west to north-east, from Alabama to New-Brunswick, a distance of 1,100 miles, with a breadth varying from 100 to 150 miles, and a mean elevation of 2,000 or 3,000 feet. They are almost everywhere clothed with forests and interspersed with delightful and fertile vallies. They present their steepest sides to the east, and the transition from their base to the maritime plain, which skirts the Atlantic, is very distinctly marked by a rocky ledge, over which the rivers fall, and to the foot of which, in the northern section, the tide penetrates. Trenton, Philadelphia, Baltimore, Richmond, Columbia, Augusta, Milledgeville, and Columbus, stand on or near the edge of this ledge, which from the last named place recedes to the north-west through Alabama and Mississippi, till the Atlantic plain merges in the Mississippi valley.

Between the Alleghanies and the Rocky Mountains, the OZARK MOUNTAINS extend along the middle of the great valley of the Mississippi in a northerly and southerly direction. The Arkansas and the Red River are the only streams that have forced a passage through these mountains, which, though low, occupy a great extent of country, and are covered with wood. The greater rivers of Eastern Texas have their rise in the southern declivities of these elevations.

From Labrador, westward, a line of elevated ground, not entitled to be called mountainous, as its greatest known elevation does not exceed 2,000 feet, forms the water-shed between the basin of the St. Lawrence and the great lakes, and the streams which flow northward to Hudson's Bay. It is, however, cut through by the Nelson River; and after separating the vallies of the Saskatchawan and the Churchill, it either sinks down into the great plains of this region, or extends north-eastward between Hudson's Bay and Great Slave Lake.

The following table will exhibit the points of culmination of the different peaks of the North American system of mountains:

Principal Chains.	*Peaks.*	Height above the Sea. *Feet*
Cordillera of the Isthmus	*Silla de Veragua*	9,000
" Guatemala	*Volcano d'Agua*	14,900
	" *Fuego*	14,700
" Mexico	" *of Popocatepetl*	17,735
	" *Orizaba*	17,388
	Istaccihuatl	15,700
	Nevado de Toluca	15,156
	Coffre de Peroté	13,514
Rocky Mountains	*Spanish Peak*	11,000
	James' Peak	11,320
	Long's Peak, or Bighorn	13,575
	Mount Hooker } 52° N.	15,700
	" *Brown* } 52° N.	16,000

Principal Chains.	*Peaks.*	Height above the Sea *Feet.*
Californian, or Maritime Range	*Mount Hood*	12,000
	" *Rainier*	10,000
	" *St. Helen's*	12,000
	" *Baker*	10,000
	" [illegible]	[illegible]

GOLD.—Mexico, (*North-western Provinces;*) United States, (*California, N & S Carolina and Georgia;*) Central America, (*passim.*)
SILVER.—Mexico, (*Central Provinces;*) Central America, (*passim;*) United States, (*in the Lead Districts of Lake Superior, &c.*)
TIN.—Mexico; United States, (*California.*)
MERCURY.—Mexico; United States, (California.)
COPPER.—Mexico; United States, (*New-Jersey, New-York,* and *in the regions of Lake Superior, &c.*)
LEAD.—Mexico; United States, (*Illinois, Missouri, New-York, &c.*)
IRON.—United States, (*New-Jersey, Pennsylvania, Massachusetts, Connecticut, South Carolina, New-York, Maryland, &c.;*) Mexico; Canada, (*mines of St. Maurice &c.*) and Central America, (*passim.*)
COAL.—Cape Breton; Nova Scotia; United States, (*Pennsylvania, &c.*)
SALT.—United States, (*New-York, Massachusetts, Kentucky, Illinois, Missouri and California;*) Central America, (*Honduras, &c.*) Mexico, (*Oaxaca, &c.;*) &c.

North America, noted for the vastness of its physical features, almost outdoes itself in the immensity of its plains: in no other part of the world are they so extensive. The enormous space from the outlet of the Mackensie River to the delta of the Mississippi, and between the central chain of the Mexican system and Rocky Mountains and the Alleghanies, forms the largest plain, not of America alone, but of the world. It embraces the basins of the Mississippi, the St. Lawrence, the Churchill or Nelson, almost the whole basin of the Missouri, nearly the whole basins of the Saskatchawan and Mackensie Rivers, and the entire basin of the Coppermine River. Four-fifths of that portion of this vast plain, which lies beyond the 50th parallel of latitude, is a bleak and barren waste, overspread with innumerable lakes, and bearing a striking resemblance to Northern Asia; but its more southerly portion, or that lying west of the Alleghany chain and north from the Gulf of Mexico, differs widely in character from the other, being well wooded and fertile on the east side; bare of wood but fertile in the middle, and becoming almost a desert in the extreme west. In some of the flat parts of North America, large tracts of territory are met with, which, in respect to aridity of soil and of the sand by which they are covered, may be compared to the deserts of Asia and Africa. The most extensive and remarkable of these tracts, is the Desert of Nuttal, at the eastern foot of the Rocky Mountains, between the Upper Arkansas and Paduka, forming part of the great central plain.

The plain east of the Alleghanies, running along the coast of the Atlantic Ocean, is a region of forests, of great variety of soil and much broken in surface, but in the main a fertile, and in the southern parts an exuberant, tract of territory. Here the first discoveries and settlements were made, and the first tree of liberty in America planted, which, watered by the blood of patriots, has spread its branches over the whole continent, from the Atlantic to the Pacific, and is still expanding, and will expand, till he whole earth is overshadowed by its blossoms. This territory constiutes the old states of New-England, and part of the middle and southern United States, and is separated from the great basin of the Mississippi by he range of the Alleghany Mountains.

The country beyond the Rocky Mountains, and north and west of the elevated plateau of Mexico, is second only to the Atlantic plain in all the requisites for the progress of civilization. Scarcely discovered, and just emerging, as it were, from the darkness of ages, it has become the residence of thousands of our citizens, and is looked upon as the germ of future empires, such as exist in the other portions of our Union. Already the axe and hammer are heard in its midst, and smiling cities and peaceful homes are dotted over the land, that but yesterday was the haunt of the Red Man, and the lair of the wild beast. The laws of civilization have taken root, and the American eagle, perched on the heights of the mountains, watches over the interests of its republican sons on the far-distant shores of the Columbia and Colorado. The country has a climate as mild and beneficent as that of the Middle and Eastern States, and its soil is fruitful in all that can make life happy and homes cheerful.

The Rivers of North America form one of its most prominent features; and it is a remarkable characteristic, that almost all are navigable throughout the greater part of their course.

I.—The great central river, the Mississippi, has its sources in the brooks which form the small Lake Itaska, about 47° 10′ north latitude, on a high table-land, 1,500 feet above the level of the sea, and 3,200 miles from the mouth of the river, following the windings of the stream, but only 1,250 in a straight line. Rising in a region of swamps and wild rice lakes, it flows at first through low prairies, and then in a broken course through forests of elm, maple, birch, oak, and ash, till at the Falls of St. Anthony, 1,100 miles from its source, it tumbles over a limestone ridge with a fall of 17 feet. The river is here 600 yards wide. Below this point it is bounded by limestone bluffs, from 100 to 400 feet high, and first begins to exhibit islands, drift-wood and sand-bars. Its current is slightly broken by the Rock River and Desmoines Rapids, which, however, present no very considerable interruption to navigation; and 850 miles below the Falls of St. Anthony it receives from the west the stream of the Missouri. Between the mouth of the Missouri and the sea, a distance of 1,220 miles, it receives its principal tributaries;—the Ohio from the east, and the Arkansas and Red River from the west, and immediately below the mouth of the latter, it gives off, in times of flood, a portion of its surplus waters to the Atchafalaya. Below the Atchafalaya it discharges a portion of its waters by the Lafourche and the Iberville; but the greater part of its contents flows on in the main channel, which passes through a flat tract, and reaches the Gulf of Mexico at the end of a long projecting tongue of mud, formed by the deposites of the current. Near the sea it divides into several channels, here called passes, with bars at their mouths, on which are from 12 to 14 feet of water. Before the introduction of steam vessels, the river was navigated by keel-boats, which, in going upward, were rowed along the eddies of the stream, or drawn by ropes along the shore; and by this tedious process more than three months were consumed in ascending from New-Orleans to the Falls of the Ohio, a passage which is now made in five or six days. The first steamboat was introduced in 1811; there are now upwards of 700 on the river.

The tributaries of the Mississippi are:—

The Missouri, which is navigable to the foot of the great falls, and steamboats have gone up the stream 2,200 miles from its junction with the Mississippi. It rises in the Rocky Mountains, and some of its sources are within a mile of those of the Columbia. The falls in several parts of this river are only inferior to those of the Niagara. In a course of 17 miles it has a descent of 360 feet, and in that space, besides the Great Falls, of 90 feet perpendicular and 300 yards wide, and a fine fall of 50 feet, there are several others of from 12 to 20 feet. The Missouri hence flows through vast prairies, and soon after receiving the Yellow Stone, a large, navigable stream, takes a south and south-east course to the Mississippi. Its principal tributaries from the west are the Platte, the Kansas, and the Osage. The obstructions to the navigation of the Missouri are the same as those of the Lower Mississippi, but they are more numerous and formidable. Islands and sand-bars make the channels intricate, and in many places navigation is hazardous, from the rafts, snags, falling banks, &c. The other tributaries of the Missouri, not hitherto mentioned, are the Little Missouri, Shienne, Quicourt, Gasconade, Jaques, Sioux, Grand and Chariton, the length of the streams of which average from 500 to 800 miles, and are of great volume.

The OHIO is, next to the Missouri, the most important of the tributaries of the Mississippi. This river is formed by the union of the Alleghany, 350 miles long, and the Monongahela, 300 miles, at Pittsburg, from which place to the Mississippi it has a course of 950 miles, receiving, in its progress, numerous navigable streams from both sides; from the north the Muskingum, the Big Beaver, Sciota, Miami and Wabash, and from the south, the Kanhawa, Big Sandy, Kentucky, Greene, Cumberland and Tennessee. The whole region drained by this fine river includes an area of 200,000 square miles, rich in the most useful natural productions, and enjoying a mild and healthful climate. The breadth of the stream varies from 400 to 1,400 yards, and the annual range between mean water and flood is more than 50 feet. The floods occur in December and on the melting of the snow in spring. The navigation is usually impeded by ice in the winter, and, in the upper part of the river, by drought in summer; but during the other seasons the stream is covered with steamers and river craft, carrying on an active trade.

The ARKANSAS exceeds the Ohio in size, but its course is generally through an almost desert country, which diminishes its importance. The navigation is insecure, and in summer, in many parts, the stream is dried up. Steamboats ply only from its mouth to Fort Gibson, 420 miles, while its whole length is estimated to be 2,500 miles. Its source is in the mountains of New Mexico, whence its course, in which it receives the Canadian and other great rivers, is eastward and south to the Mississippi, which it joins near the 34th parallel.

The RED RIVER rises in the Mexican Cordillera, and hence pursues a course south and east to the Mississippi, forming in part the north boundary of the State of Texas. The obstructions which formerly impeded navigation have been partly removed; steamboats ply on its bosom the whole length of its navigable course.

The ILLINOIS is formed in the north part of the state of the same name, by the junction of the Kankakee from Indiana and the Des-Plaines from Wisconsin, from which it flows 200 miles to the Mississippi. It is navigable to the Falls of Ottawa. In some places the river expands to such a width as to have the appearance of a lake; and one expanse of this kind, 20 miles long, has received the name of Lake Peoria. The Kankakee rises within two miles of the St. Joseph, which falls into Lake Michigan, and in the wet season boats may pass from the one to the other. The Des-Plaines runs for some distance along the shores of the lake, with which there is a natural communication through Chicago, which has been improved by a canal, finished in the year 1848. Boats now pass regularly from the lake to the Illinois River, and so communicate with the rivers of the west.

The *other tributaries*, which debouch into the Mississippi, and not hitherto mentioned, are the St. Peter's (500 miles long;) the Penaca or

Turkey (200;) Iowa (350;) Chacaguar (200;) Desmoines (600,) St. Croix (300;) Chippewa (300;) Wisconsin (600;) Rock River (450;) Kaskaskia (300;) Salt (250;) Maramec (200;) St. Francis (450;) White (600;) Hatchy (200;) Yazoo (300;) and Big Black River, 200 miles in length.

II. The mighty St. Lawrence, the outlet of the great northern lakes and receptacle of all the rivers of Canada, will next claim description. It flows from the north-east extremity of the Lake Ontario, where its stream, for the first forty miles, is divided by a multitude of islands, some merely bare rocks, some covered with pines, and others presenting the richest meadows and verdant pastures. This space is termed the *Lake of the Thousand Isles;* but the real number of islands is said to be 1692. About 100 miles from the lake, a number of rapids interrupt navigation, but they are now passed by the Cornwall Canal, and below the Lake St. Francis, are the Cedar Rapids and the Cascades, difficulties, which are surmounted by the Military Canal. The Ottawa now meets the St. Lawrence, and forms, at their junction, the Islands of Montreal, Jesus and Perrot. Between Montreal and the southern shore, is the Sault St. Louis, which is passed by means of the Lachine Canal. From this point there is no material obstruction, but the current is, in some places, still rapid. Midway, between Montreal and Quebec, the river expands into the Lake St. Peter, but further down the width continues regular, till it passes Quebec, below which it encircles the Isle of Orleans, and then gradually and regularly expands into a wider estuary, which terminates with the Island of Anticosti, about 700 miles from Lake Ontario. At Quebec, the river is only 1314 yards wide; at the mouth of the Sanguenay, 120 miles further down, it is 18 miles; at Cape de Monts, 130 miles more eastward, 25 miles, and where at last it opens into the gulf, the estuary is nearly 105 miles across. The tide is perceptible 450 miles above Anticosti: vessels of 600 or 700 tons reach Montreal. In winter, the river, in its upper course, is frozen over; but below Quebec, the navigation is never obstructed, except by the large masses of ice brought down by the current. The principal tributary of the St. Lawrence, is the Ottawa, which flows from Lake Temiscaming, and much resembles the St. Lawrence itself in its great breadth and lake-like expanses. At its union with this river, it spreads out into the Lake of the Two Mountains, and 30 miles up its stream are the Long Sault Rapids, which are passed by the Grenville Canal. Steamers ascend to Bytown and Hull, at the foot of the Chaudieres or Kettle Falls, the principal of which is 60 feet high. Above these are numerous rapids. The other affluents are: *on the left bank*—the St. Maurice; the Batiscan; the St. Anne; the Jaques Cartier and the Sagueney, a large and broad river, the outlet of Lake St. John; and *on the right bank*—the Oswegatchie, La Grasse, the Raquette, and St. Regis, from New-York; the Chateauguay, above Montreal; the Richelieu or Sorel, the outlet of Lake Champlain; the Yamaska, the St. Francis and Nicolet, at Lake St. Peter; the Besancour, Gentilley, Du-Chêne, Chaudière and Etchemin, between St. Peter's and Quebec.

III. The other rivers of North America, which are neither so immense nor important as the Mississippi and St. Lawrence, will be fully examined under the descriptions of the several nations through whose territories they have their course. The principal of these streams, are:

Those *flowing into the Atlantic*, or the gulfs and bays intersecting he lands which border on that great ocean, proceeding from north to south they are:

Miramichi, } In New-Brunswick,
St. John's, } falling into the Bay of
St. Croix, } Fundy.
Penobscot.
Kennebec.
Merrimack.
Connecticut.
Hudson.
Delaware.
Susquehanna.
Potomac.
Rappahannock,
York River, { *Matapony,* *Pamunkey.*
James River.
Chowan.
Roanoke.
Pamlico, *Tar* or *Taw.*
Neuse.
Cape Fear, or Clarendon River.
Little Pedee.
Great Pedee.
Lynch's.
Santee.
Edisto, or Pompon.
Combahee.
Savannah.
Ogechee.
Cannouchee.
Alatamaha.
St. Mary's.
St. John's, and
St. Lucia.

All which, except the three first, are within the territories of the United States.

The rivers *flowing into the Gulf of Mexico,* proceeding from east to west, are:

Oscilla, or Ausilla.
St. Mark's.
Ocklockonee.
Apalachicola.
Econfina.
Choctawhatchie.
Perdido.
Mobile, { *Alabama,* *Tombigbee.*
Pascagoula.
Pearl.
Atchafalaya.
Sabine.
Trinity.
Brazos.
Colorado.
Guadaloupe.
Nueces.
Rio Grande del Norte,

which, in its course, divides Mexico from the United States. There are few others, of any magnitude, emptying into the gulf. The rivers of Eastern Mexico have, in general, short courses, and chiefly rise from the table lands formed by the Cordilleras. The principal are the San Fernando; the Santander; the Tampico, formed by the union of the Panuca and Montezuma; the Alvarado; the Huascualco; the Tobasco, all in Mexico; and the Rio Hondo, which separates Yucatan from the British settlements at Balize, and the Balize River, wholly within the British possessions. The rivers of Central America are inconsiderable streams, except the San Juan, which connects Lake Nicaragua with the Caribbean Sea, and which, at some future day, may become a part of the water communication projected between the two oceans.

The *rivers flowing into the Pacific Ocean,* from the mountain chains of Western America. The largest, beginning at the south, are as follows:

Chimalapa, or Tehuantepec,
Rio Verde,
Rio Yopez,
Zacatula,
Santiago,
Rosario,
Hiaqui,
Guayamas.
Ascension,
Rio Gila,
} in Mexico.

Colorado, Sacramento, etc } in California.
Columbia, in Oregon.
Frazer's River, and several smaller streams, north of Observatory Inlet, in the American possessions of Russia.

The *rivers which fall into the Arctic Ocean* and Hudson's Bay. These are but little known, and can never be extensively used for the purposes of commerce. They are.

The Mackensie, Coppermine River, Thlew-ee-cho-dezeth,	Flowing into the Arctic Ocean.	Churchill, Nelson's, Severn,	Flowing into Hudson's Bay.

The COASTS OF NORTH AMERICA are more indented than any other of the great divisions of the globe, with immense gulfs and arms of the sea. One of the principal of these, in the north-east part of the continent, consists of what Balbi has not unaptly termed the Sea of the Esquimaux, from its coasts being everywhere occupied by tribes belonging to this peculiar race: it consists of two great divisions, Davis' Straits and Baffin's Bay, separating Greenland from the main land, and Hudson's Bay lying more to the south and west, but connected with the former by numerous channels, some of which have been only recently discovered. The navigation of these seas and inlets, even in the most favorable seasons, is extremely difficult, from their being constantly encumbered with ice; and it is only during a short period of the year that it can be attempted. The next great inlet of the sea is the Gulf of St. Lawrence, so called from the great river of the same name which falls into its south-west extremity. Passing over the numerous inlets and noble bays on the coast of the United States, we come to the Gulf of Mexico and the Caribbean Sea. This vast Mediterranean is separated from the Atlantic by the Peninsula of Florida and the islands of the West Indies. The latter are, as it were, a continuation of Florida, and are, it is probable, the only remaining points of what was once a broad belt of land, which has been broken to pieces and partly submerged in some of those tremendous convulsions to which the earth has been subject. But however this may be, this great inland sea is divided into two portions by the Peninsula of Yucatan and Cape San Antonio, at the western extremity of the Island of Cuba, which approach within a comparatively short distance of each other; that to the north being called the Gulf of Mexico, and that to the south the Caribbean Sea, or the Sea of the Antilles. The Gulf of Cortez or California, separating the peninsula of that name from the main land, is the most important inlet of the sea on the west coast of North America.

To abridge the tedious and dangerous voyage round Cape Horn, and give to navigation a direct and safe access to the eastern shores of the Pacific, has been a favorite scheme, for centuries, of scientific exploration and of mercantile hope. For a long time its practicability at any point was disputed. The best inquiries left it in doubt. Every narrow portion of the continent of America has undergone examination, and has for a while been regarded with preference, and has been again abandoned. Difficulties sprang up as to each; and a comparison of their relative advantages, affected more or less by the desire of the respective inquirers and explorers, to render the junction of the two seas specially serviceable to their own countries, excited apprehensions as to all. Still all are satisfied that the project is not only practicable, but practicable at a comparatively small amount of labor, and at a moderate cost.

Five principal routes for crossing the isthmian portion of the continent have been especially regarded with favor, and have received the highest testimonials as to practicability:—

First—By the Isthmus of Panama.

Second—By the Isthmus of Darien.
Third—By the Lake Nicaragua and River San Juan.
Fourth—By the river Atrato, in New Granada; and
Fifth—By the Isthmus of Tehuantepec.

The present day has been reserved for the accomplishment of the great works the plans of inter-oceanic communication involve. The construction of the first, third, and fifth of these have been undertaken, and already are the highways of travel and commercial activity.

The Isthmus of Panama will be surmounted by a railroad, which has already been commenced and partially completed by an American company. No portion of the line is so formidable as to oppose any serious obstacles to the attainment of the proposed mode of transit, and for the greater part of its length the levels are remarkably favorable.

The route by the Rio San Juan is regularly traversed by steamers belonging to an American company, and the short distance between the lake and the ocean will be overcome either by railroad or canal. This is the only serious difficulty encountered in the transit, and is at the present time overcome by a mule ride of a few hours. The Pacific terminus of the route is San Juan del Sul, at which point the Pacific lines of steamships touch on their passages to and from the Isthmus and our Pacific ports.

Americans have also undertaken the Tehuantepec route, and surveying parties have been on the ground. The American company derives its charter from Garay, to whom the Mexican Government had some years ago granted the right of way. Some difficulties, indeed, have sprung up between the present authorities of Mexico and the parties undertaking the works, which has caused a temporary suspension of operations. The completion of the route, however, is too important to admit of long delay, and there is little doubt but that the Mexican Government will eventually yield to the desire of commercial nations to have the passage effected.

The routes proposed to be carried over the Isthmus of Darien and by the Rio Atrato, are at present in abeyance. Both could be easily constructed. It is improbable, however, that any steps will at the present day be taken towards opening them, as the routes now in course of construction are perhaps more eligible, and at least are sufficient for the present amount of transit and transportation from the Atlantic to the Pacific.

The relative merits of the three routes which American citizens have undertaken, can scarcely be defined—each has its advantages and disadvantages. The Panama route is short, but on the eastern side of the country, the climate is hot, moist, and deadly; the San Juan route is through a luxurious country, and its climate is comparatively healthy, but the river is beset with difficult falls and rapids, and there is no good port on the Pacific; and the Tehuantepec route is rugged and much longer than that of Panama, it is nearer, however, to the United States, and through a country as salubrious as could be desired. These advantages and disadvantages will be considered, and the merits of one or the other must be deduced therefrom; but a great deal will depend on individual preference and prejudice, not on rational deduction, for their paying success.

Of the cost of completing these works, no close calculation has been made. Their importance to commerce would warrant any expense, nor is it to be supposed that expense could become an element in retarding their progress. If the cost of the works should amount to hundreds of millions, the commercial intercourse they would initiate with the isles of the Pacific and the rich countries of Asia would fully repay the outlay.

From this digression, we must again proceed to describe the great physical features of this continent.

North America is pre-eminently the country of lakes, and exhibits masses of fresh water, unequalled in any other part of the world. The great northern lakes are the most remarkable, as well for their extent as for their utility, as channels of navigation; and form just so many inland seas

LAKE SUPERIOR, the largest and most northerly of the lakes of Canada bordering on the United States, has a length of 420 miles, and an extreme breadth of 165 miles; its circuit is about 1,750, and its area has been estimated at 32,000 square miles. Its surface is 596 feet above the level of the sea; but as its depth varies from 500 to 900 feet, and is even supposed to be in some places 1,200 feet, its bottom lies far below the level of the ocean. The basin which is drained by this great lake is estimated at 100,000 square miles, and has 220 rivers and streamlets to convey the waters deposited within it. Some of these rivers are of considerable size, and though their sources are seldom more than 60 or 70 miles distant from the lake, they are in general from 500 to 600 feet above its level, and their currents are much broken by falls and rapids. The water is very pure and cold; the bottom consists of adhesive clay. The shore on the north consists of lofty rocks, from 300 to 1,500 feet high, and is lined with numerous islands, which afford shelter for vessels; the southern shore is chiefly low and sandy, interrupted here and there by limestone rocks, and is wholly destitute of bays or any other shelter. There are several large islands, beside those on the north coast, of which Maurepas and the Carebow Islands belong to Britain, and Isle Royale, in the western part, to the United States.

LAKE HURON receives the waters of Lake Superior through the River St. Mary's, which is about 30 miles in length, with falls of 30 feet, 22½ of which occur at the Sault or Rapids of St. Mary's, extending over a space of two miles. Greatest length 250, and breadth 220 miles; its circuit is 1,200 miles, and its area about 20,000 square miles. The surface of this lake is 578 feet above the level of the sea, and its average depth is 1000 feet. The shores are much similar to those of Lake Superior; high and rocky on the north, and low and swampy on the south. The long chain of the Manitoulin Islands has the same broken appearance as the northern coast. These islands almost completely divide the great expanse called the Georgian Bay from the body of the lake. On the west side of the lake is a large inlet called Saginaw Bay.

LAKE MICHIGAN lies in the same level with Huron, and indeed is properly a part of it, the two being connected by the Straits of Michilimackinac, which is four miles wide at the narrowest part. Length 300 and breadth from 80 to 90 miles; area 22,000 square miles, and the greatest depth 900 feet. Green Bay, on its west side, is nearly detached from the lake by a long narrow peninsula, and several islands.

LAKE ERIE is connected with Lake Huron by the rivers St. Clair and the Detroit, the former of which, after a course of 30 miles from that body of water, expands itself into a small shallow lake of the same name, about 100 miles in circumference, and is thence continued under the name of the Detroit to Lake Erie. These two rivers, with the intervening lake, are navigable for vessels of 7 or 8 feet draught. Lake Erie is 265 miles long and 63 in breadth at the middle. Its surface is 565 feet above the level, and has an area of 9,600 square miles. The shores are low, but in a few places interrupted by rocky cliffs: towards the west there are extensive marshes on both sides. The want of sheltered bays has rendered it necessary to resort to pier harbors; the mouths of the rivers are also obstructed by sand-bars. The islands, 26 in number, are all on the south-western portion of the lake: the largest are Palee, belonging to Canada, and Cunningham, belonging to the United States; as also do the Bass Islands.

The River Niagara, 33 miles in length, forms the outlet of Lake Erie, and has a descent of 334 feet to Lake Ontario. Of this, 165 feet form one perpendicular fall, and 51 the descent of the rapids in the half mile immediately above the falls. Below the falls, the Niagara flows through a deep rock-bound chasm, the sides of which are formed by mural precipices, nearly 300 feet high, as far as Queenston, where the ground sinks down almost to the level of the river. The great fall, 20 miles from Lake Erie, is divided by Goat Island into two portions, one of which, named the Horse Shoe Falls, from its semi-circular form, has a lineal extent of 600 yards on the Canadian side; the other, an extent of 300 yards, on the American side. For grandeur and sublimity, the Falls of Niagara are unequalled and unsurpassed by any other natural scene in the world. President Dwight estimated the quantity of water precipitated over the falls at 11,524,375 tons an hour; Darby at 1,672,704,000 cubic feet per hour; and Pickens at 113,510,000 gallons, or 18,524,000 cubic feet a minute. The river contains several islands; one of which, Grand Island, contains 18,000 acres of rich fertile soil, covered with forests. This island is celebrated as the "El Dorado" of Major Noah, of New-York, who designed to collect the remnants of Israel here, previous to their return to the tents of Jacob, now occupied by the Infidel Musselman; and another, Navy Island, which acquired some notoriety in the late Canadian insurrection. Grand Isle is on the American, and Navy Island on the Canadian side.

Lake Ontario is about 200 miles in length; its greatest breadth is 60; its circuit 470; its area 6,300 square miles; its surface 232 feet above the level of the sea, and its depth from 300 to 600 feet. The shores are generally low, but between Toronto and the Bay of Quinte they are higher. The harbors are Toronto and Kingston on the north and Sackett's Harbor on the south-east. There are about 20 small islands in the eastern part of the lake. It emits its waters by the River Kataraqui and the Lake of the Thousand Isles, which afterwards become the St. Lawrence.

The other principal lakes of the north are:—*In Canada*, St. John's, Nipissing, Mississagua, Muskoka, Trading, Simcoe, Cameron's, Sturgeon, Pidgeon, Shemong, Trout, Rice, Rideau, and Mississippi;—*in the British Territory North-west of Canada*, Lake of the Woods, Winnipeg, Winnepegoos, Athabaska, Great Slave Lake, Abbitibbi and Misstassin;—*in the United States*, Champlain, George, Oneida, Otsego, Skaneateles, Owasco, Cayuga, Seneca, Crooked, Canandaigua, Honedoye, Hemlock, Chatauque and Canesis, all in New-York; Temiscouta, Baamchenungamock, Pongokwahem, Moose, Chesuncook, Pemadumcook, Moosetogmaguntic, Umbagog, Schoodic, and Upper Schoodic, in Maine; Winnipiseogee, in New-Hampshire; and Memphremagog, between Canada and Vermont. There are numerous others which it is impossible to mention. In Louisiana, are the great lakes of Pontchartrain, Borgne, Ouacha, Grand, and others formed by the waters of the Mississippi; Bodeau, Cado, Bistinoe, Caunisnia, Bayou-Pierre, Spanish, Black, and others formed by the Red River and its branches. In Wisconsin, is Lake Winnebago, formed by Fox

River; the Four Lakes, Kushkaning, Geneva and Red Lake. There are several extensive lakes also in Florida.

The LAKES OF CALIFORNIA will next claim our attention, which, though situated within the United States, will, from their location in a different physical region to that which has been already described, warrant a separate paragraph. The Tule Lakes extend in the direction of the coast, from south-east to north-west, for about 200 miles; they are by no means so capacious or deep as some of the smaller northern lakes; the Pyramid Lake, in the centre of which a natural pyramid erects its granite sides, was but lately discovered by Capt. Fremont, and is fully described in his "*Expedition*, &c." There are several others of considerable size, among which the Great Salt Lake of the desert is pre-eminent.

The LAKES OF MEXICO are situated on the plateau of the mountains: the Zumpango, Christoval, Tezcuco and Chalco, are small bodies of water in the elevated plain of Mexico; but the largest lake in the country is that of Chapala, in the plain of Xalisco, which is traversed by the River Santiago. It is about 90 miles long and from 12 to 18 wide.

The LAKES OF CENTRAL AMERICA are of great importance to that country, and furnish valuable means of transporting merchandise from one part to another. Lake Nicaragua, between 10° and 12° north latitude, and 84° and 86° west longitude, is 95 miles long and 30 in breadth. At a little distance from the shore it is from six to ten fathoms deep, and in some places more; it contains several islands, chiefly of volcanic formation, the most remarkable of which is Ometepe, not far from the north-west shore, which contains a lofty volcano. The surface of the lake is 128 feet above the level of the sea. It discharges part of its waters by the River Tepitapa into the Lake of Managua or Leon, which is 45 miles long and 15 wide, and deep enough for the largest vessels, but has no navigable outlet; the greatest part of the waters of the Lake Nicaragua are discharged through the San Juan. There is some probability that this river and lake may be fixed upon for a communication between the Atlantic and Pacific, (see p. 19;) at the present time but small boats of two or three tons are able to navigate the river. There are some other lakes in Central America: Itza, in Guatemala, about north latitude 16° 8′, and west longitude 91° 16′, is thirty miles long and six broad, containing eleven islands, and surrounded with lands fertile in the extreme. Golfo Dolce, also in Guatemala, is 28 miles long by 12 miles broad.

A multitude of ISLANDS belong to North America. We shall briefly notice the principal, in the order of the seas in which they are situated. In the Atlantic Ocean there is the Archipelago of St. Lawrence, at the mouth of the Gulf of St. Lawrence; its principal islands are Newfoundland, Anticosti, Prince Edward's Island, and Cape Breton. The great Columbian Archipelago or West Indies, though properly belonging to North America, will be treated of in the second division of this work. The Bermuda Islands are off the coast of Carolina, and consist of a great number of small islets, few of which are habitable. These will be described under the head of "*British North America.*" In the Pacific Ocean, the largest islands are in the Archipelago of Quadra or Vancouver; and that of King George III., on the north-west coast, with the Aleutian Archipelago in Russian America. In Behring's Sea, are the group of Pribylof and Nounivok, also belonging to Russia. The ARCTIC ARCHIPELAGO, in the Arctic Ocean, presents a vast number of islands, the majority of which, previously to the later voyages of discovery, were regarded as part of the American Continent. Balbi proposes to subdivide them as follows:—1. Eastern or Danish Arctic lands, comprising the great group of Greenland and Iceland, belonging to Denmark, and Jan Mayen's Land, without stationary inhabitants. 2. The West or British Arctic lands, extending to the west and north of Baffin's and Hudson's Bays, the principal groups of which are New Devon, North Georgia, with the islands of Cornwallis, Melville, &c. And 3. The Archipelago of Baffin, consisting of Parry's Land, with the Islands of Cockburne, Southampton, New Galloway, &c. However plausible this may appear, such a division, with the progress of discovery, will soon be insufficient, and require modifying; and even at present it can be of no practical use

North America abounds in what are termed natural wonders and curiosities. Natural bridges, mammoth caves, petrefactions, Indian antiquities, &c., are by no means uncommon. This, however, is not the place to describe these marvellous creations; but full accounts will be found of each in the description of their several localities.

The climate of North America is almost as celebrated for its preponderance of cold as Africa is for the preponderance of heat. With the exception of the maritime coast of the Pacific, beyond the Rocky Mountains, the temperature in the same latitude is everywhere inferior to that of the old world. Countries which, from their geographical position, we should suppose to be temperate and mild, are exposed to long and severe winters, and in point of fact, countries in the same parallel with England, are almost entirely too rigorous for the habitation of man; and even in the 45th parallel on the north side of the great lakes, winter enshrouds more than one half of the year. Frost is no unfrequent visitant on the low shores of the Gulf of Mexico, which are on the same parallel with Morocco, Cairo and Suez. This predominance of cold has been ascribed to a variety of causes: one, and not the least, is the greater elevation of the surface. Not only is the continent traversed by immense mountains, covered with perpetual snow, but in Mexico very extensive plains are found at an elevation of from 6,000 to 10,000 feet above the level of the ocean. In some parts, where the plateaux rise rapidly, there is often within a few leagues, an extraordinary change of temperature. At Vera Cruz and the whole eastern coast of Mexico, northward to the Rio Grande, the heat is generally quite oppressive, while a few hours' journey brings the traveller to the "tierra templada," where the air is clear and the heat moderate, and thence is but a short distance to the high plateau, where an overcoat and blanket would not be found uncomfortable. Such is the rapid succession of climate, that within a short time and distance, the polar cold and the tropic heat may be successively experienced.

These different climates have different vegetable productions. "Hence, the traveller journeying down the deep descent of one of those magnificent ravines, (leading from the plateau of Mexico,) through forests of birches, oaks and pines, finds himself suddenly on the level shores, surrounded by palms, and has an opportunity of seeing the animal products of the north and south, of the Alpine regions and tropics—nay, of the eastern and western hemispheres, mingled together. Wolves of northern aspect dwelling in the vicinity of monkeys; humming-birds returning periodically from the borders of the frozen zone, with the northern bunting and soft feathered tit mice, to nestle near parrots; and the common European whistling-duck and teal, swimming in lakes which swarm with syrens and Brazilian parras and boat bills."

Another cause of the inferior temperature of the new world may be partly ascribed to the great indentation of the sea between North and South America, and the absence of those extensive sandy deserts in the tropical regions, which, by reflecting the rays of the sun, render Africa so uncommonly heated. The place of these is supplied by dense forests, and traversed by the largest rivers of the world, which powerfully diminish the influence of the solar beams. A strong and abundant vegetation is, in fact, the distinguishing characteristic of North as well as South America, and to this fact may be attributed much of the difference which distinguishes the old from the new world.

And with respect to North America, we may add, that while but a small portion of it is within the torrid zone, it reaches far within the Arctic circle, where it also attains to a great breadth. The north-west wind prevails in the winter. This wind, sweeping over a desolate country, overspread with marshes, forests, frozen lakes, and mountains buried under eternal snow, contracts an intense degree of cold, and in its progress southward, passing over a wilderness, where the forests shade the earth from the sun, its original character is in no respect changed. It slowly yields to the dominion of latitude, and retains its boreal character long after it has penetrated into the natural regions of heat. Throughout North America the north wind is accordingly felt to be keen and piercing. It increases the rigor of the seasons, and extends the influence of winter far into those latitudes, which, in the other hemisphere, are blessed with perpetual spring.

The countries lying within the tropics are exposed to the inroads of the northern blasts; and the great heats felt at Vera Cruz and other sea-board cities, are often suddenly reduced by strata of cold air brought by the north winds from the polar regions. These winds blow from October to March, frequently bursting forth in tremendous hurricanes—"northers," and cooling the air to such a degree, that at Vera Cruz the thermometer very frequently falls to 60° *Fahr.* In the basin of Mexico, the temperature has sometimes marked the freezing point, and thin ice has been formed on stagnant pools.

To the prevalence of these north winds, therefore, combined with the extraordinary elevation of the surface and the yet uncultivated state of the country, overspread with vast forests, the inferior temperature of North America seems ascribable. But with this great inconvenience, the climate of the continent is healthy, and the rate of mortality not greater, in the more elevated regions, to that of the old world, and in some of the middle districts longevity is a distinguishing feature in its vital statistics.

Stretching, as North America does, from the Arctic regions to far within the tropics, and possessing soils of every elevation and quality, her vegetable productions are necessarily of varied character. Owing to the humidity and comparative coolness of the climate and the natural richness of the land, fertilized by the successive decays of ages, her forests and pastures are of unrivalled extent, luxuriance and magnificence.

The forests consist, generally, of very heavy timber, including many species of pines and larches, unknown to the old world, with an endless variety of oaks, maples, cypresses, tulip trees, mahogany, log-wood, &c., &c.; nor are the agricultural products less peculiar or less diversified. The potatoe is eminently an American tuber, and tobacco, now the greatest luxury of both worlds, though its cultivation is extended to almost all countries, was indigenous to North America alone. Indian corn, millet, cocoa, vanilla, pimento, copaiba, jalap, sassafras, nux vomica, and many other drugs and medicines important in the arts and pharmacy, are all American. The coccus cochinilifer, which produces the cochineal of commerce, is peculiar to Mexico. These all grow wild, in a state of nature, or are cultivated for the convenience of collection, and have been a great source of wealth to the country.

The forests and fields of North America, however, have been enriched by contributions from the old world, and many plants, hitherto unknown to American soil, have, since Europeans settled in the country, been introduced and become valuable adjuncts to her already varied products. At the head of these may be placed wheat, barley, oats and rice, all of which find a congenial soil and succeed to perfection. The sugar cane, originally from the East Indies or Madeira, and the coffee plant, have become staple products; and oranges, lemons, peaches and most descriptions of fruit trees, are of eastern origin. American apples, though now superior to the apples of England, are derived from trees carried from that country; and the vine, the cultivation of which has of late years been much attended to, seems to flourish in many parts of the country almost as well as in its native soil in Western Europe.

The Zoology of North America, though as yet but little known, presents a vast catalogue of the different families of animated nature. The animals differ in many important respects from those of Europe, and of the useful kinds there are singularly few. Neither the horse, the ox, nor the hog were found on the American continent when discovered, and the want of them must, no doubt, have been a considerable obstacle to the advancement of the natives in the career of civilization. The elephant and camel were also unknown to America, and in fact the aborigines appear to have had no substitute for these essentially valuable animals. The Bison, or American ox, (*Bos Americanus*,) the largest native quadruped of the New World, is principally found on the vast western prairies. It is rarely, if ever, seen east of the Mississippi, and it has never been found on the Atlantic plain. The Bos Moschatus, or musk ox, is found only in the most northerly parts of America, to the west of Hudson's Bay, from 60° to 73° north latitude. Its horns, which cover all its forehead, are often of great weight. The Rocky Mountain goat, remarkable for the fineness of its wool, inhabits the Rocky Mountains from Mexico to the extremity of the range. Several species of deer are also found in various parts. The rein-deer is the most northern ruminating animal, being found in Greenland and the most northerly of the Arctic Islands, and on the west coast it descends as far as the Columbia River.

The canine race of North America is of several species, some of which are peculiar to the New World. The physiognomy of the American wolf, when contrasted with that of Europe, is very distinct. There is a great variety of foxes. The fur of the *canis lagopus*, or Arctic fox, and of some other varieties of the same genus, is of considerable value. The best known variety of the American dog is the *canis familiaris*, found in Newfoundland. This animal is now common, from the northern settlements of Canada to the shores of Florida, and has become deservedly a great favorite. It is strong and active, has long and fine glossy hair, a curved, bushy tail, and webbed toes, by means of which it swims admirably well. The color of the back and sides is generally black, with a white belly and legs, and frequently a white spot at the tip of its tail. It is naturally fitted, by its thick covering of hair, for a cold climate, and is more active and in better health in this country in winter than in summer.

The beaver, (*castor*,) is more abundant, perhaps, in the north-western parts of North America, than in any other part of the globe. But the great demand for and high price of its fur, has led to a great diminution of its numbers, and to its nearly total extinction in the more accessible parts of the country; and its entire extermination at a no very distant day may be calculated upon, if means are not taken for its preservation and increase.

North America has but few beasts of prey. The *felis discolor*, or puma, is found on both the northern and southern continents; though denominated the American lion, it is neither so large nor fierce as the jaguar. A number of bears, some of them of the largest and most formidable description, are found in Arctic America, two of which are peculiar to those inhospitable regions.

Tropical America has a great variety of apes and monkeys, but none of them approach so nearly to the human form as the ourang-outang or chimpanzee; and none of them have the ferocity of the baboon. Many, however, have prehensile tails, endowed with so great delicacy of touch, that they have been compared to the trunk of the elephant. This fits them admirably for travelling from tree to tree, and sporting in the vast forests which they inhabit.

Portions of North America are infested by a great variety of reptiles. The rattle-snake is as common as its bite is dangerous, but there are many others whose attacks are little less venomous. The true *boa-constrictor* is found of enormous size in the marshes and swamps of tropical America. Centipedes, sometimes a yard in length, enormous spiders, scorpions, &c., are also found in these regions.

Among the insects of North America are many of large size and beautiful colors; the butterflies are truly gorgeous, and the bug-tribe as varied as extensive. No country in the world presents such a field for the entomologist or amateur collector. The mosquito, in the middle and southern regions, is a prolific and most annoying creature, and in some places in Mexico and Central America is in such numbers and so vicious, as to render whole districts uninhabitable. According to Humboldt, white ants and termites are even more destructive here than their congeners in the old world.

The birds of North America are exceedingly numerous, and are at the present day as fully known to Europe as to Americans themselves, through the labors of the indefatigable Audubon, whose works on natural history have a world-wide celebrity. The birds of prey are of a great number of species, including eagles, vultures, hawks, falcons, owls, &c. The white-headed or bald eagle is well-known as the national emblem of the United States. The vultures are the great Californian vulture, the black vulture, and the turkey-buzzard; the latter is well-known and numerous in the Southern United States, where, *maugre* their filthy habits, they are protected by law as useful denizens, being of great benefit in consuming decaying animal matter, which would otherwise pollute the atmosphere, and render a locality offensive and dangerous to the health of the people. The wild turkey of America is a noble bird, of brilliant, blackish plumage; and of this bird Dr. Franklin has observed: "It would have been a much fitter emblem for our country than the white-headed eagle, a lazy, cowardly, tyrannical bird, living on the labors of others, and more suited to represent an imperial despotic government than the Republic of America." The duck tribe is very numerous. Canvas-backs are peculiar to America, and are esteemed a great luxury by the gourmand; they are found mostly on Chesapeake Bay and the neighboring rivers. But the most characteristic of American birds is the humming-bird, remarkable alike for its small size and the brilliant metallic lustre of its plumage; it is found south of the 45th parallel, but is more numerous towards the southern coasts. Vast flights of pigeons, in their periodical migrations, frequently darken the sun, and often require, such is their countless number, four or five days in passing over one particular spot. Their course is marked by millions of those who have fallen from exhaustion or pressure, and the ground for miles is frequently covered with such as have perished. Of the game species there are partridges, grouse, pheasants, &c.; in general, however, these are distinct in species to those of Europe. The mocking-bird, the blue-jay and whip-poor-will, are all peculiar to America. Robins of large size, sparrows, and the smaller birds, are everywhere in great numbers. The American robin is four times the size of that of Europe.

The waters of North America swarm with a great variety of the finny tribes. The cod, the mackerel, the shad, &c., are delicious, and very abundant on the coast and in the great rivers. The lakes produce enormous sized pike, pickerel and other fresh water fish, and the salmon inhabits the rivers in the north and the Columbia River on the western coast. Shell-fish are nowhere so abundant as here.

The cetaceous family inhabit the more northerly seas; the most useful and remarkable, are the common and spermaceti whales and the narwhale. The common seal is abundant on all the coasts and islands of America, but it is more common in the high latitudes than elsewhere, and is of essential use to the Esquimaux and other original tribes, furnishing them with almost all the necessaries of life, both as regards clothing and food.

Nothing, however, is so worthy of remark in relation to the zoology of North America, as the wonderful increase of horses and cattle, brought by the first settlers from Europe. Had we not been fully aware of all the circumstances in regard to their immigration, it would certainly have been supposed that they were indigenous to America, and that it in fact was their native country. They here rove about in immense herds in a state of pristine freedom; and so numerous have they become, that the slaughter of oxen, not for the carcass, but merely for the hide, is the principal business of several extensive districts. In consequence of the extraordinary increase of horses, the mode of existence of the natives, especially in California, has been wholly changed; they have become expert horsemen, and pass considerable part of their time on horseback, approaching in this respect the Tartars and Arabs of the old world. Sheep, however, have not succeeded so well in America as cattle and horses, and their wool, in most parts, is of an inferior quality to that of the European stock, and the mutton ranker in flavor.

The Aborigines or Native Indians are a distinct race, differing altogether in physical form, in language, and, perhaps, in intellectual character, from every other variety of the human race. Probably, however, the general agreement which exists among themselves, is even more remarkable than their disagreement from other races. The *Red* men, as the Americans call themselves, in contra-distinction to the *Whites* of Europe and the *Blacks* of Africa, exhibit surprisingly little difference, although extending over 70°

on the north side, and 54° on the south side of the equator. Heat or cold, drought or moisture, elevation or depression of surface, have certainly no effect in the production, even in the smallest variations, occasionally discoverable among them. "The Indians of New-Spain," says Humboldt, "bear a close resemblance to those who inhabit Canada, Florida, Peru and Brazil: over 1,500,000 square leagues, from Cape Horn to the St. Lawrence and Behring's Straits, we are struck at the first glance with the general resemblance in the features of the inhabitants. We think we perceive them all to be descended from the same stock, notwithstanding the prodigious diversity of their languages. In the portrait, drawn by Volney, of the Canadian Indians, we recognize the tribes scattered over the savannahs of the Apure and the Carony. The same style of feature exists in both Americas."

The general physical conformation of the American Indian may be briefly summed up. Their skin is dark, having more or less of a red tinge, usually called copper-colored, but thought to be more correctly characterized by that of cinnamon; the hair of the head is black, coarse, lank, shining, long, but not very abundant, and the hair on the other parts of the body is very deficient. The beard is seldom altogether wanting, but it is so uniformly scanty, as often to present the appearance of its being so. The forehead is long, and the eyes are deep sunk, small and black. The face is broad across the cheeks, which are round and prominent; nose well raised and round at the apex; the mouth is large and the lips black; the chest high, thighs massy, legs arched, feet large, hands and wrists small. The height is nearly the mean European stature, but the body is usually more squat and thick-set. The countenance is hard-favored and the look stern, yet, with a certain sweetness in the expression of the mouth, which contrasts strongly with the rest of the features. It will appear from this statement, that the races which the American most nearly resembles, are the Mongul, Malayan and Indo-Chinese. The features of the face, are, however, more amply chiselled than in any of these; the frontal bones are more flattened than in any of them, and the stature is greater than it is, at least, in the Malayan race. Although in the tropical regions of America there are no black men, as in Asia and Africa, nor in the temperate regions any whites, as in Europe, still varieties do exist in an inferior degree, which may be compared to those which exist among Europeans and among negroes. The most striking of these are found in the short, squat and tallow-colored Esquimaux, about the polar regions of the north, and the tall Patagonians in the extreme south of the southern continent. The first of these differ in no respect, as far as physical form is concerned, from the people of the same name in Asia and Europe. In point of height, the several Indian nations differ materially even on the same continent: and upon the whole, it may be remarked, that the American race exhibits a wider difference in stature than any other family of mankind, while this difference, at the same time, would not seem to be productive of any essential variation in either physical or intellectual capacity. In point of color, there is no material difference, except in shade. The probability is, after all, the number of races of men in America is at least as great as in any other part of the world, but still, throughout the whole, the contour of a distinct family is perceptible, and the same features are alike recognized from the north to the south, and from the Atlantic to the Pacific Ocean.

The intellectual faculties of this great family are decidedly inferior. They are not only averse to the restraints of education, but are incapable of abstract reasoning. Their minds seize on simple truths, but reject all investigation and analysis. Their long proximity to Europeans has caused little change in their mode of thinking or in their manner of life, and their social condition is consequently not far removed from the primitive barbarism in which they existed on the first visits of civilized man. They have made few improvements in the construction of their houses or boats; their inventive and imitative faculties appear to be very humble, nor have they the smallest taste for the arts and sciences. One of the most prominent of their mental defects, is the difficulty with which they comprehend the relation of numbers, and to this defect is to be attributed many of their disputes with the Europeans who have purchased their lands.

With respect to the American languages, it may be sufficient to state, that they exhibit resemblances not less remarkable than those which we have noticed in the physical and mental characteristics of the people. All nations have languages which possess a common distinctive character, but still apparently differing from all those of the old world with which we are acquainted. This resemblance is not of an indefinite kind, but consists, generally, in the peculiar modes of conjugating verbs by the insertion of syllables, which gave rise to the remark of Lavater, that this wonderful uniformity "favors in a singular manner the supposition of a primitive people, which formed the common stock of the American indigenous nations." History and physical science, however, have hitherto completely failed to throw any light upon the origin of the North American Indians; and it is needless to repeat the numerous hypothesis and conjectures which have been hazarded. On this subject, the work, "*The Origin of the North American Indians, by John Mackintosh*," is very concise, and as a book of great value and interest, it is highly recommended to the reader's perusal. The whole number of pure Indians in North America may be set down at about 7,000,000, of which the greater part inhabit Mexico and Central America. The numbers in the British Possessions and the United States are comparatively few.

The several principal nations inhabiting North America, and all speaking a different language, are as follows:

In *Central America*:—The Changuenes; the Taukas; the Mosquitoes, and the Poyais, &c.

In *Yucatan*:—The Chols or Choles; the Lacaudones and the Maya-Quiche family, consisting of the Mayas or Yucatans, the Mames or Pacomams, the Quiches, Kachiqueles and Kachis, &c.

In *Mexico*:—The Chapanegues, in Chiapa; the Mixteques and Zapoteques, in Oaxaca; the Totomaques, in Vera Cruz and Puebla; the Mexicans or Aztecs; the Othoms, the Tarasques, in Mechoacan; the Tarahumara, in Durango; the Yaquis, in Sonora; the Moquis; and the Apaches, of which there are numerous tribes.

In *the United States*:—The Panis-Arrapahoes family, comprising a number of subdivisions, which inhabit the country drained by the Platte; the Columbian family, which possess the valley of the Columbia River; the Sioux-Osage family; the Mobile-Natchez family; the Mohawk, Huron or Iroquois family; the Lenappe family; and innumerable tribes belonging to these great families, which will be further noticed elsewhere.

In *the British and other Northern regions*:—The Wakash or Nootka; the Kalriche family, and the several nations of the Esquimaux.

The Caucasian or White Races, who have settled in America, belong chiefly to the nations of Western Europe. The Spaniards colonized Mexico and Florida; the English colonized the Eastern portions of North

America, from Florida northward; the Danes settled Greenland, Iceland, &c.; the French were the first settlers of the St. Lawrence and the Mississippi. Numerous Dutch colonists settled at New-York and in New-Jersey. To these have been added Swedes, Germans, Swiss, Scotch, both Celtic and Saxon, and Irish in great numbers; and out of all these has been formed the great Anglo-American family, which is now rapidly spreading over all the habitable portion of North America, subduing nature and nations in its progress to universal dominion. The Russians have some settlements in the extreme north-west, but these being merely temporary sojourners, cannot be taken into a general account of the population.

AFRICAN NEGROES have, for the last two centuries, been imported into North America, and are now continued in the Southern United States as slaves. Pure negroes still form about one-eleventh of the population; while the races sprung from intermixtures are also very numerous. These have never attained to excellence, either in literature or the arts, but are still looked upon as an inferior race; and even where slavery does not exist, their social condition is not one of the happiest description.

All the European colonists, and many of the aboriginal inhabitants, profess Christianity; but several of the independent tribes are still addicted to *Fetichism*, or to what may be called Sabeism or Dualism. It is very remarkable, that among all the tribes, however savage, we find an idea, more or less clear, of a Supreme Being, who governs the heaven and the earth; of an evil spirit, who shares with him the dominion of nature; and of the immortality of the soul, or rather of a future state of existence. Several of the tribes have priests or conjurors; some have neither; but all believe in the existence of invisible beings, and of a future life. Some represent God under the form of a star; some as an animal; some, on the contrary, see him only in the phenomena of nature. A great number of religious creeds, based on supposed revelations, as well as the religion of the ancient Mexicans, have disappeared with the conversion to Christianity of those who professed them; but some part of the creed or religious practices of the Aztec nation, seem still to be preserved among their descendants. It is even curious to observe in the creed of the Tlascalteks the doctrine of transmigration; and to find among the Mexicans, traditions of the mother of mankind having fallen from her estate of innocence and happiness; of a great flood, in which a single family escaped on a raft; and of a pyramidal edifice raised by the pride of mankind, and destroyed by the wrath of the gods; ceremonies of purification at the birth of children; images, made of maize flour, and distributed in portions to the people assembled in the temples; confession of sins made by penitents; and religious associations, resembling those of the monks and nuns of Catholic countries. At the arrival of the Spaniards human blood flowed in the *teocallis*, or temples, of the Mexicans.

The Sioux, the Chippeways, the Sakis, the Foxes, the Winnebagoes, the Menomenes, and other tribes of North America, all believe, perhaps, in a Great Spirit; but there is no individual among them who has not a favorite object of reverence, in some animal, tree, herb, or root. Every chief of a family, every old woman, and almost every individual, has a collection of herbs and medicinal roots, which they call the medicine bag, and regard as a sanctuary of so many divinities. They keep it carefully in their tents, and never separate from it when they are at war or on a journey. Among several of these tribes, when they are settled for a portion of the year, there are huts, where girls are placed to watch over the fire which is kept burning in the centre, like the Roman vestals, the Peruvian Virgins of the Sun, the guardians of the Prytaneum at Athens, and the Guebres of Persia and India. It seems to be considered as an emblem of the sun, or at least is consecrated to that vivifying luminary.

The religion of the Natches, Choctaws, and some other tribes, is a kind of Sabeism. The Cahans make the most extravagant gestures in addressing the Supreme Being. The Knisteneaux regard as spirits the fogs which cover the marshes of their country. The Chippewas believe they are descended from a dog, and, consequently, regard that animal as sacred; they represent the Creator of the World under the form of a bird, whose eyes flash lightning and whose voice produces thunder. They have also traditions of a great flood, and of the long life of the primitive human race.

Among several of the North American tribes fanaticism occasions scenes not less cruel, than those with which the Hindoos celebrate their Curracksûja; but our space does not allow us to enumerate ceremonies which are almost as various as the tribes that practice them.

North America is politically divided into a number of independent states, and the colonial possessions of several European nations. These we shall describe in the following order:—1. *Danish Possessions.* 2. *French Possessions.* 3. *Russian Possessions.* 4. *British Possessions,* (with *Mosquitia.*) 5. *The United States of America.* 6. *The United States of Mexico.* 7. The Independent States of Central America, viz.: *Guatemala, San Salvador, Honduras, Costa Rica* and *Nicaragua.*

DANISH POSSESSIONS IN NORTH AMERICA.

Greenland, with Iceland, Jan Mayen's Land, &c., form the possessions of Denmark in North America. The following table will exhibit the extent and population of each separately:

Names.	Discovered.	Extent.	Population.	Chief Places.
Greenland	911	350,000?	15,000	Uppernavic.
Iceland	874	30,000	56,000	Reikiavik.
Spitzbergen, &c.	1533	26,000	——	——
Jan Mayen's Land	1611	200	——	——
Total		406,200	71,000	

Greenland lies to the north-east of the continent, having Davis' Straits on the west, and the Atlantic Ocean on the east; how far it extends north has never been ascertained—Cape Farewell, in latitude 59° 49′ north, is its most southerly point. This country is of a triangular shape, with its apex to the south, and was for a long time supposed to be united to the continent on the north-west; but further researches of navigators have ascertained this to be untrue, and it is probable that Greenland will eventually be found to be a large island.

The whole country is high and rocky; its surface presenting a chaotic assemblage of sterile mountains, bare or covered with ice, which also covers the intervening vallies. A range of lofty mountains are said to traverse its centre, dividing it into East and West Greenland. The east shore, above 65° north, is an impenetrable accumulation of ice, and is much colder, more barren and miserable than the transmontane districts. It may be said to consist of one uninterrupted glacier. The western shore is high, rugged and barren, and rises close to the water's edge in cliffs and mountains, which are seen from sea at the distance of 60 miles. The whole coast is indented with a number of bays or *fiords*; and interspersed with innumerable islands: the principal of these is the island of Disco, in the bay of the same name. The coasts and islands are the only parts of Greenland ascertained to be inhabited.

The rocks are principally of granite, gneiss, clay-slate, porphyry, pot-stone, &c. Rich copper ore, black lead, marble, asbestos, serpentine, garnets, crystals, and some other valuable stones, are found in abundance. There are no volcanoes, but hot springs are found on the coasts. Coal is obtained on the island of Disco.

Vegetation, even in the south, is almost suspended; a few stunted birch, alders and willow trees, with mosses, lichens, grasses, and fungi, form its whole *fauna*. On the west coast, however, the cultivation of culinary vegetables has succeeded, and several kinds of wild berries have attained considerable perfection.

Among the animals, are the rein-deer in the south, and the polar bear in the north; white hares, foxes, of various colors, and dogs; seals abound on the southern coasts, where also the walrus is met with. In the north seas are whales of several species, and in the sea, rivers and fiords an abundance of fish: turbot, herrings, salmon, halibuts, rays, &c., with a great variety of *crustacea*. Fishing and sealing are the principal occupations of the natives. Sea-fowl, eagles, ravens, and other birds of prey, are very numerous.

The climate is intensely cold. The sun has considerable power, however, during the summer, but fine weather never continues long. Violent storms are frequent in autumn; rain or hail are unfrequent, the latter seldom falls. The aurora-borealis has sometimes a light equal to that of the full moon. In these latitudes there is no night in summer and no day in winter.

There are in West Greenland thirteen colonies, fifteen minor commercial and ten missionary establishments; the most northerly of these is Uppernavic, in latitude 72° 50′; Godt-haab, or Good Hope, the most ancient of the settlements, in latitude 64° 10′, has a good harbor.

The commerce of Greenland is, of course, very limited. The trade gives employment to five or six vessels. Whale oil, seal, bear and rein-deer skins, eider-down, &c., form the catalogue of its exports; the imports consist of such manufactures as are required by the peculiarities of the country, among which are woollens, blankets, coffee, spirits, &c. &c.

The Greenlanders are believed to be of the same race as that which inhabits Northern Asia and America, from whom they differ little in person, manners, or language: those inhabiting the west coast are short in stature, and have long, black hair, small eyes, and yellow or brown skins; but those living on the east coast, only a few hundreds in number, are taller, fairer, more active and robust. These people display skill in the construction of their fishing-boats and hunting implements, which are made of the drift-wood which is brought in vast quantities to the coast. Many have embraced a species of Christianity, and their superstitions are now giving way to a rude sort of civilization. In their homes and persons they are more remarkable for want of cleanliness than anything else. The food of the natives is principally the dried flesh of the seal, with a little game and fish; coffee, tobacco, snuff, and brandy, are esteemed great luxuries. The whole population numbers about 15,000 souls, of which the Danish and Norwegian colonists form about one-half; the native population, which once numbered 20,000, has been gradually diminishing, and will, no doubt, in the process of a few years, become extinct.

Greenland is said to have been discovered by an Icelander in the first part of the 10th century, and the first colony was formed in 923. Under the Norwegian colonists the country was governed by Icelandic laws, and had a bishop of its own. MSS. have been recently discovered which throw much light on the history of these primitive colonies. Of the subsequent history, however, we have no account, and the fate of the colonists is uncertain. Several expeditions have, from time to time, been undertaken for their discovery, but hitherto without success.

The first of the modern settlements was established in 1721, under the auspices of the Danish crown, by Hans Egede, a Norwegian, who has written an interesting work on Greenland.

Iceland is a large island in the North Atlantic, on the confines of the Arctic Circle, generally considered as belonging to Europe, but which should rather be reckoned as belonging to America. It is between 63° 30′ and 66° 40′ north latitude, and 16° and 23° west longitude, and is of an irregular triangular shape, having an area of about 30,000 square miles, and a population of 56,000.

This land appears to owe its existence to submarine volcanic agency, and to have been upheaved at intervals from the bottom of the sea. It is traversed by ranges of mountains, the principal ridge running east and west, and from these other chains are given off, which terminate on the coast in bold and rocky headlands. The coast is indented with *fiords*, and presents much similarity to that of Norway. In the south-east there is an extensive tract of level country, covered with vegetation, but two-thirds of the island is buried under lava and snow. The general aspect of the country is rugged and desolate in the extreme The height of the mountains has not been well-ascertained, but some have an elevation of more than 7,000 feet. The Yökuls or enormous ice mountains are the highest; the most extensive of these is the Klofa-Yökul, which covers an area of 3,000 square miles. The Snafel-Yökul in the west is 4,580 feet high, and Oreefa-Yökul in the east, 6,280 feet, being the highest culmination in Iceland. The celebrated volcano, Hecla, is in the south-west, and about 30 miles inward. It is more remarkable for the frequency and violence of its eruptions than its height, being only 5,200 feet above the level of the ocean. There are upwards of 30 other volcanoes in existence, which occasionally spread frightful desolation over the land. Twenty-three eruptions of Hecla are recorded by Europeans since their settlement in Iceland.

The bays and harbors along the coast are numerous and secure, but little known or frequented; those of Eyafiords on the north, Eyrarbacka on the south, and Reikiavik on the west, are best known. The rivers, which are numerous and comparatively large, have almost a north and south course. There are several lakes, of which Myvatn is the most considerable; it is 40 miles in circumference, and contains upwards of 30 islands composed of lava. Numerous other islands line the whole coast of this inhospitable country, all presenting the same desolate appearance.

The geological character of the island is various; the rocks not bearing external marks of heat, are mostly of trap, and contain all the varieties of

3

zeolite, chalcedony, greenstone, porphyry, slate, &c.; the celebrated double refracting calcareous spar is found chiefly on the eastern coast. Basaltic columns, similar to the Giant's Causeway in Ireland, occur in many parts, especially on the west coast, where they form several grottos, and that of Stappen bears a great resemblance to the cave of Fingal, in the Island of Staffa.

Few metals are met with; iron and copper have been found, but the mines have not been wrought. Sulphur is abundant everywhere, and formerly was largely exported. The intermitting hot springs form the greatest wonder of these polar regions, and are used by the natives for domestic purposes; food is cooked by them, and huts built over small fountains to form steam baths. In some parts of the island vast cauldrons of boiling mud are in a state of constant ebullition, sending up columns of dense vapor, which obscure the atmosphere a great way around.

The extensive forests with which tradition invests Iceland, no longer exist, and nothing but stunted shrubs, little better than underwood, are now found. Vast quantities of *surturbrand*, or fossil wood, are frequently found at a great depth beneath the surface.

Of wild animals, foxes are most numerous, and bears of northern aspect brought down on the ice, frequent the shores. The reindeer, introduced from Norway, has greatly multiplied, and is entirely wild. Nearly all kinds of sea-fowl inhabit the coasts and islands, and plovers, curlews, snipes, &c., are found in the interior. The eider-duck abounds, and its feathers form a staple export. The coasts, lakes and rivers produce fine fish, and the seal inhabits the coasts, off which are also vast supplies of cod, haddock, herring, &c. The fisheries are extensive, and employ a great portion of the people, who exist principally on their produce. Large quantities of pickled fish are also exported.

The climate is variable: great and sudden changes of temperature often occur. The cold is much increased by large masses of floating ice, which accumulate on the coasts, and fogs are perpetual. Thunder is seldom heard, but storms of wind and rain are frequent, and the *aurora borealis* and other meteors are much more common and brilliant than in more southern climates. The sun is visible at midnight at the summer solstice from the hills, in the north part of the island, but the summers are very short, and are succeeded by a cold, dark and dreary winter, not enlivened by a single ray of the great luminary.

Agriculture is on a very limited scale, being confined mostly to the growing of grass and hay for the herds of black cattle with which the island abounds. Potatoes and some culinary vegetables have been introduced, but nothing but the red cabbage succeeds well. In 1834, there were 500,000 sheep, 36 or 40,000 head of black cattle, and from 50 to 60,000 horses on the island. The wool is of fine descriptions, and about 3,00 or 4,00 skuppunds (skuppund= 6,400 lbs.) are annually exported. The whole population is employed in feeding cattle or in fishing, or in both: those who breed cattle, being, as compared with those who live by fishing, nearly as three to one. There are no manufactures, except of a domestic nature, carried on; every man makes his own shoes and clothes, in which employment the bishop and other high functionaries are frequently engaged. Barter is the prevailing system, little or no money being possessed by the inhabitants. The peasantry assemble annually at Reikiavik and other principal settlements, and bring down with them wool, butter, skins, tallow, Iceland moss and some fine cattle, and in return for these, take back coffee, sugar, tobacco, snuff, brandy, rye, wheat, salt, soap, &c. The better class purchase linens and cotton goods, which have latterly come more in use. Those who live near the coasts bring dried cod and stock fish, dried salmon, whale, shark and seal oils, seal skins, &c. The domestic exports have been inconsiderable of late.

The Icelanders are chiefly of Norwegian origin, and have a frank, open countenance, florid complexion and flaxen hair. They have retained, with few innovations, the ancient modes of life and the costume of the Scandinavian race. Their dwellings are filthy, and like those of the Irish, repulsive to strangers. The people have retained, in all its purity, their ancient language, and are very attentive to their religious and moral duties. Domestic education is universal, and there are few who cannot read and write. Many of the peasants are well versed in the classics, and the Latin language is frequently used as a medium of communication with foreigners. They are very fond of their *sagas* or ancient traditional tales, which are read aloud in their families during the long winter evenings.

The affairs of the island are presided over by a governor, with the title of *Sliftamtman*, who is sometimes a native, but more frequently a Dane. Under him are *amtmen*, or provincial governors, and each province, of which there are three, is divided into *syssels* or shires, presided over by *sysselmen* or sheriffs: these collect taxes, hold petty courts, regulate assessments, &c. The *tatsroed* or chief justice, holds, with two assistants, a criminal court at Reikiavik, but capital offences are sent to Copenhagen for trial. Crimes, however, are rare: petty theft and drunkenness are the most common.

The island constitutes a bishopric. There are 194 parishes, but the clergy amount to about 300, and are very poor. There are four charity hospitals, but no work-houses. The principal school is at Bessestadt, and has three masters, who teach the classics, theology, and the Danish language: the youth finish their studies at Copenhagen. Domestic education is much attended to, and is productive of much good.

Reikiavik, the capital, on the south-west coast, has little more than 500 resident inhabitants, chiefly Danes. Most of the villages are situated on the coasts, at convenient spots, for the receipt and transport of merchandise.

Iceland was discovered by a Norwegian pirate, in 860, but the earliest permanent settlement was effected in 874. In little more than half a century, all the coasts were occupied by settlers; and about 928, the inhabitants formed themselves into a republic, and established the *Althing*, or General Assembly of the Nation, which was held annually at Thingvalla, in the south-west, and not abolished until 1800. The Icelanders maintained their independence for nearly 400 years, but during the 13th century became subject to Norway; and on the annexation of that kingdom to Denmark, Iceland was transferred along with it, and has since remained a colonial dependence of that nation.

Spitzbergen, or pointed mountains, (formerly known as East Greenland,) is the most northerly land hitherto discovered, and lies between the 76th and 81st degrees of north latitude, and the 9th and 3rd of east longitude, or about midway between Nova Zembla and Greenland. The group consists of four principal islands, viz.: Spitzbergen Proper, North-east Land, South-east Land and Charles' Foreland, the last on the west of the others. Besides these, there are some others of considerable extent, as the Ryke Yse Island and the Ice Islands on the east, which were discovered in 1645; the Hope or Sea Horse Island; and the Bear or Cherry Island, on the south, discovered by Barentz, in 1596. The Thousand Islands, an archipelago of some magnitude, lie south of South-east Land. Innumerable smaller inlets and rocks surround the whole coast, which is indented with capacious bays and fiords, in some parts almost dividing the country. Little, however, is known of the topography of these northern regions, nor has their extent been at all accurately ascertained, but it is stated that the actual superfices, though occupying a larger space, is smaller than that of Iceland. These islands rise in many places into mountains, of from 1000 to 3700 feet in height, the peaks of which are covered with snow, coeval, perhaps, with their creation. The coasts are iron-bound, presenting only a few tolerable harbors: the best of these is Smeerenberg, on the west coast, where the Dutch had once a considerable establishment. The surface, for the most part, is destitute of any vegetable or animal products, but there are a few bears and foxes, which live upon fish, &c. Spitzbergen was formerly a principal station for the whale fisheries, but the whales have been for some time past very scarce in the surrounding seas, and it is now but seldom visited. These lands were originally discovered by Sir Hugh Willoughby, in 1533; were first visited by the Dutch, in 1595, and surveyed by Captain Phipps, in 1773. The sovereignty of Denmark over Spitzbergen, is of course only nominal. It is also claimed by the Autocrat of Russia. There is no stationary population.

Jan Mayen's Land, in latitude 71° and longitude 7° west, is a small island, also nominally under the crown of Denmark. It is similar in character to the other arctic islands, and of no possible use, except as a harbor for whale ships. It is generally about 7,000 feet above the ocean. Beerenberg, a lofty hill, in the northern part of the island, is seen at the distance of 30 leagues from land. It was discovered in 1611.

Several other mountainous and sterile islands, in the Arctic Seas, belong also nominally to Denmark. They are productive of nothing but a few precious stones, minerals and volcanic matters, and are wholly useless to commerce. Whales and other valuable oil-producing animals frequent their inhospitable shores, which afford good harbors.

FRENCH POSSESSIONS IN NORTH AMERICA.

The only colonies held by the French in North America are the Islands of St. Pierre, Grand and Petit Miquelon, which lie on the south of Newfoundland. Formerly, however, this nation owned nearly one-half of the whole continent; but all, except these small, and almost unheard-of islands, has been wrested from it, either by conquest, cession, or purchase. Newfoundland passed from French authority in 1713; Cape Breton and Prince Edward's Island, in 1745; Canada and Nova Scotia, in 1763; and in 1803, the extensive territory of Louisiana. This latter was purchased by the United States, and now forms the flourishing states of Louisiana, Arkansas, Missouri and Iowa, and is inhabited by a large, industrious and thriving population.

These islands, which were ceded to France in 1763, are used only as fishing stations for French vessels; they have otherwise no importance, commercial or military. In 1847 the governments of the French and the

United States entered into a treaty of reciprocity in regard to these dependencies. They are under the charge of a governor, who resides at the town of St. Pierre, on the island of the same name. The population is only temporary.

RUSSIAN POSSESSIONS IN NORTH AMERICA.

This territory comprehends the north-western portion of the continent of North America, extending from Behring's Straits eastward to the meridian of Mount St. Elias, along both the Arctic and Pacific Oceans; and from that mountain southward, along the coast chain of hills, till it touches the coast about 54° 40′ north latitude, forming an area of about 394,000 square miles.

The Aleutian Islands, stretching from the Peninsula of Kamskatka, in Asia, to Cape Alaska, in North America, though comprised in the government of Irkutsk, may be considered as belonging to this region. These are very numerous, occupying a circular arc, extending from 165° to 195° east longitude. Apparently, this insular chain consists of the summits of a range of submarine mountains. They are of volcanic origin, and at the present day are subject to eruptions. Earthquakes are common and frequently violent. Behring's Island, Attoo and Oonalashka are the largest; the first being 104 miles in length; but many are only inconsiderable rocks, intersected by channels, varying in width and safety, and generally exhibit a barren aspect; high conical mountains, covered with snow, being their most prominent features. Vegetation is scanty; there are no trees or plants surpassing the dimensions of low shrubs and brushes, but abundance of fine grass is observed in the more sheltered vallies, and different roots, indigenous or transplanted, are there found. Oonimack, one of the islands, contains enormous volcanos, one of which, Chichaldinsk, is about 8,083 feet above the level of the sea. The seas abound in fish; and wild birds are plentiful. The hunting the sea-otter, the skin of which affords a fur of the finest quality, was formerly carried on to a great extent, but an indiscriminate destruction has greatly reduced the number, and comparatively few are now taken. The seal is also a valuable animal, affording the inhabitants a constant supply of food and clothing: the thin membrane of the entrails is also used in the place of glass. Foxes are the principal quadrupeds. The natives, a grade between the North American Indian and Mongol Tartar, are of middle size and of a dark brown complexion; their features are strongly marked, and have an agreeable and benevolent expression. Their hair is strong and wiry; beard scanty and their eyes black. They are not devoid of ingenuity: they are, however, indolent but peaceable, and extremely charitable, and at the same time stubborn and revengeful. Tattooing is practised among them; but the young ladies finding the Russians do not approve of these disfigurations, are gradually abolishing the custom. The laws of matrimony are very loose: a man may have as many wives as he can maintain, and a woman may have two husbands; it is not an uncommon affair, indeed, for men to exchange their wives with each other. The principal subsistence of the Aleutians is derived from fishing and hunting: their habitations are spacious excavations in the earth, roofed over with turf, and sometimes as many as 100 to 150 persons occupy an apartment. Only a few of these islands are inhabited, and it is stated that the population has decreased since the Russians possessed the country: at the present time it is variously estimated at from a few hundreds to 6,000. The islands were partially discovered by Behring, in 1741, and were afterwards visited by a number of explorers. There is, however, as yet, but little known concerning them further than their existence.

The possessions of Russia, on the continent, are chiefly mountainous, and along the coasts several culminations attain great elevation, and are perpetually covered with snow. Mount St. Elias is the most lofty, being elevated 17,900 feet above the ocean. Little or nothing is known of the interior. The line of the coast is very irregular, being indented by large bays, formed by bold promontories and peninsulas: the Peninsula of Alaska forms the south-west point of the country from which the Aleutian Islands begin. There are several extensive islands along this coast, which are included in the Russian territory: the principal of which, commencing at the north, are—Kodiak, Sitka, Admiralty, Prince of Wales', and Queen Charlotte or Washington Island.

The climate of Russian America is very severe, though by no means so extreme as experienced in similar latitudes of the eastern continents. The mean temperature of the winter months is about 34° Fahr.: in January and February, the thermometer ranges below—28°, but in August, the hottest month, it has a mean of 57°, and frequently rises to 70°. The country is subject to sudden changes, and frequent falls of rain in summer and snow in winter.

The Russian American Company* had formerly possession of the whole territories. The settlements originated with an association of merchants formed at Irkutsk, who obtained from the Emperor Paul exclusive privilege of trading for peltry in the Aleutian Islands and adjacent coasts. This privilege was extended by the Emperor Alexander over all Russian America. The capital and principal factory was first established at Kodiak; but the increasing scarcity of sea-otters in the Aleutian Islands, and the necessity of pursuing them further south, led the then governor to lay the foundation of New-Archangel, which has now become the chief depôt. The Russian dominion, however, over the vast solitudes of this region, is merely nominal: some of the tribes, who live along the coast, sell and barter furs with the Russians, and acknowledge the sovereignty of the empire; but most of them, as well as those in the interior, are quite independent. The interior, indeed, is, in the main, quite unknown to the Russians, who possess merely small establishments on the coast and some posts surrounded with ditches and palisades, which are dignified with the title of forts. In 1824, a treaty between Russia and the United States of America was ratified, defining the boundary of the former, and limiting the Russian settlers to the country north of 54° 40′; and in 1825, another between Great Britain and Russia, still further limiting the Russian settlements. By this treaty, the extreme east line was fixed at the meridian of Mount St. Elias, northward to the Arctic Sea, (about 141° west longitude,) and southward along the range of coast hills to 54° 40′, or about the entrance to Observatory Inlet. The British have since obtained a twenty years' lease of the continental portion of these territories, and the exclusive privilege of supplying the Russians with agricultural produce and provisions. The Russians, at the present day, only occupy the islands off the coast. New-Archangel, the capital, is situated on the coast of the Island of Sitka, in 57° 30′ north latitude and 135° 13′ west longitude. It is a town of about 1,000 inhabitants, and contains the boards and warehouses of the company. The habitations

* Charter renewed 1849.

are of wood and well built. The whole country is under the surveillance of a governor, who derives his authority from the company at Irkutsk he resides in the capital, and controls all the actions of the colonial serfs and employées. The total population of Russian America is estimated at 60 or 70,000, including the aborigines.

The commerce of this country is chiefly confined to the exportation of furs to Canton, and the import of provisions and agricultural supplies from the British possessions. It is of little value, being less than $300,000 a year, and is constantly declining, consequent on the extinction of the seal and otter.

Russia also claims Spitzbergen; but by general assent, those desolate regions are considered as forming a part of the Danish Possessions.

BRITISH POSSESSIONS IN NORTH AMERICA.

These enormous, but scattered and ill-defined territories, sufficient of themselves to form several empires of vast dimensions, are, with small exceptions, situated in the more northern portions of America, and are naturally comprehended under the two heads of *Continental and Insular*. The *first* comprises New-Britain, the United Canadas, New-Brunswick and Nova Scotia, (which includes Cape Breton,) all lying contiguous to the northern United States;) and the territory of Honduras in Central America; and the *second*, the islands of Newfoundland and Prince Edward on the confines of the Gulf of St. Lawrence, and the Bermudez' or Somers' Islands, in the Atlantic Ocean. Each of these has a separate local executive and legislature, and forms a distinct colonial dependence. The extent, population, &c., of these several political divisions are exhibited in the annexed table:

Name.	Date of Settlement or Acquisition.	Extent in Sq. Miles.	Approximate Population.	Capitals.
1. New-Britain	s. 1670	2,000,000	60,000	York Factory.
2. United Canadas	a. 1763	349,300	1,600,000	Quebec.
3. New-Brunswick	a. 1763	27,700	220,000	Fredericton.
4. Nova Scotia, &c.	a. 1763	18,746	310,000	Halifax.
5. Prince Edward's Isl'd.	a. 1745	2,134	50,000	Charlottetown.
6. Newfoundland	a. 1713	35,913	100,000	St. John's.
7. Bermudez' Islands	s. 1609	47	14,000	Hamilton.
8. Honduras	a. 1670	62,740	4,000	Balize.
Total		2,497,080	2,358,000	

NEW-BRITAIN.

(HUDSON'S BAY COMPANY'S TERRITORIES.)

The immense regions comprehended under this title, extend from the Russian Possessions and Pacific Ocean on the west, to Baffin's Bay and Davis' Straits on the east, and from the northern line of Canada and the 49th parallel far into the polar regions, terminating in that direction only with the bounds of discovery. Naturally, these territories are divided into three sections: one drained by the rivers flowing into the great lakes and Hudson's Bay; another, by those flowing into the Pacific Ocean; and the third, by those which, rising in the high lands which bound the great central valley, by a northerly course empty themselves into the Arctic Ocean. The *first*, comprehends the "Hudson's Bay Territory Proper:" a region of lakes and marshes, and rivers, where a few mountains rise above the savage and icy plain; the *second*, and more northern, has been little explored, nor is it probable that it will contribute much to the purposes of commerce, being ice-bound and uninviting, and inhabited by a half-starved race, whose only means of subsistence is fishing and hunting; the *third*, which lies west of the Rocky Mountains, though more promising, is nevertheless an inhospitable region, except a small slip along the Pacific, and in the more southerly portions of the country. These regions are occupied by the Hudson's Bay Company, and used for the purpose of trapping and hunting. For the convenience of transactions, the country has been divided into the following districts:

1. Labrador.
2. Rupert River.
3. Abbitibbee.
4. Moose.
5. Albany.
6. Severn.
7. York.
8. Nelson.
9. Churchill.
10. Rainy Lake.
11. Red River.
12. Swan River.
13. Norway.
14. Island.
15. Cumberland.
16. English River.
17. Athabasca.
18. Saskatchawan.
19. Lesser Slave Lake.
20. Greater Slave Lake.
21. Coppermine.
22. New Georgia, &c.

The great features of this country have been described in the general article on North America. It is a region of ice and eternal snow, where the beams of the sun scarcely ever penetrate, and where nature seems to hold strife with chaos. The winters are severe in the extreme; ice on the rivers is eight feet thick; brandy freezes; and in consequence of the cold, rocks split with a tremendous noise, fully equal to that of heavy artillery, and the scattered fragments fly to an astonishing distance. The temperature, however, is subject to the most capricious variations. Rain suddenly falls while the beholder is admiring the cloudless sky; while, on the other hand, the sun will as suddenly burst forth in the midst of the heaviest showers. The *aurora borealis*, sometimes mild and serene, sometimes dazzling and agitated, equals the light of the full moon, and is frequently resplendent and corruscating.

These imposing scenes, however, serve only to augment the solemn melancholy of the desert. Nothing can be more frightful than the environs of Hudson's Bay. To whichever side we direct our view, we perceive nothing but land incapable of cultivation, and precipitous rocks, that rise to the clouds, and yawn into deep ravines and barren valleys, into which the sun never penetrates, and which are rendered inaccessible by masses of ice and snow, which never melt. This sea-like bay is open only from July to September, and even then is much obstructed by icebergs.

Hudson's Bay affords only a small quantity of fish: but the lakes, even those farthest north, abound in excellent pike, sturgeon, and trout; and their banks are inhabited by aquatic birds, among which are observed several species of swans, geese, and ducks. The Coppermine and other northern rivers, swarm with vast shoals of fish in great varieties.

The principal quadrupeds are the buffalo, musk-ox, moose, deer, beaver, wolf, foxes of different colors, the lynx or wild cat, white, black and brown bears, the wolverine, otter, jackash, wejack, pine-marten, ermine, skunk, muskrat, porcupine, hare, rabbit, wood-squirrel, climbing-squirrel, and different species of mice.

The world of vegetation almost terminates in these northern solitudes, and except near the lake and rivers has scarcely an existence. The banks of the Churchill produce some berry-bearing shrubs, the gooseberry bush, three species of vaccinium, the black currant, strawberry, and a small species of wild rose, the burdock, woodsorrel, dandelion, a species of cistus, a species of box, different kinds of moss, several grasses and peas. The trees which compose the forests of this savage country, present very few species: the pine, dwarf larch, poplar, willow and dwarf birch, complete the catalogue. These trees, however, are much influenced in their growth by locality and soil, and are, in some of the southern parts and near the great lakes, of great size, but in the north gradually dwindle down and finally disappear. The banks of the rivers, in the districts bordering on the United States, seem to be susceptible of several kinds of cultivation: barley and rye have ripened there, and hemp becomes very fine; but it will not be long before the progressive advancement of the Canadian population will require these lands for agricultural purposes.

On Winnepeg Lake there is a hardy set of colonists, who were conducted there by Lord Selkirk, and which consists almost entirely of Scotch Highlanders. In this rigorous climate, they exert their energies to *live*, and seem in some manner to succeed in their laudable design: but away from all civilization, they will, no doubt, return to the savage state and herd with the natives of the forests, or sink under the blight of expatriation.

The following historical sketch is from Mr. Farnham's late work on the Oregon Territory, and will be read with interest:

"A charter was granted by Charles II., in 1670, to certain British subjects, associated under the name of 'The Hudson's Bay Company,' in virtue of which they were allowed the exclusive privilege of establishing trading factories on the Hudson's Bay and its tributary rivers. Soon after the grant, the company took possession of the territory, and enjoyed its trade without opposition till 1787; when was organized a powerful rival under the title of the 'North American Fur Company of Canada.' This company was chiefly composed of Canadian-born subjects—men whose native energy and thorough acquaintance with the Indian character, peculiarly qualified them for the dangers and hardships of a fur trader's life in the frozen regions of British America. Accordingly, we soon find the North-west outreaching in enterprize and commercial importance their less active neighbors of Hudson's Bay; and the jealousies naturally arising between parties so situated, leading to the most barbarous battles, and the sacking and burning each other's posts. This state of things, in 1819, arrested the attention of parliament, and an act was passed in 1821, consolidating the two companies into one, under the title of 'The Hudson's Bay Company.'

"This association is now, under the operation of their charter, in sole possession of all that tract of country bounded north by the northern Arctic Ocean; east by the Davis' Straits and the Atlantic Ocean; south and south-westwardly by the northern boundary of the Canadas and a line drawn through the centre of Lake Superior; thence north-westwardly to the Lake of the Woods; thence west on the 49th parallel of north latitude to the Pacific Ocean; and on the west by a line commencing at the last mentioned point, and running northwardly parallel to the Pacific coast to 54° 40′ north latitude, and thence along the maritime range of hills till it intersects the 141st parallel of longitude west from Greenwich, Eng., and thence due north to the Arctic Sea. In this territory, Vancouver's Island, &c., is included.

"They have also leased for twenty years, commencing in March, 1840, all of

Russian America, except the post of Sitka; the lease renewable at the pleasure of the H. B. C. Its stockholders are British capitalists, resident in Great Britain. From these are elected a board of managers, who hold their meetings and transact their business at 'The Hudson's Bay House,' in London. This board buys goods and ships them to their territory, sells the furs for which they are exchanged, and does all other business connected with the company's transactions, except the execution of their own orders, the actual business of collecting furs, in their territory. This duty is entrusted to a class of men who are called partners, but who, in fact, receive certain portions of the annual net profits of the company's business, as a compensation for their services.

"These gentlemen are divided by their employers into different grades. The first of these is the Governor-general of all the company's posts in North America. He resides at York Factory, on the west shore of Hudson's Bay. The second class are chief factors; the third, chief traders; the fourth, traders. Below these is another class, called clerks. These are usually younger members of respectable Scottish families. They are not directly interested in the company's profits, but receive an annual salary of £100, food, suitable clothing, and a body servant, during an apprenticeship of seven years. At the expiration of this term they are eligible to the traderships, factorships, &c., that may be vacated by death or retirement from the service. While waiting for advancement they are allowed from £80 to £120 per annum. The servants employed about their posts and in their journeyings are half-breed Iroquois and Canadian Frenchmen. These they enlist for five years, at wages varying from $68 to $80 per annum.

"An annual Council, composed of the Governor-general, chief factors and chief traders, is held at York Factory. Before this body are brought the reports of the trade of each district; propositions for new enterprises, and modifications of old ones; and all these and other matters deemed important, being acted upon, the proceedings had thereon and the reports from the several districts are forwarded to the Board of Directors in London, and subjected to its final order.

"This shrewd company never allow their territory to be overtrapped. If the annual return from any well trapped district be less in any year than formerly, they order a less number still to be taken, until the beaver and other fur bearing animals have time to increase. The income of the company is thus rendered uniform, and their business perpetual.

"Some idea may be formed of the net profit of their business, from the facts that the shares of the company's stock, which originally cost £100, are 100 per cent. premium, and that the dividends range from ten per cent. upward, and this too, while they are creating out of the net proceeds an immense reserve fund, *to be expended in keeping other persons out of the trade.*

"They also have two migratory trading and trapping establishments of fifty or sixty men each.—The one traps and trades in Upper California; the other in the country lying west, south, and east of Fort Hall. They also have a steam vessel heavily armed, which runs along the coast, and among its bays and inlets, for the twofold purpose of trading with the natives in places where they have no post, and of outbidding and outselling any American vessel that attempts to trade in those seas. They likewise have five sailing vessels, measuring from 100 to 500 tons burthen, and armed with cannon, muskets, cutlasses, &c. These are employed a part of the year in various kinds of trade about the coast and the islands of the North Pacific, and the remainder of the time in bringing goods from London, and bearing back the furs for which they are exchanged.

"One of these ships arrives at Fort Vancouver in the spring of each year, laden with coarse woollens, cloths, baizes and blankets; hardware and cutlery; cotton cloth, calicoes and cotton handkerchiefs; tea, sugar, coffee and cocoa; rice, tobacco, soap, beads, guns, powder, lead, rum, wine, brandy, gin and playing cards; boots, shoes and ready-made clothing, &c.; also, every description of sea stores, canvas, cordage, paints, oils, chains and chain cables, anchors, &c. Having discharged 'supplies,' it takes a cargo of lumber to the Sandwich Islands, or of flour and goods to the Russians at Sitka or Kamskatka; returns in August; receives the furs collected at Fort Vancouver, and sails again for England.

"The value of peltries annually collected in Oregon, by the Hudson's Bay Company, is about $140,000 in the London or New-York market. The prime cost of the goods exchanged for them is about $20,000. To this must be added the per centage of the officers as governors, factors, &c., the wages and food of about 400 men, the expense of shipping to bring supplies of goods and take back the returns of furs, and two years' interest on the investments. The company made arrangements, in 1839, with the Russians at Sitka, and at other ports, about the sea of Kamtskatka, to supply them with flour and goods at fixed prices. And as they are opening large farms on the Cowlitz, the Umpqua, and in other parts of the Territory, for the production of wheat for that market; and as they can afford to sell goods purchased in England under a contract of 50 years' standing, 20 or 30 per cent. cheaper than American merchants can, there seems a certainty that the Hudson's Bay Company will engross the entire trade of the North Pacific, as it has that of Oregon.

"Soon after the union of the North-west and Hudson's Bay Companies, the British Parliament passed an act extending the jurisdiction of the Canadian courts over the territories occupied by these fur traders, whether it were 'owned' or 'claimed by Great Britain.' Under this act, certain gentlemen of the fur company were appointed justices of the peace, and empowered to entertain prosecutions for minor offences, arrest and send to Canada criminals of a higher order, and try, render judgment, and grant execution in civil suits where the amount in issue should not exceed £200; and in case of non-payment, to imprison the debtor at their own forts, or in the jails of Canada."

The northern shore of Lake Superior, eastward of Pigeon river, is a region rich in minerals of the most useful descriptions. The highlands, forming the coast, abound in the finest of copper-ore, and are much similar in geological construction to the northern peninsula of Michigan. The islands, also, which line the shore, are metaliferous, and contain mines of copper, iron, and a variety of basaltic and porphyritic formations. As yet, however, the interests of commerce and manufactures have not demanded very extensively the wealth of this distant region: but capital is flowing in gradually, and every day developes, more and more, its resources. There are no permanent settlements in this portion of the British territory, if we except a few factories belonging to the Hudson's Bay Company, nor is it probable, that, for a long time to come, any considerable immigration will be directed to this desolate wilderness.

The subject of annexing Vancouver's Island to the Hudson's Bay Company's territories, is now being discussed by the imperial parliament, and if the votes given indicate the destiny of that fine country, there can be no doubt but that it will eventually come into its possession. Whether it will be opened for settlement, or not, is questionable: but the probability is, that it will share the fate of New-Britain, generally, and be sealed to the enterprize of both British subjects and citizens of the United States. Thus one of the most beautiful and fertile islands in the world will be doomed to remain a wilderness for centuries yet to come, if not wrested from the hand of monopoly by the strong arm of popular resentment.

The Moravian brethren have established several settlements in the eastern sections of this country, and besides preaching the gospel, have taught the Esquimaux many of the useful arts of life, and thereby partially civilized all within their influence.

The area of this country has been estimated to contain somewhat less than 2,000,000 square miles; but it is difficult, in the present state of our geographical knowledge, to approach to exactness on this point. The population is reckoned, including the Indians, at from 50 to 60,000.

THE UNITED CANADAS.

This country is situated between 42° and 51° north latitude, and 61° and 81° west longitude; being about 1,400 miles in length from east to west, and varying in breadth from 200 to 400; its area is 349,821 square miles. In 1791 it was divided into the two provinces of Upper and Lower Canada, but was again united, for legislative purposes, in 1841. Canada forms a long, narrow tract of country, extending south-westward from the Atlantic, along both sides of the River St. Lawrence, as far as the 45° of north latitude, and from the point where that parallel crosses the river, it stretches westward along the northern bank of the Kataraqui and the northern shores of the Lakes Ontario, Erie, Huron and Superior, including the peninsula formed by Lake Huron on the west, and Erie and Ontario on the south and south-east. The River Ottawa forms the common boundary between the two provinces through the greater part of its course.

Canada is intersected by a number of chains or ridges of mountains, extending from the coast far into the interior, and between these lie extensive and fertile vallies, equal in soil and productiveness to any lands in the New World. North of the St. Lawrence, and near the eastern extremity of Lower Canada, rises a ridge of heights, and which stretches close to the river for upwards of a hundred miles, and forms its rugged banks as far as Cape Tourment, about thirty miles below Quebec. Here the ridge, taking a direction west-south-west, terminates on the River Ottawa, about thirty-eight leagues above its confluence with the St. Lawrence, after extending from Cape Tourment along the course of the river about 300 miles. The country between it and the St. Lawrence, from 15 to 30 miles in breadth, is beautifully picturesque, well-watered and level; towards the west especially, this tract may be considered as the choicest part of the province.

North of this ridge, and between the Ottawa River and the 81st meridian and the 52d parallel, the country is intersected by another and higher range of mountains, which runs into the interior in a north-west direction, at about the distance of 200 miles from the former ridge, and which forms the watershed between the St. Lawrence and Hudson's Bay. This is an immense wilderness, and, as far as known, is covered with dense forests, whose solitudes are only disturbed by the native hunters.

South of the St. Lawrence a ridge commences about 100 miles below Quebec, which takes a south-west course, and opposite this city is about ten leagues distant from the river. The intervening country is fertile and well-wooded, and capable of a high state of cultivation. Continuing in the same direction, this chain crosses the boundary line between the Canadas and the United States, and proceeds on the same course until it meets with the Hudson River. The level tract from the St. Lawrence northward, rich in soil and with a climate favorable to health and plenty, forms the site of the most flourishing and populous settlements in the country.

The "Land's Height," which divides the tributaries of the St. Lawrence from those of the Atlantic Ocean, commences near Cape Rosier, and stretching into the interior in a direction nearly parallel with that river, and with the former chain, from which it is nearly fifty miles distant, terminates on the eastern bank of the Connecticut River, about 400 miles from its beginning. The valley between these two ridges varies much in quality of soil and fertility. From the 45th parallel to the Chaudiere and St. Lawrence there is a tract of excellent and highly-productive land, occupied by a thriving population, and well-cultivated. This part of the country, from its luxuriant soil and its contiguity to the United States, and also from containing the main roads and principal points of communication between the two territories, will, probably, become the most flourishing part of the Canadas. From the River Chaudiere eastward the land is more broken, irregular, and of indifferent quality, interspersed with some good lands, however, which are already settled. The country still farther east, and as far as Cape Rosier, is yet a wilderness, and being in appearance unfertile and barren, offers little encouragement to settlers. South of the heights, however, and as far as Chaleur's Bay, though the lands are of the same character, the districts, especially near the margin of the bay, are thickly settled, but the inhabitants, being employed in the fisheries, bestow little attention upon agricultural pursuits.

The country, from the eastern frontier along the northern shores of the St. Lawrence and the great lakes, in length about 570 miles, and in breadth from 40 to 50 miles, has an excellent soil and climate, and is not exceeded in fertility by any part of the American continent. It generally consists of a fine dark loam, mixed with rich vegetable mould; but it is so happily varied as to present situations adapted to every species of produce. The land eastward of the Bay of Quinté, on Lake Ontario, is a uniform level of great beauty, and is well-watered by numerous streams, which are generally navigable for boats and canoes, and supply an immensity of water-power. From the Bay of Quinté, at a distance of about 40 miles from the eastern shores of Lake Ontario to its western extremity, runs a longitudinal ridge, of no great elevation, and of inconsiderable breadth. Another ridge, called the Queenstown Heights, extends from this point eastward along the southern shores of Lake Ontario, between these and Lake Erie, into the State of New-York. This range never rises in any part more than 480 feet above the level of the lake.

The country which lies between the Lakes Ontario and Erie, and which extends around the western extremity of Lake Ontario to the Bay of Quinté, is watered by a number of large and small streams. The land throughout is uncommonly rich and fertile, and already contains a number of flourishing settlements.

The remaining part of the tract we have been describing, which extends along the shores of Lake Erie from the River Ouse to the Lake and River of St. Clair, is an uninterrupted level, and is as fertile as any lands in Canada. That portion of the country which lies between Lake Erie and Lake St. Clair is perhaps the most delightful in the provinces. The luxuriance of the soil, the diversified and warm scenery which everywhere opens to the view, the excellent fish which abounds in the river, and the profusion of game to be found in the woods, combine to attract a continual supply of new settlers to this highly-favored tract.

The northern shores of Lake Huron and Superior are yet but the home of the trapper, and little settled; the country, however, is promising, though broken by ragged steeps and ridges, and will, with the progress of emigration, soon be overspread with all the exterior signs of civilization and a thriving population.

The topographical contour of the Canadas and their geographical position, exposes them to all the extremes of climatic influences. In summer the thermometer frequently marks from 98° to 105°, but the mean range is about 80° Fahr., while in winter the cold is so severe as to freeze the mercury; this, however, is an occurrence rarely happening, and the mean of this season is about 20° or 25° below zero. The weather during these cold days is unusually clear and healthy. The warm season endures about five months, from May to September, when the snow begins to fall, and in a short time lays thick upon the lands, protecting them from the severity of the weather until the return of spring. In the eastern sections of the country dense fogs, brought by the winds from the regions of Newfoundland, overshadow the face of the earth, and this gloomy and disagreeable state of things continues to December, when the severe frosts set in, and the atmosphere again becomes clear and bracing, and the sky is of a bright azure blue until the opening May. During the long winters of Canada the inhabitants use the sleigh instead of wheel carriages, with which they travel with great rapidity; so light is the draught that the same horse will go in one day from 80 to 90 miles. About the beginning of December all the small rivers are frozen up, from their sources, and even the St. Lawrence is interrupted in its course, and in many parts strongly bound up with ice, and becomes a high road for travellers from one shore to another.

The snow begins to melt in April, and the thaw is so rapid, that it generally disappears by the end of the second or third week. Vegetation then resumes its suspended powers; the fields are clothed with verdure, and spring can scarcely be said to exist before summer arrives. In the upper the winter is much shorter than in the lower province, nor is the cold so intense, being tempered by its proximity to the great lakes. The spring opens, and the labors of the farmer commence six weeks or two months earlier than in the neighborhood of Quebec: the climate is not liable, indeed, to the same extremes, either of heat or cold, and the weather, in autumn, is usually more favorable for securing the late crops.

Most of the causes which contribute to make the climate of the northern part of America more severe and subject to greater extremes than that of Europe on the same parallel, bear with especial force on the Canadian regions, and it is to these causes that the great length of the winters, which prove such a drawback to the country, must be mainly attributed.

The greater portion of these provinces is covered with dense forests; the trees composing which, especially on the more northern and eastern parts, do not, generally speaking, attain the same lofty size as those of the United States, nor flourish with the same exuberant vitality. The pine family and various species of evergreens, are the most numerous and predominant. Among various other kinds of trees, are the silver and American firs, Weymouth and Canadian pines, white cedar, maple, birch, American ash, basswood, hickory, two or three species of wild cherry, and numerous varieties of oak. Like the rest of the American continent, most of the plants and animals differ specifically from those of the Old World. Many of the smaller kinds of annual and perennial plants are common to Canada and regions lying much further south, which may be accounted for by the high summer temperature, while the deep snows of winter effectually protect their roots through the severest seasons; but the trees and larger shrubs, which find no shelter, belong, for the most part, to more northern and arctic regions. Of the smaller plants, the *Zizania aquatica* may be noticed as peculiar to Canada, and abounding in most of the swamps, (a grass, not unlike rice, and affording food to herds and occasionally to the Indian natives,) and the gensing and Canadian lily, common to this country and Kamtschatka. The sugar maple is abundant, and supplies the settlers with a cheap and useful substitute for the sugar of tropical regions. Most of the oak growing in the woods is unfit for ship-building, and the greater part of the timber used for that purpose is cut in New-Brunswick and the New-England States. The species called the live oak, which grows in the warmer parts of the colony, is, however, said to be well adapted for ship timber; the various kinds of wood, available for no other purpose, serve to supply the pot and pearl ash manufactories.

Among the wild animals ranging through the unreclaimed regions, are the American elk, fallow deer, bear, wolf, fox, wild-cat, raccoon, marten, otter, and various species of *viverræ* and *mustelæ;* the beaver, hare, grey and red squirrel, and in the more southern parts, the buffalo and roe-buck. The bears usually hybernate, if the season has enabled them to get sufficiently fat for the purpose; if not, they migrate to a warmer climate.

Among the birds may be mentioned the wild-pigeon, quail, partridge and different kinds of grouse; water-birds are very numerous, as might be inferred from the general character of the region, where, in the basin of the St. Lawrence and the numerous lakes occupying the elevated table-lands around it, half the fresh water in the surface of the globe is collected. A humming-bird, the smallest of its species, is also indigenous, and may be seen in the gardens of Quebec, flitting round the flowers and constantly on the wing.

The race of reptiles, though not so numerous or prolific as in the more southern regions of the continent, is well represented, and rattlesnakes, copperheads, &c., are occasionally met with. Fish, in great variety and abundance, swarm in the lakes and rivers, in which respect few rivers can rival the St. Lawrence. The sturgeon is common, and the salmon and herring fisheries are considerable. Seals are also occasionally met with in large shoals, in the lower parts of the river.

Forests can only exist where the prevailing winds bring with them sufficient moisture, but they may usually be taken as a measure of the fertility of the soil, no less than of the humidity of the climate. In this respect, therefore, taken generally, the Canadas must be considered as occupying a region of fertility and unusual productiveness, the upper province much more so than the lower one. Tobacco, hemp, flax, and the different kinds of grain and pulse, are successfully cultivated, as are all the common fruits and vegetables of England and the United States. Melons of different species abound, and are probably indigenous; as are also the strawberry and raspberry: these last flourish luxuriantly in the woods, and on the plains of Quebec are gathered in great quantities and carried to that market. Pears and apples succeed well, both there and about Montreal, and on the shores of Lake Erie the grape, peach and nectarine, as well as all the hardier kinds of fruit, arrive at the greatest perfection.

Canada does not appear to be rich in mineral products, but iron abounds in some districts: veins of silver-lead have been met with in St. Paul's Bay, (some fifty miles below Quebec,) and coal, salt and sulphur are also known to exist in the country. No volcanos have been discovered, but authentic accounts are preserved of several violent earthquakes; among others, one in 1663, when tremendous convulsions, lasting for six months, extended from Quebec to Tadeausac, (130 miles below that town,) which broke up the ice of the rivers and caused many great landslides and dislocations; in 1791, earthquakes were also frequent and violent in the same region, and the shores, both of the gulf and the river St. Lawrence, present many proofs of former convulsions in the horizontal banks of recent shingles and shells, and in an elevated limestone strata, with wave-scooped marks and lithodomas perforations, that occur in various parts of the shores.*

* Lyell's Geology, vol. ii.

Great excitement was lately produced by the discovery of some gold mines, near Quebec, on the lordship of M. de Lery. The gold is usually found in the bed of some stream, either in the form of dust or in rounded masses of various sizes, associated and frequently cemented with the gravel which forms the bed of the river. This gravel is collected and submitted to the process of riddling, by which a portion of the mineral, in the form of dust, gravitates to the bottom of the sieve and escapes into a trough underneath, which is gently filled with crude mercury, with which it amalgamates. The amalgam is then put into a retort and a slow heat applied, by which the mercury is volatilized, and the pure gold remains at the bottom of the retort. It is now ready for the mint, and its transportation to market is unattended with any further expense. The amount collected has not been made known, but it is probable that but little has, as yet, been gathered from its native beds. The district in which this gold is found has long been called *Le Val d'Or*.

Canada is divided into two provinces, named Upper or West and Lower or East. Lower Canada is divided into the four districts of Quebec, Montreal, Three Rivers and Gaspé; Upper Canada is divided into eleven districts, named Home, Gore, Niagara, London, Western, Eastern, Johnston, Ottawa, Bathurst, New-castle and Midland. These are subdivided into counties, townships, seignories, parishes, &c. The counties are as indicated in the following lists:

Those of Upper Canada: York, Halton, Lincoln, Middlesex, Northumberland, Leeds, Durham, Wentworth, Carleton, Glenville, Lennox, (and Addington,) Prince Edward, Oxford, Frontenac, Glengarry, Hastings, Stormont, Simcoe, Lanark, Norfolk, Essex, Kent, Dundas, Prescott, Haldimand, Huron and Russell, altogether occupying 27,832 square miles; the remainder of the province being yet unappropriated and undivided.

Those of Lower Canada: Saguenay, Montmorency, Orleans, Quebec, Portneuf, Champlain, St. Maurice, Berthier, L'Assumption, La Chesnaye, Terrebonne, Two Mountains, Ottawa, Vaudreuil, Beauharnois, L'Acadie, La Prairie, Montreal, Chambly, Vercheres, Richelieu, St. Hyacinthe, Rouville, Missisquoi, Stanstead, Shefford, Sherbrooke, Drummond, Yamaska, Nicolet, Lothiniere, Megantic, Dorchester, Beauce, Bellechasse, L'Islet, Kamouraska, Remouski, Gaspé, Bonaventure, Towns of Montreal, Quebec, Three Rivers and William Henry, which occupy all the extent of the province, except 7,174 square miles, which is yet unappropriated.

The area of the United Canadas is 349,821 square miles, or 223,885,440 acres, and of this the upper province comprises 147,832 square miles, or 94,612,480 acres, and the lower one 201,989, or 129,272,960 acres. The population, by the returns of 1850, was, for Lower Canada, 770,000; for Upper Canada, 803,879, but since that period, the natural increase and the increase from emigration, which has been much pressed of late years, will authorize us in estimating the present (1852) population at nearly 2,000,000 souls: the number of emigrants landed in the several districts in the year 1851 alone was not less than 170,000 persons, besides many who passed through the United States to that country.

The people of Lower Canada are chiefly of French extraction, but those of the upper province are British, many of whom are from Scotland: comparatively small numbers of the Irish emigrate to this country. The French population cling to old customs and prejudices, but they are honest, industrious and hospitable. They retain, indeed, all the characteristics of the old French, and present the spectacle of an old, uneducated and stationary society, in the midst of a new and rapidly advancing country. A few families possess large properties, but among the mass of the *habitans*, as they call themselves, there is an almost uniform equality of condition, property and ignorance. They are a hard-working people, but few of them can read and write: those who *are* educated exercise a great influence over the masses, and take the lead in all public affairs. The rest of the population, as before stated, is chiefly British, with some slight foreign intermixture, and to them is owing the rapid development of the productive resources of the country. Their numbers are constantly receiving new acquisitions from emigration, which of late years has obtained such an impetus, that, if unrestrained by untoward causes, the whole extent of the colonies will be overspread with thriving settlements in the course of a very few years.

The aboriginal inhabitants still occupy some regions northward of the Lakes Huron and Superior, and along the whole extent of the northern boundary; but their numbers are rapidly diminishing and melting away, like snow beneath the sun, on the approach of the modern emigrant. Little or no success has attended the efforts of the philanthropist to introduce among them habits of civilization, or to improve their condition: they are still identified with the forests, and there they will live and perish.

Lower Canada is divided into counties and seignories, the latter of which were created by the French government in favor of certain leading persons, who were bound to grant or concede a portion to any applicant, the seigneur's profit being derived from payment of a small rent or from astricted services of the tenant, from one-twelfth of the corn ground at the seignorial mill and from a fine on the transference of a property otherwise than by inheritance. To this system it is owing that the French population has been confined to a comparatively small extent of territory, and has never amalgamated with the British; for by its enabling every person to obtain a portion of land without any immediate outlay, young men were tempted to remain at home, and being subject to feudal regulations and services, the occupiers were bound to a routine system of cultivation. Hence, the French Canadians exhibit a singular want of activity and enterprize, and their portion of the province has a dense and poor population, strongly attached to ancient habits. Under the British rule, various methods of granting land have been practised; but it is now all disposed of by auction sales, the minimum price being five shillings sterling or one dollar and twenty-five cents per acre, and the price is payable at the time of sale.

The French colonists are all Catholics: their clergy are numerous, and are under the spiritual jurisdiction of the Bishop of Quebec, who is paid by government. Nunneries are numerous in the different sections, and there are several public schools and colleges, at which not only the clergy but the upper classes receive their education. There is also an English Bishop of Montreal appointed by the crown, with an archdeacon and a number of clergymen in Lower Canada, and the Bishop of Toronto, two archdeacons and forty or fifty clergymen in Upper Canada. Episcopacy is not, however, the prevalent form of church government in Canada: there are a great many Dissenters, Presbyterians, &c., who, by late acts of parliament, receive government support.

We have no accurate statistics to exhibit the relative proportions of the two leading churches,*viz.: the Church of England and the Church of Rome; but the returns of the secondary denominations, which are given, are complete, and refer to the year 1850.

* In Lower Canada (1845) there were 571,714 Roman Catholics, and 43,274 Church of England.

	Churches.	Ministers.	Communicants.
Wesleyan Methodists	98	185	20,520
Baptists	143	84	8,575
Methodist Episcopalians	76	183	7,465
Universalists	10	10	1,200

The system and means of elementary education throughout the colonies are still very imperfect. The Roman Catholics have several endowed academic institutions, but there exists no means of college education in Lower Canada for Protestants, so that many young men are annually drawn for that purpose into the United States. In Upper Canada there is a college and royal grammar school at Toronto. A college, also, for the education of ministers of the Church of Scotland is established at Kingston, under the patronage and with the assistance of the General Assembly of the Church of Scotland, in which the literary classes of the institution are available for lay pupils.

The government of the provinces is vested in a Governor-General, appointed by the crown, and assisted by a council. Formerly, and since 1791, there was a legislative assembly for each province, but by an act of the British Parliament, these were re-united in 1841, and have since met at Kingston, the new capital of the United Canadas. For administrative purposes, the country is divided into districts, which are subdivided into counties, parishes and townships. Each district has its own judges, subject to the General Court of Appeal; a sheriff and grand voyer, or inspector of the roads, whose duty it is to open new roads and to keep those already established in good repair. The Legislative Assembly has the exclusive right of raising revenues for the internal expenses of the colonies.

The tide of popular sentiment has exerted a mighty influence in modifying the laws and producing a conciliatory spirit in the government. Many of the prerogatives of the British Parliament have been abrogated. The colonies have now the regulation of the customs, and the system of education. They have also been lately privileged to regulate their postal arrangements to suit themselves. By these concessions, Great Britain is gradually preparing the people to exercise aright that independent station, which they must, in the natural order of things, and at no distant period, assume; and like a good mother, points out to her children the path to honor and happiness, alike beneficial to nations and individuals.

Canada, indeed, cannot long continue to be ruled by a distant nation—already it is more so in name than in reality; and as the part of its population born in Europe must diminish with each succeeding generation, its predilections for the mother country will vanish, and either be turned to independence, or incline to an alliance with some other independent nation on the same continent; perhaps, indeed, it may at some future time think fit to annex itself to the United States of America, a result not unlooked-for by parties in both countries.

The commerce of the Canadas is of some consideration, and under the fostering care of the mother country, which has sacrificed the prosperity of her West India colonies to the avarice of the Canadians, has steadily increased in extent and importance. It is principally carried on through the ports of Quebec, Montreal, St. John's, Coteau du Lac and Stanfield. From the United Kingdom the Canadas import coal, metals, cordage, East India produce, and the various manufactures of Britain; from the British West Indies, sugar, molasses, rum, coffee, and hard woods, with other tropical productions; and from the United States, beef, pork, flour, biscuit, rice, tobacco, &c. Owing to the unjust and oppressive preference given to Canadian timber in the markets of Great Britain and the West Indies, it forms by far the principal export from the colony. The next article is grain, especially wheat, a great portion of which is derived from the United States, and only passes, under bond, through the Canadian ports; and then follows ashes, furs, fish, &c. and other raw products. The exports of bread-stuffs from the ports of Quebec and Montreal, for the seven years ending with 1846, were:

Years.	*Flour.* bbls.	*Wheat.* bush.	*Oats.* bush.	*Peas.* bush.
1840	315,612	142,059	——	59,878
1841	356,210	562,862	——	123,574
1842	294,799	204,107	5,666	78,985
1843	209,957	144,933	3.651	88,318
1844	415,467	282,183	24,574	130,355
1845	442,228	396,252	53,530	220,912
1846	555,602	534,747	46,060	216,339

The commerce between Canada and the United States has been steadily increasing for some years past, and since the commercial regulations, in regard to the navigation of the St. Lawrence, promulgated in 1847, it has assumed a promising aspect. (See *Hunt's Merchants' Magazine*, 1847, p. 94.) The imports into the British Possessions amounted, in 1846–7, to $7,985,543, and the exports to the United States to $2,343,927; and as the chief trade was carried on with the Canadas, at least two-thirds of the above may be set down to the account of these provinces. The number of clearances were, for the same year, 6,834 vessels, of 1,170,956 tons; and the number of entrances, 6,776 vessels, of 1,186,110 tons. This far exceeds the total of the tonnage employed between the United States and Great Britain.

For a full statement of the commerce between Great Britain and her North American colonies, see " Commercial Statistics," p. 72.

But the internal trade of Canada is one of the most prominent symptoms of its prosperity. The internal improvements are as yet in their infancy, and consist chiefly of a few canals by the river rapids, or as connections between other water communications. There are few rail-roads, and the common roads of the country are in a very bad state, and few and far between. The enterprise of individuals, however, is progressively developing itself, and the spirit of innovation will soon connect the several regions by those iron-bands which have so much contributed to the prosperity of other states. The most astonishing work just completed (1849) is the suspension bridge over the Niagara: a work equal in monstrosity to the celebrated Menai Bridge in Wales, which a few years ago was looked upon as one of the wonders of the world. The great highways of Canada are its system of lakes and rivers, which afford facile intercourse to the immediate trade of their neighborhood. By means of these, the timber and furs of the country are transported from their locations to the ports and harbors, and by the same means foreign produce is carried to the back-woods for distribution. The annual value of this trade counts many millions of dollars, and developes in a greater degree, than any other means, the resources and wealth of these exuberant regions. These routes, however, can only be made useful during the summer months; in winter the streams are all ice-bound, and do not permit of being navigated. During this inhospitable season the backwoodsman is at work, bringing down his timber on sleighs over ice and snow, which proves, from the ease by which it is then dragged along, a superior mode of conveyance. Two extensive lines of canal—the *Rideau,* extending from By-town to Kingston, and the *Welland,* from the south-western part of Lake Ontario to Port Maitland, are the longest and most useful works in Canada. The first is 135 miles long, and was executed by the British Government at little less than $5,600,000 expense; and the second, which is 42 miles long, and cost $2,500,000, avoids the Falls of Niagara, and is navigable for vessels of 150 tons burthen; it was executed by an incorporated company. These facilitate the connection of large tracts, and have proved of great benefit to the settlers and merchants in this vicinity.

Kingston, lately the capital of the Canadas, is very advantageously situated at the head of the Cataraqui River and of the Rideau Canal, on the site of the old Fort *Frontenac.* The harbor is well sheltered, convenient, and accessible to ships of 18 feet draught, and contains the royal naval station on the lakes. The entrance is strongly fortified. Churches of every denomination, built in a handsome style, are found in the place, and many fine stores. The population amounts to 8,399.

Toronto, formerly called York, and, until 1841, the capital of Upper Canada, contains (1850) 23,503 inhabitants, and occupies a good situation on a fine bay on Lake Ontario, which affords access to vessels drawing 15 feet of water, and is sheltered by a low, circular, sandy peninsula near the town. From Oct., 1849, to Oct., 1851, Toronto was the capital of the Canadas.

Port Hope and Coburg are thriving towns, between Toronto and Kingston, but occupy exposed situations on the shores of the lake. Brockville, Prescott and Cornwall, are considerable places on the St. Lawrence. Prescott is situated at the foot of navigation for large vessels and steamers; but small steamers ply between it and Coteau du Lac, passing the Long-Sault rapids above Cornwall by means of a canal. By-town, at the mouth of the Rideau River, on the right bank of the Ottawa, is a thriving place, with about 3,000 inhabitants. Perth is another increasing place, about midway between the Ottawa and Lake Ontario, and connected with the Rideau Canal by a lateral cut of 11 miles. Hamilton, at the head of Lake Ontario, has lately risen to importance in consequence of the rapid progress of the western settlements. Population, (in 1848,) 10,000. The town of Niagara, formerly called Newark, at the mouth of the Niagara River, has a good harbor and an active trade, though the Welland Canal diverts some of its business. Queenstown stands on the Niagara, at the foot of the ridge through which the river has cut its deep channel. Here a battle was fought in 1812, and a monumental pillar was subsequently erected to the memory of General Brock, who fell in the action; but some miscreant has lately almost destroyed it, by blowing out its inside with gunpowder.

The other places worthy of notice in Upper Canada are Chippeway, a village above the falls; Fort Erie, opposite Buffalo; Sherbrooke, at the mouth of the Ouse, on Lake Erie; Victoria, Charlotteville and Norfolk, on or near the bay formed by the Long Point in Lake Erie; Amherstburg, at the mouth of the Detroit, with a good harbor and a military post; Sandwich, opposite the city of Detroit; Goderich, on the eastern coast of Lake Huron; Chatham and London, on the River Thames, which flows through a very fertile country into the Lake St. Clair; and Guelph, 45 miles west of Toronto. There is also a fort, garrison, and naval station at Penetaugushene, on Gloster Bay, at the south-east extremity of the Georgian Bay of Lake Huron.

QUEBEC, the present capital of the Canadas, is situated partly on a bold headland rising 350 feet above the left bank of the St. Lawrence, between it and the river St. Charles, and partly on the narrow margin of the river below the rock. The principal part of the upper town is enclosed with fortifications, which are considered to be impregnable, and the summit of Cape Diamond is crowned by the citadel, a very strong fortress. Population in 1850, 39,800. The Hotel Dieu or General Hospital, the Roman Catholic and Protestant Episcopal Cathedrals, the Jesuits' Barracks, the Parliament House, and the Obelisk, erected to the memory of Wolfe and Montcalm, are the principal objects of interest. Lat. 46° 48′ N.—Long. 70° 72′ W. It is situated 420 miles from the Gulf of St. Lawrence, and is accessible to the largest ships.

MONTREAL, on an island of the same name, is situated at the mouth of the Ottawa, and at the foot of a hill which commands a delightful prospect. Population in 1850, 56,000. Though 600 miles from the Gulf, it is accessible for large ships, and its trade is very extensive. The Roman Catholic Cathedral is a very fine building, capable of containing 12,000 persons; and some of the convents and hospitals are striking objects. The island is a beautiful oval shaped tract, 32 miles long by 10 broad, with an almost level surface, there being only one hill of considerable elevation, and one or two of smaller dimensions. It forms one seignory belonging to the Catholic clergy. Montreal was the capital until October, 1849.

Lachine is a considerable village some miles above Montreal, and owes its prosperity to the rapids below, which have made it the landing and shipping place for goods passing between Montreal and the upper country; some part of the trade, however, is carried past it by boats through the Lachine Canal. Coteau du Lac, at the foot of Lake St. Francis, and above Cedar Rapids, owes its rise to similar circumstances.

La Prairie, on the south side of the St. Lawrence, a few miles above Montreal, is the great thoroughfare of traffic between that city and the United States. A railroad, 15 miles long, connects it with St. John's, on the Richelieu, at the foot of navigation for lake vessels. At Chambly, below St. John's, there is a strong military post. Sorel, or William Henry, at the mouth of the Richelieu, is a less considerable town than might be expected in such a situation. Its population is only 2,000. There are a military post and garrison at Isle aux Noix, above St. John's.

The banks of the river between Montreal and Quebec are lined with numerous pretty villages, which are rendered conspicuous by their large stone churches, with shining tin-covered roofs and spires. But there is no place of much importance except Three Rivers, at the mouth of the St. Maurice, on its left bank, which is a place of some trade and mechanical industry, and has a population of 4,000. Below Quebec the settlements are few, and consist generally of fishing villages. In the Saguenay country and the Domain, the only white occupants are found at the trading stations of the King's Posts' Company, which possesses the exclusive privilege of taking furs and fish in this quarter. Stanstead, with 1,200 inhabitants, and Sherbrooke, with 800, are the principal towns of the Eastern Townships, a tract of 6,000,000 acres, behind the French Seignoral Settlements, on the borders of New-Hampshire and Vermont; and which, during the last few years, have been colonized by upwards of 100,000 British and American subjects.

There are also some thriving little towns on the left bank of the Ottawa, in Lower Canada, where the lumber trade is actively carried on. Hull, opposite By-town, with which it is connected by a chain of remarkable bridges across the falls, is the principal, and has a population of about 2,000 or 3,000 souls.

Canada was discovered in 1497 by Sebastian Cabot; and, as early as 1508, the French had surveyed and made a chart of the Gulf of St. Lawrence. In 1525, the country was formally taken possession of by France, but the first permanent settlement was made at Quebec in 1608, under the most determined opposition from the Indians, which continued with bloody feuds for many years, but was finally terminated in a friendly treaty. In 1757, the British forces under General Wolfe captured Quebec after a tremendous fight, in which both Wolfe and the French General Montcalm fell. After this the whole country submitted, and, by the treaty of Paris in 1763, the whole of Canada, as well as Nova Scotia, &c., was formally ceded to the British, leaving undisturbed the seignorial rights and the endowments of the Catholic Church; and these concessions, by gratifying the French people, probably saved these provinces to the British crown, at the war of the American Revolution.

In the war of 1812, '13 and '14, between the United States and the British, severe contests were maintained on the borders, which, from the contiguous residences of the habitans, and the conflict of feeling among the Canadians themselves, assumed the combined character of civil and general warfare, the horrors of which were heightened by the employment of the Indians by the British, who, with all their passions roused, were sent among the republicans to wreak their barbarous vengeance.

In 1836, an attempt was made, by a large portion of the people in Upper Canada, to secure their independence of the mother country, arising partly from the onerous system of church rates, and partly from that of perpetual offices established by the crown; but the revolt was unsuccessful. The enterprise was headed by William Lyon MacKenzie, then or formerly a member of the House of Assembly, and Mayor of Toronto; and, had his skill and firmness been equal to the task, the independence of the country would probably have been established under a republican form of government. The only effect, however, of this rebellion was, to force the British government to suspend the constitution, and to other extreme measures, and thus plunge the whole country into a state of disorganization and anxiety, from which it did not recover for some time.

The re-union of the two provinces of Upper and Lower Canada, which had been divided since 1791, was effected by the Imperial Parliament in 1841; and the legislative bodies, which had heretofore been distinct, were also united and thoroughly reformed in constitution, and their powers extended; since which period, the country has made much progress in settlement and development, but has also remained subject to republican agitation, which, no doubt, is fostered by its contiguity to the United States, whose institutions are on a more liberal basis than those of Canada, and offer great temptations to those whose dispositions tend to the elevation of the people from a state of colonial dependence to one of absolute freedom from foreign control.

The only real advantage that Great Britain has obtained from her connection with the Canadas, is derived from its commerce with those colonies; otherwise, ever since they have been in possession of that nation, they have been an annual expense on the exchequer of that country, and a source of great anxiety and dispute on both sides of the Atlantic.

NEW-BRUNSWICK.

The province of New-Brunswick, lying on the main land of the continent, contiguous to the United States and Lower Canada, consists of an extensive tract, comprising 27,700 square miles, the greater part of which is still covered with dense forests; the land, however, is in general fertile, and excellently adapted for all the purposes of profitable agriculture and the settlement of emigrants.

This province is bounded north by the Bay of Chaleurs and the river Restigouche; on the south by the Bay of Fundy; on the east by the Gulf of St. Lawrence, and on the west by Lower Canada and the State of Maine, and is separated from Nova Scotia by a narrow neck of land, which divides the Gulf of St. Lawrence from the Bay of Fundy.

The face of the country is, in general, pretty level or moderately undulating; but it is diversified by several isolated groups of hills, particularly in the northern parts. Innumerable rivers and streams intersect it in all directions, which are alike suitable to navigation and manufacturing purposes. The climate, though foggy and raw in winter, is on the whole salubrious. The natural products are numerous and valuable; wild animals are plentiful, and the rivers and lakes abound in fish, while along the coasts cod, haddock, salmon and other species of the finny tribe, are yielded in plenty to the enterprising fisherman. The whale fisheries are carried on to some extent. The resources of the province are thus inexhaustible, and according to MacGregor, suitable to the maintenance of three millions of inhabitants. As yet, New-Brunswick has a small population, at most about 200,000, and the principal settlements are along the river St. John and its lakes. On the northern side of the entrance of this great river, from the Bay of Fundy, stands the town of St. John, the largest in the province, and the seat of an extensive trade. FREDERICKTON, which claims to be the capital of the colony, is situated nearly ninety miles above St. John, on the same river, and is yet, in appearance, a mere village. The chief buildings are the government-house and a college.

Bordering on the Gulf of St. Lawrence, and separated from the river of that name only by a narrow strip of the territory of Lower Canada, this province possesses great capacities for sustaining an extensive inland trade with the Canadas.

Miramichi is the next chief river to St. John. It falls into the gulf, and is navigable for large vessels for about forty miles. Along its banks, here and there, are seen the cabins of the settlers, who have not, however, made any great progress in cultivation. The cutting and export of timber form the main trade of the district. About twenty miles up, on the south bank, is the village of Chatham, where many ships load, and where many of the merchants are settled, who have erected stores and wharves. Four miles further up stands Newcastle.

The province is divided into eleven counties, which are again subdivided into townships. The geology of the country is very little known; but limestone seems to be the prevailing formation, though clay-slate, grauwacke, and even the primitive formations frequently occur. Coal is abundant, and is wrought near the Grand Lake, by a joint stock company. Iron and gypsum occur also in considerable quantities.

Agriculture, notwithstanding the rich tracts of alluvial soil skirting the rivers and large indentations of the sea, is considerably less advanced than in Nova Scotia and the Canadas. This is owing, in part, to the later settlement of the province, but chiefly to the people preferring the more profitable but far more laborious occupation of lumbering. Within the last few years, however, great improvements have taken place in this respect. Agricultural societies have been formed, new settlers have introduced the improved forms of agriculture, and emulation has been generally excited by ploughing-matches, cattle-shows and distribution of premiums. Wheat, corn, barley and oats are the principal grain crops, but by far the most important article is the produce in potatoes, the crop of which may be annually estimated at not less than 3,000,000 bushels. Red and white clover are the grasses most cultivated, and beans, peas, turnips, mangel-wurzel and beet-root thrive well, and are raised in pretty large quantities. Pasturage is followed to some extent, and it is estimated that the live-stock of the province is not less than 130,000 horses, 100,000 cattle, 150,000 sheep and 60,000 hogs. The felling and conveyance of timber constitutes, however, as before observed, the great employment of the laboring classes; but most of the lumberers are dissolute and depraved, and the occupation prevents them from paying proper attention to agriculture. Many of the trees, especially the yellow pine, attain great size, and furnish timber of good quality, though inferior to that of Norway and the Baltic. It is principally conveyed to Great Britain in the log, and some is manufactured into deals, boards, staves, &c.

Ship-building is extensively carried on, especially at St. John's. The number of ships built in 1846, was 164, of the aggregate burden of 45,864 tons. These are generally, however, of the class called "*slop-built*," and do not enjoy a high character for solidity or endurance. The trade of the country is chiefly carried on with the mother country and the United States, and employs about 4,000 ships and upwards of 450,000 tons annually. The imports consist chiefly of corn from the United States and the manufactures of England and Ireland, and West India produce, with some minor articles. The exports are lumber, whale oil and dried and pickled fish, as salmon, cod and herrings.

The colony seems, on the whole, to be improving. The Brunswick Land Company have done much to promote emigration, and several joint stock companies and banks have been established. The premium for bills on England varies from 8 to 11½, and the difference between the currency and sterling price of money, in the province, amounts to 11½ per cent. Bank paper forms largely the medium of circulation.

The form of government is much similar to that of the other British possessions. The parliament consists of 26 members, and sits at Frederickton. The judiciary courts are, the Court of Chancery, presided over by the governor; the Supreme Court, directed by four justices; Circuit Courts; a Court of Common Pleas, and numerous courts for the recovery of small debts. The revenues are raised from sale of lands, taxes and other imposts: they are small, and only capable of defraying the civil expenditure. The army is paid by Great Britain, but every man is subject to militia duty. The charge of religion is vested in the Bishop of Frederickton. The people are pretty equally divided among the different sects, and it is said that a fanatical spirit interrupts, to a great extent, the internal peace of the colonists.

In regard to education, a sufficient number of establishments exist: there is a college at the capital, several grammar schools, and common schools in every parish.

We have no authentic statistics of the Church of England, nor of the Roman Catholics, in this colony. We are enabled, however, from the accurate reports made by some of the dissenting churches, to record their present condition and numerical force. The Wesleyan Methodists and Episcopal Methodists, though not very numerous, have a respectable and efficient corps clerical and about 8,000 communicants, and the Universalists have two societies and two meeting-houses. The Congregationalists and Presbyterians have also several churches and missionary stations, and the Baptists have 92 churches, 59 ordained ministers, and 9,283 church members. Sunday-schools are attached to every society, and home-meetings, especially in remote places, are common throughout the country, evidencing a popular regard for Christian solemnities. The Church of England and the German Lutherans form a vast majority.

The population of New-Brunswick consists of a mixed race of English, Irish, Germans and Welsh, and a few Scotch and Americans. The French have also some small settlements on the east coast. The aboriginal inhabitants are few in number and live in scattered villages, in different parts, and are chiefly of the Roman Catholic religion, having been converted by the first settlers.

The country, now called New-Brunswick, was, in the early part of last century, comprised by the French within the districts of New-France, and viewed as an appendage to Acadia. During the war, the French were expelled from the country, and at the peace of 1763 it was ceded to Great Britain and constituted a part of Nova Scotia, until 1785, when it made a separate province. The country, however, was little more than a wilderness, until General Sir Guy Carleton procured for it a royal charter, and was himself appointed the governor. To his exertions it owes its rapid rise to prosperity, but it also owes many material improvements in its roads, schools, agriculture, judicial arrangements, &c., to Sir H. Douglas, governor, from 1824 to 1831. Many of the Hessians, after the war of the revolution, settled in this province on lands granted by the government.

NOVA SCOTIA AND CAPE BRETON.

The Peninsula of Nova Scotia and the Island of Cape Breton, together forming one of the provinces of British North America, are separated from each other only by the Gut of Canscaw, a narrow strait through which the waters of the Gulf of St. Lawrence partly escapes. Their relative position and similar geological features, render it probable that at some previous period they have been united, and have since been dissevered by the action of the waters of that mighty stream. It lies between 43° and 46° north latitude, and 61° and 67° west longitude, and is bounded on the north by part of the Gulf of St. Lawrence, which separates it from Prince Edward's Island; on the north-east by the Gut of Canscaw; on the west by the Bay of Fundy, which separates it from New-Brunswick, and on the south and south-east by the Atlantic Ocean. It measures about 100 miles in length, but is of unequal breadth; altogether it contains 15,617 square miles, or 7,496,160 acres. One-third of its superfices is occupied by lakes of various shapes and sizes, spread in every direction over the face of the peninsula. There is no part of the land thirty miles distant from navigable water, and in all parts there are fine streams and rivers. The southern margin of Nova Scotia is broken and rugged, with very prominent features, deep inlets and craggy islands. The features of the northern coast are soft and free from rocks. The peninsula has no elevations deserving the name of mountains; its highest point, Mount Ardoise, between Windsor and Halifax, not rising more than 700 feet above the sea. A pretty high ridge of hills skirts the shore of the Bay of Fundy.

The chief promontories are Capes George and Canscaw on the north-east side, and at the southern extremity is Cape Sable. The basin of Minas is a deep inlet on the north-west side, forming a part of the Bay of Fundy, which separates Nova Scotia from New-Brunswick. St. Mary's and Argyle bays are on the south-west side; Pictou, Antigonische and Chedebucto bays, form the chief irregularities on the northern coast; and the eastern coast, from Cape Canscaw to Cape Sable, is indented with almost innumerable small bays, harbors, and rivers. The rocks and islands which fringe the Atlantic coast are exceedingly picturesque. Deep water is found, almost without exception, close to their shores.

As regards geological constitution, the greater part of Nova Scotia may be described as a low range, running from south-west to north-east, resting on solid rocks of granite, trap and slate, alternately. Towards the east end are beds of sandstone, grauwacké, gypsum, limestone, porphyry, and many other kinds of rock; and on these strata there is usually a deep, rich soil. The barren tracts are chiefly of sand and clay; and in these parts, especially about Pictou, are the great coal-fields of Nova Scotia. Iron is abundant in the coal strata, and different varieties of lead and copper ore, though in smaller quantities. Near Pictou are several brine springs, one of which is saturated with salt, in the proportion of 12 to 88.

The climate of Nova Scotia, like that of the adjoining districts, is salubrious and pleasant; but is in a peculiar degree exposed to the extreme of summer heat and winter cold. The ground is generally covered with snow from the middle of December till the middle of March, in which respect it nearly resembles Upper Canada; and during this period the farmers draw upon sledges their wood and poles from the forest, and draw their produce to market. It is difficult to say when spring commences, as it is rather late and irregular in its approaches. When vegetation does begin, it is very rapid, and two or three days make a perceptible change in the amount of the foliage. The summer may be said to be short and powerful, and during the time it lasts, it exerts a much greater influence on vegetation than is observable in Britain. During this period the inhabitants go very lightly dressed. Altogether, the climate of Nova Scotia is as good as that of Scotland, if not superior; nor are there any of those local or epidemical disorders with which other countries are frequently afflicted. Although the winters are intensely cold, they are not so disagreeable as the raw, changeable winters of Britain, nor nearly so fatal to human life. Besides, if the settlers work during three-quarters of a year, they have ample provision for the remaining quarter, and are enabled to look forward to winter as their season of holiday enjoyment and relaxation. We have been informed by a Nova Scotian, that the improvement of the country is greatly retarded by the inactive habits of the settlers. The employment most popular is fishing, and agriculture remains so backward, that large importations of flour from the United States are constantly required, the payment of which drains the country of specie. The farmers, it seems, are in the habit of ceasing to exert themselves after attaining a moderate means of subsistence, and their sons spend the time in riding and other frivolous pursuits, which should be devoted to the improvement of the paternal acres. These half-idle habits, and also an indulgence in spirituous liquors, are described as the true cause of the backward state of the colony, as respects its territorial improvement.

Few parts of the world are so well-watered as Nova Scotia. The rivers, brooks, springs, and streams of different kinds, are very numerous. Some of the lakes are extremely beautiful, containing in general one or more small islands, which are covered with a luxuriant growth of wood, and vary in every imaginable shape. The land in the neighborhood of them is often undulated in the most romantic manner. These lakes will in time be of great service to the province. In several instances they nearly intersect the peninsula, offering scope for inland navigation.

The fruits produced in the country are numerous. Besides a great variety of wild fruits, gooseberries, strawberries, cherries, and raspberries, there are pears of various kinds, and all the varieties of English plums, apples of a very superior quality, and some other fruits. The other vegetable products are cucumbers, potatoes, artichokes, cauliflowers, cabbages, beans, and peas. Hops are an invariable and sure crop, and may be raised in great abundance. Pumpkins and Indian corn are cultivated to a great extent. Carrots, onions, parsnips, beets, celery, and most other kitchen herbs, are produced with ease. The grains cultivated by the farmers are summer and winter wheat, rye, buckwheat, barley, and oats. The natural forests are elm, cherry, white, black, yellow and gray birch, red oak, beech, white and yellow pine, white, red and black spruce, maples, &c.

The forests of Nova Scotia abound in good timber: pine and birch, oak, beech, ash and maple, are the most common trees; and many of the inhabitants have, for years, been supported by the timber trade. The principal wild animals in the province are the moose deer, carribboo, bear, loup-cervier, fox, martin, otter, mink, and squirrel. Hunting and trapping were once extensively pursued; but the decrease of animals has obliterated these employments from the industrial means of Nova Scotia. The fisheries employ many families, but the chief and most profitable pursuit is mining, the value of coal alone amounts annually to near $800,000.

Gypsum, which abounds in the western districts, is highly-prized in the United States as a manure; and a stone, which is extremely well-adapted for grind-stones, and is celebrated all over America under the appellation of "Nova Scotia blue-grits," is found in many parts. The exports of these articles alone have been estimated at the value of $100,000.

The manufactures are unimportant, and as a general thing come under the denomination of "*home-spun.*" Grist and saw-mills are numerous; besides which, there are several breweries and tan-yards.

The geographical position of Nova Scotia gives it great commercial advantages, and its trade, especially with the United States, has been for some years steadily on the increase. The exports, chiefly to Canada, Great Britain and the United States, consist of fish-oil, timber, coals, &c. The trade principally centres in Halifax.

The means of internal communication are on a respectable footing, and improvements in this respect are being rapidly made. Water communication is also on a good scale, the natural facilities being augmented by canals in one or two locations. They are fairly supported by the legislature, and the inhabitants of each district are compelled to furnish, either personally or by substitute, a certain quantity of labor for the same purpose.

The Lieutenant-Governor of Nova Scotia, who is subordinate to the Governor-General of British North America, is supreme military and civil magistrate within the province. The Council, appointed by the crown, consists of 12 members, of whom the Bishop and Chief-Justice, *ex-officio*, form a part. The Legislative Assembly is a body of 41 members, elected by the freeholders. These assemblies are constituted on the same basis as the Imperial Parliament, but all their acts require the approval of the local executive and of the British sovereign, before they can become valid in law. Each county returns two members to the legislature, the remainder are deputed by the towns. The common law of England prevails in Nova Scotia, so far as it does not conflict with local enactments.

The state religion is the Protestant Episcopal, but other sects have numerous congregations. The Established Church is supported by the crown. Nova Scotia was created a Bishopric in 1787. Presbyterians are the most numerous sect of dissenters from the national establishment. The province can boast of numerous schools, academies, and a Royal college at Windsor; the Nova Scotians are generally better educated than the Canadian population.

The colony is divided into 10 counties, of which Cape Breton is one. There are 52 parishes. The chief towns are Halifax, Truro, Londonderry, Onslow, &c. The capital, Halifax, is pleasantly situated on the slope of a rising ground, facing a fine spacious bay or natural harbor in front, on the eastern or more accessible side of the peninsula. It contains about 25,000 inhabitants, and is a central point for the foreign commerce and fishing-trade of the colony. Although possessing considerable wealth and trade, and the seat of an intelligent population, it is behind English towns of the same size and of inferior capabilities. Here, as elsewhere in the colonies, dependence on the arrangements of the home government deadens public spirit, and retards that natural tendency to advance which is so observable in the towns of the United States. Halifax is the British North American Station for the Cunard Line of Steamships which sail between Liverpool and Boston, and New-York, and the central depot for the British naval forces.

Of the population of the province, which amounts to 310,000, the aboriginal inhabitants do not exceed 600, and there are about 6,000 Acadians (or descendants of the original French settlers,) and about 2,000 negroes. The remainder consists of Germans or their descendants, British emigrants, chiefly from the north of England and Scotland, a few Irish, and the descendants of refugee loyalists from the United States. The Acadians congregate in settlements of their own, mixing little with the other classes of the inhabitants.

Cape Breton is a romantic and mountainous island, lying close to Nova Scotia on the east, and only divided from it by a narrow strait, called the Gut of Canscow. On the western side is the Gulf of St. Lawrence. The island measures upwards of a hundred miles in length by about sixty in extreme breadth, including the numerous bays which indent the land. The natural productions of this island resemble those of Nova Scotia; wheat, indeed, is less generally grown, but oats and potatoes are raised to a considerable extent. There are large tracts of good land in the lower parts, and the expense of clearing it of timber is estimated at £3 an acre. The minerals of the island are valuable. Cape Breton is politically annexed to Nova Scotia, of which it forms a county. Area, 3,129 square miles.;

Nova Scotia was discovered by Cabot, or more properly Gaboti, in 1497, and was first settled by the French, who called it Acadia. It subsequently fell under the English, having been, in 1627, granted by James I. to Sir W. Alexander, and named Nova Scotia. In 1632 it was restored to France by the treaty of St. Germain ; but it several times subsequently changed hands, and was not finally established in the quiet possession of the British until 1758. At the peace of 1758, the boundaries of this colony were so defined as to include New-Brunswick and Cape Breton ; but in 1784 the former was made a separate government, so far as local affairs were concerned, being under the superintendence of the Governor-General as well as the other colonies.

PRINCE EDWARD'S ISLAND.

This rich and productive island is situated in the Gulf of St. Lawrence, between Cape Breton on the east and New-Brunswick on the west, and is separated from Nova Scotia on the south by a strait of about nine miles in breadth. It measures 140 miles in length, and is 34 at its greatest breadth. The general appearance of this island from the sea is level, but, on landing, the scenery is varied with gentle undulations. It abounds with streams and lakes, and in many places it is indented with bays, no part being more than eight miles from the sea. The soil is in general fertile, yielding good crops of wheat and other grains ; and parsnips, turnips, carrots, potatoes, and almost all the common culinary vegetables, succeed well. The climate of Prince Edward's Island is in some respects similar to that of the neighboring countries. The winter is said to be shorter than in Lower Canada, and the atmosphere is noted for being free of fogs. Agricultural operations commence about the beginning of May, and the harvest is generally over by the end of October. The chief disadvantage this colony labors under, and which is equally applicable to the others near it, is the great length of the winter, which obliges the farmer to lay up a very large supply of hay for supporting his live-stock.

The capital of the island is Charlottetown, on the Hillsborough River, which contains about 4,000 inhabitants. The other principal towns are Gagetown, Belfast, Dartmouth, &c. The population consists chiefly of English settlers, with some few Acadians, and numbers at the present time 50,000. The chief exports are timber, deals, fish, &c., which are principally carried to England and the United States. The government and ecclesiastical affairs are similar to those of the other Anglo-American colonies

This island was taken from the French in 1756, and annexed with Cape Breton to the government of Nova Scotia in 1763, but since 1768 has formed a separate colony.

NEWFOUNDLAND.

This large and valuable island, forming another of the British North American Colonies, lies at the entrance of the Gulf of St. Lawrence and off the east coast of Labrador, from which it is separated by the narrow strait of Belle-Isle, between 46° 30′ and 51° 40′ north latitude, and the meridians of 52° 15′ and 59° 10′ west longitude. Its greatest length from north to south is 350 miles, and its average breadth 130 miles; superficial area 35,913. The fixed population is about 100,000, exclusive of those who visit the different stations during the fishing season.

The island may be described as being of a triangular shape, but is much indented by broad and deep bays, harbors, coves, rivers, and lagoons, which, besides numerous capes and projecting headlands, form two peninsulas,—on one of which called Avalon, at the south-east corner, is the town and harbor of Avalon.

Its aspect from the sea is far from prepossessing, and its surface rugged and wild in the extreme. The interior, which, until within the last twenty-five years, was generally unknown, is much broken by water; and the lakes, marshes, and scrubby trees form its essential characteristics. The only large navigable streams are the Humber and River of Exploits. Its prevalent geological constitution is of granite, on which is superimposed, in some parts, porphyry, quartz, gneiss, mica, and clay-slate, with secondary formations; coal and iron also occur in some places.

The eastern half of the interior is generally a low, picturesque country, traversed by hills and lakes, the whole being diversified by trees of humble growth. The country westward is more rugged and mountainous, with little wood, except near the shore. The mountains are not generally in ridges, but have each apparently its separate base. The highest part of the island is its northern peninsula, lying along the straits of Belle-Isle; near its centre are flats of considerable extent; swampy, unhealthy, and usually covered with peat or strong wiry grasses.

The forests abound in spruce, birch, and larch. Pine seldom occurs, and never grows to any considerable size; indeed, there is little wood of any value, except for fuel and the building of small boats. Whortleberry bushes and *wisha capuca* (Indian tea) are the principal plants on the high wooded grounds.

The best and most fertile soil is along the rivers, and at the heads of the bays fringing the island; but both the soil and the climate generally are unfavorable for raising grain, though well adapted for pasturage, and the cultivation of potatoes and other green crops and roots.

The animals peculiar to the other northern parts of the continent are common to this island. Vast herds of carriboo deer graze on the plains and woods of the interior, and their flesh constitutes nearly the sole diet of the Micmac Indians. Beavers are scarcer than formerly; but foxes are still numerous along the rivers and sea-coast. Among the other wild animals are wolves and bears. Seals abound along the northern shores. The insect tribes are well represented on the swampy places, especially during the hot months, and sometimes prove very troublesome.

The best known and most celebrated among the animals of this island, however, are its fine breed of dogs, famed for docility, intelligence, obedience, and attachment to their masters. They are remarkably voracious, and are usually fed on salted fish; but, like the aborigines of the country, they endure hunger for a lengthened period. The true breed has become very scarce, and the breed known as the "Newfoundland dog" in the United States, though equally as sagacious, hardy, and fond of water, is a cross with the mastiff, or some other specie. The true breed is web-footed, but the cross may be generally recognized, by a practised eye, in the countenance of the animal. From their peculiarities they are well adapted to their native land—a land of waters, where their webbed feet assist them in swimming—a land dreary and cold, where their thick shaggy coats protect them from the inclemencies of a long winter.

Newfoundland has long been celebrated for its fisheries, on which, indeed, the inhabitants principally depend. The Great Bank on the east side of the island is, in some places, 200 miles in breadth and 600 in length, the soundings being from 25 to 95 fathoms. There is also an Outer Bank lying between latitude 44° 10′ and 47° 30′ north, and longitude 44° 15′ and 45° 25′ west, and a continuation of banks extends southward to Nova Scotia. Fogs prevail almost without interruption on these shoals, occasioned by the meeting of the waters of the Gulf Stream from the tropics with those driven by the winds from the polar regions. A counter current from the north sweeps also along the shore of Labrador, bringing with it large icebergs, and rendering navigation dangerous, especially during foggy weather. The best fishing grounds on the Great Bank are between the 42d and 46th parallels. The cod fisheries, which commenced soon after the discovery of America, attained so high an importance during the last war with the French, that the exports of cod and cod oil, in 1814, amounted to no less than £2,604,000 sterling, or $12,500,000; but the English fisheries have since rapidly declined, and, at the present time, are not valued at more than one-fifth of that sum. In 1849, there were 6,159 boats employed in this branch of industry.

The seal fishery is conducted in boats varying from 80 to 120 tons, with crews of from 20 to 30 men. The season commences early in April; it is principally carried on close to the shore of Labrador, and has, of late years, attained considerable importance. There is also a small whale fishery conducted in boats on the south side of the island, and the salmon fisheries are said to be profitable and pretty extensive. The total value of all the fisheries in 1849 was $4,196,300.

The commercial standing of Newfoundland is secondary to that of the other British North American Colonies, but still is not despicable. Its exports average in value about $5,000,000, and consists chiefly, if not altogether, of the products of its fisheries. The principal imports are British manufactured goods, colonial produce, corn, ship-biscuit, and a variety of other articles for the consumption of the inhabitants. The trade between the island and the United States has considerably increased of late, and will no doubt eventually lead to beneficial results. One-half the shipping employed belongs to the resident colonists.

The government of Newfoundland was for a long time administered by naval commanders, who were appointed to cruize on the fishing stations, and who returned home in the winter. Within the last century, however, it was deemed necessary to have a resident governor. In 1812, in consequence of a petition from the inhabitants, a representative government was established, the elections being by almost universal suffrage. The assembly comprises 15 members, and has attached to it a legislative and executive council. The laws are generally based on the common law of England, and are administered by circuit courts; but the police is inefficient in the extreme, though greatly improved of later years. Besides the standing army, which is paid by the imperial government, there is a militia, in which all able bodied men are obliged to serve, and the other protective means are ample. An education act was passed in 1836, which has been the means of bringing within the reach of all the benefits of elementary instruction;

the population, nevertheless, is, as a general thing, extremely unlettered and ignorant.

There is no church establishment, all sects having equal privileges; but a titular Roman Catholic bishop, as well as a Protestant prelate, lately appointed, reside at St. John's. The Roman Catholics are the prevailing body; but Episcopalians, Presbyterians and Wesleyans are numerous.

The people of Newfoundland are honest and industrious, but much addicted to drunkenness, and are superstitious to a degree almost beyond belief. Crimes of any magnitude are of rare occurrence. The people, chiefly consisting of Irish, Scotch, and emigrants from Guernsey and Jersey, or their descendants, (the Indian aborigines having been long all but extinct,) are employed either wholly or occasionally in the fisheries. The breed of cattle and sheep, and the cultivation of small patches of land, are likewise partial sources of occupation. The women, besides assisting the men in catching and curing the fish, are engaged either in rural occupations or in spinning and knitting worsted stockings, mittens and socks. In winter, much time is consumed in bringing home fuel, building boats, and making or repairing fishing implements. The morals of the people are at a low ebb, and among the Irish, the rude celebrations of that people are consummated amid riotous mirth and too often horrid debauchery; but, as before observed, capital offences are seldom committed. The houses and food of the common people are alike filthy, and to the stranger almost as repulsive as those of the savages of Labrador.

Newfoundland was probably discovered by the Norwegians, in the 11th century, but if so, it was subsequently forgotten, till Cabot visited it in the summer of 1497, and named it "Prima Vista," from its having been the first land discovered by that celebrated navigator. As early as 1500, an extensive fishery was carried on by the Portuguese and French, on the neighboring banks; but though Sir Walter Raleigh and others attempted to form a colony here, no successful settlement was made until Sir G. Calvert, afterwards Lord Baltimore, in 1623, established himself in the south-east part of the island, called Avalon, and appointed his son governor. Ten years after, a colony was sent over from Ireland, and in 1654, a few English settlers came over. The French, early in the 17th century, had formed a station at Placentia, and were a constant source of annoyance to the English. At the peace of Utrecht the island was finally conceded to the English, but the fishery rights were still a *quæstio vexata* between the two nations.

With regard to the fishery in general, it was chiefly carried on during the first half of the last century by the English, Anglo-Americans and the French; but the capture of Cape Breton, and other possessions in America, gave a very severe blow to the fisheries of the latter. The American war divided the British fishery: that portion which had previously been carried on by the people of New-England, being thenceafter merged into that of the United States, but still the English contrived to preserve to themselves the largest share. During the French war, the French were entirely excluded from the fisheries, in consequence of which the English profited by a monopoly of the business: but since the peace, at the consummation of which, the islands of St. Pierre and Miquelon were ceded to the French, it has been carried on chiefly by the French and Americans, that of the English having materially declined since that period.

THE BERMUDEZ, OR SOMERS' ISLANDS.

The number of islands and cayos, composing the Bermudez group, is said to be more than 360 in all. When viewed from the ocean, they present a very picturesque appearance. Their elevation is trifling, the highest land scarcely attaining to the height of 500 feet above the level. In aspect they are similar to the West Indian groups, except that they remind the voyager, from their proximity and the sea flowing between them, of the lake scenery of North America and European climates.

They are geographically situated, centrally, in latitude 32° 20′ north, and longitude 64° 50′ west; 600 miles east from the coast of South Carolina. They are estimated to contain 47 square miles, and a population, equally of blacks and Europeans, of about 12 or 14,000.

St. George's and St. David's, with other islands of minor importance, form several bays; and the harbor of St. George's is large enough to contain the whole British navy, but is difficult of ingress and egress, in consequence of the smallness of its entrance. The principal island or main land as it is called, is about 20 miles in length, but it rarely exceeds one and a half in width. In the centre of the island, and on the north side of a beautiful bay, is the town of Hamilton, now the seat of government. The only places fortified are Ireland and St. George's Islands, where forts have been lately built, which render the islands almost impregnable. At the former of these is the naval dock-yard, off which there is good anchorage and moorings laid down for 15 or 20 ships of war, though the breakwater is extensive enough to contain a large fleet of the line. There are two other moorings for the navy, viz.: Murray's anchorage, near the ferry, and Five Fathom's Hole, off the mouth of St. George's harbor. With the exception of two or three small detachments, the chief military force is stationed at St. George's.

The legislature of the Bermudez consists of a council of eight members and an assembly of thirty-six members, each parish electing four of the latter. The executive is vested in a governor, who, with the council, is appointed by the crown. The parliaments are septennial, but are always newly elected on the accession of a new sovereign. The church establishment is under the surveillance of the Bishop of Nova Scotia. Churches and sunday-schools are well endowed, and the attendance of the congregations and scholars respectable. The school system, adopted by late enactments, is expected to work beneficially on the educational interests of the people, but at present few of the inhabitants can read or write, and a general ignorance and superstition prevail. The condition of the people has been much improved, however, by the establishment of friendly societies, which have greatly sustained the welfare of the blacks since their emancipation.

The principal exports from the Bermudez' (the produce and manufactures of the islands) are arrowroot, potatoes, onions, and palmetto and straw hats, in producing which the people excel. They possess some 100 vessels of from 120 to 150 tons, which are chiefly employed in the trade between the northern colonies and the West Indies. The whale fishery off the islands employs some of the people, and might be profitably carried on by suitable capital: at present it yields little more than 1,000 or 1,200 barrels of oil a year. The waters about the islands and reefs abound in a great variety of fish, but none are cured for exportation. Cattle and sheep are plentiful, and large quantities of poultry are fed for supplying the shipping that call at these islands. All the ordinary products of tropical climates, both animal and vegetable, are produced in abundance: the fruits are various and excellent. The arrowroot of Bermudez has a world-wide celebrity, and is fully equal to that brought from the East Indies.

We have no late returns of the commerce of these islands, but in 1837 the total value of imports amounted to £79,811, and of exports £25,275. Ships *inward*, 122, tons 11,651; *outward*, 126, tons 11,001. The revenue for the same year was £17,273, and the expenditures £19,374. The mails for England and the United States are received via Halifax and New-York monthly, by the Royal West India Mail Steamships.

The climate of the Bermuda's is delightful during the summer, neither suffering from the rigors of the north nor the fervid heat of more tropical regions. Nor in the winter is much cold experienced; but the north-west snows which rage in those latitudes in that season are awful, and lay waste the farms, and strew the shores with wrecks. The soil is deep, and much fertilized by the near proximity of the ocean and heavy dews, never suffering from drought, so common in the West Indies.

The legislatures of these islands and Antigua, were the only colonial legislative bodies that abolished slavery without the intervention of apprenticeships. The proportion of the £20,000,000 voted by parliament for compensation was £50,584 for 4,203 slaves, valued at £27 4s. 11d. each.

HONDURAS.

This settlement, on the east coast of Central America, lies between the parallels of 17° and 18° north latitude, and the meridians of 88° and 90° west longitude; and is bounded north by Yucatan; west by Vera Paz, a portion of the territory of Guatemala; south by Guatemala, and east by the Bay of Honduras. The area is 62,740 square miles, but the population is very sparse, and numbers only about 4,000, of which about 300 are Europeans.

The coast is a low flat, and surrounded by an abundance of reefs and verdant islands, called *cayos or keys*. The approach to the shore is very dangerous, especially during north winds, and the different *cayos* resemble each other so much, as to make the navigation of the channels between them extremely difficult except to experienced pilots. Proceeding inland, the surface rises gradually into an elevated region, covered with primeval forests. The rivers are numerous, and some of them large; the principal, the Balize, is navigable 200 miles.

The climate is hot and humid, but is reported to be more healthy than the lowlands of Mexico. The heat, however, is much moderated by sea breezes, which blow at regular intervals, and has an average temperature of 80°. The rains are so heavy that the Sibun River sometimes rises 50 feet in a few hours, and are frequently accompanied by violent thunder-storms.

Volcanic products and marble, and other limestone formations, are found in various parts. The shores and banks of the rivers are covered with a deep and rich alluvial soil. The forests abound with the finest timbers, mahogany, logwood, &c., which are the staple products of the colony, and their cutting the chief employment of the settlers. Every settlement at Honduras has a plantain walk. Cassava, yams, arrowroot, maize, &c., are grown, but only for home comsumption; the sugar-cane, coffee and cotton succeed well, but are little cultivated; cocoa, and an inferior kind of indigo, are indigenous.

The animal kingdom is composed of a large catalogue. European cattle, and other domestic animals, thrive exceedingly well. The American tiger, the tapir, armadillo, raccoons, grey fox, deer of various kinds, and a vast number of monkies, inhabit the country; birds and fish are in great variety, and testacea particularly plentiful. Many turtles are taken by the inhabitants upon the keys and islands of the coast, and some of those animals, so interesting to aldermen and civic bodies generally, are exported to England and the United States of America.

There are about 20,000 tons of shipping employed in the Honduras trade. The chief exports are mahogany, logwood, cochineal, hides, cocoa-nuts, cedar, &c., which are exchanged for British manufactures, and other European and colonial produce.

Honduras is governed by a superintendent, nominated by the crown, and seven magistrates, elected annually by the people. Trial by jury is in force, and the common laws of England generally; from the decisions of the courts, appeal lies to the superintendent and sovereign in council.

The amount of compensation received by the proprietors of slaves, at their emancipation, was £101,959; the average value of a slave being £120 4s. 7d., a larger sum than in any other colony.

Balize is the only town in the settlement, and is situated at the mouth of the river of the same name, in latitude 17° 29′ north, and 88° 8′ west longitude. It consists of about 500 houses, chiefly of wood; the streets are regular, and the whole town shaded by cocoa-nut and tamarind trees. Its chief edifices are the government house, a church, and several chapels; it has a public and several private schools.

The coast of Honduras was discovered by Columbus in 1502, but the date of its first settlement is uncertain. It was transferred by Spain to England by treaty in 1670, but its occupation was long contested by the Spaniards, who committed great havoc among the logwood cutters until the year 1798, since which time the sovereignty of the country has remained quietly in the hands of the British.

The government of Guatemala, in 1834, gave a charter to an English company, called "*The Eastern Coast of Central America Commercial and Agricultural Company*," for the whole of the department of Vera Paz, lying directly west of the Balize; and, subsequently, a further grant of the district of Santo Thomas, on the Bay of Honduras. This company is said to have established settlements, and made many improvements upon their grants; but it does not appear that any transfer of political authority accompanied these patents.

Further south and east of the British Possessions, in Central America, is a Kingdom of Native Indians, under the protection of the British crown, and which, from its proximity and the political connection it maintains with Great Britain, claims a next place to the colonies of that country

---

THE KINGDOM OF MOSQUITIA,

To which the above note alludes, has its existence only from the weakness of the surrounding nations, and is properly, as it was under the authority of Spain, a portion of the states of Honduras and Nicaragua. Its present position and the claims, which the government of Great Britain, in its behalf, have put forth, have concentrated the eyes of the whole world on the concerns of this *soi disant* kingdom, and rendered all intelligence, in reference to it, interesting and important. Little, however, is known respecting it, and until lately few persons were acquainted with its existence. The statements published by interested parties, every now and then, are not wholly reliable, and must be read with caution.

The country of Mosquitia forms the north-eastern projection of Central America, which lies between 11° and 16° north latitude and 83° and 86° west longitude, and extends itself from the mouth of the Roman River (exactly 15° 5′ 5″ north latitude and 85° 40′ west longitude, 19 miles eastward of Cape Honduras) along the Caribbean Sea to Punta Gorda, (exactly 11° 47′ west longitude.)

The King of Mosquitia lays claim, besides these, to the territory between Punta Gorda and Chiriqui Lagoon, and also to the Corn Islands.

The Mosquitian territory is divided from the Central American Republics by a chain of mountains, which extends from the confines of Veragua, almost in the centre of the isthmus, north-westwardly to the vicinity of Lake Nicaragua, then northerly from the Great Falls of Saint Quan to the springs of the Blewfields River, and from these north-westwardly to the neighborhood of Comalapa and Matagalpa, towns belonging to the State of Nicaragua, passing these to the Segovia River, and from this point north-westerly to the Guayapa River, from which latter point the boundary runs towards Honduras, in a direction from north-east, to the embrochurés of the Roman River.

Those territories which lie between the Punta Gorda and the Chiriqui Lagoon, and also the Corn Islands, have been hitherto contested by the States of Costa Rica and Nicaragua and the King of Mosquitia. The settling of these differences and the arrangement of the claims of the Mosquitian king, had, by the mediation of England, been attempted in 1841, for which purpose the late deceased king, ***Robert Charles Frederick,*** (!!!) accompanied by the then governor of Balize, Col. McDonald, went into the contested country, on board the English frigate the Tweed, where the negotiations were carried on with Don Quijano, the then commander of Quan Del Norte. It appears, however, that no determination was had, and the affair was transferred to the charge of the late Patrick Walker, appointed in May, 1842, British Consul-general and Political Agent, and accredited as such in the Kingdom of Mosquitia.

Setting aside these contested parts, if we take the southern boundary at Punta Gorda, the Mosquitian Territory contains a surface of 26,000 square miles; but if the contested parts are included, the superficial contents would amount to about 34,000 square miles.

It would be tiresome to wade through the labyrinth of diplomacy which has entangled the history of this territory. As a last resort, the British have determined on supporting the claims of this kingdom against the neighboring republics, and have already taken possession of the Port of San Juan de Nicaragua and secured its cession to his Mosquitian majesty. How this matter will end it is impossible to say; but it is probable that if no other nations interfere in behalf of the co-cláimants, the Kingdom of Mosquitia will be consolidated within the utmost limits claimed.

The ultimate object of the British, it is reasonable to suppose, is to secure the exclusive use of the Rio San Juan and Lake of Nicaragua, in order to communicate there-through with the Pacific Ocean, and eventually form a junction between the Atlantic and Pacific, by cutting a ship-canal through the narrow strip of land between the lake and the ocean. This has long been projected, and would be the cheapest means of effecting an object so desirable to the commercial world. The means taken to effect this are exceptionable, and will be condemned by persons of all parties as an act unworthy the magnanimity of the British nation.

The country is one of the richest in tropical America. It produces all the staples of the West Indies, and large quantities of mahogany, logwood and other cabinet materials, besides cochineal, dye-woods and medicinal drugs in abundance. The climate, however, is unhealthy, and unfit for the residence of Europeans.

CANALS IN THE CANADAS.

Names.	From	To	Length in Miles.	Cost.
*Rideau	By-Town	Kingston	135	$5,600,000
†Welland	St. Catharine's	Port Colborne	42	2,500,000
‡Lachine	Lachine	Montreal	8	625,000
Greenville	‖Overcoming Long Sault Rapids		—	——
Chambly	Chambly	St. John's	9	——
Cornwall	Cornwall	Dickinson's Landing	12	——
Beauharnois	Beauharnois	Coteau du Lac	16	——

* Connects the Ottawa and St. Lawrence Rivers. † Connects Lakes Ontario and Erie. ‡ Overcomes Sault St. Louis. ‖ 20 miles from the mouth of the Ottawa.

RAILROADS IN THE BRITISH POSSESSIONS.

There are as yet but few railroads in the British possessions: those in a finished state and in working order, are the "Niagara and Queenston," 7 miles long; the "Lachine and Montreal," 9 miles long, connecting the two places, and the "Champlain and St. Lawrence," 15 miles, from La Prairie to St. John's; from which place it will be continued to the New-York State line. There are, however, several extensive lines, either progressing to completion, or projected and definitively settled upon; some intended to connect with lines from the United States, and others with those of the interior. The principal of these are:

1. The "St. Andrew's, Woodstock and Quebec Railroad."
2. A line of railroad from Halifax, through Nova Scotia and New-Brunswick, to unite with the above at Great Falls, on the St. John's River.
3. The "St. Lawrence and Atlantic Railroad," now constructing, and which will join the Atlantic and St. Lawrence Railroad on the province line. By these, the connection between Montreal and Portland will be completed. There are also several lines in New-Hampshire and Vermont, which will ultimately be extended to Montreal.
4. A line from Quebec, via Toronto, to Hamilton, to connect with the "Great Western Railway" at that place.
5. The "Great Western Railway," which will extend from Hamilton to a terminus opposite Detroit, Michigan.
6. A line from London to Goderich.
7. A line in a south-western direction from Quebec, to connect with the "St. Lawrence and Atlantic" line, which will thus connect Quebec with Portland and the whole system of New-England lines.

There are other important lines projected, but the uncertainty of some and the non-plausibility of others, renders it unnecessary to enlarge upon our catalogue.

COMMERCIAL STATISTICS OF BRITISH COLONIES.

STATEMENT OF THE COMMERCE BETWEEN THE UNITED KINGDOM OF GREAT BRITAIN AND IRELAND AND THE BRITISH NORTH AMERICAN COLONIES FOR EACH OF THE PAST SEVEN YEARS, ENDING 5TH JANUARY, 1847.

(From Parliamentary Returns.)

I.—*An account of the declared value of the various articles of British Produce and Manufactures exported from Great Britain and Ireland to the British North American Colonies, (exclusive of Honduras.)*

Years.	Apothecary Wares.	Apparel, Slops and Haberdash'y	Arms and Ammunition	Bacon and Hams.	Beef and Pork.	Beer and Ale.	Books, Printed.	Brass and Copper Manufactures.	Butter and Cheese.
	£	£	£	£	£	£	£	£	£
1840...	9,742	250,151	12,871	3,796	4,060	10,510	15 628	30,897	2,755
1841...	10,343	293,975	12,586	301	347	8,972	16,947	29,997	2,440
1842...	11,069	282,551	9,619	62	490	7,298	17,406	8,266	4,558
1843...	13,979	201,106	11.760	100	1,282	7,180	14,332	14,127	2,032
1844...	14,638	321,908	15,365	189	456	8,415	18,097	15,723	4,169
1845...	16,629	388,269	18,339	443	690	7,912	19,843	23.744	1,670
1846...	16,332	390.022	14,163	198	1,515	7,238	19.738	25,565	2,024

Years.	Hats of all sorts.	Iron & Steel, wrought & unwrought.	Lead and Shot.	Leather, wrought & unwrought.	Leather, Saddlery & Harness.	Linen Manufactures, including Linen Yarn.	Painters' Colours.	Plate, Plated Ware, Jewellery, & Watches.	Salt.
	£	£	£	£	£	£	£	£	£
1840...	30,354	248,800	10,494	71,214	5,986	164,487	28,402	13,456	22,062
1841...	27,727	253,640	10,824	79,888	6,676	147,800	25,461	15,823	16,922
1842...	26.928	145,744	7,924	59,918	4,024	108,599	21,465	15,824	17,887
1843...	20,171	133,837	6,057	54,752	2,705	80,029	22,707	9,193	21,276
1844...	26,899	236,958	14,778	75,295	3,404	135,664	33,017	14,849	25,460
1845...	40,725	309,120	12,220	79,328	4,004	153,371	35,450	16,897	18,619
1846...	40,031	275,589	9,196	75,911	3,911	142,570	30,765	19,210	21,626

Years.	Cabinet and Upholstery Wares.	Coals, Cinders, and Culm.	Cordage.	Cotton Manufactures, including Cotton Yarn	Earthenware of all kinds.	Fishing Tackle of all sorts.	Glass.	Hardware and Cutlery.
	£	£	£	£	£	£	£	£
1840.....	5,901	21,186	103,250	611,303	44,875	37,270	42,506	131,326
1841.....	5,539	23,858	78,274	629,811	41,682	34,570	52,520	155,750
1842.....	4,976	21,740	34,758	500,391	35,152	28,762	43,259	128,181
1843.....	4,271	28,324	44,054	334,580	32,215	24,986	37,339	102,260
1844.....	4,222	24,489	62,982	702,229	50,924	34,631	58,690	167,876
1845.....	5,709	33,316	83,051	742,225	61,756	43,454	51,350	200,476
1846.....	6,034	49,520	74,933	641,455	63,085	41,950	31,868	193,880

Years.	Silk Manufactures.	Soap and Candles.	Stationery.	Sugar, Refined.	Tin & Pewt'r Wares; Tin unwrought, & Tin Plates	Umbrellas and Parasols.	Woollen Manufactures, including Yarn.	Other Articles.
	£	£	£	£	£	£	£	£
1840.....	125,880	67,991	46,001	56,248	21,106	4,374	449,111	139,092
1841.....	93,162	64,843	46,624	87,721	22,845	6,625	517,555	118,998
1842.....	74,674	56,736	44,750	55,169	13,873	4,801	426,847	104,950
1843.....	36,401	47,397	30,409	27,420	15.754	3,943	270,003	90,793
1844.....	84,113	63,323	42,179	71,558	23,086	7,648	538,929	136,005
1845.....	118,997	49,971	48,894	62,556	50,571	12,765	674,207	157,610
1846.....	130.186	40,529	47,928	59,947	38,505	13,952	637,638	135,234

Aggregate Value of British and Irish Produce and Manufactures Exported from the United Kingdom to the British North American Colonies.

1840..............	£2,847,913...	$13,669,982	1844..............	£3,044,225...	$14,611,280
1841..............	2,947,061....	14,145,892	1845..............	3,550,614....	17,042,947
1842..............	2,333,525....	11,200,920	1846..............	3,308,059....	15,878,683
1843..............	1.751.211....	8,405,812			

II.—*An account of the quantities of the various articles imported into the United Kingdom of Great Britain and Ireland, from the British North American Colonies; with the quantities so imported entered for home consumption.*

Years.	Beef, Salted.		Pork, Salted.		Fish of British taking.		Oil, Train and Sperm., of British Fishing.	
	Imported.	Home Consumption.	Imported.	Home Consumption.	Imported.	Home Consumption.	Imported.	Home Consumption.
	cwts.	cwts.	cwts.	cwts.	cwts.	cwts.	tuns.	tuns.
1840......	1,574	69	82	25	118,499	free.	12,084	11,758
1841......	2,039	145	291	55	130,374	free.	11,176	10,988
1842......	5,924	1,556	21,226	8,421	127,754	free.	8,908	9,034
1843......	15,716	2,112	13,936	4,426	78,659	free.	12,764	12,998
1844......	10,016	480	2,236	256	74,293	free.	9,593	9,646
1845......	2,676	1,188	1,552	187	135,611	free.	10,336	free.
1846......	3,539	free.	1,800	free.	86,399	free.	7,093	free.

Years.	Skins, Musquash.		Skins, Otter.		Skins, Seal of British taking.		Skins, Wolf.	
	Imported.	Home Consumption.	Imported.	Home Consumption.	Imported.	Home Consumption.	Imported.	Home Consumption.
	number.	number.	number.	number.	number.	number.	number.	number
1840......	215,538	230,225	12,351	238	523,296	525,282	8,274	322
1841......	147,835	387,264	12,387	381	279,908	277,759	10,108	479
1842......	558,227	282,132	6,743	316	316,330	318,750	8,656	466
1843......	577,295	955,512	8,633	616	653,204	650,098	10,777	1,377
1844......	282,566	410,582	8,308	157	460,150	460,761	13,231	1,839
1845......	351,826	free.	8,533	free.	438,909	free.	10,310	free.
1846......	328,129	free.	9,664	free.	258,606	free.	8,549	free.

Years.	Skins, Beaver.		Skins, Fox.		Skins, Lynx.		Skins, Marten.	
	Imported.	Home consumption.	Imported.	Home consumption.	Imported.	Home consumption.	Imported.	Home consumption.
	number.	number.	number.	number.	number.	number.	number.	number.
1840.....	55,435	56,454	18,906	3,084	36,592	10,677	61,919	60,463
1841.....	52,240	56,533	22,403	4,185	46,192	20,559	67,375	59,318
1842.....	44,810	51,534	16,645	3,965	10,995	16,942	69,972	60,629
1843.....	40,480	42,254	27,747	2,956	8,627	5,786	84,804	65,259
1844.....	39,056	37,999	21,950	1,311	7,238	1,915	76,272	68,366
1845.....	43,762	free.	25,715	free.	10,649	free.	119,106	free.
1846.....	66,098	free.	19,744	free.	21,546	free.	155,905	free.

Years.	Skins, Mink.		Skins, Bear.		Corn, Wheat of British Possessions.		Corn, Wheat Flour of British Possessions.	
	Imported.	Homeconsumption.	Imported.	Homeconsumption.	Imported.	Homeconsumption.	Imported.	Homeconsumption.
	number.	number.	number.	number.	qrs.	qrs.	cwts.	cwts.
1840.....	29,658	9,281	5,287	1,093	8,192	4,701	477,978	364,229
1841.....	22,233	12,008	5,400	1,269	68,859	64,745	626,567	650,710
1842.....	23,815	8,094	6,358	470	33,375	37,674	518,022	551,322
1843.....	32,137	9,077	6,224	712	20,256	22,149	326,101	383,679
1844.....	32,889	10,949	5,918	658	36,123	37,771	670,948	672,236
1845.....	42,592	free.	5,842	free.	38,612	34,010	667,433	614,326
1846.....	60,837	free.	6,557	free.	68,419	71,650	904,055	969,245

Years.	Deals and Battens of British Possessions.		Deals, Battens, or other Timber or Wood, of British Possessions.		Wood and Timber, Staves.			
					Imported.		Home consumption.	
	Imported.	Home consumption.	Imported.	Homeconsumption.				
	gt. hndrds.	gt. hndrds.	loads.	loads.	gt. hndrds.	loads.	gt. hndrds.	loads.
1840.....	49,704	52,183	——	——	76,261	——	76,344	——
1841.....	52,174	50,509	——	——	80,936	——	77,473	——
1842.....	23,200	15,123	109,829	170,644	26,076	14,097	21,456	19,054
1843.....	——	——	339,417	346,146	——	43,899	——	37,315
1844.....	——	——	392,757	395,787	——	44,180	——	46,396
1845.....	——	——	489,587	498,140	free.	53,582	free.	free.
1846.....	——	——	482,685	483,890	free.	45,974	free.	free.

Years.	Masts, Yards, & Bowsprits, under 12 inches in diameter.		Masts, Yards, and Bowsprits, 12 inches in diameter.		Fir Timber, 8 inches square, or upwards.		Timber, 8in. square, or upwards, other than Fir, of British Posses.	
	Imported.	Homeconsumption.	Imported.	Homeconsumption.	Imported.	Homeconsumption.	Imported.	Homeconsumption.
	number.	number.	loads.	loads.	loads.	loads.	loads.	loads.
1840.....	8,513	8,433	5,129	5,474	551,695	545,142	95,258	92,673
1841.....	7,450	7,537	6,278	6,016	540,543	521,483	92,497	88,529
1842.....	2,200	1,843	2,271	1,899	152,479	83,942	22,241	14,563
1843.....	—	—	—	—	—	—	—	—
1844.....	—	—	—	—	—	—	—	—
1845.....	—	—	—	—	—	—	—	—
1846.....	—	—	—	—	—	—	—	—

Years.	Timber of all sorts, of British Possessions.		Ashes, Pearl and Pot.	
	Imported.	Homeconsumption.	Imported.	Homeconsumption.
	loads.	loads.	cwts.	cwts.
1840.....	—	—	98,261	
1841.....	—	—	89,571	free, if of
1842.....	200,517	316,210	116,394	British
1843.....	578,169	603,251	136,880	Posses-
1844.....	545,754	550,697	147,720	sions.
1845.....	789,757	794,332	156,256	
1846.....	729,651	731,930	119,172	

N.B.—The equivalent of these articles is not declared in the return. It is impossible to give an approximate price to articles of such changeable value.

STATEMENT OF THE VALUE OF THE COMMERCE BETWEEN THE UNITED STATES OF AMERICA AND THE BRITISH NORTH AMERICAN COLONIES, (EXCLUSIVE OF HONDURAS,) FOR THE PAST FIVE YEARS, ENDING 30TH JUNE, 1847.

Years.	Exports from United States.	Imports into United States.	In favor of United States.
(9 m'ths) 1843.....	$2,724,422	$ 857,696	$1,886,726
1844.....	6,715,903	1,465,715	5,250,188
1845.....	6,054,226	2,020,065	4,034,161
1846.....	7,406,433	1,937,717	5,468,716
1847.....	7,985,543	2,343,927	5,641,616

Tonnage employed in the above trade, 1847.

Entered United States Ports.	Cleared from United States Ports.
Vessels........................6,834	Vessels........................6,776
Tonnage.......................1,170,956	Tonnage.......................1,186,110

STATEMENT OF THE VALUE OF THE COMMERCE BETWEEN THE UNITED STATES AND BRITISH HONDURAS, FOR THE PAST FIVE YEARS, ENDING JUNE 30TH, 1847.

Years.	Exports from United States.	Imports into United States.	In favor of United States.	Against United States.
(9 m'ths) 1843.....	$108,582	$1 ,688	$......	$25,106
1844.....	239,809	248,343	......	9,324
1845.....	239,915	204,818	35 097	......
1846.....	390,032	207,997	182,035	......
1847.....	301.917	197,232	104.685	......

Tonnage employed in the above trade, 1847.

Entered United States Ports.	Cleared from United States Ports.
Vessels........................45	Vessels........................55
Tonnage.......................6,522	Tonnage.......................6,453

Commercial Statistics of French Colonies.

STATEMENT OF THE VALUE OF THE COMMERCE BETWEEN MIQUELON AND THE FRENCH NORTH AMERICAN FISHERIES AND THE UNITED STATES OF AMERICA FOR THE PAST FIVE YEARS, ENDING 30TH JUNE, 1847.

Years.	Exports from United States.	Imports into United States.	In favor of United States.	Against United States.
(9 m'ths) 1843.....	$5,215	$119	$5,096	$....
1844.....	3,484	....	3,484	....
1845.....	....	151	......	151
1846.....	....	18	......	18
1847.....	....	435	......	435

Cleared for the above, 1847.................................24 vessels.
" " " ....2744 tons.

N. B. Since this period, a treaty of reciprocity has been entered into with regard to these fisheries, and it is probable that the trade may hence become of more value.

The following Tables exhibit the results of the French Fisheries in their whole extent, from the year 1842 to the year 1846, inclusive.

1. VESSELS EMPLOYED IN THE FISHERIES.

YEARS	VESSELS.	TONNAGE.	MEN.
1842..............	483	60,964	10,540
1843..............	523	64,334	12,785
1844..............	453	56,902	11,744
1845..............	455	58,441	11,923
1846..............	472	61,986	12,823

2. QUANTITY AND OFFICIAL VALUE OF FISH.

YEARS.	KILLOGRAMS OF FISH.	OFFICIAL VALUE
1842..............	32,119,022	6,437,725 francs.
1843..............	34,959,419	7,791,883 "
1844..............	37,936,235	7,587,247 "
1845..............	33,336,967	6,652,096 "
1846..............	36,951,882	7,358,816 "

The total value of fish, whalebone, cod-sounds, &c., in 1846, was 15,438,658 francs, and the total quantity of fish exported in the same year, was 8,809,346 killograms, valued at 1,737,749 francs, more than one-half of which were sent to the French colonies, and a large quantity to Sardinia.

Both the British and Americans exceed the French in the export of salted fish, despite the artificial encouragement the latter enjoy: one cause of this superiority being the facilities they possess for drying on shore at the proper time, while the French are obliged to keep it on board, salted and undried, until the end of the season—a circumstance which damages its appearance, and also its keeping properties.

THE UNITED STATES OF AMERICA.

The United States, the most interesting and influential republic of the world, and second only in importance to the great powers of Europe, occupies the central portion of the continent of North America. This confederation, consisting originally of thirteen states, now of thirty-one states, the federal district, and several territorial appendages, lies between the parallels of 24° and 49° north latitude, and the meridians of 67° and 125° west longitude: extending from the Atlantic to the Pacific Oceans, and from the British colonies on the north to the republic of Mexico and the great gulf on the south. The whole extent of this boundary is now definitely settled by treaty.* The greatest width of this country, from east to west, is 2,900 miles, and the greatest depth, from north to south, 1,700 miles: its area may be estimated at 3,260,000 square miles, including California, Texas, &c., recently acquired. It has a frontier of about 10,000 miles; of which 4,400 is sea-coast, and 1,500 lake-coast.

The territory of the United States is traversed by two principal chains of mountains: the Alleghanies, on the east side, and the Rocky Mountains, on the west. These divide the country into three distinct regions: the Atlantic slope, the valley of the Mississippi, and the declivity from the Rocky Mountains to the Pacific.

The Alleghanies are less a chain of mountains than a long plateau, crested with several chains of mountains or hills, separated from each other by wide and elevated vallies. East of the Hudson the mountains are chiefly granitic, with rounded summits, often covered at their tops with bogs and turf, and distributed in irregular groups without any marked direction. Some peaks of the Green Mountains, in Vermont, and the White Mountains, in New-Hampshire, rise to the height of 5,000 or 6,000 feet above the sea. After passing the Hudson the structure of the mountains seem to change. In Pennsylvania and Virginia they assume the form of long parallel ridges, varying in height from 2,500 to 4,000 feet, and occupying a breadth of one hundred miles. In the northern part of Georgia, where they terminate, they again lose the form of continuous chains, and break into groups of isolated mountains, touching at their base, some of which attain a considerable elevation.

The Rocky Mountains are on a much grander scale than the Alleghanies. Their base is 300 miles in breadth, and their loftiest summits covered with everlasting snow, rise to the height of 10 or 12,000 feet. These vast chains may be considered as a continuation of the Cordilleras of Mexico. They are distant from the Pacific Ocean from 5 to 600 miles, but between them and the coast several minor ranges intersect the country, but of which few particulars are known.

* The treaties relative to these boundaries are, 1. Treaty of Paris, 1783. 2. Treaty of London, 1794. 3. Louisiana Treaty, 1803. 4. Treaty of Ghent, 1814. 5. Convention of London, 1818 and 1828. 6. Florida Treaty, 1819. 7. Treaty with Mexico, 1828. 8 Treaty with Russia, 1824. 9. Ashburton Treaty, 1842. 10. Texas Annexation Resolutions, 1845. 11. Oregon Treaty, 1846. 12. Treaty of Guadalupe, 1848.

The immense valley included between these two ranges of mountains, is intersected by the Mississippi River, which runs, from north to south, all through the United States. The country west of the Mississippi, with little exception, is yet a wilderness, inhabited by roving bands of Indians, and beyond the limits of the organized states the whites have scarcely a settlement; but the country east of that river is thickly populated, and in the highest state of cultivation. The most remarkable feature in the face of the country is the low plain, from 50 to 100 miles wide, which extends along the Atlantic coast. Beyond this plain the land rises towards the interior till it terminates in the Alleghanies. The rest of the country east of the Mississippi is agreeably diversified with hills and vallies, plains and mountains. The soil of the low country, except on the banks of creeks and rivers, is sandy, and comparatively unproductive; but the remainder has a strong, fertile soil, capable of supporting a dense population.

The shores of the United States are washed by three seas: the Atlantic Ocean on the east, the Gulf of Mexico on the south, and the Pacific Ocean on the west. The principal bays and sounds on the Atlantic border are Passamaquoddy Bay, which lies between the State of Maine and the British Province of New-Brunswick; Massachusetts Bay, between Cape Ann and Cape Cod; Long-Island Sound, between Long-Island and the coast of Connecticut; Delaware Bay, which sets up between Cape May and Cape Henlopen, separating the States of New-Jersey and Delaware; Chesapeake Bay, which communicates with the ocean between Cape Charles and Cape Henry, extending in a northern direction for 200 miles, through the States of Virginia and Maryland; Albemarle Sound and Pamlico Sound, on the coast of North Carolina. There are no large bays or sounds on the coast of the Gulf of Mexico. On the Pacific coast, however, there are several excellent bays, but the principal and only one necessary to mention is the Bay of San Francisco, in the newly-acquired territory of California. It is one of the finest bays in the world, and capable of containing the navies of all the European powers at one time.

With the exception of Michigan and Lake Champlain, none of the great lakes of North America lie wholly within the territory of the United States; the rest are on the northern boundary, where they form a connected chain, extending through a distance of more than 1,200 miles. The first in the chain is Lake Superior, the largest body of fresh water on the globe. Few persons are really aware of the magnitude of these great lakes; they are truly inland seas, and navigation is as dangerous, and subjected to all the vicissitudes, which are connected with the navigation of the Baltic, the Black Sea, or the Mediterranean.

The following is an authentic tabular statement of the extent of these fresh water seas, as represented in a report of the State Geologist of Michigan:

	Mean Length.	Mean Breadth.	Area in Square Miles.
Lake Superior	400	80	32,000
" Michigan	220	70	22,000
" Huron	240	80	20,000
" Green Bay	100	20	2,000
" Erie	240	40	9,600
" Ontario	180	35	6,300
" St. Clair	20	14	360
			92,260

The same tabular statement exhibits, also, the depth and elevation of each above tide water:

	Mean Depth.	Elevation.
Lake Superior	900 feet	596 feet.
" Michigan	1,000 "	578 "
" Huron	1,000 "	578 "
" Erie	84 "	565 "
" Ontario	500 "	232 "
" St. Clair	20 "	570 "

Lake Champlain, lying between Vermont and New-York, is 128 miles long, and from 1 to 16 miles wide, and discharges its waters through the Sorel into the St. Lawrence. It is computed that the lakes contain above 14,000 cubic miles of water; a quantity more than five-sevenths of all the fresh water on the earth. The extent of country drained by the lakes, from the north-western angle of Superior to the St. Lawrence, including also the area of the lakes themselves, is estimated at 335,515 square miles.

The principal rivers of the United States may be divided into four classes. *First*, the Mississippi and its wide-spread branches, which drain the waters off the whole country included between the Alleghany and Rocky Mountains; *second*, the rivers east of the Alleghany Mountains, which, rising from their eastern declivity, water the Atlantic plain, and hence flow into the ocean; *third*, the system of rivers flowing into the Gulf of Mexico, which may be subdivided into those flowing from the southern slope of the Alleghanies, and those having their source in the highlands of Texas; and *fourth*, those streams on the west of the Rocky Mountains, which flow into the Pacific Ocean.

The Mississippi rises west of Lake Superior, in latitude 47° 47′ north, amidst lakes and swamps, dreary and desolate beyond description; and, after a south-east course of about 500 miles, reaches the falls of the St. Anthony, where it descends perpendicularly 16 feet, and where are numerous rapids. From these falls it pursues, at first, a south-easterly, and then a southerly direction; and, after forming the boundary between Iowa, Missouri, and Arkansas on the west, and Wisconsin, Illinois, Kentucky, Tennessee, and Mississippi on the east, passes through Louisiana, and discharges itself through a delta of many mouths into the Gulf of Mexico. It is nearly 3,200 miles in length, and is navigable, with few obstructions, to the Falls of St. Anthony.

The following are the principal tributaries of the Mississippi from the east:—1. The Wisconsin, which joins it between the parallels of 42° and 43° north latitude. 2. The Illinois, a navigable river, which joins it near latitude 38° 40′ north. 3. The Ohio, which itself is formed by the junction of the Alleghany and Monongahela rivers at Pittsburg. It flows in a south-westerly direction for 945 miles, separating the north-western states from Virginia and Kentucky, and falls into the Mississippi in 37° north latitude. The chief tributaries of the Ohio are the Wabash, the Cumberland, and the Tennessee, which last is formed of several streams from the western parts of Virginia and the Carolinas, which unite a little west of Knoxville, in the State of Tennessee, and runs at first south-west into Alabama, where it turns and runs north-west, through Tennessee into Kentucky, and joins the Ohio 10 miles below the mouth of the Cumberland; and 4. The Yazoo, which rises in the northern part of the State of Mississippi, and running south-west, joins the Mississippi 100 miles above Natchez.

The principal tributaries of the Mississippi, from the west, are—1. The St. Peter's, which joins it about nine miles below the Falls of St. Anthony, after a south-east course of several hundred miles. 2. The River Des-Moines, which joins it near the parallel of 40° north latitude, after a south-easterly course of more than 800 miles. 3. The Missouri, which is formed by three branches, called Jefferson's, Madison's and Gallatin's Rivers, all of which rise and unite in the Rocky Mountains. The whole length, from the highest point of Jefferson's River, to the confluence with the Mississippi, is, by actual course, about 2,500 miles, and to the Gulf of Mexico nearly 3,500 miles; during the whole of which distance there is no cataract or considerable impediment to the navigation, except at Great Falls, which are above 2,000 miles from the Mississippi. At these falls the river descends, in the distance of 18 miles, 362 feet. The principal tributaries of the Missouri are the Yellow Stone, which rises in the Rocky Mountains, and joins it after a north-easterly course of nearly 600 miles; the Nebraska or Platte, which rises also in those mountains, and, after an easterly course of 800 miles, joins the Missouri in latitude 41° north; and the Kansas, which joins it near latitude 39° north, after an easterly course of more than 600 miles. 4. The Arkansas, which rises in the Rocky Mountains, and pursuing a south-easterly course, forms, for some distance, the boundary between the Indian Territory and Texas; after which its course lies principally in the State of Arkansas, till it joins the Mississippi in 34° north latitude. Its length is more than 1,300 miles. 5. The Red River, which also rises in the Rocky Mountains, below Santa Fé, and, after a south-easterly course of more than 1,000 miles, falls into the Mississippi in latitude 31° north.

The principal rivers east of the Alleghanies are:—1. The Connecticut, which rises in the highlands separating the United States from Canada, and running southerly, divides New-Hampshire from Vermont, and passing through Massachusetts and Connecticut, falls into Long Island Sound. It is navigable for sloops for fifty miles, to Hartford, and by means of canals and other improvements, has been rendered passable for boats 250 miles further. 2. The Hudson, which rises west of Lake Champlain, and, pursuing a southerly course of more than 300 miles, falls into the Bay of New-York, after receiving numerous affluents. It is navigable for ships to Hudson, 130 miles; and for sloops and steamboats to Troy, 40 miles further. It is connected with Lake Champlain by means of a canal from Albany. 3. The Delaware, which rises in New-York, and flowing southerly, separates Pennsylvania from New-York and New-Jersey, and falls into Delaware Bay, after a course of 300 miles. It is navigable for ships of the line 40 miles, to Philadelphia; and for sloops 35 miles further, to the head of the tide at Trenton Falls. 4. The Susquehannah, which also rises in New-York, and pursuing a southerly zig-zag course through Pennsylvania, falls into the head of Chesapeake Bay, near the north-east corner of Maryland. During the last 50 miles the navigation is obstructed by an almost continued series of rapids. 5. The Potomac, which rises in the Alleghanies, and, after forming, during its whole course, the boundary between Maryland and Virginia, falls into Chesapeake Bay. It is navigable for ships of the largest dimensions to Washington, the federal capital, about 200 miles from the ocean; but in the upper part of its course there are numerous obstacles, many of which, however, have been overcome by canals. 6. James' River, which rises in the mountains, and falls into the southern part of Chesapeake Bay; and 7. The Savannah, which forms the dividing line between South Carolina and Georgia, and falls into the Atlantic in latitude

32° north. It is navigable for large vessels to Savannah, 17 miles; and for boats to Augusta, 130 miles further.

The principal rivers which rise south of the Alleghanies, and fall into the Gulf of Mexico, are: 1. The Appalachicola, which discharges itself into Apalachy Bay, in Florida. It is formed by the union of the Chatahouchee and Flint rivers, the former of which rises in the northern part of Georgia, and flowing south, receives the Flint at the south-west extremity of the state. During the latter part of its course, the Chatahouchee forms the boundary between Georgia and Alabama. 2. The Mobile, which discharges itself into Mobile Bay. It is formed by two large rivers, the Alabama and Tombigbee, which unite near latitude 31° north, after having pursued each a separate course of many hundred miles. There is another system of rivers flowing into the Gulf from the highlands of northern Texas, consisting of the Sabine, Trinity, Brazos, &c., which need only be mentioned here, as the property of Texas will be minutely described elsewhere.

The rivers flowing from the Rocky Mountains to the Pacific, consist of 1. The Columbia, which rises near latitude 55° north, and running southwest, falls into the ocean in latitude 46° 15′, after a course of 1500 miles. Its principal tributaries are Clark's River, Lewis' River, and the Multnomah or Willamet, all of which join it on its left bank. This river was discovered in 1792, and settlements were made in the neighborhood by Americans in 1810. The mouth of the river is obstructed by flats, but vessels of 300 tons can ascend to the distance of 125 miles, and large sloops further. 2. The Sacramento, emptying into the Bay of San Francisco. 3. The Buenaventura, rising in the coast range of the California Mountains, empties into Monterey Bay. 4. The Colorado, and River Gila, (which separates Mexico from the United States,) flow from the mountains near Santa Fé, and would, if not received by the Gulf of California, empty into the Pacific; they belong, however, to the same system of rivers.

In a country so extensive, and stretching over so many degrees of latitude, there must, of necessity, be a great diversity of climate, and interminable differences in its physical appearance. The climate of the United States is variable and inconstant; subject alike to extremes of heat and cold. It passes rapidly from the frosts of Norway to the scorching heats of Africa, and from the humidity of Holland to the droughts of Castile. In the central districts it is not uncommon to experience within a few hours, a variation of 25° to 30° *Fahr.* The annual extremes are more marked in the northern states, and progressively approximate on approaching the southern coast, till reaching the extreme point of Florida the thermometer is almost stationary the whole year round, and at most does not vary 12°. Locality however, in the United States as elsewhere, in a great measure determines the character of the climate; on the Atlantic coast the modifying influence of the ocean is recognized, and the severity of the climate much remedied. Inland, beyond the mountains, and throughout the whole valley of the Mississippi, the climate is purely that of latitude, and subject to exact seasonal influences; while the lake region, like the Atlantic coast, is modified by the near vicinity of those large inland seas. The region skirting the Pacific from the 49th parallel to San Diego, has a climate peculiarly mild; the winters are neither long nor severe, nor the summers fraught with that intensity peculiar to the latitudes. With these exceptions, the general character of the climate is "inconstancy." Even the Indians complain of the sudden variations of the temperature.

The mineral resources of the United States are as abundant as various.

In Pennsylvania, and some other states, iron and anthracite form the great staples, and vast beds of bituminous coal are found in almost all the western states. Copper abounds especially in the north-western states, and along the coast of Lake Superior; vast boulders of copper, some tons in weight, have been found in the Wisconsin region, and such has of late years been the activity of mining operations, that the market has been almost entirely supplied with these metals from the west. The lead mines of Missouri and Illinois are inexhaustible. New York, Virginia, and Pennsylvania, and the whole north-west produce salt in abundance; and in Utah territory, the Great Salt Lake and its valley contain salt sufficient to preserve, if salt will preserve it, the integrity of the Union to the crack of doom.

The United States, indeed, possesses mines of every metal or mineral known to the arts. It has all the useful and all the precious metals. California has eclipsed all known mineral regions in the abundance of its gold, quicksilver, and other minerals; and gold is mined in considerable quantities in the states of Virginia, North Carolina, South Carolina, Georgia, and Alabama. New-Mexico and the neighboring regions likewise abound in the precious metals. With regard to marbles, building stones, slates, clays for brick and pottery, no country is better supplied. New-England rests on a bed of granite and marble; the middle states overlie sandstone and freestone bases, and most part of the Ohio region has a foundation of limestone. Granite pervades the whole country from the crest of the Rocky Mountains to the Pacific. Such resources are of incalculable value to a state, and have ever been the staples of national wealth. And if an illustration be required to show that Americans can develope the great resources of the country Providence has given them, we need only point to Pennsylvania, which, since 1840, has quadrupled the production of her coal mines; to the activity of the miners in the bleak region of Lake Superior; and to the shores of the Pacific, whither they have voyaged for the purpose of reaping the hidden treasures of the land; and it may here be stated, that the aggregate annual value of minerals produced in 1850, was at least tenfold that of the products of 1840.

In commercial affairs, the country enjoys great advantages; the extent of the coast, the energy of the people, and above all, the unrestrained liberty enjoyed in this as in all other departments of life by the Americans, have tended to such a result. In commerce the United States is second only in prosperity and extent to Great Britain. It has attained an amazing magnitude; there is no part of the globe which is not visited by American merchantmen; and the foreign and coasting trade, and the inland trade carried on over an unequalled extent of artificial and natural lines of communication, are all on an equal scale. The domestic commerce may be divided into three branches: 1. That which is carried on coastwise, up the bays and large rivers, and on the great lakes by schooners, sloops, and steamboats. 2. That which is carried on chiefly in steamboats, but partly in rude flat-bottom boats on the affluents of the Mississippi. The natural centre of this trade is New-Orleans; which, situated at the outlet of the valley, is necessarily the great entrepot of all the produce destined for exportation, and of all the foreign articles required to supply the wants of the people of the western states.* 3. The overland trade between the western and At-

* A great portion of this commerce has been transferred from New-Orleans to the Atlantic ports, by means of the lines of railroad and canal which have been opened within the past few years in a direction east and west.

lantic states, consists principally of hogs, horses, cattle and mules, which are driven every year to the Atlantic states to the value of many millions of dollars; but the difficulty of conveyance has hitherto prevented any other return than money. To obviate this difficulty, many canals and railroads have been constructed, which will be used to transport return merchandise as well as travellers across the mountains. The four maritime states of New-England are those most devoted to navigation and trade; and Massachusetts, though it contains less than one twenty-fifth of the population of the United States, owns more than one-fourth of the shipping tonnage. The next to New-England the people of New-York, Pennsylvania and Maryland, are the most commercial. Such of the inhabitants of those states and of the Atlantic states to the south of them, as live near the mouths of rivers, or on the great bays or estuaries, are generally of seafaring habits. They are extremely skilful in naval architecture; and there are no class of mariners more capable of endurance and management than the far-famed "yankee captain"—in all weathers he is on deck, never seems to sleep, nor ever loses a breath of wind that may fill his sail: on these peculiarities has depended the success of Americans, and they now rank as the ablest seamen of the world.

The exports of the United States to foreign countries, consist principally of agricultural products, with some naval stores, lumber, and other productions of the forests. Considerable quantities of cotton goods are sent to foreign parts, as also various manufactured articles of minor consideration. The value of exports for the year ending 30th June, 1850, compared with those of 1845, was as herewith exhibited:

Products of the Fisheries	$2,824,818
" " Forest	7,442,503
" " Agriculture	108,482,797
" " Manufactures	13,374,059
Articles not enumerated	4,822,735
	$136,946,912
" exported in 1845	99,299,776

The imports are European manufactured goods of all sorts, particularly the finer descriptions; tropical staples, as coffee, sugar, spices, wines, spirits, etc.; with considerable quantities of Asiatic productions, as teas, silks, etc. For the same years named above, the description and value of imports were as follows:

Articles free of duty	$22,710,382
" duty *ad valorem*	155,427,936
	$178,138,318
" imported in 1845	117,254,564

The vessels and tonnage employed in foreign commerce during the year 1849–50, amounted in the aggregate to

	American.		Foreign.		Total.	
	Vessels.	Tonnage.	Vessels.	Tonnage.	Vessels.	Tonnage.
Entrances	8,412	2,573,016	10,100	1,775,623	18,512	4,348,639
Clearances	8,379	2,632,788	9,816	1,728,214	18,195	4,361,002

And with the same vessels entering and clearing, the crews amounted to

	American. Men.	American. Boys.	American. Total.	Foreign. Men.	Foreign. Boys.	Foreign. Total.	Total.
Entering	100,637	3,732	104,369	89,618	2,183	91,801	196,170
Clearing	102,888	3,865	106,753	86,886	2,232	89,118	195,871

The average burden of each American vessel is 309 tons, and of each foreign vessel 176 tons—difference in the average burden of American and foreign vessels 133 tons; one man is employed to every 24.6 tons American, and one to every 19.3 tons of foreign shipping, facts exhibiting the superior economy of large over small vessels.

The fisheries of the United States are extensive and very valuable, and this branch of industry has been pursued with a hardy daring from the earliest colonial times. The foreign or whale fishery is pursued in all the great seas; in the Atlantic from pole to pole, but chiefly south of the equator for the black whale, and in the southern Indian and Pacific Oceans for the spermaceti whale. The shipping employed in the whale fishery in 1850, amounted to 146,017 tons—all from the states of Massachusetts, Rhode Island, Connecticut and New-York, and from the following ports—Fall River 928 tons, New Bedford 96,419 tons, Barnstable 3,853 tons, Edgartown 2,420 tons, and Nantucket 19,055 tons; Providence 499 tons, Bristol 3,814 and Newport 1,516; New London 2,622, and Stonington 8,861; Sag Harbor 2,574 tons, Greenport 253 tons, New-York 465 tons, and Cold Spring 2,736 tons. About 12,000 seamen and landsmen are employed in this business, and as a maritime school it is one of the most efficacious—many of our most experienced liner captains and coast pilots owe their subsequent usefulness to the training they have had in the whaler. The returns from this fishery, for the year 1850–51, amounted to 98,534 barrels sperm, and 341,945 barrels whale oil, and a commensurate quantity of bone, etc. The arrivals at each of the whale shipping ports were in the following proportions:

Ports.	Vessels.	Sperm Oil. Barrels.	Whale Oil. Barrels.	Ports.	Vessels.	Sperm Oil. Barrels.	Whale Oil. Barrels.
New-Bedford	94	46,966	150,156	Newport	2	1,130	1,650
Nantucket	14	15,500	3,405	Mystic	5	131	12,803
Fairhaven	13	9,491	14,145	Stonington	8	1,235	15,550
New-London	28	2,799	64,317	Provincetown	23	2,805	307
Sag Harbor	4	110	10,970	Cold Spring	3	—	8,850
Greenport	7	857	13,844	Truro	1	202	—
Warren	8	3,552	1,774	Beverly	1	260	—
Boston	9	7,871	—	Dartmouth	1	50	10
Edgartown	4	3,150	4,100	Falmouth	1	—	2,800
Westport	1	45	2,650	Lynn	1	120	2,600
New-York	5	2,308	1,924				
Mattapoisett	3	1,385	30	Total	236	98,534	341,945

The products of this fishery brought home for a series of years have been as follows:

Years.	Vessels.	Sperm.	Whale.	Years.	Vessels.	Sperm.	Whale.
1839–40	213	156,445	203,441	1845–6	199	92,877	219,763
1840–1	222	157,643	205,164	1846–7	252	121,410	320,545
1841–2	207	163,697	163,816	1847–8	196	108,531	243,876
1842–3	147	167,134	205,861	1848–9	188	99,433	256,183
1843–4	231	138,585	267,082	1849–50	177	86,157	191,152
1844–5	242	158,484	274,843	1850–1	236	98,534	341,945

The barrel averages about 31¼ gallons.

Seal oil and furs are also obtained in the polar regions, and are annually brought home by the whaling ships to a large amount.

The cod fishery is pursued off the coasts of New-England, and as far north as Labrador, and east as far as the Great Bank of Newfoundland. It is engaged in chiefly from the New-England ports, and from one or two ports in New-York, and in 1849–50 employed 85,646 tons of shipping, of which 13,982 tons were from Gloucester, 12,308 tons from Barnstable, 11,462 from Penobscot, 6,092 tons from Wiscasset, 4,789 tons from Plymouth, and more or less from other ports. The mackerel fishery employs 58,111 tons shipping.

The United States have already made astonishing progress in industry and wealth. In every department of industry; in agriculture, the manufactures, fisheries and commerce, the movement is equally rapid and sustained. Agriculture has ever been the staple pursuit of the North Americans, and agricultural products have always constituted their principal articles of export. The first exports of the early colonists were the natural products of the forest: firs, lumber, pitch and tar; pot and pearl ashes, with some cattle and provisions, constituted the chief articles of trade from the northern provinces in the early part of the eighteenth century; but rice and tobacco had even then become important items of exportation from the southern colonies. At a later period, wheat became the great staple of the middle and western states, and cotton that of the more southern sections of the country. Flax and hemp thrive, particularly in the rich soil of Kentucky and Missouri. Maize, being suited to a great variety of soils and situation, is so universally cultivated, as to have received the name of "corn," as a distinctive appellation. Oats for horses, and rye for distillation, are the prevalent species of grain in the northern states, while in the extreme south the sugar cane is found to flourish, and to supply almost all the demand for this article for home consumption. Grapes for wine, and beets for sugar, are articles of prospective culture, regarding the value of which sanguine expectations are entertained. Cotton, the great staple of the United States, is raised in small quantities in Virginia and Kentucky, but is chiefly produced in the country further south. It is the produce of the herbaceous or annual cotton plant, and is of two kinds—the Sea Island or long staple, and the Upland or short staple. The former, which is of a superior quality, is grown chiefly in the Carolinas and Georgia, on the Atlantic, and in some parts of the State of Texas. Cotton was first sown in the United States in or about 1787, and was first exported in small quantities in 1790; since then its culture has become enormous. Tobacco has been the staple of Virginia and Maryland since their first settlement, and is also extensively grown in Kentucky, Ohio, Missouri, and other states; besides the quantities required for domestic use, large amounts are exported. Rice was first cultivated in South Carolina, in 1694, since which time its culture has been so successful, that, in addition to supplying the home consumption, it affords an annual surplus for the purposes of commerce. Indigo was formerly produced in large quantities in the Carolinas and Georgia, but since the introduction of cotton, its cultivation has almost ceased. The culture of the tea plant is being attempted.

The principal productions of agriculture, as exhibited in the census of 1850, are noted in the following table, which also shows the states (arranged in reference to the quantity of production) in which the several staples are produced in the greatest quantities:

Wheat........	*bushels*	104,799,230	—Pennsylvania, Ohio, Virginia, New-York, Illinois, Indiana, Michigan, Wisconsin, etc.
Indian Corn...	"	591,586,053	—Ohio, Kentucky, Illinois, Indiana, Tennessee, Missouri, Virginia, Georgia, Alabama, North-Carolina, etc.

Tobacco ......*pounds*	199,532,494	—Virginia, Kentucky, Maryland, Tennessee, Missouri, North Carolina, Ohio, Connecticut, etc.
Cotton..*bales*, 400 *lbs.*	2,474,214	—Alabama, Mississippi, Georgia, South Carolina, Tennessee, Louisiana, North Carolina, Arkansas, Texas, Florida, Virginia, and Kentucky.
Wine.........*gallons*	141,295	—Ohio, Pennsylvania, Indiana, North Carolina, Missouri, etc.
Hay.............*tons*	13,605,384	—New-York, Pennsylvania, Ohio, etc.
Hemp (dew-rotted) "	62,182	Kentucky, Missouri, Virginia, Illinois, Iowa, Indiana, Ohio, etc.
" (water-rotted) "	13,059	
Flaxseed.......*bushels*	567,749	—Ohio, Kentucky, Virginia, North Carolina, New-York, etc.
Maple Sugar...*pounds*	32,759,263	—New-York, Vermont, Ohio, Indiana, etc.
Cane Sugar.... "	318,644,000	—Louisiana, Florida, Texas, Georgia, etc.
Wool.......... "	52,422,797	—New-York, Ohio, Pennsylvania, Vermont, Virginia, Indiana, etc.
Butter........ "	312,202,286	—New-York, Pennsylvania, Ohio, etc.
Cheese........ "	103,184,585	—New-York, Ohio, Massachusetts, Vermont, etc.

The value of live stock is stated at $552,705,238.

The following table shows the number of farms and plantations under cultivation in each state, in 1850, and the quantity of improved land in each:

States, etc.	No. of Farms.	Acres Improved.	States, etc.	No. of Farms.	Acres Improved.
Maine	46,760	2,019,593	Louisiana	13,422	1,567,998
New-Hampshire	29,229	2,251,388	Texas	12,198	635,913
Vermont	29,687	2,322,923	Arkansas	17,758	780,333
Massachusetts	34,235	2,127,924	Tennessee	72,710	5,087,057
Rhode Island	5,385	337,672	Kentucky	74,777	6,068,633
Connecticut	22,445	1,734,277	Ohio	143,887	9,730,650
New-York	170,698	12,285,077	Michigan	34,089	1,923,582
New-Jersey	23,905	1,770,337	Indiana	93,896	5,019,822
Pennsylvania	127,577	8,619,631	Illinois	76,208	5,114,041
Delaware	6,063	524.364	Missouri	54,458	2,911,422
Maryland	21,860	2,797,905	Iowa	14,805	814,173
Dist. of Columbia	264	17,083	Wisconsin	20,177	1,011,308
Virginia	77,013	10,150,106	California	500	34,312
North Carolina	56,916	5,443,137	Minesota	157	5,035
South Carolina	29,969	4,074,855	Oregon	1,164	135,357
Georgia	51,759	6,323,426	Utah	300	15,319
Florida	4,304	349,423	New-Mexico	3,750	161,296
Alabama	41,964	4,387,088			
Mississippi	23,960	3,489,640	Total	1,327,249	112,042,600

During the war of the Revolution some manufactures sprung up in the states; and on the adoption of the Constitution, provision was immediately made for the support of the manufacturing industry of the country, by protecting duties. Under the ægis of this salutary provision these interests have flourished, every undertaking has prospered, and the United States will, no doubt, soon outstrip all other countries in the march to distinction in this branch of industry. From the endless variety of soil and climate, which produce in abundance every species of raw material, the cheap and inexhaustible supply of moving power furnished by the rivers and torrents, combined with the improvements which are daily taking place in machinery, this result is indicated as an unerring destiny. At present, however, the industry of the country is chiefly applied to agriculture, but the progress of manufactures obtains footing day by day, and extends their limits to every part of the country.

The entire capital invested in the various manufactures in the United

States on the first of June, 1850, not including any establishments producing less than the annual value of $500, amounted in round numbers to

	$530,000,000
Value of raw material	550,000,000
Amount paid for labor	240,000,000
Value of manufactured articles	1,020,300,000
Number of persons employed....1,050,000.	

The capital invested in 1840 amounted to $267,726,579, and hence the capital employed in manufactures has almost doubled in the ten subsequent years.

The number of manufacturing establishments in each of the states and territories in 1850, was as follows:

Alabama	1,622	Louisiana	1,021	North Carolina	2,523
Arkansas	271	Maine	3,682	Ohio	10,550
California	—	Maryland	3,863	Oregon, *Ter*	51
Columbia, *Dist.*	1,427	Massachusetts	9,637	Pennsylvania	22,036
Connecticut	3,963	Michigan	1,979	Rhode Island	1,144
Delaware	513	Minesota, *Ter.*	5	South Carolina	1,473
Florida	121	Mississippi	866	Tennessee	2,798
Georgia	1,407	Missouri	3,030	Texas	307
Illinois	3,099	New-Hampshire	3,301	Utah, *Ter.*	—
Indiana	4,326	New-Jersey	4,374	Vermont	1,835
Iowa	482	New-Mexico, *Ter.*	20	Virginia	4,433
Kentucky	3,471	New-York	23,985	Wisconsin	1,273

The manufacture of iron is very important to each of the states, and in several, as in Pennsylvania, New-York, Ohio, Massachusetts, New-Jersey, etc., forms one of the most valuable branches of their industry. In Pennsylvania nearly one-tenth the whole population derive their subsistence from the iron manufactures.

The census of 1850 returns 21 states as making pig iron, and in these there are 773 establishments for its production. The capital invested amounted to $17,346,425; the value of raw material and fuel, etc., used was $7,005,289; the number of hands employed, 20,448; monthly wages, $422,219, and the products 564,755 tons pig iron, etc., valued at $12,748,777.

In the manufacture of castings all the states except Florida and Arkansas are more or less engaged, and in these there are 1,391 establishments; the capital invested is $17,416,361; the value of raw material, fuel, etc., used, $10,346,353; the number of hands employed, 23,599; castings, etc., made 322,745 tons, valued at $25,108,155.

Nineteen states manufacture wrought iron, in which there are 422 establishments, 231 of which are in Pennsylvania. The capital invested is $13,995,220; the value of raw material, fuel, etc., $9,518,109; number of hands employed, 12,978; wrought iron made, 272,044 tons, valued at $16,387,079. This great interest of iron manufacture as compared with its condition in 1840, is exhibited in the following summary:

		1850.	1840.	Increase.
Capital invested	*dollars*	48,758,206	20,432,121	28,326,085
Hands employed	*number*	57,025	30,497	26,528
Iron produced	*tons*	594,789	484,136	110,653
Value of products	*dollars*	54,244,011	—	—

The cotton manufacture is carried on in all but seven states, but the great manufacturing states are Massachusetts, Pennsylvania, Rhode Island, Connecticut and New-York. The whole number of establishments manufacturing cotton goods in 1850 was 1,094, of which 213 were in Massachusetts, 208 in Pennsylvania, 158 in Rhode Island, 128 in Connecticut, 86 in New-York, and 47 in New-Hampshire. Georgia had at the same date 35 establishments, and the other states from 2 to 33 each. The entire capital invested in this branch was $74,504,031; the cotton consumed, 641,240 bales; value of all raw material, fuel, etc., $34,835,056; hands employed—males, 33,151, and females, 59,136; monthly wages, $1,357,292; products—763,678,407 yards sheeting, and 27,873,600 pounds yarn and thread, valued together at $61,869,184. The relative importance of this manufacture in the several states is as follows:

STATES.	Capital Invested.	Value of all Raw Material.	No. of Hands Employed.	Value of Products.	Cap. Invested in 1840.
Massachusetts	$23,455,630	$11,289,309	28,730	$19,712,461	$17,414,099
New-Hampshire	10,950,500	4,839,429	12,122	8,830,619	5,523,200
Rhode Island	8,675,100	3,484,379	10,875	6,447,120	7,326,000
Pennsylvania	4,528.925	3,152,530	7,663	5,322,262	3,325,400
Connecticut	4,219,100	2,500,062	6,186	4,357,522	3,152,000
New-York	4,176,920	1,985,975	6,330	3,591,989	4,900,772
Maine	3,329,700	1,573,110	3,739	2,596,356	1,398,000
Maryland	2,236,000	1,165,579	3,022	2,120,504	1,304,400
All other States	12,932,156	4,844,683	13,620	8,890,351	6,758,488
Total, 1850	$74,904,031	$34,835,056	92,287	$61,869,184	
" 1840	51,102,359	—	72,119	46,350,453	51,102,359
Increase	$23,781,672	—	20,168	$15,518,731	

The first cotton mill erected in the United States was located at Providence, R. I., in 1790, and power-looms were introduced at Waltham in 1815. The cottons manufactured are principally shirtings, sheetings and calicoes, for printing, carpetings, jeans, etc., and in the south the goods are principally heavy domestics for negro wear. There are very few establishments manufacturing fine goods on account of the expense of labor.

Twenty-five states have woollen manufactures, but only eight have invested in this branch a capital of above $500,000, and in nine the capital invested is less than $100,000. The aggregate capital invested is $28,118,-650; the quantity of wool used, 70,862,829 lbs.; the value of all raw material, $25,755,988; the number of hands employed, 39,252; monthly wages paid, $699,940; cloth manufactured, 82,206,652; and value of all products, $43,207,555. The states having the largest interest in this branch, with the statistics of each in this relation, compared with those of 1840, are as follows:

STATES.	Capital Invested.	Value of all Raw Material.	Hands Employed.	Value of all Products.	Capital Inv. in 1840.
Massachusetts	$9,089,342	$8,671,671	11,130	$12,770,565	$4,179,850
New-York	4,459,370	3,838,292	6,674	7,030,604	3,469,349
Connecticut	3,773,950	3,325,709	5,488	6,465,216	1,931,335
Pennsylvania	3,005,064	3,882,718	5,726	5,321,866	1,510,546
New-Hampshire	2,437,700	1,267,329	2,127	2,127,745	740,345
Rhode Island	1,013,370	1,163,900	1,758	2,381,825	685,350
Vermont	886,300	830,684	1,393	1,579,161	1,406,950
Ohio	870,220	578,423	1,201	1,111,027	537,985
All other states	2,583,334	2,197,262	3,755	4,419,931	1,303,414
Total, 1850	$28,118,650	$25,755,988	39,252	$43,207,940	
" 1840	15,765,124	—	21,342	20,696,999	15,765,124
Incr'e in 10 years	$12,353,526	—	17,910	$22,510,941	

The manufacture of woollens has been carried on in families for domestic wants from an early period, but it is only within the past 20 years that large establishments have been formed, and still later since the improved machinery has been introduced.

The manufactures of the United States, otherwise than those of iron, cotton and wool, are very various, and embrace almost every article known to commerce. The manufactures of machinery, of hardware, and metallic articles generally, are extensive branches; those of silk, of flax, and of mixed fabrics, are also considerable. Then there are tanneries, saddleries, soap and candle houses, distilleries and breweries, powder mills, paint and dye factories, glass houses, potteries, brick yards, sugar houses, paper mills, cordage factories, flouring, grist, saw, oil, etc., mills, and an infinite number of others, each employing large capitals, and manufacturing to an immense money value. The aggregate capital invested in all otherwise than those previously excepted, was, in 1850, about $378,000,000; the hands employed about 862,000, and the value of goods manufactured about $860,000,000.

Internal communication is munificently provided for. Besides roads of the ordinary construction, which are generally as well made as those in older countries, the several states have constructed a series of rail-roads and canals which, in length are unequalled in the world.

No sooner had the subject of rail-roads evidenced a practicability in England, than their importance as a means of travel and conveyance recommended them to the people of this country, and measures were at once taken to give their advantages to our internal traffic. The Quincy R. R. was the first laid in the Union. Since that period they have been extended from every important point. Such, indeed, has been the rapid progress of rail-road making, that at the present day all the great cities of the Atlantic communicate by this means, not only with each other, but also with the most distant west, and it is now in contemplation to extend the lines northward into the British Possessions, and to Oregon and California on the Pacific. The aggregate length of all the completed rail-roads in the United States, on the 1st January, 1852, was about 12,000 miles; of those in progress, about 8,000 miles, and of those in contemplation, the majority of which will no doubt be put in operation, some thousands of miles more. The comparative cost of rail-roads in Europe and the United States, per mile, including right of way, is as follows: In Massachusetts, $36,000; in the other Eastern States, $24,000; in New-York, $26,000; in New-Jersey and Pennsylvania, $40,000; and in the Western States, $11,000—but the small cost in these districts is owing to the natural facilities of the country and the mode of construction: in England, $175,000; in France, $107,500; in Belgium, $80,000; in Germany, $40,000, (owing to the low price of labor and land;) and in Prussia, $47,000.

Canals in the United States are comparatively few, and with the exception of the New-York and Erie, the Miami, the Wabash and Erie, the Illinois and Michigan, and some others, have been constructed more for the improvement of pre-existing avenues of commerce than with a view of opening new ones. There are many, however, highly important in their local bearings, and have proven advantageous to the states through which they pass. The aggregate length of all the canals is upwards of 6,000 miles, one-half of which amount is in New-York, Pennsylvania and Ohio, alone. The necessity for canals, however, has become, with the increase of rail-roads, an obsolete idea; indeed, in the eastern states canals have been entirely abandoned as a means of intercourse, and it is probable that hereafter as "the slow coaches of olden times," they will be entirely suspended, as inappropriate to the genius of the age and the wants of the people.

The great mass of the people of the United States are descendants of emigrants from Great Britain and Ireland, but a considerable portion are also of French, German, and Dutch extraction, particularly in the States of Louisiana, Pennsylvania, and New York, and daily accessions are making to their numbers by immigration from every part of Europe: during the year 1850, indeed, little less than half a million foreigners landed at the various ports of the Union. But the English language and literature are universally pursued; the children of immigrants, from other nations, soon lose their national peculiarities, language, and character, by intermarriages and a common education; and the Anglo-Saxon spirit completely preponderates throughout the heterogeneous mass, except in the eastern parts of Pennsylvania, where a large community of German settlers have long clung, with imperturbable pertinacity, to the language and habits of their fatherland: they have, however, of late years, found out the inconvenience of retaining their nationality in a foreign country, and are beginning to join in the feelings and habits of the general mass. The total population of the United States, according to the census of 1850, was 23,288,565; and when we consider that this civilized and industrious multitude exists in a region which, only two centuries ago, supported only a few hundred thousands of half-clad and half-fed savages, and look at the rapid and steady increase which has marked its progress, we see a new and most striking phenomena in the history of the human race. Though there has been a great accession of numbers by immigration from Europe, ever since the first settlement of the country, yet there is no reason to doubt that the growth of the population is chiefly owing to the natural increase of a community, multiplying itself without any check from difficulty of subsistence or want of unoccupied lands. Nor is it a less interesting consideration, that this same facility of self-multiplication will continue to exist for an indefinite period; and that should no external or accidental cause interfere, the United States will, before the end of the present century, form the most numerous Christian community, speaking one language, in the world. The first census was taken in 1790; since which period there have been six decennial enumerations; their results are stated in the following table:

Number and Classes of Population.

Census Year.	White Persons.	Colored Persons. Free.	Colored Persons. Slave.	Total Population.
1790	3,172,464	59,466	697,897	3,929,827
1800	4,304,505	108,395	893,041	5,305,941
1810	5,862,004	186,446	1,191,364	7,239,814
1820	7,861,907	238,156	1,538,128	9,638,191
1830	10,526,248	319,599	2,009,043	12,866,020 *
1840	14,189,695	386,303	2,487,355	17,069,453 *
1850	19,662,448	427,819	3,198,298	23,288,565

Absolute Decennial Increase.

Census Year.	White Persons.	Colored Persons. Free.	Colored Persons. Slave.	Total Population.
1790-1800	1,132,041	48,929	195,144	1,376,114
1800-1810	1,557,499	78,051	298,323	1,933,873
1810-1820	1,999,903	51,710	346,764	2,398,377
1820-1830	2,664,341	81,443	470,915	3,227,829
1830-1840	3,663,447	66,704	478,312	4.208,433
1840-1850	5,472,753	41,516	710,943	6,225,212

Including seamen, soldiers, etc.—in 1830, 11,130; and in 1840, 6,100—not otherwise accounted for.

Relative Decennial Increase—per centum.

Census Year.	White Persons.	Colored Persons. Free.	Colored Persons. Slave.	Total Population.
1790–1800	25.68	82.28	27.96	35.02
1800–1810	36.18	72.00	33.40	36,50
1810–1820	34.30	27.75	29.57	33.35
1820–1830	34.52	34.85	30.75	33.92
1830–1840	34.72	20.88	23.81	32.67
1840–1850	38.20	10.95	28.58	36.18

The colored population of the United States, in which are included not only the negro, but also the mulatto and mixed races, forms somewhat more than one-sixth of the total population. The free blacks are not generally admitted to political equality with the whites; in some states, indeed, their testimony is not admitted against a white man, and they are subject to some other civil disabilities. Slavery has been abolished in all the Eastern states, and prospectively in Pennsylvania and New-Jersey, and its establishment was forbidden, by the ordinance of 1787, in all the states north-west of the Ohio, and subsequently in those north of 36° 30' beyond the Mississippi, except the State of Missouri. Maritime slave-trade has been declared piracy; but a great and active inland trade is carried on from the Atlantic slave states to the new states in the south and west, and it is believed that the number clandestinely introduced from Africa has also been considerable, even since the trade was declared illegal. The non-slaveholding states are: Maine, New-Hampshire, Vermont, Massachusetts, Rhode Island, Connecticut, New-York, New-Jersey, Pennsylvania, Ohio, Indiana, Illinois, Michigan, Wisconsin, Iowa, and California, and the territories north of these. The slave-holding states are: Delaware, Maryland, Virginia, North Carolina, South Carolina, Georgia, Florida, Alabama, Mississippi, Louisiana, Arkansas, Tennessee, Kentucky, Missouri, and Texas. In the District of Columbia slavery is tolerated, and the Indians, in the territories west of Arkansas, hold a number of slaves. New-Mexico, Utah, and Oregon, are, at present, free from this institution, but the two first named territories may be admitted as states with or without slavery. The slaves form rather more than one-third part of the population of the slave-holding states, but they are unequally distributed, and the whites generally preponderate.

The aboriginal races or Indians resident within the territories of the United States are not included in any of the enumerations. Perhaps the whole number in the Union may be 500,000.

There is in the United States no national or established religion. It is expressly provided, (*Amend. to Const.* Art. I.) that "Congress shall make no law respecting the establishment of religion or prohibiting the exercise thereof.

The "Baptists" are the most numerous in every portion of the Union, but on a diversity of minor topics, this denomination has been split into several sub-sections, which will be noted in the nomenclature of the following statistics. In 1847, there were in the United States:

	Churches.	Ordained Ministers.	Church Members.
Regular Baptists	7,883	4,641	655,536
Anti-Mission do.	1,912	913	67,868
Six Principle do.	20	22	3,400
Seventh Day do.	63	58	6,943
Church of God do.	130	90	8,000
Free Will do.	1,165	771	63,372
Campbellites do.	1,800	1,000	160,000
Christian Connection do.	650	782	35,600
Total	13,623	8,287	1,000,719

The Regular Baptists have fourteen colleges and eight theological schools under their charge. The colleges have 67 professors, 2041 graduates, 720 ministers, and libraries containing 63,800 volumes; and the theological schools 30 professors, 294 graduates and ministers, 150 students and 13,750 volumes in eight libraries. In connection with the Baptists are several Missions, home, foreign and Indian; Bible Societies and a Publication Society. They have also, espousing their peculiar views, 20 weekly, one semi-monthly, 11 monthly, three quarterly and one annual periodicals. This denomination preponderates in Rhode Island, Virginia, Kentucky, and most of the states further south. The estimated total of persons connected, otherwise than by church membership, with the Baptists, is about 4,500,000.

The "Presbyterians" are numerically second only to the Baptists. Their statistics exhibit the following classification and numbers:

	Churches.	*Ministers.*	*Church Members.*
Old School Presbyterians	2,376	1,715	179,543
New do. do.	1,581	1,430	145,416
Cumberland do.	570	300	60,000
Associate and other do.	530	290	45,500
Total	5,057	3,735	430,459

The total, in connection with these churches, may be set down at 2,400,000. The old school Presbyterians have, under their supervision, several of our oldest and most respectable colleges, especially in the southern and western states; also theological schools at Princeton, N. J., Alleghany City, Pa., Prince Edward County, Va., Columbia S. C. and New-Albany, Ind., and a large number of parochial and Sunday schools. They support missions to the United States Indians, and in Western Africa, India, Siam, China and Papal Europe, and domestic missions throughout the States. The number of periodicals devoted to old Presbyterianism, is one annual, one quarterly, two monthly and seven weekly newspapers. There are, in connection with the General Assembly, 22 synods, 118 presbyteries, 343 candidates for the ministry, 231 licenciates, 1715 ministers and 2376 churches, with an aggregate of communicants, numbering 179,543. During the ecclesiastical year 1846–7, the amount contributed for religious purposes, was $310,104 91. We have no statistics other than given above, in reference to the other denominations. The Presbyterians are the pervading sects in New-York, New-Jersey, Pennsylvania and the western parts of Maryland and Virginia: they are also numerous in the north-western states.

The "Congregationalists" are the next in point of numbers. According to the statistics of 1847 they had:

Churches.	*Ministers.*	*Church Members.*
1,867	1,612	177,668

and about 2,000,000 otherwise in connection. The churches planted by the Pilgrims, soon after their arrival at Plymouth, were all of this denominaton. Their progress has been rapid: in 1648, there were in Massachusetts 39 churches; in 1696, they had increased to 74; in 1767, to 280; in 1790, to 332; and in 1800, to 352. In the other New-England States, the growth of Congregationalism has been nearly as follows: in 1648, there were five churches in Connecticut and three in New-Hampshire; in 1696, there were 36 in Connecticut, five in New-Hampshire, and three in Maine; in 1760, in Connecticut, 153—in New-Hampshire, 40—in Maine, 20—and in Rhode-Island, 10 churches. The present number, in all New-England, is 1,353. In this estimate the evangelical churches only are included. In the states out of New-England, Congregationalism had scarcely an existence prior to the present century; it is estimated that now there are not less than 514 evangelical churches in the Middle and Western states. The Congregationalists have under their charge 18 Colleges, and a number of Theological Seminaries; besides Missions, Bible, and Publication Societies, in every part of the Union.

The "Episcopal Methodists" are more generally diffused throughout the states than any other denomination. They are least numerous in Louisiana, and most numerous in the Middle States. This church is divided into "North" and "South," being disagreed on the question of slavery. In the "North Church" there are 3,245 travelling, 318 superannuated, and 4,962 local preachers—609,670 white, and 30,750 colored church members, and 6,182 Sunday Schools, with 62,533 teachers, and 329,633 scholars. The "South Church" has 1,433 travelling, 86 superannuated, and 2,833 local preachers; 327,284 white, and 127,933 colored church members; and 1,262 Sunday Schools, with 7,409 teachers, and 44,500 scholars. The "North Church" is under five, and the "South" under four Bishops. The Episcopal Methodists have seven Colleges and 23 Seminaries and High Schools. Missions are supported in Liberia, Oregon, South America, China, Germany, India, Sweden, and throughout the new states, and among the United States Indians. They have also numerous periodicals and newspapers in furtherance of their own views. The first Methodist Society was founded in America in 1766, by Philip Embury, a local preacher from Ireland, in the city of New-York, and the first church was erected in the same place two years afterwards; in 1773, the date of the first published "Minutes," there were ten travelling preachers, and 1,160 church members; and in 1784, when this church was organized, there were 82 preachers, and 14,988 church members. The total of this church may be about 1,800,000 persons, inclusive of communicants.

The "Protestant Episcopal," or Anglican church, which sprang from the old English church, as established by law, previous to the Revolution, is the wealthiest of all other denominations, and is constituted of the older classes of American society; but in point of numbers it is far inferior to the Baptists, Congregationalists, Methodists, &c., and has lately been outstripped by the Catholics. It is more stationary than any other denomination: being more exclusive and less given to proselytism than any other; and while other churches are recruited by constant immigrations, this has no such accessions, the people of "England proper," who would adhere to this church, being but a small portion of those leaving the old countries. The Catholics are almost entirely dependent on this means for their increase. The number of churches in this connection is 1,232; of ministers, 1,373; and of communicants or church members, 72,099. The total nominally belonging to this church may number about 1,500,000 persons. They have eight Colleges under their charge, and numerous Theological Seminaries and High Schools. Their provisions for Missions, Bible Societies, Sunday Schools, &c. are ample. The dioceses are 31 in number, being coextensive with the states, except in the State of New-York, which has two Bishops. Missionary Bishops superintend the ecclesiastical affairs in the Territories, which comprise two divisions, "the Northern" and "the Southern," which are separated by the compromise line of Missouri, viz. 36° 30′ north latitude. In the new states it sometimes happens that the same Bishop presides over one, two or more dioceses. The first Episcopal Church in America was founded in New-York, on the site of the present

"Church of the Holy Trinity," and is still the most wealthy of all the American Churches.

The "Roman Catholics" have rapidly increased of late years, in consequence of the influx of immigrants from Ireland, and other Catholic countries. By comparing the statistics of 1837 and 1847, we find that during the last ten years the dioceses and bishops have doubled, and that the churches and priests have nearly tripled. The annexed will show this remarkable increase more clearly:

	Dioceses.	*Bishops.*	*Churches.*	*Priests.*	*Communicants*
1837	13	12	300	373	600,000
1847	26	24	812	864	1,173,600

The Catholics have 13 Colleges; 43 "Female Religious Institutions," (*nunneries;*) 66 "Female Academies;" 244 Clerical Students, and 88 Charitable Institutions. They are most numerous in the Atlantic cities, in which are most French and Irish; they are spread over Maryland, where, perhaps, they form a majority of the people; have many congregations in Missouri, Illinois, and part of Kentucky, and predominate in Louisiana. The accession of New Mexico and California, (which are not included in the above statistics,) will have added largely to the Catholic strength. There seems, indeed, to be a likelihood that, at no distant day, the Catholic population will become a majority in some of the states, and as there is no express provision in the several Constitutions against the establishment of state religions, it is to be feared that the Catholics will take advantage of this omission, and proclaim a spiritual supremacy wherever it is possible. It is high time, however, for the people of this highly-favored and Protestant country to remedy these defects in their fundamental laws, and forever exclude the baneful influence of Papal authority from our land. The statistics of the past ten years are a sufficient warning, and ought not to be slighted.

The relative importance of the remaining sects are exhibited in the following table:

Denominations.	*Churches.*	*Ministers.*	*Members*
Dutch Reformed	279	271	31,214
German Reformed	750	191	75,000
Evangelical Lutherans	1,232	501	146,300
Moravians	22	24	6.000
Protestant Methodists	—	740	64,318
Reformed do.	—	75	3,000
Wesleyan do.	—	600	20.600
German do.	1,800	500	15,000
Albright do.	600	250	15,000
Mennonites	400	250	58.000
Unitarians	300	250	30,000
Universalists	I,194	700	60,000
Swedenborgians	42	30	5,000
Mormons, (now chiefly in California)			15,000
Quakers, (in Pennsylvania, New-York, &c.)			150,000

The above comprise the chief Christian sects. Besides those enumerated as distinct sects, schisms frequently arise, by which congregations become separated into sections, each following its favorite pastor, without change of denomination, discipline or form of worship. As a general fact, indeed, it may be said that all the evangelical churches stand upon the same platform, and differ little but in name, and there seems to be a general agreement, each with the other, in all essential points of doctrine, and, to some extent, of discipline likewise. A stranger visiting an evangelical church could not, by any visible means, determine to which denomination it appertained. The religious societies of America have done much towards the establishment and consolidation of the Sunday School system: all have united in the good work, and there is now scarcely a child who has not the benefit of these institutions, and the amount of good they are influential in bringing forth will, no doubt, be exhibited in the well-being of the whole future people.

The only anti-Christian sect, in the civilized portion of the United States, is the "Jews," which number about 50 or 60,000, and are chiefly confined to the large Atlantic cities. They are an inoffensive people, and make good citizens, but in their private morals have been considered exceptionable. The proscription they have everywhere suffered, may have had a great influence on their present debasement; and it is to be hoped that the enlightened philanthropy, which is now abroad, will shortly ameliorate their condition and reverse the general opinion.

The Indian tribes, though in some measure under the influence of the Christian religion, cannot be said to have advanced much in its civilization. As a body they still adhere to the Paganism in which they were originally found, and still practice their barbarous rites and ceremonies. Their superstitions are sometimes of the most ridiculous description, but have a powerful influence over their actions, for good or for evil, as the case may be.

The United States have fully comprehended the maxims, that "uneducated mind is educated vice," and that "education is the cheap defence of nations." Various provisions have, as a sequence, been made in all the states for the literary and scientific education of their citizens: in most of them common and primary schools are widely distributed, and high schools and colleges are numerous. The necessary expense is provided for either by means of "school funds," accumulated from various sources, or by taxation; and in the new states and territories a thirty-sixth part of the public lands is reserved for the purposes of education. In the latter, however, no general system of instruction has yet been introduced; and, indeed, throughout the Union, there is neither any general system, nor is education carried to that extent and degree of efficiency which seems necessary, under the forms of government which prevail, to render the people capable of beneficially exercising and performing their important political duties and privileges. "One of the most common errors, in my opinion," says Mr. Combe, "committed by foreigners who write about America, as well as by the Americans themselves, is greatly to over-estimate the educational attainments of the people. The provision in money made by law for the education of all classes is large, compared with such countries as Britain and Austria; but, contrasted with what is necessary to bestow a really good education, it is still very deficient." And owing to various causes, which he specifies, the education received by nine-tenths of the children, in the agricultural districts, is extremely defective, and if the common education of America generally be analyzed, it will be found to comprise little beyond the mere acquisition of reading, writing and cyphering. From the best and fullest data we can obtain, there were, in 1840, in the United States, 3,546,643 white children, between the ages of 4 and 16, fit subjects for the school; and of these, 891,000 have not, or do not use the means even of a primary or common school education! From the same sources we also learn, that there are 549,693 white adults, over twenty years of age, who can neither read nor write. The chief part of these, however, are said to be foreigners, especially the Irish immigrants: if this be so, the number at the present date must be much larger, in consequence of the unparalleled immigration of the last few years. In the higher schools and colleges, however, matters are essentially different, and the educations there are as sound and extended, as in the former cases they are found to be deficient and superficial. The classics, the sciences and belles-lettres, are as well taught as in the most celebrated European universities and colleges. from these sources have sprung the Jeffersons, the Adamses, the Hamiltons, the Winthrops, the Wheatons, and other great scholars of America, whose works will endure as long as the language in which they are written. Lecturing to the people, in lyceums and society-halls, on every topic that can prove instructive or entertaining, has, for some years, been extensively practiced; and, as a mode of public instruction, is well-calculated to advance popular intelligence, if properly regulated; but hitherto this method, in consequence of deficiency in primary education, has not yielded any great advantage, and from the subjects chosen by the lecturers, which are commonly of an exciting character, it may be questioned whether or not they have been of any benefit whatever to the morals of the community.

The only educational institution, solely under the supervision of the supreme government, is the "Smithsonian Institution," lately founded and not yet in operation. Being localized at the seat of government, it can have no general effect on the educational progress of the people. The funds for its support were bequeathed by the late Mr. Smithson, of England, to the people of the United States, and for the "diffusion of knowledge among mankind;" the Congress has chosen to confine this knowledge to a favored section of the country, evidently in contravention of the intention of the donator.

There are in the United States 131 colleges and universities; sixty-one principal theological seminaries; eleven law schools, and forty-four medical schools. These will be fully described under the several states in which they are located. The number of students, who annually receive their education at these establishments, does not fall much short of 40,000.

Beside the above, there are 5,000 academies and high schools, distributed through the states, at which, in the year 1850, there were 250,000 students The ancient and modern languages, grammar, history, logic, rhetoric, moral and natural philosophy and the sciences, are taught in these institutions; they are generally considered as "select schools" for the more wealthy classes.

The common and primary schools, in 1850, numbered 70,000, with an aggregate of scholars amounting to 2,500,000. Evening schools are also established in some of the large cities, for the benefit of those whose occupations demand their attention during the day.

Closely connected with the religious and educational communities of the United States, are the great social instrumentalities, comprehended under the titles of benevolent societies, or such as by various means pertain to the progress of the people, in their religious, literary, and other duties of life. They naturally divide themselves into three distinct denominations: the first contains the Missionary, Bible and Tract societies; the second consists of the learned and scientific societies; and the third comprehends those societies of a miscellaneous character, all having a philanthropic view of improving the social condition of the inhabitants.

Societies of these descriptions are essentially of British origin, and are still maintained in that country, on a scale of munificence unparalleled in the history of any people. The people of the United States, as true descendants of the English, inherit from them, as well as many other peculiarities, the virtues which inculcate the necessity and advantage of providing means for the support of institutions of this description. That the people of the United States have comprehended, in its full spirit, their renovating and reforming influences, is evidenced in the multiplicity and complete organization, on a sound basis, of such societies, and in the support they individually and collectively receive among all classes.

The "American Bible Society," whose head-quarters are in the city of New-York, was instituted in 1816, and has more than two thousand auxiliary societies in all parts of the Union. Since that period to the present year, 1848, it has issued no less than 5,780,095 copies of the Bible, or parts of the Bible; of which 655,066 copies were issued during the year 1847–48. It has also published it in nearly all the languages of the world, among which are enumerated the Dutch, French, Italian, Swedish, Welsh, Portuguese, Danish, Irish, German, Spanish, Ojibwa, Hebrew, Latin, Polish, Gaëlic, Syriac, Greek, Arabic, Mohawk, Russian, Indian, Chinese, Delaware, &c., languages. The receipts of this society, for the year ending 30th April, 1848, amounted to $254,337 18, being the largest sum ever received in any single year, fully showing the increased spirit of the people in aid of the institution. The British and Foreign Bible Society, the parent of all similar consociations, was established in 1804, from which time it has issued 19,741,770 copies of the Bible, in *one hundred and thirty-eight* different languages. The receipts for the year 1846–7, were £117,440 9*s*. 3*d*., or a sum equal to $563,714; and the total expenditures £128,525 5*s*. 3*d*., or $616,921. Since the organization of the British society, it is calculated that the total issues of *all* societies have amounted to 30,000,000 Bibles and Testaments!!

Missionary societies are supported by the members of the several religious denominations, on separate footings, each having in view the religious conversion of the heathen, and the supplying of distant parts, which may be away from the influence of a regular ministry, with religious instruction; and the general diffusion throughout the world of a knowledge of the Christian doctrine. The present missionary societies, other than those supported by the Roman Catholics, are numerous and efficient. In Asia, Africa, Australia, and, indeed, in every part of the world, the great work of evangelization is going on apace. The Turk is throwing aside his deadly hatred; the inhabitants of China, so tenacious of forms and ceremonies, are embracing the new doctrines; the wild and untamed nations of Tartary, Arabia and Africa, and the people of the isles of the Indian and Pacific Ocean, are all overshadowed with the influence of Christianity, and are embracing, through the perseverance of the missionary, the forms and spirit of civilized societies. It would be impossible to indicate, by statistical detail, the amount of good that has been accomplished through these institutions; those interested in the matter will find all that is requisite for information, in the numerous publications issued by the several societies. These works contain, not only accounts of the progress of the missionary enterprises, but are replete with the most useful and valuable accounts of the nations among whom the missions are planted, contributing much to our general knowledge of the world, and the habits and customs of its various people. Domestic missions, and many other societies of a like kind might here be noticed, but the space allotted to this subject, which is a theme that volumes could not exhaust, must here be closed. As complete a list of the Protestant Missionary Stations, in every part of the world, as could possibly be got together, will be found near the conclusion of these volumes.

The literary and scientific societies of the United States, are established, not only in large communities, but are co-extensive with the limits of the country. In the most remote village or settlement, lyceums, lecture-rooms, debating-societies, &c., are as common for the improvement of the grown, as elementary schools are for children. Libraries and museums of natural history, medical, legal and general scientific associations, mechanics' institutes, &c., are universally a part of the organization of American society, and their effects on the people are fully exhibited in their inventive genius, their facility of appliance, and their peculiar aptness in accommodating themselves to circumstances; all, the legitimate result of a pre-existing knowledge, acquired at these institutions, and without which, the comforts and conveniences of life, in many of its phases, and especially in the newer regions, would be materially curtailed, and, perhaps, be altogether wanting. Apart, however, from the immediate and more practical benefits derived from these societies, who can compute their amount and value in enlarging the mind and elevating the character of a people?

The societies of a more miscellaneous, but no less worthy, useful and benevolent description, are the "American Colonization Society," the various "Prison Societies," the "Immigrant Societies" of the larger cities, and a host of others, even to mention which would occupy volumes. These names fully denote their several objects, and indicate the benevolent provisions for which they have been instituted. The numerous temperance societies are not only a blessing to individuals and families, but to the community at large, and are a means of saving, in a pecuniary point of view, immense sums, which, before their institution, were annually disbursed in all that was destructive to social order and the moral discipline of the nation. Their influence over every department of life, and the universal happiness they have diffused, has marked the present age as a peculiar era in the history of the human family, and will ever tend to elevate the renown of a people who fully and energetically embrace the principles of their organization.

Thus, the United States, in all that developes the religious tendencies, the morality and the physical superiority of the people, stands in the foremost rank; and if these societies, of which we have briefly spoken, continue to receive the aid and support of Americans, as they have hitherto done, the future destiny of our Union, which is prospectively one of mighty influence, will be secure, and Americans, as a nation, will receive the homage and reverence of all the good of the earth; and as the bright star of the west, herald the morning of liberty and happiness to a world, which yet lies in the gloom of superstition, ignorance and oppression.

The government of the United States is a federal democratic republic. It is based on the constitution of 1787, and amendments thereto.

The electors of the most numerous branch of the several state legislatures are qualified electors in the states respectively for all elective officers of the general government.

All legislative powers are vested in Congress, which consists of a Senate and House of Representatives.

The "House of Representatives" is composed of members chosen every second year by the people of the several states, and in number in accordance with the population of each, and in order to ascertain the number each state is entitled to, a census is taken every ten years, excluding from the enumeration for this object two-thirds of the slaves, and all Indians not taxed. Each state is entitled to at least one representative. Vacancies are filled by intermediate elections. The House chooses its speaker and other officers. No person under twenty-five years of age, who has been less than seven years a citizen of the United States, and who is not a resident of the state electing him, is qualified for representative.

The constitution provided for a specific number of representatives from each state to compose the House until the ascertainment of the population under the census of 1790; but since then legislation has decennially fixed the number to be elected. From the 3d March, 1793, the apportionment was one representative to every 33,000 of the representative population; after 1803, one to every 33,000 also; after 1813, one to every 35,000; after 1823, one to every 40,000; after 1833, one to every 47,000; after 1843, one to every 70,680; and after 3d March, 1853, there will be 233 representatives to be divided *pro rata* to the several states. The following table shows the number of representatives to which each state has been entitled since the establishment of the government:

STATES.	1787.	1793.	1803.	1813.	1823.	1833.	1843.	1853.
Maine	—	—	—	—	7	8	7	6
New Hampshire	3	4	5	6	6	5	4	3
Massachusetts	8	14	17	20	13	12	10	11
Rhode Island	1	2	2	2	2	2	2	2
Connecticut	5	7	7	7	6	6	4	4
Vermont	—	2	4	6	5	5	4	3
New York	6	10	17	27	34	40	34	33
New Jersey	4	5	6	6	6	6	5	5
Pennsylvania	8	13	18	23	26	28	24	25
Delaware	1	1	1	2	1	1	1	1
Maryland	6	8	9	9	9	8	6	6
Virginia	10	19	22	23	22	21	15	13
North Carolina	5	10	12	13	13	13	9	8
South Carolina	5	6	8	9	9	9	7	5
Georgia	3	2	4	6	7	9	8	8
Alabama	—	—	—	—	3	5	7	7
Mississippi	-	—	—	—	1	2	4	5
Louisiana	-	—	—	—	3	3	4	4
Tennessee	—	—	3	6	9	13	10	10
Kentucky	—	2	6	10	12	13	10	10
Ohio	—	—	—	6	14	19	21	21
Indiana	—	—	—	—	3	7	10	11
Illinois	—	—	—	—	1	3	7	9
Missouri	—	—	—	—	1	2	5	7
Arkansas	—	—	—	—	—	—	1	2
Michigan	—	—	—	—	—	—	3	4
Florida	—	—	—	—	—	—	—	1
Texas	—	—	—	—	—	—	—	2
Iowa	—	—	—	—	—	—	—	2
Wisconsin	—	—	—	—	—	—	—	3
California	—	—	—	—	—	—	—	2

In addition to these representatives from states, the House admits a delegate from each organized territory, who has the right to debate on subjects in which his territory is interested, but cannot vote.

The "Senate" consists of two members from each state, elected by the Legislatures thereof respectively for six years. One-third the whole body is renewed biennially, and if vacancies happen, by resignation or otherwise, during the recess of the legislature of any state, the executive of such states makes a temporary appointment until the next meeting of the legislature, which fills such vacancy. Senators must be at least thirty years old, must have been citizens of the United States for nine years, and be residents of the state by which chosen. Each senator has one vote. The Vice-President of the United States is *ex officio* President of the Senate, but a President *pro tempore* is elected by and from among the Senators, who in the absence of the President, acts in his stead.

The constitutional government went into operation on the 4th March, 1789, but a quorum of the first Congress, which met at the City of New York, was not formed until the 6th April, nor was the first President of the United States inaugurated before the 30th April. The following is a complete list of sessions of Congress held up to the present time:

Congress.	Session.	Commenced.	Terminated.	Days of Duration.	Speaker of House.	No. of Acts Passed.
1st	1st	6 April, 1789	29 Sep., 1789	176	Frederick A. Muhlenburg, *Pa.*	107
	2d	4 Jan., 1790	12 Aug., 1790	221		
	3d	6 Dec., 1790	3 Mar., 1791	88		
2d	1st	24 Oct., 1791	8 May, 1792	198	Jonathan Trumbull, *Conn.*	97
	2d	5 Nov., 1792	2 Mar., 1793	118		
3d	1st	2 Dec., 1793	9 June, 1794	190	Frederick A. Muhlenberg, *Pa.*	119
	2d	3 Nov., 1794	3 Mar., 1795	121		
4th	1st	7 Dec., 1795	1 June, 1796	178	Jonathan Dayton, *N. J.*	85
	2d	5 " 1796	3 Mar., 1797	89		
5th	1st	15 May, 1797	10 July, 1797	57	do. do. *do.*	156
	2d	13 Nov., 1797	16 " 1798	246		
	3d	3 Dec., 1798	3 Mar., 1799	91		
6th	1st	2 " 1799	14 May, 1800	165	Theodore Sedgewick, *Mass.*	112
	2d	17 Nov., 1800	3 Mar., 1801	107		
7th	1st	7 Dec., 1801	3 May, 1802	148	Nathaniel Macon, *N. C.*	95
	2d	6 " 1802	3 Mar., 1803	88		
8th	1st	17 Oct., 1803	27 " 1804	163	do. do. *do.*	108
	2d	5 Nov., 1804	3 " 1805	119		
9th	1st	2 Dec., 1805	21 April, 1806	141	do. do. *do.*	95
	2d	1 " 1806	3 Mar., 1807	93		
10th	1st	26 Oct., 1807	25 April, 1808	183	Joseph B. Varnum, *Mass.*	106
	2d	7 Nov., 1808	3 Mar., 1809	117		
11th	1st	22 May, 1809	28 June, 1809	38	do. do. *do.*	113
	2d	27 Nov., 1809	1 May, 1810	156		
	3d	3 Dec., 1810	3 Mar., 1811	91		
12th	1st	4 Nov., 1811	6 July, 1812	246	Henry Clay, *Ky.*	208
	2d	2 " 1812	3 Mar., 1813	122		
13th	1st	24 May, 1813	2 Aug., 1813	71	do. do. *do.*	271
	2d	6 Dec., 1813	18 April, 1814	134		
	3d	19 Sep., 1814	3 Mar., 1815	165	Langdon Cheves, *S. C.*	
14th	1st	4 Dec., 1815	30 April, 1816	149	Henry Clay, *Ky.*	298
	2d	2 " 1816	3 Mar., 1817	92		
15th	1st	1 " 1817	30 April, 1818	151	do. do. *do.*	256
	2d	16 Nov., 1818	3 Mar., 1819	108		
16th	1st	6 Dec., 1819	15 May, 1820	162	do. do. *do.*	208
	2d	13 Nov., 1820	3 Mar., 1821	111	John W. Taylor, *N. Y.*	
17th	1st	3 Dec., 1821	8 May, 1822	157	Philip P. Barbour, *Va.*	239
	2d	2 " 1822	3 Mar., 1823	92		

Congress.	Session.	Commenced.	Terminated.	Days of Duration.	Speaker of House.	No. of Acts Passed.
18th	1st	1 Dec., 1823	27 May, 1824	179	Henry Clay, *Ky.*	336
	2d	6 “ 1824	3 Mar., 1825	88		
19th	1st	5 “ 1825	22 May, 1826	169	John W. Taylor, *N. Y.*	265
	2d	4 “ 1826	3 Mar., 1827	90		
20th	1st	3 “ 1827	26 May, 1828	176	Andrew Stevenson, *Va.*	225
	2d	1 “ 1828	3 Mar., 1829	93		
21st	1st	7 “ 1829	31 May, 1830	176	do. do. *do.*	369
	2d	6 “ 1830	3 Mar., 1831	88		
22d	1st	5 “ 1831	14 July, 1832	223	do. do. *do.*	458
	2d	3 “ 1832	3 Mar., 1833	91		
23d	1st	2 “ 1833	30 June, 1834	211	do. do. *do.*	390
	2d	1 “ 1834	3 Mar., 1835	93	John Bell, *Tenn.*	
24th	1st	7 “ 1835	4 July, 1836	211	James Knox Polk, *Tenn.*	458
	2d	5 “ 1836	3 Mar., 1837	89		
25th	1st	4 Sept., 1837	16 Oct., 1837	43	do. do. *do.*	537
	2d	4 Dec., 1837	9 July, 1838	218		
	3d	3 “ 1838	3 Mar., 1839	91		
26th	1st	2 “ 1839	21 July, 1840	233	R. M. T. Hunter, *Va.*	157
	2d	7 “ 1840	3 Mar., 1841	87		
27th	1st	31 May, 1841	13 Sept., 1841	106	John White, *Ky.*	515
	2d	6 Dec., 1841	31 Aug., 1842	263		
	3d	5 “ 1842	3 Mar., 1843	88		
28th	1st	4 “ 1843	17 June, 1844	196	John W. Jones, *Va.*	281
	2d	2 “ 1844	3 Mar., 1845	91		
29th	1st	1 “ 1845	10 Aug., 1846	253	John W. Davis, *Ind.*	309
	2d	7 “ 1846	3 Mar., 1847	87		
30th	1st	6 “ 1847	14 Aug., 1848	252	Robert C. Winthorp, *Mass.*	311
	2d	4 “ 1848	3 Mar., 1849	89		
31st	1st	3 “ 1849	30 Sept., 1850	301	Howell Cobb, *Ga.*	367
	2d	2 “ 1850	3 Mar., 1851	91		
32d	1st	1 “ 1851	1852	—	Linn Boyd, *Ky.*	—
	2d	“ 1852	3 Mar., 1853	—		

Besides its ordinary legislative capacity, the Senate is vested with certain judicial functions, and its members constitute a High Court of Impeachment. No person can be convicted by this court unless on the finding of a majority of Senators, nor does judgment extend further than to removal from office and disqualification. Representatives have the sole power of impeachment.

The Executive Power is vested in a President, who is elected by an Electoral College, chosen by popular vote, or by the legislature of the state, the number of electors being equal to the number of Senators and Representatives from the states to Congress. His term of office is four years, but he is eligible for re-election indefinitely. The electors forming the college, are themselves chosen in the manner prescribed by the laws of the several states. A majority of the aggregate number of votes given is necessary to the election of President and Vice-President, and if none of the candidates has such a majority, then the election of President is determined by the House of Representatives, and that of the Vice-President by the Senate, from among the three candidates having the highest number of electoral votes, and in doing so, the vote is taken by states, the representatives of each state having only one vote, which must, of course, be determined by a majority of their number. No person can be President or Vice-President who is not a native born citizen, of the age of thirty-five years, and who has been a resident of the United States for fourteen years. The President is commander-in-chief of the army and navy, and of the militia when in the service of the Union. With the concurrence of two-thirds of the Senate, he has the power to make treaties, appoint civil and military officers, levy war, conclude peace, and do all that rightly belongs to the executive power. He has a veto on all laws passed by Congress, but so qualified, that notwithstanding his disapproval, any bill becomes a law on its being afterwards approved of by two-thirds of both houses of Congress. The President has a salary of $25,000 per annum, and "the white house" at Washington, for a residence during his official term. The Vice-President is *ex-officio* President of the Senate; and in case of the death, resignation or other disability of the President, the powers and duties of that office devolve upon him for the remainder of the term for which the President had been elected. This provision of the constitution, for the first time since the foundation of the government, came into operation in 1841, on the demise of the late lamented General Harrison, who died 4th April, just one month after his inauguration, when John Tyler, the Vice-President, succeeded. In case of the disability of the Vice-President, the President of the Senate *pro tempore*, takes his place. The offices of President and Vice-President have been occupied by the following gentlemen since the adoption of the constitution:

	Presidents.	Vice-Presidents.	Term of Office.			
1.	George Washington	John Adams	30th Ap.,	1789,	to 4th Mar.,	1793
2.	Do. do.	Do. do.	4th Mar.,	1793,	to 4th Mar.,	1797
3.	John Adams	Thomas Jefferson	"	1797	" "	1801
4.	Thomas Jefferson	Aaron Burr	"	1801	" "	1805
5.	Do. do.	George Clinton	"	1805	" "	1809
6.	James Madison	Do. do. (d. 20 Ap., 1812)	"	1809	" "	1813
7.	Do. do.	Elbr. Gerry (d. 23 Nov., 1814)	"	1813	" "	1817
8.	James Monroe	Daniel D. Tompkins	"	1817	" "	1821
9.	Do. do.	Do. do.	"	1821	" "	1825
10.	John Quincy Adams	John C. Calhoun	"	1825	" "	1829
11.	Andrew Jackson	Do. do.	"	1829	" "	1833
12.	Do. do.	Martin Van Buren	"	1833	" "	1837
13.	Martin Van Buren	Richard M. Johnson	"	1837	" "	1841
14.	Wm. Henry Harrison	John Tyler	"	1841	" 4th Apr.,	1841
15.	John Tyler (on the death of Gen. Harrison)		4th Apr.,	1841	" 4th Mar.,	1845
16.	James K. Polk	George M. Dallas	4th Mar.,	1845	" "	1849
17.	Zachary Taylor	Millard Fillmore	"	1849	" 9th June,	1850
18.	Millard Fillmore (on the death of Gen. Taylor)		9th June,	1850		

The administrative business of the nation is conducted by several officers, with the title of Secretaries, etc., and who form what is termed the "Cabinet." These are the Secretary of State, the Secretary of War, the Secretary of the Navy, the Secretary of the Treasury, the Post Master General, the Secretary of the Interior, and the Attorney General—the last being the official law authority for advisement in administrative affairs. Each of these presides over a separate Department.

The "Department of State" was created by an act of Congress of the 15th of September, 1789; by a previous act of the 27th July, 1789, it was denominated the Department of Foreign Affairs. It embraced, until the establishment of the Department of the Interior in 1849, what in some other governments are styled the Department of Foreign Affairs and Home Department; but the duties now being divided, it confines its operations almost entirely to foreign matters, and hence its original title might with propriety and convenience be restored.

The *Secretary of State* conducts all treaties between the United States and foreign powers, and corresponds officially with the public ministers of the government at foreign courts, and with ministers of foreign powers, resident in the United States. He is entrusted with the publication of all treaties with foreign powers, preserves the originals of all treaties and of the public correspondence growing out of international intercourse; grants passports to American citizens visiting foreign states, etc. He has charge of the Great Seal of the United States, but cannot affix it to any commission until signed by the President, nor to any instrument without authority of the President.

Secretaries of State—Salary $6,000 per Annum.

Thomas Jefferson, *Va.*	26 Sep.,	1789
Edmund Randolph, *Va.*	2 Jan.,	1794
Timothy Pickering, *Pa.*	4 Feb.,	1795
John Marshall, *Va.*	13 May,	1800
James Madison, *Va.*	5 Mar.,	1801
Robert Smith, *Md.*	6 "	1809
James Monroe, *Va.*	25 Nov.,	1811
John Quincy Adams, *Mass.*	5 Mar.,	1817
Henry Clay, *Ky.*	8 "	1825
Martin Van Buren, *N. Y.*	6 "	1829
Ed. P. Livingston, *La.*		1831
Louis McLane, *Del.*	7 Mar.,	1833
John Forsyth, *Ga.*		1834
Daniel Webster, *Mass.*	5 Mar.,	1841
Hugh S. Legaré, *S. C.*	9 May,	1843
Abel P. Upshur, *Va.*	24 June,	1843
John Nelson, *Md.*	29 Feb.,	1844
John C. Calhoun, *S. C.*	6 Mar.,	1844
James Buchanan, *Pa.*	5 "	1845
John M. Clayton, *Del.*	6 "	1849
Daniel Webster, *Mass.*	20 July,	1850

This department has subject to it the Diplomatic Bureau, the Consular Bureau and a Home Bureau. The United States are represented by Ministers Pleni-potentiary at the courts of Great Britain, France, Russia, Prussia, Spain, Mexico, Brazil and Chili; by Commissioners at the court of Pekin, China, and at the Sandwich Islands; by a Minister Resident at the Sublime Porte, and at other courts by Chargés des Affaires; and United States' Consuls are stationed at all the important commercial ports in the world. Foreign Ministers accredited to the government of the United States are—Envoys Extra-ordinary and Ministers Pleni-potentiary from Great Britain, Russia, the Argentine Republic, France, Spain, Chili, New-Grenada, Brazil, Mexico and Peru; Ministers Resident from Portugal, Prussia and Belgium; and Chargés des Affaires from Denmark, Austria, Holland, Sweden, Naples, Sardinia, Venezuela and Nicaragua. Foreign Consuls from all commercial nations reside in the several Collection Districts of the Union.

The "Department of the Interior" was established by an act of Congress of the 30th March, 1849. The *Secretary of the Interior* is entrusted with the supervision and management of all matters connected with the public domain, Indian affairs, pensions, patents, public buildings, the census, the penitentiary of the District of Columbia, the expenditures of the Federal Judiciary, etc. Each of these interests is managed in a separate bureau or office, the immediate head of which is styled Commissioner, Superintendent, or Warden, as the case may be.

Secretaries of the Interior—Salary $6,000 per Annum.

Thomas H. Ewing, *Ohio*	6 Mar.,	1849
James A. Pearce (declined)	20 July,	1850
T. M. T. McKennon (dec.)	8 Aug.,	1850
Alex. H. H. Stuart, *Va.*	10 Sep.,	1850

The "Department of the Treasury" was created by an act of Congress of the 2d of September, 1789. The *Secretary of the Treasury* superintends all the fiscal concerns of the government, and upon his own responsibility recommends to Congress measures for improving the condition of the revenue. All public accounts are finally settled at this Department; and for this purpose it is divided into the office of the Secretary who has the general superintendence, the offices of the two Comptrollers, the offices of the Six Auditors, the office of the Commissioner of Customs, the Treasurer's office, the Register's office, the Solicitor's office, and the office of the Coast Survey. Assistant Treasurers' offices are also established at Boston, New-York, Philadelphia, Charleston, New-Orleans and St. Louis.

Secretaries of the Treasury—Salary $6,000 *per Annum.*

Alex. Hamilton, *N. Y.* .....12 Sep., 1789		William J. Duane, *Pa.*...... 1833
Oliver Wolcott, *Ct.*......... 4 Feb., 1795		Roger B. Taney, *Md.*....... 1833
Samuel Dexter, *Mass.* ......31 Dec., 1800		Levi Woodbury, *N. H.* .... 7 Mar., 1833
Albert Gallatin, *Pa.* ....26 Jan., 1802		Thomas Ewing, *Ohio* ...... 5 " 1841
George W. Campbell, *Ct.*... 9 Feb., 1814		Walter Forward, *Pa.*.......13 Sep., 1841
Alexander J. Dallas, *Pa.* .. 6 Oct., 1814		John C. Spencer, *N. Y.* ... 3 Mar., 1843
William H. Crawford, *Ga.* . 5 Mar., 1817		George M. Bibb, *Ky.*.......15 June, 1844
Richard Rush, *Pa.*......... 7 " 1825		Robert J. Walker, *Miss.* ... 5 Mar., 1845
Samuel D. Ingham, *Pa.*..... 6 " 1829		William M. Meredith, *Pa.* . 6 " 1849
Louis McLane, *Del.*........ 1831		Thomas Corwin, *Ohio*......20 July, 1850

The "Department of War" was created by an act of Congress of the 7th of August, 1789, and at first embraced not only military, but also naval affairs. The *Secretary of War* superintends every branch of military affairs, and has under his immediate direction the Adjutant General's office, the Quartermaster General's Bureau, the Paymaster's Bureau, the Subsistence Bureau, the Medical Bureau, the Engineer Bureau, the Topographical Bureau, the Ordnance Bureau, etc.; and the department has the superintendence of the erection of fortifications, of making public surveys, and other important services.

Secretaries of War—Salary $6,000 *per Annum.*

Henry Knox, *Mass.*........12 Sep., 1789	Peter B. Porter, *N. Y.* ....26 May, 1828
Timothy Pickering, *Pa.*..... 2 Jan., 1795	John H. Eaton, *Tenn.*...... 9 Mar., 1829
James McHenry, *Md.* .....27 " 1796	Lewis Cass, *Mich.*......... 1831
Samuel Dexter, *Mass.* ......13 May, 1800	Joel R. Poinsett, *S. C.*..... 7 " 1837
Roger Griswold, *Ct.*........ 3 Feb., 1801	John Bell, *Tenn.*.......... 5 " 1841
Henry Dearborn, *Mass.* ... 5 Mar., 1801	John McLean, *Ohio* ....13 Sep., 1841
William Eustis, *Mass.*...... 7 " 1809	John C. Spencer, *N. Y.* ...12 Oct., 1841
John Armstrong, *N. Y.*....13 Jan., 1813	James W. Porter, *Pa.* ..... 8 Mar., 1843
James Monroe, *Va.* ....27 Sep., 1814	William Wilkins, *Pa.*.......15 Feb., 1844
William H. Crawford, *Ga.*.. 2 Mar., 1815	William L. Marcy, *N. Y.*.. 5 Mar., 1845
Isaac Shelley, *Ky.* .... 5 " 1817	George W. Crawford, *Ga.*.. 6 " 1849
John C. Calhoun, *S. C.*.....16 Dec., 1817	Edmund Bates (declined)..20 July, 1850
James Barbour, *Va.* ...... 7 Mar., 1825	Charles M. Conrad, *La.*.... 8 Aug., 1850

The "Department of the Navy" was created by an act of Congress of the 30th of April, 1798. The *Secretary of the Navy* issues all orders to the naval forces and superintends naval affairs generally. Attached to the Department are—a Bureau of Docks and Navy Yards, a Bureau of Ordnance and Hydrography, a Bureau of Construction, Equipment and Repairs, a Bureau of Provisions and Clothing, a Bureau of Medical and Surgical Instruments, etc.; and the National Observatory at Washington is under the control of the Navy Department. The ministerial duties of these several Bureaux were formerly exercised by a Board of Navy Commissioners.

Secretaries of the Navy—Salary $6,000 *per Annum.*

George Cabot, *Mass.* .... 3 May, 1798	Mahlon Dickerson, *N. J.*... 1834
Benjamin Stoddart, *Md.*....21 " 1798	James K. Paulding, *N. Y.*..30 June, 1838
Robert Smith, *Md.*.........26 Jan., 1802	George P. Badger, *N. C.* .. 5 Mar., 1841
J. Crowningshield, *Mass.* .. 2 Mar., 1805	Abel P. Upshur, *Va.* ....13 Sep., 1841
Paul Hamilton, *S. C.*...... 7 " 1809	David Henshaw, *Mass.* ....24 July, 1843
William Jones, *Pa.* ....12 Jan., 1813	Thomas W. Gilmer, *Va.* ...15 Feb., 1844
B.W. Crowningshield, *Mass.*19 Dec., 1814	John Y. Mason, *Va.* ....14 Mar., 1844
Smith Thompson, *N. Y.* ...30 Nov., 1818	George Bancroft, *Mass.* ...10 " 1845
Samuel L. Southard, *N. J.* . 9 Dec., 1823	John Y. Mason, *Va.* 1846
John Branch, *N. C.* ...... 9 Mar., 1829	William B. Preston, *Va.*... 6 Mar., 1849
Levi Woodbury, *N. H.*.... 1831	William A. Graham, *N. C.*..20 July, 1850

The "Department of the Post Office" was established under the authority of the Old Congress. The *Postmaster General* has the chief direction of all postal arrangements with foreign states as well as within the federal limits. The general business is managed by three Assistant Postmasters General, who preside respectively over the Contract office, the Appointment office, and the Inspection, etc., office.

Postmasters General.—Salary $6,000 *per Annum.*

Samuel Osgood, *Mass.*......26 Sep.,	1789	Amos Kendall, *Ky*......... 1 May,	1835
Timothy Pickering, *Pa.* ... 7 Nov.,	1791	John M. Niles, *Ct.*.........25 "	1840
Joseph Habersham, *Ga.* ... 2 Jan.,	1795	Francis Granger, *N. Y.* ... 6 Mar.,	1841
Gideon Granger, *Ct.* ....17 Mar.,	1802	Charles A. Wickliffe, *Ky.* ..13 Sep.,	1841
Reuben J. Meigs, *Ohio* .... "	1814	Cave Johnson, *Tenn.* ..... 5 Mar.,	1845
John McLean, *Ohio* .... 9 Dec.,	1823	Jacob Collamer, *Vt.*........ 6 "	1849
William J. Barry, *Ky.*..... 9 Mar.,	1829	Nathan K. Hall, *N. Y.*....20 June,	1850

The "Attornies-General," who are considered as forming a part of the Cabinet, and who are the constitutional advisers and defendants of the government, are generally men of the greatest acquirements in their profession. The gentlemen who have held this office, are enumerated in the annexed list:

Attornies-General.—Salary $4,000 *per Annum.*

Edmund Randolph, *Va.*..26th Sept.	1789	Benj. F. Butler, *N. Y* ..25th Dec.	1835
William Bradford, *Pa.*...27th Jan.	1794	Felix Grundy, *Tenn.* .... 1st Sept.	1838
Charles Lee, *Va.*.........10th Dec.	1795	Henry D. Gilpin, *Pa.* ....11th Jan.	1840
Levi Lincoln, *Mass.*....... 5th Mar.	1801	John J. Crittenden, *Ky.*. 5th Mar.	1841
Robert Smith, *Md.* ...... 2d "	1805	Hugh S. Legare, *S. C.*...13th Sept.	1841
John Breckenridge, *Ky.*..23rd Dec.	1806	John Nelson, *Md*........ 1st July	1843
Cæsar A. Rodney, *Del.*...21st Jan.	1807	John Y. Mason, *Va.*..... 5th Mar.	1845
William Pinckney *Md.*....11th Dec.	1811	Nathan Clifford..........	1847
Richard Rush, *Pa.* ......10th Feb.	1814	Isaac Toucey, *Ct.*.......	1848
William Wirt, *Md.*........16th Dec.	1817	Reverdy Johnson, *Md.*... 6th Mar.	1849
John McPh. Berrien, *Ga.*. 9th Mar.	1829	John J. Crittenden, *Ky.*.20th July	1850
Roger B. Taney, *Md.*....	1831		

The Judicial powers of the United States are vested in a Supreme Court and in such other inferior Courts as Congress may from time to time establish. The present judicial establishment consists of a Supreme Court, Circuit Courts, and District Courts.

The "Supreme Court," the highest judicial tribunal of the Union, is composed of a Chief Justice and eight Associate Justices, the Attorney General, a Reporter and Clerk. This court is held in Washington, and has one session annually, commencing on the first Monday in December.

The Supreme Court has exclusive jurisdiction in all controversies of a civil nature where a state is a party, except between a state and its citizens, and except also between a state and citizens of other states or aliens—in which latter case it has original but not exclusive jurisdiction. It has exclusively all such jurisdiction of suits and proceedings against ambassadors or other public ministers, or their domestics or domestic servants, as a court of law can have or exercise consistently with the law of nations; and original, but not exclusive jurisdiction of all suits brought by ambassadors or other public ministers, in which a consul or a vice-consul is a party. It has appellate jurisdiction from final decrees and judgments of the circuit courts in cases where the matter in dispute, exclusive of costs, exceeds the sum or value of 2,000 dollars, and from final decrees and judgments of the highest courts of the several states in certain cases. It has power to issue writs of prohibition to the District Courts, when proceeding as Courts of Admiralty and maritime jurisdiction; and writs of mandamus in cases warranted by the principles and usages of law to any courts appointed or persons holding office under the authority of the United States. The trial of issues in fact in the Supreme Court in all actions at law against citizens of the United States is by jury.

A final judgment or decree in any suit, in the highest court of law or equity of a state in which a decision in the suit could be had, where is drawn in question the validity of a treaty or statute of, or an authority exercised under the United States, and the decision is against their validity; or where is drawn in question the validity of a statute of, or an authority exercised under any state, on the ground of their being repugnant to the constitution, treaties, or laws of the United States, and the decision is in favor of their validity; or where is drawn in question the construction of any clause of the constitution, or of a treaty or statute of, or commission held under the United States, and the decision is against the title, right, privilege, or exemption, specially set up or claimed by either party, under such clause of the constitution, treaty, statute, or commission; may be re-examined, and reversed or affirmed, in the Supreme Court of the United States, upon a writ of error, the citation being signed by the Chief Justice, or Judge, or Chancellor of the court rendering or passing the judgment or decree complained of, or by a Justice of the Supreme Court of the United States, in the same manner, and under the same regulations, and the writ has the same effect, as if the judgment or decree complained of had been rendered or passed in a Circuit Court; and the proceeding upon the reversal is also the same, except that the Supreme Court, instead of remanding the cause for a final decision, may, at their discretion, if the cause shall have been once remanded before, proceed to a final decision of the same, and award execution. But no other error can be assigned or regarded as a ground of reversal in any such case, than such as appears on the face of the record, and immediately respect the before-mentioned questions of validity or construction of the said constitution, treaties, statutes, commissions, or authorities, in dispute.

Chief Justices of the Supreme Court.—Salary $5,000 per Annum.

John Jay, *N. Y.*	26th Sept.	1789
John Rutledge, *S. C.*	1st July,	1795
William Cushing, *Mass.*	27th Jan.	1796
Oliver Ellsworth, *Conn.*	4th Mar.	1796
John Jay, *N. Y.*	19th Dec.	1800
John Marshall, *Va.*	27th Jan.	1801
Roger B. Taney, *Md.*	28th Dec.	1835

The "Circuit Courts" are held by a Justice of the Supreme Court assigned to the Circuit and by the Judge of the District in which the Court sits conjointly. The United States is divided into nine judicial Circuits, in each of which a Court is held twice a year. The Circuits are as follows:

I. Maine, New-Hampshire, Massachusetts, and Rhode Island.
II. Vermont, Connecticut, and New-York.
III. New-Jersey and Pennsylvania.
IV. Delaware, Maryland, and Virginia.
V. Alabama, Louisiana, and Kentucky.
VI. North-Carolina, South-Carolina and Georgia.
VII. Ohio, Indiana, Illinois, and Michigan.
VIII. Kentucky, Tennessee, and Missouri.
IX. Mississippi and Arkansas.

The states of Florida, Texas, Iowa, Wisconsin and California have not yet been attached to any circuit; but the District Courts have the power of Circuit Courts. There is a local Circuit Court held in the District of Columbia by three judges specially appointed for that purpose. The Chief Justice of that court sits also as District Judge of that District.

The Circuit Courts of the United States have original cognizance, concurrent with the courts of the several states, of all suits of a civil nature, at common law, or in equity, where the matter in dispute exceeds, exclusive of costs, the sum or value of 500 dollars, and the United States are plaintiffs or petitioners, or an alien is a party, or the suit is between a citizen of the state where the suit is brought and a citizen of another state. They have exclusive cognizance of all crimes and offences cognizable under the authority of the United States, (except where the laws of the United States otherwise direct,) and concurrent jurisdiction with the District Courts of the crimes and offences cognizable therein. But no person can be arrested in one district for trial in another, in any civil action, before a Circuit or District Court. No civil suit can be brought, before either of said courts, against an inhabitant of the United States, by any original process, in any other district than that whereof he is an inhabitant, or in which he shall be found at the time of serving the writ; and no District or Circuit Court has cognizance of any suit to recover the contents of any promissory note, or other *chosé* in action, in favor of an assignee, unless a suit might have been prosecuted in such court to recover the said contents, if no assignment had been made, except in cases of foreign bills of exchange.

The Circuit Courts have appellate jurisdiction from final decrees and judgments of the District Courts, in all cases where the matter in dispute exceeds the sum or value of fifty dollars. They also have jurisdiction of certain cases, which may be removed into them before trial from the state courts. But no District Judge, (sitting in the Circuit Court,) can give a vote in any case of appeal, or error, from his own decision; but may assign the reasons of such his decision. The trial of issues in fact in the Circuit Courts, in all suits, except those of equity and of admiralty and maritime jurisdiction, is by jury.

The "District Courts" are held respectively by a district judge alone. Each state is one district for the purposes of holding District or Circuit Courts therein, with the exception of New York, Pennsylvania, Virginia, Georgia, Florida, Mississippi, Louisiana, Arkansas, and California, each of which is divided into two districts; and of Alabama, Tennessee, and Iowa, each of which are divided into three districts. There are besides these, Territorial Courts, which are temporary, and lose that character whenever a territory becomes a state.

Each court has a clerk, a public attorney or prosecutor, and a marshal—all of which are appointed by the President of the United States, with the exception of the clerks, who are appointed by the courts severally.

The District Courts of the United States have, exclusively of the courts of the several states, cognizance of all crimes and offences that are cognizable under the authority of the United States, committed within their respective districts, or upon the high seas, where no other punishment than whipping, not exceeding thirty stripes, a fine not exceeding one hundred dollars, or a term of imprisonment not exceeding six months, is to be inflicted, and also have exclusive original cognizance of all civil causes of admiralty and maritime jurisdiction, including all seizures under the laws of impost, navigation, or trade, of the United States, where the seizures are made on waters which are navigable from the sea by vessels of ten or more tons' burthen, within their respective districts, as well as upon the high seas, saving to suitors, in all cases, the right of a common law remedy, where the common law is competent to give it; and also have exclusive original cognizance of all seizures on land, or other waters than as aforesaid, made, and of all suits for penalties and forfeitures incurred, under the laws of the United States. And they also have cognizance, concurrent with the courts of the several states, or their circuit courts, as the case may be, of all causes where an alien sues for a *tort* only in violation of the law of nations, or a treaty of the United States. They also have cognizance, concurrent as last mentioned, of all suits at common law, where the United States sue, and the matter in dispute amounts, exclusive of costs, to the sum or value of one hundred dollars. They also have jurisdiction, exclusively of the courts of the several states, of all suits against consuls or vice-consuls, except for offences above the description aforesaid. The trial of issues in fact, in the District Courts, in all causes, except civil causes of admiralty and maritime jurisdiction, is by jury.

An act of the 18th of December, 1812, requires the district and territorial judges of the United States to reside within the districts and territories, respectively, for which they are appointed; and makes it unlawful for any judge, appointed under the authority of the United States, to exercise the profession or employment of counsel or attorney, or to be engaged in the practice of the law. And any person offending against the injunction or prohibition of this act, shall be deemed guilty of misdemeanor.

Appeals are allowed from the District to the Circuit Courts in cases where the matter in dispute, exclusive of costs, exceeds the sum in value of $50, and from the Circuit Courts to the Supreme Court in cases where the matter in dispute exceeds the sum, or value, of $2,000; and in some cases where the inconvenience of attending a court by a justice of the Supreme Court is very great, the District Courts are invested with Circuit Court powers.

The appointment of all judges of the United States is made by the President, by and with the advice of the Senate; and the judges hold their several offices during good behavior, and can be removed only on impeachment. Their compensation is fixed by law, and cannot be diminished during their period of office.

The defensive means of the United States, though scattered over a vast extent of country, and though still in their infancy, are adequate to all its wants, and are progressively increased, year by year. The chief harbors are strongly secured by fortifications sufficient to repel any immediate attack from without, and the Indian frontiers and lines of commerce in the interior are protected from savage incursions by stockade and other detached forts.

The army consists of two distinct classes, viz.: a small regular force, and the militia or national guards. The first, styled the army of the United States, comprises the engineers, topographical engineers, and the ordnance, two regiments of dragoons, one of mounted riflemen, four of artillery, and eight of infantry. Several additional regiments were organized during the Mexican war, but on the conclusion of hostilities were again disbanded. The effective force of the regular army, including the staff officers, is 10,317 men. The volunteers are only called into service during a state of hostilities or insurrection, and are merely a substitute for the necessity of enforcing the services of the militia. The numerous independent companies, now organized voluntarily in all thickly-populated cities, may be classed under this head. These are all uniformed, drilled, and kept together without any aid from the states, and can only be called out on an emergency, trusting to their patriotism for the fulfilment of their duties, in which, however, we ought to state they have never as yet failed. The militia is properly the force of the state in which it resides, and is composed of all, with some legal exceptions, between the ages of 18 and 45. The present number is 1,858,534, of which 747 are general officers, 2,374 general staff-officers, 16,392 field-officers, 50,945 company-officers, and 1,704,942 non-commissioned officers, musicians, privates, etc. The pay of the officers is much higher than the same classes in European armies. There can be no doubt of the efficiency of the United States military; the successive triumphs of the American arms on the fields of the Revolution, in the hard-fought battles of the last war with Britain, and on the bloody plains and ravines of Mexico, fully attest their superiority of *morale* and organization, and the acquirements of the officers. It would be hard to give a preference to one arm of the service over another—each has displayed a valor and discipline equal to any emergency, and both have succeeded in routing the enemy; and the Mexican war, conducted, as it has been, by the union of regulars and citizen-soldiers, has stamped with lasting fame the whole physical force of the Union.

The army is under the command of a major-general, who is styled General-in-chief, and who resides at Washington, except when called to take the field. The President is, *ex-officio*, Commander-in-Chief of the Army of the United States. The states are divided into three military divisions, under the command of two brigadiers-general, who are commonly majors-general by brevet. These are subdivided into eleven departments, viz.: 4 in the eastern, 5 in the western, and 2 in the Pacific divisions.

There is a Military Academy at West Point, on the Hudson River, for the education of youth intended for the army. The branches taught are engineering and fortifications, mathematics, natural and experimental philosophy, ethics, drawing, sword exercise, and all the sciences which contribute to the utility of a gentleman and soldier. The cadets are appointed by the President, on presentation by the Senators of the several states, and a certain number is only allowed to each state. They are engaged to remain at the Academy for five years, and receive, during their educational course, a pay of $16 per month, and two rations, or a commutation of forty cents per day. When any cadet has received a regular degree from the academic staff, after going through all the classes, he is considered as among the candidates for a commission in any corps, according to the duties he may be judged competent to perform; and if there is not, at the time, a vacancy in such corps, he may be attached to it, at the discretion of the President, by brevet of the lowest rank until a vacancy shall happen. From this school has emanated some of the greatest military talent of the country—men now renowned in arms, the sciences, and the fine arts. Many of the elevês of this institution, though yet young men, have, from their recent exploits and scientific acquirements, exhibited to the country the benefit this establishment is likely to confer on the nation.

The Navy acquired great reputation during the war with Britain, and augmented its claim to honor during the protracted blockade of the ports of Mexico. In foreign parts it has been equally successful. Algiers and the Barbary States, generally, can attest its prowess, and the great powers of Europe confess its superiority in both talent and force. Unlike the forces of those countries, the seamen of the United States fight as patriots, and not as prisoners, and feel that the honor of their country requires their endeavors. The Navy consists of 11 ships of the line, 12 first class frigates, 2 second class frigates, 22 sloops of war, 5 brigs, 8 schooners, 4 bomb vessels, 1 ordnance transport, 13 steamers, and 6 store-ships and brigs; but of these, five of the ships and three frigates are yet on the stocks, and three of the ships are employed as receiving ships, at New York, Boston, and Norfolk. The navy, however, is rapidly increasing, and several large mail steamers are capable of being converted into war-ships, and liable to be called into service whenever required. The United States, indeed, are in such a position as to be able to raise in twelve months, a larger navy from her commercial marine, than any that has yet swept the seas.

The marine corps is organized as a brigade, and numbers at the present time 75 commissioned officers and 2,320 non-commissioned officers, musicians, and privates: in all 2,395 men. This force is subject to the laws and regulations of the navy, except when detached for service with the military. The marines are enlisted for five years.

The Navy is divided into the home squadron, the Brazil squadron, the Pacific, the Mediterranean, and Coast of Africa squadrons. There are seven navy yards, viz.: Portsmouth, Charlestown, New York, Philadelphia, Washington, Norfolk, and Pensacola. The naval asylum, at Philadelphia, and the naval school, at Annapolis, are of great benefit to this arm of the service. The organization of the naval force exhibits the following numbers: 68 captains (the highest grade), 97 commanders, 327 lieutenants, 69 surgeons, 29 passed assistant surgeons, 36 assistant surgeons, 64 pursers, 22 chaplains, 181 passed midshipmen, 264 midshipmen, 28 masters, 22 professors of mathematics, 3 naval school teachers, 31 boatswains, 42 gunners, 36 carpenters, and 34 sailmakers. The number of men and boys, of course, varies with the number of ships in commission; the seamen are engaged for three years, and are paid at the rate of twelve dollars a month, out of which, however, they have to find the chief portion of their clothing.

From the above, it is evident that the defensive means of the United States are superior to those of any country of the world. Every ship owned could be converted into a ship of war; every man, except foreigners, is liable to do military duty, and with patriotic hearts they *would* do it with that spirit and energy that liberty may depend on; the pecuniary means of the government are sufficient for all purposes; and should an enemy be rash enough to invade our shores, there is no doubt but that he would return with the same conclusive ideas of the invincibility of the Union as that entertained by the people of this favored country themselves.

The policy of the United States has hitherto been against the maintenance of a standing army, as dangerous to the public weal. That such is a tenable objection, let Mexico, Austria, France, Italy, and even the people of Great Britain attest. Besides the expense of its equipment and support, it has ever tended to coerce and tyrannize over the people, and been a cause rather than a preventive of war. The United States, however, is able to entrust the liberties of the country to its free citizens, who require not pay, but that glory and fame that ever attends the victory of liberty over despotism.

Judging from the market value of United States stocks, it is evident that the national finances are in a favorable condition. At the present time, they range at from nine to eleven per cent. premium; and although burdened with the extraordinary expenses of a long and costly war on a foreign republic, the resources have been more than sufficient to meet all engagements. The revenues of the country are drawn from customs, sales of public lands, and some miscellaneous sources. There is at present no direct taxation. By means of these, the old debt incurred during the revolutionary war and the last war with Great Britain, were totally expunged in 1837, and after reserving a large sum for contingencies, a surplus, amounting to $28,209,230, has been deposited with the several states, according to the ratio of their electoral votes, with the proviso that it be liable to be recalled whenever necessity should demand. This necessity, however, has not yet occurred, though the burden of the Mexican war has weighed heavily on the resources of the treasury, and it is even probable that its reimbursement may never be required. Since the extinction of the debt, commercial embarrassments have, in some measure, affected the resources of the country, and many causes have tended to render the creation of a new debt indispensable; but up to the present time it is small, and as stated by the President, in his message to Congress, in 1850, amounts only to $64,228,238—a sum insignificant when compared with the immense income of the government and the rapidly-increasing tide of prosperity which is flowing over our glorious republic. The annexed tables will exhibit the aggregate receipts and expenditures of the federal government for the years ending 30th June, 1849 and 1850 comparatively:

I. RECEIPTS INTO THE TREASURY.

	1849.	1850.
From Customs	$28,346,738 82	$39,668,686 42
" Sales of Public Lands	1,688,959 55	1,859,894 25
" Miscellaneous sources	1,038,649 13	1,847,218 33
Total receipts exclusive of loans	$31,074,347 50	$43,375,798 90
Balance in the Treasury	153,534 60	2,184,964 28
Total exclusive of loans, etc.	$31,227,882 10	$45,560,763 18
Loans, deposits, Treasury notes, etc.	28,588,750 00	4,045,950 00
Total means of Treasury	$59,816,632 10	$49,606,713 18

II. EXPENDITURES, EXCLUSIVE OF TRUST FUNDS.

	1849.	1850.
For Civil list	$2,865,615 88	$3,042,770 07
" Foreign intercourse	7,972,832 01	4,838,594 76
" Miscellaneous items	3,179,192 66	6,958,360 24
" Department of Interior	——	3,400,524 87
" War Department	17,290,936 68	9,401,239 16
" Navy do.	9,869,818 20	7,923,313 18
On account of Public Debt	16,453,272 39	7,437,366 41
Total expenditures	$57,631,667 82	$43,002,168 69
Balance	2,184,964 28	6,604,544 49

Since the refusal of Congress to re-charter the Bank of the United States, no banking institutions of a national character have been established. The banks of the Union are generally, with few exceptions, joint stock companies, with fixed capitals, incorporated by the respective states. They are all banks of issue, and their notes form the principal circulating medium.

The condition of all the banks making returns, according to the official statements made on or near the 1st of January, of each year, is exhibited in the annexed table:

Liabilities.	1849. 654 banks, 128 br'n'es.	1850. 685 banks, 139 br'n'es.	1851. 724 banks, 148 br'n'es.
Capital	$207,309,361	$217,317,211	$227,555,594
Circulation	114,743,415	131,366,526	155,058,581
Deposits	91,178,623	109,586,595	127,570,791
Due other banks	30,695,366	36,717,451	46,362,995
Other liabilities	6,706,357	8,805,309	6,379,464
Total	$450,033,122	$503,793,092	$562,927,425
Resources.			
Loans and Discounts	$332,823,195	$364,204,078	$412,733,004
Stocks	23,571,575	20,606,759	22,459,421
Real Estate	17,491,809	20,582,166	20,195,761
Other Investments	7,965,463	11,949,548	8,935,872
Due by other banks	32,228,407	41,631,855	50,425,632
Notes of other banks	12,708,016	16,303,289	17,189,826
Specie Funds	8,680,483	11,603,245	15,275,277
Specie	43,619,368	45,379,345	48,671,133
Total	$478,088,316	$532,260,285	$595,883,926

The specie currency of the country consists of gold, silver, and copper coins. The gold is in pieces of the denomination of double eagles ($20), eagles ($10), half-eagles, quarter-eagles, and dollars. The silver is in dollars (100 cents), half-dollars, quarters, dimes (10 cents), half-dimes, and three-cent pieces. The copper coins are cents and half-cents. Accounts are kept in dollars ($), cents (c.), and mills (m.=1,000th part of a dollar). The amount of this specie in circulation cannot be ascertained. The Director of the Mint furnishes an annual statement of the amounts coined, etc., from which it appears that in 1850 there were coined, of gold, 2,701,764 pieces, valued at $31,981,733; of silver, 7,419,800 pieces, valued at $1,866,100; and of copper, in cents, 4,566,656, valued at $44,467, or a total of 14,588,220 pieces, and $33,892,301. A little more than twenty-eight-thirtieths of the gold was from the mines of the United States. The total quantity and value of the coinage, from 1793 to the end of 1850, is stated at 370,536,129 pieces, and $195,074,718; of this, $117,330,935 was gold, $77,447,565 silver, and $1,296,211 copper.

The great confederacy, of which we have been endeavoring to exhibit a bird's-eye view, though of recent date, supplies sufficient material for the historian. We can afford, however, but small space for the remarks we intend to offer on its career, from infancy to comparative maturity—from the period, scarcely twenty-five decades past, when it was first trod by the white man, to the present time, when it numbers thirty-one independent states, and several territorial appendages. It has passed through all its trials—war, pestilence, and famine—and now, unscathed and whole, it is presented to the world as the abode of liberty and the seat of a mighty empire of freemen. In the few short years of its existence, indeed, it has accomplished the work of ages, and not only surpassed the old states of Europe in civilization and wealth, but is viewed by them as a "bright star," going before them through the wilderness of anarchy and social disorganization, leading them forth to the accomplishing of their high destinies, as cosmopolitan heroes, and arbitrators of their own liberties and nationalities. The ultimate supremacy of the United States, in all that tends to elevate man, is inevitable, and, come weal or woe to other nations, this country will ever be a refuge and home to the wanderers of the earth; and seek its reward alone in the good citizenship of those who find repose from their toils and oppressions within its borders.

The United States, as a nation, may now be regarded as the most interesting and important of all the nations of the earth. It has fully established the principle, that man is capable of political self-government, and proven by an adequate test that the Democratic republican system is best adapted to the happiness of a people, provided that its beneficent principles be exercised and employed by intelligent and patriotic minds. Originally subject to the crown of Great Britain, denied representation, goaded by onerous taxation, the people of the colonies unitedly protested, petitioned and entreated for redress, but in vain; and finally, after having exhausted all gentler means in their efforts to obtain fair justice, resisted the orders of the government and placed themselves in opposition to the royal armies. The first battle was fought at LEXINGTON, 19th April, 1775, in which the American colonists lost, in killed and wounded, 84 men, and the British 245 men. Previous to this, however, a congress of representatives from all the colonies had convened at Philadelphia, for the purpose of protecting their collective interests, and on the 5th September, 1774, elected Peyton Randolph, their first president. On the 17th June, in the year 1775, the contending parties again met at BUNKER HILL, near Boston, at which encounter the Americans lost 453 and the British 1054 men. At this battle, the Americans were led by the brave General Prescott, and the British by Lord Howe. General Warren, then president of the provincial congress of Massachusetts, was killed in this engagement, which he had entered as a volunteer.

On the 4th day of July, 1776, the congress then assembled at Philadelphia, signed and promulgated to the world, the DECLARATION OF INDEPENDENCE; each member pledging his life, his fortune and his sacred honor on the issue; but it was not until after a long and bloody struggle that this declaration was fully established. George Washington was appointed commander-in-chief of the American forces, and it is, perhaps, to his virtues, more than any other cause, that the United States are indebted for their nationality. It has been justly remarked, that "the world never produced but one Washington," and certainly no other man has been known to unite all the good qualities of this ONE. Devoted, soul and body, to the cause of liberty, he refused all compensation for his services; endured toil, privation, danger and evil slander; restored the fallen energies of his barefooted and often discontented troops; encouraged the desponding; won the disaffected, and with judgment and skill seemingly beyond the lot of man, guided his little army of ill-provided and undisciplined men, without the necessary means of war, against a powerful and scientific foe, through a long succession of victories, until the surrender of Cornwallis and the suspension of hostilities which then ensued. This crowning event in the revolution occurred on the 19th of October, 1781, on which occasion 7,073 British soldiers laid down their arms and were made prisoners of war, and the British power was thus finally and effectually crushed.

The era of the Revolution is replete with ideas and actions, that in conception and pursuit will ever present a glowing page in the history of our country. The principles contended for, the indomitable courage and persevering endurance which signalized the progress of the revolt, the success that crowned the patriotic endeavors of the actors in the glorious strife, and more than all, the vast importance, not only to America, but to all the world, of the result of these transactions, will ever be looked upon as the commencement of a new phase in national policy, and must, as a matter of course, sympathetically lead the minds of men, individually and collectively, to those inquiries which infallibly tend to liberality in governments, to the social progress of the people, and to a just perception of the beneficent influences of democratic principles, and actions based on popular assent. Awake to the justice and policy of the same ideas and the same principles of action which governed our revolutionary fathers, Europe is now endeavoring to disenthral her destinies, and cast off the despotism and tyranny which, like an incubus, has long disturbed her repose and disabled all her energies; and the people of the United States may, in scanning the mighty upheavings of society in France, Germany, Italy, and even in England herself, now congratulate themselves that their institutions are understood and appreciated, and accept as a tribute highly complimentary to their principles, these manifestations of popular power and of the incipient sovereignty of the people.

The principal battles fought during the Revolution, with the results of each, are shown in the annexed tabular statement:

Battles.	*Dates.*	*American Commanders.*	*Loss.*	*British Commanders.*	*Loss.*
Lexington	19th April, 1775	———	84	Pitcairn	245
Bunker Hill	17th June, "	Prescott	453	Howe	1,054
Flatbush	12th Aug. 1776	Putnam	2,000	Do.	400
White Plains	28th Oct. "	Washington	300	Do.	300
Trenton	25th Dec. "	Do.	9	Rahl	1,000
Princeton	3d Jan. 1777	Do.	100	Mawhood	400
Bennington	16th Aug. "	Stark	100	Baum	600
Brandywine	11th Sept. "	Washington	1,200	Howe	500
Saratoga	17th Oct. "	Gates	350	Burgoyne	*600
Monmouth	25th June, 1778	Washington	230	Clinton	400
Rhode Island	29th Aug. "	Sullivan	211	Pigott	260
Briar Creek	30th March, 1779	Ash	300	Prevost	16
Stoney Point	15th July, "	Wayne	100	Johnson	600
Camden	16th Aug. 1780	Gates	720	Cornwallis	375
Cowpens	17th Jan. 1781	Morgan	72	Tarlton	800
Guildford	15th March, "	Greene	400	Cornwallis	523
Eutaw Springs	8th Sept. "	Do.	555	Stewart	1,000
Yorktown	19th Oct. "	Washington	—	Cornwallis	†—

This table is, of course, made independent of numerous skirmishes and battles of less importance.

* 5,752 prisoners. † 7,073 prisoners.

A definitive treaty of peace was signed, and the independence of the country recognized by England, on the 13th September, 1783, provisional articles having been agreed upon and signed 30th November, 1782. The British eventually evacuated all their strong-holds and sailed from the city of New-York 25th November, 1783, leaving the whole country, east of the Mississippi and south of Canada, in possession of their republican conquerors.

Having established its rank among the nations of the world, the United States experienced great difficulties and party opposition in the formation of a new government. Hitherto it had been ruled by the continental congress at Philadelphia, but the new position of the country claimed for its defence a more intimate union and a more balanced understanding, than the articles of confederation, which yet banded the several states together, could pretend to sustain. It was found necessary to draw closer the ties of relationship, and at length, on the second Monday in May, 1787, a convention, composed of delegates from the several states, assembled in Philadelphia, for the pupose of forming a constitution, which should effectually supply the wants of the nation. General Washington was called upon to preside over its deliberations, and on the 17th September a constitution was adopted and submitted to the states, severally, for their decision. It was finally ratified by each, but not without a warm opposition and much delay: Rhode Island prolonged the issue until 29th of May, 1790, and was the last to give its consent. The instrument, however, had been ratified on the 14th July, 1788, and became the fundamental law of all the acceding states.

The progressive increase of the dimensions of this country by conquest and cession, has been rapid. At the termination of the revolution, in 1783, it was confined to the territories east of the Mississippi and south of the Canadas. In 1803, it was augmented, by the purchase from France, of Louisiana, a country now occupied by the thriving States of Louisiana, Arkansas, Missouri and Iowa, and several territories, extending over many hundreds of thousands of square miles of the fairest of lands. Florida was purchased of Spain in 1819, and at the same time the Spanish claim to the "Oregon" was transferred to the Republic. In 1845, Texas voluntarily annexed itself to the Union; and by the treaty of 2d February, 1848, on the conclusion of the Mexican war, the extensive territories of New-Mexico and Alta California were ceded by our southern neighbors, and are now a portion of the United States.

The subsequent history of the Union has been as glorious as its inception. In war, the Americans have ever been victorious—in agriculture, manufactures and commerce, industrious and successful—in the arts and learning, pre-eminently advanced—and as a people, they have sustained themselves valiantly against the arts and prejudices of the old-school politicians, thereby fully proving the capacity of man for self-government and the falsity of the "divine right" doctrines of monarchists and despots. Their social position is one to be envied; their homes are replete with all necessaries and every comfort, and the utmost freedom of speech and religion is enjoyed by all. From one end of the country to the other, happiness and content—peace and plenty—and unbounded liberty are depicted in the countenance and bearing of man in every station of life. The millionaire and the mechanic have an equal share and are equally potent in framing the laws which assure to them the blessings they enjoy. What a contrast to the pitiful condition of the people of down-trodden Europe, and the despot-swayed hordes of Asia and Africa!

"I appeal to history," says Philips; "Tell me, thou reverend chronicler of the grave, can all the illusions of ambition realized, can all the wealth of a universal commerce, can all the achievements of successful heroism, or all the establishments of this world's wisdom, secure to empire the permanency of its possessions? Alas! Troy thought so once; yet the land of Priam lives only in song! Thebes thought so once; yet her hundred gates have crumbled, and her very tombs are but as the dust they were vainly intended to commemorate! So thought Palmyra—where is she? So thought the countries of Demosthenes and the Spartan; yet Leonidas is trampled by the timid slave, and Athens, insulted by the servile, mindless and enervate Ottoman! In his hurried march, time has but looked at their imagined immortality; and all its vanities, from the palace to the tomb, have, with their ruins, erased the very impression of his footsteps! The days of their glory are as if they had never been; and the island, that was then a speck, rude and neglected in the barren ocean, now rivals the ubiquity of their commerce, the glory of their arms, the fame of their philosophy, the eloquence of their senate and the inspiration of their bards! Who shall say, then, contemplating the past, that England, proud and potent as she appears, may not, one day, be what Athens is, and the young America soar to be what

Athens was! Who shall say, that when the European column shall have mouldered, and the night of barbarism obscured its very ruins, that mighty continent may not emerge from the horizon, to rule, for its time, sovereign of the ascendant!"

THE NORTH-EASTERN STATES,

(NEW-ENGLAND.)

New-England is that portion of the United States lying east of the State of New-York, and comprises the several states of Maine, New-Hampshire, Vermont, Massachusetts, Rhode Island and Connecticut. This region is comprised between the latitudes 41° and 47° 20′ north and the longitudes 66° 49′ and 73° 15′ west, and is bounded on the north by the British Provinces, on the east by New Brunswick and the Atlantic Ocean, on the south by the Atlantic Ocean and Long Island Sound, and on the west by the State of New-York and Lake Champlain. Within these limits the superficies is about 66,000 square miles.

The surface of New-England is infinitely varied. Mountain ranges, bold spurs and solitary eminences, rising from the moderate elevation of the New-Haven bluffs to the lofty grandeur of Mt. Washington are everywhere dispersed. Beautiful swells of land of every form are innumerable. No valleys of great extent occur, but intervales are ever recurring. Few countries are better watered; rivers, brooks and mill-streams, issuing from the mountains and hill-sides traverse the valleys, or dashing over the precipice glide swiftly towards the ocean, and many of the streams are little more than a succession of cascades. To the mill-power afforded by these New-England owes much of its greatness. Numerous lakes too are found in the landscape, and nothing can be more cheerful than the aspect they impart. Such is the interior. Its coasts are bold and rocky, but everywhere indented with inlets and the mouths of rivers, which afford almost every town lying near the sea the conveniences of commerce. Portsmouth, Boston and Newport harbors are equal to any in the world. With regard to climate and soil the region is unblessed. Extremes press upon extremes, winter upon summer, and in the short space of 24 hours the colds of Lapland and the heats of the tropics may be experienced; and with little exception the lands are sterile and require the persistent toil of man to make them yield their fruits. But with all these drawbacks the New-England farmer is prosperous, and his lands the best cultivated of any in the United States.

New-England, however, is more manufacturing and commercial in its industry than it is agricultural. Here is the great workshop of the Union and the centre of a vast foreign and domestic commerce. Its internal trade and transportation are equally magnificent. Its railroads interlace in every section and extend beyond the state for hundreds of miles. Few countries of the same extent, indeed, have more energetically sought pre-eminence in useful employments, and none has been more successful in realizing the aims of its ambition.

But the character of the New-Englander is solid, and his endeavors are guided by principle. Religion and education he fosters as the source of all his welfare in life, and armed with these he fears not whatever may oppose. As a young giant he grapples with his destiny, and in the midst of his toils only looks to the end. It is men with such characters that have developed the resources of the country, and subdued the sterile soils and barren mountains, the rivers, and even the elements, to their will and purpose.

The population of New-England now amounts to 2,727,597, and its distribution to its several constituent states is in the following proportions:

STATES.	White Persons.	Colored Persons.	Total Population.
Maine	581,763	1,325	583,088
New-Hampshire	317,389	475	317,864
Vermont	312,902	709	313,611
Massachusetts	985,704	8,795	994,499
Rhode Island	144,000	3,544	147,544
Connecticut	363,305	7,486	370,791
Total	2,705,063	22,334	2,727,597

And its increase from 1790 to 1850 has been as indicated in the annexed table:

Date of Census.	Maine.	New Hampshire.	Vermont.	Mass.	Rhode Island.	Conn.
1790	96,540	141,899	85,416	378,717	69,110	238,141
1800	151,719	183,762	154,465	423,245	69,122	251,002
1810	228,705	214,360	217,713	472,040	77,031	262,042
1820	298,335	244,161	235,764	523,287	83,059	275,202
1830	399,455	269,328	280,652	610,408	97,199	297,675
1840	501,793	284,574	291,948	737,699	108,830	309,978
1850	583,088	317,864	313,611	994,499	147,544	370,791

THE STATE OF MAINE.

Maine, the north-easternmost of the United States, lies between the latitudes 43° 5′ and 47° 20′ north, and the longitudes 66° 49′ and 71° 4′ west, and is bounded on the north-west and north by Canada; east by New-Brunswick and the River St. Croix; south by the Atlantic Ocean, and west by the State of New-Hampshire. The boundary on the side of Canada is a conventional line, agreed upon between the British and United States' governments in 1842, and embodied in the Treaty of Washington. The mean length, from north to south, is 235 miles, and the breadth from east to west, 140 miles. The area is variously estimated, at from 30 to 32,628 square miles, or 20,881,920 acres.

The surface of Maine is diversified, and generally uneven, but with few exceptions, cannot be said to be mountainous. In the western part of the state is an irregular chain of hills springing from the White Mountains, which passes north of the sources of the Kennebec and Penobscot rivers, and thence running eastward, terminates in a single peak called Mars Hill, 1,683 feet high. The highest point of land in the state is Mount Katahdin, which rises between the two principal branches of the Penobscot, and has an elevation of 5,300 feet above tide-water. From the chain above alluded to, hills covered with the finest of pine and other timbers, traverse the state in every direction. The intervening valleys have an excellent soil, and afford the chief arable districts of the country. Within a distance of 15 or

20 miles from the coast the hills subside, and the quality of the soil becomes much inferior to that of the mountain valleys. The tracts on the margins of the great rivers, however, are equal in richness and fertility to any in the New-England States.

It is estimated that about one-tenth of this state is covered with water. The principal rivers are the Penobscot and the Kennebec, both of which are upwards of 250 miles long, but navigable for no great distance from the ocean. Next in size and importance to these is the Androscoggin, which has numerous falls, affording favorable sites for manufacturing purposes. The Saco and Sheepscot are also considerable streams. The largest lake is the Moosehead, which is 50 miles long, and 10 to 12 broad. The Umbagog is 18 miles long and 10 broad. There are numerous smaller lakes in other portions of the state, and many are surrounded with beautiful and picturesque scenery. The sea-coast, which is 210 miles in extent, has several excellent bays and harbors. Penobscot Bay and Casco are magnificent, and of great dimensions, and may be reckoned as equal to any in the Union. The tides rise to a great height along all the coast.

The climate of this state is one of extremes. The average range of the thermometer during the year is about 125° *Fahr.*, the heat of summer often marking 96° or 98°, while in winter the temperature sinks to 25° and 27° below zero. These are extremes, and are never of long continuance. The season of vegetation commences about the middle of April, and ends with September, when the fall sets in and is succeeded by a long winter.

Maine is divided into thirteen counties, and contained, in 1850, a population of 583,088, or one person to every 36 acres. The inhabitants are chiefly settled near the Atlantic coast, the northern portions of the state being, as yet, a wilderness, and scarcely less so than when first trod by the white man. The population of the counties is exhibited in the following table:

COUNTIES.	White Persons.	Free Colored Persons.	Total Population.
Aroostook	12,529	6	12,535
Cumberland	78,956	593	74,549
Franklin	20,007	20	20,027
Hancock	34,343	29	34,372
Kennebec	62,379	142	62,521
Lincoln	74,616	259	74,875
Oxford	39,658	5	39,663
Penobscot	63,026	63	63,089
Piscataquis	14,732	3	14,735
Somerset	35,577	4	35,581
Waldo	47,191	39	47,230
Washington	38,684	126	38,810
York	60,065	36	60,101
Total	581,763	1,325	583,088

CLASSES AND SEXES OF POPULATION.

Classes.	Males.	Females.	Total.
White Persons	296,635	285,128	581,763
Colored " —free	705	620	1,325
" " —slave	—	—	—
Total	297,340	285,748	583,088

PROGRESSIVE MOVEMENT OF POPULATION.

Date of Census.	White Persons.	Colored Persons. Free.	Colored Persons. Slave.	Total Population.	Decennial Increase. Numerical.	Decennial Increase. Per 100.
1790	96,002	538	—	96,540	—	—
1800	150,901	818	—	151,719	55,179	57.1
1810	227,736	969	—	228,705	76,986	50.7
1820	297,340	995	—	298,335	69,630	30.4
1830	398,263	1,190	2	399,455	101,120	33.9
1840	500,438	1,355	—	501,793	102,338	25.6
1850	581,763	1,325	—	583,088	81,295	16.2

The number of families in the state, in 1850, was 103,787, and hence there were 5.6 persons to each family; and at the same date there were 95,797 dwelling-houses, which contained, on the average, 6.1 persons each. These proportions are nearly uniform throughout the counties. The mortality in the year 1849–50 amounted to 7,545 deaths, or one death to every 77 persons. In Aroostook the rate of mortality was only one death in each 109 persons, while in Cumberland it was as high as one in every 59 persons, being there at its maximum.

Agriculture and commerce are the prominent branches of industry in this state. About three fourths of the whole population derive their support from the former pursuit. Mining and manufactures are rather incidental than proper occupations. Considerable numbers are engaged in navigation and the fisheries.

Agriculture is here pursued with much care, and the farmers, generally, are thrifty, and in some cases wealthy. Cattle and sheep are now raised in large numbers, and the crops, though not so profuse as in the valley of the Ohio, are very fair and of excellent quality. Sometimes, however, the grain suffers from the shortness of the season, and this is especially the case with Indian corn. The live stock consists of some 65,000 horses and mules, 400,000 neat cattle, 750,000 sheep, and 200,000 swine, with an abundance of poultry. Oats and Indian corn form the largest crops, and next in amount are those of wheat, barley, and rye. The wheat crop is about 400,000 bushels annually. Potatoes are planted widely, but the crop is not so large as formerly, being now only about 8,000,000 against 10,000,000 bushels in 1840. Perhaps 800,000 tons of hay are cured in the season. The products of the forest are large, but the orchard and garden yield comparatively little to the general stock. The number of farms, in 1850, was 46,760.

Mining is chiefly confined to the production of building materials, lime, &c. Mining for metals is scarcely known, and employs but few persons.

The whole number of manufacturing establishments, in 1850, was 3,682, besides which a considerable number of small manufactories, not enumerated, existed, and household industry was largely productive of domestic fabrics, &c. Some few cotton mills, several paper mills, numerous tanneries, brick fields, &c., with furnaces, rope-walks, lime-kilns, carriage factories, and mills of various descriptions, give employment to about 20,000 persons. Ship building is also carried on to a great extent, and in this respect Maine is the first state of the Union. The capital invested in manufactures may be estimated at twelve millions of dollars.

The commerce and navigation of Maine is chiefly confined to coasting and fishing, and a trade in lumber, lime, and a few other staple articles. There is little or no intercourse between the ports of this state and the countries of Europe. The value of commerce with foreign states for the year ending 30th June, 1850, amounted to $2,413,323; *viz.*, value of exports, $1,556,912, and of imports, $856,411. The tonnage employed in the foreign trade was as follows:—

Nationality.	Entered.	Cleared.	Total.
American	53,309	111,123	164,432
Foreign	89,877	91,014	180,891
Total	143,186	202,137	345,323

The total amount of shipping owned within the state was 510,421 tons, and of this 211,087 tons were engaged in coasting. The mercantile steam marine amounted to 5,580 tons. The quantity of shipping employed in the cod fisheries was 37,347 tons, and in the mackerel fisheries 12,249 tons.

During the year ending as above, 326 vessels, of an aggregate burden of 91,212 tons, were built in the state.

Maine has little transit trade, but the commerce between the ports and the interior is considerable. Transit trade, however, will enlarge when the system of railroads, now progressing, is completed. The Cumberland and Oxford Canal is the only work of the kind in the state, and is of purely local advantage. It was completed in 1829, and connects Portland with Sebago Pond, a distance of 20½ miles, and by a lock in Songo river the navigation is extended to Brandy and Long Ponds, 31 miles farther. The canal is 34 feet wide at the surface, and 18 feet at the bottom; with 26 wooden locks. Its construction cost about $250,000. The railroads finished, progressing, and proposed, are numerous, and open up a large country. When completed to Montreal and Halifax, as designed, they will be of essential value to the interests of the state. The cost to complete the whole system as now proposed, is estimated at from $12,000,000 to $15,000,000. The lines completed and in progress, to 1850, were, the Portland, Saco, and Portsmouth Railroad, 51 miles long; the Boston and Maine Railroad (3 miles only in this state); the Atlantic and St. Lawrence Railroad, from Portland to Montreal, 150 miles, (about 70 miles in Maine); the Androscoggin and Kennebec Railroad, 55 miles; the Kennebec and Portland Railroad, 68 miles; the York and Cumberland Railroad, from South Berwick to Portland, 52 miles; the Bangor and Oldtown Railroad, 11 miles; the Androscoggin Railroad, from Greene to Farmington, 37 miles; the Buckfield Branch Railroad, 13 miles; the Calais and Baring Railroad, 6 miles; the Machias Port Railroad, 8 miles; the Penobscot and Kennebec, 54 miles, &c. The following are the lines proposed, and which will probably be completed at an early date:—the Belfast and Waterville Railroad, 33 miles; the Kennebec and Franklin Railroad, 37 miles; the Somerset and Kennebec Railroad, 40 miles; the Penobscot, Lincoln, and Kennebec Railroad; the European and North American, from Bangor to Halifax (90 miles in Maine), &c.; and besides these there are some short and local roads, both completed, progressing, and contemplated.

At the commencement of 1850 there were 32 banks in this state, and according to the Bank Commissioner's Report, made in May, 1850, the capital of these amounted to $3,586,100, the circulation to $2,994,905, debts to other banks to $111,727, the deposits to $1,380,137, and profits undivided to $169,390—total liabilities, $8,251,260. The assets consisted of specie $630,296, real estate $102,570, bank notes $254,701, due from banks $813,232, and other assets, including loans and discounts, $6,450,450. The average rate of dividends was about 8 per centum.

Education in this state is respectably provided for. Bowdoin College, at Brunswick, is the oldest literary institution of the state, having been founded as early as 1794, and has been in operation since 1802. Among its alumni are many names that have obtained distinction in every department of life. It has 8 professors, 997 alumni, of which 176 are ministers, and in 1850 it had 104 students. The library contains 25,590 volumes. Waterville College, at Waterville, under the direction of the Baptists, was founded in 1820, and has now 5 professors, 267 alumni, of which 82 are ministers; and in 1850 it had 76 students. Its library numbers 8,100 volumes. The total expenses incurred by students during their studies amounts to about $150 per annum. The Maine Medical School at Brunswick was founded in 1820, and in 1850 counted 596 graduates. It had in that year 5 professors, and 74 students. There are also theological seminaries at Bangor and Redfield. The seminary at Bangor dates from 1816, and is under the charge of the Congregationalists. In 1850 it had 3 professors and 37 students, and the number to which it had given education amounted to 202. The library has 7,000 volumes. The seminary at Redfield is under Wesleyan authority; it was founded in 1822. Academies and grammar schools are numerous, and common schools are found throughout the state. From the official school report, made up to the 1st April 1850, it appears that the number of persons between the ages of 4 and 21 years in the districts making returns, (about seven eighths of the whole) was 194,095; that the average attendance at the common schools was, in summer, 110,609, and in winter, 102,485. The number of school districts returned was 3,350, of school houses 3,063, and the average length of schools for the year was 19.2 weeks. These schools were taught by 5,989 persons, 2,454 males, and 3,535 females, and the average wages for teachers were—for males $16.66, and for females $5.84, per month. The amount raised by taxes for the support of common schools was $221,923.

There is a hospital for the insane, at Augusta, which is one of the most reputable establishments in the Union, and has accommodations for about 150 patients. During the year 1849–50, 253 patients were under treatment, 66 of which were recovered, and 22 improved; and on the 31st March of the latter year 136 remained in the hospital. The ordinary expense to patients is about $2.50 per week, and for this they have board, &c.

At Thomaston is the State Prison. During the year ending 30th April, 1850, 31 convicts were sent in. Of these 4 were committed for arson, 5 for burglary, 2 for forgery, 49 for larceny, 5 for murder, and 1 for passing spurious coin. These statistics, indicating the moral condition of the people, are very satisfactory, and exhibit a very small ratio of crime in relation to the population. Since the 2nd July, 1824, the date of the foundation of the establishment, 981 convicts had been received, or 27 per annum, on the average.

The Congregationalists, Baptists, and Methodists, are the numerically preponderating religious denominations in this state. The Universalists are also numerous, and of late years the Catholics have greatly increased in numbers. The Protestant Episcopalians, in point of numbers, rank low, as do also the Free-Will Baptists, Friends, and Unitarians.

The Constitution of Maine was adopted by a Convention held at Portland, on the 29th of October, 1819, and went into operation in 1820. The government consists of a governor, senate, and house of representatives. The governor is chosen by the people for one year. Seven councillors are also chosen annually, to assist and advise the governor. The house of representatives cannot have less than 100 nor more than 200 members, and the senate is limited between 20 and 31; both houses are elected annually. The qualifications for the above offices have merely reference to age and nativity. The right of voting is conceded to every male citizen of 21 years of age, who is not a pauper or criminal, and who has resided in the state three months previous to the election. Elections are taken by written ballot.

The judiciary of Maine consists of a Superior Court, three District Courts, and fourteen Courts of Probate, one for each county, except the county of Lincoln, which is divided. Portland, Bath and Bangor, have special municipal courts. All judicial officers are appointed by the governor, with the advice and consent of the council, and hold office for seven years after their appointment.

The militia of the state amounts to 44,665, of which number 39,256 are infantry, 1,456 cavalry, 2,028 artillery, and 1,925 riflemen. Shakers, Quakers, Judges and Ministers of the Gospel, are exempt from bearing arms.

The finances of the state are in a very flourishing condition. The receipts into the Treasury for the year ending 30th April, 1850,

Amounted to	$525,688
To which may be added balance in Treasury 30th April, 1846	79,038
	$604,726
Expenditures in 1849–50	478,802
Balance 30th April, 1850	$125,924

The public debt, in 1846, amounted to $1,274,285, and in 1850, to $854,750; $419,535 having been paid in the interval. The annual interest on this sum is about $55,000. The resources of the state are set down at $860,781 11.

The principal sources of income are direct taxes, which, in 1849–50, amounted to $190,996—sale of public lands, school funds, county taxes, etc. The principal items of expenditure are the redemption and interest of the public debt, salaries, education, charitable institutions, Indian annuities, pensions, and premiums to agricultural societies.

Maine was visited for the purposes of settlement as early as any of the New-England States, but, from various causes, the progress of improvement was much impeded. The French attempted to settle on the Kennebec as early as 1604. In 1607, Sir John Gilbert, under a grant from Queen Elizabeth, brought out a colony, which, however, returned after wintering at the mouth of the same river. They represented the country as a cold, barren, mountainous desert, which discouraged the English from making further efforts for some time. Meanwhile the French established themselves on the St. Croix, and the Dutch had a colony at New-Castle, which was under the jurisdiction of the New Netherlands. After the establishment of the Plymouth Company, more effectual efforts were made by the English to colonize this portion of their dominions; but, although some trading-houses were established near the Penobscot, no permanent settlement was made previous to 1635. In that year the Company granted a charter to Sir Ferdinand Gorges for the country between the Piscataqua and the Kennebec, and in his name the government was administered. In 1652, the province was made a county of Massachusetts, and called Yorkshire; but in 1665 it again fell into the hands of the heirs of Gorges, of whom it was ultimately purchased by Massachusetts, in 1677, for £1,200. At this period it was divided into two parts, of which Gorges' grant was one, and the country lying between the St. Croix and the Kennebec, known by the ancient French name of Acadie, was another. The whole country, however, was granted to Massachusetts in 1691.

From its first settlement to the middle of the 18th century, the inhabitants suffered severely from the Indians. In 1675 almost the whole settlements were destroyed. From 1692 to 1702, the province presented an uniform scene of rapine and destruction. In 1720, the conflict was renewed, and the settlers suffered grievously until 1726, when a treaty was concluded with the Indians, which was observed for some years. Eventually the savages became reduced in number, and few now remain in the state.

From the year 1791 until 1820, the history of Maine is merged in that of Massachusetts. We hear little of it in the Revolutionary War, or subsequently. In the last war, however, a portion of the state was obliged to submit to the English, and remained under the British authority until the conclusion of peace. The separation of this district from Massachusetts was frequently attempted. In Oct., 1785, a convention met at Portland to consider the subject, and in the following year the project was submitted to the people of Maine; but it appears that a majority of the voters decided against the measure. In 1819, numerous petitions having been presented to the legislature of Massachusetts, an act was passed for ascertaining the wishes of the people. A large majority voting in favor of separation, a convention was called, under the authority of Massachusetts. A Constitution was formed and adopted, and on the 2d March the District of Maine became an independent state, and a member of the confederation.

Augusta, the capital of the state, lies on both sides of the Kennebec River, 43 miles from its mouth, and at the head of sloop navigation: latitude 44° 18′ 33″ north, and longitude 69° 47′ west. Population, 8,231. The two portions of the town are united by a handsome stone bridge. The city is regularly laid out, and has many elegant dwellings. It contains the state-house, court-house, jail, United States arsenal, and several hospitals and churches. The state-house is situated on an eminence, a little south of the city, on the west side of the river. Its central part is 84 feet long and 56 feet deep, with two wings, each 34 feet long by 54 deep. It has a Doric portico of eight granite columns, one stone each, 21 feet high, and weighing 10 tons. The dome and cupola are handsome structures. Before it is a spacious park, ornamented with walks and trees. The United States Arsenal, on the east side of the river, is a large and elegant stone edifice, and the Lunatic Asylum is a fine granite building, with wings, and is surrounded with 70 acres of ground. It is also on the east side of the river. The High School is a brick edifice, 65 by 50 feet, two stories high. Half a mile above the city is a splendid dam across the river, with locks to facilitate navigation. The cost of this great work was between $300,000 and $400,000. There were in Augusta, in 1850, ninety-four stores; four grist-mills; four saw-mills: two oil-mills; one distillery; two academies, with 150 students; and thirty-six schools, with 2,129 scholars. The growth of the place has been rapid since it became the seat of the government.

Portland City, which is the largest and most important town of the state, is finely situated on an elevated peninsula, projecting into Casco Bay. It is well laid out, and neatly built. The harbor is deep, safe, spacious, easily accessible, and always open. The shipping belonging to the port amounts to about 140,000 tons. Population, 26,816.

The City of Bangor, at the head of the navigation of the Penobscot River, 60 miles from the sea, communicates with an extensive interior country by means of the wide-spreading branches of the Penobscot, and possesses on the falls, immediately above the town, every facility for manufacturing purposes. Population, 14,441. It is the seat of a Theological Seminary, and, as a whole, is one of the pleasantest situated and most elegantly-built cities in the Union. Its commerce is extensive, and its coasting-trade superior to most of the northern ports.

THE STATE OF NEW-HAMPSHIRE.

THIS state lies immediately west of Maine. It is bounded on the north by Lower Canada; south-east by the Atlantic Ocean, on which it has a sea-coast of eighteen miles; south by Massachusetts, and west by Vermont, from which it is separated by the Connecticut River. It lies between the meridians of 70° 40′ and 72° 28′ W. long., and 42° 41′ and 45° 11′ N. lat., and is 168 miles long, and from 19 to 90 miles broad, having an area of 9,411 square miles, or 6,023,040 acres, of which 110,000 acres are estimated to be covered with water.

The Atlantic shores of New-Hampshire are in most places but a sandy beach, and bordering upon them are extensive salt marshes. They are penetrated by numerous creeks and coves which accommodate vessels of small size, but with the exception of Portsmouth, at the mouth of the Piscataqua, there is no harbor sufficient for merchantmen. For twenty or thirty miles from the coast the country is either level or variegated with small hills and vallies. Beyond this the hills increase in size, and in many parts of the state swell into lofty mountains, particularly in the north and along the height of land between the Merrimack and the Connecticut. The highest summits between these rivers are Grand Monadnock, near the south-west corner of the state, which is 2,354 feet above the level of the sea; Sunapee mountain, near the lake of the same name, and Mooseheloc, still further north, the height of which is estimated at 4,636 feet. But the White Mountains are more celebrated than either of these. They lie about thirty miles north of Lake Winnipiseogee, and with the exception of the Rocky mountains, are the loftiest in the United States. Mount Washington, the highest summit, is 6,428 feet high. The mountains, lakes, vallies, and cataract of New-Hampshire abound with sublime and beautiful scenery, and have acquired for the state the title of "the Switzerland of America." The White Mountains, though not an uninterrupted range, are sometimes regarded as a continuation of the Alleghanies. The "Notch" in these mountains is regarded as a great natural curiosity, being in some places not more than 22 feet wide, with lofty precipices on both sides, and affording some of the wildest and grandest scenery in nature. A road passes through this "Notch," being the only place in which the mountains can be passed. By this road the products of northern New-Hampshire and the north-east part of Vermont find a market at Portland, in the State of Maine; and so important is this communication regarded by that state, that its Legislature has frequently made grants for its improvement. The other more elevated peaks in this state are Mount Adams, 5,960 feet high; Mount Jefferson, 5,860; Mount Madison, 5,620; Mount Monroe, 5,510; Mount Franklin, 5,050; Mount Pleasant, 4,920; and the Kearsarge Mountains, 2,460 feet above the level.

The soil of New-Hampshire is generally fertile. The intervales on the large rivers are the richest and best fitted for tillage, but the uplands having a warm, moist soil, are best fitted for grazing and pasturage. Indian corn, wheat, rye, oats and flax are produced, and the pork, beef, mutton, cheese and butter are largely exported. The natural growths are the oak, elm, birch, maple, pine and hemlock. Sugar is extensively made from the hard maple trees: the amount, as estimated by the "Commissioner of Patents" for 1847, was 2,225,000 pounds.

New-Hampshire enjoys a very healthy climate, and the weather is generally serene. In summer the heat is great, sometimes rising to 95°, and the winters, during which the thermometer sometimes marks 15° below zero, are often very severe. These extremes, however, seldom occur, and are of short duration. In the neighborhood of the White Mountains, the peaks of which are almost always covered with snow, the winters are excessively cold, but they temper the air and render summer delightful and cool. Longevity of the inhabitants is notorious in this state, and it is not unfrequent to find persons enjoying good health at the age of 100 years and upwards. The cold weather sets in about the middle of September and continues till May; the severity of winter, however, does not set in before November, from which to the opening of spring the country is clothed in a thick mantle of snow, and the rivers frozen up from their sources.

Among the beautiful lakes of this state are Lake Umbagog, on the eastern state line, and Winnipiseogee, near the centre, which is a highly picturesque body of water, twenty-two miles long, and contains a number of romantic islets. The country around is mountainous, and abounds in the most exquisite scenery. Squam Lake lies a little northward, and Lake Sinapee to the south-west, running between the Merrimack and Connecticut. The Androscoggin River rises in Lake Umbagog, and after a northerly course of twenty miles, turns to the east and passes into Maine. The Piscataqua is the boundary between this state and Maine from its source to its mouth, and in the first part of its course is called Salmon Fall River. The Merrimack rises in the White Mountains, near the sources of the Saco, and running south through the centre of the state, passes into Massachusetts, where it turns and runs in a north-easterly direction and falls into the Atlantic. The Connecticut rises in the highlands which separate this state from Canada, and passing through the lake of the same name, and running south between Vermont and New-Hampshire, passes into Massachusetts. The principal tributaries of the Connecticut, commencing at the south, are Ashuelot, which empties itself near the south-west corner of the state; Sugar River, which is the outlet of the Sunapee Lake; lower Ammonoosuck, which rises in the White Mountains, near the sources of the Merrimack, and falls into the river near Bath and upper Ammonoosuck, which empties itself at Northumberland. The principal tributaries to the Merrimack from the west are the Nashua, which comes from Massachusetts and empties itself near the southern boundary of the state; the Cootoocook, which empties itself at Concord; and Baker's River, which rises in Moose-heloc mountain, and empties itself at Plymouth. The tributaries from the east are Winnipiseogee River, the outlet of the lake, and Squam River, which is the outlet of Squam Lake. The principal branches of the Piscataqua are the Swamscot or Exeter and Cocheco rivers, both of which join it near its mouth.

The Isle of Shoals, eight in number, lie in the ocean eleven miles south-east of Portsmouth. A part belong to Maine and a part to New-Hampshire. They consist of barren rocks, and are inhabited by a few fishermen.

The State of New-Hampshire possesses many remarkable peculiarities which are considered as natural curiosities. The "Notch" has been adverted to before. Bellows' Falls are in the Connecticut River at Walpole. The whole descent of the river in the space of a hundred yards, is forty-four feet. There are several pitches, one above another, at the highest of which a large rock divides the stream into two channels, each about ninety feet wide. When the water is low, the eastern channel is dry, being crossed by a bar of solid rock, and the whole stream falls into the western channel, where it is contracted to the breadth of sixteen feet, and flows with astonishing force and rapidity.

The White Mountains are frequently visited by travellers. Mount Washington is usually ascended from the south-east. After climbing the sides of the mountain for some distance, the forest trees begin to diminish in height, till at the elevation of about 4,000 feet, a region of dwarfish evergreens surrounds the mountain with a formidable hedge a quarter of a mile in thickness. After this, the bald part of the mountain, which is very steep, and consists of naked rocks, presents a scene of desolation; but the labors of the aspirant are recompensed for his toil, if the sky be serene, by a most noble and extensive prospect. On the south-east there is a view of the Atlantic, the nearest part of which is distant sixty-five miles in a right line; on the south, Winnipiseogee Lake lies in full view; on the south-east the summit of Mooseheloc, and far away on the verge of the horizon is Grand Monadnock. The barren rocks which extend a great distance in every direction from the summit, add a melancholy cast to the grandeur of the scene.

The recent geological survey of this state by Dr. Charles F. Jackson, has resulted in the discovery of extensive copper and iron mines. A copper-mine, in Coos county, yields an ore of 33 per cent. of pure copper. New-Hampshire also abounds in granite and marble, with many other mineral substances of equal value.

The aggregate population of New Hampshire in 1850 was 317,864, or one person to every 19 acres; and its distribution into the ten counties into which the state is divided, was as follows:

COUNTIES.	White Persons.	Free Col'd Persons.	Total Popula.
Belknap	17,693	28	17,721
Carroll	20,154	2	20,156
Cheshire	30,117	27	30,144
Coos	11,849	4	11,853
Grafton	42,316	7	42,343
Hillsboro'	57,359	118	57,477
Merrimac	38,364	81	38,445
Rockingham	50,869	117	50,986
Strafford	29,327	37	29,364
Sullivan	19,341	34	19,375
Total	317,389	475	317,864

CLASSES AND SEXES OF POPULATION.

Classes.		Males.	Females.	Total.
White Persons		155,902	161,487	317,389
Colored "	—free	243	232	475
" "	—slave	—	—	—
Total		156,145	161,719	317,864

Dwellings	57,339	Deaths in 1849–50	4,268	Farms in cultivation	29,229
Families	62,287			Manufactories	3,301

PROGRESSIVE MOVEMENT OF POPULATION.

Date of Census.	White Persons.	Colored Persons. Free.	Colored Persons. Slave.	Total Population.	Decennial Increase. Numerical.	Decennial Increase. Per 100.
1790	141,111	630	158	141,899	—	—
1800	182,898	856	8	183,762	41,863	29.5
1810	213,390	970	—	214,360	30,598	16.9
1820	243,236	925	—	244,161	29,801	13.9
1830	268,721	604	3	269,328	25,167	10.2
1840	284,036	537	1	284,574	15,246	5.6
1850	317,389	475	—	317,864	33,390	11.7

The industry of New-Hampshire is chiefly agricultural, but of late years manufactures have sprung up, and are now making considerable progress. Commerce and internal trade have likewise received an impetus since the introduction of railroads, while all minor employments are prospering.

Agriculture employs three fourths of the whole population. The products of the soil are similar in every respect to those ordinarily grown in northern latitudes. In this state, however, the ruggedness of the country and austerity of the climate, is prejudicial to some growths. The great crops are Indian corn and oats, about 1,500,000 bushels of each being the average annual product; wheat is next in extent, yielding about 200,000 bushels; rye about two thirds that amount, and then buckwheat and barley, which are comparatively small crops. The potato crop yields about 5,000,000 bushels annually, and about half a million tons of hay are cured. Maple sugar is produced to a very large amount. The live stock consists of about 48,000 horses, 262,000 neat cattle, 800,000 sheep, and 140,000 swine, and poultry to the value of $120,000. The product of wool is at the rate of 1,200,000 pounds per annum. Lumber is also largely produced.

The capital invested in manufactures is about $16,000,000, showing an increase of 75 per cent. since 1840. The chief manufactures are cotton and woollen goods, in the production of which three fourths the factory capital of the state is employed. The minor manufactures are paper, hats and caps, glass and crockery, bricks and lime, etc. There are also considerable numbers of tanneries and other leather manufactories, carriage factories, powder mills, and mills of other descriptions. The value of home-made goods averages annually about $1 per head of the population.

Mining and the fisheries are comparatively of small account. On the coast, however, a number of fishing stations have long been established, and some tonnage is employed in the mackerel and cod fisheries.

New Hampshire has but one port on the Atlantic, and as far as its direct foreign commerce is concerned it might as well be without any. In 1849–50 the total value of its exports to foreign countries was only $8,927, and for the same year its imports amounted only to $49,079. The amount exported, however, does not indicate that it has no exportable produce, but that what it has is carried to ports of other states. The shipping employed in the foreign trade was 19,257 tons, as follows:

Nationality.	Entered.	Cleared.	Total.
American	3,572	682	4,254
Foreign	7,472	7,531	15,003
Total	11,044	8,213	19,257

The shipping owned within the state on the 30th June, 1850, was 23,093 tons, of which 14,979 tons were registered, and the remainder licensed, etc. The proportion of the latter employed in the coasting trade was 4,025 tons; in the cod-fisheries, 2,664 tons; and in the mackerel-fisheries, 1,204 tons. The number of ships built in 1849–50 was 10, and the tonnage, 6,914 tons; but the greater part of this was built for other states. In 1805 the exports of New Hampshire were valued at $608,408, and in 1810 at $234,-650. To 1825 they averaged $200,000, but since that period have rapidly declined. The coasting trade, however, has greatly increased.

There are 22 banks in the state, with an aggregate capital of $2,375,900, the capital of the banks varying from $50,000 to $200,000. The circulation amounted in December, 1850, to $1,897,111, and the deposits to $566,634. The principal assets were specie, $129,399; debts due, $4,328,120; real estate, $43,670, etc.

The means of internal communication are being rapidly improved. At the close of 1850, 16 railroads had been built, with an aggregate length of

513 miles. The principal of these are: the Eastern Railroad, 16.8 miles; the Nashua and Concord Railroad, 35 miles; the Northern Railroad, 81.7 miles; the Manchester and Lawrence Railroad, 23.5 miles; the Sullivan Railroad, 25.6 miles; the Concord and Montreal Railroad, 69 miles; the Portsmouth and Concord Railroad, 40 miles: the Concord and Claremont, 50 miles; and others, as the Ashuelot, the Contoocook Valley, Central, Cocheco, and Great Falls and Conway, etc. The navigation of the Merrimac has been improved by dams, locks, and short canals; these are at Bow Falls, Hookset Falls, Amoskeag Falls, Union Falls, and Sewall's Falls. The Middlesex Canal affords a boatable communication between Boston and Concord. The effect these lines have had on the interests of the state are apparent in the rapid progress made of late years in every department of industry. With one exception their seaward terminus is at Boston.

Education in New Hampshire is liberally provided for, and its Common Schools have long been fostered by the state. The whole number of school districts, in 1850, was 2,167, and the average attendance at these was, in summer, 46,225, and in winter, 60,271, each season averaging about nine weeks. The number of teachers employed was 1,246 males, and 961 females; the monthly wages of the first was $14 73; and of the latter, $6 21, varying, however, in the several districts. The whole amount expended in the support of these schools was $174,518, of which sum $145,892 were raised by tax, and the remainder either contributed by the state or received from the proceeds of local funds. The teachers have an Institute. The schools have hitherto been under a State Superintendent, but in 1850 were placed under the charge of County Superintendents. There is an asylum for the Insane at Concord, but the Deaf and Dumb are provided for at the American Asylum at Hartford, and the Blind at the Asylum at Boston.

The only collegiate institution is Dartmouth College, at Hanover, founded in 1769. It has 9 professors, and in 1850 had 221 students. Its library contains 16,500 volumes. The New Hampshire Medical School, attached to this institution, was founded in 1797. In 1850 it had 7 professors and 52 students; its graduates at the same date numbering 758. This school has a good apparatus for philosophical and chemical purposes, and a valuable anatomical museum. There are three theological schools: the Methodist General Biblical Institute, at Concord, founded in 1847, had in 1850, 3 teachers, 40 students, and a library of 2,000 volumes; the Gilmanton Theological Seminary, founded in 1835, is under the direction of the Congregationalists, and in 1850 had 3 professors, and 23 students, and its library contained 4,300 volumes; and the New Hampton Theological Seminary, under Baptist direction, was founded in 1825; in 1850 it had two teachers, and 36 students, and in its library, 2,000 volumes.

The principal religious denominations are the Baptists, Congregationalists, and Methodists: in 1850 the Baptists had 7 associations, 96 churches, 73 ordained and 14 licensed ministers, and 8,526 church members; the Congregationalists, 211 churches, 192 ministers, and 24,629 church members; and the Methodists, 181 ministers, and 9,123 church members. Of the other denominations, the Protestant Episcopalians, Universalists, Unitarians, etc., are the most prominent. Roman Catholics are few in number, and are excluded by the Constitution from political power. New Hampshire is the only one of the United States that gives to one religious sect a preference over another.

New Hampshire was granted in 1622 to John Mason and F. Gorges, and the first settlements were begun in 1623, at Dover and Portsmouth. In

1641 it was annexed to Massachusetts, but in 1679 it again became a separate province. New-Hampshire, with the other New-England States, in 1686, was placed under the government of Sir Edmund Andross; the union with Massachusetts was revived in 1689, and continued until 1692. From 1699 to 1702 it was united to Massachusetts and New-York. In the latter year it was wholly under Massachusetts, but in 1741 a final separation took place. After the revolutionary war, to which it raised a subsidy of 12,409 men, it formed a constitution, and has since been an independent member of the union. The English authority was extinguished in this state in 1775, and in 1776 a temporary government was established, which continued during the war, a president being annually elected.

CONCORD, the capital, lies on both sides of the Merrimack, which is spanned by two bridges. Lat. 43° 12′ 20″ N., and long. 71° 29′ W. The city lies chiefly on two streets, one of which extends nearly two miles. The public buildings are a state-house, a court-house, jail, state prison, &c.; there are also numerous churches and many elegant private buildings. The state-house is a beautiful structure of hewn granite, 126 feet long and 49 feet wide, with a projection of four feet on each front, and cost over $80,000. It is surmounted by a fine cupola. The hall of the representatives and sen ate chamber are spacious and elegant rooms. The city contained in 1850, fifty-six stores; produced hardware and cutlery to the amount of $40,810; it had one fulling mill; one wool factory; and three tanneries, &c. There were published at that date six weekly newspapers and one periodical. The academy contained 180 students, and thirty-six common and primary schools educated 2,180 scholars. Population, 8,584. By locks and canals around the falls of the Merrimack and the Middlesex Canal, a valuable communication exists with Boston; there is also a communication by railroad. Turkey Pond, containing an area of 700 acres, and Long Pond, 500 acres, are in the immediate vicinity, on the west side of the city.

PORTSMOUTH, near the mouth of the Piscataqua, is the largest and most commercial town in the state. Its harbor is unsurpassed in the world, being safe, easily defended, and having forty feet of water at the lowest tides. It is completely land locked, and protected by several large islands from the winds. The town is neatly built, and has a population of 9,739 inhabitants, who carry on the coasting trade and fisheries with some activity, and prosecute some branches of manufactures. The navy station of Kittery is on the opposite shore of the river. Lat. 43° 4′ 35″ N., and long. 70° 45′ 50″ W. Portsmouth was first settled in 1623, under the auspices of Mason and Gorges. It has several times been destroyed by fire.

The other principal places are Dover, Nashua, Keene, Exeter, Manchester, Peterborough, Walpole, Claremont, Gilmanton, Meredith, Hanover and Haverhill.

THE STATE OF VERMONT.

VERMONT is the north-westernmost of the New-England States, and lies between the parallels of 42° 50′ and 45° north latitude, and the meridians of 71° 33′ and 73° 25′ west longitude. The state is bounded north by Lower Canada, as settled by the treaty of 1842; east by the western bank of the Connecticut River, which separates it from New-Hampshire; south by Massachusetts, and west by New-York, from which it is separated chiefly by Lake Champlain. It is 157½ miles long, from north to south, and 61 wide, from east to west, and contains a superficial area of 10,212 square miles, or 6,535,680 acres.

The surface of Vermont is, with little exception, hilly and mountainous. The Green Mountains, from which the state derives its name, come from Massachusetts, and run through its centre. In the southern part of Washington county they divide into two chains: the western and principal chain continuing in a northerly direction, and terminating near the northern boundary of the state; the eastern, or as it is sometimes called, the "height of land," strikes off to the north-east, dividing the waters which fall into Lake Memphremagog and Lake Champlain. The western range presents the highest summits, but has inequalities, which afford a passage for Onion and La Moelle rivers. The loftiest culminations in the Green Mountains, are Killington Peak, a few miles east of Rutland, 3,675 feet high; Camel's Rump, about half-way between Burlington and Montpelier, 4,190 feet; and Mansfield Mountain, a few miles farther north, 4,280 feet above the level of the sea. Ascutney is a single mountain, five miles south-west of Windsor, 3,320 feet in height.

The soil of Vermont is in general fertile, being for the most part deep and of a dark color, moist, loamy, and well-watered. The intervale lands are esteemed best; bordering on these is a strip, one or two miles wide, which is comparatively poor; but beyond this the land possesses a fertility nearly equal to that on the rivers. The soil is peculiarly well-adapted for the cereal grains, especially on the margins of the lakes and rivers. Grazing is also extensively engaged in by the inhabitants, and even on the Green Mountains are fine grazing farms. The natural growths east of the mountains are birch, beach, maple, ash, elm, and butternut, and on the west the growth of the hard woods is intermixed with pine and other evergreens.

The climate is nearly assimilated to that of New-Hampshire. The winter commences in November, and snow lies from the middle of December to the middle of March. On the side of the hills it is often from four to six feet deep The thermometer ranges from 94° to 15° or 20° below zero; the mean annual temperature is about 43½° Fahr. Trees bud from the 6th to the 20th April, and flowers from the close of May. Wheat and oats are sown about the middle of April, and ripen about the middle of August. The first frost appears from the middle of September to the commencement of October, but is light until November.

Lake Champlain lies between New-York and Vermont. Its length, from Whitehall, at its southern extremity to its termination, 24 miles north of the Canada line, is 128 miles; its breadth varies from half a mile to sixteen miles, and its surface covers about 600 square miles. There are several large islands in the northern part of the lake, the principal of which are North and South Hero and Isle La Motte. The outlet of the lake is the River Sorelle, which runs north into the St. Lawrence. Lake Memphremagog is partly in this state, but principally in Canada. It is 30 miles long, and discharges its waters through the St. Francis River into the St Lawrence. Lake Champlain is connected with the Hudson River by a canal 64 miles long, which joins the river a little north of Albany, and also forms a junction with the Erie Canal. There are several good harbors in Vermont on this lake, the principal of which are Burlington, St. Albans, Vergennes, &c. &c.

The Connecticut receives several streams, flowing from the eastern declivity of the mountains, the principal of which, commencing at the south, are the West River, Queechy, White River, and the Passumsic. The rivers which fall into Lake Champlain, beginning in the north, are Missisque, which rises south-west of Lake Memphremagog, and discharges itself into Missisque Bay; La Moelle, which rises south of the same lake, and running west, empties itself 10 miles north of Burlington; Onion River, which rises still farther south, and running nearly parallel with La Moelle, passes by Montpelier, and joins the lake four miles north-west of Burlington; Otter Creek, which rises in the south-western part of the state, and, running west of north, passes by Rutland, Middlebury, and Vergennes, and empties itself twenty miles south of Burlington. None of the rivers of Vermont are navigable, except for a few miles from their mouths; but they abound with valuable mill-sites.

The population of Vermont, in 1850, amounted to 313,611, or in the proportion of one person to every 21 acres; and was thus distributed among the 14 counties into which the state is divided:

COUNTIES.	White Persons.	Free Colored Persons.	Total Population.	COUNTIES.	White Persons.	Free Colored Persons.	Total Population.
Addison	26,441	108	26,549	Orange	27,277	19	27,296
Bennington	18,512	77	18,589	Orleans	15,693	14	15,707
Caledonia	23,081	5	23,086	Rutland	32,939	120	33,059
Crittenden	28,927	109	29,036	Washington	24,710	14	24,654
Essex	4,647	3	4,650	Windham	29,025	37	29,062
Franklin	28,500	86	28,586	Windsor	38,208	112	38,320
Grand Isle	4,142	3	4,145				
Lamoelle	10,869	3	10,872	Total	312,902	709	313,611

CLASSES AND SEXES OF POPULATION.

Classes.		Males.	Females.	Total.
White Persons		159,374	153,528	312,902
Colored "	—free	366	343	709
" "	—slave	—	—	—
Total		159,730	153,871	313,611

PROGRESSIVE MOVEMENT OF POPULATION.

Date of Census.	White Persons.	Colored Persons. Free.	Colored Persons. Slave.	Total Population.	Decennial Increase. Numerical.	Decennial Increase. Per 100.
1790	85,144	255	17	85,416	—	—
1800	153,908	557	—	154,465	69,049	80.8
1810	216,963	750	—	217,713	63,248	40.8
1820	234,846	918	—	235,764	18,051	8.2
1830	279,771	881	—	280,652	44,888	19.0
1840	291,218	730	—	291,948	11,296	4.0
1850	312,902	709	—	313,611	21,663	7.4

The number of dwelling-houses in the state, on the 1st June, 1850, was 56,548, and the number of families 59,665, and hence the ratio of families to each dwelling is 1.06, and the ratio of persons 5.5, indicating a ratio of about five persons to each family. The deaths occurring in 1849–50 amounted to 3,130, or a ratio of one death to each 100 persons. The returns giving this result, however, are probably incorrect.

The industry of this state is essentially agricultural, no less than three fourths of the whole population being engaged in farming and grazing. The whole number of farms in 1850 was 29,809. The live stock is estimated at 420,000 neat cattle; 67,000 horses and mules; 200,000 sheep; 320,000 hogs; and poultry to the value of about $180,000. Oats yield the largest cereal crop, the production being upwards of 4,000,000 bushels; of Indian corn about 1,600,000 bushels are produced; of wheat 500,000 bushels; of rye and buckwheat about 450,000 bushels each; and of barley 70,000 bushels. The potatoe crop varies from seven to eight millions of bushels, and that of hay is about 800,000 tons. Animal products, and the products of the dairy, are large and valuable; and the forest yields exportable articles in the shape of lumber, pot and pearl ashes, &c.

Manufactures in this state are confined chiefly to the production of coarse and bulky articles, as leather, bricks and lime. paper, woollen goods, &c. The woollen trade employs fully one fourth of the whole manufacturing capital of the state. Domestic, or home-made articles, are produced largely, and perhaps few states, in this respect, exhibit a greater thrift and industry than Vermont. Mining, except in a very few localities, is but little attended to, although many of the useful metals, and much fine building material, are found in the state.

The foreign commerce of Vermont is very limited. Its only direct outlet is Burlington, on Lake Champlain, and hence the eastern portions of the state must depend on other states for a market. The value of exports in 1849–50 was $430,906, and of imports $463,092, but this year was one of more than average prosperity. The entrances amounted to 99,435 tons, and the clearances to 82,856 tons. The shipping owned within the state on the 30th June, 1850, was 4,530 tons, 3,096 tons of which was navigated by steam.

The transit and internal trade of Vermont is considerable, and is constantly being extended. This state has of late years progressed wonderfully, and has now several long lines of railroad, extending from the borders of Massachusetts and New-Hampshire to Burlington and Canada; and lines also extend south-west from Rutland to Whitehall and Troy, in New-York. More than 300 miles of road are now in working order within the state.

Vermont has 23 banks, and it is a highly creditable fact that they are all solvent, and well managed. Their condition in 1850 was as follows:—Liabilities: capital stock $1,829,395; circulation $2,321,808; other liabilities $351,659—total liabilities $4,502,862. Resources: specie $129,811; discounts $3,541,081; deposits $606,320; other assets $346,519—total $4,623,731.

The means of education in this state are ample, but nevertheless the system cannot compete with that pursued in Massachusetts or New-York. The oldest collegiate institution is the University of Vermont, founded in 1791. Its library contained about 12,000 volumes. Middlebury College was finished in 1800; it has six professors, and in 1850 had 63 students. Its library counts 7,054 volumes. Norwich University, founded in 1834, has also six professors, and in 1850 had 59 students. There are two medical schools in the state. The Castleton Medical College was founded in 1818, and has seven professors, and in 1850 had 104 students. The Vermont Medical College, at Woodstock, dates from 1835, and in 1850 had 90 students attending its courses. Theological seminaries are numerous. Academies and grammar-schools are from 50 to 60 in number, and in these between 4,000 and 5,000 students are constantly being educated. The common schools of the state are under the charge of a state superintendent. According to the School Report of 1850 the number of school districts was 2,647, and the number of scholars 95,616. The state gave for the support of these $74,180, but the whole cost, the balance of which is raised by tax in the several districts, amounted to $204,695. The teachers' wages averaged, for males, $13.78 per month, and for females, $5.60 per month. The number of weeks taught by males was 19.125, at a total cost of $65,896, and by females 41.721, at a cost of $58,475. There was formerly a separate fund for the support of schools, but this was abolished in 1845, and appropriated to pay off the state debt. They are now supported by an annual appropriation and district taxation. The Vermont Asylum for the Insane, at Brattleboro', is an institution of great value, and in August 1849 had under treatment 448 patients. Up to that date 1459 had been treated, of which 666, or 58.4 per cent., were recovered. The average charge for patients is $100 per annum. The deaf and dumb of this state are educated at Hartford, Connecticut, at the American Asylum. The State Prison is self-supporting, and during the year ending Sept. 1849 it received 34 convicts, only one of whom was a female.

The religious denominations having the largest numbers, are the Baptists, Congregationalists, and Methodists. Roman Catholics and Protestant Episcopalians, are also numerous, and there are several churches belonging to the minor sectaries, as Unitarians, &c. The following table exhibits the statistics of the condition of each denomination in 1850.

Denomination.	Churches.	Ministers.	Communicants.
Baptists	112	81	8,092
Congregationalists	194	190	20,209
Methodists	—	134	7,849
Protestant Episcopalians	19	23	1,000
Unitarians	4	2	—
Universalists	84	39	—

The Roman Catholics are under the jurisdiction of the Bishop of Boston, and the Protestant Episcopalians under that of the Bishop of Vermont, whose diocese is co-terminous with the state.

The State of Vermont was first settled at Fort Dummer, by emigrants from Massachusetts. From 1741 to 1764, New-Hampshire claimed the territory of Vermont, and made several grants of land therein. New-York also claimed the territory, and obtained a grant from Parliament, in the year 1764. At the commencement of the revolution, Vermont declared itself independent, yet, on account of the conflicting claims of New-York and New-Hampshire, the Congress feared to admit it into the Union as a separate independency. In this state of affairs, the British were in the hopes of detaching Vermont from the revolting states, but she was true to herself through all her difficulties: "the Green Mountain boys," as they were called, were found among the foremost in repelling the common enemy, and all attempts, either to persuade or coerce her into allegiance to the crown, proved abortive. In 1790, a treaty was made, by which New-York relinquished her claim to the territory, receiving a consideration of $30,000, and in the following year Vermont was admitted to full fellowship as an independent member of the United States.

The present constitution was framed in 1793, but has since been amended. The government consists of a governor, executive council, senate and assembly, all chosen annually by the people. The senate consists of 30 members, and the assembly of one member from each town. Every adult male citizen, of quiet and peaceable behavior, may vote. The executive committee, which has 12 councillors, are elected annually, and have a co-ordinate jurisdiction with the governor, who cannot act without their consent. The provisions of the constitution, in regard to negroes and aliens, are liberal and just. Once in seven years a "council of censors" is appointed, whose duty it is to inquire "whether the constitution has been preserved inviolate, and whether the executive and legislative branches have performed their duties as guardians of the commonwealth; whether taxes have been justly laid and collected, the public moneys properly disposed of, and the laws duly executed."

The judiciary powers are vested in a Supreme Court, consisting of six judges; in County Courts or Courts of Common Pleas, comprising six circuits, each County Court being composed of one judge of the Supreme Court, who is *ex officio* chief justice of the County Courts of his circuit, and two assistant judges for each county, and in Justices of the Peace. All the judges and justices are chosen annually by the legislature.

The finances of the state are in a very flourishing condition ; the receipts for the fiscal year ending Sept. 1st, 1849, were $119,386, and the expenditures, $111,056. The principal income is from taxes, which amounted, in 1849, to $87,135.

MONTPELIER, the state capital, is situated at the union of the branches of the Onion or Winooski River, in latitude 44° 16′ N., and longitude 71° 32′ W. Its site is a plain of moderate extent, surrounded by elevated hills. The great road from Boston to Burlington passes through the town and makes it a great thoroughfare. It contains a beautiful state-house, a court-house, jail, several churches, 15 stores, several mills and manufactories, and about 4,000 inhabitants. The state-house is built of granite, 72 feet wide in the centre, with two wings, and is each 39 feet, making a whole length of 130 feet. It has a projecting portico in the centre of six Doric columns, 6 feet in diameter and 36 feet high. The centre building is 100 feet deep, and the wings 50 feet deep. The whole is surmounted by a fine dome, 100 feet high from the ground to the top. In the interior are rooms for various offices, and elegant halls for the senate and representatives. Its architecture is much admired.

BURLINGTON, on Lake Champlain, is the largest city within the state. Lat. 44° 27′ N. and long. 73° 10′ W. It is built on a fine bay, which sets up between two points on the east side of the lake and forms a regular curve. Near the centre of the town is the public square, on which the court-house is built, and which is surrounded by brick stores and the principal hotels. It contains many neat and some splendid dwellings, surrounded with shrubbery, and generally having fine gardens in the rear. Some of the public buildings are spacious and elegant, the churches especially are beautiful specimens of architecture. The harbor of Burlington is the best on the lake, and is of easy access. It has been much improved by the government, which has erected a noble breakwater to protect it from the west winds. Steamboats stop here daily on their way from Whitehall to St. John's. A steam ferry-boat crosses at this place to Fort Kent, on the opposite side of the lake, to Plattsburg. The university of Vermont is located here. About a mile and a half north-east is the flourishing manufacturing village of Winooski, on Onion River. The river here has a fall of 20 feet, nearly perpendicular, which affords a great water-power, easily available. The first settlement in Burlington was made after the peace of 1783, and it was first organized in 1787. Population 5,211.

The other principal towns are St. Alban's, Swanton, Vergennes, in the lake ; Middlebury, the seat of a college ; Pittsford, Rutland, Manchester, Bennington, Newbury; Brattleboro' which contains the state lunatic asylum; Rockingham, Windsor, Woodstock ; Norwich, the seat of a university, and Danville.

THE STATE OF MASSACHUSETTS.

Massachusetts, the parent state of New-England, and the chief manufacturing district of the United States, is bounded on the north by Vermont and New-Hampshire; east by the Atlantic; south by the Atlantic, Rhode Island and Connecticut; and west by the State of New-York. It lies between 41° 23′ and 42° 52′ N. latitude, and the meridians of 69° 50′ and 73° 30′ W. longitude. It is about 190 miles long from east to west, with an average breadth of 90 miles, and contains about 7,500 square miles, or 4,800,000 acres.

The face of the country is diversified. There are several ranges of mountains in the western part of the state, continued from Vermont and New-Hampshire, and running across the state into Connecticut. The first is the Taghkanic range, which may be regarded as a branch of the Green Mountains. It leaves the range at Williamstown, in the north-west corner of the state, and traversing the county of Berkshire, divides the waters of the Hudson from those of the Housatonic, and passes into Connecticut. The second is the Green Mountain range, which runs on the east side of the Housatonic, and pursues a course east of south, between the waters of the Housatonic and those of the Connecticut. The third is the Mount Tom range, which commences in New-Hampshire, and running south-west, crosses Connecticut River at Northampton, and then proceeds in a southerly course on the west side of the river. The Lyme range leaves Mount Tom range, about ten miles east of Northampton, and proceeds in a southerly course on the east side of Connecticut River. The part of the state east of these mountains is hilly, except in the south-eastern counties, where it is level and sandy. On the sea-coast the land is generally poor, particularly in the south-east. The rest of the state has generally a strong good soil, well adapted to grazing and grain. The valleys of the Connecticut and the Housatonic, especially, have a fine soil, and embrace many flourishing and pleasant towns. The improvements in agriculture made in this state are highly respectable and laudable. The farms around Boston are literally gardens, from which the capital is supplied with the finest fruit and vegetables. The principal agricultural productions are grass, Indian corn, rye, wheat, oats, and potatoes. Apples are abundant, and large quantities of cider are made annually. Beef, pork, butter and cheese are also abundant and of excellent quality. Among the mineral products are iron ore, which is found in large quantities in Bristol and Plymouth; and marble, quarries of which have been opened in Stockbridge and other towns of Berkshire county. At Chelmsford and Quincy great quantities of beautiful granite are found, which is much used for building in Boston and New-York.

The greatest elevation in Massachusetts is Saddle Mountain, on the Taghkanic range, 4,000 feet high. Mount Holyoke, near Northampton, is more than 1,200 feet, and Wachussett mountain, in Princeton, is an isolated summit, from 2 to 3,000 feet above the level of the sea.

The county of Barnstable is a peninsula, commonly called the peninsula of Cape Cod. Its shape is that of a man's arm bent inwards both at the elbow and the wrist. A great part of this peninsula is sandy and barren, and in many places wholly destitute of vegetation; yet it is populous. The inhabitants derive their support almost entirely from the ocean; the men being constantly employed at sea, and the boys at a very early age being put on board the fishing boats. In consequence of the violent east winds, it is supposed that the cape is gradually wearing away. Nantucket Island lies south of Cape Cod. It is fifteen miles long, and contains about fifty square miles. The soil is light and sandy, but in some parts rich and productive, particularly in hay. The inhabitants are principally of the denomination of Friends. The men are generally robust, enterprising seamen, extensively engaged in the whale fishery, and are as skilful and adventurous as any in the world. To the south-east of this island are the Nantucket shoals, where many vessels have been shipwrecked. They extend about fifty miles in length and forty-five in breadth. Martha's Vineyard lies west of Nantucket. It is twenty miles long, and from two to ten broad. There is a spacious harbor on the north side of the island, called Holmes' Hole. Vessels bound to Boston or the eastward are frequently seen here in great numbers, waiting for a wind to enable them to double Cape Cod. It is calculated that more than 1000 vessels anchor here in the course of a year. Elizabeth Islands are small islands, extending in a row about eighteen miles in length, along the south-east side of Buzzard's Bay. Plum Island extends along the coast from Newburyport, south, to Ipswich. It is nine miles long and one broad, and is separated from the main land by a narrow sound, over which a bridge has been built. In the season, when plums are ripe, this island is the resort of the neighboring inhabitants, and a scene of lively amusement. The principal capes are Cape Ann and Cape Cod, on each side of Massachusetts Bay; Cape Malabar, at the south-east extremity of the peninsula of Cape Cod; Sandy Point, on the north side of Nantucket Island; and Gay Head, at the western extremity of Martha's Vineyard.

Connecticut River crosses the western part of the state from north to south, intersecting the counties of Franklin, Hampshire and Hampden, and passes into Connecticut. The Merrimack comes from New-Hampshire, and running north-east, empties at Newburyport. Ipswich River is a small stream which falls into Ipswich harbor, at the south end of Plum Island. Charles River falls into Boston harbor, between Boston and Charlestown. Neponset River falls into Boston harbor on the south side of the town. Taunton River rises in Plymouth county, and runs southwest into Narragansett Bay. It is navigable for vessels twenty miles, to Taunton. The principal branches of the Merrimack are the Concord and Nashua Rivers. The principal branches of the Connecticut are Miller's River and the Chicapee from the east, and Deerfield and Westfield from the west. The Housatonic rises in the northern part of Berkshire county, and flows south in the State of Connecticut.

Massachusetts Bay, that gives name to the state, which is often called the Bay State, extends from Cape Ann on the north, 40 miles, to Cape Cod on the south, and includes Boston and Cape Cod Bays. Buzzard's Bay, on the south shore, is 30 miles in length. Boston Harbor is one of the finest in the world: capacious, safe, easy of entrance, and easily defended, but in the winter season is often ice-bound. New-Bedford, on Buzzard's Bay, has a fine harbor.

The climate of Massachusetts differs little from that of the New- England States in general. On the coast, and within the range of sea-influence, it is much more equable and mild than in the interior, but is subject to fogs. The severe cold of winter is only of short duration, and that season can scarcely be said to be set in before December. The harbors, however, are frequently closed by ice for several weeks together. In the interior the rivers are usually frozen over for weeks at a time, and the roads are blocked up with snow. The reign of winter terminates with March, although sometimes prolonged far into April. It is succeeded by a season of rapid vegetation, and by the middle of June, the summer season, which is as hot and sultry as in Florida, has fairly commenced. The heat of July and August is often excessive, but the nights are cool, and for a great part of the time the air is temperate, clear, and elastic. The sea breezes prevail in this section in winter, bringing cold, sleety weather, but in summer a moist coolness that gratefully relieves the heats. Rain falls on the average about 60 days in the year, and in amount varies from 46 to 52 inches. The endemic diseases of the climate are affections of the lungs; but consumption is not more prevalent than in other parts.

The state is divided into 14 counties, and in 1850 contained a population of 994,499 inhabitants. The distribution of these into the several counties was in the following proportions:

COUNTIES.	White Persons.	Free Col'd Persons.	Total Popula.	COUNTIES.	White Persons.	Free Col'd Persons.	Total Popula.
Barnstable	35,153	123	35,276	Middlesex	160,694	689	161,383
Berkshire	48,259	1,333	49,592	Nantucket	8,110	342	8,452
Bristol	74,746	1,431	76,577	Norfolk	78,661	231	78,892
Duke's	4,487	533	4,540	Plymouth	55,220	477	55,697
Essex	130,682	618	131,300	Suffolk	142,484	2,023	144,507
Franklin	30,779	91	30,870	Worcester	130,167	622	130,789
Hampden	50,778	503	51,281				
Hampshire	35,405	327	35,732	Total	985,704	8,795	994,499

CLASSES AND SEXES OF POPULATION.

Classes.		Males.	Females.	Total.
White Persons		484,284	501,420	985,704
Colored "	—free	4,314	4,481	8,795
" "	—slave	—	—	—
Total		487,808	505,081	992,889

PROGRESSIVE MOVEMENT OF POPULATION.

Date of Census.	White Persons.	Colored Persons. Free.	Colored Persons. Slave.	Total Population.	Decennial Increase. Numerical.	Decennial Increase. Per 100.
1790	373,254	5,463	—	378,717	—	—
1800	416,793	6,452	—	423,245	44,528	11.9
1810	465,303	6,737	—	472,040	48,795	11.5
1820	516,419	6,868	—	523,287	51,247	10.8
1830	603,359	7,048	1	610,408	87,121	16.6
1840	729,030	8,669	—	737,699	127,291	20.1
1850	985,704	8,795	—	994,499	256,800	34 8

The total number of dwellings in the state, in 1850, was 152,359, and of families 191,243, or in the ratio of 6.5 persons to each dwelling, and 5.2 persons to each family; and the relative proportion of dwellings and families was as 1 to 1.26. The deaths amounted to 19,485, exhibiting a ratio of mortality equal to 1.96 per cent., or 1 death to every 50.9 inhabitants. The density of the population in Massachusetts is 1 person to every 4.9 acres.

The industrial employments of Massachusetts permeate every branch of national industry, but manufactures, agriculture, and commerce give support to a great majority of the people. Its ever-increasing ratio of population is a true index to its prosperity. Agriculture alone employs about two-fifths of the whole number of inhabitants. This branch is pursued with increasing energy; and the aid it has had from the establishment of agricultural societies, and the fostering care of the government, has been the means of establishing the farming interest on a sound basis. The best breeds of cattle have also been introduced. Massachusetts, indeed, is now the best cultivated state in the Union, and has, perhaps, the most improved live stock. The crops taken from the land, although falling short of the demand, are unusually large, and relatively to the area and character of its soils, surprisingly large. Indian corn is grown to the amount of between 2,000,000 and 2,500,000 bushels, and oats yield about 3,000,000 bushels. Rye, wheat, barley, and buckwheat are comparatively small crops, that of wheat being not more than 28,487 bushels, against 101,178 in 1840. Potatoes are widely planted, and the crop of hay reaches at least 600,000 tons. Hemp and flax are grown to some small amount, and hop fields are frequently met with throughout the state. The products of the forest are necessarily small, but orchard and garden products are valuable. The live stock numbers about 50 asses and mules, 74,060 horses, 299,600 neat cattle, 179,537 sheep, and 120,000 swine, in all valued at $12,000,000. Poultry is also plentiful. The state, with this vast amount of stock and produce, is yet an importing state, the wants of the population in the manufacturing towns being always in advance of production. There are 33,989 farms in the state, or 1 to every 29 persons; and the condition of the land in 1850, was as follows: 300,000 acres tillage land, 1,311,220 acres pasture land, 715,000 acres unimproved land, 257,000 acres unimprovable land, 98,539 acres used as roads, and 169,117 acres covered with water. The number of barns and store-houses was 74,765.

Massachusetts manufactures more fibrous materials than all the rest of the Union together. It is one great industrial province, scarcely a square mile of which is destitute of its workshop. The capital invested in manufactures is not far under $100,000,000. For the manufacture of cotton goods there are 3,337 mills, and 32,559 looms; and 1,220,752 spindles are employed. The annual product of this branch is about 200,000,000 yards of cotton cloth. Lowell and Lawrence are the great centers of the cotton enterprise; the former town alone has a manufacturing capital of $13,260,000. It contained, in 1850, 40 mills, 325,520 spindles, and 9,906 looms; and gave employment to 12,000 operatives, the products of whose labor amounted to a weekly average of 2,135,500 yards of fabrics. The manufacturing interests of Lawrence are to about one half the amount of those of Lowell. The woollen manufacture is second only to that of cotton. There are 191 mills, 4,943 looms, and 208,884 spindles employed in this branch. The consumption of wool amounts annually to about 18,000,000 pounds, and the capital invested in its manufacture is $9,500,000. The goods turned out are cassimeres, broad cloths, satinets, Kentucky jeans, flannels, blankets, and a variety of other pure and mixed articles; and carpets are produced to an immense extent. Worsted goods, hosiery, silks, linens, etc., are also largely manufactured.

Besides the above, which constitute the staple manufactures, large establishments are engaged in the various mechanic arts, and in the manufacture of domestic articles. The machine shops are extensive, as also the manufactories of iron, steel, brass, and other metals. Forges and furnaces are numerous. The principal metalic staples are farming implements, axes, engines, and boilers, and machinery of all kinds, for which the demand is great. Edged tools and cutlery general are made to a large amount.

Another of the great manufactures of this state is that of leather. Whole villages are frequently devoted to this branch, and it is estimated that $20,000,000 is under the annual value of the products of the boot and shoe manufactures alone.

The minor manufactures embrace every description of goods, from the most substantial to the most worthless, and from the rude tool of the laborer to the most finished mathematical instrument. Glass, hats, salt, and paper are manufactured extensively; and large numbers of persons are employed in the refining of sugars, in powder making, and in the manufacture of paints and colors. The number of distilleries has decreased from 78 in 1840, to 43 in 1850: a fact attributable to the progress of temperance principles, and the moral resistance of the people to the debasing influence of the ancient rum-drinking habits of our pious forefathers.

In 1850 the total number of workshops amounted to 25,684; and there were besides 19 breweries, 388 tanning houses, 5,312 warehouses and stores, 71 rope-walks, 718 grist mills, 330 carding mills, 99 fulling mills, 1,605 saw mills, 16 small-arm manufactories, 836 slitting mills and nail shops, 13 printing and dying establishments, 9 linen factories, with 3,984 looms, etc., 114 paper mills, 423 other mills, 204 iron works and furnaces, 68 oil factories, 8 glass factories, 47 card factories, 23 bleacheries. There are also in the state, salt works extending over a superfice of 5,358,587 square feet; and the extent of wharf accommodation is 14,834,350 square feet.

As a commercial state Massachusetts holds the third rank in the Union. In 1849–50 the value of its exports amounted to $10,681,763, and of its imports to $30,374,684; and the shipping employed in the carrying trade for the same period, was as in the annexed table of tonnage:

Nationality.	Entered.	Cleared.	Total.
American	339,508	272,278	611,786
Foreign	271,941	274,674	546,615
Total	611,449	546,952	1,158,401

Of this aggregate, Boston entered 478,859 tons, and cleared 437,760 tons. The shipping owned within the state, in 1850, amounted to 685,442 tons, of which 477,328 tons were in the foreign trade and whale fisheries, and the remainder in the coast trade and coast fisheries. Boston owned 320,687 tons, and New Bedford 127,960 tons. The proportion of shipping employed in the whale fisheries was 122,676 tons, and the proportion employed in the coasting trade was 115,846 tons, in the cod fisheries 41,470 tons, and in the mackerel fisheries 42,895 tons. The amount of shipping propelled by steam-power was 7,903 tons. During 1849–50, 121 vessels, of an aggregate burden of 35,836 tons were built in the state. The capital invested in the whale fisheries is about $12,000,000, and that in the cod and mackerel fisheries about $2,000,000; the returns of the whale fisheries alone is estimated at about $15,000,000 annually. Massachusetts, indeed, has ever been the foremost state of the Union in respect of the foreign fisheries. Her vessels penetrate every ocean for the whale, and are found from Greenland and Behring's Straits to the confines of the pole south; nor is it less noted for the extent of its coast fisheries, which are carried on from the Gulf of St. Lawrence to the capes of Virginia.

Massachusetts is not more celebrated for her manufactures, commerce, and fisheries, than for the moral qualities of the people engaged in these departments of industry. The intelligence, character, and happiness of the operatives are well understood, and contrast essentially with the supineness and misery of the same class in foreign countries. The young women who are employed in the cotton and woollen factories are noted for their many virtues, and industrious and economical habits. The CITY OF LOWELL, which is justly entitled to the appellation of the "Manchester of America," employs in its factories 10,000 females, many of whom devote their leisure hours to literature and the fine arts, and publish a highly creditable monthly periodical, entitled the "Lowell Offering," which is supplied with matter from their own pens. In 1820, the population of the township of Lowell was less than 200; in 1850, it had increased to 32,620! The city is situated on the south side of the Merrimack, below Pawtucket Falls, and the mills are supplied with water from that river, through a canal 1½ miles long, 60 feet wide, and 8 deep; from the main canal the water is conveyed through lateral canals to the various mills. All children, under 15 years of age, engaged in these factories, are required by law to have three months schooling each year. A rail-road and canal connects the city with Boston, and the Merrimack River with Newburyport.

Another great manufacturing town is SPRINGFIELD. At this place is located the United States' Armory, the machinery of which is driven by water-power: 18 water-wheels keep in active operation 11 trip-hammers and 28 forges, and from the work-shops are produced in one year, in the article of muskets alone, the value of $154,000. Besides the armory, there are several extensive cotton and other factories, employing a large capital and a commensurate number of hands. Population in 1850, 20,721.

Other manufacturing places, notable for a variety of productions, but chiefly cotton goods—are Fall River, Taunton, Worcester, Northampton, Pittsfield, Adams, and LAWRENCE, which has lately been incorporated as a city. The latter place, from the numerous facilities, artificial and natural, which it enjoys, will eventually become one of the most celebrated manufacturing places in the state. The population in 1850 was 8,341.

BOSTON is the principal seaport and capital of the state. It is celebrated in history as being the scene of the first regular battle fought during the American Revolution, and the first point of resistance to British authority. Latitude 42° 21′ 23″ north, and longitude 71° 4′ 9″ west. It is beautifully situated, principally on a peninsula at the head of Massachusetts Bay, and had in 1850 a population of 138,788. The city consists of three parts, namely, Old Boston, on the peninsula; South Boston, which was formerly a part of Dorchester, and East Boston, formerly Noodles' Island. The isthmus which connects the peninsula with the main land is about a mile in length, and was originally in some parts very narrow, but has been much improved, and forms the main avenue from the city towards the south, leading direct to Roxbury. Various bridges now lead to the beautiful towns in the environs, as Charlestown, Cambridge, &c., and a solid causeway of earth leads to Brookline on the west.

At Charlestown, on the summit of Bunker Hill, stands a monument in commemoration of the battle fought at that place. The structure is built entirely of granite, in a most substantial manner, to a height of 220 feet from its base; it is a plain obelisk. At the top, under the apex, is a room of about 18 feet in diameter, in which is deposited two of the only six cannon owned by the continental congress at the opening of the revolutionary war. They are of the calibre of three pounders, made of brass, and one of them has been burst near the muzzle. The place where these relics are deposited is attained by a circular stone stair-case, and the windows at that elevation command a beautiful panorama of the country for many miles around.

The state-house, which is the principal public building, is located on

Beacon Hill, the highest point of the city, and fronts on the "Common," a public park covering an area of 75 acres of beautiful undulating land, and surrounded with an iron fence about a mile in length. The state-house is 173 feet long and 61 feet wide, and is capitol of the state. The most imposing building, perhaps, on account of its associations, is Faneuil Hall, celebrated in history as the spot where the orators of the revolution stimulated the people to a resistance of British oppression. It is appropriately called the "Cradle of Liberty," and is held in almost sacred veneration. The building is 100 feet long by 80 feet wide, and three stories high. The great hall is on the second story; it has a spacious gallery on three sides, and is exceedingly well adapted for popular demonstrations.

The city-hall or old state-house is 110 feet long, 38 feet wide, and three stories high. It is at the head of State-street, and contains the offices of the city government. Besides these, there are the Merchants' Exchange, the Faneuil Hall market, (585 feet long,) the court-house, custom-house, Athenæum, hospital, &c., &c.; all buildings which would do honor to the most magnificent of European cities.

Boston has contributed much toward the elevation of native literature. It has a large number of literary and philosophical institutions, and furnishes some of the best periodicals and newspapers in the country.

As a commercial town, Boston is second only to New-York. The shipping belonging to the port in 1850, amounted to 320 687 tons, and the value of imports from foreign countries are about $26,000,000 annually, and the exports about $10,000,000. The amount of trade coastwise is three or four times as great as that to foreign ports.

Boston is the centre of the railroad system of New-England, and from it the iron band diverges to all parts. It is also accommodated with canals and roads, and every facility is given for inter-communication. The city of Boston, indeed, might be considered as a little world within itself, and would occupy many volumes in the description of its parts.

Cambridge is the seat of Harvard University, which is only about four miles from Boston city, and has a permanent fund of $60,000 in property, and a yearly income of about $22,000, besides students' fees. About a mile further is the beautiful cemetery of Mount Auburn, in a lovely and picturesque situation, and in which rest many of the great and virtuous sons of New-England. Population, 14,624.

Salem, 15 miles north-east of Boston, is a considerable town of 21,220 inhabitants, who have always been distinguished for their commercial enterprise, frugality and industry. Newburyport, a prettily situated and neatly built town at the mouth of the Merrimack, carries on a considerable trade, especially in the cod, mackerel, and whale fisheries. Fall River Village, at the mouth of the Taunton River, 45 miles south of Boston, is largely engaged in the cotton manufactures, and further up the river, at the head of sloop navigation, is Taunton, also a manufacturing town. Plymouth, on the coast, 36 miles south-east of Boston, is memorable as the spot where the exiled Independents of Yorkshire, usually called "the pilgrim fathers," founded the first settlement in New-England, 22d December, 1620. Worcester is a rapidly increasing town on the railroad, 45 miles west of Boston. The population of Newburyport, in 1850, was 9,974; of Fall River, 11,805; of Plymouth, 7,088, and of Worcester, 16,852.

The internal improvements, consisting of canals, railroads, &c., are very extensive. The Quincy Railroad, which was finished in 1827, was the first built in the United States. It is three miles long, and runs from the granite quarries to Neponset River. In 1850 there were 36 separate railways traversing within the state, which, with their branches, had a total length of 1,142 miles, and had been built at a gross cost of $51,873,985, or at the rate of $45,424 per mile. The principal lines are, the Berkshire Railroad, 21 miles long; the Boston and Lowell, 26 miles; the Boston and Maine, 74 miles; the Boston and Providence, 41 miles; the Boston and Worcester, 45 miles; the Cape Cod, 28 miles; the Connecticut River, 51 miles; the Eastern, 38 miles; the Fall River, 42 miles; the Fitchburg, 49 miles; the Fitchburg and Worcester, 12 miles; the Lawrence, 12 miles; the Nashua and Lowell, 9 miles; the New Bedford and Taunton, 20 miles; the Newburyport, 16 miles; the Norwich and Worcester, 66 miles; the Old Colony, 37 miles; the Pittsfield and North Adams, 19 miles; the Providence and Worcester, 43 miles; the Salem and Lowell, 16 miles; the Taunton, 12 miles; the Western, 112 miles; the Worcester and Nashua, 46 miles, and several others. The railroads of Massachusetts are always well built and substantial. They intersect the state like network, and bring together every principal place, and extend to the south and west, and to Canada. The chief centers are Boston, Worcester, Springfield, Fitchburg, Lowell, etc. The aggregate results of the operations of these roads for 1849 and 1850, are summed up in the following comparative statement:

	1850.	1849.	Increase.	Decrease.
Number of Railways	36	31	5	—
Miles of road and branches	1,142	1,070	72	—
Gross cost	$51,873,985	$51,801,126	$72,859	—
Average cost per mile	45,424	47,388	—	$1,964
Gross receipts, 1850	6,466,872	6,102,014	364,858	—
Gross expense	3,142,945	3,100,694	42,251	—
Net income	3,323,902	3,061,320	262,382	—
Average net income per cent. on cost	6.41	6.03	0.38	—
Gross number of miles run	4,278,240	4,271,930	6,310	—
Average receipts per mile run	$1.51	$1.41	$0.10	—
Average expenses per mile run	0.73	0.71	0.02	—
Average net income per mile run	0.78	0.70	0.08	—
Number passengers carried	8,856,656	8,788,589	68,067	—
Number passengers carried 1 mile	147,888,327	144,305,281	3,583,046	—
Tons of merchandise carried	2,219,050	2,167,751	51,299	—
Tons of merchandise carried 1 mile	72,573,280	70,848,225	1,725,055	—
Total weight of passenger trains, in tons, hauled 1 mile, not including passengers	100,383,950	114,962,615	—	14,578,665
Total weight of freight trains, in tons, hauled 1 mile, not including freight	130,571,531	135,285,563	—	4,714,032
Total number of tons, not including passengers, hauled 1 mile	303,528,761	321,078,871	—	17,550,110

Massachusetts has no general system of canals. Those which have been constructed are chiefly to overcome obstacles in river routes. The Middlesex Canal, connecting the Merrimack River, two miles above Lowell, with Boston Harbor at Charlestown, is 27 miles long, and was the first canal of any length completed in the United States. Hampshire and Hampden Canal continues the Farmington Canal from the north line of Connecticut, 22 miles, to Northampton, making the whole line from New Haven, Conn., 76 miles. This, however, is now in disuse. Blackstone Canal, 45 miles long, connects Worcester with Providence, R. I. The Montague Canal, round Montague Falls, in the Connecticut River, is three miles long, and overcomes by eight locks a fall of 75 feet. South Hadley Canal, along South Hadley Falls, in the same river, is two miles long, and has five locks, and the Pawtucket Canal, a mile and a half, connects Lowell and Chelmsford. The number of miles of post-roads in Massachusetts in 1850, was 1,811, they are all of the finest quality, and perhaps better constructed than any others in the United States.

The educational conveniences in this state are ample, and all the institutions are flourishing, and in great repute for learning and science. Harvard University, at Cambridge, is the oldest and best endowed seminary in the country. It was founded in 1638, about 18 years after the first landing of the Pilgrims. It has lately been endowed largely by Mr. Lawrence, of Boston, for the purpose of establishing a school of practical science. Williams' College, at Williamstown, in the north-west corner of the state, was founded in 1793, and is in a flourishing condition. Amherst College was founded in 1831, and has had an unexampled growth, and now ranks with the first colleges in New England. The Congregationalists have a seminary at Andover, the Baptists at Newton, and the Catholics at Worcester. The following are the statistics of these colleges in 1850:

Names.	Instructors.	Alumni.	Ministers.	Students.	Volumes.
Harvard University	29	6,203	1,628	273	82,000
Williams' College	9	1,213	373	180	9,643
Amherst "	12	870	388	166	16,000
Holycross "	14	9	—	120	4,220
Andover Theological Seminary	6	1,006	1,006	87	21,259
Divinity School (Harvard)	2	238	238	19	3,000
Newton Theological Institute	3	201	201	33	5,500
Law School (Harvard)	4	—	—	94	—
Medical " "	6	575	—	139	—
Berkshire Medical School	5	473	—	103	—

Besides these, academies and grammar schools are numerous, and there are some other establishments for instruction in the higher branches. Mechanics' institutions, and scientific and literary societies also exist in all the large towns, and are well attended.

The public schools are free to all, the teachers, etc., being supported by a tax on each township. About $800,000 is annually raised for this purpose. The average attendance is about 142,000, but in the winter season about 30,000 more attend than at other times. The male teachers have wages averaging $33 per month, and females, $14 per month.

There are 67 incorporated academies in the state, with about 3,800 pupils, and 1,096 unincorporated academies and private schools, with 28,000 scholars. The value of permanent property belonging to the schools is—school fund, $850,000; local academy fund, $365,000; value of libraries, $45,000; value of apparatus, $26,000; value of school houses, $2,750,000. The total sums expended annually for education in this state cannot be less than $3,500,000. There are 3 normal schools which are supported by the state.

The great mass of the people adhere to the congregational form of Christianity, but there are numerous other denominations, among which the Baptists and Methodists are numerically preponderant. The Universalists have also a firm footing in the state; while the Episcopal sections, Roman Catholic, and Protestant, are but a small minority. Besides these there are churches belonging to the Unitarians, Presbyterians, Christians, Swedenborgians, Shakers, etc.

From an abstract of the returns of the banks published in the "American Almanac for 1851," it appears that in 1849, there were 119 banks in the state, besides 42 Savings' banks. The capital in the banks amounted to $34,680,000; circulation, $15,700,935; and a total debit due from the banks to $68,685,490. The specie in their vaults, was $2,749,917; real estate, $1,098,000, etc. The aggregate average dividends of all the banks, for the year, was a fraction over $6.76 per cent. The Savings' banks had 71,629 depositors, and a deposit of $12,111,554; more than one-third of which was deposited in the two banks at Boston. The average rate of dividends for the last five years, was 5¼ per cent. With these statistics in view, it will be evident that pauperism is on a limited scale. In 1849, the whole number of persons relieved was only 24,892, of which 10,251 were foreigners; and of these 9,128 were from Ireland! The expense of supporting this class was $441,675.

The provisions of the constitution are much similar to those of the other states, but, perhaps, more liberal to the negro people, who are considered as qualified voters. The governor and legislature are elected annually. The judiciary consists of a Supreme Judicial Court, with a chief and three associate judges; of Courts of Common Pleas, with a chief and five associate justices; County and Probate Courts, and Municipal Courts

The finances of this state, Jan. 1st, 1847, were as follows:

Total Receipts in 1846, including Money Borrowed	$563,272 88
" Expenses	555,065 31
Cash on hand Jan. 1st., 1847	$8,658 57

The public debt of the state, at the same period, was $999,654, and the credit of the commonwealth lent to rail-roads $5,049,555, making a total indebtedness of $6,049,209. As security for the redemption of the scrip lent to rail-roads, the state holds a mortgage on all the roads, and also 3,000 shares in the Eastern, 4,000 in the Norwich and Worcester, and 1,000 in the Andover and Haverhill. Besides these, the commonwealth owns various stocks and funds to the amount of $2,650,180.

The territory of Massachusetts comprised, for many years after its settlement, two separate colonies, styled Plymouth Colony and the Colony of Massachusetts Bay. The first English settlement that was made in New-England was formed by one hundred and one persons, "the pilgrim fathers," who fled from religious persecution in England; landed at Plymouth on the 22d December, 1620, and laid the foundation of the colony. The settlement of Massachusetts Bay was commenced at Salem in 1628. Boston was settled in 1630. The two colonies continued separate, and elected their own governors till 1685–6, when they were deprived of their charters, and were placed under the government of Joseph Dudley, and afterwards of Sir Edmund Andros. In 1692, they were united into one colony, under a new charter, and the governors were afterwards appointed by the king In 1774 a Provisional Congress assumed the government, and in July, 1775, elected councillors. In 1780, the constitution was formed, but was thoroughly amended in 1821.

THE STATE OF RHODE ISLAND.

Rhode Island is the smallest of the United States, and is situated between 41° 22′ and 42° 3′ N. lat., and the meridians of 71° 6′ and 71° 38′ West longitude. It is about 49 miles long and 32 miles broad, containing a superficial area of 1,340 square miles. Bounded on the north and east by Massachusetts, west by Connecticut, and south by the Atlantic Ocean.

The northern part of this state is hilly and broken; the remainder is in general level. About one-tenth of its surface is covered with the waters of Narragansett Bay. The soil in the northern section is thin and barren; but the islands and the country bordering on the bay are very fertile, and celebrated for their fine cattle, their numerous flocks of sheep, and the abundance and excellence of their butter and cheese. The southern part of the state is an excellent grazing country.

Pawtucket, the principal river, rises in Massachusetts, and running south-east into this state, falls into Providence river, one mile below the city of Providence. There are falls of about fifty feet descent four miles from its mouth; below the falls the river is called Seekonk. Providence river is formed by the Wauasquiatupcket and Moshasuck, two small streams which unite just above Providence. The other rivers are the Pawtuxet—which falls into Providence River from the west, five miles below Providence; it abounds with falls which furnish fine situations for mills and manufacturing establishments—and the Pawcatuck, which falls into Stonington harbor. In the latter part of its course it is the boundary between this state and Connecticut.

Narragansett Bay is a fine body of water dividing the state into two parts. It communicates with the ocean between Point Judith on the west and Point Seaconet on the east. It is 30 miles long and 15 broad, and embraces several beautiful islands. The north-east arm of the bay is called Mount Hope Bay, the north-west arm Greenwich Bay, and the Northern arm Providence Bay. The principal rivers which fall into it are the Providence and Taunton. It is accessible at all seasons, and affords a splendid and secure harbor for vessels.

Rhode Island, from which the state takes its name, is in Narragansett Bay. It is fifteen miles long, and on an average, three-and-a-half broad, containing about 50 square miles. Its climate and soil are delightful; the summers remarkably pleasant, and the winters milder than on the continent. It is well adapted for invalids from southern countries. Travellers call it the "Eden of America." Canonicut is a beautiful island lying west of Rhode Island. It is about seven miles long and one broad. Providence Island lies on the north-east of Canonicut, and Block Island about 10 miles south-west of Point Judith. The inhabitants are chiefly occupied in the fisheries.

The climate is much similar to that of Massachusetts, but in consequence of the proximity of Rhode Island to the sea, is milder and more equable. The spring commences with March, and the summer reigns through June, July, and August. The autumn weather in September and October is delightful, and the winters are pretty regular and steady from November to March. The air is pure and salubrious.

The state is divided into five counties, the population of which in 1850 was 147,654, or in the ratio of one person to every 5.9 acres. The distribution of the population into the five counties of the state was as exhibited in the annexed table:

COUNTIES.	White Persons.	Free Colored Persons.	Total Population.
Bristol	8,190	324	8,514
Kent	14,821	247	15,068
Newport	19,341	676	20,017
Providence	85,837	1,788	87,625
Washington	15,911	519	16,430
Total	144,000	3,544	147,544

CLASSES AND SEXES OF POPULATION.

Classes.	Males.	Females.	Total.
White Persons	70,417	73,583	144,000
Colored " —free	1,660	1,884	3,544
" " —slave	—	—	—
Total	72,077	75,467	147,544

PROGRESSIVE MOVEMENT OF POPULATION.

Date of Census.	White Persons.	Colored Persons. Free.	Colored Persons. Slave.	Total Population.	Decennial Increase. Numerical.	Decennial Increase. Per 100.
1790	64,689	3,469	952	69,110	—	—
1800	65,437	3,304	381	69,122	12	0.0
1810	73,314	3,609	108	77,031	7,909	11.4
1820	79,413	3,598	48	83,059	6,028	7.9
1830	93,621	3,561	17	97,199	14,140	17.0
1840	105,587	3,238	5	108,830	11,631	11.9
1850	144,000	3,544	—	147,544	38,874	35.6

The number of dwellings in 1850 was 22,379, and of families 28,488; and hence the number of persons to each dwelling was 6.6, and to each family 5.2; and the proportion between dwellings and families was as 1 to 1.2, nearly. The deaths in 1849–50 amounted to 2,241, or in the ratio of one death to every 66 persons.

As an industrial state Rhode Island stands pre-eminent. Its soils are not of the richest, but it has many good farms, and produces all the staples of New England. Indian corn and oats form the largest crops, next barley and rye, and lastly wheat and buckwheat. Of the latter two grains, however, the yield is small, and, in all, the annual production does not amount to more than 1,300,000 bushels. The live stock amounts as follows: 9,000 horses and mules, 40,000 neat cattle, 100,000 sheep, and 35,000 swine, &c. Wool is produced to the amount of nearly 120,000 lbs, and the value of the dairy is $260,000. The number of farms in 1850 was 5,385.

Manufactures are the great interest of the state, and, in relation to its size, no other has been more successful, or has so numerous and varied productions. It is full of mills and factories, and employs in its various workshops some 40,000 persons. Cottons and woollens form four-fifths of its productions, but almost all descriptions of heavy goods are manufactured. The number of productive establishments in 1850 was 901, but in this number none are reckoned the annual value of which did not exceed $500. The capital employed in manufactures in 1840 amounted to ten millions of dollars—it now amounts to almost double that sum.

The direct foreign commerce of Rhode Island, once considerable, is now comparatively small, and not at all commensurate with its population and industry, but this is owing to the greater eligibility of neighboring ports, from which it exports and imports largely. The value of its commerce in 1849–50 was—exports $216,265, and imports $258,303. The shipping employed in carrying the merchandize representing these sums was as follows:

Nationality.	Entered. Tons.	Cleared. Tons.	Total. Tons.
American	17,847	16,770	34,617
Foreign	2,075	1,705	3,780
Total	19,922	18,475	38,397

Divide the commerce of the state into seven parts, and the relative importance of Providence will be 4, of Bristol 2, and of Newport 1. The shipping owned in the state amounted in 1850 to 26,068 tons: 5,829 tons were engaged in the whale fisheries, and in cod and mackerel fisheries 543 tons. The coasting trade employed 13,177 tons, and the shipping navigated by steam amounted to 432 tons. In 1806 the direct exports from Rhode Island were valued at $2,091,835.

There are 61 banks in Rhode Island, 23 of which are located in Providence. Their condition in April 1850 is thus stated: capital $11,297,552; circulation $2,525,549; deposits on interest $126,035; deposits not on interest $1,282,715; due banks $588,295; dividends unpaid $28,396; and net profits on hand $684,566—total liabilities $16,533,108. The assets were—dues from directors $729,251; dues from other stockholders $538,079; other dues $13,555,170; specie $291,295; real estate $236,610; and stocks, bills of and deposits in other banks, &c., in all balancing the liabilities. The number of Savings' Institutions in June, 1850, was eight, the whole number of depositors 7,983, and the deposits and profits amounted to $1,283,935.

Brown University, at Providence, founded in 1764, is the only collegiate institution in the state: it has eight professors, and in 1850 had 125 students. Its library numbers 12,000 volumes. The library of the Providence Athenæum contains 16,000 volumes. Academies are numerous, and well conducted. There are in the state 332 public school districts, and the number of children under 15 years of age is 38,052. The average attendance is 16,590, and the cost of educating them was, in the year 1849–50, $86,554, of which sum $25,330 was granted by the state, and $54,844 was raised by town taxation. The number of convicts sent to the State Prison at Providence, 1849–50, was 16, and there were 80 persons imprisoned in Providence County Jail. In the former the prisoners are employed at stave making, and in the latter at cabinet work.

The most prominent religious denominations are the Baptists, Congregationalists, Episcopalians, and Methodists. Besides these there are some Friends, Unitarians, Roman Catholics, and Jews.

Providence and Newport are the principal seats of government, but the legislature sometimes meets at South Kingston, Bristol and East Greenwich.

PROVIDENCE is one of the capitals, and had a population, in 1850, of 41,513. The city contains an area of about nine square miles, which is divided by Providence River; the two parts being connected by convenient bridges. Among the principal buildings are a state house, city hall, court-house, custom-house, Brown University, the Athenæum, six public schools, a hospital, and a number of churches. The Athenæum is a beautiful structure of the Grecian Doric order, 40 feet front by 78 feet deep. The cost of the building was $20,000, and it has a library that cost about the same sum. Its harbor is at the head of Narragansett Bay, and is of very considerable commercial importance. Lat. 41° 49′ 22″ N., and long. 71° 24′ 48″ W.

NEWPORT, the next city of importance, and one of the capitals, had a population of 9,568, in 1850. Its harbor is one of the best in the United States, and it has some, but no considerable foreign commerce, its capital being principally invested in manufactures and the whale fisheries. The site of the town is beautiful—rising gently from the shore, it presents from the bay a most pleasing aspect. The state-house is located in Washington Square; the houses of the town are neatly and regularly built, and the place has, of late years, become a fashionable summer resort. The Redwood Library, which was founded in 1747, has a neat building, and a select collection of about 4,000 volumes. The principal public buildings are the state-house and churches, including one Jews' Synagogue. Lat. 41° 28′ 20″ N. and long. 71° 21′ 14″ W.

BRISTOL, on Warren River, a creek of Providence Bay, a neat and busy commercial town, is distinguished for the enterprise of its inhabitants, who are actively engaged in foreign commerce, the coasting trade, and the whale and seal fisheries in the Pacific Ocean. Population 4,616.

KINGSTON, EAST GREENWICH, both towns of some distinction, and several others of minor note, complete the catalogue of Rhode Island towns.

RHODE ISLAND was first settled in 1636, by Roger Williams, who located with a small colony at Providence. He had been banished from Salem, Mass., for his religious opinions. In 1638, he purchased the territory from the Narragansett Indians, and in the same year was joined by William Coddington and 17 others, who also had fled from religious persecution. In 1647, a code of laws and civil government was established by permission from England, and an assembly of six persons as representatives from each town, was created. Some difficulties having arisen in regard to the grant to Williams and Coddington, upon an application to King Charles II., a charter was granted, incorporating "Rhode Island and Providence Plantations." It was provided that no person should be molested or called in question for differences in matters of religion, and the supreme power was vested in a governor, deputy-governor, ten assistants and representatives of the several towns chosen by the freemen. Until the year 1841, this charter was the only constitution of the state, though for more than 20 years past efforts had been made to form a constitution under the sanction of the general assembly, but without effect. In the spring of 1840, an association was formed with a view of extending the right of suffrage to every white male citizen of the United States residing in the state, and in the spring of 1841, this association took the responsibility of calling a convention for the purpose of forming a constitution according to their peculiar views. Such convention was held, and such constitution formed and submitted to the people; but on account of the informality under which it was prepared, only a portion of the people recognized or voted on the question. Those who did vote being in favor of the constitution, it was declared to be adopted as the supreme law of the land. The government, however, refused to recognize it, and in the meantime, had taken legal measures for the calling of a convention for a similar object. Another constitution was prepared by that convention, and submitted to the people, who adopted it, with a majority of more than two to one. Two separate forms of governments were now recognized by two different portions of the people; the "suffrage party" proceeded to elect their governor and public officers under their constitution, and claiming them as the legitimate officers, they were organized at Providence under the protection of an armed force on the 3d of May, 1841. Owing to the public excitement, the government under the legitimate constitution, had not been able to organize, and the charter government organized as usual at Newport, on the 4th May, 1842. On the 18th, the governor elected by the "suffrage party" attempted to capture the state arsenal at Providence, but failed in the attempt. Desirous of meeting the views of all parties, the general assembly provided for another convention to form another constitution, and about the same time another attempt was made to overthrow, by force of arms, the charter government of the state. The insurgents, led by their governor, took up a position at Chepachet, from which, however, they were easily driven by the state troops, and completely dispersed. The convention last provided for by the charter government, met in September of the same year, and framed another constitution, which, on being submitted to the people, was adopted almost unanimously, the "suffrage party" protesting against it, yet subsequently voting under it.

By the present constitution the government is vested in a governor, senate, and assembly, elected annually by the people. The lieutenant-governor is also a member of the Senate, and the governor presides over that body. The senate otherwise consists of one member from each town or city. The judicial power is vested in a supreme court, and such other courts as the general assembly may ordain.

Every citizen of the United States, 21 years of age, one year a resident in the state, and six months in the town or city where he offers his vote, owning real estate to the amount of $134, or renting for seven dollars above all incumbrances, is entitled to the rights of suffrage. The name of each voter must be enrolled one year previous to his ability to vote, and he must have paid a tax of one dollar, and performed military duty. A residence at any garrison or naval station is not considered as a legal residence.

The government finances are in a very good condition. When the state first received the deposit fund or surplus revenue from the United States, they invested it for schools. For the state prison and the "Dorr War," the state has since used $152,919 of it, and this is sometimes spoken of as a debt. There is also a claim of about $40,000 for some old revolutionary certificates. There is no state debt, properly speaking, The ordinary annual expenditure, exclusive of debts and schools, is about $48,000, which is raised by personal taxes, fines, &c.

This state has several works of internal improvement, important not only to its own immediate interest, but also highly advantageous to the neighboring states. The Blackstone Canal, a part of which is in this state, connects Providence and Worcester. The same is true as regards the Providence and Boston Railroad. With the latter is connected a daily line of steamboats, which ply to New-York City. The Providence and Stonington Railroad lies principally in this state, and is also connected with New-York by a splendid line of mail steamboats. Both Stonington and Providence communicate with Green Port, the eastern terminus of the Long Island Railroad, and hence with New-York, which it more direct. The passenger and traffic business on all these lines, each being a central link in the chain uniting the north-east with the south, is immense; and when some lines which are now in progress, become completed, there will be no more remunerative highways than those of Rhode Island. The length of post-roads within this state is 444 miles. Magnetic telegraphs traverse it in every direction.

THE STATE OF CONNECTICUT.

CONNECTICUT, the southernmost of the New-England States, is situated between 41° and 42° 2′ N. lat. and 71° 20′ and 73° 15′ W. long. It is bounded north by Massachusetts; east by Rhode Island; south by Long Island Sound, and west by the State of New-York. It is about 96 miles in length from east to west, and about 78 from north to south, with a superficial area of 4,764 square miles, or 3,048,960 acres.

The surface of this state, though not mountainous, is traversed with several considerable elevations. In passing across the country, from east to west, hills occur very frequently; but much less so in passing from north to south. One elevated range occurs eight or ten miles east of the Connecticut River, which it crosses at Chatham and terminates near East Haven. Another higher range commences at a bluff, 370 feet high, called East Rock, a little north-east of New-Haven, and proceeds northwardly through the state into Massachusetts; on the west of Hartford it is denominated Talcott Mountain, and the whole Mount Tom Range. The Blue Hills, in Southington, in this range, have an elevation of 1,000 feet, and are said to be the highest land in the state. At a bluff, 400 feet high, called West Rock, two miles north-west of New-Haven, a considerable range takes its rise, and proceeds thence into Massachusetts and Vermont. This constitutes the southern portion of the Green Mountain range; and in the north part of the state produces a very broken country. The Taghkanic range runs on the west side of the Housatonic River, and terminates at Ridgefield.

The great body of the state is excellent land, fitted for all the purposes of agriculture. Much of it has been under actual cultivation for upwards of 150 years, and still retains its original strength. The County of Fairfield and the intervale lands on the Connecticut River, are the best in the state. The country along the Quinebaug is also very fertile. The principal productions are Indian corn and oats; next to these are rye, hay and potatoes. Flax is also raised extensively. Almost every farm has one or more orchards, and great quantities of cider are annually made. The crops of pumpkins, onions, parsnips and beans, are also of great consequence to the Connecticut farmer. In some parts of the state, the soil is comparatively thin and barren.

Though subject to great extremes and sudden changes of temperature, the climate is generally healthy. Near the coast, the weather is extremely variable, changing according to the direction of the wind. In the interior, it is more steady, and the influence of the seasons more marked. The thermometer, in summer, sometimes rises to 92°, and in winter falls to 10° or 12° below zero, and except on the sea-coast, snow lies on the ground three months. The spring is often backward, but the summer and autumn are delightful.

Numerous bays and creeks, affording excellent harbors, penetrate the southern shore. The principal seaports are New-London, New-Haven, Stonington and Bridgeport on the coast, and Middletown in the interior. The harbor of New-London is the best in the state: it is spacious, safe and deep, and not liable to be frozen over in winter. New-Haven harbor is less deep, and seems to be gradually filling up. Stonington has a good harbor, protected by a breakwater, and Bridgeport also may boast of a like convenience. Connecticut River is navigable for vessels drawing 10 feet of water to Middletown. Long Island Sound, which forms the southern boundary of the state, is a fine body of water, 140 miles long from the Harbor of New York to the Atlantic Ocean, and 25 miles in its broadest part. It has all the advantages of an inland sea in regard to a protection from the storms of the ocean, and its shores present a delightful scene.

The principal river is the Connecticut, the finest river in New England: its whole course from north to south, is 410 miles, 70 of which are in this state. It is navigable for ships to Middletown and Hartford, and for 20 ton boats its navigation is extended by means of canals to the mouth of Wells River, Vermont, 300 miles in all. The Housatonic is 150 miles long, and navigable for sloops to Derby. It affords, in its course, extensive water-power, and between Canaan and Salisbury, it has a fall of 60 feet perpendicular. The Thames, in the eastern part of the state, is formed by the junction of Shetucket and Yantic Rivers, at Norwich, and is navigable for small sea vessels. All these rivers are celebrated for their shad-fisheries. The state is abundantly supplied with smaller streams, which afford extensive water-power, and is everywhere well watered by brooks and springs.

Connecticut produces some valuable minerals. Iron ore is found in Salisbury and Kent, and bog iron ore, excellent for castings, at Stafford. "Verde antique" marble is found at Milford; freestone is also found in abundance. A copper-mine exists in Simsbury, and at Stafford and Suffield there are several mineral springs, which are frequented by invalids.

Connecticut contains a population of 370,791 inhabitants, or one person to every eight acres; and its distribution into the eight counties was, in 1850, in the proportions as follow:

COUNTIES.	White Persons.	Free Col'd Persons.	Total Popula.
Fairfield	58,370	1,405	59,775
Hartford	68,756	1,210	69,966
Litchfield	44,266	987	45,253
Middlesex	30,397	283	30,680
New Haven	60,730	1,396	62,126
New London	50,328	1,493	51,821
Tolland	19,946	145	20,091
Windham	29,512	567	30,079
Total	363,305	7,486	370,791

CLASSES AND SEXES OF POPULATION.

Classes.		Males.	Females.	Total.
White Persons		180,001	183,304	363,305
Colored "	—free	3,749	3,737	7,486
" "	—slave	—	—	—
Total		183,750	187,041	370,791

Dwellings	64,016	Deaths in 1849–50	5,781	Farms in cultivation	22,445
Families	73,448			Manufactories	3,913

PROGRESSIVE MOVEMENT OF POPULATION.

Date of Census.	White Persons.	Colored Persons. Free.	Colored Persons. Slave.	Total Population.	Decennial Increase. Numerical.	Decennial Increase. Per 100.
1790	232,581	2,801	2,759	238,141	—	—
1800	244,721	5,330	957	251,002	12,861	5.4
1810	255,279	6,453	310	262,042	11,040	4.4
1820	267,161	7,944	97	275,202	13,160	5.0
1830	289,603	8,047	25	297,675	22,473	8.0
1840	301,857	8,104	17	309,978	12,303	4.1
1850	363,305	7,486	—	370,791	60,813	19.2

Connecticut, in reference to its extent and population, is one of the most wealthy states of the Union, and in every department of industry has largely developed its resources. It stands pre-eminent in both agriculture and manufactures, and as a commercial state occupies the third position in New England. The great agricultural staples are Indian corn, oats, and rye; and the small crops are wheat, buckwheat, and barley. It produces, also, considerable crops of tobacco and hemp. The live stock is proportionably larger than in any of the other north-eastern states. The manufactures embrace almost every description of goods, but its great staples are cotton and woollen fabrics, and articles from leather. Paper is also extensively manufactured. The capital employed in all the manufactures amounts to over $18,000,000. There is little mining carried on, but the fisheries are as zealously pursued as in the neighboring states of Rhode Island and Massachusetts.

The commerce of the state is chiefly with the West Indies and the states southward. The direct foreign exports amounted in 1849–50 to $241,930, and the imports to $372,390, and employed in their transportation the following amounts of shipping in tons:

Nationality.	Entered.	Cleared.	Total.
American	22,510	17,515	40,095
Foreign	11,572	9,802	21,374
Total	34,152	27,317	61,469

About one half the foreign trade centers at New Haven, and one fourth at New London. The other ports of entry, viz., Fairfield, Stonington, and Middletown, are of little importance as relates to foreign trade. The shipping owned within the state on the 30th June, 1850, was 113,086 tons, of which 42,511 tons were registered shipping, and of this 11,483 tons were employed in the whale-fisheries, chiefly from Stonington and New London. The employments of the enrolled and licensed shipping was as follows: in the coasting trade, 61,361 tons; in the cod-fisheries, 4,249 tons; and in the mackerel-fisheries, 1,577 tons. The steam marine amounted to 8,355 tons. During the year '47 vessels were built, the aggregate burden of which was 4,819 tons. The direct exports from this state have greatly diminished: in 1796 they were valued at $1,452,793; in 1806 at $1,715,828; in 1816 at $593,806; in 1826 at $708,893; in 1836 at $438,199; and in 1846 at $775,912. The returns for 1849–50 exhibit a much less value than at any former period; a fact, probably, accounted for by the completion of the railroads to New York and Boston, which afford such easy transport for merchandize to the chief commercial marts of the Union, where it finds a greater competition and cheapness in freights than at its own ports.

In 1850 there were 41 banks in the state, which were, according to the commissioner's report, well managed and in a sound condition, having kept their notes at par at the Suffolk Bank of Boston, and paid average dividends of 7½ per cent. the past year. Their principal features on the 1st April were as follows: capital, $9,907,503; circulation, $5,253,884; deposits, $2,357,939; and other liabilities, $1,602,881—total liabilities, $19,122,207; and their resources were—real estate, $389,982; specie, $640,622; discounts, $15,607,315, and other items to a balance.

At the same date there were 15 savings' institutions, in which 32,966 depositors had placed $4,746,692, of which $1,051,300 was deposited in 1849–50; and the amount withdrawn in that year was $719,898. The expenses of management were $10,837, and the dividends varied from 5 to 7½ per cent. The securities are loans on real estate and personal property, and stocks and investments in banks, stocks, and bonds.

There were also at same date 8 General Stock Insurance Companies, with an aggregate capital of $1,400,000; 11 Mutual General, with a capital of $1,487,025; 6 Life Mutual, with a capital of $1,400,000; 2 Health, with a capital of $203,175; and 1 Life and Health, with a capital of $100,000.

Internal improvement has gone on apace in this state. Its railroads extend in all directions, and in 1850 there were 551 miles completed, and 65 miles in progress. The cost had been to the last of December, $17,498,-599. The principal of these are the Housatonic, 73 miles; the Norwich and Worcester, 58 miles; the New Haven and Hartford, 36 miles; the Hartford and Springfield, 20 miles; the New York and New Haven, 46 miles; the Hartford, Providence, and Fishkill; the Naugatuck; the New London, Willimantic and Palmer, etc. There are others projected, and which will be finished at an early date. The canals of this state have been principally filled in, but there are several short cuts on the Connecticut River, which have been built to improve its navigation. The turnpikes and other roads are generally well kept.

Education in this state is universal, and the system of common schools very perfect. In 1850 there were 217 school societies and 1,649 school districts. The number of children attending them was 92,055. The teachers, etc., are paid from the proceeds of the school fund, which now amounts to $2,076,602, and yields interest to the amount of $137,449 annually, or about $1 50 to each child educated. A Normal School has lately been founded for the training of teachers, the attendance on which is free to one pupil from each school society. Schools or conventions for the same purpose are also held in each county annually. The whole system is under the direct supervision of a State Superintendent.

The American Asylum for the Deaf and Dumb, and the Retreat for the Insane, both at Hartford, are supported chiefly by the state. In May, 1850, the former had 210 inmates, of which 32 were from Maine, 23 from New Hampshire, 19 from Vermont, 75 from Massachusetts, 7 from Rhode Island, 8 from South Carolina, and 26 belonged to this state. Each of the states named supports its own afflicted. The Retreat for the Insane is also open to patients from other states.

Yale College, at New Haven, is one of the oldest literary institutions in the United States, and numbers among its alumni the greatest names of American history. It was founded in 1700, and derived its name from one of its earliest patrons. In 1850 it had 23 professors, and an aggregate of 555 students, viz., in the Academic department, 432, of which 93 were seniors, 91 juniors, 122 sophomores, and 126 freshmen; in the Theological department 38; in the Law department 26; in the Medical department 38; and in the department of Philosophy and Arts 21. From its foundation to 1850 it had graduated 5,932, of which 2,962 were then alive; and of the total graduates, 1,562 had been ministers, and of these 724 were still living. Trinity College, at Hartford, is an Episcopal institution, and was founded in 1824. In 1850 it had 9 professors and 74 students. Its library contained 9,000 volumes. The Wesleyan University, at Middletown, was founded in 1831, and had in 1850, 8 professors and 124 students, with a library of 11,123 volumes. The Theological Institution, at East Windsor, is directed by the Congregationalists, and represents the old school elements of Connecticut theology. It was founded in 1822, and had in 1850, 4 professors, 52 students, and to that period had educated 596 persons. A professor of Ecclesiastical History has since been added. There are, besides these colleges and schools, a large number of acadamies, seminaries, and grammar schools, which have a good reputation, and attract to their sphere students from the adjoining states. Some of these are endowed establishments.

The principal religious denominations are the Congregationalists, Baptists, Methodists, and Episcopalians. The Congregationalists have 206 ministers, 267 churches, and 35,158 communicants; the Baptists, 111 churches, 89 ministers, and 16,230 communicants; the Episcopal Methodists have 148 ministers, and about 22,000 church members; and the Protestant Episcopalians have 106 ministers, and 9,360 communicants. The denominations having smaller numbers are the Universalists, 14 churches; the Roman Catholics, 9 churches; the sects of Methodists (otherwise than Episcopal), in all, 8 churches; the Second Adventists, 8 churches; the Christians (*par excellence*), 5 churches; the Freewill Baptists, 1 church; the Presbyterians, 5 churches; and the Unitarians, 4 churches. The Jews have two synagogues.

The Constitution of Connecticut, framed in 1818, grants to every white male citizen of the United States, 21 years of age, who has resided six months in his town, and who is seized of a freehold of the annual value of $7, the right of voting, and every voter is eligible to any elective offices not expressly excepted. The elections take place on the first Monday in April, annually.

The Legislature, or General Assembly, is composed of a Senate, to consist of not less than 18 nor more than 28 members, chosen by districts, and a House of Representatives, the members of which are chosen by towns. No special qualification is needed for membership, only that those chosen must have also the right to vote. Senators and Representatives are elected by a majority of votes. The Legislature meets alternately at New Haven and Hartford, annually, on the first Monday in May.

The executive authority is vested in a governor, who must be a voter, and 30 years of age or upward. He is chosen annually by a majority of votes. A lieutenant governor is also chosen at the same time in the same way; as also a secretary, treasurer, and comptroller. The powers of the governor extend only to granting reprieves, and he may veto a bill of the Legislature, but a majority of both houses may pass it subsequently and make it law.

The Militia of the state numbers 57,719 rank and file, of which 53,240 are infantry, 692 cavalry, 2,083 artillery, and 1,704 riflemen. It forms one division, two brigades, and eight regiments; one regiment being apportioned to each county.

The total resources of the Treasury in 1849–50 amounted to $122,346, of which sum $73,557 was raised by tax, and $37,053 from bank dividends. The expenditures amounted to $118,392, viz., General Assembly, $25,986; executive salaries, $14,150; contingent expenses of executive, $15,399; judiciary, $49,002; and other salaries and contingencies, $13,821. Connecticut has no public debt, except one to the school fund amounting to $58,212, against which the state holds productive bank stock to the amount of $406,000. The counties and towns assess their own taxes.

The eight counties of Connecticut are subdivided into 147 townships, and contain six cities, viz., Bridgeport, Hartford, Middletown, New Haven, New London, and Norwich; and also 12 boroughs, viz., Danbury, Essex, Guildford, Litchfield, New Britain, Newtown, Norwalk, Southport, Stamford, Stonington, Waterbury, and Willimantic. New Haven and Hartford are alternate capitals of the state.

New Haven lies on the sea coast, and is a place of considerable commercial and manufacturing importance, and one of the most beautiful cities of the Union. It is laid out in two parts: the old town and new township. The streets are so arranged as to form regular squares, and in those parts appropriated exclusively to residences, almost every house has a garden in front, with flowers, vines, and overhanging trees. The State House and Yale College are the most conspicuous of the public buildings; but New Haven is no less renowned for the number than for the taste and elegance displayed in its church buildings. Population, 22,539.

HARTFORD is situated on the Connecticut River, 50 miles from its mouth. The city is beautifully located, but not very regular in its street lines. It is a place of considerable trade, and on the lines of several railroads. The State House and City Hall are the prominent buildings; but Washington College, the American Asylum, the Retreat for the Insane, the Athenæum, etc., claim alike the attention of the traveler. The American Asylum for the Deaf and Dumb is the oldest institution of the kind in the United States. Besides these, the city contains a large number of church buildings, much admired for their architectural chasteness. The old Charter Oak is still standing here, a historic relic of much interest to the sons of New England. The trunk of this venerable tree, which sheltered the colony from the tyranny of Andros, now measures 21 feet in girth. Population in 1850, 17,966.

MIDDLETOWN, 14 miles south of Hartford, is a port of entry, at the head of ship navigation on the Connecticut. It is a beautiful city, and contains, besides the Court House, and a number of handsome church edifices, the Wesleyan University, which occupies a commanding site in the upper part of the city. The place was first settled in 1651, and was incorporated in 1784. In 1850 it contained 9,211 inhabitants.

BRIDGEPORT, situated on the Sound, is the southern terminus of the Housatonic Railroad, and has hitherto been the starting point of winter travel to Albany and the north from New York City. Population, 7,558.

NEW LONDON and NORWICH, both on the Thames, are also important places, and have considerable commerce. New London is one of the principal whale-fishery stations in New England, and in 1850 had 9,006 inhabitants. STONINGTON, farther east, lies on the Sound, and is also a great fishing station. Regular communication by steamboat is kept up with New York from all the cities above-mentioned, and with the interior, and New York and Boston by Railroads. The principal towns in the interior are chiefly engaged in the manufactures, and all are distinguished for their neatness, cleanliness, and that civic order which has ever marked the condition of the inhabitants.

The territory of Connecticut originally comprised two colonies, that of "Connecticut and that of New Haven." The Connecticut colony was first settled at Hartford, by emigrants from Massachusetts, in 1735, and the colony of New Haven, in 1638, by emigrants from England. In 1662, a charter was granted by Charles II., with ample privileges, uniting the two colonies under one government; but the colony of New Haven refused, for some time, to accept the charter, and the union did not take place until 1665. The charter was suspended in 1687 by Sir Edmund Andros; but was again restored after the Revolution of 1688, and formed the basis of the government until 1818, when the present constitution was framed.

THE MIDDLE STATES.

THE geographical position of the states comprised in this section of the Union, has determined its nomenclature. With some exception, this territory was formerly known as the New-Netherlands, and was first planted by the Dutch. On one side were the colonies of New-England, and on the other those of Virginia, a country originally co-extensive with what are now termed the Southern States. Thus centrally dividing the two great English settlements, and occupied by a nation not always at peace with Great Britain, the interests of the English settlers became identified with the occupation by them of the whole, and, as a consequence, it was not long before the British government determined upon taking possession of the country, and destroying a competitor and an enemy at one and the same time. This act was consummated in 1664; after which period to the conclusion of the peace of 1783, the whole Atlantic region remained, with little exception, in the undisputed occupation of the "mother of nations."

This section is bounded on the north by the great lakes, the St. Lawrence River and the provinces of Canada; south by "Mason & Dixon's Line," which divides it from Virginia; east by the states of New-England and the Atlantic Ocean, and west by portions of Virginia and Ohio. It lies between the latitudes of 38° and 45° north, and the longitudes of 72° and 81° west, and comprises the states of New-York, New-Jersey, Pennsylvania, Delaware and Maryland. Its length, from north to south, is 460 miles, and its breadth, from east to west, 370 miles; the area is about 114,484 square miles, or 73,269,760 acres.

The advantageous situation of the section—the beautiful diversity of features which distinguishes it—the natural facilities for intercommunication which it enjoys, and the energy which has ever prompted the inhabitants in their several callings, have unitedly elevated the states comprised within its borders to a proud pre-eminence in all that conduces to wealth and national grandeur. Without derogating the substantial interests of the surrounding states, those of the middle section may claim the combination of all that is useful and artistic, which cannot but influence their social and industrial position. While the states to the north and east are confined to the production of one description of staples, and those of the south and west to others, the middle states, enjoying a climate intermediate, and other sectional advantages, produces alike those of each, and with these and the uninterrupted facilities they enjoy in their relation with all the states and with foreign countries, their continued and ever increasing prosperity has been assured.

Mountains, vallies and plains,—lakes, rivers and capacious bays, diversify the topography of this section, and combine in grandeur and magnificence to promote the great interests of the inhabitants. Running from the north-east to the south-west are the Alleghanies,—a mine of inexhaustible wealth, producing coal, iron and other useful minerals. On the north and west the great lakes and the St. Lawrence form an outlet for commerce; and the rivers flowing in a southern direction to the Atlantic, convey to the coast the productions of the interior, which are received by the merchants of the large Atlantic cities, and transported hence from the magnificent harbors, which indent the shores, to supply the commerce of the world with the varied wealth of this bountiful region.

The Middle States, though originally peopled by the Dutch, whose descendants still form a large moiety of the inhabitants in the older settled parts, have a most heterogeneous population. Every nation of the world has contributed its quota, but the chief portion of the aggregate of the inhabitants is of British origin, and the institutions of the country are essentially a counterpart of the institutions of that enlightened nation. Society, however, in these states cannot be said, except generally, to possess any distinctive aspect, and not unfrequently whole localities may be found in which the immigrant inhabitants still retain all the habits and peculiarities of the nation from which they sprung: thus, in some parts of Pennsylvania the people are decidedly Dutch, using their primitive language, and tenaciously adhering to the habits and feelings of "faderland,"—while in other sections the descendants of other nations still retain *their* several and ancient customs. This state of society, however, though it has some inconveniences, is not irreconcilable with harmony, and the utmost friendship exists among this variety of nationalities; and that fraternization, which liberty and a community of rights engenders, tends to cement a compact of peace and congenial intercourse which, in other countries, is frustrated by the devices of despotism and conflicting interests. These elementary contributions of the people of all nations must eventually coalesce and form a body, compact and whole, and a new nationality possessing in combination the knowledge, the genius, and the talents, in learning and the arts, of the whole civilized world, and that commixture of physical essences which are believed to improve the race in which the combination is effected: the steady industry of the German family, the quick perception and martial energy of the Celt, the commercial spirit and the prudence of the English, and the patriotism of the whole, will be combined in the future races who will inhabit these states, and be productive of a unity that will eclipse in physical and moral power the unmixed nations of the world, and assume a destiny grand and imposing, and to which no equal shall elsewhere be known. The advantages of this commixture of nationalities will be felt throughout the whole confederacy; and while we see the countries further south, from which hitherto the civilizing influence of foreign immigration has been excluded by the policy of selfish rulers, subject to all the horrors of national incapacity, and liable to ever-recurring internal hostilities, we shall behold in these states that power and harmony which are the inheritance of a physical and moral completeness, and the birthright of freemen.

The progress which the people have already made in every department of life, and the increase of their numbers, has been rapid and astonishing. The few who first settled at New-Amsterdam, now New-York, at the commencement of the 17th century, and at Philadelphia and other places, at a later period, have extended their limits to their present dimensions, and increased to a population of 6,500,000 souls. They have rapidly passed from the hardships of settlement and colonial servitude, and now enjoy all the facilities and conveniences of older nations, and have in prospect all the glories which are sure to attend the progress of a people who are devoted to liberty, and a reciprocal communion with the world at large.

The several states forming this section will be considered separately.

THE STATE OF NEW-YORK.

New-York, the most populous as well as the most important and influential of the United States, is the most northerly of the Middle Division, and lies between 40° 30′ and 45° north latitude, and 71° 56′ and 79° 56′ west longitude. It is bounded north by Lake Ontario, the St. Lawrence, and Lower Canada; east by Vermont, Massachusetts and Connecticut; south by the Atlantic Ocean, New-Jersey and Pennsylvania, and north-west by Pennsylvania and Lake Erie. Exclusive of Long Island, it is 320 miles long and 312 broad, and contains, in the whole, 46,085 square miles, or 29,494,400 acres, of which 11,755,276 are devoted to cereal agriculture.

In a country like this, with an area almost equal to that of all England and Wales, there must of necessity be a great diversity of surface, climate and productions. The south-eastern angle of the state is mountainous, being traversed by several ridges proceeding from the State of New-Jersey, one of which crosses the Hudson River at the Highlands, presenting a bold and lofty face along both margins of the river, and abounding in the most magnificent scenery. The Catskill Mountains, as a range, are the most elevated, and have several culminations, as Round Top, (3,084 feet high,) of considerable size; but the greatest elevation in the state is Mount Marcy, in the Adirondack group, which rises 5,467 feet above the level of the ocean. The country of Lake Champlain is hilly, and becomes mountainous on approaching the highlands which divide the waters of the lake from those which flow into the St. Lawrence and Lake Ontario. The western part of the state lying between Lake Ontario and Pennsylvania is principally level, except near the state line, where it becomes more broken and abrupt. From Genessee river, near its mouth, to Jamestown, on the Niagara, there is a remarkable ridge, running almost the whole distance, which is 78 miles long, and in a direction from east to west. Its general altitude above the neigh boring land, is 30 feet, and its width in some places is not more than 120 feet. The elevation of this ridge is 160 feet above the level of Lake Ontario, to which it descends by a gradual slope, and its distance from that water is from six to ten miles. There is every reason to suppose that this ridge was once the margin of the lake. About 20 miles south and parallel to the above, there is another ridge, which runs from Genessee River to Black Rock,—the country between being called the Tonawanda valley, and there is the same reason to believe that it was formerly the bed of the waters of Lake Erie.

The great northern lakes, viz.: Ontario, Erie and Champlain, are partly in this state. Lake George, south of Lake Champlain, communicates with it by a short outlet. It is 37 miles long, and from one to seven broad, and embosoms more than 200 beautiful islets. Its waters are so clear and transparent, that the bottom is visible at almost any depth; and on each side it is skirted with mountains, abounding in the most romantic scenery. There are numerous small lakes in the western part of the state, which discharge their waters into Lake Ontario, either directly or indirectly through the Seneca and Oswego Rivers, and being connected by canals and railroads, afford peculiar facilities to transportation and travel. These, with their extent, &c., are as follow:

Lake	Length	Breadth
Lake Oneida	length 22 miles	breadth 4 to 6 miles.
" Cazenovia	" 4 "	" 1 "
" Otsego	" 9 "	" 1 to 2 "
" Canaderaga	" 5 "	" 1½ "
" Otisco	" 5 "	" 2 "
" Skaneateles	" 15 "	" ½ to 1 "
" Owasco	" 12 "	" 1 "
" Cross	" 4 "	" ½ "
" Cayuga	" 40 "	" 1½ to 3½ "
" Seneca	" 40 "	" 2 to 4 "
" Crooked	" 22 "	" 1½ "
" Canandaigua	" 14 "	" 1 to 1½ "
" Hemlock	" 6 "	" 1 "
" Conesus	" 9 "	" 1 "
" Chautauque	" 18 "	" 1 to 3 "

Beside the above, numerous smaller lakes are distributed over the western portion of the state; and in the north are the Fulton chain of lakes, and others, which form the sources of the tributaries of the Mohawk and the Hudson rivers.

The rivers of New-York have contributed much to its present importance and wealth. The Delaware forms part of the boundary between this state and Pennsylvania; and the Niagara River connects Lake Erie with Ontario, forming part of the western boundary. The St. Lawrence separates New-York from the Canadas. The Hudson rises in the mountainous regions in the west of Lake Champlain, and pursuing a southerly course of more than 300 miles, communicates with the Atlantic below the city of New-York. It is navigable for ships to Hudson, for large sloops to Albany, and for small sloops to Troy, the head of tide-water. The state dam, a little north of the last city, secures a further navigation of some miles. The whole is navigated by numerous steamboats, the magnificence of which is unparalleled, and the commerce of the Hudson is immense, it being the outlet of the canal and railroad traffic from the west and that of both sides of the river. The Mohawk is the principal branch of the Hudson: it rises 20 miles north of Rome, and running south of east, passes Rome, Utica and Schenectady; and after a course of about 135 miles, falls into the Hudson by several mouths between Troy and Waterford. The navigation of this river is interrupted by numerous falls and rapids, the most remarkable of which are at Cohoes, where the water falls over a perpendicular rock, and are little inferior to those of Niagara. The scenery is bold, and when the waters are high, presents a sublimity and magnificence seldom witnessed. The rivers running into Lake Ontario are the Genessee, Oswego and Black. The Genessee rises in Pennsylvania and pursues a northerly course: there are four great falls in this river—two within five or six miles from its mouth and the others about 70 miles further up. The Oswego is the outlet of Oneida Lake, and falls into Ontario, at Oswego. The Seneca receives the waters of the Canandaigua, Seneca, Cayuga, and several other lakes, and runs into Oswego River, at Three River Point. Black River rises south-east of Rome, and after a northerly course of 120 miles, runs into Lake Ontario, near Sackett's Harbor. The rivers which empty into the St. Lawrence, are the Oswegatchie, Grass, Racket and St. Regis. The Big Chazy, Saranac and Sable, fall into Lake Champlain. The Susquehannah and Alleghany Rivers rise in this state and run into Pennsylvania. The Tioga and Chenango are branches of the Susquehannah.

The bays and harbors of New-York are magnificent sheets of water. The Bay of New-York is nine miles long and four broad, having three fine islands in its centre. It spreads before the city, on the south side, having Long Island on the east and Staten Island and New-Jersey on the west. On the north it receives the Hudson, and on the east it communicates with Long Island Sound, through the East River; on the west with Newark Bay, through the Kills, and on the south with the Atlantic Ocean, through the Narrows and the Lower Bay. It is deep enough for the largest vessels, well secured from winds and storms, sufficiently spacious for the most numerous fleets, and the currents are so rapid that it is seldom obstructed by ice.

In physical enormities New-York is pre-eminently favored. The falls of Niagara are, perhaps, the greatest wonders of the world. They are in the Niagara River, about half way between Lakes Erie and Ontario. This immense river here rushes over a precipice, and falls perpendicularly to the depth of 176 feet. The tremendous roar of the waters can sometimes be heard at a distance of 40 miles; and the vapor, which continually rises in clouds from below, and which in the sun presents all the colors of the most beautiful rainbow, can be seen at a distance of seventy miles. In the Mohawk River, about two miles from its mouth, are the Falls of Cohoes, which are second only to those of Niagara, and have been much admired for their beauty and sublimity. The scenery around is enchanting. The river, which is here between 300 and 400 yards wide, descends, at high water, in one sheet, to the depth of 70 feet. About three-fourths of a mile below, a bridge has been thrown across the river, from which a view of the falls is inexpressibly grand.

The Saratoga and Ballston Springs are the most celebrated in America. Saratoga is about 30 miles north of Albany, with which it communicates by railroad, and a few miles to the west of the Hudson. Ballston is 12 miles south-east of Saratoga. These springs, during the summer months, are the resort of the gay and fashionable as well as of invalids from all parts of the Union. The waters, which contain considerable quantities of iodine, afford relief in many obstinate diseases. The warm springs of New-Lebanon, south-east of Albany, are visited for medicinal bathing. At Salina are the celebrated salt-springs, owned by the state, where sufficient fine salt is manufactured to supply all Western New-York and Canada. The falls at Trenton and those of Genessee are also of considerable magnitude, and much admired for their picturesque and beautiful scenery.

The climate of the state is much modified by local circumstances. In the southern section, the influence of the ocean is very perceptible, and the climate is changeable, but the annual range of the thermometer is not so great as in the north and north-east, nor are either heat or cold so intense. The counties bordering on the eastern states, partake of their characteristics. In the west again, the climate is moderated by the proximity of the great lakes, which, in some degree, assimilate it to that of the Atlantic section. The following table will illustrate the thermometric differences of the three sections:

	Max.	*Min.*	*Range.*	*Mean.*
New-York City	+ 94°	+ 6°	88°	50° 31
Albany	+104°	—17°	118°	46° 00
Rochester	+ 96°	+ 1°	95°	48° 33

As a general thing, however, it may be remarked, that the climate is exceedingly healthy, and with few local exceptions, altogether exempt from endemic diseases.

The 59 counties into which the state is partitioned contained, in 1850, a population of 3,097,095, or one person to every 9.5 acres, and the distribution of the inhabitants was as follows:

COUNTIES.	White Persons.	Free Colored Persons.	Total Population.
Albany	92,110	1,169	93,279
Alleghany	37,683	125	37,808
Broome	30,241	419	30,660
Cattaraugus	38,848	102	38,950
Cayuga	54,924	534	55,458
Chautauque	50,358	135	50,493
Chemung	28,537	284	28,821
Chenango	40,051	260	40,311
Clinton	39,935	112	40,047
Columbia	41,776	1,297	43,073
Cortland	25,103	37	25,140
Delaware	39,628	206	39,834
Duchess	57,022	1,970	58,992
Erie	100,214	779	100,993
Essex	31,098	50	31,148
Franklin	25,043	59	25,102
Fulton	20,079	92	20,171
Genessee	28,416	72	28,488
Greene	32,232	894	33,126
Hamilton	2,186	2	2,188
Herkimer	38,062	182	38,244
Jefferson	67,971	182	68,153
King's	134,897	3,984	138,881
Lewis	24,424	40	24,464
Livingston	40,690	185	40,875
Madison	42,783	289	43,072
Monroe	86,973	677	87,650
Montgomery	31,579	413	31,992
New-York	502,027	13,520	515,547
Niagara	41,959	301	42,260
Oneida	98,913	653	99,566
Onondaga	85,285	605	85,890
Ontario	43,418	499	43,917
Orange	54,783	2,362	57,145
Orleans	28,399	102	28,501
Oswego	61,980	218	62,198
Otsego	48,481	157	48,638
Putnam	14,008	130	14,138
Queen's	33,389	3,444	36,833
Rensellaer	72,337	1,026	73,363
Richmond	14,307	586	14,893
Rockland	16,368	594	16,962
St. Lawrence	68,581	36	68,617
Saratoga	45,066	580	45,646
Schenectady	19,667	387	20,054
Schoharie	33,092	456	33,548
Seneca	25,261	180	25,441
Steuben	63,409	362	63,771
Suffolk	34,809	2,113	36,922
Sullivan	24,966	92	25,088
Tioga	24,683	197	24,880
Tompkins	38,448	298	38,746
Ulster	57,804	1,581	59,385
Warren	17,152	46	17,198
Washington	44,402	348	44,750
Wayne	44,701	252	44,953
Westchester	56,216	2,045	58,261
Wyoming	31,935	46	41,981
Yates	20,442	148	20,590
Total	3,049 457	47,937	3,097,394

CLASSES AND SEXES OF POPULATION.

Classes.	Males.	Females.	Total.
White Persons	1,54[illegible],052	1,504,405	3,049,457
Colored " —free	22,9[illegible]8	24,959	47,937
" " —slave	—	—	—
Total	1,567,868	1,529,526	3,097,394

PROGRESSIVE MOVEMENT OF POPULATION.

Date of Census	White Persons.	Colored Persons. Free.	Colored Persons. Slave.	Total Population.	Decennial Increase Numerical.	Decennial Increase Per 100.
1790	314,142	4,654	21,324	340,120	—	—
1800	556,039	10,374	20,343	586.756	246,636	72.5
1810	918,699	25,333	15,017	959,049	372,293	63.4
1820	1,330,744	31,980	10,088	1,372 812	413,763	43.1
1830	1,868,061	44,870	75	1,913.006	540,194	32.0
1840	2,378,890	50,027	4	2,428,921	515,915	26.9
1850	3,049,457	47,937	—	3,097,394	668,473	27.5

The total population of the state on the 1st June, 1850, was comprised in 566,959 families, and hence the average size of each family was about 5½ persons. The number of dwelling-houses was 472,151, and hence, on the average, each dwelling covered 6½ persons. The housing of families, however, varies considerably in the several counties—in New-York there are 13.6 persons to each house, while in most other counties 5 and 6 appears to be the general average; but it must be remembered that in New-York the dwellings are larger than in the agricultural towns. The average mortality in all the state, for the year 1849–50, was in the ratio of one in every 66 persons. In New-York the mortality was one in every 44, and in some of the counties as low as one in 75, 100, 112, and even 122. A large portion of the mortality attributed to New-York and vicinity, and also to the towns on the main lines of travel, must, however, have resulted from deaths of emigrants on their way to the states to the westward, thousands of whom are annually destroyed from the combined effects of disease, want, and the abuses which beset their journeyings.

Industrial pursuits are nowhere more various or generally extensive than in New-York, and in many of the branches the people of this state are, perhaps, more advanced and perfected than in any other parts of the Union. Agriculture is in a most flourishing condition, and has, of late years, been beneficially influenced by the establishment of promotive associations. Numbers of the more wealthy farmers are pursuing their occupations under a skillful and scientific management; and to improve their stock the best breeds of cattle, horses, &c., have been imported. About two-thirds of the total population are engaged in this branch of industry. The stock existing in the state may be set down at 540,000 horses, 2,350,000 neat cattle—one half milkers, producing annually from 80 to 85 million pounds of butter, and from 48 to 52 million pounds of cheese—7,500,000 sheep, producing from 4¾ to 5 million fleeces—and nearly 2,000,000 hogs. Poultry is very plentiful. The annual production of the cereals is not very large in proportion to the extent of land covered, but the grain, especially the wheat, of New-York, is notably fine. Oats form the largest crop, averaging 30 million bushels; next Indian corn, 16 to 18 millions; wheat 14 millions; and from three to four million bushels each of barley, buckwheat, and rye. Potatoes and flax are grown to some extent, and minor crops in various quantities. The forest, orchard, and garden, afford adequate returns to labor, and the market for the products of the two latter is near, and always ready. The average yield of the several staples of agriculture is approximately as follows: barley 16 bushels, wheat 14, peas 15, beans 10, buckwheat 14 to 15, turnips 88, potatoes 93, Indian corn, 55, rye 10, and oats 27 bushels to the acre.

Mining occupies, in New-York, but a secondary position, and although 37 of the counties have mines of iron, lead, and other minerals, there is, nevertheless, but a small prospect of any extended operations being undertaken. Iron is the most widely diffused, and occurs in every known form and combination. The principal lead mines are those of St. Lawrence and Sullivan counties. Copper and zinc are also mined. Marble, granite, sandstone, freestone, gypsum, ochres, &c., are abundant, and are mined for the purposes of agriculture and architecture. The average value of all mining operations may be estimated at 16 million dollars. The salt works of Onondaga are very valuable, and afford a revenue to the state.

In the manufacture of fibrous fabrics Massachusetts and Rhode Island excel New-York, and Pennsylvania excels it in the manufactures of iron; but in most other branches of manufacturing industry, this state is pre-eminent. Flour, leather, spirits, agricultural implements, and a thousand other articles of domestic utility, are manufactured in large quantities. Engines and machines are chiefly made in the large cities, in which also may be found persons pursuing every grade and kind of manufactures known to civilization. About 200,000 persons are occupied in these pursuits, and the capital invested for manufacturing purposes amounts to nearly $80,000 000. The number of establishments in which the value of goods annually turned out exceeds $500, according to the census of 1850, was 23,985, of which about 100 were cotton mills, 260 woollen factories, and 85 silk factories; 2,000 grist mills, 7,800 saw mills, and a large number of oil, fulling, and carding mills.

The foreign commerce of New-York is equal to a full third of the whole commerce of the Union, and as a port New-York city occupies a proud position among the great commercial marts of the world, being second only to London. Her lake and interior commerce is equally immense, and in all the kindred departments of industry a steady increase has been going on for many years. In 1849–50 the imports from foreign countries amounted in value to $111,123,524, and the exports to $52,712,789. The shipping employed in carrying this mighty bulk of merchandize amounted to 4,426,816 tons, as exhibited in the following aggregates:

Nationality.	Entered.	Cleared.	Total.
American	1,502,290	1,411,557	2,913,847
Foreign	775,430	737,539	1,512,969
Total	2,277,720	2,149,096	4,426,816
Atlantic Ports	1,145,835	983,289	2,129,124
Lake Ports	1,131,885	1,165,807	2,297,692

In 1840–41 the exports amounted to $33,139,833, and the imports to $75,713,126. The shipping now owned within the state is 944,349 tons, and of this 485,109 tons were engaged in coasting. The mercantile steam marine amounted to 130,957 tons, of which 94,809 tons were coasting and river vessels. The whale fisheries employed 6,029 tons, and the cod fisheries 337 tons. About one-fourth the coasting tonnage is employed on the lakes.

The internal commerce of the state, carried on chiefly by means of railroads and canals, in conjunction with the Hudson River, is as extensive as that of the whole Mississippi valley. The external points from which it diverges are New-York on the Atlantic, Dunkirk and Buffalo on Lake Erie, Sackett's Harbor, Oswego, &c., on Lake Ontario, and Whitehall on Lake Champlain. The greater portion of the merchandize carried over the several lines is merely in transit from tidewater on the Hudson to the States north and west of New-York, or *vice versa.* It is almost impossible to estimate the amount of this, or to distinguish the transit from the domestic movement. The average commerce of the canals is about $120,000,000 per annum, and perhaps, since the completion of the New-York and Erie Railroad, that of the railroads may be to the same amount. Beside the merchandize transported over the various lines there is a large amount of business done in transmitting the western immigration landing at New-York city to its destination, and in accommodating ordinary travel. Hundreds of thousands annually take advantage of these means of transport, and the number of travellers is constantly on the increase.

The canals, railroads, plank roads, and turnpikes of the state exhibit no less the foresight than the energy of the people. The canals are, with one exception, the property of the state. These have been chiefly built with the view of uniting, by a water communication, the navigation of the lakes with the Hudson River, and thus opening up the States beyond New-York to the commerce of the world. In this they have been eminently successful. The railroads have a like purpose in view. But besides this, these works have been eminently beneficial to the state itself, and have done more than all else in fostering its material development, and increasing its population.

The main canal of the state is the Erie Canal, stretching from Albany to Buffalo. Lateral canals, some of great length, diverge north and south, thus connecting large sections of country, and concentrating to general depôts a vast commerce. The whole length of canal in the state, including the magnificent work of the Delaware and Hudson Canal Company, is not far short of 1,000 miles. Of the railroads the principal are the Hudson River Railroad, and the New-York, Harlaem, and Albany Railroad, both connecting the Atlantic with Albany. From Albany railroads extend northward and eastward, into Massachusetts and Vermont, to Canada; and westward from Albany to Buffalo, with many branches extending northward to the St. Lawrence, and Lake Ontario; southward to the New-York and Erie Railroad, which latter is also one of the great continuous roads, built to accommodate travel from the Hudson, at Piermont, to Dunkirk on Lake Erie. The Long Island Railroad and the New-York and New-Haven Railroad accommodate communication eastward. There are numerous other completed railroads, not here mentioned, and many other roads are in progress, or have been definitely proposed. The plank road system is accommodating localities in many directions, and has been very successfully commenced. Its advantages are numerous, and in a few years hence its application must become very general. In relation to turnpikes no state is better supplied, and indeed roads of every description are generally well kept, and suitable for the most extensive travel. Internal communication by natural waters, except so far as regards Long Island Sound, the Hudson River, and the Lakes, is of no great extent. On these, however, a large trade is carried, and as a whole the accommodation in the numerous steamboats and other craft, is efficient and even magnificent.

According to the State Comptroller's Report in June, 1850, there were in the state 191 banks, and one branch. The leading features of the condition of these institutions in the aggregate, at that date, are exhibited in the following abstract:

Liabilities.	N. Y. City Banks.	Country Banks.
Capital stock	$27,300,330	$20,479,397
Profits	4,302,450	3,810,614
Circulation	6,209,387	18,104,954
Due State Treas.	12,475	1,461,427
Deposits	35,955,549	10,735,416
Due Banks	17,402,377	5,559,412
Other liabilities	610,845	1,563,629
Total	$91,793,447	$61,301,840

Resources.	N. Y. City Banks.	Country Banks.
Loans & Discounts	$52,983,659	$36,209,886
Loans, &c. to Directors	2,921,512	1,887,712
Loans to Brokers	2,172,985	314,925
Real Estate	1,943,166	1,401,358
Bonds and Mortgages	223,527	2,845,741
Stocks	2,149,029	9,478,465
Specie	10,739,957	913,382
Cash items	8,336,149	845,332
Other resources	9,723,443	9,415,039
Total	$91,793,447	$61,301,840

namely—

	N. Y. City Banks.	Country Banks.
Incorporated Banks	$59,552,219	$32,762,910
Associated Banks	32,241,228	21,346,210
Individual Banks	—	7,192,720

The Schools of New-York are essentially a feature in its social condition, and whether we consider the subject in relation to the sums expended in their support, or to the system of instruction afforded, this state is equally pre-eminent. In January, 1850, it contained 11,397 organized public school districts, and reports had been received from 11,173. The whole number of children in the state, at that time, between the ages of five and 16 years, was 735,188, and of this number 9,079 had been under instruction for the entire year, 18,455 for 10 months, 59,315 for 8 months, 106,100 for 6 months, 167,732 for 4 months, and the rest for periods of shorter duration. The total expenses of supporting these schools amounted to $1,766,668, of which $859,845 was produced from the school fund. In many of the large cities the schools are free to all, and of late years evening-schools for apprentices have been supported.

The number of private schools was 1,697, and the number attending such schools was 70,606.

Connected with the common schools there are two Normal schools, for the education of teachers, and, of late, Teachers' Institutes have been established in each county. The teachers also hold a convention annually for the purpose of consultation and exchange of ideas respecting education.

But the crowning glory of the School System is the Free Academy in New-York City. This is open to pupils from the common schools, who, on examination, are found to possess superior abilities. They receive, free of all expense, a full course of collegiate instruction, and on leaving the institution are well fitted to undertake the highest offices, and thus the avenue to distinction is open to all who merit it.

Besides these institutions there are numerous incorporated academies, seminaries, and schools of a high order, and the state makes efficient provision for the support and education of the deaf and dumb, the blind and the insane. The establishments for these purposes are truly magnificent, and an honor to the state and humanity. The academies are under the charge of the Regents of the University, and the common schools of county superintendents, and a general state superintendent.

There are also several Universities and Colleges in the state, which have generally a high celebrity for efficiency. The following are the principal.

Colleges.	Location.	Founded.	Professors.	Students.	Libraries.
Columbia College . . .	N. York City	1754	8	130	17,000
Union College	Schenectady	1795	12	230	15,000
Hamilton College . .	Clinton	1812	10	149	10,000
Madison University . .	Hamilton	1819	9	127	7,000
Geneva College . . .	Geneva	1823	5	42	5,000
New-York, University of	New-York City	1831	11	151	4,000
St. John's College . .	Fordham	1841	16	110	12 000
St. Paul's College . .	College Point	1837	11	29	2,000

The Public Libraries, especially those in New-York City, are on a large scale, and of great advantage to those whose researches require much reference. But as yet there are no libraries to compare with even the small ones of Europe, and in many departments of literature they are extremely deficient, so much so, indeed, that it would be impossible to prosecute particular studies even within the limits of the Union.

The several religious denominations of this state are generally well provided with church room, and the means of educating their clergy. The Protestant Episcopal Church, which previous to the revolution was the church established by law, is still the most influential and wealthy. It has two bishoprics within the state, namely, that of New-York, and that of Western New-York. The first contains 299 churches and 264 clergymen, and the latter 135 churches and 118 clergymen. The Roman Catholics have three dioceses, namely those of New-York, Albany, and Buffalo. The first is an archbishopric, the territory of which includes the two last, as also the dioceses of Hartford and Boston. Within the diocese of New-York they have 70 churches and 60 other stations, with 109 clergy, and 202,000 people: within that of Albany there are 70 churches and 40 other stations, with 61 clergy, and 80,000 people, and within that of Buffalo 58 churches, and 53 clergy, with 70,000 people. The Catholics count every member of their churches in these figures, and not as other sects, their communicants only.

Of the evangelical churches the Episcopal Methodists are very numerous, and have seven conferences. The Baptists have 41 associations, 794 churches, 705 ordained and 132 licensed ministers, and 85,000 members. The Anti-Mission Baptists have two associations and 1,200 members. The Presbyterians (O. S.) have 187 churches and 25,000 members. The Presbyterians (N. S.) have about the same numerical strength; and the Congregationalists number about 12,000. The Universalists, Unitarians, Dutch and German Churches, and the Quakers, are less numerous than the above, but are, nevertheless, influential bodies severally; and besides these there are other sects, as Lutherans, Moravians, Christians, &c., which, if not numerically strong, exercise an influence in their proper spheres. The Jews have about 20 synagogues, and in all the large trading cities are found in crowds. New York City, however, is the Jews' paradise, and Chatham street their Holy of Holies. Sabbath schools are attached to most of the churches.

Almost every religious body has its own theological schools. The Episcopalians have the Theological Institution of the City of New-York; the Presbyterians the Union Theological Seminary at New-York, and the Theological Seminary at Auburn; the Baptists have the Literary and Theological Institute at Hamilton; the Lutherans have a seminary at Hartwick; the Associated Reformed Church has a seminary at Newburg, and there are others.

Law schools are attached to Columbia College, and the University at New-York, and there is also a school of this description at Ballston.

Medical schools are established at several points. The most noted are the Medical School of the University, and the College of Physicians and Surgeons at New-York; the Medical Institute of Geneva College, and the Medical School at Albany. The *esprit de corps* of the profession is kept alive by medical societies in the counties, cities, &c. In some instances the curriculum of studies is as abstruse as at London and Paris, and the conditions of admission to practise equally stringent. The law, however, leaves the doors of the profession open to all, and in this does infinite injustice to the regular practitioner, and an irreparable injury to the public. Quackery is thus on a par with science, and safe from legal censure as long as it forbears from absolute murder. The democratic idea is here too closely followed, and the "abstract liberty" of the French put in practice.

The right to vote is conceded to every white male citizen 21 years of age and upwards, but he must have been such for ten days at least, and have been a resident of the state for one year. Colored citizens to be eligible to vote must possess a freehold of $250 value, and have been residents three years. Convicts, and persons betting on the result of an election, are by law deprived of the suffrage. The general election is held on the Tuesday succeeding the first Monday of November, annually.

The legislature consists of a Senate and Assembly. The Senators, 32 in number, are elected from districts of equal population, for two years, and Assemblymen, 128 in number, are elected annually from like districts, but each county, except that of Hamilton, is entitled to one member. The legislature assembles annually at Albany on the first Tuesday in January.

The Governor is elected for two years, and must be at least 30 years old a citizen of the United States, and have resided in the state for five years The Lieutenant Governor, with the same qualifications, is elected for the same term, and is, *ex officio*, President of the Senate. A subsequent two-thirds vote in favor of any legislative act, vetoed by the Governor, becomes law. The chief executive officers are also elected by the people.

The court for the trial of impeachments, consists of the Senate and Justices of the Court of Appeals. The Court of Appeals consists of eight judges, who are elected for eight years, and so classified that two are elected every second year. The state is divided into eight judicial districts, of which the city of New-York is one, and in this city the number of justices is fixed by a special law. In each of the other districts, four justices of the Supreme Court are elected to serve eight years. The justices have general jurisdiction in law and equity. Each county, except New-York, elects one county judge for four years, who also acts as surrogate; but counties having more than 40,000 inhabitants, may elect a separate surrogate. Towns elect justices of the peace to serve four years. Cities may have inferior local courts, of civil and criminal jurisdiction. Tribunals of conciliation may be established, whose decisions shall be binding only upon parties who voluntarily submit their disputes and agree to abide the result.

The constitution is very concise on the financial movements of the state. It provides for the payment of the public debt by a sinking fund, etc.; forbids the state to give its credit to any individual or corporation, and denies the further accumulation of indebtedness, except for casual deficits, or in case of insurrection or invasion, until the present debt is extinguished.

The general fund and railroad debt of the state at the close of the fiscal year ending 30th September, 1849, was $6,389,693, and the canal debt at the same period was $16,414,524—total $22,804,217, on which accrues annually $1,259,036 interest. There was also a contingent debt, consisting of state stock and Comptroller's bonds of $1,233,905, upon which the state did not pay interest. The aggregate debt amounted to $24,038,122.

The property of the state consisted at the above date of its public works, on the construction of which $33,214,158 had been expended; but the nett amount of tolls during the year had been $2,757,103, which is six per cent. interest on $45,951,712, which may be taken as the actual value of the works. The taxable property in the state was assessed at $666,089,526, and the state taxes were $278,843; the county taxes, $3,895,434; and the town taxes, $1,374,703—total $5,548,981, or 83 mills on the dollar.

The general fund revenue for the year ending 30th September, 1849, amounted to $902,688, and the expenditures for the same period to $842,316, leaving a surplus of $150,371. This expenditure does not include the payments on account of the public debt, but only the ordinary and extraordinary expenses of the government. The debt is fully provided for by the canal, etc., receipts, and from the same sources $200,000 are annually available to the general fund.

The state holds other funds than the above; the school fund, which amounted in 1849 to $5,018,563, and produced $301,114 annual interest; the United States deposit fund, all of which is devoted to educational purposes; and the bank fund, which has been established for the security of the bank circulation in the state.

The cities of the state are New-York, Brooklyn, Albany, Hudson, Troy, Buffalo, Rochester, Utica, Schenectady, Syracuse, and Oswego. There are also 167 incorporated villages, and between 700 and 800 other villages.

New-York, the Empire City, and commercial capital of the Union, is located in the southern part of the state, on Manhattan Island, at the confluence of the Hudson and East Rivers. The East River and a small strait called the Harlem River, divides the island from the main land. The city, which is co-extensive with the county, occupies the whole island, and is 13 miles long, with an average width of one and three-quarters of a mile. Its greatest breadth is 2½ miles, and contains an area of 14,200 square acres. The surface is very irregular, and consists chiefly of sand, in which are imbedded rocks of various species.

The population, in 1850, was 515,547, of which 254,106 were males, and 261,441 females.

There are several smaller islands belonging to the city, which are located in the Bay and East River, fronting its eastern and southern portions, the principal of which are Governor's Island, Bedlow's, Blackwell's, Randal's, &c.; the two first of which are used by the United States as strongholds, and the others by the city authorities for Almshouse and Hospital purposes.

The Bay and Harbor of New-York is one of the most beautiful and safest in the world, and gives free ingress and egress to vessels of the largest class at all seasons of the year. On the Long Island side, east, lies the city of Brooklyn; at a distance of 8 miles from the Battery, south, is Staten Island, with its highlands and neat villages, and on the west the Jersey shore, with Jersey City, Hoboken and Weehawken in sight, presenting a view of unsurpassed beauty and magnificence. The Battery is a public promenade, embowered in trees, and laid out in grass with gravel walks. It is at the extreme southern point of the city, and overlooks the bay, the Hudson and East River. Castle Garden is built at the mouth of the Hudson, and is connected with the western point of the battery by a bridge of about 100 yards long. For several years past it has been used as a place of public resort. At the entrance of the harbor are the narrows formed by the approximation of Staten and Long Islands. This pass is about three quarters of a mile wide, and is strongly fortified. Fort Diamond is built on a reef, 200 yards from the eastern shore, and is covered by Fort Hamilton, which stands on an elevated site directly in its rear. Fort Tompkins and Richmond, both strong works, defend the pass on the western side. In the bay are three Islands, Governor's, Bedlow's, and Ellis's, all of which are well fortified, and together afford a safe protection from their respective directions; while at Throg's Neck, about 14 miles east, the eastern passage is protected by fortifications, upon the very guns of which the vessels of an enemy must pass before entering the harbor. Shipping from every maritime nation, and merchantmen of every size, line the wharves of the city on both sides, for the distance of three miles, presenting a continuous forest of spars and cordage, mingled with the chimneys of numerous steamboats. Upwards of 1000 sail vessels, 80 steamboats and steamships, 70 or 80 tow-boats, and 200 canal boats, may usually be found in the harbor of New-York during the business season. In the coldest winter this harbor is never obstructed by ice, so that vessels bound out or in are never delayed on that account.

The dense and populous part of the city has a circumference of about nine or ten miles. The lower part, or that originally built, is irregularly laid out, but the upper portion has been laid out in a rectangular form. The public buildings, which are generally of a costly nature, are numerous, including many magnificent churches and places of popular amusement.

The "City Hall" stands in the Park, three quarters of a mile from the Battery. It is built on three sides, of white marble, and in the rear of red free stone. The building is entered from the front by twelve marble steps.

A double circular stair-case, also of marble, leads to the second story, through the centre of the building; at the top of the stairway is a circular gallery, with marble floor, from which rise 10 marble columns of the Corinthian order, supporting a splendid dome and sky-light. On this floor are the chambers of the two boards of the Common Council; the governor's room, hung with national portraits; and the chambers occupied by the city courts. The rooms on the first floor are occupied by the Mayor and other officers of the corporation, and the basement is appropriated as a Mechanic's Institution, the grand jury rooms, and other public offices. The building is surmounted by a cupola, in which is placed a clock; there is also a room, constantly occupied, night and day, by a watchman, whose duty it is to keep a constant look-out for fires, and give notice of their occurrence and location by a given number of strokes on an immense bell which hangs in a belfry in the rear of the cupola, and which is used for no other purpose. Its sound may be heard from one end of the city to the other, and is immediately responded to by a hundred others in every direction.

This building was commenced in 1803, and completed in 1812, at a cost of $583,734.

The "Merchants' Exchange" is located in Wall-street, extending through to Exchange-street, and from William to Hanover streets. It is built of Quincy granite, and is 200 feet long by 171 to 144 wide, 77 feet high to the top of the cornice, and 124 feet to the top of the dome. The front has a recessed portico with 18 Grecian Ionic columns, 38 feet high, and four feet four inches thick, each one solid block of stone weighing 43 tons. The building occupies the site of the exchange destroyed in the great fire of 1835. It is entirely fire-proof, having no wood-work in its construction, except the doors and window frames. The cost of the present building was $1,800,000.

The "Custom House" is situated on the corner of Nassau and Wall streets, and extends through to Pine-street. It is 200 feet long and 90 feet wide, and 80 feet high, and is built in the most substantial manner, of white marble. The entrance to the portico, on Wall-street, is reached by 18 marble steps, and the portico is embellished with eight Grecian Doric columns, of the same material, 32 feet high, and 5 feet 8 inches thick. The rear portico, on Pine-street, is similarly ornamented, but in consequence of the rise of land from Wall to Pine-street, the ascent is only by three steps. The great business hall is a rotunda, 60 feet in diameter, with recesses and galleries; it is surmounted by an elaborate stuccoed dome, supported by 16 elegant Corinthian columns, 30 feet high. The cost of the building and ground was $1,175,000; of the building alone, $950,000. This building is also perfectly fire-proof, and stands on the site of the old city hall, on the steps of which General Washington was inaugurated first president of the United States.

The "Halls of Justice" occupy the square bounded by Centre, Franklin, Elm, and Leonard streets. It is 253 feet long, by 200 wide, and is built in the massive and purely Egyptian style of architecture, from granite quarried at Hallowell, in Maine. The heavy style of architecture, coupled with the sombre color of the stone, gives the building a gloomy aspect quite in keeping with its purpose as a prison, and which has obtained for it the name of the "Tombs." In this building is held the Court of Sessions, and the principal police court; it contains also the city prison or house of detention, with 148 cells for different classes of prisoners. The front of the building on Centre-street is entered by eight steps, leading to a portico with four immense Egyptian columns; from this there is another ascent by 12 steps, between massive columns, to an area of 50 feet square, the ceiling of which is supported by eight large columns.

The above are only a few of the principal buildings appropriated to public business. There are numerous others, as the University, the Lyceum of Natural History, Columbia College, the City Hospital, several Asylums, the Astor House, and other hotels, the new Post-office, the Revenue office, and a great number of splendid private mansions.

Of the churches, many of which are superb specimens of architectural taste, the "Church of the Holy Trinity" is the most magnificent. It stands on Broadway, opposite the head of Wall-street, and having a large open space about it, presents its symmetrical and elaborate structure to advantage on every side. It is built of brown free stone to the very pinnacles of the spire, which is surmounted by a gilded cross, at the height of 264 feet. The building is of Gothic structure, ornamented with elaborate and costly sculpture. The effect of the interior is grand and imposing, the windows being of stained glass, admitting only a subdued light; but the convenience of the worshippers has in some degree been sacrificed to the symmetry of the building, the location of the pulpit and the massive pillars which extend to the fretted roof, shutting the speaker from the view of great numbers of the congregation. The new "Grace Church" is the next in point of magnificence. It is built of white marble, in the Gothic style, and while the exterior will not compete with that of Trinity in costliness or beauty, the interior is arranged with more elegance and taste. It is located on the east side of Broadway, nearly three miles from the Battery. "St. Thomas" is a beautiful structure of rough stone. The Reformed Dutch Church on Washington Square, is a beautiful building in the Gothic style. The new Unitarian Church on Broadway, near Prince-street, is also a fine specimen of taste; as also many others of the various denominations. The whole number of churches is 172, of which 23 are Baptist, 33 Protestant Episcopal, 30 Presbyterian, 6 Congregational, 30 Methodist, 13 Roman Catholic, 23 Reformed Dutch, 3 Universalist, 1 Unitarian, 6 Jewish, and 4 Quaker.

New-York has few public grounds, but those are beautiful and well appreciated by the public. They are the Battery, Bowling Green, the Park, St. John's Park, Washington Square, Tompkins' Square, Gramercy Park, and Union Place; all these are beautified with ornamental trees, and some with splendid fountains. These are the principal resort of the citizens during the cool evenings and mornings of the summer months, and are truly the lungs of the city.

The city is supplied with an abundance of pure and wholesome water through an aqueduct of stone masonry, laid in hydraulic cement, under ground, from Croton River, a distance of 40 miles, to the receiving reservoir, (which is five miles north of the City Hall,) from which the water is conveyed through two lines of iron pipes to the distributing reservoir, 3 miles from the City Hall, and thence through iron pipes throughout the city. These pipes extend in all directions, a distance of 183 miles. The cost of this work has been a little less than $16,000,000. The receiving reservoir covers an area of 35 acres, and will contain water sufficient to supply the present wants of the city, without waste, for a period of five or six weeks. The water is almost perfectly pure, and notwithstanding the immense cost of obtaining it, the convenience, health, and safety from fire, of the citizens, are so far enhanced by its use, that none hesitate to contribute their proportion to the expense.

New-York has numerous literary, scientific and benevolent institutions, each of which is of great utility in its peculiar modes of doing good. It has also several well regulated theatres and operas, the principal of which are the Park, Bowery, Broadway, Astor, Chatham, with the Castle Garden, and some others of minor importance.

New-York, in short, may be considered as a world within itself. People of every nation, kindred and tongue, and exercising every art and profession known to man, are its inhabitants. Churches of every persuasion—people of all creeds—institutions of every imaginary shade, and man in all his phases, and in every condition, are all agglomerated within the circuit of this, the Empire City of the western world, and form a most heterogeneous compound of all that is extreme. New-York has suffered much from fire. The great fires of 1835 and 1845 are matters of history.

Brooklyn is the next city in point of population, and may be considered as a suburb of New-York. The population, in 1850, was 96,852, being an increase of 60,619, from 1840. This city is situated on Long Island, opposite the city of New-York, with which it has constant and rapid communication, by means of 5 ferries. The East River, between the two cities, is only about three-quarters of a mile wide, and, as a consequence, their business is much blended. Brooklyn, however, has considerable commerce of its own, and good wharfage for vessels of the largest class. The Atlantic Dock in South Brooklyn, is a work of some magnitude, and will eventually become of great advantage to the commerce of the place. At the upper or northern part of the city is the Wallabout, at which the British prison ships were moored during the revolution, and where ELEVEN THOUSAND FIVE HUNDRED American prisoners died from starvation, confinement, and other inhuman cruelties practised upon them by their captors. At that place is one of the United States' Navy Yards, from which some of the largest ships in the service have been launched. Greenwood Cemetery, one of the most beautiful burying places in the country, is situated in the south section of the city, a short distance from the bay, and contains 200 acres, diversified with hill and dale, wood, plain and lake. Brooklyn has 42 churches, but although the city is beautifully situated and exceedingly well built, there are no public buildings except the new City Hall (now being erected) to vary the monotony of its long lines of private mansions. Some of the churches are handsome structures, and unique in external appearance, and the Brooklyn Female Academy and the Savings' Bank are also neat buildings, but they have nothing to distinguish them particularly from ordinary structures built for the same purposes. There are, however, in Brooklyn, some of the most magnificent and costly private mansions, the residences chiefly of the merchant princes of the commercial emporium.

Albany is the capital of the state. It is situated on the west bank of the Hudson, 145 miles from its mouth. The population, in 1850, was 50,771, being an increase in ten years, of 17,050. It is handsomely located upon a gentle rise of land, and with its gilded domes, presents an imposing appearance from the river. The capitol is the principal public edifice ; it is built of stone, in a square surrounded by an iron railing, and occupies a commanding and elevated position at the head of State-street. The building is 115 feet long by 90 feet in width, and contains elegant and richly furnished apartments for the Senate and Assembly and other state officers. The City Hall is a superb building of white marble, and is surmounted with a large gilded dome. Besides these are the Exchange, the Albany Academy, the Female Academy, Medical College, and a num ber of churches of beautiful construction. Albany enjoys a large commerce, being the entrepôt between the north-west and New-York city, and its manufactures are considerable, amounting to upwards of $2,000,000 per annum. Two ferries cross the river to Greenbush, and numerous steamboats, some of the most splendid and largest in the world, with an endless number of towboats, ply between this city, New-York, and the intermediate places. The Erie Canal and the Champlain branch terminate at Albany, producing a large forwarding commission business. Railroads also connect it with Boston and Buffalo; and a similar connection will soon be completed to New-York by means of the Hudson River and the Harlaem roads. A tremendous fire, which consumed one-eighth part of the city, broke out on the 17th August, 1848. The property burnt covered 200 acres, and is variously estimated at the value of from $3,000,000 to $5,000,000. Many vessels and boats, and large quantities of merchandize, were also destroyed by the devouring element. This catastrophe has done more damage than the great fire of 1845, in New-York.

Troy is on the east side of the Hudson, 10 miles above Albany. It is a thriving city, and even now a rival to Albany in business and enterprise. Manufactures of various descriptions occupy one-third of the people. The population, according to the census of 1850, was 28,785, and is rapidly increasing.

Rochester, on the line of the Erie Canal, had a population of 36,561, in 1850. It is connected with the cities in every direction, by means of railroads or canals, and with the lakes through Genessee River, on which it is built.

Buffalo, on Lake Erie, is the western terminus of the Erie Canal and the great chain of railroads which connect with Albany. It is a place of great activity and considerable commercial importance. Buffalo is destined to be one of our most flourishing cities. The population, in 1840, was 18,213, and in 1850, 40,266, being an increase in ten years, of 22,053, or more than 120 per cent.

Among the larger villages may be mentioned Williamsburg, adjoining Brooklyn on the East; Jamaica, Sag Harbor, Sing-Sing, Newburg, Poughkeepsie, Waterford, Herkimer, Lyons, Palmyra, Batavia, Lockport, &c., &c.; all flourishing places.

It is said that New-York was first discovered by Verazzano, an Italian, but history generally attributes that honor to Hendrick Hudson, an English-navigator, then in the service of the Dutch West Indian Company. He sailed up the Hudson river, which still bears his name, in 1609, and subsequently sold his claim to the Dutch Government. A colony of that nation settled at Fort Orange, in 1613, and in the following year built some fortifications on the south point of Manhattan, now New-York Island, to which they gave the name of New-Amsterdam. The territory claimed by the Dutch extended from Fort Good-Hope, on the Connecticut River, to Fort Nassau on the Delaware, and undefinedly northward. To this they gave the name of New-Netherlands. The English laid claim also to these lands, and in 1664, Charles II. granted the whole country to his brother, the Duke of York and Albany, and sent an army under Col. Nicholls to enforce a surrender and expel the Dutch. The name of Fort Orange was now changed to Albany, and New-Amsterdam to New-York, the whole territory also taking the latter name in honor of the patentee. The colony was recaptured in 1673, and remained in the hands of the Dutch until the ensuing year, when it was restored to the English. During the seven years' war with the French, New-York suffered much from their incursions, accompanied with the Indian savages, and the country was almost desolate, when the peace of Paris restored tranquillity, and gave Canada to the British. During the revolution which soon followed, it was the scene of warlike commotion, and some of the most glorious victories the American arms wrested from the foe. It was one of the original thirteen, and during that momentous period, sent 17,781 soldiers into the field. New-York city was held by the British after the battle of Long Island until the final evacuation on the 25th November, 1783, a day which relieved the citizens from their old task-masters, and which has ever since been celebrated as a national anniversary by the inhabitants of the whole Union.

THE STATE OF NEW-JERSEY.

New-Jersey, one of the oldest states of the Union, and now one of the most prosperous, enjoys peculiar advantages from its geographical position, and the necessity of extending all the great lines of communication from north to south through its territory. Topographically, it has little to boast of; its soil is of but middling fertility, and a large extent of its surface is covered with salt marshes or sandy plains, but little suited for extensive agricultural operations. Nor is it capable of fostering commerce, although the ocean washes its entire eastern and southern shores; and except one or two ports, which, however, are but little frequented, there are altogether wanting those deep, capacious harbors which have contributed so much to the prosperity of its neighbors. New-Jersey lies between 38° 57′ and 41° 22° N. lat. and between 73° 58′ and 75° 29′ W. long. It is bounded north by the State of New-York; East by the Hudson River and the Atlantic Ocean; South by the Atlantic Ocean, and West by Delaware Bay and River, which separates it from the States of Delaware and Pennsylvania. In length it is 183 miles, and in breadth from 40 to 72 miles: the area being 8,320 square miles, or 5,324,800 acres.

The northern section of this state is traversed by some elevations, and may be termed mountainous, being crossed by the Blue Ridge and other rugged heights. Fronting on the Hudson, the "Palisades" present a perpendicular wall, in some places rising to the height of 200 feet, and extending 20 miles along the shores. From these precipitous cliffs the view of New-York, its magnificent harbor and the whole country around, is truly grand, and full of the most picturesque and varied scenery. The intervales and slopes are well adapted to grazing, and the soil is more fertile than in the more southern parts. The hills are highly metaliferous, and mining operations are extensively carried on in several parts of the district. The central section has an undulating, and in some localities a plane surface, and is agreeably diversified. The soils are good, and celebrated as wheat lands. The farmers have paid great attention to the cultivation of fruits and vegetables, which are disposed of in the markets of New-York and Philadelphia. The apples are especially fine, and are much inquired after for exportation to Europe, where, under the name of "Newtown Pippins," they enjoy great celebrity and bring a high price. The southern counties, including all the coast from Sandy Hook to Cape May, are level, and principally, as before observed, barren, producing little but scrub oaks and yellow pines. Of late years, however, these, formerly considered as almost worthless, have come into use for steamboats and the supply of glass houses, and, as a consequence, the value of the country where they abound has been much increased. The highlands of Navesink, near Sandy Hook, are the only elevations of note in this section, and are the first land seen by seamen approaching the coast. In this vicinity there are several beautifully located watering places, which attract to the shores during the hot months of summer, large numbers of visitors and invalids.

Excepting the Hudson and Delaware, which enclose the state east and west, no rivers of much importance traverse the country. The Raritan, which empties into the Bay of the same name, and the Passaic, which falls into Newark Bay, and some few others, as the Hackensack and Great Egg Harbor River, are the principal, and are all navigable for a few miles from their mouths. The Passaic and Hackensack supply immense water power, having several falls and rapids, and their margins are now covered with a succession of factories and mills of various descriptions. The Great Falls above Paterson, on the Passaic, have a perpendicular descent of 70 feet, and in seasons of flood, present a most magnificent and singularly thrilling scene. Newark Bay, which connects with the Bay of New-York through a narrow strait or "*Kill*," and Raritan Bay, further south, are the only indentations of any extent along the eastern shore: the whole coast from Sandy Hook, southward, being a dangerous sand beach, on which the surf beats violently, and which has long been notorious to, as it has been dreaded by, navigators approaching New-York from the ocean.

The climate of New-Jersey is similar principally to that of southern New-York, but varies somewhat in different places, being influenced by local causes. Cape May is a place of much resort during summer, and is esteemed one of the healthiest bathing stations in the Union. In those parts, under the influence of the mephitic vapors of the swamps, agues and fevers of great malignancy prevail, but generally the state, especially in the higher portions, is very healthy.

The number of inhabitants in New-Jersey in 1850 was 489,555, or one person to every 11 acres; and their distribution to the several counties in the proportions as follows:—

COUNTIES.	White Persons.	Colored Persons. Free.	Colored Persons. Slave.	Total Popula.
Atlantic	8,750	210	1	8,961
Bergen	13,094	1,590	41	14,725
Burlington	41,194	2,009	—	43,203
Cape May	6,190	243	—	6,433
Camden	23,325	2,097	—	25,422
Cumberland	16,170	1,019	—	17,189
Essex	71,783	2,161	6	73,950
Gloucester	14,035	620	—	14,655
Hudson	21,319	500	2	21,821
Hunterdon	28,212	769	8	28,989
Mercer	25,987	1,999	6	27,992
Middlesex	27,255	1,369	11	28,635
Monmouth	27,927	2,311	75	30,313
Morris	29,146	993	19	30,158
Ocean	9,883	149	—	10,032
Passaic	21,922	630	23	22,575
Salem	17,415	2,052	—	19,467
Somerset	17,965	1,696	27	19,688
Sussex	22,678	310	1	22,989
Warren	21,990	366	2	22,358
Total	466,240	23,093	222	489,555

CLASSES AND SEXES OF POPULATION.

Classes.	Males.	Females.	Total.
White Persons	233,746	232,494	466,240
Colored " —free	11,542	11,551	23,093
" " —slave	102	120	222
Total	245,390	244,165	489,555

PROGRESSIVE MOVEMENT OF POPULATION.

Date of Census.	White Persons.	Colored Persons. Free.	Slave.	Total Population.	Decennial Increase. Numerical.	Per 100.
1790	169,954	2,762	11,423	184,139	—	—
1800	195,125	4,402	12,422	211,949	27,810	15.1
1810	226,861	7,843	10,851	245,555	33,606	15.8
1820	257,409	12,609	7,557	277,575	32,020	13.0
1830	300,466	18,103	2,254	320,823	43,248	15.5
1840	351,588	21,044	674	373,306	52,483	16.3
1850	466,240	23,093	222	489,555	116,249	31.1

The number of dwelling houses in the state in 1850 amounted to 81,064, or one to every six persons, and the number of families amounted to 89,080, or each family to an average of 5.5 persons. The deaths during 1849–50 numbered 6,467, or one death to every 75 of the population, being about 1.33 per centum.

The industry of New Jersey is devoted alike to mining, agriculture and manufactures. Mining is at present carried on with energy and success both by companies and individuals. The whole series of hills in the northern half of the state are full of metallic ores, which from their proximity to the great mart of commerce, New-York City, are incalculably valuable. Iron is mined extensively, also zinc, copper and other minerals. The Franklinite, an ore of iron, much superior as a basis for paints to the oxides of lead, is very abundant, and is manufactured by the New-Jersey Mining Company for that purpose. Building material of the best descriptions also abounds, and a number of other materials useful in the arts. In agriculture New Jersey has long enjoyed a prominent position, and the great body of the people are engaged in one or other of its various departments. Indian corn, oats, rye and wheat form the great cereal crops. The Indian corn crop averages eight million bushels, and that of wheat about two million bushels. Buckwheat is also extensively grown. On the 1st June, 1850, there were 23,905 farms in cultivation, and hence the average size of a farm is about 220 acres. The market gardens and orchards of New-Jersey supply the markets of New-York and Philadelphia with an abundance of the finest kinds of vegetables and fruits. The peaches of this state have a world-wide celebrity. The manufactures of New-Jersey are extensive, and embrace almost every description of goods: machinery, hardware, fire-arms, jewelry, etc., are made chiefly at Newark; and Paterson is celebrated for its cottons, and other fabrics. Here also are the works at which Colt's revolvers are manufactured. Silk, flax, woollen and mixed goods are also produced to a considerable amount. The best saddlery in the world is made at Newark, and in almost every part of the state there are extensive tanneries and other manufacturies of leather. Whole villages are employed in boot and shoe making. In the southern parts of the state the manufacture of glass, earthenware, fire-brick, etc., are the great manufactured staples. Paper is also extensively produced, and there are also several large factories at which carriages and locomotives are built. The whole number of manufacturing establishments within the state on the 1st June, 1850, amounted to 4,374, but in this number only those producing to the value of $500 and upwards annually are included.

The direct foreign commerce of New-Jersey is very small, on account of its proximity to the port of New-York, from which the great bulk of its products is exported. In 1849–50 its exports amounted to but $1,655 and its imports to $1,494. The coasting trade however is extensive. The registered tonnage owned within the state is 201 tons, and the enrolled and licensed 77,725 tons, of which latter 5,489 tons are navigated by steam. In regard to shipbuilding the state occupies the seventh place. In 1849–50 there were built 57 vessels of an aggregate burden of 6,201 tons. This branch is chiefly carried on at Perth Amboy and Great Egg Harbor. The coast fisheries are extensive, and are carried on chiefly to supply the neighboring markets.

The *internal* trade and transportation of New-Jersey are on an extensive scale, and with regard to *internal improvements* few states occupy a higher position. The geographical situation of the state has favored this development. The great lines of railroad between New-York and Pennsylvania, which form the connecting link between the north-east and the south and west, of necessity pass through it. Branch roads have also been constructed from all the central roads to meet the wants of the manufacturing towns. Few states indeed have greater facilities for travel or traffic. The Delaware and Hudson Canal and the Morris Canal are also important channels of transport, and are mainly useful for coal transportation. The common roads throughout the state are generally well kept.

According to the official returns, January, 1850, there were in New-Jersey twenty-four banking institutions, and their condition at that date was as follows :—Capital $3,596,720, circulation $2,548,352, deposits $1,886,-595, surplus $543,776, bills receivable $6,192,575, due from other banks $1,452,057, specie $630,734, real estate $300,037, bonds and mortgages, etc., $257,568. Suspense account $21,889.

Education is well provided for in this state. It has three collegiate institutions, two theological seminaries, and one law school. The College of New Jersey, which was founded 1738, is located at Princeton, and in 1850 had 15 professors and 243 students. Its library contains 16,000 volumes. Rutgers' College at New Brunswick was founded in 1770, and has now 9 professors and 76 students; and Burlington College, founded 1846, has 5 professors and 42 students. The libraries of the two latter do not exceed 1,500 volumes each. The Seminary of the Dutch Reformed Church at New Brunswick dates from 1784, and in 1850 it had three teachers and 36 students. The Presbyterian Seminary at Princeton, founded 1812, has 5 teachers and 153 students; and its library contains 12,000 volumes. The Law School at Princeton forms a department of the College, and had in 1850 three professors and eight students. For medical education the state depends on the schools of New-York and Philadelphia. There are in the state, besides the above, a considerable number of academies and grammar schools, at which many of the higher branches of learning are taught. The common schools of the state are distributed into 1,561 districts. The returns for 1850, however, only report from 1,465 districts. These contained at that period 118,992 children between the ages of 5 and 16 years; and the number attending school was 70,053, of which 7,525 attended for a less time than four months, 8,319 for less than eight months, and 8,107 for less than twelve months. The average duration of schools was nine months. The average price of tuition per quarter to each pupil was $2 06. The total amount appropriated or received for school purposes was $119,351. The state owns a school fund which in 1850 amounted to $388,582.

The state supports in part its infirm. The Lunatic Asylum at Trenton, built by the government, was opened for the admission of patients in May, 1848. On the 1st January, 1849, there were in the institution 83 patients—46 males and 37 females; and during the year ensuing 96 others—55 males and 41 females, were received and 69 were discharged, leaving, 1st January,

1850, 110—62 males and 48 females, under treatment. The charge for patients supported by the public is $3 per week. For the deaf mutes and the blind there is no separate establishment, but the state makes an annual grant for the support of those who may be indigent, or such as may be placed for education in the institutions of other states.

The State Prison is located at Trenton. The statistics of this institution up to 1st January, 1850, exhibited the following details. On the 31st December, 1848, it contained 176 prisoners, and during the year ensuing received 108, making a total of 248; and the number discharged was, by expiration of sentence 79, by pardon 17, by death 3, (one killed and one suicide)—in all 99, which left in prison on 1st January, 1850,—white males 125, and white females 9; colored males 51, or a total of 185. Of these, 4 were for manslaughter, 6 for murder in 2d degree, 4 for rape, 4 for forgery, 32 for burglary, 34 for larceny, 38 for violent assaults, and 4 for arson; and 90 were natives of New-Jersey, 27 of New-York, 19 of Pennsylvania, and 39 were foreigners. The longest sentence is for 20 years, and two are under that sentence. These statistics would indicate a ratio of higher grades of crime very favorable to the morality of the people.

Among the religious denominations the Methodists are the strongest numerically. The Presbyterians, both of the old and new schools, however, are also large and respectable bodies, and the Protestant Episcopalians have many churches. There are also a considerable number of Roman Catholics (especially in the manufacturing towns), Baptists, Congregationalists, Dutch Reformed and other Churches; and in some districts the Quakers have congregations. The following are some of the principal statistics of the churches:—

Denominations.	Churches.	Clergy.	Communicants.
Protestant Episcopalians	47	59	3,054
Roman Catholics	23	27	20,000
Episcopal Methodists	—	361	33,812
Baptists	89	102	12,121
Baptists—Anti-Mission	8	7	300
Presbyterians (O. S.)	142	157	19,827
" (N. S.)	(About as numerous as O. S.)		
Universalists	3	3	100

The constitution under which this state is now organized, went into operation on the 2d day of September, 1844. The Governor is elected by the people for three years, but is ineligible for re-election for the ensuing term. He must be thirty years of age, and must have been a citizen of the United States for twenty years, and a resident for seven years previous to his election. The legislative power is vested in a Senate and General Assembly. The Senate is composed of nineteen members, or one from each county, elected for three years, one-third of their numbers being elected annually. Senators must have attained the age of thirty years, and have been citizens of the state four years, and inhabitants of the county for one year next preceding election. The General Assembly consists of fifty-eight members, elected by the people of the counties, according to their ratio of population. Members must have attained the age of twenty-one years, and must have been citizens of the state four years and residents one year, and must also be entitled to the rights of suffrage. The powers and privileges of the legislative body are similar in every shape to those of any other state.

The judicial power belongs to a Court of Appeals, a Court of Chancery, a Supreme Court, Circuit Courts, and other inferior courts. The Judges of the Court of Errors and Appeals are appointed by the Governor, with the advice and consent of the senate, and hold their offices for six years; the Judges of the Supreme Court and the Chancellor are appointed for seven years, and the Judges of the Courts of Common Pleas are appointed by the Senate and General Assembly, unitedly, and hold their offices for five years. The Secretary and the Attorney-General are appointed by the Governor, with consent, for five years, but the State Treasurer is appointed annually by the Senate and General Assembly in joint meeting.

The right of suffrage is enjoyed by every white male citizen of the United States, of the age of twenty-one years, who has resided in the state one year, and in the county in which he votes five months next preceding the election. Paupers, idiots, insane persons, and persons convicted of crimes which preclude them from giving evidence in judicial proceedings, are not permitted to vote. Colored persons are also incapable. The elections take place annually, on the second Tuesday of November, and the legislature meets at Trenton on the second Tuesday of January.

The militia of the state numbers 39,171 men of all arms, and the Governor is *ex-officio* commander-in-chief of the forces of the state.

The public burdens of this state are very light, and its income is derived from sources which accident has placed in the way of the government, and without resorting to taxation. The chief sources of income are transit duties on railroads and canals, dividends on stock, taxes on railroad stock, interest on bonds of Camden and Amboy railroad, special loans, proceeds of labor of state prisoners, etc., and the principal expenses are for the support of lunatics, deaf mutes and the blind, salaries of executive, legislative and judicial officers, support of state prison, pensions, etc. The receipts for the year ending 1st January, 1850, including a balance from former years of $10,823, amounted to $136,514, and the whole amount expended was $126,553, leaving a balance of $9,961 to the credit of 1851. About one-third of the expenditures were extraordinary, and hence the ordinary expenses may be estimated at less than $100,000 per annum.

The public debt owing by this state amounts to $67,595, and the annual interest on this is $4,075, or less than 6 per cent. Against this debt the state owns productive property to the value of $262,396, and property not now productive, consisting of U. S. surplus revenue which has been lent to the counties without interest to the value of $764,670, being a total of productive and non-productive property amounting to $1,026,066. The whole amount of the School Fund owned by the state in 1850 was $388,583, of which there is unavailable the sum $11,169 and available $377,414. From these figures it is shown that the financial condition of the state is good, but at the same time it must be owned that many items of its income are derived from objectionable sources, one of the most impolitic of which is the tax on transit through its territory.

Trenton, the capital of the state, is situated on the east shore of the Delaware, at the head of steamboat navigation. Lat. 74° 39′ N. and long. 4° 58′ 36″ W. The city is regularly laid out, and has many fine stores and private dwellings. The state-house is a handsome stone building, 100 feet long and 60 feet broad; it is beautifully situated on the Delaware, and commands a fine view of the surrounding river scenery. The Delaware is crossed by an elegant covered bridge, 1,100 feet long and 36 feet wide, being supported by five arches resting on stone piers. This is one of the finest specimens of bridge architecture in the United States, and is much admired by men of science as a work of consummate skill. The railroad passes over it. The Delaware and Raritan Canal passes through Trenton to the river at Bordentown. The trains for Philadelphia and New-York pass through the city twice a day. The population, in 1840, was 4,035, and is now estimated at 7,000, having increased rapidly in consequence of its position as an entrepôt. Trenton is celebrated in history as the site of a battle between the British allies and the Americans, December 25, 1776, in which the former were almost entirely captured.

NEWARK, on the west bank of the Passaic, is the most populous city of the state, and celebrated for its manufacture of leather and some other articles. Its population is about 38,885. The city, which is elevated 30 or 40 feet above the level of the river, is regularly laid out and well built. There are numerous public buildings and churches, which render its appearance lively, and at a distance, somewhat imposing. The court-house is a handsome stone building in the Egyptian style, and stands on the north side of the city. Newark is well supplied with pure water from a never failing spring about a mile distant. Several literary institutions supply the people with books, and are a resort to which they adjourn after the arduous toils of the day. Steamboats ply daily between this city and New-York, and it is also connected with that city and Philadelphia by a fine line of railroad. The commerce of Newark is considerable, and a number of small craft is owned by its inhabitants.

ELIZABETHTOWN, five miles south of Newark, is an ancient borough, and a railroad centre of some consideration, being on the intersection of the New-Jersey and the Elizabethport and Somerville railroads. Population, 3,600. RAHWAY is a manufacturing village on the river of the same name. Population, 3,000. JERSEY CITY, nine miles east of Newark, on the Hudson River, opposite New-York, is the commencing point of Southern travel from that city, and is connected therewith by two ferries. It has considerable trade and manufactures. The New-Jersey R. R. and Morris Canal, and also the Paterson R. R. terminate here; and it has lately become the dock station of the Cunard line of steam-ships. Population, 6,856. HOBOKEN, a pleasant village three miles north, also on the Hudson, is a favorite summer resort of the citizens of New-York. NEW-BRUNSWICK, at the head of navigation on the Raritan, is the seat of Rutger's College, one of the most flourishing institutions in the United States. It is an old town and badly laid out; but in the newer portions the buildings are neat and elegant, being surrounded with beautiful gardens. The prospect from the college is extensive, and the scenery, comprising a view of the mountains in the north, and Raritan Bay, is very impressive. It is connected with the Delaware River by a canal to Bordentown, forty-two miles long.

PRINCETON is the seat of the College of New-Jersey and a Theological Seminary belonging to the Presbyterians. Both institutions are in a flourishing condition. It has a population of about 1,600 inhabitants. A battle in which the Americans were victorious, was fought here, January 3, 1777.

PATERSON, at the falls of the Passaic, is a flourishing city, and is chiefly engaged in manufactures, being highly favored with water-power and other advantages in location. The Morris Canal passes south of the city, and railroads communicate with New-York, and also connect northward with the New-York and Erie Railroad. The latter work is not yet finished, but when completed will form a new, convenient and direct route through Jersey City to New-York, and divert much of the business which is now inconvenienced by a transhipment at Piermont, the terminus of the New-York and Erie Railroad on the Hudson. Paterson contains a number of beautiful churches, and in the suburbs are many elegant and well located private residences surrounded by gardens and shrubberies. The principal manufactures are cotton goods, machinery, carriages, and fire-arms. The population of the city in 1850 was 21,341. There are a number of manufacturing villages in the neighborhood, as New-Manchester, etc. The Passaic Falls are a great resort for the New-Yorkers in summer and are certainly worthy a visit.

The territory comprised within this state was originally a portion of the New-Netherlands, and was under the Dutch Governors until the capture of New-York by the British, in 1664. It was afterwards included in the extensive grants to the Duke of York by Charles II., and was conveyed by him to Lord Berkeley and Sir George Carteret. In 1665, Philip Carteret was appointed first governor. In 1676, New-Jersey was divided into two provinces, respectively styled East Jersey and West Jersey; the former constituting the government of Carteret, and the latter being held for a time, as a dependency of New-York. In 1682, East Jersey was transferred to William Penn and eleven associates, and Robert Barclay, the celebrated author of the "Apology for the principles of the Quakers," was appointed Governor.

The reünion of the two provinces was effected in 1702, and the country now styled as New-Jersey, was placed under Lord Cornbury, the then Governor of New-York. In 1738, this connection was dissolved and a separate government instituted, which lasted until the war of the revolution. New-Jersey furnished subsidies to the number of 18,736 during that eventful struggle, and her sons were always found foremost in defence of the liberties of their native soil. William Temple Franklin, a son of the celebrated Dr. Benjamin Franklin, was the last royal governor of the province.

THE STATE OF PENNSYLVANIA.

Pennsylvania, a part of that extensive country which was granted to the celebrated William Penn, and from whom it derives its name, is situated between 39° 43′ and 42° 17′ N. latitude, and between 74° 44′ and 80° 34′ W. longitude; being bounded north by the State of New-York and Lake Erie; east by New-York and New-Jersey, from which it is separated by the Delaware River; south by Delaware, Maryland and Virginia, and west by Virginia and Ohio. It is 310 miles in extreme length, and 162 miles in breadth—having a superficial area of 44,000 square miles, or 28,160,000 acres.

The surface of Pennsylvania is essentially mountainous, few level tracts of any extent being met with in any portion of the state. In the south-eastern section, however, the mountains subside, and the lands are more undulating than hilly. The Alleghany Mountains run across the state from south-west to north-east, and there are many smaller ranges on each side of the principal ridge, and generally parallel with it. These have local names, and are known as the Blue Mountains, Sideling Hill, Laurel Hill, &c. The eastern ascent of the Alleghanies is rugged and steep, but on the north and west these elevations gradually sink and form an extensive table land.

The soil of this state is well adapted for agricultural operations. The richest tract is on the south-east of the mountains, on both sides of the Susquehannah, extending from the Blue Ridge to the Delaware. This part has long been settled and is highly cultivated. The tract between Lake Erie and the Alleghany River has also a very superior soil, but being as yet sparsely settled, its progress in improvement is more backward.

The minerals which abound in the mountain regions have been a source of unprecedented wealth to the inhabitants. Coal, iron and salt are in inexhaustible profusion. West of the mountains are vast fields of bituminous coal, which is used at Pittsburg and other places for manufacturing purposes. In this region salt springs occur, which yield a strong brine. The anthracite coal region extends from the Susquehannah, and occupies the whole mountain districts to the south and east. The quality of the mineral varies much, and each district produces specific kinds, which, however, are respectively preferred for the purposes to which they are severally applicable. It has been calculated that the anthracite beds in Pennsylvania cover an area of 975 square miles, or 624,000 acres, and in some places have a depth of sixty or seventy feet; and as each cubic yard is estimated to contain about one ton of the coal, the quantity must be sufficiently large to supply the country for ages to come. The bituminous coal region, or that over which the veins are scattered, occupies an area of about 21,000 square miles. The coal from this region constitutes the great resource of the steamboats on our western rivers, and has, more than any other agent, tended to facilitate the settlement of the fertile lands, and the development of the commercial prosperity, of the great west.

The Delaware River forms the eastern boundary of the state, and is deep enough for ship-navigation to Philadelphia. The Lehigh falls into the Delaware, at Easton, after a course of seventy-five miles. The Schuylkill rises in the Blue Ridge, and after a south-east course of 120 miles, also joins the Delaware, opposite Mud Island, six or seven miles below Philadelphia. Falls and rapids interrupt navigation in several places, but have been overcome by numerous improvements, which render it serviceable nearly to its source.

The Susquehannah river is formed by the union of its two principal branches, viz: the eastern and western: the eastern branch rises in Otsego Lake, in the State of New-York, and running south-west, receives the Tioga, near the boundary line. It then flows first south-east and then south-west, until it receives the western branch at Northumberland, after which the course of the river is first south and then south-east until it falls into the head of Chesapeake Bay, near the north-east corner of Maryland. The navigation of the last fifty miles is interrupted by an almost continuous series of rapids, but further up, to the union of its two branches, no obstruction, which cannot be surmounted, occurs. The tide water canal, however, supplies all the demands of commercial interests, and overcomes all the natural disabilities of the river.

The Alleghany River rises in this state, and runs first north-west into New-York, and thence, by a bend to the south-west, again enters Pennsylvania, and at Pittsburg, uniting with the Monongahela, forms the Ohio. It is a steady stream, and navigable for keel boats of ten tons, to Hamilton, 260 miles from its mouth. In its course it receives several fine streams, chiefly flowing from the eastern highlands. The Monongahela rises at the foot of the Laurel Hills, in Virginia, and joins the Alleghany, after a northerly course of 300 miles. It is navigable for large boats and steamers to Brownsville, sixty miles, and for small boats to Tygart's Valley, 200 miles from the junction of the two rivers.

Pennsylvania has a climate intermediate between the extremes of the northern and southern sections of the country. The south-eastern part, in which Philadelphia is situated, has a changeable climate, and the annual extremes of temperature are great. Among the mountains and in the northern counties the climate is more settled, but much colder, particularly in the winter season. To the west of the Alleghany Mountains the weather is generally milder than to the eastward, owing principally to the prevalence of south-east winds; and the annual mean temperature of Philadelphia and Pittsburg are almost similar, though somewhat varied in distribution throughout the year from local causes. The temperature of Philadelphia during the year varies from about 98° to 6° Fahr., and at Pittsburg the extremes are about 94° and 10°. The winters and summers are decidedly marked, but the spring is short, variable, and uncertain. The fall, however, is the pleasantest part of the year, and the weather in that season, though sometimes interrupted by excessive heat, is serene and delightful. The state is considered one of the healthiest of the continent, and on the whole the climate is favorable for agriculture and the collection of produce.

In 1850 Pennsylvania contained 2,311,786 inhabitants, or one to every 12½ acres; and the proportional population of the counties was as follows:

EASTERN DISTRICT.

COUNTIES.	White Persons.	Colored Persons.	Total Popula.
Adams	25,426	555	25,981
Berks	76,576	553	77,129
Bucks	54,366	1,725	56,091
Carbon	15,656	30	15,686
Chester	61,209	5,229	66,438
Cumberland	33,370	957	34,327
Dauphin	33,491	1,263	35,754
Delaware	23,120	1,559	24,679
Franklin	37,956	1,948	39,904
Lancaster	95,318	3,626	98,944
Lebanon	25,985	86	26,071
Lehigh	32,431	48	32,479
Monroe	13,170	100	13,270
Montgomery	57,442	849	58,291
Northampton	40,099	136	40,235
Perry	19,953	135	20,088
Philadelphia	389,224	19,438	408,782
Pike	5,692	189	5,881
Schuylkill	60,307	406	60,713
Wayne	21,841	49	21,890
York	56,324	1,126	57,450
Total	1,180,056	40,007	1,220,063

WESTERN DISTRICT.

COUNTIES.	White Persons.	Colored Persons.	Total Popula.
Alleghany	134,827	3,463	138,290
Armstrong	29,431	129	29,560
Beaver	26,444	245	26,689
Bedford	22,637	415	23,052
Blair	21,517	260	21,777
Bradford	42,634	197	42,831
Butler	30,262	84	30,346
Cambria	17,645	128	17,773
Centre	23,112	243	23,355
Clarion	23,448	117	23,565
Clearfield	12,482	104	12,586
Clinton	11,055	152	11,207
Columbia	17,607	103	17,710
Crawford	37,750	99	37,849
Elk	3,529	2	3,531
Erie	38,593	149	38,742
Fayette	37,443	1,669	39,112
Fulton	7,474	93	7,567
Greene	21,660	476	22,136
Huntingdon	24,461	325	24,786
Indiana	26,916	254	27,170
Jefferson	13,421	97	13,518
Juniata	12,904	125	13,029
Lawrence	20,947	132	21,079
Lucerne	55,699	373	56,072
Lycoming	25,890	367	26,257
Mercer	32,881	291	33,172
Mifflin	14,570	410	14,980
Montour	13,155	84	13,239
McKean	5,218	36	5,254
Northumberl'd	23,180	92	23,272
Potter	6,042	6	6,048
Somerset	2,317	99	24,416
Sullivan	3,683	11	3,694
Susquehanna	28,529	159	28,688
Tioga	23,889	98	23,987
Union	25,982	101	26,083
Vanango	18,270	40	18,310
Warren	13,593	78	13,671
Washington	43,380	1,559	44,939
Westmoreland	51,280	446	51,726
Wyoming	10,650	5	10,655
Total	1,078,407	13,316	1,091,723
Grand T'l	2,258,463	53,323	2,311,786

CLASSES AND SEXES OF POPULATION.

Classes.	Males.	Females.	Total.
White Persons	1,142,863	1,115,600	2,258,463
Colored " —free	25,057	28,266	53,323
" " —slave	—	—	—
Total	1,167,920	1,143,866	2,311,786

PROGRESSIVE MOVEMENT OF POPULATION.

Date of Census.	White Persons.	Colored Persons. Free.	Colored Persons. Slave.	Total Population.	Decennial Increase. Numerical.	Decennial Increase. Per 100.
1790	424,099	6,837	3,737	434,373	—	—
1800	586,098	14,561	1,706	602,365	167,992	38.7
1810	786,804	22,492	795	810,091	207,726	34.4
1820	1,019,045	30,202	211	1,049,458	239,367	29.5
1830	1,309,900	37,930	403	1,348,233	298,775	28.4
1840	1,676,115	47,854	64	1,724,033	375,800	27.8
1850	2,258,463	53,323	—	2,311,786	587,753	34 1

The total number of dwellings in the state, in 1850, was 386,216, or one to every 5.9 persons, and the number of families, 408,497, or one to every 5.6 persons. The deaths in 1849–50 amounted to 28,318, or one in every 82 persons, being a ratio of 1.19 per cent. on the whole population.

Mining is by far the most important interest in Pennsylvania, and next to England, this state produces more iron and coal than any other country. Of the whole number of counties, 45 actually contain iron works, and of the remaining number nine abound in iron and coal, and only eight can be regarded as not suited to the manufacture of iron. The number of works in Eastern Pennsylvania is 364, and in Western Pennsylvania 140.

Production of Iron from the Ore.

BLAST FURNACES.	Number of Iron Works. E. Penn.	W. Penn.	Total.	Capital Invested.	Capacity. Tons.	Make, 1849. Tons.
—using Anthracite coal	57	—	57	$3,221,000	221,400	109,000
" Bituminous "	—	7	7	223,000	12,600	4,900
" Coke "	—	4	4	800,000	12,000	—
" Charcoal—hot blast	67	18	85	3,478,000	130,700	58,800
" " —cold blast	60	85	145	5,170,000	173,600	80,600
Total	184	114	298	12,892,000	550,300	253,300
Bloomeries	6	—	6	28,700	600	335

Conversion of Cast into Wrought Iron.

WORKS.	Number of Works. E. Pen.	W. Pen.	Total.	Capital Invested.	Forge Fires.	Puddling Furnaces.	Capacity. Tons.	Make, 1849. Tons.
Charcoal forges	118	3	121	$2,026,300	402	—	50,250	28,495
Rolling mills	56	23	79	5,554,200	—	436	174,400	108,358
Total	174	26	200	7,580,500	402	436	224,650	136,853

The amazing difference between the capacity of the works and the amounts produced, is the result of foreign competition—all the markets accessible from the sea or the lakes, being supplied with English iron, at a much cheaper rate, than the same qualities can be manufactured at in this country. The rolling mills, which formerly manufactured considerable quantities of railroad iron, are now almost entirely employed in making boiler plates and cut nails, with which the English can compete neither in quality or price. All this has resulted from the free-trade tariff of 1846, at which time the iron works of the state were enjoying a high degree of prosperity, and in 1847, the aggregate production of furnaces was 358,500 tons, and of forges and rolling mills 203,700 tons. Since this period the production has rapidly declined.

There are 604 nail machines in the state, each averaging annually 1,000 kegs of 100 pounds each, or a total of 30,300 tons. Of the product of the forges, two-thirds is sold in the form of blooms to the rolling mills, and manufactured into plates, rods, and bars, and the remaining one-third is sold in the form of hammered bar iron. Of works engaged in the manufacture of steel there are 7 in Eastern, and 6 in Western Pennsylvania—producing together 6,078 tons; in the eastern district 3,278 tons, and in the western district 2,800 tons. The total number of iron works of all kinds is 504, the capital invested $20,501,200, and men employed 30,103. Probably 15,000 persons are otherwise incidentally employed, which will make the total number about 45,000; and thus, allowing to each laborer "five in family," we have a population of 225,000, or about one-tenth the inhabitants of the state, dependent on the manufacture of iron for a living.

The production of anthracite coal has almost quadrupled in the past ten years—in 1840 the product was 867,045 tons, and in 1850, 3,242,641, viz.:

Years.	Lehigh.	Schuylkill.	Lackawanna.	Shamokin.	Wyoming.	Total.
1840	225,591	452,291	148,470	15,928	—	867,045
1850	801,246	1,683,425	454,240	19,650	259,080	3,242,641

And a like increase is observable in the production of bituminous coal.

The agricultural position of Pennsylvania is a high one, and the state enjoys in its soil and climate every advantage. It is noted for its wheat, oats, and rye. The crops of grain in millions of bushels average—wheat, 16; oats, 21; rye, 13; buckwheat, 4; and Indian corn 22. Barley is a very small crop. The various crops are, potatatoes, about 10,000,000 bushels; hay, 1,800,000 tons; tobacco, 900,000 pounds; and maple sugar, 2,000,000 pounds. Live stock is abundant, and considerable amounts of cheese, butter, wool, and the products of the hog are exported. The cheese and butter of Pennsylvania are highly prized. Flax is grown to some extent. In 1850 there were in the state 127,577 farms under cultivation.

The manufactures of Pennsylvania, otherwise than those of iron, are very various and extensive. The two most important are those of woollen and cotton goods; the woollen manufactures, in 1850, employed a capital of $3,005,064, and the raw material—wool, 7,560,379 pounds, and coal, 10,777 tons, was valued at $3,282,718. The number of hands employed was 5,726; 10,095,234 yards of cloth were made, and the value of the whole product was $5,321,866. The capital invested in cotton manufactures was $4,528,925; the cotton used annually, 44,162 bales, valued at $3,152,580; hands employed, 7,649, and the products, 45,746,790 yards, valued at $5,322,269. In these two branches, only three other states of the Union manufacture to a greater extent than Pennsylvania. In comparison with the statistics of 1840 no material alteration has taken place in cotton manufactures, but in those of wool the capital invested and the product have more than doubled. The whole number of productive establishments in 1850 amounted to 22,036, but in this number none producing less than $500 annually are included.

The completion of many of the most important works of internal improvement in this state have given to internal trade an unwonted vigor. Commencing at Philadelphia, the lines have a general direction westward, and at Pittsburg they communicate with those of Ohio and the country as far west as the Mississippi, and north to the Great Lakes. These works consist of an immense length of canal and of railroads, which when completed will form as judicious a system of improvements as could possibly be devised. The great central line of communication commences at Philadelphia, whence the Columbia Railroad, 82 miles long, carries it to the Susquehanna, thence the eastern and Juniata sections of the Pennsylvania Canal, in all 172 miles long, carries it to Hollidaysburg; thence by the Alleghany Portage Railroad, 36 miles long, it reaches Johnstown, and thence Pittsburg is reached by the western division of the canal, 104 miles—a total distance from Philadelphia of 394 miles; and from Pittsburg the Beaver Canal runs into Ohio 31 miles, and the Erie Extension Canal will continue the line to Erie on the lake, 105 miles. The French Creek Feeder, 27 miles long, and Franklin line, 22 miles, the latter joining the Feeder seven miles below Meadville, unite with the Erie Extension Canal at Conneaut Lake. The other principal canals are—(1) the Delaware Division, from Bristol on the Delaware, 60 miles, to Easton, the western terminus of the Morris Canal of New-Jersey, where it joins the Lehigh Navigation, 46½ miles long, to Mauch Chunk, and to the falls at Stoddartsville, 41½ miles further; (2) the Lackawaxen Canal, an extension of the Delaware and Hudson Canal into Pennsylvania, to Honesdale, 25 miles long; (3) the Schuylkill Navigation, from Philadelphia *via* Reading to Port Carbon, 108 miles; (4) the Union Canal, from Reading westward to the Susquehanna, 82 miles; (5) the Susquehanna or Tidewater Canal, from Wrightsville, opposite Columbia, 45 miles, to Havre de Grace on Chesapeake Bay; (6) the Susquehanna section, which diverges from the Central Canal at Duncan's Island, 39 miles, to Northumberland—with its north branch, 73 miles, and extension, 90 miles, which will terminate at the New-York State line, and its western branch, to Farrandsville, 75 miles; (7) the Chesapeake and Ohio Canal, from Pittsburg to the Atlantic coast, and a number of lateral and local canals, finished and unfinished. The whole length of canal in the state is 1,280 miles—848 miles of which are owned by the state and 432 by companies. The principal railroads are—the Columbia and the Alleghany Portage Railroads, before mentioned, both state works; the Reading Railroad, 92 miles long; the Pennsylvania Railroad, 135 miles long; the Philadelphia and Baltimore Railroad, 98 miles long; the Cumberland Valley Railroad, 77 miles long, etc. In all there are from 45 to 50 railroads in the state, with an aggregate length of 1,625 miles, of which 1,087 are in operation, and 538 in course of construction. The railroads and canals of Pennsylvania have been built at a cost of little less than $80,000,000, of which the cost of railroads was about $45,000,000.

In November, 1850, there were in Pennsylvania 46 banks and 5 branch banks; the aggregate liabilities of these at that period were—capital, $17,701,206; circulation, $11,798,906; deposits, $17,689,212; due other banks, $5,811,157; and sundries, $93,015; and the assets consisted of specie, $4,337,394; specie funds, $2,787,565; loans and discounts, $38,-423,274; stocks, $1,417,078; real estate, $1,114,738; other investments, $1,230,064; due from other banks, $4,244,194; and notes of other banks, $2,570,139.

For the year ending 30th June, 1850, Pennsylvania exported to foreign countries merchandize to the value of $4,501,606, of which $4,049,464 was the value of domestic products. The direct imports for the same year were valued at $12,066,154. The shipping inward amounted to 539 vessels and 132,370 tons, of which 352 vessels and 100,009 tons were American, and that outward to 479 vessels and 111,618 tons, of which were American 309 vessels and 81,276 tons. All this commerce belonged to the collection district of Philadelphia. The total shipping of the state amounts to 258,939 tons, of which 64,205 tons is registered for foreign trade. The steam shipping amounts to 50,809 tons.

The number of vessels built in the state, 1849–50, was 185, with an aggregate burden of 21,409 tons—166 and 18,150 in the district of Philadelphia, 1 and 21 in that of Presque Isle, and 18 and 3,238 in that of Pittsburg.

The Common Schools of Pennsylvania, exclusive of those of Philadelphia, numbered in the year 1849, to 8,278, to which were attached 10,050 teachers, and the average number of scholars was 43 in each school. The aggregate cost of instruction, etc., was $562,930, and there was paid for school houses, repairs, etc., $146,144, of which sum the state appropriation amounted to $156,487—the residue being raised by tax from 460,782 persons liable. The public schools of Philadelphia form a separate system, and are supported by the city. The principal collegiate institutions in the state are, the University at Philadelphia, founded 1755, which has a medical department; Dickinson College at Carlisle, founded 1783, to which is attached a law department; Jefferson College at Canonsburg, founded 1802; Washington College, founded 1806; Alleghany College at Meadville; Pennsylvania College at Gettysburg; Lafayette College at Easton; Marshall College at Mercersburg; and the Western University at Pittsburg. Jefferson Medical College and Philadelphia Medical College are both located at Philadelphia. There are also Theological Schools situated at Gettysburg, Mercersburg, Alleghany, Canonsburg, Pittsburg, Meadville, and Philadelphia.

The Methodist form the most numerous of Christian denominations, next the Presbyterians and Baptists, and in order of precedence, the Episcopalians, the Roman Catholics, and Congregationalists. The Society of Friends, by which the state was founded, is yet very numerous in Pennsylvania; and the Universalists and Jews have several churches.

The constitution allows the right of suffrage to every adult white freeman who has resided in the state for one year, and in his district ten days before an election; but voters must have paid a state or county tax. Elections are held on the second Tuesday in October.

The Legislature consists of a Senate of 33 members, and a House of Representatives of 100 members. Senators are chosen for three years, one-third being renewed annually, and Representatives for one year. There are the usual qualifications as to age, citizenship, and residence.

The Governor is elected by the people, and may hold office six out of nine years. He must be a citizen, at least 35 years of age, and have resided in the state seven years.

The Judiciary consists of a Supreme Court, with four judges, who hold courts in banco, once a year, in four several districts—for the eastern district at Philadelphia, for the middle at Harrisburg, for the northern at Sunbury, and for the western at Pittsburg—the judges are elected by the people of the districts severally; District Courts in the four districts; and Courts of Common Pleas, which are held in 24 districts, each comprising one or more counties.

The public debt of Pennsylvania, on the 31st December, 1849, amounted to $40,511,173 92, viz:

Six per cent. stocks	$2,041,022 51
Five " "	37,336,716 90
Four and a half per cent. stocks	200,000 00
Total funded debt	$39,577,739 44

Relief notes in circulation	653,164 00
Interest certificates outstanding	179,422 91
" " unclaimed	4,448 38
Interest on outstanding and unclaimed certificates	11,294 34
Domestic creditors	85,104 88
Total unfunded debt	$933,434 51
Total funded and unfunded debt	$40,511,173 92

And the regular interest on this is $1,988,616. During the year past $521,465 86 was also paid in reduction of the principal debt, and $51,500 arrears of interest, etc. These sums together make an aggregate of $2,040,116 99 paid on account of the public debt. The value of productive property held by the state at this time amounted to $31,152,754, consisting chiefly of the state canals, railroads, and turnpikes.

The revenue and expenditure for the two years ending 30th November, 1849 and 1850, compare as follows:

REVENUES.				EXPENDITURES.			
Years.	State Tax.	Can. & RR. Tolls.	Total.	Years.	State Works.	Debt.	Total.
1849,	$1,293,921	$1,628,860	$5,010,978	1849,	$951,249	$2,040,117	$4,084,772
1850,	1,317,822	1,713,848	5,644,338	1850,	1,488,799	2,004,714	4,569,054

The principal cities and towns in the state are—

HARRISBURG, the capital, situated in Dauphin county, on the Susquehanna, and near the junction of Union Canal with the Tidewater Canal, latitude 40° 2′ 36″ north, and longitude 76° 20′ 33″ west. The State House is a handsome building, and from its location on an elevation facing the river, commands a fine view. The County Court House, Jail, and Masonic Hall are also substantial buildings, and with the churches, 16 or 17 in number, constitute the principal buildings. Population 1840, 5,980, and in 1850, 8,163.

PHILADELPHIA, the commercial emporium, situated chiefly between the Schuylkill and Delaware, and extending from river to river. It consists of one city, seven incorporated districts, seven boroughs, and ten townships, and covers an area of 76,800 acres. The aggregate population in 1850, was 409,045. In 1800 it was 81,005; in 1810, 111,210; in 1820, 137,097; in 1830, 188,961, and in 1840, 258,037—increase from 1840 to 1850, 151,008, or 58.5 per centum. Philadelphia is a most regularly planned city, and is at the same time the best built and most cleanly place in the United States. Its fine squares and streets being mostly lined with shade trees and shrubbery, the city has a rural aspect of surpassing beauty, and many of the main streets are named from the indigenous sylva of the state. The public buildings of Philadelphia are more than ordinarily costly and grand, and many of them are intimately connected with the history and traditions of the Union. The most celebrated structure is the old State House, held in veneration as the witness of the signing of the Declaration of Independence. It is situate on the north side of Independence Square, and fronts on Chestnut Street. The old U. S. Bank, the Exchange, the Bank of Pennsylvania, the U. S. Mint, etc., are other prominent buildings; and Girard College, for the secular education of orphans, stands as a lasting monument to the philanthropy of Stephen Girard, its illustrious founder. The churches of the city are also very fine, and exhibit varied and beautiful designs, highly creditable to the architectural genius of the inhabitants. The city is supplied with water by the Fairmount Waterworks; and the city proper and many of the outlying districts are lighted with gas.

The railroads centering in Philadelphia carry to and from its market an immense amount of merchandize, and the coastwise commerce employs about 15,000 vessels, of all sizes, annually. The coal trade is also principally carried on at this place.

Pittsburg, situate at the head of the Ohio, at the confluence of the Alleghany and Monongahela Rivers. It is the seat of extensive manfactures, and has with propriety been termed the "Birmingham of America." It is surrounded by several populous villages, as Alleghany, Manchester, Birmingham, Lawrenceville, and other suburbs. The city has been lighted with gas since 1836, and it is supplied with water, raised by steam-power, from the Alleghany, and distributed through iron pipes. In 1845 the city suffered severely from fire.

Other principal places are Easton, Reading, Lancaster, York, Carlisle, Hollidaysburg, Beaver, Erie, Washington, Chambersburg, etc. In the anthracite region, Pottsville, Mauch Chunk, and Honesdale, are the most noted places.

In 1638, a company of Swedes purchased a tract of land from the Indians on the west side of the Delaware River, and there made the first settlement of the state. The Dutch subsequently possessed the territory, but in 1664, when the English captured New-Netherlands, this colony also fell into their hands, and for several years it was held subject to the Governors of New-York. In 1681, William Penn, the celebrated Quaker, obtained the grant of a charter for the territory from Charles II., and proceeded to settle the country. In 1768, the boundary known as Mason and Dixon's line was run between Pennsylvania and Virginia. William Penn died in 1718, and his heirs continued to hold his interests until the revolutionary war, when they sold their claims to the commonwealth for the sum of $580,000. In 1775, an addition, by purchase of the Indians, was made in the north-west. The first constitution of the state was adopted in 1676, the second in 1790, and the present in 1838, and the last has been amended.

Delaware was originally a part of Penn's patent, and for a long period formed a component part of Pennsylvania.

During the seven years' war with France and the revolutionary war, this state took an active position, and to the latter supplied a subsidy of 25,678 men. It was several times occupied by the royal forces, and for some months Philadelphia was made their head-quarters. Though actually settled by Quakers, an anti-war sect, Pennsylvania has ever been the first to assert the military glory of the Union, and has been honored with many scenes which have since been exhibited on the page of history as the most brilliant of our national exploits.

THE STATE OF DELAWARE

Delaware, next to Rhode Island, is the smallest state in the Union. It is situated between 38° 27′ and 39° 50′ north latitude, and between 74° 50′ and 75° 40′ west longitude; and is bounded on the north by Pennsylvania; on the east by Delaware Bay and the Atlantic Ocean; and on the south-west by Maryland. Its length from north to south is 98 miles, and its greatest breadth 32 miles; area 2,120 square miles, or 1,356,800 acres.

In the north this state is somewhat hilly, but otherwise level and low. Large tracts are sometimes immersed under water, which renders them swampy and unfit for agriculture. Some fine grazing farms are found in Sussex county, and wheat yields a comparatively large crop.

The principal rivers are the Brandywine and Christiana, small streams indeed, but well remembered in history. These unite below Wilmington, and fall into the Delaware. They afford many valuable mill sites. The Appoquinimink, Duck Creek, Jones' River, Mispillion, Broadkill, and Indian River fall into Delaware Bay and the ocean. The Nanticoke River rises in the southwestern part of the state and flows into Maryland.

The climate is assimilated to that of southern Jersey, but the proximity to the ocean renders the winters mild and moist. The state is not very healthy, especially in the low lands, which emit a miasm from the stagnant pools, and create fevers and fluxes which prove very fatal.

Delaware, in 1850, had 91,528 inhabitants, or one person to every 14½ acres; and the distribution of the population into the three counties into which the state is divided was as follows:

COUNTIES.	White Persons.	Colored Persons. Free.	Colored Persons. Slave.	Total Population.
Kent	16,119	6,350	347	22,816
New Castle	34,822	7,568	394	42,784
Sussex	20,348	4,039	1,548	25,935
Total	71,289	17,957	2,289	91,535

CLASSES AND SEXES OF POPULATION.

Classes.	Males.	Females.	Total.
White Persons	35,771	35,518	71,289
Colored " —free	8,989	8,968	17,957
" " —slave	——	——	2,289
Total	——	——	91,535

PROGRESSIVE MOVEMENT OF POPULATION.

Date of Census.	White Persons.	Colored Persons. Free.	Colored Persons. Slave.	Total Population.	Decennial Increase. Numerical.	Decennial Increase. Per 100
1790	46,314	3,899	8,887	59,096	—	—
1800	49,852	8,268	6,153	64,273	5,177	8.7
1810	55,361	13,136	4,177	72,674	8,401	13.7
1820	55,282	12,958	4,509	72,749	75	0.1
1830	57,601	15,855	3,292	76,748	3,999	5.4
1840	58,561	16,919	2,605	78,085	1,337	1.7
1850	71,289	17,957	2,289	91,535	13,450	17.2

The industry of this state is devoted chiefly to agriculture, but in the northern section a considerable amount of manufacturing is carried on. The agricultural staples are Indian corn, oats, and wheat. Of the other crops but little is raised. The live stock amounts to about 16,000 horses and mules, 57,000 neat cattle, 42,000 sheep, and 84,000 swine. The manufactures employ a capital of about two and a half millions of dollars, and consist of woollens, cotton goods, paper, leather, and some few other articles. Iron is manufactured to some extent, but the state is more noted for its gunpowder and wheaten flour than any other staple. The flouring mills on the Brandywine are numerous and extensive, and their brand is favorably known in the market. There are between 30 and 40 mills in operation.

Delaware can scarcely be said to possess any direct foreign commerce.

Not a single arrival or departure is chronicled for the year 1849–50. In former years, however, it appears to have had some small share, as at the commencement of the present century (1801), it exported merchandise to the value of $662,042, and in 1806, to the value of $500,106. In 1846 the exports amounted to $146,222, and its imports to $11,215; but in that year the exports more than doubled the average annual value for the past 40 years.

The tonnage owned in the state was, in 1850, 16,719 tons, of which 15,067 tons were engaged in the coasting trade. The proportion navigated by steam-power was 2,774 tons. In 1849–50 there were built 16 vessels of an aggregate burden of 1,848 tons—12 schooners, 3 sloops, and 1 steamer. The chief commercial port is Wilmington.

There are nine banks in the state, with a total capital of $1,391,100. The amount in circulation was in 1850, $651,121; deposits, $290,556, and dues to other banks, $410,535. The assets were loans and discounts, $1,653,595; stocks, $1,928; real estate, $85,024; dues from other banks, $218,341; notes of other banks, $72,992; specie funds, $17,727; and specie, $147,512.

The northern part of Delaware lies on the great line of travel from the northern to the southern Atlantic states; but with the exception of a few miles of railroad and canal is almost destitute of internal improvement. The Chesapeake and Delaware Canal is, however, an important work, uniting, as it does, the two great bays from which it takes its name. It is 14 miles long, and extends from Delaware City to Back Creek. The New Castle and Frenchtown Railroad connects the steam navigation of the Delaware and Chesapeake; and the Philadelphia and Baltimore Railroad, which passes northward of this through the state, forms a link in the great southern line.

Education is miserably conducted, and, as a consequence, there were in 1850 no less than 19,523 persons of the age of 20 years and upward who were unable to read and write—nearly one fourth of the whole population! The number of Common Schools at that date was 209, and the number of children attending them, 13,288. This is a cheering fact, and indicates that the next generation will be better educated than the present. In 1840 there were only 6,924 scholars attending 152 schools. The cost of tuition in 1850 was $38,462, and the total cost, including contingencies, $44,209, of which sum, $27,508 was received from the school fund, and the remainder raised by contributions and tax. There is a college at Newark, and about 30 academies in the state.

The great bulk of the people are Presbyterians and Methodists. The Episcopalians are also numerous. Baptists and Roman Catholics have a few churches. The Quakers form a small but respectable body of people.

In religious affairs, however, the statistics of Delaware are usually included in those of the neighboring districts, and hence they cannot be determined with exactness from the synodal reports. The Protestant Episcopalians and Baptists are the only denominations that give their statistics separately, these are as follows:

Denominations.	Bishops.	Clergy.	Churches.	Communi.
Protestant Episcopal	1	15	17	590
Baptist	0	3	2	352

Delaware has no public debt, but possesses funds, exclusive of the school funds, to a considerable amount. The finances of the government for the year 1847 exhibit the following figures:

Receipts.		*Expenditures.*	
State Treasury	$38,031 65	State	$33,500 33
School Fund	44,837 03	Schools	28,403 43
Total receipts	$82,868 68		$61,904 76
Excess of Income,			$20,964 76

The Governor is elected by popular vote for a term of four years, and is ineligible for re-election. He must be a citizen of the United States, 30 years of age, and have resided in the United States twelve, and in the state six years previous to his election. The legislative power is vested in a general assembly, consisting of a SENATE and HOUSE OF REPRESENTATIVES. The Senate is composed of nine members, three from each county, who are elected by the people for four years. A Senator must have attained the age of 27 years—must have an estate in the county for which he is elected, of the value of $1,000—must have resided in the county one year and in the state three years next preceding. The House of Representatives has twenty-one members, seven from each county, elected annually. Members must have attained the age of twenty-four years, and have resided in the state three, and in the county one year preceding their election.

The judiciary is vested in a Supreme Court, a Court of Chancery and Orphans' Court, &c. All judges are appointed by the Governor, and hold their offices during good behavior.

Every free white male citizen of the age of twenty-two years and upwards, having resided in the state one year and in the county one month next previous to the election, and having paid a poll tax within two years, enjoys the right of suffrage. No person in the military, naval or marine service of the United States can obtain the right by being quartered within the state, and no idiot, insane person, pauper or convicted felon can vote. The legislature has a right to impose disfranchisement as a punishment for crime. The elections are held on the second Tuesday in November, and the General Assembly meets at Dover on the first Tuesday of January, biennally.

DOVER, the capital of the state and seat of government, is situated on Jones' Creek, about five miles from its mouth. Lat. 39° 10′ N., and long. 75° 30′ W. It is a well laid out town, and has a vicinity highly picturesque. The state-house is a fine building, situated on a large public square in the centre of the place. There are also three churches.

WILMINGTON is the principal seaport, and the largest city in the state. The population, in 1850, was 13,931. It is situated between the Brandywine and Christiana Creeks, about one mile from their confluence. The principal part of the town is laid out in a rectangular plan, and on the south-west side of a hill which rises 109 feet above the tide. On the north-east side of the hill, at a village on the Brandywine, which forms a beautiful appendage to the town, is the finest collection of flouring mills in the Union. The principal buildings of Wilmington are the city-hall and some few others. It contains also 16 churches of various denominations. The Christiana admits vessels drawing 14 feet of water to the town, and those drawing only eight feet can ascend several miles further up. The Brandywine has seven feet of water to the mills. The shipping belonging to Wilmington is between 7,000 and 8,000 tons. A fair amount of commerce is attracted to this port, but the main business depends on the coastwise trade, The fisheries are in some degree attended to.

NEWCASTLE, on the Delaware, a few miles south of Wilmington, carries on a considerable trade with Philadelphia. Lewistown, on Lewis' Creek, is celebrated for its extensive salt works.

This state was originally settled in 1627, by a party of Swedes and Finns, and was called New Swedeland. They built forts at Wilmington and Lewiston. In 1655, the colony was captured by the Dutch from New-York, under old Governor Stuyvesant, and after the subjugation of New-Netherlands by the British, the Dutch, in their turn, were expelled from Delaware, and that country was included in the jurisdiction of the Governor of New-York. In 1682, the Duke of York relinquished his claim to William Penn, who consolidated it with his colony at Philadelphia. Then, as now, it was divided into three counties, which were styled the "three lower counties on the Delaware." In 1701, the representatives from Delaware withdrew from those of Pennsylvania, and convened in assembly at Newcastle, in 1704. After this period it remained separate from Pennsylvania, though the same Governor presided over both colonies until the 4th of July, 1776.

This state took an active and honorable part in the revolution, by which it suffered severely. It subsidized 2,386 men for the revolutionary army, and also advanced large sums of money during that eventful struggle.

The first constitution was framed in 1776, the second in 1792, and the present amended constitution, in 1838.

THE STATE OF MARYLAND.

Maryland is situated between 38° and 39° 43′ N. lat., and 75° 10′ and 79° 20′ W. long.; being bounded on the north by Pennsylvania; east by Delaware and the Atlantic Ocean, and south and west by Virginia. It is 110 miles long and 106 broad, and has an area of 13,959 square miles, or 8,933,760 acres.

The country on the eastern shores of Chesapeake Bay is low and level, partaking of all the characteristics of Delaware. On the western shore, below the falls of the rivers, it is principally level, but above the country gradually becomes uneven and hilly, and in the western part of the state is mountainous, being intersected by several ridges of the Alleghanies.

The soil of Maryland is well adapted to the cultivation of tobacco and wheat, which are the staple productions of the state. Some cotton, of an inferior quality, is raised, and in the western counties considerable flax and hemp. The forests abound with various kinds of nuts, used for fattening hogs, which run wild, and are killed in considerable quantities for packing. Iron ore abounds in various parts of the state, and coal is found in inexhaustible quantities and of a superior quality, on the Potomac, in the neighborhood of Cumberland.

The Potomac, which forms the western boundary of Maryland, is the largest river in the state. It rises in the Alleghany Mountains and falls into Chesapeake Bay, between Point Lookout and Smith's Point. This river is seven and a half miles wide at its mouth, and navigable for ships of the greatest burden 300 miles, three miles below the head of tide-water.

Above this point the navigation is obstructed by a succession of falls, around which, however, canals have been dug, and the navigation improved so far as to render the river passable for boats, to Cumberland, 191 miles above Washington. The whole descent of the Potomac, from the mouth of Savage River to Cumberland, a distance of 31 miles, is 445 feet; from Cumberland to the Shenandoah Falls, 130 miles, it is 490 feet; hence to Great Falls, 39 feet in 40 miles; and between these and tide water, 12 miles, 143 feet—making the whole descent from the mouth of the Savage River to tide water, 219 miles, 1,160 feet.

The Elk, Chester, Choptank, Nanticoke Wicomico and Pokomoke all rise in Delaware, and flowing south-west through Maryland, empty from the eastern shore into Chesapeake Bay. The rivers flowing from the west are the Pawtuxent, a navigable stream; the Severn, on which Annapolis stands, and the Patapsco, on which the city of Baltimore is situated.

Chesapeake Bay divides this state into two unequal portions, and is one of the finest bodies of water in the world, affording good anchorage and free admission to its ports of the largest class of vessels.

The climate in the northern parts of the state is much similar to that of southern Pennsylvania. South of Baltimore there is a considerable change, and the atmosphere is more moist and warmer. The annual average temperature is about 58°, with a range of about 80°. The thermometer seldom falls below 14° or rises higher than 98°. Some parts of the state, being swampy and low, are subject to intermittents and bilious affections, but in the north and more elevated districts it is generally healthy.

The State of Maryland contained, in 1850, a population of 583,035, or one person to every 15.3 acres; and the distribution of the inhabitants into the several counties was in the following proportions:

WESTERN SHORE.

COUNTIES.	White Persons.	Colored Persons. Free.	Slave.	Total Population.
Alleghany	21,633	412	724	22,769
Anne Arundel	16,542	4,602	11,249	32,393
Baltimore	175,358	28,570	6,718	210,646
Calvert	3,630	1,530	4,486	9,646
Carroll	18,667	974	975	20,616
Charles	5,665	913	9,584	16,162
Frederick	33,314	3,760	3,913	40,937
Harford	14,413	2,777	2,166	19,356
Montgomery	9,435	1,311	5,114	15,860
Prince George's	8,901	1,139	11,510	21,550
St. Mary's	6,225	1,631	5,842	13,698
Washington	26,929	1,829	2,090	30,848
Total	340,712	49,448	64,371	454,531

EASTERN SHORE.

COUNTIES.	White Persons.	Colored Persons. Free.	Slave.	Total Population.
Caroline	6,096	2,788	808	9,692
Cecil	15,472	2,623	844	18,939
Dorchester	10,788	3,807	4,282	18,877
Kent	5,616	3,143	2,627	11,386
Queen Anne's	7,040	3,174	4,270	14,484
Somerset	13,385	3,483	5,588	22,456
Talbot	7,080	2,597	4,134	13,811
Worcester	12,401	3,014	3,444	18,859
Total	77,878	24,629	25,997	128,504
Western Shore	340,712	49,448	64,371	454,531
Grand Total	418,590	74,077	90,368	583,035

CLASSES AND SEXES OF POPULATION.

Classes.	Males.	Females.	Total.
White Persons	211,495	207,095	418,590
Colored " —free	34,914	39,163	74,077
" " —slave	—	—	90,368
Total	—	—	583,035

PROGRESSIVE MOVEMENT OF POPULATION.

Date of Census.	White Persons.	Colored Persons. Free.	Slave.	Total Population.	Decennial Increase. Numerical.	Per 100.
1790	208,649	8,043	103 036	319 728	—	—
1800	216,326	19.587	105,635	341,548	21,820	6.8
1810	235,117	33,927	111,502	380 546	38.998	11.4
1820	260,222	39,730	107,398	407.350	26 804	7.0
1830	299,020	45,026	102,994	447,040	39 690	9.7
1840	318,204	62,078	89,737	470,019	22,979	5.1
1850	418,590	74,077	90,368	583,035	113,016	24.0

The whole number of dwellings in the state, in 1850, amounted to 81,708, and of families to 87,384, and hence the number of persons to each dwelling was 7.1, and to each family 6.6. The proportion between dwellings and families was as one to 1.06. The total number of deaths in 1849–50 was 9,594, or in the ratio of one death to every 60.7 persons, the rate of mortality varying from one in 49.6, in Baltimore county, to one in 106 in Caroline county.

Agriculture and mining, with some manufactures, and a good share of the commerce of the Union, employ the majority of the inhabitants. The mineral productions of Maryland consist chiefly of iron and coal. The coal fields which lie in the Cumberland Valley are large and valuable, and since the completion of the great internal improvements to their locality, have become scenes of busy industry. Iron abounds in every section, and sulphuret of copper, ochres, chromes, &c., have been discovered. Porcelain earth and coarser clays occur abundantly in the north-east, and building material is found everywhere. The forests yield timber and wild fruits, the latter of which afford the hogs a plentiful and fattening subsistence. Agriculture flourishes in all sections—tobacco and wheat forming the great staples. As a tobacco growing state Maryland is the fourth in importance. In 1850 there were 21,860 farms and plantations in the state. Manufactures employ a capital of ten or twelve millions of dollars; those of cotton and wool have of late years become very extensive, and in the cotton manufacture this state has progressed wonderfully. Silk, flax, and mixed goods, are also made to some extent. The flouring mills, however, are perhaps the cynosure of Maryland, and certainly no other State of the Union has become so celebrated for its brands, which are appreciated in every market. Tanning and leather factories are numerous, and sugar refining is extensively engaged in. Ship-building is also a considerable branch of industry.

In regard to commerce Maryland enjoys the fifth or sixth position. The exports in 1849–50 amounted in value to $6,967,353, and the imports to $6,124,201, while the shipping employed in the foreign trade for the same period was as follows:

Nationality.	Cleared. Tons.	Entered. Tons.	Total. Tons.
American	89,296	70,427	159,723
Foreign	37,523	29,161	66,684
Total	126,819	99,588	226,407

which was navigated by 9,386 men and boys. The shipping owned within the state in 1850 amounted to 193,087 tons, of which 100,513 tons (13,451 tons navigated by steam power) were engaged in the coasting trade. The ports are Baltimore, Vienna, Oxford, Snow Hill, Annapolis, Town Creek, and St. Mary's—their priority in the list determining their relative importance. The number of vessels built in 1849–50 was 150, and their tonnage 15,964 tons. In 1806 the exports from Maryland were valued at $14,580,905, but in 1821 they had decreased to less than $4,000,000; since that period they have rapidly increased.

The internal trade is considerable; its course being from Baltimore towards the mining regions, and as soon as the railroad to Wheeling is completed, this will be one of the great transit states from the Atlantic to the Valley of the Ohio. The Chesapeake and Ohio Canal, and the Baltimore and Ohio Railroad, are two of the most magnificent works ever undertaken. The canal extends from Georgetown, in the District of Columbia, to Pittsburg, 342 miles, and the railroad from Baltimore to Wheeling. These works are incorporated by the states, Maryland, Virginia, and Pennsylvania. When completed, they will open a vast outlet for the products of the country through which they pass, and be especially useful to the coal mines of Pennsylvania and the northern counties of Maryland and Virginia. The great chain of southern railroads traverses this state in a south-westerly direction, passing through Elkton, Baltimore, Bladensburg, to Washington, &c. Other lines, built and being built, intersect the state in other directions.

Maryland has 24 banks; 12 in Baltimore, and 12 in the rural districts. The condition of those of Baltimore in January, 1850, was as follows:—capital $7,101,056; circulation $2,073,578; deposits $3,648,819; specie $2,113,758; and discounts $10,925,106. The returns of January, 1851, show an increase in the circulation of $208,340, in the deposits of $880,147, in the discounts of $858,680, and in the specie of $196,416, which amounts, added to those of 1850, exhibit the standing of the banks in 1851. The twelve country banks have an aggregate capital of about $1,500,000.

The higher classes of schools are numerous in this state, and in regard to subjects taught their standing is superior, in many respects, to other southern schools. The oldest institution is Washington College, at Chestertown, founded in 1783, which in 1850 had 70 students, and five professors. St. John's College, at Annapolis, which dates from 1784, in 1850 had 30 students, and six professors. St. Mary's, at Baltimore, was founded in 1799, and in 1850 had 122 students, and 20 professors. At Emmetsburg is Mount St. Mary's College, founded in 1830. It had, in 1850, 126 students, and 24 professors. The two last are Roman Catholic Institutions. St. James' College, near Hagerstown, a Protestant Episcopal Institution, founded 1844, had, in 1850, 10 professors, and 32 students. The library of Mount St. Mary's contains upwards of 20,000 volumes, but none of the other College libraries number more than 5,000 volumes. The Medical Schools are—that attached to the University of Maryland, and Washington Medical College, both at Baltimore. In 1850 the former had about 100 students, and the latter 26: at each there are six professors. There are in the state about 200 academies and grammar schools, and about 700 common and primary schools, at which poor children are educated without expense. The amount of public funds distributed to the colleges, academies, and schools in 1850 was $20,099, besides which $1,906 was granted for the support of the indigent deaf and dumb.

The Roman Catholics form a large majority of the people. The Archbishop of Baltimore is the oldest metropolitan of the United States. They have 70 churches, and 10 other stations. The Episcopalians are also very numerous, and have 123 ministers, and 88 churches, which, however, are not so numerously attended as those of the Catholics. The Baptists have 22 churches, 20 preachers, and about 2,000 communicants, and the Anti-Mission Baptists have 24 churches and 17 preachers. The Presbyterians have several churches, and there are some few Methodists, Unitarians, Universalists, and other denominations.

BALTIMORE is the largest city of the state, and the third in point of population in the United States. It is situated on a bay that sets up from the Patapsco River, 14 miles from its entrance into Chesapeake Bay. This is the city of monuments. The "Washington Monument," which stands on an elevation of 150 feet, is a most imposing structure. It is a column, 200 feet high, including the base, surmounted by a colossal statue of Washington, 13 feet high. The monument is built of white marble; the base is 50 feet square, and the column 20 feet in diameter, with a spiral staircase in its interior. The "Battle Monument" is also constructed of white marble, with a base of Egyptian architecture. The column is in the form of a Roman fascis, on the bands of which are encircled the names of those who fell in defending the city when attacked by the British, in 1814. The entire height of the monument is fifty feet. Baltimore has several public buildings and churches of much beauty, among which are the City Hall, Court-House, and the Penitentiary. The Roman Catholic Cathedral, and the Unitarian Church, corner of Charles and Franklin streets, are both elegant specimens of architecture.

The commerce of Baltimore is extensive, embracing, as it does, besides that of Maryland, a large portion of the trade of north-western Pennsylvania and other interior states. In 1850, its tonnage was 86,022. It is the greatest flour market in the Union, and has a large export trade in tobacco. Its manufactures have, however, become as important as its commerce. The amount of capital employed in this branch of industry, is upwards of $4,000,000. The products are chiefly flour, tobacco, cigars, cotton and woollen goods, powder, paper, iron and copper ware, glass, machinery, &c.

The city was chiefly laid out in 1729, and as it was settled principally by Catholics, that denomination is still the most numerous. The population in 1840, was 134,379, and in 1850, 169,054.

ANNAPOLIS, a small city on the Severn River, two miles from its entrance into Chesapeake Bay, is the capital of the state. Lat. 38° 58′ 35″ N., and long. 76° 33′ W. This city derives all its claim to notice from the fact that it contains the state buildings; otherwise it would be hidden among the obscure villages of the country. Population, in 1850, 4,198. There are some interesting scenes connected with Annapolis, however, and it was several times occupied by the old Congress during the revolution. Here Washington resigned his commission to that august body.

FREDERICK is a city of some importance, and ranks as second in the state. The Baltimore and Ohio Railroad passes through it. Population, 6,037.

Hagerstown, Williamsport, Bladensburg, Westminster, Cumberland, &c., are all places of some consideration, and important as entrepôts of commerce.

The ports of delivery, besides Baltimore and Annapolis, are St. Mary's, on the Potomac; Nottingham, on the Pawtuxent; Havre de Grace, at the mouth of the Susquehannah; Chestertown, on the Chester River; Oxford, on Treadhaven Creek, which flows into the Choptank, near its mouth; Vienna, on the Nanticoke; and Snowhill, on the Pocomoke. Considerable shipping is owned at all these places.

In Maryland the Governor is elected by the people triennially. The state is divided into three districts—the Eastern, Southern, and Northwestern. The Governor is elected from the districts alternately. He must be at least thirty years of age, and must have resided in his own district three years next preceding his election.

The legislature consists of a SENATE and HOUSE OF REPRESENTATIVES. The Senate is composed of twenty-one members, elected by the people for six years, one-third being renewed every two years. Members must have attained the age of twenty-five years, and have resided in the city or county for which they are chosen, three years next preceding their election. The House of Delegates consists of seventy-eight members, elected annually. Delegates must be at least twenty-one years of age, and have resided in their own county one year previous to election.

The judiciary power is vested in a Court of Appeals, a Court of Chancery, and several inferior courts. All judges have their appointment from the Governor, with the consent of the Senate, and hold their offices during good behavior.

The right of suffrage belongs to every white male citizen of twenty-one years of age and upwards, who has resided in the state one year, and in the county where he votes, six months next preceding the election. The elections take place annually, on the first Wednesday in October, and the legislature meets at Annapolis on the last Monday of December.

The resources of the state treasury for the year ending 1st December, 1849, amounted to $1,631,385, of which $315,945 was a balance from last financial year, and the expenditures amounted to $1,146,492, leaving in the treasury $484,893. The chief sources of income were from direct taxes $531,598, licenses $135,834, railroads $127,019, and in lesser sums—auction duties, bank dividends, fines, stamps, canal revenues, tobacco inspection and taxes on stocks, inheritances, commissions, insurances, protests commissions, &c., and tax for colonization of colored persons. The expenditures were—for the support of the executive, legislature and judiciary, state colonization society ($10,000), interest on public debt ($715,556), funded arrears of interest ($260,308), colleges, &c., and several contingent and miscellaneous expenses.

The nominal amount of State Debt, Dec. 1, 1849, was		$15,909,981
From which deduct Balt. & Ohio R. R. Loan	$4,197,000	
" " Tobacco Loan, . . .	163,689	
" " Susquehannah and Tide Water Canal Loan . .	1,000,000	
		5,360,689
And an actual debt remains of		$10,549,292

which includes $618,619 funded arrears of interest. The sinking fund at this period amounted to $1,892,837, which, deducted from the above debt, will exhibit the actual liabilities of the state. To meet these liabilities, in addition to the proceeds of an annual tax, the state holds $5,292,225 of productive property, consisting of stocks, bonds, &c., and $15,495,452 of unproductive property. Since 1846, Maryland, which had suspended payment of interest on her public liabilities, has resumed, and, besides paying up accruing interest, will, early in 1854, by means of the sinking fund, have paid off all arrears. Much of the debt cannot be redeemed for 20 or 40 years, on account of the terms of the loans, but will be purchased in the market by the state long before maturity. The action of this state in reference to its liabilities is worthy of imitation in other portions of the Union.

The militia of the state consists of five divisions, and the whole number of men enrolled is 46,864, of which number the infantry comprises 41,952 men, the cavalry 2,594, the artillery 1,640, and the riflemen 678. The governor is *ex officio* Commander-in-chief.

Maryland was the third English colony planted in America. In 1632, this territory was granted by Charles I. to Sir George Calvert, Lord Baltimore, a Roman Catholic and an eminent statesman, who had been secretary to James I.; but before the patent was completed, Lord Baltimore died, and the instrument, dated 20th June, 1632, was given to his eldest son Cecil, who succeeded to his titles, and who, for upwards of forty years, directed, as proprietor, the affairs of the colony.

Leonard Calvert, brother of Cecil, Lord Baltimore, was appointed first Governor; and he, together with about 200 persons, Roman Catholics, commenced the settlement of St. Mary's, in 1634. A free toleration of religion was established, and a system of equity and humanity was practised with regard to the Indian tribes.

Maryland was one of the foremost of the revolutionary states, and supplied to the army during that eventful struggle, 13,912 men. In the last war with England this state suffered severely, and was devastated by fire and the sword. Baltimore commemorates the patriotism of her brave citizens who fell defending the liberties of their country, by a splendid monument.

THE DISTRICT OF COLUMBIA.

Or, Federal District of the United States, as originally laid out, and as it remained until 1846, occupied an area of ten miles square on both sides of the Potomac, about 120 miles from its mouth, and was ceded to the United States by Virginia and Maryland, in 1789, of which states respectively it had hitherto formed parts. It was thus granted for the purpose of establishing therein a Federal Capital and a seat for the General Government. In 1846, the portion on the Virginia shore of the river was retroceded to that state, so that at the present time the district comprehends only one county, that of Washington, in which are situated the cities of Washington and Georgetown.

The population of the district in 1850 was 57,687, or 820 persons to each square mile; and its general statistics were as follows:

Cities, etc.	Dwellings.	Families.	White Persons.	Colored Persons. Free.	Colored Persons. Slave.	Total Popula.	Farms in culti.	Produc. Estab.
Washington	6,345	6,679	29,815	8,073	2.113	40,001	29	356
Georgetown	1,174	1,215	6,081	1,569	725	8,366	9	59
Country parts	398	398	2,131	340	849	3,320	226	12
Total	7,917	8,292	38,027	9,973	3,687	51,687	264	427

CLASSES AND SEXES OF POPULATION.

Classes.	Males.	Females.	Total.
White Persons	18,548	19,479	38,027
Colored " —free	4,210	5,763	9,973
" " —slave	1,422	2,265	3,687
Total	24,180	27,507	51,687

PROGRESSIVE MOVEMENT OF POPULATION.

Date of Census.	White Persons.	Colored Persons. Free.	Colored Persons. Slave.	Total Population.	Decennial Increase. Numerical.	Decennial Increase. Per 100.
1800	10,066	783	3,244	14,093	—	—
1810	16,079	2,849	5,395	24,023	9,930	70.4
1820	22,614	4,048	6,077	33,039	9,016	37.5
1830	27,563	6,152	6,119	39,834	6,795	20.6
1840	30,657	8,361	4,694	43,712	3,878	9.7
1850 *	38,027	9,973	3,687	51,687	7,975	18.2

The government of the district is vested entirely in Congress; but the laws of the state from which it was taken, with few exceptions, are continued in force, as they existed at the period of the cession. A Circuit Court, consisting of a Chief Justice and two associate Judges is established, which sits at Washington. Appeals and writs of error go from this court directly to the Supreme Court of the United States. An orphan's court is also instituted. The county has justices of the peace, and there is a mar-

* The county of Alexandria, which was re-annexed to Virginia in 1846, contained in 1850 10,108 inhabitants; and the population in the district, had it remained in tact, would now have been 61,695, and the increase 18,008, or 41.2 per centum. The population of Alexandria in 1840 was 9,967.

shal and attorney for the district. The Supreme Court sits at Washington on the first Monday in December, annually.

The **CITY OF WASHINGTON**, the Federal Capital and seat of the supreme government, is situated on the east bank of the Potomac. Lat. 38° 52′ 43″ N., and long. 76° 55′ 30″ W. Population, in 1840, 23,364; and in 1850 40,001.

The situation is one of the most picturesque and beautiful in the Union. The city stands at the junction of the Potomac and Anacosta, and is encompassed by forest clad hills, from which the view of the surrounding country and the silvery wanderings of the rivers, interspersed with numerous villas and shady retreats, is truly enchanting, and in every way worthy to be the metropolitan district of a nation of freemen.

The city itself is planned out on a most magnificent scale, and if ever completed as designed, it must eventually become one of the finest cities of the world. The ground on which it is built is elevated about 40 feet above the river, from which it has a gradual ascent. It is regularly laid out in streets running due north and south, intersected by others at right angles. Besides these streets, which are from 80 to 110 feet wide, there are avenues from 130 to 160 feet wide, which diverge from centres in various parts of the city, crossing the other streets transversely. The avenues are named after the several states of the Union; the streets which run east and west after the letters of the alphabet, as A street east, and B street west, &c., and those which run north and south are numbered 1, 2, 3, &c., as First street north, and Second street south, &c. At the points from which the avenues diverge, are spacious squares. The ground embraced in the plan of the city is very extensive, but only a small portion of it is yet occupied by buildings. Five of the avenues radiate from the president's house, and five from the capitol, which afford ready communication from all parts to these central and important points. Pennsylvania avenue, extending between these edifices, is the most compactly built and the handsomest thoroughfare of the city.

The "CAPITOL," which is finely situated on an eminence, commands a view of every part of the city and a considerable portion of the adjacent country. This is a grand and imposing structure, and a fitting place for the meeting of the nation's representatives. It stands on an elevation 72 feet above tide water, and is the first object that attracts the eye on approaching the city. The building is of white free-stone, and occupies an area of one and a half acres. Including the wings, which are each 100 feet front, it is 362 feet long, and 121 feet in depth. The projection on the east or main front, inclusive of the steps, is 65 feet, and on the west, 83 feet. The first is ornamented with a splendid portico of 22 lofty Corinthian columns, and the latter with a like portico, supported by ten columns. The building is surmounted by a splendid dome, 120 feet high, under which, in the middle of the building, is the rotunda, 95 feet in diameter and 95 feet in height, and on the walls the magnificent national paintings of Trumbull are hung. The room is also adorned with various *alto-relievo* groups, each representing some great national event. The colossal statue of Washington, by Greenough, is now placed in the rotunda. The congressional library-room, on the west of the rotunda, is 92 feet long, 34 feet broad, and 36 feet high, and contains from 30,000 to 40,000 volumes, and a large collection of medals, paintings, statuary, &c. The Senate chamber, in the north wing of the building, is 78 feet long and of a semi-circular form. Under this is the room in which the Supreme Court sits. The House of Representatives is in the opposite wing, and is somewhat larger than the Senate chamber, and semi-circular. These several apartments are gorgeously furnished and ornamented with statuary and paintings, presenting to the eye a splendid realization of national extravagance.

The "WHITE HOUSE," the residence of the President of the United States, is situated at the junction of Pennsylvania, New-York, Connecticut and Vermont avenues, and is a splendid free-stone built edifice. The building is 170 feet long and 85 feet deep, and two stories high. It is ornamented on the front, facing on La Fayette Square, with a beautiful Ionic portico, and the garden front is embellished by a circular colonnade of six Ionic columns. The interior is splendidly arranged, and furnished in a style becoming the chief magistrate of a great nation.

Adjoining the president's mansion are the extensive buildings appropriated by the department of war, navy, state and treasury. The new treasury building is 300 feet long, and in the rear is a wing 100 feet long. Along the front is a splendid colonnade supported by thirty-two columns of massive dimensions. The "General Post-Office is a large and beautiful marble building, with two wings, and is highly adorned by large fluted columns of marble. It is situated corner of North and Seventh streets. The Patent-Office is also a large and splendid building, and exhibits great architectural skill. The upper part is at present appropriated as a depository of the National Institution. The Smithsonian Institute, when completed, will be a splendid edifice, and add greatly to the importance of Washington, and, at the same time, be a lasting monument of the munificence of the man, whose treasure was bequeathed for its foundation and endowment.

The navy-yard, about three-quarters of a mile from the capitol, has an area of 27 acres, and is enclosed by a substantial brick wall. Within this enclosure are the officers' quarters, shops, warehouses, two large ship houses, and an armory. These are all fine establishments of their kind, and are kept in the best of order. The navy magazine is an extensive building of brick, in which are employed a large number of artisans for the manufacture of combustibles for warlike purposes.

Within the limits of the city there are 27 churches, belonging to the different denominations. The variety, skill and taste in their architectural designs are highly creditable, and conduce much to the general symmetry of the city, and its appearance from a distance.

Numerous institutions of a benevolent, religious, educational and philanthropic character dignify the moral aspect of the capital. There are two orphan asylums, the Washington and St. Vincent's, which are supported, one by the ladies of the city and the other by the Sisters of Charity. The Howard Society is an establishment for supplying poor females with work at equitable prices.

Among the public buildings of Washington the theatres and places of amusement are not the least important. The Washington Theatre, the National Theatre, the Assembly Rooms, King's Picture Gallery, &c., are the most conspicuous of this class.

Columbia College is an excellent institution, and the building is an ornament to the city. It is situated on an elevation, commanding a splendid view of the surrounding country. The Theological Seminary, the Columbian Institute, the American Historical Society, the Columbian Horticultural Society, the City Library, the Athenæum, the National Institution for the promotion of science, and some others, afford to the citizens every advantage in the pursuit of knowledge, and the edifices are highly ornamented and rich in taste and design.

The "City-Hall," intended for the use of the corporate authorities of Washington, is yet in an unfinished state, but when completed, will furnish another magnificent structure in addition to the many which now adorn the metropolis. The penitentiary and city jail are large buildings.

The "Congressional Cemetery" is worthy of note. This last resting place of the "Worthies of America," occupies an area of ten acres, near the eastern branch of the Potomac, and about a mile and a half from the capitol. The grounds are surrounded by a high brick wall, and have a considerable elevation above the river, commanding an extensive prospect of the beautiful scenery which surrounds the city. They are tastefully laid out with ornamental trees and shubbery, and many of the tombs, enclosing the ashes of the eloquent dead, are remarkable for taste and appropriateness. Here rest some of the noblest and bravest of patriots and statesmen, whose voices have re-echoed through the land the watchword of freedom, and whose history is blended with the fairest page of their country's annals.

Washington is connected with the north and south by railway, and is accessible from the Atlantic for ships of the largest class.

During the last war with Great Britain this city was destroyed by fire, and many of the public records and works of art either consumed or carried off by the soldiers. This wanton act, perpetrated by Gen. Ross, who soon after met a retributive death at Baltimore, will ever remain a record of disgrace and infamy against a nation boasting of the highest civilization and humanity. No sophistry can palliate—no necessity could justify so foul a deed. Washington, however, soon recovered from the disaster, and is now advancing with rapid strides, and its population is increasing in a steady progression.

GEORGETOWN is divided from Washington by Rock Creek, and is distant from the capitol three miles. It is beautifully located, and from its elevated position commands a view of the splendid panorama of the Potomac and the surrounding country. It is a place of some consideration, enjoying a fair share of manufactures and commerce. The public buildings consist chiefly of some educational establishments, churches and public offices; the private residences are generally well built, and have a new and clean appearance. The Roman Catholic College is the most extensive building, and holds a high station for efficiency. The city is laid out regularly. Georgetown may be considered as a suburb of Washington. The Chesa peake and Ohio Canal commences at this place. The population has been almost stationary for twenty years, during which it has varied only from 7,360 in 1830, to 7,312, in 1840, being a diminution of 48. In 1850 it had increased to 8,366.

THE SOUTHERN STATES.

UNDER this head are included the States of Virginia, North Carolina, South Carolina, Georgia, and the new state of Florida. These occupy a territory of 998 miles in length, from the line of Mason and Dixon to the southern point of Florida, and lie between the latitudes of 40° and 25° 30′ N., and the meridians of 74° and 89° W. longitude. They are bounded north by Pennsylvania; north-east and east by Maryland and the Atlantic Ocean; south by the Gulf of Mexico, and west by the Gulf and the States of Alabama, Tennessee, Kentucky and Ohio. The area of the whole is 251,786 square miles, or 161,143,055 acres.

The coasts of this region from the Potomac on the Atlantic, round the peninsula of Florida, to the Pearl River, on the Gulf of Mexico, are about 1,150 miles in length, and are indented with numerous inlets and bays, and lined with a large number of islands and reefs, which render navigation difficult and dangerous. No rivers of much commercial importance are found south of Chesapeake Bay, and few that furnish channels sufficiently capacious and deep for large shipping, and, as a consequence, little foreign commerce belongs directly to this section. The coasting trade, however, is very extensive, and somewhat compensates for these deprivations.

The inhabitants of the Southern States may be said to be entirely devoted to agricultural pursuits. Some manufactures, however, exist, and manufacturing industry is steadily progressing, especially in the more northerly of these states. The great staples are cotton, rice and tobacco. Some wheat and corn, perhaps sufficient for home consumption, are raised. The whole region being extensively covered with pine, is rich in pitch, tar and turpentine, which are sent northward in large quantities, and lumber is an article of export. In several of the states gold has been discovered, of which no inconsiderable amount is annually sent to the mint for coinage; and in Virginia, coal fields of a vast area exist, and in many parts this combustible is used as a common fuel, and for manufacturing purposes.

The Southern States were settled somewhat earlier than the northern and middle districts, and in the main by persons from the same countries. The increase of population, however, has not been so rapid as in either. The annexed table, the result of decennial cenuses, will exhibit with precision the amount of population at each period:

Date.	Virginia.	N. Carolina.	S. Carolina.	Georgia.	Florida.	Total.
1790	748,308	393,751	249,073	82,548	—	1,473,680
1800	880,200	478,103	345,591	162,101	—	1,865,995
1810	974,622	555,500	415,115	252,433	—	2,197,670
1820	1,065,379	638,829	502,741	340,987	—	2,547,876
1830	1,211,405	737,987	581,185	516,823	34,730	3,082,130
1840	1,239,797	753,419	594,398	691,392	54,477	3,333,483
1850	1,421,661	868,072	668,507	905,999	87,401	3,951,640

It is a remarkable fact that, with the exception of the few cities on the Atlantic coast, there are in these states no collections of people into villages exceeding in number 5,000. They are scattered over the country, or aggregated in small masses on plantations. This disposition of the population has a decided effect on their character, and tends to that personal independence we observe in all their actions. Without systematic organization, each inhabitant is free to act for himself, and, untrammelled by the usages of society, enjoys almost a primitive state of existence.

Some few Indians still remain in these states, but the bulk of the tribes have been transported to the west of the Mississippi.

THE STATE OF VIRGINIA.

Virginia, or the "Old Dominion," as it is popularly termed, is the largest of the Atlantic states, and has been the longest time settled by Europeans of any portion of the present United States, with the exception of those parts settled by the Spaniards. It is situated between 36° 33′ and 40° 43′ N. lat., and between 75° 25′ and 83° 40′ W. long., and is bounded north by Pennsylvania and Maryland; east by the Atlantic Ocean; south by North Carolina and Tennessee, and west by Kentucky and Ohio, the three last of which formerly constituted portions of its territory. It is 408 miles long and 212 broad, and has an area of 64,000 square miles, or 40,960,000 acres.

This extensive state may be divided into four parts, essentially differing from each other. The first, extending from the sea-coast to the termination of tide-water, at Fredericksburg, Richmond, &c., is low and flat—in some places fenny, and others sandy; and on the margins of the rivers composed of a rich loam, covered with a luxuriant, and even rank, vegetation. This division has been formed by a comparatively recent alluvion; marine shells and bones are everywhere found near the surface of the earth. The next division extends from the head of tide-water to the Blue Ridge. The surface, near tide-water, is level; higher up the rivers, it becomes swelling, and, near the mountains, often abrupt and broken: the soil is divided into sections of very unequal quality, parallel to each other, and extending across the state. The parallel of Chesterfield, Henrico, Hanover, &c., is a thin, sandy, and, except on the rivers, an unproductive soil. That of Goochland, Cumberland, Prince Edward, Halifax, &c., is generally fertile: Fluvanna, Buckingham, Campbell, and Pittsylvania, are but poor; and Culpepper, Orange, Albemarle, Bedford, &c., have a rich, though frequently a stony and broken soil, on a substratum of tenacious, red-colored clay. The scenery of the upper part of this section is highly picturesque and romantic. The third division is the valley between the Blue Ridge and North and Alleghany Mountains, and extends, with little interruption, from the Potomac to Tennessee and North Carolina. It is narrower, but of greater length than either of the preceding sub-divisions; the soil is a mould formed on a bed of limestone, which often appears above the surface, in veins parallel to the mountains, and making every possible angle with the horizon. The surface of this valley is sometimes broken by sharp and solitary mountains, detached from the general chain, the sides of which, nearly bare, or but thinly covered with blasted pines, form disagreeable objects in the landscape. The bed of the valley is fertile, producing good crops of Indian corn, wheat, rye, oats, buckwheat, hemp, flax, &c. The fourth and last division extends from the Alleghany Mountains to the Ohio River, and is wild and broken, being in some places fertile, but generally barren. Here are mines of lead, iron, coal, and salt.

The forest, near the sea, is composed of pine, oak, cypress, cedar, juniper, holly, &c.; above tide-water, of pine, oak, poplar, hickory, locust, chesnut, gum, ash, sycamore, elm, &c.; in the valley, of nearly the same, with maple, scaly-bark hickory, fir, arbor vitæ, &c. In the more western parts of the state, buck-eye, sugar maple, and some other trees become common; but the body of the forest is the same as between the mountains and tide water; except, indeed, that the western forests are far more heavy, more lofty, and less intermixed with copse. In respect to mineral productions, few are found in the first zone, the soil being alluvial; the second section contains pit-coal of a good quality, within 20 miles of Richmond, on James River; the third region has many inexhaustible mines of iron ore, of a fine quality; and the fourth is distinguished for its various mineral treasures.

The Alleghany Mountains pass through the western part of the state, from south-west to north-east; the Blue Ridge is east of the Alleghany range, and runs parallel with it, dividing the state into two parts, nearly equal. The peaks of Otter, in the Blue Ridge, are 4,260 feet high, and are the highest land in the state.

The principal rivers are Potomac, Rappahannock, York, and James, which rise east of the Alleghany Mountains, and flow into Chesapeake Bay; and the Big Sandy, the Great Kanawha, and the Little Kanawha, which rise west of the mountains, and flow into the Ohio; the Shenandoah runs between the mountains, and discharges itself into the Potomac.

The natural bridge over Cedar Creek, in Rockbridge county, is one of the most magnificent curiosities in the world. It is a huge rock, in the form of an arch, 90 feet long, 60 wide, and from 40 to 70 feet deep, thrown over the river more than 200 feet above its surface, and supported by abutments so gracefully curved, so long and light, and springing, as to appear scarcely more heavy than the capital of a Corinthian pillar. There is another natural bridge in Scott county, of nearly the same height, but less beautiful. The falling spring, in Bath county, forms a beautiful cascade, streaming from a perpendicular precipice 200 feet high. The passage of the Potomac through the Blue Ridge at Harper's Ferry, is celebrated for its grandeur and magnificence. There are many mineral springs in Virginia. The hot and warm springs of Bath county, the sweet springs of Monroe, the sulphur springs of Greenbriar, those of Montgomery, and the baths of Berkely county, are much frequented.

In consequence of the great extent and varied surface of Virginia, the climate is very different in different situations. In the greater part of the country, below the head of tide-water, the summers are hot and sultry, and the winters are mild, though the cold is sometimes severe. From the head of tide-water to the mountains, the air is more elastic and pure, and both summers and winters are several degrees of temperature below that of the low country. Among the mountains, the summer weather is generally fine, though the heat is sometimes very oppressive; to the westward the climate is more mild than to the eastward. Except in the neighborhood of stagnant waters in the low country, Virginia has, upon the whole, a salubrious climate; the greatest heat at Monticello, near the middle of the state, has been 98°, and the greatest cold 6° below 0. The mean annual temperature at Williamsburg is about 57°.

Virginia is divided into two districts and 140 counties, and in 1850 contained 1,421,081 inhabitants, or one person to every 28 acres; and their distribution to the several counties was in the following proportions:

EASTERN VIRGINIA.

COUNTIES.	White Persons.	Colored Persons. Free.	Colored Persons. Slave.	Total Popula.
Accomac	9,742	3,161	4,987	17,890
Albemarle	11,876	586	13,338	25,800
Alexandria	7,218	1,408	1,382	10,008
Amelia	2,794	157	6,819	9,770
Amherst	6,350	393	5,953	12,699
Appomattox	4,210	184	4,799	9,193
Bedford	13,556	463	10,061	24,080
Brunswick	4,895	543	8,456	13,894
Buckingham	5,426	250	8,161	13,837
Campbell	11,538	841	10,866	23,245
Caroline	6,892	903	10,661	18,456
Charles City	1,664	772	2,764	5,200
Charlotte	4,605	362	8,988	13,955
Chesterfield	8,402	468	8,616	17,486
Culpepper	5,111	488	6,683	12,282
Cumberland	3,083	339	6,329	9,751
Dinwiddie	10,985	3,253	11,468	25,706
Elizabeth City	2,341	97	2,148	4,586
Essex	3,025	419	6,762	10,206
Fairfax	6,835	597	3,250	10,682
Fauquier	9,875	643	10,350	20,868
Fluvanna	4,533	217	4,737	9,487
Franklin	11,638	66	5,726	17,430
Gloucester	4,290	680	5,557	10,527
Goochland	3,854	653	5,845	10,352
Green	2,667	34	1,699	4,400
Greensville	1,731	123	3,785	5,639
Halifax	11,006	504	14,462	25,972
Hanover	6,541	219	8,393	15,153
Henrico	8,548	1,272	6,135	15,955
Henry	5,324	208	3,340	8,872
James City	1,489	663	1,868	4,020
Isle of Wight	4,724	1,234	3,395	9,353
King & Queen	4,094	461	5,764	10,319
King George	2,304	265	3,403	5,972
King William	2,702	346	5,371	8,419
Lancaster	1,805	263	2,640	4,708
Loudon	15,081	1,354	5,641	22,076
Louisa	6,423	404	9,864	16,691
Lunenburg	4,310	195	7,187	11,692
Madison	4,458	149	4,724	9,331
Mathews	3,644	147	2,923	6,714
Mechlenburg	7,256	912	12,429	20,597
Middlesex	1,903	149	2,342	4,394
Nansemond	5,425	2,143	4,715	12,283
Nelson	6,478	138	6,142	13,258
New Kent	2,221	433	3,410	6,064
Norfolk City	9,113	912	4,295	14,320
Norfolk Co.	4,907	823	4,354	10,084
Northampton	3,105	745	3,648	7,498
Northumberl'd	3,072	519	3,755	7,346
Nottoway	2,251	136	6,050	8,437
Orange	3,902	184	5,921	10,007
Patrick	7,197	88	2,324	9,609
Pittsylvania	15,263	735	12,798	28,796
Portsmouth	6,345	530	1,751	8,626
Powhattan	2,532	364	5,282	8,178
Prince Edward	4,177	488	7,192	11,857
Prince George	2,670	518	4,408	7,596
Prince William	5,081	530	2,498	8,129
Princess Ann	4,280	259	3,130	7,669
Rappahannock	5,642	296	3,844	9,782
Richm'd City	15,184	2,391	9,907	27,482
Richmond Co.	3,462	709	2,277	6,448
Southampton	5,971	1,795	5,755	13,521
Spottsylvania	6,903	527	7,481	14,911
Stafford	4,415	318	3,311	8,044
Surry	2,215	985	2,479	5,679
Sussex	3,086	742	5,992	9,820
Warwick	598	43	641	1,282
Westmorland	3,410	1,113	3,557	7,080
York	1,825	454	2,181	4,460
Total, E. Vir.	401,617	45,786	409,295	856,698

WESTERN VIRGINIA.

COUNTIES.	White Persons.	Colored Persons. Free.	Colored Persons. Slave.	Total Popula.
Alleghany	2,763	58	694	3,515
Augusta	19,024	533	5,053	24,610
Barbour	8,671	221	113	9,005
Bath	2,436	43	947	3,426
Berkeley	9,566	249	1,956	11,761
Boone	3,054	—	183	3,237
Botetourt	10,749	423	3,736	14,908
Braxton	4,123	—	89	4,212
Brooke	4,923	100	31	5,054
Cabell	5,904	6	389	6,299
Carroll	5,726	29	154	5,909
Clarke	3,615	123	3,614	7,352
Doddridge	2,639	80	31	2,750
Fayette	3,782	17	156	3,955
Floyd	6,000	15	433	6,448
Frederick	12,769	912	2,294	15,975
Giles	5,859	54	657	6,570
Gilmer	3,403	—	72	3,475
Grayson	6,142	36	499	6,977
Greenbrier	8,549	156	1,317	10,022
Hampshire	12,389	214	1,433	14,036
Hancock	4,040	7	3	4,050
Hardy	7,930	353	1,260	9,543
Harrison	11,214	26	488	11,728
Highland	2,853	10	364	3,227
Jackson	6,480	11	53	6,544
Jefferson	10,476	540	4,341	15,357
Kanawha	12,002	201	3,140	15,353
Lee	9,440	40	787	10,267
Lewis	9,621	42	368	10,031
Logan	3,533	—	87	3,620
Marion	10,438	20	94	10,552
Marshall	10,050	39	49	10,138
Mason	6,843	49	647	7,539
Mercer	4,018	27	177	4,222
Monongahela	12,092	119	176	12,387
Monroe	9,062	81	1,061	10,204
Montgomery	6,822	66	1,471	8,359
Morgan	3,431	3	123	3,557
Nicholas	3,889	1	73	3,963
Ohio	17,609	235	164	18,008
Page	6,332	311	957	7,600
Pendleton	5,443	30	332	5,805
Pocahontas	3,308	23	267	3,598
Preston	11,574	47	87	11,688
Pulaski	3,613	34	1,471	5,118
Putnam	4,693	10	632	5,335
Raleigh	1,735	7	23	1,765
Randolph	5,003	39	201	5,243
Ritchie	3,886	—	16	3,902
Roanoke	5,813	154	2,510	8,477
Rockbridge	11,484	364	4,197	16,045
Rockingham	17,408	465	2,331	20,204
Russell	10,867	70	982	11,919
Scott	9,325	31	473	9,829
Shenandoah	12,595	262	911	13 768
Smythe	6.901	197	1,064	8,062
Tazewell	8,807	75	1,060	9,942

COUNTIES.	White Persons.	Colored Persons. Free.	Slave.	Total Popula.
Taylor	5.030	69	168	5,267
Tyler	5.456	4	38	5 498
Warren	4,492	367	1,748	6.607
Washington	12,372	109	2,131	14,612
Wayne	4,654	7	189	4,850
Wetzel	4,261	6	17	4,284
Wirt	3,319	2	32	3,353
Wood	9,008	69	373	9,450
Wyoming	1,583	1	61	1,645
Wythe	9,618	221	2,185	12,024
Total W. Vir.	493.687	8,043	63,233	564,963
Total E. Vir.	401,617	45,786	409,295	856,368
Grand Total	895,304	53,829	472,528	1,421,661

CLASSES AND SEXES OF POPULATION.

Classes.	Males.	Females.	Total.
White Persons	451,552	443,752	845,304
Colored " —free	25,843	27,986	53,829
" " —slave	—	—	472,528
Total	—	—	1,421,661

PROGRESSIVE MOVEMENT OF POPULATION.

Date of Census.	White Persons.	Colored Persons. Free.	Slave.	Total Population.	Decennial Increase. Numerical.	Per 100
1790	442,115	12,766	293,427	748,308	—	—
1800	514,280	20,124	345,796	880,200	131,892	17.6
1810	551,534	30,570	392,518	974,622	94,422	10.7
1820	603,087	37,139	425,153	1,065,379	90,757	9.3
1830	694,300	47,348	469,757	1,211,405	146,026	13.7
1840	740,958	49,852	448,987	1,239,797	28,392	2.3
1850	895,304	53,829	472,528	1,421,661	181,864	14.6

The number of dwellings in the state in 1850 was 165,815, and of families 167,530, being a proportion of about 8.8 persons to each dwelling and family. The deaths in 1849–50 averaged one in every 72 persons. The relative social and industrial statistics of the two divisions of the state are exhibited in the annexed table:

District.	Dwellings.	Families.	Inhabitants.	Farms.	Manuf.	Deaths, 1849–50.
Eastern Virginia	82,691	83,729	856,698	37,741	2,293	13,465
Western "	83,124	83,801	564,963	39,272	2,140	5,888
Total	165,815	167,530	1,421,661	77,013	4,433	19,053

If the population of Virginia be divided into 100 parts, it will be found that about 76 parts obtain their subsistence from agriculture, 12 from manufactures and trades, 2 from mining, 4 from commerce, and the residue from other employments.

The mines of Virginia have of late years become very productive. Coal is principally found in the western counties, and is of every quality, from anthracite to the highly bituminous and cannel; and iron of the finest description is found in the same district. In 1840 the production of wrought iron from all the forges and rolling mills was 5,886 tons, but in 1850 it had increased to 15,328 tons, in the manufacture of which, 17,296 tons pig iron, 2,500 tons blooms, 66,515 tons mineral coal, and 103,000 bushels of charcoal, in all valued at $591,448, had been used, and employment given to 1,295 hands. The capital invested in this interest is $791,211, and the value of the product set down at $1,254,995. The amount of pig and cast iron produced from the furnaces is about 28,000 tons annually. The salt works of the Kanawha are more extensive than any others of the Union. Gold is also found at the base of the Blue Ridge, and lead, plumbago, etc., are in abundance. Gypsum, porcelain, and other clays, with building material, etc.; slate, and indeed almost all the more useful minerals are produced in one or other part of the state.

The grain crop of Virginia consists principally of Indian corn, wheat, and oats; little of rye, barley, or buckwheat is grown. The finest wheat is that produced west of the mountains; but the best brands of flour are those of Richmond. Of the staple crops, tobacco is by far the most important; cotton and flax, however, are by no means of trifling amount, though not produced in so large quantities as in some other states. The cotton crops average 23,000 bales; live stock, which in this state finds noble ranges of pasture land and a congenial climate, is abundant; and the products of animals are large and valuable. The wool of Virginia is excellent, and stands well in the markets. Virginia is also a great "hog state," and in the western district the annual slaughter is immense. Bacon, cheese, and butter are largely exported. In 1850 there were 77,013 farms under cultivaion—37,741 in the east, and 39,272 in the west.

As a manufacturing state, Virginia holds the fifth or sixth rank in the United States. Its iron manufactures are the most important, and embrace machinery, hardware, cutlery, fire-arms, etc. Cotton and woollen manufactures are also important. In 1850 there were in the state 27 cotton mills, the capital invested therein amounted to $1,908,900, and the number of hands employed was 2,963; the raw material used was valued at $828,375, and the product at $1,486,880. There was also manufactured 1,755,915 pounds of yarn. The capital invested in woollen manufactures was $392,640, the raw material was valued at $488,899; hands employed, 668; value of products, $841,013. Mixed goods and manufactures of silk, flax, etc., are made to a considerable amount. In the manufacture of tobacco about $2,000,000 are invested. The number of productive establishments, manufacturing to the value of $500 and upwards annually, was in 1850, 4,433—2,293 in the eastern district, and 2,140 in the western.

Virginia exported directly to foreign countries in the year ending 30th June, 1850, domestic articles to the value of $3,413,158, and foreign articles to the value of $2,488—total $3,415,646; and its imports from foreign countries were valued at $426,599. The shipping entered amounted to 30,965 tons—12,190 American and 18,775 foreign, and the shipping cleared amounted to 65,458 tons—42,091 American and 23,367 foreign. The chief ports are Richmond, Norfolk, and Alexandria—Petersburg, Tappahannock, and Cherrystone are of minor importance. The registered shipping owned in the state amounts to 18,042 tons. The coasting trade is considerable, and perhaps three times the amount of the foreign trade; the imports coastwise are not less than $12,000,000, and the exports are little less in value. The principal articles exported are tobacco and flour, also firewood, rosin, turpentine, etc. The enrolled and licensed shipping owned at the several ports, including those on the Ohio River, amounted in 1850, to 55,007 tons. Eight states export to foreign countries more than Virginia, and eleven import to a greater amount. The shipping built in Virginia in 1849–50 amounted to 3,584 tons in 34 vessels.

In 1850 there were completed in this state 565 miles of railroads, and 418 miles of canals and navigation improvements; and there were in course of construction 390 miles of railroads, and upwards of 200 miles of plank-roads. The principal railroads were the Richmond, Fredericksburg, and Potomac, 76 miles long; the Richmond and Petersburg, 22 miles; and the Petersburg and Roanoke, 62 miles, which together form a portion of the great southern line. The Seaboard and Roanoke Railroad runs from Weldon, N. C., to Norfolk. The other lines are, the Appomattox, 10 miles; the Alexandria and Orange, 75 miles; the Central, 98 miles; the Chesterfield, 12 miles; the Greenfield and Roanoke, 21 miles; the Manasses Gap, 107 miles, etc.; and many lines are projected or being constructed, to unite with the railroad systems of neighboring states. The Virginia canals consist of the James' River and Kanawha, which extends along the bank of the river from Richmond to Lynchburg, 146 miles; the Dismal Swamp Canal, which extends from Deep Creek to Joyce's Creek, a branch of the Pasquotank River, which flows into Albemarle Sound, 23 miles; and several short cuts, branches, etc.

In October, 1850, there were in the state 6 banks and 31 branches—liabilities: capital $9,814,545, circulation $10, 256,967, deposits $4,717,732, and other items $338,841; assets: specie $2,928,174, loans and discounts $19,646,777, stocks $269,914, real estate $764,282, other investments $210,498, due from and notes of other banks $1,925,652, and $552,153.

Virginia formed a new constitution in 1851. The right of suffrage is conferred on every white male citizen 21 years of age and upwards, who has resided two years in the state and one year in the place he may offer his vote. The General Assembly is composed of a Senate of 50 members, elected for four years, and House of Delegates of 152 members, for two years. This legislature meets biennially at Richmond, and a majority of each house constitutes a quorum. The Governor is chosen for four years, and is ineligible for the succeeding term. He must be a native of the United States, a citizen of Virginia of five years' standing, and 30 years of age. A Lieutenant-Governor, with the same qualifications, is elected at the same time and for a like term, and is *ex-officio* President of the Senate. All administrative officers are also elected by the people. The constitution provides for a Supreme Court of Appeals, District Courts, Circuit Courts, and County Courts—the state to be divided into 21 circuits, 10 districts, and 5 sections; and for each circuit a judge is elected by the people thereof for eight years, and for each section a judge for 12 years. These last constitute the Court of Appeals, any three of whom constitute the court. County courts are held by justices of the peace chosen for four years.

The public debt and resources of Virginia, 1st February, 1850, amounted to the following sums:

PUBLIC DEBT.			
Revolutionary war debt,	6 per cent.		$24,039
1812 war debt,	7 "		319,000
Internal improv. debt,	6 "		7,503,917
" " "	5 "		1,065,600
" " "	5½ "		25,300
Bank subscription debt			450,107
			$9,387,962
Of this there is held by state agents under the control of the legislature—			
—by Literary Fund		$1,096,106	
—by Board of Public Works.		366,862	1,462,966
Actual outstanding debt			$7,924,994
Add contingent debt			6,039,292
Actual and contingent debt			$13,964,286

RESOURCES.	
Stocks and debts due and productive	$7,379,455
Property not now productive	4,475,359
Total funds held by state	$11,854,814

N.B.—The internal improvement debt consists of—

Debt incurred for	James River, etc.	$4,505,583
" "	other river imp.	464,614
" "	railroads	2,251,116
" "	turnpike and bridges	476,496
" "	state and county roads	897,008
Total		$8,594,817

The annual interest on the absolute debt is $555,685. The ordinary expenses of the government amount to about $570,000, and the ordinary revenue and taxation amounted in 1849–50 to $632,756.

The permanent literary fund capital amounts to $1,561,160, and the revenue derived therefrom for the year ending 1st October, 1849, was $95,935; the total sum expended in the education of 30,387 poor children was

$70,111. The University and the Military School at Lexington also received in part their support from the state. Virginia's principal colleges are:

Colleges.	Founded.	Location.	Profs.	Students, 1850.
William and Mary	1692	Williamsburg	6	—
Hampden Sidney	1783	Prince Edward's Co.	6	25
Washington	1812	Lexington	6	81
University	1829	Charlottesville	10	212
Randolph	1832	Boydstown	11	145
Emery and Henry	1839	Glade Spring	4	55
Rector	1839	Taylor Co.	3	50
Bethany	1840	Bethany	6	113
Richmond	1832	Richmond	6	72
Military Institute	1839	Lexington	6	120
Medical College	1838	Richmond	6	75
" "	—	Winchester	5	—

Law departments are attached to the University and to William and Mary College, and a medical department to the University. The Episcopalians have a Theological School in Fairfax county; the Presbyterians control the Union Theolgical Seminary in Prince Edward's county; and the Virginia Baptist Seminary is located at Richmond. The aggregate libraries attached to the above contain 57,000 volumes.

Of the religious denominations in Virginia, the Baptists, Methodists, and Presbyterians are numerically preponderant, and count respectively 47,000, 34,000, and 17,000 communicants. The Protestant Episcopalians are also numerous in this state.

Richmond, the state capital, is situated on the north side of James' River, immediately below the falls, 150 miles from its mouth, and in latitude 37° 32′ 17″ north, and 79° 26′ 28″ west. It is the depot of a fine back country, and contains within itself unsurpassed facilities for manufacturing. The capitol is one of the most beautiful edifices in the Union, and its churches, public buildings, and private residences will compare well with those of any other city. Population, 27,483. Manchester, on the opposite bank of the river, and which is connected therewith by a bridge, has considerable manufactures.

Norfolk is the chief seaport. It is situated on the east bank of Elizabeth River, a few miles above its entrance into Hampton Roads, and has a commodious and safe harbor. Gosport navy yard, on the opposite side of the river, is an important station, and contains a magnificent dry dock, which cost nearly $1,000,000. Dismal Swamp Canal opens an extensive communication from Norfolk to the south, and the Seaboard and Roanoke Railroad connects it with the railroad systems of the south and west. Population 14,320. Petersburg, a port of entry on the Appomattox, has a population of 14,603; Fredericksburg, on the Rappahannock, is an important commercial depot, and contains about 5,000 inhabitants; Charlottesville, on Moore's Creek, is chiefly noted as the location of the University of Virginia; Lynchburg is a great tobacco market; Harper's Ferry, at the junction of the Shanandoah with the Potomac, is noted for its majestic scenery, and contains an arsenal and armory of the United States; Winchester occupies the site of old Fort Loudon, and is otherwise an important town; and there are others of importance along the courses of the rivers. Wheeling is the most flourishing of the Ohio towns.

In this connection we may mention, that in Westmorland county, on the Potomac, is the spot where the illustrious Washington was born. The house, which stood on Pope's Creek, about half a mile up the stream, on a plantation called Wakefield, is now in ruins. A stone, with the simple inscription, "HERE, ON THE 11TH FEBRUARY, 1732, GEORGE WASHINGTON WAS BORN," indicates the hallowed spot. Mount Vernon, higher up the river, was his residence in life and tomb in death. Here is the Mecca of America. The house in which he resided is a simple frame building, and his tomb a plain structure of red brick. Many a pilgrim has sought this sacred retreat, to pay a tribute of gratitude to the memory of the immortal Washington.

The first European settlement made in the original United States was at Jamestown, in Virginia, in the year 1607. The country was granted by Queen Elizabeth to Sir Walter Raleigh, who named it Virginia, in honor of his virgin (?) sovereign. The grant was vacated by the execution and attainder of Raleigh under James I., and the territory was then granted to the London company. Jamestown was then settled, and the name given in honor of the reigning monarch. Virginia was conspicuous for her loyalty as a colony, and was among the last to acknowledge the commonwealth, and the first to proclaim Charles II. at the Restoration. The state has produced a number of eminent statesmen and warriors, among whom were Washington, Jefferson, Monroe, Madison, and Chief-Justice Marshall.

The early history of this state is replete with numerous romantic and highly affecting incidents occasioned by dangers and calamities,—by sickness, want, and contests with the Indians.

The government of the colony was originally administered by a council of seven persons, with a president chosen from among themselves, but afterwards it was administered by a Governor, appointed, except during the commonwealth, by the crown. The first President was E. M. Wingfield, and the first Governor, appointed 1610, was Lord De la War, from whom Delaware derives its name.

Shortly after the war of the revolution broke out, a Provisional Government was established, and Peyton Randolph chosen President. A constitution was formed in 1776, which was the fundamental law of Virginia until 1830, when it was superseded by the present constitution. Patrick Henry was the first constitutional Governor.

THE STATE OF NORTH CAROLINA.

NORTH CAROLINA is situated between 33° 53′ and 36° 33′ N. latitude, and between 75° 45′ and 84° W. longitude. It is bounded north by Virginia; east by the Atlantic Ocean; south by South Carolina, and west by Tennessee. Length, 430 miles, breadth, 198; area, 43,800 square miles, or 28,032,000 acres.

Along the whole coast of this state is a ridge of sand, separated from the main land in some places by narrow sounds, in others by broad bays. The passages and inlets through it are shallow and dangerous, and Ocracoke Inlet is the only one north of Cape Fear through which vessels can pass. In the counties on the sea-coast the land is low and covered with extensive marshes and swamps, and for 60 or 80 miles from the shore is a dead level. Beyond this the country swells into hills, and in the more western parts of the state rises into mountains. Mitchell's Peak is the highest culmination east of the Mississippi, being 6,720 feet above the level of the sea. In the low country the soil is generally sandy, and covered with immense forests of pitch pine; in the swamps, rice of a fine quality grows in abundance, and in the upper country wheat and other cereals, with hemp and flax.

Cape Hatteras, Cape Lookout, and Cape Fear are the most celebrated in the state. All of them are dangerous to mariners, but particularly Cape Hatteras, where storms of unusual violence prevail. Numerous vessels are every year wrecked on this coast. The principal inlets are Currituck, Roanoke and Ocracoke. Albemarle Sound, in the north-east part of the state, is 86 miles long, and from 10 to 20 broad. The Great Dismal Swamp extends northward into Virginia. It is 30 miles long from north to south, and 10 miles broad, and embraces about 150,000 acres, generally covered with trees. In the centre is Drummond's Pond, 15 miles in circumference. The Little Dismal or Alligator Swamp lies between Albemarle and Prentice Sounds.

The Chowan River rises in Virginia and falls into Albemarle Sound. The Roanoke, formed by the Staunton and Dan, both of which rise in Virginia, is navigable for 70 miles, to the falls, and by means of a canal around the falls, is further continued to Danville, in Virginia. The Pamlico rises in the northern part of the state. The Neuse rises also in the northern part of the state, and after a course of 500 miles, falls into Pamlico Sound, 70 miles below Newbern. It is navigable 12 miles above Newbern for sea vessels, and 200 miles further for boats. Cape Fear River has 18 feet of water on the bar: large vessels can ascend to Wilmington. The Yadkin is a tributary of the Great Pedee; it rises in the mountains in the west, and after pursuing a south-east course, enters South Carolina. In Montgomery county are the narrows, where the river descends 321 feet in 24 miles. The Catawba also rises in the west and passes into South Carolina, where it takes the name of Wataree.

The climate of the coast section is subject to great and sudden changes, and is often unhealthy in the fall. The winters are mild but boisterous;—the spring, however, soon appears, and vegetation much earlier than in the west on the same parallel. The summers are hot and sultry, but the autumns serene and beautiful. The exhalations from the swamps are very pernicious and destructive to life. The climate of the upper country is more steady, and generally colder. Among the mountains the summer is pleasant, but in winter a great degree of cold is experienced. At the University of North Carolina, Chapel Hill, the hottest day exhibited a temperature of 96°, and the coldest 10°, and the usual average was 59° 7. Peaches blossom in February, and the first frost occurs generally in October. Rainy days, 98; cloudy, 333; clear, 32.

The total population of North Carolina, in 1850, was 868,072, averaging one person to every 32 acres, and its distribution to the several counties was in the following proportions:

COUNTIES.	White Persons.	Colored Persons. Free.	Colored Persons. Slave.	Total Populat'n.
Alamance	7,924	324	3,196	11,444
Alexander	4,653	24	543	5,220
Anson	6,556	101	6,832	14,489
Ashe	8,096	86	595	8,777
Beaufort	7,663	904	5,249	13,816
Bertie	5,344	313	7,194	12,851
Bladen	5,055	354	4,358	9,767
Brunswick	3,651	319	3,302	7,272
Buncombe	11,601	107	1,717	13,425
Burke	5,477	163	2,132	7,772
Cabarras	6.943	119	2,685	9,847
Caldwell	5,006	108	1,203	6,317
Camden	3,572	290	2,187	6,049
Carteret	5,167	149	1,487	6,803
Caswell	7,081	418	7,770	15,269
Catawba	7,272	21	1,569	8,862
Chatham	12,164	300	5,985	18,449
Chowan	2,944	104	3,673	6,713
Cleaveland	8,579	57	1,747	10,383
Columbus	4,257	149	1,503	5,909
Craven	7,222	1,536	5,951	14,709
Cumberland	12,447	946	7,217	20,610
Currituck	4,600	189	2,447	7,236
Cherokee	6,493	8	337	6,838
Davidson	12,139	189	2,992	15,320
Davie	5,613	82	2,171	7,866
Duplin	7,165	342	6,007	13,514
Edgecomb	8,365	277	8,547	17,189
Franklin	5,685	521	5,507	11,713
Forsyth	9,663	152	1,353	11,168

COUNTIES.	White Persons.	Colored Persons. Free.	Colored Persons. Slave.	Total Populat'n.
Gates	4,158	397	3,871	8,436
Granville	10,296	1,088	9,865	21,249
Green	3,259	116	3,244	6,619
Guilford	15,859	694	3,186	19,739
Gaston	5,928	33	2,112	8,073
Halifax	5,763	1,872	8,954	16,589
Haywood*	5,931	15	418	6,364
Hertford	3,553	873	3,716	8,142
Hyde	4,798	211	2,627	7,636
Henderson	5,892	37	924	6,853
Iredell	10,547	30	4,142	15,019
Johnston	8,900	163	4,663	13,726
Jones	2,139	142	2,757	5,038
Lenoir	3,567	145	4,116	7,828
Lincoln	5,661	30	2,055	7,756
Martin	4,615	325	3,367	8,307
McDowell	4,777	207	1,262	6,246
Mecklenburg	8,284	157	5,473	13,914
Montgomery	5,055	44	1,773	6,872
Moore	7,197	169	1,976	9,342
Macon†	5,705	135	549	6,489
Nash	5,972	629	4,056	10,657
New Hanover	8,190	897	8,581	17,668
Northampton	5,994	830	6,511	13,345
Onslow	5,005	170	3,108	8,283
Orange	11,330	481	5,244	17,255
Pasquotank	4,611	1,234	3,105	9,950
Perquimans	3,629	450	3,252	7,331
Person	5,593	295	4,893	10,781
Pitt	6,664	100	6,633	13,397
Randolph	13,795	397	1,640	15,832
Richmond	4,890	224	4,704	9,618
Rowan	9,901	115	3,854	13,870
Robeson	7,244	1,217	4,365	12,826
Rockingham	8,747	419	5,329	14,495
Rutherford	10,425	220	2,905	13,550
Sampson	8,424	476	5,685	14,585
Stokes	7,264	149	1,793	9,106
Surry	16,171	272	2,000	18,443
Stanley	5,437	49	1,436	6,922
Tyrrell	3,296	130	1,702	5,028
Union	8,018	51	1,928	9,997
Wake	14,177	1,301	9,409	24,887
Warren	4,604	441	8,867	13,912
Washington	3,216	235	2,215	5,766
Watauga	3,242	29	129	3,400
Wayne	7,802	664	5,020	13,486
Wilkes	10,746	211	1,142	12,109
Yancy	7,809	50	346	8,205
Total	552,464	27,196	288,412	868,072

*710 and †120 Indians reside in this county.

CLASSES AND SEXES OF POPULATION.

Classes.	Males.	Females.	Total.
White Persons	272,369	280,095	552,464
Colored " —free	13,226	13,970	27,196
" " —slave			288,412
Total			868,072

PROGRESSIVE MOVEMENT OF POPULATION.

Date of Census.	White Persons.	Colored Persons. Free.	Colored Persons. Slave.	Total Population.	Decennial Increase. Numerical.	Decennial Increase. Per 100.
1790	288,204	4,975	100,572	393,751	—	—
1800	337,764	7,043	133,296	478,103	84,352	21.4
1810	376,410	10,266	168,824	555,500	77,397	16.1
1820	419,200	14,612	205,017	638,829	83,329	15.0
1830	472,843	19,543	245,601	737,987	99,158	15.5
1840	484,870	22,732	245,817	753,419	15,432	2.1
1850	552,464	27,196	288,412	868,072	114,653	15.2

Of the population in 1850 there were employed in agriculture 217,095 persons, in commerce 1,734, in trade and manufactures 14,322, in navigating the ocean 327, in sailing on canals, rivers, &c., 379, and 1086 in the learned professions. The increase of the population in this state has been greatly retarded during the last 50 years by the drain of emigration, first to Kentucky and Tennessee, and lately to the States of the south-west.

The industry of North Carolina is chiefly agricultural, and the great staples of the South—cotton, tobacco, and rice, are cultivated extensively. Indian corn forms the largest cereal crop, next oats and wheat, but the crops of rye, buckwheat, and barley, are very small. The live stock numbers about 192,000 horses and mules, 850,000 neat cattle, 730,000 sheep, and 2,000,000 swine. The yield of wool is between eight and nine hundred thousand pounds, and the value of the dairy about $800,000. The state has valuable mines of iron and coal, and a considerable deposit of gold is found at the base of the Alleghanies; but mining is not prosecuted to any great extent. The gold mines of North Carolina are richer than those of the other Atlantic States, and the deposit seems to have here a wider range. The greater part of the gold is taken to the mint for coinage, but the quantity thus disposed of by no means indicates the quantity yielded. The gold is found chiefly in scales flattened and broken, but in several instances lumps (one weighing 28lbs *avoird.*) have been exhumed. The usual currency in the gold region is "dust," contained in goose quills, and each man carries his scale and weights.

Manufactures are in a more flourishing condition, and of late years have decidedly progressed. The manufacturing capital cannot now (1850) be less than $6,000,000, and a considerable portion of this has been invested in the manufacture of cotton goods. In 1850 there were 31 mills, and about 52,000 spindles; and the annual consumption is about 13,000 bales of 4000 lbs. each. The fisheries are of little consequence, although fish is plentiful in the rivers and bays.

The direct foreign commerce of the state is small, but the coasting trade is considerable and prosperous. The latter is carried on chiefly with the northern ports. The value of exports to foreign countries, in 1849–50, was $416,501, and of imports $323,692, and in this business 28,300 tons of shipping were entered, and 42,232 tons were cleared. Three-fourths of this commerce is transacted at Wilmington. The shipping owned within the state, on the 30th June, 1850, amounted to 45,016 tons, of which 30,284 tons were employed in coasting. The steam marine was 3,232 tons, and there were built, during the year, 23 vessels, of an aggregate burden of 2,650 tons. In 1816 the exports were valued at $1,328,755, but since then the annual value has seldom exceeded that of 1849–50. The exports of the latter year, indeed, are much above the average.

The state has completed some great works of improvement, and when the system of projected railroads is finished, few other districts will have better means of transport and transit. It is cut through by the great road, north and south, and the enterprise of the people is pressing towards the west—towards Tennessee and the Mississippi River. At the present time (1851) 240 miles of railroad are in working order, and 385 miles in course of construction.

There are 18 banks in the state, the capital stock of which amounts to $3,825,000, and the circulation, in April, 1850, was $3,542,448. The specie held by these institutions amounted to $1,682,410.

North Carolina has made great improvement in its educational facilities of late years, but still the destitution of the state in this respect is lamentable. Of common schools there are about 1,200, and there are 180 or 200 academies in the state. The institutions of a higher grade are the University at Chapel Hill, Davidson College in Mecklenburg county, and Wake Forest College. In 1850 these had together 247 students. The Law School of the University had 10 students. The state provides institutions for the deaf and dumb, and also for the insane.

Methodists and Baptists are the leading religious denominations. The number of Presbyterians, Anti-Mission Baptists, and Episcopalians is also respectable. The state is eminently Protestant, the whole Catholic diodiocese of Charleston, which includes both the Carolinas, not counting more than 5,000 Roman Catholics.

The government is vested in a Governor, a Council of seven persons, a Senate and House of Commons. The Governor, Senators and Representatives are elected by the people, and hold their offices for two years. The Council is chosen every two years by the General Assembly. The General Assembly also appoints the judiciary. Every white male of 21 years of age, having resided in the county one year and paid taxes, is entitled to vote for Governor and members of the House of Commons.

To vote for a Senator he must, in addition to these, own fifty acres of land.

The public debt of this state is contingent, and arises from endorsements by the state, of bonds of railroad companies to the amount of $1,100,000, from which sum, however, must be deducted $13,000 for bonds not used, and $110,000 for bonds paid. This reduces the amount for which the state is liable, to $977,000.

The income into the state treasury, in 1847, amounted to $251,717 00, and the expenditures to $175,402. There was a balance in the treasury of $76,315, on the 30th October, 1847. The chief sources of income are from taxes, profits on railroads, &c. The ordinary expenses of the government are about $55,000 annually.

Very early after the discovery of North America several essays were made to settle on the coast of Carolina, but without success. A company of emigrants who fled from Virginia on account of religious persecution, founded the first permanent colony at a place called Albemarle, on the eastern branch of Chowan River. In 1663, Charles II. granted a charter for the Carolinas, to the Earl of Clarendon and others, who proceeded in an effort to settle there, first taking command of the colony at Albemarle. A colony was sent from Barbadoes and located near Cape Fear. William Sayle was appointed first Governor in 1669. In 1729, the crown purchased the whole of the Carolinas for $17,509, and they were divided into two provinces, called North and South Carolina. In 1769, the oppression of the British Minister caused a rebellion, which was successful at the time, but two years after, Governor Tryon, at the head of his troops, defeated the "Regulators," as the armed inhabitants called themselves, killing 300 in battle, and taking several prisoners, of whom twelve were condemned for high treason, and six executed. During the war of the revolution, the Carolinas took an active part, and as early as 1775, a declaration was put forth by a sort of congress at Mecklenburg, which breathed the true spirit of independence. In 1776, the constitution of North Carolina was adopted, and with some amendments made in 1835, has continued to the present time as the fundamental law of the land.

Raleigh, the capital, is situated in the centre of the state, near the river Neuse. It contains a beautiful granite state-house, and other public buildings, and had, in 1850, a population of 3,091. Lat. 35° 47′ N. and long. 78° 43′ W.

Newbern, on the same river, is a place of considerable business, and has a good share of commerce. Population, in 1850, 4,722

Wilmington, the largest town in the state, contained, in 1850, a population of 6,218. It is situated on the east side of Cape Fear River, 35 miles from the Atlantic, and is very unhealthy. It enjoys considerable coasting business. More produce is exported from this place than any other in the state.

Fayetteville, the next in population, is situated near the west branch of Cape Fear River. Population, in 1850, 4,285. It has some commerce, and perhaps is better situated and provided with better facilities for trade, than any other town in the state.

THE STATE OF SOUTH CAROLINA.

South Carolina lies between the latitudes 32° 2′ and 35° 10′ N., and between the longitudes 78° 24′ and 83° 30′ W., and is bounded north and north-east by North Carolina; south-east by the Atlantic Ocean; and south-west by Georgia, from which it is separated by the Savannah River. In length 262 miles, and breadth 200, it has an area of 28,200 square miles, or 18,048,000 acres.

The coast is lined with a chain of fine islands, between which and the shore the navigation is convenient. The main land is naturally divided into the upper and lower country. The low country extends 80 or 100 miles from the coast, and is covered with pine forests, interspersed with swamps and marshes, having a rich soil. Succeeding this region is an undulating country, chiefly of sand, which extends about 50 or 60 miles westward. Proceeding further inland the mountains become abrupt, but on advancing, the country displays an elevated level, and is succeeded by a fine country of hills and dales, which, in the western extremity of the state, rise into lofty mountains. The banks of the rivers of the low country are extremely fertile, and produce large crops of cotton and Indian corn. The marshes and swamps are the finest rice lands in the Union. Many parts in the central district are susceptible of agricultural improvement, and afford ample pasturage. However, the whole country east of the first heights is comparatively barren and worthless. The soil of the upper country is strong and fertile. Cotton and rice are the staples of South Carolina, but the soil and climate are well adapted to tobacco and indigo, and these were formerly cultivated to a great extent, but the cultivation of the present staples now engrosses the whole attention of the planter.

The climate of the upper country is healthy at all seasons. In the low country the summer months are sickly, particularly August and September and at this season, the climate proves destructive to the unacclimated.

The principal rivers are the Savannah, Pedee, and Santee. The Savannah rises in the Alleghanies, and taking a south-eastern course, divides this state from Georgia. It is navigable 18 miles to Savannah, and for small vessels to Augusta, 140 miles further. Boats proceed above the falls 60 miles, without interruption. The Pedee rises in North Carolina, where it has the name of Yadkin; it is navigable nearly to the northern boundary. The Santee, the great river of South Carolina, is formed by the union of the Congaree and Wateree, near the centre of the state. It is navigable through its whole length, and as far as Camden, on the Wateree, and Columbia, on the Congaree. Cooper and Ashley Rivers fall into Charleston Harbor. Edisto River empties itself at Edisto Island, 20 miles further south, and Combahee, still lower down. There is a canal 22 miles long, connecting the Santee and Cooper rivers, by which the produce of a large section of this state, and of a part of North Carolina, is brought to the city of Charleston.

The population of South Carolina, in 1850, was 668,507, or in the ratio of one person to every 28 acres; and its distribution to the 29 districts into which the state is divided was in the following proportions:

DISTRICTS.	White Persons.	Colored Persons. Free.	Slave.	Total Popula-
Abbeville	12,693	363	19,262	32,318
Anderson	13,871	90	7,514	21,475
Barnwell	12,289	311	14,008	26,608
Beaufort	5,945	581	32,279	38,805
Charleston	24,586	3,843	44,376	72,805
Chester	8,005	146	9,887	18,038
Chesterfield	6,678	218	3,894	10,790
Colleton	7,404	330	31,771	39,505
Darlington	6,750	39	10,041	16,830
Edgefield	16,275	262	22,725	39,262
Fairfield	7,076	82	14,246	21,404
Georgetown	2,193	201	18,253	20,647
Greenville	13,372	93	6,691	20,156
Horry	5,521	50	2,075	7,646
Kershaw	4,681	214	9,578	14,473

DISTRICTS	White Persons.	Colored Persons. Free.	Slave.	Total Popula.
Lancaster	5,861	113	5,014	10,988
Laurens	11,371	83	11,953	23,407
Lexington	7,352	21	5,557	12,930
Marion	9,784	103	7,520	17,407
Marlboro'	5,033	156	5,600	10,789
Newbury	7,243	212	12,688	20,143
Orangeburg	8,120	78	15,384	23,582
Pickens	13,105	120	3,679	16,904
Richland	6,764	501	12,978	20,243
Spartanburg	18,312	49	8,039	26,400
Sumpter	9,815	340	23,065	33,220
Union	9,322	138	10,392	19,852
Williamsburg	3,902	37	8,508	12,447
York	11,300	126	8,007	19,433
Total	274,623	8,900	384,984	668,507

CLASSES AND SEXES OF POPULATION.

Classes.	Males.	Females.	Total.
White persons	137,773	136,850	274,623
Colored " —free	4,110	4,790	8,900
" " —slave	—	—	384,984
Total	—	—	668,507

PROGRESSIVE MOVEMENT OF POPULATION.

Date of Census.	White Persons.	Colored Persons. Free.	Slave.	Total Population.	Decennial Increase. Numerical.	Per 100.
1790	140,178	1,801	107,094	249,073	—	—
1800	196,255	3,185	146,151	345,591	96,518	38.7
1810	214,196	4,554	196,365	415,115	69,524	20.1
1820	237,540	6,726	258,475	502,741	87,626	21.1
1830	257,863	7,921	315,401	581,185	78,444	15.6
1840	259,089	8,271	317,038	594,398	13,213	2.3
1850	274,623	8,900	384,984	668,507	74,109	12.4

The number of dwellings and families in this state are nearly equal, the former being 51,450, and the latter 51,739; and the number in each family is 12.5 persons, including slaves. The deaths during the year 1849–50 amounted to 7,842, or in the proportion of one death to every 83 persons.

Agriculture is the absorbing pursuit, and employs more than three-fourths of the people. In 1850 there were 27,868 plantations and farms. The great crops are those of cotton and rice; the yearly product of the cotton fields averages 140,000,000 lbs., and the products of the rice plantations is more than 80,000,000 lbs. annually. Tobacco is grown, but the crop is small. The cereals, which are cultivated chiefly on the western uplands, are Indian corn, the annual yield of which is from twelve to fifteen million bushels, wheat about two million bushels, and oats about half that number. Rye and barley are little attended to. The potatoe crop averages three million bushels. The live stock consists of about 162,000 horses and mules, 620,000 neat cattle, 275,000 sheep, 950,000 swine, and poultry to the value of half a million dollars. Wool is produced to the amount of 350,000 lbs., and the produce of the dairy may be valued at $750,000. Bees and silk-worms flourish in this climate, and yield valuable returns in honey, wax, and cocoons. The tea plant and indigo have lately been introduced to South Carolina agriculture.

South Carolina is not a manufacturing state, yet it has a fair number of industrial establishments. In 1850 there were 1,439, exclusive of those the products of which were not valued at $500 per annum. The manufacturing of cotton goods has of late years been firmly established, and in 1850 there were in the state 16 mills and 36,500 spindles, which consumed 10,000 bales annually: they are chiefly devoted to the production of coarse fabrics. The capital employed in manufactures is about four millions dollars. Domestic goods are made to a large amount. Mining, except for gold at the base of the Alleghanies, is almost unknown, nor are the fisheries made a source of profit.

The commerce of South Carolina has increased immensely within a few years. In 1849–50 its exports were valued at $11,447,800, and its imports at $1,933,785, being nearly double the value of its commerce in 1845–6.

Charleston is the principal port, and enjoys fully nine-tenths of the commerce. The shipping owned within the state on the 30th June, 1850, amounted to 36,072 tons. The coasting trade employed 18,944 tons, of which 7,454 tons were navigated by steam power. The internal trade of the country has increased wonderfully since the opening of the railroads, and to the same cause the increase of exportations from Charleston ought to be attributed, since much of the products of Tennessee and northern Georgia now seek that port for an outlet for the northern and foreign markets.

The railroads of the state stretch from the sea-board to the Savannah, and there connect with the systems of Georgia and Tennessee, and will ultimately form a part of the trunk roads to the states north of the Ohio, and to the Mississippi. There are also several local railroads. The principal lines are the State Road from Charleston to Hamburg, 136 miles long, with a branch 68 miles long, to Columbia, and one to Camden, 44 miles long; and the Greenville and Columbia Railroad, 22 miles long. The whole length of completed railroad is 292 miles, and there are about 135 miles in the course of being constructed. Up to 1850 the total cost of railroads had been $7,243,000. There are also several short canals in the state; the Santee Canal is 22 miles long, and the Winyaw Canal 7½ miles; and the Catawba River has been improved by several cuts, in all 11 or 12 miles in length. Post roads are numerous, but indifferently kept.

The banking capital of the state amounted, in Aug. 1850, to $5,991,856; the circulation was $2,788,600, and the total liabilities were $15,530,934. The securities were ample, viz., specie on hand $1,153,772; real estate $282,877; discounts $5,830,171; and other assets to a balance.

South Carolina cannot boast of a very extended system of education, but it has several excellent colleges and seminaries, at which the higher branches are taught. The College of South Carolina is the most important of these. The College at Charleston, and Erskine College, are also valuable foundations. In 1850 they had an aggregate of 377 students, and from six to eight professors each. The Theological Seminaries are—the Southern, at Columbia, attached to the College, and under the Presbyterians; that at Lexington (Lutheran), and the Furman Seminary in Fairfield district (Baptist); together these had, in 1850, 774 students. The Medical College at Charleston, a school of high repute, had 158 students, and eight professors. There are, besides, about 160 academies in various parts of the state, and between 600 and 700 primary and common schools. About 25,000 youths and children are constantly being educated, yet a large portion of the inhabitants are destitute of even the advantage of elementary knowledge.

The Methodists and Baptists are numerically the preponderating denominations in this state. The Protestant Episcopal churches are likewise numerous, and there are also a goodly number of Presbyterians. The Unitarian and Universalist sects are scarcely known here, and there are very few Roman Catholics.

COLUMBIA, the capital and seat of government, is situated in Richland District, on the east bank of the Congaree River, and had, in 1850, a population of 6,060 souls. Lat. 33° 57′ N., and long. 81° 7′ W. The state-house is a plain wooden edifice, but the village is handsomely laid out and well built, with some elegant mansions. A steamboat plies from Columbia to Charleston, passing through the Santee Canal, and a communication is kept up by railroad. The business of the place is in a flourishing condition.

CHARLESTON is the principal commercial city, and most populous in the state. It is situated at the confluence of the Ashley and Cooper rivers, which unite in Charleston harbor, seven miles from the ocean. The population of the city proper was, in 1850, 29,261, and in connection with St. Phillip's, which is actually a suburb, though not embraced in the chartered limits, the population is 41,137. The city is pleasantly located, and the tide, which rises and flows with considerable rapidity, contributes much to the health of the location. It is, however, so low, that parts of the town have been, at different periods, overflown. The principal public buildings are the city-hall, exchange, court-house, custom-house, and guard-house, besides which there are several handsome churches. Charleston has the principal commerce of the state. Its shipping, in 1850, amounted to 33,292 tons. The harbor is spacious and well protected by Fort Moultree and Fort Sumter, at the mouth; by Castle Pinckney, on an island in the harbor, and by Fort Johnson, on the south side of the harbor, nearly opposite the city. There are two arsenals in the city, and in the vicinity, about two miles out of town, are nine fire-proof magazines.

GEORGETOWN, on Winyaw Bay, near the mouth of the Pedee, is 13 miles from the ocean. It is well situated for trade, being in the neighborhood of fertile lands, and connected with an extensive back country. There is a bar at the entrance of the bay, which prevents vessels drawing more than 11 feet of water from entering. Population, 2,100.

The other principal towns are CHERAW, on the Pedee, which has considerable trade; BEAUFORT, south of Charleston, on Port Royal Island, in the harbor, which has a fine anchorage; GREENVILLE, in the north, a neat town with about 1,000 inhabitants, situated in a fertile and healthy district; and HAMBURG, on the Savannah, opposite Augusta. This place is connected with Charleston by the South Carolina Railroad, and with Crawford, Atlanta and Harrison, by the Georgia Railroad.

The present constitution was formed in 1790. The Governor and Lieutenant-Governor are elected for two years by the Legislature in joint ballot. The Senators are elected for four years, and the members of the House of Representatives for two years, by the people. One-half of the Senators are elected biennially. Every citizen who has resided in the state one year, and in the county where he offers his vote six months previous to an election, and who has paid taxes, is entitled to the rights of suffrage. No colored person can vote.

South Carolina is the only state that does not consider its citizens competent to choose their representatives to the presidential electoral college. They are appointed by the Legislature.

The judicial power is vested in such superior and inferior courts of law and equity as the legislature may from time to time institute. The judges are appointed by joint ballot of the General Assembly, and hold their seats during good behavior. Sheriffs hold office for four years, and are ineligible for the succeeding four years.

The public debt amounts to $2,310,896.

In 1670, this state was permanently settled by a small body of English emigrants under William Sayle, who remained about nine years at Port Royal Island. In 1679, they removed to the present site of Charleston. In 1706, the French and Spaniards made an attack on Charleston, but were repulsed. Hitherto the colony had been under a proprietory government; but in 1720 it became a crown colony. In 1775, the importation of British goods was prohibited, and a military force raised to defend the colony against the royalists. Several battles were fought in this state during the period of the revolution; the most important was that of Eutaw Springs, in 1781. South Carolina raised 6,617 men for the continental army.

In 1833, the state placed itself in opposition to the general government, and threatened a withdrawal from the Union, in consequence of the existing tariff, but through the influence of Henry Clay and others in the United States Senate, the difficulty was arranged without proceeding to forcible measures. A like threat is now held out as a terror to all abolitionists who desire the exclusion of slavery from the newly-acquired territories

---

THE STATE OF GEORGIA.

Georgia is situated between 30° 19′ and 35° N. lat., and between 80° 50′ and 85° 40′ W. long. This state is bounded on the north by Tennessee and North Carolina; on the north-east by South Carolina; south-east by the Atlantic Ocean; south by Florida, and west by Alabama. Length, 314 miles,—breadth, 248 miles; area, 62,000 square miles, or 39,680,000 acres.

The topography of Georgia, both as regards the arrangement of its coasts and the whole inland country, is much similar to that of South Carolina; and the staples are the same, with the addition of some of the tropical fruits, as figs, oranges, olives, lemons, &c. The forests abound in timber, chiefly oaks and pines.

The Savannah separates this state from South Carolina, under which head it is described. The Ogeechee falls into the ocean 15 miles south of the above. The Alatamaha is formed by the Oconee and Ockmulgee: it runs south-east, and discharges itself into the Atlantic through several mouths, sixty miles south-west of the Savannah. It is navigable for small vessels to Milledgeville, on the Oconee, 200 miles from the ocean. The bar at the mouth has 14 feet at low water. The St. Mary's is a deep river. It rises in Eokefanoke swamp, and after a very crooked course of 150 miles, falls into the ocean between Cumberland and Amelia islands. It is navigable to its source. Flint River joins the Chattahouchee in the south-west corner of the state, and hence the united streams take the name of Apalachicola. The Chattahouchee rises in the northern part of the state, and in the lower part of its course, forms the boundary between Georgia and Alabama.

The low country has an agreeable, healthy climate for eight or nine months of the year; but in the latter part of the summer and fall it is sickly, except on the sea-islands, which are comparatively healthy. The climate of the upper country is agreeable; and in the north-west, at the foot of the mountains, (which, indeed, terminate in Georgia,) it is esteemed one of the healthiest in the Atlantic states.

The principal islands of the coast are Tybee, Ossabaw, St. Catherine's, Sapello, St. Simon's, and Cumberland. These are the sea islands, so celebrated for the beautiful texture of their cotton. Eokefanoke swamp, part of which is in Florida, is 180 miles in circumference, and abounds with alligators, snakes, and swarms of insects, which render it uninhabitable by human beings. Cypress Swamp is near the mouth of Satilla River.

The population of Georgia, according to the census of 1850, amounted to 905,999 souls, being then one person to every 44 acres; and was distributed into the counties in the following proportions:—

COUNTIES.	White Persons.	Colored Persons. Free.	Colored Persons. Slave.	Total Popula.
Appling	2,521	24	404	2,949
Baker	4,355	—	3,765	8,120
Baldwin	3,522	24	4,602	8,148
Bibb	7,009	53	5,637	12,699
Bryan	1,164	15	2,245	3,424
Bullock	2,840	—	1,460	4,300
Burke	5,116	152	10,832	16,100
Botts	3,680	3	2,805	6,488
Camden	2,069	4	4,246	6,319
Campbell	5,718	7	1,507	7,232
Carroll	8,252	4	1,101	9,357
Cass	10,271	21	3,008	13,300
Chatham	9,161	722	14,018	23,901
Chattooga	5,131	4	1,680	6,815
Cherokee	11,629	14	1,157	12,800
Clark	5,515	15	5,589	11,119
Cobb	11,568	3	2,272	13,843
Columbia	3,617	72	8,272	11,961
Coweta	8,202	18	5,415	13,635
Crawford	4,342	13	4,629	8,984
Dade	2,532	—	148	2,680
Decatur	4,618	5	3,639	8,262
De Kalb	11,372	32	2,924	14,328
Dooly	5,580	6	2,775	8,361
Early	3,716	1	3,529	7,246
Effingham	2,009	7	1,848	3,864
Elbert	6,676	16	6,267	12,959
Emanuel	3,591	24	962	4,577
Fayette	6,740	4	1,965	8,709
Floyd	5,202	4	2,999	8,205
Forsyth	7,812	11	1,027	8,850
Franklin	9,076	55	2,382	11,513
Gilmer	8,236	4	200	8,440
Glynn	698	3	4,232	4,933
Gordon	5,156	—	828	5,984
Greene	4,744	58	8,266	13,068
Gwinnett	8,953	10	2,294	11,257
Habersham	7,675	2	1,218	8,895
Hall	7,370	7	1,336	8,713
Hancock	4,212	60	7,306	11,578
Harris	6,709	30	7,982	14,721
Heard	4,520	3	2,400	6,923
Henry	9,743	14	4,969	14,726
Houston	6,512	14	9,934	16,450
Irwin	2,883	1	450	3,334
Jackson	6,808	19	2,941	9,768
Jasper	4,323	29	7,134	16,486
Jones	3,899	46	6,279	10,224
Jefferson	3,717	47	5,367	9,131
Laurens	3,459	9	2,974	6,442
Lee	3,025	8	3,626	6,659
Liberty	2,002	16	5,908	7,926
Lincoln	2,187	31	3,780	5,998
Lowndes	5,845	22	2,484	8,351
Lumpkin	7,993	22	939	8,954
Macon	4,090	1	2,961	7,052
Madison	3,767	3	1,933	5,703
Marion	6,568	8	3,604	10,180
McIntosh	1,327	72	4,629	6,028
Meriwether	8,481	2	7,993	16,486
Monroe	6,810	5	10,170	16,985
Montgomery	1,541	—	613	2,154
Morgan	3,634	16	7,094	10,744
Murray	12,492	11	1,930	14,443
Muscogee	10,360	62	8,156	18,578
Newton	8,079	30	5,187	13,296
Oglethorpe	4,382	3	7,874	12,259
Paulding	5,560	2	1,477	7,039
Pike	8,686	61	5,558	14,305
Pulaski	3,784	39	2,804	6,629
Putnam	3,300	26	7,468	10,794
Rabun	2,338	—	110	2,448
Randolph	7,857	3	5,008	12,868
Richmond	8,152	282	7,812	16,246
Scriven	3,173	1	3,673	6,847
Stewart	8,649	5	7,373	16,027
Sumter	6,469	18	3,835	10,322
Talbot	7,793	18	8,723	16,534
Taliaferro	2,051	51	3,044	5,146
Tatnall	2,378	18	831	3,227
Telfair	2,096	—	930	3,026
Thomas	4,943	4	5,156	10,103
Troup	7,789	42	9,048	16,879
Twiggs	3,517	42	4,620	8,179
Union	6,955	1	278	7,234
Upson	4,720	—	4,704	9,424
Walker	11,408	37	1,664	13,109
Walton	6,896	16	3,909	10,821
Ware	3,597	3	288	3,888
Warren	6,168	149	6,108	12,425
Washington	5,993	35	5,738	11,766
Wayne	1,088	5	406	1,499
Wilkinson	5,467	—	2,745	8,212
Wilkes	3,805	21	8,281	12,107
Total	521,438	2,880	381,681	905,999

CLASSES AND SEXES OF POPULATION.

Classes.	Males.	Females.	Total.
White Persons	266,496	255,342	521,438
Colored " —free	1,368	1,512	2,880
" " —slave	—	—	—
Total	267,864	256,854	905,999

PROGRESSIVE MOVEMENT OF POPULATION.

Date of Census.	White Persons.	Colored Persons. Free.	Colored Persons. Slave.	Total Population.	Decennial Increase Numerical.	Decennial Increase Per 100.
1790	52,886	398	29,264	82,548	—	—
1800	101,678	1,019	59,404	162,101	79,553	96.3
1810	145,414	1,801	105,218	252,433	90,332	55.7
1820	189,564	1,767	149,656	340,987	88,554	35.1
1830	296,806	2,486	217,531	516,823	175,836	51.5
1840	407,695	2,753	280,944	691,392	174,569	33.7
1850	521,438	2,880	381,681	905,999	214,607	31.0

The number of dwelling houses in the State in 1850, was 91,001; and the number of families, 91,471. In these numbers, however, the slave residences and families are not counted, being considered as parts of the estate and family of their owners; and hence the ratio of persons to the house and family, which in the above returns is nearly 10 persons to each, is actually much less, but there are no means to ascertain it correctly. The same mode of taking the census has been observed throughout all the slaveholding States. The number of deaths during 1849–50 amounted to 9,920, or in the ratio of one in 91.3, or a little more than one per cent.

The productive industry of Georgia is chiefly agricultural, mining and manufactures being still in comparatively a rudimentary condition. Some iron, however, is made, and from time to time considerable quantities of gold have been collected. The great agricultural staple is cotton, which is extensively grown throughout the State, and on the islands along the coast. The latter, usually called *Sea-Island staple*, bears a high price in the market, and is the finest and best produced. About 490,000 or 500,000 bales are produced annually, each bale averaging 375 lbs. Rice may also be considered as a staple produce, the annual crop of which is now about 18,000,000 lbs. The other southern crops, as tobacco, sugar, etc., are small comparatively. The cereals, with the exception of Indian corn, are little attended to. The crop of Indian corn averages about 30,000,000 bushels, while that of wheat is scarcely 1,200,000, and of oats much less in amount. Barley, rye, and buckwheat are scarcely known to the planters. The live stock is ample, the horned cattle averaging one and swine averaging two to each inhabitant. The stock of sheep, however, is small. The orchards and gardens produce little, but there is abundance of fruit, as figs, oranges, melons, pomegranates, citrons, peaches, etc. In 1850–51, 51,759 farms and plantations were under cultivation. The manufactures of Georgia are progressing. The state, in this respect, takes the lead among the Southern states, and has commenced an era of manufacturing prosperity which promises great results. It has a number of large cotton mills, which are worked by slave-labor, and which produce the coarser description of goods much cheaper than the same qualities can be made in the North. It has also extensive tanneries and mills of various descriptions. The manufactures generally, however, are such only as are positively necessary for the country, and all goods of a fine texture and quality are imported. The whole number of manufacturing establishments producing annually $500 and upwards in 1850 was 1,407.

The foreign commerce of Georgia has doubled since 1840, owing, no doubt, to the completion of its system of railroads. In 1849–50, it exported to the value of $7,551,943, and imported to the value of $636,964. In 1841, the exports were valued at $3,696,513, and the imports at $449,007. The coasting and internal trade has increased in like proportion.

Georgia has adopted a liberal policy in respect of internal improvement. Its railroad system, starting from Savannah and Charleston, S. C., traverses the state westward to Alabama and Tennessee, tapping the west and southwest, and attracting to the seaboard a large portion of the traffic which formerly sought an outlet at New Orleans and Mobile. The great railroad from New York to Mobile and New Orleans, also passes through Georgia, and, when completed, will tend greatly to enhance the prosperity already enjoyed by the inhabitants. There are also a number of local railroads and branches diverging from the main lines. The whole length of completed railroad in the state in 1850, was 784 miles, and about 220 miles more were in course of construction. The cost of these works, up to that period, had been $13,922,000. Georgia has also several canals and some river improvements of great value to internal trade. In December, 1850, there were 10 banks and 11 branches in the state. The official returns made to the secretary of state, at that period, exhibited their condition in the aggregate as follows:—*Liabilities:* Capital, $13,482,198; circulation, $9,898,827; deposits, $2,580,826; due other banks, $483,422; and other items, $1,452,121. *Resources:* Loans and discounts, $11,421,626; stocks, $1,574,349; real estate, $7,195,063; other investments, $2,377,716; due by other banks, $3,117,466; notes of other banks, $535,593; specie fund, $141,300; specie, $2,112,446. In 1846 the capital of the banks amounted only to $6,519,400; and in 1848, to $8,035,070; and the circulation, which in 1846 was only $2,907,778; and in 1848, $2,784,446; had in 1850, increased as above exhibited to upwards of $9,000,000.

The University of Georgia, located at Athens, is the principal literary institution in the state, and was designed to have an academic branch in each county. It was founded in 1788, and has been well endowed. There are several other colleges of note. In 1850, there were in the state about 200 academies, with 9,000 students, and 1,200 primary and common schools, with 35,000 scholars.

The Baptists, Methodists and Presbyterians are the most numerous religious denominations. The Baptists have 620 churches, 298 ordained ministers, and 47,151 church members; and the Anti-Mission Baptists, 348 churches, 116 ministers, and 23 preachers, with 11,603 church members. The Methodists have 54,521 communicants. The Presbyterians, (O. S.) have 95 churches, and 4,338 members; the other Presbyterian sects are numerous. The Protestant Episcopalians have 23 churches, and a large body of adherents. The Catholics, Unitarians, and Universalists have also some congregations, and there are some Jews.

SAVANNAH, the largest and most important city in Georgia, in latitude 32° 4′ 56″ N., and longitude 81° 8′ 18″ W., has a population of 27,841. The city is built on a low sandy plain, on the south bank of the Savannah River, 18 miles from its mouth. Vessels drawing fourteen feet can come up to the wharves, but those of a large size are obliged to anchor about three miles down the river. The streets and buildings are regular and well planned, and, being decorated with trees, give to the city a rural and healthy appearance. There are several public buildings, churches &c., and immense piles of substantial warehouses line the wharves. The trade of Georgia centres in this place. It is now connected with the west, and north by lines of railroad which terminate only with the boundaries of the state; and it is in contemplation to extend these in other directions, and thereby open to the city a larger share of western business. Communication by steamboats is kept up with Charleston and other Atlantic cities, and a line of sailing vessels runs regularly to New-York. Possessing a fine harbor, and with these artificial advantages, this city must eventually become a great commercial emporium, and rapidly increase in population and wealth.

AUGUSTA, on the Savannah, below the falls, 127 miles from Savannah, is an entrepôt for the produce of a large district. This is brought down the river to Savannah and exported in large quantities to foreign ports. The population, in 1850, was 9,376.

MILLEDGEVILLE, the capital, is on Oconee River, near the centre of the state. Lat. 33° 7′ N., and long. 83° 20′ W. Population, in 1850, 4,095. It contains a state house, penitentiary, arsenal, &c. ATHENS, the seat of the University of Georgia, is a thriving village. DARIEN, on the Alatamaha River, 12 miles from its mouth, is a place of some considerable trade, and a depôt for the produce of the river valley. It is rapidly increasing in population and wealth. SUNBURY, BRUNSWICK and ST. MARY'S are small ports south of Savannah. PETERSBURG and WASHINGTON, in the interior, are also places of some consideration. MACON, on the Ockmulgee, and COLUMBUS, on the Chattahouchee, at the head of steam navigation, are depôts of populous and productive regions. The former, in 1822, consisted of only one log cabin: it now contains about 6,000 inhabitants, and the latter was a primitive wilderness in 1828, but now contains at least 8,000 souls. DAHLONEGA is the seat of a branch United States mint. A number of new towns have of late sprung up along the lines of the railroads, which are rapidly increasing and becoming important and wealthy.

The first constitution of Georgia was framed in 1777; a second in 1785; and the present one in 1798. Many amendments have been made.

Suffrage belongs to every white adult male citizen who has resided in the state six months, and paid all taxes demanded. The General Assembly consists of a SENATE and HOUSE OF REPRESENTATIVES. The former consists of 47 members chosen by districts, and the latter of 130 members. Both are elected biennially. The representatives are appointed in districts every seven years, according to the result of the state census. The Governor is also elected every two years. He must have attained the age of 30 years, and have been a citizen of the United States nine years, and an inhabitant of the state six years. He must also be possessed of a freehold of 500 acres, or $4,000 in other property, above all debts. Should there be no choice by the people, the election is decided by the General Assembly in joint ballot. The President of the Senate succeeds to the gubernatorial chair, in case of the death or disability of the Governor. A two-thirds vote disarms the Governor's veto.

The judiciary consists of a Supreme and Superior Court, and Circuit Courts. The Supreme Court for the Correction of Errors consists of three justices, who are appointed by the General Assembly, and may be removed by a two-thirds vote. The Superior Court has exclusive jurisdiction in criminal cases and land suits, and concurrent in all civil cases. The judges are appointed for six years. Justices of the inferior courts are elected by the people, and act as probate judges. Justices of the peace are also elected by popular vote in districts. All judges have fixed salaries. Sheriffs are appointed for two years, but are ineligible for a second appointment. Imprisonment for debt, except in cases of fraud, is abolished.

The constitution provides that there shall be no importation of slaves from Africa or any foreign place, after October, 1798. The legislature shall have no power to free slaves without the owners' consent, or to prevent immigrants from bringing with them persons deemed slaves by any one of the United States. Slaves are protected in their persons like free whites, except in case of insurrection, or unless their "death should happen by accident in giving such slaves MODERATE CORRECTION."

The finances of Georgia for the year ending October 1st, 1847, exhibited the following results:—Total receipts into the state treasury, $316,014, to which must be added $395,536 58 balance from previous year, making total means, $711,550 58. The expenditures for the year amounted to $349,299 28 : a balance of $362,251 30 being left in the treasury, of which $298,704 61 were in unavailable funds, and $63,546 89 in available funds. The estimated expenditures, for 1848, are $289,775, and the estimated receipts, $276,679, showing a deficiency for the year of $12,996.

The public debt of the state stands thus :

Sterling bonds (at $4 80)	$144,625 61
Federal bonds	1,435,250 00
Total	$1,579,875 61

The sterling bonds at 5 per cent. pay an annual interest of $7,231 28, and the federal bonds at 6 per cent, $86,115. One-half the sterling bonds will be liquidated this year (1848) from the sinking fund and surplus of 1847.

Georgia was the last settled of the thirteen original states forming the American Union. Previous to 1732, Georgia was a wilderness, and, though within the chartered limits of Carolina, was claimed by Spain as a part of Florida. At this period, this territory was granted to a company whose object was to transport gratuitously such persons as were seeking a subsistence. In honor of the grantor, George II., it was called Georgia. In November of that year, 160 persons arrived under Gen. James Oglethorpe, and a large quantity of land was purchased of the Cherokee Indians. The town of Savannah was now settled. Emigrants from Scotland and Germany arrived at successive periods. In 1742, the Spaniards attacked the settlement, but were repulsed. Georgia was preserved on this occasion by the skill and address of the Governor. Many restrictions retarded the prosperity of the colony, and so trifling were the productions, that, in 1750, the exports did not exceed £10,000. The government was ceded to the crown in 1752, and all the privileges and regulations of the other colonies extended to Georgia. A general assembly was established in 1755. From this period Georgia began to make rapid progress in prosperity and population. The rich swamps and lowlands on the rivers were brought into cultivation, and the effects of judicious government were soon visible in the increased amount of exports. In 1763, they had increased to £27,000, but in 1773, the value had risen to £121,000.

In the revolutionary war, Georgia, though not suffering under the grievances endured by the northern colonies, joined its sisters in the struggle, and was several times overrun by the British troops, and the principal inhabitants were obliged to abandon their possessions and fly into the neighboring states. In proportion to their numbers, the exertions and losses of her citizens were as great as in any of the states.

After the termination of the war, Georgia suffered from the incursions of the Creek Indians. In 1790, a treaty was concluded with this nation, by which the boundaries of Georgia were established. Georgia possessed, as included within her limits, a claim to an immense body of western land, of which, in 1795, the legislature sold a large portion, said to contain 22,000,000 acres, to a company, which company sold it to a second party. In the succeeding year the legislature declared the sale unconstitutional, and, on this ground, and that it had been obtained through bribery, they declared it to be void, and ordered all the records to be burnt. In 1802, Georgia ceded all the lands west of the Chattahouchee River and of a certain line, including the contested lands; and in 1814, Congress passed an act by which a compromise was made with the Yazoo purchasers, who received a certain amount of public stock. The recent history of Georgia is barren of important events, but the state is making rapid strides in prosperity and population.

THE STATE OF FLORIDA.

Florida, the most southerly state in the Union, is bounded north by Georgia and Alabama; west by Alabama; south and west by the Gulf of Mexico, and east by the Atlantic Ocean. It is situated between 25° and 31° N. lat., and between 80° and 87° 30′ W. long. This state is 400 miles long and 340 in extreme width, having an area of 53,786 square miles, or 34,423,055 acres, of which only about one-half is as yet surveyed and occupied.

A spur from the Alleghanies entered the original limits of Florida in the north-west, from which the French and Spaniards gave the name of Apalachian to the whole range of the Alleghanies. But by the sub-division of the states the mountains have been partitioned off, and the country in this state is generally level, or with but slight undulations. There is much good soil in Florida, and much that is sandy and unfit for agriculture, bearing only pines and shrubs. A large portion also consists of swamps and everglades. The shores are indented with bays and lagoons, and are lined with numerous islands. The climate is such that vegetation is perennial, and many of the tropical fruits grow luxuriantly. It is healthy, except in the vicinity of the lowlands and swamps, the temperature seldom varying more than 60 degrees between summer and winter, and seldom rising above 90°. Some of the islands, and especially those south of the southern point, enjoy a very equable climate, the annual range never being more than 12 or 15 degrees.

The St. John's is the principal river on the Atlantic coast. It is supposed to be almost 300 miles long in its various windings: vessels of eight feet draught have navigated it 150 miles from its mouth, and entered Lake George and Dunn's Lake. In some parts of the river it is four miles wide, and in others not more than a quarter of a mile wide. It flows parallel with the coast from north to south, and empties into the Atlantic. The St. Mary's, which rises in Georgia, passes through a part of Florida and enters the Atlantic. The Appalachicola, formed by the union of the Flint and Chattahouchee, which rise in Georgia, empties into the Gulf of Mexico, and is navigated through its entire length and far up its tributaries. It is a fine river. The Withlacoochee, Escambia, Suannee, Oscilla, Ocklocony, and Choctawatchie are the other principal rivers. The Perdido divides the state for a short distance from Alabama. There are several small lakes in Florida, some of which are noted for the quiet and wild beauty of their scenery.

The climate of Florida is essentially tropical. From October to June, it is generally mild and pleasant, but the summer months are extremely hot and sultry, and during this season fevers are prevalent, and dysentery and diarrhœa very destructive to life. St. Augustine and the islands, however, enjoy a good climate, and are often resorted to by invalids.

Salt is made in small quantities, and some granite is quarried: otherwise no minerals of importance are produced in this state.

The natural productions of Florida are live oak timber, which is unequalled in quality, and a great variety of other useful and ornamental woods. The fig, orange, date, etc., are among its fruits. Cotton is one of its most profitable staples, and sugar is extensively grown. Rice, indigo, etc., are furnished to a considerable value. The lands of Florida, however, are best suited for grazing, and vast herds of cattle and swine roam over its illimitable pastures. Sponges of fine quality are collected on the reefs.

The aggregate population of Florida in 1850 was 87,401, or one person to every 394 acres; and its distribution to the several divisions and counties in the following proportions:

I.—NORTHERN DISTRICT.

1.—WESTERN FLORIDA.

COUNTIES.	White Persons.	Colored Pesons. Free.	Slave.	Total Popula.
Calhoun	886	38	453	1,377
Escambia	2,644	375	1,332	4,351
Franklin	1,184	—	377	1,561
Holmes	1,481	—	163	1,644
Jackson	3,075	30	3,534	6,639
Santa Rosa	2,095	4	784	2,883
Walton	1,037	6	336	1,379
Washington	1,434	12	504	1,950
Total	13,836	465	7,483	21,784

2.—MIDDLE FLORIDA.

COUNTIES.	White Persons.	Colored Persons. Free.	Slave.	Total Popula.
Gadsden	3,900	4	4,879	8,783
Hamilton	1,775	9	685	2,469
Jefferson	2,775	5	4,938	7,718
Leon	3,183	56	8,203	11,442
Madison	2,802	—	2,688	5,490
Wakulla	1,164	1	790	1,955
Total	15,599	75	22,183	37,857

3.—EASTERN FLORIDA.

COUNTIES.	White Persons.	Colored Persons. Free.	Slave.	Total Popula.
Alachua	1,617	1	906	2,524
Benton	604	—	322	926
Columbia	3,541	1	1,266	4,808
Duval	2,338	95	2,106	4,539
Hillsboro'	1,711	6	660	2,377
Levi	320	—	145	465
Marion	2,069	—	1,269	3,338
Nassau	1,061	26	1,077	2,164
Orange	238	2	226	466
Putnam	473	10	204	687
St. John	1,417	115	993	2,525
St. Lucie	110	2	27	139
Total	15,499	258	9,201	24,958

II.—SOUTHERN DISTRICT.

4.—SOUTHERN FLORIDA.

COUNTIES.	White Persons.	Colored Persons. Free.	Slave.	Total Popula.
Dade	147	1	11	159
Monroe	2,086	126	431	2,643
Total	2,233	127	442	2,802
Grand Total	47,167	925	39,309	87,401

CLASSES AND SEXES OF POPULATION.

Classes.	Males.	Females.	Total.
White Persons	25,674	21,493	47,167
Colored " —free	420	505	925
" " —slave	—	—	39,309
Total	—	—	87,401

PROGRESSIVE MOVEMENT OF POPULATION.

Date of Census.	White Persons.	Colored Persons. Free.	Colored Persons. Slave.	Total Population.	Decennial Increase. Numerical.	Decennial Increase. Per 100.
1830	18,385	844	15,501	34,730	—	—
1840	27,943	817	25,717	54,477	19,747	56.9
1850	47,167	925	39,309	87,401	32,924	60.4

The number of dwellings in the state in 1850 amounted to 9,022, and the number of families to 9,107, or about 9.6 persons to each dwelling and family; and in 1849–50 the mortality amounted to 933 deaths, or in the ratio of one death to every 93.7 of the whole population.

The industry of Florida is almost entirely devoted to agriculture, the mechanic arts having progressed but slightly. In 1850 there were in the state 4,304 farms and plantations under cultivation, and only 121 manufacturing establishments, the annual products of which were valued at $500 and upwards, and these latter were only such as are incidental to an agricultural country. Indian corn is the great cereal crop and averages about 2,300,000 bushels annually; oats is next in amount but is very limited, and the cultivation of wheat, barley and rye is scarcely at all attended to. The crops of potatoes and hay are comparatively large. The staples or crops peculiar to the country are cotton, rice, sugar, tobacco, etc. The cotton crop averages some 48,000 bales; and Florida yields considerable lumber, chiefly live oak, which is highly estimated for ship-building.

The foreign commerce of Florida has materially increased of late years. In 1840 the exports were valued at $1,858,850, and in 1850 at $2,623,624; and the imports in 1840 were $190,728, and in 1850 $95,709. Imports to a very large amount, however, are made indirectly from domestic ports, and the same remark also applies to exports, the chief bulk of which pass through New Orleans and the Atlantic ports. The coasting and interior trade are of considerable value. The shipping owned within the state in 1850 amounted to 11,273 tons, of which 5,636 tons were registered for the foreign trade, and the residue of which, 2,185 tons, were navigated by steam, was employed in coasting. The entrances and clearances of shipping employed in the foreign trade in 1849–50 were as follows:

	Am. ships	For. ships	Total
ENTRANCES	7,518 tons	10,462 tons	17,980 tons.
CLEARANCES	" 10,022 "	" 12,134 "	" 22,156 "

of which shipping Appalachicola cleared 17,192 tons and entered 12,196 tons; Key West cleared 3,723 tons and entered 5,379 tons; and the small remainder was cleared and entered in the districts of Pensacola and San Augustine.

There are no railroads or canals in operation in this state, and the common roads are nowhere of a very high character for efficiency. The Legislature of 1848–49 chartered three companies for the establishment of railroads, viz., the Atlantic and Gulf Railroad Company, to connect the waters of the Atlantic and Gulf of Mexico upon such route as may be deemed most advisable and judicious; Florida and Georgia Railroad Company, for constructing a line between the Chattahoochee river and Gulf of Mexico at some point on St. Andrew's Bay, and the Pensacola Railroad Company for the purpose of constructing a road from some port on the St. Mary's river to Pensacola. Some short railroads, worked by horse power, were formerly in operation; one connecting St. Mark's and Tallahassee, and lines from St. Joseph's to Iola and Appalachicola.

Education is as yet but little attended to, and the scattered condition of the settlements will long retard its progress. The government, however, has ample means for its support in the school lands, etc., and the constitution provides for the organization of common schools throughout the country. There are academies and grammar schools in the cities, chiefly private, but there are no institutions where a collegiate course can be had.

The following are the principal provisions of the present constitution of the state:

Representatives, not more than 60 in number, must be 21 years old, white citizens of the United States, two years resident of the state, and one year of the county, and be elected for one year. In 1845, and every tenth year thereafter, a census shall be taken, and the representatives shall be apportioned by adding three-fifths of the slaves to the whole number of free whites. Senators are elected for two years; they must be 25 years old, and otherwise have the same qualifications as representatives. The General Assembly, chosen on the first Monday of October, shall meet on the first Monday in November of each year.

The Governor shall be elected by a plurality of votes for four years, and shall be ineligible for the four years next after his term. He shall be 30 years old, ten years a citizen of the United States or an inhabitant of Florida at the adoption of the constitution, and a resident thereof for five years next before the election. He may *veto* a bill; but a majority of those elected to both houses may pass it again, notwithstanding his *veto*. If the office be vacant, the president of the Senate, and after him the speaker of the House, shall act as Governor. No officer in a banking company, while he serves in a bank, or for twelve months afterwards, shall be eligible for the office of governor, senator, or representative. No duellist, or second in a duel, shall hold any office under the state. The secretary of state shall be elected by the legislature for four years.

The Supreme Court, having appellate jurisdiction only, shall be composed of the circuit judges for five years after the election of these judges, and thereafter until the General Assembly shall otherwise provide. The circuit courts shall have original common law jurisdiction in all matters, civil and criminal. They shall also have original equity jurisdiction, until a separate chancery court be established by the Legislature. The judges shall be elected by concurrent vote of a majority of both houses, and shall be chosen at first for five years; after that term, during good behavior. They may be removed by impeachment, or by address of two-thirds of each house. An attorney-general shall be elected by joint vote of the two houses for four years; also a solicitor for each circuit for the same term. No act of incorporation shall be passed or altered, except by the assent of two-thirds of each house, and by giving three months' notice. No bank charter shall be for more than 30 years, nor shall it ever be extended or renewed. The capital of a bank shall not exceed $100,000, nor shall a dividend be made exceeding 16 per cent. a year. Stockholders shall be individually liable for the debts of the bank, and no notes shall be issued for less than $5. The credit of the state shall not be pledged in aid of any corporation whatsoever. No law shall be passed to emancipate slaves, or to prohibit the immigration of persons bringing slaves with them; but free colored persons may be prevented from entering the state. For an amendment of this constitution, two-thirds of both houses must assent: the proposed alteration must then be published six months before the succeeding election, and then be again approved by a two-thirds vote in the succeeding assembly.

The finances of the government, for the year 1846, were as follow:—The principal items of expenditure were, for the legislative department, $14,724 33; executive, $5,838 56; judicial, $9,263 76; printing laws, &c., $1,690 69; criminal prosecutions, $6,606 26; contingent expenses of courts, $1,756 05, and contingent fund, $1,705 85. Taxes to the amount of $39,500 were the principal sources of income. Florida has a considerable public debt, chiefly contracted for banking purposes.

St. Augustine, the oldest town in Florida, as it is in the United States, is situated two miles from the Atlantic, on the south side of a peninsula, and is protected from the ocean by Anastasia Island. In 1850 it had a population of 2,993. Its climate is pure and healthy, and the town is embowered in orange groves. Like all old places, the streets are narrow, but the buildings, which are two stories high, are handsome and picturesque, having around them balconies and piazzas. The public buildings are the United States barracks, the land office, and several churches. Fort Marion, standing at the mouth of the harbor, protects the town.

Tallahassee, the seat of government, lies on the northern part of the state, upon an elevated site, and is a place of considerable business. Lat. 30° 28′ N., long. 84° 36′ W. A railroad runs from this town to St. Mark's, a seaport on the gulf, 22 miles distant. It contains a bank, the state-house, a jail, a market, and several churches. The permanent population is about 2,000, but in winter is much increased by accessions of visitors.

Pensacola is situated in Escambia county, and is the most westerly of the Florida towns. It lies on Pensacola Bay, 10 miles from the Gulf. The United States navy-yard at this place is one of the most useful in the Union. Population about 2,800. The harbor is accessible to vessels drawing 8 feet of water.

Jacksonville, on St. John's River, is a thriving seaport and depôt for a large and fertile district. Apalachicola, on the river of the same name, has a good harbor, and considerable trade in cotton. About 20 steamboats navigate the river. It is connected with St. Joseph's by railroad. St. Joseph's, a little west of Apalachicola, and on the Bay of St. Joseph, has a deep, capacious harbor, and is well sheltered from the winds. It is connected with Iola, on the Apalachicola River, and with the town of Apalachicola by railroad. Quincy, Lancaster, Smyrna, and some other places are rapidly progressing to importance. Smyrna, from its situation, must eventually become the depôt of an immense and fertile agricultural country.

Key West, one of the islets of the southernmost extremity of the peninsula, has a fine harbor, and can accommodate the largest class of ships. It is an important naval station, and the seat of the Wrecker's Court, to which all cases of salvage are brought for adjudication. The wreckers of Key West are said to be a most daring set of men, and fully capable of aiding and recovering vessels stranded on the reefs.

Florida was discovered by Cabot in 1496, and first visited by Ponce de Leon in 1512. In 1562, we find the French and Spaniards contesting their respective rights to the country. Subsequently the English from Georgia and Carolina attempted to gain possession, but unsuccessfully. In 1763, Florida was ceded to England in exchange for Cuba, and was divided into two provinces. Spain recovered it in 1781, and her possession was confirmed at the peace of 1783. The United States purchased the territory in 1819, and paid the Spanish government in spoilation claims! After the usual territorial probation, Florida was admitted into the Union in 1845.

THE WESTERN STATES.

The states comprised under this caption are those of Ohio, Indiana, Illinois, Michigan and Wisconsin on the north of the Ohio and east of the Mississippi rivers; Kentucky south of the Ohio, and the states of Missouri and Iowa on the west of the Mississippi. The immense territories westward of these will be described hereafter. The whole region is included in the great basins of the St. Lawrence, Ohio, Mississippi and the Missouri, and together occupy an area of 399,395 square miles, or 255,612,819 acres, all of which, excepting 48,709,283 acres, have been surveyed and partially settled. The population of these vast regions, which, in 1790, was only 73,077, had increased, in 1840, to 4,131,370, and the census of 1850, made it 6,379,801 souls.

If we except a few isolated elevations, the whole extent of the Western States presents a series of plains inclining only in the direction of the great lakes and rivers which form the chief features of this prolific country. No continuous chain or any hill approaching the semblance of a mountain, interrupts the vision, and the far horizon alone arrests the powers of sight. Along the rivers, indeed, some few ragged bluffs occasionally occur, but so limited is their extent and so small their occupancy, that they are lost in the universality of the pervading characteristics of the whole, and can only claim a notice in a minute topographical description of the locality in which they exist.

The soil of these prairies is infinite in variety, of great depth, and fertile beyond description. Naturally they are clothed with a strong sward, bearing a tall, coarse grass, and in some places extensive tracts are covered with forests of oak, pine, walnut and other valuable trees. Here are found some of the most lovely landscapes, and for miles and miles, a varied scenery of natural growth, with all the diversity of gently swelling hill and dale—here trees grouped or standing singly alone; and there arranged in long avenues, as though planted by human hands, with strips of open prairie intervening. Sometimes the "openings" are dotted with numerous clear lakes and form scenes of enchanting beauty. 'Tis in these regions the bison roams, and here the red hunter formerly delighted to pursue his game amid the primeval developments of nature.

But the most important features of this country are the giant rivers which, with a thousand branches, penetrate to every portion of the land, and lead off the surplus waters to the vast central trunk which traverses it from north to south. Without these and those vast lakes which lie on the north, the whole region must forever have remained an impenetrable wilderness. These are now the great avenues of commerce, and have contributed more than all the artificial constructions of man to develope the teeming wealth of the regions watered by their courses. Craft of every description, from the primitive flat bottom boat to the magnificent steamboat, the acmé of mechanical skill, bear upon their bosoms the staples and productions of every land, endowing with riches the whole country, and adding daily to the necessities and luxuries of the thriving people who by their presence and perseverance have caused the wilderness to smile and the nakedness of the earth to be clothed in perennial harvests.

Nor is all the wealth of this prolific region in the surface. In the bowels of the earth unbounded supplies of the most valuable minerals exist. Lead, iron, coal and lime are here imbedded, and by the untiring industry of man are made to contribute to his convenience and use. Salt, too, is found in abundance in all the states.

Here, then, we have a country rich in the produce of the mines—rich in the great staples of agriculture—prolific beyond comprehension, and supplied with every accommodation for the transportation of man and merchandize, and of an extent equalled by few of the great empires of either ancient or modern times. The prospects of such a country, how grand! and its destiny, how mighty! Its progress from a wilderness to a garden has been rapid. Untrod by man within a century, it now maintains its millions, and exports a surplus to feed the starving nations of Europe. Unscathed by slavery, it is the home of the freeman, and its lands are tilled by unshackled hands, and in this we discover the great secret of its prosperity.

THE STATE OF OHIO.

This flourishing and populous state is the most easterly of the western division of the Union, and is bounded north by the State of Michigan and Lake Erie; east by Pennsylvania; south-east and south by the Ohio River, which separates it from Virginia and Kentucky; and west by the State of Indiana. It lies between the latitudes of 38° 34′ and 42° N., and between the longitudes of 80° 35′ and 84° 57′ W. In length it is 230 miles, and in mean breadth, 210 miles. Its area is 39,628 square miles, or 25,361,593 acres.

The northern parts of the state bordering on Lake Erie, and the interior, are generally level, and in some places wet and marshy. The eastern and south-eastern parts, near the Ohio River, are very uneven, often rising in abrupt and broken hills—this section, however, cannot properly be termed mountainous. On the margin of the Ohio and several of its tributaries, are strips of alluvial of great fertility. The valleys of the Sciota and the Great and Little Miami, are the most extensive sections of level, rich, and fertile lands in the state. In a state of nature, Ohio was, with the exception of some central prairies, covered with a dense forest, to which the fertility of the soil gave a stupendous development. The most extensive prairies are found on the head waters of the Muskingum and Sciota; also near the sources of the Miami River, and the north-western parts of the state. The forest trees most abundant are the oak of several species, black and white walnut, hickory, maple of different kinds, ash of various species, beech, birch and poplar, sycamore, linden, chestnut, locust, elm, buck-eye, with numerous others. The agricultural productions are wheat, rye, Indian corn, oats, buckwheat, barley, potatoes, and all kinds of garden vegetables. Considerable attention has been of late paid to the cultivation of hemp and tobacco. The raising of horses, sheep, cattle, and swine, for exportation, engages the attention of a large proportion of the farmers. The amount of agricultural products of this state, including provisions, flour, wheat, etc., annually sent to other states of the Union, and exported to foreign countries, is greater than from any part of the United States, and Ohio may emphatically be termed an agricultural state.

The principal rivers in Ohio, besides the great and beautiful river which gives its name to the state, and forms part of its eastern and its entire southern boundary, are the Mahoning, Beaver, Muskingum, Hockhocking, Sciota, and Little and Great Miama, which flow south into the Ohio River. Those which flow northward into Lake Erie, are the Maumee, Portage, Sandusky, Huron, Cuyahoga, Grand and Ashtabula. Lake Erie forms the northern boundary of the state for 160 miles, and is navigable for the largest class of vessels.

The climate of Ohio is one of the most healthy in the United States. Free from extremes of heat or cold, it is peculiarly well adapted to agriculture. The southern parts are generally warmer than on the Atlantic in the same latitude, while the tracts in the more northerly districts are in winter somewhat colder. The new settlers in the marshy and low locations and near stagnant waters, are liable to fevers and fluxes of various types, and require acclimatizing before they can enjoy health. These, however, are only exceptions to the general salubrity of the state. Nine tenths of the surface of the state are susceptible of agricultural improvement. The river bottoms are highly fertile, and the rich level uplands of the interior are unsurpassed as farming lands. Fine prairies, interspersed with groves of timber, sometimes marshy, but more frequently dry and elevated, occupy a considerable area. The southeastern and eastern parts are hilly, but the lands are by no means poor even on the hills, and the slopes are always excellent. On the whole, Ohio may be considered as one of the most productive countries of the world.

The most important and useful minerals are abundant. Coal, iron, salt and limestone, the two first in the northeast chiefly, are found in most parts of the state; and marble and freestone, when adapted for architectural purposes, and gypsum, are of frequent occurrence. Chalybeate springs, useful for medicinal purposes, are numerous. The forests produce black walnut, various species of oak, hickory, sugar maple, beech, birch, poplar, ash, sycamore, pawpaw, buckeye, cherry, dogwood, elm, hornbeam, and many other timbers valuable for cabinet work, building, and other purposes. The country abounds in game of every sort.

In 1850, Ohio had a population of 1,980,408 souls, or one inhabitant to about every thirteen acres; and its distribution to the several counties was in the following proportions:

COUNTIES.	White Persons.	Colored Persons.	Total Popula.	COUNTIES.	White Persons.	Colored Persons.	Total Popula.
Adams	18,828	55	18,883	Butler	30,429	360	30,789
Allen	12,085	24	12,109	Carroll	17,633	52	17,685
Ashland	12,789	3	23,792	Champaign	19,272	490	19,762
Ashtabula	28,725	41	28,766	Clark	21,855	323	22,178
Athens	18,119	96	18,215	Clermont	30,044	411	30,455
Auglaise	11,251	87	11,338	Clinton	18,247	591	18,838
Belmont	33,766	834	34,600	Columbiana	33,444	177	33,621
Brown	26,520	812	27,332	Coshocton	25,630	44	25,674

COUNTIES.	White Persons.	Colored Persons.	Total Popula.
Crawford	18,167	10	18,177
Cuyahoga	47,745	354	48,099
Darke	20,111	163	20,274
Defiance	6,947	19	6,966
Delaware	21,682	135	21,817
Erie	18,366	202	18,568
Fairfield	29,984	280	30,264
Fayette	12,456	270	12,726
Franklin	41,310	1,600	42,910
Fulton	7,780	1	7,781
Gallia	15,865	1,198	17,063
Geauga	17,827	—	17,827
Greene	21,460	486	21,946
Guernsey	30,273	165	30,438
Hamilton	153,423	3,420	156,843
Hancock	16,725	26	16,751
Hardin	8,237	14	8,251
Harrison	19,870	287	20,157
Henry	3,435	—	3,435
Highland	24,952	829	25,781
Hocking	14,002	117	14,119
Holmes	20,448	4	20,452
Huron	26,167	36	26,203
Jackson	12,330	391	12,721
Jefferson	28,526	606	29,132
Knox	28,811	62	28,873
Lake	14,616	38	14,654
Lawrence	14,920	326	15,246
Licking	38,731	115	38,846
Logan	18,631	531	19,162
Loraine	25,824	262	26,086
Lucas	12,220	140	12,363
Madison	9,946	69	10,015
Mahoning	23,646	89	23,735
Marion	12,597	21	12,618
Medina	24,411	30	24,441
Meigs	17,924	47	17,971
Mercer	7,401	311	7,712
Miama	24,398	598	24,996
Monroe	28,281	70	28,351
Montgomery	37,973	246	38,219
Morgan	28,515	70	28,585
Morrow	20,270	10	20,280
Muskingum	44,421	628	45,049
Ottawa	3,307	1	3,308
Paulding	1,765	1	1,766
Perry	20,746	29	20,775
Pickaway	20,595	413	21,008
Pike	10,327	629	10,953
Portage	24,337	82	24,419
Preble	21,662	74	21,736
Putnam	7,210	11	7,221
Richland	30,834	45	30,879
Ross	30,207	1,867	32,074
Sandusky	14,257	48	14,305
Sciota	18,274	154	18,428
Seneca	26,954	151	27,105
Shelby	13,634	324	13,958
Stark	39,733	145	39,878
Summit	27,422	63	27,485
Trumbull	30,455	35	30,490
Tuscarawas	31,672	89	31,761
Union	12,076	128	12,204
Van Wert	4,766	47	4,813
Vinton	9,246	107	9,353
Warren	24,960	601	25,561
Washington	29,149	391	29,540
Wayne	32,953	28	32,981
Williams	8,018	—	8,018
Wood	9,139	18	9,157
Wyandott	11,243	49	11,292
Total	1,956,108	24,300	1,980,408

CLASSES AND SEXES OF POPULATION.

Classes.	Males.	Females.	Total.
White Persons	1,004,111	951,997	1,956,108
Colored " —free	12,239	12,061	24,300
" " —slave	—	—	—
Total	1,016,350	964,058	1,980,408

PROGRESSIVE MOVEMENT OF POPULATION.

Date of Census.	White Persons.	Colored Persons. Free.	Colored Persons. Slave.	Total Population.	Decennial Increase. Numerical.	Decennial Increase. Per 100.
1800	45,028	337	—	45,365	—	—
1810	228,861	1,899	—	230,760	185,395	408.7
1820	576,572	4,862	—	581,434	350,674	151.9
1830	928,329	9,568	6	937,903	356,469	61.3
1840	1,502,122	17,342	3	1,519,467	581,564	62.0
1850	1,956,108	24,300	—	1,980,408	460,941	30.3

The number of dwelling-houses in the state in 1850 was 336,098, or one dwelling to every 5.9 persons; and the families numbered 348,523, or 5.7 to each family. The deaths in 1849–50 amounted to 28,949, or one in 68.4 of the whole people.

Mining, though not a principal occupation in Ohio, is nevertheless an extensive one; and in the development of its mineral resources the state has been eminently progressive. The principal minerals produced are iron, bituminous coal, and salt, but it has abundance of others, of which the future will take advantage. The production of pig iron in 1850 amounted to 52,658 tons, of iron castings to 37,399 tons, and of wrought iron to 14,416 tons; in 1840 the production was 35,236 tons cast iron, and 7,466 tons wrought iron: and the capital, etc., at both periods as follows:

Kinds of Metal Made.	Number of Works.	Capital Invested.	Value of Raw Material, etc.	Hands Employed.	Value of Products.
Pig iron	35	$1,503,000	$630,037	2,415	$1,255,850
Cast iron	183	2,063,650	1,199,790	2,758	3,069,350
Wrought iron	11	620,800	604,493	708	1,076,192
Total	229	$4,190,450	$2,434,320	5,881	$5,301,392
Total, 1840	91	1,161,900	—	2,268	—

The agricultural capacities of Ohio are surpassed by those of no other state. It is decidedly the finest wheat country in the world, and for grazing and cattle and sheep feeding it has scarcely an equal. The cereal crops in millions of bushels may be estimated—wheat at 15, oats at 22, Indian corn at 63, and the crops of buckwheat and rye each at two million bushels. Barley is rarely produced, and may be said to be unknown to Ohio agriculture. Hemp and flax, tobacco, potatoes are valuable crops, and are grown in considerable quantities. Live stock consists of 513,625 horses, 2,180 mules, 1,103,811 cattle, 3,812,707 sheep, and 1,672,178 hogs, valued at $33,269,135. The wool, pork, beef, and other animal products from this state are of a very superior quality; the slaughter of hogs for packing in Cincinnati and some other towns is immense. The forest, orchard, and garden contribute also materially to the general wealth. In 1850 there were 143,887 farms under cultivation.

The manufacturing industry of Ohio permeates almost every branch of the mechanic arts. Machinery is made on an extensive scale; hardware of all kinds is manufactured, and metal workers generally form a numerous class. In the manufacture of woollen goods 130 factories are employed, and a capital of $870,220 invested; the quantity of wool consumed in 1850 was 1,657,726 lbs., and the value of all raw material, fuel, etc., was $578,423; the hands employed numbered 1,201, and the products were 1,374,087 yards of cloth and 65,000 pounds of yarn, together valued at $1,111,037. There were at the same period eight cotton factories in the state, with an aggregate capital amounting to $279,000; cotton consumed 4,270 bales, which with fuel, etc., was valued at $227,060; hands employed 401; products 280,000 yards sheeting, and 433,000 pounds of yarn and thread, valued at $394,790. The capital invested in the woollen manufactures in 1840 was $537,985, and in those of cotton goods $113,500. Silk, flax and mixed goods are also made to some extent, and a large capital is employed in the leather trade. Distilleries, flouring mills, paper mills, etc., are established in most of the counties. The number of productive establishments, manufacturing to the value of $500 and upwards annually, in 1850, was 10,550, of which number nearly one-sixth were located in Hamilton county.

The direct foreign commerce of Ohio is comparatively small; but it has nevertheless a considerable trade with Canada. The value of the exports in the year ending 30th June, 1850, amounted to $217,632, and of the imports to $582,504. The coastwise trade of Ohio on the lakes, and its trade on the Ohio River, and by the course of its railroads and canals, is immense. The shipping enrolled in the several districts amounted in 1850 to 62,462 tons.

In November, 1850, there were in the state 57 banks and branches, the condition of which in the aggregate presented the following features: liabilities—capital $8,718,866, circulation $11,059,760, deposits $5,310,555, and other items $1,649,745; and assets—loans and discounts $17,039,593, stocks $2,220,891, real estate $451,593, other investments $460,892, due by other banks $3,373,272, notes of other banks $1,195,655, specie funds $98,460, and specie $2,750,537. The banks of Ohio consist of three classes, viz.: Independent Banks, of which there are eleven, Old Banks, five, and the State Bank and branches, forty-one.

Ohio has completed several magnificent works of internal improvement. Railroads and canals traverse it in every direction. The Ohio Canal connects the waters of Lake Erie at Cleveland with those of the Ohio at Portsmouth, and is 309 miles long; the Walhonding Canal extends along the valley of the river of the same name, from Roscoe on the Ohio Canal to Rochester, a distance of 25 miles; the Hocking Canal leaves the Ohio Canal at Carroll, and traverses the left bank of the Hocking River to Athens, 56 miles; the Miami Canal and extension extends from Cincinnati to its junction with the Wabash and Erie Canal, 181 miles; the Warren county Canal, 19 miles long, the Sidney Feeder, 13 miles long, and the St. Mary's Feeder, 11 miles long, are branches of the Miami Canal, and extension; the Muskingum Improvement extends from the Ohio Canal at Dresden to the mouth of the Muskingum River, 91 miles; and the Sandy and Beaver Canal (Mahoning) extends from the Ohio Canal at Bolivar to the Ohio River, a distance of 86 miles, and unites with the Pennsylvania Canals at the state line. The tolls collected on all the canals in 1849 amounted to $740,463. The principal railroads in the state are as follows:

Railroads.	Miles.	Railroads.	Miles
Belfontaine and Indiana	118	Lake Shore	165
Central	137	Little Miami	84
Cincinnati and Belpre	121	Mad River and Lake Erie	134
Cincinnati and Dayton	60	Mansfield and Newark	60
Cincinnati and Hillsboro'	37	Ohio and Indiana	126
Cleveland and Erie	80	Ohio and Mississippi	20
Cleveland and Pittsburg	98	Ohio and Pennsylvania	135
Cleveland and Wellsville	30	Sandusky and Mansfield	56
Columbus and Cleveland	149	Scioto and Hocking Valley	110
Columbus and Lake Erie	39	Toledo and Cleveland	86
Dayton and Springfield	24	Western	37
Findlay	16	Xenia and Columbus	54
Greenville and Miami	20	Xenia and Dayton	16
Hamilton and Eaton	20		

Of these 27 roads, 690 miles were in operation in 1850, and 1,341 in course of construction. The cost so far as completed had been up to June of that year $12,768,000. Besides these highways the state has a number of fine macadamized roads, plank-roads, and ordinary roads traverse every county.

The schools of Ohio are scarcely inferior in efficiency to those of Massachusetts and New-York. The common school fund amounts to $615,626; the greater portion of school moneys, however, are derived from taxation. In 1849, the amount distributed to the several districts was $293,159. The whole number of school districts is 6,826, and of common schools 5,042, which have on their rolls 90,464 scholars. The principal collegiate institutions are—the University at Athens, founded 1804; Miami University at

Oxford, founded 1809; Franklin College at New Athens, Western Reserve College at Hudson, Kenyon College at Gambier, Granville College, Marietta College, Oberlin College, Cincinnati College, to which medical and law schools are attached; St. Xavier's College, and Woodward College, also at Cincinnati, Ohio Wesleyan University at Delaware, etc. Theological schools are attached to Kenyon College, the Western Reserve College, and several others. Lane Seminary at Cincinnati is a celebrated institution belonging to the Presbyterians. Several of these institutions are in high repute.

The most numerous religious denominations are the Episcopal Methodists, Baptists and Presbyterians. The Episcopalian Protestants, the Congregationalists, and Roman Catholics have also many communicants, and the minor churches are represented in the larger cities.

The constitution of Ohio grants the right of voting to all male citizens 21 years of age. The legislature consists of a Senate and House of Representatives; Senators, who must be citizens of the United States, 30 years of age, are chosen for two years, and Representatives, who must be 25 years of age, for one year. The General Assembly has the sole power of enacting all the state laws, the assent or signature of the Governor not being necessary in any case whatever. The Governor is chosen biennially. The Judiciary consists of a Supreme Court with four Judges, Courts of Common Pleas, for the holding of which the State is divided into 19 circuits, and several inferior and local courts. Justices are elected by the legislature for seven years. Cleveland and Cincinnati have Special Superior Courts, and Cincinnati has also a Commercial Court. The institutions supported by the state are the Lunatic Asylum and the Deaf and Dumb Asylum at Columbus.

The total revenue of Ohio for the fiscal year ending 15th November, 1849, amounted to $2,937,571, and the disbursements to $2,383,136; surplus $554,435. The chief sources of income are taxes on property, canal tolls, dividends, rents, interests, etc. The chief expenses are interest on foreign and domestic debt, repairs of canals, schools, and legislative appropriations. The public debt consists of domestic bonds outstanding, $529,592 38, bearing interest $28,557 96 annually, school and trust funds $1,615,625 59—interest $96,937 54, and the foreign debt $16,880,982 50; interest $1,022,358 95; total $19,026,200 47—interest $1,147,854 45. The state has assets—$2,007,260 34, surplus revenue, and public property in canals, railroads, etc., $3,011,858 71. The value of real and personal property in the state, in 1849, was $430,839,085, on which the state tax was $1,296,347 56.

Columbus, the capital of the state, is situated on the left bank of the Scioto River, immediately below the junction of the Olentangy or Whitestone. The State capitol is a very handsome building. The streets are laid out rectangularly, and in the centre of the city is a public square of ten acres, handsomely enclosed. Franklinton, on the opposite bank of the river, is connected with Columbus by a bridge. Railroads connect it with Cincinnati and Cleveland. Population in 1850, 17,367; in 1840 it was 6,048.

Cincinnati, the Queen city of the West, is beautifully situated on the north bank of the Ohio. The shores of the river at this point afford good landing. The city, except on the margin of the river, is laid out in streets crossing at right angles; it has many handsome public buildings, including more than 100 churches, several colleges, spacious school houses, etc. The commerce of Cincinnati is immense, and it is likewise the principal seat of Ohio manufacturing industry. In 1795 it was a mere village of 500 inhabitants; in 1810, it had 2,540; in 1820, 9,642; in 1830, 24,831; in 1840, 48,338, and in 1850 116,108.

SANDUSKY, on the lake shore, is the terminus of the Mad River and Erie Railroad, and otherwise a point of importance connected with the lake and interior trade of the state. In 1850, its population was 5,434, and in 1851, 7,901, having increased in one year 45 per centum.

CLEVELAND, also on the lake, and a great railroad centre, is situated on an elevated plain at the mouth of Cuyahoga River; it has a spacious and safe harbor, and may be considered as the principal port of the state. Its population has increased rapidly; in 1840 it was 6,071; in 1850, 17,074, and in 1851, 21,034. The great increase in 1850–51 may be attributed to the completion of several lines of railroads terminating at this point.

Fairfield, Astabula, etc., are ports of consideration, and have good harbors. Toledo is the eastern terminus of the Michigan railroads. Hamilton and Dayton are important interior towns. Springfield has several large manufacturing establishments; and Zanesville, Portsmouth, Marietta, Chillicothe, etc., are also flourishing places, on the great thoroughfares.

Ohio, previous to 1788, was an entire wilderness; in that year a settlement was made at Marietta, and in 1789, the country was placed under a territorial government, and called the "Western Territory." This name applied not only to Ohio, but to all the district north-west of the Ohio River to the Mississippi, and included the present states of Indiana, Illinois, Michigan and Wisconsin. At a subsequent period it was known as the "Territory North-west of the Ohio." The ordinance by which this territory was established forbids "slavery" in any future state that may be formed within this district. Ohio became a state in 1802.

THE STATE OF INDIANA.

INDIANA lies between the latitudes of 37° 45′ and 41° 52′ north, and between the longitudes of 84° 42′ and 88° 12′ west. It is bounded on the north by the lake and State of Michigan; east by the State of Ohio; south by the Ohio River, which separates it from Kentucky; and west by the State of Illinois. The state is 246 miles long and 160 miles broad, and has an area of 36,580 square miles, or 23,411,431 acres.

Indiana is in no part mountainous, but that portion bordering on the Ohio contains much broken, hilly land. The interior parts, the valleys of the east and west forks of White River, present a gently undulating country, generally timbered, with occasional strips of rich bottom on the margin of the streams. The valley of the Wabash, in the lower part, is an undulating surface of forest and prairie. North of Terre Haute, the land is of the first quality, fine forest, occasionally opening into beautiful and fertile prairies. On the St. Joseph's, and across to the head waters of the Maumee, are extensive wet and dry prairies, and heavily timbered lands, with a soil of exhaustless fertility. On the shore of Lake Michigan are sand hills, and along the Kankakee extensive swamps and marshes. The kinds of timber most abundant are, oaks of various species, ash, beech, buckeye, walnut, cherry, sugar tree, hickory, elm, sassafras, honey-locust, with some cotton-wood, sycamore, hackberry and mulberry. The principal productions are wheat, rye, Indian corn, oats, buckwheat, barley, potatoes, etc.

The climate of Indiana is favorable and agreeable. The winters are milder and shorter than in the Atlantic states, and the summers are, in general, not warmer. The spring commences about the middle of February.

The peach blossoms in March, and the woods are green in April. The country in the upper parts of the state is healthy, and the districts along the rivers, except in the neighborhood of swamps and marshes, are not considered insalubrious.

In 1850 Indiana contained 988,416 inhabitants, or one person to every 24 acres; and these were distributed to the several counties in the following proportions:

COUNTIES.	White Persons.	Colored Persons.	Total Popula.
Adams	5,789	8	5,797
Allen	16,817	102	16,919
Bartholomew	12,336	92	12,428
Benton	1,144	—	1,144
Blackford	2,849	11	2,860
Boone	11,611	20	11,631
Browne	4,827	19	4,846
Carroll	10,982	33	11,015
Cass	10,936	85	11,021
Clark	15,246	582	15,828
Clay	7,926	18	7,944
Clinton	11,845	24	11,869
Crawford	6,523	1	6,524
Daviess	10,308	44	10,352
Dearborn	20,021	145	20,166
Decatur	14,951	156	15,107
De Kalb	8,241	10	8,251
Delaware	10,839	4	10,843
Dubois	6,300	21	6,321
Elkhart	12,674	16	12,690
Fayette	10,145	72	10,217
Floyd	14,305	570	14,875
Fountain	13,201	52	13,253
Franklin	17,760	208	17,968
Fulton	5,980	2	5,982
Gibson	10,554	217	10,771
Grant	10,945	147	11,092
Greene	12,238	75	12,313
Hamilton	12,504	180	12,684
Hancock	9,595	103	9,698
Harrison	15,206	80	15,286
Hendricks	14,047	36	14,083
Henry	17,380	225	17,605
Howard	6,615	42	6,657
Huntingdon	7,847	3	7,850
Jackson	10,837	210	11,047
Jasper	3,539	1	3,540
Jay	7,017	30	7,047
Jefferson	23,348	568	23,916
Jennings	11,773	323	12,096
Johnson	12,086	15	12,101
Knox	10,546	538	11,084
Kosciusko	10,242	1	10,243
La Grange	8,369	18	8,387
Lake	3,990	1	3,991
La Porte	12,070	75	12,145
Lawrence	12,003	94	12,097
Madison	12,358	17	12,375
Marion	23,363	650	24,013
Marshall	5,346	2	5,348
Martin	5,844	97	5,941
Miami	11,293	11	11,304
Monroe	11,259	27	11,286
Montgomery	17,955	129	18,084
Morgan	14,502	74	14,576
Noble	7,940	6	7,946
Ohio	5,297	11	5,308
Orange	10,559	250	10,809
Owen	11,950	156	12,106
Parke	14,741	227	14,968
Perry	7,259	9	7,268
Pike	7,210	10	7,220
Porter	5,229	5	5,234
Posey	12,451	98	12,549
Pulaski	2,595	—	2,595
Putnam	18,581	34	18,615
Randolph	14,064	661	14,725
Ripley	14,724	96	14,820
Rush	16,226	219	16,445
Scott	5,870	15	5,885
Shelby	15,484	18	15,502
Spencer	8,615	1	8,616
Stark	557	—	557
Steuben	6,102	2	6,104
St. Joseph	10,925	29	10,954
Sullivan	10,110	31	10,141
Switzerland	12,866	66	12,932
Tippecanoe	19,218	159	19,377
Tipton	3,525	7	3,532
Union	6,906	38	6,944
Vanderburgh	11,187	227	11,414
Vermillion	8,643	18	8,661
Vigo	14,556	733	15,289
Wabash	12,124	14	12,138
Warren	7,381	6	7,387
Warrick	8,789	29	8,811
Washington	16,788	252	17,040
Wayne	24,323	997	25,320
Wells	6,141	11	6,152
White	4,752	9	4,761
Whitley	5,095	95	5,190
Total	977,605	10,811	988,416

CLASSES AND SEXES OF POPULATION.

Classes.	Males.	Females.	Total.
White Persons	506,400	471,205	977,605
Colored " —free	5,480	5,331	10,811
" " —slave	—	—	—
Total	511,880	476,536	988,416

PROGRESSIVE MOVEMENT OF POPULATION.

Date of Census.	White Persons.	Colored Persons. Free.	Colored Persons. Slave.	Total Population.	Decennial Increase. Numerical.	Decennial Increase. Per 100.
1800	4,577	163	135	4,875	—	—
1810	23,890	393	237	24,520	19,645	402.9
1820	145,758	1,230	190	147,178	122,658	500.2
1830	339,399	3,629	3	343,031	195,853	133.8
1840	678,698	7,165	3	685,866	342,835	99.9
1850	977,605	10,811	—	988,416	303,550	44.6

The number of dwellings in the state in 1850 was 170,178, and of families, 171,564, nearly equal, or in the ratio of about 5.7 persons to each dwelling and family. The deaths in 1849–50 amounted to 12,728, or one death to every 77.7 persons.

The number of blind persons, according to the new census, was 278, of deaf and dumb 517, of insane 442, and of idiotic 617; of paupers there were 861, of convicts 81, and of persons of all ages unable to read and write 75,017.

The number of farms was 101,973, valued at $128,325,552, and the value of farming utensils was $6,684,799. The principal agricultural productions, compared with the same of 1840, exhibit the following results:

PRODUCTIONS.		Quantity. 1840.	Quantity. 1850.	PRODUCTIONS.		Quantity. 1840.	Quantity. 1850.
Wheat	*bush.*	4,049,376	6,457,965	Hay	*tons*	178,029	400,064
Rye	"	129,621	80,948	Tobacco	*lbs.*	1,820,306	1,058,879
Indian corn	"	28,155,887	51,449,668	Hops	"	38,591	124,685
Oats	"	5,981,605	5,269,645	Hemp	*tons*	8,605 (Hemp and Flax)	120
Barley	"	28,015	39,815	Flax	"		279
Buckwheat	"	49,019	174,972	Maple sugar	"	3,727,795	2,634,787
Peas and beans	"	—	38,109	Orchard products		$110,055	$339,000
Potatoes	"	1,525,794	2,181,618	Garden products		$61,212	$68,134

And in 1850 there was also produced 13,366 gallons of wine, 17,591 bushels clover seed, 16,986 bushels grass and other seeds, 35,677 bushels flax seed, 181,518 gallons maple molasses. The live stock consisted of 310,475 horses, 7,068 mules and asses, 280,052 milch cows, 37,108 working oxen, 385,969 other horned cattle, 1,068,413 sheep, and 2,314,909 hogs, in all valued at $23,002,978; and the products of animals were as follows—wool 2,679,909 lbs., butter 12,787,547 lbs., cheese 654,808 lbs., and the value of animals slaughtered was $5,668,374. The yield of silk cocoons was 1,591 lbs., and of bees' wax and honey 830,261 lbs.

The manufactures of Indiana are on a respectable footing, and are continually being extended, both in kind and amount. In 1850 the capital invested in this branch of industry amounted to $7,235,220, being an increase over that of 1840 of $3,103,177, or 75 per cent. The condition of the cotton, wool and iron manufactures is exhibited in the annexed table:

Cotton.		*Wool.*		*Wrought Iron.*	
Capital invested	$43,000	Capital invested	$171,545	Capital invested	$17,000
Cotton used, *bales*	675	Wool used, *lbs.*	413,350	Pig metal used, *tons*	50
Coal consumed, *tons*	300	Coal, *tons*	190	Ore used, *tons*	3,150
Value of all raw material	$28,220	Value of raw material	$120,486	Coke and charcoal, *bush.*	85,000
Hands—38 m. and 57 f.	95	Hands—189 m. and 57 f.	246	Value of raw material, etc.	$4,425
Monthly wages (av. $13 m. and $6.77 f.)	$881	Monthly wages (av. $21 81 m. and $11 3 f.)	$4,461	Hands	22
Value of product	$44,200	Value of products	$205,802	Monthly wages, average	$27.45
Yarn manufactured, *lbs.*	300,000	Cloth manufactured, *yds.*	235,500	Tons wrought iron made	175
		Yarn manufactured, *lbs.*	404,000	Value of products	$11,760

The total number of manufacturing establishments producing annually $500 and upwards was 4,326, and the value of goods manufactured was $19,199,681. The value of home-made goods was $1,682,918.

Indiana does not enjoy a direct foreign commerce, and is dependent on ports of other states for outlets. Most of its surplus products are now carried to the states eastward, via. the lakes, Ohio River and railroads. Its exports consist of pork, lard, grain, etc. Considerable amounts of produce are also sent to New-Orleans for shipment. The interior trade is rapidly increasing.

There is only one chartered bank in Indiana—the State Bank at Indianapolis In November, 1850, its capital amounted to $2,082,958, its circulation to $3,422,455, its deposits to $630,335, and other liabilities to $112,175. Its securities consisted of loans and discounts $4,395,099, real estate $364,233, other investments $108,485, due by other banks $815,062, notes of other banks $224,842. It had branches at Bedford, Evansville, Fort Wayne, Indianapolis, Lafayette, Lawrenceburg, Madison, Michigan city, New Albany, Richmond, South Bend, Terre Haute and Vincennes.

Indiana has numerous magnificent public works. The Wabash and Erie Canal connects the waters of Lake Erie with those of the Ohio, and has a total length of 458 miles. Eastward it also connects with the canal system of Ohio. The White Water Canal extends from Lawrenceburg to Cambridge, 76 miles. These great works have been made at an immense expense, and their completion has created a commensurate debt, but the state has lately surrendered the works to the bond holders on their assuming one-half the state debt. The railroads completed and in operation are—the Madison and Indianapolis line, 86 miles long, with a branch to Shelbyville, 16 miles, and thence branches to Rushville, 20 miles, and Knightstown, 27 miles; the New Albany and Salem line to Crawfordsville, 125 miles; the Lafayette and Crawfordsville, 28 miles; the Columbus, Nashville and Bloomington line, 42 miles; the Martinsville line, 29 miles; the Indianapolis and Bellefontaine line, 76 miles; the Indianapolis and Peru line, 76 miles; the Indianapolis and Lafayette line, 69 miles; the Terre Haute and Richmond line, via. Indianapolis, 145 miles; the Jeffersonville and Columbus line, 66 miles; the Lawrenceburg and Greensburg line, 42 miles; and the Northern Indiana line, 76 miles. Numerous others are projected.

A new constitution has been lately provided for this state; it secures to every white male adult citizen and to foreigners who have resided one year in the United States and declared their intention to become citizens, the right of voting. No negro or mulatto is allowed to vote, and duellists, public defaulters, etc., are disfranchised, as are also those who bribe, threaten, or reward any elector. Elections are held on the second Tuesday of October.

The Legislature consists of not more than 50 senators and 100 representatives; senators are elected for four, and representatives for two years, and the former must be at least 25 years of age, and the latter 21, at the time of election. Sessions are held biennally, commencing on the Thursday next after the first Monday in January, 1853.

The Governor must be at least 38 years of age, a citizen of the United States, and a resident of Indiana of five years' standing. He is elected for four years. The Governor's *veto* to any legislative act can only be annulled by a subsequent majority vote of *all* the members of both houses acting separately. The Lieutenant Governor must be qualified as the Governor. The people at large elect a Secretary, Auditor, and Treasurer of State.

The Judicial power is vested in a Supreme Court, in Circuit Courts, and such inferior Courts as the Legislature may establish. The Justices and other officers are elected by the people.

The revenue of the state for the year ending 31st Oct., 1849, including $694,096 balance from former years, amounted to $1,566,339, and the disbursements to $1,137,398, leaving $428,941 in the treasury.

Since the adjustment acts of 1846 and 1847 the state debt amounts only to $6,816,600, of which $4,941,000 bear interest at the rate of 5 per cent., and the residue interest at the rate of 2 1-2 per cent. The canal bond holders assume an equal amount of debt.

The State Institutions are the Asylum for the Deaf and Dumb, the Institute for the Blind at Indianapolis, and the Hospital for the Insane.

The School Fund amounts to $715,748. The common schools are under the charge of a State Superintendent, and in 1850 numbered 5,899 schools, and the number of scholars was about 375,000. The census states that Indiana has 83 colleges at which 5,290 students were under tuition. In this number many academies must be counted. The principal are the Indiana State University at Bloomington, St. Gabriel's College at Vincennes, Hanover College at South Hanover, Wabash College at Crawfordsville, Indiana Ashbury University at Greencastle, and Franklin College, which together had in 1850, 339 students. There is a law department to the State University and Medical Colleges at La Porte and Indianapolis. The Indiana Theological Seminary, a Presbyterian school, is located at South Hanover. The total number of libraries in the state is 1,017, and of volumes 75,416; and the press consists of 98 publications, which have an aggregate circulation of 17,892 copies, chiefly issued weekly.

The Methodists, Baptists and Presbyterians are the numerically preponderating religious denominations. The Episcopalians and Catholics also have numerous churches. The whole number of churches are stated at 1,892, and the value of church property is assessed at $1,499,718.

Indianapolis, the capital of the state, is situated on the left bank of the west fork of White River, and is the centre of the state system of railroads. The state-house is one of the most splendid buildings in the west. It is 180 feet long, by 80 feet wide, and 45 feet high, with an appropriate dome. It is built after the model of the Parthenon at Athens, with a portico on each front, having 10 Doric columns, and has elegant halls for the two houses of the legislature, a court-room and rotunda. Population 8,034.

La Fayette is situated on the left bank of the Wabash River, at the head of steamboat navigation, and is a place of commercial importance.

New-Albany, on the Ohio, is a large and flourishing town, containing a number of manufacturing establishments. Jeffersonville, opposite Louisville, is the site of the state-prison. Madison is a large and flourishing village, with great natural facilities. Population in 1850, 8,037. Evansville is also an important point, and the southern terminus of the canal. Vevay, a Swiss colony, has a fine location, and is prettily laid out, being surrounded by vineyards; Lawrenceburg, below the mouth of the Whitewater, has an extensive trade, and is now a place of some importance; New-Harmony, founded by the German Harmonites, and subsequently purchased by Mr. Owen, the eminent socialist, is a flourishing settlement. Vincennes is the oldest town in the state. Terre Haute, on the national road, and Logansport, on the Wabash, are considerable towns. Richmond, on the western state line; Michigan City, at the base of Lake Michigan, and the only lake port in the state; Covington, on the Wabash, are places of note.

Vincennes was originally settled by French soldiers from Canada. This occurred in 1702. Separated from the world, they became assimilated to the savages, by whom they were surrounded, and with whom they intermarried. In 1763, Indiana came into possession of the British. The revolution gave it to the United States, the government of which granted it to the inhabitants who had taken sides with the patriots. The fort on the opposite side of the river was built in 1778, as a protection against the savages. The inhabitants at that time, consisted of French, Canadians and Indians. Wayne's victory and the treaty of 1797, put an end to hostilities. Incited by the British, the Indians commenced depredations, and committed a number of murders in 1810–11, in consequence of which Gen. Harrison was despatched to subjugate these savage marauders. The battle of Tippecanoe compelled them to sue for peace. In 1816, Indiana took her place as a state of the Union, and formed a constitution for its own government. Since that period it has rapidly progressed in population and wealth, but unfortunately has contracted a large public debt which still continues to enthrall the energies of the people, and must for a long time to come, remain unpaid. The resources of the state, however, are ample, and full provision has been made for its ultimate liquidation.

THE STATE OF ILLINOIS.

Illinois, so celebrated for the extent of its prairies, is situated between 37° and 42° 30′ N. latitude, and between 87° 49′ and 91° 30′ W. longitude; and is bounded north by the State of Wisconsin; east by the Lake Michigan and the State of Indiana; south-east and south by the Ohio River, which separates it from Kentucky, and west by the Mississippi River, which flows from the north southward between it and the states of Iowa and Missouri. In extreme length it is 372 miles, and in extreme breadth 210 miles; having an area of 55,055 square miles, or 35,235,209 acres.

The surface is generally level; the southern and the northern parts of the state are somewhat broken and hilly, but no where rising to an elevation deserving the name of a mountain. That portion of the state south of a line from the mouth of the Wabash to the mouth of the Kaskaskia, is mostly covered with timber; thence northward, prairie predominates. "The eye sometimes wanders over immense plains covered with grass, finding no limit to its vision but the distant horizon; while more frequently it wanders from grove to grove, and from one point of woodland to another, charmed and refreshed by an endless variety of scenic beauty." A range of bluffs commences on the margin of the Mississippi (a short distance above the mouth of the Ohio,) and extends north of the Des Moines Rapids, sometimes rising abruptly from the water's edge, but most generally at a few miles distance, having, between the bluffs and the river, a strip of alluvial formation of most exhaustless fertility. The soil throughout the state is generally very fertile. The forest trees most abundant are oak, of various kinds, walnut, ash, elm, sugar-maple, locust, hackberry, buckeye, sycamore, &c. Lead is a very important mineral production of this state; copper and iron ores exist. Coal abounds in the bluffs: and several fine salt springs exist in the southern part of the state. Vegetable productions are Indian corn, wheat, rye, oats, buckwheat, potatoes, turnips, cotton, hemp, flax, tobacco, the castor bean, &c.

A large part, probably two-thirds of the surface of the state, is covered with prairies. A common error has prevailed that the prairie land is wet. Much of it is undulating and entirely dry. *Prairie* is a French word signifying *meadow*, and is applied to any description of surface that is destitute of timber and brushwood, and clothed with grass. Wet, dry, level and undulating are terms of description merely, and apply to prairies in the same sense as they do to forest lands.

Level prairie is sometimes wet: the water not running off freely is left to be absorbed by the soil, or evaporated by the sun. Crawfish throw up their hillocks in this soil, and the farmer who cultivates it will find his labors impeded by the water.

In the southern part, that is, south of the national road, leading from Terré Haute to the Mississippi, the prairies are comparatively small, varying in size from those of several miles in width, to those which contain only a few acres. As we go northward, they widen and extend on the more elevated ground between the water courses to a vast distance, and are frequently from six to twelve miles in width. Their borders are by no means uniform. Long points of timber project into the prairies, and line the banks of the streams, and points of prairie project into the timber between these streams. In many instances are copses and groves of timber, from one hundred to two thousand acres, in the midst of prairies, like islands in the ocean. This is a common feature in the country between the Sangamon River and Lake Michigan, and in the southern parts of the state. The lead mine region, both in this state and the Wisconsin Territory, abounds in these groves.

The *origin* of these prairies has caused much speculation. We might as well dispute about the origin of forests, upon the assumption that the natural covering of the earth was grass. Probably one-half of the earth's surface, in a state of nature, was prairies or barrens. Much of it, like our western prairies, was covered with a luxuriant coat of grass and herbage. The *steppes* of Tartary, the *pampas* of South America, the *savannas* of the southern and the *prairies* of the western states, designate similar tracts of country. Mesopotamia, Syria and Judea had their ancient prairies, on which the patriarchs fed their flocks. Missionaries in Burmah and travellers in the interior of Africa mention the same description of country. Where the tough sward of the prairie is once formed, timber will not take root. Destroy this by the plough, or by any other method, and it is soon converted into forest land. There are large tracts of country in the older settlements, where, thirty or forty years since, the farmers mowed their hay, that are now covered with a forest of young timber of rapid growth.

Extensive prairies existed in the Atlantic states at the period of the first visits of Europeans. Captain John Smith noticed them when he visited the Chesapeake. The late Mungo Park describes the annual burning of the plains of Mandingo in Western Africa, in the same manner as one would describe the prairie fires of the western states.

The term *barrens*, in the western dialect, does not indicate *poor land*, but a species of surface of a mixed character, uniting forest and prairie. These are called "openings" in Michigan and northern Illinois. The timber is generally scattering, of a rough and stunted appearance, interspersed with patches of hazel and brushwood, and there the contest between the fire and timber is kept up, each striving for the mastery.

In the early settlements of Kentucky, much of the country below and south of Green River presented a dwarfish and stunted growth of timber, scattered over the surface or collected in clumps, with hazel and shubbery intermixed. This appearance led the first explorers to the inference that the soil itself must necessarily be poor, to produce so scanty a growth of timber, and they gave the name *barrens* to the whole tract of country. Long since it has been ascertained that this description of land is amongst the most productive soil in the state. The term barren has since received a very extensive application throughout the west. Like all other tracts of country, the barrens present a considerable diversity of soil. In general, however, the surface is more uneven or rolling than the prairies, and sooner degenerates into ravines and sink-holes. These tracts are almost invariably healthy; they possess a greater abundance of pure springs of water, and the soil is better adapted for all kinds of produce, and all descriptions of seasons, wet and dry, than the deeper and richer mould of the bottoms and prairies.

The Mississippi, Ohio and Wabash rivers form more than two-thirds of the boundary of the state. The Big Muddy, Kaskaskia, Illinois and Rock rivers, and many smaller streams, empty themselves into the Mississippi River. Chicago River empties into Lake Michigan. Vermillion, Embarras and Little Wabash into the Wabash, and Saline and Big Bay Creeks into the Ohio River.

The climate of Illinois is, in general, excellent. In the south it is sufficiently mild to raise cotton, and peaches come to maturity in the most northerly districts. Except on the river-bottoms and in the neighborhood of swamps, the state is healthy and free from endemic diseases.

The minerals of Illinois are various. Iron and bituminous coal are abundant, and native copper, in small quantities, has been found in the southern counties. The most important of these productions, however, is the vast quantities of lead which exist in the neighborhood of Galena, the mines of which are the richest in the world. The ore is generally found in horizontal strata, of various depths, and the yield of pure metal averages 75 per cent. The lead region extends from Galena, beyond the limits of the state, being found on both sides of the Mississippi, and is supposed to occupy a district 200 miles long and 60 broad. Mining operations have been carried on in this region for the last quarter of a century, and the quantity of lead smelted has been immense. Salt is manufactured on the Saline River, and in the neighborhood of Brownsville, on Muddy Creek.

Illinois contained, in 1850, a population of 851,470, or one person to every 41 acres; and its distribution to the several counties was in the following proportions:—

COUNTIES.	White Persons.	Colored Persons.	Total.
Adams	26,170	138	26,508
Alexander	2,464	20	2,484
Bond	6,136	8	6,144
Boone	7,621	5	7,626
Browne	7,184	14	7,198
Bureau	8,831	10	8,841
Calhoun	3,230	1	3,231
Carroll	4,583	3	4,586
Cass	7,248	5	7,253
Champaign	2,647	2	2,649
Christian	3,202	—	3,202
Clarke	9,494	38	9,532
Clay	4,268	21	4,289
Clinton	5,002	137	5,139
Coles	9,299	36	9,335
Cook	42,999	386	43,385
Crawford	7,118	17	7,135
Cumberland	3,720	—	3,720
De Kalb	7,539	1	7,540
De Witt	5,001	1	5,002
Du Page	9,287	3	9,290
Edgar	10,641	51	10,692
Edwards	3,490	34	3,524
Effingham	3,792	7	3,799
Fayette	8,027	48	8,075
Franklin	5,646	35	5,681
Fulton	22,492	16	22,508
Gallatin	5,109	339	5,448
Greene	12,369	60	12,429
Grundy	3,021	2	3,023
Hamilton	6,310	52	6,362
Hancock	14,633	19	14,652
Hardin	2,808	79	2,887
Henderson	4,610	2	4,612
Henry	3,807	—	3,807
Iroquois	4,072	77	4,149
Jackson	5,829	33	5,862
Jasper	3,206	14	3,220
Jefferson	8,083	26	8,109
Jersey	7,300	54	7,354

COUNTIES.	White Persons.	Colored Persons.	Total.
Jo Daviess	18,386	218	18,604
Johnson	4,096	17	4,113
Kane	16,697	6	16,703
Kendall	7,724	6	7,730
Knox	13,221	58	13,279
Lake	14,187	39	14,226
La Salle	17,799	16	17,815
Lawrence	5,843	278	6,121
Lee	5,288	4	5,292
Livingston	1,552	—	1,552
Logan	5,128	—	5,128
McDonough	7,611	5	7,616
McHenry	14,977	2	14,979
McLean	10,121	42	10,163
Macon	3,988	—	3,988
Macoupin	12,272	83	12,355
Madison	19,990	446	20,436
Marion	6,716	4	6,720
Marshall	5,178	2	5,180
Massac	4,070	22	4,092
Mason	5,898	23	5,921
Menard	6,328	21	6,349
Mercer	5,244	2	5,246
Monroe	7,633	46	7,679
Montgomery	6,258	18	6,276
Morgan	15,939	125	16,064
Moultrie	3,225	9	3,234
Ogle	9,990	30	10,020
Peoria	17,461	86	17,547
Perry	5,267	11	5,278
Pike	18,785	34	18,819
Pope	3,871	104	3,975
Piatt	1,606	—	1,606
Pulaski	2,257	8	2,265
Putnam	3,920	4	3,924
Randolph	10,697	382	11,079
Richland	4,002	10	4,012
Rock Island	6,936	1	6,937
St. Clair	19,606	575	20,181
Saline	5,495	93	5,588
Sangamon	18,983	245	19,228
Schuyler	10,547	26	10,573
Scott	7,902	12	7,914
Shelby	7,762	45	7,807
Stark	3,710	—	3,710
Stephenson	11,658	8	11,666
Tazewell	12,016	36	12,052
Union	7,570	45	7,615
Vermillion	11,482	10	11,492
Wabash	4,640	50	4,690
Warren	8,162	14	8,176
Washington	6,929	24	6,953
Wayne	6,822	3	6,825
White	8,916	109	8,925
Whiteside	5,359	2	5,361
Will	16,670	33	16,703
Williamson	7,149	67	7,216
Winnebago	11,761	12	11,773
Woodford	4,416	—	4,416
Total	846,104	5,366	851,470

CLASSES AND SEXES OF POPULATION.

Classes.	Males.	Females.	Total.
White Persons	445,644	400,460	846,104
Colored " —free	2,756	2,610	5,366
" " —slave	—	—	—
Total	448,400	403,070	851,470

PROGRESSIVE MOVEMENT OF POPULATION.

Date of Census.	White Persons.	Colored Persons. Free.	Colored Persons. Slave.	Total Population.	Decennial Increase. Numerical.	Decennial Increase. Per 100.
1810	11,501	613	168	12,282	—	—
1820	53,788	506	917	55,211	42,929	349.5
1830	155,061	1,637	747	157,445	102,234	185.2
1840	472,254	3,598	331	476,183	318,738	202.3
1850	846,104	5,366	—	851,470	375,287	78.9

The whole number of dwelling houses in the state on the 1st June, 1850, amounted to 146,544, or a ratio of one house to every 5.8 persons, and the number of families was 149,150 or 5.7 persons to each family. The aggregate number of deaths during the year 1849–50 was 11,619, or a relative mortality of one death to every 73.3 persons.

The industrial pursuits of the people are chiefly agricultural, but there are large numbers employed in mining, especially in the north-west, and still larger numbers employed in manufactures and commerce. The commerce of Chicago alone is greater than that of several of the maritime states, and the interior trade thence permeates to the Ohio and back to its western limits. The industry of this state, indeed, is of the most varied description.

Mining is chiefly confined to the production of lead and iron; the former in the north-west corner of the state near Galena, and the latter in a majority of the counties. Coal is mined in the southern counties. Copper, zinc, etc., also are abundant.

The fine prairies of Illinois form the best of agricultural lands, and are equally adapted to cattle raising and sheep farming. The crops from the virgin soils are immense, and the quality of the several grains produced compares favorably with the best in the United States. The wheat crop of 1850 is estimated to have been 9,800,000 bushels, that of oats 6,200,000 bushels, and of Indian corn 58,000,000 bushels. The crops of barley, rye, and buckwheat are very small, and average less than 200,000 bushels each. Hemp and flax are grown to a considerable amount; also tobacco. Live stock is abundant, and the products of the dairy very valuable. Animal products, as beef, pork, wool, etc., are exported largely. In 1850, the number of farms under cultivation within the state was 76,208.

The manufactures of Illinois have been constantly increasing. They comprise all the principal articles of domestic use, and machinery, farming implements, saddlery, and almost every requisite. In 1850 there were in the state 3,099 establishments producing annually $500 and upwards, and of course a large number of those small, irregular establishments which are so frequently found in new countries. The woollen manufacture is perhaps as important as any other, but in all, the prosperity is great. Grist, flouring, saw and other mills are found in every section.

The navigable rivers which bound the state and penetrate it in every direction, together with the internal improvements that have been completed, give great facilities to the prosecution of internal trade. The trade on the Mississippi and Ohio to and from Illinois ports, is large, but it is at Chicago on Lake Michigan that the bulk of commercial material is collected and distributed. From this point the internal trade diverges in every direction, and extends to the Ohio River through the Illinois and Michigan Canal; and from this city the travel eastward is now complete by railroad as well as by water to Buffalo and the Atlantic coast.

The value of the direct foreign commerce of Illinois is very small, and its sphere confined to the ports of Canada on the lakes. In 1848 the exports to Canada were valued at $70,496, and consisted of wheat, flour, pork, beef, corn, etc., and the imports were valued at $10,731, consisting chiefly of salt, pig iron, pine lumber, etc. For the same year the exports coast-wise amounted to $10,709,330, and the imports to $7,838,640. The exports consisted chiefly of agricultural produce, machinery, furs, tallow, tobacco, etc., and the imports of groceries, dry goods, hardware, crockery, coal and manufactures generally. The greater portion of the exports were destined for New-York, via. the lakes and Erie Canal, but considerable quantities were dispatched to the south.

The Illinois and Michigan Canal, one of the most magnificent works of the age, is the most important undertaking that has been completed in this state. It connects the navigation of Lake Michigan at Chicago with that of Illinois River at La Salle, 212 miles from its mouth, whence to the Mississippi the course is free to steam vessels of ordinary draft. The canal is 60 feet wide at the surface, 36 at the bottom, and is six feet deep; and the locks, 17 in number, are of the same size with those of the "enlarged Erie"—designed for boats carrying from 100 to 120 tons. The railroad system proposed for Illinois is at once extensive and judiciously demarked. The great line of the State will be the Central Railroad which, having its southern terminus near the mouth of the Ohio, will pass northward and give off branches to Chicago on the east and Galena on the west, in its course uniting with and intersecting all the main roads of the country. For the building of this road Congress has made large grants of land. Several lines are also to pass in a direction east and west, and form links in the great chain of railroads which will ultimately extend from the Atlantic to the Pacific Ocean. The railroads already completed, or partially so, are—the Chicago and Galena Union Railroad, with branches, to Aurora and St. Charles; the Chicago branch of the Northern Indiana Railroad; the Chicago and Rock River Railroad; the Sangamon and Morgan Railroad; the Springfield and Alton Railroad, etc. In 1850, the whole length of railroad completed was 149 miles, and the length in course of construction was 1,126 miles. Illinois has also a large number of plank-roads, and the system is daily being extended. By this means Chicago is connected with the principal towns of the interior, and no small share of its prosperity dates from the establishment of roads of this description to the agricultural centres of the country.

The number of common school districts in Illinois is 2,002, and of schools 2,317. The number of children under 20 years of age in the state is 209,639, and the average number attending school 51,447. The principal collegiate institutions are—Illinois College at Jacksonville, founded 1829; Shurtleff College at Upper Alton, founded 1835; McKendree College at Lebanon, founded 1835, and Knox College at Galesburg, founded in 1837. The aggregate number of professors in these is 22, and of students 162; and their libraries contain about 12,000 volumes. At Alton there is a Baptist Seminary and at Chicago a Medical School.

The Methodist and Baptists form in this state the largest denominations; next the Presbyterians and Roman Catholics; and in smaller numbers there are Episcopalians, Congregationalists, etc. About one-half the whole population may be considered as belonging to the Methodist Church.

The constitution of Illinois was adopted in convention 31st August, 1847, and ratified by the people 7th March, 1848.

The right of voting is conceded to every white male citizen, 21 years of age, and resident in the state the year next before an election.

The Legislature consists of a Senate of 25 members and a House of Representatives of 75 members. Senators are elected for 4 years, one-half the number biennially—they must be 30 years old, citizens of the United States, and residents of 5 years' standing. Representatives must be 25 years old, citizens, and have resided in the state 3 years. In forming electoral districts, the number of *white* inhabitants alone is to be regarded.

The Governor (and Lieutenant-Governor) must be 35 years of age, a citizen of the United States of 14 years' standing, and a resident in the state for 10 years. He is chosen for four years, and must reside at the seat of Government. He possesses the qualified *veto* power.

The Judiciary consists of a Supreme Court, Circuit Courts, and County Courts. For the election of Supreme Court Judges the state is divided into three divisions, each of which elects a judge for nine years, one judge retiring every three years. This court has original jurisdiction in cases relating to revenue, cases of mandamus and habeas corpus, and some impeachments, and appellate jurisdiction in all. One session is held in each division annually. For the election of Circuit Court Judges the state is divided into nine circuits, each of which elects one judge for six years. County Courts for the transaction of county and probate business, with limited civil and criminal jurisdiction, are held by judges elected for four years.

On the 1st January, 1851, the public debt of Illinois amounted to $16,-627,509 86, viz: State debt $8,784,481 43, and Canal debt $7,843,028 43.

To meet the Canal debt, besides the revenue derived from tolls, the state has pledged the lands and town lots originally granted by the general government, appraised at $2,126,355. These assets are in the hands of trustees. The Canal tolls in 1850 amounted to $119,406 97 net. The principal of the state debt is provided for by a constitutional tax of two mills on each dollar of taxable property.

SPRINGFIELD, the capital of the state, is centrally situated, about 14 miles south of the Sangamon River, an affluent of the Illinois. The country around is beautiful prairie land and exceedingly fertile. The State House, a handsome building, is of hewn stone, and there are several churches of architectural pretensions. It is connected with the navigation of the Illinois by means of a railroad terminating at Naples.

JACKSONVILLE, in the line of the Sangamon Railroad, is a flourishing place, and there are a number of other interior cities and towns with populations varying from 3,000 downwards, but which require no particular notice. The cities on the lines of the rivers are more important.

On the Mississippi are Galena, Rock Island City, Nauvoo, Warsaw, Quincy, Alton, Kaskaskia, etc. GALENA, on Fever River, 7 miles from its mouth, is the chief depot of the lead mining region. ROCK ISLAND CITY, at the junction of Rock River with the Mississippi, is a place rapidly rising to importance, and forms a depot for an extensive country watered by that river. It is the site of Fort Armstrong, the foundation of which is laid upon rocks rising some 20 feet out of the river. NAUVOO City, formerly the chief city of the Mormons, has become decayed since the expulsion of those unfortunates, and the grand temple, one of the most substantial and elegant structures on the continent, has been destroyed by fire. The city is now occupied by the followers of the French socialist, Mons. Cabet, and has been partially revived. Under the Mormons it contained 25,000 inhabitants—its population in 1850 was less than 1,000.

WARSAW, opposite the mouth of the Des Moines, and QUINCY, the capital of Adams county, have good prospects, and as the country fills up may become places of note. ALTON, situated a little north of and opposite to the mouth of the Missouri River, is a very thriving town, and in a region rich in timber and bituminous coal. KASKASKIA, on the river of the same name, 11 miles from its mouth, stands on an extensive plain. It was originally settled by the French of Canada. Shelbyville, Vandalia, etc., on the Kaskaskia River, are also considerable places.

CAIRO, at the confluence of the Ohio with the Mississippi, occupies a site most appropriate for a great commercial city, but in consequence of the lowness of the ground on which it is located, and its liability to be overflown, its progress has been slow. Immense sums of money have been expended in raising levies to protect it from inundations, yet its population is very small, and there seems to be little prospect of this age enjoying its advantages.

SHAWNEETOWN, on the Ohio, is the only place of any degree of importance on that river. The towns on the Wabash are Mt. Carmel, Lawrence, etc., but none of these claim especial notice. On the Indiana side of the river are the important towns of Vincennes, Terre Haute and Covington.

CHICAGO, the principal lake port of Illinois, is situated on the river of the same name, which empties into Lake Michigan in its south-western corner. The location is a low flat, almost level with the lake, and no elevation is discernible for an extent of many miles back. It has many advantages, and is destined to become a most important city. Already it is the centre of travel and transportation between the states east of it and the upper valley of the Mississippi, and the depot of an extensive inland range.

The harbor of Chicago is formed by two small streams, which uniting a short distance from the lake form a river, of perhaps 100 feet wide. This is docked and wharfed all along on both sides for a distance of about half a mile or more, and a protecting dock extends several hundreds of feet into the lake. Two or three schooners may lie along side of this harbor, and leave a passage for a steamer or other craft. Chicago is no less a depot for the extensive agricultural country lying back of it, than it is an entrepot between the east and west countries. Its trade on the lakes and by railroads and canal is immense, and it seems almost impossible to estimate the vastness it may attain to. Grain and lumber form its chief exports, while the imports embrace every species of goods known to civilization. The distribution of these gives rise to a vast inland trade, radiating for hundreds of miles. The coasting trade is scarcely inferior to that of Buffalo, and is constantly increasing.

The favorable position of this city for commerce, however, has been greatly enhanced by artificial means, and the completion of numerous works of internal improvement. It is connected with every part of the Union by railroad, while numerous railroads, plank-roads, etc., penetrate hence to all points of importance within the state itself; and its magnificent canal, connecting it with the navigable waters of the Illinois, and through that river with the whole central valley, has opened up to its use the treasures of a country unsurpassed in fertility and natural wealth.

In 1830 Chicago was a mere trading post; in 1840 it had a population amounting to 4,479, and in 1850 it contained 28,269 inhabitants. Its present population cannot be far from 40,000. Waukeegan, about 10 miles from the northern state line, and several other places intermediate between that town and the city of Chicago, are attaining importance.

Illinois was explored by La Salle, the enterprising French traveller, in the early part of the 17th century, and French settlements were formed at Kaskaskia, Cahokia, and some other places soon afterwards. These settlements never became important, and at the peace of Paris, in 1763, the whole country was ceded to the British. The present population has immigrated during the current century, and consists chiefly of Europeans, and some few persons from New-England and the Middle States. In 1809, the country was placed under a territorial government, and in 1818, was admitted as a state of the Union. The Indians have several times risen against the whites, but the entire body is now removed to the west of the Mississippi. Illinois was comprised in the original "Territory North-west of the Ohio."

THE STATE OF MICHIGAN.

Michigan, situated on the four great Lakes of Huron, Superior, Michigan and Erie, has unsurpassed advantages for an extended commerce; and the fertility of its soil and the fresh energy of its people, promise fair to make it one of the finest of agricultural states. It occupies two large peninsulas, and lies between the latitudes of 41° 48′ and 47° 30′ N., and between the longitudes of 82° 20′ and 90° 10′ W. This state is 344 miles long and 300 miles broad: occupying an area of 60,042 square miles, or 38,426,294 acres, of which 10,428,338 acres remain to be surveyed. It is bounded north by Lake Superior; east by Lake Huron, the St. Clair River and Lake, the Detroit River and Lake Erie—all which separate it from the British possessions; south by the States of Ohio and Indiana; and west by Lake Michigan and the Menomonee and Montreal Rivers.

The surface of the lower or southern peninsula is generally level, having very few elevations which may be termed hills. The interior is gently undulating, rising gradually from the lakes to the centre of the peninsula, and is mostly covered with fine forests of timber, interspersed with "oak openings," "plains," and beautiful "prairies." Along the eastern shore of Lake Michigan, are sand hills, thrown by the winds into innumerable fantastic forms, sometimes covered with stunted trees and scanty vegetation, but most generally bare. On the shore of Lake Huron, are some high sand cliffs. The point formed by Lake Huron and Saginaw Bay is generally low and swampy. The forest trees are the same as in Ohio, with the addition of white and yellow pine; fruit trees produce abundantly. The soil is well adapted to wheat, rye, oats, barley, flax, hemp, Indian corn, buckwheat, &c. All kinds of garden vegetables, and the various species of grasses, thrive well.

The southern peninsula of Michigan is drained by several large rivers and numerous smaller streams, which rise near the centre and pass off in an easterly and westerly direction, with the exception of the Cheyboygan and three or four smaller streams, which flow in a northerly direction; the larger streams are navigable for boats and canoes nearly to their sources. Raisin and Huron Rivers flow into Lake Erie; Rouge into the *Detroit* strait; Clinton, St. Clair and Black River, into the lake and strait of St. Clair. Saginaw River, formed by the junction of the Tittibawassee, Hare, Shiawassee, Flint and Cass Rivers, falls into Saginaw Bay. Thunder Bay River and Cheyboygan flow into the northern part of Lake Huron. St. Joseph, Kalamazoo, Grand and Maskego rivers, and several smaller streams, flow in a westerly direction into Lake Michigan. Many parts abound with small clear lakes, from which are taken great quantities of fish of various kinds, and of most exquisite flavor.

The northern peninsula, between Lakes Michigan and Superior, occupies about 12 millions of acres. Portions of it are the mere development of sublime scenery, which appertains to that comparatively elevated portion of the continent. Mountains and lakes, plains, rivers and forests, spread over it with a boldness of outline, which may be said to constitute almost a peculiar type in North American geography. This division embraces the mineral district of Michigan. Much of it falls under the influence of causes which render it of little or no value in an agricultural point of view. Accuracy, with respect to the extent of the different kinds of soil, either in acres or miles, must be the result of explanation and survey. The northern shores of Lake Michigan and Huron, as far as Point Detour, are exclusively limestone, where rock is at all visible, and this rock is characterised by the usual indications of gypsum and saline springs. The growth of trees is as various as the soils, and is, in general, an accurate index of its fertility. The sugar maple is interspersed throughout the tract, being separated by the sand plains, the mountain masses, and by tracts of spruce lands. This tree forms, however, so considerable a proportion of the growth, that the natives can always, by a timely removal of their camps, rely on the manufacture of sugar. The beech tree is found as far north as Point Iroquois, at the outlet of Lake Superior. The white oak, however, may be regarded as a surer test of soil and climate together, than any other of our forest trees. It is doubtful whether this tree ever attains its full size in a climate that is not decidedly congenial to agriculture. The rock maple and red oak are found, at intervals throughout the north-west; both species are seen at the sources of the Mississippi, but the beech has not been observed north of the locality mentioned, nor the white oak north of the straits of Mackinac. The interior abounds in minor lakes, and enjoys a singular advantage of inter-communication by its streams and portages. Taking the whole extent of the territory from Menomonee river, following the curves of the coast to the north-west limits of the state at the mouth of the Moniaw or Montreal river of Lake Superior, it affords not less than 720 miles of coast navigation; and embraces, in this distance, several large bays and excellent harbors. About forty large and some sixty small streams discharge their waters into the three lakes constituting portions of the boundary.

The mineral region of this district, in the neighborhood of Lake Superior, is rich in copper of the finest quality, and which is frequently found in its native state. The extreme length of the region is about 135 miles, and it has a width varying from one to six miles. The mineral, however, does not exist in every portion of this district, for miles may intervene and no trace be ascertained. In some of the river beds, large boulders of native copper are frequently met with.

No state in the Union is more bountifully supplied with wild animals, game, fish, and aquatic fowl. The beaver frequents the rivers, and in the forests bears, wolves, elk, deer, and foxes abound. The trout of Michilimackinac are large and well-flavored, and are plentiful at all seasons. White fish are taken in large quantities in the River Detroit and Lake St. Clair, as well as at the Falls of St. Mary's. Sturgeon are abundant in the lakes, which also contain pike, pickerel, etc.

The climate of Michigan is much modified by the waters, which on three sides form its boundaries, and though naturally situated in the regions of intense cold, the state is rendered pleasant and agreeable in temperature and weather. The range of the thermometer approximates to that observed on the sea-coast, and the atmosphere is moist and equable at all seasons of the year. The grains and fruits of Europe grow luxuriantly in the rich alluvial deposits, and grazing and sheep farming are highly favored by the mildness of the climate, the housing of cattle being seldom required even in the dead of winter. In the northern peninsula, the seasons are more marked, and the extremes of temperature greater; but even there, no material obstruction to profitable husbandry is experienced.

Michigan had in 1850 a population of 397,654 souls, or one person to every 91 acres; and its distribution to the several counties was in the following proportions:

COUNTIES.	White Persons.	Colored Persons.	Total.	COUNTIES.	White Persons.	Colored Persons.	Total.
Allegan	5,120	5	5,125	Hillsdale	16,153	6	16,159
Barry	5,033	39	5,072	Houghton	707	1	708
Berrien	11,178	239	11,417	Huron	210	—	210
Branch	12,456	16	12,472	Ingham	8,606	25	8,631
Calhoun	18,965	197	19,162	Ionia	7,589	8	7,597
Cass	10,518	389	10,907	Jackson	19,346	85	19,431
Chippeway	890	8	898	Kalamazoo	13,070	109	13,179
Clinton	5,100	2	5,102	Kent	11,982	34	12,016
Eaton	7,055	3	7,058	Lapeer	7,007	22	7,029
Genesee	12,003	28	12,031	Lenawee	26,282	90	26,372

COUNTIES.	White Persons.	Colored Persons.	Total.
Livingston	13,481	4	13,485
Macomb	15,516	14	15,530
Marquette	136	—	136
Mason	93	—	93
Michilimackinac and 21 unorganized counties	3,561	37	3,598
Midland	64	1	65
Montcalm	891	—	891
Monroe	14,642	56	14,698
Newago	509	1	510
Oakland	31,207	63	31,270
Oceana	281	19	300
Ontonagon	383	6	389
Ottawa	5,532	55	5,587
Saganaw	2,609	—	2,609
Sanilac	2,112	—	2,112
St. Clair	10,396	24	10,420
St. Joseph's	12,699	26	12,725
Schoolcraft	16	—	16
Shiawassee	5,230	—	5,230
Tuscola	291	—	291
Van Buren	5,800	—	5,800
Washtenaw	28,343	224	28,567
Wayne	42,035	721	42,756
Total	395,097	2,557	397,654

CLASSES AND SEXES OF POPULATION.

Classes.	Males.	Females.	Total.
White Persons	208,471	186,626	395,097
Colored " —free	1,412	1,145	2,557
" " —slave	—	—	—
Total	209,883	187,771	397,654

PROGRESSIVE MOVEMENT OF POPULATION.

Date of Census.	White Persons.	Colored Persons. Free.	Colored Persons. Slave.	Total Population.	Decennial Increase. Numerical.	Decennial Increase. Per 100.
1810	4,618	120	24	4,762	—	—
1820	8,591	305	—	8,896	4,134	86.8
1830	31,346	261	32	31,639	22,743	255.6
1840	211,560	707	—	212,267	180,628	570.8
1850	395,097	2,557	—	397,654	185,387	87.2

The number of dwelling houses in the state in 1850 was 71,616, and of families 72,611, or a ratio of about 5.5 persons to each dwelling or family; and the number of deaths is stated to have been in the year preceding the 1st June, 1850, 4,520, or one death in every 99 of the population, being a little over one per centum.

Agriculture is the branch of industry generally pursued in Michigan, and perhaps the country is more favorably situated for carrying it on successfully than most of the other states. Its soil and climate are genial to the growth of all the cereals, and all the vegetation of temperate regions flourishes luxuriantly. The great crops are those of wheat, for which Michigan is famous, oats, and Indian corn. Barley, rye, and buckwheat have received but little attention. The fine grasses, native and foreign, afford a plentiful pasturage for the live stock, which is sufficiently abundant for domestic purposes. The flocks of sheep in the southern counties are large, and sheep-farming generally has become a favorite pursuit. This employment, indeed, has increased wonderfully within the past few years in this and all the adjoining states, and the production of wool for export has been very large and is increasing with every season. In 1850 the number of farms of all descriptions under cultivation was 34,089, and the farming population included fully five sixths of the whole number of inhabitants.

The manufactures of Michigan are as yet on a limited scale and confined chiefly to the fabrication of articles of immediate necessity. Lumbering is one of the great employments, and it is estimated that Michigan produces in sawed timber alone 150 millions of feet per annum. Saw, flouring, grist, etc., mills are numerous, as also are tanneries, distilleries, etc. The mineral region situated in the northern peninsula is now the scene of great mining operations and is becoming very productive. Large amounts of copper ore are raised and smelted, and with the progress of settlement the country must become very valuable. The iron mines in this region are also attracting attention. The whole number of manufacturing establishments in the state producing $500 and upwards annually in 1850 was 1,979.

The foreign commerce of Michigan is very limited, being confined to an intercourse with the British Provinces. Its coastwise trade, however, is commensurately large, and its sphere only bounded by the limits of the great lakes and the navigation of the western waters. Detroit is its great port, and from this district alone the exports amount to upwards of four million dollars annually, while its imports are little less than that in value. The principal exports are flour and grains, the product of the state, and its imports consist of the manufactures of the Atlantic states and Europe. The transportation trade is also one of vast extent—the great north-western lines of railroad passing through the southern district, being the principal channels through which the commerce of the north-west has its course.

The principal works of internal improvement, to which allusion is made above, are the Central Railroad and the Southern Railroad, with their connexions and branches. The former traverses the state east and west from Detroit to New Buffalo, and thence is continued via. Michigan City to Chicago, and the latter extends from Monroe and Toledo, and is continued to Chicago by the Northern Indiana Railroad.

In January, 1851, there were in Michigan eight banks and one branch bank with an aggregate capital of $764,022, and their financial condition at that date was as follows—loans and discounts $1,319,303, stocks $420,521, real estate $221,626, other investments $65,033, due by other banks $404,691, notes of other banks $109,086, specie funds $195, specie $125,722, circulation $897,364, deposits $416,147, due other banks $42,559, other liabilities $342,816.

The government is based on the constitution of 1850. Generally every white male citizen who has attained his majority is eligible to vote at all elections. The Legislature consists of a Senate and House of Representatives; the Senate has 32 members and the House not less than 64 nor more than 100 members. Senators are elected, one half annually, from single districts and for two years, and Representatives annually in ratio of population, but each organized county is entitled to at least one. Both must be citizens of the United States and qualified electors in the respective districts and counties which they represent. The chief executive power resides in the Governor, who with a Lieutenant-Governor is elected by a plurality of votes for two years; these officers must be at least 30 years of age, must for five years have been citizens of the United States, and for two citizens of Michigan. The Judiciary consists of a Supreme Court, District Courts, Probate Courts and Justices of the Peace, and Municipal Courts of civil and criminal jurisdiction may be established in cities. All judges and justices of the peace are elected by the people. Administrative officers, viz., the Secretary of the State, Superintendent of public instruction, State Treasurer, Commissioner of Land Office, Auditor General and an Attorney General, are also elected by the people and hold office for two years.

The public debt amounted to $2,812,717 on the 31st December, 1849, most of which draws interest at 6 per centum, and at the same date the resources of the state amounted to $740,754. The value of real and personal property was $28,999,202, and the amount of taxes collected thereon was $102,406. The total resources of the treasury for the year ending 30th November, 1849, were $545,846, and the expenditures $490,399—surplus $55,-447. The ordinary annual expenses exclusive of interest on debt and school moneys are under $100,000.

The common schools of Michigan are supported partly by the state and partly by local taxation. In 1849 the school money apportioned amounted to $52,305, and $73,805 was raised by taxes. There are 3,060 school districts in the state and the number of scholars is 125,218. Unincorporate, private and select schools educated 4,788 scholars. Besides the above sums $51,085 were raised for purchasing, building and furnishing school houses, and the township tax for the support of libraries amounted to $17,630. The number of volumes in township libraries was 67,877. A state normal school, endowed from the school lands, has been established at Ypsilanti. A State University at Ann Arbor has also been recently founded; and there is a Catholic College near Detroit. For the education of the blind and the deaf and dumb there is an Asylum at Kalamazoo, and at Flint there is an Asylum for the insane. All these institutions are of recent date.

The State Prison is located at Jackson.

The Methodists in numbers outweigh all other religious denominations; the Baptists and Presbyterians are numerically the next, and there are also several churches belonging to the Congregationalists, Protestant Episcopalians and Roman Catholics.

The principal cities and towns in Michigan are Lansing, Detroit, Pontiac, Monroe, Ann Arbor, Ypsilanti, Adrian, Marshall, Kalamazoo, Niles, New Buffalo, all in the southern portion of the state; Grand Rapids and Maskegon, on the rivers of the same name; Saginaw, on Saginaw river; Port Huron, at the N. entrance of St. Clair river, etc.

Lansing, the capital, is situated in Ingham county, on Grand river, 117 miles from Detroit, and has been the seat of government since Dec. 1847. It is centrally situated in reference to the settlements. Though but a few years have elapsed since the place was a wilderness, it now contains upwards of 400 houses and several large hotels. The State House is a spacious and handsome building, in the centre or an enclosure overlooking the town, and on an elevation of about 50 feet above the river. Several saw and flouring mills, propelled both by steam and water power, have been erected, and there seems to be every prospect of its becoming a flourishing place. Population 1,600.

Detroit, the former capital, and the largest and most flourishing town in Michigan, is well situated for trade on the W. side of Detroit river, seven miles S. of Lake St. Clair, and 18 N. of Lake Erie. It stands on an elevated site, about 30 feet above the water. It is regularly laid out, and has many excellent public buildings and private residences. It enjoys great facilities for an extensive commerce, and few cities have better prospects for future eminence. Pop. 21,057. The Central railroad extends hence to New Buffalo, 221 miles, and another to Pontiac, 25 miles. Detroit was formerly a military post of the French, and a great depot of the fur-traders.

The first permanent settlement in this state was made at Detroit by the French, in 1670, but at the peace of Paris, 1763, the country was ceded to the British, and at the close of the Revolutionary war, transferred to the United States. In 1805, the country was erected by Congress into a separate territorial government. During the last war (1812) with England, Michigan fell into the hands of the enemy through the treason of Gen. Hull, but was retaken under Gen. Harrison in the following year. In 1836, it was admitted into the Union as a state.

THE STATE OF WISCONSIN.

Wisconsin, one of the most flourishing and healthy states of the Union, lies between the latitudes of 42° 30′ and 47° N., and between the longitudes of 87° and 92° 40′ W., and is bounded north by the territory of Minesota, Lake Superior and the northern peninsula of Michigan; east by Lake Michigan; south by the State of Illinois and west by the Mississippi River, which separates it from the State of Iowa and Minesota territory. It is 300 miles in length and 240 miles broad, with an area of 53,924 square miles, or 34,511,360 acres, of which only 13,955,825 are surveyed.

Wisconsin is one vast plain, varied only by river hills, and the gentle swells and undulations of the country, usually called "rolling." This plain is elevated from 600 to 1,500 feet above the level of the ocean. The highest lands are those dividing the waters of the lakes from those of the Mississippi. From these there is a gradual descent towards the south and west, which, however, is several times interrupted by ridges and mounds, the latter of which, rising above the general landscape, present an anomaly in the contour of the country, and in the unsettled parts serve as guides to the traveller. The slope towards Lake Superior is very abrupt, and as a consequence, the rivers are short, rapid, and broken by falls. They are unfit for navigation, but possess abundance of water-power, which, at no distant period, will become useful to the settler. There is another ridge of broken land, running from Green Bay south-westerly, forming the "divide" between the waters of Lake Michigan and those of the Bay and the Neenah. After pursuing a similar direction, this ridge passes into the State of Illinois.

Besides the great lakes on the north and east, a vast number of smaller ones are scattered over the northern portion of the state. They are from one to twenty miles in extent, and many are amid the most beautiful and picturesque scenery, abounding in fish of various kinds, and having a rich supply of fine specimens of agate, cornelian and other precious stones on their shores. In the shallow water of the bays, the "*zigania aquatica*," a species of wild rice, is abundant, and attracts immense flocks of water-fowl to these localities, and even affords a nutritious aliment for man. Among the small lakes may be mentioned Lakes Winnebago, St. Croix, Cass, Pepin, Four Lakes, the Mille Lac, Ottawa, Pewaugau, Pewaukee, Geneva, Greene, and many others.

The Mississippi, as before observed, forms the western boundary. It is augmented from this state by the waters of the Chippewa and Wisconsin, which, though themselves considerable rivers, scarcely perceptibly increase the volume of the "Father of Waters." Innumerable smaller streams and branches run through the whole extent of the state, so that no portion of it is without a plentiful supply of good and generally pure water. The Mississippi is navigable as far up as the Falls of St. Anthony, and small steamboats ply on the Wisconsin and some other rivers.

The rivers running into the Mississippi take their rise in the vicinity of the sources of those running into the lakes, and they often originate in the same lake or swamp, so that the communication from the Mississippi to the lakes is rendered comparatively easy at various points. Some of the rivers are supplied from the Tamarack Swamps, from which the water takes a dark color.

All kinds of crops which are raised in northern latitudes may be cultivated with success; and owing to the great range of pasturage on the prairies, it is an uncommonly fine grazing country. The counties of Grant and Iowa abound with lead and copper ore. Bordering the Mississippi and Wisconsin rivers the soil is rich, and the surface most generally covered with a heavy growth of timber.

The proximity of Wisconsin to the Great Lakes ensures it a softer climate than its geographical position would assign to it. The extremes, however, are great—the thermometer sometimes during the summer marking 100°, and in winter receding to 40° below zero. The mean temperature of the year is, in different parts, from 46° 6′ to 47° 4′; and of spring, 43° 4′ to 48° 6′; summer, 67° 3′ to 71° 1′; autumn, 45° 5′ to 48° 2′; and winter, 17° 3′ to 27° 3′. The lowest mean monthly temperature is 13° 58′ in January; and the highest 75° 47′ in July. The annual amount of rain falling is from 27.96 to 38.83 inches. The north and north-west, and the south and south-west winds are those most prevalent; the former in the winter and the latter in the summer season.

The salubrity of the climate, the purity of the air, and of the water; the coolness and short duration of the summers, and the dryness of the winters, conspire to render Wisconsin one of the most favored regions of the United States. The swamps, marshes, and wet meadows are constantly supplied with pure water from springs; and as they are seldom exposed to long continued heats, they do not send forth those noxious vapors so much dreaded in the more southern sections of the Union. Many of the most flourishing towns are in the immediate vicinity of large swamps, yet no injurious effect on the general health is experienced.

Wisconsin contained in 1850, according to the census of that year, 305,191 inhabitants, or one person to every 113 acres; and these were distributed to the several counties in the following proportions:

COUNTIES.	White Persons.	Colored Persons.	Total Popula.
Adams	187	—	187
Brown	6,173	42	6,215
Calumet	1,621	122	1,743
Chippewa	614	—	614
Crawford	2,481	17	2,498
Columbia	9,547	18	9,565
Dane	16,618	23	16,641
Dodge	19,069	69	19,138
Fond du Lac	14,465	3	14,468
Grant	16,140	30	16,170
Greene	8,563	—	8,563
Iowa	9,502	28	9,530
Jefferson	15,314	3	15,317
Kenosho	10,714	18	10,732
Lafayette	11,527	14	11,541
La Pointe	483	6	489
Manitouwoc	3,702	—	3,702
Marathon	508	—	508
Marquette	8,620	20	8,640
Milwaukie	30,967	110	31,077
Portage	1,249	1	1,250
Racine	14,907	66	14,973
Richland	902	1	903
Rock	20,686	22	20,708
Sauk	4,370	1	4,371
Sheboyan	8,371	7	8,378
St. Croix	619	5	624
Walworth	17,858	3	17,861
Washington	19,484	—	19,484
Waukesha	19,136	38	19,174
Winnebago	10,107	18	10,125
Total	304,565	626	305,191

CLASSES AND SEXES OF POPULATION.

Classes.	Males.	Females.	Total.
White Persons	164,221	140,344	304,565
Colored " —free	365	261	626
" " —slave	—	—	—
Total	164,586	141,605	305,191

PROGRESSIVE MOVEMENT OF POPULATION.

Date of Census.	White Persons.	Colored Persons. Free.	Colored Persons. Slave.	Total Population.	Decennial Increase. Numerical.	Decennial Increase. Per 100.
1840	30,749	185	11	30,945	—	—
1850	304,565	626	—	305,191	274,246	886.2

The number of dwellings in the state in 1850, was 56,316, or one dwelling for every 5.4 inhabitants, and the families numbered 57,608, or in the proportion of 5.3 persons to every family. The number of deaths was 2,884, or in the ratio of one to every 105.8 inhabitants.

The industry of the people embraces mining, agriculture, manufactures, commerce, etc., and in each of these branches the state has made astonishing progress. Twenty years ago the state, within its present limits, contained only 3,245 inhabitants, but such has been its facilities for prosecuting all kinds of industry, that in the ten years ending 1840, it increased 853.6 per cent., and in the ten years ending 1850, 886.2 per cent. Mining is generally confined to the lead region of the Galena country in the south-west; but copper and iron are also extensively mined in other parts—copper in the north-east, and iron, more or less, in almost every county. Agriculture employs about nine-tenths of the whole population, and much attention is given to grazing, for which, indeed, the greater portion of the country is better adapted than to grain growing. In 1850 there were in the state 20,177 farms under cultivation, or one farm to every 15 of the whole population. The manufactures of the state are yet but in embryo, and are chiefly incidental. At the date above named there were 1,273 establishments, at which productions to the value of $500 and upwards annually, were turned out. In commerce the state is scarcely second to any of those north-west of the Ohio. It has an extensive front on Lake Michigan, and an outlet on Lake Superior, besides its fine navigable rivers, which, but for a short portage, would afford a natural passage from the Lakes to the Mississippi. Such advantages, especially those peculiar to the front on Lake Michigan, have been very favorable to the development of the resources of the country, and have invited to it a commerce which the most extravagant visionary could not have dreamed of ten years ago. Milwaukie and other towns have sprung up as if by magic, and have already become ports of considerable importance. In regard to Milwaukie, indeed, it is the rival of Chicago, and with the progress of settlement must become a great entrepôt between the north-west and the states to the eastward.

Wisconsin is engaged in several works of internal improvement which will add essentially to the commercial facilities of the state. The most important of these, perhaps, is the Portage Canal, which will, when completed, open a navigable channel from Green Bay to the Mississippi by way of the Fox and Wisconsin Rivers. The canal is very short, and its cost as nothing compared with the benefit it will afford to the neighboring communities. From Milwaukie, on Lake Michigan, railroads are being built towards the interior, and many others, chiefly connecting with these, are projected. The Milwaukie and Galena Railroad is about 70 miles long, and will form a junction with the Chicago and Galena Union Railroad; and the Rock River line from Chicago will, following the valley of the Rock River, terminate at Fon du Lac. Plank-roads and macadamized-roads are already numerous, and in reference to plank-roads, few other states have greater means for making them, or a surface more fit for their establishment.

MADISON, the capital, is 159 miles from Chicago, and pleasantly situated on a peninsula between two lakes, on a gentle swell of ground from which there is a regular descent to the water. It is well laid out, the streets crossing each other at right angles, and having in their centre a large square, in the middle of which is the state-house, a handsome stone edifice. The town contains about 1,500 inhabitants.

MILWAUKIE is the largest and most important town in the state. It is situated on both sides of the Milwaukie River, near its entrance into Lake Michigan, 90 miles above Chicago, and is a very flourishing city. Previous to 1835, this city was a wilderness; its population in 1850 was 21,000. Constant steamboat communication from Milwaukie to Buffalo and other lake ports, is maintained, and the interior is reached by railroads and plank-roads.

GREEN BAY, on the bay of the same name; RACINE and SHEYBOYGAN, on Lake Michigan; PRAIRIE DU CHIEN, on the Mississippi River, are growing towns, and will eventually become important to the commerce of the state.

Wisconsin originally belonged to the French, and formed part of that vast territory called New-France. It was ceded to Great Britain in 1763, and acquired by the United States at the close of the revolution. Few settlements were made in the territory previous to 1836, when it was erected into a separate territorial government. In 1848, having, after a prolonged opposition, voted itself a constitution, it was admitted into the Union as an independent state.

THE STATE OF KENTUCKY.

KENTUCKY, formerly a part of Virginia, and until explored by Daniel Boone, in 1770, a wilderness, is now one of the most populous and prosperous of the states of the American Union. It lies between the latitudes of 36° 30′ and 39° 10′ North, and between the longitudes of 82° and 80° 35′ West. It is bounded on the north and north-west by the windings of the Ohio River, which separates it from Ohio, Indiana, and Illinois; east by the Big Sandy River, and the Cumberland Mountains, which separate it from Virginia; south by Tennessee, and west by the Mississippi, which separates it from Missouri. From east to west, it is 400 miles long, and from north to south, 175 broad; its area occupies 40,500 square miles, or 25,920,000 acres.

The outline of Kentucky, except on its southern border, is very irregular, and, as delineated on maps, has the appearance of a cumulated mountain. The only mountains are the Cumberland range, on the western borders of Virginia. The eastern counties are hilly, and the tract from five to twenty miles wide along the margin of the Ohio River, extending through the whole length of the state, is of a similar character, and much broken. The soil of these regions is good, and a part of this tract lying immediately on the Ohio, averaging one mile in width, consists of bottom lands, and is subject to periodical inundations. Between this tract, the eastern counties and Green River, lies the "garden of the state." It is about 150 miles long, and from 50 to 100 miles wide. The surface of this district is agreeably undulating, and the soil black and friable. The natural growths are the black-walnut, black-cherry, honey-locust, buck-eye, paw-paw, sugar-maple, mulberry, elm, ash, cotton-wood, white thorn, &c. The country between Green and Cumberland rivers is called the "barrens." In 1800, the legislature of the state bestowed this tract gratuitously on actual settlers, under the impression that it was of little value; but it proved to be excellent grain land, and peculiarly well adapted to grazing and the rearing of cattle.

The whole state, below the mountains, rests on an immense bed of limestone, usually about eight feet below the surface. There is everywhere apertures in this formation called "sinkholes," through which the waters of the rivers disappear into the earth. The waters for this reason are more diminished during the dry season than those of any other portion of the Union, and the small streams are entirely dried up and disappear. The banks of the rivers are natural curiosities; the streams have generally worn very deep channels in the calcareous rock over which they flow. The precipices formed by Kentucky River are, in many places awfully sublime, presenting perpendicular banks of 300 feet of solid limestone. In the southwest part of the state, between Green River and the Cumberland, there are several wonderful caves. One called the "Mammoth Cave," is said to be eight or nine miles long.

The staple productions of Kentucky are hemp, tobacco, wheat and Indian corn. Salt springs are numerous, and supply not only this state, but also Ohio and Tennessee with that mineral. Iron, bituminous coal, and granite are mined in considerable quantities in the eastern districts.

Kentucky is almost insulated by navigable rivers. The Big Sandy, which rises in the Cumberland Mountains, near the sources of the Tennessee and Cumberland rivers, forms the eastern boundary for nearly 200 miles. The Ohio forms the northern boundary for nearly 600 miles, and the Mississippi the western boundary. The Cumberland River rises in the mountains, and passes into the State of Tennessee, where it makes a circular bend, and returning to Kentucky, falls into the Ohio, 60 miles from its mouth. It is 600 miles long, and navigable for boats of 15 tons, 500 miles up. The Tennessee falls into the Ohio after winding southward from its source in Alabama, returns through Tennessee, and hence flows northward until it meets the Ohio, into which it falls, about 12 miles west of the Cumberland River. The principal rivers which lie wholly within the state are Green, Kentucky, and Licking, all of which fall into the Ohio, and are navigable for a considerable distance for boats.

Situated in the centre of the United States, on the table land of the western country, with the Alleghany Mountains to the eastward, and the high lands of Tennessee on the south, Kentucky enjoys a climate protected from all extremes, and is not excelled in salubrity by any other portion of North America. In Lexington, near the centre of the state, the heat of summer seldom exceeds 80° Fahrenheit, and in winter the temperature scarcely ever recedes below 25°. The average annual temperature is about 58°. The whole of the state being, as above remarked, on a bed of limestone, and considerably elevated above the rivers, there are no swamps or bodies of stagnant waters, except in a very few locations, and as a consequence, the atmosphere is generally pure and sweet, and remarkably free from misasmatic emanations.

Kentucky contained in 1850 a population of 982,405 souls, or one person to every 26 acres; and its distribution among the several counties was in the following proportions:

POPULATION OF COUNTIES.

COUNTIES.	White Persons.	Colored Persons. Free.	Colored Persons. Slave.	Total Popula.
Adair	8,083	108	1,707	9,898
Allen	7,389	39	1,314	8,742
Anderson	4,948	30	1,282	6,260
Ballard	4,628	26	842	5,496
Barren	15,543	113	4,584	20,240
Bath	9,479	103	2,535	12,115
Boone	9,044	37	2,104	11,185
Bourbon	7,158	242	7,066	14,466
Boyle	5,379	313	3,424	9,116
Bracken	7,948	115	840	8,903
Breathitt	3,603	12	170	3,785
Breckenridge	8,616	11	1,966	10,593
Bullitt	5,392	27	1,355	6,774
Butler	5,056	18	681	5,755
Caldwell	9,809	132	3,107	13,048
Callaway	7,094	10	992	8,096
Campbell	12,871	79	177	13,127
Carroll	4,552	25	949	5,526
Carter	5,961	23	257	6,241
Casey	5,863	59	634	6,556
Christian	11,309	131	8,140	19,580
Clark	7,709	134	4,840	12,683
Clay	4,739	167	515	5,421
Clinton	4,591	36	262	4,889
Crittenden	5,474	29	848	6,351
Cumberland	5,477	43	1,485	7,005
Daviess	9,423	50	2,880	12,353
Edmondson	3,753	10	325	4,088
Estell	5,568	6	411	5,985
Fayette	11,180	666	10,889	22,735
Fleming	11,628	147	2,139	13,914
Floyd	5,503	62	149	5,714
Franklin	8,741	356	3,365	12,462
Fulton	3,499	4	943	4,446
Gallatin	4,399	34	704	5,139
Garrard	7,036	25	3,176	10,237
Graves	9,949	9	1,439	11,397
Grant	5,994	5	532	6,531
Greenup	8,998	50	606	9,654
Grayson	6,512	5	320	6,837
Green	6,335	117	2,608	9,060
Hancock	3,216	15	622	3,853
Hardin	12,023	43	2,459	14,525
Harlan	4,109	36	123	4,268
Harrison	9,739	140	3,185	13,064
Hart	7,740	52	1,301	9,093
Henderson	7,654	120	4,397	12,171
Henry	8,376	53	3,013	11,442
Hickman	3,932	18	841	4,791
Hopkins	10,199	50	2,192	12,441
Jefferson	47,329	1,591	10,911	59,831
Jessamine	6,289	135	3,825	10,249
Johnson	3,843	—	30	3,873
Kenton	16,116	92	830	17,038
Knox	6,239	199	612	7,050
Laurel	3,946	7	192	4,145
La Rue	5,176	10	672	5,859
Lawrence	6,143	1	137	6,281
Letcher	2,440	10	62	2,512
Lewis	6,869	11	322	7,202
Lincoln	6,635	103	3,355	10.093
Livingston	5,404	56	1,118	6,578
Logan	10,751	363	5,467	16,581
Madison	10,270	64	5,393	15.727
Marion	8,599	80	3,086	11,765
Mason	13,675	385	4,284	18.344
Marshall	5,020	—	249	5,269
McCracken	5,241	18	808	6,067
Meade	5,799	21	1,573	7,393
Mercer	10,472	335	3,260	14,067
Monroe	6,902	23	831	7,756
Montgomery	6,671	159	3,073	9,903
Morgan	7,395	38	187	7,620
Muhlenburg	8,250	37	1,522	9,809
Nelson	9,550	109	5,130	14.789
Nicholas	8,683	165	1,513	10,361
Ohio	8,568	49	1,132	9,749
Oldham	5,156	49	2,424	7,629
Owen	8,900	30	1,514	10,444
Owsley	3,616	22	136	3,774
Pendleton	6,230	35	509	6,774
Perry	2,972	3	117	3,092
Pike	5,250	17	98	5,365
Pulaski	12,861	27	1,307	14,195
Rock Castle	4,289	33	375	4,697
Russell	4,901	13	435	5,349
Scott	8,891	219	5,836	14,946
Shelby	10,288	190	6,617	17,095
Simpson	5,755	43	1,935	7,733
Spencer	4,659	32	2,151	6,842
Taylor	5,463	147	1,640	7,250
Todd	7,361	97	4,810	12,268
Trigg	7,252	80	2,797	10,129
Trumble	4,997	25	941	5,963
Union	6,704	16	2,292	9,012
Warren	10,597	209	4,317	15,123
Washington	9,086	63	3,045	12,194
Wayne	7,856	6	830	8,692
Whitley	7,227	19	201	7,447
Woodford	5,882	165	6,376	12,423
Total	761,688	9,736	210,981	982,405

CLASSES AND SEXES OF POPULATION.

Classes.	Males.	Females.	Total.
White Persons	392,840	368,848	761,688
Colored " —free	4,791	4,965	9,736
" " —slave	—	—	210,981
Total	—	—	982,405

PROGRESSIVE MOVEMENT OF POPULATION.

Date of Census.	White Persons.	Colored Persons. Free.	Colored Persons. Slave.	Total Population.	Decennial Increase. Numerical.	Decennial Increase. Per 100.
1790	61,133	114	11,830	73,077	—	—
1800	179,871	741	40,343	220,955	147,878	202.8
1810	324,237	1,713	80,561	406,511	185,556	84.0
1820	434,644	2,941	126,732	564,317	157,806	38.8
1830	517,767	4,037	165,213	687,917	123,600	21.9
1840	590,253	7,317	182,258	779,828	91,911	13.3
1850	761,688	9,736	210,981	982,405	202,577	25.9

The number of dwelling houses in the state on the 1st June, 1850, was 130,769, and the number of families 132,920, and hence the number of persons to each house or family was about 7 1-2, but in this reckoning the slave dwellings and families are set down as a part of the estate of their owner. The mortality amounted to 15,206, or a ratio of deaths in the proportion of one to every 64 persons, being about 1.5 per cent.

The industry of Kentucky is chiefly agricultural, but manufactures have of late years made great advance. In 1850 there were in the state 74,777 farms under cultivation, and the crops of grain in millions of bushels amounted—Indian corn to 58, oats to 18, wheat to 2½, rye to 3, but those of barley and buckwheat were very small. The great staples of the state are hemp and flax, and tobacco, of which articles an immense amount is annually produced. Live stock is abundant, and vast numbers of cattle are exported annually, chiefly to the southern states, for consumption. The hog trade is immense, and its products, as lard, lard-oil, candles, prussiate of potash, etc., form a material item in the general wealth. Large amounts of wool and of the products of the dairy are also produced.

The number of manufacturing establishments in the state, producing not less than $500 annually, was in 1850, 3,471. The cotton manufactures employed a capital of $239,000, and consumed 3,760 bales of cotton, worth $180,000, gave employment to 891 operatives, and yielded 1,003,600 yards of goods, valued at $274,000; beside which 725,000 pounds of yarn was produced. The woollen manufactures employed a capital of $249,820, and consumed 673,000 pounds of wool, worth $205,287; hands employed, 382; value of products, $318,819; goods manufactured, 878,034 yards. The capital invested in the manufacture of iron was $176,000, and the value of raw material used, viz.: 2,000 tons pig metal, 1,600 tons blooms, and 280,000 bushels of charcoal, amounted to $180,805; hands employed, 183; wrought iron made, 3,070 tons; and value of products, $299,700. The manufactures of tobacco, cordage, bagging, and some other articles are very extensive.

Kentucky has no direct foreign trade, but exports and imports through New Orleans or the Atlantic ports. The river and internal trade of the state, however, is considerable, and the latter has progressed of late years with great rapidity. The chief exports of Kentucky are its tobacco, flax and hemp, some cotton, wool, grain, and dairy products; also cattle and hogs, with immense amounts of animal products. The shipping owned within the state in 1850, amounted to 14,820 tons, all of which was navigated by steam-power. The chief shipping port is Louisville on the Ohio.

The state has several lines of railroad in operation, and has projected a system that will embrace the whole surface. The existing railroads are—the Lexington and Frankfort line, 29 miles long, and the Frankfort and Louisville line, 49 miles long; and the projected railroads are—the Tennessee and Cincinnati line, from Nashville, Tenn., *via* Frankfort; the Nashville and Louisville line; the Nashville and Mississippi line, terminating at Columbus; the Covington and Lexington line; the Maysville and Danville line, etc. The Mobile and Ohio railroad will traverse this state in its western part. There are also in the state several short canals and river improvements, and a bridge over the Ohio river at Louisville is talked of.

Kentucky has 5 banks and 21 branch banks. The banking capital of the state amounted, at the close of 1850, to $7,536,927; the circulation to $7,613,075; deposits to $2,323,607; and other liabilities to $1,256,589. At the same date the loans and discounts amounted to $12,506,305; stocks to $694,962; real estate to $419,070; other investments to $440,127; specie to $2,791,351; and other assets to $3,002,034.

The first constitution of Kentucky was framed in 1790, the second in 1799, and the present one in (11th June) 1850. This latter constitution secures the *right of voting* at all elections to every free white male citizen 21 years of age and upward, and who has resided in the state two years, in the county, town, or city one year, and in the precinct 60 days next preceding the election. Elections are held on the first Monday in August.

The Legislature consists of a Senate and House of Representatives. Senators, 35 in number, are elected from single districts for four years, and must have attained to the age of 30 years, have resided in the state six years, and in the district from which they are elected, the last year. Representatives, 100 in number, are chosen from single districts for two years, and must have attained the age of 24 years, and have resided in the state two years, the last thereof in the district. Sessions are biennial, commencing 1st November, 1851. No session is to continue more than 60 days.

The Governor (and Lieutenant-Governor) is chosen for four years by a plurality of votes. He must be 35 years old at the least, and have resided in the state the six years immediately anterior to his election. A majority of both houses of the Legislature may annul any veto he may place on a bill. All executive officers, except the Secretary of State, who is appointed by the Governor, are elected by the people.

The Judiciary consists of a Court of Appeals, District and Circuit Courts, and County Courts. The four judges of appeals are elected by the people for eight years, the 12 district and circuit judges for six years, and the county judges (three for each county) for four years. Each county elects also two justices of the peace for four years. Attorneys, clerks, coroners, jailors, and assessors are elected for the same term as the judges to whose court they are attached. Sheriffs are elected for two years.

The receipts into the public treasury for the year ending 10th Oct. 1850, amounted to $598,602 29, and the total resources, including a balance, to $619,611 84. The total disbursements amounted to $522,754 78, leaving a balance of $86,857 06 in the treasury. The expenses of this year included the pay of the convention for framing the new constitution, and the payments to the sinking fund. On the 31st December, 1850, there was a balance to the credit of the sinking fund of $78,225 35; its total resources for the year then ending were $444,113 74, and its disbursements on account of the public debt, payment of interest, etc., amounted to $365,888 39. The public debt at the time above stated consisted of the following items: bonds bearing 5 per cent. interest, $536,545; bonds bearing 6 per cent. interest, $3,661,092; total, $4,248,637.

The value of taxable property was $299,381,809, and the government owns $1,270,500 in bank stock, 400 miles of turnpike, 29 miles of railroad, and 290 miles of slack-water navigation, which together yield about $100,000 annual revenue.

The school fund held by the state amounts to $1,299,268, but is not available on account of the government using a portion of the interest for ordinary expenses, but is annually increased by so much as the amount thus withheld. Reports were received from 71 counties, and 5 cities and towns; and the number of children reported was 87,498—average attendance at public schools 42,736. The money distributed to such counties, etc., amounted to $51,040, of which $29,116 was from the permanent school fund, and $21,874 from the two cent tax. These statistics embrace only the district schools connected with the state system. The number of children in the state between 5 and 16 years of age was 192,990.

Institutions for the higher grades of education are numerous, and of these the following are the principal:

Colleges, etc.	Location.	Pro.	Stu.	Colleges, etc.	Location.	Pro.	Stu.
Transylvania	Lexington	7	50	Western Military	Blue Lick Springs	9	218
St. Joseph's	Bardstown	17	126	Shelby	Shelbyville	4	95
Centre	Danville	5	114	Baptist Theo. Inst.	Covington	4	13
Augusta	Augusta	4	51	Law Department	Univ. of Louisville	3	77
University	Louisville	—	—	Law Department	Transylvania Univ.	3	50
Georgetown	Georgetown	7	77	Medical Department	Univ. of Louisville	7	376
Bacon	Harrodsburg	4	60	Medical Department	Transylvania Univ.	7	214

The aggregate number of volumes in the college libraries is about 75,000.

The institutions of the state for the relief of the unfortunate are, the State Lunatic Asylum at Lexington; the Deaf and Dumb Asylum at Danville; the School for the Blind at Louisville; and the Marine Hospitals at Smithland and Louisville. The State Penitentiary is located at Louisville.

The Baptists, Methodists, and Presbyterians are the most numerous of religious denominations, and have respectively about 69,000, 31,000, and 13,000 church members. The Episcopalians have a bishop and about 30 clergy, and the Catholics a bishop and several churches.

The militia of the state consists of 85,619 infantry, 1,560 cavalry, 679 artillery, and 771 riflemen.

Frankfort is the state capital. It is situated on the Kentucky river, 60 miles from its mouth, at the base of the lofty hills through which the waters pass. Lat. 38° 14′ N., long. 84° 40′ W. The state-house, built of white marble, is a handsome edifice, and the penitentiary, conducted on the Auburn plan, is a strong and durable structure. Steamboats come up to the city, and keel-boats navigate the river above. Population 4,372.

Louisville is the chief commercial city of the state, and lies on the south bank of the Ohio river, immediately above the falls. The canal, from Portland, enables steamboats to come to the wharves. The trade is extensive and valuable, and manufactures of various descriptions are carried on with great spirit. Founderies, steam-bagging factories, cotton and woollen mills, flouring mills, etc., are numerous. The city has many handsome public buildings, and the private residences are comfortable and well built. Population in 1850, 43,217.

Lexington is the oldest city in Kentucky. It is surrounded by a most beautiful and fertile country. The Transylvania University, the State Lunatic Asylum, and several other public buildings, are important adornments to the city. Population, 7,500. The Hon. Henry Clay, the illustrious statesman, resides at Ashland, near this place.

Maysville, on the Ohio, with a population of 4,255; Augusta, the seat of a college; Newport and Covington, on the opposite banks of Licking River; Harrodsburg, Bardstown, etc., are the other most important cities.

The first permanent settlement within the present limits of Kentucky, was made by the celebrated Daniel Boone, in 1775. Until 1790, it was an integral portion of Virginia, but in that year it became detached and formed for itself a constitution. In 1792, it took its station as an independent member of the United States. Since this period, it has rapidly progressed in population, wealth and standing as a state, and now claims as its citizens some of the most patriotic statesmen that ever sounded the tocsin of liberty. Among these, the names of Clay and Crittenden are pre-eminent—names as much revered at home as they are respected and confided in by all foreign nations.

THE STATE OF MISSOURI.

Missouri is situated between 36° 30′ and 40° 30′ North latitude, and between 89° 20′ and 96° West longitude. It is bounded on the north by the State of Iowa; on the east by the Mississippi, which separates it from Illinois and Kentucky; on the south by the "compromise line" of 36° 30′, and on the west by the Indian territory and the Missouri River. Length, from north to south, about 315 miles: breadth, 280 miles. The superficial area is 67,451 square miles, or 43,169,028 acres, all of which, except 2,680,857, have been surveyed.

With the exception of the alluvial bottoms, Missouri is rolling or hilly; yet no part rises to an elevation deserving the name of a mountain. No other state in the Union is so greatly diversified as respects soil and external features. The south-eastern corner is almost entirely alluvial. A range of hills commences in François county, and extends in a south-westerly direction to the southern boundary of the state. Another range of a larger class, commencing near the Missouri, and between the waters of the Gasconade and Osage, continues through the state, increasing in magnitude until far within the State of Arkansas; these are termed the Ozark Mountains. This ridge is frequently very abrupt near the water courses, and often retiring from them, with strips of rich alluvial between. In St. François county exists the celebrated mountain of the micaceous oxide of iron, which has an elevation of 350 feet above the surrounding plain, is a mile and a half across its summit, and yields eighty per cent. of pure metal. Five miles south is another magnificent pyramidal mountain of the micaceous oxide of iron, known as the Pilot Knob, 300 feet high, with a base of a mile and a half in circumference. This pyramid is not in plates, but huge masses of several tons in weight, and yields also eighty per cent. Copper is found in Missouri, and its inexhaustible lead mines are well known. The "Pine Ridge," in this region, furnishes that lofty timber in abundance; many of the trees being ninety feet high, and four feet in diameter. Washington county is a perfect bed of metallic treasures,—lead and copper, copperas, chalk, black lead and brimstone, cornelian and other precious stones, free-stone, grind-stone, and burr-stone. St. Genevieve county has numerous quarries of magnificent marble, and vast caverns of beautiful white sand, resembling snow, much prized for the manufacture of flint glass. "Throughout the mineral district is found, on searching the bowels of the earth for ores, beds of rich red marl clay, which has been proved to be the very best manure for the soil. These beds are inexhaustible; and some years hence, that portion of Missouri which is considered a sterile, mineral region, will be found as fertile as any portion of the state. Between the waters of the Osage and the Missouri, is a fine tract of country, celebrated for its fertility, agreeably diversified with woodland and prairie, and abounding with coal, salt springs, etc. The country north of the Missouri is emphatically a fine district. There is no part of the globe where greater extent of country can be traversed more easily when in its natural state. It has for the most part a surface delightfully rolling and variegated, sometime rising into picturesque hills, then stretching far away into the sea of prairie, occasionally interspersed with shady groves and sparkling streamlets. Almost every acre of this fine region of country is susceptible of agricultural improvement, and is unusually productive. The products consist of tobacco, cotton, hemp, corn, wheat, rye, oats, barley, and the grasses. All the garden vegetables thrive well. Large quantities of horses, mules, horned cattle, sheep, and hogs are raised annually for exportation.

The Mississippi meanders along the entire eastern boundary of the state, for a distance of 400 miles, receiving in its course the waters of the Missouri. Through the center and the richest part of the state the wild Missouri pours out its never ceasing currents, being navigable for steamboats far westward, for four or five months in the year. The Lamine, Osage, and Gasconade on the right, and the Grand and Chariton on the left, are the navigable tributaries of the Missouri. Salt River, a navigable stream, falls into the Mississippi 86 miles above the Missouri. Maramec River, also navigable, enters the Mississippi 18 miles below St. Louis. The White and the St. François drain the south-eastern portion, and the Six Bulls and tributaries the south-western part of the state. The climate of Missouri is remarkably serene and temperate, and very favorable to longevity.

The state is divided into 100 counties, and in 1850 contained an aggregate of 682,044 inhabitants, or one person to every 66 acres. The distribution of the population to the several counties was in the following proportions:

COUNTIES.	White Persons.	Colored Persons. Free.	Slave.	Total Popula.
Adair	2,283	8	51	2,342
Andrew	8,758	13	662	9,433
Atchison	1,641	7	30	1,678
Audrain	3,048	1	457	3,506
Barry	3,317	—	150	3,467
Bates	3,520	8	141	3,669
Benton	4,546	9	3,460	5,015
Boone	11,300	13	3,666	14,979
Buchanan	12,072	1	902	12,975
Butler	1,563	—	53	1,616
Caldwell	2,176	4	136	2,316
Callaway	9,898	22	3,907	13,827
Camden	2,208	—	130	2,338
CapeGirardeau	12,203	35	1,674	13,912
Carroll	4,812	8	621	5,441
Cass	5.610	2	478	6,090
Cedar	3,278	1	82	3,361
Chariton	5,688	48	1,778	7,514
Clarke	5,013	10	504	5,527
Clay	7,585	5	2,742	10,332
Clinton	3,346	1	439	3,786
Cole	5,699	18	979	6,696
Cooper	9,837	22	3,091	12,950
Crawford	6,112	—	285	6,397
Dade	3,976	1	269	4,246
Dallas	3,552	8	88	3,648
Daviess	5,056	1	241	5,298
De Kalb	2,008	2	65	2,075
Dodge	351	—	2	353
Dunklin	1,205	11	13	1,229
Franklin	9,542	20	1,459	11,021
Gasconade	4,884	—	112	4,996
Gentry	4,195	3	50	4,248
Greene	11,548	7	1,230	13,785
Grundy	2,856	1	149	3,006
Harrison	2,434	—	13	2,447
Henry	3,377	3	672	4,052
Hickory	2,143	1	185	2,329
Holt	3,827	3	127	3,957
Howard	9,040	39	4,890	13,969
Jackson	10,992	39	2,969	14,000
Jasper	4,009	1	213	4,223
Jefferson	6,407	9	512	6,928
Johnson	6,573	12	879	7,464
Knox	2,626	2	266	2,894
La Clede	2,357	1	140	2,498
La Fayette	9,005	70	4,615	13,690
Lawrence	4,607	4	248	4,859
Lewis	5,364	8	1,206	6,578
Lincoln	7,389	5	2,027	9,421
Linn	3,681	—	377	4,058
Livingston	3,933	6	308	4,247
Macon	6,262	—	303	6,565
Madison	5,278	29	696	6,003
Marion	9,322	76	2,832	12,230
McDonald	2,132	21	83	2,236
Mercer	2,671	6	14	2,691
Miller	3,654	—	189	3,834
Mississippi	2,373	4	746	3,123
Moniteau	5,434	4	566	6,004

COUNTIES.	White Persons.	Colored Persons. Free.	Slave.	Total Popula.
Monroe	8,464	29	2,048	10,541
Montgomery	4,449	3	1,037	5,489
Morgan	4,192	5	453	4,650
New Madrid	4,057	3	1,481	5,541
Newton	4,013	14	241	4,268
Nodaway	2,048	—	70	2,118
Oregon	1,392	22	18	1,432
Osage	6,434	—	270	6,704
Ozark	2,279	—	15	2,294
Perry	6,395	26	794	7,215
Pettis	4,261	5	884	5,150
Pike	10,299	35	3,275	13,609
Platte	13,997	50	2,798	16,845
Polk	5,804	13	369	6,186
Pulaski	3,885	—	113	3,998
Putnam	1,638	—	19	1,657
Ralls	4,777	6	1,368	6,151
Randolph	7,265	18	2,156	9,439
Ray	8,834	25	1,514	10,373
Reynolds	1,824	—	25	1,849
Ripley	2,731	13	86	2,830
Saline	6,108	16	2,719	8,843
Schuyler	3,230	2	55	3,287
Scotland	3,631	—	151	3,782
Scott	2,773	16	393	3,182
Shannon	1,190	—	9	1,199
Shelby	3,744	11	498	4,253
St. Charles	9,492	13	1,949	11,454
St. Clair	3,107	1	448	3,556
St.Genevieve	4,636	61	616	5,313
St. François	4,233	51	680	4,964
St. Louis	97,577	1434	5,967	104,978
Stoddard	4,221	6	50	4,277
Sullivan	2,895	—	88	2,983
Taney	4,274	—	99	4,373
Texas	2,270	—	42	2,312
Warren	4,291	4	935	5,860
Washington	7,713	23	1,075	8,811
Wayne	4,152	6	360	4,518
Wright	3,305	—	82	3,387
Total	592,078	2,544	87,422	682,044

CLASSES AND SEXES OF POPULATION.

Classes.	Males.	Females.	Total.
White Persons	312,996	279,082	592,078
Colored " —free	1,339	1,205	2,544
" " —slave	43,508	43,914	87,422
Total	357,843	324,201	682,044

PROGRESSIVE MOVEMENT OF POPULATION.

Date of Census.	White Persons.	Colored Persons Free.	Slave.	Total Population.	Decennial Increase. Numerical.	Per 100.
1810	17,227	607	3,011	20,845*	—	—
1820	56,081	283	10,222	66,586	45,741	219.9
1830	114,803	561	25,091	140,455	73,869	110.9
1840	323,838	1,574	58,240	383,702	243,247	173.2
1850	592,078	2,544	87,422	682,044	298,342	101 6

The number of dwellings in the state in 1850 amounted to 96,805, and of families to 100,834; and hence each dwelling covered 7 persons, and each family consisted of 6.8 persons. The deaths during the year 1849–50 numbered 12,217, or in the ratio of 1 to every 55 persons. The mortality was greatest along the Mississippi; in St. Louis county it was 1 death in 22 persons, but here the mortality is greatly increased by the influx of diseased immigration.

Missouri is one of the richest states of the Union, and its resources have been rapidly developed. Mining is carried on with great success, and agriculture, nowhere finding more suitable climate and soils, yields vast amounts of produce for export. The crop of Indian corn is estimated at 35,000,000 bushels, and the crops of oats and wheat are also large. Flax and hemp, tobacco, etc., are staples of great and increasing importance. The amount of live stock is immense; and wool-growing and hog-fattening have become sources of great wealth to those engaged in such occupations. The whole number of farms and plantations in the state in 1850, was 54,458. Manufactures are carried on, but except at St. Louis there are few establishments of any extent. The number of factories in 1850 at which goods to the annual value of $500 and upwards were manufactured, amounted to 3,030, and of these, 1,309 were located in the city of St. Louis alone, and 100 more in the county.

The state has little direct foreign commerce, but its river trade is very great. St. Louis is perhaps the most important port on the line of the river above New Orleans, and is the general depot for the whole extent of the upper valley of the Mississippi, as also of a great part of that of the Ohio. The shipping owned in the state amounts to 28,907 tons, of which 24,955 tons are navigated by steam, and all is employed in the river trade. The trade with the interior follows chiefly the courses of the larger streams. There are as yet no railroads, and the ordinary roads are none of the best. Efforts, however, are now being made to build railroads from the Mississippi westward, to accommodate the ever increasing population in that direction.

The State Bank is the only incorporated banking institution in the state. The parent bank is located at St. Louis, but there are branch banks in other places. In June, 1850, its condition in the aggregate was as follows: *Liabilities*—Capital owned by state, $954,205; capital owned by individuals, $245,546; deposits, $988,220, and circulation $2,396,500, which with other items make up a total of $5,232,680. *Assets*—Specie, $1,452,886; discounts, $1,869,690; exchanges matured and maturing, $1,008,342; real estate, $117,980, and other items to a balance.

Missouri is well supplied with literary institutions in which the higher grades of learning are taught, but its common school system, although it is being gradually improved, is still very defective. There are probably 1500 common schools in the state, and there are also a number of academies. The oldest collegiate institution in the state is the University of St. Louis, established in 1832; Missouri University was founded in 1840; St. Vincent's College in 1843; Masonic College in 1834; St. Charles' College in 1839, and Fayette College in 1846. The condition of these in 1850 is exhibited in the following table:

Name of College.	Location.	Professors.	Alumni.	Students.	Volumes in Library.
University of St. Louis	St. Louis	17	25	160	12,000
Missouri University	Columbia	12	26	52	—
St. Vincent's College	Cape Girardeau	12	—	90	5,000
Masonic "	Marion Co.	5	13	45	—
St. Charles "	St. Charles	3	20	20	390
Fayette "	Fayette	2	—	75	—

Medical schools are attached to the University of St. Louis and Missouri University; the first had in 1850, nine professors and 112 students, and the latter seven professors and 92 students. The Baptists and Methodists are numerically the strongest religious denominations, but the Presbyterians and Roman Catholics have numerous and large congregations. The Catholics form a large portion of the people of St. Louis. Other denominations have scattered congregations, but with the exception of the Protestant Episcopalians, have scarcely a recognized existence.

All citizens, 21 years of age, and who have resided in the state one year, and three months in the place where they vote, are electors. The General Assembly consists of a House of Representatives, the members of which are elected for two years; and a Senate, the members of which are chosen for four years, one-half going out every second year.

The Governor and Lieutenant-Governor, the latter of whom is, *ex-officio*, President of the Senate, must be 35 years of age, and natives of the United States. They are elected by a plurality of votes. The governor has the *veto* power, but the legislature may pass a bill by a majority of both houses. In case of the governor's death or disability, the lieutenant-governor, president of the senate, or speaker of the house, as the case may be, take his place; but if the term has more than 18 months to run before completion, three months' notice may be given, that a new election will take place.

The constitutional provisions in regard to slavery, are similar to those of Kentucky.

The Judiciary consists of a Supreme Court, and Circuit Courts; the Common Pleas and Criminal Courts of St. Louis, and the Common Pleas Court of the city of Hannibal. The judges of these courts are appointed by the governor. The jurisdiction of the county courts is limited to matters of probate and local affairs, as roads, &c. The judges of these are elected by the people, and hold office for four years. Appeal lies from these to the circuit courts.

JEFFERSON CITY, the capital, is situated on the south bank of the Missouri River, near the centre of the state. Latitude 38° 36′ north—longitude 92° 8′ west. The state-house and penitentiary are located here. Population in 1850, 3,721.

ST. LOUIS, the commercial emporium of the west, and the largest city in the state, was founded in 1764, by the French. It is situated on the Mississippi, below its junction with the Missouri, and 1,200 miles above New-Orleans. The city consists of two parts, built on different elevations. The lower part, or that on the margin of the river, is laid out in narrow streets, and is chiefly occupied by those engaged in business. The more elevated portion is different in appearance, and is laid out regularly in broad, handsome streets, lined with the splendid mansions of the rich. A variety of public buildings beautify this locality. The population is composed of men of all nations, but the predominant races are Americans, French, and Germans. In 1840, it numbered 16,469; but in 1845, had increased to 34,140; and, in the year 1850 it had swelled to 97,860. The city is supplied with water from the river, which is raised to a reservoir by steam-power, and thence distributed through iron pipes to every part. The streets are lighted with gas. St. Louis is the principal depôt of the American Fur Company. Jefferson Barracks are 11 miles below the city. Upwards of 2,800 steamboats arrive at St. Louis annually, conveying to and fro vast quantities of merchandize.

ST. CHARLES, formerly the capital of the state, lies on the Missouri, about 20 miles from its junction with the Mississippi, and is a considerable town. The inhabitants, numbering in 1850, 4,102, are chiefly of French origin. INDEPENDENCE, on the south side of the river, near the western boundary, is the starting-point or rendezvous for the Santa Fé traders and emigrants to Oregon. The other towns of importance are New Madrid, Jackson, St. Genevieve, Herculaneum, Hillsborough, Bowling-Green, Hannibal, Palmyra, St. Francisville, &c., on the Mississippi; Hermona, Boonesville, Franklin, Fayette, Brunswick, Lexington, &c., on the Missouri; Warsaw, Oseola, &c., on the Osage; Platte City on the River Platte; &c.

Missouri was originally a portion of the extensive Territory of Louisiana, as purchased by the United States in 1803. Settlements had been made at St. Louis, St. Genevieve, and elsewhere, about the middle of the last century, but the population never counted more than a few hundreds. In 1804, the Territory of Orleans, now Louisiana, was separated from the bulk of the new purchase, and a separate territorial government erected for each, the latter successively bearing the title of Territory of Louisiana and that of Missouri. In 1821, the portion of this vast territory within the present limits of Missouri, was erected into an independent state, and became a member of the American Union. The remaining portions of this territory have since become the states of Arkansas and Iowa, and Minesota Territory, and there are yet some immense districts not appropriated.

THE STATE OF IOWA.

Iowa, formerly a portion of the Missouri Territory, lies immediately north of the state of that name, and is geographically situated between the latitudes of 40° 30′ and 43° 30′ N., and between the meridians of 90° 20′ and 96° 50′ W. longitude. This large and fertile state is bounded on the north and west by the Western Territories; east by the Mississippi River; and south by the State of Missouri and the lower course of the Des Moines River. It is 270 miles long, and about 200 miles in breadth, having an area of 46,428 square miles, or 29,913,920 acres.

The general features of this state present much of what is called "rolling," without being mountainous or even hilly. An elevated table-land or plateau, however, extends through a considerable portion of the country, dividing the streams which flow respectively into the Missouri and Mississippi rivers. The margins of the rivers and streams are thickly timbered, but the rest of the state is open prairie, with alternations of woodland of some extent, which diversify and enliven the scenery. The varieties of the prairie lands are endless: some are level and others rolling; some clothed in thick grass, suitable for grazing farms, while hazel thickets and sassafras shrubs invest others with a perennial verdure, and in spring and summer they are superbly decorated with flowers. The soil of Iowa is universally good, being of a rich black mould; and in the prairies this is sometimes mixed with sandy loam, and sometimes with red clay and gravel.

The Mississippi River borders the east of this state, and is navigable for the entire distance. The Des Moines waters the southern section of the country, and falls into the Mississippi, after forming, for some distance, the south-western boundary of the state. It is navigable for 100 miles from its mouth. The Iowa River, a navigable stream, also traverses a large portion of the state. Besides these, there are numerous minor rivers and streams falling into either the Missouri or Mississippi, and which are highly beneficial to the fertility and productiveness of the land, as well as being available for transportation and internal communication.

The buffalo, which formerly roamed over the flowery prairies, is now almost extinct, but the elk, though much diminished in numbers, is still hunted in the recesses of the state. Panthers and wild cats are sometimes seen, and the grey wolf still lurks about the remote settlements. The common prairie wolf is a denizen of these regions, and proves mischievous among the sheep and hogs. In the wooded districts the black bear is found. Foxes, raccoons, opossums, gophars, porcupines, and squirrels of various kinds, are also numerous. The otter and bear still inhabit the unsettled parts about the rivers and lakes. Deer are also quite numerous—the flesh affording food and the skins clothing to the pioneer of the wilderness.

"A review of the resources and capabilities of this country," says Dr. Owen, "induces me to say with confidence, that *ten thousand* miners could find profitable employment within its confines." The lead mines alone afford as much of that metal as the whole of Europe, excepting Great Britain, and their capabilities are unbounded. Zinc occurs in fissures along with the lead. It is chiefly in the form of electric calamine, and is found in the form of cellular masses. In some "diggings" this mineral is found in a state of carbonate, and in others as a sulphuret. Iron ore is abundant, but as yet, on account of the sparsity of population and want of capital, but little iron, either bar or cast, has been manufactured. The mineral region is principally confined to the neighborhood of Dubuque, and along the river heights of the Upper Mississippi.

The population of this state in 1850 amounted to 192,214 souls, or one person to every 276 acres; and its distribution to the several counties was in the following proportions:

COUNTIES.	White Persons.	Colored Persons.	Total Popula.
Allamakee	777	—	777
Appanoose	3,124	7	3,131
Benton	672	—	672
Black Hawk	135	—	135
Boone	735	—	735
Buchanan	517	—	517
Cedar	3,939	2	3,941
Clarke	79	—	79
Clayton	3,871	2	3,873
Clinton	2,802	20	2,822
Dallas	854	—	854
Davis	7,257	7	7,264
Decatur	964	1	965
Delaware	1,759	—	1,759
Des Moines	12,963	24	12,987
Dubuque	10,816	25	10,841
Fayette	825	—	825
Frêmont	1,244	—	1,244
Henry	8,685	12	8,707
Iowa	822	—	822
Jackson	7,201	9	7,210
Jasper	1,280	—	1,280
Jefferson	9,903	1	9,904
Johnson	4,450	22	4,472
Jones	3,006	1	3,007
Keokuk	4,822	—	4,822
Lee	18,809	51	18,860
Linn	5,441	3	5,444
Louisa	4,913	26	4,939
Lucas	471	—	471
Madison	1,179	—	1,179
Mahaska	5,988	1	5,989
Marion	5,453	29	5,482
Marshall	338	—	338
Monroe	2,884	—	2,884
Muscatine	5,663	68	5,731
Page	551	—	551
Polk	4,515	—	4,515
Pottawattomie *	7,828	—	7,828
Poweshiek	615	—	615
Scott	5,972	14	5,986
Tama	8	—	8
Taylor	204	—	204
Van Buren	12,266	4	12,270
Wapello	8,466	5	8,471
Warren	961	—	961
Washington	4,957	—	4,957
Wayne	339	1	340
Winneshiek	546	—	546
Total	191,879	335	192,214

CLASSES AND SEXES OF POPULATION.

Classes.	Males.	Females.	Total.
White Persons	100,885	90,994	191,879
Colored " —free	168	167	335
" " —slave	—	—	—
Total	101,053	91,161	192,214

PROGRESSIVE MOVEMENT OF POPULATION.

Date of Census.	White Persons.	Colored Persons. Free.	Colored Persons. Slave.	Total Population.	Decennial Increase. Numerical.	Decennial Increase. Per 100.
1840	42,924	172	16	43,112	—	—
1850	191,879	335	—	192,214	149,102	345.7

The number of dwelling houses in the state in 1850 was 32,962, and the number of families 33,517, or about 6 persons to each; and the number of deaths in 1849–50 amounted to 2,044, or 1 in every 94 inhabitants, somewhat less than one per centum.

* Pottawattomie County, which occupied the great bulk of the western half of the state, has been divided into the following counties since the above returns were made; Adair, Adams, Audubon, Bancroft, Bremer, Buena Vista, Buncombe, Butler, Carroll, Cass, Cerro Gordo, Cherokee, Chickasaw, Clay, Crawford, Dickinson, Emmett, Floyd, Fox, Franklin, Greene, Grundy, Guthrie, Hancock, Hardin, Harrison, Howard, Humboldt, Ida, Kossuth, Manona, Mills, Mitchell, Montgomery, O'Brien, Oceola, Palo Alto, Plymouth, Pocahontas, Potawattomie, Risley, Sac, Shelby, Sioux, Union, Wahkow, Winnebago, Worth, Wright, and Yell.

This young state, scarcely escaped from the wilderness, has rapidly assumed an importance which augurs favorably of its future greatness. Its position in relation to the great trunk stream of the continent, and the numerous navigable waters traversing its interior, make it accessible to emigration, and form highways of an active commerce. Few districts are remote from a water course, and steamboats already penetrate to its western borders, carrying to and fro the ever-increasing commercial material of the country.

As yet, however, the state is strictly an agricultural region; the trades and manufactures, indeed, are on a very small scale, and other cognate branches of industry have scarcely gained a footing; but the many facilities it enjoys in its streams and general resources, favor the opinion that a varied and prosperous industry will, at no distant period, overspread its surface. The grains and other agricultural productions are similar to those grown in the valley states generally; and the soil and climate are highly favorable for grasses of every species. On the rich alluvial borders of the Des Moines River, the cultivation of tobacco has been very successful; and in the same region, the castor bean (*ricinus communis*), from which the castor oil of commerce is expressed, succeeds well. Wool-growing has also become a remunerative employment; thousands of sheep, instead of being slaughtered as formerly, are now annually imported, and as fast as their increase exceeds the pasture range, are driven further into the wilderness. Nothing, indeed, pays labor so well in the great interior as does this occupation—little care is required, and it is a suitable and reliable source of profit. The raising of hogs is also largely engaged in—they find here a boundless range of forest and prairie, and feed upon the natural products of the soil. The capacities of the country for all such employments are immense, and it may be truly said of this state, that "no country in the world is more promising to the emigrant than that comprising the great valley of the Upper Mississippi, of which Iowa forms so important a part." The whole number of farms under cultivation in 1850 was 14,805.

The galena country, in the north-east part of the state, has long been attractive to the miner. Mines were wrought here by the French, and to some considerable extent the present race of inhabitants continue the production of this mineral. The lead found here is similar in its origin and quality to that of Illinois and Wisconsin. Iron is also extensively deposited, and though not yet much sought after, is a valuable resource for the future. Some castings, however, are annually manufactured, but to no appreciable amount. It is needless to enumerate the other manufactures, as none further than those incidental to an agricultural country exist. In 1850 the whole number of establishments manufacturing to the value of $500 and upwards was 482.

Iowa has neither canals nor railroads, but it has good turnpikes, and its common roads, easily constructed in so level a country, are numerous. Several plank-roads are also in use. The state, however, will ultimately be crossed by lines of railroad, which will form parts of the great highway from the lakes to the Pacific Ocean, and branches from these main trunks are projected to every important centre. The most important of these projected railroads will be the line continuous of the Chicago and Rock Island Railroad, now building in Illinois; it will cross the Mississippi near the mouth of Rock River, and passing almost east and west through the state, will strike the western border at Council Bluffs, and thence be carried *via* the South Pass of the Rocky Mountains, through the Mormon settlements in Utah Territory and along Humboldt's River to some Pacific port.

The constitution of Iowa provides that every adult white male citizen, idiots, insane, and persons convicted of infamous crimes, excepted, and who has resided in the state six months, and in the county in which he offers his vote, shall enjoy suffrage. The General Assembly consists of a Senate and House of Representatives, and holds its sessions biennially, commencing on the first Monday in December. The Representatives must be at least 21 years of age, and have resided in the state one year, and in the district one month previous to election; Senators must be 25 years of age; one half their number being elected biennially.

The Governor is chosen by a plurality of all the votes, for four years; he must be at least 30 years old, and have resided in the state two years next preceding his election. In case of the death or disability of the Governor, the Secretary of State is invested with his powers. A Secretary of State, Auditor and Treasurer, are chosen by the people for the term of two years; and a Superintendent of Public Instruction, for three years.

The Judiciary consists of a Supreme Court and Circuit Courts. The Supreme Court consists of a Chief-Justice and two associate justices, elected by the joint vote of the General Assembly, for six years. This court has only appellate jurisdiction, and the power to correct errors in law. The judges of the lower courts are elected by the voters of each district, for five years. There are also county courts and justices of the peace.

The constitution makes ample provision for common schools. All lands granted by Congress, all escheats, and other specified avails, are to constitute a perpetual fund to be applied to education. A special fund is also provided for the support of a State University. The permanent school fund, in 1848, amounted to $132,908.

The absolute debt of the state, in 1848, was $55,000, on which the interest was $5,500 per annum. The revenue is derived from taxes on real and personal property, the aggregate value of which was $15,471,103, and the tax $37,884. The total expenditure was $32,514, which sum includes interest, school moneys, public buildings, etc. The ordinary expense of the state government is $19,000.

Iowa City is the capital and seat of government. It is situated on the east side of the Iowa River, which is navigable at all seasons for keel-boats. This place was the hunting-ground of the Indian until 1839. The location is beautiful, rising on a succession of plateaux, or elevated terraces, overlooking a splendid country. The capitol is in the Grecian Doric style of architecture, measuring 120 feet long and 60 feet wide, and is two stories high above the basement. It is surmounted by a dome supported by 22 Corinthian columns. The present population is about 1,600, and is daily increasing from the influx of emigrants.

Dubuque, Muscatine, Burlington, Keokuk, etc., near the Mississippi, are also places of considerable population and trade. There is a Quaker settlement at Salem, in Henry county, which is said to be in a very flourishing condition.

New-Buda, a Hungarian settlement, recently established under General Ujhazy, is situated in Decatur county, on the Crooked Fork River, an affluent of the Missouri. The country these heroic patriots occupy is one of the finest agricultural plots in the state.

Iowa, formerly a portion of French Louisiana, came into the possession of the United States in 1803. It was erected into a separate territorial government in 1838, and having formed for itself a constitution, and performed all the other requirements of the national laws, was admitted as a state of the Union in December, 1846. It has of late rapidly filled up, and the stream of immigration, which is now flowing westward, will, at no distant period, if not arrested, swell the population of this state to millions. The extent, variety of soil, the treasures confined in the bowels of the earth, and its whole physical capacities, combine as many requisites for human enterprise, as are developed in any other tract of country of equal size, and invite an early development of its resources, with the promise of wealth and happiness to the necessitous people of Europe, who are daily seeking homes within the borders of this highly eligible state.

THE SOUTH WESTERN STATES.

Under this caption are included the states of Tennessee, Alabama, Mississippi, Louisiana, Arkansas, and Texas. These states are geographically situated between the latitudes of 36° 40′ and 26° north, and between the longitudes of 81° 30′ and 106° west. They are bounded on the north by Virginia, Kentucky, Missouri and the Indian Territory; on the east by North-Carolina, Georgia, and Florida; on the south by the Gulf of Mexico; and on the west by the Rio Grande del Norte, which separates the United States from the Republic of Mexico. The superficial area of the territory included in these states is about 564,327 square miles, or 361,169,876 acres, of which 216,753,271 acres are yet unsurveyed, and but partially settled, the population being only six inhabitants to the square mile.

The whole of this region, excepting the State of Texas, lies in the lower valley of the Mississippi, and is watered, principally, by the tributaries flowing into that mighty stream. Texas is geographically separate from the central valley, and depends on rivers entirely within itself for irrigation and conveyance. The whole section now under consideration, is much assimilated in surface and quality of soil, and all the included states are equally rich in the productions of the peculiar staples of the southern United States.

The institutions of these several states are also much akin the one to the other, and slavery, in a greater or less degree, is common to all.

With the exception of a few scattered settlements along the Mississippi and Gulf of Mexico, the commencement of the present century found these states a wilderness, inhabited only by the savage Indian and the wild animals of the forest. The rapid increase in their population, and the immense wealth that has been developed in these states in so short a period, has excited the wonder of the world, though in these respects they cannot compare with the progress of the new states in the north-west.

The original settlers of the whole of this region, included in these states, were Frenchmen, either from Canada, or otherwise. The territory of the states east of the Mississippi was ceded by France to England in 1763, and came into the possession of the United States on the conclusion of the

Revolutionary War. The Louisiana purchase, in 1803, gave to the United States all the lands west of the Mississippi to the Spanish boundary; and Texas was voluntarily annexed to the United States in 1845. There is yet an immense unoccupied territory to the west, as far as the Rocky Mountains, which also formed a part of the Louisiana purchase. This territory, however, though partly belonging to this region, will be more conveniently described in a separate section.

THE STATE OF TENNESSEE.

TENNESSEE, once a part of North Carolina, is now the most populous and thickly settled of the South-Western states. It lies between the latitudes of 36° and 37° 42′ North, and between the longitudes of 81° 30′ and 90° 10′ West. On the north, it is bounded by the States of Kentucky and Virginia; on the east by North Carolina, from which it is separated by the Smoky Mountains: on the south by Georgia, Alabama, and Mississippi, and on the west by Arkansas and Missouri, from which it is divided by the Mississippi River. In extreme length, it is 440 miles, and in breadth, 116 miles. It has an area of 45,000 square miles, or 28,800,000 acres.

This state is divided centrally from north-east to south-west, by the Cumberland Mountains, and the territories lying on the respective sides are termed East and West Tennessee. East Tennessee is intersected by several ranges of hills, and the elevated vallies between are highly fertile, and the climate congenial to the growth of the various cereal crops and fruits of more northern regions. West Tennessee is chiefly level, but towards the central range of hills, becomes first undulating, and then more abrupt and elevated. In this region, the soil, especially in parts bordering on the rivers, is deep, rich and fertile, and is well adapted for grazing and rearing cattle. Tennessee produces cotton, tobacco, hemp, and a variety of other staples, both of the north and south.

The rivers of this state are, the Mississippi, which runs the whole length of its western line; the Cumberland, partly in Tennessee, but which rises in Kentucky and runs its principal course within that state; and the Tennessee, which is formed by several branches which rise in western Virginia and the Carolinas, and unite a little west of Knoxville. It runs south-west into Alabama, where it makes a circular bend, and reëntering, passes through Tennessee into Kentucky, and falls into the Ohio, 12 miles from the mouth of the Cumberland. Its course resembles the letter U. This river is navigable to Muscle Shoals, 248 miles, at all seasons of the year. Here it spreads out and becomes so shallow that it is difficult for boats to pass when the water is low. Above the shoals there is no obstruction for 250 miles, till arriving at the "Suck" or "Whirl," where the river breaks through the Cumberland Mountains: here the river is compressed to a width of 70 yards. Just as it enters the mountains a large rock projects from the northern shore, which causes a sudden bend in the river, and throws the water with great violence against the southern shore, when it rebounds around the point of the rock and produces the whirl. Boats, however, ascend and descend the whirl with little danger or difficulty. The principal branches of the Tennessee are the Clinch and Holston, both of which rise in Virginia, and running south-west, unite at Kingston, the latter having received French Broad River four miles above Knoxville. The Hiwassee rises in Georgia, and joins the Tennessee about 70 miles above the "Suck." Duck River rises in the Cumberland Mountains, and joins the Tennessee 57 miles above Nashville. Several considerable rivers flow into the Mississippi.

The climate of Tennessee is generally healthy, and vegetation commences from six to seven weeks earlier than in the New England States. The winters are neither long nor severe. The snow is regarded as deep at ten inches, and does not usually remain on the ground more than eight or ten days. Cattle require no housing. Since the settlement of the country, the Cumberland River has been frozen over but two or three times.

Like the State of Kentucky, Tennessee has numerous caves of great extent, some of which contain human skeletons and the bones of various animals. One cave has been explored to the distance of ten miles. It contains many vaulted compartments, glittering with stalactites, and when viewed by torchlight, the scene is most magnificent. Petrifactions of various kinds are found in many places. Petrified trees and animals are abundant, and among these are the bones of the Mastodon, and the organic remains of animals long since extinct. In the Cumberland Mountains are some very singular impressions of the feet of men, horses, and other animals, as distinctly marked in the solid limestone as if made on moist clay. No satisfactory explanation has hitherto been given respecting the existence of these relics of a past age, but it is probable, nay, certain, that at the time the rocks were impressed, they were in a soft state, and have since become hard by the petrifying influences which surrounded them. Immense banks of oyster shells, of enormous size, have been found in the southern parts of the state.

Tennessee, in 1850, contained 1,002,625 inhabitants, or about one person to every 28 acres, and the proportionate distribution of these to the several districts and counties was as follows:

EASTERN TENNESSEE.

COUNTIES.	White Persons.	Colored Persons. Free.	Colored Persons. Slave.	Total.	COUNTIES.	White Persons.	Colored Persons. Free.	Colored Persons. Slave.	Total.
Anderson	6,391	41	506	6,938	Knox	16,337	225	2,193	18,755
Bledsoe	5,042	90	827	5,959	Marion	5,720	43	557	6,314
Blount	11,173	125	1,084	12,382	Meigs	4,483	1	395	4,879
Bradley	11,478	37	744	12,259	Monroe	10,623	63	1,188	11,874
Campbell	5,653	99	318	6,068	Morgan	3,271	28	101	3,400
Carter	5,911	32	353	6,296	McMinn	12,286	52	1,568	13,906
Claiborne	8,609	100	660	9,369	Polk	5,986	52	400	6,338
Cocke	7,502	79	719	8,300	Rhea	3,951	28	436	4,415
Granger	9,170	165	1,035	12,370	Roane	10,526	115	1,544	12,185
Green	16,522	209	1,093	17,824	Scott	1,868	—	37	1,905
Hamilton	9,216	187	672	10,075	Sevier	6,451	66	403	6,920
Hancock	5,448	10	202	5,660	Sullivan	10,605	133	1,004	11,742
Hawkins	11,573	107	1,690	13,370	Washington	12,672	259	930	13,861
Jefferson	11,479	107	1,628	13,204					
Johnson	3,485	14	206	3,705	Total	235,361	2,455	22,487	260,303

MIDDLE TENNESSEE.

COUNTIES.	White Persons.	Colored Persons. Free.	Colored Persons. Slave.	Total.	COUNTIES.	White Persons.	Colored Persons. Free.	Colored Persons. Slave.	Total.
Bedford	15,938	71	5,503	21,512	Grundy	2,522	15	236	2,773
Cannon	8,115	24	843	8,982	Hickman	7,559	22	1,816	9,397
Coffee	7,061	23	1,267	8,351	Humphreys	5,304	21	1,097	6,422
Davidson	23,858	848	14,175	38.881	Jackson	13,900	115	1,558	15,673
Dickson	5,885	1	2,118	8,004	Lawrence	8,095	23	1,162	9,280
De Kalb	7,335	13	668	8,016	Lewis	3,697	5	736	4,438
Fentress	4,305	1	148	4,454	Lincoln	17,809	62	5,621	23,492
Franklin	10,096	49	3,623	13,768	Macon	6,137	45	766	6,948
Giles	16,519	72	9,358	25,949	Marshall	11,916	66	3,634	15,616

COUNTIES.	White Persons.	Colored Persons. Free.	Slave.	Total.
Maury	16,760	90	12,670	29,520
Montgomery	20,000	74	9,071	21,045
Overton	10,086	60	1,065	11,211
Robertson	11,504	25	4,616	16,145
Rutherford	17,014	130	11,978	29,122
Smith	13,709	186	4,517	18,412
Stewart	7,017	127	2,575	9,719
Sumner	16,511	200	8,006	22,717
Van Buren	2,481	18	175	2,674
Warren	8,416	83	1,710	10,209
Wayne	7,232	8	930	8,170
White	10,028	132	1,284	11,444
Williamson	14,267	70	12,864	27,201
Wilson	19,915	402	7,127	27,444
Total	341,331	3.181	132,847	477,359

WESTERN TENNESSEE.

COUNTIES.	White Persons.	Colored Persons. Free.	Slave.	Total.
Benton	5,931	21	363	6,315
Carroll	12,814	18	3,135	15,967
Decatur	5,263	17	723	6,003
Dyer	4,883	10	1,468	6,361
Fayette	11,420	35	15,264	26,719
Gibson	15,296	58	4,194	19,548
Henderson	10.571	1	2,592	13,164
Haywood	8,713	48	8,498	17,259
Hardeman	10,310	38	7,108	17,456
Harden	9,040	31	1,257	10,328
Henry	13,392	20	4,821	18,233
Lauderdale	3,397	6	1,766	5,169
Madison	12,861	57	8,552	21,470
McNairy	11,447	24	1,393	12,864
Obion	6,572	4	1,057	7,633
Perry	5,504	4	314	5,822
Shelby	16,591	206	14,360	31,157
Tipton	4,673	22	4,192	8,887
Weakly	11,523	15	3,070	14,608
Total	180,201	635	84,127	264,963
Grand Total	756,893	6,271	239,461	1,002,625

CLASSES AND SEXES OF POPULATION.

Classes.	Males.	Females.	Total.
White Persons	382,270	374,623	756,893
Colored " —free	3,072	3,199	6,271
" " —slave	—	—	239,461
Total	—	—	1,002,625

PROGRESSIVE MOVEMENT OF POPULATION.

Date of Census.	White Persons.	Colored Persons. Free.	Slave.	Total Population.	Decennial Increase. Numerical.	Per 100.
1790	32,013	361	3,417	35,791	—	—
1800	91,709	309	13,584	105,602	69,811	195.0
1810	215,875	1,317	44,535	261,727	156,125	147.8
1820	339,927	2,779	80,107	422,813	161,086	61.5
1830	535,646	4,655	141,603	681,904	259,091	61.2
1840	640,627	5,524	183,059	829,210	147,306	21.6
1850	756,893	6,271	239,461	1,002,625	173,415	20.9

In 1850 there were in the state 129,420 dwelling houses and 130,005 families, and hence the average of persons to each dwelling and family was 7.7, but in these numbers the slave dwellings and families are reckoned as parts of the estate of their owners and not separately. The deaths in 1849-50 amounted to 11,759, exhibiting a mortality of one person to every 84 of the population, or about 1.2 per cent.

Agriculture is the leading industrial employment in Tennessee, but other branches, as manufactures and mining, have also obtained a sound footing. In 1850 there were within the limits of the state 72,710 farms under cultivation, viz.: 21,232 in Eastern, 32,545 in Middle, and 18,933 in Western Tennessee; and there were at the same date 2,798 manufacturing establishments, the annual products of which were valued at $500 and upwards, viz.: in the east 941, in the middle 1,297, and in the west section 551.

Indian corn, oats, and wheat are the great grain crops—that of corn averages 52, that of oats 4, and that of wheat 2 millions of bushels. Rye, buckwheat and barley are little grown and cannot enter into an estimate of the crops. Cotton and tobacco are the southern staples, and hemp and flax are annually produced in an increasing quantity. The forests are also very valuable and yield large quantities of lumber, turpentine, etc. But within the United

States scarcely any other state is so peculiarly adapted in climate and grasses for the raising and fattening of cattle, and the abundance of mast and nuts makes it very eligible for hog feeding. Live stock is numerous and requires little care the year round.

The minerals of Tennessee are iron and coal, with some lead, with building material in abundance. The mining interest is in a flourishing condition, and in the eastern and middle sections of the state there are numerous bloomeries, forges, and rolling mills. Saltpetre and salt is also abundant.

The manufactures consist of woollens and cottons, chiefly of the coarse descriptions, and a large number of tanneries, potteries, rope-walks, flouring-mills, etc., are established in every section. Water power is abundant, and is the principal motive agent used to propel machinery.

The trade of this state is chiefly with the South, to which it exports large quantities of live stock, grain, beef, pork, etc.; it has also considerable commerce with the Atlantic states *via.* the railroads terminating at Charleston and Savannah; and many of its staples are carried down the rivers to the Ohio. It has little or no direct foreign commerce.

The means of transportation in Tennessee are being rapidly developed by the building of railroads. The only lines yet complete are those from the Georgia state line to Chattanooga, and the Memphis and Charleston railroad, but the lines in progress are numerous and important. Nashville will be the great centre of railroads in Western Tennessee, and from this city lines are projected to Cincinnati and to Louisville on the Ohio, to Columbus and Memphis on the Mississippi, and a line in a direction south to the state line where it will join the Mobile and Ohio railroad, and another to Chattanooga. These will all interlock at Nashville. The Mobile and Ohio road will also pass through the western district, taking Jackson and Trenton in its course. In Eastern Tennessee there is a line from Chattanooga to Knoxville, and lines are projected from this latter place to Virginia and North Carolina.

There are in the state 4 banks and 19 branch banks. On the 1st June, 1851, the aggregate condition of these institutions was as follows:—Capital $6,881,568, loans and discounts $10,992,139, stocks $432,902, real estate $662,520, due by other banks $1,559,418, notes of other banks $729,186, specie $1,458,778, circulation $6,814,376, deposits $1,917,757, due other banks and other liabilities $71,638.

Tennessee has ample funds for educational purposes, but as yet its common schools are not very numerous. It has, however, several colleges which for efficiency will compare well with any in the new states; and academies and high schools are established in all the cities and larger villages.

The principal collegiate establishments are as undernamed—

Names.	Location.	Founded.	Profs.	Students, 1850.	Volumes in Library.
Greenville College	Greenville	1794	2	41	3,000
Washington College	Washington Co.	1794	2	42	1,500
University	Nashville	1806	7	75	9,500
Franklin College	Near Nashville	1845	6	75	2,200
East Tennessee College	Knoxville	1792	5	57	5,000
Cumberland University	Lebanon	1844	9	47	4,200
Jackson College	Columbia	1833	5	26	2,600
Union College	Murfreesboro'	1848	5	65	1,000
Southwestern Theol. Sem.	Maryville	1821	2	90	6,000
Law School	Lebanon	—	3	56	—
Medical College	Memphis	—	7	—	—

The numerically preponderating religious sects are the Methodists, Baptists and Presbyterians; the Methodists have about 600 preachers and 90,

000 members; the Baptists about 460 churches, 270 ministers, and 40,000 church members; and the Presbyterians (O. S.) about 20,000 church members. The Presbyterians (N. S.) and Anti-Mission Baptists are also numerous; and there are some Unitarians and Universalists. The Protestant Episcopal Church has a Bishop and 17 pastors, and the Roman Catholics have a Bishop, who is suffragan to the archdiocese of St. Louis, 6 churches, 2 chapels, 20 stations, 9 clergy and about 4000 communicants.

The Constitution of Tennessee was adopted at Knoxville, in 1796; but in 1834, underwent a thorough revision. Every free white citizen of the United States, 21 years of age, and who has resided in the county where he offers his vote six months, is eligible to vote at all elections. Every man is considered white who is a competent witness, in court, against a white man. All free colored men are exempt from military duty in time of peace, and from poll taxes. The government consists of an Executive, Legislature, and Judiciary. The Executive is vested in a Governor, who must be at least 30 years of age, a citizen of the United States, and a citizen of the state of at least seven years' standing; he is elected by a plurality of votes, for two years. The Senators must be 30 years of age, and the Representatives at least 21 years of age. Any qualified voter is eligible to these offices. The general elections take place biennially, on the first Tuesday in August, and the sessions (every second year) commence on the first Monday of October. No person who denies the being of a God, or a future state of rewards and punishments, can hold any civil office.

The Judiciary consists of the Supreme Court, with three Judges, one for each district; a Court of Chancery, with four Chancellors, one for each chancery district; Circuit Courts, with a Judge for each of the fourteen circuits; and the Criminal Court of Davidson County, and the Commercial and Criminal Courts of Shelby County. The Judges of the Supreme Court are elected by a joint vote of the two Houses of the General Assembly, and hold office for 12 years except removed therefrom before the expiration of that term for cause. The judges of the inferior Courts are elected in like manner for a term of eight years. All judges have a fixed compensation, unalterable during their tenure of office. Justices of the Peace are elected in districts, by the people, for six years.

The constitution forbids lotteries, and the sale of lottery tickets; and the emancipation of slaves by the legislature, without the consent of the owners.

The condition of the finances, for the year ending October, 1850, is exhibited in the annexed. The total receipts, in that year, were $790,693; and the expenditures, $802,436. The income is derived from taxes on property, privileges, and banks; entries of public lands; dividends of State Bank, applied to academies and schools; surpluses of penitentiary, and internal improvement dividends. The principal items of expenditure were for the Legislature, Judiciary, and Executive; state prosecutions, common schools, and academies; internal improvements; charitable institutions, etc., etc. The public debt at the same period, amounted to $3,352,857, and the productive property held by the state to $4,894,922. The annual interest on the debt is $179,176. The state holds for school purposes $1,321,655. Exclusive of the debt and schools the ordinary expenditures are $290,000 per annum.

Tennessee was originally included in North Carolina. Fort Loudon was built in 1757, on the Little Tennessee River; but in 1760, the garrison and settlers were massacred by the Cherokees. The next attempt at settling was made in Carter's Valley; but the first permanent settlement was effected in 1768, by immigrants from Virginia. In 1776, the boundaries of the territory were settled by North Carolina and Virginia; and, in 1784, the territory was ceded, conditionally, by North Carolina to the United States; and the same year the act of cession was repeated, when a portion of the people announced themselves independent of North Carolina, and prepared a constitution for a state government. which caused much confusion. In 1789, the legislature of North Carolina required their senators in Congress to execute deeds for the cession of the territory, which was accordingly complied with in 1790, and a territorial government erected. In 1796, the territory was admitted into the Union, and a state constitution adopted. The early history of Tennessee is marked, throughout, up to 1794, with wars and contentions between the whites and Cherokees, and Creek Indians. Nothing, however, of importance has occurred since it became a state, nor can a single date be fixed upon to record a historical incident, further than to record its rapid progress, and its civil condition from period to period. Tennessee has given two presidents to the United States, in the persons of Andrew Jackson, the Hero of New-Orleans, and James K. Polk.

The principal cities and towns in the state, are Nashville, Memphis, Knoxville, Greenville, Athens, Columbia, Franklin, Bolivar, La Grange, &c., &c.

Nashville, the capital, is the largest city, and enjoys an extensive commerce. It is situated in Davidson County, on the south bank of the Cumberland, 122 miles from its mouth, and, in 1850, had 10,000: and, including the suburbs, 17,502 inhabitants. This city is rapidly increasing, and at the present day probably numbers at least 20,000. Latitude 36° 9′ 33″ north, and longitude 86° 49′ 3″ west. It is the seat of the University of Tennessee. Nashville is named in honor of General Nash, who fell at the battle of Germantown, 1776. The city is built on an elevated and uneven site, but the streets are laid out in regular squares, lined with handsome buildings, occupied as stores and private dwellings. The public buildings are the state-house, market, lunatic asylum, penitentiary, three banks, 13 churches, the University buildings, various schoolhouses, &c. Water is supplied to the city from Cumberland River, being raised by steam machinery into a reservoir, 66 feet above high-water mark. Numerous steamboats ply to and from Nashville. Clarkesville, on the north bank of the river, below Nashville, is a flourishing town. Lebanon, the capital of Wilson County, is the seat of Cumberland University. Franklin, south of Nashville, is a considerable village, and carries on some important manufactures. It is the seat of a college. Population, 1,500.

Knoxville, on the north bank of the Holston River, was formerly the seat of government, and a town of some consideration. East Tennessee College is located here. The Hiwassee Railroad terminates at this city. Population, about 4,600. The vicinity is thickly settled, and a number of large villages occupy the surrounding country.

Fayetteville, at the head of navigation on the Elk River, is a considerable village. Chattanooga, on the south bank of the Tennessee, and the present terminus of the Western and Atlantic Railroad, is a thriving place; and Savannah, Perrysburg and Reynoldsburg, also on the same river, are important towns. COLUMBIA, on Duck River, is the seat of Jackson College; MURFREESBORO', on Stone River, was formerly the capital of the state; GREENVILLE, is the seat of a college. On the Mississippi, MEMPHIS is the largest city. It is situated on the site of old Fort Pickering. The commerce of this place is greater than any other in the state. A railroad extends from Memphis to La Grange, and is intended to connect with Charleston, S. C. BOLIVAR, RANDOLPH, COVINGTON, and some other extensive villages, lie on the river to the north of Memphis.

THE STATE OF ALABAMA.

ALABAMA is situated between 30° 17′ and 35° North latitude, and between 84° 58′ and 88° 26′ West longitude. It is bounded on the north by Tennessee; on the east by Georgia, from which the River Chattahouchee separates it as far north as West Point; on the south by Florida to the Perdido, and thence by the Gulf of Mexico; and west by the State of Mississippi. Length, 325 miles—breadth, 200 miles: area, 50,781 square miles, or 32,499,872 acres.

The northern districts of this state are mountainous, being crossed from east to west by the south-western extremity of the Alleghanies. In the south the country is generally level. The two divisions differ essentially in soil, climate aud natural productions. The north has a fine fertile soil, and the mountains and hills are covered with immense forests of oak, hickory, ash, elm, cedar and poplar. The central region is comparatively sterile, and covered with pine. Forests of cypress, gum, swamp-oak, holly and live oak diversify the south, and the soil is rich and deep, and peculiarly well adapted to the growth of cotton, sugar, rice, and tobacco. Here groves of orange trees, the lemon, and a variety of fruit trees flourish luxuriantly, and afford in their shade seclusion from the burning sun, which in summer is oppressive and powerful. The climate in the northern district resembles that of the middle States, and here the seasons are well marked, but never severe. In the south, snow and ice are seldom seen, and the seasons are only diversified by small extremes.

The country between the Alabama and Tombigbee is the best part of the state. That east of the Alabama consists of good land, a considerable portion of it of the first quality. Of the lands lying north and west of the Alabama and Coosa rivers, the soil is generally good, and well adapted to cotton and sugar growing, and there are some fine cotton lands on the Tallapoosa, in the lower part of its course.

The state is traversed by several fine rivers. The Tennessee passes through the northern sections, draining in its course all the country north of the mountains. The southern parts are drained by the tributaries of the Alabama and Tombigbee, which unite about latitudes 31° N., and form the Mobile, which, after a short course, falls into Mobile Bay, an arm of the Gulf of Mexico. The Alabama is formed by the Coosa and Tallapoosa rivers, which rise in Georgia, and running west, unite in 32° 30′ N. latitude. It is navigable for steam-vessels to the junction, but neither the Coosa nor Tallapoosa are navigable for a great distance except by flat-bottom boats.

The Cahawba falls into the Alabama at the town of the same name. The Tombigbee, the western branch of the Mobile, rises in the State of Mississippi, and pursues a southerly course of nearly 500 miles, before it joins the Alabama. It receives many fine streams, and is navigable to Columbus in Mississippi. The Black Warrior, one of its tributaries, is navigable for boats nearly to its source. This river is of importance, because it will probably become the channel of communication between the immense fertile country in the northern part of the state and the sea-ports on Mobile Bay. The Chattahouchee, which lies on the eastern line of the state, is navigable for steamboats to Columbus, Georgia, and by river craft nearly to its source. The Perdido separates the parts south of 31° N. lat. from Florida.

The Bay of Mobile, which receives the main body of the waters of the state, is 30 miles long and 12 miles broad, and affords some of the best harbors on the Gulf of Mexico. It is of a triangular shape, having its base on the south, half of which consists of a narrow strip of land protecting it from the perturbations of the sea, and the influence of the southern winds. The waters, except at its entrance, are deep, and the anchorage safe.

Alabama is divided into 52 counties, and in 1850 contained an aggregate population of 971,671 or one person to every 42 acres. The distribution of this population to the several counties was in the following proportions:

SOUTHERN ALABAMA.

COUNTIES.	White Persons.	Colored Persons. Free.	Colored Persons. Slave.	Total Popula.
Antauga	6,274	19	8,730	15,023
Baldwin	2,100	96	2,218	4,414
Barbour	12,842	10	10,780	23,632
Bibb	7,097	11	2,861	9,969
Butler	7,162	35	3,639	10,836
Chambers	12,784	18	11,158	23,960
Choctaw	4,620	—	3,769	8,389
Clarke	4,901	9	4,876	9,786
Coffee	5,382	1	557	5,940
Conecuh	4,922	6	4,394	9,322
Coosa	10,414	9	4,120	14,543
Covington	3,077	88	480	3,645
Dale	5,623	2	721	6,346
Dallas	7,461	8	22,258	29,727
Greene	9,265	49	22,127	31,441
Henry	6,776	1	2,242	9,019
Lowndes	7,258	8	14,649	21,915
Macon	11,280	22	15,596	26,898
Marengo	7,101	37	20,693	27,831
Mobile	17,306	938	9,356	27,600
Monroe	5,648	40	6,325	12,013
Montgomery	10,172	112	19,511	29,795
Pike	12,102	24	3,794	15,920
Pickens	10,972	6	10,534	21,512
Perry	8,342	26	13,917	22,285
Randolph	10,616	29	936	11,581
Russel	8,405	32	11,111	19,548
Shelby	7,153	7	2,376	9,536
Sumter	7,369	50	14,831	22,250
Talladega	11,618	35	6,971	18,624
Tallapoosa	11,511	—	4,073	15,584
Tuscaloosa	10,553	26	7,479	18,056
Wilcox	5,516	1	11,835	17,352
Washington	1,293	24	1,496	2,713
Total	274,817	1,777	280,411	557,005

NORTHERN ALABAMA.

COUNTIES.	White Persons.	Colored Persons. Free.	Colored Persons. Slave.	Total Popula.
Benton	13,397	3	3,763	17,163
Blount	6,941	—	426	7,367
Cherokee	12,170	23	1,691	13,884
De Kalb	7,730	9	506	8,245
Fayette	8,450	10	1,221	9,681
Franklin	11,399	14	8,197	19,610
Hancock	1,480	—	62	1,542
Jackson	11,766	30	2,292	14,088
Jefferson	6,714	8	2,267	8,989
Lauderdale	11,097	60	6,015	17,172
Lawrence	8,343	63	6 852	15,258
Limestone	8,405	15	8,063	16,483
Madison	11,937	164	14,326	26,427
Marion	6,922	3	908	7,833
Marshall	7,953	25	868	8,846
Morgan	6,638	50	3,437	10,125
St. Clair	5,501	7	1,321	6,829
Walker	4,857	1	266	5,124
Total	151,690	495	62,481	214,666

RECAPITULATION.

DISTRICTS.	White Persons.	Colored Persons. Free.	Colored Persons. Slave.	Total Popula.
Northern	151,690	495	62,481	214,666
Southern	274,817	1,777	280,411	557,005
Total	426,507	2,272	342,892	771,671

CLASSES AND SEXES OF POPULATION.

Classes.	Males.	Females.	Total.
White Persons	219,728	206,779	426,507
Colored " —free	1,047	1,225	2,272
" " —slave	—	—	342,892
Total	—	—	771,671

PROGRESSIVE MOVEMENT OF POPULATION.

Date of Census.	White Persons.	Colored Persons. Free.	Colored Persons. Slave.	Total Population.	Decennial Increase. Numerical.	Decennial Increase. Per 100.
1820	85,451	571	41,879	127,901	—	—
1830	290,406	1,572	117,549	309,527	181,626	142.8
1840	335,185	2,039	253,532	590,756	281,229	90.8
1850	426,507	2,272	342,892	771,761	180,915	30.5

The number of dwelling houses in Alabama in 1850 was 72,070, of which 25,426 were in North, and 47,644 in South Alabama; and the number of families was 73,786, of which 25,521 were in northern and 48,265 in southern district, or an average of about 10.5 persons to each dwelling and family—in the north 8.6 and in the south 11.6. The slave dwellings and families are reckoned as a part of their owner's estate and not here counted. The deaths in 1849-50 numbered 6,656 in the south, or a proportionate mortality of one in every 83 of the population, and in the north the number of deaths was 2,428, or one in every 89 persons. For the whole state the mortality amounted to 9,084, or about one death in every 84 inhabitants.

Alabama is eminently an agricultural state and produces all the staples of the south. Its great staple however is cotton, the annual crop of which is now about 220,000,000 lbs. Tobacco and rice are likewise grown, and also some sugar. In the northern part of the state there is much land devoted to cereal grains; of these Indian corn is the largest crop, averaging about 28,000,000 bushels yearly; the crops of oats and wheat are also comparatively large, but that of rye is small, and barley and buckwheat are scarcely known. The garden and orchard are of little account. The forest furnishes considerable timber, and some rosin and turpentine, but little if any for export. The farms under cultivation number 41,964. The quantity of live stock is large in proportion to the population. In manufactures this state has made only a slight advance. It has however all the pre-requisites for this branch of industry, *viz.*, motive power, the raw-material, coal for fuel, and cheap labor; and if capital were turned in this direction much progress might be made. Besides the ordinary number of tanneries and leather factories there are already several cotton mills in various parts, but as yet these have essayed to manufacture only the coarse goods demanded for domestic use. Flouring, grist and saw-mills are numerous; and the products of family industry amount to a considerable sum. The manufacturing capital used in the state may be estimated at $4,500,000. Manufacturing establishments producing annually $500 and upwards number 1,022. The mines of iron and coal in the north mountain region might supply an abundance of of those useful minerals, but there does not appear to be as yet much effort made to work them. Some small quantities of both however have been annually taken out. Granite, marble, lime and gypsum are also plentiful and are used to some extent. On the whole, little can be said of Alabama mining industry, but the time is not far distant when the railroads now being built will stimulate the people to action and call forth the latent treasures for which under present circumstances there is no demand. Gold is also found in this state, and from time to time the production has been considerable.

Mobile City is the great commercial depot of the state. Perhaps the northern part of the country may depend on the Georgia lines of railroad and the Atlantic ports for an outlet, but for all the central and southern districts Mobile is the natural port. The exports to foreign countries for the year 1849–50 amounted in value to $10,544,858, all domestic produce, and the imports to $865,362; and the foreign carrying trade employed 209,005 tons of shipping, of which 96,020 tons entered and 112,985 tons cleared. The coasting trade however is much more extensive than the foreign, and is principally carried on with the northern Atlantic states.

In January, 1851, there were three banks, with numerous branches in this state, the aggregate capital of which amounted to $1,800,580, the circulation to $3,568,535, deposits to $1,474,963, and all other liabilities to $857,633. The assets at the same date were, loans and discounts $4,670,458, stocks $70,361, real estate $125,697, other investments $81,000, due by other banks $969,334, notes of other banks $63,865, and specie $1,938,820.

The works of internal improvement completed in Alabama consist of several canals, as that at the Muscle Shoals of the Tennessee, and the Huntsville Canal, both of which are important to the northern section of the state. The railroads completed are the Tuscumbia and Decatur railroad, 44 miles long, and that from Montgomery to West Point, 87 miles long, at which latter place it unites with the systems of Georgia and South Carolina. The first named road will form a link in the great line from Memphis on the Mississippi to Charleston on the Atlantic, and the latter road will be continued from Montgomery through Selma to Jackson and Vicksburg. The Mobile and Ohio Railroad will have its southern terminus at Mobile, and though running but a short distance within this state will be of inestimable value to its commerce. This road it is intended shall be carried north to Cairo at the mouth of the Ohio river. Numerous other lines are proposed and some of them will no doubt be completed in course of time; the most important of these are, the Mobile and Huntsville road, which will be extended into Tennessee; the Alabama and Tennessee road from Selma to Gunter's Landing, the Pensacola road from Montgomery to Pensacola; a road from Blakely on Mobile Bay to Columbus in Georgia, and a road from Mobile to New Orleans. By these lines the north will have ready access to the Gulf ports, and the Great South-west will be united to the ports of the Atlantic.

Alabama is respectably provided with educational institutions, and has several seminaries which have attained celebrity. Of the collegiate establishments the State University at Tuscaloosa is the principal; it was founded in 1831 and has been endowed with a fund amounting to $250,000, on which the state pays interest $15,000 annually. In 1850 it had 9 professors and 92 students; and its library contained 7,123 volumes. La Grange College, founded 1831, Spring Hill College, founded 1830, and Howard College at Marion, founded 1841, have efficient corps of teachers, and average from 60 to 75 students each annually. There is also at Marion a Theological Seminary under the charge of the Baptist denomination. Academies and grammar schools are numerous, and common schools have of late years been extended over the whole state.

The Baptist and Methodist denominations are the strongest in point of numbers; but the Presbyterians, Catholics and Episcopalians constitute a respectable moiety of the people.

Tuscaloosa, the former capital, is situated at the head of steam navigation, on the Black Warrior River. It is a small but thriving town, being the centre of a considerable agricultural district. Latitude 33° 12' North, longitude 87° 42' West.

Mobile, at the mouth of the Mobile river, has become the seat of an extensive trade, and is the most commercial city in the state. The population, which, in 1830, was only 3,194, had increased in 1840 to 12 672, and in 1850 it had further increased to 20,513. It is the chief outlet of the commerce of the state, and immense quantities of cotton and other staples are brought down the rivers to this point from the upper districts, and also from the western parts of Georgia and from the state of Mississippi. The harbor is good, and is well protected by fortifications. The city was founded by the Spaniards in 1700, but it did not become a place of much importance until captured by the Americans in 1811. Mobile is frequently visited with the yellow fever, and is subject to other diseases peculiar to low and hot situations.

BLAKELEY stands opposite Mobile, at the mouth of the Tensaw. It has many advantages as a commercial point, but has never been able to supersede Mobile, although it enjoys a finer climate and is more healthy. MONTGOMERY on the Alabama, the present state capital, has a large trade, being the centre of an extensive cotton region. It is connected by railroad with West Point on the Georgia state line, and steamboats ply regularly between here and Mobile, &c. ST. STEPHENS, on the Tombigbee, is a flourishing place, surrounded by a fertile and beautiful country. CAHAWBA, at the confluence of the Alabama and Cahawba rivers, was laid out in 1818, and was formerly capital of the state. It is connected with Marion by a railroad. WETUMPKA, at the union of the Coosa and Tallapoosa; FLORENCE, at the head of steam navigation, on the Tennessee; WATERLOO, HUNTSVILLE, TUSCUMBIA, &c. are all important places, and chiefly connected with the commerce of the state.

The constitution of this state is dated 1819. It provides for an Executive, Legislature and Judiciary. The Executive is vested in a Governor, who is chosen, by a plurality of the popular vote, for the term of two years. He must be at least 30 years of age, a native of the United States, and have resided in the state four years. The General Assembly consists of a Senate and House of Representatives. Representatives must be white citizens of the United States; resident the last two years in the state, and one year in the place they represent; they are chosen for two years, and number not less than forty-four, nor more than sixty, until there are one hundred thousand white inhabitants in the state, and thereafter not less than sixty nor more than one hundred. Senators must not be more than one-third, nor less than one-fourth, of the number of the representatives, and have all their qualifications, and must also be twenty-seven years old: they are chosen for four years —one-half every second year. The sessions of the General Assembly are biennial. A census is taken every six years to apportion senatorial and representative districts, and every county must have at least one representative.

Every white male person, twenty-one years old, a citizen of the United States, resident in the state one year next preceding an election, and three months in his county, city, or town, may vote.

The Judiciary consists of a Supreme Court, and such other courts as the legislature may ordain. The Supreme Court has appellate jurisdiction only, but its judges (unless otherwise provided by law,) must sit at "*nisi prius*," as a Circuit Court, and have original jurisdiction in all criminal cases, and in civil suits above fifty dollars. Judges are appointed by the General Assembly, have a fixed salary, and hold office six years, but may be removed by address of two-thirds of both houses, after notice and a hearing.

The State Treasurer and Comptroller are chosen annually, and an Attorney General and County Solicitor once in four years, by the General Assembly

The state debt amounted in 1849 to $9,170,555, and there was a contingent debt of $4,438,522, or a total of $13,609,077. The annual interest on the absolute debt is $469,000, which is punctually paid. The school fund amounted to $927,850, and the other productive property of the state to $6,300,000. The ordinary expenses of the government are about $130,000. The taxes amount to upwards of $482,000.

Mobile was the first place settled in the state, at which period it belonged to Florida. At the time it came into possession of the United States very few inhabitants were found in all the district. The rapid increase it has maintained since then is shown elsewhere. In 1817, Alabama was erected into a territorial government, and in 1820 was admitted as an independent state of the Union.

THE STATE OF MISSISSIPPI.

Mississippi is situated between 30° 10′ and 35° north latitude, and between 88° 10′ and 91° 35′ west longitude; and is bounded north by Tennessee; east by Alabama; south by the Gulf of Mexico and Louisiana, and west by the Pearl River, which separates it from Louisiana, and the Mississippi, which separates it from Louisiana and Arkansas. This state is 325 miles long, and 192 miles in extreme breadth; containing an area of 47,114 square miles, or 30,153,054 acres.

In the south, for about 100 miles from the Gulf of Mexico, the country is almost a dead level, covered chiefly with forests of pine, cypress swamps, prairies, and inundated swamps and marshes. Further north the surface becomes more elevated, and in many places hilly and broken, but in no part of the state are there any elevations approaching the character of mountains. A range of bluffs stretch along the Mississippi, at various distances, in some places reaching almost to the margin of the river. They are an extension of the table-lands, which extend over a portion of the state into the low grounds of the river, and are in general possessed of a fertile soil. The low alluvial, on the margin of the rivers, is the richest land in the state. These, however, are frequently overflowed during the season of flood, and devastation is spread far and wide in the cultivated districts. The lands bordering on the Yazoo, in the north-west part of the state, are very fertile, with a fine, rich and black mould; but the pine regions, on the contrary, are comparatively barren, and have a light and unproductive soil. The great staple of Mississippi is cotton, but Indian corn, bananas, sweet potatoes, tobacco, indigo, and great varieties of fruit, are cultivated; and the natural growths, consisting of valuable timber, and spices, fruits, &c., yield considerable wealth to the inhabitants.

The Gulf of Mexico skirts the southern shore of this state for 70 or 80 miles, and a chain of low and sandy islands stretches along the coast. The principal of these are Cat Island and Ship Island, the former of which has lately become a depôt of the "British and West India Royal Mail Steamships." The Bay of Pascagoula, lying between these and the main land, is 65 miles long and from seven to eight miles wide, and forms an inland navigation from Mobile Bay to Lake Borgue and Lake Pontchartrain. No harbor admitting vessels of more than eight feet draught, is found in all this distance.

The Mississippi River winds along the western borders for 530 miles. The banks of this river, except where approached by the bluffs, consist of inundated swamps, covered with cypress. The Yazoo is the largest river entirely within the state. It has a course of more than 200 miles from north to south, 50 of which are navigable; and, after passing through a most fertile and elevated district, enters the Mississippi 12 miles north of Vicksburg. The Big Black is also a large river, falling into the Mississippi near 32° north latitude. It is as long, but not so capacious, as the Yazoo. The other rivers emptying into the Mississippi are of small account, and, except the Homochitto, incapable of navigation. The Tombigbee rises in the north-east part of this state, and flows into Alabama. The rivers flowing into the Gulf of Mexico are: the Pearl, which rises in the centre of the state, and, passing south, forms, in its lower course, the dividing line of the states of Mississippi and Louisiana, and, at length, enters the Rigolets between lakes Pontchartrain and Borgue. It is navigable for vessels drawing six feet of water for about 50 miles, and for boats, 100 miles further up; but the bay, at its mouth, has only four feet of water.

The climate of this state is more mild and agreeable than Louisiana. In the north the temperature ranges between 26° and 94°, which may be considered as extremes, but the southern portion, below 31°, is both uncomfortably hot and unhealthy. In these regions the lime and the orange flourish luxuriantly.

The productions of Mississippi are chiefly those of the tropics, but in the northern part of the state many of the growths are cognate with those of the more temperate regions of North America. The natural scale of vegetation ranges from the heliconias and the banana to the hardy trees of the forest. In the neighborhood of the Gulf we have, mingled with deciduous trees and plants, the pine, the cypress, magnolia, and sweet gum. A great variety of forest trees flourish in the north, among which may be mentioned several kinds of oak, walnut, hickory, dog-wood, elm, maple, and cottonwood. The wild animals of this state are those common to the whole valley of the Mississippi; but confined to the more southern portion we find all those which are generally considered as tropical. The birds are mostly migratory, moving northward in the summer. The paroquet is found throughout the southern region; and venomous snakes are very common. The turtle-dove, mocking-bird, quail, and humming-bird, are also denizens of this state.

Mississippi is divided into two districts, viz., "Northern Mississippi," containing 23 counties, and "Southern Mississippi," containing 36 counties. In 1850 it had an aggregate of 606,555 inhabitants, or a ratio of one person to every 49 acres, which was distributed in the following proportions:

NORTHERN MISSISSIPPI.

COUNTIES.	White Persons.	Colored Persons. Free.	Colored Persons. Slave.	Total Popula.
Attala	7,578	9	3,412	10,999
Bolivar	395	2	2,180	2,577
Carroll	8,661	18	9,812	18,491
Chickasaw	9,886	2	6,480	16,368
Choctaw	8,420	4	2,978	11,402
Coahoma	1,387	2	1,391	2,780
De Soto	9,487	2	9,553	19,042
Itawamba	11,395	6	2,127	13,528
Lafayette	8,346	4	5,719	14,069
Lowndes	6,523	28	12,993	19,544
Marshall	14,271	1	15,417	29,689
Monroe	9,417	38	11,717	21,172
Noxubee	4,976	—	11,232	16,208
Oktibbeha	4,309	18	4,844	9,171
Panola	5,021	3	6,420	11,444
Pontotoc	12,136	8	4,968	17,112
Sun Flower	348	—	754	1,102
Tallahatchee	2,096	—	2,547	4,643
Tippah	15,808	5	4,928	20,741
Tishemingo	13,528	1	1,961	15,490
Tunica	396	1	917	1,314
Winston	5,178	10	2,768	7,956
Yallabusha	8,652	9	8,597	17,258
Total	168,214	171	133,806	302,191

SOUTHERN MISSISSIPPI.

COUNTIES.	White Persons.	Colored Persons. Free.	Colored Persons. Slave.	Total Popula.
Adams	3,952	255	14,415	18,622
Amité	3,643	3	6,050	9,696
Claiborne	3,449	42	11,450	14,941
Clark	3,823	6	1,648	5,477
Copiah	6,303	11	5,480	11,794
Covington	2,222	2	1,114	3,338
Franklin	2,540	14	3,350	5,904
Green	1,379	1	638	2,018
Hancock	2,444	12	1,216	3,672
Harrison	3,378	56	1,441	4,875
Hinds	8,690	25	16.625	25,340
Holmes	5,547	4	8,377	13,928
Issaquena	366	7	4,105	4,478
Jackson	2,271	100	825	3,196
Jasper	4,296	1	1,887	6,184
Jefferson	2,657	43	10,493	13,193
Jones	1.887	3	274	2,164
Kemper	7,738	1	5,378	12,517
Lauderdale	6,029	27	2,661	8,717
Lawrence	3,549	—	2,929	6,478
Leake	3,982	2	1,549	5,533
Madison	4,328	2	13,843	18,173
Marion	2,215	—	2,195	4,410
Neshoba	3,393	—	1,335	4,728
Newton	3,432	1	1,032	4,465
Perry	1,679	10	749	2,438
Pike	4,225	33	3,102	7,360
Rankin	3,945	6	3,276	7,227
Scott	2,778	1	1,182	3,961
Simpson	3,190	3	1,541	4,734
Smith	3,073	—	998	4,072
Warren	5,998	27	12.096	18,121
Washington	553	—	7,836	8,389
Wayne	1,499	—	1,393	2,892
Wilkinson	3,624	30	13,260	16,914
Yazoo	4,069	—	10,349	14,418
Total	127,544	720	176,092	304,364
Grand Total	295,758	899	309,898	606,555

CLASSES AND SEXES OF POPULATION.

Classes.	Males.	Females.	Total.
White Persons	156,260	139,498	295,758
Colored " —free	473	426	899
" " —slave	—	—	309,898
Total	—	—	606,555

PROGRESSIVE MOVEMENT OF POPULATION.

Date of Census.	White Persons.	Colored Persons. Free.	Colored Persons. Slave.	Total Population.	Decennial Increase. Numerical.	Decennial Increase. Per 100.
1800	5,179	182	3,489	8,850	—	—
1810	23,024	240	17,088	40,352	31,502	355.9
1820	42,176	458	32,814	75,448	35,096	86.9
1830	70,443	519	65,659	136,621	61,173	81.1
1840	179,074	1,366	195,211	375,651	239,030	175.3
1850	295,758	899	309,898	606,555	230,904	61.6

The number of dwellings in the state in 1850 was 51,681, and of families 52,107, or in the ratio of about 11½ persons to each dwelling and family. The deaths amounted to 8,711, or one in every 69.9 of the population.

The great body of the people pursue agriculture as an occupation—few are engaged either in manufactures or commerce. The cereals are not cultivated to a great extent. Cotton is the great staple, and rice and tobacco, though not largely grown, enjoy here a congenial soil and climate. Sugar growing is also a staple occupation. The whole number of farms and plantations under cultivation in 1850 was 23,960. Manufactures, which in 1850 were pursued in 866 establishments, are chiefly those incidental to an agricultural country. The capital invested in the iron manufacture amounted to $100,000, and the value of the entire products to $117,400. The raw material used cost $50,370, and there were employed in the several establishments 112 hands. In the cotton manufactures $38,000 were invested, and the value of the goods produced was $30,500. Mississippi has no direct foreign commerce, but exports through the neighboring ports. The shipping owned within the state, and engaged in the coasting trade, amounted on the 30th June, 1850, to 1,496 tons, of which 675 tons were navigated by steam power.

The internal improvements of Mississippi are not extensive. The Vicksburg and Jackson railroad, 46 miles, has been extended to Brandon, 13 miles further: cost together about $500,000. It has a branch road to Raymond. The Mississippi Railroad (Natchez and Malcolm) is completed 22 miles. It is intended to unite Canton with Natchez by railroad via Jackson, but as yet little progress has been made in the matter. The railroad from St. Francisville to Woodville is 28 miles long, and cost $168,000:—the greater part of this line is in Louisiana. Several other railroads are projected, and on some the work has been commenced.

Mississippi University, at Oxford, founded in 1846, though not fully organized, is expected to become an institution of great value. The Centenary College and Oakland College are in a flourishing state. In 1850 there were, besides seven collegiate institutions, 71 academies for the higher branches of education, in which 2,553 young persons were being taught; and 382 common and primary schools, with 8,236 scholars. The number of adult white persons unable to read or write was 8,360.

The Methodists and Baptists are the most numerous religious denominations. In 1847 the Methodists had 76 travelling, 3 superannuated, and — local preachers, with 15,949 church members; and the Baptists, at the same period, 15 associations, 326 churches, 147 ordained ministers, 35 licensed preachers, and 19,539 communicants. There were also some Anti-Mission and other Baptist sects. Presbyterians were also numerous. The Anglican Church had a Bishop and 17 clergymen; and the Roman Catholics had also a Bishop and several congregations.

The constitution of this state is dated 1817. Every free white male person, twenty-one years of age, a citizen of the United States, a resident of the state for one year, and of the town or county in which he offers his vote for four months next preceding an election, is entitled to suffrage. The Legislature consists of a Senate and House of Representatives. Representatives not less than 36 nor more than 100 in number, and not less than one for each county are chosen every second year. They must be qualified voters, and have resided in the state two years, and in the county for which they are elected one year last past. The Senate must consist of not less than one-fourth nor more than one-third the number of representatives. Senators must be at least 30 years old, citizens of the United States of four years standing, and have resided in the district they represent one year. They are elected for four years, one-half being renewed every two years. The Executive is vested in a Governor, chosen by a plurality of votes for two years. All officers are elected by the people in districts or counties. No person denying the being of a God or a future state of rewards and punishments can hold office. The legislature has no power to emancipate slaves without the owner's consent, except on account of great public services, and then must pay for them; nor can it prevent immigrants from importing slaves of the same description with those already in the state, if they be *boná fide* property and not criminals. The introduction of slaves as merchandize is prohibited; but settlers, previous to 1845, might import them for their own use. No grand jury is necessary to prosecute slaves for crimes not capital.

The judiciary consists of a high court of Errors and Appeals, a Superior Court of Chancery, District Chancery Courts, and District or Circuit Courts.

The public debt* of Mississippi, in 1847, amounted to an aggregate of $7,271,707, of which $5,000,000 is contingent, having been incurred for banking purposes. The annual interest on the $2,271,707 of absolute debt is $128,000. The ordinary expenses of the government are about $155,000 exclusive of interest on public debt.

JACKSON, in Hinde's county, and on the west bank of the Pearl River, is the capital of the state. Lat. 32° 23′ N., long. 90° 8′ W. The city is located on a plain about one mile square, and contains a state-house, the penitentiary, and several other public buildings. It has about 3,000 inhabitants.

NATCHEZ is the largest and most commercial town in the state. It is situated on the east bank of the Mississippi, about 121 miles below the mouth of the Yazoo River, and 300 above New-Orleans. It is divided into two parts: the lower town, which is situated immediately on the river, and extends back some 200 yards; and the upper town, which is built on a bluff which rises abruptly 300 feet above the river. The first is devoted to conveniences for those trafficking on the river, and the latter for the residences of the better classes of society. The streets are wide, regular, and adorned with shade trees. Natchez contains many elegant public buildings, and during a part of the year is a pleasant and not unhealthy abode. It is the great cotton mart for the lower Yazoo district, and the whole country northward and east. The population, in 1850, was 5,239.

VICKSBURG, 106 miles north of Natchez, lies on the western declivity of the Walnut Hills, and presents from the river a picturesque attitude. It contains several public buildings. Population, in 1850, about 4,211. Vicksburg is the depôt of an extensive back country, and the steamboat traffic in the cotton season is immense.

PORT GIBSON, on Bayou Pierre, and between Natchez and Vicksburg, is a flourishing village. Grand Gulf, its port, is situated on the Mississippi.

The other considerable towns in the state are YAZOO CITY, on the Yazoo River; COMMERCE, on the Mississippi; MONTICELLO, the former capital; WOODVILLE, in the south-west corner of the state; and MISSISSIPPI CITY and SHIELDSBORO', on the gulf shore. COLUMBUS, at the head of steam navigation on the Tombigbee River, is also a prominent town, and, of late years, has increased wonderfully in population and wealth. With one or two exceptions, indeed, it is now the largest city in the state.

The discovery of this portion of the Union is attributed to De Soto, a Spaniard, who, in 1540, landed in Florida, and afterwards traversed the country as far as the Mississippi, in search of gold, and died on the banks of that river in 1542. The first settlement was made by the French at Natchez, in 1716, but in 1729, the whole colony was massacred by the Indians. In 1763, this territory, together with all the vast possessions claimed by the French east of the Mississippi, was ceded to Great Britain, and claimed by Georgia. In 1783, peace being consummated, the country fell into the hands of the United States. In 1802, Alabama and Mississippi were purchased by the general government, and were then named the Mississippi Territory. In 1817, Mississippi was portioned off as a state, and Alabama erected into a separate territorial government. The southern portion of the state, below 31° N. lat., belonged to Florida, but was captured by the United States in 1811, and attached to Mississippi by President Madison.

THE STATE OF LOUISIANA.

Louisiana, one of the most important of the United States, lies between 29° and 33° North latitude, and between the meridians of 88° 40′ and 94° 25′ West longitude. It is bounded north by Arkansas and Mississippi; east by the Mississippi and Pearl rivers, which separate it from the State of Mississippi, and by the Gulf of Mexico, into which its southern extremity projects; south by the Gulf of Mexico; and west by Texas, from which it is divided chiefly by the Sabine River. This state is 340 miles long, and 228 miles wide,—with a superficial area of 44,215 square miles, or 28,297,602 acres, of which only 20,231,897 had been surveyed in 1847.

The whole southern portion of Louisiana, from the Pearl to the Sabine, consists of low swampy marshes or vast prairies. The tract about the delta is one continued swamp, destitute of trees, and covered with strong reeds five or six feet high. Along the gulf or sea, marsh extends far into the country, and passing this the land gradually rises, and here the prairies commence. A large portion of this tract is annually overflowed by the rivers. By a survey made by order of the general government, in 1828, it was found that five millions of acres, or a little more than one-sixth of the state, was subject to this periodic inundation, and that but a small portion of this was fit for cultivation. In the alluvial territory are small bodies of prairie lands, slightly elevated, and of great fertility. More extended prairies constitute a large portion of the state. Pine woods, which have a rolling surface, are extensive, and have generally a poor soil. The greater part of the prairies has a second-rate soil, but some parts of those of Opelousas, and particularty those of Attakapas, are extremely rich, and feed large herds of cattle. The lands along the Mississippi are considerably higher than those further off, in consequence of the river depositing more largely on its banks, and it has become necessary to raise artificial embankments or *levees* to protect the rear settlements from inundation. On the east bank, the levees commence sixty miles above New-Orleans, and extend down the river more than 130 miles. On the west shore, it commences 172 miles above New-Orleans. The northern part of the state has an undulating surface, and is covered with a heavy natural growth of white, red and yellow oak, hickory, black-walnut, sassafras, magnolia and poplar. The bottoms along the Red River are from one to ten miles broad, and are of great fertility. On the uplands, which are sandy and less fertile, pines and various kinds of oak are found. The lower courses of the Red River have been denominated the "cotton planter's paradise."

The staple productions of Louisiana are sugar, cotton and rice. Sugar-cane grows chiefly on the shores of the gulf, and especially on the bayoux and mouths of the delta and Mississippi. None is grown north of 31° N. lat. Cotton is grown everywhere. Rice is principally confined to the banks of the rivers, where irrigation is easy. The quantity of land adapted to sugar has been computed at 250,000 acres; the rice lands at 250,000 acres, exclusive of submerged districts which might be improved; and cotton lands at 2,400,000 acres.

The climate of Louisiana is more extreme than in the same latitudes on the Atlantic. The summer heats are higher, and the cold of winter more severe, owing to the cold "northers" which sweep over the frozen countries northward. The southern portions of the country, being wet and marshy, are very unhealthy in summer and autumn, and the cities are frequently scourged with the yellow fever. The more elevated parts of the state have a climate pleasant and salubrious.

The Mississippi River runs through the centre of southern Louisiana, and being there divided into several mouths, forms of the land a number of large and small islands. The Atchafalaya leaves the Mississippi a little below Red River, and is supposed to carry off as much water as that river brings in. The Plaquemine, La Fourche, Iberville and other outlets, leave the Mississippi in like manner at various points, and carry off considerable waters to the Gulf. The Red River crosses the state from west to east, and enters the Mississippi 240 miles above New Orleans. The Washita runs in a southerly direction, and falls into the Red River a little above its entrance into the Mississippi. The other rivers are the Tensas, Sabine, Vermillion, Leche, Pearl, Amitė, etc. The largest lakes are those of Pontchartrain, Maurepas, Borgue, Chetimaches, Mermenteau, Calcasieu and Sabine—all south of 31° N. lat. The coasts are indented with numerous large bays, and lined with islands and sandbars.

Louisiana is divided into two districts, and each of these into several parishes. In 1850 it contained 511,974 inhabitants, or one person to every 55 acres; and these were distributed in the following proportions:

EASTERN DISTRICT.

PARISHES.	White Persons.	Colored Persons. Free.	Colored Persons. Slave.	Total Popula.
Ascension	3,339	147	7,266	10,752
Assumption	5,170	27	5,341	10,538
Baton Rouge, East	5,347	279	6,351	11,979
Baton Rouge, West	1,818	102	4,350	6,270
Feliciana, East	4,061	23	9,514	13,598
Feliciana, W.	2,473	106	10,666	13,245
Iberville	3,568	104	8,542	12,214
Jefferson	18,021	874	6,196	25,091
La Fouche	5,143	22	4,368	9,533
Livingston	2,523	20	842	3,385
Orleans	91,355	10,038	18,068	119,461
Plaquemines	2,221	390	4,779	7,390
Point Coupee	2,967	561	7,811	11,339
St. Bernard	1,406	73	2,323	3,802
St. Charles	867	121	4,132	5,120
St. Helena	2,354	11	2,196	4,561
St. James	3,285	62	7,751	11,098
St. John Baptist	2,586	191	4,540	7,317
St. Tammany	3,642	359	2,363	6,364
Terre Bonne	3.324	72	4,328	7,724
Washington	2,367	4	1,037	3,408
Total	167,837	13,586	122,764	304,187

WESTERN DISTRICT.

PARISHES.	White Persons.	Colored Persons. Free.	Colored Persons. Slave.	Total Popula.
Avoyelles	4,066	99	5,161	9,326
Bienville	3,623	21	1,895	5,539
Bossier	2,507	—	4,455	6,962
Caddo	3,637	39	5,208	8,884
Calcasieu	2,716	241	957	3,914
Caldwell	1,584	—	1,231	2,815
Carroll	2,336	10	6.443	8,789
Catahoula	3,585	19	3,378	6,982
Claiborne	4,949	—	2,522	7,471
Concordia	823	1	6,934	7,758
De Soto	3,548	25	4,446	8,019
Franklin	1,664	14	1,573	3,251
Jackson	3,406	2	2,158	5,566
La Fayette	3,390	160	3,170	6,720
Madison	1,416	4	7,353	8,773
Morehouse	1,877	30	2,006	3,913
Nachitoches	5,466	881	7,854	14,201
Rapides	5,037	184	11,340	16,561
Sabine	3,347	—	1,168	4,515
St. Landry	10,139	1,243	10,871	22,253
St. Martin	4,741	531	5,835	11,107
St. Mary	3,423	424	4,961	8,808
Tensas	900	2	8,138	9,040
Union	4,778	—	3,425	8,203
Vermillion	2,328	14	1,067	3,409
Wachita	2,293	7	2,708	5,008
Total	87,579	3,951	116,257	207,787
Grand Total	255,416	17,537	239,021	511,974

CLASSES AND SEXES OF POPULATION.

Classes.	Males.	Females.	Total.
White Persons	141,059	114,357	255,416
Colored " —free	7,598	9,939	17,537
" " —slave	—	—	239,021
Total	148,657	124,296	511,974

PROGRESSIVE MOVEMENT OF POPULATION.

Date of Census.	White Persons.	Colored Persons. Free.	Slave.	Total Population.	Decennial Increase. Numerical.	Per 100.
1810	34,311	7,585	34,660	76,556	—	—
1820	73,383	10,960	69,064	153,407	76,851	100.4
1830	89,231	16,710	109,588	215,529	62,122	40.5
1840	158,457	25,502	168,452	352,411	136,882	63.5
1850	255,416	17,537	239,021	511,974	159,563	45.2

The number of dwellings in the state in 1850, amounted to 49,101, or one to every 10.3 persons; and the number of families 54,112, or each family contained 9.4 persons. The difference in the proportion of the dwellings and families throughout the state is 5,011, and of this difference 4,144 occurs in the parish of Orleans. The deaths in 1849–50 numbered 11,948, or one in every 47.9 of the inhabitants—in the eastern district, one in 40.5, and in the western district, one in 46.7; in Orleans, the mortality was one in every 32.7 of the inhabitants.

The agriculture of Louisiana is devoted chiefly to the production of cotton, sugar, rice, etc., which articles constitute the staples of the state. Of cotton the present annual production amounts to over 266 million pounds, of sugar not less than 300 million pounds, and of rice perhaps six million pounds. Indian corn is the only grain planted, and the annual crop of this is not more than ten million bushels; nor are the miscellaneous crops either much varied or large. Of live stock the state has an abundance, and, except in respect of sheep, these all thrive well. In 1850, there were within the limits of Louisiana 13,422 farms and plantations under cultivation. The manufactures of the state, except in the large cities, are of little consequence: of the 1,021 establishments producing $500 dollars and upwards annually in 1850, no less than 900 were in Eastern Louisiana, and of this number 521 were in Orleans parish, 147 in that of West Feliciana, and respectively 54, 49, 36, and 33 in the parishes of Jefferson, East Feliciana, Livingston and St. Tammany. Seven parishes had none. In Western Louisiana, the parishes of Madison, St. Landry, Rapides and Carroll had respectively 24, 18, 11, and 10 such establishments, and in nine parishes in this district there were none. The articles of manufacture are various, but chiefly such as are incidental to an agricultural country, and to the necessities of the commercial towns. Nothing, however, is manufactured for export, except the sugars. The forests produce little or nothing, nor are there any mines wrought; and hence the only exchangeable articles produced in this state are its agricultural staples, sugar and cotton.

The prosperity of Louisiana, however, depends mainly on its commercial facilities. Its own products, compared with those which are deposited at its ports from other states and countries, constitute but a small moiety of the aggregate of its commercial material. The value of merchandize deported on the Mississippi alone to and from New Orleans is immense, although its increase has been materially checked by diverting the current of the trade of the upper valley to the Atlantic ports by means of railroads. The character and value of goods received at New Orleans from the interior for the year ending with August, 1851, were as follows, and it may here be premised that more than one-fourth is transported to the Atlantic ports coastwise, and is thence exported to foreign countries:

Cotton	$48,756,764	Bale Rope	804,180
Sugar	12,678,180	Butter	342,835
Tobacco	7,736,600	Hay	144,843
Flour	4,234,977	Hides	140,388
Pork	4,134,632	Coal	250,000
Lard	4,381,404	Potatoes	325,744
Lead	1,041,616	Staves	315,000
Molasses	2,625,000	Tallow	147,936
Bacon	5,879,470	Feathers	127,535
Corn	1,726,881	Oats	479,741
Whisky	1,621,928	Corn Meal	10,986
Wheat	177,594	Other articles	8,302,306
Bagging	903,800		
Beef	541,511	Total	$106,924,083
Hemp	452,088		

Total in 1849–50	$96,897,873	Total in 1845–46	$77,193,464
" 1848–49	81,989,695	" 1844–45	57,196,122
" 1847–48	79,779,151	" 1843–44	90,991,716
" 1846–47	90,033,256	" 1842–43	53,782,045

The goods sent to the interior consist of various manufactured articles, foreign and domestic, West Indian produce, the sugars and rice of Louisiana and other states, and such other staples as are not produced therein.

The commerce maintained directly with foreign countries, amounted in 1849–50 to the following values: exports, $38,105,350, and imports, $10,760,499. The exports are those named in the above tables. The imports are chiefly from Europe, South America, the West Indies, etc. The shipping employed in the foreign carrying trade in the same year, amounted to 1,741 vessels, and 720,790 tons, viz., 898 vessels, and 350,850 tons entered, and 843 vessels, and 369,937 tons cleared the ports. The registered shipping owned within the state amounts to 83,668 tons, and the coasting shipping to 160,631 tons, of which latter 144,723 tons are navigated by steam. The shipping built in 1849–50 amounted to 1,592 tons.

Of late years the trade of Louisiana has been diverted from its natural channel by the enterprise of the North in building railroads from the seats of production to the Atlantic ports, and by this means affording a more easy and expeditious mode of transport to the markets than by the rivers. The merchants of this state, however, have determined to compete in this respect with their northern brethren, and although so well supplied with navigable channels, they are now canvassing the propriety of extending lines of railroad from New Orleans in all directions. It is apparent, indeed, that without these the commercial superiority of New Orleans must wane. The principal lines proposed will extend from New Orleans through Mississippi, Tennessee, and Kentucky, uniting with the several systems completed and progressing within those states. Direct lines will also communicate with the Atlantic states, and also westward, penetrating Texas, and ultimately extending to San Francisco. Many of the proposed lines will no doubt be completed within the next few years, and all may, in course of time, be brought into operation. At present the state contains only a few miles of local railroads. It has also several canals, and quite a number of excellent turnpikes.

In December, 1850, there were in the state five banks and 29 branches, the aggregate capital of which was $12,370,890, the circulation $5,059,229, deposits $8,464,389, and other liabilities $1,334,232. The assets consisted of specie, $5,716,001, specie funds $1,200,000, loans and discounts $19,309,108, real estate $2,255,169, and other items $4,268,045.

The principal provisions of the new constitution of this state are as follow: The three departments of the government, Legislative, Executive, and Judicial, are to be kept entirely and for ever distinct. No citizen can be at the same time clothed with functions pertaining to two of them. The Legislature is to consist of a Senate and House of Representatives. The Senate will consist of thirty-two Senators, elected for four years. The House of not more than one hundred, nor less than seventy Representatives, chosen for two years.

No minister of religion is eligible to the legislature. The pay of members is fixed at $4 per day; but no session shall extend beyond sixty days; any action at a later period of the session is absolutely void. No member is eligible, except by popular election, to any office which may have been created, or its emoluments increased, while he has been a member.

The Executive department consists of a Governor and Lieutenant Governor each chosen for four years. Each must be at least 35 years of age when chosen, and must have been for fifteen years a citizen of the United States and a resident of the state. The Governor cannot be re-elected while in office. No member of Congress, officer of the United States, or minister of religion, is eligible to the office of governor or lieutenant-governor. The latter presides over the Senate, and has a casting vote (only) therein; and, in case of the death or incapacity of the governor, succeeds to his functions. The governor has the Veto Power, which can only be overruled by a vote of two-thirds of each branch of the legislature. The Secretary of State shall hold during a term of the governor.

The right of suffrage is extended and restricted as follows:—Every free white male, twenty-one years of age, who has been for two years a citizen of the United States and a resident of the state, is entitled to vote. Absence from the state for ninety days (except of a continuous householder) interrupts and vitiates the acquisition of residence. No soldier or sailor of the United States, pauper or criminal, shall be entitled to vote.

A state census was taken in 1847, preliminary to a new apportionment; the next in 1855; thence every tenth year. The sessions are to be held at New-Orleans till 1848; afterward at such place as the legislature shall designate.* Once fixed, this place shall not be changed, except by the consent of four-fifths of the legislature. Elections are to be held on the first Monday in November, on each alternate year. One-half the Senators first chosen, (to be designated by lot,) go out at the expiration of two years; and half a Senate with a whole House are to be chosen every second year thereafter. The legislature is to assemble on the third Monday in January, and to proceed to choose a United States Senator, if there be any vacancy, on the next Monday thereafter.

The Judiciary is to comprise a Supreme Court, composed of a Chief-Justice, appointed for eight years, at a salary of $6,000 per annum,—and three Associate Justices, also appointed for eight years, with an annual salary of $5,500. Those first appointed will go out, respectively, in two, four, and six years, so that, while judges thereafter shall hold for eight years each, there shall be a new one chosen by each legislature. The legislature is to divide the state into Judicial Districts for six years, not less than twelve nor more than twenty in number, each presided over by a District Judge, not less than thirty years old—six years a resident of the state, and five a practitioner of law; salary, $2,500 each.

---

* Baton Rouge has been chosen as the seat of government.

The financial condition of Louisiana is one of prosperity. The public debt amounts to $16,238,131; of which $1,380,566 is absolute, and $14,857,565 contingent, and will probably never fall upon the treasury. The interest on the absolute debt is $78,914. The ordinary expenses of the government amount to about $515,207.

Baton Rouge, the new capital, is situated on the east bank of the Mississippi, and lies chiefly on one street, 30 or 40 feet above high water mark, from which the land rises by a gradual and gentle swell. Among its public buildings the United States' Barracks are the most imposing. Baton Rouge is also the seat of a flourishing college. When the new state buildings are erected, the importance of the city will be much increased. The population, in 1850, was 4,262.

New-Orleans, the former capital, and, after New-York, the most commercial city in the Union, stands on the east bank of the Mississippi, 100 miles from the sea, and four from Lake Pontchartrain. The city is built on a plain, inclining from the river towards the swamp in the rear, so that when the Mississippi is full the streets are inundated; the *levee*, however, prevents the great body of water from overwhelming the place, and, at the same time, affords a pleasant promenade for the citizens.

The position of New-Orleans, in a commercial point of view, is unrivalled. The Mississippi, and its numerous tributaries, brings to its market the products of 20,000 miles of navigation, through one of the most fertile countries of the world; and carries back the contributions of every country and climate. The city proper is in the form of a parallelogram, running along the river 1,320 yards, and extending back 700 yards. The whole extent of the city, including its incorporated faubourgs, is not less than five miles, parallel with the river. The houses are principally of brick, and built in an elegant and substantial style. The buildings in the city are especially conspicuous for their elegance, and many houses in the suburban districts are surrounded with gardens, and ornamented with orange and other beautiful trees. The view from the river is splendid beyond description.

During the business season, or from November until July, the port is crowded with vessels, of all sizes and of every nation, with hundreds of large and splendid steamboats, and a multiplicity of river craft, consisting of barges, flat-bottom boats, &c. Nothing can present a more busy scene than the *levee* at this time; the loading and unloading of steamboats and vessels of various descriptions, and the throng of drays, transporting tobacco, sugar, cotton, and the varied and immense products of the whole central valley.

The city since 1836 has been divided into three separate municipalities, each having a distinct Council, for the management of its own affairs. The "First Municipality" includes the city proper, extending from the river back to Lake Pontchartrain, and occupying the centre; the "Second," adjoining it above; and the "Third," below, both extending from the river to the lake. The inhabitants of New-Orleans are composed chiefly of Americans, French, Spaniards, Creoles, and the colored races of every shade; and almost every other nation is well represented in this modern Babylon. The French and Spaniards occupy chiefly the central and lower parts of the city, where the buildings are of an ancient and foreign construction, and where the manners, customs and languages of those nations are preserved in their purity. On entering this portion the stranger would find it hard to believe he was in an American city.

The public buildings of New-Orleans form conspicuous objects, and are in many respects *sui generis*. The Cathedral or Church of St. Louis, on the Place d'Armes, strikes the stranger forcibly by its venerable and antique contour. It was founded in 1792. Every Saturday evening, by the conditions of its erection, masses are offered for the soul of Don André, its founder; and, at sunset of that day, the tolling of the bell reminds the inhabitants of the stipulation. On the right and left of the cathedral are buildings devoted to public offices. The old State-House, formerly the Charity Hospital, occupies a whole square, fronting on Canal-street, and is surrounded by ornamental pleasure-grounds. Previous to the removal of the capital the centre building was occupied by the legislature, and the wings by offices for the governor and chiefs of departments. The new Charity Hospital is 290 feet long, and three stories high, and is entered on Common-street, under a Doric portico. The lower part of the building is occupied by the resident physicians, and as lecture-rooms, &c., for medical students; while the second and third stories are divided into wards for the patients and rooms for the Sisters of Charity, who devote themselves to attendance on the sick. The hospital is calculated to hold 540 patients. The grounds around are handsomely laid out, and kept in good order. This is truly the Charity Hospital, and is peculiarly well-adapted for the reception of those who are attacked with virulent fevers, which annually invade the city, and cause such devastation among the people, especially unacclimated foreigners. The Franklin Infirmary, fronting on Pontchartrain Railroad, is a private hospital, and capable of accommodating 200 patients.

There are many churches worthy of notice, and which are alike conspicuous for their varied styles of architecture and the substantial manner in which they are built. Many have the sombre tint and gloomy aspect of ancient times, while others exhibit the decorative, but flimsy style, of modern taste.

The markets of New-Orleans are large and convenient. Poydras-Street Market is 402 feet long, and 42 feet wide. The Vegetable Market is 172 feet long. The Meat Market, on the *levee*, is built of brick, and extends from Ann to Main-street. St. Mary's Market, in the Second Municipality, is a noble structure, built of brick, and covered over in imitation of granite. It is 480 feet long and 42 feet wide. Washington Market is in the Third Municipality, and is a fine structure. All these markets are well supplied with both the necessaries and luxuries of life, and the taste and means of every one can be suited.

The theatres of the city are conspicuous buildings, and, for the purposes to which they are applied, celebrated throughout the world for their elegance and accommodations. The most magnificent of these is the "St. Charles," which is 132 feet front by 175 feet deep. In the centre of the dome is suspended a chandelier, 12 feet high and 36 feet in circumference, weighing 4,200 pounds, and lighted by 176 gas jets. It contains 23,300 cut glass drops, weighing together 900 pounds. The other fittings are on an equally magnificent scale. The "Orleans" is a spacious edifice, of the Roman Doric and a mixture of the Corinthian and composite orders. The performances in this theatre are in the French language. The "Campbell-Street or American Theatre," is 160 by 60 feet. It is in the Second Municipality, and can accommodate 1,100 persons.

Among the buildings of New-Orleans, the various cotton presses are not the least imposing in appearance. The Orleans Cotton Press extends over an area of 194,656 feet, which is nearly covered with buildings. On an average it presses 200,000 bales of cotton annually, but its capacity is much larger. The banks, hotels, &c., are also immense edifices. The St. Charles' Hotel is world-renowned for its magnificence, and the sumptuous fare it provides for its visitors. The United States Branch Mint is a noble structure, 282 feet long and 108 feet deep, with two wings, each 29 by 81 feet, and the whole three stories high. The building cost $182,000.

New-Orleans is supplied with water from the Mississippi, the water of which is raised into a reservoir 250 feet square. The water works belong to the Commercial Bank, and cost $722,000. Mains are laid in all the streets to lead the water; and a large pipe, a mile long, is used to distribute water to clean and cool the streets in hot weather. There is also a draining company, with a capital of $640,000, for the purpose of draining the marshes about the city. The Custom-House is also an ornament to the place.

The harbour of New-Orleans is one of the most capacious and deep in the world, and the local conveniences for shipping and the transaction of an extensive business, are unsurpassed. The number of vessels, of all kinds, visiting New-Orleans during the year, is immense, and a regular communication by packets is kept up with all the large Atlantic cities, and those on the gulf. It is, in fact, the great receiving and distributing depôt of the whole west, and the greatest cotton mart in the world. The unhealthiness of the location, however, is against it, but no doubt the fears of northerners have greatly exaggerated this drawback, and the same may be said of the moral atmosphere; the people are represented as polite, hospitable and kind, to the stranger and the distressed; indeed, its numerous charitable institutions are a full guarantee of these qualities; and if some looseness of morals is perceptible, the mixed and transitory character of the population must have prepared the mind to expect little better.

The newspapers of New-Orleans are the best conducted, most spicy, and readable sheets produced from the American press. The "Picayune," the "Delta," and the "Crescent;" the "Bulletin," the "Times," the "Bee," "Courier" and "National;" the "Mercury," and the "Prices Current," are all admirable in their various objects. The French, Germans, and Spaniards, have their daily sheets, and the several religious denominations issue their weekly bulletins to their supporters. The "Medical Review," than which no periodical is better conducted, or more prized by the profession, is published tri-monthly, and has a large subscription; "De Bow's Commercial Review of the South and West," is one of the best statistical works in the country, and alike creditable to the learned editor, and beneficial to all interested in southern and western business.

There are, besides the new University, two Colleges in New-Orleans, ten academies, and thirty or forty primary and common schools. A special session of the legislature was called, in 1848, to take into consideration the extension of schools throughout the state, and to regulate other matters connected with the education of the people. Lectures on a variety of useful and interesting subjects are to be delivered in the several departments of the university during the winter season, which will, no doubt, tend to enlighten and prove beneficial to the morals and habits of the people. An "Historical Society" has been lately founded, but as yet little has been done to give it stability, except the sending a commissioner to Europe to search out documents relating to Louisiana while under the French and Spaniards.

The history of New-Orleans is replete with stirring incident and adventure, and with the city is connected many scenes which have become portions of our national story. The "battle of New-Orleans," fought on the 8th January, 1815, will ever glow on the page of our annals as one of the most glorious victories of the American arms. The city was founded in 1718, by Bienville, the French Governor of Louisiana. The population, in 1840, was 103,193, and at the present time, may be set down at 120,000.

The other principal towns in Louisiana are—DONALDSONVILLE, 90 miles above New-Orleans, on the west bank of the Mississippi, and for some time capital of the state; MADISONVILLE, on Lake Pontchartrain, a healthy pleasant resort for the inhabitants of New-Orleans during the hot season; ALEXANDRIA, on the Red River, 120 miles from its mouth, and in the centre of a rich cotton district. It is well laid out, and contains a population of 2,000 inhabitants, chiefly Americans; NATCHITOCHES, on the west bank of the Red River, 200 miles up, is the largest town west of the Mississippi, and was formerly a French military post of great strength: the population is a mixture of French, Spaniards, Indians and Americans; WALLACE and SHREVEPORT are towns further west; ST. FRANCISVILLE, OPELOUSAS, ST. MARTINSVILLE, &c., are also towns of considerable note, and all enjoy large trade with the districts in their immediate vicinity.

The State of Louisiana comprises the southern part of an immense territory, which formerly belonged successively to France and Spain. This country, in its original integrity, extended north to the 49th parallel of latitude, and was confined only by the Mississippi on the east, and the Rocky Mountains and New-Spain, on the west. The river was discovered by Marquette and Joliette, two French missionaries from Canada, in 1673, and explored by La Salle, in 1682. The name of Louisiana was given it in honor of Louis XIV. In 1699, the first settlement was made at Iberville. In 1718, the city of New-Orleans was founded. In 1763, Louisiana was ceded to Spain, but in 1801 it was again given up to the French, and Napoleon considering it impossible or impolitic to retain it, sold the whole country to the United States for $15,000,000. The portion of the territory now forming the State of Louisiana, was erected into a separate territorial government, in 1804, under the title of the Territory of Orleans, the former title remaining to the country north and west, or that which now constitutes the states of Arkansas, Missouri, Iowa, and the vast unsettled west. In 1812, the Territory of Orleans was admitted into the Union as an independent state, under the title of the State of Louisiana. It is now one of the most prosperous states in the Union.

THE STATE OF ARKANSAS.

ARKANSAS is situated between 33° and 36° 30′ North latitude, and between the meridians of 89° 30′ and 94° 30′ West longitude. It is bounded on the north by the State of Missouri; east by the Mississippi River, which separates it from Tennessee and Mississippi; south by Louisiana; and west by Texas and the Indian territory. This state is about 270 miles long, and 240 in extreme breadth,—having an area of 51,697 square miles, or 33,086,548 acres.

The surface of Arkansas is extremely diversified, and the soil of very unequal quality. The eastern portion of the country, bordering on the Mississippi, is an extended plain, and so low as to be frequently inundated during the seasons of flood. In the central districts the lands are undulating and in some portions broken. The western section is mountainous, being traversed by the Ozarks, which attain a general altitude of 2,000 feet above the level of the Gulf of Mexico. The Black Mountains, north of the Arkansas River, and the Washita Hills, at the head waters of the Washita, are considerable elevations. The principal staple is cotton, which is largely grown in the eastern districts. Corn is also cultivated with much success, but the cereal crops generally are not so abundant as in the other western states. Grapes, plums, etc., grow wild in profusion.

The principal rivers, besides the Mississippi, which washes its eastern border and receives all the streams from the state, are the Arkansas, St. Francis, White, Washita, and the Red River. The Arkansas rises in the mountains of New Mexico, whence its course is eastward to the Mississippi, which it enters near the 34th parallel. Steamboats ascend the stream as far as Fort Gibson, but the navigation is insecure, and in summer the waters are almost dried up. The White River, a considerable stream, joins the Arkansas near its mouth, after a southerly course of 300 miles, during which it is nourished by several large rivers. The Red River passes through the south-west angle of the state, and forms its southern boundary for a few miles. The St. Francis passes from north to south in the north-east part of the state, and falls into the Mississippi about 34° 40′ N. lat.

The climate of this state, except in the low, marshy lands, is generally salubrious and pleasant. The temperature is neither so high as in Louisiana, nor so low as in the states north-west of the Ohio, nor are the extremes so wide apart. In the north-western districts, however, the winters are severe, and a large quantity of snow falls, and lays on the lands for a much longer period than in Tennessee and the country east of the Mississippi. This is owing to the cold north winds which sweep over the country, and at times lay waste vast districts.

The ban of an unaccountable prejudice has hitherto weighed heavily upon the prosperity of Arkansas, and as a state it is too frequently looked upon as the most resourceless of the Union. That such is not the case is now satisfactorily proved. Much of its soil is rich and fertile, and its river bottoms teem with luxuriant vegetation. In its minerals, however, centers the glory of its future. It has all that are deemed useful and precious: it has coal and iron in inexhaustible quantities, and both gold and silver are found within its borders. The coal field commences about 40 miles above Little Rock, on the Arkansas River, and extends up the river on both sides, far beyond the limits of the state. It is from 20 to 30 miles wide, and the average thickness of the veins is from 4 to 9 feet. Every known description of coal is found here, and it is probable that in a very short time the whole lower valley of the Mississippi will be supplied from this source. The iron beds lie in close neighborhood, and can be worked at a small expense. Zinc and manganese are also plentiful. The zinc is in the form of a sulphuret, which yields 45 per cent. of pure metal. The deposits of lead ore are eastward of the coal region. The principal veins contain an argentiferous galena. Some of the ores are very pure, and yield about 80 per cent. of metal, and from others as much as 112 ounces of silver have been extracted from the ton weight. The average yield of silver varies from 44 to 64 ounces per ton in the various mines. The mineral wealth of the country, however, is only begun to be known, but enough has been ascertained to place Arkansas in the first rank of mineral producing districts.

The population of Arkansas in 1850 amounted to 209,639, or one person to 159 acres; and was distributed into the several counties into which the state is divided in the following proportions:

COUNTIES.	White Persons.	Colored Persons. Free.	Slave.	Total Popula.
Arkansas	1,695	13	1,412	3,120
Ashley	1,405	5	644	2,058
Benton	3,508	1	201	3,710
Bradley	2,601	2	1,226	3,829
Carroll	4,390	11	213	4,614
Chicot	1,122	9	3,984	5,115
Clark	3,129	7	875	4,011
Coward	3,339	4	240	3,583
Crawford	6,935	92	933	7,960
Crittenden	1,842	5	801	2,648
Dallas	4,333	2	2,542	6,877
Desha	1,695	56	1,169	2,920
Drew	2,361	—	917	3,278
Franklin	3,497	3	—	3,500
Fulton	1,768	1	50	1,819
Green	2,530	10	53	2,593
Hempstead	5,180	32	2,460	7,672
Hot Springs	3,237	11	361	3,609
Independence	6,927	12	828	7,767
Izard	3,016	—	196	3,212
Jackson	2,517	6	563	3,036
Jefferson	3,197	16	2,621	5,834
Johnson	4,489	7	731	5,227
Lafayette	1,900	—	3,320	5,220
Laurence	4,882	4	385	5,271
Madison	4,659	—	164	4,823
Marion	2,047	129	126	2,302
Mississippi	1,496	7	865	2,368
Monroe	1,652	2	—	1,654
Montgomery	1,891	1	56	1,948
Newton	1,704	7	47	1,758
Ouachita	6,285	2	3,364	9,591
Perry	957	6	15	978
Philips	4,341	3	2,591	6,925
Pike	1,751	—	110	1,861
Poinsett	2,026	3	279	2,308
Polk	1,196	—	67	1,263
Pope	4,231	—	479	4,710
Prairie	1,812	12	273	2,097
Pulaski	4,526	13	1,119	5,658
Randolph	3,029	3	243	3,275
Sabine	3,392	6	503	3,901
St. Francis	3,770	2	706	4,479
Scott	2,920	17	146	3,083
Searcy	1,950	—	29	1,979
Servier	2,836	32	585	3,453
Tell	2,902	15	424	3,341
Union	5.526	5	4,767	10,298
Van Buren	2,761	—	103	2,864
Washington	8,757	14	1,199	9,970
White	2,309	2	149	2,460
Total	162,068	589	46,982	209,639

CLASSES AND SEXES OF POPULATION.

Classes.	Males.	Females.	Total.
White Persons	85,699	76,369	162,068
Colored " —free	318	271	589
" " —slave			46,982
Total			209,639

PROGRESSIVE MOVEMENT OF POPULATION.

Date of Census.*	White Persons.	Colored Persons. Free.	Slave.	Total Population.	Decennial Increase. Numerical.	Per 100.
1820	12,579	77	1,617	14,273	—	—
1830	25,671	141	4,576	30,388	16,115	113.2
1840	77,174	465	19,935	97,574	67,186	217.4
1850	162,068	589	46,982	209,639	112,065	114.8

The number of dwellings in the state in 1850 was 28,218, and the number of families, 28,371, or in the proportion of 7.3 persons to each dwelling or family, the two being nearly equal. The deaths in 1849–50 amounted to 2,987, indicating a mortality of one in every 69 persons, or 1.45 per cent.

Agriculture employs nearly the whole population, and is devoted chiefly to the production of southern staples. The cereal crops, except, perhaps, that of Indian corn, which averages 8,800,000 bushels, are unusually small; wheat only yielding about 250,000 bushels, and oats about twice that amount, while the crops of rye and barley are scarcely worth mentioning. The cotton crop, to which the greatest attention is given, amounted, in

* In 1810 the population of Arkansas was included in that of Missouri.

1840, to 6,028,624 pounds only, but it is now about 35,000,000 pounds; and the crop of tobacco averages 300,000, and has been gradually increasing from year to year. Hemp and flax, sugar, etc., are grown to a considerable amount. The products of the forest are valued at $260,000 annually, and consist chiefly of lumber and peltry. The state is singularly destitute of fruit trees, and market gardens are things scarcely known to the people. The whole number of farms and plantations under cultivation within the state, in 1850, was 17,712, or 1 to every 12 or 13 of the inhabitants. The mineral resources of the state are yet to be developed.

The manufactures of Arkansas are chiefly confined to the preparation of staples for market, or of articles of immediate necessity to the farmer, as leather, soap and candles, with agricultural implements, etc. Grist and saw mills employ one half the manufacturing capital of the state, which does not, however, amount to over a $1,000,000. The number of productive establishments in the state, producing $500 annually, according to the census of 1850, was only 271, but there were a number of smaller ones not enumerated. Arkansas has no direct commerce, but exports its staples through New Orleans. The river trade is large, and employs a considerable tonnage of steam and sail craft; and the internal trade of the state has been increasing at a rapid rate. Arkansas has no banks, or at least any that issue money for circulation; nor has the state made any effort to improve its means of intercommunication, except, perhaps, in the clearing of the rivers.

There is no collegiate institution in the state, and there are but few common schools. Toward the establishment of the first, Congress granted 500,000 acres of land, but the state authorities diverted this grant from its original purpose, and distributed it among the counties, in utter defiance to the intention of the grantor. The common schools are supported by the proceeds of the sale of the *sixteenth section* lands of each township and the revenue arising from leases of salt springs, etc., which form the school fund. These sources, however, are inadequate, and the legislature does little to remedy the deficiency. There are academies and high schools at Little Rock, Fayetteville, Washington, Camden, and some other places, but we have no means of ascertaining their condition or the number of scholars attending them. Perhaps no state in any part of the world is so destitute of the means of education, or so careless of its benefits, as Arkansas. The principal religious denominations are the Methodists and Baptists, and there are also considerable numbers of Catholics.

The constitution was formed in 1836. The Governor is chosen by the people for four years, but cannot hold office more than eight in every twelve years. The Senate can never consist of less than 17, nor more than 33 members, and the House of Representatives of less than 54, nor more than 100 members. Senators are chosen for four years, and Representatives for two years. The General Assembly meets once in two years, at Little Rock. Every white male citizen of the United States, who has resided in the state six months, may vote. The constitution abolishes all lotteries, and forbids the sale of lottery tickets. The Legislature has power to establish one bank, with branches, and one banking institution to promote agricultural interests. It cannot emancipate slaves without the consent of their owners. In respect to trial for crimes and punishment, they are placed on the same footing with the whites; otherwise the provisions respecting slaves are similar to those of Louisiana and the other southern states. Courts of justice are obliged to assign council to indicted slaves.

The Judiciary consists of a Supreme Court, with a Chief Justice and two Associate Justices, and six Circuit Courts. The Judges of the Supreme Court are appointed for eight years, and those of the Circuit Court for four years: the first are chosen by the Legislature, and the latter by the people. Judges of the county courts are chosen by the Justices of the Peace.

Arkansas has a debt of $3,617,227, of which $2,769,336 belongs to the absolute, and $848,891 to the contingent debt. The annual interest on the absolute debt is $164,660. The ordinary expenses of the government, exclusive of interest, amounted, in 1848, to $31,974.

Little Rock, the capital, stands on a high bluff on the south bank of the Arkansas river, and at the head of steamboat navigation. Lat. 34° 40′ N., and long. 92° 12′ W. It is regularly laid out, and contains the state-house, court-house, United States' arsenal and land office, the state penitentiary, with a number of churches, two banks, a theatre, an academy, and other public buildings. The population is 4,138. Helena, Columbia, Osceola, Marion, Napoleon, &c., are considerable villages on the Mississippi; Belleville, Arkansas, Pine Bluff, Dardanelles, Van Buren, &c., on the Arkansas; Fulton, Lewisville, Laynesville, &c., on the Red River; &c. These contain from 300 to 1,200 inhabitants, and are all favorably situated for commerce. There are also a number of populous villages in the interior of the country. The Red River district, especially, has much improved and increased in population.

Arkansas was a part of the Louisiana purchase. Previous to 1819, it was attached to the Missouri territory, but in that year was formed into a separate territorial government. In 1836, it formed a constitution, and was admitted into the Union as an independent state.

THE STATE OF TEXAS.

Texas, formerly a province of Mexico, and more recently an independent republic, is situated between latitudes 26° and 36° 30′ north, and longitudes 93° 20′ and 107° west from Greenwich or 16° 19′ and 29° 59′ from Washington. It is bounded on the north by New Mexico, the Indian Territory, from which it is separated by the Red River, and the state of Arkansas; east by Arkansas and Louisiana, from the latter of which the Sabine River chiefly divides it; south by the Gulf of Mexico, and west by the northern states of Mexico, and New Mexico. The boundary established by Congress in 1850 runs from the Red River northward, on the 100th meridian to 36° 30′ N. lat., thence along that parallel to the 103d meridian, thence south on that line to 32° N. lat., and on that to the Rio Grande, and down that River to the Gulf of Mexico. The extent of the state east and west is 600 miles, and north and south 400 miles, with a superficial area of 237,321 square miles, or 151,885,440 acres.

The country presents a surface varying from the low plains which border the Gulf of Mexico, to the rolling and hilly regions of the centre and north. In the north-west there are hills of considerable elevation. The flat maritime region extends inland from 20 to 80 miles, being narrowest near the

San Antonio river, and widest near the Brazos. It is furrowed by deep ravines, and the streams which course through these, are of considerable volume. Dense forests border their margins for a great distance back, but the intervening country is mostly open prairie. The forests do not extend quite to the coast, but terminate at a distance of about five miles from it. Beyond this level region the surface gradually becomes undulating, and presents a succession of broad swelling knolls and wide shallow valleys. The prairies and woodlands in this region alternate in the most picturesque manner; the prairies are generally of small extent and interspersed with groves, or "islets in the grassy lake;" and the forest trees here attain a larger growth than those of the level country, and the forests are more widely diffused over the surface. The whole region is irrigated by frequent springs and streams of the purest water. The width of this zone varies from 30 to 50 miles. A hilly region succeeds, and although much less fertile than that below, it abounds in the grandest scenery, and is watered by innumerable beautiful streams flowing over pebbly beds and forming cascades that would afford excellent mill sites. Few of these hills exceed in elevation 500 feet; their summits are generally flat and tufted with dense thickets of cedar. Beyond this is another undulating region which terminates on the Red river. This section is about 100 miles broad on the meridian of Austin, gradually widening to the east and narrowing to the west, and encloses the Saline lake of the Brazos. It is bounded north-west by ranges of mountains which extend across the north-western portion of Texas, and which furnish the sources of the Red river, the Brazos, the Colorado, and other streams on the east, and the Rio Puecro and other tributaries of the Rio Grande on the west. Many of these mountains are of considerable height, and some are snow-capped throughout the greater portion of the year.

The rivers of Texas, following the general slope, traverse the country in a southerly direction. Few countries of the world are better provided with water communication, but in none of the rivers is steam navigation practicable for more than from 100 to 200 miles. The clearing of some, however, may open a passage further up. The principal, beginning at the east, are the Sabine, which separates Texas from Louisiana and the Neches, both emptying into Sabine Lake which is reached from the sea by a narrow inlet; the Trinidad, a large and long stream, the San Jacinto, famous for the decisive battle fought on its banks, and Buffalo Bayou, on which stands Houston and Harrisburg, all emptying into Galveston Bay; the Brazos, which with numerous tributaries, waters so large a surface and empties directly in the sea; the Colorado, a splendid stream which flows into the eastern portion of Matagorda Bay; the Guadaloupe and San Antonio, which unite near their entrance into Espiritu Santo Bay; the Neuces, formerly considered as the western limit of the republic, and the Rio Grande, a large navigable stream, the present western limit of the state. The Red river winds along the northern frontier and forms the great outlet for the produce of Upper Texas. Long, narrow sand islands line the Gulf coast, and form within them lagoons and bays of great extent. Galveston Bay is by far the most important of these bodies of water; it is about 35 miles long, north and south, and from 12 to 18 miles broad, with an average depth of nine feet, but in the channel there is water sufficient for vessels of large tonnage; its entrance, however, is obstructed. The Bay of Matagorda is also an extensive water sheet, and has many fine streams debouching into it. The bays named Espiritu Santo, Aransa, etc., are of less extent, but in process of time must become of great importance to the commerce of the state.

Nearly the whole coast admits of inland navigation, being protected by the before-mentioned sand islands.

The geological structure of the country has been little examined. In the north-west many of the primitive and oldest sedimentary rocks are found, but the general character of the formations would indicate that the middle and plain regions are of diluvial origin. Along the coast a series of superficial accumulations extend inland for 100 to 150 miles, and these consist of calcareous, arenaceous, and argillaceous substances generally intimately blended, but sometimes one or the other may preponderate, and the thickness of the beds becomes gradually less on approaching the higher portions of the undulating region. Fossil bones, skulls of various species, etc., are found throughout this region. These accumulations rest upon a coarse sandstone, and in some of the ravines worn by the rivers a marly or rotten limestone is found beneath the sandstone. In the higher portions of the undulating region the sandstone crops out, and is frequently seen in long irregular ridges, resembling a rocky beach. This sandstone varies infinitely in texture; in some places it is composed of coarse sand and comminuted shells, and incloses round silicious pebbles, and in others it is quite fine grained and resembles freestone. Beyond the undulating region the secondary rocks begin to appear in horizontal strata, forming hills with flat summits 400 or 500 feet high. These strata consist chiefly of limestone, containing organic fossils and nodular masses of iron pyrites.

The sections of the state which by their geological features indicate that they contain valuable minerals, have been little explored. The mountains traversing the north-west are probably connected with the ranges of Chihuahua and New Mexico which contain valuable mines of gold and silver. Sulphuret of lead has been found on the San Saba, and tradition says that the Spaniards formerly worked a silver mine near this stream. Copper is found on the Brazos, and beds of coal exist in several places. The hilly and undulating counties contain immense deposits of iron ore and valuable quarries of freestone and limestone. Beds of lignite, and saline and sulphur springs occur in these sections—also gypsum. The level region affords hardly any minerals worthy of notice—indeed throughout its whole extent scarce a stone can be found. The islands lying off the coast contain vast pans of natural salt evaporated from the waters of the Gulf which the tides throw up and leave to the influence of the sun. On Padre Island the salt is several inches thick in these reservoirs, and many tons weight are thus formed every summer.

The composition of the soils of Texas is as various as the extent of surface over which it is spread. In the level and undulating sections it consists of a rich deep calcareous loam, in which sandy and clayey particles are combined with a carbonaceous vegetable mould. On several of the rivers iron oxides mingle in the soil, and this is especially the case near the Red River, the Brazos, and Colorado, which are deeply tinged with this ferruginous formation. These soils are extremely fertile, but there seems to be a preference in this regard to the soils of the undulating regions. The soils of the hilly regions differ widely; in the valleys the alluvial accumulations are very deep, but the hills have generally a very light thin soil, consisting of a layer of vegetable mould only a few inches deep, resting on the limestone. As a whole, Texas in its conformation and character of soils resembles much the fertile regions of northern Italy. It has been called the Garden of America, and certainly it may be admitted that if its soils and climates are equalled by any other, they are surpassed by none in the world.

The productions of Texas vary nothing from those of the Middle and Southern states generally; in the hilly sections, wheat, rye, oats, and barley thrive well; in the level and undulating regions, maize, cotton, sugar, tobacco, etc., are grown luxuriantly, and through all the southern part peaches, figs, and other tropic fruits. Apples, pears, cherries, and the fruits generally found in the gardens of temperate climates, flourish best in northern Texas. Grapes grow everywhere, and the orange and lemon have been planted on the shores of Galveston Bay. Wild fruits of various descriptions are abundant in every region. The forests consist of live oak, pine, cedar, mesquit and other timbers, many of which are highly valued for cabinet furniture. The live oak of Texas would suffice for the world's navy. The staples of agriculture are cotton, sugar, and tobacco; and both the cotton and sugar of Texas are considered as superior to those of Louisiana. The tobacco is said to equal the best grown in Cuba. The climate is also well adapted for silk culture. The mulberry abounds, and the worm is enabled to continue its operations throughout nearly the whole year.

All the animals of the temperate regions of America are found in Texas. Vast droves of buffaloes frequent the whole unsettled portion. At the sources of the Brazos and Colorado the droves often cover the whole face of the country for miles, and are the chief dependence the Commanche and other Indian tribes have for subsistence. Deer are so numerous as to be found in herds of several thousands, and in the frontier settlements venison can be procured more readily than mutton. Mustangs, or wild horses, are found in the western prairies, and these animals are seen moving in dense columns four or five miles long, and the horses eight or ten abreast. They are smaller than the domestic horse, but are easily tamed and subdued to labor. The stampede or tremendous trampling made by these herds when in motion is often heard for several miles, and resembles the sound of distant thunder. Bears, wolves, opossums, hares, and other similar animals are found in all the forests. Every species of wild fowl and game is plentiful. Bees are very numerous in many places, and vast quantities of wild honey are procured from the forests. There are but few venomous reptiles or insects in the country; rattle snakes and moccassin snakes are occasionally met with, but are not numerous; and scorpions, of a harmless nature however, are found in the western counties. Excellent fish frequent the bays and rivers. Among these are red-fish, grundiquoit, mullet, sea-perch, sea-trout, etc. The red-fish is often caught in great quantities, and is highly esteemed. Buffalo and cat-fish are found in all the rivers, and on the coast, turtle in abundance. Galveston Bay is famed for its oysters, and this bivalve is also plentiful in all the inlets along the coast.

The aboriginal tribes of Texas consist of several nations, but with the exception of the Commanche Indians these are insignificant in point of numbers. The Commanches can muster 3000 warriors, and their whole population is about 13,000. The Lipans number less than 300 warriors, and the other tribes known as the Tonkewas, Carancuawas, Towaccanies, Levies, Cashattas, Alabamas, Caddos, Cherokees, etc., are only known in small localities. These Indians are all in a wretched and destitute condition, and range through the wilds in search of plunder. Occasionally they have proved troublesome to the frontier settlements, but they can no longer be considered as dangerous foes. Perhaps the whole number within the limits of the state may count 25,000, but during a greater portion of the year most of these are on hostile or hunting excursions in the northern states of Mexico, where the sparsity of the population allows of their indulging in their barbarous pursuits without any effectual molestation. The Indians indeed have ever been more troublesome to the Mexicans than to the Texans.

Texas is divided into seventy-eight counties, and in 1850 these in the aggregate contained 212,592 inhabitants, being a ratio of one person to every 714 acres. The distribution of the population to the several counties was in the following proportions:

COUNTIES.	White Persons.	Colored Persons. Free.	Colored Persons. Slave.	Total Popula.
Anderson	2,284	—	600	2,884
Angelina	945	24	196	1,165
Austin	2.286	6	1,549	3.841
Bastrop	2,180	—	919	3,099
Bexar	5,635	28	389	6,052
Bowie	1,271	—	1,641	2,912
Brazoria	1,329	5	3,507	4,841
Brazos	466	—	148	614
Burleson	1,213	—	500	1,713
Caldwell	1,054	1	274	1,329
Calhoun	876	—	234	1,110
Cameron*	8,469	19	53	8,541
Cass	3,089	—	1,902	4,991
Cherokee	5,389	1	1,283	6,673
Collin	1,816	—	134	1,950
Colorado	1,534	—	723	2,257
Comal	1,662	—	61	1,723
Cook	219	—	1	220
Dallas	2,536	—	207	2,743
Denton	631	—	10	641
De Witt	1,148	—	568	1,716
Fannin	3,260	—	528	3,788
Fayette	2,740	—	1,016	3,756
Fort Bend	974	5	1,554	2,533
Galveston	3,785	30	714	4,529
Guadalupe	1,171	5	335	1,511
Gillespie	1,235	—	5	1,240
Goliad	435	—	213	648
Gonzales	891	—	601	1,492
Grayson	1,822	—	186	2,008
Grimes	2,328	—	1,680	4,008
Harris	3,755	7	905	4,668
Harrison	5,604	5	6,213	11,822
Hays	259	—	128	387
Henderson	1,155	1	81	1,237
Hopkins	2,469	—	154	2,623
Houston	2,036	12	673	2,721
Hunt	1,477	2	41	1,520
Jackson	627	30	339	996
Jasper	1,226	—	541	1,767
Jefferson	1,504	63	269	1,836
Kaufman	982	—	65	1,047
Lamar	2,893	—	1,085	3,978
Lavacca	1,139	—	432	1,571
Leon	1,325	—	621	1,946
Liberty	1,623	7	892	2,522
Limestone	1,990	—	618	2,608
Matagorda	913	3	1,208	2,124
Medina	881	—	28	909
Milan	2,469	2	436	2,907
Montgomery	1,439	—	945	2,384
Nacogdoches	3,758	31	1,404	5.193
Navarro	3,444	11	388	3,843
Newton	1,255	8	426	1,689
Nueces	650	1	47	698
Panola	2,676	2	1,193	3,871
Polk	1,544	—	805	2,349
Red River	2,493	7	1,406	3,906
Refugio	269	—	19	288
Robertson	670	—	264	934
Rusk	6,012	—	2,136	8,148
Sabine	1,556	—	942	2,498
San Augustin	2,984	—	1,561	3,647
San Patricio	197	—	3	200
Shelby	3,278	—	961	4,239
Smith	3,575	—	717	4,292
Starr	(With Cameron.)			
Titus	3,168	1	467	3,636
Travis	2,336	11	791	3,138
Tyler	1,476	—	418	1,894
Upshur	2,712	—	682	3,394
Van Zandt	1,308	—	40	1,348
Victoria	1,448	—	571	2,019
Walker	2,663	—	1,301	3.964
Washington	3,166	—	2,817	5,983
Webb	(With Cameron.)			
Wharton	510	—	1,242	1,752
Williamson	1,410	3	155	1,568
Total	154,100	331	58,161	212,592
Viz.—Males	84.863	171	—	—
Females	69,237	160	—	—

The number of dwelling houses in the state in 1850 was 27,988, and the number of families 28,377, or a ratio of 7.6 persons to each dwelling and family, the two being nearly equal. The deaths occurring in 1849–50 amounted to 3,046, which exhibits a mortality equal to one death in every 69 of the inhabitants, or 1.45 per centum.

Agriculture is almost the sole occupation in Texas. Every one is engaged either in planting, grain growing or cattle raising. No other state combines so intimately facilities for all these sources of wealth. Her two most important staples are cotton and sugar, both of which are cultivated on the coast lands and for 100 miles up the principal rivers. Superior lands, it is said produce upwards of a bale of cotton per acre. The crop of 1850 amounted to 45,820 bales—in 1847 it was only 8,317 bales. Sugar growing has been until lately only an experimental interest, but it has succeeded so well, and so fine has been the crop for several years back that capital now seeks an investment in Texas sugar lands in preference to those of Louisiana. Good lands yield about half hogshead per acre. Corn and oats grow luxuriantly, and excellent vegetables are reared with scarcely any effort in

* With *Starr* and *Webb* counties.

every section of the state; 50 to 75 bushels of corn to the acre are frequently produced, and this without any preparation of the land, but the average is not more than 40 bushels. Wheat is also grown extensively in the higher sections. With regard to cattle breeding no state has greater facilities—its rich spontaneous grasses are perennial, and cattle roam abroad the year round without requiring attention on the part of their owner. Climate and soil are, indeed, benificent. Suitable locations can be found for every staple, and if any attention was paid to agriculture as a science, Texas might then claim with a truth to be the *Garden of America.* The number of farms under cultivation in 1850 was 12,198.

The manufactures of Texas are purely incidental, or such only as are absolutely requisite for an agricultural population. The number of establishments producing $500 and upwards annually was in 1850 only 307. The state however possesses every pre-requisite for entering on a prosperous career of manufacturing industry. Its water-power is boundless. The undulating regions of New-England scarcely furnish a more extensive water-power than may be afforded by the rivers of Texas, especially from the table-lands along her large streams up to their sources in the mountains; the Upper Brazos with its tributaries, the Colorado with its beautiful arms, the Concho, Llano, San Sabar, and Perdinales; the Guadalupe with its San Marcos and Blanco; the San Antonio with its Salado, Cibolo, Leon and Medina, and the Leona of the Nueces, possess eminent advantages in their power to propel machinery, and seem to have been providentially located in the vicinity of the great staples of manufacturing industry. The cotton and iron of this state, indeed, may at no distant future period become the materials of a local industry that shall furnish the state with its great wants. The cheapness of labor, too, must enter largely into any estimate that may be formed of the development of the manufacturing destiny of the state—a population of Mexicans could be brought over the river and employed even at a cheaper rate than would remunerate slave labor.

The amount of industry expended in mining, fishing, and some other productive employments is as yet small, but the future is full of great hope, and to the far-seeing the prospect is at least a fair one.

Texas has an extensive coasting trade, but its commercial dealings with the foreign world are limited. In 1849–50 its exports direct to foreign countries amounted only to $24,958, and its imports to $25,650. The shipping entered was 16 vessels of 3,671 tons in the aggregate, and 15 vessels of 3,608 tons cleared, chiefly foreign bottoms. The registered tonnage of the state amounts to 415 tons. In the coasting trade, however, the Texan shipping amounts to 38,198 tons, of which 979 tons are navigated by steam power. The coasting trade is chiefly with New-Orleans, but New-York and some other of the Atlantic ports carry on considerable trade with the state. All the cotton finds its way to New-Orleans.

Works of internal improvement have as yet received but a small share of attention. Several great works, however, have been proposed, as harbor works, railroads and canals. It is proposed to build a railroad from the Red River to the Gulf, and also to extend a line or lines with branches from New-Orleans westward. Western Texas is also indicated as a starting point for the great Pacific railroad, but the attainment of these objects are so uncertain as to admit of scarcely more than a passing mention. The ordinary roads of the state are respectable, but in the rainy season are liable to inundation, and hence for a portion of the year the rivers seem to be the only avenues of commerce.

The present constitution was adopted in convention at Austin, 27th August, 1845, and ratified by the people, 13th October, of the same year. Every white male inhabitant, 21 years of age, being a citizen of the United States or of Texas, who has resided in the state one year, and six months in the district, county, city or town where he offers his vote, is invested with the suffrage. Electors absent from home, but within their own district, may vote for district officers, and any where in the state for state officers.

The General Assembly consists of a Senate and House of Representatives: the Senate is composed of not less than nineteen nor more than thirty-three members. Senators are elected for four years, one-half going out every two years—they must be qualified voters, at least thirty years of age, and have lived in the state three years, the last year thereof in the district for which they are chosen. Representatives, of whom there shall not be less than forty-five, nor more than ninety, are chosen for two years:—they must be qualified voters, having lived in the state two years, and the last year thereof in the place where they are chosen. The legislature meets biennally at the city of Austin, which is to continue the state capital until 1850, and at that period a more suitable place is to be selected by the vote of the people. The members of the legislature receive each $3 per diem, and $3 for every 25 miles of travel to and from the capital.

The Governor and Lieutenant-Governor are chosen by a plurality of the popular vote for two years, and are ineligible to serve for more than four years out of any six years. The Governor must have the same qualifications as a Senator, and receives $2,000 per annum. The Lieutenant-Governor is *ex-officio* president of the Senate. The Secretary of State is nominated by the Governor, and his nomination confirmed by the Senate for two years. The State Treasurer and Comptroller are chosen biennially by joint vote of both houses. The Governor may *veto* a bill, but by a two-thirds vote of both houses in its favor, it becomes law.

The Judiciary consists of a Supreme Court, with a Chief-Justice and two Associate Justices, appointed for six years. There are eight District Courts, with one judge to each district. These courts have original jurisdiction both in civil and criminal suits. In criminal cases, if the punishment be not specifically determined by law, the jury determine it. An Attorney-General is appointed for two years by the Governor, and confirmed by the Senate, and district attornies are chosen by joint ballot of both houses of the Legislature, also for two years. In equity causes, either party may demand a jury-trial.

The constitution has several peculiar provisions. It renders duellists ineligible to public offices; forbids grants of money for any purposes than the ordinary expenses of government, except by a two-thirds vote; provides for the revision of the laws, civil and criminal, every ten years; makes a wife's property, real and personal, her separate property, not liable for the husband's debts; protects the homestead to the value of $2,000; forbids the creation or extension of corporations for banking or other purposes; forbids the creation of a debt of more than $100,000, except in case of war, insurrection or invasion, etc., etc. The provisions with regard to slavery are similar to those of the other southern states. No law of emancipation shall be passed without the owner's consent, and by paying full compensation for the slaves liberated; nor shall emigrants to Texas be prevented from bringing their slaves with them, but bringing them as merchandize is forbidden. The slave-holder is prevented from injuring them, and in case of disobedience to the laws, they are liable to have them sold, but for their own benefit.

Slaves are entitled to a jury in criminal suits, and all crimes against a slave are punishable as if against a white person.

The public debt of Texas amounts ostensibly to $12,435,982 68—a debt which was contracted chiefly for the prosecution of the war of Independence, and which was taken at exorbitant rates and far below its cash value. Since becoming a state of the Union, the legislature has thought fit to revise this amount and reduce it to its absolute value, which the Auditor of the state estimates on the following basis:

	Ostensible Debt.	Specie Estimate.
Principal	$8,700,305 11	$4,965,394 15
Interest	3,735,699 57	1,881,928 08
Total	$12,435,982 68	$6,847,322 23

The details of this arrangement, as reported by the Auditor of the state, are as follows:

—Issues under act, 7th June, 1837, and the subsequent explanatory acts of 19th Jan., 1839, and 11th May, 1846:
Principal $825,795 01
Interest at 10 per cent. .... 825,795 01—1,657,590 02
which Texas estimates in specie value—
— $1,623,693 38 at 70 cents $1,136,585 36
— 27,896 64 at 100 " .... 27,896 64—1,164,482 00

—Issues under acts, 18 Nov., 1836, 16 May, 1838, 22 Jan., 1839, and 14 Jan., 1840:
Principal $1,213,287 00
Interest at 10 per cent. .... 1,369,615 70—2,582,902 70
which is estimated in specie value—
— Principal $777,953 50
— Interest .... 873,248 85—1,651,202 35

—Issues under act, 5 Feb., 1840:
Principal $817,000 00
Interest at 10 per cent. $790,920 00
" 8 " .... 20,516 26— 811,936 26—1,628,936 26
which in specie value is estimated—
— Principal at 30 cents $245,100 00
— Interest at 30 cents .... 243,430 00— 488,530 00

—Issues under act, 5 Feb., 1840:
Principal $836,800 00
Interest .... 636,028 80—1,472,908 80
which is estimated in specie value—
— Principal at 20 cents $167,376 00
— Interest at 20 cents .... 127,205 76— 294,581 76

—Issues under act, 9 June, 1837:
Principal—1st Issue $50,000 00
2d Issue 370,000 00
3d Issue .... 2,077,546 00—2,497,546 00
Interest —1st Issue $15,000 00
2d Issue .... 74,000 00— 89,000 00—2,586,547 00
which is estimated in specie value—
— 1st Issue—Principal at par . $50,000 00
Interest " . 15,000 00— 65,000 00
— 2d Issue—Prin. at 50 cts. .. $185,000 00
Interest " .. 37,000 00— 222,000 00
— 3d Issue at 25 cents .... 519,386 50— 806,386 50

—Issues under act, 28 Nov., 1835, and 5 Feb., 1840 (audited drafts):
Principal $331,653 70
" estimated in specie value 326,957 07

—Issues under acts, 20 March, 1848, and 8 Feb., 1849:
Principal $2,178,143 40
Interest .... 3,801 60—2,181,945 00
which is estimated in specie—
— Principal $2,130,318 08
— Interest .... 3,801 60—2,117,181 68

All this debt is amply secured. Texas has an immense wealth in her public lands, and resources to the amount of $10,000,000 in U. S. bonds, and the United States holds in reserve one-half of this fund until the creditors of the state file a release of their claims in the office of the Secretary of the Treasury. The payment then does not altogether rest with Texas, but is guaranteed by the Union, and it now only remains for the creditors to adjust their demands. Those who wish to know more of the details of the finances of Texas are referred to the report of the U. S. Secretary of the Treasury, made to the President in September, 1851.

The average annual expenses of carrying on the state government amount to about $100,000. The receipts and expenditures for the year ending 31st October, 1848, were as follows:

Receipts.		Expenditures.	
Direct and license taxes	$82,522 86	Executive	$24,790 41
Miscellaneous	3,974 65	Legislative	48,356 88
Revenue accrued under late Republic	10,713 54	Judiciary	25,962 53
Balance from last year	51,238 05	Miscellaneous	17,451 79
		Total	116,161 61
Total available means	$148,449 10	Balance in Treasury	32,287 49

Amount in the Treasury to the credit of School Fund......$17,071 86

The City of Austin, the capital of the state, is situated on the north bank of the Colorado, and until lately, was an uninhabited wilderness. Lat. 30° 24′ N., and long. 95° 42′ W. The city consists chiefly of frame houses, and a few brick buildings, occupied by the wealthier classes and tradesmen. The country in the neighborhood is becoming settled, and quite a number of farm houses have been built. Population, about 5,000.

Sabine, at the outlet of the Sabine Lake, is a port of entry. Galveston, the chief port in Texas, is situated at the eastern extremity of the island of the same name. It is the depot of a vast and fertile region, watered by the Trinidad and other rivers. The commerce of this port has increased to something considerable, and its prospects are, at the present time, more encouraging than those of any others of the sea-board towns. Galveston has at the present period about 4,600 inhabitants. Houston, the former capital, is situated at the head of navigation of Buffalo Bayou, a small tributary of Galveston Bay, and is a place of little consideration. Velasco, on the north bank of the Brazos River, at its mouth, is a pleasant town, and said to be very healthy. Matagorda, at the mouth of the Colorado, near the head of Matagorda Bay, is a considerable town. Goliad is an old Spanish town on the north bank of the San Antonio, 40 miles from its mouth. It is noted for the massacre of Col. Fannin and 400 prisoners, by the Mexicans. San Antonio de Bexar, also an old Spanish town, is situated higher up the river, and is celebrated in history as the scene of several battles and the gallant defence of the Alamo, by Col. Travis, for two weeks. Zodiac is a new town on the Pedernales and four miles from Fredericksburg, the seat of Gillespie county, and sixty miles north of San Antonio. The Germans and Mormons are the principal settlers, who live together in perfect harmony.

The Mormons number about 200, and though they have been there only a short time, have already made great improvements. They have all kinds of useful mechanics, who make every thing they want. About 500 acres have been enclosed, a good part of which is cultivated in gardens. They raise Egyptian and English wheat, and it is said that the soil is well adapted to its culture. The town consists of 60 or 70 frame houses, and a church and school-house have lately been constructed. This is the most northerly settlement in western Texas. There is a prophecy among these enthusiasts, and which is fully believed by the "faithful," that western Texas is the place destined to witness the final triumphs of the Mormon churches.

The following account of the Germans at New-Braunfels, is contained in a letter to the *New-York Journal of Commerce*, and will be read with interest:

New-Braunfels, (Texas) March 29, 1848.

This seems purely a German town, although there are several artisans, merchants, lawyers and doctors who are Americans. The town is settled by and is mostly under the influence of the German company, and has a sort of German nobleman for Mayor—a very fine man. The site of the city is beautiful, on the west bank of the Guadalupe and Comal rivers, at their junction. The banks at this point are elevated, though the town is in the valley properly, and a beautiful ridge of rolling land runs along in the rear for miles, commanding a scenery of the country, town and river, where there are already several out-of-town residences occupied by the "upper ten."

The Comal, called by many the most beautiful little river in Texas, rises about three miles above, and is augmented by tributaries gushing through the bed, till its magnitude, on reaching the Guadalupe, is astonishing. It must be twenty feet wide, with a depth of five feet. The Messrs. Torry are building flour, corn, and saw mills on the margin of the river, close to the town, and as they are the first in the field, will make a fortune by the operation—or at any rate, add to that already made. It seems almost a pity that the transparent, crystal-like Comal should be turned to such "base use." The bed of the stream seems to be a sort of soapstone, very soft, while the banks below the surface are limestone. The water is very limy, (as are all the rivers in this section); still it seems perfectly healthy, and is esteemed by the adjacent settlers as superior. Fish—perch, cat, trout, and those of other names—are abundantly taken.

The Guadalupe rises many miles above, supposed 300, near the head waters of the Rio Grande, in the mountains, and is a clear, handsome stream, but subject to great diminution and overflows. It is believed that it will be navigated, with the assistance of slack water, in a few years, up to this point, at least for a portion of the year—the Comal itself always supplying its quota. The town is so unlike any Texas-made that I had seen, that on first reaching the elevation from the river, which gives a full view, it appeared to me that I was out of my own country. There are the mud hovels, with thatched roofs, and earth floor—the little neat white plastered cottages, made of stone, also with the thatched roof made of long prairie grass,—the little buildings, with one room, made of a sort of tiles, stuck into the earth close enough together to make the mud adhere, with which they are completely plastered. The doors are made of different materials, but mostly of suspended cloth of some kind. Windows they have none, except from a hole left in the side of the house.

The German women usually sit out of doors, even to do their sewing. They do all the gardening, and often as much field-work as the men. I saw one woman, less than thirty-five years old, who was called from the spade—where, with her two girls, she was hard at work—with their peculiar style of short dress—to entertain her husband and friends with a song, accompanying herself on the piano. If she has as much credit in the field as at the piano, her accomplishments are such as few of our American women can boast. Her's was a cottage of the better class, with a little window glass, and an air of tidiness about it. Indeed, there is a prevailing neatness about the whole complexion of the town, and a few fine foreign-style dwellings. Almost every little hovel or cottage has a small patch of ground highly cultivated, fenced in with brush. It is wonderful how experience has taught these people to love and cherish their stinted lot of ground, where you can see them morning, noon, and evening, carefully plucking every weed, and nursing with a mother's care, the peeping vegetation—measuring with nice precision that more matured, and calculating the few dimes that it will bring when ready for market.

How different the Texans! With them it is thought of "no account to raise garden stuff"—and very seldom do you find it in the country. With them it is "hog and hominy," with a rude log house, often entirely open to the winds and rain. I have stayed at a "planter's," who had five hundred cattle in the yard and in sight, with probably three hundred ranging, whose house was made of logs, badly spliced or dove-tailed—any two being of sufficient distance apart to admit of easy ingress and egress all under fifteen years. The house was *divided into one room!* The cooking was done out of doors. With fifty cows and calves, not a pound of butter or a spoonful of milk on the table. "'Twas of no account." This man, in our section, would be called worth $50,000. But 'tis their way—they like it, grow fat and yellow.

The German companies continue emigration from their country to this as fast as possible, notwithstanding their pecuniary troubles, which have caused great embarrassment to all parties, there being now many protested bills. A short time back the whole "Grant" was threatened, but a recent law of the Legislature has given them two years longer to fulfil the contract of introducing the required number of emigrants, and has ratified the claims of the married emigrants to 640 acres each, and 320 to the unmarried. One-half of this amount goes to the German Emigration Company.

The religion of the Germans here is the Lutheran; so much so that I am told there is scarcely a dozen Catholics in the place. The inhabitants are quiet, prudent and industrious, mostly; although there is some complaint by Americans of losing cattle, all of which is charged upon the Dutch.

The first settlements in Texas were made by the French at Matagorda, but the settlers were soon after expelled by the Spaniards, who, in 1690, extended their cordons from New-Spain over the whole territory. Previous to this time, the Indians held undisputed sway over this fine country. Spanish forces were stationed at Goliad, Bexar, Nacogdoches, etc., and held military possession until the revolution which overthrew the Spanish power in Mexico. On the consummation of Mexican Independence, Texas became, in connection with the adjoining State of Coahuila, a state of the Republic. Soon after this period, several colonies of Americans, who had been invited into the territory by the Mexicans, settled in the eastern section, and were for a long time secured from the onerous burdens of Mexico proper. For some time previous to 1835, however, serious complaints against the central government were uttered, and in the following year open rebellion was rife. The Mexican President invaded Texas with a large army, and was successively victorious and defeated in a number of skirmishes. The American settlers declared their independence in March, 1836, and the defeat of the Mexicans and the capture of Santa Anna at San Jacinto, (21st April, 1836,) secured to the "patriot party" the acknowledgment of their independent position by the Mexican President, and the whole country east of the Rio Grande was acceded to them. The acts of Santa Anna, however, were never confirmed by the Senate, and of course their authority was, to say the least, equivocal. No serious attempt having been made by the Mexicans to regain Texas, for eight or nine years, the political nationality of the country was considered as consolidated, and in 1845, under this supposition, the

United States of America admitted the young republic as a state of the Union. The consequence of this act was war with Mexico—a war which the United States assumed by the annexation of Texas at a time when that country was at war with Mexico. The history of this war is recent and well known : the arms of the United States were everywhere victorious, and when peace returned, not Texas alone, but New-Mexico and Alta California, were parcelled off to the Americans, and forever lost to the Mexican republic.

The joint resolutions of Congress admitting Texas into the Union, were signed by the President of the United States, 1st March, 1845, and ratified by the Congress of Texas on the 4th of July, 1845. The presidents of the Republic of Texas from the period of its independence to its annexation to the American Union, were—Sam Houston, 1836; Mirabeau B. Lamar, 1838; Sam Houston (2d term,) 1841, and Anson Jones, 1844. The first Governor, under the new order of affairs, was J. Pinckney Henderson, who entered into office in January, 1846.

On the annexation of Texas to the Union, her western boundary towards New-Mexico was undefined, and its settlement was left to the United States' authorities. The claim of Texas to the whole line of the Rio Grande, however, was still substantially maintained, and on the conclusion of the war that state sought to extend its authority over all the region east of the river. This the federal authorities appear to have frustrated, but the boundary was not settled definitely until Congress passed an act by which all the claims of Texas beyond a certain line were purchased for the sum of $10,000,000. The act was satisfactory to the Texans, and has been the means of averting a danger which threatened the integrity of the Union. From this "indemnity" Texas is bound to pay all her debts for which the proceeds of the custom duties of the late republic had been pledged, and one-half of it is to be retained by the United States until a sufficient release is filed with the Secretary of the Treasury by the creditors claiming.

THE INDIAN TERRITORY.

Included under this head is all that vast region immediately north of Texas and west of the State of Arkansas. It lies between the latitudes of 33° 50′ and 40° North, and the longitudes of 94° 20′ and 100° West. In length, 310 miles, and breadth 290 miles. It has an area of 248,851 square miles, or 159,264,640 acres.

The lands of this region, especially those adjoining the states of Missouri and Arkansas are represented to be fertile, and the climate well adapted to agricultural pursuits. It is watered by numerous fine rivers which rise in the Mexican Cordilleras, and traverse the country in a direction east and west, falling into the Mississippi. Iron, lead, coal and salt are abundant. The vast prairies which here stretch over thousands of miles, are almost destitute of timber, but covered with long grass. The Indians have, in numerous instances, converted their settlements into well cultivated farms, and the various grains, vegetables, and other agricultural products of corresponding latitudes in the states east of the Mississippi are raised in profusion.

This territory was set apart by Congress for the permanent residence of the Indian tribes which have been removed from the states east of the Mississippi. Here they are secured a refuge from the progressive encroachments of the white races, and allowed to live under governments of their own choice, subject to no other control of the United States than such as may be necessary to preserve the peace of the frontier and harmony among the several tribes.

The inhabitants of the Indian Territory consist of tribes indigenous to the country, and the emigrant tribes, transported under the authority of the United States' Congress. The designation and present enumeration of each tribe is exhibited in the annexed table:

Indigenous Tribes.		Transported Tribes.	
Pawnees	12,500	Cherokees	29,911
Osages	4,102	Creeks	24.594
Kansas	1,700	Choctaws	12,410
Omahas	1,301	Seminoles	3,136
Otoes and Missouris	931	Chippewas, Ottawas, etc	2,028
Puncahs	777	Chickasaws	4,111
Quapaws	400	Delawares	1,059
		Kickapoos	505
		Peorias and Kaskaskias	150
		Piankeshaws	98
		Senecas from Sandusky	125
		Senecas and Shawnees	211
		Shawnees	887
		Stockbridges, Munsees, etc	278
		Swan Creek, etc	62
		Weas	176
		Winnebagoes	2,182
		Wyandots of Ohio	385
Total	21,711	Total	78,309

Besides the above, there are about 5,000 Indians of various tribes yet on the east side of the river Mississippi, and which are now in process of removal. With these, the total population of the Indian Territory will be near 105,000. The several tribes maintain their national distinctions.

The Choctaw nation occupies about 19,500 square miles of territory between the Red River and Arkansas. This domain consists of fine arable land, diversified in surface and enjoying a salubrious climate. Their government is thoroughly republican, being modelled after that of the United States. Their constitution is of their own framing, and their laws of their own enactment. Through the exertions of the missionaries, these Indians have progressed rapidly in morality, intelligence, and skill in the mechanic arts. The Choctaws are chiefly engaged in the growing of wool and culture of cotton, which they manufacture into fabrics suitable for apparel. Boarding schools and academies, in which are a large number of the young, are established, and supported from the annuity funds, amounting to $26,000 annually, from the United States. The New Testament and several valuable works have been translated into their language, and it is in contemplation to publish a weekly newspaper.

The Creeks are situated in a beautiful and fertile country north of the lands occupied by the Choctaw nation. The spirit of improvement has here, as with their neighbors, effected much among this celebrated tribe, and their physical and moral condition is not essentially inferior to the intelligent Choctaws. Their fields produce all the cereal grains and some cotton, and their homesteads are well-built, and generally surrounded by gardens and orchards. They have a written constitution and laws, and are governed by the national council.

The Cherokees, the most numerous tribe in the territory, occupy lands north and east of the Creeks. They are good agriculturists, and have large herds of horses and cattle. A well conducted paper, called the "Cherokee Advocate," is published in this nation.

The other transported tribes are said generally to have improved in their condition since their removal from the east. They occupy various determined sections, and are not allowed to interfere with each other's governments. They have each their own laws, and are regarded as so many distinct nations. The villages occupied by the Indians are generally well located, and their houses built in a substantial manner. Their fields are well cultivated, and produce all the staples of the country. Some considerable cotton has of late years been received from this territory at New-Orleans.

The indigenous tribes have not, as a general thing, improved in the same degree as their brethren from the east. They still cling to their wild pleasures, and prefer the excitement of the hunt and war to the peaceful monotony of civilization. Some tribes, however, are settling into habits of industry, and have become good farmers, and attentive to the teachings of the missionaries. There is every prospect, indeed, that before any long lapse of years, the barbarism of the Indian tribes will have given way, and the symbols of civilization have taken its place. Nor is it improbable that when sufficiently advanced in intelligence, these Indians, among whom there are orators of no mean calibre, and men of some learning, will be admitted through their representatives into our national congress, and become constituents of our great commonwealth.

THE TERRITORY OF MINESOTA.

Minesota is situated between the latitudes 43° 30′ and 49° north, and the longitudes 89° 30′ and 102° 12′ west from Greenwich, or 12° 29′ and 25° 11′ from Washington; and is bounded north by British America, east by Lake Superior and Wisconsin, south by Iowa, and west by the vast unoccupied country which stretches to the crest of the Rocky Mountains. Its extent north and south is about 360 miles, and its greatest width about 480 miles, and within its limits contains an area of about 83,000 square miles, or 53,120,000 acres.

Throughout the whole of this territory scarcely an elevation that could be dignified with the name of mountain occurs. The surface is in general level or undulating, but varies considerably in elevation, and in the ascents and descents of its plateaux. In some parts, especially in the neighborhood of the Mississippi and St. Peter's, the ground is much broken, and their margins lined with high bluffs of various formations; while in others the rivers flow through deep channels, seemingly worn into the earth by the force of their waters. Every portion of Minesota may be reached by inland navigation. The traveller will meet constantly with springs and small lakes, the sources of mighty rivers, whose waters are discharged thousands of miles to the north into Hudson's Bay; as many to the east into the Gulf of St. Lawrence, or to the south into the Gulf of Mexico. Springs are often seen within a few feet of each other, the sources of rivers, whose outlets in the ocean are some six thousand miles apart. In almost every direction canoe navigation, with short portages, is practicable by means of the numerous rivers, whose sources are nearly interlocked or connected by chains of lakes. The Mississippi has its source here, some 3,000 miles from its mouth. Nine hundred miles of the length of this majestic river are embraced in this territory, and its numerous tributaries course through its fertile plains. The north-east portion is washed by the crystal waters of Lake Superior, which is of itself an inland sea for the prosecution of trade and commerce, and opens an avenue to the Atlantic. The Missouri, after having flowed nearly 1,000 miles from the base of the Rocky Mountains, sweeps along its whole western boundary, ensuring navigation almost to Oregon. Its large tributaries, James and Big Sioux Rivers, water valleys of great beauty and fertility. Extensive prairies, blooming with flowers and covered with luxuriant grasses, affording sustenance to immense herds of buffalo, saying nothing of elk, deer, antelopes, and other small game. Red River, which discharges itself into Lake Winnipeg, has its sources near those of the Mississippi. Beautiful lakes of transparent water, well stocked with fish, and varying in size from ponds to inland seas, are profusely scattered over the territory. Forests of pine and other evergreens, orchards of sugar-maple, groves of hard and soft woods of various species, wild rice and cranberries, and various species of wild fruit, copious springs of pure water, a fertile soil, and water-power, easily improved and abundantly distributed, render this region peculiarly adapted to the wants of man. Add to these a salubrious climate, and Minesota appears to enjoy eminent capacities for becoming a thriving and populous state. Its mineral resources are unknown, but indications and discoveries have been made that certify its wealth in copper and lead. Building stone of every description, limestone, etc., are found everywhere underlying the soil, while many valuable and precious stones are found on the shores of the lakes. For a country so overspread with lakes, and traversed by such a number of rivers, it is astonishingly free from marsh and morass. The land has a great elevation above the Gulf of Mexico, and the waters of the north and east, and as a consequence is easily and perfectly drained; and moreover, the margins of the lakes and rivers themselves are generally surrounded by hills and bluffs, which protect their neighborhoods from inundation. The whole country is thus eligible for agriculture.

The census of 1850 gave a population of 6,077, or one person to every 13.8 square miles, and its distribution to the several counties was as follows:

COUNTIES.	White Persons.	Free Col'd Persons.	Total Popula.
Benton	416	2	418
Dakotah	582	2	584
Itaska	97	—	97
Mahkatah	158	—	158
Pembina	1,134	—	1,134
Ramsay	2,197	30	2,227
Wabashaw	242	1	243
Wahnahta	160	—	160
Washington	1,052	4	1,056
Total	6,038	39	6,077

CLASSES AND SEXES OF POPULATION.

Classes.	Males.	Females.	Total.
White Persons	3,695	2,343	6,038
Colored " —free	21	18	39
" " —slave	—	—	—
Total	3,716	2,361	6,077

The number of dwelling-houses in the territory in 1850 was 1,002, and of families 1,016, or about six persons to each dwelling and family; and the deaths in 1849–50 numbered 30, or one to every 200 inhabitants. In June, 1850, there were 157 farms under cultivation; also five manufacturing establishments, producing annually $500 ana upwards.

A census of the territory taken on the 11th June, 1849, exhibited a population of 4,780, of which 3,667 were males, and 1,713 females; and hence the increase in one year was 1,297, or 27 per centum.

The settlements as yet made in the territory are chiefly confined to the peninsula between the Mississippi and St. Croix on the south, and on the Red River on the north. Otherwise the country is inhabited only by the aboriginal hunters, the Chippewas and Sioux Indians. Their numbers are not ascertained, but may approximate to about 12,000. With some of the tribes treaties have been made for the purchase of their lands, and for their removal, which, when effected, will open to the white settler immense tracts of rich and fertile soils, productive of every species of grain and fruits usually grown in northern climates. The Indians have long been in connection with the whites, and have for more than two centuries carried on with them a profitable trade in furs and peltries. Their hunting-grounds are now chiefly confined to the vast prairies west of the Mississippi. The white inhabitants are from almost every portion of the world: the Canadian, the sons of New-England and the Middle States, with English, French, and Germans, are all intermingled; and not a few of the citizens consist of half-breeds, who chiefly reside on the Red River, and have settlements for some distance on both sides of our northern boundary. These are descendants of the original settlers at Lord Selkirk's colony, and Indian women of the Chippewa family. Their village is called Pembina. Hardy and hard-working, prudent as the New-England farmer, religious and intelligent, they form no mean class in the general community. They trade with the southern settlers, exchanging furs and pemmican for the superfluities of the South. They rear cattle and sheep, weave their own clothing, and live in a middle state of civilization. They have churches and schools, and many of the better class are educated at a collegiate establishment which has long been maintained among them. As a consequence, however, of their ostracized situation, they still retain many of the peculiarities of their original nations, modified indeed by the circumstances that surround them, and their connection with savage life. In the new settlements, the industry of the whites is almost entirely agricultural. They have mills on a number of the streams, and steamboats ply regularly on their waters. They are building roads, and from the energy they exhibit in overcoming natural obstacles, the real prosperity of the territory seems to be ensured. A large business has been already done by the steamboats that sail regularly between Galena and St. Paul and Stillwater. The products of the chase, and the fruits of the field, are exported in considerable quantities. With regard to immigration, the prospects are favorable. Farmers, laborers, and professional men, are daily ascending the rivers in search of a new home. The day, indeed, is not distant when the forests will be laid low, and the flowery prairies be converted into fields and gardens, producing every necessary to the use and enjoyment of man. Earth, air, and water abound in the prerequisites of man's happiness and enjoyment, and are only waiting his advent to yield up their now unused abundance.

The organization of the government of the territory having been so recent, it is impossible to exhibit by statistics the resources of this new and almost untouched country. The first legislature, which adjourned after a session of sixty days, on the 1st November, 1849, was chiefly employed in organizing the government, and dividing the territory into suitable civil districts, and appointing officers to enforce the laws. Among its most important acts were those establishing a judiciary, a school system, and relative to the improvement of roads. All these will have a paramount influence over the future destiny of the country. Perhaps one of the most humane and politic acts of the legislature was the admission to citizenship of "all persons of a mixture of white and Indian blood, who shall have adopted the habits and customs of civilized men;" and not less politic is that law which requires the establishment of schools throughout the territory. The act of the General Government organizing the territory appropriates two sections of land in every township for the support of common schools. No other state in the Union has received more than one section of land in each township for such purpose. The present population (Jan., 1852) is probably not far from 12,000 souls.

The principal settlements are St. Paul, Stillwater, Mendota, Fort Snelling, Pembina, etc.

St. Paul, the capital, is situated on the left bank of the Mississippi, 15 miles by water, and 8 miles by land, below the Falls of St. Anthony. The town is situated on a plateau terminating on the river in a precipitous bluff 80 feet elevation above the river. The bluff recedes from the river at the upper and lower ends of the town, forming two landings, from both of which the ascent is gradual. The first store or trading-house was built in 1842. In June, 1849, the town contained 142 houses, all of which, with the exception of perhaps a dozen, had been built within the year previous. This number included the government house, three hotels, four warehouses, ten stores, several groceries, two printing-offices (from which two newspapers are issued weekly), several mechanics' shops, a school-house, etc. There was not a brick or stone house in the town. Since the period above-mentioned, however, several churches and many durable houses, built of stone and brick, from materials in the vicinity, have been erected. The population in June, 1850, was 1,294. St. Paul is well located for commerce, and from its being at the head of navigation below the Falls, must necessarily become not only the political, but the commercial capital of the territory. In the neighborhood of St. Paul there is an extensive settlement of Canadians, chiefly persons formerly employed by the Hudson Bay Company, called Little Canada. Population 600.

Stillwater is situated on the west side of Lake St. Croix, near its head, on ground having a gentle ascent from the shore to a high bluff in the rear, which extends in the form of a crescent, and nearly encloses the town. The first settlement was made in 1843. It contains a court house, several hotels and stores, and many neat dwellings. Steamboats seldom ascend higher than this place. The environs consist of a beautiful prairie country, and are being rapidly brought under cultivation. Population in June, 1850, 822. Marine Mills is a flourishing settlement on St. Croix River, a few miles above its entrance into the lake. The precincts contain about 200 inhabitants. Its water-power and the fine country which surrounds it must enforce its speedy increase and prosperity. Several villages on the Wisconsin side of the St. Croix River have been established, and are rapidly increasing in importance. Indeed, the resources of the vicinity on both sides are such as to ensure to the villages considerable commerce.

Fort Snelling is situated on the high rocky promontory, 106 feet above the water, at the confluence of St. Peter's River with the Mississippi. The military works were commenced in 1819. The fort is in the form of a hexagon, and surrounded by a stone wall. From the river its appearance is imposing and seemingly impregnable. It is, however, within the reach of cannon from higher ground; but the object for which the site was selected—the protection of the frontier from savage incursion—is well attained by its situation. The garrison usually consists of three companies of dragoons. The view from these fortifications is extensive. The military reservation of the establishment embraces an area of 10 miles square, of which the fort is near the center. The settlement in the neighborhood contains only about 40 inhabitants. In the fort there were 267 males and 50 females in June, 1849. Mendota, or St. Peter's, on the western bank of the Mississippi, south of the confluence of St. Peter's River, has been occupied for several years by the American Fur Company as a depot for their trading establishments with the Indians of the north-west. Two stores and two or three houses constitute the village. It is, however, a fine town site; and being situated at the junction of two great rivers, and near the head of steam navigation, its importance in a commercial point of view has not been overlooked. Whites are not allowed to reside here without special permission from the U. S. government, the village being in the military reservation. It will ultimately command the trade of the St. Peter's River. Population in June, 1849, 122.

Some other small villages exist in this neighborhood, but of their importance or present state little is known. Kaposia, from its situation near the point of land opposite St. Paul, though yet little more than an Indian town, may ultimately become of consequence. St. Anthony, at the Falls, and Sauk Rapids, opposite the mouth of Osakis River, are both on the east bank of the Mississippi; and higher up, on both sides of Nokay River, is Fort Gaines, the most northerly military establishment in the country. The supplying of these remote stations with provisions, etc., creates considerable traffic and traveling both by land and water. The return traffic consists of furs and peltry, with other Indian contributions.

The territory of Minesota derives its name from *Mini-sotah*, the Indian name for St. Peter's River; *mini* in their language meaning "water," and *sotah* "muddy or slightly turbid." The country originally belonged to the French by priority of discovery. At an early period their traders, missionaries, and soldiers had penetrated into the western wilderness. The United States had little authority over this region until 1812. In 1816 a law of Congress excluded foreigners from the Indian trade; and for the encouragement of our citizens the military post at Fort Snelling was established in 1819. Among the explorers of this country the names of Carver, Pike, Cass, Long, Beltrami, Schoolcraft, Nicollet, Owen, etc., will ever be intimately connected with its history. The honor of verifying the sources of the Mississippi belongs to Schoolcraft. The present territory was established by act of Congress, 3d March, 1849, and shortly after Alexander Ramsay was appointed Governor, and made St. Paul his capital, where the government was organized. "Congress may hereafter divide said territory, or annex any portion of it to another state or territory."

THE WESTERN TERRITORY.

This territory comprises the remaining unorganized portion of Louisiana, as purchased by the United States in 1803. It extends from the Nebraska or Platte River northward to the 49th parallel, and from White Earth and Missouri Rivers westward to the Rocky Mountains. The territory has an area of 579,584 square miles.

The greater part of this immense territory is watered by the Missouri River and its numerous tributaries. The Yellow Stone, the largest tributary, extends its branches to the very base of the Rocky Mountains, and to near the sources of the Nebraska. A mountain ridge, which branches from the great Rocky Mountains, in about 42° N. lat., traverses the country in a N. E. direction towards Lake Winnipeg. In the E. portion of the territory the country is partly covered with forests, but beyond this commences a vast ocean of prairie, almost level, and clothed in grass and flowers. Approaching the mountains, however, the country gradually assumes a barren aspect. Countless droves of buffalo, elk, and deer, range upon the vast plains, but even these are fast diminishing before the attacks of the hunter.

In a country of such extent, generally level, naked, and open, the climate must in a great measure correspond to the latitude. Immediately on the borders of the settled states it is mild and temperate; beyond, it gradually becomes more extreme, and towards the mountains cold, bleak, and polar. Travellers speak of encountering storms of hail and sleet in the summer. When the winds blow from the W. over the mountain summits, the cold they occasion is intense.

As yet the whole territory is inhabited by Indians, but the time is not far distant when the pioneer will penetrate its forests and prairies, and bring under cultivation the soil that from its creation has not been turned by the labor of man. The wild herds will be replaced with the ox, the horse, and the sheep, and golden crops will succeed the flowers and grasses that now only bloom in useless luxuriance, and wither with the first frosts of autumn, without contributing to the necessity or comfort of civilized man.

That portion of the country lying in the valley of the Platte is sometimes termed "*Nebraska Territory*," and as such it has been proposed to organize it. A bill for the purpose of defining its boundaries was introduced into Congress, 7th January, 1845, but no action was had on the subject. The country north of this valley still retains the name of "*North-West Territory*," from the fact that it formerly belonged to the extensive territory under that name, from the which so many states have already been set off.

The boundaries of the territories occupied by the several Indian nations residing in this region, as defined in the treaty of Laramie, made in Sept., 1851, are as follows:

The Sioux or Dacotah Nation—"Commencing at the mouth of *White Earth River*, on the Missouri River; thence in a south-westerly direction to the forks of the Platte River; thence up the north fork of the Platte River to a point known as the Red Bute, or where the road leaves the river; thence along the range of mountains known as the Black Hills to the head waters of Heart River; thence down Heart River to its mouth, and thence down the Missouri to the mouth of White Earth River."

The Gros Ventre, Mandan and Arrickera Nations (in common)—"Commencing at the mouth of Heart River; thence up the Missouri River to the mouth of Yellow Stone River; thence up the Yellow Stone River to the mouth of Powder River; thence from the mouth of Powder River, in a south-easterly direction to the head waters of Little Missouri River; thence along the range of the Black Hills to the head waters of Heart River, and thence down Heart River to the place of beginning."

The ASSINABOIN Nation—"Commencing at the mouth of Yellow Stone River; thence up the Missouri River to the mouth of Muscle Shell River; thence from the mouth of the Muscle Shell River in a south-easterly direction, until it strikes the head waters of Big Dry Creek; thence down that Creek to where it empties into Yellow Stone River, nearly opposite the mouth of Powder River, and thence down the Yellow Stone to the place of beginning."

The BLACK FEET Nation—"Commencing at the mouth of Muscle Shell River; thence up the Missouri River to its sources; thence along the main range of the Rocky Mountains in a southerly direction, to the head waters of the northern sources of Yellow Stone River; thence down the Yellow Stone River to the mouth of Twenty-Five Yard Creek; thence across to the head waters of Muscle Shell River, and down Muscle Shell River to the place of beginning."

The CROW Nation—"Commencing at the mouth of Powder River and the Yellow Stone; thence up Powder River to its source; thence along the main range of the Black Hills and Wind River Mountains to the head waters of Yellow Stone River; down the Yellow Stone River to the mouth of Twenty-Five Yard Creek; thence to the head waters of the Muscle Shell River; thence down Muscle Shell River to its mouth; thence across the head waters of Big Dry Creek and down to its mouth."

The CHEYENNE and ARRAPAHOE Nations (in common)—"Commencing at the Red Bute, or where the road leaves the north fork of Platte River; thence up the north fork of Platte River to its source; thence along the main range of the Rocky Mountains to the head waters of the Arkansas River; down the Arkansas River to where the main Santa Fe road crosses it; thence in a north-westerly direction to the forks of the Platte River, and up the Platte River to the place of beginning."

Each of these tribes recognizes a Head, or Principal Chief, through whom all transactions with the government of the United States are conducted.

The United States have also the reserved right to build forts, make roads, and march armies in and through the country. And it is specially ordained, that although the several nations have allotted territories, they shall each and all have the natural right to hunt over the whole territory.

PACIFIC COUNTRY.

IN this division of the United States are included the Territory of Oregon, and the extensive regions recently acquired from the Mexican Republic, known as California Alta and Nuevo-Mexico. It lies generally to the west of the Rocky Mountains, and between the latitudes of 32° and 49° north, but as a matter of convenience the whole territory of New-Mexico, as it now exists, although not properly or altogether within the geographical limits of the country, will be described under this section.

THE TERRITORY OF OREGON.

OREGON is a large and compact quadrangle of land, situated between latitudes 42° and 49° north, and longitudes 109° and 124° west from Greenwich, or 31° 59' and 46° 59' from Washington; and is bounded north by British America, east by the Rocky Mountains, south by Utah and California, and west by the Pacific Ocean. Its extent from north to south is about 480 miles, and from east to west 600 miles, and its limits contain an area of 341,463 square miles, or 218,536,320 acres.

Oregon is a country of huge mountains, and wide, elevated plateaux. It is divided by two great ranges into three distinct portions. From the Pacific Ocean to the Cascade range, a distance of from 100 to 150 miles, includes the first; from the Cascade range to the Blue mountains, the second; and from these to the Rocky Mountains, the third. Considerable diversity in soil, climate, and productions, characterizes these several regions. The southern portion of the Pacific section is supposed to be that best adapted to agriculture. The middle section has a light, sandy soil, except near the streams, where a rich alluvium prevails. The mountains are almost barren. The third, or eastern section, is a rugged country, but in its intervales contains much grass lands, which renders it peculiarly suited to the rearing of cattle and for sheep-farming. Some parts of the Cascade Mountains rise 4,000 feet above the sea-level. The Rocky Mountains, many culminations of which attain 6,000 feet, present a serious barrier to communication with the old states. Only three passes have been found which admit of travel: the first in 46° 22' N.; the second in 44° 30' and the third, the South Pass, discovered by Fremont. The usual overland route to Oregon is through the last. A range of mountains, called the "Klamet," runs from the Rocky Mountains westward toward the Pacific. The climate on the Pacific is temperate, and much milder than near the Atlantic in the same latitude. In the interior, it becomes more extreme; and in the mountains, varying with their elevation, winter is almost perpetual, and many of the higher culminations are capped with snow throughout the year. The greatest quantity of rain falls between November and March.

The Pacific coast of Oregon is generally rugged, and extends 650 miles along that ocean. Only three or four harbors occur in its whole length. The Columbia, or Oregon, is the principal river; and into this, which has a S. W. and W. course from the Rocky Mountains, all the main streams of the territory empty. The navigation of this river is frequently obstructed by falls and rapids, and there is only an uninterrupted passage from the ocean, for large ships, of about 120 miles. The principal tributaries are Willamette River, Lewis or Saptin River, and Clarke's or Flathead River, all of which receive numerous fine streams, that water an immense surface. There are a number of small lakes in the country.

There is no material difference in the natural productions of Oregon and those of the Eastern States. Vegetation is, however, more developed. The fir has been found 46 feet in circumference and 300 feet in height, and pines from 200 to 250 feet high, and from 20 to 40 feet in girth. The mineral resources of the country are almost unknown, but there is no reason to suppose that the earth here is less metalliferous than in the more southern portion of the Pacific region. Wild animals, in great numbers and variety, inhabit the recesses of the mountains, and the valleys and plains.

The trapper and hunter have explored the country with profit in peltry and furs. The cultivated portions, as yet confined chiefly to the banks of the lower Columbia and to the neighborhood of Puget's Sound, are very productive. The cereal crops have been abundant, and fruit trees, vines, and culinary vegetables thrive well. Since the discovery of gold in California, a great demand has arisen for the agricultural products of Oregon, and, as a consequence, a commercial connection has been the result. The export of lumber has been large. This incipient commerce will not be transitory—the demand for building materials is constantly on the increase, and that for breadstuffs and provisions will last as long as mining is the chief em ployment in California. Some commercial intercourse is maintained also with the Sandwich Islands, and the Russian settlements on the north. But with all these fortuitous circumstances that have attended the first settlement of the territory, it must still remain much as it is—a mere agricultural and pastoral country—unless some means of easy and rapid communication can be maintained with the Western States and the Atlantic coast. A railroad is the only solution of this difficulty. The one proposed by Mr. Whitney seems to have some claims to consideration, and by its means the shores of Lake Michigan would be brought in a juxtaposition with the mouth of the Columbia River. The details for the construction of such an avenue, chiefly through a country infested with hostile Indians, and through mountain passes almost inaccessible, have been laid before Congress, and are favorably spoken of; but to mature plans, and obtain capital for such a work, seems to offer insuperable difficulties even to its commencement. It is almost too great a work for individual enterprise. If a railroad is to be built, let it be a national work.

The total number of inhabitants in Oregon, in 1850, was 13,293, and the distribution of these to the several counties was in the following proportions:

COUNTIES.	Area: Sq. M.	White Persons.	Col'd Persons.	Total.
Benton	16,000	810	4	814
Clackamas	141,000	1,836	23	1,859
Clarke	40,000	592	51	643
Clatsop	6,000	458	4	462
Linn	18,000	994	—	994
Lewis	90,000	457	101	558
Marion	21,000	2,740	9	2,749
Polk	2,400	1,046	5	1,051
Washington	5,000	2,643	8	2,651
Yam Hill	2,600	1,511	1	1,512
Total	341,000	13,087	206	13,293

CLASSES AND SEXES OF POPULATION.

Classes.	Males.	Females.	Total.
White Persons	8,142	4,945	13,087
Colored " —free	119	87	206
" " —slave	—	—	—
Total	8,261	5,032	13,293

The number of dwellings and families was equal, being 2,374, or 5.6 persons to each. The farms in cultivation numbered 1,164, and there were 51 manufacturing establishments producing annually $500 and upward.

There are several villages and settlements of considerable pretensions in Oregon. Oregon City, the territorial capital, is situated about 30 miles up the Willamette river, and two miles above the Clackamas rapids, which prevent all navigation to the city. Perhaps no other place in the Union has such immense water privileges, and many large saw-mills are already in operation. PORTLAND, 12 miles below the falls, may be considered as the port of Oregon City. Its trade with the Pacific towns, and also with those of the Atlantic, especially with New York, is prosperous and increasing. ASTORIA, near the mouth of the Columbia River, on its south bank, has a good harbor and other natural advantages for becoming a great commercial depot. At present there are not 20 buildings in the place. It is the only port of entry in the territory. PACIFIC CITY, on the north shore of the entrance to the Columbia, is yet a new place, but has bright prospects. Its harbor is said to be excellent. FORT VANCOUVER, on the north bank of the Columbia River, 100 miles from its mouth, is the principal trading post of the Hudson Bay Company west of the mountains. Ships drawing 14 feet of water can ascend 20 miles further up the river. The establishment consists of about 100 houses enclosed by picket-fences, and defended by armed bastions and a block-house. A Catholic church is the only building of note. The inhabitants are chiefly South Sea Islanders in the employ of the company. The establishment is on an extensive scale, and the center of vast interests—all the company's Indian trade being conducted here. Extensive agricultural operations for the support of the traders, are carried on. The farm contains about 3,000 acres. The stock of cattle and sheep is very large, and is rapidly increasing in numbers and improving in breed from the importation of European stock. The mixed breed of sheep yields from 12 to 18 pounds of fleece. The mills and outposts of the fort extend several miles above on the river. Other settlements on the Columbia are, WALLA-WALLA, a little below the confluence of Lewis River; FORT OKENAGAN, at the mouth of the river of the same name; FORT COLVILLE, below the union of Clarke's River with the Columbia.

FORT NESQUALLY, on Puget's Sound, is occupied by the "Puget's Sound Agricultural Company." Their farms are very extensive, and are kept in a high state of cultivation. They supply provisions to the Hudson Bay Company's servants west of the mountains, and export largely to the Sandwich Islands and the Russian post of Sitka. The company has also extensive farms on the Cowlitz River.

Oregon, in its entirety, extends between 42° and 54° 40′ north latitude, but by the treaty of 1846, all the territory north of 49° was ceded to Great Britain. Perhaps the greatest defect in this treaty was the ceding of Vancouver's Island to the British—an island notoriously the finest portion of the disputed country, both in regard to its agricultural capacities, its commercial position, and its mineral productions. The retention of this alone would have been preferable to our possession of the whole mainland. This country was not discovered until nearly two centuries after the occupation of Mexico by the Spaniards, nor was it at all known until late in the 18th century. In 1792 the discovery of the mouth of the Columbia River by Capt. Grey gave to the United States a claim to sovereignty over the country watered by that river and its branches. Settlements, however, had previously been made by the English at Nootka Sound, and on the upper waters of the Columbia, and on these facts the British based their claim. The Louisiana Treaty of 1803 transferred the claims preferred by France to the United States, and presuming that Louisiana really did extend to the Pacific, this formed a most important point in the controversy. In 1804–5–6, Captains Lewis and Clarke explored the country from the head waters of the Missouri River to the mouth of the Columbia. Trading houses were subsequently erected by Americans on Lewis River and at Astoria. The fort at Astoria was taken by the British in the last war, but restored on the conclusion of peace. To adjust, or rather suspend, the conflicting claims of each, the United States and Great Britain, in 1818, agreed to a suspension of sovereign occupancy for ten years, which agreement was extended indefinitely in 1828, with a proviso that either party might recede from the agreement on giving one year's notice to that effect. The treaty of 1819 with Spain, in which that nation withdrew its claims to the territory in favor of the United States, greatly strengthened the presumptions of the Union; but still, no immediate measures were resorted to. The disputes respecting the sovereignty were renewed in 1845, and the President was authorized by Congress to give the notice required. This step led to the final settlement of the question, and a partition of the territory by the line of 49° north latitude. In 1848 a bill passed both Houses of Congress, and was approved by the President on the 14th August, by which Oregon was erected into a territorial government, and soon after the necessary officers were sent out, and the government organized.

By the treaty of partition, the Hudson Bay Company retained possession of their farms, etc., in Oregon. They have now made the offer to the United States, of all their right and title in these occupancies, for the sum of $1,000,000. Should this be accepted, both parties will, no doubt, be satisfied, and all future cause of disagreement be prevented.

THE STATE OF CALIFORNIA.

CALIFORNIA occupies all that portion of California Alta* westward of the following line, to wit—beginning at the intersection of 42° north latitude, and 120° longitude west from Greenwich, or 42° 59′ from Washington; thence south in a direct course to 39° north latitude; thence south-east to where the Rio Colorado intersects the parallel of 35° north latitude, and thence down the mid channel of that river to the boundary between the United States and Mexico. Within these limits the surface measures 188,981 square miles, or 120,947,840 acres.

This grand division of California (the only part, indeed, to which the name properly applies) is traversed from N. to S. by two principal ranges of mountains, called respectively the *Sierra Nevada*, which divides the region from the great basin, and the *Coast Range*, running almost parallel to and at a short distance from the Pacific coast. The main feature of this region is the long, low, broad valley of the San Joaquin and Sacramento Rivers—the two valleys forming one—500 miles long and 50 miles broad. Lateral ranges, parallel with the Sierra, make the structure of the country, and break it into a surface of valleys and mountains—the valleys a few hundreds, and the mountains 2,000 to 4,000 feet above the sea. These form greater masses and become more elevated in the north, where some peaks,

* California Alta in its full extent, as acquired of Mexico, lies between 32° and 42° N. lat. and 106° and 124° N. long., and is bounded north by Oregon, east by the crest of the Rocky Mountains, south by the Rio Gila and California Baja, and west by the Pacific Ocean, on which it has a front of 900 miles. The area included within these limits is 448,691 square miles. This extensive territory is now divided into the state of California, Utah Territory and (in part) the territory of New Mexico.

as the Shaste, enter the regions of perpetual snows. The great valley is discriminated only by the names of the rivers that traverse it. It is a single geographical formation, lying between the two ranges, and stretching across the head of the Bay of San Francisco, with which a delta of 25 miles connects it. The two rivers rise at opposite ends of this long valley, receive numerous affluents—many of them bold rivers, become themselves navigable rivers—flow towards each other, meet half way, and enter the bay together in the region of tide water; making a continuous water line from one end to the other. The resources of this valley, mineral and agricultural, are immense, and perhaps no part of the world affords greater facilities for easy development. Gold and quicksilver are the most valuable of its mineral products. The soil and climate, though varying much with locality, are generally well suited for agriculture. Westward of the rivers, the soil is chiefly dry and unproductive; but on the east side the country is well watered and luxuriantly fertile, being intersected by numerous fine streams, forming large and beautiful bottoms of rich land, wooded principally with white-oaks. The foot hills of the Sierra which limit the valley make a woodland country, diversified with undulating grounds and pretty vales. Near the Tulare Lakes, and on the margins of the Sacramento and San Joaquin Rivers, the surface is composed of level plains, gradually changing into undulating, and rolling towards the mountains. The region W. of the Coast Range to the Pacific—the only portion inhabited before the discovery of gold—has long been the seat of numerous missions; and around these, generally situated in the most lovely vales, agriculture has converted the country into a perfect garden. All the cereals of temperate regions are cultivated, and the olive and grape thrive luxuriantly. Wheat is the first product of the north. The moisture of the coast seems particularly suited to the cultivation of roots, and to vegetables used for culinary purposes, which in fact grow to an extraordinary size. Few localities indeed can produce in such perfection so great a variety of grains and fruits.

The coasts of California are generally precipitous and rugged; and in relation to their extent present few good harbors. The bays of San Diego, Monterey, and San Francisco, are the finest, and their capacities extensive. San Francisco Bay is one of the most important in the world, not merely as a harbor, but also and mainly from the accessory advantages which belong to it—fertile and picturesque dependent country, general mildness of climate, connection with the great central valley, etc. When these advantages are taken into account, with its geographical position on the line of communication with Asia, its importance rises superior to all contingencies. Its latitudinal position is that of Lisbon; its climate that of Italy; bold shores and mountains give it grandeur; the extent and resources of its dependent country are the cynosure of the world. The bay is separated from the sea by low mountain ranges, and only a narrow gate, about a mile wide, affords an entrance. It is land-locked in every sense of the word, and protected on all sides from the weather. Passing through this narrow entrance, the bay opens to the right and left, extending in each direction about 35 miles, having a total length of 70 and a coast of 275 miles. It is divided by projecting points and straits into three separate compartments, of which the northern two are called San Pablo and Suisson bays. The surface is much broken by numerous islands—some mere rocks, and others grass-covered, rising to the height of 300 to 800 feet. Directly fronting the entrance, mountains, a few miles from the shore, rise about 2,000 feet above the water, crowned by forests of lofty cypress, which are visible from the sea, and make a conspicuous landmark for vessels entering the bay. Behind, the rugged peak of Mt. Diavolo, 3,770 feet high, overlooks the surrounding country of the bay and the San Joaquin.

The shore presents a varied character of rugged and broken hills, rolling and undulating land, and rich alluvial tracts, backed by fertile and wooded ranges, suitable for towns, villages, and farms, with which it is beginning to be overspread. Such is the bay and proximate country and shore of San Francisco. It is not a mere indentation of the coast, but a little sea to itself, connected with the ocean by a defensible gate. The head of the bay is about 40 miles distant from the sea, and there commences its connection with the noble valley of the San Joaquin and Sacramento.

The climate of California is remarkable in its periodical changes, and for the long continuance of the wet and dry seasons, dividing as they do the year into two nearly equal parts, which have a most peculiar influence on the labor applied to agriculture and the products of the soil, and in fact connect themselves inseparably with all the interests of the country. The dry season commences with May. The north-east winds, following the course of the sun's greatest attraction, then commence to blow, and in their passage across the snow-clad ridges of the Rocky Mountains and the Sierra Nevada, become deprived of all their moisture. They therefore pass over the hills and plains of California, where the temperature is very high in the summer, in a very dry state, and absorb like a sponge all the moisture the atmosphere and surface of the earth can yield. The dry season commences much earlier in the south than towards the north, and continues some time after the sun repasses the equator at the autumnal equinox. About the middle of November, the climate being relieved from these N. E. currents, the S. W. winds set in from the ocean, surcharged with moisture; the rains commence and continue to fall, not constantly, but with sufficient frequency to designate the period of their continuance. Cold winds and fogs render the climate of San Francisco, and in fact the whole coast, somewhat irksome. A few miles inland, however, where the heat of the sun modifies and softens the ocean wind, the weather is delightful. The heat in the middle of the day is not too great to retard labor. The nights are cool and pleasant. This is the climate which prevails in all the valleys of the Coast Range, and extends throughout the country north and south as far eastward as the valley of the Sacramento and San Joaquin. In this vast plain, the sea breeze loses its influence, and the degree of heat in the middle of the day during the summer months is much greater than on the Atlantic coast in the same latitude. It is dry, however, and perhaps not more oppressive. The thermometer sometimes ranges from 110° to 115° in the shade, during three or four hours, say from 11 to 3 o'clock. In the evening as the sun declines, the radiation of heat ceases. The cold, dry atmosphere from the mountains spreads over the whole country, and renders the nights cool and invigorating. No general description of the climate of California will cover the whole land; it varies with the latitude. The climate of the coast and interior, of the mountain and valley, etc., differ widely; and it is perhaps to these circumstances that the opinions and statements respecting it are so conflicting. Each writer has noted his own impressions.

The greater portion of the returns of the census of 1850 were destroyed at San Francisco, in one of the great fires that have visited that city; and those portions which were received at the census office at Washington are thought to be very imperfect—hence no exact account of the population can be had. The number of inhabitants, however, may be estimated at not less than 155,000, and their distribution to the several counties is nearly as follows:

COUNTIES.	Population.	COUNTIES.	Population.
Butte	4,786	San Luis Obispo	1,521
Calaveras	16,894	Santa Barbara	1,185
Centra Costa	722	Santa Clara	3,502
Colusi	115	Santa Cruz	643
El Dorado	20,785	Shasté	378
Los Angelos	8,000	Solano	589
Marin	323	Sonoma	560
Mariposa	4,400	Sutter	3,466
Mendocino	56	Trinity	659
Monterey	1,872	Tuolumne	7,000
Napa	405	Yolo	1,124
Sacramento	16,000	Yuba	19,032
San Diego	1,644		
San Francisco	36,000	Total	155,617
San Joacquin	4,000		

To this total at least 50 per cent. ought to be added, as it is estimated that not more than two-thirds of the population was reached by the census takers. This would make the population 233,425; the truth, however, cannot be attained until further returns are obtained. The majority of these are occupied in the mining districts. It is impossible to form any estimate of the number of mountain Indians. Some suppose there are as many as 300,000 in the country. These inhabit the foot hills of the Sierra, and the valleys between them and the coast. They seem to be of the lowest grade of human beings. They live chiefly on acorns, roots, and insects, and the kernel of the pine burr; occasionally they catch fish and game. They exhibit no inclination to cultivate the soil, neither do they pretend to hold any interest in the lands, nor have they been treated by the Spanish or American immigrants as possessing any. They are lazy—idle to the last degree. Formerly, at the missions, those who were brought up and educated by the priests made good servants. Many of those now attached to families seem to be faithful and intelligent; but those who are at all in a wild and uncultivated state, are most degraded objects of filth and sloth. They are invariably hostile to the whites, and have already committed many aggravated murders and depredations on the persons and property of the immigrants and gold-hunters.

Previous to the treaty of peace with Mexico and the discovery of gold, the exportable products of the country consisted almost exclusively of hides and tallow. The Californians were a pastoral people, and paid much more attention to the raising of horses and cattle than the cultivation of the soil. Wheat, barley, maize, beans, and edible roots, were cultivated only in sufficient quantities for home consumption. The destruction of cattle for their hides and tallow has now ceased in consequence of the demand for beef. The number of cattle now in California is estimated only at 500,000 head—a supply inadequate to the wants of the beef eaters now in the country for more than five or six years. The great bulk of animal food must therefore come from the Atlantic Coast and the Western States. The time is not far distant when cattle from the Mississippi valley will be driven by tens of thousands to supply this new market. The climate and soil of California are well suited for the cereals; but the temperature along the coast is too cool for the successful culture of maize as a field crop. The root crops thrive luxuriantly. Apples, pears, and peaches are cultivated with facility; and there is no reason to doubt that all the fruits of the Atlantic States can be produced in great plenty and perfection. The grasses are very luxuriant and nutritious, affording excellent pasturage. Oats spring up spontaneously the whole length of the coasts, and from 40 to 50 miles inland. The dry season matures and cures these grasses and oats, so that they remain in an excellent state of preservation during the summer and autumn, and afford an ample supply of forage. While the whole surface of the country appears parched, and vegetation destroyed, the numerous flocks and herds which roam over it continue in excellent condition. Irrigation would become necessary in many parts during the dry season, to improve the products of the soil and increase their quantity. The farmer derives some important advantages from this season. His crops are never injured by rain, and he can with perfect confidence permit them to remain in his fields as long after they have been cut down as his convenience may require. Agriculture, however, must continue for some time to come as of secondary consideration. Men will not submit to its toils while they can gather a harvest of gold. Commerce must supply almost every species of food, until the thirst for metal becomes satiated, or the supply exhausted.

The commercial resources of California are at the present founded entirely on its metallic wealth. Gold is the staple product of the country, and is immediately available in an uncoined state for all the purposes of exchange. It is not here as in other countries, where the products of the earth and of art are sent to markets—foreign and domestic—to be exchanged for the precious metals. Here gold not only supplies the medium of domestic trade, but is the staple of foreign commerce. A large trade has consequently sprung up, and, centering at San Francisco, is thence distributed into the interior. The whole world is competing for its market. Vessels of all nations have their prows directed to this *Dorado*. Gold is the sun that attracts them. The whole trade of the Pacific—that of China and the islands—will centre at San Francisco, for no other countries on the west coast have exports which find a market in the ports of Asia. Important as the commerce of the Pacific is and will be to California, it cannot now, nor will it ever, compare in magnitude and value to the domestic trade between it and the older States of the Union. In 1848, California did not probably contain more than 25,000 people. That portion of it which has since been so wonderfully peopled was comparatively without resources. Notwithstanding the great distance emigrants have been compelled to travel, more thaa 200,000 have already overcome the difficulties, and spread themselves over the hills and plains. They have been supplied from distances as great, not only with necessaries but the comforts and many of the luxuries of life. Houses have been imported from China, Chili, and the Atlantic States. All materials required in building cities and towns have been added to the wants of a people so numerous, destitute, and remote from the sources of supply. Those wants will exist as long as emigration continues to flow into the country, and labor, employed in collecting gold, shall be more profitable than the mechanic arts. The value of the trade between the old States and California for the year 1850, is estimated at $25,000,000; and if the emigration and general movement continues for five years longer, this trade may amount to $100,000,000 per annum.

The gold region of California is between 400 and 500 miles long, and from 40 to 50 miles wide, following the line of the Sierra Nevada. Further discoveries may, and probably will, increase the area. The metal is found in the beds of the rivers, and in the gullies formed by the action of waters during the rainy season. The original seat of this metal is in the quartz rock of the mountains, and it is there that the veins will be ultimately found. Hitherto it has been gathered chiefly from the surface, in the form of dust, but of late scientific mining operations have been initiated. What the production will eventually be, no one can foresee. The value of the metal gathered in 1849 is estimated at $40,000,000, and this only from the surface; in 1850 not less than $80,000,000 were gathered, and in 1851 the value will exceed $100,000,000. There does not seem to be any special deposits in the rivers—gold is found everywhere east of the Sacramento and San Joaquin rivers. A great part of the immense amount gathered is carried away by foreigners, and perhaps not more than two-thirds reaches the Atlantic ports. About $81,000,000 have been coined at the United States' mint up to October 1st, 1851. Quicksilver is found in the form of cinnabar in several districts, and must soon become valuable for the purpose of extracting the gold from its matrix. The mineral resources of California are not confined to these metals—coal, iron, etc., are known to exist; but these will not be worked so long as gold hunting is remunerative.

The principal towns in California previous to the occupation of the country by the Americans, and the discovery of the rich gold deposits in the valley of the Sacramento, were Monterey, the ancient capital, San Diego, a port in the south, Los Angeles, San Jose, San Francisco, etc. None of these were of much importance, nor was their connection with the commercial world otherwise than very limited. Since these great events, however, a new era has commenced, and the whole region has experienced one of the mightiest revolutions in the history of mankind. The old settlements above alluded to have become large cities—new towns have sprung up with almost fabulous rapidity—a living tide has inundated the country from all parts of the habitable globe. Wherever a site eligible for commerce or trade is found, there we now see the germ of a future city, or perhaps a city grown to considerable proportions. Every thing is progressive; and where a year or two ago the population could be numbered by thousands it now numbers its tens of thousands, and yet the tide flows, and every day witnesses new arrivals of hardy immigrants—the fathers of a future state, whose wealth and position in the world will vie with that of Tyre in the days of its greatest glory. VALLEJO, a new city, is the present capital of the State. It is here that the governor resides, and here the legislature of the state holds its sessions. SAN JOSE, the old capital, is a town founded on the ancient mission of the same name, in a pleasant valley opening on the southern extremity of the Bay of San Francisco. A railroad is proposed to be built between this town and SAN FRANCISCO, which latter is situated not far from the entrance to the bay, on its south shore, and has an excellent harbor and every accommodation for an extensive commerce. From the geographical position of this place, and its proximity to the gold regions, which must supply all the exports, it will eventually become the mart of an extensive commerce with Asia and the islands of the Pacific. Never in the annals of a nation has any city risen to importance at such a rate as this. At the commencement of 1849 it was a mere village—in 1850 it had a population of 30,000, and had during the intervening period received more than 200,000 immigrants from all parts, whose destination was the great mineral region of the valley above. Steam communication has been established between New York, *via.* Panama and the San Juan route and this city, and regular lines of steamboats sail between it and the new towns on the Sacramento. Its commerce with Oregon has also been greatly developed, and will no doubt be much enlarged in the future. Among the new cities are NAPA, SONOMA, BENICIA, etc., on the north shore of Pablo Bay, and MARTINEZ on its south shore. On the Sacramento and its tributaries, are NEW YORK *of the Pacific*, STOCKTON, SUTTER, SACRAMENTO, FREMONT, VERNON, YUBA, NICOLAUS, etc.; and on the San Joaquin, the city of SAN JOAQUIN, near the mouth of the Stanislaus river. HANGTOWN, WEAVERSVILLE, MARYSVILLE, and numerous other places are mentioned; but so rapidly are they, one and all, increasing in extent and population, that it is futile to attempt to describe their present condition—every new arrival from this wonderful country bringing information that renders the most recent previous information obselete and nugatory. Each successive day indeed witnesses the foundation of some future city. Nothing is here stationary. San Francisco in one season increased its population from hundreds to thousands, while in a shorter period Sacramento City and Stockton became the depots of an extensive inland commerce, and rose to an importance to which few cis-montane cities can boast after a whole century of existence. With such results and with comparatively small means, what great ends must we not anticipate, since the inhabitants have acquired almost every thing adapted to facilitate their labors?

The history of California previous to its occupation by the Americans has little to interest the general reader. It was discovered by Cobrillo, a Spanish navigator, in 1542; and the northern part of it having been visited by Sir Francis Drake, in 1578, he gave it the name of New Albion. The first colonies were planted in 1768, by the Spaniards—chiefly by priests of the order of St. Francis, whose object was to convert the Indians to the Catholic faith. The mission stations which are found in the country were established by this renowned order. The revolution which separated Mexico from Spain annexed California to that republic. The country has several times since the Spanish power was exterminated suffered from revolution; and for the last ten or twelve years of its connection with Mexico, the authority of that nation over it was very loose. Its distance from the metropolis indeed would tend to such a result. The people more than once declared themselves independent, and as often rejoined the confederacy. In 1846 California was occupied by the United States' forces; and by the treaty of Guadalupe Hidalgo, 2d Feb., 1848, the whole country was ceded to that government. In the latter part of the same month, a mechanic, named James W. Marshall, was employed in building a saw-mill for Captain Sutter, on the south branch of a river known as the American Fork. On Fremont's map, the river is called "Rio de los Americanos." While cutting a mill-race for this improvement, Mr. Marshall discovered the scales of gold as they glistened in the sunlight at the bottom of the sluice. Pieces of considerable size were taken out, and in a few days gold to the amount of $150 was gathered. The laborers soon became satisfied of its precious nature, and the news spread rapidly about the country. Examinations were prosecuted at other points along the stream, and almost everywhere with success. The result has been extraordinary. Thousands have flocked to the scene from all parts of the world, and a lively commerce has thus been initiated, which bids fair in a few more years to become more extensive and valuable than all the present foreign trade of the United States together. In 1849, in consequence of the disorganized condition of things and the insecurity which generally prevailed, the people, by their delegates, met in convention, and formed a constitution, under the provisions of which the commonwealth is now organized and governed. The main feature of this document is its exclusion of slavery from the state—otherwise it is not much different from those of the generality of the older states. California was admitted as a state of the Union in 1850.

THE TERRITORY OF UTAH.

UTAH, the "Deseret" of the Mormons, lies between the latitudes of 37° and 42° north, and the longitudes 106° and 120° west from Greenwich; and is bounded on the north by Oregon, on the east by the Indian Territory and New-Mexico, from which it is separated by the crest of the Rocky Mountains, on the south by New-Mexico, and on the west by California. From east to west its length is 620 miles, and its depth from north to south 345 miles—its superficies contain an area of 187,923 square miles, or 120,270,720 acres.

This territory occupies the northern portion of the great interior basin of California Alta, lying between the Sierra Nevada and the Rocky Mountains. This basin is some 500 miles diameter every way, between 4,000 and 5,000 feet above the sea-level, shut in all around by mountains, with its own system of lakes and rivers, and having no connexion whatever with the sea. Partly arid, and sparsely inhabited, its general character is that of a desert, but with great exceptions, there being many parts of it very fit for the residence of a civilized people, and of these parts the Mormons have lately established themselves in some of the largest and best. Mountain is the predominating structure of the interior of the basin, with plains between—the mountains wooded and watered, the plains arid and sterile. The interior mountains range nearly north and south, in line with the Sierra Nevada and Rocky Mountains, and present a very uniform character of abruptness, rising suddenly from a narrow base of from ten to twenty miles, and attaining an elevation of two to five thousand feet above the level country. They are grassy and wooded, showing snow on their summit peaks, and affording small streams of water, which lose themselves, some in lakes, some in the dry plains, and some in the belt of alluvial soil at their bases. Between these mountains are the arid plains which receive and deserve the name of desert. The whole region is more Asiatic than American in its character, and much resembles the elevated country between the Caspian Sea and northern Persia. The rim of the basin is massive ranges of mountain, of which the Sierra Nevada on the west, and the Wah-satch and Timpanogos chains on the east, are the most conspicuous. On the north it is separated from the waters of the Columbia by a branch of the Rocky Mountains, and from the Gulf of California on the south by a bed of mountain ranges, the existence of which has only recently been determined. Snow abounds on them all, and benches of good alluvion, the wash and abrasion of their sides, are usually found at their bases.

The Great Salt Lake and the Utah Lake are in this basin, towards its eastern rim, and constitute its most interesting feature—one a saturated solution of common salt, and the other a fresh water lake. Lake Utah is about 100 feet above the level of the Salt Lake, which is itself 4,200 feet above the sea level, the two being connected by a strait about 35 miles in length. These lakes drain an area of 12,000 square miles, and have on the east, along the base of the mountains, the usual bench of alluvion, which extends to a distance of 300 miles. Utah Lake is 35 miles long, and remarkable for the numerous and bold streams which it receives from the mountains on the south-east. It abounds with trout and other fish, which constitute the food of the Indians during the fishing season. The Great Salt Lake has a very irregular outline, and is about 70 miles in length. The shores of the lake in the dry season are whitened with incrustations of salt, and every thing within reach is covered with crystallizations. No fish or animal life is found in it. Five gallons of water evaporated by Fremont in September, gave 14 pints of salt, and a part, on being analyzed, afforded 97.8 per cent. of chloride of sodium, and 2.2 per cent. of the chlorides of calcium and magnesium, and sulphate of soda and lime. Southward of Utah are other lakes, but of these little is known beyond their position.

The most considerable river of the basin is that named Humboldt's River. It is a very peculiar stream, and has many of the characteristics of the Jordan, although twice as long—rising in mountains, and losing itself in a lake of its own, after a long and solitary course. It rises in two streams from the mountains west of the Great Salt Lake, which unite after some 50 miles, and bears westwardly along the northern side of the basin towards the great Sierra Nevada, which it is destined never to reach, much less to pass—it loses itself by absorption and evaporation as it goes, and terminates in a marshy lake with low shores, fringed with bulrushes, and whitened by saline incrustations. The country through which it passes (except its immediate valley) is a dry, sandy plain, from 4,700 feet (at the forks) to 4,200 feet (at the lake) above the level of the sea, and varying from a few miles to 20 miles in breadth, being bounded by broken ranges of mountain. Its own immediate valley is rich alluvion, covered with nutritious grasses, and the course of the river through the plain is marked by a line of willows and cottonwood trees. This river is on the best travel route from the Mormon settlements at the lake to California. Its termination is within 50 miles of the base of the Sierra Nevada, and opposite the Salmon Trout River pass—a pass only 7,200 feet above the level of the sea, and less than half that amount above the level of the basin, and leading into the valley of the Sacramento.

The other principal rivers in the basin are found on its circumference, collecting their waters from the snow-clad mountains which surround it, and are—*first*, Bear River, rising in the massive ridge of the Timpanogos mountains, and falling into the Great Salt Lake, after a doubling course through a fertile and picturesque valley 200 miles long; *second*, Utah River and Timpanogos River, discharging themselves into Utah Lake after gathering their copious streams in the adjoining parts of the Wah-satch and Timpanogos mountains; *third*, the Nicollet River, rising south in the long range of the Wah-satch mountains, and falling into a lake of its own name after making an arable and grassy valley 200 miles in length through a mountainous country, and *fourth*, Salmon Trout River, which falls into Pyramid Lake. Carson and Walker's Rivers and Owen's River, issuing from the Sierra Nevada, are bold rivers of considerable length, and are lost in lakes beyond the base of the mountains. Besides these principal rivers issuing from the mountains, there are many others all around, all obeying the general law of losing themselves in sands or lakes or belts of alluvion, and almost all of them indices to some arable land with grass and wood.

The mountain ranges of this remarkable country are thinly covered with some varieties of pine, cedar, aspen, and a few other trees, and afford an excellent quality of bunch grass equal to any in the Rocky Mountains. Black-tailed deer and mountain sheep are frequent in these solitudes. The plains, unlike the hilly country, are sterile—no wood, no water, no grass—the artemisia the prevailing herb; nor do they support animals, except hares, which shelter in these gloomy shrubs, and the fleet and timid antelope. No birds are seen on the plains and few on the mountains. Even the Indian is here degenerate, and what few roam over them exist in the lowest state of human degradation. On the margins of the lakes their condition is more elevated, and living in small tribes, they have attained something of the human attribute.

The climate of the Great Basin does not present the rigorous winter due its elevation and mountain structure. The temperature is little inferior to that incident to the latitude, and the warm summer is scarcely expended before the beginning of November. In the valleys the greatest mildness prevails the whole year, and it is not unfrequent that two crops are housed during the summer. In fact there is nothing in the climate of this great interior region, elevated as it is, and surrounded and traversed by snowy mountains, to prevent civilized man from making it his home and finding in its arable portions the means of a comfortable subsistence, and this the Mormons of the valleys have infallibly proved.

The country above delineated is one new to civilization—it is yet almost an unknown desert, and though inhabited in some parts, and having been traversed annually by the California emigration, it will require extensive explorations before its true character can be ascertained, and what has been told of it must then necessarily demand the qualification of great exceptions. It is not presumed, however, that its general characteristics are falsely, although imperfectly depictured, yet it is probable that further investigations may result in modifying all our preconceptions, and changing the whole current of its destiny. Humboldt gave us the first glance of its physical organization; Fremont gave us the first details, and the Mormons, who are colonizing in its fertile valleys, are constantly adding to our knowledge of its remarkable physiognomy, and yet it is so little known. The position of the country, however, is as interesting as its formation. It lies between two seats of civilization, and forms between them the only means of communication by land. Through this country will be formed a great highway, and before the lapse of many years the steam-horse will be ploughing through the mountains and awaking their echoes with its sonorous breath, and along with this will come the rapid settlement of all its habitable parts. Already even, in anticipation of such a result, the pioneer is abroad, and the hand of industry is preparing for the coming event, to the successful issue of which the Mormons have done and are doing a mighty work, and their history will ever be closely identified with the progress of civilization in these parts.

A census of the country was taken in 1850, but hitherto the marshals have failed to make returns to the appropriate office, and hence the results are not made public. It is presumed that the population is about 12,000.

This portion of California Alta was never settled by the Spaniards, nor was it ever more than a nominal dependency of that nation, nor of the Mexican Republic. Previous to the Mexican war, indeed, few white men, except those engaged in scientific explorations, had entered the country. About the period when that war broke out, the Mormons were driven from their city of Nauvoo, in Illinois, by mob violence, and shortly afterwards emigrated to the borders of the Great Salt Lake. Their settlements soon became prosperous and populous, and within the four years after the first pioneers had entered the country their numbers had increased to about 12,000. The ratification of the treaty of Guadalupe Hidalgo, by which the United States became possessed of the country, found them without the pale of the Mexican law, and as yet the laws of the United States had not been extended over the new acquisitions, and they were virtually without government and without protection for person and property. In this anomalous condition of affairs, and in the exercise of an inherent political right, they established for themselves a form of government suited to their immediate wants. The constitution of the "State of Deseret," for so they styled the new nationality, was similar in its general aspects to the constitutions of the other states of the Union; it recognized a Governor, a Legislature and Judiciary, and gave the suffrage to all citizens of a proper age. In its provisions it was essentially liberal and contained no sectarian prohibitions. The destiny of the country, however, was to be decided by Congress: and in virtue of its authority, that body passed an act defining and organizing the "Territory of Utah," which received the President's approval on the 9th September, 1850. It has since been carried into effect.

The government as organized under the above-named act, and which is the same as that applied to the Territory of New-Mexico, secured to every free white male inhabitant, above the age of 21 years, who was a resident of the territory at the time of the passage of said act, the right to vote and of eligibility for any elective office at the first election, but the qualifications at all subsequent elections are to be prescribed by the Territorial Legislature.

The Legislative Assembly consists of a Council and House of Representatives. The Council consists of 13 members, elected for two years, and the House of Representatives, of 26 members, elected for one year. The apportionment of Councillors and Representatives is based on population. All laws passed by the Legislature are to be submitted to Congress, and if not approved, will be of no effect.

The Governor is the chief executive officer, and is appointed by the President for four years, and until his successor is qualified. He must reside within the Territory, is *ex-officio* Superintendent of Indian Affairs, may pardon offences against the Territorial laws, and grant reprieves to offenders against the laws of the United States, and he appoints to all offices created by the Territorial Legislature. A Secretary of State is appointed in like manner, and in the absence or disability of the Governor this officer acts in his stead.

The Judiciary is vested in a Supreme Court, District Courts, Probate Courts, and in Justices of the Peace; the justices are appointed by the President, and have in general the same extent of jurisdiction as like courts in the District of Columbia. The township and county officers are appointed or elected as the Legislature may provide.

A Delegate to Congress is elected by a plurality of all qualified voters.

The same act appropriates $20,000 to the erection of public buildings, and $5,000 for the establishment of a library.

The metropolis of the Territory is Great Salt Lake City, situated 22 miles south-west of the lake from which it takes its name, and about one mile and a half east of the Jordan River, 4,300 feet above the level of the sea, and in 40° 45′ 44″ north latitude, and 111° 26′ 34″ west longitude. It is laid out in large squares, and one acre and a quarter of land is allotted to each family for garden purposes. A council house has been erected; and the citizens have it in view to build another temple, larger and more magnificent even than that of Nauvoo. The houses are as yet small, but very commodiously built, the material being adobes, or sun-dried brick. The population of the city is about 6,000, but it is so laid out as to admit of its becoming one of the largest and most convenient cities in the world. Being on the highway to California, thousands of emigrants from the states find in this settlement a place to rest themselves and cattle, and recruit their stores of provisions, previous to entering the desert they have to cross before reaching the goal of their desires. Some settlements of Mormons have also been made on the borders of Utah Lake.

The prospects of these settlements are very encouraging. They are on all sides surrounded by a labyrinth of mountains, which are supposed to be very rich in mineral wealth. Rock salt is very abundant in the neighborhood, and the Great Lake is saturated with salines, which concrete spontaneously on its shores and incrust its bottom. Otherwise they are possessed of vast resources. The soil is exceedingly rich, and when irrigated, which is of easy accomplishment, yields fine crops of grain and other agricultural staples. Add to these natural advantages the industry to appropriate them, which is a portion of the religion of the settlers, and what shall stay the onward progress of this colony, the location of which within a few years was scarcely known to civilized man?

TERRITORY OF NEW-MEXICO.

NEW-MEXICO, as now established, consists of the country which has from time immemorial been known as such, and the southern half of the great interior desert of Alta California, which is temporarily attached to it. It is bounded north by the parallel 38° latitude north, as far west as the Rocky Mountains, and from thence to the California line by 37° latitude north; west by the eastern line of California; south by the Rio Gila, and the 32d parallel, and east by the 103d meridian west from Greenwich. In its greatest length it is 720 miles, and in its greatest breadth 417 miles; and its surface has an area of 210,744 square miles, or 134,876,160 acres.

New-Mexico west of the Rocky Mountains.—This portion of the Territory lies principally in the great California basin, which has been fully described under the head of "Utah Territory." Outside the basin and towards the Rio Gila, the country is generally hilly and broken, and along the whole line of that river there are but few spots susceptible of agricultural improvement. As yet, however, little whatever is known of the country, and hence it seems most proper to forego a further consideration of it in this connexion. It has no stationary population.

New-Mexico Proper.—The general aspect of this portion of the country is mountainous, with a large valley in the middle, running north and south, formed by the Rio Grande del Norte. This is generally about 20 miles wide and bordered on the east and west by mountain chains—continuations of the Rocky Mountains. The height of these south of Santa Fé, may, upon an average, be from 6,000 to 8,000 feet, while near that city and further north, some snow-capped peaks are seen which rise from 10,000 to 12,000 feet above the sea-level. The mountains are chiefly composed of igneous rocks, as granite, sienite, diorite, basalt, etc., and are highly metalliferous. On the higher ranges excellent pine timber grows; on the lower, cedars and sometimes oaks, and in the central valley, mesquite, etc.

The main artery of this country, the Rio Grande, is a large and long river. Its head waters are found between 37° and 38° latitude north, in the recesses of the Rocky Mountains. Its course is generally south and south-east; and its principal affluents are the Chames, Pecos, Conchos, Salado, Alamo, and San Juan. The length of the river in a straight line is about 1,200 miles; but from the meanderings of its lower course it runs at least 2,000 miles—from the regions of eternal snows to the almost tropical climate of the Gulf of Mexico, which it enters in 25° 50′ latitude north. The elevation of the river above the sea is 4,800 feet at Albuquerque; 3,800 at El Paso; but at Reinosa, 300 or 400 miles from its mouth, only 170 feet. The fall of the river is seldom used as a motive power. The principal advantage at present derived from its waters is for agriculture, by a well managed system of irrigation. In its upper course it is shallow and interrupted by banques and sand bars. The lower course of the river, however, is open to navigation, and steamboats ascend up it as far as Laredo, 700 miles from the Gulf.

The climate of New-Mexico is generally temperate, constant, and salubrious. Considerable atmospheric differences, however, are experienced in the mountain districts and in the low valleys of the rivers. In the latter it is often confined and sultry, and the summer heat frequently rises to 100° Fahr., but the nights are always cool and pleasant. The winters are comparatively of long duration, and in the mountains severe. Owing, however, to the condensation of the moisture on the frozen hills, the sky is always clear and dry. The months of July and October inclusive, constitute the rainy season; but the rains are neither so heavy nor so regular in their annual returns as on the more equatorial parts of the continent. Disease is little known, except some inflammations and typhoid fevers, which prevail during the winter, and the general salubrity of the climate is substantiated by numerous cases of longevity. According to the census of 1850, there were in the territory 314 persons between 80 and 90 years of age; 90 persons between 90 and 100, and 40 persons over 100. Of those over 100, one was 103, one 106, two 110, and one 130—the last was Candelario Agular, a farmer in Valencia county.

The mineral resources of New-Mexico are various and very extensive. Gold, silver, iron, and copper abound. Gold is found in the Santa Fé district as far south as Gran Quivira, and north as far as the Rio Sangre de Cristo. Mining, however, has been long neglected, and many of the *placeros*, which were formerly worked, have been entirely deserted. The mines in the neighborhood of Santa Fé are the only ones worked at the present time, but gold has ever been collected from the mountain streams, and many poor persons are still engaged in such occupation. Silver mines were worked by the Spaniards at Avo, at Cerillos, and in the Nambé Mountains. Copper is abundant throughout the country, and iron is equally so. Coal has also been discovered in a number of places; and gypsum, both common and selenite, are found in large deposits—the common is used as lime for white-washing, and the crystalline or selenite instead of window glass. On the high table lands between the Del Norte and Pecos Rivers are some extensive *salinas* or salt lakes, from which all the domestic salt used in the country is procured.

The celebrated copper mines near the head waters of the Rio Gila, are thus described by Mr. Theo. F. Morse, geologist of the Boundary Commission on the part of the United States. "These mines," he says, "situated near 108° longitude west, and 32° 40′ latitude north, in the western extremity of the Sierra de Mogovon, from the most authentic resources, are said to have been long known to the Apache Indians, but were first worked by the Spaniards about the commencement of the present century, with various success, till 1828, when they fell into the hands of Mons. Coursier, and were managed by McKnight, who was also a partner; but were at last abandoned, about 1837, on account of the hostility of the Indians, who cut off the provision trains and killed some of the herders. At one time as many as 500 men were engaged in the mines, which are said to have yielded abundantly, and made the fortune of the proprietors. The ground, in a small extent, is riddled over with shafts and huge excavations.

"The ore is a red oxide of copper, with native copper disseminated through it, occurring in nests and seams through a decomposed feldspathic porphyry, which rock or gangue is, from its softness, easily worked with the pick, and needs no blasting, thus essentially reducing the cost of mining. From the purity and easy reduction of the ore, the expense of producing the metal by the smelting operation was small and easily effected, in a very rude furnace, the cinders of which contain a great deal of reduced copper. At the time the mine was worked, the State of Chihuahua was coining a great deal of copper currency, for which they paid a high price, and for which purpose the copper from this ore, from its purity, was admirably suited, and supplied the mint. An erroneous impression exists that the gold, said to be contained in the copper, paid for its transportation to the city of Mexico, which, however, is not the case, as the gold is not separated from the copper in that city. On examination of some copper found about the furnace, I was unable to detect a trace of gold.

"The mines are very much fallen in, and some of the works, said to be the richest deposits, are entirely inaccessible. But at the English price of copper ore, many thousands of dollars' worth are lying in heaps about the premises, and the old slags and scoria would richly repay the labor of re-working. I think, however, at the high price of provisions and labor, the mines, rich as they seem to be, would not yield much profit. When some of the fertile valleys in the neighborhood are cultivated, labor and provisions will be cheaper.

"Within half a mile of the Presidio are several large hills of magnetic iron ore, similar to the Pilot Knob and Iron Mountain of Missouri. This ore could be, at a small cost, converted into bar-iron, heated in a Catlin forge, the hills abounding in timber fit for fuel.

"About four miles south-west of the mine of copper, formerly were worked some gold mines, which are said to have yielded well, but which were never extensively worked, on account of the Indians. Some of the old shafts have been recently opened by some Americans, who are said to be making an ounce per diem. The gold occurs in scales and plates, in a quartz vein, which very much resembles the auriferous quartz of Georgia. Parallel with the gold vein is a vein of sulphuret of lead (galena), which, on reducing to lead, I found to contain sixteen ounces to the cwt., which is considered a rich ore.

"When the command under Brevet Lieutenant-Colonel Craig arrived here in January last, there were then standing the ruins of about sixty adobe houses, including a triangular Presidio, flanked with round towers. This has been repaired by Colonel Craig, as a barrack for his men, and the best of the remaining houses have been repaired for the officers and men of the U. S. Mexican Boundary Commission, who have established here their headquarters; the material of the more dilapidated houses having been used for rebuilding the latter. The place now bears quite an active appearance—trains are arriving and departing frequently, and the hum of voices is now heard where a few months ago none but the Apache roamed. Should a permanent post be established here, and protection thus afforded to the miner and agriculturist, this region of country will attract many from the states of Sonora and Chihuahua, as well as Americans. Never-failing springs are found among the hills, which are thickly timbered with scrub-oak, walnut, cedar, and lofty pines, fit for fuel and building purposes. The valley of the Miembres, which, at its nearest point, is seven miles distant, contains many acres of land which could be irrigated by that river. In the immediate vicinity of the mines are small patches capable of irrigation, fit for garden spots."

The soil of New-Mexico is generally sandy and looks poor, but by irrigation it produces abundant crops. Indian corn, wheat, beans, onions, and fruits are raised in large quantities, and the grape-vine is largely cultivated, producing wines of excellent quality. The most fertile part of the valley begins below Santa Fé, and it is no uncommon occurrence in the southern districts to raise two crops in the year. The general dryness of the climate and aridity of the soil, however, will always confine agriculture to the valleys of the water courses. The inhabitants have no system in their farming —the plough is a rough machine and made entirely of wood, and the fields are generally without fences. The best cultivated lands are those of the *estancias* or large estates; these are apparently a remnant of the old feudal system, and were granted, with the Indians and all other appurtenances, by the Spanish monarch to favorite vassals. The inhabitants pay considerable attention to cattle-raising, and are possessed of large flocks and herds. In 1850 the live stock of New-Mexico, in the several counties, consisted of:

COUNTIES.	Horses.	Asses and Mules.	Milch Cows.	Working Oxen.	Other Cattle.	Sheep.	Swine.	Total Val. of Live Stock.
Ariba	940	1,800	814	1,743	1,951	52,993	1,585	$266,586
Valencia	1,026	973	4,990	3,351	1,684	62,879	1,482	312,795
Bernalilla	568	1,937	787	1,633	1,928	123,046	880	312,066
Santa Anna	785	777	189	817	1,741	32,075	328	109,100
Taos	1,002	1,219	738	2,055	1,182	23,685	1,438	170,075
Santa Fé	332	1,161	757	1,117	1,281	23,766	329	127,707
San Miguel	433	681	2,351	1,433	319	26,726	381	206,169
Total	5,086	8,548	10,626	12,149	10,086	345,170	6,423	1,504,497

These, however, are generally of small size. The pasturage is extensive in the wild country, and thousands of stock graze thereon the year round. The Indians prove the greatest enemies to the farmers, and frequently carry off whole herds.

Previously to the taking of the census of 1850, the population of New-Mexico was variously computed at from 60,000 to 90,000. At that period it was ascertained to be 61,505, or one person to every 3.4 square miles of the whole territory; and the distribution of the inhabitants to the several counties was in the following proportions:

COUNTIES.	White Persons.	Colored Persons.	Total Popula.
Bernalillo	7,749	2	7,751
Rio Ariba	10,667	1	10,668
Santa Anna	4,644	1	4,645
Santa Fé	7,704	9	7,713
San Miguel	7,070	4	7,074
Taos	9,507	—	9,507
Valencia	14,147	—	14,147
Total	61,488	17	61,505

CLASSES AND SEXES OF POPULATION.

Classes.	Males.	Females.	Total.
White persons	31,706	29,782	61,488
Colored " —free	14	3	17
" " —slave	—	—	—
Total	31,720	29,785	61,505

Of the white persons above accounted for, the proximate composition is—Spaniards about 2,600, creoles about 10,000, mixed (Indian and Spaniard) about 13,000, Puebla Indians about 27,000, and the residue Americans and other foreigners.

The above enumeration is exclusive of the independent tribes of Indians which exist in the territory. The Navajos are a powerful tribe inhabiting a fine country west of the Rio Grande, and number about 7,000; the Eutaws inhabit the north-west frontier, and number 4,000 or 5,000; the Apaches about 5,000, roam over the vast regions east of the Rio Grande and north of El Paso; the Jicorilles, a branch of the Apache family, 500 in number, are neighbors of the Eutaws, etc. To these must be added large parties of Camanches, Arrapahos, and Cheyennes, perhaps 36,000 in number, which infest the borders of the north and east, and lay the unwary traveller under contribution—frequently committing the foulest murders, or carrying off the women and children into captivity. Numerous tribes are also found in the vast territory west of the mountains.

The social and industrial statistics of New-Mexico, as exhibited in the census, are as follows: number of dwellings 13,453, and of families 13,502, or about 4.5 persons to each dwelling and family; and the number of deaths in 1849–50 was 1,157, or one in every 53.2 inhabitants. There were at the same period 3,750 farms under cultivation, and 20 productive establishments, the annual products of which were valued at $500 and upwards.

The constitution of society in New-Mexico is similar, in most respects, to that of all Indo-Spanish countries. While the rich conform to the dictates of modern fashion, the mass of the people adhere to the manners and customs of former times. The men retain their *serapes*, or colored blankets, and wide trousers, trimmed with glittering buttons; and the ladies, of all classes, their *rebozo*, or small shawl, drawn over their heads, which gives them so coquettish an appearance. Both sexes enjoy their *cigarittos*, their *siesta*, and their evening amusement at *monte* or *fandango*. Their dances are very graceful, and combine the quadrille and waltz. The prominent ingredient in the Mexican race is their Indian blood—it is visible in their features, complexion, and in all their acts and disposals. The men are ill-featured, but the women are graceful and winning. The differences in the sexes are nowhere more observable. The men are lazy, mendacious, treacherous, and cruel, while the women are affectionate, open-hearted, and active. Education is by no means common, but there is a strong common sense, and natural aptness in the people, which are frequently of more practical use than the most refined book-learning, especially in a country so circumstanced as this. Many of the evils of this condition of New-Mexican society will, no doubt, be eradicated by the contact of civilization, and education will become an indispensable requisite in order to keep up with the progress of commerce, and the influx of an educated population from the east.

New-Mexico, previous to the late war, was a state of the Mexican Re-

22

public, and its rulers consisted of a governor and legislature (*junta departmental*); but as the latter was more an imaginary than a real power, the governor was, in fact, despotic, and subject only to the laws of revolution, which, in this state, were very freely administered by upsetting the gubernatorial chair as often as the republic did the presidential. Well knowing the favors of fortune were at all times precarious, the governors have, in general, during their terms of office, plundered the treasury and provided against contingencies. The people, credulous and easily deceived, had to submit to every outrage, and should one more courageous than his fellows assert the profligacy of the government, his doom was as certain as speedy. Thus has New-Mexico dragged on its existence—the sport of despots and the foot-ball of fortune. The judiciary was as dependent as the executive was independent, and all law succumbed to the dictates of one man. Besides these, the clergy, as well as the military classes, had their own courts of justice. In relation to the confederacy, however, New-Mexico always maintained greater independence than any other of the states—partly from its distance from the capital, but more from the spirit of opposition in the people, who derived no advantage from the connection, and suffered much from its taxation without an equivalent protection. The supreme government never succeeded here in imposing upon the people the *estranquillas*, or monopoly of the sale of tobacco, and New-Mexico was free from some other enormities. In the same way the people resisted the introduction of copper coin. This loose connection with the central power will aid much in the assimilation of the people with the emigrants from the United States, provided the government of the latter will bestow upon them—what the former could not—stability, safety, protection, and those just rights which are enjoyed by all persons under the ægis of American principles.

The present form of government is such as that generally applied to territories of the United States. All citizens of proper age are voters, and elect councillors and representatives, who together form the legislature. The governor and judges are appointed by the president with the consent of the senate. (See Utah, *antea*.)

The principal city of New-Mexico is Santa Fe, one of the oldest Spanish settlements. Its elevation above the sea is 7,047 feet. Santa Fé is about 20 miles east, in a direct line, from Rio del Norte, and lies in a wide plain, surrounded by lofty mountains. A small creek, rising in the hills, and flowing past the city, supplies it with water. The land around is sandy, poor, and destitute of timber; but the mountains are covered with pine and cedar. No pasturage is observed about the settlements, and as a consequence stock is driven to the mountains. The climate is delightful and free from extremes. The sky is clear and cloudless, and the atmosphere dry. The houses are built of *adobes*, but one story high, with flat roofs. The streets are narrow and irregular. The *plazza* is spacious, and one side is occupied by the official residence of the executive. The palace is, without being extraordinarily grand, a good building, and exhibits two curiosities, viz., windows of glass and *festoons of Indian ears*. Among the public buildings there are two churches with steeples, but of an ordinary construction. There are 30 or 40 stores in the city, principally kept by Americans. The inhabitants, excepting the Americans, are Spaniards and Indians, and the castes sprung from an indefinite amalgamation of the two races. Society is in a deplorable condition. They spend their time in card-playing, drinking, smoking, and at fandangoes. They are expert thieves, and live in a miserable state of ignorance, superstition, dirt, and poverty.

The city proper contains 4,000 or 5,000 souls, and as many more are settled within its jurisdiction. Santa Fé is the depôt of a considerable commerce, carried on between Northern Mexico and the Western States, and is generally visited by the overland emigrants to California.

There are a number of other towns along the course of the Rio Grande, chiefly inhabited by Indians. These are styled *Pueblos*, and the inhabitants *Pueblo Indians*, to distinguish them from the same races that infest the open country. The principal are Taos, Canada, San Miguel, Paso del Norte, etc. None of these, however, demand more than a passing notice.

New-Mexico became known to the Spaniards about the year 1581, and formal possession was taken of the country in 1598. Christianity and slavery were early and simultaneously introduced among the Indians, and conversion and personal service enforced by the sword. The converted Indians were made to live in villages, and were distinguished from the roving bands by the title of *Pueblos.* Many towns, of which only the ruins now remain, were established at that time. Many mines were worked, and the occupation of the country seemed to be secured, when, quite unexpectedly, in 1680, a general insurrection of all the Indian tribes broke out against the Spanish yoke. The Spaniards were either massacred or driven southward, where they founded Paso del Norte. The country was not recovered for 10 or 12 years. Several insurrections have since occurred, but none so universal or disastrous as this one. The deep rancor of the Indian, however, bequeathed from sire to son for successive generations, still animates the race, and is often displayed in the most bloody and cruel outbreaks. This country followed the fate of Mexico after the revolution that overthrew the Spanish power, and since that period has been silently degenerating. The history of New-Mexico previous to the invasion of the Americans, has little to arrest attention. It is a continuous record of barbarism and tyranny. On the 8th of September, 1846, Santa Fé was captured by the Americans under General Kearney, and soon after several of the river towns were visited on his route to California. A civil government was now established. On the 19th of January, 1847, an insurrection broke out against the Americans, and in several pueblos many Americans were murdered; among whom was Governor Bent and Sheriff Lee. Taos, Arroya-Hondo, and Rio Colorado were the chief scenes of strife. The battles of La Canada and El Embudo also occurred in this month, and in February the battle of Taos; in all of which the Mexicans were completely vanquished. Some few skirmishes occurred after these, but none of importance. From this period the United States authorities exercised exclusive power. On the 2d of February, 1848, a treaty of peace and cession was signed at Guadalupe Hidalgo, by which New-Mexico was assigned to the Union. On the 9th of September, 1850, the country within its present limits, was erected into a Territory, the claim of Texas to the east bank of the Rio Grande having been adjusted.

STATISTICAL RECAPITULATION.

I.—STATISTICS OF POPULATION.

1.—PROGRESSIVE MOVEMENT OF POPULATION FROM 1790 TO 1850.

STATES.	Census, 1790.	Census, 1800.	Census, 1810.	Census, 1820.	Census, 1830.	Census, 1840.	Census, 1850.
New England States.							
Maine	96,540	151,719	228,705	298,335	399,455	501,793	583,188
New Hampshire	141,899	183,762	214,360	244,161	269,328	284,574	317,964
Vermont	85,416	154,465	217,713	235,764	280,652	291,948	313,611
Massachusetts	378,717	423,245	472,040	523,287	610,408	737,699	994,499
Rhode Island	69,110	69,122	77,031	83,059	97,199	108,830	147,544
Connecticut	238,141	251,002	262,042	275,202	297,675	309,978	370,791
Total	1,009,823	1,233,315	1,471,891	1,659,808	1,954,717	2,234,822	2,727,597
Middle Atlantic States.							
New York	340,120	586,756	959,049	1,372,812	1,913,006	2,428,921	3,097,394
New Jersey	184,139	211,949	245,555	277,575	320,823	373,306	489,555
Pennsylvania	434,373	602,365	810,091	1,049,458	1,348,233	1,724,033	2,311,786
Delaware	59,096	64,273	72,674	72,749	76,748	78,085	91,535
Maryland	319,728	341,548	380,546	407,350	447,040	470,019	583,035
Total	1,337,456	1,806,891	2,467,915	3,179,944	4,105,850	5,074,364	6,573,305
Southern Atlantic States							
Virginia	748,308	880,200	974,622	1,065,379	1,211,405	1,239,797	1,421,661
North Carolina	393,751	478,103	555,500	638,829	737,987	753,419	868,903
South Carolina	249,073	345,591	415,115	502,741	581,185	594,398	668,507
Georgia	82,548	162,101	252,433	340,987	516,823	691,392	905,999
Florida	—	—	—	—	34,730	54,477	87,401
Total	1,473,680	1,865,995	2,197,670	2,547,936	3,082,130	3,333,483	3,952,471

Western States.							
Ohio	—	45,365	230,760	581,434	937,903	1,519,467	1,980,408
Indiana	—	4,875	24,520	147,178	343,031	685,866	988,416
Illinois	—	—	12,282	55,211	157,445	476,183	851,470
Michigan	—	—	4,762	8,896	31,639	212,267	397,654
Wisconsin	—	—	—	—	—	30,945	305,191
Kentucky	73,077	220,955	406,511	564,317	687,917	779,828	982,405
Missouri	—	—	20,845	66,586	140,455	383,702	682,043
Iowa	—	—	—	—	—	43,112	192,214
Total	73,077	271,195	699,680	1,423,622	2,298,390	4,131,370	6,379,801
South-Western States.							
Tennessee	35,791	105,602	261,727	422,813	681,904	829,210	1,002,625
Alabama	—	—	—	127,901	309,527	590,756	771,671
Mississippi	—	8,850	40,352	75,448	136,621	375,651	606,555
Louisiana	—	—	76,556	153,407	215,529	352,411	511,974
Arkansas	—	—	—	14,273	30,388	97,574	209,639
Texas	—	—	—	—	—	—	212,592
Total	35,791	114,452	378,635	793,842	1,373,969	2,245,602	3,315,056
California	—	—	—	—	—	—	188,981
Organized Territories.							
Minesota	—	—	—	—	—	—	6,077
Oregon	—	—	—	—	—	—	13,293
Utah	—	—	—	—	—	—	18,792
New Mexico	—	—	—	—	—	—	61,505
Total	—	—	—	—	—	—	99,667
District of Columbia	—	14,093	24,023	33,039	39,834	43,712	51,687
Grand total	3,929,827	5,305,941	7,239,814	9,638,191	12,866,020*	17,069,453*	23,288,565
Decennial increase—numerical	—	1,376,114	1,933,873	2,398,377	3,227,829	4,203,433	6,219,112
" " per cent.	—	35.02	36.50	33.35	33.92	32.67	36.43

* Including seamen, soldiers, aliens, etc., not otherwise accounted for—in 1830, 11,130; and in 1840, 6,100.

2.—POPULATION CLASSIFIED IN RELATION TO CASTE AND SEX—Census of 1850.

STATES.	WHITE PERSONS.			COLORED PERSONS.					Total Population.
				FREE.			SLAVES.	TOTAL.	
	Males.	Females.	Total.	Males.	Females.	Total.			
New England States.									
Maine	296,635	285,228	581,863	705	620	1,325	—	1,325	583,188
New Hampshire	155,902	161,587	317,489	243	232	475	—	475	317,964
Vermont	159,374	153,528	312,902	366	343	709	—	709	313,611
Massachusetts	484,284	501,420	985,704	4,314	4,481	8,795	—	8,795	994,499
Rhode Island	70,417	73,583	144,000	1,660	1,884	3,544	—	3,544	147,544
Connecticut	180,001	183,304	363,305	3,749	3,737	7,486	—	7,486	370,791
Total	1,346,613	1,358,650	2,705,263	11,037	11,297	22,334	—	22,334	2,727,597
Middle Atlantic States.									
New York	1,545,052	1,504,405	3,049,457	22,978	24,959	47,937	—	47,937	3,097,394
New Jersey	233,746	232,494	466,240	11,542	11,551	23,093	222	23,315	489,555
Pennsylvania	1,142,863	1,115,600	2,258,463	25,057	28,266	53,323	—	53,323	2,311,786
Delaware	35,771	35,518	71,289	8,989	8,968	17,957	2,289	20,246	91,535
Maryland	211,495	207,095	418,590	34,914	39,163	74,077	90,368	164,445	583,035
Total	3,168,927	3,095,112	6,264,039	103,480	112,907	216,387	92,879	309,266	6,573,305
Southern Atlantic States.									
Virginia	451,552	443,752	895,304	25,843	27,986	53,829	472,528	526,357	1,421,661
North Carolina	272,789	280,506	553,295	13,226	13,970	27,196	288,412	315,608	868,903
South Carolina	137,773	136,850	274,623	4,110	4,790	8,900	384,984	393,884	668,507
Georgia	266,096	255,342	521,438	1,368	1,512	2,880	381,681	384,561	905,999
Florida	25,674	21,493	47,167	420	505	925	39,309	40,234	87,401
Total	1,153,884	1,137,943	2,291,827	44,967	48,763	93,730	1,566,914	1,660,644	3,952,471
Western States.									
Ohio	1,004,111	951,997	1,956,108	12,239	12,061	24,300	—	24,300	1,980,408
Indiana	506,408	471,220	977,628	5,472	5,316	10,788	—	10,788	988,416

Illinois	445,644	400,460	846,104	2,756	2,610	5,366	—	5,366	851,470
Michigan	208,471	186,626	395,097	1,412	1,145	2,557	—	2,557	397,654
Wisconsin	164,221	140,344	304,565	365	261	626	—	626	305,191
Kentucky	392,840	368,848	761,688	4,771	4,965	9,736	210,981	220,717	982,405
Missouri	312,986	279,091	592,077	1,338	1,206	2,544	87,422	89,966	682,043
Iowa	100,885	90,994	191,879	168	167	335	—	335	192,214
Total	2,135,506	2,889,640	5,025,146	27,521	27,731	56,252	298,403	354,655	6,379,801
South-Western States.									
Tennessee	382,270	374,623	756,893	3,072	3,199	6,271	239,461	245,732	1,002,625
Alabama	219,728	206,779	426,507	1,047	1,225	2,272	342,892	345,164	771,671
Mississippi	156,260	139,498	295,758	473	426	899	309,898	310,797	606,555
Louisiana	141,059	114,357	255,416	7,598	9,939	17,537	239,021	256,558	511,974
Arkansas	85,699	76,369	162,068	318	271	589	46,982	47,571	209,639
Texas	84,863	69,237	154,100	171	160	331	58,161	58,492	212,592
Total	1,069,879	980,863	2,050,742	12,679	15,220	27,899	1,236,415	1,264,314	3,315,056
California	—	—	188,000	—	—	981	—	981	188,981
Organized Territories.									
Minesota	3,695	2,343	6,038	21	18	39	—	39	6,077
Oregon	8,142	4,945	13,087	119	87	206	—	206	13,293
Utah	—	—	11,381	—	—	—	—	—	11,381
New Mexico	31,706	29,782	61,488	14	3	17	—	17	61,505
Total	43,543	37,070	99,405	154	108	262	—	262	99,667
District of Columbia	18,548	19,476	38,027	4,210	5,763	9,973	3,687	13,660	51,687
Grand total	—	—	19,662,448	—	—	427,819	3,198,298	3,626,117	23,288,565

3.—Land Area* and Population to Square Mile, 1850.

STATES, ETC.		Area, Square Miles.	Aggregate Population.	Population to Square Mile.
New-England States.	Maine	30,000	583,188	19.44
	New-Hampshire	9,280	317,964	34.26
	Vermont	10,212	313,611	30.07
	Massachusetts	7,800	994,499	126.11
	Rhode Island	1,360	147,544	108.05
	Connecticut	4,674	370,791	79.33
	Total	63,326	2,727,597	43.07
Middle States.	New-York	46,000	3,097,394	67.66
	New-Jersey	8,320	489,555	60.04
	Pennsylvania	46,000	2,311,786	50.25
	Delaware	2,120	91,535	43.64
	Maryland	9,356	583,035	62.31
	Total	111,796	6,573,305	58.77
Southern States.	Virginia	61,352	1,421,661	23.17
	North Carolina	45,000	868,903	19.30
	South Carolina	24,500	688,507	27.28
	Georgia	58,000	905,999	15.68
	Florida	59,268	87,401	1.47
	Total	247,620	3,952,471	16.00
Western States.	Ohio	39,964	1,980,408	49.55
	Indiana	33,809	988,416	29.23
	Illinois	55,405	851,470	15.36
	Michigan	56,243	397,654	7.07
	Wisconsin	53,924	305,191	5.65
	Kentucky	37,680	982,405	26.07
	Missouri	67,380	682,043	10.12
	Iowa	50,914	192,214	3.77
	Total	395,319	6,379,801	16.13
South-Western States.	Tennessee	45,600	1,002,625	21.98
	Alabama	50,722	771,671	15.21
	Mississippi	47,156	606,555	12.86
	Louisiana	46,431	511,974	11.02
	Arkansas	52,198	209,639	4.01
	Texas	237,321	212,592	0.89
	Total	479,428	3,315,056	6.91
California		188,981	188,981 †	1.00
Organized Territories.	Minesota	83,000	6,077	0.07
	Oregon	341,463	13,293	0.03
	Utah	187,923	11,381	0.11
	New-Mexico	210,744	61,505	0.28
	Total	823,130	99,667	0.12
Unorganized Territories.	North-Western	587,564	Indians	
	Nebraska	136,700		
	Indian	187,564		
	Total	911,828		
District of Columbia		60	51,687	861.45
Grand total		3,221,595	23,288,565	7.21

* In the body of the book the total area is given—here only the land area, as estimated by the superintendent of the United States census.

† Estimated for comparison.

COLLEGES AND SCHOOLS.

II.—PRINCIPAL COLLEGES OF THE UNITED STATES, JANUARY, 1848.

NAME.	LOCATION.	Founded.	Instructors	No. of Alumni.	Students.	Volumes in Library.	COMMENCEMENT.
Bowdoin	Brunswick, Me.	1794	10	941	123	21,000	1st Wed. in Sept
Waterville	Waterville, do	1820	6	240	74	7,000	2d Wed. in Aug.
Dartmouth	Hanover, N.H.	1769	14	2,480	200	15.000	Last Tues. in Aug.
University of Vermont	Burlington, Vt.	1791	6	441	97	11,000	1st Wed. in Aug.
Middlebury	Middlebury, do	1800	5	852	60	7,000	4th Wed. in July.
Norwich University	Norwich, do	1834	5	107	88	1,000	2d Thurs. in July.
Harvard University	Cambridge, Mass.	1638	35	6,062	270	79,200	4th Wed. in Aug
Williams	Williamstown, do	1793	8	1,581	177	8,500	3d Wed. in Aug.
Amherst	Amherst, do	1821	11	858	150	20,000	2d Thurs. in Aug.
Holy Cross	Worcester, do	1843	14	none.	117	4,300	Last week in July.
Brown University	Providence, R.I.	1764	7	1,613	141	27,500	1st Wed. in Sept.
Yale	New-Haven, Conn.	1700	34	5,678	379	47,000	3d Thurs. in Aug.
Trinity	Hartford, do	1824	8	136	74	9,500	1st Thurs. in Aug.
Wesleyan University	Middletown, do	1831	7	306	110	12,000	1st Wed. in Aug.
Columbia	New-York, N.Y.	1754	13	1,384	124	14,000	Wed. af. 1st Mon. in J'ly
Union	Schenectady, do	1795	13	2,762	257	16,000	4th Wed. in July.
Hamilton	Clinton, do	1812	10	551	178	10,000	4th Wed in July.
Madison University	Hamilton, do	1819	8	200	140	7,000	3d Wed. in Aug.
Geneva	Geneva, do	1823	8	....	66	5,400	1st Wed. in Aug.
University of New-York	New-York, do	1833	7	323	151	4,000	Wed. prec. 4th July
St. Paul's	College Point, do	1837	11	380	29	2,800	Last Thurs. in June
St. John's	Fordham, do	1841	14	10	110	10,000	About 15th of July
College of New-Jersey	Princeton, N.J.	1746	15	2,867	240	14,500	Last Wed. in June
Rutgers	N. Brunswick, do	1770	9	513	76	15,000	4th Wed. in July.
Univ. of Pennsylvania	Philadelphia, Penn.	1755	7	531	88	5,000	15, 16 or 17th July.
Dickinson	Carlisle, do	1783	12	579	142	12,000	2d Thurs. in July.
Jefferson,	Canonsburg, do	1802	9	1,000	93	10,000	2d Wed. in June.
Washington	Washington, do	1806	8	441	105	3,300	Last Wed. in Sept.
Alleghany	Meadville, do	1815	5	82	67	9,009	3d Thurs. in July.
Pennsylvania	Gettysburg, do	1832	11	121	81	2,300	3d Thurs. in Sept.
Lafayette	Easton, do	1832	7	101	82	5,000	3d Wed. in Sept.
Marshall	Mercersburg, do	1835	9	83	75	13,000	2d Wed. in Sept.
West'rn Univer. of Penn	Pittsburgh. do	1819	8	....	130	small.	Last Wed. in June.
St. Thomas of Villanova	nr. Philadelphia, do	....	5	....	30	.....	3d Wed. in July.
Delaware	Newark, Del.	1833	6	71	48	3,500	3d Wed. in July.
St. John's	Annapolis, Md.	1784	6	143	71	3,300	The 22d February.
St. Mary's	Baltimore, do	1799	9	....	150	.....	4th July.
Mount St. Mary's	Emmetsburg, do	1830	24	137	126	4,000	Last Wed. in June.
St. James	nr Hagerstown, do	1842	10	3	32	8,750	Th. bef. 1st Mon. in Aug
Georgetown	Georgetown, D.C.	1789	12	180	89	22,000	Near last of July.
Columbian	Washington, do	1821	10	174	50	6,000	2d Wed. in July.
William and Mary	Williamsburg, Va.	1693	5	....	68	5,000	July 4th.
Hampden Sidney	P. Edward co. do	1783	6	1,500	25	7,000	Wed. bef. 4th July
Washington	Lexington, do	1812	6	600	81	5,000	3d Thurs. in June.
University of Virginia	Charlottesville, do	1819	9	730	73	17,500	20th June, if not S.
Richmond	Richmond, do	1832	6	none.	43	1,200	3d Wed. in Dec.
Randolph-Macon	Boydton, do	1832	11	124	145	6,000	2d Wed. in June.
Emory and Henry	Glade Spring, Va.	1839	4	....	44	2,800	Last Wed. in June.
Rector	Taylor co., io	1839	3	none.	...	2,500	Last Wed. in Sept.
Bethany	Bethany, o	1840	6	16	128	....	4th July.
Univers. of N. Carolina	Chapel Hill, N.C.	1789	9	905	55	12,000	1st Thurs. in June.
Davidson	Mecklenberg co. do	1838	3	4	44	1,500	Last Thurs. in June
Wake Forest	Wake Forest, do	1838	3	11	24	4,700	3d Thurs. in June.
College of Charleston	Charleston, S.C.	1795	4	121	44	3,000	Last Tues. in March
Erskine	Abbeville Dist., do	....	..	....	88	.....	....
South Caroliaa	Columbia, do	1804	8	....	219	19,000	1st Mond. in Dec.
Franklin	Athens, Ga.	1785	9	558	147	13,000	1st Wed. in Aug.
Oglethorpe	Milledgeville, do	1836	5	53	45	3,000	Wed af. 2d M'd Nv

COLLEGES IN THE UNITED STATES—*Continued.*

NAME.	LOCATION.	Founded	Instructors	No. of Alumni.	Students.	Volumes in Library.	COMMENCEMENT.
Emory	Oxford, Ga.	1837	6	78	91	4,000	Wed. af. 3d M. in J'y
Mercer University	Penfield, do	1833	6	16	61	3,000	Last Wed. in July.
Christ Coll. and Ep. Ins.	Montpelier, do	1839	4	....	35	.....	....
University of Alabama	Tuscaloosa, Ala.	1828	9	149	82	9,000	2d Mon. in July.
La Grange	La Grange, do	1831	6	120	62	3,000	1st Wed. in June.
Spring Hill	Spring Hill, do	1830	12	....	70	4,000	1st day of February
Howard	Marion, do	1841	6	none	40	1,500	4th Thurs. in July.
Centenary	Rankin co., Miss.	1841	8	18	37	1,850	1st Wed. in June.
Mississippi University	Oxford, do	1846	..	....	...	.....	Not fully organized.
Oakland	Oakland, do	1830	5	69	64	7,000	First Thurs. in April
Centenary of Louisiana	Jackson, La.	1841	5	9	49	4,400	Last Wed. in July.
St. Charles	Grand Coteau, do	1833	21	2	103	4,000	15th July.
Baton Rouge	Baton Rouge, do	1838	4	....	45	300	December.
Franklin	Opelousas, do	1839	4	70	...	.....	1st November.
University of Louisiana	New-Orleans, do	....	..	....	—.	.....	Not fully organized.
Greenville	Greenville, Tenn.	1794	2	110	41	3,000	3d Wed. in Sept.
Washington	Washington co., do	1794	2	110	42	1,000	....
University of Nashville	Nashville, do	1806	6	377	92	9,700	1st Wed. in Oct.
Union	Murfreesboro, do	1842	4	none	70	300	1st Wed. in Nov.
Franklin	near Nashville, do	1844	6	6	44	1,000	1st week in Oct.
East Tennessee	Knoxville, do	1807	7	112	81	3,980	1st Wed. in Aug.
Cumberland University	Lebanon, do	1844	5	4	80	1,000	Last Thurs. in July.
Jackson	Columbia, do	1830	4	43	44	2,000	2d Wed. in Aug.
Transylvania	Lexington, Ky.	1798	16	610	91	14,000	3d Wed. in Aug.
St. Joseph's	Bardstown, do	1824	17	150	126	5,000	Last Thurs. in July.
Centre	Danville, do	1819	5	237	130	4,500	Last Thurs. in June.
Augusta	Augusta, do	1825	4	60	51	2,500	Th. af. 1st Wed. in Aug
Georgetown	Georgetown, do	1830	7	65	120	5,200	Last Wed. in June.
Bacon	Harrodsburg, do	1836	4	....	60	1,800	Last Friday in June.
University of Ohio	Athens, Ohio	1821	6	151	66	3,500	1st Wed. in Aug.
Miami University	Oxford, do	1809	5	343	137	8,000	2d Thurs. in Aug.
Franklin	New Athens, do	1825	4	90	80	2,200	Last Wed. in Sept.
Western Reserve	Hudson, do	1826	11	138	71	6,000	2d Thurs. in Aug.
Kenyon	Gambia, do	1826	6	146	49	8,800	1st Wed. in Aug.
Granville	Granville, do	1832	5	30	26	4,000	3d Wed. in July.
Marietta	Marietta, do	1832	5	91	49	6,300	Last Thurs. in July.
Oberlin Institute	Oberlin, do	1834	10	164	93	4,000	4th Wed. in Aug.
Cincinnati	Cincinnati, do	1819	8	....	84	.....	....
St. Xavier	Cincinnati, do	1840	14	....	270	6,000	2d Wed. in July.
Woodward	Cincinnati, do	1831	5	17	15	1,400	Friday bef. 4th July
Wittenberg	Springfield, do	....	..	....	...	.....	....
Ohio Wesleyan Univer.	Delaware, do	1844	5	4	31	2,000	1st Wed. in Aug.
Indiana State University	Bloomington, Ind.	1827	5	231	46	2,500	Last Wed. in Sept.
Hanover	South Hanover, do	1829	6	92	41	2,200	3d Thurs. in Aug.
Wabash	Crawfordsville, do	1833	6	49	40	4,800	4th Wed. in July.
Indiana Ashbury Univ.	Greencastle, do	1839	5	....	112	.....	....
St. Gabriel's	Vincennes, do	1843	7	....	50	.....	....
Franklin	Franklin, do	1837	5	1	14	200	4th Wed. in July.
Illinois	Jacksonville, Ill.	1329	10	81	38	3,000	Last Thurs. in June.
Shurtleff	Upper Alton, do	1835	4	4	3	1,600	4th Thurs. in July.
McKendree	Lebanon, do	1834	4	25	80	700	3d Wed. in July.
St. Mary of the Lakes	Chicago, do	1846	8	....	...	.....	15th July.
Knox Manual Labor	Galesburg, do	1837	5	....	48	3,000	4th Wed. in June.
St. Louis University	St. Louis, Mo.	1832	17	25	160	12,000	15th July.
St. Vincent's	Cape Girardeau, do	1843	12	....	90	5.000	Last Thurs. in July.
Masonic	Marion county, do	1831	5	13	45	.....	Last Thurs. in Sept
Missouri University	Columbia, do	1840	11	26	52	.....	4th Thurs. in Aug.
St. Charles	St .Charles, do	1889	5	19	60	.....	2d Wed. in Aug.
Michigan University	Ann Arbor, Mich.	1837	7	....	89	5,000	1st Wed. in Aug.
St. Philip's	near Detroit, do	1839	4	....	30	.....	1st Mond. in Oct.
Iowa University	Iowa City, Iowa.	1840	..	....	...	.....	....
Franklin	Franklin, do	1844	4	....	38	500	....
Beloit	Beloit, Wisc.	1847	..	....	...	.....	....
Baylor University	Independence, Tex.	1844	..	....	...	.....	....

2.—ROMAN CATHOLIC ECCLESIASTICAL SEMINARIES, 1848.

NAMES.	LOCATION,	No. of Instructors	No. of Pupils.	Under care of the
St. Mary's Theological Seminary............	Baltimore, Maryland	5	20	Sulpitians.
Mount St. Mary's Theological Seminary	near Emmetsburg, do	3	10	....
Theological Seminary of St. Charles Borromeo	Philadelphia, Penn.	4	30	Lazarists.
Ecclesiastical Seminary........................	Fordham, New-York	7	25	Jesuits.
Theologica. Seminary of St. Francis de Sales.	Milwaukie, Wisconsin	2	6	....
St. Louis Theological Seminary.............	St. Louis, Missouri	5	20	Lazarists.
St. Michael's Theological Seminary..........	near Birmingham, Penn.	1	12	....
Theological Seminary of St. Athanasius......	Nashville, Tennessee	3	10	....
Ecclesiastical Seminary......................	Spring Hill, Alabama	..	..	Jesuits.
Ecclesiastical Seminary of St Vincent of Paul	Assumption, Louisiana	6	11	Lazarists.
Ecclesiastical Seminary of Bardstown........	Bardstown, Kentucky	..	5	....
St. Mary's Ecclesiastical Seminary..........	Chicago, Illinois	3	..	....
Ecclesiastical Seminary of St. Francis Xavier	Cincinnati, Ohio	2	10	Jesuits.
Ecclesiastical Seminary......................	Huron county, do	4	7	....
Seminary of St. Thomas.......................	Detroit, Michigan	2	7	....
Theological Seminary.........................	Vincennes, Indiana	..	2	....

3.—PROTESTANT THEOLOGICAL SEMINARIES, 1848.

NAMES.	LOCATION,	Denomination.	Founded.	No. Profes.	No. of Students.	No. of Alumni.	Volumes in Library.
Bangor Theological Seminary...	Bangor, Me.	Congregational..	1816	3	37	202	7,000
Theological Seminary	Concord, N. H.	Methodist.......	....	..	..	....	....
Gilmanton Theol. Seminary.....	Gilmanton do	Congregational..	1835	3	..	69	3,000
New-Hampton Theol. Seminary.	New Hampton, do	Baptist	1825	2	36	....	2,000
Andover Theol. Seminary.......	Andover, Mass.	Congregational ..	1807	6	93	1006	21.250
Divinity School, Harvard Univ..	Cambridge do	Unitarian.......	1816	3	23	238	3,000
Newton Theological Institution..	Newton, do	Baptist.........	1825	4	30	201	5,500
Theol. Department Yale College.	New-Haven, Conn.	Congregational..	1822	4	35	515	900
Theol. Institution of Connecticut..	East Windsor, do	Congregational..	1833	3	17	151	5,000
Theol. Sem. Prot. Epis. Church..	New-York, N. Y.	Prot. Episcopal..	1821	5	64	336	10,000
Union Theological Seminary.....	New-York, do	Presbyterian....	1836	5	106	211	18,000
Auburn Theological Seminary...	Auburn, do	Presbyterian....	1821	4	30	580	6,000
Theol. Depart. Madison Univer..	Hamilton, do	Baptist.........	1820	4	41	133	4,000
Hartwick Seminary.............	Hartwick, do	Lutheran........	1815	2	1	52	1,250
Theol. Sem. Asso. Ref. Church..	Newburgh, do	Asso. Ref. Ch...	1804	1	11	143	3,200
Theol. Sem. Dutch Ref. Church..	N. Brunswick, N. J.	Dutch Reformed.	1784	..	..	....	....
Princeton Theological Seminary.	Princeton, do	Presbyterian....	1812	5	153	1626	11,000
Seminary Lutheran Church......	Gettysburg, Penn.	Lutheran........	1826	3	30	195	7,500
German Reformed...............	Mercersburg, do	G. Ref. Church..	1825	2	18	121	6,000
Western Theological Seminary..	Alleghany, do	Presbyterian....	1825	2	48	252	5.000
Western Theological School.....	Meadville, do	Unitarian	1844	4	40	9	8,000
Theological Seminary	Canonsburg, do	Asso. Presbyter..	1792	2	33	147	2,000
Theo. Sem. Asso. Ref. Church..	Pittsburgh, do	Asso. Reformed.	1825	3	35	85	1,500
Theological Seminary...........	Philadelphia, do	Reformed Presb.	....	3	13	....	....
Episcopal Theological Seminary.	Fairfax co., Va.	Prot. Episcopal..	1822	4	38	229	5,000
Union Theological Seminary....	Pr. Edward's co. do	Presbyterian....	1824	..	..	....	....
Virginia Baptist Seminary.......	Richmond, do	Baptist.........	1832	..	..	....	....
Southern Theological Seminary.	Columbia, S. C.	Presbyterian....	1831	..	..	....	....
Theological Seminary...........	Lexington, do	Lutheran.......	1830	1	10	29	1,500
Furman Theological Seminary...	Fairfield Dist., do	Baptist	1826	3	15	120	1,500
Theol. Sem. Asso. Ref. Church..	Abbeville Dist., do	Asso. Reformed.	....	..	..	....	....
Mercer Theological Seminary...	Penfield, Ga.	Baptist	1833	3	4	....	1,000
Howard Theological Institution..	Marion, Ala.	Baptist	1843	2	10	....	1,000
Western Bap. Theol. Institution.	Covington, Ky.	Baptist	1840	4	18	9	2.000
Southwest Theological Seminary	Maryville, Tenn.	Presbyterian....	1821	..	..	....	....
Lane Seminary..................	Cincinnati, Ohio.	Presbyterian....	1829	3	36	218	10,000
Theol. Depart. Kenyon College..	Gambia, do	Prot. Episcopal..	1828	5	4	....	4,500
Theol. Depart. Western Res. Coll.	Hudson, do	Presbyterian....	1836	3	22	80	80
Granville Theol. Department....	Granville, do	Baptist	1832	..	..	....	....
Oberlin Theological Department.	Oberlin, do	Presbyterian....	1834	4	27	97	400
Theol. Sem. Asso. Ref. Church..	Oxford, do	Asso. Reformed.	1839	1	12	....	....
Indiana Theological Seminary...	S. Hanover. Ind	Presbyterian....	....	..	..	....	....
Alton Theological Seminary.....	Upper Alton, Ill.	Baptist.........	1835	..	..	....	....
Kalamazoo Theol. Seminary.....	Kalamazoo, Mich.	Baptist-.........	1846	..	..	....	....

4.—LAW SCHOOLS.

PLACE.	NAME.	PROFESSORS.	STUDENTS.
Cambridge, Mass.	Harvard University	2	102
New-Haven, Conn.	Yale College	3	52
Princeton, N. J.	College of New-Jersey	3	..
Carlisle, Pa.	Dickinson College	1	6
Williamsburg, Va.	William and Mary College	1	32
Charlottesville, Va.	University of Virginia	1	72
Chapel Hill, N. C.	North Carolina University	.	..
Tuscaloosa, Ala.	Alabama University	1	..
Lexington, Ky.	Transylvania University	3	75
Cincinnati, Ohio	Cincinnati College	3	25
Bloomington, Ind.	Indiana State University	1	15

5.—MEDICAL SCHOOLS.

NAME.	PLACE.	Found'd	Profes's.	Stude'ts	Gradat's	Lectures commence.
Maine Medical School	Brunswick	1820	4	81	581	February 15th.
N. H. Medical School	Hanover	1797	6	50	735	1st or 2d Thurs. in August.
Castleton Med. College	Castleton	1818	7	104	555	4th Thursday in August.
Vt. Medical College	Woodstock	1835	7	96	332	1st Thursday in March.
Med. School, Har. Univ.	Cambridge	1782	6	164	547	1st Wednesday in November.
Berkshire Med. School	Pittsfield	1823	5	103	473	1st Thursday in September.
Med. Instit. Yale College	New-Haven	1810	6	52	830	6 weeks after 3d Th. in Aug.
Coll. Phys. and Sur., N. Y.	New-York	1807	6	219	852	1st Monday in November.
Med. Inst. Geneva Coll.	Geneva	1835	6	158	98	1st Tuesday in October.
Med. Faculty, Univ., N. Y.	New-York	1837	6	410	597	Last Monday in October.
Albany Medical College	Albany	1839	8	114	58	1st Tuesday in October
Medical Dep. Univ., Penn.	Philadelphia	1765	8	411	4.774	1st Monday in November.
Jefferson Med. College	Do.	1824	8	493	1,232	1st Monday in November.
Med. Dep. Penn. Coll.	Do.	1839	8	60	....	1st Monday in November.
Franklin Medical College	Do.	1846	8	..	....	2d Monday in October.
Med. School, Univ. Md.	Baltimore	1807	6	100	909	October 31st.
Washington Med. Coll.	Do.	1827	6	25	....	1st Monday in November.
Med. School, Columb. Col.	Washington	1825	6	40	81	1st Monday in November
Med. School, Univ. Va.	Charlottesville	1825	3	45	....	1st Monday in October.
Richmond Med. College	Richmond	1838	6	75	14	1st Monday in November.
Winchester Medical Coll.	Winchester		5	..	....	1st Monday in October.
Med. Coll. State of S. C.	Charleston	1833	8	158	124	2d Monday in November.
Med. College of Georgia	Augusta	1830	7	115	....	2d Monday in November.
Med. Coll. of Louisiana	New-Orleans	1835	7	30	....	3d Monday in November.
Memphis Med. College	Memphis, Ten.		7	..	....	....
Med. Dep., Transyl. Univ.	Lexington	1818	7	214	1,351	1st Monday in November.
Louisville Med. Instit.	Louisville	1837	6	242	53	1st Monday in November.
West'n Reserve Med. Coll.	Cleveland, O.	1844	8	216	96	1st Wednesday in November.
Medical College of Ohio	Cincinnati	1819	8	130	331	1st Monday in November.
Rush Medical College	Chicago, Ill.	1842	6	70	16	1st Monday in November.
Med. Dep. of Kemp. Coll.	St. Louis, Mo.	1841	9	75	19	Last week in October.
Med. Coll., St. Louis Univ.	Do.	1836	8	50	14	1st Monday in November
Willoughby Med. College.	Willoughby	1834	6	126	57	Last Monday in October.
Med. Coll., Missouri Univ.	Columbia	1840	7	92	....	1st Monday in November.

III.—STATISTICS OF THE ARMY.

1.—ORGANIZATION OF THE REGULAR ARMY OF THE UNITED STATES.

Staff Departments and Regiments.	Major Generals.	Brigadier Generals.	Adjutant General.	Asst. Adjt. Gen. (Lieut. Col.)	Asst. Adjts. Gen. (Majors bvt.)	Asst. Adjts. Gen. (Capts. bvt.)	Inspectors General.	Quartermaster General.	Asst. Quartermasters General.	Dep. Quartermasters General.	Quartermasters.	Assistant Quartermasters.	Com. Gen. of Subsistence.	Asst. Com. Gen. of Subsistence.	Commissaries of Sub (Majors.)	Commissaries of Sub (Capts.)	Surgeon General.	Surgeons.	Assistant Surgeons.	Paymaster General.	Deputy Paymasters General.	Paymasters.
General Staff	*2	3*	1	†1‡	‡4	*8‡	2	1	2	2	*8	*38‡	1	1	2	4						
Medical Department																	1	*21	*59			
Pay Department																				1	†2	*28
Military Storekeepers																						
Corps of Engineers																						
Corps Top. Engineers																						
Ordnance Department																						
Two reg'ts Dragoons																						
Reg't Mount. Riflemen																						
Four reg'ts Artillery																						
Eight reg'ts Infantry																						
Grand Aggregate	2	*3	1	†1‡	‡4	*8‡	2	1	2	2	*8	*38‡	1	1	2	4	1	*21	*59	1	†2	*28

Staff Departments and Regiments.	Colonels.	Lieutenant Colonels.	Majors.	Adjutants.	Regimental Quartermasters.	Captains.	First Lieutenants.	Second Lieutenants.	Sergeant Majors.	Quartermaster's Sergeants.	Principal or Chief Musicians.	Chief Buglers.	Sergeants.	Corporals.	Buglers.	Musicians.	Farriers and Blacksmiths.	Artificers.	Privates.	Enlisted men of ordnance. (*Number not limited.*)	Total commissioned officers.	Total non-commissioned officers, musicians, artificers, and privates.	Aggregate.
General Staff																					51		51
Medical Department																					81		81
Pay Department																					31		31
Military Storekeepers																					17		17
Corps of Engineers	1	2	4			*12	12	12					10	10		2			78		43	100	143
Corps Top. Engineers	1	1	4			*11	10	10													37		37
Ordnance Department	1	1	4			*13	12	6					53							495	37	548	585
Two reg'ts Dragoons	2	2	4	2	‡2	20	20	20	2	2	2	4	80	80	40		20		1,000		70	1,230	1,300
Reg't Mount. Riflemen	1	1	2	1	‡1	10	10	10	1	1	1	2	40	40	20		20		640		35	765	800
Four reg'ts Artillery	4	4	8	‡4	‡4	48	96	48	4	4	§		192	192		96		96	2,016		208	2,600	2,808
Eight reg'ts Infantry	8	8	16	‡8	‡8	80	80	80	8	8	16		320	320		160			3,360		276	4,192	4,464
Grand Aggregate	18	19	42	‡15	‡15	*194	240	186	15	15	19	‡6	695	642	60	258	40	69	7,094	495	886	9,435	10,317

* Vacancies in these grades, under act of June 19, 1848, are not to be filled until by casualties the numbers are reduced to—1 Major General, 2 Brigadier Generals, 6 Assistant Adjutants General, (Captains by brevet,) 4 Quartermasters, 28 Assistant Quartermasters, 20 Surgeons, 50 Assistant Surgeons, 18 Paymasters, (the additional Paymasters appointed under the Act of 3d March, 1847, "to be retained in service until 4th March, 1849,) 10 Captains of Topographical Engineers, and 12 Captains of Ordnance.

† Under the same act, vacancies happening in these grades are not to be filled.

‡ Nine of the Assistant Adjutants General, and twenty of the Assistant Quartermasters, holding also Regimental Commissions, and being accounted for in their regiments, are, to avoid counting them twice, excluded as *Staff* officers from the columns of the "total commissioned officers" (886) and aggregate (10,317.) The two commissions held by these officers are of unequal grades, and hence they are not affected by the 7th section of the Act of June 16, 1846.

The Adjutants of Artillery and Infantry (12,) and all the Regimental Quartermasters, (15,) being taken from the Subalterns, and accounted for in their several regiments as belonging to companies, to avoid counting them twice, are excluded as regimental staff officers from the columns of total commissioned officers, and aggregate of their respective regiments.

§ The 3d regiment of Artillery having two principal musicians enlisted under the Act of 3d August, 1847, retain them under the Act of June 19, 1848. When by casualties their places become vacant, they are not to be filled.

2.—Table of Pay of Army Officers.

Rank and Classification of Officers.	PAY.	SUBSIST'CE		FORAGE.		SERVANTS.		Total Monthly Pay
		20 cts. for each ration.		$8 per mo. for each horse.		Pay, etc, of a Private.		
	Per month.	No. of rations.	Monthly commutation value	No. of Horses.	Monthly commutation value.	No. of Servants.	Monthly commutation value.	
Major-General	$200 00	15	$90	3	$24	4	$62 00	$376 00
Aid de-camp, besides pay of Lieutenant	24 00	1	6	1	8	..	....	38 00
Brigadier-General	104 00	12	72	3	24	3	46 50	246 50
Aid de camp, besides pay of Lieutenant	20 00	....	....	1	8	..	....	28 50
Adjutant-General—Colonel	90 00	6	36	3	24	2	33 00	183 00
Assistant Adjutant-General—Major	60 00	4	24	3	24	2	33 00	141 00
" " " —Captain	50 00	4	24	1	8	1	16 50	98 50
Inspector General—Colonel	90 00	6	36	3	24	2	33 00	183 00
Quartermaster-General—Brigadier General	104 00	12	72	3	24	3	46 50	246 50
Assistant Quartermaster-General—Colonel	90 00	6	36	3	24	2	33 00	183 00
Deputy Quartermaster Gen.—Lt. Colonel.	75 00	5	30	3	24	2	33 00	162 00
Quartermaster—Major	60 00	4	24	3	24	2	33 00	141 00
Assistant Quartermaster—Captain	50 00	4	24	1	8	1	16 50	98 50
Commissary Gen. of Subsistence—Colonel	90 00	6	36	3	24	2	33 00	183 00
Assistant Commissary Gen.—Lt. Colonel	75 00	5	30	3	24	2	33 00	162 00
Commissary of Subsistence—Major	60 00	4	24	3	24	2	33 00	141 00
" " —Captain	50 00	4	24	1	8	1	16 50	98 50
Assistant Commissary, besides pay of Lt.	20 00	....	....	....	....	..	....	20 00
Paymaster-General, $2,500 per annum	....	....	....	....	....	..	....	208 33
Paymaster	60 00	4	24	1	8	2	33 00	125 00
Surgeon General, $2,500 per annum	....	....	....	....	....	..	....	208 33
Surgeons of 10 years' service	60 00	8	48	1	8	2	33 00	149 00
Surgeons of less than 10 years' service	60 00	4	24	1	8	2	33 00	125 00
Assistant Surgeons of 10 years' service	50 00	8	48	1	8	1	16 50	122 50
Assistant Surgeons of 5 years' service	50 00	4	24	1	8	1	16 50	98 50
Assistant Surgeons of less than 5 y. service	33 33	4	24	1	8	1	16 56	81 83
Engineers—Topographical Engineers. Ordnance Department.								
Colonel	90 00	6	36	3	24	2	33 00	183 00
Lieutenant-Colonel	75 00	5	30	3	24	2	33 00	162 00
Major	60 00	4	24	3	24	2	33 00	141 00
Captain	50 00	4	24	1	8	1	16 50	98 50
First Lieutenant	33 33	4	24	1	8	1	16 50	81 83
Second Lieutenant	33 33	4	24	1	8	1	16 50	81 83
Mounted Dragoons.								
Colonel	90 00	6	36	3	24	2	33 00	183 00
Lieutenant-Colonel	75 00	5	30	3	24	2	33 00	162 00
Major	60 00	4	24	3	24	2	33 00	141 00
Captain	50 00	4	24	2	16	1	16 50	106 50
First Lieutenant	33 33	4	24	2	16	1	16 50	89 83
Second Lieutenant	33 33	4	24	2	16	1	16 50	89 83
Adjutant, besides pay of Lieutenant	10 00	....	....	....	....	..	....	10 00
Artillery—Infantry.								
Colonel	75 00	6	36	3	24	2	31 00	166 00
Lieutenant-Colonel	60 00	5	30	3	24	2	31 00	145 00
Major	50 00	4	24	3	24	2	31 00	129 00
Captain	40 00	4	24	....	....	1	15 50	79 50
First Lieutenant	30 00	4	24	....	....	1	15 50	69 50
Second Lieutenant	25 00	4	24	....	....	1	15 50	64 50
Adjutant, besides pay of Lieutenant	10 00	....	....	1	8	..	....	18 00

3.—MILITARY GEOGRAPHICAL DIVISIONS.

(———) *General Orders, No.* 40, 31*st August*, 1848.

I. EASTERN DIVISION—The country east of a line drawn from Fond du Lac, Lake Superior, to Cape Sable, Florida, comprising four departments.

Department No. 1—Maine, New-Hampshire, Vermont, Massachusetts, Rhode Island, and Connecticut.

Department No. 2—Michigan, Wisconsin, (part) Ohio, and Indiana.

Department No. 3—New-York, New-Jersey, Pennsylvania, Delaware, and Maryland.

Department No. 4.—Virginia, North Carolina, South Carolina, Georgia, and Florida, (part.)

II. WESTERN DIVISION—The country west of a line drawn from Fond du Lac to Cape Sable, comprising five departments

Department No, 5—Florida, (part) Alabama, Mississippi, Louisiana, Tennessee, and Kentucky.

Department No. 6—Wisconsin, (part) Illinois, Iowa, and Missouri above 37° N. lat.

Department No. 7—Country west of the Mississippi, south of 37° N. lat., and north of Texas and Louisiana.

Department No. 8—Texas, south of 32° N. lat., and Colorado or Red River.

Dapartment No. 9—New Mexico and the territory of Texas north of 32° N. lat.

III. PACIFIC DIVISION.

Department No. 10—Territory of California.

Department No. 11—Territory of Oregon.

4.—Militia Force of the United States.

STATES.	General Officers.	General Staff Officers.	Field Officers, &c.	Company Officers.	Total Commissioned Officers.	Non-commissioned Officers, Musicians, Privates, &c.	Aggregate.
Maine	26	95	540	1,659	2,320	42,345	44,665
New-Hampshire	8	37	333	1,228	1,606	28,033	29,639
Massachusetts	8	38	96	426	568	95,271	95,839
Vermont	12	51	224	801	1,088	22,827	23,915
Rhode-Island	6	33	57	27	123	15,663	15,786
Connecticut	11	38	292	983	1,324	56,395	57,719
New-York	130	360	3,204	3,953	7,647	157,897	165,544
New-Jersey	19	58	435	1,476	1,988	37,183	39,171
Pennsylvania	56	164	1,523	6,054	7,797	263,890	271,687
Delaware	4	8	71	364	447	8,782	9,229
Maryland	22	68	544	1,763	2,397	44,407	46,864
Virginia	28	58	1,336	5,211	6,633	114,703	121,336
North Carolina	28	133	657	3,449	4,267	75,181	79,448
South Carolina	19	101	452	2,026	2,598	52,107	54,704
Georgia	36	98	746	2,212	3,092	54.220	57,312
Alabama	32	102	671	2,173	2,978	58,358	61,336
Louisiana	10	46	183	542	781	14,027	14,808
Mississippi	15	70	392	348	825	35,259	36,084
Tennessee	25	79	859	2,644	3,607	67,645	71,252
Kentucky	44	115	1,112	3,601	4,873	86,103	90,975
Ohio	91	217	463	1,281	2,051	174,404	176,445
Indiana	31	110	566	2,154	2,861	51,052	53,913
Illinois	....	......	......	......	......	....	83,234
Missouri	45	94	790	2,990	3,919	57,081	61,000
Arkansas	8	29	310	762	1,109	16,028	17,137
Michigan	28	148	382	2,116	2,674	58,212	60,886
Florida	3	14	95	508	620	11,502	12,122
Texas	....	......	......	......	......	....	....
Iowa	....	......	......	......	......	....	....
Wisconsin	1	6	36	126	169	5,054	5,223
District of Columbia	1	3	24	68	96	1,153	1,249
Total	746	2,374	16,392	50.945	70,458	1,704,842	1,858,534

IV.—STATISTICS OF THE NAVY.

1.—Vessels of War of the United States Navy.

Name and Rate.	Where and when built.
Ships of the Line—11. Guns.	
Pennsylvania.....120	Philadelphia....1837
Franklin..........74	Philadelphia....1815
Columbus........74	Washington.....1819
Ohio..............74	New-York.......1820
North Carolina....74	Philadelphia....1820
Delaware.........74	Gosport, Va.....1820
Alabama..........74	Portsmouth.........
Virginia..........74	Boston............
New-York.........74	Norfolk...........
New-Orleans......74	Sackett's Harbor....
Vermont...........	Charlestown.....1819
Independence, *Razee*,...........54	Boston..........1814
Frigates, 1*st Class*, 12.	
United States......44	Philadelphia....1797
Constitution.......44	Boston..........1797
Potomac..........44	Washington.....1821
Brandywine.......44	Do. 1825
Columbia.........44	Do. 1836
Congress.........44	Portsmouth.....1841
Cumberland.......44	Boston..........1842
Savannah.........44	New-York.......1842
Raritan...........44	Philadelphia....1843
Santee...........44	Portsmouth........
Sabine...........44	New-York.........
St. Lawrence.....44	Norfolk...........
Frigates, 2*d Class*—2.	
Constellation......36	Baltimore.......1797
Macedonian.......36	Captured 1812, rebuilt in 1836....
Sloops of War—22.	
Saratoga..........20	Portsmouth.....1842
John Adams.......20	Charleston, S. C. '90, rebuilt, 1820.
Vincennes........20	New-York.......1826
Warren...........20	Boston..........1826
Falmouth.........20	Do. 1827
Fairfield.........20	New-York.......1828
Vandalia..........20	Philadelphia....1828
St. Louis.........20	Washington.....1828
Cyane............20	Boston..........1837
Levant...........20	New-York.......1837
Portsmouth.......20	Portsmouth.....1843
Plymouth.........20	Boston..........1843
St. Mary's........20	Washington.....1844
Jamestown........20	Norfolk.........1844
Albany...........20	New-York.......1846
Germantown.......20	Philadelphia....1846
Ontario...........18	Baltimore.......1813
Decatur..........16	New-York.......1839
Preble............16	Portsmouth.....1839
Yorktown.........16	Norfolk.........1839
Marion...........16	Boston..........1839
Dale.............16	Philadelphia....1839
Brigs—5.	
Boxer............10	Boston..........1831
Dolphin..........10	New-York.......1836
Porpoise.........10	Boston..........1836
Bainbridge.......10	Do. 1842
Perry............10	Norfolk.........1843
Schooners—8.	
Flirt..............	Transferred from War Department.
Wave.............	
Phenix............	
On-ka-hy-e.........	Purchased.........
Bonito............1	Do. 1846
Reefer............1	Do. 1846
Petrel............1	Do. 1846
Bomb Vessels—5.	
Stromboli.........1	Purchased......1846
Vesuvius..........1	Do. 1846
Ætna.............1	Do. 1846
Hecla.............1	Do. 1846
Electra, *Ordnance transport*	
Steamers—13.	
Mississippi.......*10	Philadelphia....1841
Fulton............4	New-York.......1837
Union.............4	Norfolk.........1842
Princeton.........9	Philadelphia....1843
Michigan..........1	Erie, Pa........1844
Alleghany..........	Pittsburg, Pa........
Spitfire...........3	Purchased......1846
Vixen.............3	Do. 1846
Scorpion...........	Do. 1846
Scourge...........	Do. 1846
General Taylor......	Transf'd fm War Dep.
Water Witch........	Washington.....1845
Engineer..........	Purchased.
Store Ships and Brigs—6.	
Relief.............6	Philadelphia....1836
Erie...............8	Baltimore.......1813
Lexington.........8	New-York.......1825
Southampton.......6	Norfolk.........1845
Supply............	Purchased......1846
Fredonia..........	Do. 1846

* Paixham.

2.—OFFICERS OF THE NAVY.

	Number.		Number.
CAPTAINS	68	MIDSHIPMEN	264
COMMANDERS	97	MASTERS	28
LIEUTENANTS	327	PROFESSORS OF MATHEMATICS	22
SURGEONS	69	TEACHERS OF NAVAL SCHOOLS	3
PASSED ASSISTANT SURGEONS	29	BOATSWAINS	31
ASSISTANT SURGEONS	36	GUNNERS	42
PURSERS	64	CARPENTERS	36
CHAPLAINS	22	SAILMAKERS	34
PASSED MIDSHIPMEN	181		

3.—PAY OF THE NAVY.

PER ANNUM.

	Pay.		Pay.
CAPTAINS, Senior, in service	$4,500	SURGEONS, &c., at navy yards, &c.	$2,250
Do. do. on leave	3,500	Do. in sea service	2,400
Captains of Squadrons	4,000	Do. of the fleet	2,700
Do. do. on other duty	3,500	PASSED ASSISTANT SURGEONS.	
Do. do. off duty	2,500	ASSISTANT SURGEONS, waiting	
COMMANDERS, in sea service	2,500	orders	650
Do. at navy yards, or on		Do. at sea	950
other duty	2,100	Do. after passing, &c.	850
Do. on leave, &c.	1,800	Do. at sea after passing	1,200
LIEUTENANTS, commanding	1,800	Do. at navy yards	950
Do. on other duty	1,500	Do. do. after passing	1,150
Do. waiting orders	1,200	PURSERS.	
SURGEONS, 1st 5 years in commission	1,000	CHAPLAINS, in sea service	1,200
Do. in navy yards, &c.	1,250	Do. on leave, &c.	800
Do. in sea service	1,333	PASSED MIDSHIPMEN, on duty	750
Do. of the fleet	1,500	Do. waiting orders	600
Do. 2d 5 years	1,200	MIDSHIPMEN, in sea service	400
Do. at navy yards, &c.	1,500	Do. on other duty	350
Do. in sea service	1,600	Do. on leave, &c	300
Do. of the fleet	1,800	MASTERS,	
Do. 3d 5 years	1,400	of ship of the line at sea	1,100
Do. at navy yards, &c.	1,750	Do. on other duty	1,000
Do. in sea service	1,866	Do. on leave, &c	750
Do. of the fleet	2,100	PROFESSORS of Mathematics	1,200
Do. 4th 5 years	1,600	TEACHERS at naval schools, &c	480
Do. at navy yards, &c	2,000	BOATSWAINS, } of a ship of the line	750
Do. in sea service	2,133	GUNNERS, } of a frigate	600
Do. of the fleet	2,400	CARPENTERS, } on other duty	500
Do. 20 years and upwards	1,800	SAILMAKERS, } on leave, &c	360

NOTE.—One ration per day, only, is allowed to all officers when attached to vessels for sea service, since the passage of the law of the 3d of March, 1835, regulating the pay of the navy. *Teachers* receive two rations per day, at 20 cents each.

4.—THE MARINE CORPS.

The Marine Corps has the organization of a brigade, and numbers now 75 commissioned officers, and 2,320 non-commissioned officers, musicians, and privates, in all, 2,305 men. The pay and allowances of the officers of the marine corps are the same as those of officers of the same grades in the infantry of the army, except the adjutant and inspector, who have the same pay and allowances as the paymaster of the marines. The marine corps is subject to the laws and regulations of the navy, except when detached for service with the army by the order of the President of the United States. The head-quarters of the corps are at Washington.

V.—STATISTICS OF COMMERCE AND NAVIGATION.

EXPORTS AND IMPORTS,

From and to the United States from the 1st day of July, 1846, to the 30th June 1847.

(From the Report of Register of Treasury.)

1. EXPORTS—DOMESTIC.

Countries.	Cotton.	Rice.	Flour.	Corn and Meal.	Sugar.	Tobacco.	Total Exports.
1. Russia	$523,616	$30,205	$ 17	$	$	$49,305	$626,332
2. Prussia	....	43,430	....	....	....	....	182,252
3. Sweden and Norway	300,277	20,161	3,390	....	....	30,151	391,847
4. Swedish West Indies	....	2,278	45,312	12,935	297	6,287	110,062
5. Denmark	62,609	115,525	731	....	....	210	198,152
6. Danish West Indies	....	10,481	288,784	199,631	3,326	15,851	836,672
7. Hanse Towns	1,069,095	424,550	51,029	639	....	1,502,655	4,068,413
8. Hanover	....	....	....	....	....	6,469	6,469
9. Holland	195,108	46,598	99,032	1,748	....	661,686	1,885,398
10. Dutch East Indies	....	....	5,931	....	....	69	91,902
11. Dutch West Indies	....	5,378	63,096	12,123	89	15,971	217,216
12. Dutch Guiana	....	1,956	2,725	....	....	1,297	43,840
13. Belgium	1,003,519	149,099	306,697	16,994	....	185,113	2,874,367
14. England	34,519,231	1,145,135	11,933,723	8,055,142	1,146	2,558,002	70,223,777
15. Scotland	1,277,712	46,390	915,130	382,824	....	112,098	3,645,460
16. Ireland	44,322	30,707	2,255,721	8,685,326	....	578	12,297,698
17. Gibraltar	6,716	2,620	146,217	2,877	336	144,240	365,360
18. Malta	....	....	700	....	....	11,109	25.096
19. British East Indies	....	....	15,847	...	1,164	27,223	287,783
20. Cape of Good Hope	....	....	23,705	...	505	27,307	106,172
21. Mauritius	....	....	4,140	196	....	2,887	36,275
22. Australia	....	....	....	....	....	11,466	33,289
23. Honduras	....	8,862	62,773	2,408	1,424	2,886	261,378
24. British Guiana	....	18,036	232,637	48,284	....	9,148	621,903
25. British West Indies	7,739	94,553	1,457,552	456,078	847	56,850	3,973,252
26. British American Colonies	17,996	67,017	1,452,986	249,776	22,947	308,229	5,819,667
27. France on the Atlantic	9,937,465	570,952	3,412,522	26,461	....	663,502	17,420,385
28. France on Mediterranean	443,853	1,918	252,484	967	....	222,730	1,172,146
29. French African Ports	....	157	1,126	....	....	...	5,491
30. Bourbon	....	....	15,236	300	....	4,283	52,557
31. French West Indies	284	19,983	160,811	26,307	462	52,864	569,126
32. French Guiana	....	1,947	10,060	465	...	3,888	58,287
33. Spain on the Altantic	311,704	419	459	1,565	....	365,961	770,748
34. Spain on Mediter'n	1,014,929	....	....	....	....	98,372	1,188,340
35. Teneriffe and Canaries	....	124	449	294	....	....	15,148
36. Manilla and Phillipines	....	....	130	....	....	99	32,480
37. Cuba	303,551	647,377	296,654	399,441	....	15,255	6,005,617
38. Other Spanish West Indies	....	33,427	103,549	57,078	....	20,095	025,079
39. Portugal	....	1,771	11,175	....	....	....	56,893
40. Madeira	....	5,153	31,073	25,921	....	9,612	105,031
41. Fayal and other Azores	....	151	2,270	....	....	330	9,466
42. Cape de Verd Islands	....	787	12,602	....	2,350	8,656	71,084
43. Italy	750,567	....	12,177	....	....	227,821	1,056,022
44. Sardinia	414,931	....	10,100	....	....	194,795	630,232
45. Sicily	28,978	....	....	....	....	....	56,899
46. Trieste and Austrian Ports	1,117,159	....	320	....	....	....	1,175,385
47. Turkey, Levant, &c	....	....	180	....	....	178	61,570
48. Hayti	....	22,901	239,996	5,642	19,898	39,668	1,187,017
49. Mexico	....	655	29,857	....	627	9,545	209,841
50. Central Repubs. of America	....	....	3,150	1,350	763	1,947	73,232
51. New Granada	....	150	12,019	362	....	90	53,655
52. Venezuela	....	7,316	210,197	14,069	49	16,332	571,474
53. Brazil	....	96	1,562,979	194	....	23,279	2,566,938
54. Uruguay	....	6,339	88,917	329	3,056	6,810	180,536
55. Argentine Republic	....	4,611	53,723	....	4,334	299	123,954
56. Chili	33,087	10,462	32,411	324	74,164	5,185	1,461,347
57. Peru	....	....	8,414	....	....	111	192,978
58. Ecuador	....	....	5,340	....	313	....	27,253
59. China	...	....	10,668	80	373	9,727	2,708,655
60. West Indies generally	....	2,026	27,752	8,036	...	1,438	118,137
61. South America generally	....	1,701	10,567	....	3,236	57	44,427
62. Asia generally	....	....	335	....	2,727	1,138	161,679
63. Africa generally	....	1,361	134,164	510	4,251	144,331	700,431
64. S. Seas & Pacific Ocean	41,391	1,161	5,670	....	2,620	5.671	310,187
Total	$53,415,848	3,605,896	26,133,811	18,696,546	150,307	7,901,036	150,637,464
Government Stores to the Army, from New-York							326,800
Total Foreign Exports							8,011,158
Grand Total							$158,648,622

2. IMPORTS FROM FOREIGN COUNTRIES.

	Countries.	5 *months*, 1846.*	7 *months*, 1846-7†	*Total.*
1	Russia	$561,878	$362,795	924,673
2	Prussia	7,608	....	7,608
3	Sweden and Norway	291,154	322,544	613,698
4	Danish West Indies	184,248	662,500	846,748
5	Hanse Towns	1,557,922	2,064,263	3,622,185
6	Holland	376,576	870,633	1,247,269
7	Dutch East Indies	590,364	304,618	894,982
8	Dutch West Indies	195,354	173,684	279,038
9	Dutch Guiana	17,542	41,813	59,355
10	Belgium	314,289	634,036	948,325
11	England	15,578,727	49,591,647	65,170,374
12	Scotland	345,472	1,491,542	1,837,014
13	Ireland	27,922	562,318	590,240
14	Gibraltar	8,060	18,909	26,969
15	British East Indies	663,570	982,887	1,646,457
16	Cape of Good Hope	20,871	15,170	36.041
17	British Honduras	63,596	133,636	197,232
18	British Guiana	3,875	15,250	19,125
19	British West Indies	349,824	598,108	947,932
20	British American Colonies	955,926	1,388.001	2,343,927
21	France on the Atlantic	10,172,159	13,726,917	23,399,076
22	France on the Mediterranean	472,187	529,578	1,081,765
23	French West Indies	60,571	90,795	151,366
24	Miquelon and French fisheries	162	273	435
25	French Guiana	6,596	41,179	47,755
26	Spain on the Atlantic	152,138	122,570	274,708
27	Spain on the Mediterranean	397,897	618,654	1,016,561
28	Teneriffe and other Canaries	44,503	17,361	61,364
29	Manilla and Phillipine Islands	65,215	428,841	491,656
30	Cuba	2,837,693	9,557,174	12,394,867
31	Other Spanish West India Islands	269,416	1,872,513	2,141,929
32	Portugal	277,777	5,553	283,330
33	Madeira	95,097	760	95,857
34	Fayal, and other Azores	19,964	14,600	34,564
35	Cape de Verds	120	2,279	2,399
56	Italy	415,221	864,715	1,279,936
37	Sicily	170,894	380,094	550,988
38	Trieste	98,040	89,301	187,341
39	Turkey	306,758	270,952	577,710
40	Hayti	421,029	970,551	1,391,580
41	Mexico	265,069	481,749	746,818
42	Central Republic of America	65,900	14,681	80,581
43	New Grenada	69,885	86,769	156,654
44	Venezuela	504,116	818,380	1,322.496
45	Brazil	2,740,167	4,355,993	7,096,160
46	Uruguay	29,965	82,845	112,810
47	Argentine Republic	104,199	137.010	241,209
48	Chili	487,702	1,229,201	1,716,903
49	Peru	316,854	79,369	396,223
50	China	1,722,354	3,860,989	5,583,343
51	Asia generally	70,637	237,844	308,481
52	Africa generally	288,223	321,619	559,842
53	South Seas and Pacific Ocean	40,824	3,764	44,588
54	Sandwich Islands	....	21,039	21,039
55	South America generally	....	10,500	10,500
56	Denmark	....	475	475
57	Sardinia	....	287	237
		$44,964,110	$101,581,528	

Total for year ending June 30, 1847 .... $146,545,663

* Under Tariff of 1842. Under Tariff of 1846.

3.—VALUE OF EXPORTS

OF THE GROWTH, PRODUCE, AND MANUFACTURE OF THE UNITED STATES.

THE SEA.			
Fisheries—			
Dried fish, or cod fisheries-	......	$659,629	......
Pickled fish, or river fisheries, (herring, shad, salmon, mackerel.)	......	136,221	......
Whale and other fish oil	......	1,170,659	......
Spermaceti oil	......	788,456	......
Whalebone	......	671,601	......
Spermaceti Candles	......	191,467	......
			$3,468,033
THE FOREST.			
Skins and furs	......	747,145	......
Ginseng	......	64,466	......
Products of Wood—			
Staves, shingles, boards, hewn timber	$1,849,911	......	......
Other lumber	342,781	......	......
Masts and spars	23,270	......	......
Oak bark and other dye	95,355	......	......
All manufactures of wood	1,495,924	......	......
Naval stores, tar, pitch, rosin & turpentine	759,221	......	......
Ashes, pot and pearl	618,000	......	......
		5,184,462	......
AGRICULTURE.			5,996,073
Products of Animals—			
Beef, Tallow, hides, horned cattle	2,434,003	......	......
Butter and cheese	1,741,770	......	......
Pork, (pickled,) bacon, lard, live hogs	6,630,842	......	......
Horses and mules	277,359	......	......
Sheep	29,100	......	......
Vegetable Food—		11,113,074	......
Wheat	6,049,350	......	......
Flour	26,133,811	......	......
Indian corn	14,395,212	......	......
Indian Meal	4,301,334	......	......
Rye meal	225,502	......	......
Rye, oats, and small grain and pulse	1,600,962	......	......
Biscuit, or shipbread	556,266	......	......
Potatoes	109,062	......	......
Apples	92,961	......	......
Rice	3,605,896	......	......
		57,070,356	......
			68,183,430
Tobacco	......	......	7,242,086
Cotton	......	......	53,415,848
Wool	......	......	89,460
All other Agricultural Products—			
Flaxseed	......	1,346	......
Hops	......	150,654	......
Brown sugar	......	25,483	......
Indigo	......	10	......
			177,493
MANUFACTURES.			
Soap and tallow candles,	......	606,798	......
Leather boots and shoes	......	243,816	......

Household furniture	$......	$225,700	$........
Coaches and carriages	......	75,369	....
Hats	......	59,536	....
Saddlery	......	13,102	....
Wax	......	161,527	....
Spirits from grain	......	67,781	....
Beer, ale, porter and cider	......	68,114	....
Snuff and tobacco	......	658,950	....
Linseed oil and spirits of turpentine	......	498,110	....
Cordage	......	27,054	....
Iron—pig, bar, and nails	......	168,817	....
castings	......	68,889	....
all other manufactures of	......	929,778	....
Spirits from molasses	......	293,609	....
Sugar, refined	......	124,824	....
Chocolate	......	1,653	....
Gunpowder	......	88,397	....
Copper and brass	......	64,980	....
Medicinal drugs	......	165,793	....
Cotton, piece goods—			4,612,597
printed and colored	281,320	....	....
white	3,345,902	....	....
nankeen	8,794	....	....
twist, yarn, and thread	108,132	....	....
all other manufactures of	338,275	....	....
Flax and hemp—		4,082,523	....
cloth and thread	......	477	....
bags and all other manufactures of	......	5,305	....
Wearing apparel	......	47,101	....
Combs and buttons	......	17,026	....
Brushes	......	2,967	....
Billiard tables and apparatus	......	615	....
Umbrellas and parasols	......	2,150	....
Leather and morocco skins not sold per pound	......	29,856	....
Fire engines and apparatus	......	2,443	....
Printing presses and type	......	17,431	....
Musical instruments	......	16,997	....
Books and maps	......	44,751	....
Paper and stationery	......	88,731	....
Paints and varnish	......	54,115	....
Vinegar	......	9,526	....
Earthen and stone ware	......	4,758	....
Manufactures of glass	......	71,155	....
tin	......	6,363	....
pewter and lead	......	13,694	....
marble and stone	......	11,220	....
gold and silver, and gold leaf	......	4,268	....
Gold and silver coin	......	62,620	....
Artificial flowers and jewelry	......	3,126	....
Molasses	......	26.959	....
Trunks	......	5,270	....
Brick and lime	......	17.623	....
Domestic salt	......	42,333	....
			4,692,403
Lead	......	....	124,981
Articles not enumerated—			
Manufactured	......	1,108,984	....
Other articles	......	1,199,276	....
			2,308,260
Government stores to the army, from New-York	......	....	326,800
Total Domestic Produce and Manufactures	......	......	$150,637,464
" Foreign " "			8,011,158
Grand Total			$158,648,622

Districts.	Entrances.		Clearances.	
	No.	Tons.	No.	Tons.
Passamaquoddy	868	70,504	877	75,050
Machias	2	92	13	1,606
Penobscot	11	3,343	12	2,026
Waldoboro	6	1,285	3	600
Wiscasset	5	1,745	23	3,955
Belfast	17	2,436	103	19,232
Bath	43	10,736	95	15,992
Bangor	8	1,060	53	9,300
Portland	200	28,265	299	44,964
Saco	2	113	7	1,042
Portsmouth	44	4,409	32	1,902
Vermont	250	69,014	268	72,064
Newburyport	15	1,664	29	3,753
Gloucester	125	8,288	117	6,388
Salem	197	20,539	211	23,524
Boston	2,120	325,426	2,060	281,874
Marblehead	114	5,906	114	5,518
Plymouth	9	783	8	675
Barnstable	9	531	7	378
Fall River	96	9,815	23	4,565
New-Bedford	144	33,628	136	36,863
Edgartown	85	14,234	6	1,261
Nantucket	—	—	14	4,605
Providence	78	14,168	54	9,409
Bristol	24	4,086	31	5,192
Newport	33	5,225	14	1,962
Middletown	5	616	1	67
New-London	40	12,702	18	5,168
New-Haven	74	13,522	66	11,968
Stonington	5	1,302	10	3,366
Fairfield	16	2,297	13	1,935
Champlain	236	45,443	239	46,492
Oswegatchie	565	161,288	563	160,559
Sackett's Harbor	206	78,115	204	78,269
Oswego	647	88,923	547	83,744
Niagara	525	115,692	519	117,547
Genesee	111	21,379	108	24,311
Cape Vincent	836	256,880	827	255,465
Sag Harbor	8	2,814	21	6,963
New-York	2,738	853,668	2,401	758,745
Newark	24	2,663	11	1,167
Philadelphia	621	139,774	583	142,143
Presque Isle	9	679	—	—
Delaware	6	1,377	20	4,935
Baltimore	511	123,065	668	169,930
Annapolis	—	—	1	109
Georgetown	3	516	13	2,421
Alexandria	66	13,131	95	17,787
Norfolk	181	42,162	235	53,250
Petersburg	2	935	6	3,386
Richmond	14	4,397	81	24,225
Rappahannock	2	185	5	474
Cherrystone	—	—	1	63
Wilmington	117	18,812	166	28,676
Newbern	13	1,750	15	1,983
Camden	10	1,492	14	1,693
Beaufort, N. C	4	401	4	384
Washington, N. C	11	1,196	16	1,964
Plymouth, N. C	5	340	13	1,086
Charleston	276	74,146	308	91,286
Georgetown	7	1,089	31	4,935
Savannah	108	48,602	125	55,818
Key West	114	5,950	117	7,290
Apalachicola	40	15.045	25	12,008
Pensacola	3	465	7	1,238
Mobile	129	59,758	134	66,238
New-Orleans	1,075	402,536	1,138	440,878
Teché	10	1,362	—	—
Cuyahoga	112	12,683	120	14,120
Sandusky	24	3,552	21	3,247
Detroit	205	36,160	208	36,311
Michilimackinac	3	650	2	300
Chicago	5	2,208	6	1,552
Texas	42	12,987	25	5,704
Total	14,229	3,321,705	14 370	3,378,998

5.—ENTRANCES AND CLEARANCES.

Countries.	Entrances.		Clearances.	
	No.	Tons.	No.	Tons.
Russia	19	6,801	14	5,497
Prussia	3	675	19	5,127
Sweden and Norway	48	14,189	22	6,263
Swedish West Indies	—	—	10	1,607
Denmark	3	717	11	2,490
Danish West Indies	173	26,798	157	26,471
Holland	91	35,855	95	31,887
Dutch East Indies	18	6,583	14	5,370
Dutch West Indies	102	14,699	36	4,483
Dutch Guayana	22	4,180	22	4,381
Belgium	122	48,480	120	45,369
Hanse Towns	300	110,466	193	68,761
Hanover	—	—	1	246
England	1,340	752,332	1,332	758,153
Scotland	161	63,567	111	40,945
Ireland	395	117,269	815	225,667
Gibraltar	16	3,896	48	9,932
Malta	1	221	5	1,066
British East Indies	24	12,683	29	12,909
Mauritius	—	—	4	1,397
Cape of Good Hope	3	675	8	2,287
British West Indies	805	113,773	813	113,072
British Guayana	57	9,159	96	15,345
British Honduras	45	6,522	55	6,453
British American Colonies	6,834	1,170,956	6,776	1,186,110
Other British Colonies	—	—	2	725
France, on the Atlantic	333	154,363	344	166,075
France, on the Mediterranean	38	14,844	61	17,689
French West Indies	118	22,442	155	25,242
French Guayana	10	1,491	12	1,808
Miquelon and French Fisheries	—	—	24	2,744
Bourbon	—	—	4	1,492
Spain, on the Atlantic	46	19,191	31	10,759
Spain, on the Mediterranean	103	23,720	96	23,592
Teneriffe and the Canaries	10	2,445	5	856
Manilla and Philippine Islands	13	5,816	9	3,189
Cuba	1,465	244,014	1,516	262,008
Porto Rico	248	39,809	177	28,646
Portugal	24	5,385	19	4,420
Madeira	12	2,589	23	4,394
Fayal and the Azores	11	1,899	8	1,108
Cape de Verd Islands	1	167	11	2,038
Sicily	111	30,377	8	2,072
Tuscany	14	5,915	8	2,531
Sardinia	10	3,380	38	13,548
Trieste and other Austrian Ports	12	5,134	36	13,140
Turkey	18	5,014	8	1,118
Mexico	66	9,400	55	12,871
Central America	13	1,822	7	1,345
New Granada	14	2,530	10	1,299
Venezuela	84	13,913	68	11,430
Brazil	290	65,849	204	42,648
Argentine Republic	4	693	10	2,237
Cisplatine Republic, (Uruguay,)	19	4,378	21	4,322
Chilé	21	8,508	23	8,262
Peru	4	919	6	1,770
Equador	—	—	1	168
China	38	17,775	23	12,334
Hayti	227	28,785	239	30,459
South America generally	2	550	1	186
Europe generally	—	—	1	326
Asia generally	4	1,081	2	448
Africa generally	58	12,247	62	11,570
West Indies generally	—	—	80	9,971
Liberia	2	428	1	180
Pacific Ocean, Whaling Vessels	116	39,042	97	33,066
Atlantic Ocean, Whaling Vessels	22	3,546	27	5,175
Indian Ocean, Whaling Vessels	14	3,015	43	11,395
Sandwich Islands	2	760	5	1,978
North-West Coast	—	—	6	2,284
Total	14,229	3,321,705	14,370	3,378,998

6.—STATEMENT EXHIBITING THE FOREIGN COMMERCE AND NAVIGATION OF EACH STATE.*

	STATES.	VALUE OF EXPORTS.							VALUE OF IMPORTS.		
		DOMESTIC PRODUCE.			FOREIGN PRODUCE.			Total American and Foreign Produce.			
		In American Vessels.	*In Foreign Vessels.*	*Total.*	*In American Vessels.*	*In Foreign Vessels.*	*Total.*		*In American Vessels.*	*In Foreign Vessels.*	*Total.*
1	Maine	$1,453,809	$160,262	$1,614,071	$4,755	$15,377	$20,132	$1,634,203	$445,745	$128,311	$574,056
2	New-Hampshire	....	1,407	1,407	....	283	283	1,690	13,150	3,785	16,935
3	Vermont	231,985	....	231,985	282,313	....	282,313	514,298	239,641	....	239,641
4	Massachusetts	7,942,656	1,320,121	9,262,777	1,534,580	451,105	1,985,685	11,248,462	18,189,238	16,287,770	34,477,008
5	Rhode Island	190,596	838	191,434	935	....	935	192,369	301,075	4,414	305,489
6	Connecticut	563,848	34,854	598,702	490	....	490	599,192	271,870	3,953	275,823
7	New-York	32,513,500	12,302,980	44,816,480	3,577,741	1,450,117	5,027,888	49,844,368	71,084,398	13,082,954	84,167,352
8	New-Jersey	18,428	....	18,428	....	700	700	19,128	4,066	771	4,837
9	Pennsylvania	6,146,513	2,116,798	8,263,311	273,466	7,614	281,080	8,544,391	8,843,773	743,743	9,587,516
10	Delaware	185,013	50,446	235,459	....	....	....	235,459	12,452	270	12,722
11	Maryland	6,796,076	2,836,284	9,632,360	94,539	35,345	129,884	9,762,244	3,928,643	503,671	4,432,314
12	District of Columbia	108,894	15,375	124,269	....	....	....	124,269	25,049	....	25,049
13	Virginia	3,499,110	2,146,558	5,645,668	10,740	1,966	12,706	5,658,374	333,091	53,036	386,127
14	North Carolina	261,949	22,970	284,919	....	....	....	284,919	136,483	5,901	142,384
15	South Carolina	6,058,387	4,369,759	10,428,146	475	2,896	3,371	10,431,517	1,201,911	378,747	1,580,658
16	Georgia	2,050,360	3,661,789	5,712,149	....	....	....	5,712,149	147,514	59,666	207,180
17	Florida	722,821	1,085,356	1,808,177	1,900	461	2,361	1,810,538	103,180	40,118	143,298
18	Alabama	3,197,209	5,857,371	9,054,580	....	....	....	9,054,580	80,492	309,669	390,161
19	Louisiana	25,609,818	16,178,485	41,788,303	193,204	70,126	263,330	42,051,633	7,437,995	1,784,974	9,222,969
20	Mississippi	....	....	....	....	....	....	....	81	255	336
21	Tennessee	....	....	....	....	....	....	....	1,256	....	1,256
22	Missouri	....	....	....	....	....	....	....	167,195	....	167,195
23	Ohio	203,102	575,842	778,944	....	....	....	778,944	88,381	2,300	90,681
24	Kentucky	....	....	....	....	....	....	....	26,956	....	26,956
25	Michigan	47,098	46,697	93,795	....	....	....	93,795	37,369	234	37,603
26	Illinois	40,100	12,060	52,100	....	....	....	52,100	266	....	266
27	Texas	....	....	....	....	....	....	....	20,087	9,739	29,826
	Total	$97,841,272	52,796,192	150,637,464	5,975,138	2,036,020	8,011,158	158,648,622	113,141 357	33,404,281	146,545,638

*Arkansas, Iowa, Wisconsin, and Indiana have no direct foreign commerce.

7.—TONNAGE EMPLOYED IN UNITED STATES TRADE, 1846–7.

STATES, ETC.	AMERICAN Total Crews.	AMERICAN TONNAGE. For. trade.	AMERICAN TONNAGE. Dom. trade.	FOREIGN. Total Crews.	FOREIGN. Tonnage.	TOTAL Tonnage.
1 New-York	54,056	1,086,744	750,951	30,944	537,458	2,375,153
2 Massachusetts	1,368	291,410	568,513	8,641	129,404	989,327
3 Louisiana	8,624	233,839	213,537	6.684	170,059	573,957
4 Pennsylvania	4,412	102,055	182,996	1,833	38,338	313,449
5 Maryland	3,520	82,099	139,119	1,685	40,966	262,184
6 Vermont	4.551	69,044	2,560	....	....	71,604
7 Maine	2,099	50,156	384,167	4,027	69,483	503,806
8 South Carolina	1,282	38,974	27,017	1,561	36,261	102,252
9 Connecticut	1,910	29,073	102,888	71	1, 366	133,327
10 Virginia	691	21,677	73,401	1,738	39,045	134,122
11 Rhode Island	1,102	21,149	48,011	134	2.330	71,497
12 North Carolina	960	20,850	24,488	150	2,840	48,179
13 Alabama	609	16,596	18,030	1,568	43,162	77,388
14 Florida	534	11,256	12,559	833	10,204	34,019
15 Georgia	390	9,553	21,023	1,391	39,049	69,625
16 Ohio	289	5,962	50,779	476	10,273	67,014
17 Texas	223	5,119	2,487	479	7,868	15,474
18 New-Hampshire	71	2,141	20,426	148	2,268	24,838
19 Illinois	72	1,858	3,251	17	350	5,459
20 Delaware	30	639	14,761	26	738	16,138
21 New-Jersey	23	613	83,644	93	2,850	86,307
22 District of Columbia	28	516	23,457	....	....	23,971
23 Michigan	4	35	28,452	17	36,795	65,262
24 Mississippi	....	....	391	....	....	391
25 Missouri	....	....	31,635	....	....	31,635
26 Kentucky	....	....	10,388	....	....	10,338
27 Tennessee	....	....	2,707	....	....	2,707
Total	99,345	2,101,359	2,839,045	64,364	1,220,346	6,160,750

In the above table the states are arranged in the order of their foreign trade, in American bottoms.

TONNAGE OF THE UNITED STATES IN SUCCESSIVE YEARS.

Years.	Registered tonnage.	Enrolled and licensed tonnage.	Total tonnage.	Registered tonnage in the whale fishery.	Proportion of the enrolled and licensed tonnage employed in the Coasting trade.	Cod Fishery.	Mackerel fishery.	Whale fishery.
1815	854,294	513,833	1,368,127	....	435,066	26,570	....	1,229
1816	800,759	571,458	1,372,218	....	479,979	37,879	....	1,168
1817	809,724	590,186	1,399,912	4,874	181,457	53,990	....	349
1818	606,088	619,095	1,225,184	16,134	503,140	58,551	....	614
1819	612,930	647,821	1,260,751	31,700	523,556	65,044	....	686
1820	619,047	661,118	1,280,166	35,391	539,080	60,842	....	1,053
1821	619,896	679,062	1,298,958	26,070	559,435	51,351	....	1,924
1822	628,150	696,548	1,324,699	45,449	573,080	58,405	....	3,133
1823	639,920	696,644	1,336,565	39,918	566.408	67,620	....	585
1824	669,972	719,190	1,389,163	33,165	589,223	68,419	....	180
1825	700,787	722,323	1,423,110	35,379	587,273	70,626	....	....
1826	737,978	796,211	1,534,189	41,757	666,420	63,761	....	226
1827	747,170	873,437	1,620,607	45,653	732,937	74,048	....	338
1828	812,619	928,772	1,741,391	45,621	758,922	74,947	....	180
1829	650,142	610,654	1,260,797	56,284	508,858	101,796	....	....
1830	576,675	615,311	1,191,776	38,911	516,978	61,554	35,973	792
1831	620,451	647,394	1,267,846	82,315	539,723	60,977	46,210	481
1832	686,989	752,460	1,439,450	72,868	649,627	54,027	47,427	377
1833	750,126	856,123	1,606,149	101,158	744,198	62,720	48,725	478
1834	857,438	901,468	1,758,907	108,060	783,618	56,403	61,082	364
1835	885,821	939,118	1,824.940	97,640	792,301	72,374	64,443	....
1836	897,774	984,328	1,882,102	144,680	873,023	63,307	64,424	1,573
1837	810,447	1,086,238	1,896,685	127,241	956,980	80,551	46,810	1,894
1838	822,591	1,173,047	1,995,639	119,629	1,041,105	70,064	56,649	5,229
1839	834,244	1,262,234	2,096,478	131,845	1,153,551	72,258	35,983	439
1840	899,764	1,280,999	2,180,764	136,926	1,176,694	76,035	28,269	....
1841	945,803	1,184,490	2.130,744	157,405	1,107,067	66,551	11,321	....
1842	975,358	1,117,031	2,092,390	151,612	1,045,753	54,804	16,096	377
1843	1,009,305	1,149,297	2,158,801	152,374	1,076,155	61,224	11,775	142
1844	1,068,764	1,211,330	2,280,095	168,293	1,109,614	85,224	16,170	320
1845	1,095,171	1,321,829	2,417,002	190,695	1,190,898	69,825	21,413	206
1846	1,130,286	1,431,798	2,562,084	186,980	1,289,870	72,516	36,463	439
1847	1,241,312	1,597,732	2,839,095	193,858	1,452,623	70,177	31,451	....

8.—STATISTICS OF SHIP BUILDING IN THE UNITED STATES.

VESSELS BUILT IN 1846–7.

States.	Ships.	Brigs.	Sch'rs.	Sloops and canal boats.	Steamers.	Total vessels built.	Total tonnage.
Maine	73	120	151	1	1	346	63,548
New Hampshire	7	1	2	....	...	10	5,288
Vermont	....	....	1	2	...	3	135
Massachusetts	33	13	84	5	3	138	27,769
Rhode Island	3	2	3	1	1	10	2,110
Connecticut	3	....	30	8	1	42	6,027
New-York	17	5	88	138	23	371	50,994
New-Jersey	....	....	70	26	5	101	9,830
Pennsylvania	8	2	31	121	66	228	24,126
Delaware	....	....	17	6	2	25	2,279
Maryland	5	17	108	....	1	131	12,691
District of Columbia	....	1	2	19	...	22	801
Virginia	....	....	25	....	2	27	1.524
North Carolina	1	....	27	6	...	34	2,384
South Carolina	....	....	3	....	...	3	161
Georgia	....	....	....	1	...	1	25
Ohio	1	6	29	10	37	83	18,191
Missouri	....	....	1	43	16	60	6,073
Tennessee	....	....	....	....	1	1	167
Kentucky	....	....	1	....	30	31	5,424
Louisiana	....	....	9	-	2	12	493
Florida	....	....	....	....	2	2	387
Michigan	....	1	7	4	5	17	3,293
Alabama	....	....	....	....	...	....	.....
Total	151	168	689	392	198	1,598	243,732

VESSELS BUILT IN SUCCESSIVE YEARS.

States.	Ships.	Brigs.	Sch'rs.	Sloops and canal boats.	Steamers.	Total vessels built.	Total tonnage.
1815	136	224	680	274	...	1,314	154,624
1816	76	122	781	424	...	1,403	131,668
1817	34	86	559	394	...	1,073	86,393
1818	53	85	428	332	...	898	82.421
1819	53	82	473	242	...	850	79.817
1820	21	60	301	152	...	534	47,784
1821	43	89	248	127	...	507	55,856
1822	64	131	260	168	...	623	75,346
1823	55	127	260	165	15	622	75,007
1824	56	156	377	166	26	781	90,399
1825	56	197	538	168	35	994	114,997
1826	71	187	482	227	45	1,012	126.438
1827	58	133	464	241	38	934	104,342
1828	73	108	474	196	33	884	98,375
1829	44	68	485	145	43	785	77,098
1830	25	56	403	116	37	637	58,094
1831	72	95	416	94	34	711	85962
1832	132	143	568	122	100	1,065	144.539
1833	144	169	625	185	65	1,188	161,626
1834	98	94	497	180	68	937	118,330
1835	25	50	302	100	30	507	*46,238
1836	93	65	444	164	124	890	113,627
1837	67	72	507	168	135	949	122.987
1838	66	79	510	153	90	898	113,135
1839	83	89	439	122	125	658	120,988
1840	97	109	378	224	64	872	118,309
1841	114	101	312	157	78	762	118,893
1842	116	91	273	404	137	1,021	129,083
1843	58	34	138	173	79	482	*63,617
1844	73	47	204	279	163	766	103,537
1845	124	87	322	342	163	1,038	147,018
1846	100	164	576	355	225	1,420	188,202
1847	151	168	689	392	198	1,598	242,732

* For 9 months.

Table of Mail Service for the year ending June 30, 1846.

States and Territories.	Length of Routes.	Annual Transportation.			Total Transportation.	Total Cost.
		Mode not specified.	In Coaches.	Railroad and Steamboat.		
	Miles.	Miles.	Miles.	Miles.	Miles.	
Maine	3,955	784,728	258,870	70,824	1,114,422	$40,791
New-Hampshire	2,384	242,684	400,264	62.400	705,348	25,409
Vermont	2,530	280,696	444,928	2,100	727,724	26,723
Massachusetts	3,618	376,980	811,626	722,204	1,910,810	105,898
Rhode Island	385	58,250	74,880	30,264	158,394	9,102
Connecticut	1,788	363,896	156,936	211,176	732,008	43,863
New-York	13,304	1,812,529	1,678,318	1,453,652	4,944,499	237,918
New-Jersey	2,021	106,097	404,456	229,288	733,841	58,850
Pennsylvania	10,276	902,060	1,603,056	359,216	2,864,332	155,304
Delaware	605	66,040	84,874	....	150,914	7,887
Maryland	2,351	228,956	302,276	391,768	923,000	138,679
Virginia	110,02	1,048,260	857,177	515,112	2,420,549	193,586
North Carolina	7,323	582,524	666,952	337,272	1,586,748	172,557
South Carolina	4,605	366,548	421,220	229,820	1,017,088	117,959
Georgia	5.782	475,566	422,336	230,720	1,228,622	150,162
Florida	2,937	86,216	173,861	87,984	348,061	44,909
Ohio	11,337	911,599	1,569,496	617,344	3,098,412	166,954
Michigan	4,073	334,384	300,456	195,312	830,152	48,288
Indiana	6,855	617,906	594,670	....	1,212,576	68,875
Illinois	8,473	563,262	1,285,496	35,776	1,884,534	125,291
Wisconsin	2,881	210,792	91,312	....	302,104	15,691
Iowa	1,409	110,344	64,064	....	174,408	8,658
Missouri	7,909	576,072	427,400	473,616	1,477,088	68,875
Kentucky	7,613	570,448	655,724	1,056,016	2,282,188	125,850
Tennessee	6,906	622,076	704,292	....	1,326,368	91,160
Alabama	6,728	607,684	650,936	197,704	1,456,354	227,412
Mississippi	4,361	484,328	318,240	28,704	881,272	95,109
Arkansas	4,458	438,412	105,456	46,800	590,668	56,264
Louisiana	2,806	225,216	7,488	108,256	365,960	42,670
Total*	149,679	14,179,553	15,537,033	7,781,828	37,398,414	
Cost		$629,018	$1,164,590	$870,570		2,665,079†

* Add Texas, 3,186 miles; in all, 152,865 miles.
† Also, expenses of mail agencies, $42,406; service in Texas, from Feb. 16, 1846, $9,189 making in all $2,716,673.

Number of Post-Offices, &c., at various periods.

Year.	Number of Post Offices.	Extent of Post Roads.	Revenue of the Department.	Expenditures of the Department.	Amount paid for	
					Compensat. of Postmasters.	Transport'n of the Mail.
		Miles.	Dollars.	Dollars.	Dollars.	Dollars.
1790	75	1,875	37,935	32,140	8,198	22,981
1795	453	13,207	160,620	117,803	30,272	75,359
1800	903	20,817	280,804	213,994	69,243	128,644
1805	1,558	31,076	421,373	377,367	111,552	239,635
1810	2,300	36,406	551,684	405,969	149,438	327,966
1815	3,000	43,748	1,043,065	748,121	241,901	487,779
1820	4,500	72,492	1,111,927	1,160,926	352,295	782,425
1825	5,677	94,052	1,306,525	1,229,043	411,183	785,646
1830	8,450	115,176	1,850,583	1,932,708	595,234	1,274,009
1835	10,770	112,774	2,993,356	2,757,350	945,418	1,719,067
1840	13,468	155,739	4,539,265	4,759,110	1,028,925	3,296,876
1845	14,183	143,940	4,289,842	4,320,732	1,409,875	2,905,504
1846	14,601	152,865	3,487,199	4,084,297		2,716,673

VII.—THE UNITED STATES MINT.

Coinage of the Mint of the United States, from 1792, *including the coinage of the Branch Mints from the commencement of their operations, in* 1838.

Years.	GOLD.	SILVER.	COPPER.	WHOLE COINAGE.	
	Value.	Value.	Value.	No. of Pieces	Value.
1793-5........	$71,485 00	$370,683 80	$11,373 00	1,834,420	$453,541 80
1796..........	102,727 50	79,077 50	10,324 40	1,219,370	192,129 40
1797..........	108,422 50	12,591 45	9,510 34	1,095,165	125,524 29
1798..........	205,610 00	330,291 00	9,797 00	1,368,241	545,698 00
1799..........	213,285 00	423,515 00	9,106 68	1,365,681	645,906 68
1800..........	817,760 00	224,296 00	29,279 40	3,337,972	571,335 40
1801..........	422,570 00	74,758 00	13,628 37	1,571,390	510,956 37
1802..........	423,310 00	58,343 00	34,422 83	3,615,869	516,075 83
1803..........	258,377 50	87,118 00	25,203 03	2,780,830	370,698 53
1804..........	258,642 50	100,340 50	12,844 94	2,046,839	371,827 94
1805..........	170,367 50	149,388 50	13,483 48	2,260,361	333,239 48
1806..........	324,505 00	471,319 00	5,260 00	1,815,409	801,084 00
1807..........	437,495 00	597,448 75	9,652 21	2,731,345	1,044,595 96
1808..........	284,665 00	684,300 00	13,090 00	2,905,888	982,055 00
1809..........	169,375 00	707,376 00	8,001 53	2,861,834	884,752 53
1810..........	501,435 00	638,773 50	15,660 00	3,056,418	1,155,868 50
1811..........	497,905 00	608,340 00	2,495 95	1,649,570	1,108,740 95
1812..........	290,435 00	814,029 50	10,755 00	2,761,646	1,115,219 50
1813..........	477,140 00	620,951 50	4,180 00	1,755,331	1,102,275 50
1814..........	77,270 00	561,687 50	3,578 30	1,833,859	642,535 80
1815..........	3,175 00	17,308 00	....	69,867	20,483 00
1816..........	....	28,575 75	28,209 82	2,888,135	56,785 57
1817..........	....	607,783 50	39,484 00	5,163,967	647,267 50
1818..........	242,940 00	1,070,454 50	31,670 00	5,537,084	1,345,064 50
1819..........	258,615 00	1,140,000 00	26,710 00	5,074,723	1,425,325 00
1820..........	1,319,030 00	501,680 70	44,075 50	6,492,509	1,864,786 20
1821..........	189,325 00	825,762 45	3,890 00	3,139,249	1,018,977 45
1822..........	88,980 00	805,806 50	20,723 39	3,813,788	915,509 89
1823..........	72,425 00	895.550 00	....	2,166,485	967,975 00
1824..........	93,200 00	1,752,477 00	12,620 00	4,786,894	1,858,297 00
1825..........	156,385 00	1,564,583 00	14,926 00	5,178,760	1,735,894 00
1826..........	92,245 00	2,002,090 00	16,344 25	5,774,434	2,110,679 25
1827..........	131,565 00	2,869,200 00	23,557 32	9,097,845	3,024,342 32
1828..........	140,145 00	1,575,600 00	25,636 24	6,196,853	1,741,381 24
1829..........	295,717 50	1,994,578 00	16,580 00	7,674,501	2,306,875 50
1830..........	643,105 00	2,495,400 00	17,115 00	7,357,191	3,155,620 00
1831..........	714,270 00	3,175,600 00	33.603 60	11,792,284	3,923,473 60
1832..........	798,435 00	2,579,000 00	23,620 00	9,128,387	3,401,055 00
1833..........	978,550 00	2,579,000 00	28,160 00	10,307,790	3,765,710 00
1834..........	3,954,270 00	3,415,002 00	19,151 00	11,637,643	7,388,423 00
1835..........	2,186,175 00	3,443,003 00	39,489 00	15,996,342	5,668,667 00
1836..........	4,135,700 09	3,606,100 00	23,100 00	13,719,333	7,764,900 00
1837..........	1,148,305 00	2,096,010 00	55,583 00	13,010 721	3,299,898 00
1838..........	1,809,595 00	2,333,243 00	53,702 00	15.780,311	4,206,540 00
1839..........	1,355,885 00	2,189,296 00	31,286 61	11,811,594	3,576,467 61
1840..........	1,675,302 50	1,726,703 00	24.627 00	10,558,240	3,426,632 50
1841..........	1,091,597 50	1,132,750 00	15,973 67	8,811,968	2,240,321 17
1842..........	1,834,170 50	2,332,750 00	23,833 90	11,743,153	4,190,754 40
1843..........	8,108,797 50	3,834,750 00	24,283 20	114,640,582	11,967,830 70
1844..........	5,428,230 00	2,235,550 00	23,987 52	9,051,831	7,687,767 52
1845..........	3,756,447 00	1,873,200 00	38,948 04	11,806,196	5,668,595 54
1846..........	4,034,177 06	2,558,580 00	41,208 00	20,133,515	6,633,965 00
Total,.......	52,344,542 50	69,052,014 90	1,083,774 52	315,239,616	122,480,321 92

VIII.—ECCLESIASTICAL STATISTICS

1.—EPISCOPAL DENOMINATIONS.

PROTESTANT EPISCOPAL,* (Anglican.)

DIOCESES.	Founded.	BISHOPS.	Consecrated.	Number of Clergy.	Number of Churches.	Communicants.
Maine	1847	George Burgess	1847	10	7	560
New-Hampshire	1844	Carlton Chase	1844	8	10	515
Vermont	1832	John Henry Hopkins	1832	20	19	1,497
Massachusetts	1797	Manton Eastburn	1842	73	43	4,715
Rhode Island	1843	John O. K. Henshaw	1843	28	19	2,348
Connecticut	1784	Thomas C. Brownell	1819	101	86	7,467
New-York	1787	Benjamin T. Onderdonk	1830	230	193	15,000
Western New-York	1839	William H. De Lancy	1839	103	47	6,000
New-Jersey	1815	George W. Doane	1832	57	40	2,274
Pennsylvania	1787	Alonzo Potter	1845	129	76	10,053
Delaware	1841	Alfred Lee	1841	11	14	515
Maryland	1792	William R. Whittingham	1840	120	85	6,639
Virginia	1790	William Meade John Johns, Asst. Bp	1829 1844	114	76	6,000
North Carolina	1823	Levi S. Ives	1831	38	21	1,850
South Carolina	1795	Christopher E. Gadsden	1840	65	42	4,324
Ohio	1819	Charles P. McIlvaine	1832	64	46	4,000
Georgia	1841	Stephen Elliot	1841	24	12	894
Kentucky	1832	Benjamin B. Smith	1832	22	13	730
Tennessee	1834	James H. Otey	1834	16	10	545
Mississippi	....	*Vacant*	....	17	8	450
Louisiana	1844	Leonidas Polk	1838	27	13	724
Michigan	1836	Samuel A. McCoskry	1836	27	18	1,200
Alabama	1844	Nicholas H. Cobbs	1844	24	11	663
Illinois	1832	Philander Chase	1819	25	14	973
Florida	....	*Vacant*	....	6	4	220
Indiana	1825	Jackson Kemper	1835	18	2	552
Missouri	1825	Cicero S. Hawks	1844	14	10	537
Wisconsin	....	Jackson Kemper	1835	23	24	969
Iowa	....	Jackson Kemper	1835	3	3	
Arkansas	1838	George W. Freeman	1844	4	4	1,000
Texas	1846	George W. Freeman	1844	4	2	
Aggregate of Church				1,425	972	83,214

Total population connected with this church about 1,500,000.

ROMAN CATHOLIC.†

DIOCESES.‡§	BISHOPS.‡	Consecrated.	Places of Worship: Churches.	Places of Worship: Other Stations.	Clergy: In the Ministry.	Clergy: Otherwise employed.	Ecclesiastical: Institutions.	Ecclesiastical: Students.	Religious Institutions: Males.	Religious Institutions: Females.	Catholic Population of Dioceses
BALTIMORE....*Md.*	SAMUEL ECCLESTON	1834	65	10	48	34	4	50	5	7	100,000
New-Orleans...*La.*	Anthony Blanc	1835	49	-	51	14	1	11	-	4	160,000
Louisville.....*Ky.*	Bened Joseph Flaget	1810	40	75	32	9	2	-	1	4	30,000
Boston........*Mass.*	John Fitzpatrick	1844	52	25	44	5	-	-	-	-	80,000
Philadelphia...*Pa.*	Francis Patrick Kenrick	1830	74	-	55	8	1	25	-	2	120,000
New-York....*N. Y.*	John Hughes	1838			71	17	1	22	1	3	
Albany.........."	John McCloskey	1844	130	100	34	-	-	-	-	-	230,000
Buffalo.........."	John Timon	1847			18	-	-	-	-	-	
Charleston..*S. Car.*	Ignatius Reynolds	1844	25	50	21	-	1	3	-	2	7,000
Richmond.....*Va.*	Richard V. Wheelan	1841	14	-	10	-	-	6	-	-	20,000
Cincinnati....*Ohio.*	John B. Purcell	1833	50	10	46	12	1	10	1	3	50,000
Cleveland......"	Amedeus Rappe	1847	33	20	17	-	1	7	-	2	30,000
ST. LOUIS......*Mo.*	PETER R. KENRICK	1841	51	25	54	27	3	23	2	16	50,000
Mobile.........*Ala.*	Michaël Portier	1826	12	30	19	-	1	-	1	1	11,000
Detroit.......*Mich.*	Peter P. Lefevere	1841	28	20	27	-	1	9	-	2	75,000
Vincennes.....*Ind.*	John Stephen Bazin	1847	51	-	38	8	1	17	2	1	30,000
Dubuque.....*Iowa.*	Mathias Loras	1837	13	9	8	-	-	-	-	1	6,500
Nashville.....*Ten.*	Richard P. Miles	1838	6	20	7	-	1	-	1	-	1,500
Natchez.....*Miss.*	John J. Chanche	1831	7	14	5	-	-	-	-	-	6,500
Pittsburg.......*Pa.*	Michael O'Connor	1843	57	-	41	-	-	25	2	2	35,000
Little Rock.....*Ill.*	Andrew Byrne	1844	6	10	6	1	1	3	-	-	700
Chicago........"	William Quartier	1844	60	50	46	2	1	-	-	1	50,000
Hartford.....*Conn.*	William Tyler	1844	12	14	10	-	-	-	-	-	20,000
Milwaukie.....*Wis.*	John P. Henni	1844	37	42	36	-	1	6	2	-	40,000
Galveston.....*Tex.*	John M. Odin	1842	12	37	14	-	-	-	-	1	20,000
OREGON CITY..*Or.*	FRANCIS N. BLANCHET	1845									
Walla-Walla...."	Magloire Blanchet	1846	13	1	24	-	-	-	1	1	7,500
Fort Hall........"	........do.	....									
Colville.........."	........do.	....									
Nesqually........"	Francis N. Blanchet	.....									
Aggregate of Church			907	562	782	137	22	27	19	53	1,190,700

* Church Almanac. † Catholic Directory. ‡ Arch-dioceses and Arch-bishops are printed in SMALL CAPITALS. § The dioceses of Vancouver's Island, Princess Charlotte's, and New Caledonia are administered by the Right Rev. Niddeit Demers.

2.—PRESBYTERIAN DENOMINATIONS.

OLD SCHOOL.*

Names of Synods.**	No. of Presbyteries.	No. of Churches.	No. of Ministers.	No. of Communicants.
Albany .... N.Y.	4	50	79	7,197
Buffalo, ... "	4	33	36	2,754
New-York.... "	6	89	104	11,604
New-Jersey	7	130	146	17,826
Philadelphia, Pa.	8	221	176	25,655
Pittsburg .... "	7	196	131	19,558
Wheeling .... O.	4	103	65	9,657
Ohio.......... "	7	141	84	10,100
Cincinnati.... "	6	126	83	8,820
Indiana.........	5	104	64	5,288
Northern Indiana	4	55	31	1,927
Illinois..........	8	126	65	3,936
Missouri.	5	76	40	3,074
Kentucky.......	6	133	73	7,224
Virginia..	6	151	118	10,081
North Carolina..	3	145	85	8,846
West Tennessee.	5	77	48	4,460
South Carolina..	4	95	70	7,431
Georgia.........	5	95	59	4,338
Alabama.........	3	85	52	4,280
Mississippi......	8	138	87	5,513
Total.........	115	2,373	1,696	179,371

NEW SCHOOL.†

Names of Synods.	No. of Presbyteries.	No. of Churches.	No. of Ministers.	No. of Communicants.
Genessee ...... N.Y.	6	145	136	16,046
Albany .... "	7	106	124	13,409
Utica............. "	5	98	90	9,780
Geneva.. .... "	10	195	197	20,790
New-York & New-Jersey.......	9	118	158	21,971
Pennsylvania	5	68	66	10,889
Western Pennsylvania.	3	35	19	2,366
Western Reserve, O.	8	146	130	9,625
Ohio .... "	5	70	54	5,218
Cincinnati ...... "	3	49	40	3,889
Indiana.	7	101	60	4,460
Illinois.............	5	62	53	3,407
Peoria. .... Ill.	4	46	52	2,230
Missouri...........	4	50	33	1,832
Michigan..........	7	106	84	6,591
Kentucky	3	21	14	954
Virginia...........	3	39	39	3,659
Tennessee.........	5	73	40	5,422
West Tennessee....	3	34	28	2,021
Mississippi.........	3	19	13	857
Total.............	105	1,581	1,430	145,416

Cumberland.¶

This church, in the aggregate, consists of 570 congregations, 300 ministers, and about 60,000 communicants. Its operations are chiefly confined to the Western States, where it took its rise a few years past. Its doctrines are substantially those of the new school, with which, as with all the other Presbyterian sects, it holds friendly correspondence.

ASSOCIATE.‡

Synod	Names of Presbyteries.	No. of Congregations.	No. of Ministers.	No. of Families.	No. of Communicants.
First Synod.	Cambridge..	11	7	367	887
	Ohio........	15	7	603	1,260
	Chartiers...	17	11	1,007	2,246
	Miami.......	22	9	404	854
	Philadelphia	16	6	237	790
	Alleghany..	23	10	649	1,892
	Muskingum.	22	11	720	1,670
	Albany.....	7	3	244	633
	Chenango...	23	10	1,005	2,180
	Stamford. ..	6	3	35	521
	Indiana.....	14	5	250	850
	Illinois......	13	2	139	311
	Richland. ..	16	4	295	661
	Iowa........	9	4	99	229
	Itinerating..	-	26	-	-
	Total.........	118	213	6,054	14,984
2d Synod.	Cambridge..	3	6	177	419
	New-York ..	8	6	576	1,783
	Vermont ...	3	2	133	345
	Illinois.....	4	2	124	302
	Total........	16	18	1,010	2,850
	Grand Total	231	134	7,064	17,834

ASSOCIATE REFORMED.§

Names of Synods.	No. of Presbyteries.	No. of Churches.	No. of Ministers.	No. of Members.
Synod of New-York	5	40	44	4,600
First Synod of the West—(*Pennsylvania and Ohio*).....	5	111	67	9,660
Second Synod of the West—(*Ohio and Indiana*)..	8	118	69	6,490
Synod of the South—(*North and South Carolina*)......	6	45	35	5,500
Total......	24	314	215	26,250

Reformed, &c.‖

The Reformed Presbyterian is a small church under a general Synod. It consists of 5 Presbyteries, 33 ministers, 7 licensed preachers, 15 theological students, 56 congregations, and about 6,000 communicants. It has a Theological Seminary at Philadelphia, and supports a mission in Northern India. There are several other denominations of Presbyterians but so insignificant are they in extent and influence, that it has been impossible to find any one acquainted with their statistics.

* Presbyterian Almanac. † Minutes of General Assembly. ‡ Communicated by Dr. Stark. § Communicated by Rev. William McLaren, D.D. ‖ Communicated by Rev. John N. McLeod, D.D. ¶ American Almanac. ** Also one Synod in Northern India, consisting of the Presbyteries of Lodiana, Furrukhabad and Allahabad; three churches, nineteen ministers, and eighty-two communicants.

3.—BAPTIST DENOMINATIONS.

NAME OF STATES.	Regular.*					Anti-Mission.*				
	No. of Associations.	No. of Churches.	No. of Ministers.	No of Licentiates.	Number of Church Members.	No. of Associations.	No. of Churches.	No. of Ministers.	No. of Licentiates.	Number of Church Members.
Maine	13	300	218	23	21,475					
New-Hampshire	7	102	83	15	9,577					
Vermont	9	112	90	3	9,183					
Massachusetts	12	234	213	18	30,088	2	8	6	2	245
Rhode Island	2	43	44	6	6,943					
Connecticut	6	108	102	20	16,212					
New York	43	811	730	116	87,776	2	25	14	3	964
New Jersey	4	86	92	17	11,454	1	6	4	1	246
Pennsylvania	15	302	208	43	27,873	3	23	14	2	868
Delaware	—	1	2	—	342	1	10	3	3	335
Maryland	2	22	13	2	1,960	2	24	8	3	404
Dis. of Columbia	—	4	5	1	706	—	—	—	—	—
Virginia	23	498	237	66	78,645	9	98	44	—	4,461
North Carolina.	22	454	231	80	32,671	9	162	105	10	5,815
South Carolina.	13	389	190	42	40,237	2	15	6	1	289
Georgia	26	620	298	103	47,151	17	348	116	23	11,603
Florida	1	32	18	8	1,333	—	12	4	—	509
Alabama	17	427	195	47	28,210	12	185	86	6	6,417
Mississippi	15	326	147	35	19,539	7	49	19	3	1,679
Louisiana	5	73	42	8	3,311	1	4	2	—	80
Texas	2	24	13	1	672	1	8	3	—	132
Arkansas	6	67	23	1	2,015	3	27	13	2	517
Tennessee	18	440	240	52	32,159	19	286	134	12	10,186
Kentucky	42	685	344	105	60,371	16	192	74	12	7,085
Ohio	26	477	195	62	25,766	10	139	58	5	3,456
Indiana	22	364	175	51	18,366	7	104	42	8	3,870
Illinois	20	292	171	54	12,342	15	158	92	5	4,382
Missouri	21	334	155	57	16,366	11	118	67	7	4,336
Michigan	10	162	105	12	8,431	—	—	—	—	—
Wisconsin	2	40	38	3	1,740	—	—	—	—	—
Iowa	2	36	14	5	913	1	10	9	2	189
Indian Territory	—	16	18	8	1,671	—	—	—	—	—
Oregon Territory	—	2	2	1	40	—	—	—	—	—
Total	406	7,883	4,651	1,065	655,536	151	1,912	913	110	67,868

*Baptist Almanac.

Other Sects.

The statistics of the minor sections of the Baptist Church cannot be obtained in detail. The following exhibits the aggregate of each, as stated in the Baptist Almanac for 1847:

SIX PRINCIPLE BAPTISTS have 20 Churches, 22 ordained ministers, and 3,400 communicants.
SEVENTH DAY Do. " 63 " 58 " " 6,943 "
CHURCH OF GOD, Do. " 130 " 90 " " 8,000 "
FREE-WILL, Do. " 1165 " 771 " " 63,000 "
REFORMERS, (Campbellites,) " 1800 " 1,000 " " 160,000 "
CHRISTIAN CONNECTION, do. " 650 " 782 " " 35,000 "

In connection with the two first of these churches, are several valuable societies, viz:

1. THE AMERICAN BAPTIST MISSIONARY UNION.—Missions are sustained in Europe, Asia, Africa, and North America. In EUROPE—France. Denmark, Prussia, Germany and Greece. In ASIA—Burmah, Siam, Assam, China and Hindostan. In AFRICA—Among the Bassas on the west coast. And in NORTH AMERICA—Among the Ojibwas, Ottawas, Tuscaroras, Shawsnes, Stockbridges, Delawares and Cherokees. SUMMARY—16 Missions, embracing 56 stations and 87 out-stations; 99 missionaries, of whom 42 are preachers; 155 native preachers; 82 churches and 50 schools. Receipts for the year ending 1st April, 1846, $112,619 94.

2. THE AMERICAN AND FOREIGN BIBLE SOCIETY.—Organized 17th Feb., 1846.—Receipts in 1845-6. $36,971 76c. Issued 10,413 Bibles and 25,314 Testaments.

3. THE AMERICAN BAPTIST HOME MISSION SOCIETY.—Organized 1832.—Receipts for the year ending April 1st, 1846, $40,588 Employed 106 missionaries, supplying 472 stations; churches organized, 33; ministers ordained, 15 Auxiliaries employ 241 missionaries, supplying 640 stations. Its missionaries have organized 564 churches, and ordained 430 ministers.

4. THE AMERICAN BAPTIST PUBLICATION SOCIETY.—Organized 1839.—Receipts for 1845-6, $22,728. This society has published 45 bound volumes and 171 tracts.

5. THE SOUTHERN BAPTIST CONVENTION.—Organized 1843.—The first triennial meeting was held at Richmond, Va., June 10, 1846. Receipts for *Foreign Missions*, $11,735, and *Domestic Missions*. $7,493. Foreign Stations—China and Africa. Domestic Sta. in 14 Southern States.

6. THE AMERICAN INDIAN MISSION ASSOCIATION.—Organized 1842. Receipts 1845-6, $4,769 Has 19 missionaries, of which 9 are ordained preachers laboring among the Pottawatamies, Weas, Shawnees, Tuscaroras, Delawares, Stockbridges, Choctaws and Creeks. Churches, 5; communicants, 300.

4.—METHODIST DENOMINATIONS.

EPISCOPAL.*

	CONFERENCES.	PREACHERS. Travelling.	PREACHERS. Superannuat'd	PREACHERS. Local.	Church Members.
NORTH CHURCH.	Baltimore,...Md.	229	19	280	68,725
	Philadelphia, Pa.	156	4	291	50,123
	New-Jersey....	152	4	186	30,156
	New-York......	254	30	220	47,107
	Providence, R.I.	112	13	72	13,357
	New-England ..	108	19	76	13,305
	Maine..........	161	30	167	20,281
	New-Hampshire	81	17	64	10,384
	Vermont........	71	14	46	7,953
	Troy,......N. Y.	174	16	138	25,327
	Black River, do.	112	11	145	15,917
	Oneida.... do.	164	23	203	26,181
	Genessee, do.	188	22	254	27,305
	Erie, ...Pa.	123	16	170	20,437
	Pittsburg,....Pa.	162	15	274	42,052
	Ohio............	238	11	525	65,984
	North Ohio.....	132	6	288	27,161
	Michigan........	116	10	188	16,768
	Indiana	116	3	309	32,530
	North Indiana...	106	8	267	27,336
	Rock River.....	125	14	252	18,219
	Iowa............	53	..	95	7,717
	Illinois..........	97	12	433	25,216
	Total.........	3230	317	4943	639,541
SOUTH CHURCH.	Kentucky	96	1	145	26,710
	Missouri........	51	3	93	10,636
	St. Louis,...Mo,	60	3	138	13,890
	Louisville,..Ky.	61	1	....	18,210
	Holston, ...Te.	88	7	327	38,605
	Tennessee......	150	3	....	41,255
	Virginia.........	97	7	166	30,373
	Indian Mission..	30	..	27	3,155
	Arkansas........	49	3	144	9,068
	Memphis, ...Te.	96	5	310	29,114
	North Carolina..	73	13	133	26,648
	Mississippi......	76	3	....	15,949
	Georgia	120	14	444	54,521
	Louisiana.......	52	1	57	8,044
	South Carolina..	111	12	278	73,124
	Alabama.........	126	9	429	42,431
	Florida..........	36	1	70	6,558
	Texas, West....	32	..	39	2,545
	" East.....	29	..	33	4,386
	Total,........	1433	86	2833	455,217
	Grand Total....	4663	403	7776	1,094,758

BISHOPS.

Church	Bishop	Entered traveling min.	Elected bp.
North	Elijah Hedding...Entered traveling min. 1801—elect'd bp. 1824	1801	1824
North	Beverly Waugh	1809	1836
North	Thos. A. Morris	1816	1836
North	Leonidas L. Hamline	1832	1844
North	Edmund S. Janes	1830	1844
South	Joshua Soule...Entered trav. min. 1799—elected bp. 1824	1799	1824
South	James O. Andrew	1812	1832
South	William Capers	1808	1846
South	Robert Paine	1818	1846

WESLEYAN.†

CONFERENCES.	No. of Ministers.	Licentiates.	Church Members.
New-York ...	26	20	945
New-England	40	10	1,991
Champlain ...	25	13	1,300
St. Lawrence.	35	36	1,150
Rochester....	83	42	2,716
Alleghany....	40	25	3,278
Miami........	55	34	2,110
Michigan.....	50	17	1,566
Illinois.......	8	15	568
Wisconsin....	8	10	250
Total........	370	222	15,874

PROTESTANT

Churches, so far as reported.................438
Communicants.....................................80,000

Annual Conferences.............................30
Stationed Ministers..............................700
Unstationed Ministers and Preachers..........800

OTHER CHURCHES.

		Churches.	Ministers.	Members.
REFORMED METHODISTS		——	75	3,000
GERMAN	do.	800	500	15,000
ALBRIGHT	do.	600		13,000

* Methodist Almanac.
† Communicated by Lucius C. Matlack, Publishing Agent for Methodist Connection.
‡ Communicated by Rev. J. J. Smith, of New-York.

5.—CONGREGATIONAL DENOMINATIONS.

ORTHODOX.*

GENERAL ASSOCIATIONS.	No. of Churches.	No. of Ministers.	Church Members.
Massachusetts....	478	473	56,103
Maine............	217	166	17,504
Connecticut......	256	239	36,380
Rhode Island.....	20	16	2,770
New-Hampshire..	188	181	22,790
Vermont.........	194	190	20,209
New-York........	130	123	6,719
Pennsylvania.....	16	9	456
Ohio.............	94	15	5,506
Indiana..........	9	6	†
Illinois..........	75	50	3,471
Michigan........	70	50	2,114
Wisconsin........	86	68	2,736
Iowa............	34	26	910
Total,.........	1867	1612	177,668

UNITARIAN.‡

STATES.	No. of Congregations.	No. of settled Pastors.	No. of Ministers without Parishes.	No. of Communicants.	No. in Connection.
Maine...........	15	Estimated at about 200	Estimated at about 60	Estimated at about 30,000	Estimated at about 300,000
New-Hampshire..	24				
Vermont	6				
Massachusetts....	162				
Connecticut......	4				
Rhode Island....	3				
New-York........	13				
Pennsylvania.....	3				
Maryland........	1				
Dist. of Columbia	1				
South Carolina...	1				
Georgia..........	2				
Louisiana........	1				
Kentucky	1				
Ohio............	1				
Indiana	2				
Illinois..........	8				
Missouri.........	1				
Wisconsin	1				
Alabama	1				
Total	251				

This Church has two Theological Schools, one at Cambridge, Mass., and one at Meadville, Pa. There are also several incipient or feeble societies throughout the United States, carrying the entire number of congregations beyond three hundred.

* Congregational Almanac † Not reported.

‡ The whole number of Anti-Trinitarian Churches in the United States, including
Hicksite Quakers or Friends;
Campbellites, (Reformed Baptists ;)
Christians, (Baptists;)
Universalists;
Seventh Day Baptists, (in part;) and
Unitarians (Congregationalists.)
exceeds one million of persons. *Rev. Frederick A. Farley.*

PROGRESS OF CONGREGATIONALISM.

The churches planted by the Pilgrims, soon after their arrival at Plymouth, were all Congregational. When the Synod met at Cambridge, in 1648, there were thirty-nine Congregational Churches in Massachusetts. In 1767, they nnmbered two hundred and eighty. In 1790, they amounted to three hundred and thirty-two. In 1800, there were three hundred and fifty-two. The present number in Massachusetts is 478.

In the other New-England states, the growth of Congregationalism has been nearly as follows:

In 1648, there were four churches of this order in Connecticut, and three in New-Hampshire. In 1695, there were thirty-six in Connecticut, five in New-Hampshire, and three in the Province of Maine. In 1760, there were in Connecticut, one hundred and fifty-three; in New-Hampshire, forty; in Maine, twenty; and in Rhode Island, ten. The present number in all the New-England States is one thousand three hundred and thirty-three. In this estimate, the Evangelical churches only are included.

In the states out of New-England, Congregationalism, as a form of church polity separate from Presbyterianism, scarcely had an existence prior to the commencement of the present century. It is estimated, that there are now not less than five hundred and fourteen Evangelical Congregational churches in the Middle and Western States, besides many others in which there is a large infusion of the Congregational principles of church government.

6.—GERMAN AND DUTCH CHURCHES.

REFORMED DUTCH CHURCH.*

The Reformed Dutch Church in North America derives its origin from the Reformed Church of Holland, which still preserves its doctrinal standards and form of church government. The first churches were planted during the Dutch Colonial government. Churches were afterwards formed in the range of the Dutch settlements on Long Island, along the Hudson River and the Mohawk, and in the northern and middle counties of New-Jersey. Of late the number of churches considerably increased, and a few churches have been organized through missionary effort in the states of Michigan, Illinois and Indiana. These churches are under the care of a General Synod, the two particular Synods of New-York and Albany, and twenty-four classes, twelve of them attached to the particular Synod of New-York, and twelve to the particular Synod of Albany. The statistical returns for 1847 show the following results:—

Numbers of Churches, 282; Ministers, 298; Families, 24,141; Congregation, 110,308; Communicants, 34,100.

No returns were received from a few congregations, so that the full number would reach somewhat higher. Of the churches, 212 are in the state of New-York, 52 in New-Jersey, 6 in Pennsylvania, 7 in Illinois, and 5 in Michigan.

Rutger's College. a literary institution, founded under the auspices of the Reformed Dutch Church, and the Theological Seminary, are both located at New-Brunswick, N. J.

GERMAN REFORMED CHURCH.*

The German Reformed Church in the United States was formed among the first emigrants from Germany in Pennsylvania. A large proportion of these emigrants came in the early part of the last century from the Palatinate in Germany, where the German Reformed Church took its rise. The first ecclesiastical organization took place between 1730 and '40. The churches first planted were in Eastern Pennsylvania, though settlements were made at an early period in North Carolina, Virginia, Maryland, &c. It is now, in the extended growth of the German population, spread over the whole of Pennsylvania and Ohio, and over portions of Maryland, Virginia, North Carolina, Missouri, Indiana, Illinois, Michigan, &c. The church is divided into two bodies, which maintain a correspondence, but are independent of each other.

The Eastern portion of the church is the original and parent body, and bears the title of "The Synod of the German Reformed Church of the United States." Its territory extends westward in Pennsylvania to the Alleghany Mountains, to portions of Maryland, Virginia, North Carolina, and a few churches in New-York. It has under its jurisdiction eleven classes, seven of which are in Pennsylvania, one in Maryland, one in Virginia, one in North Carolina, and one in New-York. The statistical reports of the classes to the General Synod in 1847 exhibit:—

Numbers of Ministers, 163; Churches, 495; Members, or Communicants, about 37,000. A large number of churches failed to report the number of members, the aggregate must, therefore, be much larger. I have seen their numbers stated in a condensed statistical account of the various denominations, at 75,000. This, however, must be a vague computation.

The General Synod of the Western body is termed "The Synod of the German Reformed Church of Ohio and adjacent States." It is located principally in Western Pennsylvania and Ohio, but is extending into the adjoining States, and has for its field the whole Valley of the Mississippi. The minutes of their General Synod of last year exhibit:—

Numbers of Ministers, 63; Churches, 179; Members, 9,030.

A few churches had not reported the number of members. There is a literary institution named Marshall College, under the auspices of the German Reformed Church, and a Theological Seminary located at Mercerburg, Franklin County, Pennsylvania, and is in a very prosperous condition.

EVANGELICAL LUTHERANS.†

SYNODS.	No. of Ministers.	No. of Congregations.	No. of Communicants.
New-York	36	40	7,000
Hartwick ..... N.Y.	20	29	2,800
Franckean ..... "	13	33	2,500
Pennsylvania	67	224	31,181
West Pennsylvania	50	114	13,000
East Pennsylvania	26	49	5,200
Alleghany ..... Pa.	20	72	5,200
Pittsburg ..... "	23	75	5,000
Maryland	35	74	9,000
Virginia	17	39	1,700
Western Virginia	8	21	1,500
North Carolina	12	24	2,000
South Carolina	33	47	3,500
Tennessee	14	40	5,000
Missouri	68	98	9,000
South-West	6	10	500
Ohio	28	111	5,000
Miami ..... Oh.	20	37	2,100
Wittemberg ..... "	16	54	2,300
Eastern Ohio, Western Ohio, English Synod, Oh.	70	245	30,000
Tuscarawas	3	7	800
Illinois	8	12	700
Indiana	12	35	2,500
Indianapolis. (Ger.)	9	18	1,600
Michigan	10	20	1,700
Total	626	1,518	150,781

* Communicated by the Rev. Thomas De Witt. † Communicated by the Rev. Charles Martin, Pastor of St. James's Ch., N. Y.

7.—MISCELLANEOUS DENOMINATIONS.

NAMES OF STATES.	UNIVERSALISTS.* Associations.	Societies.	Churches.	Meeting-houses.	Preachers.
Maine	8	127	45	103	70
New-Hampshire.	6	96	13	53	38
Vermont	4	102	—	76	50
Massachusetts.	5	145	64	124	132
Rhode Island.	1	10	—	4	5
Connecticut	3	31	—	22	19
New-York	16	252	—	163	144
New-Jersey	—	4	—	2	3
Pennsylvania	5	33	—	15	29
Ohio	12	131	—	73	70
Michigan.	2	31	—	6	24
Indiana	9	53	—	12	29
Illinois	5	35	—	3	22
Kentucky	3	17	—	13	20
Wisconsin	1	7	—	1	14
Iowa	1	4	—	—	4
Missouri.	1	5	—	1	8
Tennessee	1	—	—	—	6
Maryland	1	3	—	2	3
Virginia	1	3	—	3	4
North Carolina	1	—	1	17	1
South Carolina	1	4	—	9	5
Georgia	1	1	—	4	3
Alabama.	1	3	—	2	3
Mississippi.	—	—	—	—	1
Louisiana	—	—	—	—	1
Total	89	1097	123	708	708

QUAKERS OR FRIENDS.†

The SOCIETY OF FRIENDS has eight yearly meetings, viz:—NEW-ENGLAND, held at Newport, R. I.; NEW-YORK, held in the city of New-York; PENNSYLVANIA and NEW-JERSEY, held at Philadelphia; MARYLAND, held at Baltimore; VIRGINIA, held at Cedar Creek and Summerton, alternately; NORTH CAROLINA, held at New-Garden; OHIO, held at Mount Pleasant, and INDIANA, held at Richmond, in Wayne county: these include from 120,000 to 150,000 members.

The HICKSITES, or Unitarian section of the Quakers, seceded from the original body in 1827. Their doctrines are certain opinions promulgated by Elias Hicks, of Long Island, denying or invalidating the miraculous conception, divinity and atonement of Christ, and also the authenticity and divine authority of the Holy Scriptures. In this secession some members in New-York, Philadelphia, Baltimore, Ohio and Indiana yearly meetings, went off from the original society. They number altogether from 20,000 to 30,000.

Total: From 150 to 180,000

UNITED BRETHREN.‡ CONGREGATIONS.	Date of Settlement.
I.—PENNSYLVANIA.	
Bethlehem	1741
Nazareth.	1744
Schoeneck.	1747
Emmans.	1762
Philadelphia.	1741
Lancaster	1749
Litiz	1756
York.	1751
Hebron	1750
Lebanon.	1847
Hopedale	1837
II.—NEW-YORK.	
City of New-York	1742
Staten Island.	1763
Camden	1832
III.—MARYLAND.	
Graceham.	1758
IV.—NORTH CAROLINA	
Salem.	1766
Bethabara.	1753
Bethania.	1760
Friedberg	1773
Friedland.	1775
V.—OHIO.	
Gnadenhuetten.	1799
Sharon.	1843
Canal Dover	1839
VI.—INDIANA.	
Hope	1830
Enon	1847
VII.—ILLINOIS.	
New-Salem.	1844
Total 26	....

Statistics: The Moravians, or United Brethren, in the United States are said to number about 6,000: these are all considered as missionaries, and are liable to be sent to any part of the world to preach the Gospel. Total: 6,000

There are a great number of other minor denominations, chiefly of local origin and influence, the proper names of which are indistinctly known to the general reader. These we must omit in detail. The most conspicuous among them are as follow:—

1.—Disciples of Christ.
2.—Evangelical Asssociation.
3.—Latter Day Saints, or Mormons.
4.—Mennonite Society.
5.—Reformed Mennonite Society.
6.—Millenarians.
7.—New Jerusalem, or New Christian Church.
8.—Omish or Amesh Church.
9.—Restorationists.
10.—Shakers, or Shaking Quakers.
11.—Schwenkfelders.
12.—Second Advent Believers.
13.—United Brethren in Christ, and a number of others.

* Universalist Almanac. † Rupp's Religious Denominations. ‡ Reichel's Hist. Sketch of the Church and Missions of the United Brethren.

CANALS OF THE UNITED STATES.

Names of Canals.	*Extending*				Length in Miles.
MAINE:					
Cumberland and Oxford,	*from*	near Portland	*to*	Sebago Pond,	20.5
Songo River Improvement,	"	Sebago Pond	"	Long Pond,	30.
NEW-HAMPSHIRE:					
Bow Falls,	Constructed to overcome these difficulties.				.75
Hookset Falls,					.13
Amoskeag Falls,					1.
Sewell's Falls,					.25
Union Falls,					9.
Middlesex,	(*See* Massachusetts.)				
VERMONT:					
White River Falls,	Around Falls.				..5
Bellow's Falls,					.16
Waterquechy,					.4
MASSACHUSETTS:					
Middlesex,	*from*	Boston	*to*	Middlesex,	27.
Pawtucket,	"	Lowell	"	Chelmsford,	1.6
Blackstone,	"	Worcester	"	Providence, R. I.	45.
Hampshire and Hampden,	"	Northampton	"	Farmington Canal.	22.
Montague Falls,	Around Falls.				3.
South Hadley Falls,					2.
RHODE ISLAND:					
Blackstone,	(*See* Massachusetts.)				
CONNECTICUT:					
Farmington, (filled in,)	*from*	New-Haven	*to*	Hamp.&Hamp.canal.	56.
Enfield Falls,	Around Falls.				5.5
NEW-YORK:					
Erie,	*from*	Albany	*to*	Buffalo,	364.
Champlain Junction,	"	West Troy	"	Whitehall,	64.
Waterford Junction,	"	Waterford	"	Cohoes Village,	2.
Oswego,	"	Syracuse	"	Oswego,	38.
Cayuga and Seneca,	"	Montezuma	"	Geneva,	21.
Crooked Lake,	"	Penn Yan	"	Dresden,	8.
Chemung,	"	Elmira	"	Jefferson,	39.
Chemung Feeder,	"	Corning	"	Fairport,	16.
Chenango,	"	Utica	"	Binghamton,	97.
Genesee Valley,	"	Rochester	"	Olean,	108.5
Danville Branch,	"	Mt. Morris	"	Danville,	11.
Black River,	"	Rome	"	Carthage,	77.5

Names of Canals.	Extending		Length in Miles.
NEW-YORK:—*Continued.*			
Feeder,	*from* Black River	*to* Boonville,	10.
Delaware and Hudson,	" Roudout	" Lackawaxen creek,	83.
Harlaem, (not used,)	" Hudson River	" East River,	3.
Croton Aqueduct,	" Croton River	" New-York,	40.5
Oneida,	" Higgins	" Oneida Lake,	8.
NEW-JERSEY:			
Delaware and Raritan,	*from* Bordentown	*to* New-Brunswick,	42.
Morris,	" Jersey City	" Easton, Pa.,	101.7
Salem,	" Salem Creek	" Delaware River,	4.
PENNSYLVANIA:			
Delaware Division,	*from* Bristol	*to* Easton,	59.7
Eastern do.	" Columbia	" Millersburg,	44.5
Susquehannah do.	" mouth ofJuniata	" Northumberland,	39.
Juniata,	" do.	" Hollidaysburg,	127.5
West Branch,	" Northumberl'd	" Farrandsville,	75.
North Branch,	" do.	" Wilkesbarre,	73.
Western Division,	" Johnstown	" Pittsburg,	105.
Franklin,	" Franklin	" Meadville,	22.
Erie and Beaver,	" Beaver River	" Erie,	136.
French Creek Feeder,	" French Creek	" E. & B. Canal,	27.
Lackawaxen,	" Delaware Riv.	" Honesdale,	22.
Bald Eagle,	" West Br. Canal	" Bellefonte,	25.
Susquehannah, or Tide water	" Wrightsville	" Havre deGrace, *Md.*	45.
Conestoga,	" Lancaster	" Safe Harbor,	18.
Codorus,	" York	" Susquehannah Riv.	11.
Union,	" Reading	" Middletown,	82.
Schuylkill,	" Philadelphia	" Port Carbon,	108.
Lehigh Navigation,	" Easton	" White Haven,	47.
DELAWARE:			
Chesapeake & Delaware,	*from* Delaware city	*to* Back Creek,	14.
MARYLAND:			
Chesapeake and Ohio,	*from* Georgetown, DC	*to* Cumberland,*	184.
Chesapeake & Delaware,	(*See* Delaware.)		
DISTRICT OF COLUMBIA:			
Chesapeake and Ohio,	(*See* Maryland.)		
VIRGINIA:			
Alexandria,	*from* Ches.& O.Can.	*to* Alexandria,	7.2
James River & Kanawha,	" Richmond	" Lynchburg,	148.
Dismal Swamp,	" Chesap'ke Bay	" Albemarle Sound,	23.
Branches,	" Dismal Swp. C.	"	11.
NORTH CAROLINA:			
Weldon,	Around Falls in the Roanoke,		12.
Club Fort and Harlow,	*from* Club Foot Cr.	*to* Harlow Creek,	1.5
Dismal Swamp,	(*See* Virginia.)		

* To be continued to Pittsburg, 341½ miles.

Names of Canals.	*Extending*		Length in Miles.
SOUTH CAROLINA:			
Santee,	*from* Charleston	*to* Santee River,	22.
Winyaw,	" Winyaw Bay	" Kinlock Creek,	7.5
Saluda,	" Shoals	" Granby,	6.2
Drehr's,	At Saluda Falls,		1.3
Lorick,	" Broad River	*to* Head of Falls,	1.
Lockhart's,	Around Falls of Broad River,		2.7
Wateree,	" Jones' Mill	*to* Elliot's,	4.
Catawaba,	At various points of Catawaba River,		7.8
GEORGIA:			
Savannah and Ogeechee,	*from* Savannah	*to* Ogeechee River,	16.
Brunswick,	" Alatamaha	" Brunswick,	12.
ALABAMA:			
Muscle Shoal,	*from* Head of Shoals	*to* Florence,	35.7
Huntsville,	" Triaria	" Huntsville,	16.
LOUISIANA:			
Orleans Bank,	*from* New-Orleans	*to* LakePontchartrain,	4.2
Canal Carondelet,	" do.	" Bayou St. John,	2.
Barataria,	" do.	" Berwick Bay,	85.
Lake Veret,	" Lake Veret	" La Fourche Riv.,	8.
KENTUCKY:			
Kentucky Riv. Navigation,	Improvements by dams and locks.		100.
Licking do.,			94.
Green do.,			190.
Barren do.,			100.
Louisville & Portland,	Around Falls of the Ohio,		2.5
ILLINOIS:			
Illinois & Michigan,	*from* Chicago	*to* La Salle,	113.
INDIANA:			
Wabash and Erie,	*from* Toledo, Ohio,	*to* Evansville, Ind.,	458.7
Whitewater,			
OHIO:			
Ohio and Erie,	*from* Cleveland	*to* Portsmouth,	307.
Zanesville Branch,	" Canal	" Zanesville,	14.
Columbus do.,	" do.	" Columbus,	10.
Lancaster do.,	" do.	" Lancaster,	9.
Hocking Valley,	" Lancaster	" Athens,	56.
Walhonding Branch,	" Canal	" Walhonding Riv.,	25.
Eastport do.,	do.	" Eastport,	4.
Dresden do.,	" do.	" Dresden,	2.
Miami and Branches,	" Cincinnati	" —	87.7
Miami Extension & do.,	" —	" Defiance,	139.
Wabash and Erie,	*See* Indiana.	(91 mls. in Ohio)	
Muskingum Improvement,	" —	" —	91.
Sandy and Beaver, (Mahoning,)	" O. & E. Canal at Bolivar	" Mouth of Little Beaver Creek,	86.

RAILROADS OF THE UNITED STATES.

Lines.		*Extending*		Length in Miles.
Maine:				
Portland, Saco, & Portsm'th,	*from*	Portland	*to* Portsm'th, N. H.	51.7
Kennebec, Bath, & Portland,	"	Portland	" Augusta,	—
Bath Branch,	"	Brunswick	" Bath,	—
Atlantic and St. Lawrence,	"	Portland	" Canada line, 45°	156.
Buckfield Branch,	"	Mechanic's Falls	*to* Buckfield,	12.
Androscoggin & Kennebec,	"	Danville	*to* Waterville,	54.5
Waterville and Bangor,	"	Waterville	" Bangor,	—
Bangor and Piscataquis,	"	Bangor	" Oldtown,	11.7
Calais,	"		" Calais,	2.
Boston and Maine,		(*See* Massachusetts,)		
New-Hampshire:—				
Great Falls Branch,	*from*	Somerworth	*to* Great Falls Vil.	2.7
Nashua and Lowell,*	"	Nashua	" Lowell, Mass.,	14.5
Concord,	"	Nashua	" Concord,	35.
Northern,	"	Concord	" West Lebanon,	69.
Bristol Branch,	"	Franklin	" Bristol,	13.
Concord and Portsmouth,	"	Concord	" Portsmouth,	—
Concord and Montreal,	"	Concord *via* Meredith	" Canada line, 45°	—
Cheshire,	"	S. Ashb'nham	" Bellow's Falls,	54.
Sullivan,	"	Bellow's Falls	" Hartford,	28.
Eastern,		(*See* Massachusetts,)		
Boston and Maine,		(*See* Massachusetts,)		
Vermont:				
Vermont Central,	*from*	W. Lebanon	*to* Burlington,	115.
Conn. & Passumpsic Rivers,	"	W. Lebanon	" Canada line, 45°	114.
Rutland,	"	Bellow's Falls	" Burlington,	117.
Vermont and Massachusetts,		(*See* Massachusetts,)		
Massachusetts:*				
Eastern (part in N. Hamp.)†	*from*	Boston	*to* Portsmouth,	55.
Salisbury Branch,	"	Salisbury	" Salisbury Mills,	3.
Essex Branch,	"	Salem	" South Danvers,	22.5
Gloucester Branch,	"	Beverley	" Gloucester,	16.
Marblehead do.,	"	near Salem	" Marblehead,	3.
Boston & Me.†(pt.N.H.&Me.)	"	Boston	" S. Berwick, Me.	74.5
Lawrence Branch,	"	N. Andover	" Lawrence,	2.
Medford do.	"	Malden	" Medford,	2.
Lowell and Lawrence,	"	Lowell	" Lawrence,	12.3
Boston and Lowell,†	"	Boston	" Lowell,	26.
Woburn Branch,	"	S. Woburn	" Woburn Centre,	2.
Nashua and Lowell,		(*See* New-Hampshire,)		

* The total length of Railroads in Massachusetts in January, 1849, was 1,040½ miles, and 317¼ double tracks, or a total of 1,357¾ miles of single track. The total cost is stated at $49,298,183, of which $8,884,119 were expended in 1848.

† Double tracks or part double tracks.

Lines.		Extending.		Length in Miles.
Nashua and Worcester,	*from*	Nashua, N.H.	*to* Worcester,	39.
Worcester and Norwich, and Branch,	"	Worcester	" Norwich & Allyn's Pt., Ct.	66.
Fitchburg,†	"	Boston	" Fitchburg,	49.3
Fitchburg and Worcester,	"	Fitchburg,	" Worcester,	14.
Vermont and Massachusetts,	"	Fitchburg	" Brattleboro', Vt.	58.7
Watertown Branch,	"	Railroad	" Watertown,	5.
Lexington,	"	W.Cambridge	" Lexington,	6.6
Stoney Brook Branch	"	Groton	" Chelmsford,	13.
Boston and Worcester,†	"	Boston	" Worcester,	44.
Worcester Branch,	"	Railroad	" Worcester,	.5
Saxonville do.	"	Nantick	" Saxonville,	4.
Millbury do.	"	Grafton	" Millbury,	3.2
Milford do.	"	S.Farmington	" Milford,	12.
Brookline do.	"	Railroad	" Brookline,	3.
Brighton do.	"	Railroad	" Brighton,	5.
Newton Lower Falls Branch,	"	Railroad	" Lower Falls,	5.
Western,†	"	Worcester	" W. State Line,	118.
Pittsfield and North Adams,	"	Pittsfield	" North Adams,	18.6
Peterboro' and Shirley,	"		"	12.
Berkshire,	"	S. State Line	" W. Stockbridge,	38.
Hartford and Springfield,	"	Hartford	" Springfield,	6.
Connecticut River,	"	Springfield	" N. State Line,	50.
Chicopee Branch,	"	Cabotsville	" Chicopee Falls,	2.
Boston and Providence,†	"	Boston	" Providence, R.I.	43.
Providence and Worcester,	"	Prov., R. I.	" Worcester,	43.5
Dedham Branch,	"	Low Plain	" Dedham,	2.4
Norfolk County,	"	Dedham	" Blackstone,	26.
Stoughton Branch,	"	Canton	" Stoughton,	4.
Taunton do.	"	Mansfield	" Taunton,	11.
New-Bedford and Taunton,	"	New-Bedford	" Taunton,	20.
Old Colony,†	"	Boston	" Plymouth,	37.
Milton Branch,	"	Neponset	" Milton,	3.
Bridgewater Branch,	"	S. Abington	" Bridgewater,	6.7
Quincy,	"	Neponset Riv.	" Quincy Quarry,	3.
South Shore,	"	Quincy	" Cohasset,	22.
Dorchester Branch,	"		" Dorchester,	3.
West Stockbridge,		(*See* New-York,)		
Fall River,	"	Braintree	" Fall River,	42.5
Cape Cod Branch,	"	Middleboro	" Sandwich,	27.
Cheshire,		(*See* New-Hampshire,)		
RHODE ISLAND:				
Boston and Providence,		(*See* Massachusetts,)		
Providence and Worcester,		(*do.* do.)		
Stonington and Providence,		(*do.* Connecticut.)		
CONNECTICUT:				
Stonington and Providence,	*from*	Stonington	*to* Providence, R.I.	50.
Norwich and Worcester,		(*See* Massachusetts,)		

† Double tracks or part double tracks.

Lines.		*Extending.*			Length in Miles.
Hartford and Springfield,	*from*	Hartford	*to*	Springfield, Mass.	26.
New-Haven and Hartford,	"	New-Haven	"	Hartford,	36.
New-Haven Canal,	"	New-Haven	"	Plainville,	28.
New-York and New-Haven,	"	New-Haven	"	New-York,	77.
Housatonic,	"	Bridgeport	"	N. State Line,	74.
New-York:					
Long Island,	*from*	Brooklyn C'y	*to*	Greenport,	96.
Hempstead Branch,	"	Railroad	"	Hempstead,	2.5
N. Y., Haerlem, & Albany,	"	New-YorkC'y	"	Chatham 4 Cor's	80.5
Hudson River,	"	New-YorkC'y	"	Greenbush,	144.
Hudson and Berkshire,	"	Hudson City	"	Berkshire,	31.5
Albany & W. Stockbridge,	"	W. Stockb'ge	"	Greenbush,	38.
Troy and Greenbush,	"	Troy	"	Greenbush,	6.
Schenectady and Troy,	"	Schenectady	"	Troy,	20.5
Rensselser and Saratoga,	"	Troy	"	Balston Spa,	25.
Saratoga and Schenectady,	"	Schenectady	"	Saratoga,	22.
Washington and Saratoga,	"	Saratoga	"	Whitehall,	40.
Whitehall and Plattsburg,	"	Whitehall	"	Plattsburg,	
Mohawk and Hudson,	"	Schenectady	"	Albany,	17.
Utica and Schenectady,	"	Schenectady	"	Utica,	78.
Syracuse and Utica,	"	Utica	"	Syracuse,	53.
Oswego and Syracuse,	"	Syracuse	"	Oswego,	35.
Auburn and Syracuse,	"	Syracuse	"	Auburn,	26.
Skaneateles and Jordan,	"	Jordan	"	Skaneateles,	5.5
Auburn and Rochester,	"	Auburn	"	Rochester,	78.
Syracuse&Rochester(direct)	"	Syracuse	"	Rochester,	—
Tonawanda,	"	Rochester	"	Attica,	43.5
Attica and Hornellsville,	"	Attica	"	Hornellsville,	—
Attica and Buffalo,	"	Attica	"	Buffalo,	31.
Buffalo and Niagara Falls,	"	Buffalo	"	Niagara Falls,	22.
Lockport and Niagara Falls,	"	Lockport	"	Niagara Falls,	23.
Lewiston Branch,	"	Railroad	"	Lewiston,	3.3
Ithaca and Owego,	"	Ithaca	"	Oswego,	29.
Ogdensburg,	"	Ogdensburg	"	Rouse's Point,	117.5
Chemung,	"	Elmira	"	Seneca Lake,	—
New-York and Erie,	"	Pierpont	"	Dunkirk,	450.
Newburg Branch,	"	Chester	"	Newburg,	19.
New-Jersey:					
Paterson and Hudson River,	*from*	Jersey City	*to*	Paterson,	17.
Paterson and Ramapo,	"	Paterson	"	Ramapo,	16.
New-Jersey,	"	Jersey City	"	N. Brunswick,	34.
New-Brunswick Branch,	"	N. Brunswick	"	Trenton,	28.
Trenton Branch,	"	Trenton	"	Bordentown,	8.
Camden and Amboy,	"	Camden	"	South Amboy,	61.
Camden and Woodbury,	"	Camden	"	Woodbury,	9.
Elizabethport & Somerville,	"	Elizabethport	"	Somerville,	26.
Morris and Essex,	"	Newark	"	Morristown,	20.

Lines.		*Extending.*			Length in Miles.
PENNSYLVANIA :					
Philadelphia and Trenton,	*from*	Philadelphia	*to*	Trenton,	26.2
Philadelphia, Germantown, and Norristown,	"	Philadelphia	"	Norristown,	17.
Germantown Branch,	"	P.G.&N.R.R.	"	Germantown,	4.
Philadelphia & Wilmington,	"	Philadelphia	"	Wilmington, Del.	27.
Phila., Reading, & Pottsville,	"	Philadelphia	"	Pottsville,	95.
Little Schuylkill,	"	Port Clinton	"	Tamaqua,	23.
Mill Creek,	"	Port Carbon	"	Coal Mines,	9.
Schuylkill Valley & Branches,	"		"		25.
Schuylkill,	"	Schuylkill	"	Valley R. R.	13.
Mine Hill & Schuylkill Hav.	"	do. Hav.	"	Mine Hill,	20.
Pottsville and Danville,	"	Pottsville	"	Danville,	44.5
Little Schuylkill & Susqueh.	"	Sunbury	"	Pottsville,	104.
Lehigh and Susquehannah,	"	Wilkesbarre	"	White Haven,	20.
Mauch Chunk & Branches,	"	Mauch Ch'k	"	Coal Mines,	25.
Room Run,	"	Mauch Ch'k	"	Coal Mines,	5.2
Lyken's Valley,	"	Millersburg	"	Broad Mountain,	$16\frac{1}{2}$
Pine Grove,	"		"		4.
Columbia,	"	Philadelphia	"	Columbia,	82.
Westchester Branch,	"	Paoli	"	Westchester,	10.
Valley,	"	Col'a R. R.	"	Morristown,	20.5
Philadelphia City,	"		"		6.
Harrisburg and Lancaster,	"	Harrisburg	"	Lancaster,	35.5
Carbondale,	"	Carbondale	"	Honesdale,	18.
Williamsport and Corning,	"	Williamsport	"	Corning,	73.5
Wrightsville, York, and Gettysburg,	"	Wrightsville and York	"	Gettysville,	
York and Maryland,	"	York	"	Strassburg,	
Cumberland Valley,	"	Harrisburg	"	Chambersburg,	
Franklin,	"	Chambersb'g	"	Hagerstown, Md.	22.
Alleghany Portage,	"	Hollidaysburg	"	Johnstown,	39.6
Beaver Meadow,	"		"		20.
Beaver Meadow Branch,	"		"		12.
Hazelton and Lehigh,	"		"		8.
Nesquehoning,	"		"	Lehigh River,	5.
Lackawana,	"		"		
Cleveland & Pittsburg,		(*See* Ohio,)			
	"		"		
	"		"		
	"		"		
DELAWARE :					
Frenchtown,	*from*	Newcastle	*to*	Frenchtown,	16.
Philadelphia & Wilmington,		(*See* Pennsylvania,)			
Wilmington and Baltimore,		(*See* Maryland,)			
	"		"		
MARYLAND :					
Wilmington and Baltimore,	*from*	Wilmington	*to*	Baltimore,	70.
Baltimore and Ohio,	"	Baltimore	"	Cumberland,	178.

Lines.		*Extending.*			Length in Miles.
Washington Branch,	*from*	Relay House	*to*	Washing., D. C.	31.
Elkridge and Annapolis,	"	Elkridge	"	Annapolis,	21.
Baltimore & Susquehannah,	"	Baltimore	"	Strasburg, Pa.	58.
Owen's Mills,	"		"		—
	"		"		
	"		"		
VIRGINIA :					
Winchester and Potomac,	*from*	Harper's F'y	*to*	Winchester,	32.
Richm'd, Fred'k, & Potomac,	"	Aquia Cr. L'g	"	Richmond,	76.
Louisa,	"	Taylorsville	"	Gordonsville,	58.
Richmond and Petersburg,	"	Richmond	"	Petersburg,	22.5
Chesterfield,	"	Richmond	"	Coal Mines,	13.
City Point, (Appomattox,)	"	Petersburg	"	City Point,	12.
Petersburg,	"	Petersburg	"	Weldon, N. C.,	63.
Seaboard and Roanoke,	"	Portsmouth	"	Weldon, N. C.,	78.5
Greensville and Roanoke,	"	Hicksford	"	Gaston, N. C.,	18.
	"		"		
	"		"		
	"		"		
NORTH CAROLINA :					
Raleigh and Gaston,	*from*	Raleigh	*to*	Gaston,	87.
Wilmington and Weldon,	"	Weldon	"	Wilmington,	167.
Central, (Chartered,)	"		"		
	"		"		
	"		"		
	"		"		
SOUTH CAROLINA :					
South Carolina,	*from*	Charleston	*to*	Hamburg,	136.
Columbia Branch,	"	Branchville	"	Columbia,	68.
Camden Branch,	"		"		
	"		"		
	"		"		
	"		"		
GEORGIA :					
Georgia,	*from*	Augusta	*to*	Atalanta,	172.
Athens Branch,	"	Union Point	"	Athens,	40.
Warrenton Branch,	"	Oamak	"	Warrenton,	3.
Central,	"	Savannah	"	Macon,	192.
Macon and Western,	"	Macon	"	Atalanta,	—
Western and Atlantic,	"	Atalanta	"	Dalton & R'd Clay,	
	"		"		
	"		"		
	"		"		
FLORIDA :					
Tallahassee and St. Mark's,	*from*	Tallahassee	*to*	St. Mark's,	26.
St. Joseph's,	"	St. Joseph's	"	Jola,	28.
Pensacola and Montgomery,	"	Pensacola	"	Montgomery,	40.
	"		"		

Lines.		Extending.			Length in Miles.
Tennessee:					
	from		*to*		
	"		"		
	"		"		
Alabama:					
Montgomery & West Point,	*from*	Montgomery	*to*	West Point,	87.
Tuscumbia and Decatur,	"	Tuscumbia	"	Decatur,	44.
	"		"		
	"		"		
Mississippi:					
Vicksburg and Jackson,	*from*	Vicksburg	*to*	Jackson,	46.
Raymond Branch,	"	V. & J. R. R.	"	Raymond,	8.
Jackson and Brandon,	"	Jackson	"	Brandon,	14.
Mississippi,	"	Natchez	"	Malcolm,	22.
St. Francisville,	"	St. Francisv'e	"	Woodville	28.
Grand Gulf,	"		"		7.
	"		"		
	"		"		
Louisiana:					
St. Francisville,		(*See* Mississippi,)			
Mexican Gulf,	*from*	New-Orleans	*to*	Proctersville,	27.
New-Orleans and Carrolton,	"	New-Orleans	"	Carrolton,	—
	"		"		
	"		"		
Texas:					
Red River,	*from*		*to*		
	"		"		
	"		"		
Kentucky:					
Lexington and Ohio,	*from*	Lexington	*to*	Frankfort,	29
	"		"		
	"		"		
Ohio:					
Little Miami,	*from*	Cincinnati	*to*	Springfield,	84.
Mad River,	"	Springfield	"	Sandusky	135.
Sandusky and Mansfield,	"	Sandusky	"	Mansfield,	55.

The following railroads (July, 1849) are in course of construction, viz.:—
Zenia and Columbus, 53 m.; Cleveland and Columbus, 135 m.; Mansfield and Newark, 52 m.; Hancock and Findly, 18 m.; Iron, 26 m.; Dayton and Springfield, 24 m.; Greenville and Dayton, 30 m.; Cleveland and Pittsburg, 145 m.; Wellsville and Mansfield, 105 m. Total miles in progress, 595. Capital, $9,100,000.

Lines.		Extending.			Length in Miles.
Indiana:					
Madison and Indianapolis,	*from*	Madison	*to*	Indianapolis	57.
	"		"		
	"		"		
Illinois:					
Meredosia,	*from*	Meredosia	*to*	Springfield,	66.
Galena and Chicago,	"	Galena	"	Chicago,	
	"		"		

Lines.	Extending.		Length in Miles.
MICHICAN.			
Southern,	*from* Monroe	*to* Hillsdale,	70.
Adrian and Toledo,	" Adrian	" Toledo,	33.
Central,	" Detroit *via* Kalamazoo	" New-Buffalo,	221.
Tecumseh Branch,	" Ypsilanti	" Tecumseh,	10.
Detroit and Pontiac,	" Detroit	" Pontiac,	25.
Detroit and Shelby,	" Detroit	" Shelby,	—
	"	"	
	"	"	
	"	"	
	"	"	

PROGRESS OF RAILROAD-BUILDING IN THE UNITED STATES.

	Opened during the year.	Total at the end of the year.	Cost each year.	Total Cost at the end of each year.
1827	3	3	$50,000	$50,000
1829	9	12	450,000	500,000
1830	155	167	2,500,000	3,000,000
1831	17	184	1,450,000	4,450,000
1832	29	213	500,000	4,950,000
1833	151	364	4,100,000	9,050,000
1834	86	450	2,850,000	11,900,000
1835	287	737	11,750,000	23,650,000
1836	316	1,053	7,600,000	31,250,000
1837	237	1,290	6,700,000	37,950,000
1838	571	1,861	14,500,000	52,450,000
1839	240	2,101	12,750,000	65,200,000
1840	279	2,380	4,500,000	69,700,000
1841	183	2,463	5,000,000	74,700,000
1842	277	2,740	6,650,000	81,350,000
1843	509	3,249	11,200,000	92,550,000
1844				
1845	410	3,659	19,000,000	111,550,000
1846	485	4,144	9,200,000	120,750,000
1847	205	4,249	2,400,000	123,150,000
1848	1,009	5,258	30,270,000	153,420,000
1849				

AVERAGE COST OF RAILROADS.

In the United States	$29,200	per mile.
Great Britain	175,500	"
France	107,500	"
Belgium	80,000	"
Germany	40,000	"
Prussia	47,000	"

TELEGRAPH LINES IN THE UNITED STATES AND THE CANADAS,

(USING MORSE'S INVENTION.)

Completed, in progress, or contemplated, 1st March, 1849.

COMPLETED.	NAME OF THE LINES.	EXTENDING.		NO. OF STATIONS.	MILES IN LENGTH.
June 6th, 1844, the whole finished in 1846.	Washington and Baltimore line now merged in the Magnetic Telegraph Company	from Washington, D. C. / " Washington, D. C	to Baltimore, Md. / " New-York City	10	365
"	New-York, Albany and Buffalo Telegraph Company	" New-York City	" Buffalo, N. Y	16	506
"	New-York and Boston	" New-York City	" Boston, Mass.	8	240
"	Buffalo and Canada Junction	" Buffalo, N. Y	" Lockport & Queenstown, UC	3	48
1847.	Queenstown and Niagara River	" Queenstown, U. C	" Niagara River	2	7
"	Toronto, Hamilton, and Niagara River	" Toronto, U. C	" Niagara River	5	88
"	Montreal Telegraph Company	" Toronto, U. C	" Quebec, L. C	13	556
"	Queenstown and Chippewa	" Queenstown, U. C	" Chippewa, U. C.	2	10
"	Western Telegraph Company	" Hamilton, U. C	" London, U. C.	4	78
"	Syracuse and Oswego	" Syracuse, N. Y.	" Oswego, N. Y	2	38
"	Auburn and Elmira	" Auburn, N. Y.	" Elmira, N. Y.	4	75
"	Ithaca and Binghampton	" Ithaca, N. Y.	" Binghampton, N. Y.	3	48
"	Philadelphia and Pittsburg	" Philadelphia, Pa.	" Pittsburg, Pa.	7	309
"	Pittsburg and Louisville	" Pittsburg, Pa	" Louisville, Ky	9	418
1848.	Louisville and St. Louis	" Louisville, Ky	" St. Louis, Mo.	4	271
"	Boston and Newburyport	" Boston, Mass.	" Newburyport, Mass.	3	34
"	New-London, Norwich and Worcester	" New-London, Ct.	" Worcester, Mass	3	74
"	Rhode Island Telegraph Company	" New-Bedford, Mass.	" Worcester, Mass	6	97
"	Washington and New-Orleans	" Washington, D. C.	" New-Orleans, La.	20	1716
"	Philadelphia and Pottsville	" Philadelphia, Pa	" Pottsville, Pa.	8	92
"	Troy and Montreal	" Troy, N. Y.	" Montreal, U. C.	14	278
"	Ocean Telegraph Company	" Wilmington, Del.	" Lewes, Del	10	97
"	Erie and Michigan Telegraph Company	" Buffalo, N. Y	" Milwaukie, Wis.	26	812
"	Sciota Telegraph Company	" Columbus, Ohio	" Portsmouth, Ohio	4	90

"	American Telegraph Company	"	Baltimore, Md.	"	Lancaster, Pa	4	83
"	Boston and Portland	"	Boston, Mass	"	Portland, Me.	3	110
"	Lake Erie Telegraph Company	"	Pittsburg, Pa.	"	Cleveland, Ohio	6	—
"	" " "	"	Buffalo, N. Y.	"	Detroit, Mich.	9	—
"	New-Orleans and Ohio	"	Wheeling, Va.	"	Waynesborough, Tenn.	17	—
"	Waynesborough and Memphis	"	Waynesboro', Tenn.	"	Memphis, Tenn.	4	—
"	Maysville and Cincinnati	"	Maysville, Ky.	"	Cincinnati, Ohio	4	—
"	Western Telegraph Company	"	Baltimore, Md.	"	Wheeling, Ohio	9	277
"	" " "	"	Frederick, Md.	"	Washington, D. C.	3	43
"	Winchester and Harper's Ferry	"	Winchester, Va	"	Harper's Ferry, Md	3	32
"	Dayton and Logansport	"	Dayton, Ohio	"	Logansport, Ind	7	251
"	Baltimore and North Point	"	Baltimore, Md.	"	North Point, Md.	2	7
"	New-Orleans and Balize	"	New-Orleans, La.	"	Balize, La.	2	100
"	Brownsville and Pittsburg	"	Brownsville	"	Pittsburg, Pa.	2	35
1849.	Troy and Whitehall	"	Troy, N. Y.	"	Whitehall, N. Y.	8	65
"	Bridgeport and Bennington	"	Bridgeport, Ct.	"	Bennington, Vt.	11	154
"	New-York and Erie Telegraph Company	"	New-York City	"	Fredonia, N. Y	18	—
"	Portland and Halifax	"	Portland, Me	"	Halifax, N. S.	10	—
"	St. Louis and Chicago	"	St. Louis, Mo	"	Chicago, Ill	—	—
"	Dubuque and Ottawa	"	Dubuque. Iowa	"	Ottawa	—	—
"	Jacksonville and Bloomington	"	Jacksonville, Ill	"	Bloomington, Iowa	—	—
"	Vincennes and Evansville	"	Vincennes, Ind	"	Evansville, Ind.	—	—
	Lines Building and contemplated.	"	Waynesboro', Tenn.	"	New-Orleans, La.	—	—
		"	Newark, N. J	"	Easton, Pa.	—	—
		"	Philadelphia, Pa.	"	Wilkesbarre, Pa	—	—
		"	Providence, R. I.	"	Bristol, Ct.	—	—
		"	Harrisburg, Pa	"	Reading, Pa.	—	—
		"	Galliopolis, Ohio	"	Charleston, S. C.	—	—
		"	Portsmouth,	"	Hanging Rock	—	—
		"	Louisville, Ky	"	Hopkinsville	—	—
		"	Nashville, Tenn.	"	St. Louis, Mo.	—	—
		"	Columbus, Ohio	"	Apalachicola, Flo	—	—
		"	Macon, Geo.	"	Milledgeville, Geo.	—	—
		"	Quebec, L. C.	"	Halifax, N. S.	—	—
		"	Cahaba	"	Tuscumbia, Ohio	—	—
		"	Macon, Geo.	"	Atlanta, Geo.	—	—
		"	Boston, Mass.	"	New-York City	—	—
		"	Newburgh, N. Y	"	Albany, N. Y.	—	—

N. B.—There is no line using any instrument but Morse's, except House's, between Philadelphia and New-York. It is contemplated to erect another line, (O'Reilly's, with Bain's Printing Apparatus,) from New-York, via Albany, to Buffalo.

STEAMBOAT DISTANCES ON THE MISSISSIPPI RIVER.

(BETWEEN FORT SNELLING AND BALIZE.)

West Bank.		Miles from Mouth.	Miles from Fort Snelling.	*East Bank.*		Miles from Mouth.	Miles from Fort Snelling.
Fort Jackson,	*La.*	27	2151	Balize,	*La.*	0	2178
Donaldsonville,	"	187	1991	South East Pass,	"	10	2168
Plaquemine,	"	222	1956	Fort St. Philip,	"	32	2146
Iberville Bayou,	"	230	1948	Battle Ground,	"	101	2077
Point Coupee,	"	281	1897	New-Orleans,	"	105	2073
Red River, (mouth)	"	341	1837	Lafayette,	"	107	2071
Vidalia,	"	404	1774	Carrollton,	"	111	2067
St. Joseph,	"	432	1746	Baton Rouge,	"	245	1933
Carthage,	"	494	1684	Port Hudson,	"	270	1908
Milligan's Bend,	"	545	1633	St. Francisville,	'	281	1897
Tompkins' Bend,	"	571	1607	Fort Adams,	"	352	1826
Providence,	"	586	1592	Homochitto River,	*Miss.*	362	1816
Louisiana Line, 33°N.	"	616	1562	Natchez,	"	404	1774
Grand Lake Land'g,	*Ark.*	618	1560	Grand Gulf,	"	457	1721
American Bend,	"	635	1543	Big Black River,	"	458	1720
Point Chicot,	"	655	1523	Warrenton,	"	503	1675
Columbia,	"	660	1518	Vicksburg,	"	513	1665
Napoleon,	"	725	1453	Yazoo River,	"	525	1053
Arkansas River,	"	725	1453	Princeton,	"	615	1563
White River,	"	739	1439	Egg Point,	"	630	1548
Old Town,	"	791	1387	Cypress Bend,	"	703	1475
Helena,	"	821	1357	Bolivar,	"	713	1465
Sterling,	"	831	1347	Montgomery Point,	"	744	1434
St. Francis River,	"	831	1347	Victoria,	"	745	1433
Greenock,	"	937	1341	Delta,	"	811	1367
Osceola,	"	991	1187	Peyton,	"	845	1333
Little Prairie,	*Mo.*	1040	1138	Walnut Bend,	"	855	1323
Riddle's Point,	"	1068	1110	Commerce,	"	876	1302
New-Madrid,	"	1070	1108	Norfolk,	"	892	1286
Norfolk,	"	1140	1038	Memphis,	*Tenn.*	903	1275
Cape Girardeau,	"	1183	995	Randolph,	"	970	1208
Perryville,	"	1249	929	Hatchee River,	"	971	1207
St. Mary's,	"	1264	914	Fulton,	"	981	1197
St. Genevieve,	"	1278	900	Ashport,	"	1003	1175
Herculaneum,	"	1292	886	Obion River, (mouth)	"	1011	1167
St. Louis,	"	1315	863	Hickman,	*Ky.*	1112	1066
Mouth of Missouri R.	"	1335	843	Columbus,	"	1127	1051
Clarkesville,	"	1378	800	*Mouth of Ohio River,*	"	1145	1033
Louisiana,	"	1397	781	Breeseville,	*Ill.*	1224	954
Palmyra,	"	1444	738	Kaskaskia,	"	1257	931
La Grange,	"	1462	716	Harrison,	"	1287	891

West Bank.		Miles from Mouth.	Miles from Fort Snelling.	East Bank.		Miles from Mouth.	Miles from Fort Snelling.
Winchester,	*Mo.*	1492	686	Waterloo,	*Ill.*	1302	876
Desmoines River,	"	1522	656	Alton,	"	1337	841
Fort Madison,	*Ia.*	1553	625	Gilead,	"	1349	829
Burlington,	"	1563	615	Quincy,	"	1458	720
Bloomington,	"	1615	563	Lima,	"	1479	999
Davenport,	"	1636	542	Warsaw,	"	1522	656
Camanche,	"	1657	521	Nauvoo,	"	1539	639
Charleston,	"	1676	502	New-Boston,	"	1593	585
Bellevue,	"	1698	480	Illinois City,	"	1623	555
Dubuque,	"	1712	468	Rock Island,	"	1636	542
Peru,	"	1723	455	Port Byron,	"	1642	536
Winchester,	"	1741	437	Fulton,	"	1661	517
Prairie la Porte,	"	1757	421	Savannah,	"	1678	500
Fort Snelling,	*Mta.*	2178	0	Galena,	"	1710	468
				Cassville,	*Wisc.*	1751	427
				Fort Crawford,	"	1766	412
				Prairie du Chien,	"	1773	405
				Chippeway River,	"	2082	96
				St. Croix River,	*Mta.*	2137	41
				Falls of St. Anthony,	"	2178	0

STEAMBOAT DISTANCES ON THE OHIO RIVER.

(BETWEEN CAIRO AND PITTSBURG.)

North Bank.	Miles from Mouth.	Miles from Pittsburg.	South Bank.	Miles from Mouth.	Miles from Pittsburg.
Cairo, at mouth of Ohio,	0	1019	Paducah, ...	49	970
Caledonia, ...	13	1006	Tennessee River, (mouth)	49	970
Fort Massac, ...	39	980	Smithland, ...	61	958
Belgrade, ...	42	978	Cumberland Riv., (mouth)	61	958
Golconda, ...	84	935	Raleigh, ...	141	878
Cave in Rock, . . .	112	907	Carthage, ...	147	872
Shawneetown, . . .	136	883	Henderson, ...	187	832
Wabash River, (mouth)	141	878	Green River, (mouth)	206	813
Mount Vernon, . . .	161	858	Owenboro, ...	234	785
Evansville, ...	198	821	Hawesville, ...	268	751
Rockport, ...	243	776	Flint Island, ...	303	716
Troy, ...	262	757	Brandenburg, . . .	354	665
Rome, ...	293	726	Salt River, (mouth) .	372	647
Fredonia, ...	328	691	Portland, ...	391	628

North Bank.	Miles from Mouth.	Miles from Pittsburg.	*South Bank.*	Miles from Mouth	Miles from Pittsburg.
Leavensworth, . . .	333	686	Louisville, ...	394	625
Mauksport, ...	351	668	Westport, ...	419	600
New-Albany, . . .	391	628	Milton, ...	445	574
Jeffersonsville, . . .	395	226	Kentucky River, . .	457	562
Utica, ...	404	615	Ghent, ...	465	554
Bethlehem, ...	425	594	Warsaw, ...	473	546
Madison, ...	445	574	Bellevue, ...	509	513
Vevay, ...	465	554	Petersburg, ...	514	505
Rising Sun, ...	503	516	Covington, ...	535	484
Aurora, ...	512	507	Licking River, (mouth)	536	483
Lawrenceburg, . . .	517	502	Newport, ...	537	482
Miami River, (mouth)	529	490	Augusta, ...	579	440
Cincinnati, ...	535	484	Dover, ...	588	431
Columbia, ...	542	477	Charleston, ...	592	427
New-Richmond, . . .	557	462	Maysville, ...	599	420
Mount Pleasant, . .	562	457	Concord, ...	617	402
Moscow, ...	565	454	Vanceburg, ...	629	390
Neville, ...	569	450	Greenupburg, . . .	669	350
Chilo, ...	578	441	Big Sandy, ...	688	331
Higginsport, ...	584	435	Catletsburg, ...	688	331
Ripley, ...	590	429	Guyandot, ...	702	317
Aberdeen, ...	599	420	Kanawha River, (mouth)	741	278
Manchester, ...	611	408	Point Pleasant, . . .	742	277
Rome, ...	625	394	Letartsville, ...	772	247
Rockville, ...	633	386	Belleville, ...	804	215
Sciota River, (mouth) .	648	371	Blennerhassett's Island,	820	199
Portsmouth, ...	649	370	Little Kanawha River,	821	198
Hanging Rock, . . .	675	344	Parkersburg, ...	822	197
Burlington, ...	694	325	Vienna, ...	829	190
Gallipolis, ...	738	281	Sistersville, ...	866	153
Pomeroy, ...	758	261	Lanesville, ...	897	122
Troy, ...	808	211	Elizabeth, ...	909	110
Muskingum River, (mouth)	834	185	Wheeling, ...	922	97
Marietta, ...	835	184	Martinsville, ...	923	96
Newport, ...	854	165	Wellsburg, ...	938	81
Bridgeport, ...	922	97	Georgetown, ...	974	45
Warren, ...	931	88	Beaver, ...	987	32
Steubenville, ...	945	74	Economy, ...	999	20
Wellsville, ...	965	54	Middletown.	1007	12
Liverpool, ...	969	50	Pittsburg, ...	1019	0

STEAMBOAT DISTANCES ON THE MISSOURI,

FROM THE MOUTH OF THAT RIVER TO COUNCIL BLUFFS.

North Bank.	Miles from Balize.	Miles from Mouth of Missouri.	Miles from Council Bluffs.	*South Bank.*	Miles from Balize.	Miles from Mouth of Missouri.	Miles from Council Bluffs.
Five Barrel Island, . .	1935	600	67	Council Bluffs, ...	2002	667	0
Upper Oven Island, . .	1923	588	79	Bellevue, ...	1962	627	40
Lower Oven Island, . .	1919	584	83	Platte River, ...	1950	615	52
Fair Sun Island, . . .	1868	533	134	Little Nemaha River, .	1880	545	122
Nishnabotna River, . .	—	—	—	Big Nemaha River, . .	1843	508	159
Wolf River, ...	1825	490	177	Weston, ...	1735	400	267
Nodaway River, ...	1809	474	193	Fort Leavenworth, . .	1728	393	274
Little Platte River, . .	1708	373	284	Kansas Landing, . . .	1698	363	304
Liberty Landing, . . .	1683	348	319	Independence, ...	1686	351	316
Richmond, ...	1630	295	372	Lexington, ...	1625	290	377
Grand River, ...	1575	240	427	Boonville, ...	1525	190	277
Chariton River, ...	1555	220	447	Marion, ...	1488	153	404
Franklin, ...	1525	180	487	Jefferson River, . . .	1472	137	430
Griswold, ...	1411	76	591	Osage River, ...	1462	127	440
Newport, ...	1403	68	599	Pinckney, ...	1411	76	591
St. Charles, ...	1355	20	647	Mouth of Missouri, . .	1335	0	667

Probable extent of Steam Navigation on the Western waters, including the rivers, bayoux, &c., connected with the Mississippi by channels navigable for steamers: 16,674 *miles.* By Col. Long, Top. Eng., U. S. A.

MISSISSIPPI AND BRANCHES, BAYOUS, &C.

	Miles.		*Miles.*		*Miles.*
Mississippi Proper, .	2,000	Obion, ...	60	Big Sunflower, . .	80
St. Croix, ...	80	Forked Deer, . . .	195	Little Sunflower, . .	70
St. Peter's, ...	120	Big Hatchee, . . .	75	Big Black, ...	150
Chippeway, . . .	70	St. Francis, ...	300	Bayou de Glaze, . .	90
Black, ...	60	White, ...	500	Do. Care, . . .	140
Wisconsin, . . .	180	Big Black, ...	60	Do. Rouge, . . .	40
Rock, ...	250	Spring, ...	50	Do. La Fourche, .	60
Iowa, ...	110	Arkansas (nav. high water, 850,) . .	600	Do. Plaquemine, .	12
Cedar, ...	60	Canadian, ...	60	Do. Teche, . . .	96
Des Moines, . . .	250	Neosho, ...	60	Grand River, . .	12
Illinois, ...	245	Yazoo, ...	300	Bayou Sorrele, . . .	12
Maremec, ...	60	Tallahatchee, . . .	300	Do. Chien, . . .	5
Kaskaskia, ...	150	Yalabusha, ...	130		
Big Muddy, . . .	5				

MISSOURI AND BRANCHES.

	Miles.		*Miles.*
Missouri Proper (during a part of the year),	1800	Kansas, ...	150
Yellow Stone, ...	300	Osage, ...	275
Platte or Nebraska, ...	40	Grande, ...	90

OHIO AND BRANCHES.

	Miles.		*Miles.*		*Miles.*
Ohio Proper, . . .	1,000	Big Sandy, ...	50	Barren, ...	30
Alleghany, . . .	200	Scioto, ...	50	Wabash, ...	400
Monongahela, . . .	60	Kentucky, ...	62	Cumberland, . . .	400
Muskingum, . .	70	Salt River, ...	35	Tennessee, . . .	720
Kanawha, . .	65	Green, ...	150		

RED RIVER AND BRANCHES, BAYOUS, &C.

	Miles.		*Miles.*		*Miles.*
Red River Proper, .	1,500	Bayou Bœuf, . . .	150	Sulphur Fork, . . .	100
Washita, . . .	375	Bayou Macon, . . .	175	Little River, . . .	65
Saline, ...	100	Bayou Louis, . . .	30	Kiamichi, ...	40
Little Missouri, .	50	Tensas River, . . .	150	Boggy, ...	40
Bayou D'Arboune, .	60	Lake Bistenaw, . .	60	Bayou Pierre, . . .	150
Bayou Bartholomew	150	Lake Caddo, . . .	75	Atchafalaya, . . .	360

POPULATION, DEBT, LOAN, ETC., UNITED STATES.

STATEMENT, exhibiting the population of the United States, the Public Debt, the receipts from Loans and Treasury Notes, the receipts, exclusive of Treasury Notes and Loans, and the payments on account of the debt each year, from 1791, *to June,* 1848, *inclusive.*

Years.	Population.	Debt.	Receipts from Loans and Treas. Notes.	Revenue exclusive of Loans & Treas. Notes.	Principal and interest of debt paid.
Census of 1791	4,067,371	$75,463,476 52	$5,791,112 56	$4,418,913 19	$5,287,949 50
2	4,205,404	77,227,924 66	5,070,806 46	3,669,960 21	7,263,665 99
3	4,343,457	80,352,684 04	1,067,701 14	4,652,923 14	5,819,505 29
4	5,481,500	78,427,404 77	4,609,196 78	5,431,904 87	5,801,578 09
5	4,619,543	80,747,587 39	3,305,268 20	6,114,834 59	6,084,411 61
6	4,757,586	83,762,172 07	362,800 00	8,377,549 65	5,835,846 44
7	4,895,629	82,064,479 33	70,135 41	8,688,780 98	5,792,421 82
8	5,033,672	79,228,529 12	308,574 27	7,900,495 80	3,990,294 14
9	5,171,715	78,408,669 77	5,074,646 53	7,546,813 31	4,596,876 78
Census of 1800	5,309,758	82,976,294 35	1,602,435 04	10,848,749 10	4,578,369 95
1	5,502,772	83,038,050 80	10,125 00	12,935,330 95	7,291,707 04
2	5,695,787	80,712,632 25	5,597 36	14,994,793 95	539,004 76
3	5,888,801	77,054,686 30		11,064,097 63	7,256,159 43
4	6,081,816	86,427,120 88	9,532 64	11,826,307 38	8,171,787 45
5	6,274,830	82,312,150 50	128,814 94	13,560,693 20	7,369,889 79
6	6,467,845	75,723,270 66	48,897 71	15,559,931 07	8,989,884 61
7	6,660,859	69,218,398 64		16,398,019 26	6,307,720 10
8	6,853,874	65,196,317 97	1,882 16	17,060,661 93	10,260,245 35
9	7,046,888	57,023,192 09		7,773,473 12	6,452,554 16
Census of 1810	7,239,908	53,173,217 52	2,759,992 25	9,384,214 28	8,008,904 46
11	7,479,729	48,005,587 76	8,309 05	14,423,529 00	8,009,204 05
12	7,719,555	45,209,737 90	12,837,900 00	9,801,133 76	4,449,622 45
13	7,959,381	55,962,827 57	26,184,435 00	14,340,409 95	11,108,123 44
14	8,199,208	81,487,846 24	23,377,911 79	11,181,625 16	7,900,543 94
15	8,439,034	99,833,660 15	35,261,320 78	15,696,916 82	12,628,924 35
16	8,678,860	127,334,933 74	9,494,436 16	47,676,985 66	24,871,082 93
17	8,918,687	123,491,965 16	734,542 59	33,099,049 74	25,423,036 12
18	9,158,513	103,466,633 83	8,765 62	21,585,171 04	21,296,201 62
19	9,398,339	95,529,648 28	2,291 00	24,603,374 37	7,703,926 29
Census of 1820	9,638,166	91,015,566 15	3,040,824 13	17,840,669 55	8,628,494 28
1	9,959,965	89,987,437 66	5,000,324 00	14,573,379 72	8,367,093 62
2	10,281,765	93,546,676 98		20,232,427 94	7,848,949 12
3	10,603,565	90,875,877 28		20,540,666 26	5,530,016 41
4	10,925,365	90,239,777 77	5,000,000 00	19,381,212 79	16,538,303 76
5	11,247,165	83,788,432 71	5,000,000 00	21,840,858 02	12,095,344 78
6	11,568,965	81,054,059 99		25,260,434 31	11,041,032 19
7	11,890,765	73,987,357 20		22,966,363 96	10,003,668 35
8	12,212,565	67,475,043 87		24,763,629 23	12,163,438 07
9	12,534,365	58,421,413 67		24,827,627 38	12,383,867 78
Census of 1830	12,856,165	48,565,406 50		24,844,116 51	11,355,748 22
1	13,277,415	39,123,191 66		28,526,820 82	16,174,378 22
2	13,698,665	24,322,235 18		31,665,561 16	17,840,309 29
3	14,119,915	7,001,032 88		33,948,426 25	1,543,543 38
4	14,541,165	4,760,082 08		21,791,935 55	6,176,565 19
5	14,962,415	351,289 05		35,430,187 10	58,191 28
6	15,383,665	291,089 05		50,826,796 08	
7	15,804,915	1,878,223 55	2,992,989 15	24,890,864 69	21,822 91
8	16,226,165	4,857,660 46	12,716,820 86	26,303,561 74	5,605,720 27
9	16,647,415	11,983,737 53	3,857,276 21	30,023,966 68	11,117,987 42
Census of 1840	17,068,665	5,125,077 63	5,589,547 51	19,442,646 08	4,086,613 70
1	17,560,082	6,737,398 00	13,659,317 39	16,850,160 27	5,600,689 74
2	18,051,499	15,028,486 37	14,808,735 64	19,965,009 25	8,575,539 94
June 30 3	18,542,915	27,748,188 23	12,551,409 19	8,231,000 26	861,596 55
4	19,034,332	24,748,188 23	1,877,847 95	29,320,707 78	12,991,902 84
5	19,525,749	17,093,794 80		29,941,853 90	8,595,049 10
6	20,017,165	16,750,926 33		29,699,967 74	1,213,823 31
7	20,508,582	38,956,623 38	28,900,765 36	26,437,403 16	6,719,282 37
8	21,006,000	58,526,349 37	21,256,700 00	*35,425,750 59	*15,249,197 21

Present debt, including the amount to be realized on the 1st of May, 1848, of the Loans of 1846, 1847 and 1848, $65,787,008 92

TREASURY DEPARTMENT,
Register's Office, August 5, 1848.

DANIEL GRAHAM, *Register.*

* Estimated returns not completed.

THE UNITED STATES OF MEXICO.

The Republic of Mejico, or Mexico by the treaty of 1848,* has been much curtailed in its dimensions, and the secession of Texas, and the cession of California, &c., to the United States, have confined it to the narrow strip of land between the Gulf of Mexico and the Pacific. Its present boundaries are the Rio Bravo or Rio Grande del Norte and the Gulf of Mexico on the east and north-east; the State of Guatemala on the south-east: the Pacific Ocean on the west and south-west; and the Rio Gila, &c., on the north. Within these boundaries the superficial area is estimated at about 1,100,000 square miles :—the extreme length is about 1,400 miles from north-west to south-east, and the greatest breadth about 650 miles. With reference to its geographical position, Mexico lies between the latitudes of 15° 20′ and 33° 30′ North, and between the meridians of 90° and 117° West from Greenwich.

Nothing can be more unsatisfactory than our acquaintance with this country. Few even of the principal towns and rivers are correctly laid down, except indeed, within the small circle personally visited by Humboldt, or those regions explored by the officers attached to the invading army of the United States of America, so that even the elements of a good map do not exist; and with respect to population and other statistics, the unsettled, disorderly and almost lawless state of the country makes enquiry useless and all but nugatory.

That portion of the country lying south of the tropic of Cancer is the most populous and rich, both in vegetable and mineral productions, and nearly all the information gained respecting Mexico has been collected in that part, to which, consequently, it is primarily applicable. The regions lying north of the tropic become less populous as we proceed northward, and many large districts claimed by the republic and divided into states and territories, are almost unknown, being inhabited only by wild Indian tribes, baffling all the attempts of their nominal masters to subdue them.

The surface of Mexico is very varied, and to this circumstance must be attributed, as much as to the difference of latitude, that singular variety of climate which distinguishes it from almost all other countries. The great

* The northern boundary of Mexico, according to the treaty of 1848, commences " in the Gulf of Mexico, three leagues from land, opposite the mouth of the Rio Grande, otherwise called Rio Bravo del Norte, or opposite the mouth of its deepest branch, if it should have more than one branch emptying directly into the sea; from thence up the middle of that river, following the deepest channel, where it has more than one, to the point where it strikes the southern boundary of New-Mexico; thence westwardly, along the whole southern boundary of New-Mexico (which runs north of the town called *Paso*,) to its western termination; thence northward along the western line of New-Mexico, until it intersects the first branch of the River Gila, (or if it should not intersect any branch of that river, then to the point on the said line nearest to such branch, and thence in a direct line to the same); thence down the middle of the said branch and of the said river, until it empties into the Rio Colorado, following the division line between Upper and Lower California to the Pacific Ocean.

chain of mountain plateaux which commences in the Isthmus of Panama and runs northward, diverges, after leaving Central America, into two great arms, like the upper part of the letter Y, following the coast on either side. The western arm has some very high summits, and preserves its mountainous character until it reaches the Rocky Mountains; the eastern arm begins to subside after reaching the 21st or 22d parallel, and is subsequently lost in the vast plains of western Texas. The whole of the vast tract between these mountains forms the high table-lands of Mexico—the Plateau of Anahuac—elevated from 6,000 to 8,000 feet above the ocean's level. Hence, though a large portion of this plain is south of the tropic, it enjoys a moderate climate—inclining, indeed, more to cold than an excess of heat. Some very high culminations are dispersed over the surface of these table-lands, and in some parts well-defined ridges are recognized, which divide it into sub-plateaux, which are known under a variety of local names. But few vallies, however, interrupt the general level, and in some districts it is quite unbroken by depressions or hills.

The most remarkable tract in this elevated region is the plain of Tenochtitlan, (in which is the capital) surrounded by porphyritic and basaltic rocks. It is of an oval form, 54 miles long and 37 miles broad, occupying an area of 1,700 square miles, of which about 160 square miles are covered with water. More elevated on the south-east side, here are seen towering above the plain, the volcanos of Popocatepetl, 17,735 feet, Iztaccihuatl, 15,700 feet, Cittalapetl or Orizaba, 17,388 feet, and Nauhcampapetl or the Coffre de Perote, 13,514 feet above the sea.

The waters of the valley of Mexico are deposited in five principal lakes, situated on different levels:—that of Tezcuco, which is near the centre of the valley, and covers 70 square miles, is the least elevated. Further north are the lakes of St. Christoval and Tonanitla—while south is the lake Chalco, occupying an area of 51 square miles; and these three are five feet higher than that of Tezcuco. The most elevated, however, of the whole, though the smallest, is Zimpango, the level of which is 30 feet above that of Tezcuco. These lakes are fed by numerous small rivers, and having no natural outlet, are drained by the Desague of Huchuetoca, an artificial canal cut through the rock, 12 miles in length, 150 feet deep and 300 feet wide—having its embouchure in the River Panuco, which flows eastward to the Gulf of Mexico. This great work, completed in 1789, at an expense of £1,292,000, was undertaken to obviate the frequent inundations, some of which did great damage to the capital. The water of Lake Tezcuco is salt, that of the rest is fresh; but from those to the south sulphuretted hydrogen is copiously disengaged, the stench of which is often perceptible in the city of Mexico.

Beside the volcanoes already mentioned, those of Tuxtla, Jorullo and Colima, in the table land, are at present in a state of activity, and there are several others now extinct. Jorullo, which rises west of the capital, first broke out in 1759, when a tract of land three or four miles square, swelled up like an inflated bladder, emitting flames and fragments of rock through a thousand apertures. These active volcanos seem to be connected with others parallel to them, and obviously of similar origin. Earthquakes are frequent in Mexico, but it is seldom they create much mischief.

The geological characteristics of the mountains of Mexico are essentially different from those of the great ranges of Europe and Asia, in which granite is overlaid with gneiss, mica and clay-slate—for here we seldom meet with granite, as it is covered with porphyry, green-stone, amygdaloid, basalt, obsidian and other rocks of igneous origin. Granite, however, appears on the surface in the Pacific chain, and the port of Acapulco is a natural excavation in that species of rock. The plateau of Anuhuac, from the 14th to the 20th parallel, is a mass of porphyry, characterized by the constant presence of horn-blende and the entire absence of quartz, and in it are deposited large quantities of the ores of the precious metals. These ores, however, are found in various rocks;—in the mines of Comanja, rich veins of silver occur in sienite; in those of Guanaxuato, which are the richest in Mexico, the metal lies in primitive slate-clay, passing into talc-slate; and those of Real del Cardonal, Xacala, and Somo del Toro, are situated in a bed of transition limestone. Humboldt says that, at the time of his visit, there were 3,000 mines of gold and silver in Mexico; but the ignorance and misrule which prevail in the country have greatly diminished their importance as a source of wealth.

The mineral wealth of Mexico is not altogether confined to the precious metals. Iron is found in great abundance in Guadalajara, Mechoacan and Zacatecas:—but no mines of this metal were worked before 1825. Copper is raised in Mechoacan and Guanaxuato. Tin is obtained partly from mines, but principally from the washings of the ravines. The lead mines, though rich, are entirely neglected. Zinc, antimony and arsenic have been found, but neither cobalt nor manganese. A quicksilver mine is wrought in the State of Queretaro, but the greater quantity used in the extraction of the precious metals, is obtained from Spain, and, in a great measure, the quantity of the metals produced depends on the supplies of quick-silver from that country. At the present time, these are under lease to the Rothschilds, and consequently, they are able to regulate the production of gold in Mexico, which frequently acts banefully on the interests of the country. Carbonate of soda, used in smelting the silver ore, is found in great abundance, crystallized on the surface of several of the lakes.

The theory of mining is little understood in Mexico, the oldest modes of working being still generally practised, notwithstanding the improvements introduced by the English—and the machinery for draining the mines and raising the ore is of the most primitive character. Indeed, many of the mines have been abandoned on this account, which, under more favorable circumstances, might again be worked advantageously. The ignorance of the miners is only equalled by their obstinate adherence to exploded practices. But this should not be a matter of surprise, when the condition of the *Mineria*, or School of Mines, is taken into account. Without necessary implements, with bad regulations, and the minerals unclassified, and all in a deplorable state of disorder, this splendid institution, which cost upwards of $600,000 to erect, is irretrievably lost to the interests for which it was founded.

Compared with the vast extent of Mexico, her rivers are few and unimportant, and great disadvantages are suffered for want of water communication. The Rio Grande del Norte, which separates the United States from Mexico, has a long course, but the trade on that river must ever be sequestered by the superior ability and energy of the Americans. The Rio Grande de Santiago, called by the natives Tolototlan, rises in the centre of the republic, not far from the capital, and, after traversing the Lake Chapala, falls into the Pacific at San Blas. The Balsas or Zacatula, and the Yopez, are the only other rivers on the west side of the plateau, and on the east side are the Tula, Tampico and Tobasco, flowing into the Gulf; but they have bars at their mouths which prevent the entrance of large ships. The other rivers are short, and might more properly be called torrents. The lakes are numerous and extensive, and the principal, besides those in the valley of Mexico, already mentioned, are Chapala, in Xalisco, which, according to Humboldt, covers an area of 1,300 square miles; Pascuara, in Mechoacan—Mextitlan, Cayman, and Parras, the last two being in the tract called the *Bolson de Mapimi.*

In regard of climate, the country is divided into three regions, named respectively—the *Tierras Calientes*, or Hot Regions; the *Tierras Templadas*, or Temperate Regions; and the *Tierras Frias*, or Cold Regions. The first include the low grounds of the coasts, under the elevation of 2,000 feet; the mean temperature is about 77°, and the country is especially suited to the growth of sugar, indigo, cotton and bananas, which all flourish luxuriantly; but this district is almost inaccessible by sea for one-half the year, owing to the prevalence of north winds and boisterous gales, and during the other half are extremely unhealthy from the oppressive heat, and the great quantity of rain that falls. The coast then becomes the seat of pestilence, and the stranger, from more northern regions, arriving for the first time at Vera Cruz, or any other part of the coast within the tropics, in Aug., Sept. or Oct., has little chance of escaping the yellow fever, and fluxes, peculiar to these regions. But at the height of 2,000 to 2,500 feet, these scourges are quite unknown. The temperate regions, which are of comparatively small extent, occupy the slopes of the great plateau, and range from 2,500 to 5,000 feet in elevation above the sea. The mean annual temperature is from 68° to 70°, and the extremes of heat and cold are alike unknown. The Mexican oak, and most of the fruits and cereals of Europe, flourish in this genial climate. Fogs, however, are frequent, occasioning excessive humidity, but producing great beauty and strength of vegetation. The cold regions include the high table-lands, and mountains of upwards of 5,000 feet in elevation. The mean temperature of this plateau is generally about 62°, but in the city of Mexico it sometimes, though rarely, falls below the freezing point. In the cold season the mean heat of the day varies from 55° to 70°; while in the summer, it seldom rises in the shade above 75°. At a greater elevation than 8,000 feet, the climate is severe and disagreeable, and under the parallel of Mexico the snow-line varies from 12,000 to 15,000 feet above the level of the sea. The climate of the table-lands, on the whole, is favorable to human life, and the prevalent diseases are believed to be more owing to the bad habits of the people, than to the qualities of the soil and climate. Indeed, owing to the improvidence of the people, famine, and its concomitant privations, have thinned the population more than epidemic complaints.

The zoology of Mexico is but little known. Many species analogous to those with which we are acquainted, differ from them, nevertheless, in important characters. Among the species that are decidedly new and indigenous, are the *coendue*, a species of porcupine; the apaxa, or Mexican stag; the conepatl, of the weasel tribe; the Mexican squirrel, and another striated species, the cayopollin, and the Mexican wolf, inhabit the forests and mountains. Among the four animals classed as dogs by the Mexican Pliny, Hernandez, one, denominated *zolo itzcuintli*, is the wolf, distinguished by its total want of hair. The *techichi*, is a species of dog without voice, which was eaten by the ancient Mexicans. This kind of food was so necessary to the Spaniards themselves, before the introduction of cattle, that in process of time the whole race was destroyed. Linnæus confounds the dumb dog with the *itzcuinte-potzoli*, a species of dog very imperfectly described, and distinguished by a short tail, a very small head, and a large hump on its back. The bison and the musk ox wander in immense herds in Northern Mexico. The elks, according to the testimony of Clavigero, are sufficiently strong to have been employed in dragging a heavy carriage. We still know very little of the great wild sheep, or of the *berendos*, which, it would appear, resemble antelopes. The *jaguar*, and the *cougar*, which, in the New World, represent the tiger and lion of the old continent, are met with in the lower and hot part of Mexico; but they have been little observed by scientific naturalists. Hernandez says, that the *miztli* resembles the lion without a mane, but that it is of greater size. The Mexican bear is the same as that of the United States and Canada.

The domestic animals of Europe conveyed to Mexico, have prospered there, and multiplied in a remarkable degree. The wild horses, which gallop in immense herds over the plains of Mexico, are descended from those brought thither by the Spaniards. The breed is equally beautiful and vigorous. That of the mule is not less so. The transportation of goods between Mexico and Vera Cruz occupies 70,000 mules. The sheep are a coarse and neglected breed. The feeding of cattle is of great importance on the eastern coast, and in the state of Durango, &c. Families are sometimes met with who possess herds of 40 or 50,000 head of cattle and horses. Former accounts speak of herds two or three times more numerous. Carnivorous animals are not numerous.

The bird and insect tribes of Mexico are of beautiful colors, and in immense variety and number, and some are common to all latitudes, from the equatorial to the higher regions of the north. Parrots and parroquets, and other tropical birds, inhabit the groves of the tierras callientes, which are also infested with venomous insects, as centipedes, mosquitoes, &c., and a great variety of serpents, which, however, are not generally very formidable. Here, in some shape, is found all the birds, insects, and creeping things, of tropical climates. Higher up, in the more elevated regions, the character changes; and still more elevated, class on class of animated nature, each different from the other, is successively developed. The nature and variety differs with the elevation, which, in its effect on the living machine, acts in a known ratio with variety in latitude. Hence the animal indigenous to the polar regions, is not unfrequently met with in the elevated regions of Mexico.

Vegetation varies also with the elevation and temperature, from the burning shores of the ocean, to the icy summits of the Cordilleras. In the hot region, as high as 1,200 feet, the fan-leaved palms, the *miraguama* and *pumos* palms, the white *Oreodoxa*, the *Tournefortia velutina*, the *Cordia gerascanthus*, the willow-leaved *Cephelanthus*, the *Hyptis bursata*, *Salpianthus arenarius*, *Gomphræna globosa*, pinnated calabash tree, or *Crescentia pinnata*, the *Podopterus Mexicanus*, willow-leaved bignonia, *Salvia occidentalis*, *Perdicium Havanense*, *Gyrocarpus*, *Leucophyllum ambiguum*, *Gomphia Mexicana*, *Panicum divaricatum*, *Bauhinia aculeata*, *Hæmatoxylon radiatum*, *Hymenæa courbaril, foliis retusis*, *Swietenia Mexicana*, and the sumac-leaved *Malpighia*, predominate in the spontaneous vegetation. On the confines of the temperate and torrid zone are cultivated the sugar-cane, and the cotton, cacao, and indigo plants; but they rarely ascend above the elevation of 1,800 or 2,400 feet. The sugar-cane, however, prospers well in the sheltered valleys, at an elevation of 6,000 feet above the level of the sea. The banana tree extends from the shores of the sea, to a height of 4,350 feet. The region, from 1,200 to 6,600 feet of elevation, presents the *Liquidamber Styraciflua, Erythroxylon Mexicanum, Aralia digitata, Chicus pazcuarensis, Guardiola Mexicana, Tagetes tenuifolia, Psychotria pauciflora, Ipomæ cholulensis, Convolvulus arborescens, Veronica xalapensis, Globularia Mexicana,* stachys of Actopan, *Salvia Mexicana, Vitex mollis,* thick-flowered arbutus, *Eryngium protæflorum, Laurus Cervantesii,* willow-leaved daphne, *Fritillaria barbata, Yucca spinosa, Cobæa scandens,* yellow sage; four varieties of Mexican oaks, (commencing at an elevation of 2,820 feet, and ending at 9,720 feet;) the mountain-yew, and the corrugated angular Banisteria. In the cold region, at a height of from 6,600 to 14,100 feet, we meet with the thick-stemmed oak, (*Quercus crassipes,*) the Mexican rose, the alder, which disappears at the height of 11,100 feet; the wonderful *Cheirostemon platanoides,* the *Krameria,* the *Valeriana ceratophylla,* the *Datura superba,* the cardinal sage, the dwarf potentilla, the myrtle-leaved arbutus, the *Cotoneaster denticulata,* and the Mexican strawberry. The pines, which commence in the temperate zone at the height of 5,700 feet, disappear in the cold region at 12,300 feet. Thus the *coniferous trees,* unknown in South America, here terminate, as they do in the Alps and Pyrenees, the scale of vegetation in the larger plants. At the very limit of perpetual snow, we find the *Arenaria bryoides,* the *Cnicus nivalis,* and the *Chelone gentianoides.*

Among the Mexican vegetables, that furnish abundant alimentary supplies, the banana occupies the first rank. The two species, called the *Platano-arton,* and *Dominico,* appear to be indigenous; the *camburi,* or *Nusa sapientum,* has been brought thither from Africa. One single cluster of bananas often contains from 160 to 180 fruits, and weighs from 60 to 80 pounds. A piece of land of 120 yards of surface, easily produces 4,000 pounds weight of fruit, whilst the same extent will scarcely produce more than thirty pounds weight of wheat, or eighty pounds of potatoes. The manioc occupies the same region as the banana. The cultivation of maize is still more extended. This indigenous vegetable succeeds on the sea-coast, and in the valley of Toluca, at the height of 8,400 feet above the ocean. Maize commonly produces in the proportion of 150 to 1. It forms the principal nourishment both of men and animals. Wheat, rye, barley, and the other cerealia of Europe, are cultivated nowhere but on the plateau in the temperate region. Wheat commonly produces at the rate of twenty-five or thirty for one. In the coldest region, they cultivate the potato, originally from South America, the *Tropæolum esculentum,* a new species of *nasturtium,* or Indian cress, and the *Chenopodium quinoa,* the seeds of which are an equally agreeable and healthy aliment. In the temperate and cold regions we also meet with the oca, (*Oxalis tuberosa;*) the sweet potato and the yam are cultivated in the hot region. Notwithstanding the abundant produce of so many alimentary plants, dry seasons expose Mexico to periodical famine.

This country produces indigenous species of the cherry-tree, apple, walnut, mulberry, and strawberry. It has likewise made the acquisition of the greater part of the fruits of Europe, as well as those of the torrid zone. The *maguey,* a variety of the agave, furnishes a drink denominated *pulque,* of which the inhabitants of Mexico consume a very great quantity. The fibres of the maguey supply hemp and paper; and the prickles are used for pins and nails.

The cultivation of sugar increases, although, generally speaking, it is confined to the temperate region; and, in consequence of the scanty population, the hot and moist plains of the sea-coasts, so well adapted for the growth of this plant, continue in a great measure uncultivated. The sugar-cane here is cultivated and manufactured by free people.

In this burning climate are produced the best indigo and the best cacao. It is from the Mexican language that we have derived the term chocolatl, of which, however, we have softened the final syllable. The nuts of the cacao, considered in Mexico as an article of the first necessity, are used instead of small coin; six nuts being equivalent to one sous.

The state of Oaxaca is at present the only province where they cultivate, on a large scale, the *Nopal* or *Cactus coccinellifer*, upon which the insect that produces the cochineal delights to feed. Cochineal is annually exported to the value of £500,000 sterling. Among the other useful vegetables, we must notice the *Convolvulus jalapa*, or true jalap, which grows naturally in the district of Xalapa, to the north-west of Vera Cruz; the *Epidendrum vanilla*, which, as well as the jalap, loves the shade of the liquid-amber and the amyris; the *Copaifera officinalis*, and the *Toluiferum balsamum*, two trees which produce odoriferous resins, known in commerce by the name of the balsams of Capivi and of Tolu.

The shores of the bays of Honduras and Campeachy have been celebrated, since the period of their first discovery, for their rich and immense forests of mahogany and logwood, so useful in manufactures; but the cutting and selling of which has been seized upon by the English. A species of acacia affords an excellent black dye. The guaiacum, the sassafras, and the tamarind, adorn and enrich these fertile provinces. The pine apple is found wild in the woods; and all the shallow rocky soils are covered with different species of Aloe and Euphorbia.

The gardens of Europe have made various acquisitions of new ornaments from the Mexican flora, and, amongst others, the *Salvia fulgens*, to which its crimson flowers give so much brilliance, the beautiful dahlia, the elegant *Sisyrinchium striatum*, the gigantic *Helianthus*, and the delicate *Mentzelia*. M. Bonpland, M. Humboldt's companion, discovered a species of bombax, which produces a cotton, possessing at once the brilliance of silk and the strength of wool.

The population of Mexico is almost a matter of conjecture, or only an approximation to the truth, no census having been taken since 1793, at which period it amounted to 4,483, 529. In 1803 Humboldt, from sufficient data, estimated it at 5,837,100; in 1818 it was stated at 6,500,000, and in 1820, Malte Brun supposed it to amount to 8,000,000. These estimates cover a space of 27 years, and show the following rates of increase:

From 1793 to 1803	10	years	32	per cent., or	3.2 per annum.
" 1803 to 1808		"	12	" "	2.4 "
" 1808 to 1820	12	"	23	" "	1.9 "
" 1793 to 1820	27	"	78	" "	2.8 "

This ratio of increase would double the population of Mexico in about 36 years, and consequently in 1829 or 1830 it would have numbered 8,977,058, and at the present date, under the same ratio of progress, it must have been 13,465,587. But what is the fact? If we are to trust to late official announcements, it appears that a retrogradation has occurred. It is now stated to amount to a little less than 7,000,000. From these contradictory facts, we must conclude that little is known respecting the numbers in Mexico, or that the government of that country have motives for concealing the truth.

The following table is founded on a report of the "National Institute of Geography and Statistics," made for the use of the supreme government in 1839, and may be considered as official:

States.	*Area in sq. miles.*	*Population.*	*Capitals.*	*Pop. of Capital.*
Federal District	100.	1,389,520	Mexico	300,000
Mexico	25,450.		Tlalpan	12,000
Xalisco	73,000	679,111	Guadalajara	60,000
Puebla	18,440	661,992	Puebla	95,000
Guanaxuato	8,000	513,666	Guanaxuato	60,000
Oajaca	32,650	500,278	Oajaca	40,000
Mechoacan	22,468	497,906	Valladolid	25,000
San Luis Potosi	19,000	331,840	San Luis Potosi	50,000
Zacatecas	19,950	273,575	Zacatecas	25,000
Vera Cruz	27,660	254,380	Vera Cruz	15,000
Durango	54,500	162,618	Durango	25,000
Chihuahua	107,500	147,600	Chihuahua	30,000
Sinaloa	54,700	147,000	Sinaloa	13,000
Chiapas	18,750	141,206	Cuidad Real	3,000
Sonora	200,000	124,000	Arispe	5,000
Queretaro	7,500	120,560	Queretaro	40,000
Neuvo Leon	21,000	101,408	Monterey	15,000
Tamaulipas	35,100	100,068	Neuvo Santander	4,000
Coahuila	93,600	75,340	Coahuila	4,000
Aquas Calientes	new state ?*	—— ?	Aquascalientes	20,000
Tobasco	14,676	63,580	Villa Hermosa	5,000
Yucatan	79,500	580,984	Merida	15,000
Baja California	57,029	33,439	Loreto	500
Alta California (now detached)	376,344	15,000	Los Angelos	2,000
Neuvo Mexico (now detached)	200,000	57,026	Santa Fé	4,000

Beside the above there are the territories of Colima and Tlascala, the extent and population of which are not stated; it is probable, however, that they may be included in that of the neighboring states. Thus stood things in 1839. Since that period, the diminishing forces of foreign and civil war have existed, and even if the natural rate of increase has not been disturbed it is nevertheless probable that these destructive agencies and their concomitant miseries have at least suspended any actual increase. The sum then of about 7,000,000 may be taken more or less as the approximate population of the republic at the present time; whereas, had all circumstances been favorable, the natural increase must have augmented it to nearly 12,000,000, excluding the population of those territories which have become detached.

This population consists of Indians, native born Spaniards, Indo-Spanish or mixed races, negroes and Europeans and other foreigners. The Indians are by far the most numerous class, and from them is derived that large numerical force of serfs, called *peons*, atttached to the soil, and far more degraded than the slaves in the Southern United States. Slavery as a principle is abhorrent to Mexicans, and none of the negro race, who are found in the country, are held in servitude; yet *in fact*, slavery, and slavery in its worst shape, exists in every state of the republic. The lands are held by the church or wealthy proprietors, in haciendas or plantations, embracing

* Included in the states of Zacatecas, Xalisco and Guanaxuato.

many square leagues. These lands are sometimes divided into farms or *ranchos*, and leased to tenants at a certain rent. On these plantations are the peons, who acknowledge the owner as their master. With their clothing scant, their food coarse but abundant, they seem contented with their lot. Ignorant, superstitious, patient, they pass their harmless lives in a state of melancholy existence, but slightly removed in their enjoyments from the cattle they feed or the mules they drive. One day in the week is allowed to them for their own benefit, and that is devoted by them to cultivating vegetables, &c., or gathering fruit for the city markets, which they can attend. The Indians, who are free, inhabit ranchos and villages, or in the northern states remain in tribes isolated from the population pretending to civilization. Those who have been reared upon the farms, and mixed up with that mongrel breed, part native, part negro and part Spanish, are the class from which the bands of robbers and the guerrillas, which have proved so annoying to our armies in Mexico, are formed. Fierce, cruel, vindictive and cowardly, they are implacable in their enmities and treacherous in their friendships. With many of the vices and none of the virtues of civilization, they are willing to adopt any pursuit that will exempt them from labor, equally willing to plunder a neighbor, rob a traveller, or murder an enemy.

The Indians and Creoles of the villages are a far different description of people; they are industrious, peaceable and harmless, engaged chiefly in agriculture or the mines. In the cities the large mass of the inhabitants are of the same classes, and resemble the villagers, with that modification only which a city life is sure to produce. Here, however, the innocence of the rural population is merged into cunning, craft, falsehood and treachery; yet they are industrious and peaceable among themselves, but violent towards those they suppose to be enemies. In the various trades in which they are engaged they are skilful artisans, and exhibit specimens of handiwork which would compare favorably with any in Europe or America. Deceit and falsehood, however, are the characteristics of the Mexican, but it is deceit and falsehood engendered in an atmosphere where truth, and frankness and honesty, lead the possessor of these virtues to certain and condign punishment These remarks are not applicable to all. There are exceptions, rare, but still they exist; and in these, men of education and moral worth, every confidence can be placed, and who, rather than lay themselves open to suspicion of wrong, would sacrifice everything. These are the merchants of Mexico and the more respectable tradesmen. With such exceptions, the Mexicans are a vile race.

The influence of government in producing this state of things is acknowledged; a terror constantly occupies the minds of the people, and an apprehension of coming evils and an anxiety to avoid them, overcome all sense of moral uprightness, and convert the people into a nation of serfs, amenable to the nod of the taskmaster. Every political and civil ability that ought of right to belong to the people, is suppressed to the masses, and is exercised by the few. The church, too, acts wofully on the reasoning faculties, and holds over the head of the recusant the rod of oppression. The poor are the sport of the rich, and the weaker of the stronger party. Hence a constant struggle of interests is maintained, and the country at any moment ready to rise in rebellion at the word of the strong, the designing and the mean.

The foreigners, consisting of French, German, English, Irish and some Americans, are residents of the cities and seaports. They are for the most part very intelligent and a better class of people, who have sought their fortunes in Mexico, with the intention of returning to their own countries after acquiring the wealth they seek. They are principally engaged as merchants, factors, bankers, some few as manufacturers and miners; and some are employed in various trades. They are generally an influential class, and have acquired considerable power over the government. Their desires tend towards peace, and their interests are identified with the interests of the country; hence they are advocates of law and order; and their presence, more than any other influence, will tend to civilize and enlighten the dark creeds and political manifestations of the country. They are a nucleus, around which constitutionalism will entwine, and through which the protection of persons and property will become developed.

Agriculture, as before observed, forms a principal ingredient in the industrial economy of the Mexicans. Seven-eighths of the people are farmers. The soil and climate are peculiarly well-adapted to such pursuits; there is scarcely a plant in the known world that will not find a congenial soil and locality, or which is not susceptible of cultivation in one or other part of this vast territory. But agriculture is still in a very primitive condition; it acknowledges no science in its prosecution; nor are any of the new modes or implements now generally used in other countries, known in Mexico. The great fertility of the soil, however, in some measure counterbalances the absence of these, and where production, in other countries depends on intelligence and industry, here it is a natural, and almost spontaneous tribute, and, as a consequent, the necessity to labor is greatly abridged. Hence man, ever in his original state at war with toil, retreats into his primitive condition of idleness and luxury; and hence the indolence attributed to the denizens of the exuberant regions of tropical countries, and especially of inter-tropical Mexico. It is said, but with what degree of truth it is hard to tell, that agriculture has retrograded since the revolution, and that lands that were once under the best cultivation, are now lying waste. Even some large farms near the capital have been abandoned. On this subject M. Chevalier, who visited Mexico in 1835, thus expresses himself: "Agriculture," says he, "is neglected. No law, indeed, prevents the planting of the vine and olive tree; not only, however, has no advantage been taken of this change,* but the very lands which were cultivated in the time of the Spaniards, are now lying fallow. In a circle of a few leagues round Mexico, I have seen large villages almost abandoned. In this delightful climate, the only manure the land ever requires, is water; this is rather scarce, yet many of the hydraulic constructions, raised by the Spaniards at a great cost, are in ruins, and seem likely to remain so. The lands which, by means of this artificial irrigation, were the most fertile in the world, are gradually becoming completely sterile. Their ploughs, and other agricultural implements, are of the rudest description. No one troubles himself to introduce European improvements, or even to import better tools from the United States."

The mines of Mexico have ever been considered the main source of its wealth, and, unquestionably, its mineral riches far exceed those of any part of America, except, perhaps, Peru. Before the revolution, there were in the 37 mining districts, into which New Spain was divided, no less than 3,000 mines of gold or silver, producing annually 21,000,000 dollars in

* The Spaniards, for reasons well understood, interdicted the cultivation of the vine and olive.

silver, and about $2,000,000 in gold. Since that period this great interest has become diminished in importance; not on account of exhaustion of the mines, but from the insecurity and expenses attending operations. We must here again refer to M. Chevalier. "How," asks he, "can the mines be worked with any feeling of security, when it requires a little army to escort the smallest portion of the precious metal to its place of destination? Between the mine of Real del Monte and the village of Tezeyuco, is a mountain-pass, where a grand battle was fought between the miners and the banditti of the country. The former were defeated, overpowered by numbers, but not without having sold their lives as dearly as possible. The mine is now guarded by artillery and grape-shot, and the Englishmen employed there are regularly drilled in the use of the musket." In such a state of things, the wonder is, not that the produce of the mine has declined, but that it continues to be so great as we find it to be.

The annual yield of the gold and silver mines can never be ascertained with accuracy, in consequence of the amount secretly exported, to avoid the export and transit duties, being unknown—as well as from the quantity retained in the country, without being coined or put in circulation. The most authentic work on the mines and precious metals of Mexico, is that of M. St. Clair Duport, published in Paris, in 1843, and can be consulted by those who desire a more extensive acquaintance with the subject. He estimates the quantity of coin struck in 1841, as follows:

Silver Coin	$12,731,747
Gold "	751,058
	$13,482,805
And in the year 1842	13,979,714

The exports of the precious metals, annually, he states to be:

From Vera Cruz	$3,500,000
Tampico	6.500,000
Matamoras, &c.	1,000,000
The Ports on the Pacific	7,000,000
	$18,000,000

Of these eighteen millions, one million is sent to China, four millions to the United States and Continental Europe, and thirteen millions to England. To this can be added what is in deposit and circulation in Mexico, which may safely be calculated at two millions, thus making, in all, $30,000,000, as the annual product of the mines.

The manufacturing industry of Mexico has ever been suppressed by prohibition and bad government, consequently few, even of the absolute necessaries of life, are manufactured within the republic. The factories, in general, are so many prisons, in which the work people, taken from the jails, or from the most debased classes of society, are used with the greatest rigor. Criminals and insolvent debtors are made to labor in these prisons as a punishment. The only articles produced on a large scale are hats, glass, segars, and earthenware. Mexican leather is very indifferent; paper is of a poor quality; cutlery and hardware is scarcely attempted; the use of cast iron and tin for culinary utensils, is almost unknown, and within a few years there was but one manufacturer of watches and optical instruments in the whole country. "The Spaniards," says M. Chevalier, "are bad mechanicians, and no efforts of foreigners have been able to prevail on the Mexicans to deviate from the routine of their forefathers. All their tools are wretched; the common wheelbarrow, even, is unknown. Some merchants had imported two models, to be used in moving the bales of goods out of the custom-house, but the workmen refused to make use of them."

Nor is it possible to alter the system which now prevails in this country. Few foreigners would be so rash as attempt to introduce a foreign manufacturing community into Mexico. A more than ordinary display of industry would excite the jealousy of the natives; for nothing exasperates a Mexican more than to see Europeans and North Americans growing rich before his face, A flourishing factory, established by a foreigner, would be very likely to be pillaged during the first popular tumult. Instances of the kind have already occurred. The only European manufactory existing at Mexico, is one founded by M. Duport, a French merchant, for making *mantas*, a coarse cotton stuff much worn in the country. The looms were made at Paterson, in New-Jersey, and are the only articles of the kind in Mexico.

The following table will exhibit the total number of spindles for spinning cotton yarn in the several manufacturing states:

	Number of Spindles.		
States.	*At work.*	*Being erected.*	*Total.*
Mexico	30,156	—	30,156
Puebla	35,672	12,240	47,912
Vera Cruz	17,860	5,200	23,060
Guadalaxara	11,312	6,500	17,812
Queretaro	7,620	—	7,620
Durango	2,520	—	2,520
Guanajauta	1,200	—	1,200
Sonora	1,000	—	1,000
Total	103,340	23,940	131,280

When the Mexicans had achieved their independence, and were organizing their government, they created a fund for the encouragement of national industry, and endowed it with an additional duty of two and a-half per cent. on foreign importations. In this way, a few hundred thousand dollars was soon procured, which were expended in the vain attempt to establish manufactures. At present, the receipts of this fund are thrown into the abyss of the national deficit, which every year increases in depth, and where it is lost, like a drop of water in the sea.

An individual looking at the map of the world would be apt to conclude that Mexico must of necessity be a commercial nation. In some respects this is true: but her trade labors under serious disadvantages, which tend to restrain the development of her resources. Though washed by both oceans, neither of her coasts are accessible for a greater part of the year. On the east coast there is not a single good harbor, and in the winter months they are dangerous to navigate, on account of the "northers" which prevail at that season, and in summer they are too unhealthy for the approach of Europeans. The sphere of commerce is also circumscribed by bad laws and severe exactions, and is carried on at great risk. Under the rule of Spain it had an extensive commerce with the mother country, but that failing, it was thrown back on its own capacities. It is now, as before stated, hampered much with heavy duties, and the internal transportation of goods suffers under similar disabilities. We have no late statistics of the amount carried on. Since the occupation of the country by the United States' forces, the legitimate interests of commerce have been either entirely suspended, or the tariff regulations so modified, as to afford no just criterion of its past or future capabilities. The amount of trade between this country and the United States is exhibited in the following table:—

	Value.	
	Imports.	*Exports.*
1843 (nine months),	$1,471,937	$3,782,406
1844	1,794,833	2,387,002
1845	1,152,331	1,702,936
1846	1,531,180	1,836,621
1847	692,428	746,818

The chief article of export is bullion; but some considerable quantities of the raw productions of the country, as cochineal, drugs, dye stuffs, &c., are sent to England, the United States and other countries. The imports are foreign manufactures, cotton fabrics, linen, hosiery, yarn, woollen and silk goods, hardware, cutlery, iron, machinery, tin, earthenware and glass, &c., and colonial and foreign produce, quicksilver, cinnamon, raw silk, wines, spirits, &c. Before the revolution, the ports of Vera Cruz and Acapulco had a monopoly of all the foreign trade; but at the present time, a considerable business is done at other ports, as Tampico, Soto la Marina, Tobasco, and Matamoras, on the Gulf of Mexico; San Blas and Mazatlan, on the Pacific, and Guayamas, on the Gulf of California.

The form of government in Mexico is a problem. Ever changing in form and principle—now based on constitutional principles, and anon the sport of a dictator—it is impossible to daguerreotype its numerous phases. Fundamentally and nominally, however, it is republican, and is vested in a President and Congress, which latter consists of a Senate and House of Deputies, as in the United States of America. The Vice-Presidency has been abolished, and the alternate of the President is the Chief Justice of the Supreme Court. The Senate consists of two members, elected by each of the state legislatures. The deputies are elected by popular vote, in number according to the population, the electoral ratio being 70,000 or 80,000 inhabitants. The number of Deputies is about 100. Congress assembles on the 1st January, and sits until the 15th April, in each year. A council of government, consisting of delegates from the senate, sits during the recess of congress.

The legislative and executive departments of the several states are modelled after those of the federal constitution, and exercise all the rights not recognized as belonging to the national government. They manage their own internal resources, and have supreme power in all civil and criminal matters occurring in their respective courts. This is the case, however, only when they are able to maintain their independence:—the supreme government, under the auspices of Santa Anna, did not scruple to suspend all state functions, and by centalizing power, converted the states into departments, presided over by the nominees of the supreme executive. At the present period, however, they are in the exercise of all their attributions, and will so remain until the federal government recruits its shattered constitution, when it is probable these democratic institutions will again become offensive to the central power, and again be suppressed. The liberties of the states are ever at the mercy of the power, and on this slender guarantee the lives and properties of the people depend.

The city of Mexico, in the Federal District, is the seat of supreme power, and capital of the confederation.—*Vide* State of Mexico.

No satisfactory account has hitherto been given respecting the revenues and expenditures of the federal government. All is an enigma which has never yet been solved by either native or foreign financiers, but it is generally understood that the finances are in a deplorable state, and liable to many abuses. It is impossible, in the small space allotted to the description of each country, to develope even an insight into the working of the Mexican system, and we can only find room for a few facts connected with this topic. The revenue of Mexico is derived from a variety of sources; the customs, the per centage on mineral products, licences, special duties, transit and export duties, the tobacco monopoly, forced loans and contributions, voluntary and involuntary, and others, which are alike onerous and burthensome on the people, who derive no real advantage from the immense sums collected and disbursed.

The following exhibits the total receipts into the treasury from 1824 to 1844, a period of 20 years:

For the fiscal year,	1824			$9,770,371
" 8 months,	1825			9,720,771
From Septr. 1st,	1825	to July 1st,	1826	13,848,257
"	1826	"	1827	—
June 30th,	1827	to June 20th,	1828	11,640,737
"	1828	"	1829	12,815,009
"	1829	"	1830	11,200,020
"	1830	"	1831	17,256,882
"	1831	"	1832	16,338,860
"	1832	"	1833	—
"	1833	"	1834	10,798,464
"	1834	"	1835	—
"	1835	"	1836	26,478,509
For the fiscal year,	1837			18.477,979
"	1838			25,159,597
"	1839			27,518,577
"	1840			19,886,306
"	1841			—
"	1842			—
"	1843			—
"	1844			25,905,348

According to the report on Mexican revenue belonging to 1844, and presented to the Congress by Luis de la Rosa, the revenues of the Mexican Government were divided into seven distinct branches:

1. Duties on exterior commerce	$7,033,720
2. Duties on interior commerce	4,161,128
3 Taxes on real estate, industrial establishments, professions and trades	2,869,495
4. Rents administered for account of government	2,388,045
5. Replevins and balance of accounts	714,669
6. Extraordinary resources	6,280,634
7. Deposits	2,501,533
	$25,949,226
Charges to be deducted	43,878
Net Total	$25,905,348

The principal portion of this revenue is expended in paying interest on the national debt*, disbursing the expenses of the army and navy, and other general objects, not the least expensive of which is the support of a numerous body of officials, and peculating hangers-on to the national government. Not one cent is used for the benefit of the people :—but, on the contrary, it is expended in means of their oppressions. "Who can therefore wonder," exclaims Col. Ramsay, in his *Field Notes*, reiterating at length the condition and practices of the treasury department, "that the government of Mexico is bankrupt. With corruption in the executive and in the judiciary—with a band of peculating favorites—a host of monopolizing contractors, and an army of custom-house employeés—with a systematic contraband trade by smugglers, and equally systematic swindling by public officers—with depreciated and protested drafts—with ruinous discounts on loans—with cash charged that has never been collected—with disbursements credited that have never been made, and accounts mixed up with a carelessness that would not be tolerated by those kept with a slate and pencil."

The defensive means of the Mexicans have been hitherto sufficient for the protection of the country from foreign invasion. They were sufficient indeed, to act against the Spaniards in 1825–'29, and against the French in 1838 ; but in the American campaigns against this country in 1846–'47–'48, their impracticability was tested and shown to be illusive. The strong fortress of San Juan d'Ulloa, off Vera Cruz, was taken after a few days resistance, and all the fortified points along the line—Perote, Cerro Gordo, Puebla, &c.,—to the city of Mexico, and those of the capital itself, were successively captured by the gallant armies under General Scott. In northern Mexico the strongholds yielded with the same facility—Metamoras, Monterey, Buena Vista and Chihuahua (twice taken possession of,) attest the bravery of the Americans and the weakness of Mexico in every point of view. The armies of Mexico, though numerous, are incapable of defence ; drawn from the serfs of the soil and from the dungeons of the prison, they feel no interest in the exploits of war, well knowing that neither honor nor emolument will accrue to them, whatever be the result otherwise. They are thoroughly demoralized as a body, and prove more annoying to the peaceful inhabitants of the country than destructive to the enemy. In not one battle among the hundred fought during the late hostilities were they successful. The number of men in the Mexican army in times of peace is about 20,000, exclusive of an active militia of about 30,000. In periods of war and invasion the force is augmented *ad libitum*, and all are liable to serve. When the government is able, it pays the soldiers liberally—when the treasury is empty they liberally pay themselves from the first private house they come across, and exact forced loans with the same impunity as that enjoyed by the supreme head of the nation. The guerrillas have no other hope of remuneration or means of living but in clandestine robbery, and it is not seldom that the people are made to feel the authority of these *promising* gentlemen in matters of this sort. The

* The public debt on the 1st of June, 1848, is exhibited in the following recapitulation :—

Foreign debt (with interest to date),	$56,329,075 00
Interior do. (contracted before Independence),	39,606,695 00
do do. (contracted after Independence),	47,907,791 87
	$143,843,561 87

navy of Mexico is now extinct. It was formerly composed of several fine steamships and other vessels. A short time previous to the breaking out of hostilities the navy had been reduced to the following vessels, to be located at the places indicated:

Vera Cruz.—Brigs, Veracruzana Libre and Mexicana, and a gun boat, with 62 men in each of the two brigs.

Tabasco.—Schooners, Aguila with 53 men, and the Libertad with 30 men.

Tampico.—Gun boats, Queretaro Poblana and Victoria, with 30 men each.

Matamoras.—Gun boats, Guerrero and Union, with 30 men each.

The Mexican navy never acquired distinction, and was even beaten by the gallant but unjustly treated Commodore Moore of the Texas marine, in a naval battle off Yucatan. In this battle, with a handful of men, in a small brigantine, the two largest steamships in the Mexican service were disabled and beaten off!

The Roman Catholic is the only public recognized religion, but some others are tolerated and allowed to be exercised in private, or so as not to conflict with the pretensions of those who profess the national creed. The church establishment consists of the Archbishop of Mexico and nine Bishops, having an aggregate income of 539,000 dollars, with 3,677 parochial clergy. There are also 10 cathedrals having 168 canons and other dignitaries, and one collegiate church. The regular clergy comprise 1,998 monks, chiefly Franciscan; and there are 156 convents. Ecclesiastical property is constitutionally free from taxation, and they have the sole management of all money bequeathed for pious uses. Of late, however, and especially during the late war, they were compelled to contribute largely to the support of the army. The annual income of the ecclesiastics is nominally 12 or 13,000,000 dollars; but considering the peculations of the monks and begging brethren, it is supposed to amount actually to double that sum. The Spanish monks and priests were expelled during the revolution; and their places are filled by creoles, whose morals are anything but reputable. Religion has little influence over the white population, and the hold of the church over the Indians, never complete, is now fast loosening; for they are all more or less inclined to idolatry, and the small learning and talents possessed by this mongrel priesthood is incapable of reforming either their morals, or cleansing them of the ignorance and superstition which veils from them the light of the Gospel.

Education is entrusted to the priests, not one in twenty of whom have received an elementary education themselves. They are required by the constitution to teach the people to read and write, but this requirement has no practical effect. Ignorant and besotted, the priests are either too lazy or too incompetent to give instruction of any sort. Under the old regime, botanical pursuits were much encouraged; chemistry and mineralogy were taught in the school of mines; but the progress of science, literature and the arts, have all been checked by the unsettled state of the country since the revolution, and the expulsion of those who alone were acquainted with science and learning. The only school of any reputation in all Mexico is the Military Academy at Chapultepec, and that has been suspended since the entrance of the American armies into Mexico, perhaps never to be revived. Schools of law and medicine there are none deserving of the name, and it may be well imagined that schools of industry or commerce are wholly unknown.

Humboldt, Bullock and other European travellers have furnished excellent descriptions of numerous ancient monuments, which show that the native Mexicans, before the loss of their independence, had been in some respects a comparatively civilized and ingenious people. Among the most extraordinary are pyramids somewhat similar in exterior form to those of Egypt, and in some instances even of larger dimensions. The base of the Pyramid of Cholula is a square of 1,423 feet on each side, and its height is estimated at 177 feet. A far more elegant building of similar shape is situated in the north part of the State of Vera Cruz; it is formed of large blocks of porphyry highly polished and arranged in six stages, diminishing in size with the elevation, and having all its materials most nicely adjusted. The base is a square of 82 feet on the sides and 65 feet high, and the ascent to the top is by a flight of 57 stairs; the front is richly adorned with hieroglyphics and curious sculpture.

The mountains of Tezcuco are nearly covered with the remains of ancient buildings and cities. The ruins of Palenque in Chiapas, near the Rio Chacamas, a branch of the Usumasinta, extend upwards of 20 miles along the ridge of a mountain; and their architecture resembles more that of Europe than Mexico. The remains of the Aztec city, called by the Spaniards "La Casa Grande," are to be seen about a league to the south of the Rio Gila in the State of Sonora. They are spread over a space of more than a square league. In the centre is the Teocalli, laid down according to the cardinal points, its sides being 445 feet by 276 feet. It has three stories and a terrace, but no stairs. Within are five apartments, each 27 feet long, 11 feet broad, and 11 feet high. A wall with towers surrounds the main building. The traces of an artificial canal to the river are visible. The neighboring plain is strewed with red, blue and white earthenware, and pieces of obsidian, which prove that the Aztecs had passed through a country abounding in this volcanic substance before they dwelt on this spot, previous to their final settlement in Mexico. In the western part of the state of Chihuahua are similar ruins of great extent, which are also considered to have been the site of one of the temporary stations of the Aztecs in their migration southward. Besides sculptures, vases of different forms, sometimes even elegant, have been found similar to those of Etruria and Egypt. Roads formed of large hewn blocks of stone may be traced, not only in the neighborhood of those ruined cities, but at great distances from them.

Near San Domingo de Palenque, a village in Las Chiapas, are the imposing ruins of an ancient city named Culhuacan, which, after having been buried for ages in the thick forest, were first discovered in 1787. The ruins present the most curious and most remarkable monuments of the new world, consisting of temples, fortifications, tombs, pyramids, bridges, aqueducts, houses, vases, idols, medals, musical instruments, colossal statues, and well-executed figures in low reliefs, (*basso relievo,*) adorned with characters which appear to be real hieroglyphics. Everything announces that the city was formerly the residence of a people far advanced in architectural skill, in sculpture and painting, a people whose tall and elegant figures and fine proportions, bear no resemblance to anything Asiatic, African or Malay. The ruins, as previously remarked, extend for more than 20 miles along the summit of a mountain ridge, which separates the country of the Mayas from the state of Chiapas, and must, anciently, have included a city and the suburbs.—(See *Stephens' Central America.*)

The earliest traditions preserved respecting Mexico, inform us that in the year 648 it was settled by the Toltecans, a tribe of Indians from the Rocky Mountains, who fixed themselves, after several migrations, near the present city of Mexico. They named the country the Anahuac, and, after flourishing here for near 400 years, they were either exterminated or abandoned the country, not, however, before having imparted some degree of civilization to the barbarous Chichemecas, who arrived about 1170, and who were the next possessors of the soil. These were again displaced by the Acolhuans, who appeared about the year 1200, and drove out the last occupants. The Aztecs arrived in California in 1196, and gradually found their way southward, and in 1325 founded their chief city, on the Island of Tenochtitlan, and called it Mexico, in honor of Mexitli, their god of battles. This nation rapidly increased in power, and if the remains of monuments and large cities were a just test of civilization, the Aztecs might claim to rank high among the nations of antiquity. But they had invented no alphabet, and had nothing better than a rude species of picture writing to record events, and were ignorant even of the use of metals. Their barbarism was conspicuous in their sacrifices of the human species; no grand event of joy or grief could be complete without the flowing of human blood and roasting the dead carcase on the fires of the teocallis. Montezuma I., one of their greatest kings, extended his empire from the Gulf to the Pacific; but it must be stated, at the same time, that many of the conquered nations reluctantly obeyed his sway, and were ever ready to revolt. Such, briefly, was the state of the country on the first arrival of the Europeans.

The conquest of this mighty empire was completed by Fernandez Cortez, who arrived at Vera Cruz in 1521, with a small, but resolute force. Here he was met by a messenger from the great monarch, who had been despatched to ascertain his motives, and to command him to withdraw. But Cortez refused to return until he had communicated with Montezuma himself; and at once set out for the capital. His next step was to form a junction with the Tlascalans, who were at war with Mexico. This effected, he continued his journey, and having got the king into his possession, used him as a means to subjugate the empire. Outraged at the conduct of the Spaniards, the Mexicans flew to arms, and succeeded in driving the invader from the Aztec territory, but in the melee the emperor himself was killed. Cortez retreated to Tlascala to recruit his forces. Returning with a large body of Indians, and brigantines to navigate Lake Tezcuco, he recommenced the siege, and after a desperate resistance of seventy-five days, succeeded in capturing the city, and on the fall of the city the empire was at an end. Province after province submitted, and the Spanish power, in an incredible short time, was established from Vera Cruz to the Pacific. Cortez, on his return to Spain, was received with the highest honors, but he was ultimately neglected by the emperor; and, alas! for the gratitude of princes! the great conqueror of Mexico died at Seville in obscurity and want, while his enemies were reaping the benefit of those gallant deeds, which have rendered the name of Cortez famous in American history.

Under the Spanish arrangements, Mexico was, as a subordinate kingdom, governed by a viceroy, with powers nearly equal to those of the sovereign, checked only by the *residentia*, or court of investigation, before which he was liable to be called to account for his administration on his return home, and by the *audiencia*, or court of final appeal, in Mexico. By these arrangements, also, the natives were to be considered as freemen and vassals of the crown; and the Spanish discoverers, settlers, and their posterity, were to have a preference in all civil and ecclesiastical appointments. The natives were thus, in fact, excluded from holding all offices of trust or profit. The great object of the Spanish government was to keep the country in the hands of the European or white population; and the means adopted to effect this purpose, were, 1st. To discourage native manufactures, for the benefit of those belonging to the mother-country. 2dly. To make all the ecclesiastical establishments wholly dependent on the king, without any interference of the Pope. The growth of hemp, flax, and saffron, was prohibited, under severe penalties; that of tobacco was made a government monopoly. The cultivation of the vine and olive was likewise prohibited; that of coffee, cocoa and indigo, tolerated only under certain restrictions, and in such quantities as might suffice for the demands of the mother country. This system was retained nearly three centuries; during which Mexico continued to be a blank in the history of nations, and known only by the issue of the precious metals.

The entrance of the French into Spain, and the abdication of Charles VI., gave the death-blow to the Spanish authority in America. The natives and colored population saw in this that the time was at hand for them to assert their rights to be freemen, which was opposed by the audiencia, by whom also the viceroy was arrested, sent to Spain, and confined in prison until the general amnesty. An open insurrection against the European authority broke out in 1810, at the head of which were Hidalgo and Morelos, two priests of New Spain; and under the auspices of the latter, the first national Congress assembled at Chilpanzingo, in 1813. One of its earliest acts was to declare the independence of Mexico.

For several years the history of the Mexican Revolution is only a record of sanguinary struggles leading to no decisive result. At length in 1821, Augustin Iturbide, who had previously been a royalist, declared suddenly in favor of the liberals, and published his famous PLAN OF IGUALA, in favor of a constitutional monarchy. His cause met with a favorable reception, and he succeeded, not only in installing a National Congress, but also prevailed on that body to raise him to the throne, under the title of Augustin I. His arbitrary acts, after his elevation, however, soon caused a revulsion in the minds of the people, which, finding it impossible to repress, he abdicated. He was not only allowed to withdraw from the country, but rewarded for his past services by an annual allowance of £5,000, accompanied, however, with an edict of outlawry in case of return. In spite, however, of this prohibition, he returned clandestinely, and was soon discovered, apprehended, and shot.

On the downfall of Iturbide the Congress re-assembled, and appointed a provisional executive of three persons: Victoria, Bravo, and Negrete, all men of approved patriotism. The government was remodelled, and a constitution formed on principles much similar to those of the constitution of the United States. This was completed and published 2d Feb., 1824, and Mexico commenced anew a promising career.

The internal history of Mexico, from this period, presents one continued theme of revolution, rapine and bloodshed. War has been the every-day employment of the several political parties, whose sole object has been to gain the victory for the sake of the spoils, not for the benefit of the country; and such has been the arbitrary acts of the mushroom governments that have sprung from the revolutions of the day, and such has been the general disgust, that state after state seceded from the confederacy California, Yucatan and Texas, led the way—others followed, and eternal war was the result, now one party and then the other, being successively victorious. Finally, Texas not only asserted her independence, but maintained it, and in 1846 was annexed to the United States. Mexico madly proclaimed war with that nation also, and was well-chastised for its presumption, by the invasion of her territory and the conquest of the whole country. Peace, however, has returned; but, as an indemnity, the American Union has seized on California and New Mexico, and have effected a treaty of cession by the payment of a small amount of money. Such is the sad history of this pseudo republic. Can any one wonder at the debasing picture presented of her condition and resources—the laxity of the people's morals—the bankruptcy of her treasury—and all the evils by which she is beset? The only wonder is that, as a state, she yet encumbers the map of nations.

The following complete list of the chief executives, since the revolution, will tend to exhibit, in the rapid succession of rulers, the disturbances which must have occurred to produce such a result:

1821, *August*	Augustin Iturbide,	*President of Regency*
1822, *May* 18th	Augustin I., (Iturbide,)	*Emperor of Mexico.*
1823 — 27th	Fernandez Guadalupe Victoria, Nicolas Bravo, ——— Negrete,	*Provisional Executive.*
1825, *April*	Fernandez Guadalupe Victoria,	*President of Mexico.*
1829, —	Vicente Guerrero,*	"
— *December*	Anastasio Bustamente, (acting,)	"
1832, *March*	Gomez Pedraza,	"
1833, *May*	Antonio Lopez de Santa Anna,	"
1836, —	——— Barragan, (acting,)	"
— —	Anastasio Bustamente,	"
1840, —	Valentin Gomez Farias,	"
— —	Anastasio Bustamente,	"
1841, *May*	Antonio Lopez de Santa Anna,	"
1843, —	——— Canalizo, (acting,)	"
1845, *January*	Jose Joaquin de Herrera, (ad interim,)	"
— *June* 12th	do. do.	"
— *Dec.* 30th	Mariano Paredes y Arrillaga,	"
1846, *January*	Nicolas Bravo, (ad interim,)	"
— *June* 12th	Marino Paredes y Arrillaga,	"
— *August*	Jose Maria de Salas, (pro tempore,)	"
— *Dec.* 24th	Val. Gomez Farias, (V. P. & acting,)	"
1847, *March* 23d	Ant. Lop. de Santa Anna, (provisional,)	"
— *April* 1st	Pedro Maria Anaya (substitute,)	"
— *May* 19th	Ant. L. de Santa Anna, (provisional,)	"
— *Sept.* 14th	Manuel Pena y Pena, (acting,)	"
— *Nov.* 11th	Pedro Maria Anaya, (ad interim,)	"
1848, *Jan.* 8th	Manuel Pena y Pena, (acting,)	"
— *June* 3d	Jose Joaquin de Herrera,	"

The several states composing the Mexican confederacy will now claim a short notice.

* Gomez Pedraza had been elected, but Guerrero, who headed a revolution, overthrew the election, and caused himself to be proclaimed. Pedraza was restored by Santa Anna, in 1832.

THE STATE OF TAMAULIPAS.

This state stretches along the Gulf of Mexico from the Rio Grande del Norte to the Rio Tampico, and from the coast from 100 to 150 miles inland, within which limits is a superficial area of 35,100 square miles and a population of more than 100,000 persons. Previous to the late war with America, the northern boundary of Tamaulipas was the Rio Nueces, but by the treaty of 1848, the Rio Grande was made the dividing line between this and the State of Texas, now one of the United States.

The surface of the country is generally level, and with the exception of the hill near the mouth of the Santander, on its southern bank, no considerable elevation occurs. Tamaulipas is well adapted for commerce and agriculture: it has an extensive sea-board, and were it not for the bars at the entrances of the rivers, ships of considerable burden might enter its streams. In the western parts of the state, the chief occupation of the inhabitants is farming and cattle feeding: the soil and climate are well adapted for the production of both tropical fruits and the cereals of more temperate regions. Besides the cattle on the ranchos, vast herds roam over the common lands, and are hunted by the half-Indians for the spoils of skin and tallow.

The principal ports of Tamaulipas are Matamoras, on the Rio Grande, and Soto la Marina and Tampico, on the gulf, but they are all difficult of access, from their bars as well as the continual surf and the 'northers' which prevail during the winter season. The Port of Matamoras, perhaps the best in the state, is about 70 miles up the Rio Grande, on its west bank, and was, during the late war, in the occupation of the Americans from its capture, in 1846, to the conclusion of peace, in 1848. The capacities of this port have been highly spoken of, and were it not for the obstructions at the mouth of the river, it might become the centre of great trade. The town is handsome and well built, and at a distance, appears as a succession of fortified castles. It contains numerous churches and convents. Many of the peculiarities of the Americans have been adopted by the people: they have established schools for the education of all, and much improved on the old method of police and cleansing the streets. Population, 20,000.

Tampico de Tamaulipas, on the river of the same name, and near its mouth, is a town of recent date, but the commercial advantages of its position have caused its rapid rise and prosperity. Several English and Amercan houses are established at this port, and a trade of some extent is carried on both with Great Britain and the United States. The town as yet is of small dimensions, and contains a limited population, but when its capacities are better understood, its progress will be greatly accelerated. The River Panuco is navigable for 70 or 80 miles above Tampico.

Soto la Marina is a port on the Santander River, and is chiefly the resort of coasters. The trade here carried on is of little consideration.

Victoria, or New-Santander, the capital, is situated about 30 miles up the Santander, and has a population of about 4,000. Its commercial capacities are very limited.

THE STATE OF NUEVO LEON.

The territories included in this state lie immediately west of Tamaulipas, and extend from the Rio Grande to the Rio Santander.

The interior is rugged and mountainous, and much broken up by ravines. The table land of Mexico commences its rise in the western part. The country is well watered by several streams, which intersect this state as well as Tamaulipas, but it has no ports except some small landing places on the Rio Grande, and perhaps one or two on the Santander. The people in general follow farming and grazing, which are carried on with considerable energy. Nuevo Leon has been the scene of many gallant exploits in the American war, and has suffered, perhaps, as much as any state, from its effects.

Monterey, the capital, is a well-built town, with about 15,000 inhabitants, many of whom are extremely wealthy. It is celebrated as a place besieged and captured by the American forces, in 1846. The country around is very fine, and dotted over with prosperous ranchos and the mansions of the rich. It is built on sufficiently high ground to make it healthy, and it enjoys a beautiful climate the whole year round.

Linares is also a handsomely built place, in a highly cultivated district, and contains 5,000 or 6,000 inhabitants.

Revilla, on the Rio Grande; Natividad, on the eastern boundary; Florida, and several other towns are within this state, and enjoy a reputation for health, and industry of the people. Agua Nueva is celebrated in the military annals of the nation.

THE STATE OF COHAHUILA.

This state, one of the largest of the republic, is bounded north by the Rio Grande del Norte; on the east by Nuevo Leon; on the south by Zacatecas, and on the west by the Rio Grande de Parras, which separates it from Durango, and in part by the State of Chihuahua. Its superficial area is stated at 93,600 square miles, and its population, which is exceedingly sparse, at 73,000, the chief part of which are Indians and Indo-Spaniards.

Cohahuila has many advantages, in a commercial point of view, from its proximity to the Rio Grande, and the numerous streams which penetrate it from that river, as well as the Gulf of Mexico. It is also furnished with a superior system of roads, which were much improved by the presence of the forces of the United States during the late war. In agriculture it is preeminent, and it possesses a fine breed of horses, large droves of which run wild on the fertile plains. Manufacturing operations are limited, and confined to the larger towns, and even there, have scarcely an existence. The face of the country, though generally flat or undulating, presents some elevations, and in particular sections the ground is broken by ravines and deep sinuosities. Some silver mines exist, which are said to be very rich. This state is capable of much improvement in every department, and only wants intelligent laborers to develope its rich resources. Texas was formerly connected, politically, with this state, but revolted in 1835.

Cohahuila, the capital, is a small town in the north-east, and contains nothing remarkable to arrest further notice. Population about 4,000.

Saltillo is a city of some 12,000 population, and was, for a long period, the head-quarters of Major-General Z. Taylor during the war with Mexico. Buena Vista, the scene of a battle as glorious to the American arms as disastrous to those of Mexico, lies a few miles south of Saltillo. In this state are also the towns of Parras, Salado, Santa Rosa, Aguaverde, &c., all of which are historically connected with the military annals of the nation.

THE STATE OF CHIHUAHUA.

The situation of this state, one of the most northerly of Mexico, is between the states of Sonora and Sinaloa on the west, and the Rio Bravo and the state of Cohahuila on the east. It extends from the northern bounds of Durango to the new line between the United States and the Mexican Republic. The superficial area comprises 107,500 square miles, and the population numbers 147,000 souls. The Sierra Madre intersects the state from north to south, as in Durango; the soil and climate are much similar, and the people of the same origin as those of that state. Chihuahua is rich in mines and inexhaustible in agricultural resources.

Chihuahua, the capital, lies by the small River Sacramento, a branch of a confluent of the Rio Grande. Lat. 28° 47′ N., and long. 107° 30′ W. The population at one time is said to have been 70,000, but it is now stated at 30,000. It is a well-built town—the streets regular and at right angles, and the houses are substantial structures, and well supplied with water, which is conveyed by an aqueduct about three miles long. The cathedral, a very large and highly ornamental structure, was erected at the expense of $1,500,000, raised by a duty on the produce of the adjoining mines. The state legislature meets here in a neat building. The town is chiefly maintained as a depôt for the mining districts.

The country around the city is occupied by extensive haciendas, in which large herds of mules, horned cattle and sheep are pastured. But notwithstanding the great capabilities of the soil, agriculture is in a very depressed state, the mines being the great object of attention. Of these, the most celebrated for the quantity of the precious metals produced, is El Parral, in the south-east part of the state; but it is now in so dilapidated a condition that the amount of capital required to re-establish it, is too great to justify a well-grounded expectation of its returns being sufficient to repay the outlay.

Batopilas, eighty leagues south-west of Parral, once one of the most productive of the Mexican mines—a single mass of pure silver, weighing 425 lbs., having been found in it—is but feebly worked. Santa Eulalia has has long since been abandoned. The mine of Mordos, near Batopilas, was discovered in 1826, and has since been productive. The mine of Jesu Maria has also been abandoned on account of its inaccessibility. It is situated near the top of a mountain, and is, consequently, extremely cold in winter, the surrounding ridges being covered with snow; the village is in a temperate valley, highly capable of agricultural improvements. All the lodes near the surface contain a considerable quantity of gold, which diminishes according to the depth, while the silver proportionably increases. The immediate vicinity abounds with veins forming a circle, of which the village is the centre.

The population of the plain country is almost wholly of European descent, the natives having retired before them into the mountain recesses of the Bolson de Mapimi. The principal tribes of natives were the Apaches, Comanches and Chichimeques.

General Pike says "that the corruption of morals is universal; which is only what might have been expected from the gambling nature of the pursuits in which most part of the people are engaged; the great fortunes suddenly made by some, and the poverty of the great mass of the population; and the ignorance of all classes; and the debasing influence of the established religion." The opinion of Mr. Ward, a late traveller, does not confirm this testimony, but, on the contrary, highly lauds the morals and domestic arrangements of the people of the *Provincias Internas*.—[*See Durango*.

The other more remarkable towns in the state are San Bartolomeo, a large mart for the inland trade of the surrounding districts; El Parral, near the mine of the same name, formerly very populous, but now containing only 7,000 inhabitants; and Parras, a small town surrounded with vineyards, near the lake of the same name.

Chihuahua will ever be famous in history, which will record with enthusiasm the brilliant march of Col. Doniphan and his small band, and their gallant exploits at the capital and other places, nor will it forget to notice the later events connected with the visit of Gen. Price to that place, in 1848. Both expeditions were attended with remarkable success, and were of essential service to American interests.

THE STATE OF DURANGO.

The eastern boundary of Durango is the Rio Grande de Parras: on tne north lies Chihuahua; on the south Zacatecas and Xalisco, and on the west the State of Sinaloa. Within these limits the superficial area is 54,500 square miles, and the population 165,000, or thereabouts.

The Sierra Madre traverses the whole extent of the country, dividing it into two unequal proportions. There re, beside, several detached elevations, and the country is much corrugated by ravines and precipices. Craters of volcanos, and a mass of iron resembling erolite, excite the attention of the naturalist. Durango is rich in silver ore, and the mines have been very productive. Agriculture is in a flourishing condition, and the products, comprising cattle, mules, sheep, coffee, sugar and indigo, form the chief wealth of the people.

"To the inhabitants of the southern and central provinces," says Ward, "everything north of Zacatecas is *terra incognita*, and the traveller, after passing it, is surprised to find an improvement in the manners and character of the inhabitants. Durango, where the change first became visible, may be considered as the key to the whole north, which is peopled by the descendants of a race of settlers from the most industrious provinces of Spain, (Biscay, Navarre and Catalonia,) who have preserved their blood uncontaminated by any cross with the aborigines, and who retain most of the habits and feelings of their forefathers. They have much loyalty and generous frankness, great natural politeness, and considerable activity both of body and mind. The women, instead of passing their days in languor and idleness, are actively employed in affairs of the household, and neatness and comfort are nowhere so great and general as in the north.—(*Ward's Mexico*, ii.) This applies only to the white population. There are also many Indian tribes residing in towns and villages of their own, or hovering round the civilized settlements, and subsisting by the chase.

VICTORIA DE DURANGO, the capital, lies on the Sierra, 6,848 feet above the ocean, in lat. 24° 25′ North, and long. 108° 15′ West. Population, 25,000. It is a regularly built town, and contains a cathedral and other churches, several convents, a mint at which immense sums are annually coined, and a theatre. It is the seat of a bishopric. The inhabitants are industrious, and employed in the manufacturing of woollen articles, woodenware and leather, and have a considerable trade in cattle and mules. Iron mines are worked in the vicinity.

THE STATE OF SONORA.

THIS is a vast tract lying immediately south of the RIO Gila and east of the Gulf of California; its southern boundary is the Rio Mayo. The eastern boundary is not well ascertained. The southern coast is the only part settled by a civilized population; the central and northern regions being yet in the possession of various tribes of Indians. The coast is unhealthy, but the interior, which is more elevated, enjoys a mild equable climate, free from deleterious influences. There is an abundance of silver within the mountains, and gold is obtained in the washings of the streams and from the auriferous copper ores. This state has an area of 200,000 square miles, and its population is estimated at 124,000, but it is difficult to arrive at even an approximation to the real amount.

ARISPE is the nominal capital, and is a small town on the Rio Ures. Population 5,000.

GUAYAMAS is a port of some note, and has a good situation on the southern coast at the mouth of the River Pimas. Latitude 27° 50′ N., and longitude 112° W. Population about 5,000. It has grown up within a few years, and owes it rise to its magnificent harbor, one of the finest in Mexico. Much of the trade between Mexico and Eastern Asia centres here, this port being more accessible and covered than either San Blas or Mazatlan. Guayamas is destined to become a flourishing place.

There are several places of considerable size on the course of the rivers which run far into the country, but these are chiefly occupied by the natives.

The Indian tribes within this state are: the Apaches, who inhabit the northern sections; the Pimas, inhabiting a country called Pimeria Alta, south of the Apaches; the Opatas, in the centre of the state; and the Ceres in the south-west, and Yaquis on the south-east, bordering on Chihuahua.

THE STATE OF SINALOA,

Is situated immediately south of Sonora, fronting, also, on the Gulf of California. It is much similar in character to Sonora, and has several pearl-fisheries off the coast. Area, 54,700 square miles. Population, 147,000.

SINALOA is the capital of the state. Population, 13,000.

MAZATLAN, the chief seaport, lies on the southern part of the coast, and has a tolerably good harbor, but much inferior to that of Guayamas. Some trade, however, is centered here; and, were it not for its exposed position, it is well situated as a depôt for distributing imported articles.

CULIACAN is a considerable town on the south bank of the river of the same name. VILLA DE FUERTE was the ancient capital of Sonora and Sinaloa. ALAMOS has some 5,000 or 6,000 inhabitants, and is situated in the mining districts, of which it is the central point. All these towns, in fact, owe their rise to the mining operations carried on in this and the neighboring states.

The inhabitants, for the most part, consist of different tribes of Indians; among which are the Apaches, Mayas, Moquis, &c. Many of them are civilized and industrious, but the majority lead a nomadic life, scarcely recognizing the control of the civilized communities.

THE STATE OF SAN LUIS POTOSI.

THIS state, which contains an area of 19,500 square miles, and upwards of 300,000 inhabitants, lies west of Tamaulipas, and partly on the highest table-lands. It is rich in silver mines, and is equally celebrated for the breeding of cattle and agricultural industry. In general the surface is rugged, but extensive plains spread over the eastern portions. It is well drained by the Tampico and other rivers, which intersect it in an easterly and westerly direction.

SAN LUIS POTOSI, the capital, near the source of the Tampico River, and about 175 miles west of the port, lies in latitude 22° north, and longitude 100° 31′ west. The population of the city is 50,000 inhabitants, including the *barrios* or suburbs, which occupy a large extent of ground. It presents a fine appearance; the churches are lofty, and some of them very handsome. The streets are well-built, very clean, and intersect each other at right angles. The houses in the plaza, and in the principal avenues leading to it, are of stone, and two stories high; those in the suburbs are low, and of *adobes*, or sun-dried bricks. The government-house in the plaza, is a fine building; the front, which is of cut stone, and ornamented with Ionic pilastres, would do credit to any of the cities of Europe or America. The market-place is well-supplied with meat, fruits and vegetables. Pedlars hawk up and down the coarse manufactures of the country. Stalls are erected, and set out with *mantas*, blankets, leather-breeches, and leggings, saddles and bridles, huge wooden stirrups, and iron spurs, weight upwards of two pounds, and a great variety of manufactures from the filaments of the agave; ropes, cord, twine, and thread, matting, bagging, saddle-cloths, &c. Here, as in every part of Mexico, the venders were satisfied with one-half their asking prices, and frequently with one-third part of what they, the instant before, had sworn on their consciences the article was worth.—(*Poinsett's Notes on Mexico*, p. 242.)

From its situation, this city is the natural depôt of the trade of Tampico with the northern and western states. The foreign trade, at present, is almost wholly in the hands of natives of old Spain or of the United States. The European imports consist, principally, of French brandies, wines, silks, and cloths; English hardware, and printed cotton goods, with some mantas or ordinary cotton manufactures from the United States. In addition to its foreign trade, San Luis Potosi supplies the neighboring states of Leon and Coahuila with home-made goods of various kinds. The town abounds in tailors, hatters, leather-dressers.—(*Ward's Mexico*, p. 227, II.) The people are better dressed, and beggars are fewer, than in almost any other part of Mexico. The mines in the neighborhood have long ceased to be wrought, from exhaustion of the ores; they were, however, formerly very productive. A college, founded by voluntary subscription, and in a flourishing state, affords gratuitous instruction to poor students, in Latin, jurisprudence, theology, and constitutional rights. The city was founded in 1536.—(*Poinsett—Ward.*)

Catorce and San Juan, in the mining districts, are situated in a rugged country in the northern part of the state. The mines of Catorce are equalled only in production by the rich mineral regions of Guanaxuato. Charcas, Guadalupe, &c., are the other principal towns in San Luis Potosi.

THE STATE OF ZACATECAS,

One of the central divisions of the republic, lies west of San Luis Potosi; east of Xalisco and Aguascalentes; south of Durango, Coahuila and Nuevo Leon, and north of Guanaxuato. Its area is about 19,950 square miles, and its population 273,575 inhabitants. "As a mining district it differs materially from the neighboring state of Guanaxuato, for, in lieu of one great mother vein, it has three lodes, nearly equal in importance with many inferior lodes; upon all of which nearly 3,000 pits or shafts have been opened."—(*Ward's Mexico*, II. 323.) In the north and east the country is divided into vast breeding estates, and is very thinly-peopled. The state has no manufactures, except at the capital; the population living by mining and rural industry.

Zacatecas, the capital, is situated in a narrow valley, and is distant from Mexico, in a north-west direction, 290 miles. The population is said to be from 22 to 25,000 inhabitants, and that of its suburb, Veta Grande, 6,000. Viewed from a distance, its numerous churches and convents give it an imposing appearance; but it streets are narrow and filthy. Its markets are abundantly supplied with fish, fruits, vegetables, &c. This is one of the chief mining cities of Mexico, and has a mint, which some years ago gave employment to 300 men. The machinery in the mint is of brass, and was made by native mechanics; it is ponderous and ill-constructed;

still, however, it answers the purpose, and large sums are annually coined at the establishment. Gunpowder and some cotton fabrics are manufactured in this city.

Next to the capital, the principal towns are SOMBRERETE, FRESNILLO, JEREZ, PINOS, &c., which, according to Mr. Ward, have a population of from 12 to 18,000 each.

This state is noted for the active part the inhabitants took in securing the independence of their country, and for the jealous care it still exerts over the liberties of its people. It was the scene of many of the first struggles of the revolution.

THE STATE OF GUANAXUATO.

THIS state is the great centre of the mining districts of Mexico. Its surface is very irregular, and in some parts, especially in the north, mountainous. It abounds in mineral wealth, and constitutes the most opulent of the Mexican states, excepting the state of Mexico itself. Much of the property in this as well as the neighboring districts, belongs to the great mining families resident in Guanaxuato. Tillage land, yielding rich crops of maize, wheat, barley, &c.; orchards and gardens constitute the chief portions of the state. Area, 8,000 square miles. Population upwards of 500,000.

GUANAXUATO, the capital, in the Sierra de Santa Rosa, 6,836 feet above the level of the sea, and in the very centre of the richest mining districts of the whole country, lies in latitude 21° 0′ 15″ N. and longitude 100° 23′ 53″ W. The town is irregularly built, and the ascents and descents very steep. The open places cannot be called squares, nor can they boast of being of any particular mathematical design. The whole city, indeed, is distributed here and there, wherever an opening in the mountains permits of the erection of buildings. The churches, public buildings, and many of the private residences of the wealthy, are truly magnificent, and like the old Norman castles are often built in almost inaccessible positions.

This town was entirely created by the mines which surround it. In the vicinity of some of them are also little *pueblos*, as Valenciana, Rayas, Serena, &c., which may be considered as suburbs. These mines were first wrought in 1548, but it is only during the last hundred years that the mines of Guanaxuato have become famous. The *veta-madre* or great "mother vein" is composed of several parallel veins running N. W. and S. E. for rather more than five leagues, within which distance more than 100 shafts have been opened. According to Humboldt, this vein has furnished more than one fourth of the whole silver of Mexico, and a sixth part of the produce of America! Between the years 1766 and 1839, Mr. Ward says that it supplied bullion to the value of $225,935,736. The mine of Valencia alone, at the present day, yields an annual average of $2,000,000 to $3,000,000 net. The greater part of these mines are now worked by the "Anglo-Mexican Mining Association."

These districts suffered greatly during the revolutionary struggle, and the produce has greatly decreased since that period; whether owing to exhaustion or other causes is not told. Both Hidalgo and Mina did immense damage to the Spanish interests in Guanaxuato, from which they have never recovered; and though every exertion has been made to regain their former position, they retain but the shadow of their ancient importance.

Salamanca, on the north bank of the Rio Lerma, is also a town of some importance; also Zelaya and Irapuato. The former contains from 15 to 20,000 inhabitants.

THE STATE OF AGUAS-CALIENTES.

THIS is a new state, formed from portions of the states of Zacatecas, Jalisco and Guanaxuato, and is perhaps one of the most flourishing in the republic, in arts, manufactures and commerce. Population, 69,603.

AGUAS CALIENTES, latitude 22° N. and longitude 101° 45′ W., is situated in a fertile district, has a fine climate, and is one of the handsomest of the Mexican towns. Being intersected by several of the great roads, it has an active and considerable commerce. It is celebrated for its great cloth manufactory, which employed in 1835 three hundred and fifty hands, (*Ward's Mexico,*) and the hot springs in its vicinity, whence it derives its name. Its population may amount to 18 or 20,000.

The surrounding country is thickly peopled and dotted over with numerous towns and villages. A branch of the Rio Grande de Santiago, the outlet of Lake Chapala, penetrates this country from the south, but from its smallness can be of little use to commerce.

THE STATE OF JALISCO, OR XALISCO;

(Otherwise *Guadalaxara*, or *Guadalajara.*)

THE position of this state on the Pacific, and the advantages it gains by being traversed by the Rio Grande de Santiago, through its whole breadth, gives it an elevated station among the states of Mexico. On the north it is bounded by Sinaloa and Durango; east by Zacatecas and Aguas-Calientes; and south by Mechoacan. Its area is estimated at 73,000 square miles, and its population at 679,000. Colima, 9,000 feet high, forming the western extremity of the volcanic transverse mountains, is within the territories of this state, and is itself an active volcano, throwing out ashes and flames continually. The mines, and especially that of Bolaños, are among the richest in Mexico. The people of Xalisco are a very energetic class, and have progressed rapidly in commerce, agriculture, and the arts. Perhaps, however, these manifestations depend much on the natural advantages they enjoy.

In no part of Mexico have republican principles made such progress as in this state. It was here that the revolution was brought to maturity; that the rise and fall of Iturbide was effected, and the law, banishing Spaniards from the country, passed the senate. The government has shown a laudable desire to promote education; Lancasterian schools are established throughout the state, and it is made a qualification of voters to read and write. No part of Mexico has opposed more energetically the encroachments of the church, and no people are more worthy to enjoy their hard-earned liberties.

GUADALAXARA is the capital, and seat of government. It is situated on a rich and extensive plain, on the south bank of the Rio Santiago, 130 miles from its mouth, in latitude 21° 9′ north, and longitude 103° 2′ 15″ west. The population, which, in 1803, was only 19,500, had, in 1823, reached 46,800, and is now, probably, 60,000; so that it is, in point of population, the third city in the republic. The streets are handsomely laid out, and many of the houses elegant. There are fourteen squares. In the Plaza de Armas are the government-house, where the legislature sits, the cathedral, and the Portales de Commercio. The public promenades are ample, and the markets, shops, and other civic conveniences, are on a large scale. The college, maintained at the public expense, is a noble establishment, and has contributed much to the enlightenment of the people. The city is supplied with water from the *Cerro de Col*, three leagues distant. Many coarser kinds of manufacture are carried on within the city, which has long been celebrated for its leather and earthenware. Guadalajara was, under the Spaniards, the capital of the intendancy of the same name, and the seat of an Audiencia Real.

TEPEC, also on the Rio Grande, about 18 leagues west of the capital, is a small town, situated in a fine open plain, and is very healthy. It is a celebrated resort for the inhabitants of San Blas during the sickly season. Population, about 4,000 or 5,000.

SAN BLAS, at the mouth of the Rio Grande de Santiago, is rather a roadstead than a harbor; and is much exposed to the winds from the south and west. It is extremely unhealthy; but in the wet season, which is the most sickly, the people retire to Tepec, a small town some distance inland. The trade here carried on is very limited; and ships, finding better harbors at Guayamas and Mazatlan, generally make for those ports in preference to San Blas; and the foreign goods, which, in the time of the Spaniards, were entered here, are now brought over land by way of San Luis Potosi and Mexico.

THE TERRITORY OF COLIMA.

THIS territory occupies a few square miles around the city of Colima, and extends southward to the Pacific Ocean. Excepting the Volcano of Colima and the Paps of Tejupan, the surface presents an uninterrupted level; is very fertile, but equally unhealthy with the other sea-board districts.

COLIMA—the city—is on partially elevated ground, and out of the reach of the climactic effects of the latitude. It is a city of some 30,000 inhabitants, and lies on the east bank of the river of the same name.

The ports of Tejupan and Xala are within this territory, but are little known to external commerce. They have mere roadsteads, and the towns, in population and wealth, are insignificant.

The attributions of this territory are little known in this country, but it is supposed to exercise its political rights along with the neighboring state of Jalisco. It is not otherwise represented in the federal senate.

THE STATE OF MECHOACAN, OR VALLADOLID,

Is situated immediately west of the State of Mexico, and has a small front on the coast of the Pacific. It is one of the larger states, and occupies an area of 22,468 square miles. The population is estimated at nearly 500,000. This state formed with Jalisco and Colima, the ancient "Kingdom of Mechoacan," the name of which signifies the *country abounding in fish*, and was independent of the sway of the Aztec Emperors. The country contains several volcanoes, among which is the famous Jorullo; hot and sulphureous springs; mines, and peaks of mountains white with perpetual snow. It is, notwithstanding, one of the most agreeable and fertile regions that can possibly be conceived Numerous lakes, forests and cascades diversify the prospect. The mountains covered with wood, leave a space for meadows and fields. The air is healthy, except on the coast, where the Indians alone can resist the humid and suffocating heat.

Of all the Americans, the natives of this country were the most dexterous marksmen with the bow and arrow. The kings of Mechoacan formerly received their principal revenues in red feathers, of which carpets and other articles were manufactured.

VALLADOLID, the ancient Mechoacan and present capital of the state, a very pretty town, and enlivened by a considerable commerce, enjoys a delicious climate, and contains a population of 25,000 inhabitants. "I know of few places," says Mr. Ward, "the approach to which (from the north) is so tedious as that to Valladolid. For more than two hours you see the city apparently below you, while the road continues to wind among the surrounding trees. At length a rapid descent conducts you to the plain, where a long causeway, built across a marsh, forms the entrance to the town. The suburbs are poor and insignificant, but the high street is fine, and the cathedral, standing alone and open, has a very imposing effect. The view of the town from the Mexico side is beautiful; gardens and orchards form the foreground; while the lofty aqueduct, erected towards the end of the last century, the gorgeous churches, and a bold range of mountains behind, fill up the remaining space. Nearly all the public edifices, not immediately connected with the government, are due to the munificence of the bishops, most of whom have contributed to enrich or adorn the town. The cathedral, hospitals and aqueduct are all the works of the church. The first is a magnificent building, and wealthy, though despoiled of much of its treasures during the revolution."—(*Ward's Mexico*, ii. 374.) Valladolid has a handsome public promenade; and its climate is temperate, as it stands nearly 6,400 feet above the level of the sea. Iturbide, the short-lived emperor of Mexico, was a native of this city.

The village of Tzinzontzan, on the picturesque shores of the Lake of Patzcuaro, was the residence of the ancient kings of Mechoacan.

The Rio Balsas, which separates this state on the south from that of Mexico, is a fine river, emptying into the Pacific a little below the port of Zacatula. It has a number of fine tributaries, all rising on the western slope of the table land, but none capable of ship navigation. The port above referred to is not much frequented, though possessed of many advantages, being inland, and contiguous to a thickly populated and rich district. The Rio Lerma bounds the state on the north and east, emptying into the Lake of Xapala, and has a number of rich towns along its course both in Mechoacan and Guanaxuato.

THE STATE OF VERA CRUZ.

Vera Cruz has a great length of seaboard, lying on the Gulf of Mexico between the Rio Panuco on the north and the Rio Coatzacualco on the south, and extending inland to the margin of the high plateau or table-land. From Vera Cruz to Perote is only one day's journey, and in that short space and time the traveller experiences the suffocating heats of the coast and all the intervening climates to the poles. The lower parts of this state are almost a desert, and contain little else than sands and marshes, placed under a burning climate. Large quantities of sugar, cotton, tobacco, and other tropical products, flourish here in the greatest luxuriance. Proceeding inland the soil and climate changes, and the cereals and many of the plants and vegetables of temperate regions grow to perfection, and still further as we approach the highlands the country is covered with forests.

The beautiful town of Vera Cruz, the capital of the state and centre of a wealthy trade, which, in time of peace, Mexico keeps up with Europe and America, owes nothing to the kindness of nature, and the harbor is a mere roadstead. Latitude 19° 11′ 52″ N., and longitude 96° 8′ 45″ W. The town is well built, and its towers, cupolas and battlements give it an imposing appearance from the sea. It is, however, surrounded by barren sand hills and ponds of stagnant water, and is exceedingly unhealthy, being, in fact, the principal seat of the yellow fever. The older inhabitants, or those accustomed to the climate, are not so subject to this formidable visitation as strangers, all of whom, even if coming from the Havanna and the West India Islands, are liable to the infection. No precautions prevent its attacks, and numerous individuals have died at Jalapa on the road to Mexico, who merely passed through this pestilential focus. The badness of the water at Vera Cruz is supposed to have some share in producing the complaint. The houses of Vera Cruz are mostly large, some of them being three stories high, built in the old Spanish or Moorish style, and generally enclosing a square court with covered galleries. They have flat roofs, glass windows, and generally wooden balconies in front, their interior arrangements being the same as in Old Spain. The town and castle are built of madrepore, the lime which forms the cement being of the same material. There is one tolerably good square, of which the government house forms one side and the principal church another. The foot paths are frequently under arcades. No fewer than sixteen cupolas or domes used to be counted from the sea, but only six churches are now in use; and most of the religious buildings have been neglected or abandoned since the Spaniards were expelled from the town. Rain-water is carefully preserved in tanks; and most sorts of provisions, except fish, are dear. Crowds of vultures and buzzards perform the office of scavengers. (*Bullock in Mod. Trav.*, xxv.)

The Castle of San Juan d'Ulloa, which commands the town, is built on the small island of the same name, about 400 fathoms from the shore. It is a strong citadel, and its northwest angle supports a lighthouse with a brilliant revolving light 79 feet above the sea. The harbor of Vera Cruz is a mere roadstead between the town and castle, and is exceedingly insecure, the anchorage being so very bad that no vessel is considered safe unless made fast to brass rings, fixed for the purpose, in the castle wall; nor are these always a sufficient protection during strong north winds. But notwithstanding its numerous disadvantages, Vera Cruz maintains its commercial importance; though latterly Tampico, in a healthier situation, with a better port, has been growing into consequence.

During the period that the foreign trade of Mexico was carried on exclusively by the *flota*, which sailed periodically from Cadiz, Vera Cruz was celebrated for its "Fair," held on the arrival of the ships. It was then crowded with dealers from Mexico and most parts of Spanish America; but the abolition of the system of regular fleets, in 1778, proved fatal to this fair, as well as to the still more celebrated fair at Porto Bello. The national road from Vera Cruz to Mexico is one of the best highways in the world, and the National Bridge between Jalapa and the port is one of the finest specimens of bridge-building extant.

Vera Cruz was founded in the latter part of the 16th century, on the spot where Cortez first landed. Previously, however, there had been a small town which was called by Cortez himself Villa Rica de la Vera Cruz. It received the title and privileges of a city from Philip III., in 1615. The castle was taken by a French squadron in 1829, but was soon after abandoned and restored to the Mexicans. In 1847 it was again captured by the Americans under General Scott, and held until the ratification of peace. The city was much improved in police and health during the occupation.

Jalapa is situated in a delightful and elevated district 4,000 feet above the sea. It has 12,000 inhabitants, and is much frequented by the higher classes from Vera Cruz during the sickly season. The surrounding country is covered with dense forests, and is particularly remarkable for the medicinal article—jalap, from which the city takes its name. The ports of Alvarado and Coatzacualco on the south, are interesting only from their associations; the first was the principal entrepôt in the gulf during the occupation of Vera Cruz by the Spaniards, and has since become famed, as having been taken by Lieutenant Hunter, U. S. N. in 1847, and garrisoned by three men! and the latter derives some interest as being the eastern terminus of the proposed route across the isthmus of Tehuantepec.

THE STATE OF MEXICO,

Comprises a large district of fertile and elevated land, between Mechoacan and Queretaro on the north-west, and La Puebla on the south-east, extending from the western confines of Vera Cruz to the shores of the Pacific Ocean. Its area covers a superficies of about 25,000 square miles, on which is a population of 1,389,520 souls. Within these boundaries all the higher intelligences of the confederation concentrate, and arts and industry attain their culminating point.

The City of Mexico and some small amount of territory around it, constitutes the "Federal District," within the bounds of which the National Congress is supreme—the State of Mexico having no jurisdiction therein.

The city itself, formerly called *Tenochtitlan*, is the federal capital and seat of the supreme government of the nation. Latitude 19° 25′ 40″ N., longitude 101° 25′ 30″ W. Elevation 7,426 feet above the sea. Population, 300,000?

Mexico stands nearly in the centre of an elevated plain surrounded by mountains, and having an area of 1,700 square miles, one tenth of which is covered by four lakes, the largest of which, Tezcnco, has an area of 77 square miles. The city when taken by Cortez was built on a group of islands in this lake; but the modern city, occupying its site, owing to natural causes and drainage, is 2½ miles from its shores. The ground on which it stands, as might be anticipated, is low and swampy, and the largest buildings are erected on piles, and the roads leading thereto are "*causeways*," elevated from 8 to 10 feet above the common surface. Though within the tropics, it is so elevated that its mean temperature is only 65° *Fahr.*, coincident with that of May and September in the middle United States, and the climate throughout the year is extremely moderate and generally healthy.

"Mexico," says Humboldt, "undoubtedly is one of the finest cities ever built by Europeans on either hemisphere; being inferior only to St. Petersburg, Berlin, London and Philadelphia, as respects the regularity and breadth of its streets, as well as the extent of its public places." The architecture is generally of a very fine style, and many buildings are of truly noble construction, though usually somewhat of plain exterior. Two sorts of hewn stone, porous amygdaloid and porphyry, are used in the better parts of the city. The balustrades and gates are of Biscay iron, ornamented with bronze; and the houses, which are three or four stories high, have flat terraced roofs, like those of Italy and other southern countries, and open court yards surrounded by colonades and ornamented with plants, &c. Numbers of houses are covered with glazed porcelain in a variety of elegant designs and patterns, and the interior of the principal apartments is showily painted in mosaic and arabesque.

The *Plaza Mayor*, or grand square, is one of the finest to be seen in any metropolis; its east side is occupied by the cathedral and *segrario* or parish church, and its north side by the national palace, while on the other sides are handsome rows of shops and private dwellings. In its centre is a colossal statue of Charles IV., said to be the finest work of the kind in the New World. The national palace, a fine building, nearly square, with a front several hundred feet in extent, comprises four large courts, in which are the public offices, barracks, prison, and a large botanic garden; but almost every part of it is falling to decay. In this building also is the mint of Mexico. The cathedral, on the site of the great temple of the Aztec god Mexitli, is a heterogeneous edifice; one part of the front is low and of bad Gothic architecture, while the other and more modern part is in the Italian style, and displays much symmetry and beauty; its two towers are ornamented with pilasters and statues. The interior is imposing, lofty and magnificent; but the grandeur of the effect is much diminished by ponderous erections in different parts, and a profusion of massive carved ornaments, pictures and painted statues. The high altar and appendages are enclosed by a massive railing of mixed metal; so valuable on account of the gold it contains, that a silversmith of Mexico is alleged to have offered the bishop a new silver rail of equal weight in return for the old metal! In the interior also are some curious remains, including several idols and a "stone of sacrifice," that is, a stone on which the human victim was placed when the priest tore out his heart! On the outer wall is fixed the "*Kalenda*," a circular stone of basaltic porphyry, covered with hieroglyphic figures, by which the Aztecs used to designate the months of the year, and which is supposed to have formed a kind of perpetual calendar, (*Latrobe. p.* 175–'7; *Ward*, ii. 48.) Few monuments of antiquity, however, remain; and we may echo the exclamation of Ant. de Gama, the first among Mexican antiquaries, "*Quantos preciosos monumentos de la antiquedad, por falta de intelligenza, habran perecido en esta mañera.*" How many precious monuments of antiquity have perished through ignorance of their value! In this edifice the church services are celebrated with great magnificence; nor even in seven-hilled Rome herself is greater attention paid to the external minutiæ of religious observances. There are 50 or 60 other churches, scarcely less magnificent than the cathedral, displaying more or less the barbarous mixture of style that characterized Spanish architecture during the 16th and 17th centuries; there are also numerous religious houses, the establishments of some of which are very extensive and wealthy. The palace of the Inquisition, now applied to more useful purposes, is very elegant, exhibiting little or no appearance of the purposes for which it was intended. This tribunal was abolished by Iturbide in 1822.

Among the other remarkable public buildings of the city, the Mineria, though now in a dilapidated state, occupies the first rank. It is large and handsome, but either from defect in the foundations or from the effect of earthquakes, its front is evidently out of perpendicular. It contains a respectable, but ill arranged collection of minerals; and lectures on engineering and chemistry are sometimes given to students. The academy of fine arts, the university and public libraries, are in a similar state of confusion and neglect. The *acordada* or public prison, is a large substantial structure, fitted to contain 1,300 prisoners; the barracks, also, formerly used as a hospital, are extensive and well constructed. The theatre is a respectable building of considerable size; but the establishment has for some years had so little success, that it may be said that theatricals do not exist, and the establishment is seldom required. The Plaza del Toros, for the exhibition of bull fights, consists of a great circular enclosure, and can conveniently accommodate 3,000 spectators. The great national manufactory of tobacco stands in the south-west angle of the city; it is an immense establishment, and supplies the whole legitimate demand of the confederation for cigars.

The promenade conveniences of the city are truly a feature of Mexico. The *Alameda*, or public walk, at the west end, somewhat resembles a park, but has the stiff, formal appearance of Dutch and French grounds. In the centre is a magnificent fountain. Another open space, called the ***Passeo***, about two miles in length, planted with double rows of trees, is much frequented on holidays by persons in carriages and on horseback. In the city, also, are several *portales*, or covered colonades, lined with shops and stalls, and forming a favorite evening promenade. The environs, also, present on Friday evenings a very lively scene of bustle and gaiety; hundreds of canoes, of various sizes, mostly with awnings, and crowded with native Indians and Meztizos, are seen passing in every direction along the canals, each boat with its guitar-player at the stern, and some of the party either singing or dancing.

The manufactures carried on in the city and vicinity are not generally remarkable either for extent or fineness of workmanship. Nothing is exposed in the store windows, and most of the articles are made in the places where they are offered for sale. Gold and silver lace trimmings, epaulettes, &c., are made in great perfection; silversmith work and chasing are also well done. Jewelry and lapidary's work is made at great expense. Cabinet-ware is extremely dear, and inferior, being made with clumsy tools and bad woods; the saw is scarcely known, and the turning-lathe is of the most primitive construction. Coach-making is better understood, and extensively carried on. Hats and cloaks are made on a large scale, but are sold at high prices. Soap is a staple manufacture. Men, not women, are the milliners, and it is not uncommon to see twenty or thirty strong, able fellows, who should be employed at coal-heaving or dray-work, employed in decorating ladies' dresses, making flowers, and trimming caps and flounces! The bake-houses are large establishments, and the bread, which is excellent, is made exclusively by peons or slaves, which class also perform the work in the cloth factories. Shops, for the sale of *pulque*, a kind of beer made from the aloe, and native Spanish brandies, are very common, and have a gay appearance.

The city markets are well-supplied with animal and vegetable productions. The latter are chiefly cultivated on the *chinampas*, or floating islands, on the lakes, which are extremely fertile. Turkeys, fowls, pigeons, and many varieties of wild water-fowl, are very abundant and cheap; as are hares, rabbits, tortoises, frogs, and salamanders, all of which are esteemed good eating by the inhabitants. The meat market is well-supplied with beef, mutton, and pork, but veal is prohibited. There is a great variety of vegetables and fruits, and a most enormous consumption in proportion to the population. The vegetable market is twice the size of Washington-Market, in New-York, but yet unequal to the daily supply; and the ground is entirely covered with bananas, plantains, citrons, shaddocks melons, pomegranates, dates, mangoes, tomatoes, and all the varied productions of tropical countries.

The population of Mexico is of a very mixed character, about one-half being Creoles, or descendants of the Spaniards; one-fourth Meztizos, or half-castes, between the Europeans and Indians, and nearly another fourth copper-colored Indians, with some blacks, mulattoes, and about 6,000 or 7,000 Europeans. There is extreme disparity in the wealth of the citizens. Many of the magnates and successful speculators are immensely rich, but the mass are indolent and indigent, the lower orders being generally found loitering about the porches of churches, public buildings, and the markets. These are the *leperos*, a class somewhat similar to the *lazzaroni* of Naples; but the latter are not so notorious as the leperos of Mexico, for the crimes of robbery and murder. There is also a general torpor of the faculties, and the *dolce far niente* seems to be the *summum bonum* of all classes.

The dress of the higher order of men closely resembles that of Europeans, the large cloak being as common here as in Spain. The costume of the ladies is universally black, with the veil and mantilla; but on holidays and public occasions, their dresses are remarkable, as well for gayness of colors as for expensiveness of material. Indeed, when in their carriages on the *Passeo*, they contrast somewhat strangely with the same persons when seen at home in complete dishabile, without stockings, squatting on the floor, and either pursuing their favorite amusement of segar-smoking, or eating cakes and capsicum out of the dirty earthenware of the country.—(*Latrobe*, p. 150.)

The ladies seldom go out during the day; but after sunset, young and old come forth from their hiding-places, and the Alameda, Passeo, and Portales, swarm with the dames and signoritas of the city, chatting and smoking with their gallants. Many gentlemen belonging to the higher ranks are intelligent, and a few even fond of literature; but the city is so badly supplied with libraries, and other means of study, as to give little encouragement to such pursuits. There are three or four newspapers; but they are miserable productions, containing little besides the merest chit-chat, copiously interspersed with advertisements. The white Creoles are distinguished by their mildness, courtesy, and hospitality; their besetting sin is gambling. Female virtue is on the same low level as in old Spain; but the Mexican ladies are better educated, and would be agreeable, but for the practice of smoking, which is bad enough in men, but intolerable in women.—(*Poinsett's Notes*, p. 160.)

Tenochtitlan, the original city, as before remarked, was built on a group of small islands, in Lake Tezcuco; and was connected with the main land by three principal causeways. These still exist, and form at present paved ways over the extensive marshes of the vicinity, and protect the city from inundations, which are not unfrequent, and against an enemy they have hitherto been found convenient and useful. Mexico, when first discovered by the Spaniards, was a rich and populous city; the seat of the Aztec dynasty, religion and trade. According to Cortez, it was as large as Seville or Cordova, was well-built, and well supplied with various products. It was taken by the Spaniards in 1521, after a protracted siege, in the course of which it was nearly destroyed. It subsequently suffered much during the revolutionary struggle, and in 1847 was captured by the United States' forces, under Gen. Scott; and remained, uninjured however, in the hands of the Americans, until the return of peace.

TLALPAN is the capital of the state. It is a town of little note otherwise.

ACAPULCO is a celebrated seaport on the western coast, and the harbor is one of the finest in the world. Latitude 15° 50′ 29″ north, longitude 99° 46′ west. Population, 4,000 or 5,000. "It is familiar," says Captain Hall, "to the memory of most people, from its being the port whence the rich Spanish galleons of former days took their departure, to spread the wealth of the Western over the Eastern world. It is celebrated, also, in Anson's delightful voyage, and occupied a conspicuous place in the very interesting accounts of the Buccaniers; to a sailor, therefore, it is classic ground in every sense. I cannot express the universal professional admiration excited by a sight of this celebrated port, which is, moreover, the very *beau-ideal* of a harbor. It is easy of access; very capacious; the water not too deep; the holding-ground good; quite free from hidden dangers; and as secure as the basin in Portsmouth dock-yard. From the interior of the harbor the sea cannot be discovered, and a stranger, coming to the spot by land, would imagine he was looking over a sequestered mountain-lake."—(*South America*, ii. 172.) There are two entrances to this splendid basin, one on each side of the small island of Roqueta or Grifo, the broadest being 1½ miles across, and the other 700 or 800 feet. The town, commanded by strong forts, is small and mean, and the place lost all its importance with the loss of the Spanish trade. The climate is unhealthy. Some trade is yet carried on between Acapulco and Guayaquil, Callao, &c.; but owing to the tediousness of the voyage, this intercourse is circumscribed within narrow limits.

There are many other towns and villages in this thickly-populated state, but the length to which the description of the capital, &c., has been extended, precludes the possibility of mentioning them in detail.

Throughout this state there is much to interest. Everywhere it presents the most magnificent scenery, and remains of a splendid past. Its ancient cities and antique mementos are full of instruction, and when contrasted with its present degradation and humiliated position, leads the mind to saddened reflections on the instability of human greatness. Aye, the mighty are fallen—where the proud Aztec once swayed, and where an imperial name gave importance to power, is now the abode of a nation, whose crouching position attracts the finger of scorn to the shores of the western world! The wreck is complete, but the shame is its own.

THE STATE OF QUERETARO.

This is the smallest state in the republic, having an area of only 7,500 square miles; but it is by no means the least important. High above the level of the ocean, and with a fine soil and climate, it enjoys many immunities and advantages of which other states are destitute. It is little broken by hills or ravines, and it has scarcely an acre but is capable of cultivation. The valley of the Rio Panuco, which forms its eastern boundary, is extremely fertile, and productive of all the fruits of temperate countries; in many parts the state is covered with forests, and its mines are equal to most others in productiveness and wealth. The total population may be about 125,000, more or less.

Queretaro, the capital, lies in a rich and fertile valley, and is 110 miles north-east of the city of Mexico. Latitude 20° 36′ 39″ N., and longitude 100° 10′ 15″ W. Population 95,000. It is a well built city with three large squares, many handsome public and private edifices, and the usual excess of churches and convents. The Franciscan monastery is spacious, and surrounded with extensive gardens; and the convent of Santa Clara is an immense building, inhabited by 120 females, including many young ladies sent thither for education. The streets have side walks, laid with flags of porphyry; the city is well supplied with water, brought to it by an aqueduct about 10 miles in length, carried across the valley upon 60 arches.

Queretaro is divided into five parishes, four of which are within the city and one forms the suburbs. It has quite the air of a large manufacturing town, and enjoys an extensive trade both in foreign and domestic commodities. The large body of the people are employed in the factories and are badly paid, and suffer much from the nefarious system which obtains, not only in this city but throughout Mexico. Woollen manufactories are the most numerous, but trade of all kinds has retrograded since the expulsion of the Spaniards.

"The wool," says Ward, "is brought principally from the northern states, Zacatecas and San Luis Potosi; its price fluctuates from 16 to 24 reals the arroba of 25 lbs., including carriage; but the wool most esteemed is the produce of the state itself. It acquires its value, not from any superiority in the breed of the Queretaro sheep, but from the circumstances of the flocks being so much smaller than those of the north that they can be better attended to, fed in richer pastures, and kept more clear from thorns, which deteriorates the fleece. This wool sells at 3½ dollars (or 30 reals) the arroba."—(*Ward's Mexico*, ii. 183–'4.)

Queretaro was the temporary seat of the supreme government after the occupation of the capital by the United States forces in 1847, and there the treaty of peace, concluded 2d February, 1848, at Guadalupe Hidalgo, was ratified by the National Congress, 1848.

Pasco, San Juan del Rio, San Miguel, Alpujarras, &c., are towns in this state, but have nothing to commend them to further notice.

This state, like those of Vera Cruz and Mexico, was visited by the United States forces under General Scott, in the campaign of 1847; but with the exception of San Juan del Rio, and a few other places, was never occupied. It, therefore, felt little of the inconveniences of war. The state has been noted for its loyalty to the constitution, and was one of the confederacy formed during the war in opposition to a dishonorable peace.

THE STATE OF PUEBLA.

THE chief portion of this state is situated on the high table-land of Mexico, and, except a small strip bordering on the Pacific Ocean, enjoys a fine climate, and such a distribution of vale and mountain as to render it one of the most productive and wealthy states of the confederation. It is bounded on the west by the state of Mexico, and on the east and south-east by those of Vera Cruz and Oaxaca. The area is 18,440 square miles, and the population has been estimated at 661,902 inhabitants. The celebrated volcanoes, Popocatepetl, 17,735, and Orizaba, 17,388 feet above the level of the sea, are within the borders of Puebla. Popocatepetl and Orizaba are the highest points in North America, excepting Mount St. Elias.

LA PUEBLA, the capital, distant about 70 miles from the city of Mexico, stands on the declivity of a hill, and lies in latitude 19° 15′ north, and longitude 98° 2′ 30″ west. It is a compact and uniformly-built city. The streets, though not very wide, are straight, and intersect each other at right angles. The houses, of stone, are generally two stories high, with flat roofs, having mostly a court in the centre, surrounded by open galleries and a fountain of water, conveyed thither through earthen pipes. Many have iron balconies on the street, and their fronts are inlaid with highly-glazed tiles, or else gaudily and tastefully painted. The apartments are spacious, and are commonly paved with porcelain, and their walls are adorned in fresco.

Puebla is a perfect hot-bed of priests, and has no less than 69 churches, nine monasteries, 13 nunneries, and 23 colleges. The churches are sumptuous in the extreme. Those of Rome, Geneva and Milan, are, perhaps, built in better taste; but in expensive interior decorations, the quantity and value of the ornaments of the altar, and the richness of the vestments, they are far surpassed by the churches of Mexico and Puebla. The cathedral, which forms one side of the principal square, has nothing remarkable in its exterior, but its interior is very rich. The high altar, which, however, is too large for the building, is particularly splendid. Several of the other churches are handsome, and, with the cathedral, abound in gold and silver ornaments, paintings, statues, &c. The bishop's palace has a library 200 feet in length, which has a tolerable collection of Spanish and French books.

La Puebla is governed by four alcaldes and 16 subordinate magistrates. Its market is well supplied with all sorts of provisions, except fish. Many of the inhabitants are wealthy, and have handsome carriages, drawn by mules; but, like the capital, the city swarms with beggars. This city was formerly famous for its manufactures of coarse woollens, cottons, glass, earthenware, soap, &c., but most of these have declined, with the decrease of the trade formerly carried on with Acapulco, Callao, and other ports of the Pacific. The manufactures of glass and earthenware, however, keep up their reputation, and the soap made here is sent to all parts of the republic. The city was founded and fostered by the Spaniards.

CHOLULA, eight miles west of Puebla, and an old Aztec city, though fallen from its ancient grandeur, retains many of the attributes of splendor and wealth. Cortez, at the commencement of the 16th century, compared it to the largest cities of Spain, but since the rise of Puebla its interests have retrograded. It contains many churches, and has regular and broad streets; the houses are mostly of one story, and flat-roofed. Cholula has some manufactures. But it derives more interest from its antiquities than its present position among the cities. The principal extant relic of its ancient grandeur is a huge pyramid or *teocalli*, to the east of the town, now covered with prickly-pear, cypress, and other evergreen shrubs, and looks at a distance like a natural conical-shaped hill. As it is approached, however, it is seen to consist of four distinct pyramidical stories, the whole built with alternate layers of clay and sun-dried bricks, and crowned with a small church. According to Humboldt, each side of its base measures 439 metres, (1,440 feet,) being almost double the base of the great pyramid of Cheops; its height, however, is only 50 metres, (164 feet.) It appears to have been constructed exactly in the direction of the cardinal points. The ascent to the platform on the summit is by a flight of 120 steps. This elevated area comprises 4,200 square metres, (15,069 feet.) The chapel erected on it is in the shape of a cross, about 90 feet in length, with two towers and a dome. It was dedicated to the Virgin by the Spaniards, and has succeeded to a temple of Quetzalcoatl, the god of the air. This pyramidal pile is, however, conjectured to have served for a cemetery as well as for the purposes of religion; and Humboldt, and other authorities, regard it as bearing a remarkable analogy to the temple of Belus, and other oriental structures. The Indians believe it to be hollow, and have a tradition, that, during the abode of Cortez at Cholula, a number of armed warriors were concealed within it, who were to have fallen suddenly on the Spanish army. At all events it is certain that Cortez, having some suspicion, or information of such a plot, unexpectedly assaulted the citizens of Puebla, 6,000 of whom were killed. In making the present road from Puebla to Mexico, the first story of this pyramid was cut through, and a square chamber discovered, destitute of an outlet, supported by beams of cypress, and built in a remarkable way, every succeeding course of bricks passing beyond the lower, in a manner similar to some rude substitutes for the arch, met with in certain Egyptian edifices. In this chamber two skeletons, some idols in basalt, and some curiously-varnished and painted vases, were found.

There are, also, some other detached masses of clay and unburnt brick, in the immediate vicinity of Cholula, in one of which, apparently an ancient fortress, many human bones, earthenware, and weapons of the ancient Mexicans, have been found. The view from the great pyramid, embracing the Cordillera, the volcanoes of La Puebla, and the cultivated plain beneath, is both extensive and magnificent. Cholula is surrounded by cornfields, aloe plantations, and neatly-cultivated gardens.

MALDONADO is an insignificant port on the Pacific, and contains scarcely 500 inhabitants. There are several other large towns and villages in this state, the principal of which are HUAMANTLA, NAPOLUCAN, &c., and the CASTLE OF PEROTE, so celebrated in the annals of Mexico, as the last home of many of her gallant sons, who have either pined in its dungeons or been murdered by the political power of the day. This fortress is situated in the middle of an extensive plain, and is considered as one of the strongest in the world. It is the national prison of the republic, where all political offenders are incarcerated.

THE TERRITORY OF TLASCALA.

Though situated within the state of Puebla, this territory enjoys some immunities superior to the adjacent parts, and though not represented as an independent state, is generally described separately from all others. It was formerly the seat of an empire, but nominally subject to the Aztecs, and greatly assisted the Spaniards in the conquest of the country; hence their peculiar privileges. Area, about 100 square miles.

Tlascala, the only city within the territory, lies south of Puebla. "The town of Tlascala," says Malte-Brun, "was formerly a species of federative republic. Each of the four hills, on which it was built, had its own cacique or war-chief; but these depended on a senate, chosen by the whole nation. The subjects of this republic are said to have amounted to 150,000 families. This nation, which enjoys some peculiar privileges, is at present reduced to 40,000 persons, who inhabit about a hundred villages. One would almost feel disposed to think that a fatal destiny avenges on their heads the crime of having assisted Cortez in subjugating the independence of Mexico."—(*Syst. of Univ. Geog.*, Lib. lxxxv.)

THE STATE OF OAXACA.

This large state lies immediately south and west of Vera Cruz, and fronts on the Pacific. Its area is 32,650 square miles, and its population upwards of 500,000.

This fertile region abounds in mulberry trees, cultivated for the sake of the silk worm. A great deal of cotton, corn, cocoa and other fruits grow here, but the cochineal constitutes its principal wealth. Its granite mountains conceal mines of gold, silver and lead, which, however, are neglected Several rivers bring down gold dust, which the women are employed in collecting. Rock crystal is likewise met with. The country has numerous rivers, but the only one of importance is that on which Tehuantepec stands, and which will eventually become a place of great prosperity if the proposed inter-oceanic communication is ever completed.

Oaxaca or Guaxaca, the capital, on the Rio Verde, lies in latitude 17° 5′ N., and longitude 97° 8′ W., and has a population of 40,000. It is built in the form of a parallelogram, about two miles in length and one and a half in breadth, including the suburbs, which are laid out in gardens and planted with nopal trees. The streets, which are broad, straight, and well paved, are lined with good houses of a greenish kind of stone; and on the whole it is the neatest, cleanest and most regular built city in Mexico. The public buildings are in general handsome, solidly constructed and richly decorated; the town hall, the cathedral and bishop's palace form three sides of the principal square. There are several churches and convents, and numerous fountains are supplied with water conveyed by aqueducts across the valley from the neighboring hills of San Felipe. The climate is peculiarly good, the thermometer seldom falling below 63° or rising higher than 78°; but it is exposed to earthquakes, and suffered considerably from the last which occurred in Mexico. Oaxaca was founded by Nuno del

Mercado, one of the companions of Cortez, and received its name from the trees called *guaxes* that abound in its neighborhood.

Tehuantepec has a harbor on the Pacific Ocean, which, in spite of some natural disadvantages, derives importance from being the central depôt between Mexico and Guatemala.

The ruins of edifices at Mitla and other places indicate a very advanced state in the civilization of the former inhabitants of these beautiful regions. The walls of the palace are decorated with what architects denominate the *Grecian scroll*, and *labyrinths* or *meanders*, executed in mosaic, the design of which resembles that on the ancient Etruscan vases. Six unfinished columns of an imposing magnitude, that have been found here, are the only ones which have hitherto been discovered among the monuments of America, except those at Palenque.

THE STATE OF TABASCO.

The territories of this state, comprising an area of 14,676 square miles, and a population of 63,580 inhabitants, extends from the Rio Coatzacualco on the west, to the state of Yucatan on the east. Its coast line, on the Gulf of Mexico, extends the whole length of the state and on the south it is bounded by the state of Chiapas. The surface of Tabasco presents two essentially different districts; the low lands, on the seaboard, are like those of the other states bordering on the gulf, sandy, arid, and extremely unhealthy; but capable of being used for the purposes of tropical agriculture. Here flourishes the sugar-cane, cotton, tobacco, and a great variety of fruits peculiar to the soil and climate. In the more southern and interior parts, the highlands and mountains are covered with dense forests of mahogany, logwood, and a variety of dye-woods, medicinal plants, and drugs, for which Central America is famed; and it is here that the Mexican tiger, and other wild animals, make the night hideous with their eternal howlings.

The water-communication of this state is very extensive. Bounded by rivers at two extremities, and traversed by magnificent streams, which almost intersect the country, it possesses many advantages over the other Mexican states. The Rio Tabasco and the Usumasinta are the largest rivers, and contribute much to the prosperity of this as well as the adjoining state of Chiapas; and if the contemplated communication across the Isthmus of Tehuantepec be ever completed, Tabasco will reap essential benefits from the undertaking, and her prosperity would become identified with the interests of the commercial world. In this relation it may be mentioned that the lands on the high plateau are fertile in the extreme, and may be used for the cultivation of cereals and other products of temperate climates, whenever required, to supply the shipping that may one day pass along its western boundary, from the Atlantic to the Pacific.

Tabasco, or Villa Hermosa, the capital, lies on the west bank of the Rio Tabasco, about 60 miles from its mouth, and is a town of some 5,000 inhabitants. Frontera de Tabasco is situated on the opposite side of the river, at its mouth, and constitutes the principal port of the district. Tonala, in the lowlands of the *tierras callientes*, is also a respectable place, and is the centre of some trade. These towns, however, have little of the grandeur of the more northern cities, nor are the people endowed with any great degree of civilization. The inhabitants are chiefly Indians, and their occupations consist in cutting woods, breeding cattle, and other farming and agricultural labors. The state of Tabasco was formerly a province of the intendency of Vera Cruz, but on the adoption of the constitution, in 1824, was elevated to the dignity of a state.

THE STATE OF CHIAPAS.

THIS state lies immediately south of Tabasco and between that and the Pacific Ocean; its western boundary is the State of Oaxaca, and its eastern the Rio Pasion, (which separates it from the province of Vera Paz,) and the line between the two republics of Mexico and Guatemala. The Sierra de la Madre intersects it from east to west. The country along the coast of the pacific is a fertile region, and is very level; it partakes, however, of the same characteristics that distinguish the climate of the low lands on both oceans. North of the mountains the country has a different aspect, and is chiefly covered with forests, but has many fertile and highly cultivated spots. The only river of any consequence in Chiapas is the Tabasco, which runs through the central valley.

Chiapas is celebrated as the seat of ancient empire and civilization. The ruins of Palenque, Ocosingo and other places, attest the former existence of a race now extinct, whose advancement in the arts of life must have been far superior to that of the Indians of the present day—who, however, were not themselves in a state of barbarism when discovered. The Indians of Chiapas, indeed, formed a state which was independent of the Emperors of Mexico, and second only to Tlascala in regard to civilization. They defended themselves with courage against the Spaniards. Happily for them the soil was not rich in mines, a circumstance which has secured to the natives the preservation of their liberties. At this day even they enjoy a completely independent existence, and it is almost impossible to say that this state belongs either to Mexico or Guatemala; both nations claim it, but any authority they may assert over it is merely nominal, and has no practical result.

CIUDAD REAL, formerly *Chiapa dos Espagnos*, though nominally the capital of the country, numbers only a few families, and the total population is not more than 3,000.

CHIAPA DOS INDIOS is a much larger place, and is advantageously placed in a valley near the Rio Tabasco, 30 miles W. N. W. of the capital. It is chiefly inhabited by the Indians, whence its name, of whom there are said to be 4,000 families. It is the largest town in the state, the chief trade of which it engrosses. Its principal exports are mahogany, logwood, and cochineal, which are sent down the river to the gulf of Mexico; but a good deal of sugar is also grown in its neighborhood. Its inhabitants are said to be rich, and the town enjoys many privileges. There are many other large villages chiefly inhabited by the natives, who are in general pretty good mechanics.

The area of this state is 18,750 square miles, and the total population about 150,000. Mr. Stephens, the American traveller and archæologist, has written a fine work on this and the adjoining countries, but it is especially confined to antiquities.

THE STATE OF YUCATAN.

UNDER the old Spanish regime this country formed a Captaincy-General, and was under the dominion of the Viceroy of New Spain. The geographical position of Yucatan is favorable in a commercial point of view. It is in the form of a peninsula stretching out nearly four degrees into the Gulf of Mexico and directly opposite the city of New-Orleans. It adjoins the states of Chiapas and Tabasco, which border on the Huasacualco river, in the Isthmus of Tehuantepec, the proposed line of a ship canal and railroad to connect the Atlantic and Pacific Oceans. With these advantages it only requires energy and capital to build up a magnificent state; but it is impossible to foresee the fate of this country, surrounded as it is at present by difficulties of no little weight.

Yucatan is situated between the Gulf of Mexico and the Bay of Honduras, and between the 18° and 21° N. latitude, and the meridians of 87° and 91° W., having the territory of British Honduras on its southeast coasts. Length from north to south about 250 miles; average breadth 200 miles; area 79,500 square miles. The population is stated at 580,984. The central part of the peninsula is occupied by a ridge of high ground, which becomes gradually lower as it advances to the north; at the northern extremity its elevation is about 3,000 feet, but near Cape Catoche, it sinks to a few hundreds. The ridge in the west is skirted by an extensive plain, which towards the north is about 100 miles wide, and becomes narrower towards the south. Its surface, however, is so sandy and arid, that from the Bay of Campeaché to Cape Catoche there is not a single spring of fresh water along the coast. To the south of Cape Catoche, on the eastern side of the peninsula, and also on the west coast to the south of Rio Francisco, near Campeaché, as far as the mouth of the river Usamasinta, the country is undulating and even hilly. The soil, except on the very shores, is less sandy, and the country is chiefly covered with lofty forest trees. The climate is hot and very unhealthy along the coasts, but in the interior the atmosphere is said to be salubrious and the heat more tempered. The great productiveness of this region has been a matter of eulogy in the newspapers of the United States; but whether a mistaken notion or political bias has invested it with this property, we cannot decide. Mr. Ward, a keen observer and faithful delineator, has thus daguerreotyped its capacities. "Yucatan," says he, "is one of the poorest states in the federation. On parts of it maize, cotton, rice, tobacco, pepper and the sugar cane are produced; with dyewoods, hides, soap, &c. But the scarcity of water in the central parts of the peninsula, where not a stream of any kind is known to exist, and the uncertainty of the rainy season, render the crops very variable; and years frequently occur in which the poorer classes are driven to seek a subsistence by collecting roots in the woods, when a great mortality ensues in consequence of their exposure to a very deleterious climate. Yucatan has no mines. An active intercourse was formerly carried on with Havanna, which Yucatan supplied with Campeaché wood, salt, hides, deer skins, salted meat and the *jenequen*, a plant from which a sort of coarse thread was made and wrought up into sacking, cordage and hammocks. This trade was cut short by the war; and as few foreigners have been induced to settle in Yucatan, the inhabitants have derived but little advantage from the late change of institutions." (*Ward's Mexico*, II. p. 390–'1.)

The state is divided into 15 departments or provinces, each of which are under special officers. The principal towns are Merida, Campeaché, Bacalar, Valladolid, Vittoria, &c.

MERIDA, the capital, a very respectable city, with a splendid cathedral, is situated on the arid plain, about 24 miles from the north coast. It carries on some trade in agricultural produce by means of the small harbor of Sisal, which is formed by a sand bank and has little depth of water. Population is stated by some at 15,000, and by others at 26,000.

Campeaché is a fine handsome town, completely fortified on the west coast, and has a population of 18,000. Considerable quantities of beeswax and of the dyewood which goes by its name are exported hence. The harbor is insecure, and the adjacent waters too shoal for the convenience of the larger class of shipping.

BACALAR is a town on a small lake near the Rio Hondo, north of Balize. Considerable quantities of logwood, mahogany, dye-woods, with some valuable drugs and medicinals, form its exports, which are carried down the river to the Bay of Honduras, and principally shipped to England and the United States. VITTORIA lies on the coast near the south-west extremity of the peninsula. VALLADOLID is an inland town on the north, and has a communication by river to the Carribbean Sea.

Yucatan presents many evidences of having been the abode in former times of a race of highly civilized people, but whence they came and whither they have gone will ever remain unknown. There having existed is proved by numerous ruins of towns and villages, which exhibit much architectural beauty. The Indians of the present day are incapable of such works, nor indeed was their existence known to them previous to the researches of the European and American archæologists, whose works have created such a lively interest. In the eastern part of the state, and particularly to the south of Merida, there are the remains of several ancient stone structures; one of which, called by the natives OXMUTAL, is still in good preservation; it is about 600 feet square. The rooms, corridors and pillars are adorned with figures, in half relief, of serpents, lizards, &c., in stucco. There are also figures of men in the attitudes of dancers, and resembling in every respect those which are found in the ruins of Palenque, which proves that the same race has swayed the destinies of all the lower province of Mexico as well as Yucatan. Where are the builders?

Previous to 1821, Yucatan was, like Mexico, a Spanish colony; and on the consummation of the independence of Mexico, it became an integral portion of that nation. From the dissolution of the empire, founded by Don Augustin Iturbide, until the formation of the pact which bound together the United Mexican States, in October 1824, Yucatan maintained an independent position, administering her own government, in the meantime, on republican principles. The compact of the confederation having been accepted by her, she became incorporated in the Mexican Republic, and so remained until the consolidation of the states by Santa Anna in 1835, when a *quasi* separation took place, Yucatan standing aloof from all connection with the central power. In 1840 an actual secession was consummated, and Yucatan was proclaimed an independent republic, and the people soon after formed for themselves a constitution or fundamental law. Mexico in vain endeavored to persuade or coerce Yucatan into submission; but finally the new republic wrested from that government a peace on its own terms. This peace was based on the convention of 14th December, 1843, which secured to Yucatan many advantages she had not before enjoyed, and relieved her from many oppressions from which she had, since her first incorporation, severely suffered. By the conditions of this peace she became again incorporated with Mexico, and so remained until 1st January, 1846, when she again solemnly renounced the connection and declared anew her independence.

The chief cause which led to these results was the violation by Santa Anna of the convention of December, 1843, causing, by a decree of 21st February, 1844, the ports of the republic to be closed against the productions of Yucatan, and subjecting that state to many harrassing vexations. Another cause was the refusal of the Chamber of Deputies to recognize the convention as of any effect. These proceedings, and a renewal of the hardships she had before endured, roused Yucatan to fling off the yoke of the supreme government, and to convoke a Congress for the purpose of taking measures to secure the consolidation of her independence.

Since this period it is impossible to hazard a conjecture relative to the ultimate determination of the state. It may revert to Mexico,* remain independent, be annexed to the United States, or fall into the hands of some foreign power as a colonial dependency. Each has been projected, and the violence of party has led to many civil commotions, which have not been confined to the ruling castes, but have extended to the Indian population. All is commotion, and the destiny of the country hangs by a thread. Savage warfare desolates the land, the cities are being sacked and burnt, and the helpless women and children are slaughtered like beasts by the Indians. The whole country is now a wreck. A treaty of peace, indeed, has lately been signed between the whites and Indians, but with little prospect of its terms being adhered to by either party.

THE TERRITORY OF LOWER CALIFORNIA.

BAJA CALIFORNIA is a long narrow peninsula, extending between the parallels of 22° 48′ and 32° N. latitude, and separated from the western main-land by the Gulf of California. It is about 700 miles long; the breadth varies from 30 to 100 miles. Area, 57,000 square miles. The population has been estimated at 33,439.

The peninsula is traversed north and south by a chain of rocky hills, not more than 5,000 feet high. The surface of the country is much broken, and except in the sheltered vallies and on the margins of the streams, incapable of cultivation. There are some tolerable harbors, but in the present position of things they are useless, except as a refuge for whale ships. Lower California is said to be rich in minerals, but no mines, except those of San Antonio, about the 24th parallel, are worked, and even these produce comparatively little. The climate is excessively hot and dry; unlike Mexico, the rains, except in the most southerly part of the peninsula, occur during the winter months; summer rains seldom occur north of Loretto, in latitude 26° N. Violent hurricanes are frequent, but earthquakes seldom occur. Timber is very scarce, and except near the missions, which occupy the choicest spots, but little is done in agriculture. At these missions they

---

* Since the above was in type this state has again joined the confederation.

cultivate maize and a variety of fruits. Dates, figs, &c., are preserved, some wine is also made, and a kind of spirit is distilled from the muscat; these form articles of export. Cattle are very numerous, and feed in part on the leaves of the Moscheto, a species of acacia. Wolves, foxes, deer, goats, several lizards and scorpions are among the wild animals. The pearl fisheries in the Gulf of California are very extensive, but have caused a great sacrifice of life in prosecuting them; 600 divers were formerly employed in this perilous business, but at the present time only 16 or 17 small vessels are engaged.

Pearls, tortoise shell, a few hides, dried fruits, dried beef, cheese, soap, &c., constitute all the exports of Lower California, which are mostly sent to San Blas, Mazatlan and Guayamas in small coasting vessels. The imports are provisions, clothing, agriculture and domestic utensils, supplies for the ceremonies of the church, and a small amount of the ordinary luxuries of life.

Loretto, a small town about the centre of the peninsula, is the capital and seat of the governor, who is appointed by the federal executive, and in general belongs to the military. Population, 900 or thereabouts. La Paz, at the southern extremity of the peninsula, is another small town. Others, chiefly about the missions, exist, but are of little importance, and are peopled only by Indians who have become partly civilized.

The peninsula of California was discovered by Hernandez de Grijalva, in 1534, but no settlements were made until the latter part of the next century, when some Jesuits established themselves here with the view of converting the Indians. The exertions of these pious fathers were of little avail; and the Indians of the present day, though nominally converted to Christianity, are little removed from the barbarous state in which the holy fraternity found them. Loretto and the other towns were all founded by the Jesuits.

THE STATES OF CENTRAL AMERICA.

This country, formerly the Captaincy-General of Guatemala, is situated immediately south and east of the Mexican Republic, and occupies, with little exception, the whole of the long and narrow tract connecting the two continents. It lies between 8° 50′ and 16° 50′ north latitude, and 80° 50′ and 94° 12′ west longitude from Greenwich. The Mexican states of Tabasco and Yucatan, and the Bay of Honduras, bound it on the north; the Caribbean Sea and the territories of Mosquitia, on the east; the New-Grenadian provinces of the Isthmus on the south-east, and the Pacific Ocean on the west. The length of the country, from north-west to south-east, is about 1,200 miles, and its breadth varies from 90 to 250 miles, and the area may be estimated at 196,000 square miles.

The political condition of this country has been very unsettled since the expulsion of the Spaniards in 1822; and the states composing the confederacy were so hampered by federal restrictions, that a virtual separation took place in 1839, and was carried into effect by actual declaration in the year 1846, since which period they have existed as five separate republics. The extent, population and capitals, of each, are:

	Area in Square Miles.	Population.	Capitals.
Republic of Guatemala	28,000	850,000	New-Guatemala.
" Honduras	81,000	280,000	Chiquimula.
" Costa Rica	33,000	180,000	Cartago.
" San Salvador	24,000	330,000	San Salvador.
" Nicaragua	30,000	400,000	Leon.
Total	196,000	2,040,000	

The above table has no pretensions to accuracy; no general census having been taken since the declaration of independence. In the population of Honduras has been included that of the Mosquito Shore. In fact, there is no means of ascertaining the real condition of this country, that can be depended upon, and, as a consequence, we are obliged to give but a general outline.

The physical geography of Central America has many peculiarities. No very distinct mountain chain traverses the country, but an elevated plateau occupies the central parts, forming a kind of chain of communication between the Cordilleras of South America and the mountain-chains of Mexico. This plateau rises much more precipitously from the Pacific than from the Atlantic side, the general slope of the country being to the north-east. The table-land rises also considerably as it proceeds north-west: in Costa Rica and Nicaragua its highest parts are of very moderate elevation; and the Lake of Nicaragua, situated on a plain bounded by hills of no great height, is less than 134 feet above the level of the Pacific. In the state of Guatemala, the table-land averages perhaps 5,000 feet above the level, the loftiest summits, which are either active or extinct volcanoes, being in that republic. The water-volcano, near Guatemala, so called from its frequently emitting torrents of hot water and stones, but never fire, is 12,620 feet above the Pacific.

There are two large plains—those of Nicaragua and Comayagua, besides many of lesser size, on the banks of the larger rivers and along the shores; these principally consist of extensive savannas, with rich pasturage, interspersed with clumps of trees.

All the larger rivers of Central America flow north-east and east, the proximity of the high mountain range to the Pacific permitting but a short course to those flowing west. The chief are the Montagua, Polochie, Rio de Segovia, the San Juan, connecting the Lake of Nicaragua with the Atlantic, &c.; the banks of most of these are richly wooded. The Montagua is of considerable size, and useful for the conveyance of European goods into the interior of Guatemala.

The Lake Nicaragua is by far the most important body of water in Central America, and will probably form an important part of the projected water-communication between the Atlantic and Pacific Oceans. (For further details, see article *North-America*, p. 19.) The other principal lakes are the Golfo Dolce, 24 miles long by 10 broad, which receives several rivers, and discharges itself by the Rio Dolce into the Bay of Honduras; Lake Leon or Managua, which communicates with that of Nicaragua; and Lakes Peten, Atitan, Amatitan, &c.

Central America possesses an advantage over Mexico, in having excellent harbors on both seas; its coasts are indented by deep and capacious bays, as those of San Juan and Chiriqui, on the Caribbean Sea, and of Nicoya, Papago, and Conchagua, on the Pacific. A few islands surround the shores, and a number of small *cayos*, (low, green islets,) skirt the eastern coast, rendering navigation, from their similarity to each other, alike difficult and dangerous to shipping, except guided by an experienced pilot.

The climate of Central America is much similar to that of all tropical countries; the lowlands about the coasts are unhealthy, and fevers prevail to a great extent. The shores, however, are generally peopled by the Indian tribes, whose constitutions are more able to resist these climatic effects than those of the Europeans. The temperature of the table-land varies, according to its elevation; but an equable, moderate and agreeable temperature may be obtained there all the year round, with a perfectly healthy climate. The dry season lasts from October to the end of May, during which the north winds prevail; and in the table-lands, in November and December, water exposed to the open air at night, is sometimes, but rarely, covered with a thin pellicle of ice. The rest of the year is entitled the wet season; but the rains, though heavy, last only during the night, and the days are fair and cloudless. Earthquakes are very frequent. *Goitre* is a very common disease in Central America.

The country is rich in mineral products. The precious metals are found in great abundance in Honduras, Costa Rica, and other states; with copper, iron, lead, nickel, tin, antimony, &c.

But the vegetable productions are of far greater importance. The forests yield many valuable kinds of timber, including mahogany, cedar, ***Palo de Maria***, a species of wood well-adapted to ship-building, &c. But the logwood tree, (*hæmatoxylon campechianum*,) is by far the most valuable of the products of the forests. It is an important article of export, as well as a species of Brazil-wood, found in these regions. Among other vegetable products, may be enumerated the dragon's blood, mastic, Palma Christi, and other balsamic, aromatic and medicinal plants; with sugar-cane, cocoa, indigo, coffee, tobacco, and cotton, which are extensively cultivated. The crops vary with the elevation. Between the heights of 3,000 or 5,000 feet the *nopal*, or cochineal-plant, is a favorite object of cultivation, particularly in the neighborhood of Guatemala. Maize is generally grown, but wheat only in the high table-lands in the north; it is almost unknown in Nicaragua and Costa Rica. Flax and hemp, though well-suited to the climate, are neglected, and vanilla runs to waste for want of hands to gather and prepare it. Tamarinds, cassia, long pepper, ginger, &c., though little known to the commerce of the country, are abundant. A fruit, called *chicozapote*, yielding a great deal of substantial nourishment, supplies the place of maize, and forms a principal article in the traffic of some provinces.

Horses, asses, sheep, goats and hogs, having been introduced by the Spaniards, are now found in great abundance. Immense herds of cattle graze on the plains of Nicaragua, and Costa Rica carries on a large trade in these animals. The horses are inferior, but the mules are superior to those of other Indo-Spanish countries.

The wild animals comprise the American tiger, wolf, tapir, mountain-cow, wild goat, wild striped boar, flying squirrel, the *zorillo*, noted for its fetid odor, &c. Few of them are very formidable; but the densely wooded coasts of the Pacific are much infested by dangerous reptiles, including the cayman and several venomous serpents. The birds exhibit the most beautiful and varied plumage. Locusts and the warrior-ant are very mischievous, and often create great devastation; the latter will enter house after house, clearing them, however, of all other vermin. The pearl oyster is found on the coast.

The foreign commerce, though considerable, is small compared with what a little energy might make it. The principal exports are the precious metals, indigo, cochineal, dye-woods, sarsaparilla, balsam of Peru, hides, tortoise-shell, &c. The imports are cotton, linen and silk fabrics, hardware and cutlery; earthenware, wines, trinkets, &c. The trade is principally in the hands of the English and Americans; but being mostly carried on through Balize, its amount cannot be exactly specified. The principal ports on the Pacific are—Realejo, Calderas, La Union, Libertad, Acajutla, and Istapa. Those on the Caribbean Sea—Omoa, Truxillo and San Juan de Nicaragua, the two last being within the reputed territories of the king of Mosquitia.

Agriculture, and cattle and sheep breeding are the chief occupations of the people; but the manufactures are not unimportant. They produce some of their own cotton and woollen fabrics, and a good many hands are employed in manufacturing earthenware, furniture, cabinet work, &c.; and the Indians of the interior are proficients in making mats which are used in place of carpets.

The gold mines of Central America are not unworthy of notice. From the mine called Tisingal, in Costa Rica, says Alcedo, "not less riches have been extracted than from that of Potosi, in Bolivia." That state has also the gold mine of Aguacate, which was first wrought in 1821. Several companies have been formed at various times to work this and other mines, and the government have long been endeavoring to induce capitalists to work the silver mines of Comayagua, in Honduras; those of Chiquimula have been profitably explored, and it has been ascertained that each hundred weight of ore yields 17 marcs 6⅜ oz. (the marc is 8 oz.,) of silver. Many other mines, worked chiefly by English houses at Balize, are exceedingly productive, and when fully opened, will no doubt substantiate the assertion of Alcedo in respect to the mines of Tisingal.

The several states into which Central America is now divided, have republican forms of government, chiefly based on the constitution of the United States of America, as was also the constitution of the Confederacy. Each has a President, Vice President, Senate and House of Representatives. The judiciaries are also somewhat similar to those of the United States. But the elections take place through electoral colleges, as was formerly the case in France. Since the separation, however, it is impossible to conjecture the actual state of things, or the relative powers of the different political agencies. In some states the governments are republican only in name, as in Nicaragua, where the executive assumes dictatorial powers. In fact, to judge from the general complexion of the Indo-Spanish institutions of America, little faith can be placed in their action; it is one thing to profess but another to accord with the professions, as is daily illustrated in the actions of the despots who have ridden rough-shod over the rights of humanity. The cities, towns and villages have separate municipalities, and annually elect their alcaldes and other officers. In the State of Guatemala the Spanish laws have been entirely abolished, and a code, compiled by Mr. Livingston of the United States, substituted in its stead.

The Roman Catholic is the only religion of the state, but in some measure all other religions are tolerated. The Archbishop of Guatemala is primate; there are three bishops, those of Leon, Comayagua and Ciudad Real; and the whole country is divided into about 300 parishes, each having a curate with an income of about $1,500 a year. Monachism and personal slavery are entirely abolished, and the few nunneries which still exist are not allowed to keep their victims against their will. Education of an elementary sort is open to all, but little progress has been made in literature or the fine arts. Reading, writing and arithmetic are the principal departments taught, but instruction in the Catholic religion always goes along with these.

The population is about 2,000,000, and is divided into four grand classes, of Indians, whites, blacks and ladinos, the latter an intermixture of the Spanish and Indian races and a few mulattoes. The relative numbers of these are, Indians, 685,000; whites, 475,000; ladinos, 760,000. The number of blacks and mulattoes is inconsiderable. The constitutions of the several states grant equal rights and privileges to all. The Indians of Guatemala preserve their ancient language and customs, but in the other republics a Castilian *patois* obtains. The principal occupation of the people is agriculture; some, however, are employed in the factories and mines. They live harmoniously with the whites, but they hate inveterately the ladinos. The Indians are now the ruling race; Carrera, the last president of Guatemala, was a pure Indian, wild from the woods, but a man of genius, and much attached to study and the acquisition of civilized manners. He was a self-made man—the offspring of a revolt.

The principal cities are:—in the State of Guatemala, the city of the same name, once capital of the confederacy, but now the seat of the state government. It is situated on an undulating plain, 4,961 feet above the level of the sea, and at the distance of 26 leagues from the Pacific Ocean, in latitude 14° 37′ N., and 90° 30′ W. longitude, It is a well built town of 40,000 inhabitants, and is the see of the primate. OLD GUATEMALA (*La Antigua Guatemala, or Santiago de los Cabilleros de Guatemala,*) is also a fine town amidst ruins, in a delightful valley, eight leagues south-west of the new city. It is a place of favorite resort, and contains between 12 and 18,000 inhabitants. It has been several times destroyed by earthquakes and volcanic eruptions, and has been abandoned as the capital since the fatal earthquake of 1773. TOTONICAPAN has a population of 12,000; QUESALTENANGO, 14,000; COBAN, in Vera Paz, 14,000; SALAMA, on the POLOCHIE, 5,000; and IZABAL, a village of about forty huts, three houses and court house, on the southern shore of the Golfo Dulce. The greatest part of the export and import trade of the district is carried on by the port of Izabal and by that of Omoa, on the left of the entrance of the gulf.

The cities of *Costa Rica* are:—San José, Cartago, Esparsa, Alajuela, Eredia, Estrella, &c.

Those of *Nicaragua* are:—Leon, Grenada, and Nueva Segovia.

Those of *Honduras* are:—Comayagua, Tegusigalpa, Gracias, San Pedro, Sulaco, Olancho, Sonaguera, and Trujillo or Truxillo.

And, those of *San Salvador* are:—San Salvador, Libertad, San Vicente, San Miguel, Santa Ana, and Sonsonate. San Salvador was formerly the seat of the late general government, in the federal district, which at that time formed a circle round the city twenty miles in diameter, with a further extension of 10 miles towards the south, so as to include the road-stead of Libertad, on the Pacific.

The coasts of this country were discovered by Columbus in 1502, and most part of it was conquered by the Spaniards before 1524, and it was erected into a Captain-Generalship by the Emperor Charles V., in 1527. The policy adopted by Spain towards Guatemala, was attended with unintentional benefits to the latter. Being only a Captain-Generalship, the scale of its public expenditures was kept down in deference to the higher pretensions of the Spanish Viceroyalties, and as its financial wants were few, taxation pressed lightly on the people. It was not, however, permitted to export more of its native products than were sufficient to pay for the articles the merchants of Cadiz thought necessary to send for its consumption!

Central America was declared independent by the people, on the 15th December, 1821, and was incorporated with Mexico, which had just thrown off the Spanish yoke itself, but on the fall of Iturbide it disconnected itself from that republic, and again formed into a separate, independent government, November 22d, 1824, under the title of the "United States of Central America," and the several provinces were at the same time transformed into independent republics, as far as their own internal affairs were concerned, on the principle adopted in the states of the American Union, the Constitution of which, they chiefly copied in forming their federal fundamental law. The new federal government was organized in April, 1825, Don Manuel José D'Arcé being the first president. On the expiration of D'Arcé's term, in 1830, Gen. Francis Morazan was elected president, and again re-elected to that office in 1835.

In the early part of 1838 civil war broke out between the Indians and whites, and on the 24th of February the city of Guatemala was attacked and captured by the insurgents under General Carrera, a pure blooded Indian, and Señor Salazar, who had been vice-president since the 1st May, 1835, was killed. The government was overpowered, and Carrera ultimately succeeded in gaining the presidency, which he retained until the dissolution of the confederacy, in 1846, and continued governor of the state of Guatemala, over which he ruled with great moderation and wisdom, until 15th August, 1848, when he was overthrown by a stronger party. The dissolution was preceded by a long period of anarchy and bad feeling among the several states, which, though not actually, had been virtually dissolved since 1839. Carrera gave the death-blow to the confederacy by an actual declaration in 1846, but, at the same time, he stated that it was not impossible that, at a future time, and under favorable auspices, for a new alliance to be determined upon. The number of states are now five, viz.: Guatemala, Honduras, Costa Rica, San Salvador, and Nicaragua; all forming independent republics, and as such have been recognized by foreign powers, especially by England, which has lately concluded a treaty of alliance and commerce with the state of Guatemala.

Great agitation has lately disturbed the states of Honduras and Nicaragua, in consequence of the advances made by the boy-king of Mosquitia, an imaginary kingdom on the eastern coasts. The merits of the controversy are not as yet understood in the United States, but sufficient is known to arouse a jealous feeling towards the English, under whose protection this *soi-disant* king is placed, since it is supposed that the objects of England are sinister, and point to some act of usurpation not compatible with American interests. The latest accounts of this affair will be found under the articles "Mosquitia," (p. 67.)

THE WEST INDIES;

OR, COLUMBIAN ARCHIPELAGO.

THE Islands composing this division of the Western World are situated in the Atlantic Ocean and Caribbean Sea, extending in a curved direction from the southern coast of the United States to the north-east coast of South America. They consist of four large and a number of small islands, besides numerous rocky islets, called *cayos* or keys, surrounded by or interspersed with coral reefs and sand banks. Their geographical situation is between 10° and 28° north latitude, and 59° 30′ and 85° west longitude. They are generally divided into three groups, viz: the Lucayos, or Bahamas; the Greater Antilles; and the Lesser Antilles, or Caribbean Islands.

The "Bahamas" consist of fourteen principal and an indefinite number of smaller islands, extending in line off the coast of Florida to the Island of San Domingo, 750 miles. These are chiefly of coral formation,—low, flat, and scantily covered with soil, and most of them uninhabited. The climate is mild and agreeable, being free from the influence of tropical endemics.

The "Greater Antilles" consist of the Islands of Cuba, Porto Rico, Hayti or San Domingo, and Jamaica, the position of which is further west than either the Bahamas or Caribbean Islands.

The "Lesser Antilles" form a long chain, extending in a curved line from Porto Rico to the Gulf of Paria, usually called the "Windward Islands," and of a smaller and more scattered group, along the coasts of Venezuela, contra-distinguished as the "Leeward Islands." English writers, however, generally apply the latter name to the more northerly part of the first group, from Dominica to the Virgin Islands, restricting the appellation of "Windward Islands" to those between Dominica and Trinidad.

Most of these islands contain isolated peaks or mountain ranges, the summits of which, in the large islands, attain a great altitude. Mount Potrillo, in Cuba, has an elevation of 9,000 feet, and the Blue Mountains of Jamaica a general height of 5 to 7,150 feet above the ocean level. The following table will exhibit the culminating points of the most remarkable mountains in the several islands:

Mount Potrillo	Cuba	9,000	feet.
Sierra de Cobra, (copper mountains)	"	8,600	"
Blue Mountains	Jamaica	7,150	"
Cibao Mountains, Serranai	Hayti	8,600	"
Mount Misery	St. Kitt's	3,712	"
Central Peak	Nevis	3,000	"
Highest Peak	Dominica	6,000	"
Mont Peleé	Martinique	4,400	"
Morne Garou	St. Vincent's	4,800	"
Soufriere	Guadalupe	5,500	"
Crater of Volcano	St. Lucia	4,000	"
Sierra de Languilla	Porto Rico	3,678	"

Several of the Caribbean Islands are of volcanic origin, while others are of secondary formation, and low, rising very little above the sea. Numerous streams descend from the mountains, which, though they do not attain to the magnitude of rivers, yet serve to irrigate the fine plains and vallies through which they pass, and whose fertility is mainly owing to their influence.

The West Indies, excepting the more northerly of the Bahamas, lie between the tropics, and are, consequently, subject to great heats; yet even in the warm season, the influence of the surrounding ocean, the periodically recurring sea-breezes, and height of the land in the interior, tend to modify the climatic intensity peculiar to their geographical position. In the interior of the large islands, in which elevation is more marked, a mild and delightful temperature is enjoyed throughout the year, and several of the smaller islands possess the same advantages. The lowlands, however, in all these islands are exceedingly unhealthy, and endemic influences render them unfit for the habitation of foreigners. Here life is short, even among the native born. At an elevation of 1,200 feet, the aspect of the climate is different, nor is it liable to the propagation, and prevalence of those fevers and fluxes which prove so destructive to life in the low and swampy grounds. In the more northerly of the islands, ice sometimes forms in winter, but snow never falls. The inhabitants will complain of cold when the thermometer is ranging between 60° and 70°. The year, as in the most tropical countries, may be divided into two seasons, the wet and dry, though there is sufficient variation to mark the four seasons of more temperate regions. The spring may be said to commence in April, when the fields put forth their verdant appearance. From May to October the tropical summer reigns in all its intensity, and the heat is insupportable; the sea-breeze, however, which sets in about noon, greatly moderates the temperature. The mean height of the thermometer at this season is 80° Fah. The nights are beautiful, and are tempered by the land breeze, which blows gently off shore from about ten o'clock until day-break. With October commence the autumnal rains, when the waters pour down in torrents;—these continue until December, between which and April serene and pleasant weather prevails. The trade winds blow from an easterly direction from December to June: August is the season of hurricanes, which frequently devastate whole islands. These rarely occur, however, in Cuba, and are almost wholly unknown in Trinidad.

The rich and varied productions of these islands give them an important position in a commercial point of view. To their valuable native plants, art and industry have added others not less valuable. The sugar-cane, yielding its triplicate of sugar, molasses, and rum; the coffee-plant; pimento or allspice; the plantain and the banana; the pine-apple, anana, yam and sweet potato; maize, cassava, manioc and cocoa; the tobacco and cotton-plants; various dye-woods and stuffs, as fustic, logwood, and cochineal; and medicinal plants, as liquorice, arrow-root, jalap, and ipecacuanha; and woods for cabinet work, as mahogany and lignumvitæ;—all are either indigenous or introduced staples, and render vast contributions to commerce. To this list must be added all the varieties of tropical fruits: the bread-fruit, cocoa-nut, mango, paw-paw, guava, orange, lemon, tamarind, fig, cachew-nut, mammee, grenadilla, vanilla, &c., &c.

The cattle of the West Indies are inferior, and only a few of the islands contain sheep and goats. Very few horses, asses or mules are reared, and consequently great numbers of these animals are imported from the adjacent continents. Hogs are more abundant, and find a ready and plentiful supply of food in the woods. Wild animals are almost extinct, and consist only of a few wild boars, monkeys, rats, and the smaller species. The manati is found in Trinidad and Tobago. Reptiles and amphibious animals inhabit the shores and margins of the rivers, and fish and turtles are abundant. The bird tribe is extensive, and remarkable for beautiful plumage. Insects—mosquitos, cock-roaches, centipedes, scorpions, ants, chigos—abound in all the islands. In fact, all the abundance and all the torments of intertropical regions, prevail in the West Indies.

The original inhabitants of these islands have long been extinct, except a small remnant which still exists in the Islands of St. Vincent and Trinidad. When discovered, a dense population covered these prolific regions, but the barbarities of the Europeans, in a short space of time, destroyed these unhappy people, supplying their places with the no less unhappy African. Cuba, and the other large islands, were found in possession of the Arrawauks, a peaceful and timid race, that soon submitted to the invaders. The inhabitants of the Lesser Antilles, on the contrary, were the warlike and vigorous Caribs, who resisted the sway of the Europeans to the last. The present population is composed of white and colored persons: the former are Europeans and their descendants; while the latter consist of Africans, their descendants, and the mixed races sprung from an indiscriminate amalgamation of all. These are of every variety of color and complexion, and are variously classified as mulattoes, quadroons, &c., according to the preponderance of caste. There is also another class lately introduced into the British islands, under the name of "Coolies," who originate in the mountains of Asia, and are imported as *free laborers*, under stringent restrictions. These are intended to supply the place of the recently emancipated negroes, who, it is said,have become worthless and lazy, and a burden upon the colonist. The negro race is, however, the most numerous, forming about three-fourths of the whole population. The curse of slavery has been abolished in all the islands except those belonging to Spain. Ten years ago this barbarous institution terminated in the British Islands, and during the year 1848, the Dutch, French, and others emancipated their slaves. In Cuba and Porto Rico, the slaves yet form about two-thirds of the negro population.

With the exception of San Domingo, all the West India Islands are appropriated as colonial dependencies of European powers, and are under the surveillance of governors appointed respectively by the nations to which they belong. In the Spanish, Dutch, &c., islands, the government is of a military character, but in those belonging to the crown of Great Britain, civil constitutional governments prevail, and the institutions of the mother country, when suitable to the condition of the colonies, are the laws of the land. The French West Indies are, since the revolution of February, 1848, an integral portion of that republic, and are entitled to representation in the national councils.

The commerce of the West Indies contributes vast supplies of tropical productions, alike to the nations of Europe and America. Their colonial position, however, acts unfavorably on their prosperity, and retards that development of industry and capital they would otherwise enjoy. Nevertheless, even in a dependent state, the export and import trade is immense, and a source of wealth to those engaged in it. The chief articles of export are—sugars, molasses, rums, coffee, tobacco, cotton and cocoa; drugs, spices and dye-stuffs; mahogany and other hard woods for cabinet work; and a great variety of fruits, &c. The imports are the manufactures of Great Britain and other countries, and foreign productions generally. The United States supplies these islands with flour, and a great variety of salted provisions, and some manufactured articles. An extensive commerce is also carried on with the South American states, more especially with Venezuela and New Grenada.

The reader is referred to the separate accounts of these islands, for further and more minute information respecting their condition and resources.

The following table affords a general view of the extent and population of the principal islands, and the nations to which they pertain.

NAMES OF ISLANDS.		Area in Square miles.	POPULATION.		
			Whites.	Colored.	Total.
INDEPENDENT—San Domingo,	Republic of Hayti	29,400	——?	700,000	700,000
	" Dominica		80,000	120,000	200,000
	Total	29,400	80,000	820,000	900,000
BRITISH	Anguilla	45	365	3,235	3,600
	Antigua	108	1,980	35,000	36,980
	Bahamas	4,440	4,650	15,350	20,000
	Barbadoes	166	14,950	100,050	115,000
	Barbuda	72	....	....	1,500
	Caymans, (Dep. of Jamaica)	....	100	1,500	1,600
	Dominica	275	850	19,150	20,000
	Grenada and Grenadines	155	1,000	28,000	29,000
	Jamaica	5,468	35,000	325,000	360,000
	Montserrat	47	500	8,000	8,500
	Nevis	20	800	11,000	11,800
	St. Christopher's	68	1,700	26,000	27,700
	St. Lucia	225	1,000	15,000	16,000
	St. Vincent's	131	1,500	27,000	28,500
	Tobago	187	400	14,600	15,000
	Trinidad	2,400	5,000	42,000	47,000
	Virgin Islands	170	280	6,720	7,000
	Total	13,977	70,075	677,605	747,680
SWEDISH	St. Bartholomew's,	25	3,000	12,000	15,000
SPANISH	Cuba	43,380	425,770	482,992	908,762
	Porto Rico	3,865	127,399	229,687	357,086
	Total	47,245	553,169	712,679	1,265,848
FRENCH	Guadalupe.,	234	12,324	107,339	119,663
	Mariegalante	60	1,938	10,347	12,285
	St. Martin's, (north side)	15	....	....	3,000
	Martinique	290	13,417	106,299	119,716
	Total	599	27,679	223,985	254,664
DUTCH	Curaçoa	375	....	....	13,912
	St. Eustatius	10	....	....	12,350
	Saba	20	....	....	5,000
	St. Martin's, (south side)	11	....	....	500
	Total	416	....	....	31,762
DANISH	Santa Cruz, or St. Croix	80	2,500	31,500	34,000
	St. John's.. Virgin Isles	70	150	2,850	3,000
	St. Thomas. Virgin Isles	50	800	6,200	7,000
	Total	200	3,450	40,550	44,000
	Add for small islands omitted	600	1,500	8,500	10,000
	Grand Total	92,437	738,873	2,483,319	3,222,192

HAYTI, HISPANIOLA, OR SAN DOMINGO.

Second only to Cuba, this is the most important island of the West Indian group; its geographical and relative position, its commercial capacities, and peculiar political career, give an interest to its affairs. This island lies immediately east of Cuba, having the windward passage intervening, and west of Porto Rico, from which it is separated by the Mona Passage. It is situated between the parallels of 17° 40′ and 19° 58′ N. latitude, and between 68° 24′ and 74° 35′ W. longitude. Its shape is somewhat triangular, the apex directed eastwardly, but it has several extensive peninsulas and promontories which render it very irregular in form. The extreme length is about 400 miles, and its breadth from north to south varies from 40 to 160 miles. The small islands of Tortuga on the north, Gonaives on the west, and several others of little importance, are dependencies of Hayti. The superficial area is, according to M. Lindenau, (*Humboldt, Politic Essay,*) 2,450 square marine leagues, or nearly 29,400 English square miles.

The principal physical features of Hayti, (as its name implies,) are its mountainous regions; but in the eastern section of the island extensive plains abound; the elevated chain of the Cibao mountains stretches from Cape St. Nicholas in a south-eastern direction to Cape Espada, and many branches extending east and west intersect the country. The highest peaks of these ranges are about 8,600 feet above the level of the ocean. A chain in the north-east called Monte Christi commences at the bay of the same name, and ends at the Bay of Samana. The extensive plains in the east are occupied by immense herds of swine, horses and horned cattle; eastward of the city of San Domingo, *Los Llanos* stretch out to the extent of 80 miles in length, and from 20 to 25 in breadth. The fertility of these regions is unsurpassed, and the soil is capable, with little trouble or cultivation, of producing more sugar and other valuable commodities than all the British islands together; the inhabitants, however, are not industrious, and the whole country is still but a beautiful wilderness. North of this, enclosed between two mountain ranges, is the fertile plain of Vega Real, little inferior in extent to the *Llanos.* In the west of the island are the large plains of Artibonite, and the Cul de Sac, the last of which was formerly one vast sugar plantation, but since the overthrow of the colonial powers it has laid a waste savannah. The country is well watered. The river Yuna flows through the valley of Vega Real for upwards of 70 miles, and falls into the Bay of Samana. This river is navigable for 13 leagues from its mouth. The Yaqui, the Ozama, the Neybe and Artibonite are also large streams, and capable of navigation some distance inland. Several lakes of considerable size are also found on the south side, both of salt and fresh water; the largest of these is about 50 miles in circumference. The great Bays of Samana and Gonaives are important features in Haytian geography, and afford to the commercial world many secure harbors and ports, from which an extensive trade is carried on with the countries of Europe and North America.

Little is known of the geological structure of the island; a limestone containing vestiges of marine shells is the prevalent formation. The mines produce gold, silver, copper, tin, iron, rock-salt, &c. Those of Cibao, in the early part of the 16th century, were very productive; but the extermination of the Indian tribes, and the natural indolence of the colonists, caused an early suspension of the works. The state of the mining district, however, is improving. The principal copper mine yields an ore containing a large proportion of gold, and the sands of many of the rivers are mixed plentifully with gold grains, which are collected in small quantities by the poorer inhabitants.

Of the animals found by the first European settlers, the *Agoute* is the only one of the quadrupeds remaining. Parrots, and various species of birds of beautiful plumage, and waterfowl, are very plentiful; the alligator, cayman, turtles, &c., abound in the larger rivers, and several kinds of serpents are met with, and the testaceous and crustaceous animals form a plentiful means of support to the inhabitants of the coast.

The climate is tropical, and subject to all the various influences of location. The low lands of the coast are peculiarly unhealthy, while the more elevated regions are as bland and balmy as eternal spring. There is here, however, no sudden and violent changes of temperature, which, though high in the plains and savannas, is much moderated by the periodical recurrence of sea and land breezes. In the higher districts it is not unfrequent that a fire is found necessary. The rainy season occurs in May and June. Hurricanes and earthquakes are of frequent occurrence, and have done much damage to the island at various times. To Europeans the climate of the coast is very unfavorable—the yellow fever and dysentery are destructive agents, and during foreign invasion have been the best allies of the Haytians, and far more terrible than all the artillery of warfare. Mackenzie in his *Notes on Haiti, vol.* ii, says, that "the yellow fever would effectually secure the island in case of attack, if the policy of abandoning the coasts and destroying the towns were acted on."

The general remarks already submitted apply to the whole island. In pursuing the account it will now be necessary to recur to some historical detail respecting the rise, progress, &c., of the Spanish and French colonies, which divided the island, and the subsequent and consequent events resulting in the formation of two republics, as the separate communities now exist.

This island is memorable for having been the seat of the first European settlement and of the first independent negro government in America. It was discovered by Columbus in 1492, and settled immediately after under the guidance of his brother Diego. The avarice of the first adventurers led them to the commission of enormities towards the natives, which have left a dark blot on the Spanish name; at the present time not one aboriginal inhabitant exists from among 1,000,000 who inhabited the island at the time of its discovery. The thirst for gold and the reported wealth of the island, attracted the young and old to the scene of rapine, and while thousands were dying away, they were replaced by others willing to venture life for gold. The French Buccaneers, about the middle of the 17th century, made a footing on the west end of the island, and soon increased their colony by new acquisitions, and that part of the island was ceded to France by the treaty of Ryswick. Nothing interfered with the peace of the colonies till the breaking out of the French Revolution in 1789, when the blacks and mulattoes rose against the white population and succeeded in driving them out, or destroying them. After various conflicts, a military republic was formed under the title of the Republic of Hayti.* Hitherto the Spanish section had remained quiet, but in 1821 claimed to be independent, and in 1822 was compelled by the president of Hayti to annex itself to that republic. The whole island thus became a consolidated govern-

* President Soulouque was proclaimed *Emperor of Hayti*, 26th Aug., 1849, under the title of Faustin I.

ment, and so remained until the death of Boyer, when the political connection was dissolved and the Spanish portion again formed itself into the independent "*Republic of Dominica,*" and has been able to sustain itself ever since against the forces of Hayti.

The Dominicans hold the old Spanish portion, and are generally composed of Spaniards, creoles and some blacks. In a report made to the United States Government agent in 1845, some important historical, and statistical points are laid down, which give some idea of the importance of this division of Hispaniola. "The Dominican territory comprehends two-thirds of the island, extending from Lasabon on Massacre River in the north to the River Pedernales in the south, both falling into the sea, the latter to the windward (west) of Beata Island. The country is fertile in the productions of the West Indies, and in copper, gold, iron and coal. The pearl fisheries are carried on in the great bays. The principal ports and places are St. Domingo, Puerta de Plata, Azua, Samana, and Monte Christi.

"A constant trade is kept up with the islands of St. Thomas and Curaçoa, the United States, France, England and Germany, whither is transported a large amount of mahogany and tobacco. A sufficiency of sugar is made to supply the population and an equal amount is exported.

"The principal articles of export are mahogany, lignumvitæ, logwood, tobacco in leaf and cigars; cattle, hides, yellow and white wax, gum guiacum, honey and lumber.

"The defensive means of the republic are sufficiently ample for all immediate use. The cities are well fortified, and the frontiers protected from invasion of the blacks of Hayti. The public arsenals are well supplied with the materials of war, and they have an army of 18,000 men, of which one half is always on duty. The navy is small, consisting of only one brig and three schooners of war, all built at Caracas.

"The population is over 200,000, half of which are whites, who hold the general administration, and two thirds of the other half are mulattoes, a great portion of whom are landed proprietors, or old mechanics, and the remaining are negroes, mostly free born. Slavery has been forever abolished in the republic. Education has been very much neglected, but must now revive, as government has undertaken to supply schools in each parish at the public expense, besides which, numerous private schools for the upper classes are established in the convents, and also in the larger cities."

The government is very similar in form to that of the United States, and from appearances hitherto it seems to answer all healthful purposes. It consists of a President, Senate, and House of Representatives; and a Judiciary, with the usual powers conceded to the several departments.

The government of the ***Republic of Hayti*** is theoretically pure, but in practice it is a military dictatorship. The presidents have been mere soldiers, and held power by force of arms. Under such auspices all the prosperity the country enjoyed under France was lost, and the population is now in a state of disorganization and impending ruin. The exports are diminished, and are of *comparatively* little value; but still with ordinary exertion, with such soil and climate as the Haytians possess, prosperity may yet attend them. The population numbers about 700,000.

There is no late statistical information relative to these governments—in fact none since their separation. The commerce belonging to this island, ascertained from the returns of 1836, shows the following results: 369 ships, of 50,580 tons burden, with cargoes worth £474,782, or $2,278,954 entered;

and 395 ships of the burden of 52,485 tons, with cargoes valued at £921,-336, or $4,442,412, cleared out; thus leaving a balance in favor of the island of £446,554, or $2,163,456. No goods are suffered to remain on board vessels coming to the Haytian ports, but are warehoused on payment of one per cent. per annum. The following goods are entered free of duty: arms, ammunition, agricultural implements, horses, cattle, coin and school-books. The importation of mahogany, dye-woods and other articles produced on the island, is prohibited, as is the export of arms, coin, old or new iron or copper, horses, asses, and timber for ship-building. These regulations, however, are modified in the Dominican dominions.

San Domingo, the capital city of Dominica, and principal seaport within the Dominican territory, is situated at the mouth of the Ozama River, which forms its harbor. Latitude 18° 28′ 50″ north, longitude 69° 59′ 37″ west. This city was the first permanent settlement in America. It is surrounded by old ramparts, strengthened by bastions and outposts. Its interior is regularly laid out; the streets, which intersect each other at right angles, are spacious, but not all paved. The houses are in the Spanish style, and many of them fine, substantial buildings. Beside the cathedral, a gothic structure, built in 1540, and reported to have formerly contained the remains of Columbus, there are nine other churches, two convents, two hospitals, some large barracks, old and new national palaces, and many other public buildings, &c. The harbor is both capacious and secure; it has from 10 to 12 feet of water, but owing to a bar at the mouth of the Ozama, large ships are obliged to anchor in the outside road-stead, exposed to the south winds. St. Domingo has a considerable trade with the interior, and its external commerce is respectable. Population, 15,000.

Port-au-Prince, now Port-Republican, is the capital of Hayti, and situated in the innermost recesses of the Bay of Gonaives, on the south-west coast. It is built of wood, and has but an inferior aspect, its streets being unpaved and ill-regulated. It carries on an extensive trade with the United States and Jamaica. Population, 20,000.

The other principal towns are Cape Haytien, formerly the capital of Christophe's kingdom; Aux-Cayes, one of the most flourishing on the island; Jeremie, a place of considerable trade; Gonaives, a small town, with a good harbor, &c., &c.

The annexed transcript of a letter, published in the Turk's Island Gazette, (1848,) will give a full, and, probably, just account, of the condition of the Dominican Republic, and the vicissitudes it has undergone since its establishment, and much information important to the merchant:

"We are now in the fourth year of Dominican independence, and the third session of its legislature has drawn to a close.

If any argument can possibly prove the incompatibility of a union between the Spanish and Franco-African race; if evidence were wanting to establish the marked and distinct national characteristics of the two people, the acts of the last session of the Dominican Congress must set those questions at rest for ever.

* * * * * * * *

The Dominicans shook off the Haytien yoke because it was a violent usurpation, which strove to convert a virtuous and happy community into stupid barbarians, an usurpation which deprived them of all natural and political rights, as men, to seek their own prosperity and happiness; and the temperate, decided and judicious manner in which they have conducted this revolution, marked by no excesses, nor in which the authority of the laws, even for a moment, was suspended, eminently proves how fit they are to appreciate the privileges they have acquired.

Among the many interesting acts of the late session, I may cite the municipal law, which has been amplified, with many important additions and principles of government, already required by these Dominican communities, together with which the municipal revenues have been considerably augmented, in order to meet the extended range of the prerogatives of these useful institutions.

Amendments have likewise been introduced into the law for the improved civil government of the provinces.

Congress has also passed an act for the incorporation of a company, to form a macadamized road between Santiago and Porto Plata, which by the surveys already made, will reduce the present distance to nearly one-third.

The executive has been clothed with the most ample power for the promotion of immigration; funds have been placed at his disposal for the purpose of assisting the indigent, and authority to grant concessions of all public lands, in parcels of fifty acres, in full right and property, free of any charge whatever, to each immigrant, who is, moreover, exonerated from all military service.

That highly-impolitic vestige of Haytien legislation, that incubus upon the prosperity and advancement of any country, the imposition of patents on licenses for pursuing any kind of industry, has been quite exploded.

Licenses are now only required for merchants, shop-keepers, distilleries, and billiard-tables. All other trades and professions, of whatever nature, are free for natives as well as foreigners.

The retail trade is also open to foreigners, and all other vocations which require a license.

The foreign consignee-patent is rated at only eighty Spanish dollars—£16.

The custom-house laws have been completely remodelled, affording the utmost facilities and despatch to trade.

The import and export of gold and silver, with all other metals, and every species of mineral production, are declared free.

Vessels arriving with immigrants, and all vessels touching at any of the ports without trading, pay no port charges.

Foreign vessels can load without restriction at any place within the territory of the Dominican Republic, and in certain cases can engage in the coasting-trade.

The only articles which pay an export duty, are wax, mahogany, dye-woods, live-stock, hides, and tobacco, which duty will shortly be taken off in toto. The import duties now average twelve per cent.

But the grand and boldest measure of the session has been the reform of the currency, which has now become the law of the land.

The Dominicans, at the period when they shook off the Haytien yoke, were without a shilling in their treasury, and were suffering at the same time from a depreciated Haytien paper, current at only one-third its nominal value. They had to support an active war, build and repair extensive fortifications, equip and man a considerable naval force, supply the arsenals with warlike stores, and establish a constitutional government. All this was accomplished without difficulty by the patriotism of the citizens. New issues of paper, however, were indispensable, which, exceeding the sum required for the circulating medium of the country, caused a corresponding fluctuation and depreciation in its value. As no country can possibly improve with a fluctuating monetary system, the Dominican Congress decided at once on taking up the paper now in circulation at its intrinsic value in gold when issued, for which stock will be given, bearing five per cent. interest, redeemable in ten years, and further decreed the total reform and establishment of a new circulating medium, in sterling silver, and paper redeemable in silver on demand, at par with all other civilized nations; for the execution of which there is a considerable sum now in the treasury vaults, and any deficiency can be readily supplied by disposing of a part of the national property, for which due provision has been made.

Thus has this young republic braved all its adverse circumstances without incurring a shilling of debt, and now tenders to the world a land flowing with milk and honey, possessed of a soil unsurpassed by any in the universe; blessed with a climate that can vie with the most delicious regions; with liberty of conscience, freedom of industry, and with an enlightened government, framed to protect and respect the rights of all its inhabitants.

The rich mines which this valuable island contains, after having been closed for more than three centuries, are now revealed, and opened to the enterprise of the world.

The capitalist, the agriculturist, the artisan, will all find in this new country the most abundant resources for the advantageous employment of their active energy and talents. Add to all this, the extremely favorable position which this long-neglected country occupies, in the very centre of commercial enterprise and movement—its proximity to Europe, being, as it were, one of the outposts of the new world, stretching towards the old one, which bids fair to cause it soon to rank with the richest states of America."

THE BRITISH WEST INDIES.

The British West Indies, as exhibited in the tabular statement heretofore given, consist of a number of fine islands, situated among the several groups which together constitute the Columbian Archipelago. Though neither occupying the extent of surface, nor natural fertility of either the Spanish islands, or the independent island of San Domingo, they are remarkable as the most highly cultivated and productive of all the colonies of the British crown, and as being occupied by a wealthy, industrious and civilized race.

The institution of slavery, which for a long series of years existed in all these colonies, is now forever abolished. The British Parliament, alive to the inhumanity of the system, in 1833 passed a law, by which all the slaves were, on the 1st August, 1834, made apprenticed laborers, one portion of which were to be unconditionally liberated in four years, and the remainder in six years. At the termination, however, of the first period, such was the force of public opinion, that all, without restriction, received their liberty. To indemnify the slave-holders, the sum of £20,000,000, or $96,000,000, were granted by the mother country, and apportioned among the several colonies in a ratio in accordance with the number and value of their slaves.

The policy of this measure has been questioned, and its effect on the several islands, for good or for evil, is variously stated. There is no doubt, however, that the value of the British West Indies has greatly deteriorated since the emancipation was effected; but this may be owing to other causes, not connected with the slave-system, or over which the inhabitants could exercise no control. That the competition of countries in which slavery still exists, with these islands, is fraught with evil consequences, cannot be denied, and especially since the assimilation of duties on foreign and colonial sugars, &c., entered for consumption and export in the ports of England, the burden has fallen heavily on the non-slaveholding colonies. The system of policy adopted generally by the British Legislature, indeed, has been unwise and even inhumane towards the people of these islands. While at home she has been fostering foreign commerce, the course pursued towards her own colonies has become more galling, and the restrictions placed on West India commerce adverse to the general principles of free trade. Such alone would be sufficient to account for the decreasing value of these once productive islands; and when taken in connection with the recent disasters in the commercial world, have tested to the utmost their vast resources. The West Indians themselves are highly incensed at the conduct of the imperial government, and in the desperation of hopelessness, demand either a return to the old system of colonial protection, under which they enjoyed the highest prosperity, or the abolition of those restrictions which confine their commerce to the mother country. For the purpose of carrying out this design, the inhabitants of the several islands have banded themselves under the title of the "Loyal West Indian League,"—the object of which is to obtain redress, and in case of non-compliance with the general wishes of the people, annul British connection. The annexed abstracts from late West India papers will exhibit the feelings and wishes of the inhabitants on these points, and more fully indicate the disabilities under which the planters are laboring. The "*Barbadoes West Indian*" says:

"Why may not this system (Free Trade) be extended to us also? Why should we be compelled to suffer whatever loss or injury it inflicts upon us, by being applied to the produce which we send for sale to the British markets, and not share in the benefits to be derived from it? This is a one-sided way of dealing, where all the gains are pocketed by one party, and all the loss falls on the other, and which the colonies protest against. As England has adopted free trade, let her carry it out for the benefit of all parties of the empire. The extremities are as much a part of the body, and as useful, though not considered as vital as the head or heart; and the same blood circulates through them in as pure and healthy a state."

And the following is from the "*Jamaica Morning Journal*," which says:

"The note has been sounded, and the parishes are meeting. Saint Thomas in the Vale has passed resolutions which are before the public. Application is to be made to the Assembly of this island, and to the British Parliament, as well as to the Queen. Having lent money from the public funds for draining and improving estates in the mother country, and avowedly and ostensibly to enable the owners to compete with foreign corn-growers, we can conceive no reason which in fairness could be urged to a similar grant by way of loan for the purpose of enabling sugar-growers to contend with foreign rivals. Application for this assistance must be made, and urged on the government. The modification of the navigation laws is also deemed essential to the well-being of the colony. The merchant, as well as the planter, will desire this modification, or such an alteration of those laws as will enable him to import goods in any bottom, whether those of the country in which the goods are produced or not."

And the "*Trinidad Standard*" thus descants on the subject:

"Our prospects are, indeed, at present of the most discouraging nature, and unless Her Majesty's government shall be enabled to afford them prompt and sufficient relief, the West India Colonies will have to pass through a trying revolutionary crisis, in which, no doubt many, whose whole dependence is their precarious property in the colonies, must be plunged in irretrievable ruin, even should the colonies hereafter rally and regain any degree of prosperity. * * * In Jamaica, a proposition as been made to form a confederacy of the West Indies, and the Chamber of Commerce of that important colony have communicated the proposal in a circular addressed to the several colonies. A strong and general feeling of sympathy in this proposal has already been evinced in various significant ways."

Such are the complaints of the West India planters, and such the remedies proposed. What the next step may be it is impossible to predict; but there seems to be a general preference shown for a separate existence, and a confederation formed on the principle of the United States.

The social condition of the negroes since freed from the trammels of slavery, is said to have been much improved. Education is rapidly spreading;—the morals of the community are improving;—crime has wonderfully diminished, and Christianity is asserting a sway over the whole mass of the population, and industry has usurped the reign of sloth, idleness and bad habits, which are almost innate in the slave. Notwithstanding, however, the increased industry and improvements which have taken place, the West Indies suffer remarkably for want of laborers, and to relieve this serious difficulty, various schemes have been adopted, though without any important result. Whether from this deficiency, from the effects of the seasons or other causes, the produce and trade of the islands, as before stated, have not kept pace with their improved social condition. The importation of "Coolies" from India has been tried, but without affording any relief. Indeed, it may be said to have entirely failed in its object. These persons were imported as free laborers, under the surveillance of government: they originate in the wilds of India, and are an intractable and worthless race, and far inferior to the negro in physical powers and endurance. Many, on their arrival, refuse to work, and become an additional burden on the colonists. In many of the islands they travel in large bodies, enforcing alms; and so filthy and disgusting are they in appearance, that the inhabtants fear them as much from the diseases they may propagate, as from their sturdy mendicity.

The forms of government established in the British West Indies may be divided into two classes: those having a governor, council, and representative assemblies, and those having only a governor and legislative council. The first includes Jamaica, Barbadoes, Antigua, Tobago, Grenada, St. Vincent, Montserrat, Nevis, St. Christopher's, and the Virgin Isles; and the second, Trinidad and St. Lucia. The reason for this difference is, that most of the colonies were acquired by conquest, and the inhabitants who chose to remain in the islands were guaranteed their laws and the exercise of their religion. The governor has the chief civil and military authority; the Council is somewhat analogous to the Privy-Council of the mother country, and the House of Assembly to the House of Commons. A member of the House of Assembly, in Jamaica, must possess a freehold of £300 per annum, or a personal estate of £3,000; and an elector must have a freehold of £10 per annum, in the parish in which he votes. Some of the islands have only lieutenant-governors, who are under the governor of some adjacent island. The lieutenant-governors of St. Vincent and Tobago are under the governor of Barbadoes. Their powers, however, are nearly equal to those of a governor. In those islands which have no representative assembly, the legislative council consists of the Chief Secretary, the Treasurer, the Chief-Justice, the Attorney-General, and the commander of the troops. These are appointed by the crown; and sometimes a few of the principal landed proprietors are made members of the council. Several islands are sometimes included under one government, and send their representatives to the island which is the seat of the legislature for the time being. Thus St. Christopher, Nevis, Montserrat, and one or two other small islands, send their representatives to Antigua, which is the seat of government for them all, or, in other words, the residence of the governor.

The superior and inferior courts of judicature resemble those of England, the laws being the same, unless as they may be affected by special colonial enactments, passed from time to time. Assize courts are frequently held, to expedite the course of justice. There are likewise parish-courts, wherein justices of the peace decide summarily in small debt cases, &c. There are also offices of record, where deeds, wills, sales and patents, are recorded. All persons intending to leave the islands are obliged to give notice at the office of enrolment three weeks before they can be entitled to a pass, or to find security for what debts they may leave unpaid; and for further precautions, masters of vessels are bound, under heavy penalties, not to carry off any person without such pass. The procedure of the assemblies follows, as near as may be, the formula of the British legislature; and all their bills have the force of laws as soon as the governor's assent is obtained. The power of rejection, however, is vested in the crown, but until rejected the laws are valid. The governor can also refuse his assent to laws, and can dissolve and call together the assemblies at pleasure. Salaries are paid partly by the crown and partly from the colonial revenues.

The currency employed in the British West Indies is an imaginary money, and has a different value in the several colonies. The following are the values of £100 sterling, and of a dollar, in the currencies of the different islands:

	Sterling Currency.	Dollar Currency. s. d.
Jamaica	£100=£140	1=6. 8.
Barbadoes	100= 135	1=6. 3.
Windward Islands, (except Barbadoes)	100= 175	1=8. 3.
Leeward Islands generally	100= 200	1=9. 0.

All the West India Islands have been of incalculable utility to England, when struggling for the mastery of the world. Their consumption of British manufactures has been immense, and they have at all times furnished a supply of taxable commodities beyond the control of an enemy, and indispensable to the maintainance of the British financial system. As South America becomes more civilized, the West Indies will become extensive entrepôts for the sale of English products; and even at the present day, if properly protected, they afford abundant scope for the employment of the dormant capital of the mother country.

The several islands will now be described separately.

JAMAICA.

Jamaica, the largest and most valuable of the British islands, lies between 17° 35′ and 18° 30′ N. latitude, and between 76° and 78° 40′ W. longitude. It is 150 miles long and 55 broad, containing about 5,468 square miles.

The island is somewhat of an oval shape, with an elevated ridge called the Blue Mountains, (in some places nearly 8,000 feet above the level of the sea,) running longitudinally through it, and occasionally other ridges which traverse from north to south, approaching the sea on the south coast in gigantic spines, of sharp ascent, difficult of access, and clothed with dense and sombre forests, and on the north declining into lovely mounds, and round topped hills, covered with groves of pimento and all the exquisite verdure of the tropics—the *coup d'œil* presenting a splendid panorama of high mountains embosomed in clouds, and vast savannas or plains, hills and vales, rivers, bays and creeks. The middle part, called Pedro's Cockpit, is spread for an extent of many miles, with an infinite number of round topped hills, whose surface, covered with loose limestone, or honey-comb rock, is clothed with fine cedar and other trees of enormous bulk. The dales or cock-pits meandering between these hammocks contain a rich soil of great depth, where the succulent Guinea-grass forms a perfect carpet of ever verdant beauty.

The picturesque of the island is further enhanced by its numerous rivers, upwards of 200 of which have been enumerated. Few, however, owing to the mountainous nature of the country, are navigable for large vessels, though they are capable of great improvement. Black River, which flows for the most part through a flat country, is the deepest and most rapid, and is navigable for flat-bottom boats and canoes for about thirty miles. The other chief rivers are, on the north side the Marthabræ, White, Ginger and Great River; and on the south side the Rio Cobre and Rio Minho. The precipitate current of these streams renders them better adapted for mechanical purposes than intercourse. There are a large number of mineral and warm springs on the island, some of which are highly beneficial in cutaneous diseases, and various internal obstructions.

Jamaica has 16 principal harbors, besides 30 bays, roads or shipping stations, which afford good anchorage.

This island is evidently of volcanic origin; at the present day, however, no volcanic action is perceived. A small elevated salt lake in the mountains, 3,000 feet above the sea, has the appearance of an extinct crater, and the character of the rocks everywhere denote the powerful operation of fire. The soil is generally deep and fertile; on the north a chocolate color, in other parts a bright yellow, and everywhere remarkable for a shining surface when first turned up, and for staining the skin like paint when wetted; it appears to be of a chalky marl, containing a large proportion of calcareous matter. There is a soil on the island termed "brick mould," which is deep and mellow, on a retentive understratum—this, next to the "ash mould" of St. Christopher's, is considered the best soil in the West Indies for the sugar cane. A red earth abounds most in the hilly parts, and a purple loam, sometimes mixed with a sandy soil, in the savannas and low lands; but the highest mountains are remarkable for having on their summits a deep black rich soil.

The lead ore of Jamaica is extremely rich and heavily impregnated with silver; several varieties have been found, and, indeed, worked at Liguana, where also striated antimony is obtainable. In the low mountains of Liguana every variety of copper ore (14 different species) is in profusion, in particular the green and livid, and the shining dark copper ores; in the more mellow matrices yellow mundick (marchasites) is largely mixed. In the mountains above Bull Bay, a dark iron sand, attracted by the magnet, is found; neither gold nor silver ore has yet been discovered, though it is certain the natives possessed those metals in abundance when first visited by Columbus and the early Spanish settlers. In the river Minho particles of gold have been found after heavy rains; and Gage, (in 1655,) among other old writers, speaks of mines producing "some gold, though drossie."

The climate differs in intensity with the elevation. At Kingston, on the coast, the mean temperature is 80° Fahr, and the minimum 70°. As the country is ascended of course the heat decreases, and at the distance of 14 miles, at an elevation of 4,200 feet, the average range is from 55° to 65°; the minimum range in winter being 44° Fahr, and a fire in the evening is not only agreeable but necessary. The temperature is not subject, however, to sudden flaws, and the transitions are always slow. The air is remarkably light and enlivening, producing great cheerfulness even in old age, and so equal is its pressure, that it rarely varies more than an inch at any time of the year. From July to October is the hurricane season. The quantity of rain falling in the year is about 50 inches. The seasons are divided into four, viz: the first, the vernal and moderate rains in April and May, lasting six weeks; the second, hot and dry, including June, July and August; the third, hurricane and rainy months, embracing September, October and November; and the fourth, serene and cool, comprising December, January, February and March. There is, however, considerable difference of climate on either side of the island, and the winters on the north side are felt at least a month earlier than on the south, and the other seasons are affected in like ratio.

The natural productions of Jamaica are those of the West Indies generally. The great staples now grown by the planters are sugar canes, the coffee plant, cotton, indigo and cocoa. Sugar growing was early introduced by the Spaniards. The quantity of sugar now made is very great; and the importations into Great Britain alone have, for some years, averaged 1,500,000 cwts., which represents as many £ sterling. The sugar of Jamaica is of a very fine quality. The quantity of rum manufactured is also very large, averaging at least 4,000,000 gallons a-year. Of coffee, and that too of excellent quality, about 25,000,000 lbs. is annually exported, of which 20,000,000 lbs. is sent to England. The coffee plant was first introduced into Jamaica in 1728. It thrives in almost every soil in the mountain districts, and in the very driest places has frequently produced very abundant crops. The cultivation of cotton, indigo and cocoa was formerly more extensively engaged in than at the present day; it has principally given way to that of sugar and coffee. Jamaica produces many drugs, dyestuffs and spices. Aloes, cochineal, spikenard, canella, liquorice root, castor oil nut, vanilla, peppers, arrow-root, ginger, ipecacuanha, scammony, jalap, cassia, euphorbia, senna, &c., all attest the fruitfulness and capacities of the soil and climate.

The cultivated vegetables of Europe arrive at great perfection. Maize is the principal corn grown, and together with calavances, the yam and sweet potato, cassava, &c., forms the chief food of the negroes. The grasses thrive luxuriantly, but Guinea-grass abounds; and in consequence of its indispensable importance in feeding the cattle which supply manure for the sugar plantations, it is considered next in importance to the sugar-cane itself. The native and exotic grasses are excellent for cattle and horses, in particular that called the Scotch grass, which vegetates rapidly, and grows to the height of five or six feet, with long and juicy joints. Five horses may be fed for a year on an acre of this vegetable, allowing each every day fifty-six lbs. of grass. Of vegetables,—potatoes, yams, cassava, peas and beans of every variety, artichokes, beets, carrots and parsnips, cucumbers and tomatoes, radishes, celery, choco, ochro, Lima beans, Indian kale, calalue, various salads, cabbage trees, (200 feet high), &c., all flourish in abundance; and, indeed it may be said that harvest is perpetual in Jamaica, for every month presents a new collation of fruits and vegetables, and some spices are at maturity all the year round. The bread-fruit, cocoa-nut, plantain and banana, alligator pear, the delicious mellow fig, pine, cachew, papaw and custard apples, orange, lime, lemon, mango, grape, guava, pomegranate, soursop, shaddock, plum, tamarind, melon, wall and chestnut, mulberry, olive, date, citron, and many other delicious fruits arrive at perfection.

The population of Jamaica, which numbers about 360,000, consists of 35,000 whites, or Europeans, and their descendants; of blacks and the colored races, about 320,000; and of some Coolies, &c., which have been transported from India and other parts as free laborers. The condition of that people is the same in all the islands as regards their political and social attributes. The original Indian race is extinct. All accounts agree that the island was thickly peopled on its discovery; within half a century after, not one existed! Las Casas says, speaking of the treatment the Indians received from the Spaniards:—"*They hanged these unfortunates by thirteen, in honor of the thirteen Apostles;—I have beheld them throw the Indian infants to their dogs;—I have heard the Spaniards borrow the limb of a human being to feed their dogs, and next day return a quarter to the lender!*"

A Governor or Captain-General (appointed by the Crown) aided by an Executive and Legislative Council of 12 members, and a House of Assembly, (first convened in 1644,) form the government of the island. The Assembly consists of 45 members, each parish sending two, except Spanish-Town, Kingston and Port Royal, which send three. A representative must possess a freehold of £300 per annum, or a personal estate of £3,000, and an elector must be 21 years of age, and possess a freehold of £10 in the parish in which he votes. The Governor has a yearly salary of £4,200; the representatives receive no pay. The Judiciary consists of a Supreme Court, which sits at the capital three times a year, and has both original and appellate jurisdiction; Assize Courts, which have the same power, authority and jurisdiction, that the Justices of Assize and Nisi Prius, and Justices of Oyer and Terminer and Justices of Gaol Delivery, in England; and several inferior courts and Courts of Common Pleas. Every precinct has a Court of Sessions, held quarterly. The Governor is Chancellor, and holds a court with the same powers of judicature as the Lord High Chancellor of England. The Court of Error revises the decisions of the Supreme and Assize Courts. There are also Courts of Admiralty, a Court of Ordinary for the decision of ecclesiastical matters, and probate; and in which the Governor presides as judge—and several courts having reference to bankruptcy and insolvency. The system of jurisprudence is identical with that of England, only differing as affected by local and conventional interests.

The military establishment of this island consists, generally, of four European regiments, and one West Indian regiment, with a strong detachment of artillery, in all about 3,000 men. The colonial militia comprises three regiments of horse, well equipped and mounted, and twenty-one regiments of infantry, to each of which is attached two field-pieces and a company of artillery, in all from 10,000 to 12,000 men. All white males, from sixteen years old and upwards, are obliged by law to provide themselves with suitable clothing, and to enlist in the cavalry or infantry of the militia. Substitutes are not allowed. When on duty, each man has 2s. 6d. per day and rations; arms and ammunition are found by the government.

The trade of this important island is considerable. The shipping inward and outward varies little from seven hundred and fifty vessels of all kinds, respectively, and one hundred and fifty thousand tons annually, employing between seven and eight thousand seamen. The amount of exports is valued at between £3,000,000 and £4,000,000, and the imports at about £600,000. The principal articles of export are sugar, rum, molasses, ginger, pimento, coffee, &c., with a large variety of tropical fruits. The imports are British manufactures and colonial produce, with a variety of articles from the United States and foreign countries. Kingston is the chief port, but considerable business is done at Savannah le Mar, Morant Bay, St. Anne's, Annatto Bay, Port Maria, Port Antonio, Montego Bay and Falmouth.

The colonial revenue is derived from a variety of sources—as import and export duties, poll tax, stamps, licenses, tonnage, &c., internal duties and taxes. The annual expenditure of Jamaica is nearly £500,000, including £10,000, the perpetual revenue granted to the crown. Jamaica sustains the whole burden of its government, excepting the salary of the bishop. The local revenues, applicable for city and town purposes, amount to an additional sum of £200,000 annually.

The island is divided into three counties, viz: Middlesex, Surrey and Cornwall, each of which is subdivided into parishes, &c., as follows:—

	Area in acres.	*Towns.*	*Parishes.*	*Villages.*
Middlesex	672,616	1	9	13
Surrey	1,522,149	2	7	8
Cornwall	1,305,235	3	5	6
Total	3,500,000	6	21	27

St. Jago de la Vega, or Spanish Town, the capital, is situated at the extremity of an extensive plain, and is distant from Port Royal harbor six miles. The Cobre, a river of considerable depth, passes near the city. The barracks and hospital are excellent. The buildings of the capital are in the magnificent style of Spanish architecture, and have an imposing appearance. The population is about 5,000. The King's House is a splendid building, having cost £50,000. It is situated in the south of the great square, facing an immense pile of buildings, containing under one roof the House of Assembly, the Supreme Court, and almost all the government offices of the island.

Kingston, the chief mart of commerce, is situated on a gentle slope about a mile in length, which is bounded on the south by an extensive basin through which all vessels must advance beneath the commanding batteries of Port Royal. The harbor is one of the finest in the world. It is commanded by Fort Charles on the east, on the west by Rock Fort, and opposite its entrance by Fort Augustin. For nine miles around Kingston is an alluvial plain surrounded by a series of irregular mountains, some of which, in the east and north-east, are of considerable elevation, and interspersed with vallies and chasms, which add much to the picturesque which forms so conspicuous a feature in the landscape of Jamaica. The streets of Kingston are long and straight, the houses in general of two stories, with verandahs above and below. The English and Scotch churches are really elegant structures, particularly the former, which is built on an elevated spot, and commands a splendid view of the city, the plains around it, the amphitheatre of mountains, and the noble harbor of Port Royal.

Port Royal is situated at the extremity of a tongue of land, which forms the boundary of the harbors of Kingston and Port Royal. Towards the sea the tongue is composed of coral rocks covered with sand, which the tide frequently inundates, as a great part of the town is only a few feet above the level of the sea. The royal navy yard lies to the north; the naval hospital to the south-west, and the works of Fort Charles and the barracks to the southward. The fortifications are very strong. The harbor is capable of containing 1,000 large ships with convenience. In 1692 the whole town was destroyed by an earthquake.

The other most celebrated towns and ports are—PORT ANTONIO on the north-east, a strongly fortified place; FALMOUTH, or Marthabræ, 15 miles east of Montego Bay, built on the west side of the harbor; MAROON TOWN in the interior, on a very high mountain; MONTEGO BAY; LUCEA, or Fort Charlotte; SAVANNAH LE MAR, &c., on the western extremity of the island. Besides which, there are a number of towns and villages, all built in situations peculiarly well adapted either for internal or external commerce.

CARLISLE AND BLEWFIELD'S BAYS on the south, are worthy of notice. The roads of the island are in general good, but narrow.

Jamaica was discovered by Columbus, 2d May, 1494. It was called Xaymaca by the natives, signifying abundance of water and wood, and San Jago by Columbus, in honor of the patron Saint of Spain. The first colony was attempted in 1503, by the Spaniards. In 1558, the Aborigines had entirely perished, and slaves were then introduced. The British attacked Jamaica in 1605, but restricted their exploits to predatory warfare. The battle of Passagefort, in which the Spaniards were completely beaten, and compelled to pay a large ransom to the British for the preservation of their capital, was fought in 1638. The island remained in the hands of the Spaniards until the 3d May, 1655, from which to the present period, it has remained in the possession of Great Britain. No less than twenty-six slave insurrections have occurred in the island since occupied by England. The expense of putting down that of 1832, (exclusive of the value of property destroyed, viz. £1,154,583,) was £161,596. On this occasion, the imperial parliament granted a loan of £500,000 to assist the almost ruined colonists. The present condition of every interest in the island is said to be in an unfavorable state, consequent on several causes which seem to operate wofully on the West Indies generally.

The provisions for religion and education on this island are ample. The efforts for the extension of church accommodation by the colonial legislature has been great; and at the present time, about £25,000 is annually expended for this purpose. The Bishop of Jamaica has £4,000 per annum, and the Archdeacon £2,000. There are twenty-one rectors and about sixty clergymen belonging to the established Church. The Scotch Presbyterians have four churches; the Wesleyan Methodists, 24; the Baptists, 16, and the Moravians, eight. The crown-livings are in the gift of the bishop, but pluralities are forbidden. The value of livings is from £750 to £2,400 currency. Education is rapidly extending. Mr. Latrobe remarked universally throughout his tour of the island, that children of the colored class of every shade evinced a remarkable facility for the attainment of the rudiments of such branches of instruction as are taught them, particularly in writing and arithmetic, their progress in these being "truly extraordinary." Many of the country schools are carried on almost entirely through the agency of the more advanced scholars. The Sunday and evening schools are attended by all classes; the want of private schools of a superior order, in which the higher classes of the island could receive a liberal education, is much dwelt on by Mr. Latrobe, and the absence of a college, or some institution sanctioned by the legislature deplored. The private seminaries are little better than the "dame schools" in England.

THE CAYMANS.

The Caymans, which are dependencies of Jamaica, are three small islands in lat. 19° 20′ N., from 30 to 40 leagues N. N.W. from Point Negrill on the westward of Jamaica, the Grand Cayman being the most remote. Cayman-braque, and Little Cayman lie within five miles of each other, and about 34 miles north of Grand Cayman, which is about one mile and a half long, and one mile broad, containing about 1000 acres. Grand Cayman, the only island inhabited, is so low, that the lofty trees on it appear from ships approaching like a forest of masts peering from the waters. It has no harbor, but the anchorage on the S. W. coast is good. The inhabitants are employed in catching and feeding turtle for the markets. The soil towards the middle of the island is very fertile, producing corn and vegetables in profusion, while hogs and poultry find plenty of provender. Columbus discovered these islands on his return from Porto Bello to Hispaniola, and observing the coast swarming with turtle, like ridges of rocks, he called them Los Tortugas. The Caymans were never occupied by the Spaniards, but became the general resort of adventurers or rovers (chiefly French), for the sake of the turtle. In 1655, when Jamaica was taken by the English, these islands were still uninhabited. The present race of inhabitants are descended from the Buccaneers, and being inured to the sea, form excellent pilots and seamen. They have a chief or government officer of their own choosing, and they frame their own regulations. Justices of the peace are appointed from Jamaica; but in no other way are the inhabitants interfered with by the authorities, in the chief settlement to which they nominally, but undoubtedly belong.

TRINIDAD.

This island extends from latitude 9° 20′ to 10° 51′ north, and from longitude 60° 30′ to 61° 20′ west. The Gulf of Paria divides it from the main land. It is 90 miles long and 50 broad, having an area of 2,400 square miles. The northern front of Trinidad, as seen from the ocean, resembles an immense ridge of rocks, but on entering the Gulf of Paria, one of the most magnificent, variegated, richly-luxuriant panoramas that nature ever formed is presented to the eye; on the west is seen the mighty Orinoco, contending with the ocean, and the lofty mountains of Venezuela; while on the east, the cape, headlands, mountains, hills, vallies and plains of the island, enamelled with eternal verdure, present a *coup d'œil* truly sublime. From every elevation the scenery is transcendent, and the whole island enjoys in climate a perpetual spring. The fecundity of the soil, its gigantic and magnificent vegetation, its beautiful rivers, enchanting slopes, forests of palms, groves of citrons, and hedges of spices and perfumes—its succulent roots, delicious herbs and fruits, abundant and nourishing food, on the earth, in the air, and in the water—its azure skies and elastic atmosphere, have each and all combined to crown Trinidad with the appellation of "The Indian Paradise."

The highest land (about 3,000 feet) is to the north, near the sea; in the middle is a range of mountains less elevated, and to the south a series of lovely hills and mounds, contrasting strongly with the boldness of the northern regions. The navigable streams on the west coast are the Caroni, Chaguanas, Barrancones, Couva, Guaracara, and Sissaria; the first is navigable from its mouth, in the gulf, to its junction with the Aripo, and has several other tributaries. There are many other streams on the west coast navigable for small trading vessels. On the north and east the Rio Grande, the Oropuche, and the Nariva or Mitan, are the largest streams, and remarkable for their pure and crystalline waters. The Guatava is a large river, but not navigable, except for small boats. The Moruga is a fine stream, flowing south. In every direction limpid brooks run murmuring through lofty forests, and add beauty to the picturesque scenery through which they pass to the ocean.

The Gulf of Paria, formed by the west shore of Trinidad and the opposite shore of the main, may be said to form one vast harbor. It is thirty leagues long, and fifteen leagues from north to south. Ships may anchor safely in from three to six fathoms of water, over gravel or mud soundings. It is entered on the north by the Dragon's Mouth, and on the south-east by the Serpent's Mouth, two straits formed by projections from the island and main land. The gulf is the recipient of numerous streams from both, and several islands are embosomed in its waters.

Trinidad is evidently a section from the adjacent continent, severed either by volcanic or oceanic eruption. It has the same strata of earth, the same rocks, and in its general geological character is entirely similar. The volcanic origin of this island is indicated by several craters, and south of Cape de la Brea is a submarine volcano, which occasionally boils up, and discharges a quantity of petroleum. There is also a similar one on the east part of the island and Bay of Mayaro, which in March and June gives several detonations, resembling thunder—these are succeeded by flames and smoke, and some minutes after pieces of bitumen, as black and brilliant as jet, are thrown on shore. Near Point Icacos a number of small mounds are found, which exhale sulphureted hydrogen in abundance. In many portions of the island, indeed, volcanic action is perceptible, and frequent manifestations of its presence are experienced by the inhabitants. The island, however, is remarkably free from earthquakes; and although the whole of the West-Indies and the Spanish Main have repeatedly been devastated by these scourges, Trinidad has always been the least to suffer. The mud volcanoes, which are chiefly in the south, throw out salt water, heavily loaded with argillaceous earth, to the height of 30 feet, and are unapproachable to within fifty paces.

The minerals found in Trinidad are iron; a very brilliant white metal, more ductile and malleable than silver, supposed by M. Vauquelin to be a new metal; copper, in the form of sulphate; arsenic; plumbago and bituminous coal. But the most remarkable mineral phenomenon is the "Asphaltum, or Pitch Lake," which is situated on a head-land, jutting from the north-east corner of the island. It is elevated 80 feet above the ocean. Seen from the sea the head-land resembles a dark, scoriaceous mass, and on a nearer view it is found to consist of bituminous scoriæ, vitrified sand and earth, all cemented together. A strong sulphurous smell pervades the neighborhood for ten or twelve miles around, and is felt on approaching the shore. The usual consistence and appearance of the asphaltum, (except in hot weather, when it is actually liquid for an inch deep,) is that of pit-coal, but of a greyish color, melting like sealing-wax; ductile by a gentle heat, and when mixed with grease or oil, acquires a fluidity which adapts it well for protecting the bottoms of ships from rot, or the *teredo navalis*, a worm which proves so destructive to shipping in warm climates. Deep crevices or funnels, sometimes six feet deep, are found in various parts of the asphaltum, filled with excellent water, often containing mullet, and other small fish. Alligators are said to have been seen in these extraordinary caverns. Several of these communicate with the sea, and experience the agitation of storms that ruffle the adjacent waters, often rising and falling during a storm six or eight feet, and scattering on the land large masses of asphaltum. Pieces of what was once wood, are found completely changed into bitumen, and the trunk of a large tree on being sawn, was entirely impregnated with the pitch. When mixed with earth this substance acts as a fertilizer, and the finest fruits on the island come from the districts bordering on this singular lake. Whether this substance has been used as a manure in the United States, is not known to the writer; it would, however, be well if some horticulturist were to give it a trial.

When Trinidad was first discovered, it was inhabited by a dense population of Caribs. These unhappy people were either murdered or transported to the Hispaniola mines. The present Indian population is about 760. The inhabitants of European descent number about 5,000, and the negro and mixed races about 40,000. There are also some Chinese and a number of Coolies recently imported. The total is estimated at 47,000 souls. The Protestant interests on the island are under the surveillance of the Bishop of Barbadoes; there are ten parish churches, and a number of chapels belonging to the establishment. The Roman Catholics have four churches, and there are also several dissenters' meeting houses. The provisions for education, both of black and white persons, are ample; the Lancasterian system is generally adopted. Schools are supported either by the state or by voluntary contributions. Besides the public and free schools, there are twenty-three private academies for the education of the children of the rich.

The administrative functions are vested in a Lieutenant-Governor, and an Executive and Legislative Committee, half of which is composed of official persons, and half taken from among the people. The ancient institutions of this island are retained, else the elective system of England would long since have been introduced. The towns are governed by the Cabildo, which resembles in its functions our municipal corporations. The militia of the island numbers 4,600, and every freeman is liable to duty. The revenues of the island are derived from export and import duties, taxes, &c., and amount annually to about £40,000. The expenses of the government are principally for the civil and judicial establishments. The military expenses are borne by the mother country.

The exports of Trinidad are sugar, molasses, coffee, and some cotton and indigo. The value of exports is about £375,000 annually, two-thirds of which are carried to Great Britain, and about one-sixth to the United States. The remainder is distributed among the other West Indies, Canada and foreign states. The imports, the annual value of which is about £350,000, consist of manufactured goods, &c., chiefly from the ports of England. The weights and measures of Spain are used in all commercial transactions. The British coin of the realm, colonial coin, and the coins of Spain and Spanish America, are current in Trinidad. There are several species of base silver coin. The total value of property of all kinds in the island is about £8,000,000, and the property annually created, about £1,600,000. The amount of coin in circulation is estimated at £60,000.

Trinidad was discovered by Columbus, 31st July, 1498. It was then inhabited by a numerous race of Caribs. These fell a sacrifice to the Spaniards, who took possession of the island in 1588, and were either massacred or sent to the mines in St. Domingo. In 1775, Trinidad was captured by the French, but almost immediately afterwards delivered up again. In 1595, Sir Walter Raleigh visited the island, and committed some outrages, which were disavowed by the British government, and for which Raleigh paid the forfeiture of his life on the scaffold. On the 16th February, 1797, the British captured the island without any marked opposition, and it has since that period remained a crown colony, but retaining the constitution it had under the Spanish authority.

Puerto d'Espana, or Port of Spain, the capital, embosomed in an amphitheatre of hills, lies on the Gulf of Paria, and is one of the finest towns in the West Indies. The buildings are of massive stone, and the streets are long and wide, shaded with trees, and laid out in parallel lines from the sea, so as to catch every breeze that blows. The churches and government buildings are fine and imposing edifices. The harbor is available for the largest ships. The harbor of Port Royal, *Chagaramus*, on the west peninsula of the island, at the entrance of the Gulf of Paria, is three leagues west of Port of Spain, and comprehends a space of about 70 square miles. It is esteemed the best and safest port in the island, being in some parts 40 fathoms deep, and protected from the north by steep shores. All the western shore is a series of fine bays and harbors, in which ships may safely anchor at all times. The north and east coasts are equally well furnished with harbors and roadsteads, but those are little available on account of the prevailing winds for three-fourths of the year. The ports on the north are the Maqueribe and Las Ceuvas; to the north-east, Rio Grande, Toco and Cumana; on the east, Balandra Bay or Boat Island, Guias-Creek and Mayaro Bay. The safest port on the east is Guaiguaire., from its being sheltered by a point of land from the east winds, and from its entrance being on the south, from whence the winds are neither frequent nor violent

TOBAGO.

Tobago, or Tobacco, situated in 11° 16′ North latitude, and 60° 30′ West longitude, is the most southerly of the Caribbean Islands. In length it is 32 miles, and in breadth 12 miles, having an area of 187 square miles.

Tobago has been termed the "Melancholy Isle," because, when viewed from the north, it seems to be only a mass of lofty, gloomy mountains, with black precipices descending abruptly to the sea. The island is of a very irregular shape, and is composed principally of conical hills of basaltic formation, and of ridges which descend from the interior towards the ocean, terminating sometimes in abrupt precipices. The ravines are deep and narrow, and end generally in small alluvial plains. The north-west part is least mountainous, terminating in the south abruptly with the dark Island of Little Tobago, and the dangerous rocks called St. Giles's. The south terminates in broken plains and low lands; the whole aspect, like Trinidad, being calm and magnificent, with occasional beautiful mounds or isolated hills, so close that few levels for marsh or swamps present themselves, the delightful vales everywhere exhibiting the effect of a rotary or undulating motion of vast currents of water, and forming with the contiguous mountains truly picturesque scenery. The island is well watered by rivulets and streams arising in the interior and flowing over the lowlands to the coast, where they are occasionally obstructed, which, however, a little attention would prevent.

On a complete view of the island, as compared with the adjacent continent, the observer is impressed with the belief that it formed, at some distant day, a bold promontory of the main, from which it has been violently severed. There is, in fact, a general physiognomical resemblance between Tobago and Trinidad: in this, however, there are some exceptions, and the geological formations are not entirely the same. The soil is a rich, dark mould, and resembles, particularly in the east, that of its neighboring isle, with the advantage of its vegetable earth being deeper on the hills.

Though moist from saline impregnation, the climate of Tobago is not unhealthy. The island is out of the usual range of hurricanes, but in December and January the north winds are often strong and cold. So decidedly salubrious are the highlands, that Dr. Lloyd, the principal medical officer, reported to Sir James M'Grigor, that on some of the estates in the interior, no European resident had been buried for upwards of ten years.

The island is beset with currents, which are uncertain and dangerous to navigation. The north-east trade-wind blows all the year about the island.

The population of Tobago is about 15,000, of which only 400 or 500 are whites, the remainder are the black and mixed races. There are but two churches and two chapels belonging to the establishment, and five or six dissenter's meeting houses. Schools are established in each parish, and the Moravians and Wesleyan Methodists have schools which they have established on their own account. Tobago is entirely Protestant, and is under the diocesan surveillance of the Bishop of Barbadoes.

Tobago is ruled by a Lieutenant-governor, and by a Council of nine, and a House of sixteen members, whose powers and authority are similar to those of Jamaica, &c. The militia of Tobago consists of all adult freemen. There are at the present time no military forts or works in their charge; the batteries, houses, guns and carriages having gone to decay from inability of the colony to defray the expense of keeping them in repair.

Almost every kind of plant that flourishes in the Antilles grows in Tobago. The orange, the lemon, and the guava, pomegranate, fig and grape are in perfection; the two latter yield fruit twice a year, and all the culinary plants of Europe thrive well. The cinnamon, pimento, and nutmeg trees grow wild in some districts—and the cotton of Tobago is excellent. The staples are sugar, rum, and molasses, the chief bulk of which is carried to England. The value of exports amounts annually to about £200,000, and of imports to about £70,000 or £80,000. The weights and measures of England are used here. There is no paper currency, and but little coin on the island.

Scarborough, the capital, is situated on the south-west side of the island, along the shore. It is protected by several forts. On the windward side are numerous excellent bays, and on the north is Man-of-War Bay, capacious, safe, and adapted for the largest ships. Sandy Point forms the western extremity of the island, and is the only level land of any extent in Tobago. The other principal bays are Courland, King, Tyrrell's, Bloody, Mangrove, Englishman's and Castara, some of which are large and deep, and have good anchorage for vessels of 150 tons. Halifax Bay admits vessels of 250 tons—but a shoal at the entrance requires a pilot.

Tobago was discovered by Columbus in 1496, who found it inhabited by Caribs. In 1580, the British flag was planted on the island, but no settlement made. A small colony from Barbadoes settled here in 1625, but subsequently abandoned it. The Dutch colonized in this island in 1632. It soon after became the scene of contention, and was repeatedly sacked by both the French and English. It was declared neutral by the treaty of Aix-la-Chapelle, in 1748, but in 1763 was ceded to the British. It was captured again by the French in 1781, and ceded to that nation in 1783, but was again seized by England, in 1793, since which period it has remained unmolested in her possession.

GRENADA

Lies between the parallels of 12° 20′ and 11° 58′ N. lat., and between 61° 35′ and 61° 20′ W. long. Its greatest length, from north to south, is 25 miles, and its greatest breadth 12 miles, narrowing to a point at each extremity. Its area is about 155 square miles, and its population about 30,000, or 194 to each square mile.

Grenada is a mountainous island, the interior and north-west coast rising in successive piles of conical hills or continuous ridges, covered with forests and brushwood. From north to south, the island is traversed by one continued though irregular range, often rising to an elevation of 3,000 feet, but everywhere accessible. From this range several rivulets have their source, irrigating the country in every direction. Mount St. Catherine towers 3,200 feet above the level of the sea. Several elevations are given off from the great chain in a south-east direction, forming rich vallies. The southern portions of the island, however, are comparatively level, and consist of alluvial plains with numerous coral formations.

The principal rivers, none of which can be called navigable, are Great Bucolet, Duguisne, and Antoine, on the windward; and St. John's and Beau Sejour, on the leeward. Several hot chalybeate and sulphureous springs exist. In the centre of the island, at an elevation of 1,740 feet, amid mountain scenery, is situated the "Grand Etang," an almost perfectly circular fresh water lake, 2½ miles in circumference and fourteen feet deep. "Around this lake is a superb sylvan amphitheatre of mountains, clothed in all the verdant grandeur of the tropics." Another lake, (Antoine,) having similar characteristics, is found on the east coast, only half a mile from the sea. Both lakes are supposed to be of volcanic origin. On the south shores, near Point Saline, there are extensive salt ponds.

The geology of the island is very complicated and irregular. The mineral substances found are iron in various forms, and specimens of natural magnet. The great mass of the mountains consists of sand-stone, greywacke, hornblende and argillaceous schist. Sulphur and fuller's earth are abundant, and the bed of the adjacent ocean is of coralline formation. The soil varies with the external features of the country: in the lowlands, consisting of rich black mould on a substratum of light colored clay, while in the high and central situations, the soil is of a dingy red or brick color.

The products of this island are similar to the others composing the West Indies. The exports consist of sugar, &c., to the annual value of £200,000, and the imports amount to about £140,000 annually.

The government, at the head of which is a Lieutenant-Governor, is similar in every respect to that of Jamaica. Revenue is raised to the amount of £16,000 or £17,000 annually. The militia of the island consists of seven regiments. There is no paper money, and the annual amount of coin in circulation is only £50,000. Churches and schools are provided for the people, and in part supported by the colonial government. The Catholics and Wesleyan Methodists have establishments here.

The island is divided into six parishes, viz.: St. Patrick, St. Andrew, St. John, St. Mark, St. David, and St. George. St. George, the capital, is situated within an amphitheatre of hills, on the west side of the island. The houses are well and tastefully-built, of stone or brick, with tiled roofs. The town is divided into upper and lower—the latter, or carénage, being principally occupied with stores, ship-yards and wharves. The harbor is excellent, and well-protected with fortifications; it is said to be capable of containing 1,000 ships of 350 tons each, secure from storms. The town is supplied with water from a spring, some distance away, and is conveyed in iron pipes.

The dependencies of Grenada are the Island of Cariacou, and such of the small islands, called Grenadines, as lie between it and Grenada. Carriacou constitutes a parish, containing, according to estimate, 6,913 acres of land, and is about 19 miles in circumference.

Grenada was discovered by Columbus in 1498. It was settled by the French, from Martinique, in 1650. The British have held it since 1783.

ST. VINCENT.

This, the most beautiful of the West-India Islands, lies in 13° 10′ 15″ north latitude, and 60° 37′ 57″ west longitude. It is 18 miles long, and 11 miles broad, with an area of 131 square miles.

The island is mountainous, but the hills subside from the centre to the coast, and are capable of cultivation. Volcanic action is perceptible, and earthquakes frequent. The geological formations and soils are much similar tô those of Grenada. The island is frequently visited by hurricanes, but is generally very healthy. The dependencies within the government of St. Vincent, are:—the islands of Bequia, with its fine harbor, called Admiralty Bay; Union; Mustique and Canouan. There are also a large number of smaller islets and cayos belonging to the group.

St. Vincent is divided into five parishes, viz.: St. George, Charlotte, St. Andrew, St. David, and St. Patrick. Within the first stands the capital, Kingstown, near the south-west extremity of the island, and on a fine and deep bay, protected by fortifications. Three miles from Kingstown is Calliagua, the harbor of which is excellent. There are also the towns of New-Edinburg, Layou, Barouallie, &c. The value of exports from this island is about £350,000 annually, and the imports about £160,000.

This island was settled by the French, and during the wars of the last century very frequently changed masters. It was finally confirmed to Great Britain in 1783.

BARBADOES

Lies centrally in latitude 13° 5′ north, and in longitude 59° 41′ west, and is about 22 miles long, and 14 in breadth. Barbadoes is generally level, except in the north-east, and has a very beautiful appearance, owing to the extent of cultivation, its sloping fields and terraces. Dense forests formerly covered the island, of which portions still remain. The base of the island is calcareous rock, formed of madrepores and other marine concretions, and is probably of volcanic origin, as the majority of the adjacent islands. The soil varies much; in some districts it is sandy and light, in others a rich black earth, and in several places spongy. Clay and argillaceous deposits form extensive beds, and penetrate to a great depth. The climate is hot, but very healthy, owing to the free circulation of the sea breezes.

There are ten parishes, named after a variety of saints. BRIDGETOWN, the capital, extends along the shore of the beautiful Bay of Carlisle for two miles, and contains about 2,000 houses. The barracks are spacious and handsome. The square, on which is a statue of Nelson, is surrounded by the best buildings in the town. The government-house stands about a mile off, and is a handsome structure. The fortifications are ample and well-provided. Codrington College is the principal seat of learning—the island is well-provided with inferior schools. The government and laws are similar to those of Jamaica, and are presided over by a governor. The commerce of this island is extensive. The exports amount annually to £700,000. The annual expenses of the government is about £18,000, but including the expenses of the military, about £75,000.

Barbadoes was not marked on the maps until about 1600, and the date of its discovery is uncertain. It has always been an English settlement The island has been frequently visited by hurricanes.

ST. LUCIA.

THIS fine island is in lat. 13° 15′, and long. 60° 58′. Length 32 miles, and breadth 12 miles, having an area of 225 square miles. The approach to this island, which is divided longitudinally by a ridge of hills, from the south, is very remarkable. Two rocks, called "Sugar loaves," rise perpendicularly out of the sea, and shoot to a great height in parallel cones, standing on either side of the entrance into a small but deep bay, and are covered with evergreen foliage. Behind this, the mountains, which run north and south, rise in the most fantastic shapes. When sailing along the shore, the variety of scenery is exquisitely beautiful: coves and bays fringed with luxuriant cane-fields, and flotillas of fishing and passage boats add life and animation to the scene. On the west, there is an excellent harbor, called "Little Careenage," with three careening places, one for large ships and the others for frigates. It is accessible only to one vessel at a time, but capable of holding thirty ships of the line. The plains throughout the island are well watered, and the mountains clothed with valuable timber.

CASTRIES, the capital and only town, is situated at the bottom of a large and winding bay of the same name. Pidgeon Island is six miles distant from the harbor of St. Lucia, and in a military point of view is of great importance to the colonies, being within a short distance from Martinique, and commanding a view of every ship that may enter or depart from that island. It is, moreover, valuable for a fine and extensive anchorage between it and the northern part of St. Lucia. It is well fortified, and has good barracks.

St. Lucia is divided into Basseterre, or the Low Territory to the Leeward, and Capis-terre, the High or Windward Territory. The former is well cultivated and most populous, but the climate is unwholsome from stagnant pools and morasses. The latter division is also unwholsome, but it becomes less so, as the woods are cleared away.

The imports and exports are comparatively small: the former amount to about £90,000, and the latter to £280,000 annually. The colonial revenue amounts to £14,000 annually.

St. Lucia was settled by the English in 1635, but has frequently changed masters. Since 1803, it has remained in the hands of Great Britain.

DOMINICA.

The Island of Dominica is situated in 15° 25′ N. lat., and 51° 16′ W. long., and is about 29 miles in length and 16 in breadth, containing 275 square miles.

Dominica was the first land seen by Columbus on his second voyage, on Sunday, 3d November, 1493, from which circumstance it was so named by the great navigator. It was claimed by Spain, France and England, and for some time its occupancy remained neutral with the three powers. In 1759 it fell under the dominion of Great Britain, and was confirmed to that nation by the treaty of Paris, 1763. The lands were soon after sold under a commission from the crown, and under this measure 96,344 acres (one-half the island) was disposed of in lots of from 50 to 100 acres, producing £312,000 sterling. The lands occupied by the original settlers were confirmed to them. In 1778 the island fell into the hands of the French, but was restored in 1783. During the war of 1805, the capital was burnt by a French expedition, but the colony was saved to England by the gallantry of the inhabitants. The island has since remained in the hands of the English.

Dominica is a volcanic island, with rugged mountains and fertile intervening vallies, watered by about thirty fine rivers and numberless rivulets, springs and water-falls, which descend with great impetuosity from the hills, and under the umbrageous canopy of lofty and magnificent forests, form the most romantic cascades. The highest mountain, Morne Diablotin, is 5,314 feet above the level of the sea;—there are other elevations, but inferior to this in height. About the centre of the island, on the summit of a high mountain, there is a lake of fresh water, deep, and in some places unfathomable, and probably the site of a crater now extinct. Several mountains are continually burning with sulphur, and in numerous places warm and mineral springs issue from the hills. The sulphureous exhalations from these are very strong;—too penetrating for respiration, and the soil or sulphur and sand around these souffrieres is too hot for the feet, and scarcely firm enough to tread upon. Owing to the dense vegetation and supineness of the inhabitants, no explorations have been undertaken, and nothing is accurately known of the geology of the island. It is said that gold and silver mines exist, and that the latter metal was formerly found in abundance.

The soil, in some places, is a light brown colored mould, which appears to have washed down from the mountains and mixed with decayed vegetable matter. In the level country towards the sea, and in many districts in the interior, it is a fine, deep, black mould, peculiarly adapted to the sugar cane, coffee, cocoa, and all other articles of tropical produce. The substratum is a yellow or brick clay in some parts; in others, it is a stiff terrace, and frequently very stony. Large quantities of excellent free stone has been quarried in the Savanna, and at one time it formed an article of export to Guadaloupe and elsewhere.

The climate is much assimilated to that of the West Indies generally. Rains are very heavy here, more so than in the other island, and frequently do great damage to the plantations. Dominica, however, is very free from thunder storms and earthquakes. It is one of the best watered of the Caribbean islands, and with its rich soil, has a luxuriant vegetation. The woods afford vast supplies of valuable timber, consisting of locust, bully-tree, mastic, cinnamon, rose-wood, yellow sanders, mahogany, iron-wood, cedar, and various other sorts, useful for building, furniture, dyeing, and other purposes.

The government consists of a Lieutenant-Governor, a Legislative Council of eight, an Executive Council of twelve, and a Representative Legislative Assembly of twenty members. The general business is managed as in the other colonies. The militia consists of 1,200 men. Several churches, supported by fixed revenues, and schools, exist in the settlement. The colonial expenses are very light.

The commerce of Dominica employs about 6,000 tons of shipping. The exports amount to about £100,000, and the imports to about £80,000 sterling per annum. The United States have little connection here. The produce of Dominica consists of sugar and coffee.

Roseau, the capital, is situated on a point of land on the south-west of the island, which point forms two bays—Woodbridge's to the north, and Charlotteville to the south. "The landscape, behind the town, is beautifully grand: indeed, the whole prospect from the edge of Morne Bruce, a lofty table rock occupied by the garrison, is one of the very finest in the West Indies. The valley runs up for many miles in a gently inclined plane between mountains of irregular heights and shapes, most of which are clothed up to their cloudy canopies with rich pastures of green coffee, which perfumes the whole atmosphere, even to some distance over the sea; the river rolls a deep and roaring stream down the middle of the vale, and is joined at the outlet of each side ravine by a mountain-torrent, while at the top, where the rocks converge into an acute angle, a cascade falls from the apex, in a long sheet of silvery foam. Beneath, the town presents a different appearance from what it does at sea; the streets are long and spacious, regularly paved, and intersecting each other at right angles; there is one large square or promenade ground; and the shingled roofs of the houses, tinged with the intense blue of the heaven above them, seem like the newest slates, and remind one of that clear and distinct look which the good towns of France have when viewed from an eminence.

"The roadstead of Roseau (it can scarcely be called a harbor) is very capacious and safe, except in the hurricane months, (from the end of August to October,) when the sea, from the southward, tumbles into the Bay in a terrific manner, sometimes rising to an alarming height. On the last day of September, 1780, the sea suddenly rose to the height of 21 feet perpendicular above its usual level, destroying several houses in front of the beach, and wrecking many vessels. The fortifications of Roseau, namely, Young's Fort, Melville's Battery, Bruce's Hill and Fort Demoulin are very strong and commanding positions.

"Prince Rupert's Bay, on the north-west of the island, is three miles broad, and one and a half deep, and commodious enough for the reception of 1,000 vessels. It is surrounded by two high mountains, called the Cabriettes, the inner of which is 500 and the outer 600 feet in perpendicular height, both out of reach of any other elevated land. Fort Shirley lies between the two Cabrittes, with a rich plain of 100 acres extent at its base, and in time of war the fortifications on these heights might be rendered as strong as Gibraltar. The Grand Savanna, nine miles from Prince Rupert's Bay, and twelve from Roseau, is a fine, fertile, elevated plain, upwards of a mile in extent, and at a good distance from the neighboring mountains, whose terraces jut out from their breasts—around whose declivities flourish the richest verdure, while murmuring cascades of bubbling brooks burst through the luxuriant vegetation, or roll along the hilly avenues, surrounded by magnificent piles of rocks, sometimes black and bare, sometimes green, with countless traceries of lovely creepers interspersed with gigantic ferns and lofty palms."—[*Martin's Br. Col. p.* 74.

ANTIGUA.

THIS fertile island lies in lat. 17° 3′ N., and long. 62° 7′ W. It is 20 miles long and about 54 in circumference, containing 108 square miles. Antigua was discovered by Columbus in 1493, and named by him from a church in Seville, "Santa Maria de la Antigua." Next to Barbadoes and St. Christopher's, it is the oldest British colony in the West Indies, having been settled in 1633. In 1616 the French got temporary possession, and plundered the planters. By the treaty of Breda, 1688, the island was finally settled under British dominion, and by means of free trade, and under the auspices of the Codrington family, rapidly prospered.

Antigua is nearly oval in shape, with an extremely indented coast, and is almost surrounded by islets, rocks and shoals. In the north-east it is low and marshy. Towards the south and south-west, the elevations gradually increase, forming round-backed hills of moderate elevation, generally running east and west, intersected by cultivated vallies, and partially clothed with small trees and brushwood. Boggies' Hill, in the Sheckerley range, 1,210 feet high, is the greatest culmination. The highest district takes its rise from Falmouth, and continues to Five Island Harbor.

No island in the West Indies can boast of so many excellent bays and harbors, but they are all, except those of St. John, English Harbor and Falmouth, difficult of access. The others are St. Freeman's, (at the entrance of English Harbor,) Rendezvous Bay, Morris's Bay, Lydcsenfis Bay, Parham, Nonsuch, and Willoughby Harbors, and Indian Creek, contiguous to Freeman's Bay.

The soil of the high lands is of a red clay, argillaceous, with a substratum of marl; on the low lands it is a rich, dark mould, on a substratum of clay. In some of the formations animal remains have been found, and petrified weeds. Agate, cornelian, and chalcedony, are frequently met with. Nitrate of potash, like a hoar frost, covers the flat, oozy shore, which bounds the Bay of Falmouth. On a general view, the geological formation of the island may be said to consist of marl, conglomerate chert and trap. Marl forms the greatest part, and extends over the whole of the north and north-east; trap the south-west—conglomerate, an intervening section, extending inland from St. John's Harbor, and chert embracing a section with the latter.

Owing to the elevation of the land and the absence of forests the climate is dry, and the rainy season uncertain in its return. The temperature is less subject to variations than in other islands—the thermometer seldom ranges more than four degrees in the 24 hours. On the hills the heat is moderated by the sea breezes.

The average population of Antigua to the square mile, is 340. The great bulk of the people are employed in agriculture, and the manufactures are confined to sugar, molasses, and rum. The total inhabitants number about 37,000.

Antigua totally abolished slavery in 1834, without waiting the intermediate apprenticeship, as in the other slave colonies. It has since improved, both in physical and moral character, and the value of property is said to have been enhanced.

This island has a Governor, Legislative Council, and House of Assembly. The governor of Antigua is also governor of Montserrat, Barbadoes, St. Christopher's, Nevis, Anguilla, the Virgin Islands, and Dominica. The governor is chancellor of each of the islands, by virtue of his office. The courts of this island are a Court of King's Bench, a Court of Common Pleas, and a Court of Exchequer.

The militia consists of a brigade of artillery, a squadron of light dragoons, and two regiments of infantry, in all consisting of 945 men.

The revenue and expenditure is under £20,000 annually, exclusive of the local revenues.

Between 400 and 500 ships are entered to and depart from Antigua annually. The imports may be valued at from £90,000 to £100,000, and the exports at about £200,000.

St. John's is the capital of the island. It is regularly laid out, pretty large, and built on the north-west side, at the head of a large, but not deep harbor, the north side of which is partly formed by an elevated rock, called *Rat Island*, about midway up the harbor, and connected with the main land by a causeway, which is submerged at high water. English Harbor is a very complete dock-yard, on a small scale, surrounded by hills, on one of which, at the north-east, is the Naval Hospital.

With the exception of a few scanty rivulets amongst the hills, the whole island is destitute of running water, and the wells, heretofore dry, have proved brackish; ponds and tanks are, therefore, the mainstay of the planters. The plan of boring for water should be adopted.

BARBUDA.

This island, the property of the Codrington family, is situated 36 miles north of Antigua. It is about 20 miles broad, and contains about 1,500 inhabitants. The interior is level, the soil fertile, and the air of great salubrity. It was settled by a party of colonists from St. Christopher's, under Sir Thomas Warner, whom the Caribs compelled at first to retreat, but the English finally returned, and quickly began cultivation. The chief trade of the colonists consists in raising cattle, swine, poultry, horses and mules, for sale in the neighboring islands. There is a good roadstead; but the coast is dangerous.

NEVIS.

THIS delightful little island is separated from St. Christopher's by a strait about two miles broad, and full of shoals, in latitude 17° 14′ north, and longitude 63° 3′ west. It was first colonized by a few English, in 1628. Nevis is a single mountain, about four miles in length, three in breadth, and eight leagues in circumference, with an area of 20 square miles, springing, with an easy ascent, as it were, out of the sea, and is evidently of volcanic origin. The summit has the appearance of a crater. Hot and mineral springs are found a short distance from Clarke's Hill, the heat of which varies from 100° to 108° Fahr. At the base of the mountain is a border of level land, extremely fertile, and highly cultivated. A complete forest of evergreen trees grows like a ruff or collar round the neck of the high land, where cultivation ceases.

The island is divided into five parishes, and it has three tolerable roadsteads. CHARLESTOWN, the seat of government, lies along the shore of a wide, curving bay, and the mountain begins to rise immediately behind it, in a long and verdant acclivity. The court-house is a handsome building, with a square in front; it contains a hall on the ground-floor, for the Assembly and the courts of law, and another room up stairs for the Council. Schools and churches are provided for all.

The chief production of this island is sugar, the cultivation of which adds much to the richness of the scenery, when contrasted with the mountain forests. The value of exports is about £60,000, and of imports, £20,000 annually. The affairs of the island are managed by a Lieutenant-Governor and Council, and the House of Representatives. The laws and regulations of the island are the same as those of Antigua.

MONTSERRAT.

MONTSERRAT lies in 16° 47′ N. lat., and 62° 13′ 25″ W. long., 22 miles S. W. of Antigua, N. W. of Guadaloupe, and S. E. of Nevis, respectively. In length about 12 miles, and in breadth about 7½, it contains 47 square miles, and has a circumference of 34 miles.

The isle was discovered by Columbus, and named from its serrated mountainous appearance. It was settled by the English in 1632; in 1664 it was taken by the French, but restored at the peace of Breda, and has ever since continued under the British flag. Like many others of the West India Islands, this is probably of volcanic origin. It is very rugged, and some of the mountains are inaccessible. The same geological features mark Montserrat as are found in the neighboring isles. The hills abound with carbonate of lime, iron pyrites, and aluminous earth. The soil is in general thin, gravelly, dry, light, and thickly covered with blocks of clay and sand-stone, except in the vallies, where the loamy earth is deposited by the rains.

The coasts are generally inaccessible; on the south there is no approach, the sea for a mile or two is studded with rocks and shelving banks of coral, which prohibit even the approach of boats.

PLYMOUTH, the capital, is a small, but extremely well-built town; and the houses, constructed of a fine gray stone, have a substantial and comfortable appearance.

The church and schools are supported chiefly by the government, or the Bishop. The executive is embodied in the government of Antigua, but the islanders enjoy a separate Council and House of Assembly, The militia consists of 184 rank and file. The revenue varies from £5,000 to £6,000 annually.

The principal exports from Montserrat consist of sugar and other general produce. The imports and exports may be stated at £25,000 respectively, per annum. Cotton has been lately introduced, and is now being cultivated with success. The currency of the island is £210 = £100 sterling. There is no paper money, and the whole circulating medium is not more than £2,000 sterling.

ST. CHRISTOPHER'S.

St. Christopher's, or St. Kitt's, called by the Caribs *Licmuiga*, or *fertile isle*, is in lat. 17° 18′ N., and long. 62° 40′ W. In circumference it is 72 miles, and in area about 68 square miles, being shaped somewhat like Italy—as an outstretched leg. This singular-looking but beautiful island was discovered by Columbus in 1493, and received the name of the great navigator himself. The island was at that time densely populated. In 1623 the first settlements were formed by the English, and in 1625 a colony of Frenchmen landed here. A war with the natives ensuing, these parties united for the time, and succeeded in subduing the common enemy. In 1627 the French and English agreed to partition the island. The island was divided into upper and lower—the former and most extensive, called Capis-terre, belonging to the French; and the lower, called Basse-terre, alone inhabited by the English. The Spaniards in 1629 destroyed all the settlements, but such was the immigration to the West Indies at that period, that the next year saw 6,000 white inhabitants on the island. The French and English themselves at length disagreed, and war breaking out between the two nations, many severe and protracted battles were fought by the colonists, which ended in the subjugation of the English. The peace of Breda restored to the English their portion of the island, and peace reigned for 20 years. In 1689 hostilities recommenced, and the British colonists were forced into the sea, their property falling a prey to fire. The following year the French were driven from the island, and for many years the whole remained in the hands of the English. The treaty of Ryswick restored to the French their possessions, which they retained until 1702, when the island was captured, and, by the treaty of Utrecht in 1713, entirely ceded to the British Crown. Most of the French moved to San Domingo. After this, the island rapidly prospered. In 1782, the French squadron, under De Bouillé, attacked the colony, and captured it before relief could be afforded by the British navy. The treaty of 1783 gave the island again to Great Britain, and it has since remained a colony of that nation.

St. Christopher's is an irregular, oblong island:—through its middle runs a series of mountains from north to south, in the centre of which stands Mount Misery, 3,700 feet in perpendicular height, and, though evidently of volcanic origin, clothed with the finest wood and pasture, almost to the very summit. From the foot of the hills the country has a uniform sloping direction, stretching from a centre to a circumference bounded by a coast every inch of which is in the highest state of cultivation. There are several other peaks in the mountains, varying in height from 200 to 800 feet. There are but four streams in the island. In the lowland, springs are plentiful, but their waters are unfit for drinking, owing to strong saline impregnations; rain-water is that commonly made use of. The soil and climate is analogous to that of the adjacent islands; but from its smallness and elevation the air is perfectly dry and very salubrious.

The commerce of this island is not large. The import and export trade is nearly balanced, amounting each to about £160,000 annually, and employing, respectively, about 300 vessels, and a tonnage of 135,000 tons. The government consists of a Lieutenant-Governor, Council, and House of Assembly, to which a deputy from Anguilla is sent. Education and religion are generously encouraged. The revenue of the island is derived from customs, licenses, &c., as in other colonies The expenses of government amount to some £6,000 annually.

ANGUILLA.

ANGUILLA, or Snake Island, is situated in latitude 18° north, and longitude 64° west, being 45 miles north-west of St. Kitts, and separated only by a narrow channel from St. Martin's. The island is about 30 miles long, and scarcely three miles broad.

Anguilla was discovered and colonized by the British, in 1650, and has ever since remained with that power, subject, however, to predatory incursions of the French and pirates. The island is flat, without mountains or rivers, and has a deep, chalky soil. Nine-tenths of the country is under cultivation. In the centre of the island is a salt lake, yielding annually 3,000,000 bushels of salt, the chief portion of which is exported to the United States, and other American republics. Sugar, cotton, maize and provisions, are raised in abundance, and numbers of cattle are reared by the farmers. The climate is extremely healthy, and the people strong and active. The colonists have a chief or head magistrate, who is confirmed in his office by the government of Antigua, and a Deputy is sent to the Assembly at St. Christopher's to represent the interests of the people.

TORTOLA, AND THE VIRGIN ISLANDS.

THE Virgin Islands were discovered by Columbus, in 1493, and named in honor of the 11,000 virgins in the Roman ritual. Excepting Anegada, they are a cluster of lofty islands and rocks, about 50 in number, to the north-west of the Leeward Islands, extending about 24 leagues, east and west, and 16 north and south. Tortola, on which is the capital, is in latitude 18° 20′ north, and longitude 64° 39′ west. The English, Danes, &c., divide the sovereignty of this group. The English islands are:—Tortola, Virgin Gorda, or Penniston, (sometimes corrupted into Spanishtown,) Jos Van Dykes, Guana Isle, Beef and Thatch islands, Anegada, Nichar, Prickly-Pear, Camanas, Ginger, Cooper's, Salt, St. Peter's, and several other smaller islands.

The Dutch Buccaneers were the first occupants of these islands, having settled at Tortola in 1648. A stronger party of English Buccaneers expelled them in 1666, and they were shortly afterwards annexed to the Leeward government.

Throughout they are rugged, precipitous and rocky. The shores are indented with bays, harbors and creeks, affording good shelter to shipping. The interior is still unoccupied, being almost inaccessible.

The capital, TORTOLA, is situated on the south side of the island of the same name, close to the water's edge, on a magnificent harbor, or basin, and forms one long stretch, curving at the base of a projecting point of land. In front of the town and harbor are a number of small islets, extending far to the southward, and forming the passage called Sir Francis Drake's Channel. The harbor of Tortola is 15 miles long, and 3½ in breadth, perfectly land-locked, and has in war time sheltered 400 vessels, waiting for convoy.

Previous to 1773, the government of these islands was entrusted to a Deputy-Governor, with a Council, who exercised in a summary manner the executive and legislative authority. At that date a local legislature, similar to that of the other islands, was conferred on them, with courts of justice. They are now under the government of St. Christopher's, possessing in Tortola, however, a Council and Assembly of their own. The militia consists of about 400 men, of all grades. The revenue and commerce of these islands are insignificant.

The Virgin Islands are celebrated for their great variety of fish, which are taken in vast quantities for market. In Penniston there are between 30 and 40 mines, which have been opened, 20 of which are at present filled up; the mines appear to be principally of copper and black lead,—some gold and copper have, many years back, been taken out. They are chiefly situated in the east part of the valley, at a place called Red-Point. None have even been disturbed for 90 years, except occasionally by a few persons, who may have gone there through curiosity to see them, and take a little of the ore. The lead is of a superior quality. There is an arsenic mine on Collins' Hill. The silver mine has been worked until stopped by government. Upon the top of Red-Point Hill, there is a quantity of quartz, and crystals have been taken from this mine. No one alive at this day has been able to state the quantity of gold and silver procured from the mines.

The area of the several Virgin Isles, in acres, is as follows:—Anegada, 31,200; Tortola, 13,300; Penniston, 9,500; Jos Van Dykes, 3,200; Peter's Island, 1,890; Beef Island, 1,560; Guana Island, 1,120; and 40 other islands, with areas varying from 900 acres to five acres each, comprising, in the whole, 58,649 acres. Of these about 3,000 acres are planted with canes; 1,000 with cotton; 33,500 in pasture; 11,400 in forest and brushwood; and of barren land, 7,257 acres. The quantity of stock on the lands is given by Martin, as follows:—horses, 240; mules and asses, 529; horned cattle, 2,597; sheep, 11,442; goats, 3,225; pigs, 1,825; poultry, 44,050; and of fish, caught within the year, about 15,000,000 lbs., the whole yielding, within the year, property to the amount of £100,000 sterling. The total value of property, moveable and immoveable, is estimated at £1,000,000 sterling.

THE BAHAMA ISLANDS.

THIS multitudinous group of isles, reefs, and keys, termed Lucayos, from the Spanish words *Los Cayos*, (anglicé, the Keys,) or Bahamas, extend in a crescent-like form, from Mantilla reef, in 27° 50′ N. latitude, and 79° 05′ W. longitude, to Turk's Island, in 21° 23′ N. latitude, and 71° 55′ W. longitude, a distance of about 600 miles, not including various sand banks and coral reefs, stretching to a great extent westward.

San Salvador, Cat Island or Guanahani, one of this group, is celebrated as being the first land discovered by Columbus. This interesting event occurred on the 12th October, 1492. The Bahamas were then densely peopled by the Indian race, who were soon shipped off by the Spaniards to labor in the mines of Peru and Mexico. In 1529, New-Providence was colonized by the English, who, however, were driven off by the Spaniards, in 1641. In 1666, the English again settled here, and the islands remained in their hands until 1703, when the French and Spaniards again expelled them, destroying their plantations. The Bahamas now became the rendezvous of pirates, whose proceedings, so injurious to commerce, were eventually suppressed by the English, and themselves reduced to obedience. During the American war, the Bahamas were plundered by a squadron from Philadelphia, under Com. Hopkins, and the Governor carried off. In 1781, the Spaniards took possession of the isles, but they were restored to the British crown, in 1783, having, however, been recaptured for England by the enterprising Captain Devaux, of South Carolina. The Bahamas, since that period, have remained in the peaceful possession of Great Britain.

All these islands are little elevated above the sea, and are evidently the work of the coral insects, whose labors, though apparently insignificant, have furnished so many beautiful spots fit for the residence of civilized man. Few only are inhabited; some present to the eye a few scattered plantations, and others are tenantless. Generally speaking the Bahamas are low and flat. The ocean, close to the isles, is almost unfathomable. Reefs of rocks, or rather walls of coral, bound them after the manner observable in the South Sea isles.

New-Providence, from its harbor and relative situation in respect to the Florida channel, is considered the most important of the group, and on it is situated Nassau, the seat of government for the whole, and the head-quarters of the naval and military establishments. It is 21 miles from east to west, and seven from north to south, mostly flat and covered with extensive lagoons. A range of rocky hills runs along part of the island from east to west, at a very short distance from the sea. On this ridge many of the buildings of Nassau are erected, including the government-house, and at its extremity to the west are the barracks and Fort Charlotte. Another ridge called the Blue Hills, runs in a direction nearly parallel with the former, and 2½ miles distant.

The principal works of defence in the Bahamas are at Nassau, and have been constructed to protect the harbor and town. Fort Charlotte is the main work, which, with its several outworks, is exceedingly strong. Fort Stanley commands the western entrance to the harbor. There are other forts in the neighborhood, both on the main land and on islets in the bay. Few places, indeed, are so well fortified as this important station.

With regard to the other islands, we can do little more than specify their names. Hog Island is little more than a reef of rocks, which forms part of the N. harbor of New Providence. Rose Island, to the N. point, and E. of New Providence, is about nine miles long and a quarter broad. It affords protection to "Cochrane's Anchorage." Harbor Island is five miles long and two broad, lat. 25° 29′ N., long. 76° 34′ W., very healthy, and a favorite resort for convalescents. Turk's Island, lat. 21° 32 N., long. 71° 05′ W., principal mart for salt-making, peculiarly healthy, and a point of military importance in regard to St. Domingo. North and South Biminis. These isles are about seven miles long, in lat. 25° 40′ N. long. 79° 18′ W., healthy, well-wooded and watered, capacious anchorage, and in the event of a war, highly important for the protection of the trade of the Gulf of Florida, to the E. of which they are situate. The anchorage on the gulf side can admit any class of shipping. Those not mentioned above are in chief—ANDROS, long (22 leagues) and irregular, to the W. of New-Providence eight leagues.—Between them a tongue of ocean water runs in S. E. as far as lat. 23° 21′, called the Gulf of Providence; access difficult from reefs. Off its S. E. end are the ESPIRITO SANTO ISLES. The BERRY ISLANDS, an irregular group. Several small harbors formed by them where refreshments may he had. The S. E. of these islands are denominated the Frozen Keys, and the N. the Stirrup Keys. Off the northernmost of the latter there is anchorage on the bank, in lat. 25° 49′. The GREAT and LITTLE ISAACS. W. ¾ N., 48 miles from Little Stirrup Key, is the easternmost of three small keys called the Little Isaacs, and five miles further is the westernmost key of the same name; these are from 50 to 60 or 70 feet in length; the middle key is not so large. These keys are situated on the western end of Gingerbread Ground, which extends five leagues E by S. from the weathernmost rock, or Little Isaac, is about five miles wide near the east end, and has some dangerous sharp rocks upon it, with only seven to nine feet of water. The NARANJOS, or two ORANGE KEYS, lie four miles within the edge of the bank, in lat. 24° 55′, and long. 79° 7′. ELEUTHERA extends E. nine leagues, S. E. four leagues, and S. ½ E. twelve leagues. GUANAHANI, or CAT ISLAND, N. W. eight leagues and a half E. ½ S. from Powel's Point, in Eleuthera; it thence extends south-eastward 15 leagues, having a breadth of three to seven miles. Eleven miles south-east from Cat Island is CONCEPTION ISLAND, of about seven miles in length, N. E. and S. W., and three miles in breadth. YUMA or LONG ISLAND, 17 leagues in length from S. E. to N. W. S. by W., 17½ leagues from the S. point of Long Island, is CAYO VERDE or Green Key. From Cayo Verde, the edge of the bank forms a great and deep bay to the N. W., in the S. W. part of which is CAYO DE SAL, at the distance of ten leagues from the former. EGG ISLAND is small, in lat. 25° 31′. There are many smaller keys and rocks too numerous to mention.

An idea of the number and extent of the isles will be conveyed by the following statement of the lands in the Bahamas from an official return dated in 1827.

	Acres Granted.	*Acres Vacant.*	*Total Area.*
New Providence, Hog Island, Rose Island and Keys	33,281	31,000	64,281
Andros Islands, Sheep, Grass, and Green Keys	25,380	475,000	500,380
Berry Islands, Biminis, and Chain of Keys	2,116	18,000	20,116
Grand Bahama and its Keys	6,019	282,000	288,019
Great and Little Abaco, and Chain of Keys	24,715	296,000	320,715
Harbor Islands	—	1,000	1,0 0
Eleuthera, Royal and Egg Island, and Keys	43,922	227,000	270,922
St. Salvador, Leeward, and Little Isle	50,868	190,000	240,868
Watling's, and Windward Little Isles	18,015	10,000	28,015
Great and Little Exuma	32,876	58,000	90,876
Rum Key	15,434	5,000	20,434
Ragged Islands and Keys	—	3,000	3,000
Long Island	67,260	86,000	153,260
Crooked and Acklin's Islands and Long Keys	31,509	130,000	161,509
Atwood Keys	—	18,000	18,000
Mayaguana and French Keys	—	60,000	60,000
Great and Little Heneogue	6,210	351,000	357,210
The Calcos Islands	37,881	171,000	208,881
Turk's Island	—	9,000	9,000
Keysal and Anguilla, &c	—	10,000	10,000
Total acres	395,486	2,431,000	2,826,486

The Bahamas are formed of calcareous rocks, which are composed of corals, shells, madrepores, and various marine deposits hardened into solid masses in the revolution of ages. The deposits appear to have been thrown up in regular strata, at various periods; and their upper surface deeply honey-combed, bears evident marks of having been long covered by the waters of the ocean. No primitive formation has been found, and the bases of the islands are evidently coral reefs, originating with the Moluscæ, which, unpossessed of locomotive powers, have organic functions destined for the secretion of the lime required for their calcareous coverings. Marl is formed on many of the out islands, and here and there strata of argillaceous earth may be met with. Meteoric stones have been discovered rudely sculptured with human features by the aborigines; but whether found on the islands or brought thither, it is impossible to say; and at Turk's Island a great number of calcareous balls have been found, all bearing an indentation, as though they had been suspended to a pedicle. Their origin or nature is equally unknown. In confirmation of the idea that these islands have been raised from the bottom of the ocean on pillars of coral, after the manner of the eastern and southern hemisphere, it may be stated, many of their salt water lakes and ponds communicate with the ocean, as shown by their sea fish. Some of them are so deep as not to allow soundings; and the water in them rises and falls with the tides on the coast.

Situated at the mouth of the Gulf of Florida, placed by geographical position without the tropics, removed from the excessive heat of a vertical sun, and the intense cold of a northern winter, the Bahamas enjoy a climate mild, equable and delightful. To the islands within the torrid zone they are nearly akin—in the little variety of season, the natural productions of the earth, and the manners and customs of the people; but the decided difference in the mean annual temperature, and the more robust and healthy appearance of all classes of the community, gives to the Bahamas all the appearance of a country situated in a more temperate latitude. The summer and winter (hot and cold,) wet and dry seasons, are well marked; the cold season lasts from November to May, during which period the sky is remarkably clear and serene, the mercury at noon, Fahr., occasionally below 60°, seldom beyond 70° or 75°, while a refreshing north breeze tempers the mid-day heat, and the mornings and evenings are cool and invigorating. From May to November the heat increases and decreases as the sun advances and retires from its great northern declination. The thermometer ranges from 75° to 85° Fahr., rarely higher: a fine breeze frequently blows from the east, with cooling showers of rain, before the summer solstice and towards the autumnal equinox. The mornings then have a peculiar freshness, and the evenings a softness and beauty unknown to colder countries. From the flatness of the isles, the full benefit of the sea breezes is felt throughout every part of each island.

European and tropical vegetables and fruits thrive and are abundant; beef, mutton and poultry good and plentiful: the shores abound with fish, and there is turtle enough among the Bahamas to supply all Europe; almost every island has pretty good water; ambergris is occasionally found; cotton was formerly an abundant article of exportation, and there is scarcely a spot in any of the islands that is not covered with a luxuriant vegetation.

Ship timber, of a most excellent quality, is abundant on many of the Bahama Islands; logwood, brazilletto, fustic, green ebony and satin wood are produced in considerable quantities for building or planking vessels; the cedar, horseflesh, madeira, mastic, and other durable woods, in great plenty, and there is an inexhaustible supply of very superior firewood; sponges of good quality abound on the island shores, and the water from the wells at New Providence has the desirable quality of keeping good at sea for any length of time.

As in the other West India possessions, the government of the Bahamas is modelled after that of England: viz. a House of Assembly or Commons, consisting of 30 members, returned from the several islands; an Executive and Legislative Council of 12 members, approved by the Crown, and a Governor, who is commander-in-chief of the militia, and has the power of summoning or dissolving the legislative body, and of putting a negative on its proceedings. The electors are free white persons of 21 years of age, who have resided 12 months within the government, for six of which they must have been householders or freeholders, or in default of that have paid duties to the amount of £50. To become a representative, the person must own 200 acres of cultivated land, or property to the value of £2,000 currency.

There are several courts at law, such as the Supreme Court, which holds its sessions in terms of three weeks, with the powers of the common law courts of Westminster, and its practice modelled on that of the King's Bench, the Courts of Chancery, Error, Vice Admiralty, &c.

Nassau, in New Providence, as before observed, is the seat of government and the centre of commerce. It possesses a fine harbor, nearly landlocked, and on the south side of which the capital extends over a rather steep acclivity to the summit of a ridge, the west of which is crowned by a fortress of considerable strength, where the garrison is kept. The island is divided into parishes, each of which has its church, clergy, and school, liberally provided for. The streets are regularly laid out, the public buildings good, and activity and cleanliness immediately attracts the eye of a stranger.

Salt is manufactured on Exuma island in a pond of 223 acres; in Rugged Island in a pond of 42 acres; in Turk's Island in a pond of 130 acres; on Gunn's Key, and in a pond of 212 acres on Long Key; on Rum Key, in a pond of 650 acres; and in several ponds on Long Island, extent together, 308 acres. There are no mines in this colony.

On the island of New Providence are several private quarries of porous limestone, used in building houses, &c., and also for dripstones. It is in great abundance throughout the colony. Smacks and boats are employed in fishing, varying in size from 12 feet to 20 tons. Fish and turtle are worth, on an average, about 3½ pence per lb. There are a great abundance and variety of fish within the Bahamas Islands; there are no established fisheries, properly so called; many persons, however, get their livelihood by fishing and turtling on the coast of Cuba, and obtaining sponge on the Bahama Banks.

THE SWEDISH WEST INDIES.

The only colony belonging to the crown of Sweden in the West Indies is

ST. BARTHOLOMEW'S,

a small island about 12 miles south-east of St. Martin's, the area of which is estimated at 25 square miles, and the population at 15,000.

This island is mountainous and dangerous in approach, being beset with rocks and shoals. There is neither lake nor spring within its bounds; the inhabitants depend on the clouds for water, and when that fails, they procure it from the adjacent islands. It produces sugar, cotton, cocoa, tobacco and manioc; also iron-wood and lignumvitæ. A peculiar species of limestone, with which several of the islands are supplied, is found here, and forms an article of export.

Le Carenage is the only accessible port. It lies on the west side of the island, and is safe and commodious. Contiguous to this harbor stands Gustavia, the chief and only town. It is inhabited by Swedes, English, French, Danes, Americans, and Jews. The planters are chiefly of French origin, and about one-third the total population is composed of Irish Roman Catholics, who settled here in 1666.

St. Bartholomew's was colonized in 1648 by the French, under the direction of Poincy, the governor of St. Christopher's. The English attacked it, and plundered the settlements in 1689, from which period to 1697 it remained in their hands, and was then restored to France. Under this government the island made little advance in prosperity, and for a long time was more a resort for outlaws than a regular colony. In 1785, France ceded it to Sweden, in whose possession it still remains, and under whose government it has increased considerably in population and commercial importance. In 1848, slavery was abolished. We have no statistics of its condition.

THE SPANISH WEST INDIES.

The colonies of Spain, once stretching over more than one-half the New World, are now confined to the islands of Cuba and Porto Rico, and a few islets on the east of the latter. Her footing on the continent yielded to the force of revolution. These islands, however, are among the most fertile and valuable in the world, yielding large revenues to the mother country; and, together with the commercial advantages they afford to Spain, compensating in some degree for the loss of her former dominions.

CUBA.

This island, the largest, most flourishing, and important of the Antilles, was discovered by Columbus on the 28th October, 1492, and was first called Juanna, in honor of Prince Juan, son of Ferdinand and Isabella; afterwards Ferdinandina, in memory of the king; then successively Santiago and Ave Maria, in deference to the patron saint of Spain, and the virgin; and by Spanish geographers *La Lengua de pajaro*, as being descriptive of its form. The aboriginal name of "Cuba," however, by which it is generally known, has survived all efforts to supersede it by substitution.

Cuba is a long and narrow island, and in figure represents a crescent, having its convex to the north. Its western portion commands the entrance to the gulf of Mexico, dividing it midway between the peninsulas of Florida and Yucatan. In a military point of view it is the key to that important sea, and as such, in the possession of a large maritime power, might exert an all-powerful influence over the commerce of one-third of America. The distance from Cape Antonio, the most westerly portion of the island, (lat. 21° 54′ N. and long. 84° 57′ 15″ W.) to the nearest point of Yucatan, is 125 miles, and the distance from Point Icacos, the most northerly point, (lat. 23° 10′ N., long. 81° 11′ 45″ W.,) to Cape Sable, the most southerly point of Florida, is about 130 miles. Point Maysi, the eastern extremity of Cuba, (lat. 20° 16′ 40″ N., and long. 74° 7′ 23″ W.,) is 49 miles from Cape San Nicolas Mole, in Hayti; and Cabo de Cruz, the most southerly point of Cuba, is about 95 miles north of the most northerly point of Jamaica. The greatest length of the island, following the curve, is about 800 miles; the breadth varies from 130 to 25 miles, averaging about 80 miles. The coasts are much indented, and lined with numberless small islands, cayos, and reefs. The estimates of its area have on this account differed considerably, but including its principal dependencies it was calculated by Don Felipe Bauza at 3615 square leagues of 20 to the degree, equal to about 43,380 square miles.—(*Humboldt, Essai sur l'Isle de Cuba.*)

The physical conformation and productions of the island are second only in importance to its geographical position. Mountain chains traverse the whole length of the islands, giving off lateral ridges on both sides, with extensive intervening vallies, well watered by numberless fine streams, and fertile beyond exaggeration. Savannas and plains stretch from the mountains to the sea, and present a scene of cultivated fields clothed in perennial verdure, and producing all the staples and fruits of tropical countries. During the whole year vegetation is strong, and no season is without its peculiar fruits. So prolific indeed is the soil, that two, and sometimes three crops of grain are produced annually. The mountains are rich in minerals, particularly copper, iron, and natural magnet; and mines of gold and silver have been worked since the first period of its occupation. The copper of Cuba is very pure, and excellent in quality. Coal mines have likewise been opened, but it does not appear that they have been worked to any great extent. Marble of various kinds is met with, but from the rugged nature of the mountains, and the dense forests which everywhere loom amid the clouds, the geological structure of the island has not been well ascertained. There are several salt lakes in the interior, abounding in excellent fish, and mineral springs, impregnated with iron and iodine gush from the crevices, and up-spring from their sources in the hills. The scenery of the island is magnificent; from the elevations, the wide ocean, the multitude of islets embosomed on its surface, and the far distant shores of the adjacent continent, and large islands, and the shipping of all nations wending their pathless way through the waters, unfold to the eye such a scene as the imagination dares not to conceive. Majesty, beauty and wealth are before the spectator, and the effect is truly sublime. In the plains the scenery is changed, and the magnificence of the mountains is merged into the pastoral quietude of rural life, indicated by the teeming abundance which everywhere crowns the toil of the husbandman. Here wide plantations of sugar-cane —cotton—tobacco—and all the vigorous vegetation of the tropics, is seen to perfection, and vast herds of cattle roaming peacefnlly through the flowery savannas give token of the wealth and ease in which the people of this fine island pass their careless life.

Of the islands dependent on Cuba, the *Isla de Pinos* is the largest, and most worthy of especial notice. It lies off the south coast, near the west end of the island, being separated by a channel about 20 miles broad. The island itself is about 70 miles in circumference, mountainous, and covered with tall pines, from which it has its name. It is considered as an integral portion of Cuba, and its commerce, &c., is included in the statistics of that island. Formerly the resort of pirates, whose enormities were so dreaded by the West Indian, it is now the peaceful abode of a few fishermen, who employ themselves in the surrounding waters, and carry their productions to the markets of Cuba. Agriculture is little attended to, and the plantations are generally small. A view of any good map will show the position and names of the other islands which lie off the coast.

The progress of Cuba in population has been rapid. There have been but five or six censuses taken, the dates of which are exhibited in the annexed table. It will be observed, that an unusual increase occurs from 1827 to 1841, and from that period to 1847 a decrease of nearly 100,000. There is something wrong here, seeing that no adequate cause has operated to produce the increase from 1827 to 1841, nor yet to impede the usual increase from 1841 to 1847. The deficit in 1847 occurs among the blacks alone, and exhibits a decrease of about 25 per cent., a circumstance very improbable to occur without domestic war or pestilence. The official results, however, are below.

	1775.	1827.	1841.	1847.
Whites	96,440	311,051	418,291	425,770
Free Mulattoes	19,327	57,514	152,838	159,233
Free Blacks	11,520	48,980		
Slaves	44,333	286,942	436,624	323,759
Total	171,620	704,487	1,007,624	908,762

Censuses were also taken in 1791 and 1817, which exhibited aggregates, respectively, of 272,140 and 551,998. The following exhibits the movements in the enumerations, from period to period :

YEAR.	AGGREGATE POPULATION.			Movement. *Numerical.*	*per centum*	
1775	171,620					
1791	272,140	in 16 years	*increase*	100,520	58.5=3.6	per annum.
1817	551,998	" 26 "	"	279,858	102.8=3.9	"
1827	704,487	" 10 "	"	152,489	27.4=2.7	"
1841	1,007,624	" 14 "	"	303,137	43.0=3.0	"
1847	908,762	" 6 "	*decrease*	98,862	10.8=1.8	"

The proportion of sexes in the several races is thus—among the Europeans the males preponderate, in the ratio of 8 to 7, and among the slaves, as 9 to 5. Among the mulattoes and free negroes, the females exceed the males, respectively, in the ratio of 15 to 14, and 12 to 11. These figures indicate, in a great measure, the social position of each class, and in the results shown the philosopher may find much matter for inquiry. The wide difference between the ratios of sexes among the free and enslaved cannot be attributed to natural causes, but must result from direct murder or criminal neglect, during the infancy of the female, or both.

The people are universally Roman Catholics, and the whole island bears the impress of priestly supremacy. Churches, chapels, convents, &c., are established in all parts, and the *cross* is erected on mountain and plain. But while religion inundates the land with its sophistries and external pomp, the minds of the people are left in moral darkness; and superstition and ignorance reign supreme. There are, indeed, some 200 or 300 schools on the island, some private and others gratuitous; but all are under the charge of priests, whose object seems anything but an enlightenment of the mind. In the higher schools the classics and mathematics are taught; but in such a manner as to reduce life to an abstraction rather than a reality; and the number receiving even this education is insignificant in respect of the population. *No slave, either negro or colored, is admitted or admissible into any schools of the island*

The industry of the people is confined almost wholly to the production of the great agricultural staples. The manufactures are almost limited to the making of sugar, molasses and rum; and there has lately been established a paper-mill at Puentes Grandes. The manufacture of segars, the bleaching of wax, &c., completes the list of what may be mentioned in this connection.

The commerce of Cuba is chiefly in the hands of European merchants. The principal articles of export are sugar, coffee, rum, molasses, wax, tobacco and segars, with some honey, hides, cotton, and a variety of fruits. The imports consist of manufactured articles, chiefly from England and the United States, with corn and salted provisions, and gold, cochineal and indigo, from South America—all which, however, are transhipped to foreign countries. The exports of Cuba amount, annually, to about $20,000,000, and the imports to about $2,000,000 or $3,000,000 more. The commerce carried on between the United States and Cuba, in 1846–'7 is exhibited in the following table:

		Vessels Employed:	
	Value.	*Number.*	*Tonnage*
Exports from the United States	$6,005,617	1,516	262,008
Imports into the United States	12,394,867	1,465	244,014

This exhibits the trade of the United States in a very prosperous condition. This preponderance is ascribable principally, perhaps, to the proximity of the two nations, and the superior facilities of supplying the planters with provisions and timber; but it is no doubt owing, also, in a considerable degree, to the United States being the principal market for the sugar, coffee, and other staple productions of Cuba, the markets of England being reached chiefly through the United States. Slaves, a most important article of import, are not mentioned in the commercial statistics of Cuba. The number annually introduced is large, and has been estimated at from 2,000 to 4,000, the smaller number being more probably the truth. Mr. Turnbull, who visited Cuba in 1838–'9, estimates the annual average at 2,300. The revenue derived from commerce varies from $8,000,000 to $9,000,000 a year. There is no paper money in Cuba. The ports of the island, licensed for foreign trade, are Havanna, Santiago, Puerto-Principe, Matanzas, Trinidad, Baraçoa, Gibara, Cienfuegos, and Manzanilla.

The means of internal communication are comparatively imperfect. The common roads are badly constructed, and in the rainy season are impassable for wheels. This evil is, however, reduced in consequence of the narrowness of the island, and the nearness of all parts to the sea-coast. The principal ports and towns are united by rail-roads, and as far as they alone are concerned, little further is required. These will eventually be extended to the principal agricultural centres, and the facilities they will afford will greatly promote the interests, both of the planter and merchant. In the present state of matters, a large number of coasters are necessary to collect the produce of distant parts into the ports, and of late a number of steamboats have engaged in this lucrative business

As respects the civil government, Cuba is divided into two provinces, viz: eastern and western; Havanna being the capital of the one, and Santiago of the other. The Captain-General, governor, or supreme military chief of the island, is at the same time civil governor of the western province, but except in military matters, the governor of the eastern province is perfectly independent of the Captain-General, and responsible only to the Court at Madrid. The island is also divided into three military di visions—a western, central, and eastern; the chiefs of which are, of course, subordinate to the Captain-General. The royal court (Real Audiencia) of Puerto Principe, of which the Captain-General is *ex-officio* president, has the supreme jurisdiction in all civil and criminal affairs. In the principal cities there are "Ayuntamientos," and in the rural districts "Jueces Pedaneos," who combine the exercise of judicial functions with those of police commissioners, &c.

It is not easy to exaggerate the political importance of Cuba. Her size, geographical position, and the situation, great strength, and admirable harbor of Havanna, render her, as it were, the mistress of the Gulf of Mexico. No wonder, therefore, that her possession, and the nature of the government to which she is subject, should be objects of intense interest to the United States, and also to Great Britain and other commercial nations. On the whole it would seem to be for the common advantage of the commercial world that Cuba should continue as at present, dependent upon Spain, or that she should become independent. So long as she remains under Spain, there is but little risk of her natural capabilities being turned to the prejudice either of general commerce, or of that of any particular state. The real interests of no country require the sovereignty of this island. It is now in fact open to the commerce of the world, and in the hands of a third-rate maritime power, which precludes the idea of its becoming an oppression to commerce, or from being converted into a strong military position. Falling into the hands either of the United States, or any of the great European powers, dangers of no common occurrence might arise, not only to other portions of the world, but as referring to the internal peace of the possessory nation. Should the United States attempt to annex Cuba, the jealousy of Europe would become awakened, and perhaps negative any bargain that might be made; and in this a strong party in the United States would acquiesce on account of the existence of slavery, as well as from opposition to the acquisition of more territory. England, as its master, would emancipate the slaves, and thus destroy the productive value of the island; but by such a course the commerce of the whole West Indies would reap essential benefit, and the present ruinous competition between free and slave labor be annihilated; but should England seize or purchase the island, the United States would interfere, as of right, and protest against British occupancy. It would be dangerous in any way to alter its present condition—a condition which guarantees to the world its inoffensive existence. Spain may not have the power to protect it in case of war—but even then, would any of the great powers attack it?—if so, it would find security in the protection of every other power. Its destiny, however, is not to remain in its present position—it must eventually part from Spain; but before the period of its disruption arrives, its social condition must be essentially changed, and the relative position of other nations have undergone modification. The frequent reports of negociations between Spain and the United States, or Spain and England, for the purchase of Cuba, are, to say the least, of problematical origin; and seeing that no party could be benefited by any change in its commercial regulations, it is idle to conjecture that any nation will attempt to acquire that which, without any adequate benefit, must disturb the commercial economy of the whole world. Each may wish to possess the island, but each will oppose its acquisition by any but itself.

Havanna (Habana *Harbor*), the capital, is a large and flourishing commercial city, and perhaps, next to New-York and New-Orleans, the greatest emporium in the Western World. It stands on the north-west of the island, and on the west side of one of the most perfect harbors in the world. The population amounts to about 100,000, made up of about 45,000 Europeans and their descendants, 25,000 free mulattoes and blacks, and about an equal number of slaves. There is always a large floating population here, especially in the winter season. Previous to the relaxation of the commercial system of Spain, Havanna engrossed almost all the foreign commerce of the island, and increased rapidly in population and wealth under such favorable auspices; nor did it decline when Matanzas and other ports were thrown open, the increased trade of the island consequent on the change, being sufficient to maintain all on a liberal footing. The commerce of Havanna indeed has since greatly increased, and this must be ascribed to the freedom it now enjoys. Havanna is renowned for its harbor. The entrance is narrow but deep, without bar or obstruction of any kind, and expands into a magnificent bay. Vessels of the largest dimensions safely ride on its waters, and approach its quays. The city lies at the entrance and on the west side of the bay; its suburb, Regia, is on the opposite side. The Moro and Punta are two forts at the entrance—the Punta on the east, and the Moro on the west side; and the city is otherwise strongly defended, and fortifications have been erected on all the commanding heights in the vicinity. The city proper, which stands on level ground, is about 2,100 yards in length, and 1,200 broad. It is separated by a ditch and glacis from its suburbs, Salud, Guadalupe, Jesus-Maria, Cerro and Horcon. The streets of the city proper are narrow, crooked, and ill-regulated, but in the suburbs, especially Salud, they are wide and handsome. The houses within the walls are of stone; without, of various materials. The public edifices, such as the cathedral, government-house, admiralty, arsenal, general post-office, and royal tobacco-factory, are less remarkable for splendor than for solidity of construction. Besides the cathedral, which contains the ashes of Columbus, removed thither from San Domingo, in 1796, there are nine or ten parish churches, six others connected with hospitals and military orders, five chapels or hermitages, eleven convents, a university, two colleges, a botanic garden, anatomical museum and lecture rooms, an academy of painting, a school of navigation, and above 70 ordinary schools for both sexes. The charitable institutions consist of the "Casa Real de Beneficiencia," a penitentiary or Magdalen asylum, a foundling asylum, and seven hospitals, one of which comprises a lunatic asylum. The Casa Real has also within its walls two other lunatic asylums, a hospital for the aged and infirm, boys' and girls' schools, &c. This institution is munificently endowed with real estate, and various taxes imposed on institutions of pleasure, &c. There are three theatres, an amphitheatre for bull-fights, and several handsome public promenades. The arsenal and dockyard are at the south end of the city. In the latter large numbers of ships of the line, steamers, &c., have been built. It is perhaps equal in capacity to the most celebrated dock-yards in the world.

At the village of Casa Blanca, on the opposite side of the harbor, there are also some wharves and ship-yards, at which vessels of all sizes may be laid up, fitted out, and repaired. This village is notorious as the resort of the slavers frequenting the harbor.

The commerce of Havanna is immense, and the articles exported of the most valuable description, being as well foreign as domestic. The amount of sugar alone, exported during the year, varies from 300,000 to 400,000 boxes of 400 lbs. each, and more than one million arrobas (25½ lbs.) of coffee are despatched hence annually. The markets of the city are well furnished, and the consumption of country produce is immense, more than 2,000 beasts being constantly employed in bringing it up, besides that brought by way of railroad and other conveyances.

Havanna is the residence of the Captain-General, an Episcopal See, and seat of the government of the northern province; but Puerto Principe is the seat of the supreme judiciary. The principal nations of Europe and America have consuls resident therein. Havanna was founded in 1511, by Diego Velasquez. It has suffered several times from piratical and hostile visits. In 1762 it was captured by the British, but was restored to Spain in the following year, the whole island having been exchanged for Florida.

Next in importance to the Havanna, is Santiago de Cuba, the residence of the authorities of the eastern province. It is one of the best cities on the island, and third in commercial importance. It lies six miles from the sea, on the river of the same name, the mouth of which forms its harbor. Latitude, 19° 37′ 29″ N., and longitude 70° 3′ W. Population about 30,000. The public buildings are the cathedral, several churches, a college, a hospital, and numerous convents and schools. The port is from north to south about four miles long, with an irregular breadth, and in some places rather narrow, but it has water enough for ships of the line, and is sheltered from winds on every side. The entrance is narrow, and well defended by the Moro and Estrella castles. The city, like all the coast cities of Cuba, is very unhealthy, and frequently suffers from yellow fever; it is hemmed in on every side by mountains, which impede the circulation of the atmosphere, defying all the precautions of the strictest police. Santiago is the see of an archbishop. It was the capital of Cuba until the beginning of the 18th century, when the Havanna was raised to that dignity. Its trade is considerable, and is increasing from year to year. Santiago is the port from which the copper ore from the Sierra de Cobre is shipped. It was founded by Diego Velasquez in 1514.

Matanzas ranks next to Havanna in commercial importance. It is situated at the bottom of a deep bay, 52 miles east of the capital. Latitude 23° 2′ 28″ north, longitude 81° 37′ 44″ west. The population is estimated at 18,000 inhabitants, one-third of which is of European origin. It is well-built, partly of stone, and contains some fine public edifices. The Bay of Matanzas, defended by the Castle of San Severino, is extensive, but exposed on the north and east. The harbor in front of the city is protected by a ledge of rocks, four feet below the surface, which serves as a natural breakwater, to defend vessels at anchor within it from the swell. There are two channels by which to enter, the one by the north and the other by the south end of the ledge, but the south channel is fit only for coasting-vessels. The town is enclosed by two rivers, which bring down to the harbor so much mud as materially to injure the anchorage ground, and render it necessary to load and discharge the shipping by lighters and launches.

Matanzas, though situated in a most fertile district, had little importance until within the last 40 years. Under the old colonial system it was merely a subsidiary port to Havanna, and was not allowed to carry on any direct intercourse with foreign countries, but all impolitic restrictions having been removed in 1809, Matanzas immediately became the centre of a considerable trade, and the town and its commerce have since continued to increase, with the rapidly-increasing cultivation of sugar and coffee in the adjoining districts. A railroad connects the city with the interior.

The exports from this port in 1847, among other articles, consisted of

387,183 boxes of sugar, 3,405,777 pounds of coffee, and 54,841 hogsheads of molasses—distributed in the following proportions:

		Sugar. Boxes.	Coffee. Pounds.	Molasses. Hhds.
United States		118,102	406,479	39,398
British.	Great Britain and Ireland	68,082	32,650	5,972
	Cowes, (Isle of Wight)	50,009	5,050	31
	Gibraltar	1,697	83,400	—
	British Provinces	5,009	125,175	5,998
Other Ports of Europe		120,735	2,003,763	3,142
Havana		23,546	749,260	—

The number of vessels employed in this trade was 173 ships and barques, 294 brigs, 82 schooners, 17 polacres, and one lugger, with an aggregate burden of 123,939½ tons; of which 59,057 tons belonged to the United States, 30,697 tons to Great Britain, and the remainder to Spain, Germany, Sweden, France, Russia, Prussia, Brazil, and Norway—the relative amount according to the order of the above arrangement.

Puerto-Principe, situated in the interior, about 20 miles south-east of Neuvitas, is a small town, and derives its importance from being the residence of the Audiencia Real, and the centre of a rich district. Neuvitas, above referred to, is the port of Principe. Cardenas, east of Matanzas, has an excellent harbor, and has a considerable trade. Trinidad, on the south of the island, about its centre, is also a place of considerable commerce. Population, 15,000. It has a good harbor, but exposed from the west. Cienfuegos is rapidly rising into importance. It has a superb harbor on the Bay of Xagua, and promises to become a flourishing mart. Population, about 6,000. Several houses in New-York have transactions with this port. Manzanillo is a thriving commercial town, but small, having a population of 3,000 or 4,000 souls. Bayamo, an old town in the interior; Holguin, also in the interior, and north-west of Bayamo; El Cobre, the centre of the mining district, and Baracoa, the oldest settlement on the island, among many others, are the most noted places of Cuba.

Cuba was discovered by Columbus in 1492. It has always been held by Spain, except from 1762 to 1763, during which it was occupied by the British. In the latter year it was exchanged for Florida.

PORTO RICO,

Or Puerto Rico, is the smallest of the larger Antilles, and most eastward, lying between latitude 17° 55′ and 18° 30′ north, and between longitude 65° 40′ and 67° 20′ west. It forms part of the great wall between the Atlantic Ocean and Caribbean Sea, and is separated on the east by the Virgin Passage from the Virgin Islands, and from Hayti on the west by the Mona Passage. The island resembles a parallelogram in shape, its length, from east to west, being 100 miles, and its breadth about 38 miles—area, 3,865 square miles. The population numbers more than 350,000, of which only 127,000 are of European descent; the remainder being negroes, three-fourths of whom are slaves.

The general course of the mountains in Porto Rico is from east to west, midway between the north and south coasts. The greatest elevation is at the north-east extremity, being there about 3,000 feet above the level of the sea. Numerous rivers have their sources from this chain, which, flowing down the slopes to the Atlantic Ocean and Caribbean Sea, fertilize the soils and beautify the island. Some of these are navigable for two or three leagues for sloops and coasters. The whole coast is much indented, and the harbors are good, and fit for the reception of the largest class of shipping. The face of the island wears all the luxuriant vegetation of the tropics, and is highly cultivated, and dotted over with a number of thriving villages. The climate is said to be less unhealthy, and more desirable as a residence of Europeans, than most of the Antilles. It differs widely, however, in different parts; in the north it is liable to heavy rains, and in the south, to droughts. Violent hurricanes frequently sweep over the island, and spread devastation and ruin among the plantations.

Porto Rico is singularly destitute of wild animals. "There are almost no indigenous quadrupeds; and scarcely any of the feathered tribe are to be found in the forests. The birds are few, both in numbers and species. You may travel whole leagues without seeing a bird, or even hearing their chirp. On the rivers there are a few water-fowl, and in the forests the green parrot. Almost every other island in the West Indies is infested by snakes, and other noxious animals. Here are none. But rats, of an enormous size, and in great numbers, infest the country, and sometimes commit dreadful ravages on the sugar-canes; and although continually persecuted, their numbers do not decrease."—(*Flinter's Puerto Rico*, 53.)

The resources of Porto Rico are essentially agricultural. No minerals are found, and no manufactures exist; but one-half, however, of the available lands are cultivated. The staples produced are sugar and coffee, with the usual catalogue of West India produce. The breeding and feeding of cattle is largely attended to, and it is estimated that the number of these amounts to more than 200,000. Cattle-breeding is, perhaps, more profitable here than any other department of agriculture; but owing to the subdivision of the property, few persons own more than 1,000 cattle. The numbers of sheep, goats, hogs, mules, and asses, are, however, very limited; but there are about 80,000 horses, of tolerably good breed. The value of live stock is estimated at from $7,000,000 to $8,000,000.

Previous to 1815, Porto Rico, being excluded from all foreign countries except Spain, was either stationary or increased very slowly. But in that year a royal decree favorable to commerce, and a free trade under moderate duties, has since been permitted. In consequence of this liberal measure, the island has made rapid progress in every department of internal and external prosperity.

The following statement of the commerce of Porto Rico, in 1846, taken from *Balanza Mercantil*, published in the capital, exhibits the present condition of the colony in reference to its foreign trade.

IMPORTS AND EXPORTS.

Imports.		*Exports.*	
Articles of consumption, value	$4,429,713	Produce of island, value	$4,668,572
Gold and silver coin	586,302	Gold and siver coin	161,846
Articles on deposit	534,574	Articles from deposit	518,601
Total	$5,550,589	Total	$5,369,019
	5,369,019		
Difference in favor of imports	81,370		

The annexed statement will show the distribution of the commerce of this island.

To and from.	*Importations.*	*Exportations.*
Spain and adjacent Islands	$843,954	$712,542
Cuba	167,092	45,861
Other West India Islands	2,915,505	335,985
United States of America	1,018,711	1,644,637
Austria	—	53,166
Belgium	—	10,648
Brazil	249,128	—
Bremen and Hamburg	10,665	398,974
Sardinia	—	132,328
Denmark	—	90,795
France	49,142	1,043,439
Holland	—	4,499
England	30,099	584,872
Canada and Newfoundland	70,809	303,209
Venezuela	195,482	8,060
Total	$5,550,589	$5,369,049

The total number of arrivals were 1,135 vessels, with a tonnage of 116,623, and the total departures 1,119 vessels, and the tonnage 117,076, showing a difference in favor of arrivals of 16 vessels, and in favor of departures of 453 tons; this is owing to the fact that a larger class of vessels were used in the exporting than in the importing trade:

The carrying trade of Porto Rico is shown in the annexed table:

	Imports.	*Exports.*
Under the flag of Spain	$3,386,760	$1,064,292
" Belgium	816	10,648
" United States	1,217,032	1,654,155
" Bremen	10,825	181,316
" Denmark	70,924	20,314
" France	277,239	1,162,039
" Hamburg	22,483	258,374
" England	369,764	663,809
" Holland	27,737	6,967
" Sardinia	5,913	43,555
" Sweden	369	814
" Venezuela	159,462	2,731

The government, laws and institutions are nearly similar to those established by Spain in the rest of her transatlantic possessions. Porto Rico is governed by a Captain-General, whose authority is supreme in military affairs, and who is president of the Audiencia Real in civil affairs. In the seven towns which are capitals of departments, justice is administered by mayors; in the smaller towns and villages by inferior magistrates, called lieutenants, who determine debts under $100, act as justices of the peace, &c., &c. They are appointed by the Captain-General, who also appoints the clergy to the different livings, on the recommendation of the bishop. Public instruction is backward, but the colonies are increasing facilities in this connection. The island is divided into seven military divisions, each commanded by a Spanish Colonel. The regular military force comprises about 10,000 men, and the militia about 45,000. The naval force consists of a man-of-war, a schooner, and perhaps a dozen gun-boats. The revenue of the island amounts to about $900,000 annually.

San Juan de Porto Rico is the chief city and capital of the island, and is situated on rising ground at the extremity of a peninsula, joined to the land by a narrow isthmus. Lat. 18° 29′ 10″ N., and long. 66° 13′ 15″ W. The population is estimated at 40,000. The town, which lies on the east side of the harbor, is strongly fortified. The streets cross each other at right angles . being on a declivity, it is well drained, and is reported to be one of the healthiest cities in the new world. The public buildings are numerous, and generally built with good taste, being more solid than handsome. The harbor has a striking resemblance to that of Havanna, to which it is but little inferior. Its entrance, about 300 fathoms in width, is well defended by forts on both sides, and on small islands in the bay. Within, it expands into a capacious basin, the depth of water varying from five to seven fathoms. Porto Rico is the residence of the Captain-General, and seat of the superior courts, &c., of the island. It engrosses the larger portion by far of the commerce of the island, and has in consequence attained to considerable distinction among the emporiums of the West Indies.

The other towns of Porto Rico are comparatively insignificant. They are, MAYAGUEZ, on the west; AGUADILLA and ARECIVO, on the north; and PONCE and GUAYAMA, on the south—all of which enjoy some commerce.

Several small islands lying contiguous to Porto Rico belong to Spain, viz. Bieque, or Crab, Serpent, Great and Little Passage, the Tropic Keys, and several others. Some of these are claimed by Great Britain, but they naturally belong as here noted, and are so assigned by all geographers.

Columbus discovered this island in 1493, at which period it is said to have had a population of 800,000, all of whom were, in no very long time thereafter, exterminated by the Spaniards. In the latter part of the 17th century, it was taken by the English ; but from the prevalence of dysentery among the troops, they were soon after obliged to abandon it, since which time it has remained in the hands of Spain. A revolution broke out in 1820, but was suppressed in 1823 : the object of the people was separation from the mother country, and an independent existence. All, however, is now quiet, and a spirit of improvement has taken the place of revolutionary ideas.

THE FRENCH WEST INDIES.

THE colonial possessions of the French in the West Indies, as well as on the continent, formerly comprised an extensive and valuable domain. The revolutionary spirit which disturbed the mother country in the last decade of the 18th century and commencement of the present,, led to the total overthrow of her power in the New World. Her possessions in Hayti were then wrested from her dominion, and from inability to hold on to Louisiana, that fine country was soon after sold to the United States. Little now remained to her ; and in the prosecution of her wars with England, she even lost the last vestige of her magnificent empire in America : the superior naval force of the former having captured every island under her sway, and driven her fleets from the ocean. Such was the state of affairs in 1815. By the peace of that date, England relinquished some of the captured West Indian Islands, and at the present period, the French Republic owns only the retro-ceded islands of Guadaloupe, Marie-galante, Martinique, and the north side of St. Martin's. These, with a small fishing station in the north, and an insignificant colony in the south, now comprise the whole of the French possessions in America.

GUADALOUPE, AND ITS DEPENDENCIES.

This island lies between 15° 58′ and 16° 13′ N. latitude, and between 61° 15′ and 61° 55′ W. longitude, 40 miles south-east of Antigua, and 20 north of Dominica. Together with its dependencies, the small adjacent islands of Marie-galante, La Desirade, and Les Saintes, and a portion of the island of St. Martin's, it occupies an area of 309 square miles, and has a population of about 135,000.

Guadaloupe is divided into two unequal parts by the *riviere-salée*, or Salt river, an arm of the sea about five miles in length, and varying in width from 20 to 120 yards. The division south-west of this inlet is Guadaloupe Proper—that on the north-east is called Grand Terre. The former is of an oblong shape, and a chain of volcanic mountains covered with woods runs through the centre nearly its entire length. The medium height of its summits is about 3,000 feet, but near the south extremity the *Soufriére*, a volcano still exhibiting smouldering activity, rises to 5,108 feet above the level of the ocean. A multitude of rivulets course down the flanks of this chain, and water the slopes of the island; two of them, Goyave and Lezarde, are navigable for small craft, and highly useful for the conveyance inland of sea-mud to manure the plantations, and downwards of the produce of the island. Guadaloupe contains many mineral springs. Grand-Terre, the eastern division, is of a triangular shape. It is little raised above the level of the sea, and differs remarkably in its features from Guadaloupe Proper. It is almost a level plain, with only a few scattered hills, destitute of woods, and its rivers are insignificant.

The Saintes consist of three small islands, situated between Guadaloupe and Marie-galante. Deseada or Desirade is 10 miles long, and 5 broad. It lies 12 miles north-east of Point Chateau, the eastern extremity of Guadaloupe. Marie-galante is of a circular form, 14 miles in diameter. It is situated 15 miles east of Guadaloupe, and is traversed from east to west by a chain of hills, which, like those of Guadaloupe, abound in timber. It is very fertile, and produces large quantities of sugar, coffee, cotton, &c. These are all dependent on Guadaloupe.

The soil of Guadaloupe is light, and easy of tillage, but is inferior to that of Grand-Terre, which is rich and fertile. Almost every part of the island is capable of cultivation; and notwithstanding the deficiency of water, in some parts is very productive. The climate is extremely hot, and is only tempered by the recurrence of sea and land breezes. About 86 inches of rain fall during the year. Hurricanes and earthquakes are frequent, and have several times been attended with tragical consequences. More than one-half the cultivated land is planted with sugar-cane. The agriculture of these islands has been much improved of late, in consequence of the introduction of the new implements; and the manufacture of sugar has also improved since steam-engines were brought into use. The live stock consists principally of black cattle, sheep and mules. Guinea grass is the only forage grown.

The commerce of Guadaloupe, in which is included that of its dependencies, is considerable. The annual value of produce exported averages 25,000,000 francs, and consists of raw sugars, molasses, rum, coffee, dyewoods, cotton, copper, &c. Nearly all the exported articles are sent to France, whence also nine-tenths of the imports are derived. The imports are chiefly salt meats and fish, flour, olive oil, cotton, linen and silk fabrics, wine, perfumery, &c.; the annual value of which at least equals that of the exports. About 500 vessels, of 50,000 tons burden, enter and depart during the year. The principal roadsteads and ports are those of Basse-terre and Mahault, in Guadaloupe; Point-a-Pitre and Moule, in Grand-terre; the roadsteads of Saintes, and a few others.

Guadaloupe and its dependencies are divided into three arrondissements, six cantons, and 24 communes. The legislature consists of a governor and a colonial council of thirty members, elected for five years by the people at large. A Deputy is sent to the National Assembly in Paris, as representative of the interests of the colonists. There is a supreme court at Basse-terre. The other tribunals are two courts of assize, three of original jurisdiction, and six tribunals of justices of the peace. The colony has a military commandant, and a large armed force, and militia. Churches, schools and charitable institutions are well provided. The revenues are under 5,000,000 francs a year.

Basse-terre, the capital and seat of government, on the south-west shore, is a clean and well-built town of 5,000 inhabitants. It has two parish churches, a government house, halls of justice, a large hospital, an arsenal, some good public fountains and promenades, and a fine botanic garden. It is defended by several strong batteries facing the sea. Capisterre, on the east side of the island, is its other chief town. Point-a-Pitre, a town of some 10,000 inhabitants, is situated at the west end of Grand-terre, and owes its prosperity to its excellent port. It is regularly built, has a handsome church, and many good private edifices. This place has suffered severely from earthquakes, and a few years ago was almost entirely destroyed by one of unusual violence. The other towns are insignificant—but three of them, besides the foregoing, have their own municipal councils.

These islands were discovered by Columbus in 1493. The French took possession of them in 1635. Guadaloupe has on several occasions been taken by the English, and was occupied by British troops from 1810 to 1815, when it was restored to its ancient masters.

MARTINIQUE

This small island is situated between latitude 14° 23′ 43″ and 14° 52′ 47″ N., and between longitude 60° 46′ and 61° 15′ W., about 25 miles south-east of Dominica, and 20 miles north of St. Lucia. It is about 38 miles long, and 10 in average breadth; its area is 290 square miles.

The surface of Martinique gradually rises from the coasts inland, and mountain ranges occupy the centre of the country. Their loftiest summits are the Montagne Pelée, 4429 feet high, and Piton du Carbet, 3960 feet above the sea. These and other mountains are evidently of volcanic origin, having the characteristic conical form, and abounding in lava. Dense and luxuriant forests clothe their flanks, and in many parts cultivation is extended to the height of 1500 feet. About one-third of the island consists of level land. It is watered by numerous rivulets, but of these only three or four, disembogueing on the west, are at all navigable. At the south extremity of the island there is a small salt lake. The coasts present many bays and inlets, but the harbors on the east side are difficult of access, being obstructed by numerous islets and extensive banks of madrepore. On the south side is the Bay of Marin; on the west that of Fort Royal, one of the finest harbors in the Antilles; and in the south-west is the roadstead of St. Pierre, where ships ride safely except during west winds.

The climate of Martinique is not unhealthy, and the great heat is tempered by the sea and land breeze. The moisture of the atmosphere is excessive, and it is estimated that at the level of the sea 85 inches of rain fall during the year, most of which falls from July to October. Mineral springs are abundant, and of a chalybeate, saline, or silicious nature, and are useful in cutaneous and liver complaints.

The productions of this island differ little from those of the West Indies generally. The great staple is sugar, which is exported to France in large quantities. The average annual value of exports is somewhat under 20,000,000 francs, and the imports are to a similar amount. About 750 vessels, French and foreign, are employed in the trade. The government of the island is organized on the same principles as that of Guadaloupe. The annual expenditure is about 4,500,000 francs.

Martinique has only three towns worthy of mention. Port Royal, the capital, and seat of government, lies on the north shore of the bay of the same name, in the south-west part of the island. Population about 11,000. It is well built, and has a number of fine public edifices. The *Prefect Apostolique*, the superior ecclesiastic of the island, resides here. It is well defended on the north by Fort Bourbon, and on the south by Fort Louis. Near Fort Royal are numerous country residences. St. Pierre, also on the west coast, is the largest town in the French West Indies. It is a port of entry about 15 miles north-west of Fort Royal. The bay is of a circular shape, easy of access, but unsafe in stormy weather. Population, 15,000. La Trinite, on the bay of the same name, on the east side of the island, has a population of about 6,000. Its roadstead and harbor are secure; the latter has good holding ground, but it is difficult of access. Its entrance was formerly protected by a strong fort, now in ruins.

Martinique was discovered in 1493, and settled by the French, in 1635. In 1762, the English captured it, but restored it the following year. In 1794, it was again taken by the English, who gave it back in 1802. Again in 1807, it was captured and held until 1815. Beauharnois and his wife Josephine, subsequently the consort of Napoleon, were natives of this island. Martinique, as an integral part of the French Republic, is now represented in the National Assembly.

ST. MARTIN'S, (North Side.)

St. Martin's, one of the Virgin Islands, belonging partly to the French and partly to the Dutch, lies between Anguilla and St. Bartholomew's. It forms a commune of Guadaloupe. (*See descrip. Dutch W. I.*)

THE DUTCH WEST INDIES.

The colonial possessions of the Dutch in the West Indies are extremely limited, and consist only of a few small, but somewhat important islands. These are Curaçoa, St. Eustatius, Saba, and the southern part of St. Martin's; the first lying off the coast of Venezuela, and the three last between the islands of Anguilla and St. Christopher's

CURACOA,

OR Curassao, lies on the north coast of Venezuela, in latitude 12° 6′ north, and longitude 69° west. The shores of this island are bold, and the interior, in some parts, hilly. The soil is in general poor and rocky, and there is a great deficiency of water; but by the industry of the inhabitants some tobacco, sugar in considerable quantities, indigo, &c., are grown; and an abundance of salt is obtained from the marshes. Maize, cassava, figs, oranges, citrons, and most European culinary vegetables, are cultivated, but provisions are not produced in sufficient quantity for its inhabitants. Curaçoa was once noted for its contraband trade with the Spaniards of South America, and from this source derived immense wealth; but since Venezuela became independent, and opened her ports to the flags of all nations, Curaçoa has retired into its original insignificance.

The government is conducted by a Stadtholder, assisted by a Civil and Military Council. WILHELMSTADT, the seat of government, is one of the neatest cities in the West Indies; its public buildings are magnificent, and the private houses are commodious. The harbor is excellent, and well-protected by strong fortifications. There are several good harbors, but the principal commerce is carried on by the merchants of the capital.

The small islands of Buen Ayre and Oruba, one on each side of Curaçoa, also belong to the Dutch. They are chiefly celebrated for their fine breed and number of cattle.

ST. MARTIN'S.— (South Side.)

THIS small island, part of which belongs to the French and part to the Dutch, lies about latitude 18° north, and longitude 63° west. The southern, or Dutch division, is less fertile and less wooded than that of the French, but more profitable, on account of the salt it produces, which is sent to the neighboring isles, and to the United States. Sugar, &c., are also produced in comparatively large quantities. The Dutch portion is said to be nearly as populous as the French, and more than one-half the whites are of English origin. This island was first colonized by Spaniards, but abandoned, in 1650; after which it became an object of contention between the French and Dutch, who subsequently divided it between them

ST. EUSTASIUS

Is one of the Leeward Islands, and lies in latitude 17° 30′ north, and longitude 62° 40′ west, between St. Christopher's and Saba, nine miles north-west of the former, and 15 south-east of the latter. This island is evidently an extinct volcano; it rises from the ocean in a pyramidal form, and has a depression in the centre, apparently its ancient crater, but which now affords a plentiful cover for numerous wild animals. The coast is almost inaccessible, except on the south-west, where the town of St. Eustasius has been built. The climate is moderate, and generally healthy, but terrific earthquakes and hurricanes are frequent. The island also suffers from the scarcity of water. Almost all the land is under cultivation, and tobacco, the principal product, is raised on the sides of the pyramid to its very summit. All other West India staples are grown, and from a superabundance of hogs, rabbits, poultry, &c., the inhabitants are enabled to furnish other islands with these necessaries. Formerly St. Eustatius carried on an extensive contraband trade with South America. This island has, with little exception, belonged to the Dutch since early in the 17th century. The French and English have several times captured it.

SABA,

A small island, twelve miles in circumference, is a dependency of St. Eustatius. It consists of a delightful valley, which produces the necessaries of life, and the materials for several manufactures; but being destitute of any port, its commerce is very inconsiderable. The adjacent sea is shallow, and full of rocks, for some distance from the coast, and none but small vessels can approach very near. Access to the interior of the island is by a difficult road, cut out of the rock, by which only one person can ascend at a time.

Personal slavery was abolished in all the Dutch islands in 1848.

THE DANISH WEST INDIES.

The Danish colonies in the West Indies comprise the three islands of Santa Cruz, St. Thomas', and St. John's in the Virgin group.

SANTA CRUZ, OR ST. CROIX,

The most southerly of the Virgin Islands, is situated in latitude 17° 45′ N. and longitude 64° 40′ W., 60 miles east-south-east of Porto Rico. Its length from east to west is 20 miles, and its breadth 5 miles. The northern portion is traversed by a chain of hills, but the island is generally level. The coasts are much indented, and present numerous harbors, the best of which are Christianstadt and Friederichstadt. The rivulets are dried up during a part of the year, and water is scarce and bad, and the climate unhealthy.

The fertility of the soil is indicated by the quantity of its products. The average value of sugar amounts to about 1,200,000 rix-dollars annually, and that of its rum, celebrated throughout the world, to 50,000 rix-dollars. The principal town, Christianstadt, the capital of all the Danish West Indies, is situated on the declivity of a hill, on the north-east shore of the island. It is a well-built town of some 5,000 or 6,000 inhabitants. Its port is secure, and defended by a battery. Friederichstadt, on the west coast, has 1,500 inhabitants. Santa Cruz was discovered by Columbus in 1493. The Dutch, English, French, Spaniards and Danes, alternately possessed it until 1814, when it was finally ceded to Denmark. It also formerly belonged to the Knights of Malta.

ST. THOMAS',

Lies 36 miles east of Porto Rico, in latitude 18° 20′ N., and longitude 65° W. The surface is mountainous, and the soil less fertile than St. Croix. Sugar and cotton are the principal staples. St. Thomas has long been, and continues to be, one of the chief emporiums in the West Indies. It owes its distinction partly to its convenient situation, partly to its spacious and safe harbor at St. Thomas, on the south side of the island, and partly, and principally, to the moderation of the duties imposed on commerce. St. Thomas has in consequence become as it were a depôt for the supply of the neighboring islands, goods being sent to it until opportunity offers for conveying them to their ultimate destination. The great articles of importation are European manufactured goods, but chiefly from England, and provisions, lumber, &c., from the United States. The first-cost value of imports in 1840 amounted to $4,997,000, and the ships and tonnage inward to 368, and 58,132. In the same year the colonial arrivals were 1,563 vessels of 48,624 tons, besides a great number of vessels neither landing nor loading goods, being in that case free from port charges.

ST. JOHN'S,

Six miles east of St. Thomas, contains about 40 square miles. The soil produces sugar, coffee, tobacco, &c.

The Moravian Brethren have missions in all these islands.

In describing the West Indies, a number of small islands have necessarily been omitted. These, however, are found on any good map, and their position and proximity to the larger islands will in general indicate to what nation they belong. The number of these cannot be ascertained, but it is supposed that they may have an aggregate area of 600 or 700 square miles, and a population of 10,000. They have no commercial importance, except as dangers to be avoided by the mariner.

WEST INDIA MAIL STEAMERS.

Among the manifold advantages enjoyed by the West Indies, the British ocean mail-system is not the least. The mails from England are made up on the 2d and 17th of every month, and are conveyed to Southampton, from which they are transferred to one of the splendid steamships belonging to the "Royal Mail Steam-packet Company." This company has 15 vessels of 18,569 tons, 5,967 horse power, and 1,227 men, and two sailing vessels, 238 tons, and 30 men. They contract with the government to carry the mails between England and the West Indies and the Gulf of Mexico, from Southampton, twice a month, for £240,000 per annum, they finding 11 ocean steamers of 400 horse power, and 4 for the colonies of 200 horse power each. A West India mail steamer is capable of carrying about 80 passengers, and is fitted up in an elegant style. After leaving Southampton, the vessels proceed to Funchal, or Madeira, whence they sail for Barbadoes, and thence to Grenada; the entire distance from Southampton to Grenada, being 4,037 nautical miles, is performed in about 23 days. Every fortnight one of the colonial steamers starts from Barbadoes for Tobago, and Demerara, in Guayana, where she stops for a week, and then returns with home-mails for Tobago, Grenada, and Barbadoes. From Grenada one also starts every fortnight for Trinidad, where she remains nine days and then returns to Grenada. One also starts every fortnight from Grenada with the out-mails for St. Vincent's, St. Lucia, Martinique, Dominica, Guadaloupe, Antigua, Montserrat, Nevis, St. Christopher's, Tortola, St. Thomas, and Porto Rico; after which she returns to St. Thomas, for the purpose of procuring coal, calling at each island on her way back to Grenada. A steam-packet also starts monthly for Havanna, Vera Cruz, and Tampico, touching at Ship Island, below New-Orleans, whence mails for the United States are despatched, and the return-mails received. At Vera Cruz large shipments of specie and bullion are received, sometimes amounting to $2,500,000, which are transported from the mines in the interior for Great Britain. The vessels then proceed to Nassau and Bermuda, and then return to Southampton, calling once a month at New-York, staying only long enough to receive the mails. Another steamer starts every month from St. Thomas with the out as well as the home-mails, for Bermuda, and then proceeds to Nassau, Havanna, and Jamaica. Another steam-packet starts monthly from St. Thomas, with all the collected home-mails, proceeding by way of Fayal to Southampton. One steam-packet starts monthly from Grenada, with the out-mails for La Guayra and Porto Cabello, remains there for the period of two days, and returns to La Guayra, and thence to St. Thomas and Grenada. One steam-packet likewise starts monthly from Jamaica, with the out-mails for Santa Marta, Cartagena, Chagres, and St. Juan de Nicaragua; she then returns to Jamaica, with mails for England. Finally, another steam-packet starts monthly from Havanna for Balize and Honduras, and after stopping a few days, she returns to Havanna. This judicious system of communication by steam, between Great Britain and the West Indies, furnishes an expeditious and safe channel of trade and commerce between them, and tends to keep alive the mutual interests between the colonies, and also that between the colonies and the mother country.

The United States mail service with these countries is yet in its infancy, but a company has been formed in New-York, and already several vessels are built and in progress, for the purpose of conveying by steam the mails destined for the Pacific via Panama, calling at several of the most important West India Islands. The mails will be transported over the Isthmus, and despatched from Panama to the ports of California and Oregon, and the return mails having been collected, these vessels will return by the same route. These arrangements, however, are only the commencement of a system which, in the course of time, will be extended, and from the superior facilities enjoyed by the United States, will probably soon outstrip in efficiency and value the present magnificent provisions in mail-transportation, made by the English. The New-Orleans line of steamers from New-York call at Havanna and Balize to deliver and receive the mails.

GENERAL DESCRIPTION OF

SOUTH AMERICA.

We now enter upon the description of the richest and most fertile, the most picturesque, and, excepting Africa, the most extensive peninsula of the world. South America is situated between the parallels of 11° 20′ W. and 56° 30′ S. latitude, and between the meridians of 35° and 83° W. longitude. According to geographical writers, this vast continent contains a surface area of 6,500,000 square miles: its greatest length is 4,550, and its greatest breadth 3,200 miles. Of this extent about three-fourths lie between the tropics, and the remainder in the southern temperate zone.

South America is bounded north by the Caribbean Sea, and is connected with North America by the narrow Isthmus of Darien. On the east is the Atlantic; on the south the Antarctic, and on the west the Pacific Oceans. A number of cold and barren islands lie south of Cape Horn, the furthest extremity of the lands, which are entirely useless, and destined ever to remain in their primeval state of desolation and solitude.

From the configuration of its surface, South America may be divided into five distinct regions, each having widely-marked peculiarities, and differing essentially in their physical aspect and scenery:

First.—The low country skirting the Pacific coast, from 50 to 150 miles in breadth and 4,000 miles in length, and of which the two extremes are fertile, gradually diminishing in that respect as they approach the centre, which is a desert waste, incapable of supporting animal life or producing the most stunted shrub or germ of vegetation.

Second.—The Basin of the Orinoco, surrounded almost by lofty mountains, and forming a region of extensive plains, either destitute of wood or merely studded with brush-wood and decrepid trees; but covered with abundance of coarse long grass, in which lizards and serpents lie in a state of inactivity or torpor.

Third.—The Basin of the Amazon, a vast plain, embracing a surface of 2,000,000 square miles, and possessing a rich soil and humid climate. It is covered all over with dense forests, harboring a great variety of wild beasts, and is thinly inhabited by tribes of savage Indians, who subsist on the produce of the chase and by fishing.

Fourth.—The great southern plain, watered by the tributaries of the Rio de la Plata. Open pampas, or plains, occupy the greater portion of this region, which is dry, and in some parts barren, but in general is covered with strong weeds and grass, which furnish subsistence to prodigious herds of cattle, and afford shelter to a few wild animals of various species; and

Fifth.—The high country of Brazil, eastward of the Parana, Paraguay and Madeira, which presents a succession of ridges and vallies on the Atlantic thickly covered with wood, and in the west opens into vast plains and pasture lands, on which innumerable droves find ample subsistence.

The MOUNTAINS OF SOUTH AMERICA are of vast height, and cover a great part of the eastern and western portions of the continent.

The CORDILLERAS OF THE ANDES, or great western chain, commencing at the Straits of Magellan, on the southern extremity of the peninsula, run in a northerly direction to the Isthmus of Darien, and are generally parallel to the Pacific Ocean, at a distance of from 50 to 150 miles. Their aspect, in different parts of their course, is as various as abrupt—sometimes consisting of one entire mass, while at others two or three distinct ridges appear separated by longitudinal vallies. In Chili, the Andes are broad, and consist of a great number of mountains, all of prodigious height, and appearing to be chained to each other. In Peru, they divide into three ridges, which continue divided until within a few degrees from the equator, when they unite into a single chain. They separate again in Equador into two distinct chains, which enclose between them a spacious valley, elevated 9,000 feet above the level of the ocean. Further north, about the second parallel of north latitude, the eastern chain is subdivided into two, and in this manner the Andes enter New-Grenada, dividing its surface into three separate elevations; the western is the proper Andes, and passes towards but not into North America, over the Isthmus of Darien; the eastern, called the chain of Colombia, pursues a north-easterly course, and, winding along the shores of the Caribbean Sea, terminates on the Gulf of Paria, opposite the Island of Trinidad; the middle range runs north between the rivers Magdalena and Cauca. The most elevated part of the Andes is the double ridge in Equador, which abounds with colossal summits, the highest of which, the celebrated *Nevado de Sorato,* rises to 25,420 feet above the level of the sea. In Chili, Peru and Equador, the loftiest peaks form one row of volcanoes, many of which are in a state of constant eruption.

The EASTERN RANGE OF SOUTH AMERICAN MOUNTAINS, sometimes termed the Brazilian Andes, runs along the coast of Brazil from about 12° to 32° south latitude.

In addition to what is here called the eastern and western ranges of South American mountains, some other ridges deserve to be mentioned. The colossal trunk of the Andes sends off several branches towards the east, and besides that above noticed, which runs along the northern coast of South America, there is another which leaves the main ridge between the third and sixth degrees of south latitude. A third lateral branch makes a semicircular sweep between fifteen and twenty degrees of south latitude, and appears to connect the main body of the Andes with the mountains of Brazil and Paraguay, supplying the streams that feed the mighty Amazon on the one hand, and the sea-like Plata on the other. The particular direction, elevation, and structure of this range, however, are yet but imperfectly known.

The New World is scarcely more distinguished from the other regions of the globe by its position and magnitude, than by the majesty of its physical features. Its vast mountains, which rear their stupendous bulks above the clouds—its wide-stretching plateaux—its almost immeasurable savannas, and its mighty rivers, which roll their immense floods across these spacious plains, are all distinguishing traits of the western world. Placed amidst the summits of the Andes, the adventurous traveller seems as if surrounded with the fragments of a world destroyed, or with the materials out of which another might be constructed. There " desolation seems at perpetual strife with nature for the mastery, and vegetation lives as if in defiance of sterility." This magnificent and awfully impressive scenery of the central Andes, however, differs in several respects from that of other Alpine regions in higher latitudes. It is deficient in some of those features which not only augment its beauty and sublimity, but add majesty to horror. Glaciers, which, amidst the Alpine districts of Europe, frequently resemble a tumultuous sea suddenly congealed by the power of frost, as well as the terrible avalanches, which prove so destructive in these latitudes, are unknown in the torrid zone. But these mountains are noted for their immense chasms and cataracts. The formation of the Andes is likewise different from that of the Alps of Europe. One of the most singular circumstances in this respect is the enormous thickness and height of what geologists call the secondary formations. Baron Humboldt asserts that beds of coal have been found in the neighborhood of Santa Fé, at an elevation of 8,650 feet above the level of the sea; and even at the height of 14,700 feet, near Huanuco. The plains of Bogôta, which are about 9,000 feet above the surface of the ocean, are covered with sand-stone, gypsum, shell-limestone, and in some places rock-salt. Fossil shells have been found in the Pyrenees at the height of 11,700 feet, but in Peru at 12,800 in one place, and at 14,120 in another, where they were also accompanied with sand-stone. The basalt of Pichincha, near the city of Quito, has an elevation of 15,500, while granite, which crowns the loftiest mountains of Europe, is not found higher than 11,500 feet in the Andes, and is scarcely known in the republics either of Equador or Peru. The snow-clad summits of Sorato, Chimborazo, and the other highest peaks, consist entirely of porphyry, which there constitutes a mass of 10,000 or 12,000 feet in thickness; together with an enormous body of quartz of 9,500 feet thick. The Andes of Chili differ in their composition from the other parts of the chain; for it is in the cordillera of this part that vast blocks of crystal are found, capable of being formed into columns six or seven feet in length.

The following table is intended to exhibit the localities of the several mineralogical products of South America: though, of course, only designed as a general resumé, it will be advantageous in assisting the memory in reviewing the mineral formations on this continent:

DIAMONDS	Brazil (*Minas-Geraes*, &c.)
OTHER PRECIOUS STONES	Brazil (*Minas-Geraes*, &c.; New-Grenada, (*Cundinamarca*, &c.;) Chili; and Peru (*passim.*)
GOLD	New-Grenada (*San Juan*, *Cauca*, *Choco*, &c.;) Equador; Peru; Bolivia; Chili (*in the region of the Cordilleras*, &c.;) Brazil, (*Minas-Geraes*, *Goyas* and *Matto-Grasso*) and the Argentine Republic, (*region of the Andes*, &c.)
SILVER	Bolivia Peru; Chili; and Argentine Republic (*passim.*)
TIN	Peru.
MERCURY	Peru (*Huancavelica, mines of Santa Barbara.*)
COPPER	Peru and Chili (*passim.*)
LEAD	
IRON	Brazil (*Minas-Geraes*, *St. Paul's*, &c.;) Peru.
COAL	Peru; Chili. and several other states.
SALT	Argentine Republic; Brazil, (*Rio Grande do Norte*, *Para*, &c.;) Venezuela; New-Grenada; Bolivia; Peru, &c.
SALT-PETRE	Peru (*abundant.*)

South America is, perhaps, not more remarkable for the immensity of its mountains, than for the vast elevation of its plains. The highest cultivated land in Europe seldom exceeds 2,000 feet above the level of the sea, but much of the table land of America is from 6,000 to 10,000 feet in altitude. In Peru, extensive plains are found at the elevation of 9,000, and in Mexico not less than 500,000 square miles is from 6,000 to 8,000 feet above the sea; an elevation which rivals the celebrated pass of Mount Cenis or Mount St. Gothard. Almost interminable plains, too, stretch through the wide regions of South America, at a very slight elevation above the sea. Those of Orinoco, Amazonia and Buenos Ayres, may be mentioned as examples, and chiefly consist of extensive savannas, varied in a few places with clumps of palms, but so extremely level that the space of 800 square leagues scarcely presents any inequality.

Such a diversity of surface gives rise to a corresponding variety in the climate and vegetable productions of this continent; and all species, from the palms and other majestic trees which adorn the sultry regions of the torrid zone, to the last lichen, which creeps beneath the eternal snows that cover the summits of the Andes, are met with in these regions. In ascending from the shore to the upper ridges, the plants peculiar to the different districts of the globe appear in regular succession. At an elevation of from 3,000 to 5,000 feet, cassava, cacao, maize, plantains, indigo, sugar, cotton and coffee are produced. Both cotton and coffee also grow at a much greater elevation, and sugar is successfully cultivated in the valley of Quito. From 6,000 to 9,000 feet in elevation, the climate is best suited to the production of all kinds of European grain. Within these limits, too, are to be found the oak, and various other species of forest trees; but beyond the height of 9,000 feet large trees of all kinds begin to disappear, except dwarf pines, which are found nearly 13,000 feet above the level of the sea, and about 2,000 feet below the lower limit of perpetual snow. The space between 13,000 and 15,000 feet, grasses clothe the ground, and from this latter height, the lichen is the only plant which creeps on the rocks, and seems to penetrate under the snow.

The following is a table of the culminating points of the mountains of South America:

1. THE CHAIN OF THE ANDES:

		Feet.
In Terra del Fuego	*Cape Horn*	1,870
	Mount Darwin	6,600
	" *Sarmiento*	7,000
In Patagonia	*Corcovado*, on the W. Coast	7,500
	Yanteles	7,020
The Cordilleras, running thro' Chili, Bolivia, Equador and New Grenada	*Aconcagua*	23,944
	Descabecada	21,100
	Volcano of Maipu	12,705
	Chipicani, near Arica	18,896
	Pichu-Pichu, near Arequipa	18,600
	Volcano of Arequipa	18,300
	Nevado de Chuquibamba	21,000
	" *Sasaguanca*	17,904
	Chimborazo	21,440
	Illiniza	17,376
	Volcano of Pichincha, near Quito	15,936
	Cotocache	16,448
	Volcano of Cotopaxi	18,890
	" *Antisana*	19,150
	Cayambe	19,648

THE CORDILLERAS CONTINUED.

	Nevado de Sorato	25,400
	" *de Illimani,* 1st peak	24,450
	" " 2d peak	24,200
	Volcano de Gualatieri	22,000
	Cerro de Potosi	16,037
	Peak of Tolima	18,336
In Venezuela	*Sierra de Merida*	16,420
	Nevado de Mucachies	15,986
	Silla de Caraccas	8,632
2. THE MOUNTAINS OF BRAZIL	*Summit of the Chain of Mantiquera*	8,421
	Itacolumi, Sierra do Espinhaco	5,710
	Sierra de Piedada, near Sabara	5,818
	" *de Frio*	5,850
	" *d'Arasoiaba*	4,093
	" *Tingua,* near Rio Janeiro	3,549

The MAJESTIC RIVERS OF SOUTH AMERICA leave far behind them those of the Old World, both in the length of their course and the breadth of their streams.

Owing to the peculiar construction of South America, no rivers of any magnitude flow from it into the Pacific Ocean, the Andes forming a continued barrier along the whole western coast. From a similar reason no important stream enters the Atlantic between 12° and 32° south latitude. More than three-fourths of all the waters which fall on this continent are carried to the ocean through the channels of the Orinoco, Amazon, and La Plata.

The ORINOCO, from its position, will claim attention first. It rises in latitude 5° north, and longitude 65° west. Its course is very crooked, somewhat resembling the figure 6. For the first 300 miles it runs from north to south. It then turns, and proceeds in a westerly direction for several hundred miles, to San Fernando, where it receives from the south-west the Guaviari, a very considerable river. Here it turns northward, and, after receiving the Vichada from the west, pours its waters down the cataracts of Atures. These cataracts are 740 miles from the mouth of the Orinoco, and 760 from its source, and completely obstruct the navigation. At the distance of ninety miles below the cataracts, the river is enlarged by the junction of the Meta, one of its principal tributaries, which is 500 miles long, and navigable 370 miles. About ninety miles below the mouth of the Meta, the Orinoco receives from the west the Apure, a large and deep river, 520 miles long, having numerous and wide-spreading branches, and is more rapid than the Orinoco, into which it empties its waters by many mouths. After receiving the Apure it turns, and, running about 400 miles in an easterly direction, divides into many branches, and discharges its waters into the ocean by fifty mouths, the two most distant of which are 180 miles apart. Only seven, however, are navigable, and but one of them, the southern, called the Ship's Mouth, for vessels of more than 200 tons. All the rivers which rise on the southern declivity of the chain of Venezuela, and on the eastern declivity of the Andes, between the parallels of 2° and 9° north latitude, are tributaries of the Orinoco. It thus forms the channel which conveys to the ocean the waters of an immense basin, extending from east to west about 1,000 miles, and from north to south, in many parts, between 5 and 600.

The AMAZON, the largest river in America, rises in Peru, between two ridges of the Andes, in about latitude 16° south, under the name of the Apurimac, and, after running in a northerly direction through five degrees of latitude, is joined by other branches, and forms the Ucayale. The Ucayale runs north 6° more, and unites with the Tunguragua, and forms the Amazon. It then runs in a direction a little north of east, completely across the continent, and discharges its waters under the equator by a mouth 180 miles wide, after a course of more than 4,000 miles. The tide flows up 400 miles, and the river is navigable to the very foot of the Andes. The principal branches of the Amazon from the south, are 1. The Tunguragua and Ucayale, already mentioned. 2. The Madeira, the principal tributary of the Amazon, rises in Bolivia, near Potosi, about 20° south latitude, and passes, under various names, into Brazil, where it is joined by numerous other rivers, and makes its way in a north-easterly direction to the Amazon, into which it falls, after a course of more than 2,000 miles. 3. The Tocantins, which discharges itself into the Amazon near its mouth, after a northerly course of about 1,500 miles. Its principal tributary, the Araguay, rises between the parallels of 18° and 19° south latitude. The other principal tributaries of the Amazon from the south, are Jutay, the Juruay, and the Puros, which join it between the Ucayale and the Madeira; and the Tapajos and Xingu, which join it between the Madeira and the Tocantins. The principal rivers which fall into the Amazon on its northern bank, beginning in the west, are the Napo, the Putumayo or Ica, the Yapura and the Negro. The Negro is remarkable for sending off a branch towards the north, which, under the name of Cassiquiari, falls into the Orinoco, and thus unites the Amazon with that mighty stream. All the rivers which rise on the eastern declivity of the Andes, between the parallels of 2° north latitude and 20° of south latitude, are tributaries of the Amazon. Not a single brook rises in all this distance which does not contribute to swell its waters. The basin of the Amazon is thus more than 1,500 miles long, from north to south; from east to west, it is more than 2,000; and its area may be estimated at 3,000,000 square miles, or nearly half of South America.

The Rio de la Plata is a very broad stream, formed by the Uruguay and the Parana, which unite near latitude 34° south. It is more properly the mouth or estuary of these two rivers, as it is nowhere less than 30 miles broad, and at its entrance into the ocean, between the parallels of 35° and 36°, expands to the width of 150 miles.

The Uruguay, the eastern branch of the Plata, rises on the western declivity of the Andes of Brazil, and pursues a south-westerly course of more than 1,000 miles, for the last 200 of which it is navigable.

The Parana, or western branch of the Plata, is formed by the union of several small streams, which rise also on the western declivity of the Andes of Brazil, between 18° and 21° south latitude. It runs on the whole in a south-westerly direction about 1,000 miles, till it receives the Paraguay from the north, when it turns to the south, and after a further course of 500 miles, joins the Uruguay.

The Paraguay is formed by several streams, which rise between the parallels of 13° and 14° south latitude, near the head waters of the Tapajos, the Xingu, the Tocantins, and other tributaries of the Amazon. It pursues a southerly course through nearly 14 degrees of latitude, and joins the Parana under the parallel of 27° south latitude.

The Pilcomayo and the Vermejo, the principal western branches of the Paraguay, both rise in the Andes, between 20° and 23° south latitude, and pursue a south-easterly course of more than 1,000 miles.

The Saladillo is a considerable stream, which rises in the interior of the

Argentine province of Salta, and joins the Rio de la Plata 50 miles from its mouth, after a south-easterly course of several hundred miles. The valley of La Plata thus includes the extensive country bounded west by the Andes of Chili, and north and east by the high lands and mountains of Brazil, embracing the whole Argentine Republic and the southern part of the great empire of Brazil, and covering an area of about 1,200,000 square miles.

To complete the physical description of South America, we shall now proceed to consider the various animals that live at different heights in the Cordillera of the Andes, or at the foot of those mountains. From the level of the sea to 3,078 feet, in the region of the palms and the scitamineæ, we meet with the sloth, which lives on the *Cecropia peltata;* the boa, and the crocodile, which sleep or drag along their frightful mass at the foot of the *Conocarpus* and the *Anacardium caracoli.* It is there that the *Cavia capybara* hides himself in the marshes that are covered with the *Heliconia* and the *Bambusa*, to withdraw himself from the pursuit of the carnivorous animals. The *Tanagra*, the *Crax*, and the *Parrots*, perched on the *Caryocar* and the *Lecythis*, mingle the brilliancy of their plumage with that of the flowers and leaves. It is there that we see the glittering of the *Elater noctilucus*, which feeds on the sugar-cane; and there, too, the *Curculio palmarum* lives in the heart of the cocoa-nut tree. The forests of these burning regions resound with the howlings of the alouates, and other sapajous. The *jaguar*, the *Felis concolar*, and the black tiger of the Orinoco, still more sanguinary than the jaguar, there relentlessly chase the little stag, (*Cervus Mexicanus,*) the *Cavias*, and the ant-eaters, whose tongue is fixed to the end of their sternum. The air of these lower regions, especially in the woods and on the banks of the rivers, swarms with those countless myriads of the *mosquito*, a fly which renders a large and beautiful portion of the globe almost uninhabitable. To the mosquito is added the *Oestrus humanus*, which deposits its eggs in the skin of the human body, and occasions painful swellings; the *Acari*, which furrows the skin; venomous spiders, and ants and termites, whose formidable industry destroys the labors and the books of the inhabitants. Still higher, from 3,078 to 6,156 feet, in the region of the arborescent ferns, we seldom meet with the *jaguar*, never with the boa, alligator, or lamentin, and rarely with the monkey; but the tapir, the *Sus tajassu*, and the *Felis pardalis*, are there numerous. Man, the monkey, and the dog, are there incommoded by an infinite multitude of the *Pulex penetrans*, which is less abundant on the plains. From 6,156 to 9,234 feet, in the higher region of the cinchona, we no longer meet with the monkey or the Mexican stag; but we now find the tiger cat, the bear, and the great stag of the Andes. Lice abound in the Andes at this height. From 9,234 to 12,300 feet, is found the small species of lion, which, in the Quichua language, is known by the name of the *puma;* the lesser bear, with a white forehead; and some of the weasel tribe. Humboldt has often seen, with astonishment, the *colibri*, or humming-bird, at the height of the Peak of Teneriffe. The region of the grasses, from 12,300 to 15,400 feet of elevation, is inhabited by flocks of the *vicuna guanaco*, and *alpaco*, in Peru, and the *chili-hueque*, in Chili. These quadrupeds, which here represent the genus *Camelus* of the old continent, have not extended themselves to Brazil, because, during their journey, they must necessarily have descended into regions that were too hot for them to exist in. The *llama* is only met with in the domestic state. The vicuna prefers those places in particular where snow occasionally falls. Notwithstanding the persecution which it has experienced, flocks of 300 or 400 in number are still to be seen, at the sources of the River Amazon. This animal likewise abounds near Huancavelica, in the environs of Cuzco, and in the province of Cochabamba, near the valley of the *Rio Cocatages.* They are found then wherever the summit of the Andes rises higher than the summit of Mont Blanc. The inferior limit of perpetual snow is the higher boundary, as it were, of organized beings; some of the lichens even grow under the snow itself; but the condor, (*Vultur gryphus,*) is the only animal which inhabits these solitudes. Humboldt has seen them sailing through the air at the immense height of 21,100 feet. Some sphinxes and flies were observed at the height of 19,180 feet, and appeared to him to have been involuntarily carried into these regions by ascending currents of air.

To this distribution of the animal kingdom, according to the elevation of the country, might be joined a sketch of the purely geographical limits which certain animals never pass. It is a remarkable phenomenon that the *alpaco, viçuna* and *guanaco,* follow the whole chain of the Andes, from Chili to the 9° of south latitude, and that none should afterwards be observed north of this point. The writers of the country attribute this fact to the herb *ichos,* which these animals prefer to every other kind of food, but which they do not meet with beyond the above limits. The ostrich of Buenos Ayres presents an analogous phenomenon. This great bird is not found on the vast plains of the Parexis, where, nevertheless, the vegetation appears to resemble that of the Pampas. Perhaps, however, the saline plants may not exist there.

South America, though as yet an almost uninhabited desert, has been appropriated by its several nations. The following distinct political divisions are recognized:

1.	REPUBLIC OF NEW GRENADA.	formerly the Vice-royalty of New Grenada.	late Republic of Colombia.	All formed from the old Spanish Possessions.
2.	" EQUADOR.			
3.	" VENEZUELA: formerly Captaincy-General.			
4.	" PERU.	together the Vice-royalty of Peru.		
5.	" BOLIVIA.			
6.	" CHILI, with the Islands of Juan Fernandez, &c.			
7.	ARGENTINE REPUBLIC.	the former Vice-royalty of Buenos Ayres.		
8.	REPUBLIC OF URUGUAY.			
9.	" PARAGUAY.			
10.	EMPIRE OF BRAZIL: a colony of Portugal until 1822.			
11.	BRITISH	GUAYANA: colonies belonging to those nations.		
12.	FRENCH			
13.	DUTCH			
14.	Patagonia and Terra del Fuego: as yet only inhabited by hordes of wild Indians.			

THE REPUBLIC OF NEW GRENADA.

NEW GRENADA, formerly a vice-royalty of Spain, and also one of the states comprised in the late Republic of Colombia, extends from 12° N. to 2° S. latitude, and is bounded on the north by the Caribbean Sea and a part of Venezuela, from which it is divided by the central chain of the Andes; on the south by Equador, and on the west by the Pacific Ocean and the south-eastern extremity of Central America. It is the most important of the three independent states formed from the Colombian Confederation, and comprises an area of 380,000 square miles, and has a population, according to an official statement, of 1,687,000.

The whole country is divided into *five* principal departments, and again subdivided into *eighteen* provinces. The departments are those of

	Approximate Population.	*Capitals.*
Istmo	100,000	Panama.
Magdalena	450,000	Cartagena.
Boyaca	600,000	Tunga.
Cundinamarca	350,000	SANTA FE DE BOGÔTA
Cauca	187,000	Popayan.
Total	1,687,000=4.4 to the square mile.	

The different races are in the following proportions:

Whites and Creoles	1,058,000
Indians	376,000
Free Colored	168,000
Slaves	85,000

It must, however, be remembered, that the above representations are not founded on any census, but are given as mere estimates, and as such even for no very late date. The statistics of this country are little known, and little reliance can be placed even on the most authentic to be found.

The topographical aspect of New Grenada presents a great diversity of scenery: alpine regions and extensive plains occupy the greater portion of the country. The chain of the Andes, on the northern frontier of Equador, separates into two parallel ranges, enclosing the lofty Valley of Pastos, bounded by the still active volcanos of Azufsal, Gambal, &c., and the extinct one of Chiles. Beyond Pastos, the Cordilleras consist of three ranges: the most westerly, the elevation of which is generally less than 5,000 feet, follows the coast of the Pacific, and extends into the Isthmus of Panama; the central range is interposed between the vallies of the Cauca and Magdalena rivers, and terminates at Mompox, between latitude 9 and 10 degrees north, and the third, being the most easterly and highest range, extends to the extremity of the Parian promontory, in longitude 62° west. This last is named the Venezuelan range, and divides the waters which flow into the Orinoco, on the south-east, from the Magdalena, Zulia, Tocuyo, &c., and their affluents on its north-west side. Many of its summits reach above the limits of perpetual snow; and it has numerous lower summits, called *paramos*, which rise to 10,000 or 12,000 feet above the level of the sea, and are constantly enveloped in damp and thick fogs. The City of Bogôta, 8,100 feet above the sea, is built on a table-land formed from this mountain range, as also are the towns of Nirgua, San Felipe el Fuerte, Barquesimeto and Tocuyo; but these are at a much lower elevation than Bogôta, the mountains decreasing in height very considerably on approaching the territory of Venezuela. The mean elevation of the Andes, in New Grenada, is about 11,000 feet; their altitude is greatest on nearing the equator.

The table-lands formed between the several ranges of the mountains, constitute the most valuable portions of the country. The *Llanos*, or plains, commence at the foot of the Eastern Andes, and extend thence into the Venezuelan territories. The table-land of Santa Fé de Bogôta, being 8,100 feet above the level of the sea, is remarkable for many very striking and picturesque features; the Falls of Tequendama are said to be the most elevated in the world, though not equal in volume to the Cataract of Niagara; and the natural bridge of Icononza is certainly unequalled in magnificence. The former of these is formed by the river Bogôta, whose waters are contracted to the breadth of about 40 feet, and dashed suddenly down a precipice 650 feet high into a dark and almost fathomless abyss. The bridge of Icononza is a natural arch, crossing a chasm of 360 feet deep, and forms the only practicable passage across the gap. The plain itself is hemmed in by lofty and precipitous mountains and almost impassable abysses, with swollen and roaring torrents rushing along their frightful depths. The soil of the plain is exceedingly fertile, yielding two crops a year, and the climate is that of spring and autumn in more northern latitudes, the thermometer falling seldom below 47° or rising above 70°. The only variations are those of the two wet seasons, which are colder in a slight degree than the dry. The other table-lands partake of the same character of soil and climate, though not equally noted with that of Bogôta. The plains of the east bear all the characteristics of their tropical position: these, however, are as yet scarcely redeemed from their primitive solitude or the wilderness state in which the first discoverers found them. Their riches await as yet the hand of the bold emigrant to grasp them; and it is a pleasing reflection that the government has adopted the enlightened policy of assisting the poor of other countries to emigrate to these vast unoccupied regions, which yield spontaneously all the requirements of nature, and with little trouble would amply reward the endeavors of the husbandman. The vallies of the great rivers of this country, and these vast plains, in a few ages will teem with a busy multitude, and rival the fertility and abundance of the prolific basin of the Mississippi, in North America.

The principal rivers are the Cauca and Magdalena, which run their whole course within the territory of the republic, taking their rise in the Andes, near the southern frontier, and, after flowing nearly the entire length of the country, unite in one, and discharge their combined waters through a delta of three canals, into the Caribbean Sea, about longitude 75°. Beside these, a large number of the tributaries of the Orinoco find their sources in the different ranges of the Andes, and water the Llanos of the east: the principal of these are the Apure, Meta, &c., which are navigable almost to their sources, and in connection with the Orinoco, will eventually contribute to form lines of communication, from the Atlantic to the Pacific, by steam-boats, and be a principal means by which the resources of this wealthy country will be developed, at no very distant day. The lakes of New Grenada are of inconsiderable extent: the most celebrated is that of Guatavita, not far from the city of Bogôta, into which, it is affirmed, large treasures were thrown by the natives during the period of the Spanish conquests. Some extensive salt marshes are to be met with in different parts of the north-west coast.

New Grenada, like the other mountainous countries of South America, is rich in minerals. The Cordilleras teem with metallic wealth, and though imperfectly explored, have already produced large quantities of gold, silver, platina, mercury, copper, lead and iron; the gold is mostly obtained by washing the auriferous soils, and comes chiefly from the provinces of Choco, Antioguia and Popayan; silver is found in the province of Pamplona, and the valley of the Cauca; platina, on the coast of the Pacific; mercury and cinnabar, in several parts, as well as lead; and iron pit-coal in abundance in the plain of Bogôta. Copper, in great plenty, is found, especially at Aroa. There are mines of rock salt in the mountains north-east of Bogôta, and caves producing nitre near the Lake Guatavita. Hot sulphureous springs exist in several parts. There are also some pearl-fisheries, on both the Pacific and in the Caribbean Sea, which are prosecuted, however, with but indifferent success.

The climate of New Grenada is as diversified as the surface; on the Pacific and in the vallies of the great rivers the climatic influences of the latitude are fully recognized, and the diseases of tropical climates are very prevalent. In the mountain regions elevation demarks the peculiarities of the climate, which of course varies, and successively present the gradations between the heats of the tropics and the eternal winters of the polar regions. At an elevation from 6,000 to 10,000 feet perpetual spring sheds its balmy breath over the land, and health is the prerogative of the inhabitants. *Goitre* is the only disease indigenous to these districts, and in some cases the tumor attains an extraordinary magnitude. This disease, which is also prevalent in the mountains of Switzerland, is said to be caused by peculiarities in the water, which contains lime and other extraneous matter; but to whatever cause it may be attributed, there is no doubt but that care of diet will greatly protect the people from its attack. Iodine, and its various salts, have been found efficacious in reducing the swellings in this disease.

In order to avoid the excessive heat, and the diseases that prevail during summer on the sea-board, those Europeans who are not habituated to the climate, take refuge in the interior of the country, at the village of Turbaco, built on an eminence, at the entrance of a majestic forest, which extends as far as the River Magdalena. The houses are chiefly constructed of bamboo, and covered with palm-leaves. Limpid springs issue from a calcareous rock, which contains numerous remains of coral petrifactions; and a refreshing shade is afforded by the shining foliage of the *Anacardium Caracoli*, a tree of colossal size, to which the natives attribute the property of attracting, from a great distance, the vapors that float in the atmosphere. The surface of Turbaco being elevated more than 900 feet above the level of the sea, they enjoy a delicious coolness, especially during the night. A very curious phenomenon is observed in its neighborhood. The *volcancitos* are situated at the distance of 18,000 feet to the east of the village of Turbaco, in a thick forest, which abounds with the *Toluifera balsamum;* the *gustavia* with flowers of the Nymphea; and with the *Cavanillesia mocundo*, the numerous and transparent fruits of which resemble lanterns suspended from the extremity of the branches. The land gradually rises to a height of 120 or 150 feet above the village of Turbaco; but the soil being everywhere covered with vegetation, prevents us from distinguishing the nature of the rocks that rest upon the above-mentioned calcareous mass, impregnated with sea-shell. In the middle of an extensive plain, enclosed on all sides by the *Bromelia Karatas*, eighteen or twenty small cones are observed, the height of which is not more than from twenty to twenty-five feet. These cones are formed of a blackish-grey clay, and at the top of each is found an opening filled with water. On approaching these little craters, is heard, at intervals, a hollow and pretty loud noise, which precedes, by from fifteen to eighteen seconds, the disengagement of a great quantity of air. The force with which this air rises above the surface of the water, induces us to suppose, that, in the interior of the earth, it experiences a high degree of pressure. Humboldt generally counted five explosions in two minutes. Very frequently this phenomenon is accompanied with an ejection of mud. It is affirmed that the cones do not undergo any perceptible changes of form during the space of a great number of years; but the force with which the gas ascends, and the frequency of the explosions, appear to vary according to the seasons. The analyses of Humboldt have proved that the air thus disengaged does not contain a thousandth part of oxygen. It is azotic gas, of a purer quality than what we commonly prepare in our laboratories.

The agriculture of this state is generally much neglected, but the present government has felt itself called upon to attempt its improvement, and have concluded to forward the design by introducing foreigners from Europe and the United States of America, and the improved agricultural implements of those nations. The great variety of soil and climate renders the culture of both tropical as well as northern staples practicable. Coffee, cotton, cocoa, indigo, sugar, tobacco, &c., flourish in the savannas east of the Andes, and are considered as articles of export; the grain and nutritious roots, known in the West-Indies as ground provisions, are produced only in sufficient quantities for home consumption. Maize is grown every where, and when ripe, is pounded in wooden mortars into a coarse meal, there being no more perfect machinery for grinding it. Wheat is grown on the higher lands, and on the elevated mountain plains, where it succeeds as well as in the western parts of the United States, and often yields 40 bushels to the acre, and two crops may be produced in the year. A substitute for bread is found in *Cassava,* which is procured by a process similar to that for making starch, from the *Yuca* root; the plantain is, to the mass of the natives, what the potatoe has become to the poor of Ireland; but the rice of the lowlands of New Grenada is indifferent. Coffee is chiefly cultivated in the province of Santa Marta, but its culture is conducted with less care than in the West-India Islands. Cotton is chiefly grown in Cartagena; it is grown on the newly-cleared lands, between successive crops of maize, but the produce is said to be inferior to that from the uplands of North America, which is, in a great measure, owing to the defective mode generally followed of cleaning and depriving it of the seed. The growth of this article for export is very insignificant. The works erected in different parts of the country for the manufacture of sugar, were mostly destroyed during the revolutionary struggle, and very few of them have been repaired. No sugar is now exported, and the half-inspissated juice of the cane is only used for confectionary, or is eaten by the natives with their chocolate.

From what has been said, it will be evident that New Grenada is a country of great natural riches, suffered to lie, for the most part, waste. Were its inhabitants of an active and industrious disposition, and its resources developed, even in a moderate degree, it would be one of the richest and most important countries in the world. Previous to the discovery of the country, horses and cattle were unknown in these regions; but now, since their introduction, they have increased to such an extent as to form one of the great exports. Sheep and goats are plenty on the rich plains of Bogôta, &c.; animal food is cheap, and much consumed; and hides, wool and cheese, form a principal portion of rural produce. In some parts of New-Grenada the farms are surrounded by stone walls, which give them an air of importance not often seen, and here, in general, cultivation is in a tolerably advanced condition. Very few persons, however, have estates worth $5,000 a year; a sum which is considered in this country as a princely income.

The wild animals of New Grenada, are jaguars, tapirs, &c.; monkies are of many species, and in great numbers. Vultures, flamingoes, parrots, parroquets, &c., are abundant, and the alligator and numerous serpents are indigenous to the lower parts of the country. The rivers are well stocked with fish, and the electric eel is found in the marshes. Scorpions, millepedes, scolopendres, termites, mosquitoes, and other insects, infest the atmosphere, and prove both dangerous and annoying to the dwellers on the coasts.

The manufactures of the country are of the simplest kinds, consisting chiefly of leather, hammocks, baizes, hats and salt. None of them are of importance. The principal salt-works are at Araya and Santa Marta.

The facilities for internal communication have been very much neglected: but lately the inhabitants have been roused to the full sense of the importance of easy access to the several parts of the country. Steamboats have been established on the Magdalena and other rivers, which will much facilitate the developement of the country bordering on that great river, and open rich stores to commerce. The system of roads is altogether unavailable and bad: there is scarcely a passable road throughout the whole country. The backs of mules form the principal means of conveyance; and in places along the Andes, where even these cannot find a sure footing, men are employed to transport travellers in a rude kind of chair fastened to the back. Bridges are almost unknown: the method of crossing streams is by ropes stretched from one side to the other, with sling and basket, in which the passenger is seated, and pulled safely over the rivers or abyss, as the case may be. The spirit of improvement, however, which has lately developed itself in this country, will, no doubt, be directed to this department, and we may look at no distant day for a rectification in this matter.

There is a considerable inland trade carried on by the merchants of the coast. Foreign imports are sent by the steamboats on the Magdelena, or carried on the backs of mules into the interior, and the metals, hides and other produce are brought down and re-shipped to foreign countries in exchange. The foreign commerce is by no means insignificant. New Grenada is not outrivalled by any of its competitors of Spanish origin, nor is there any appearance that any interruption, such as is now laying waste Venezuela and Bolivia, will suspend the prosperity of the country. The ports of Santa Marta, Cartagena, Chagres, Panama and Puerto-Bello, are those most frequented by foreign traders, and the following countries are principally concerned in the trade: England, France, United States, Holland and Spain, the countries being placed in relation to the extent of their transactions.

The average annual value of the commerce of New Grenada (see *De Bow's Com. Rev.*, vol. vi., p. 19., *July*, 1848) is estimated at 40,000,000 francs. The imports, in 1840, scarcely exceeded 17,000,000 francs; in 1843, they rose to 23,000,000, and in 1844, again fell off to 22,000,000 francs. In 1843, the exports amounted to 16,000,000 francs, and in 1844, to 14,000,000 francs. The contraband trade is very large. Commercial transactions carried on with the following nations approximate to the proportions annexed:

Jamaica and England, . . .	about	13,000,000	francs.
France, ...	"	3,769,000	"
United States, ...	"	1,000,000	"
Island of Curacoâ, ...	"	820,000	"
Spain, ...	"	610,000	"
Venezuela and Peru, each	750,000=	1,500,000	"

The exports from the United States, are flour, salt, dry-goods, drugs, &c. The value of its commerce with that country during the year ending 30th June, 1846, was, imports $67,043, and exports $75,944, of which $51,849 was for domestic, and $24,095 for foreign products and merchandise. The port of Cartagena, on the northern coast, is one of the finest harbors of the world. The coasting trade is chiefly conducted from the port of Panama. A line of steamships, owned by the British, carry the mails from Chagres to Valparaiso, and the West India steamers plying between England, the United States, (New-York and Cat Island,) leave the mails at the isthmus, to be carried across to that point, and receive the return mail.

The United States have lately concluded a treaty* with this country, highly conducive to the interests of both nations, and it may be premised that the United States have secured the privilege of constructing canals or railroads across the isthmus from the Atlantic to the Pacific; but whether to the exclusion of other nations, to which the same right had been formerly conceded, is a matter of question.

---

* The following abstract contains the most important section of the Treaty of 1848:

"Article 35. The United States of America and the Republic of New Grenada desiring to make as durable as possible the relations which are to be established between the two parties by virtue of this treaty, have declared solemnly, and do agree to the following points:

"1st. For the better understanding of the preceding articles, it is and has been stipulated between the high contracting parties, that the citizens, vessels, and merchandise of the United States shall enjoy in the ports of New Grenada, including those of the part of the Grenadan territory generally denominated *Isthmus of Panama*, from its southernmost extremity until the boundary of Costa Rica, all the exemptions, privileges, and immunities, concerning commerce and navigation, which are now, or may hereafter be enjoyed by the Grenadan citizens, their vessels, and merchandise; and that this equality of favors shall be made to extend to the passengers, correspondence, and merchandise of the United States, in their transit across the said territory, from one sea to the other. The Government of New Grenada guaranties to the Government of the United States, that the right of way or transit across the *Isthmus of Panama*, upon any modes of communication that now exist, or that may hereafter be constructed, shall be open and free to the government and citizens of the United States, and for the transportation of articles of produce, manufactures, or merchandise, of lawful commerce, belonging to the citizens of the United States; that no other tolls or charges shall be levied or collected upon the citizens of the United States, or their said merchandise thus passing over any road or canal, that may be made by the government of New Grenada, or by the authority of the same, than is, under like circumstances, levied upon and collected from Grenadan citizens; that any lawful produce, manufacture or merchandise belonging to the citizens of the United States, thus passing from one sea to the other, in either direction, for the purpose of exportation to any other foreign country, shall not be liable to any import duties whatever; or, having paid such duties, they shall be entitled to drawback upon their exportation; nor shall the citizens of the United States be liable to any duties, tolls or charges of any kind, to which native citizens are not subjected in passing the said isthmus. And, in order to secure to themselves the tranquil and constant enjoyment of these advantages, and as an especial compensation for the said advantages, and for the favors they have acquired by the 4th, 5th, and 6th articles of this treaty, the United States guaranty, positively and efficaciously, to New Grenada, by the present stipulation, the perfect neutrality of the before-mentioned isthmus, with the view that the free transit, from the one to the other sea, may not be interrupted or embarrassed in any future time while this treaty exists; and, in consequence, the United States also guaranty, in the same manner, the rights of sovereignty and property which New Grenada has and possesses over the said territory."

The public revenue is raised from import and export duties, taxes,(*rentas internas,*) salt-mines, post-offices, and in times of disturbance, from voluntary and extraordinary contributions. This revenue averages about $3,500,000 a year, and the ordinary expenses do not entirely consume the amount. The national debt is not very large, and is chiefly owing to the English. The Congress has appropriated for its payment one-eighth of the customs, as well as the surplus revenue and national profits on tobacco and the sale of public lands.

The form of government of New Grenada is based upon the plan of that of the United States. The legislative function is vested in a Senate and House of Representatives, both consisting of members elected by the cantonal deputies of the provinces, in a provincial assembly, held once in four years: the Executive is vested in a President and Vice-President, the former of whom is elected for a period of four years. The constitution is, with slight variations, the same as was adopted by the former Confederation at Cucuta, on the 18th July, 1821. The departments have each an Intendente, with full powers under the General Government, save military command; the provinces are under the administration of governors, with similar powers and restrictions, and the cantons and parishes have each their own officers.

The laws, as in all the old Spanish colonies, are an ill-digested mass of the laws of Spain and the Indies, but even such as they are they would be tolerable, if they were not so badly administered. The justice of these countries is generally dearly sold, and it seems to be a maxim that justice is too precious an article to deal out cheaply to the people. The poor here, indeed, have no redress from the laws. Trial by jury, however, is allowed to all.

The Roman Catholic is the religion of the nation, and the church festivals and celebrations are conducted with extraordinary magnificence. The clergy are paid by the State, but since the revolution they have lost much of that influence they formerly possessed over the minds of the people. Education is more flourishing in New Grenada than in the other Colombian states, and as a consequence the people are more intelligent and refined. The government is making great efforts to instruct the population, and Lancasterian schools are now established in all the chief cities and towns; and elementary schools are, by law, supported in every district of the country. The fine arts of this country are chiefly confined to the capital, where some degree of architectural taste is displayed in the buildings; otherwise mediocrity in this department prevails.

The people of New Grenada, especially as refers to the whites, negroes and mixed races, are similar to the same classes throughout Spanish America. Many of the Indian tribes still enjoy their independence, and almost all of them retain their language and particular customs. The *Guairas* or *Guagniros,* occupy part of the provinces of Rio de la Hacha and Santa Marta, and live on friendly terms with the *Motilones*, who inhabit the lands watered by the Muchuchies and the St. Faustin, as far as the valley of Cucuta. They infest the passes of the mountains; pillage, conflagration and murder mark their incursions into the plains. The *Chilimes*, and another band of the Guairas, are freebooters on the banks of the Magdalena. The *Urabas*, the *Zitaras* and the *Oromisas*, form three independent states in the province of Darien, the first under a native prince called the *Playon*, the two last under a republican government. The *Curacunas* dwell on the mountains of Choco and Novita; they extend their ravages as far as Panama, and even attack small vessels in search of plunder. The ancient inhabitants of Quito are said to have spoken many different dialects. The missionaries have specified not less than a hundred and seventeen; it appears, however, that the language of the *Quitos* prevailed over the plateau, and that of the *Scires* along the coast. It is remarkable that the name of the Scires should be the same as that of an ancient European tribe, famous for its migrations and warlike exploits. They are said to have conquered the upper districts, and introduced their language into that part of Quito in the year 1000. At the time of the arrival of the Spaniards, the Peruvians were in possession of the country, and their language was generally adopted; but must we therefore conclude, with Hervas, that the Scires spoke a Peruvian dialect? In the year 1600, the *Cofanes*, one of the hundred and seventeen tribes of Quito, are said to have amounted to fifteen thousand souls; they spoke a peculiar language, which was also spoken by the inhabitants of *Anga Marca*, and in which a Jesuit has written an epitome of Christianity. Of the fifty-two tribes of Popayan, those of *Guasinca, Cocanuca* and *Paos*, had three distinct languages, which are still partly preserved in the writings of the missionaries. The *Xibaros*, the *Macas* and the *Quixos*, at one time formidable tribes, occupied the eastern declivities of the Andes, in the kingdom of Quito. Nearer the level of the sea, in the vast district of *Maynas*, are found the remains of unnumbered tribes, whose languages the missionaries have classed in the following order:—1st, Sixteen mother tongues, of which the *Andoa* has nine dialects, the *Campa* seven, and the *Mayna* four; 2dly, Sixteen scattered dialects that have no resemblance to any known mother tongue; 3dly, Twenty-two tribes, several of which are still extant, although their language is extinct; lastly, ten unknown languages. We have not included in this list the extensive tribe of the *Omaguas;* its inhabitants, spread over the whole course of the Maranon or Amazon, speak a dialect of the Guarani language in Brazil, but simpler in its grammatical forms, and more abundant in its vocabulary, from which we may infer that they had arrived at a greater degree of civilization than their kindred tribes. The migrations of this tribe of river navigators have not been clearly ascertained, but it is generally believed that they were originally from Brazil.

A civilized country, surrounded by these savage and wandering nations, is a phenomenon worthy of our particular attention. Santa Fé de Bogôta rivals Cuzco, the city of the sun, as a city of religious and civil institutions. We shall therefore proceed to illustrate this interesting problem in the history of society.

In the most remote period of antiquity, before the moon accompanied the earth, according to the mythology of the *Muyscas*, the inhabitants of Cundinamarca, on the plateau of Bogôta, lived like savages, without agriculture, laws, or religion. An aged person appeared suddenly amongst them, who came from the plains on the east of the Cordillera of Chingaza. His long and thick beard showed that his origin was not the same as that of the natives. He was known by three different names: Bochica, Nemquetheba, and Zuhé. Like Manco-Capac, he taught men to clothe themselves, to build cottages, to cultivate the ground, and to live in society. He brought with him a wife, to whom tradition has also given three names, Chia, Yubecayguaya, and Huythaca. She was remarkable for her beauty, but more so for her wickedness. She opposed all her husband's labors for the happiness of the human race; by her magic she raised the waters of the River Funzha, and inundated the whole valley of Bogôta. In this deluge, the greater number of the inhabitants were destroyed; a few only escaped to the summits of the neighboring mountains. The aged stranger, provoked by such crimes, drove Huythaca from the earth; she became the moon, and began, at that period, to illuminate our planet during the night. Bochica, pitying those that wandered in the mountains, broke the rocks which enclosed the valley on the side of Canoas and Tequendama. The waters of the Funzha having by this means subsided, he brought back the people to the vale of Bogôta, founded cities, introduced the worship of the sun, and named two chiefs, whom he invested with the religious and civil authority. He then withdrew to Mount Idacanzas, in the sacred valley of Iraca, near Tunja; having lived at this place in the exercise of the most austere devotion for two thousand years, or a hundred Muysca cycles, he disappeared at the end of that time in a mysterious manner.

This Indian fable bears an analogy to some opinions contained in the religious traditions of different nations in the old world. The good and evil principles are personified in the aged Zuhé and his wife Huythaca. The broken rocks, through which a passage is made for the waters, recalls to mind what is related of Yao, the founder of the Chinese empire. A remote period before the existence of the moon is taken notice of by the Arcadians, a people that boasted of their ancient origin. The moon was considered as a malevolent being, that increased the humidity of the earth; but Bochica, the offspring of the sun, drained the soil, protected agriculture, and was as much revered, as a benefactor, by the Muyscas, as the first Inca by the Peruvians.

There is a tradition that Bochica, observing the chiefs of the different tribes contending for the supremacy, advised them to choose *Huncahua* for their *zaque*, or sovereign, a person distinguished for his justice and great wisdom. The advice of the high priest was willingly obeyed, and Huncahua having reigned for two hundred and fifty years, made himself master of all the country from the savannas of San Juan de los Llanos to the mountains of Opon. The form of government which Bochica gave the inhabitants of Bogôta, resembled those of Japan and Thibet. In Peru, the Incas held in their own hands the ecclesiastical and secular power, and were kings and priests at the same time. At Cundinamarca, at a period probably anterior to that of Manco-Capac, Bochica appointed four electors, Gameza, Busbanca, Pesca, and Toca, the chiefs of their respective tribes; after his death, these persons and their descendants had the privilege of choosing the high priest of Iraca. The pontiffs, or lamas, being the successors of Bochica, were supposed to inherit his virtues and his sanctity. The people flocked in crowds to the Iraca, that they might offer gifts to their high priest. Many places in which Bochica wrought miracles, were visited with holy ardor. In time of war, pilgrims enjoyed the protection of the princes, through whose territory they passed to repair to the sanctuary, (*chunsua*,) and to prostrate themselves before the lama, who resided there. The secular chief was denominated the *zaque* of Tunja, to whom the *zippas* or princes of Bogôta paid an annual tribute. Thus the high priest and the zaque formed two distinct powers, like the dairi and secular emperor in Japan.

Bochica was not only regarded as the author of a new worship, and as the legislator of the Muyscas, but being the symbol of the sun, he measured the seasons, taught the Muyscas the use of their calendar, and marked the order of sacrifices to be offered at the close of the little cycles, at the period of every fifth lunar intercalation. In the dominions of the zaque, the day and night (or the *sua* and *za*) were divided into four parts: the *sua mena* lasted from sunrise to noon; the *sua meca*, from noon to sunset; the *zasca*, from sunset to midnight, and the *caqui*, from midnight to sunrise. In the Muysca language, *sua* or *zuhe* signifies the sun as well as a day. From *sua*, which is one of the surnames of Bochica, is derived *sue*, a European or white man, a word that was first applied to the Spaniards, who landed with Quesada, because the natives believed them to be the children of the sun. The Muyscas computed their time by divisions of three days; hebdomadal periods were unknown in America, as well as in a part of Eastern Asia. The year (*zocam*) was calculated by lunations; the civil year consisted of twenty moons, while that of the priests contained thirty-seven; and twenty of these great years formed the Muysca cycle. To express lunar days, lunations, and years, the people made use of a periodical series, the terms of which were denoted by numbers.

The language of Bogôta has been almost extinct since the end of the last century: it was extended by the victories of the Zaque Huncahua, by the warlike exploits of the Zippas, and by the influence of the lamas of Iraca, from the plains of the Ariari and the Rio Meta to the north of Sogamozo. This language was called by the natives, the *Chibcha*. Muysca, of which Mozca seems to be a corruption, signifies a man or person, but in general the natives applied it exclusively to themselves.

The City of Bogôta is the capital of the republic. It is situated at the foot of two mountains, which shelter it from the violent east winds, on an elevated table land, 8,650 feet above the level of the sea, in north latitude 4° 37′ and west longitude 74° 10′. The temperature of the atmosphere is fine and equable, but the climate is exeeedingly humid, though not unhealthy. Externally the city has an imposing appearance, but the streets are generally narrow, though regular, and the houses low, of ancient architecture, and of heavy and gloomy aspect. Nearly half its area is occupied by religious buildings, there being 26 churches, besides the cathedral, nine monasteries and three nunneries. The city was founded in 1538 by Quesada, and now contains 40,000 iuhabitants. Few of the dwellings display much taste or splendor; and the beauty of the city rests entirely with its ecclesiastical edifices, the tall spires and towers of which, rising amid the grandeur of the surrounding scenery, give, when viewed at a distance, a very fine appearance. Hondo, on the Magdalena, is the port of Bogôta, and is situated about 55 miles west of that city. It has a considerable trade in cotton goods, hides, grain, &c., and contains a population of about 10,000. The climate here is much warmer than at the capital, but by no means is it unhealthy. Bogôta is an archepiscopal see.

Popayan is the next city to Bogôta in size, and is more elegantly built, being the residence of many opulent merchants. It contains a mint, a university, and many magnificent religious buildings. This city is situated on the River Cauca, and has a considerable trade through the port of Cartagena. Population, 25,000.

Cartagena is the principal port of the republic, and carries on quite an extensive trade with the United States and Europe. This city was at one time of immense importance to the Spanish possessions, and is still considered as the stronghold of the republic. It is built on a sandy island of the north coast, to the westward of the Rio Magdalena, and possesses one of the finest harbors in America. It is an episcopal city—is well for tified, and has a population of 18,000. Though much decayed, it is sti.. a fine city, and the centre of trade.

PANAMA is a well built city, on a peninsula of the southern coast of the isthmus, to which it gives its name. It was formerly much frequented by Spanish merchantmen; and its importance has lately been revived by the project of making it the western depôt of interoceanic communication. Its harbor is inferior. The population fluctuates, but it is generally about 10,000.

PORTO-BELO or PUERTO-BELLO, is a very small town or village, on a fine natural harbor, but in so unhealthy a situation that it has acquired the title of the "grave of Europeans." It stands on the north side of the isthmus, opposite Panama.

SANTA MARTA is a fortified town, on the coast to the eastward of Magdalena. It possesses a considerable trade, both internal and external. Population, 6,000.

RIO HACHA, farther east, is a small town, with only 1,000 inhabitants; but is noted for the pearl-fisheries in its vicinity.

There are few other towns of consequence, except the capitals of the several departments, which have been noted before, and a few inconsiderable ports on the Pacific, which are not remarkable for anything, except want of trade.

The same style of house building is adopted throughout the republic, as is found in the capital; and the only buildings which exhibit taste or genius are those devoted to ecclesiastical purposes.

The coasts of New Grenada, which border on the Caribbean Sea, were first visited by Columbus during his fourth voyage. Sailing from Spain to the West Indies, he arrived with his fleet at St. Domingo, where having been refused permission to land, he was obliged to stand to the west; and after sailing in this direction, for a few days, discovered a small island off the Cape of Honduras, where his brother landed and traded with the natives. Prosecuting their voyage, they touched at the cape itself, on which they landed, to take possession for the crown of Spain. After performing this ceremony, the fleet proceeded along the shore, and was compelled by the easterly winds to double a cape, which the pilots performing with difficulty, gave it the name of Cape Gracias á Dios. Columbus touched in the course of the voyage at Veragua, Nombre de Dios, Belos, Porto Bello, and many other places. At Verágua he sent his brother up into the country to search for gold, and Bartholomew returning with a considerable quantity, the admiral wished to have planted a colony here: but after several fruitless attempts, abandoned the design. Ojeda and Amerigo Vespucci, as well as many other adventurous persons, followed Columbus in exploring parts of the coast of New Grenada, and Vespucci gave the first regular description of the people who inhabited its shores. In the year 1508, Ojeda and Nicuessa obtained from the Spanish crown extensive grants in this district and the adjoining country. Ojeda had the country from Cape de la Vela to the Gulf of Darien included in his charter, which tract was to be styled New Andalusia; and Nicuessa was appointed to govern from the Gulf of Darien to Cape Gracias á Dios; the territory included within these points to be named Golden Castile. Soon after the arrival of Ojeda at Cartagena, he imprudently attacked the natives, and lost the greater part of his men; but was fortunately relieved by the arrival of Nicuessa; he then went to the Gulf of Darien, and established a colony on the eastern promontory, which he named St. Sebastian. The new colony was reduced to such distress in a short time, that it was determined to proceed to Cartagena: but while on their passage, they met with two vessels bringing supplies; and returning to St. Sebastian, found their town destroyed by the natives. The whole colony then sailed to the river of Darien, where they attacked and conquered an Indian tribe, and founded a town, which they named Santa Maria del Darien. In the mean time Nicuessa endeavored to establish a colony at Nombre de Dios: but a deputation being sent to request him to assume the government, (Ojeda having died,) he repaired thither: but on his arrival, found that great dissensions had arisen among the colonists; who, instead of appointing him to the government, put him in a decayed vessel, and sent him to sea, where he is supposed to have perished. The province of Terra Firma, including both the grants of Nicuessa and Ojeda, was given by a subsequent charter, in 1514, to Pedro Arias de Avila, under whose government Vasco Nunez de Balboa, the discoverer of the South Sea, was beheaded on account of a revolt. Under the orders of Avila, the western coast of Panama, Veragua and Darien was explored as far north as Cape Blanco, and the town of Panama was founded. In 1536, Sebastian de Benalcarar, one of the officers who accompanied Pizarro in the expedition to Peru, effected the conquest and colonization of the southern internal provinces of New Grenada; whilst Gonzalo Ximenes de Quesada, who had been sent by Lugo, the admiral of the Canaries, overrun the northern districts from Santa Marta. They met with considerable opposition from the natives; but finally succeeded in reducing the country, and the whole was formed into a kingdom, and governed by a captain-general, appointed in 1547; to check whose power the royal audience was established, of which he was, however, made president.

In the year 1718, New Grenada was formed into a viceroyalty. This form of government continued until 1724, when the captain-generalship was restored; but, in 1740, the viceroyalty was re-established. Under this system, the evils of which were of a very grievous nature, the inhabitants of New Grenada continued until the invasion of Spain by the French. The desire of independence had long been prevalent; but it was not until 1806, that it began to be publicly avowed. The juntas then chosen were composed of persons generally favorable to independence. A Congress from the different provinces or departments of the viceroyalty soon afterwards assembled, and in 1811, a formal declaration of independence was made. The country has since that period passed through many vicissitudes of fortune. The cause of freedom and that of the royalists were alternately triumphant, and many frightful scenes of rapine and bloodshed occurred. In 1816, a decisive action was fought between the independents and a Spanish army under Morillo, which ended in the total defeat of the former, and the dispersion of the Congress. After remaining under the dominion of the royalists for three years, Grenada was again emancipated by the army of Bolivar, who entered Santa Fé in August, 1819. His successes, after this period, were uniform, rapid and brilliant, and the Spaniards finally evacuated the country, in the year 1823, having been confined to the Isthmus of Panama from the period of Bolivar's entrance.

The Republic of Colombia was formed in 1819, (see foot note to "Venezuela," of which New Grenada was a member: but, on the dissolution of that confederation in 1831, it became once more a separate state, and as such remains to the present time. Santander was elected first President, and took office on the 7th October, 1832, and Joaquim Mosquera was elected Vice-President. The successive Presidents to the present time have been Santander, José Ignacio de Marquez and Joaquim Mosquera. A new President was elected in 1849.

At the present day, the government of New Grenada is one of energy and enterprise. Nothing seems too much for its grasp nor anything too small for its observation. It pre-eminently excels all the others formed on the ruins of the ancient Spanish colonies, if we except that of Chili; and there is no doubt but that its present wise policy will do much to consolidate the interests of its people.

THE REPUBLIC OF EQUADOR.

THE territory of Ecuador or Equador, is that portion of the South American continent bordering on the Pacific Ocean, and lying north of Peru, and west of the empire of Brazil, being the southernmost of the three independent states formerly called the Republic of Colombia. It was anciently the Spanish Presidency of Quito, and a part of the vice-royalty of New Grenada, with the history of which it is connected until its final separation in 1831. Its present title is received from its geographical position: being situated under the equator, or that imaginary line which divides the earth into the northern and southern hemispheres.

The Republic of Equador extends from 2° north to 6° south latitude, and from 67° to 82° west longitude, comprising an area of 325,000 square miles, and a population of 600,000.

EQUADOR is situated mostly in the elevated vallies and declivities of the Andes, and enjoys a fine climate and soil. Its table lands are clothed with perpetual verdure, and the gentle gales are fragrant with the incense of ever-blooming flowers. What a wise provision of Providence, that in parts subject to the most intense climatic influences, such provision should be made for the moderation of extremes! Here, amid the heights of the table lands, the inhabitants enjoy immunity from the severity of nature, and, if willing, may enjoy a winter under the most intense sun of the equatorial regions. From the level to the summits, the temperature declines by slow gradations, and from the heats of a tropical summer to the colds of a polar winter, is but a few hours' journey.

The Andes of Equador compose the most elevated portion of the whole system, particularly between the equator and 1° 45′ of south latitude. It is only, with a very few exceptions, on this limited space of the globe, that mountains of above 19,000 feet in height have been measured with exactness; and even in this respect, there are only three peaks to which this remark can be applied; namely, Chimborazo, which would exceed the height of Mount Etna, placed on the summit of Canigou, or that of St. Gothard, piled on the Peak of Teneriffe; the other two are Cayambe and Antisana. From the tradition of the Indians of Lican, we learn, with some degree of certainty, that the Altar Mountain, called by the natives Capa-Urcu, had once a greater elevation than Chimborazo, but that, after a continual eruption of eight years, this volcano sunk to a lower altitude. In proof of this fact, the top of the mountain presents, in its inclined peaks, nothing but the traces of destruction.

The geological structure of this part of the Andes does not essentially differ from that of the great mountain chains of Europe. Granite constitutes the base, upon which the less ancient formations repose. It comes into view at the foot of the Andes, on the shores of the Pacific Ocean, as well as those on the Atlantic, near the mouths of the Orinoco. Sometimes in masses, at others in strata, (*bancs*,) regularly inclined and parallel, and containing round masses, in which mica alone prevails; the granite of Peru resembles that of the higher Alps and of Madagascar. Upon this rock, and occasionally alternating with it, is found *gneiss* or schistose granite, which passes into mica slate, and this again into primitive clay slate. Granular limestone, primitive trap, and chlorite slate, form subordinate beds in the gneiss and mica slate: while this latter, which is extensively diffused through the Andes, often encloses beds of graphite, and serves as a base to formations of serpentine, which sometimes alternate with sienite. The crest of the Andes is everywhere covered with porphyries, basalts, clink stone, and green stone. These rocks, divided into columns, present, at a distance, the appearance of an immense assemblage of dilapidated towers. The thickness and extent of the schistose and porphyritic rock is the only great phenomenon by which the Andes differ from the mountains of Europe. The porphyries of Chimborazo are 11,400 feet in thickness, without a mixture of any other rock; the pure quartz, to the west of Caxamarca, is 9,000, and the sandstone of the environs of Cuenca 4,800. These rocks form the whole of the central elevation of the Andes; while, in Europe, granite or primitive limestone constitutes the summit of the chains. Volcanoes have penetrated these immense beds, and have covered their sides with obsidian and porous amygdaloid. The lowest volcanoes sometimes throw out lava; but those of the Cordillera, properly so called, only eject water or scorified rocks, and more frequently clay, intermixed with sulphur and carbon.

Chimborazo, like Mont Blanc, forms the extremity of a colossal group. From Chimborazo, as far as 120 leagues to the south, no mountain peak attains the limit of perpetual snow. The crest of the Andes has there only from 3,360 to 3,800 yards of elevation. Beyond the eighth degree of south latitude, the snowy peaks become more numerous, especially near Cuzco and La Paz, where the peaks of Illimani and Sorata shoot up their summits to the clouds.

We should not do justice to our description of Equador, if we were to pass over in silence the terrific volcanoes which have so often overwhelmed the country, and swallowed up whole cities at a time. The majestic Chimborazo is probably nothing but an extinguished volcano. The snow, which for centuries has crowned its colossal peak, will, probably, one day or other, be melted by the remorseless fires pent up within its vast and fathomless caverns, resuming their destructive activity.

Pichincha is one of the greatest volcanoes on the surface of the globe. The height of this mountain is 15,936 feet. Its crater, hollowed out in basaltic porphyries, was compared, by La Condamine, to the chaos of the poets. This immense mouth was at that time filled with snow, but, afterwards, Humboldt found it burning. From the circumference of the crater, rise, as if shooting up from the abyss below, three rocky peaks, which are not covered with snow, because it is constantly melted by the vapors that exhale from the volcano. "In order the better to examine the bottom of the crater, we lay down flat on our breasts; and I do not believe that the imagination could figure to itself anything more melancholy, gloomy, and terrific, than what we now beheld. The mouth of the volcano forms a circular hole of nearly a league in circumference, the sides of which, a perpendicular precipice, are covered above with snow to their very edge.

The interior was of a deep black; but the gulf is so immense that we could distinguish the tops of several mountains, that are situated within it. Their summits appeared to be two or three hundred fathoms, (*toises*,) below us—judge, then, where must be their base. I myself have no doubt that the bottom of the crater is on a level with the city of Quito."

Cotopaxi is the most elevated of those volcanoes of the Andes, from which, at recent periods, there have been eruptions. Its absolute height is 18,890 feet; it would, consequently, exceed by more than 9,000 feet the height of Mount Vesuvius, even supposing that it were piled on the summit of the Peak of Teneriffe. Cotopaxi is likewise the most formidable of all the volcanoes of Equador; and its eruptions have been the most frequent and the most destructive. The cinders and fragments of rocks that have been ejected by this volcano, cover the neighboring valleys to an extent of several square leagues. In 1758, the flames of Cotopaxi shot up to a height of 2,700 feet above the edge of the crater. In 1744, the roaring of this volcano was heard as far as Honda, a town situated on the banks of the River Magdalena, at a distance of two hundred leagues. On the 4th April, 1768, the quantity of ashes vomited up from the mouth of Cotopaxi was so great, that in the towns of Hambato and Tacunga, the sky continued as dark as night until the third hour after mid-day. The eruption which took place in the month of January, 1803, was preceded by a frightful phenomenon—the sudden melting of the snows that covered the mountain. For more than twenty years neither smoke nor any distinguishable vapor had issued from the crater, and yet, in a single night, the subterranean fire had become so active that, at sunrise, the external walls of the cone, strongly-heated, had become naked, and had acquired the black color which is peculiar to vitrified scoriæ. At the port of Guayaquil, fifty-two leagues in a straight line from the edge of the crater, Humboldt heard, day and night, the roaring of this volcano, like repeated discharges of artillery.

To our description of Equador, we ought to add that of the Gallapagos Islands. This archipelago, situated under the equator, at 220 leagues to the west of the continent of America, contains volcanic peaks in the more eastern islands. The cactus and the aloe cover the sides of the rocks. In the western islands a black and deep mould affords nourishment to large trees. Flamingos and turtle-doves fill the air, and the beach is covered with enormous turtles. No trace whatever indicates the residence of man. Neither the Malays of the great ocean, nor any of the tribes of America, have ever landed on these lonely shores. Dampier and Cowley observed springs, and even rivers, in some of these islands, the peculiar Spanish names of which have given place to English appellations, at least in all our modern charts. Santa Maria de l'Aguada appears identical with York Island. The largest among the twenty-two that are known, are those of Albemarle and Narborough. Cowley describes the *enchanted island*, which presents a varied prospect of what appears to be a walled town, and a strong castle in ruins. Several harbors and roadsteads invite Europeans to form establishments there.

The river system of Equador, like that of all Western America, is divided by the summits of the Cordilleras, from which they have their rise. West of these mountains, the streams flowing into the Pacific are few, and their courses short and abrupt. The Guayaquil, at the confluence of which, into the gulf of the same name, stands the CITY OF GUAYAQUIL—is the only one of importance; it takes its rise at the base of Chimborazo, and pursuing a southerly course, empties itself in the north side of the bay. The gulf is a fine body of water, on which are embosomed several fine islands, and is capable of containing a large amount of shipping, to which it affords good and safe anchorage. The rivers eastward of the mountains are the great tributaries of the Amazon: the Negro, Napo, and the upper waters of the great Amazon itself. These all rise at the base of the mountains, and pursuing an easterly course, contribute their volumes to swell that mighty stream, which is at once the wonder and astonishment of the world. The Ucayale, and other rivers, which flow northward from Peru, join the Amazon within the territory of Equador. All these streams are navigable, and afford great facilities for the transportation of merchandise and intercommunication. The Ucayale, both under this name and that of Apurimac, traverses mountain passes almost inaccessible, where, no doubt, it winds its course amidst picturesque beauties, which await another La Condamine to describe. The Apurimac receives the Beni, which rises to the south of the city of La Chuquisaca, in Bolivia, sixty leagues further south than the sources of the Apurimac itself.

The other principal branch of the Upper Amazon is the stream which flows from the Lake Lauricocha, a lake situated very near the source of the ancient Maranon. This stream is called the New or High Maranon. It is commonly looked upon as the principal branch of the Amazon, although in reality this rank belongs to the Ucayale. The High Maranon becomes navigable near the town of Jaen, where it flows through one of those majestic narrows, called by the Spaniards *Quebrada.* Two very lofty precipices of rock, which exactly correspond with one another, have between them a narrow ravine, where, from a breadth of 250 fathoms, the river is reduced to twenty-five, without, however, its current becoming more rapid.

From San Joaquim de Omaguas, the Ucayale and the High Maranon roll their united waters across an immense plain, where, from every side, other streams bring down their tributary waters. The Napo, Yapura, Parana, Cuchivara and Putumayo would, in any other part of the world, be looked upon as considerable rivers: here, however, they belong only to the third or fourth class. The Rio Negro, which comes from New Grenada, and which merits the name of a great river, is swallowed up in the vast current of the Amazon.

The mineral products of this remarkable country are not as yet of such account as in other parts of South America and Mexico: but it is reasonable to suppose that the Cordilleras of Equador are as rich in mineral wealth as those of Peru, and that the precious metals, as gold and silver, are as plentiful in the yet hidden recesses of the mountains. Gold and silver, and the other metals, are here found at a greater elevation than in the other parts of the Andes; but there is no reason to believe that these do not exist in the lower regions, and are still hidden beneath vast masses of superficial matter, accumulated at the base of their volcanic heights. The difficulties attending the extraction has hitherto prevented the progress of mining operations; and such will, no doubt, continue to be the case, as long as a plentiful supply of mineral can be had from more accessible places.

But this country is fully indemnified for its impracticable mines. It has a mine of wealth in its agricultural resources. The soil and climate is as various as its gradation in height are capable of fostering the vegetation of every region of the world: the fruits of the luxurious tropics and the scanty shrubs and lichens of the poles, here found at different altitudes, and in soil and climate, appropriate to their economy. The temperate regions of the elevated plains, however,—where the seasons are merged into one perpetual spring, where the plough and the sickle are in use at one and the same time, and the seed-time and harvest are alike,—present the greatest luxuriance and abundant supplies. There the bud, the blossom and ripened fruit hang pendant from the same tree, and the faded flower and withered leaf yield to a perpetual succession of new creations.

The interminable forests which line the margins of the rivers and cover the mountains to their summits, abound with fine timber, which would yield a large revenue, if the means of transit to the shores were easier. Cedars, ebonies, and an infinite number of valuable woods, of great beauty and durability, are natives of these regions, and are found in profusion. Humboldt remarks, " It might be said that the earth, overloaded with plants, does not allow them space enough to unfold themselves. The trunks of the trees are everywhere concealed under a thick carpet of verdure."

Nature, in this country, has been equally prodigal in animal as in vegetable life. Jaguars, tapirs and other wild animals roam in vast numbers through the solitudes; vultures and other birds of prey inhabit the mountains; and the forests are alive with an aggregation of monkeys and parrots, and swarm with myriads of beautiful creations belonging to the bird and insect tribes. Reptiles are the dangerous denizens of the eastern departments, and exhibit themselves in great variety.

The Republic of Equador is divided into three general departments, and these are subdivided into a number of provinces and other civil partitions.

Departments.	*Area and Population.*	*Capitals.*	*Population.*
Equador	Area 325,000,	Quito	70,000
Guayaquil	and	Guayaquil	20,000
Assuay	Population ... 600,000.	Cuença	20,000

The population is merely an approximate estimate, and cannot be relied upon: it is said to be made up of the different races in the following proportions:

Whites and Creoles	157,000
Indians	393,000
Colored population	50,000

The people are of the same race, and have the same habits as those described under the head of New Grenada, and need not be further alluded to. Perhaps, however, in their moral constitution, they are inferior to the people of that state, having been more influenced by Jesuitical supervision and other debasing influences than the former; and their communication with civilized nations being inconsiderable, they can have received very little benefit from this powerful element in moral progress.

The government is in chief similar to that of the other Colombian states: and the legislative function is vested in the Senate and Deputies, and the executive power in a President and Vice-President. The political government of the departments is in the hands of Intendantes, appointed by the President, with the sanction of the Congress. The Intendante has authority over the administration of justice, police, finance and defence, but is not allowed to exercise military command. The civil and criminal codes, according to Hall, are an " ill-digested collection of the laws of Castile and of the Indies, royal ordinances and other Spanish decrees, and colonial regulations," and their administration is very unfavorably spoken of. The Roman Catholic is the state religion: other forms, though nominally tolerated, are really scarcely so save in name.

Since the freedom of the republic, considerable progress has been made in the support and encouragement of education, and in some degree the arts and sciences; but the luxurious indolence of the people, seemingly so natural to the inhabitants of the torrid zone in all countries, but in this country more especially, where the bounties of nature are showered with a lavishness that almost precludes the necessity of physical industry or mental action, is, perhaps, the greatest obstacle to their successful cultivation and to all excellence.

When the Spaniards, under Pizarro, first visited Peru, this portion of the country was under the sway of the Incas, and presents, especially in the valley of Quito, many interesting monuments of their ancient greatness and splendor, as well as traces of an advanced civilization and refinement. The progress of the invaders here was similar to their rapacious career in Peru; and the province of Quito, as they then termed it, continued in the possession of Spain, until the overthrow of the royalists in 1822, when, in consequence of the oppressions of the Spanish government, the people, headed by Gen. Sucre, rose and defeated the royalists in a decisive battle, and afterwards joined the republic formed by the union of New Grenada and Venezuela.

In 1831, however, these states were dissolved, and have since remained distinct governments. The course of events, since that time, in Equador, are little known. Personal ambition and civil war, however, have been predominant, and it is probable that its history would be but a record of successive dynasties, whose terms have been marked in blood and horror. War seems to be the ruling passion of all the Indo-Spanish nations in South America; and the prosperity of the people is made a secondary object to the success of ambitious and designing demagogues. Such, indeed, has been the story of this favored country since its emancipation from old Spain: tyrant succeeds tyrant, and the people bite the dust.

The commerce of Equador is chiefly carried on from the port of Guayaquil. The principal articles of export, are cocoa, timber, hides, cattle, tobacco, ceibo-wool, &c., but cocoa seems to be the most extensively exported, being to the annual amount of 10 or 12,000,000 pounds. The trade is chiefly confined to the United States, Mexico, Central America and Peru, in America, and England, Spain, France and Hamburg, in Europe. Manilla also takes some exports. The number of vessels in this trade, in 1835, was 123, with a burden of 21,430 tons. The value of imports were, in that year, £221,680, or 1,064,064 dollars; and that of exports, £210,429, or 1,010,059 dollars. The exports from Guayaquil of cotton and cocoa, the only items of which we have any accounts, were, in 1843 and 1844, as follow:

	Cocoa.		Cotton.	
	Quantity.	*Value.*	*Quantity.*	*Value.*
1843	15,338,970 lbs.	£170,433	80,000 lbs.	£1,920
1844	8,565,500 "	105,788	256,000 "	4,618

The principal articles of import are all kinds of manufactured goods: English broad-cloths, kerseymeres, colored broad flannels, calicos, plain and printed dimities, muslins, stockings, velveteens; Irish linens, in imitation of German *platillas;* all kinds of hardware and cutlery, and foreign silk velvets, satins, &c., as well as English ribbons and silks, &c.

The domestic manufactures of Quito, coarse cottons and woollen cloths, baizes, flannels, ponchos, &c., and its celebrated confectionary, are exported by way of Guayaquil to Central America, in exchange for indigo, steel and iron; and to Peru, in return for brandy, wine and oil, and for gold, silver and other metals, the mines of Equador not being very productive for want of energy in the people and natural difficulties.

The celebrated City of Quito is the capital of the republic. It is situated in a ravine, on the east side of Pichincha, above 9,500 feet above the sea. Lat. 0° 13′ 27″ S.—long. 78° 10′ 15″ W. The population is variously estimated at from 40,000 to 70,000. Quito, on the whole, is the best built city in South America. It has four broad, straight and well paved streets, and three large and some smaller squares, in which are the principal public buildings and the best private residences.

The houses, which are large and commodious, are mostly built of unburnt brick, cemented with a species of mortar, used by the ancient Peruvians, which soon becomes extremely hard. On account of earthquakes they are seldom more than one story high, exclusive of the ground floor or *rez-de-chaussée.* They are flat roofed, and have usually a balcony facing on the street. The city is abundantly supplied with water, and a fine brass fountain adorns the centre of the principal square.

Ecclesiastical edifices, which are numerous, form the chief ornaments of the place: the ex-Jesuits' college has a beautiful front, with Corinthian columns, finely sculptured by native artists. The interior of this edifice is very rich, and when visited by Stevenson, it had a library, said to comprise 20,000 volumes, including several rare works. All these institutions were formerly depositaries of vast quantities of gold and silver ornaments; but these of late have been turned to a better and more useful purpose by the state. The charitable institutions are numerous and well supported: there is an alms-house, an orphan asylum, hospitals, &c., which are said to be well conducted. The educational system of Quito is more perfect than most others of South America, but according to Ulloa, the students are more perfect in the exact and abstract sciences than in their knowledge of politics, history and the other departments of learning, which are more useful, and tend more to expand and vivify the intellect. The city was made a bishop's see in 1545, and is the residence of the President and seat of all the superior courts and offices of the republic.

The inhabitants of Quito, like those of other Spanish cities, make bull-fights, masquerades, dancing, gaming, music, and religious ceremonies and processions, their principal employments. Indolence is the characteristic of all classes; this, however, is in a great measure to be ascribed to the climate, and the ease with which the necessaries of life are produced. The city enjoys a perpetual spring; vegetation never ceases, but from December to March violent storms of rain and lightning almost daily occur in the afternoon. Earthquakes are also frequent; and one of these visitations, which occurred in 1797, is said to have destroyed in the province 40,000 persons, and to have had a permanent influence over the climate.

A plain, about four leagues from this city, was made choice of by the French and Spanish astronomers of 1736, for measuring a degree of the meridian; and an inscription on a marble tablet, on the wall of the ex-Jesuits church, in Quito, commemorates the event, and the labors of the commission; but the most enduring memorial of that great undertaking is to be found in the "*Historical Voyage*" of Ulloa, one of the best works of the kind that has ever been published.

Quito was founded by Sebastian Benalcasar, in 1534, and incorporated as a city by Charles V., in 1541.

Guayaquil is the principal sea-port of Equador, latitude 2° 11′ 21″ south, longitude 79° 43′ west. It is built on the north bank of the River Guayaquil, and is divided into the old and new town, the former being occupied by the poorer classes. It is a tolerably well-built city, but has frequently suffered from fires. Its private houses are mostly tiled, and furnished with arcades. The principal buildings are the custom-house, three convents, a college, hospital, &c.; but from being situated on a level, and intersected by many creeks, the drainage is bad, and the streets are so swampy as to be sometimes impassable. Many of the inhabitants live on the river in *balzas*, or rafts. The river opposite to the city is about two miles wide, and has on its south bank a dry dock, where ships of a superior construction have been built. The city is unhealthy, and infested with vermin.

The port of Guayaquil is one of the best on the Pacific, ships of large size coming close up to the town. It is defended by three forts, one being on the opposite side of the river. Ships bound for Guayaquil generally call at Puna for pilots.

The City of Cuenca, the departmental capital of Assuay, is an inland town, on a spacious plain, 9,000 feet above the level of the sea, about 186 miles south of Quito. Latitude, 2° 56′ south, longitude, 79° 12′ west. Population, about 20,000; about 3,000 of which are Indians. Its streets are broad and straight; but the houses are low, and built of unburnt brick. It contains a cathedral, two parish churches, monasteries, a college, and a hospital. Confectionary, cheese, hats, &c., are extensively manufactured here, and some trade in these, together with grain, cinchona bark, and other productions of the vicinity, is carried on. Its climate is temperate, as to heat; but it is subject to violent storms. In its neighborhood there are several remains of the Peruvian Incas. About 30 miles from Cuenca is the famous Paramo d'Assuay, where many travellers have perished from its terrible storms.

Riobamba, is another large town east of the Andes, and has about 20,000 inhabitants. Loxa is also a considerable place, which, with Valladolid, will complete the list of important towns in Equador.

THE REPUBLIC OF VENEZUELA.

The territories comprising this republic were formerly known as the Captaincy-General of Caracas, and formed more recently one of the states of the ephemeral republic of Colombia.* The coast region has, for many centuries, been styled the Spanish Main, which appellation is retained among seamen. The geographical position of Venezuela is between the latitudes of 12° north and 2° north, and the longitudes of 60° and 72° west from Greenwich. It is bounded on the north by the Caribbean Sea; on the east by the Atlantic Ocean, British Guayana, and part of the empire of Brazil; on the south by Brazil, and west by New Grenada, from which it is divided by the chain of the Andes, running to the Cape de la Vela. The island of Margarita, and some smaller islands, belong to the republic. The length, from east to west, is about 900 miles, and its greatest width about 800; the area is estimated at 450,000 square miles, and the population may be set down at 900,000; but this is evidently too small, though taken from an official statement, and it is not improbable that the actual amount will not fall far short of 1,200,000.

This republic is divided into four departments, which are again subdivided into thirteen provinces, for the purposes of local government.

Departments.		*Chief Cities.*	
1. Venezuela	Population from 900,000 to 1,200,000.	Caracas	23,000
2. Orinoco		Varinas	5,000
3. Maturin		Cumana	12,000
4. Zulia		Maracaybo	20,000

From the official statement of 1834, the different races were numerically as follows:

Whites	200,000	Free Colored	433,000
Indians	207,000	Slaves	60,000

* In this connection it will be necessary to give in brief, a history of the late "Republic of Colombia."

After the revolt of the Spanish Colonies, those in the north-west part of South America were formed into a large state, which assumed the name of Colombia, in honor of the great discoverer. This republic was formed in Dec., 1819, by the union of the Captaincy-General of Caracas, the Vice-Royalty of New Grenada, and its dependent Presidency of Quito. On the 17th of July, 1821, a General Congress met at Rosario de Cucuta, to form a constitution, which was completed and adopted on the 30th of August. The legislative power was vested in a senate of 36 members, and a chamber of deputies of 94 members; and General Simon Bolivar was elected President, and Santander, Vice-President. Bolivar and Santander were both re-elected for a second term—commencing on the 1st January, 1827. Hitherto Santander had acted as President.

In 1828 Bolivar assumed supreme power; the republic was disturbed by violent factions, and in 1829 Venezuela separated from it. In 1830, a general convention met at Bogôta, to frame a new constitution; Bolivar resigned, and took leave of public life; on the 4th May, 1830, Senor Joachim Mosquera was elected president, and General Domingo Caicedo, vice-president; but on the 4th of September Mosquera resigned, and Urdanata was appointed temporary president, until the arrival of Bolivar, whose return to power was decreed by a meeting of soldiers and citizens; but Bolivar died at Cartagena, Dec. 17th, of the same year. Venezuela again joined Colombia for a short time; but in November, 1831, a new separation took place, and since that time the late Republic of Colombia has been divided into three independent states, *Venezuela*, New Grenada, and Equador, whose constitutions are fundamentally the same as that of Colombia, formed at Rosario de Cucuta.

The superficial aspect of Venezuela is essentially different from that of the other Colombian states, and with the exception of the branch of the Andes, running between the Caribbean Sea and the basin of the Orinoco, forms an extent of unbroken and immense plains. These mountains, having very little elevation, almost everywhere admit of being cultivated, and according to the difference of level, they enjoy, in some places, the refreshing coolness of perpetual spring, while in others the influence of latitude is fully experienced. The forests covering these hills are very extensive, and would, for ages to come, supply the most extensive dock-yards; but the nature of the surface renders it too difficult an operation to remove the trees, of which, at present, navigation, possessing little activity, does not stand in need. The forests also produce a great variety of woods, admirably adapted for dying and cabinet work. Medicinal drugs, such as sarsaparilla and cinchona, are also collected.

The valley of the Orinoco, southward of these mountains, is described by Humboldt as being an awful and gloomy solitude and wilderness, almost incapable of regeneration. "I know not," he says, "whether the first sight of the *Llanos* excites less astonishment than that of the Andes. All around us the plains seemed to ascend towards the sky, and that vast and profound solitude appeared like an ocean covered with sea weeds." The phenomenon of the *mirage*, and apparitions of large lakes, with an undulating surface, are frequently to be seen, and present a very singular and surprising deception on the senses of the beholder.

The principal rivers of Venezuela are the Orinoco and its branches, flowing eastward into the Atlantic Ocean and the Rio Tucuyo, and other smaller rivers, flowing northward into the Caribbean Sea. The Orinoco is one of the largest rivers in the world, and may be navigated in connection with its great tributaries, the *Meta*, &c., almost to the foot of the Andes. The Orinoco is wholly included within the territory of Venezuela, though some of its principal branches take their rise in New Grenada and Equador. This river and the Negro, a tributary of the Amazon, are connected by the Cassiquiari, a small stream, which flows alternately into each as the waters prevail in either. There are several lakes within the republic, the largest of which is that of Maracaybo. This lake furnishes mineral pitch or asphaltes, which, mixed with tallow, is used for paying vessels. The bituminous vapours which float on the surface of the lake, frequently take fire spontaneously, especially during the great heats. The banks of this lake are so barren, and so unhealthy, that the Indians, instead of fixing their habitations there, prefer living on the lake itself. The Spaniards found many villages constructed there, without order, it is true, or uniformity, but built on solid piles. This lake, which is seventy leagues in length, and thirty broad, communicates with the sea, but its water is constantly fresh. Its navigation is easy, even for vessels of a large size. The tide is more strongly felt in it than on the adjacent coasts. The lake of Valencia, which was called by the Indians *Tacarigoa*, presents a far more attractive scene. Adorned with a luxuriant vegetation, its banks enjoy an agreeable temperature. Thirteen leagues and a half long, and four in breadth, it receives the water of about twenty rivers, and yet has no outlet itself, being separated from the sea by six leagues of country covered with rugged mountains. The adjacent scenery is picturesque, and the lake is sprinkled with numerous islets, which add much to the beauty of its expanse. The small lake, called the Ipava, forms the source of the Orinoco, which river seems to run an almost complete circuit before taking its direct course towards the sea, which it enters by a delta of about fifty canals, or channels, after flowing 1,380 miles, through an immense and fertile waste, inhabited only by savage tribes of Indians.

The climate of Venezuela is extremely hot, except in the more elevated regions, where the temperature is delightful and the weather equable. The regions about the coast and in the low marshy lands on the margins of the southern streams, are very unhealthy, and fevers and fluxes are extremely prevalent. In some parts of the valley of the Orinoco, however, although the heat is intense, the air is said to be more salubrious than on the sea-coast, in consequence of the strong breezes which prevail along its course. The soil of the plains, watered as they are by the numerous tributaries of the Amazon and the Orinoco, is exceedingly fertile in all kinds of tropical productions. Some of these immense flats are covered with interminable forests, and others with tall rank grass, over six feet in height.

The northern valleys are the most productive parts of Venezuela, because it is there that the heat and moisture are more equally combined than elsewhere. The southern plains, too much exposed to the heat of the sun, produce pasture only, in which they rear cattle, mules and horses. Cultivation ought to be flourishing in these parts, where there are no mines; but its progress is retarded from indolence and want of information.

The vast forests of Venezuela are rich in every description of valuable wood for timber, cabinet-furniture and dyes :—mahogany, cedar, a very hard species of oak, called "iron-wood," &c. Besides these, are the cocoa, which produces an article equal to that of Soconusco, in Guatemala, and other palms, bananas, plaintains, gigantic mimosas, &c. grow almost spontaneously, and in such rich profusion, that Humboldt observes, "it might be said that the earth, overloaded with plants, does not allow them space enough to unfold themselves. The trunks of the trees are everywhere concealed under a thick carpet of verdure; and if we carefully transplanted the *Orchidæ*, the *piperes* and the *popos*, which a single curbaril or American fig tree nourishes, we should cover a vast extent of ground." The *Ficus Gigantea* sometimes reaches the extraordinary height of one hundred feet. The cocoa-nut, indigo, cotton, tobacco, yam, potatoe, vanilla, cochineal, &c., are indigenous to the soil. The tobacco of Caracas is said to be superior to that of Virginia, and second only to that of Cuba and the Rio Negro. The cinchona or Jesuits' bark is almost exclusively the produce of this state and New Grenada.

The mineral productions of Venezuela form no part of its national wealth. Some gold mines have been discovered, but the disturbed state of the country for the last half century, and the disaffection of the Indians, have caused them to be abandoned. There have also been discovered some mines of copper, which produce sufficient for the service of the republic, and some little of the metal is exported. The pearl fisheries along the coasts, once so important, are now completely abandoned, but there is some hope that in a short time this profitable exploitation may be resumed under the auspices of American capitalists. The northern provinces produce a great deal of fine salt; and mineral and hot springs, although very abundant, are little visited or used as places of fashionable resort as in other countries.

The variety of animal life in such an extent of country is necessarily great: the wild animals, peculiar to tropical America, are all natives of the immense forests which clothe the mountains and vallies of Venezuela. Birds are likewise very numerous and diversified, and remarkable for the brilliancy of their plumage—the most prominent are the vulture family, parrots and paroquets, in large flocks, macaws, scarlet cardinals, flamingos, pelicans and an abundance of water-fowl. Reptiles and insects swarm in prolific broods, and the whole land teems with these beautiful but dangerous and annoying creations.

The manufactures of the country are principally a few simple articles of domestic use, and as a natural consequence foreign commerce finds a vast market for manufactured goods. Foreign manufactures, of every sort, are in active demand, and are received in exchange for the raw materials peculiar to the country—supplying the necessities and luxuries of the people, while the value of the commodities bartered, once shipped to other countries, is quadrupled, and yields an immense profit to the trade. The average annual value of imports, is estimated at about $7,000,000, and the exports at a little more; but it is impossible, at the present time, when the country is distracted by civil war and all the evils which such a state of things produces to commerce and trade, to measure its capacities by existing statistics. It is probable, that with an increased population, internal peace and other requisites to develope the resources of this country, it would be found in no wise inferior to any of the other republics of Spanish America: hitherto, however, it has enjoyed no tranquillity since it became a nation, and the consequence is that its commerce lays fallow and comparatively unprofitable.

The descendants of the Spanish settlers and the Creoles form the white population of Venezuela, and are the ruling caste. The general character of these people is the same over all South America, and indolence seems to be their besetting sin. "The Colombian who can eat beef and plantains, and smoke cigars as he swings in his hammock, is possessed of almost everything his habits qualify him to enjoy, or which his ambition prompts him to attain—the poor have little less; the rich scarcely covet more." The Negroes, and the mixtures sprung from these, which form more than half, are not a whit more active than their superiors: their only happiness is in smoking and gambling, which seems to be the only real employment the South Americans are adepts at. The fertility of the soil and the warmth of the climate have, in fact, indisposed and unfitted the people for any vigorous exertion.

The native Indians, unlike their more effeminate brethren from Europe and Asia, are endowed with strong frames, capable of much endurance, and are skilful and courageous. They live in the forests and plains, and some have attained to a semi-civilized station. Some of them, separated from each other by their languages, which have a striking dissimilarity, are a wandering people, completely strangers to agriculture, who live on ants, gum and earth; and are, in short, the very outcasts of the human species. Of this description, are the *Ottomacs* and *Yaruras*. The earth which is eaten by the Ottomacs is fat and unctuous, a genuine potter's clay, of a greyish yellow tint, owing to the presence of a little oxyde of iron; they select it with a great deal of care, and procure it from particular beds on the banks of the Orinoco and the Meta. They distinguish by the taste one species of earth from another; for it is not every kind of clay that proves equally agreeable to their palate. They knead this earth into balls of from four to six inches in diameter, and roast them before a slow fire, until their surface begins to turn red. When they are desirous of eating one of these balls they wet it again. This savage and ferocious people live on fish, lizards and fern roots, when they are to be procured; but they are so particularly fond of clay, that they every day eat a little after their food, during the very season when they have other aliments at their disposal. The missionaries, who, among the tribes to the west of the Orinoco, have converted the *Betoys* and the *Maypures*, have observed in their language, as well as in that of the *Yaruras*, a regular and even very artificial syntax. The *Achaguas* speak a dialect of the Maypure. The *Guaicas*, a very white, very diminutive, almost pigmy, but exceedingly warlike race of people, inhabit the country to the east of Passimoni. The *Guajaribes*, a deep copper-colored and extremely ferocious tribe, even supposed to be cannibals, prevent travellers from penetrating to the sources of the Orinoco. Musquitoes, and a thousand other stinging and venomous insects, swarm amidst these lonely forests. The rivers are filled with alligators, and with the little fish, called *caribes*, the ferocity of which is equally to be dreaded. Other tribes in the eastern part of the country, such as the *Maqüiritans* and *Makos*, have fixed habitations, and live on the fruits which they cultivate; they possess intelligence, and more sociable manners. The prevailing nation along the coast, from Surinam to Cape de la Vela, was formerly that of the Caribbeans, or Caribs, now almost exterminated by the Europeans. It is impossible to know whether this race originally came from the Antilles, or extended itself thither. Of all the Indian nations, the Caribbeans are most distinguished by their activity and courage; they inhabit villages governed by an elective chief, whom the Europeans denominate captain. When they proceed to battle, they assemble at the sound of the conch or sea shell. Next to the Patagonians, the Caribbeans are, perhaps, the most robust nation with which we are acquainted; according to the older travellers, they are said to be *Cannibals*, or *Anthropophagi*. At least, it appears certain that they eat their enemies, devouring their flesh with the voraciousness of vultures. The Caribbean language, one of the most sonorous, and one of the softest in the world, contains nearly thirty dialects; it even appears to be poetical, if we may be allowed to judge from the names of some of the tribes. One of them is called the *Daughter of the Palm Tree;* another, the *Sister of the Bear*. The languages spoken by the tribes of the interior, sound much harsher to the ear. With the *Salivas*, the pronunciation is completely nasal; and with the *Situfas*, entirely guttural; while the *Betoys* always sound the dental letter; and the *Quaivas*, and the *Kirikoas*, as well as the *Ottomacs*, and the *Guaranos*, emit, with incredible volubility, such peculiar sounds, that it is almost impossible to imitate them. The language of the *Achaguas*, is the only one of the interior that is possessed of any harmony. Vast tracts of country between the Casiquiari and the Atabapo, are inhabited only by gregarious monkeys, and by tapirs.

Figures engraved on rocks, prove, nevertheless, that this solitude was once inhabited by a people, who had arrived at a certain degree of civilization. Between the second and fourth parallels, in a wooded plain, surrounded by the Orinoco, the Atabapo, the Rio Negro, and the Casiquiari, rocks of sienite and granite are seen covered with colossal symbolical figures, representing alligators, tigers, domestic utensils, and images of the sun and moon. At the present day, this remote corner of the globe is uninhabited, over a space of more than five hundred square miles. The neighboring tribes are composed of savages, who are sunk to the very lowest degree in the scale of civilization, lead a wandering life, and are far from being capable of tracing the rudest hieroglyphic on these rocks. Similar monuments are met with in other parts of the republic.

The City of Caracas is the capital of the country, and is situated in a mountain valley, at the foot of the Silla de Caracas, 330 feet above the sea, from which it is eight miles inland, and twelve miles S. S. E. of its port, La Guayra. This city is finely situated, and in the enjoyment of a temperate and healthy, though variable climate; but it is much exposed to the attacks of earthquakes, by which it has frequently suffered. It is surrounded by the Guayra, and several other rivulets, which supply many public and private fountains, and wash the streets. It is a well and regularly built city: the streets are sufficiently wide, paved, and cross each other at right angles; there are, also, a number of squares, the principal of which is the Plaza Mayor. This is ornamented with several fine buildings; the cathedral, on the east side, the university on the south, and the prison on the west; but it is disfigured by ranges of low shops, collected in its centre, where the fruit, vegetable and fish markets, are held. Most of the public buildings are of a religious character; the cathedral is spacious, but heavily built, and it is probably to this circumstance that its preservation was owing during the great earthquake of 1812. Previous to that year there were eight other churches, the handsomest of which, Alta Gracia, was built by people of color; but this and the other churches, and nine-tenths of the houses, and between 9,000 and 10,000 inhabitants were destroyed, by the terrible catastrophe that then happened. There are three convents, two nunneries, and three hospitals, besides a theatre capable of containing 1,800 persons, the pit of which is not covered in. The houses of Caracas are at present inferior to those which existed previous to the great earthquake; they are now chiefly built of sun-dried clay or brick, and the roofs tiled, and the walls whitewashed. Caracas was founded in 1567, by Diego Loseda, and, under the Spanish government, was the seat of the Captaincy-General of Venezuela. In 1812, the population was 40,000, but it is now only about 24,000.

La Guayra, which is the port of Caracas, is the chief trading town of the republic; but its merchants are, for the most part, the agents of others in the capital, where all negotiations are conducted. The population is about 15,000. The harbor is but indifferent, and the climate unhealthy.

Cumana is situated on an arid, sandy plain, on the east bank of the Manzanares, and near the mouth of the Gulf of Cariaco, about one mile from the sea-shore. Latitude, 10° 28′ north, and longitude, 64° 16′ west. It is commanded by Fort San Antonio, built on an elevation to the east of the city, and the river encompasses the town, dividing it from its principal suburbs. It has two parish churches, two convents, and a theatre. The buildings are generally low, but by no means insignificant, either in extent or appearance. The roadstead is extensive, and anchorage excellent for large ships. The climate is intensely hot; the temperature being usually, in the summer months, from 90° to 95° Fahr. during the day, and seldom so low as even 80° at night. The inhabitants are distinguished for their assiduity in business, and their polished manners. This is the oldest European city on the continent, having been built by Diego Castellon, in 1523. It was totally destroyed by an earthquake in 1766.

The other principal cities of Venezuela are:—Valencia, a considerable town, with 15,000 inhabitants; Puerto-Cabello, an important seaport, in longitude 68° west, with a good harbor, and considerable trade, but in an unhealthy situation, and having only a population of 3,000; Varinas, south of the Lake of Maracaybo, once a flourishing city, but at the present day in a state of decay; Angostura or New Guayana, a small Episcopal city, on the Orinoco, with 3,000 inhabitants. It is important as a shipping station, for vessels and steamboats navigating that river, and if the American

Steam Navigation Company succeed in establishing their boats on the Orinoco, will eventually become a centre of the river-trade. MARACAYBO, a fine town, on the west side of the strait which connects the lake with the bay of the same name; it possesses a college, a pilot school, several building-slips, and is defended by three forts; population, 20,000. MERIDA, a small city, with 5,000 inhabitants, and containing a university of the second rank, and a college. Besides these, there are other important towns, and many minor ports and harbors along the coast.

The government of Venezuela is similar, in almost every aspect, to that of New Grenada; but partakes less of the energy, enterprise and liberality of that republic. It formerly consisted of the Captaincy-General of Caracas, to which has been added, however, the extensive tracts known formerly as Spanish Guayana, and now the department of Orinoco, which lies on the south of the river of the same name. The executive power is delegated to a President, whose term of office is four years; there is also a Vice-President. It is impossible, however, to form any adequate idea of the powers of the President of Venezuela, from those possessed by the President of the United States; in the one they are despotic, in the other limited; in the one all constitutional forms are mere words, in the other they are as guides and landmarks whereby the power is confined to its proper limits. The President of Venezuela is, in fact, a monarch, and all other powers are only subservient to his will. The legislative power is nominally confided to the Senate and House of Deputies, as in the United States; but such is the influence of the executive that the legislature is merely the shadow of a power. The whole government is a despotism, and the minions of the existing power distribute their oppressions among the people with an unsparing hand.

The political government of the departments is by law vested in the hands of intendantes, appointed by the president, with the sanction of Congress, with authority over the administration of justice, police, finance and defence; but without the command of an armed military force. The provinces are under the administration of governors, with powers only inferior and similar to intendantes; the cantons and parishes have each their own officers.

The civil and criminal code are an ill-digested collection of the laws of Castile and the Indies, royal ordinances, Spanish decrees, and colonial regulations; and their administration is very unfavorably spoken of. Trial by jury and liberty of the press, however, are everywhere allowed.

The religion of the country is the Roman Catholic; the ceremonies and festivals of which are celebrated with great splendor. The Inquisition was abolished in 1821, but the clergy still possess great power; and though every other creed is allowed toleration, their public rites and worship are prohibited. The clergy are paid by the state; convents are numerous, but are diminishing, and Catholicism is said to suffer to some extent by dissent. Many of the Indian tribes have embraced the Christian religion.

The armed force of Venezuela consists chiefly of Indians and the colored races. There is also a militia, which consists of the whole male population, from 16 to 40 years of age. The navy may be said to be no navy at all.

The state has made some provisions for elementary education; but, as yet, no progress has been made in this essential element in civilization. The wretched system bequeathed to all South America by the Spaniards, still exists in Venezuela; and all the important branches of useful knowledge professed at the universities, are so taught as to be really worse than useless, and, instead of expanding and enlightening the mind, serve rather to imbue it with the grossest prejudices. Primary schools are established in every parish; and Lancasterian schools exist in the principal cities. The literary talent of the country is chiefly confined to the newspapers; and on these the most lenient judgment must pronounce a most unqualified condemnation.

The fine arts are equally destitute of excellence; architecture has made but little progress, and all architectural beauty, which is found in Caracas, and the other principal cities, belongs to another race, and the old regimé. The republic cannot even boast of an ordinary portrait-painter. But, it is said, that the females of Caracas are excellent musicians, and can sing harmoniously and well. The whole scope, however, of the higher phases of the fine arts are decidedly in a backward state. The besetting sin of the Venezuelians is indolence, which retards all their social progress; they are courteous, hospitable, and when intimately known, friendly and cordial; temperate in their habits and grave in their deportment, but suspicious, reserved, slow, and imbued with an excess of national pride. The manners, dress, habits and amusements of those of European descent, much resemble those of their Spanish ancestors.

The coast of Venezuela was originally discovered by Columbus, in 1498, during his third voyage. Several voyages were afterwards made by adventurers, and some unavailing attempts having been made to colonize, the Spanish government came to the determination of settling the country under its own direction. These expeditions being managed by priests, were generally ill-conducted, and it was found necessary to subdue the natives by force. When this was partially effected, and the Spanish settlers were placed in some security, the proprietorship was sold to the Weltzers, a German Mercantile Company. Under their management, the Spaniards and natives suffered most grievous tyranny. They were dispossessed in 1750, and a supreme chief, with the title of Captain-General, was appointed. From this period until 1806, Caracas remained in the peaceful possession of Spain, and progressed in wealth and internal prosperity. In this year, a gallant, but unfortunate attempt, was made to secure the independence of the country. Gen. Miranda, a native of Caracas, formed, for this purpose, an expedition, partly from St. Domingo and partly from New-York. A landing was effected on the coast, but the forces proved wholly inadequate for the design; and many were taken prisoners, and were executed. The defeat was decisive, and for the time effectually suppressed the spirit of revolt. The entrance of the French into Spain, however, and the consequent derangement of Spanish affairs, gave the Venezuelans an opportunity to relax their bonds, and establish a free government. For this purpose a *Junta Suprema*, or Congress, was convened at Caracas, in which deputies from all the provinces, except Maracaybo, were present.

The *Junta* at first published their acts in the name of Ferdinand VII., but the captain-general and the members of the audiencia were deposed and imprisoned, and the new government received the title of the Confederation of Venezuela. The most violent and impolitic measures were now adopted by the Regency and Cortes of Spain; but the Congress finding the voice of the people decidedly in favor of independence, formally proclaimed the country a free and independent Republic, on the 5th of July

1811. A liberal constitution was formed, and affairs wore an aspect favorable to the cause of liberty until the fatal earthquake of 1812, which, operating on the superstitions of the people, led to a great change in public opinion.

Monteverde, a royalist general, taking advantage of the existing state of things, marched against Caracas, and, after defeating General Miranda, compelled the whole province to submit; in 1813, however, Venezuela was again emancipated by Bolivar, who was sent with an army from New Grenada; but, in 1814, he, in his turn, was defeated by Boves, and compelled to evacuate. In 1816, he again returned with a respectable body of troops, and was again defeated; but undismayed by reverses, he again landed in December, convened a general congress, and defeated the royalists in March, 1817, with great loss. Bolivar was now invested with dictatorial powers, the state of the country requiring unity and energy, and the contest was carried on with much spirit, and with various results. On the 17th Dec., 1819, a union of the republic with New Grenada was formed; this confederation received the title of the Republic of Colombia, and a suitable constitution was formed for the joint government. In the meantime, Bolivar was active in the field. On the 24th June, 1821, the battle of Carabobo was fought, in which the royal army was totally defeated, with the loss of their artillery, baggage, and upwards of 6,000 men; and soon after the Spaniards evacuated the country.

In the year 1829, Venezuela was separated from the Republic of Colombia, and again became an independent republic, under the presidency of Gen. Paez. In 1830, after the resignation of Bolivar, it again joined the Colombian Republic, but this union was of short duration. In November a new separation took place, and Colombia was finally divided into the three republics, Venezuela, New Grenada, and Equador.

Since this period the country has enjoyed external peace; but, within her own borders, the cauldron of political strife has been in constant ferment; and civil wars have reduced the energies of the republic, and operated heavily on its progress and prosperity.

On the 30th March, 1847,a treaty was concluded at Madrid, by which Spain renounced all sovereignty over Venezuela, and acknowledged her to be a free and independent nation.

The following persons have been successively presidents of the Republic since its separation in 1830 :—Gen. José Antonio Paez; Dr. Vargas; Gen. Soublette; and José Tadeo Monagas, the present president, whose term of service will end in 1850, if not deposed before that period.

The civil war now waging,* was commenced immediately after the massacre of several members of congress, on the 24th January, 1848, which act is said to have been perpetrated at the instigation of the president. Several battles have been fought between the popular general, Paez, and the myrmidons of Monagas, but, as yet, without result. From all appearances, the war seems to be one of *castes*, and will probably be of long continuance; it has been such pitiable outbreaks as this, that have retarded the developement of this prolific country, and such will ultimately prove its ruin if not abated.

It was in the regions of the vast plains watered by the Orinoco, that report located the fabulous "El Dorado," the golden kingdom of Manoa, which was the grand ultimatum of the Spaniards' hopes, and occasioned the fitting out of a great many expeditions in the 16th century. The Indians of Peru were continually pointing their reckless invaders to the

* This war terminated with the surrender of Paez in August, 1849.

north, and inciting their rapacious desires with stories of a more golden region, even than their own, in that direction. Whether it was that they endeavored by stratagem to rid themselves of their merciless conquerors, or that they referred to the opulent city of the Aztec Emperor, on the northern continent, has not yet been satisfactorily understood. So confident, however, were the Spaniards of the existence of such a country, that so late as the year 1780, a large expedition perished in the search, of course, fruitless, of this imaginary region.

THE REPUBLIC OF BOLIVIA.

The tract of country, occupied by the Bolivian Republic, was formerly called Upper Peru, and under Spanish dominion, formed successively portions of the viceroyalty of Lima and of Buenos Ayres. It is geographically situated between the parallels of 9° 30′ and 25° 40′ south latitude, and longitudes 58° and 71° west from Greenwich, having Peru on the north and north-west; Brazil and Paraguay on the east; the Argentine Republic and Chili on the south, and on the west the Pacific Ocean. Its extreme length from north to south is 1,100 miles, and its breadth from the Pacific to its eastern boundary is about 750 miles: the area has been estimated at 318,000 square miles.

Of all the states of South America, this, with Paraguay, is the least known to the world; whether we look for information respecting its topographical features, its social or political condition, its productions or wants, the same obscurity exists and interrupts inquiry.

The general features of the western portion of the country, however, are much similar to those of the eastern portions of Peru. It is traversed by mountains interspersed with beautiful elevated plateaux and vallies; while in the eastern provinces it stretches into a succession of immense pampas and well watered plains.

The Andes, which enter Bolivia at its southern extremity, give off near latitude 24° a lateral eastern range of no great elevation, which forms the boundary for a considerable distance between Bolivia and La Plata. About latitude 20°, the Andes divide into two great chains, which run parallel to each other to between 14° and 15° south, where they again unite. The farthest west of these chains is called the Cordillera of the coast, or of the Andes, and the furthest east the Cordillera Real: including the intermediate country, they occupy a breadth of more than 230 miles north of latitude 18° and south of that parallel of upwards of 300 miles; and cover at least 100,000 square miles of surface, which, however, is partly in Peru. Many lateral ridges, sent off by the Cordillera Real, cover the departments of Cochabamba and Chuquisaca, together with a part of those of Potosi and Santa Cruz de la Sierra: the principal of these transverse ridges branches off from the Cordillera about latitude 17° 10′, and running north past the city of Cochabamba, terminates within a few leagues of the town of Santa Cruz. The summits of the western Cordillera generally appear in the form, either of a truncated cone or of a dome, and are often volcanic: those of the eastern Cordillera, as seen from the west, offer a succession of sharp ragged peaks and serrated ridges, and are not volcanic, but in many parts highly metaliferous. The declivity of the Bolivian Cordillera is rapid on either side, but particularly so on the east: the principal elevations of both Cordilleras are about latitude 15° 19′ south, where that of the eastern chain is 24,450 feet,

(Illimani,) and of the western 25,400 feet (Sorata) above the level of the ocean. Many of the passes across both chains are between 15,000 and 16,000 feet in elevation or near the limit, in this region, of perpetual snow: while beneath the peaks of the Illimani there is a gorge or valley, perhaps 18,000 feet below the neighboring summit, probably the greatest difference in elevation that has ever yet been observed between any two similar contiguous points.

The eastern portions of the country, which is in many parts very little above the level of the sea, is watered by the Beni, Mamore, Ubahy, Pilcomayo and other considerable rivers: a few isolated ranges of hills are scattered over it, and in its southern part is the watershed between the sources of the Amazon and La Plata Rivers, both of which receive considerable affluents from Bolivia: but neither this last named track, nor the isolated hills previously mentioned, appear to rise to any great height above the sea. The whole region is extremely fertile; but it is nearly in a state of nature, and covered with vast primeval forests.

The desert of Atacama occupies the country between the Andes and the Pacific: it extends for about 250 miles along the coast, having a variable breadth of from 30 to 60 miles. It is never refreshed by rain, and is almost as sterile and worthless as the Zahara: the only habitable parts are the narrow strips which skirt the rivers.

The Beni, Mamore, and some others, unite to form the Madeira, the principal confluent of the Amazon, and have a general course from south to north. The Pilcomayo, one of the chief branches of the Plata, waters the south part of the country, running in a direction from west to east. Bolivia includes the eastern and southern shores of the largest accumulation of fresh water in South America—the Lake Titicaca, which occupies an area of 4,600 square miles, at the height of 12,798 feet above the level of the ocean, an elevation superior to that of the highest summits of the Pyrenees. In the east, lakes are numerous, and some of them, as those of Ubahy and Grande, 50 or 60 miles in length; but they have as yet been little explored. The general geological construction of the Andes applies to the western districts of Bolivia: the eastern portion consists of deluvial deposits, and in its character approaches that of the basin of the Mississippi and the other great river vallies of North and South America.

The mineral resources, especially those of the precious metals, are extensive and much celebrated. Gold is found in large quantities on the declivity of the eastern Cordillera, and in the sands of the rivers flowing thence into the Beni and its tributaries. Potosi is famous for its rich silver mines: the Cerro di Potosi, a mountain belonging to the Andes, which is 18 miles in circumference, and rises to the height of 16,037 feet, is supposed to be a solid mass of the ores or the matrix of the precious metals, of which it has produced an immense amount. Viewed from a distance, it presents all the various tints of the rainbow, and when the sun shines on the different colored ores, the effect is sublime. The first mining operations were commenced in 1545, from which time to the year 1803, it produced silver to the amount of £237,358,334 sterling, on which duty was paid, besides, perhaps, an equal amount smuggled from the country. Gold, in large quantities, was also extracted from this mountain. The revolutionary struggle, however, much retarded operations, and they have since been almost suspended, and the mines are now quite unproductive: but there is no doubt, that if capital and energy were again called into requisition, vast and uncounted treasures would flow into commerce. Copper is also abundant in the mountain regions: Corucuero and several other places owe their wealth to this source; ores of lead, tin, salt, sulphur, nitre and other volcanic formations, are collected in several districts.

The interminable forests which border the margins of the rivers of Bolivia, abound in the finest woods, fit for every purpose of ship-building, carpentry and cabinet work. The cocoa of Apolobamba and Moxas is celebrated, and is much superior to that produced in Equador: it is used by all classes as a nutritious and restorative diet. Fruits of all kinds flourish luxuriously on the Beni and other streams: tamarinds; the chirimoya, lemons, figs, sugar-canes, pine-apples, plantains, &c., grow wild in all this region.

Bolivia is very productive in medicinal plants and drugs: cascarilla, indigo, cinchona, copaiba, sarsaparilla, &c. Its agricultural products consist of rice, coffee and various grains. Cotton, gum-elastic, tobacco, dyewoods, &c., are articles of export. Among other products, is a species of cinnamon, called *canella de clava,* said to differ little from the genuine, except in the thickness of its bark. In the narrow strips along the margin of the rivers that run through the desert of Atacama, maize is much raised, with excellent fruits, cotton, sugar-cane, and the plant called *Arundodonax.*

The wild animals of the country are those peculiar to the whole central portion of South America: the tapir, jaguar, leopard, and a variety of monkies inhabit the forests on the banks of the rivers. Guanacos, alpacos, a kind of hare, and a small animal of the family *Rodentia,* whose burrowing often renders travelling on horseback unsafe, are found in the valley of Desaguadero. The llama, and other animals, mentioned in Peru, are common to this country, and the cochineal insect is raised with greater facility than in Mexico. The parrot and paroquette, as well as various singing-birds, as the thrush and whistler, are indigenous, and several kinds of turkies inhabit the woods. The rivers are well supplied with fish and amphibia, in great variety, and the eastern plains are infested with myriads of annoying reptiles and insects. Vast herds of cattle roam over the pampas, and horses, asses, mules, &c. are used as beasts of burden: sheep are only found in the mountains in the west, the eastern lands being too warm for them.

The climate of Bolivia presents several peculiarities, determined by locality. The vast desert of Atacama, on the Pacific, partakes of the characteristics of Western Peru; there it never, or but seldom rains, nor is thunder or lightning known. In the vast plains east of the Andes the rainy season, which is identical with summer, lasts from October to April, during which the rains are continuous, and the country is inundated to a great extent by the overflowing of the surcharged rivers; the temperature of these plains is very high, and throughout they may be said to be unhealthy, and productive of fevers and other endemic diseases. The banks of the Beni, however, are represented as being comparatively healthy. In the valley of Desaguadero, 1,300 feet above the level of the sea, the temperature is moderate, uniform, and the climate in the highest degree salubrious and pleasant; snow falls in November and April, the beginning and end of the summer season, but never remains on the ground for any length of time. The winter in this valley is extremely dry, and, although the nights are cool, the sky is serene and cloudless. Tremendous hail-storms are frequent in the mountains, and earthquakes on the coast. In the higher regions of the Andes the inhabitants are frequently afflicted with snow-blindness throughout the winter season; but otherwise, their exalted station is as happy as it is healthy.

Bolivia is divided into the following departments, and these are subdivided into districts and parishes:

	Departments.	*Capitals and Cities.*
1.	Potosi	Potosi, *Atacama*, *Cotagaita*, &c.
2.	Chuquisaca	Chuquisaca, *Pomabamba*, *Tomina*, &c.
3.	Cochabamba	Orepesa, *Cochabamba*, &c.
4.	La Paz	La Paz, *Apolobamba*, *Zarata*, &c.
5.	Tarija	Tarija, *Moja*, *Vehan*, &c.
6.	Santa Cruz de la Sierra, containing the territories of Santa Cruz, Moxas, and Chiquitos.	

The population of Bolivia is variously stated: Balbi estimates it at 1,300,000; Brackenridge, at 1,716,000; and some as low as 650,000. The estimate of Brackenridge is probably the most correct; he distributes it thus—Potosi and Tarija, 315,000; Chuquisaca, 246,000; Cochabamba, 530,000; La Paz, 400,000; and Santa Cruz, Moxos, and Chiquitos, 225,000. More than three-fourths of this population is composed of the aborigines, which, though in a low state of civilization, make good Catholics, and are endowed with respectable physical and mental characteristics. The foreign settlers are mostly of Spanish descent; these inhabit chiefly the mining districts and the vallies of Cochabamba, &c. The African race is not very numerous, but those of mixed blood are in considerable numbers in the Pacific districts. The Spanish creole and the negro retain their peculiarities, in disposition and physical characteristics, in all parts of South America; the creole is proud and lazy—the negro, submissive and obliged to labor; while they resemble each other in their love of dissipation, gambling, &c., and in their utter physical inability to exert themselves in their several vocations. The Indian tribes, especially those who still retain their original independence, are in natural parts far superior to the Creole and Indo-African races. Some on the Beni are wild and warlike, and go naked, even the women wearing but a few leaves bound round their waists; another tribe, the Maropas, in the immediate vicinity of the former, although a warlike and proud race, evince considerable ingenuity and aptitude for various kinds of work; they manufacture beautiful cloths, are pretty good carpenters, and are said to have shown much taste for music and painting, in which they were initiated by the Jesuits. Not a few Indians, especially in the Desaguadero valley, have been converted to Catholicity (!): these, instead of going naked or leading a roving life, have fixed dwellings, and apply themselves to agricultural pursuits, and are very ingenious in the manufacturing of fans, parasols, plumes, &c., from the feathers of the American ostrich.

The metropolis of Bolivia is the City of Chuquisaca, formerly called *La Plata;* it lies in a low plain, surrounded by hills, on the north bank of the Cachimayo, and on the high road between Potosi and Santa Cruz. Latitude 19° 29′ south, longitude 66° 40′ west. Its population amounts to 16,000, pretty equally divided between the Spaniards, Indians, and mixed races. The cathedral is a large and handsome building, and is adorned with some good paintings and decorations. The city is also provided with a university, monastic establishments, splendid churches, a conventual hospital, three nunneries, &c. The best houses are only of one story, but are roomy, and surrounded by garden-plats; they are supplied with water from the public fountains. Chuquisaca was founded in 1539; made a bishopric in 1537; the seat of an *audientia real*, in 1550; and of an archbishopric, in

1608. After the revolution it became the seat of the national government. The climate of the vicinity is mild, but the rains are of long continuance, and during the winter violent tempests are not unfrequent.

Potosi is the next city of importance, and far more populous than the capital, being the centre of the rich mining districts. It was formerly the metropolitan city. Latitude 19° 36′ south, longitude 67° 21′ 45″ west. Early in the 17th century it is said to have had a population of 150,000; but at present it amounts only to 36,000. It is built on the northern declivity of the Cerro de Potosi, on uneven ground, and has a spacious square or Plaza, in the centre of which the old Government Palace occupies one side; the treasury and public offices another; a convent and church, the third: and splendid houses of the rich, the fourth. Extensive suburbs, once inhabited by the miners, are still in existence, but are now in ruins; and nothing remains but the outline of the streets. The most remarkable edifice is the mint, built of stone, in 1751, at a cost of $1,148,000; and in the principal square is an obelisk, erected in honor of Bolivar, in 1825; it is 60 feet high. The houses of Potosi are generally of stone or brick, and of one story only, with wooden balconies, but without chimneys. The country around is perfectly barren, and the climate anything but pleasant; the rays of the sun scorching at noon, while at night the atmosphere is piercingly cold. The markets of this city are well supplied, but owing to the distance all articles have to be carried, the necessaries, as well as the luxuries of life, are comparatively high in price.

La Paz has a population of 30,000. It is situated on an eastern declivity of the Andes, at an elevation of 12,170 feet above the sea, and at no great distance from the head waters of the Beni. Latitude 17° 30′ south, longitude 68° 25′ west. It has a splendid cathedral, four churches, several convents, and is a bishop's see, with very considerable revenues. It is the centre of a considerable trade in Paraguay tea. La Paz was founded in 1548, and received its name in commemoration of the peace that ensued after the defeat of Pizarro and his comrades. It suffered considerably during the revolt of the Indians some years ago, but is still a city of some wealth and importance.

The other principal towns of Bolivia are Tarija, situated in a valley of the same name, and containing 12,000 inhabitants; Tupiza, Lipiz, Tarapaca, and San Francisco de Atacama on the Pacific, and the City of Oruro, north-west of Potosi, built at the foot of a mineral mountain of the same name. Beside these, the country is dotted over with innumerable villages of Indians, and wherever the least prospect of centralizing wealth is perceived, new settlements are made by the enterprize of capitalists.

The defensive means of Bolivia are little attended to: the standing army is limited to 2,000 men, but in case of war, the whole male population is obliged to turn out. There are, however, no sea-ports to defend, and it is very improbable that they will be attacked by a nation superior in physical power to themselves. They have no ships of war.

Agricultural industry, as a general feature of the condition of the Bolivians, is in a backward state. The natural fertility of the soil and the ease with which the necessaries of life are obtained, have, no doubt, contributed to this state of things. As in Peru, so it is in Bolivia, the inhabitants are too much engrossed in search of the precious metals. There are, however, some well supplied and extensive *estancia*, where immense numbers of cattle are bred and large crops of the various grains cultivated. The implements of husbandry are also quite unfit for the purpose to which they are applied, nor as yet are any of the new and improved ones of the United States or England introduced. The almost impossibility of weaning a people from old habits and usages has and will long contribute to retard improvement in this department of industry.

Arts and manufactures are in a like depressed state · what do exist, are manufactures of cotton cloth, the best of which is made at Oropesa; woollens of the hair of the llama and alpaca, the best at La Paz; hats of the wool of the vicuna, at San Francisco de Atacama; glass at Oropesa; vessels and ornaments of silver ware in the mining districts, and a few other articles of little importance to the general wants of the nation.

The commerce of the country is almost entirely inland: Bolivia has maintained an extensive trade with Peru, Buenos Ayres and the Republic of Paraguay. Previous to the revolution, that of Peru was maintained at the annual value of 7,000,000 dollars, and the goods received from the latter at 10,000,000 dollars. The Spaniards and Creoles, to this time, had been the only consumers of foreign goods, as the Indians and mixed races used little more than the coarse manufactures of the country. Since the separation from Spain, however, things are different: the freedom of the Indians and other inferior races has caused them to imitate the manners and extravagances of their former masters, and a consequent increased demand for foreign luxuries has ensued. The direct commerce, however, is very limited, and the chief part of the foreign goods imported are still brought by way of Buenos Ayres and Peru. The export trade of this country is all carried on from its few ports on the Pacific, to reach which they have to be conveyed first by toilsome passages against the currents of the rivers to the foot of the Andes, then across the mountains on the backs of mules, and lastly, along a miserable apology for a road, from Oruro to Cobija, the only Bolivian port of any consequence: many exporters, however, prefer to carry their goods through the southern provinces of Peru, although this incurs a transit demand of three per cent. Nothing but bullion and gems can repay these enormous expenses; and in fact, the exports of Bolivia are nearly altogether limited to the precious metals, the finer descriptions of wools and other valuables. It is probable, however, that in a few years, steam-navigation will open vast outlets for Bolivian commerce, and convey its treasures to the Atlantic coasts: the gigantic rivers flowing through the eastern and most fertile regions, are navigable almost to their sources, and the only wonder is, that the facilities they afford have not already been adopted. When this does take place—when the Amazon, Madeira and the great affluents of these rivers are navigated by steam, an era of prosperity will open to the commerce of the countries through which they run, that will astonish the world, and be productive of mighty changes in their condition. The Bolivian government has already had this subject under attention, and has offered large premiums and extensive privileges to any company that shall undertake the regular navigation of these rivers by steam.

The public revenues of Bolivia are on a respectable footing, and more than cover the expenses of government in time of peace, and pay interest on the national debt, which amounts only to about 2 or 3,000,000 of dollars.

The religious condition of Bolivia, and the condition of learning and the sciences, generally, are like those of Peru, in a state of unimpeachable inferiority: religion is a mixture of Paganism and Papistry; education, the art of confounding ideas; learning, mystification; and their sciences, the very essence of empiricism and quackery. It is probable, however, that a few years' application of the school system lately adopted, will entirely change the complexion of the inhabitants, and bring about the subversion of the present state of superstition, mummery and rottenness, that now infests the country, and reveal to the inhabitants those principles that can alone give to their land the essential benefits of liberty—that liberty, they, in their present state, are incapable of enjoying.

The weights, measures and coinage of the country, are similar, in capacity and value, to those of Spain, but bear the national impress: the silver of Bolivia, however, is of a finer character than that of Spain, and is more valuable as bullion.

The form of government is that of an elective integral republic. The constitution on which it is based, was propounded by Bolivar, in 1825, but some of the provisions of that constitution have been abandoned, and others substituted. The powers are decreed to a president, (formerly for life,) a legislature, consisting of a senate and house of deputies, and a judiciary, independent of the other divisions of the government. The whole male adult population are eligible to office, but elections are carried on through electoral colleges. Nominal liberty is also allowed to all.

The history of this country is little known: the short accounts we have are contradictory, and made to suit the interests of the writer, or his party. Bolivia, under Spain, was known as Upper Peru, and was successively attached to Peru Proper and the Viceroyalty of Buenos Ayres. It was the first to feel the effects of the revolution, and last to rid itself of Spanish oppression. Previous to the battle of Ayacucho, it was the strong-hold of General Lascerna, the Spanish Viceroy of Peru, who had fled hither on the breaking out of the revolution in Lima. The consequence of that battle, in which the Spaniards were entirely defeated, was its independence. The present name of the republic was given in 1825, in honor of the South American liberator, Simon Bolivar, and to him was entrusted its destinies. Generals Sucre, Velasco, Blanco, Santa Cruz, &c., have since successively filled the executive chair, but the state of the country has never been settled, and it is still the scene of constantly recurring revolutions: its condition is such, indeed, that he who holds power to-day has no guarantee that the morrow will not consign him to a dishonorable death, or more ignominiously to the dungeon and popular outrage. President Balivian, who has governed for some years, was driven out in 1849, and has been temporarily succeeded by Belxu, one of the generals who had revolted against his tyranny.

THE REPUBLIC OF PERU.

This republic is situated on the western side of the continent of South America, and formed a part of the ancient Spanish vice-royalty of the same name. It lies between the parallels of 3° and 22° south latitude, and 69° and 81° 20′ west longitude. On the north it is bounded by the Republic of Equador, on the south and south-east by Bolivia, and on the east by Brazil, having the Pacific Ocean lying to the west. Its extreme length, from S. S. E. to N. N. W. is about 1,500 miles; its breadth varies from 40 to 600 miles. The estimated area of Peru is 500,000 square miles.

The whole of Peru is traversed by the Cordilleras of the Andes, the eastern range of which approaches within from 30 to 100 miles of the Pacific Ocean. The country is naturally divided into three distinct regions: the slope between the Andes and the coast; the mountain regions of the Andes themselves, and that east of the Cordilleras, forming part of the great basin of the Amazon. All these divisions are widely different in character. The coast region, between the Tumbez River and the Leche, is mostly a desert, and wherever, in fact, it is not traversed by streams or is not susceptible of irrigation, it consists principally of arid, sandy wastes, and is in the last degree barren. Immediately on the coast lies all the principal settlements made by the Spaniards. The area of the mountain district has been estimated to cover about 200,000 square miles of territory. The Andes in Peru, as well as in Bolivia, consists of two main chains or Cordilleras, connected in various parts by cross ranges, and enclosing several extensive and lofty vallies. Round Cuzco is a vast knot of mountains, occupying about three times the extent of Switzerland; and round Pasco, in latitude 13° south, is another knot surrounding the plain of Bombon, 13,500 feet above the ocean level, and in which are the rich and valuable silver mines of the Cerro Pasco. The Peruvian Andes are not, in general, so elevated as the Bolivian, though many of their peaks rise above the limits of perpetual snow. The loftiest summits are towards the south where the Nevada de Chuquibamba (latitude 5°) reaches to 21,000 feet in height; and several others, surrounding the valley of Desaguadero, which belongs only partly to Peru, may at least approach this elevation. In Bolivia the east, but in Peru the west Cordillera is the highest at the mountain knot of Pasco, the Andes separating into three collateral chains, which, proceeding north, separate the basins of the Maranon, Huallaga, and Ucayale. The last range of the Andes to the east in Peru, extends between the 6th and 15th parallels, to a distance varying from 2 to 400 miles from the Pacific, and separates the basin of the Ucayale from those of the Yavari, Beni, and other affluents of the Amazon. Probably no part of the range rises above 10,000 feet.

The space enclosed between the gigantic ridges of the east and west Cordillera, called the Sierra, is partly occupied by mountains and naked rocks, partly by table lands yielding short, fine grass, and extensive hilly pasture ground, much resembling the general contour of the Highlands of Scotland, but destitute of all covering, and partly by extensive and fertile vallies, that once supported a large population. The third region or country east of the Cordilleras, is very little known; it is covered with interminable forests, and can scarcely be said to belong to Peru, being occupied only by a few missionaries and tribes of independent Indians.

The largest rivers in the world have their source from the Peruvian Andes. The Tunguragua, generally regarded as the proper source of the Amazon, and its vast confluents, Huallaga and Ucayale, (the latter formed by the junction of the Apurimac and Paro) have their sources on the east side of the western chain of the Cordilleras, between 10° 30′ and 16° south latitude, and pursue, though with many windings, a northerly course, until they pass the boundaries of the country. These great rivers are mostly navigable, and, with the assistance of steam navigation, will, no doubt, at an early period, carry the riches of this remote region across the continent to the ports of the Atlantic. There are few lakes in Peru; if we except that of Titicaca. This lake, the largest and most elevated in South America, is partly within Bolivia, being enclosed by the Cordilleras south of the table-land of Cuzco. Its outline is very irregular, being divided by a number of headlands into a main body of an oblong form, and three subsidiary portions; its area is 4,000 square miles, and its height above the ocean 12,795 feet. It is said to be in many places 500 feet deep. It contains many small mountainous islands, and from the largest, at its southern extremity, the lake has received its name, which signifies "the leaden mountain." This island is three leagues in length, and one in breadth, and about a mile from shore. It is mostly uncultivated, but very fertile. On this island tradition places the first appearance of Manco Capac; and it is yet held in great veneration by the Peruvian Indians. The other lakes of Peru are comparatively small, but are the sources from whence all the great rivers, flowing eastward, have their sources.

The rivers of the coast are of no account; they are small, shallow, and incapable of navigation. The coasts are lofty and rugged throughout. In the northern provinces, some miles of a loose, sandy desert intervene between the high lands and the ocean, but, in general, the cliffs approach close to the shore, which has not, perhaps, in an extent of 1,600 miles a dozen secure harbors. The best of these are Callao, Payta, Sechura, Salina, Pisco, Islay, and a few others; Truxillo and Lambayeque have only open road-steads. The water being almost of uniform depth, vessels are obliged to approach within a quarter of a mile of the shore before they can anchor, and the prodigious swell, which rolls unbroken from the Pacific, occasions a heavy and dangerous surf. "The operation of landing," is, except in a few places, at once difficult and hazardous; it is effected by means of *balsas* or platforms, raised on inflated skins, and differing in different parts of the coast. The *balsa* used by Capt. Hall, (see *Hall's South America,*) was made of two entire seal skins inflated, placed side by side, and connected by cross-pieces of wood and strong lashings of thongs; over all a platform of cane-mats forms a sort of deck, about four feet in width and six or eight feet in length. At one end, the person who is managing the *balsa* kneels down, and by means of a double-bladed paddle, which he holds by the middle, and strikes alternately on each side, moves it swiftly along; the passengers or goods being placed on the platform behind him. All the goods which go into the interior, at this part of the coast, are landed in this manner. The great bars of silver, and the bags of dollars also, which are shipped in return for the merchandize landed, pass through the surf, on these slender, though secure conveyances.

The mineral resources of Peru, like those of Mexico, are inexhaustible: the whole country is one vast mound of mineral wealth; the mountains, rivers and streams are glittering with gold, silver and precious stones. The very name of the country is associated in the mind with ideas of gold and silver. But though the most exaggerated notions of the value and importance of the Peruvian mines were long, and perhaps are yet, prevalent, they have no doubt furnished vast supplies of the precious metals. The greater number of mines at present being worked, are situated in the Cerro de Pisco, in the department of Junin. Their produce has materially declined since the revolutionary struggle. Humboldt, at the commencement of the present century, estimated the annual value of the gold and silver of Peru at 6,240,000 dollars, but at present, owing to the anarchy and insecurity that has prevailed, their value is probably not more than half that amount: but it is impossible to ascertain the actual amount collected, as a great quantity is smuggled out of the country to avoid the export duty. M'Culloch is disposed to estimate the average annual value of the gold and silver mines of Peru at from 7 to £750,000 sterling, or about 3,500,000 dollars. Gold is found chiefly in the district of Tarma. Huancavelica has one of the richest quicksilver mines in the world, one portion of which furnished 3,000 quintals yearly for two centuries; but such was the state of affairs in Peru, in '37 and '38, that quicksilver sold at 200 to 220 dollars per quintal, while in London, at the same time, it was sold at 65 dollars. Of course the mines were then suspended, but at the present day operations have been revived by private companies, and the mines are as productive as ever.

Exclusive of the gold and silver, Peru, like Chili, produces copper, tin, iron, coal, salt-petré, &c., in abundance. The latter, under the commercial name of nitrate of soda, has become an important article of export to the United States and England.

The vegetable products of Peru are various and very dissimilar. Sugar, rice, tobacco, yams, sweet potatoes and cocoa, are raised in the warmest situations; the vine, wheat and quinoa (*chenopodium quinoa*) are planted in the colder places, and potatoes in the most cultivated grounds. The grapes are well flavored, but the wine made from them is inferior. The sugar-cane is mostly the creole species. Maize is cultivated, and is the common diet of the people. The culture of cotton is beginning to be attended to by the Peruvians, and a very excellent article of short staple has found its way into the markets. Almost all the culinary vegetables of temperate climates may be grown in Peru. and all species of the tropical fruits find soil in which they flourish luxuriantly. Medicinal plants, drugs and dye-stuffs form a large part of the exports, and some of the hard woods abound in the forests. The cinchona, or Peruvian bark, is very plentiful in and indigenous to the country: it grows at the elevation of 10,000 or 12,000 feet: it abounds most in the northern provinces. *Coca*, the dried leaf of the *Erythroxylon coca*, is largely used by the Peruvians for chewing, much in the same way as the betel in the east. Poeppig says, that indulgence in its use brings on a gloomy kind of mania, but other authorities deny that it has any such effect.

The zoology of Peru presents a large catalogue: but it will be seen, that the animals it notices are mostly those common to the other parts of South America. The puma, or American lion; the uturuncu, (*felis onca*,) a species of tiger; the acumari, (*ursus Americanus*,) a black bear, inhabiting the mountains; the *anas*, or skunk: great varieties of deer, wild bears, armadillos, &c., form the catalogue of Peruvian wild animals, and are made objects for the chase. The llama, alpaca, guanaco, vicuna, &c., and a variety of others, have been used as beasts of burden, and are valuable for their wool and skins. Four varieties of the condor are indigenous to Peru. Alligators are found in the rivers, but the reptile tribes are not so troublesome here as nearer the equator. The cattle of Peru are not so large as the Lincolnshire breed, but are equal to the generality of those of England and Belgium: when fed on lucerne grass, the meat is tender, juicy and well flavored, and the bones very small. Black cattle thrive best in the mountains, but speedily pine and die away on the low lands of the coast. Horses and mules are of ordinary character in Peru, but goats, pigs, &c. grow to a large size, and are very fine in flavor.

Of foreign quadrupeds, acclimated in Peru, (*Stevenson's Travels*,) sheep appear to have succeeded best. They have increased in an amazing degree on the great commons and pastures of the Andes, at an elevation of 12,000 or 14,000 feet above the sea. Few sheep are bred on the coasts, but during certain months, large flocks are driven from the interior and fattened for the Lima market. Many of the ewes are in lamb, and the common bargain between the drover and the farmer is to give the lambs for the pasturage, the farmer calculating on receiving 150 lambs for every 100 ewes. Besides this increase, which is greater than in England, the ewes bear twice a year, generally in June and December. Little attention has been paid hitherto to breeding sheep, so as to improve the wool, but as the latter is now becoming an increasing article of export, more care will doubtless be bestowed on this object. The largest quantities are exported from Islay, and are chiefly produced in the neighborhood of Lampa, Puno and Cusco. It is soft, and similar in appearance to English wool, but being badly cleaned, it does not fetch more than 9d or 10d a pound; that from the mountains, between Lima and Pasco, being better cleaned, usually brings 1d per pound additional. The wool produced on the coast is of very inferior quality. Viçuna wool is exported, but only in small quantities. The average quantity of all wools exported to Great Britain and the United States, amounts annually to from 25 to 30,000 quintals.

The climate of Peru is much hotter than that of Chili. In the country included between the Western Cordillera and the coasts, rain, thunder and lightning are entirely unknown. During the winter, however, which lasts from July to November, the ground is almost constantly covered with a thick fog, which, towards the close of day, generally agglomerates into a very small mist or dew, and moistens the earth equally. During the summer, the sun's rays occasion excessive heat throughout all this region; the more so as they are received on the naked sands, whence they are strongly reflected. The entire region is unhealthy: malignant, intermittent and catarrhal fevers, pleurisies and constipations are the most common complaints, and rage constantly in Lima and other sea-board cities. A great part of Peru, between the western range of the Andes and Pacific, supplies one of the most perfect examples of what is called the *hot* and *dry* climate; as for the space of 400 leagues along the coast, rain never falls, and the parched earth is cracked asunder and plants have no existence. The summits of the Andes intercept the clouds, which pour down in torrents from the mountain districts, often accompanied by tremendous thunder and lightning, while near the sea not a drop falls to moisten the parched earth. The atmosphere, hence, in all this region, is uniformly hot. During the winter, at Lima, the thermometer never sinks below 60° *Fahr.* at noon, and it seldom rises above 85°; though it is occasionally seen at 96°. In some districts, however, the temperature is much higher, and rises over 100° or 110° in the shade. The elevated plains, between the western and central Cordilleras, called by Humboldt the high table lands of Peru, have scarcely any variation of temperature throughout the year; the mercury of Fahrenheit's thermometer always stands at about 66° or 67°: the climate is here mild and genial, and a perpetual spring exists. The only distinction of seasons arises from the rains, which prevail from November to May. The highest Andes are perpetually covered with snow, and experience an uninterrupted winter between the tropics. Here, too, amid the reign of winter, and with their sides covered with perpetual snow, volcanos, in number, pour forth their fiery lava and lurid flames.

The Republic of Peru includes seven departments, eight populous cities, and between 14 and 1500 towns and small villages; four of the departments are situated on the coast of the Pacific, and three in the interior, viz. :

	Departments.	Capitals, *Cities, &c.*
Coast.	TRUXILLO or LIBERTAD	Truxillo, *Sechura, Payta.*
	JUNIN	Huanuco, *Pasco, Junin, Banot.*
	LIMA	Lima, *Callao, &c.*
	AREQUIPA	Arequipa, *Arica, &c.*
Interior	AYACUCHO	Huamanca, *Huancavelica, &c.*
	CUZCO	Cuzco, *Abancay, Tinta, Urubamba.*
	PUNO	Puno, *Lampa, Chucuito.*

These departments are subdivided into districts, townships, and curacies or parishes, which are, or were, under the colonial system, governed by a *curate*, a *cacique*, and an *alcalde;* the first a spiritual chief, whose business it is to teach the inhabitants the Roman Catholic religion; the second, collector of revenue, and the third, civil magistrate.

The inhabitants of Peru consist, principally of Spaniards, native Indians, Africans, and the several commixtures derived from those original sources. The amount of population is left entirely to conjecture: no exact enumeration has been taken since 1802, when it amounted to 1,076,000: of these, 136,000 were Spaniards, 609,000 Indians, 244,000 Mestizos, 49,000 free Negroes and 40,000 African slaves. It was represented by Humboldt to be 1,400,000, and Balbi and the patriots of 1818, state it to have been 1,700,000. At a later date, Malté Brun gives the whole population as approximating to 1,500,000, of which the Spanish races constituted but one-fifteenth part: the Indians, Mestizos and Negroes held about the same proportions as in the census of 1802. This estimate is probably as true as circumstances would permit of; and as the affairs of the country have not been very favorable for the increase of population, it may still be considered as an approximate computation. Perhaps it may now be about 2,000,000.

LIMA, the capital of Peru, and the most splendid city of South America, is situated in the beautiful valley of the Rimac. The surrounding country is in the highest state of cultivation, and the fertile plains, crowned with the most luxurious vegetation, produce sugar, maize, rice, and the choicest of fruits in abundance. This city, which is the great emporium of trade for the whole Pacific coast of the continent of America, and the grand depôt of the metaliferous regions of South America, into which they have been pouring their wealth for nearly three centuries, is in latitude 12° 3′ south, and about six miles from Callao, its natural harbor and port, at the mouth of the River Rimac. Lima is elevated about 600 feet above the level of the sea, and is skirted by hills which overlook the city. It is surrounded by a solid wall of brick, and has seven gates. The form of the city is nearly triangular, the base extending along the margin of the river. Notwithstanding the frequent earthquakes which have destroyed this city, it occupies an area of ten miles in circumference, including he suburb of San Lazaro, situated on the north side of the city, and separated from it by the Rimac, over which there is an excellent stone bridge. The streets are paved, and through them streams of water flow, conducted from the river a little above the city; they are broad, and cross each other at right angles, forming squares of 150 yards on each side. The houses are low, but commodious and handsome, having fruit gardens attached to most of them. In the centre of the great square there is a spacious and superb fountain. The city is divided into five parishes, and contains 23 monasteries, 14 nunneries, and 16 hospitals; a cathedral and national palace. It is the seat of a university, a school of medicine, and numerous educational institutions. There is also a theatre, and other places of amusement. Its population, according to the latest census, was 54,098, of which 27,545 were males, and 26,553 females; of this number 20,000 were whites and creoles, 6,000 mestizos, from 5,000 to 10,000 were Indians, and about 2,000 negroes or blacks. The population is almost stationary, or increases very slowly; in 1793, it was stated at 52,627. Lima was founded in 1535, by Pizarro. CALLAO is situated at the mouth of the Rimac, and is strongly fortified. It is built on a low, flat point of land. The port is one of the most safe and commodious on the coast of the Pacific Ocean, and is the rendezvous of an immense amount of shipping, and a convenient depot for whaling craft. The other ports belonging to the department of Lima are Chancay and Huacho to the north, and Pisco and Chorillos to the south.*

TRUXILLO is north of Lima, in latitude 8° 6′ south, and is situated in the valley of Chono. It was one of the cities founded by Pizarro, in 1535, and lies about one and a half miles from the sea. The houses are in general built of brick, and are only one story high. Population 13,000. The port of Truxillo is Guanchaco, six miles in a northerly direction from the city. Payta, Sechura and Sana, are also ports of the department.

CUZCO, the ancient capital of the Incas, and now the capital of the department of the same name, lies in latitude 13° 32′, about 400 miles southeast from Lima. It was founded in the 11th century, by Manco Capac, the first Inca of Peru, and taken possession of by Pizarro in 1534. It stands on an uneven site, skirted by mountains on the north and west. The ruins of the famous fort, built by the Incas, are still visible on the mountains, on the north of the city. The houses are principally of stone, and its public buildings are a cathedral, nine churches, and numerous convents and hospitals. The cathedral and convent of San Augustine are said to rank among the finest buildings in the new world. The Guatanay, a small stream, runs past the town. Its population is 46,000. The people are said to be industrious, and to excel in embroidery, painting and sculpture.

HUAMANCA, or the north-west of Cuzco, is the principal city of Ayacucho, and lies in latitude 13° south, on the declivity of a mountain ridge, not remarkable for its height, but still so far above the river as to be scantily supplied with water. It was founded by Pizarro in 1539. The principal buildings of the city are a cathedral, a university, in which all the liberal professions are taught, and several churches, convents and hospitals. The surrounding country is fertile, populous, and under a high state of cultivation—the climate mild and equable—and there is an abundance of all kinds of fruit and culinary vegetables. The mines of Huamanca are reported to be very rich, but few of them are worked. The population of the city amounts to 39,000.

AREQUIPA, containing 20,000 inhabitants, is one of the best cities in Peru, and lies in the valley of Quilca, 7,700 feet above the level of the sea, from which it is 30 miles distant; latitude 16° 30′ south. ARICA, in 18° 28′, is the principal outlet of the mining districts of the south, but owing to a heavy surf, which beats upon the shore, it is always difficult, and sometimes impossible, to effect a landing, except in the *balsas* of the natives The town is a miserable agglomeration of the rudest huts, and contains a population of 400 or 500 persons. PUNO, the capital of a department of

* Wilkes, (*U. S. Explor. Exped.*,) states that Lima is fast going to decay; but that Callao is becoming a thriving place, and has usually in port about forty vessels.

the same name, contains 16,000 inhabitants, and is a well-built city. The vicinity is a most beautiful country, and its proximity to the Lake Titicaca contributes much to the romantic interest of the place. HUANUCO is the capital of the department of Junin. The cities of Peru, generally, are well-built, but the buildings are low, and seldom support a second story; this is precautionary and necessary, on account of the disasters occasioned by the frequent recurrence of earthquakes. Many of the cities that now exist, were built long before the Spanish Conquest, and, even to this day, many of the private houses belong to the early era of the first Incas.

The native Spaniards or Creoles of Peru, forming the higher and more cultivated classes, are said to be inferior to the same denominations in almost all the other South American states. Their long political degradation, the general diffusion of wealth, and the facility of procuring the necessaries of life, seem to have been the principal cause of this degradation. The males are described as being an insignificant race: destitute of all that is manly; alike enervated in body and mind, and unable to exert themselves. The trade of the country is carried on entirely by foreigners. The ladies, though more equal to the task of living than the men, are, nevertheless, destitute of that propriety which ought to distinguish their sex: they are vain, proud and profligate, and great coquettes. Both sexes are devoted to the destructive habit of gambling, and their families are consequently neglected. In the country, however, the morals of the community are better, and more restraint is maintained over the passions, but still the same bane exists among them as in the cities. Peru may be said to be one vast gambling-house.

The accounts of the Indians, given by recent travellers, are various and conflicting; however, the statement of Ulloa may, on the whole, be safely depended on. That excellent observer represents them as in the lowest stages of civilization, without any desire for the comforts and conveniences of civilized life, immersed in sloth and apathy, from which they can rarely be roused, except when they have an opportunity of indulging to excess in ardent spirits, of which they are exceedingly fond. (*Voyage II.*, liv. vi. cap. 6.) With the exception of Mr. Stevenson, most recent travellers say, that they are dirty in the extreme, seldom taking off their clothes, even to sleep, and still more rarely using water. (*Modern Traveller*, "Peru," p. 286.) Their habitations are miserable hovels, destitute of every convenience or accommodation, and disgustingly filthy. Their dress is poor and mean, and their food coarse and scanty. Their religion is still tainted with the superstitions of their forefathers, but they are great observers of the external rites and ceremonies of the church, and spend large sums of money on masses and processions; a species of profusion to which they are excited and encouraged by their priests, who profit by it. The oppressions, both in their religious and domestic connections, to which they have been subject before and after the conquest, have probably sunk them to the low point in the scale of civilization they occupy; but no doubt were proper care taken, it would be possible, materially, to improve their habits and condition.

A good deal too of their apathy and little progress in arts and industry, must be ascribed to the physical circumstances under which they have been placed: the mild languor of the climate and the fertility of the soil, which, on the one hand, by diminishing their wants, and on the other, by enabling them to supply those which they do feel, with comparatively little exertion, take away and greatly weaken some of the most powerful motives that prompt to labor and invention. The principal burden to which the Indian was subject, under Spanish rule, was that of the *mita,* or compulsory labor in the mines. All male Indians, from 18 to 50 years of age, were compelled during a certain specified period, to undergo this servitude. Its severity had, however, been materially abated previously to the revolution, and it was then entirely suppressed.

From the nature of the country, Peru labors under great disadvantages in regard to inland communication. The deep vallies that separate the elevated plains; and the lofty mountains which rise between the table land and the coast, render travelling difficult. In many parts there is a total want of roads and bridges, and in others the paths lie along the edges of steep and rugged precipices, so narrow, that mules alone pass in security. In the most mountainous districts, it is customary for those who can afford it, to travel on the backs of Indians; in this way they are carried for 15 or 20 days together, over roads winding through uninhabited forests and craggy steeps. In the lower regions, however, the means of internal communication are more attended to, and a general system of road-making has attracted the attention of government; and there is little doubt but that the progress of steam-travel in other countries will act as a stimulus to the Peruvians to build lines of railroads to connect their principal cities, but at present nothing of the kind is known in Peru.

The defensive means of the nation are chiefly confined to a few strong forts to protect its commerce on the sea-board, and one or two small armed steamers. Its standing army is a miserable mob, composed of the lowest grade of inhabitants, half clad, half fed, and would be entirely useless in case of foreign invasion. The coast, however, presents great natural features for defending the country: high bluffs and almost perpendicular walls of rocks occur, from which, with proper means and management, all the forces of the world might be kept at bay. But the general passive character of the Peruvians will ever prevent the nation from becoming even tolerable in arms.

Agriculture is quite in its infancy. The fields owe their luxuriance more to nature than man, except in the single advantage of water, which he often directs and supplies to them. Manure is a thing seldom thought of, and the implements of husbandry are of the rudest construction. The plow, slight and single-handed, is constructed altogether of wood and without a mould-board: the plow-share is a thick iron blade, (or oftener a piece of *iron-wood,*) only tied on by a lasso or thong of raw hide. Harrows they have none: a clumsy rake or bundle of brush-wood, dragged over the sown ground, supply their place. Indeed, their whole system of farming is uncouth and inconvenient in the extreme, and all their implements are of a similar description. They drive their sugar and corn mills by means of oxen, as if wind and water were not as powerful, to say nothing of the expense.

The arts and manufactures of the Peruvians are on a par with other signs of their civilization: but the natives are not destitute of ingenuity. In the district of Tarma, they make *ponchos,* or loose cloaks, of great beauty and fineness, and on the table lands warmer and coarser blankets, &c. In the vallies goat-skins are made into cordovans, cow-hides into saddle-bags and travelling cases for bed and bedding, and mats from rushes used for carpetings. Cords for packing are manufactured from the manguey. The fine silver filagree work, for which inland Peru is celebrated, is made at Hua manca. But as a general thing, the manufactures of Europe and the United States have superseded in the larger towns the rude inventions of the natives, and are supplied to Peru in exchange for bullion and raw material.

The commerce of Peru, which has been much retarded by foreign and domestic troubles, has of late considerably increased. The export trade chiefly consists of the produce of the mines and raw materials for manufacture, but is on a much more limited scale than when the country was under Spanish rule. The principal articles are gold, silver, copper and other metals; Peruvian and other barks for medicinal purposes; drugs of various descriptions; chinchilli, seal and other skins; hides, tallow, &c.; wool, cotton and some other articles of minor import. The wool of Peru is said to equal in quality that of England, but it is exported in a very dirty state, and consequently is sold at a reduced price: the greatest quantity goes from South Peru, but the Vicuna and Alpaca are the best. Some cotton is exported from Payta; some from Islay and Arica, but altogether the annual quantity does not exceed 30,000 quintals. Salt-petre has of late become an article of extensive trade. Each year manifests a considerable increase in the amount of exports. The imports into Peru are of great variety, and come chiefly from England and the United States: the Germans and French have, however, of late, made great progress in the introduction of their peculiar wares. Peru will continue for some time a vast inlet for foreign manufactured goods, especially those of the finer descriptions, while in exchange for these, the exporting nations will reap the benefit of the immense mineral wealth of the country.

The following figures* will exhibit the commercial statistics, for the years 1839 and 1840. The exports, designating the principal articles, were:

Articles,	*in* 1839,	*in* 1840.
Bullion, &c.	$6,554,141	7,810,746
Peruvian Bark	50,327	117,999
Chinchilla Skins	11,016	9,648
Copper and Copper Ore	91,089	105,210
Copper in bars	14,637	21,318
Cotton	371,800	429,444
Hides	6,859	19,090
Horns	320	—
Seal Skins	556	—
Saltpetre	299,152	454,712
Sugar	52,150	—
Tin	61,867	64,948
Wool—Viçuna	752	910
" Sheep's	252,032	295,208
" Alpaca	397,650	412,500
Sundries, &c.	—	—
Total Exports	$8,164,349	$9,741,733

The imports in 1840, designating the countries from which they were brought, were, in round numbers:

From England	$6,150,000
" France	1,450,000
" United States	1,400,000 (?)
" Canton and Manilla	300,000
" Germany	300,000
" Spain and Cuba	300 000
" Italy	200,090
Total	$10,100,000

* De Bow's Com. Rev., July, 1848.

The trade carried on between the United States and Peru* amounted, in the years, ending 30th June, 1844, 1816 and 1847, to the annexed particulars:

Exports from the United States to Peru.		*Exports from Peru received in the United States.*	
1844	$16,807	1844	$184,424
1846	none.	1846	252,599
1847	192,978	1847	396,223

The present government is founded on republican principles and popular supremacy. Under Spanish rule, the viceroys were the source of all laws, and had indefinite power over the lives, property and liberties of the people. The constitution of Peru, which was finally settled on in 1839, recognizes executive, legislative and judicial functions, which are entirely separate and independent of each other. The executive power is delegated by Congress to a President, whose term of service is six years, unless he is dismissed for cause. There is no vice-president, as in the United States, but the President of the Executive Council supplies the place of President in case of dismissal, sickness or death. This council consists of the ministers of relations and members of the senate. The legislative power resides in a Senate and an Assembly, chosen from the people through electoral colleges. The deputies are apportioned one for every 20,000 inhabitants. Judges are appointed by the Executive, and are not removable, except for misconduct. The constitution provides for the several subjudiciaries, and appropriates justices, having separate qualifications, for the departments, districts, towns and parishes; and on the whole, the operations of the courts are carried on with honor and uprightness. Knowledge of the law, however, is by no means a qualification of a Peruvian judge, and it is not unfrequent that the greatest injuries are inflicted upon applicants through the ignorance of the arbitrator and lawyers.

The established religion is the Roman Catholic, and no other is tolerated. The *morale* of the dispensers of the divine mission, however, is not very strict: the clergy are careless of their duties and lax in their habits. On this subject, a late writer has remarked, "The Indians and curates are often seen chaffering and driving hard bargains in relation to first fruits, (for tithes are collected by the state,) marriages, burials and religious festivals, which latter are closely interwoven with the entire social system of the country. The Sierra curates are men commonly much worn out in constitution at the age of 40. These gentlemen, when their home becomes irksome, start off, swayed by some sudden impulse, to the nearest town of white inhabitants, where they enjoy a finer climate and more gratifying company. The curate not unfrequently resorts to a mining village, under pretext, perhaps, of selling his *primicia* or first fruits in grain, gambling with the miners day and night, till the "primicia" be all swallowed up; and the poor residentiary returns home involved in a debt which he cannot pay for the next six months, even should his curacy be worth 4,000 or 5,000 dollars a year, though it be oftener much less."

The church is presided over by an archbishop, whose residence is at Lima, and several suffragans. It is immensely rich, and has amassed large amounts of property from pious donors. The Inquisition is entirely abolished.

* United States' Treasury Reports.

Literature, though now confined to a few of the higher classes of society, is in a progressive state of development. Schools for reading, on the Lancasterian plan, are common in the capital, and exist in the large provincial towns. Lima has a university, and several other colleges; but the former has seldom more than 50 students, and the latter are of little significance. Superior education is confined to a small number of the whites, and ornamental almost always takes precedence of useful instruction. Indians and negroes remain in almost their natural ignorance, and seldom progress further than the actual requirements of their limited transactions demand. The sciences are little cultivated, and medicine here is a system of gross quackery, and its principles entirely neglected.

The weights and measures used in Peru are those of Spain, and the coinage is of similar values and proportions as in that country.

The history of the Peruvians presents all the features of romance. When the Spaniards, under Pizarro and Almagro, arrived in Peru, in 1532, they found the country under the dominion of the Incas, who, according to the traditions of the natives, had held the sovereignty about 400 years.

If we may believe the native traditions, the Peruvians were initiated in the arts of society and government, by a man and woman who came from an island in the Lake Titicaca, in the south country. Manco Capac instructed the men in agriculture and other useful employments, while Mama Oëlla taught the women to weave and spin. The former, after collecting the savages into society, and founding a town, turned his attention to framing laws for their government. He constituted himself their sovereign and high priest, and made the office hereditary in his own family. His territories at first comprised only a few leagues around the capital, but they were rapidly enlarged under his vigorous and enlightened government. The same tradition represents the disappearance of this remarkable legislator to have been as sudden and unaccountable as his arrival. His death is supposed to have taken place about the end of the 12th or commencement of the 13th century, of the Christian era. From this period to the arrival of the Spaniards, the native historians enumerate fourteen reigns of Incas, (such was the title of these monarchs,) whose names have been preserved. It was in the latter part of the reign of Huana Capac, in 1524, that the discovery of Peru by Europeans took place.

The government and manners of the ancient Peruvians, as compared with those of the Mexicans, were mild in the extreme. Still, however, a considerable number of the attendants of the Incas were sacrificed at their death, and interred with them, that they might appear in the next world with their former dignity, and be served with the same respect. The remains of the roads, aqueducts, palaces, temples, and other structures, scattered over the country, attest the advanced state of civilization at which the Peruvians, as compared with most other American nations, had arrived. The empire of the Incas fell an easy prey to Pizarro and his blood-thirsty comrades. The relation of their barbarities is revolting, and the subsequent usage the Indians received from the hands of the Spaniards, will ever remain an indelible blot on the escutcheon of that nation.

Peru, under the government of a viceroy, continued in the hands of Spain for nearly 300 years, and was the last strong-hold of the Spaniards in South America. In 1821, however, the valiant San Martin, with the Chilian army, entered the country, and proclaimed its independence; but, like all the *ci-devant* Spanish colonies, it has been involved since then in all but perpetually-recurring vicissitudes, and a prey to civil commotions.

The following few memoranda, furnished by the Peruvian Minister at Washington, will present the leading events in the history of this country since it became an independent nation.

The declaration of the independence of Peru was made at Lima, the 28th July, 1821, after the occupation of that capital by Gen. San Martin, with the combined armies of Buenos Ayres and Chilé. Gen. Lascerna, viceroy of Peru, had retired on the 5th into the interior of the country, with the Spanish forces, and there sustained the war until the 9th of December, 1824, the date of the battle of Ayacucho, after which he was obliged to capitulate.

San Martin, under the title of "Protector," exercised power in Lima, from his entry to the 21st September, 1822, the date of the assembling of the first Congress of Peru. While he himself was occupied in forming a constitution, the powers of the government were transferred to a "Junta Gubernativa," composed of Gen. Lamar and Seignors Salazar y Baquijano and Alvarado, deputies to the same congress. Shortly after, the constitution being sanctioned, he nominated Gen. Don José de la Riva Aguero President of the Republic.

In July, 1823, some difficulties occurred between the president and congress, which resulted in the deposition of the former, and the nomination, in his room, of Gen. José Bernardo Fagle. It was about this time that Gen. Bolivar debarked at Callao, with the auxiliary army of Colombia, and, in consequence of the difficult circumstances in which the country was found, he was declared Dictator by Congress, and charged with the direction of the war against the Spaniards, and the consolidation of the independence of the republic.

Gen. Bolivar exercised power as "dictator," to the month of July, 1825, when he resigned, and placed at the head of affairs a Council of Government, composed of his own ministers. At the end of 1826, he promulgated, and made acceptable to the assemblies of electors, a new constitution, in which the executive power was decreed to a president for life. He was consequently elected such president, according to the forms adopted by the constitution.

But he was at that time at Bogôta, and the Colombian troops which he had left at Lima revolted against the new constitution, and demanded to be led back to their own country. The council of government, installed by Bolivar, finding themselves without support, were obliged to convoke a Congress, which declared the constitution, introduced by Bolivar, abolished, and promulgated another, the 18th June, 1827. The same Congress nominated Gen. Lamar, President, and Salazar y Baquijano, Vice-President, of the republic.

In the month of June, 1829, this administration was overthrown by Gen. Gamarra, who convoked a Congress, and caused himself to be nominated President: Gen. Lafuente obtained the Vice-Presidency.

Gen. Gamarra retained himself in office the four years designated by the constitution; and at the end of this term, a convention, convoked to reform the constitution, assembled. The convention nominated Gen. Orbegoso, President, and Salazar y Baquijano, Vice-President. The reformed constitution was promulgated in the month of August, 1834.

But in January, 1835, a revolution broke out in Lima, under the lead of Gen. Salaberry, who entitled himself "Supreme Chief," and deposed the

Vice-President, charged with the executive power in the absence of President Orbegoso, who at that time was travelling in the southern provinces. Gen. Orbegoso demanded the intervention and assistance of Gen. Santacruz, President of Bolivia, in order to sustain himself against Salaberry; Santacruz entered Peru with an army, and after a prolonged campaign, subdued and made Salaberry prisoner, in February, 1836. But he did not abandon Peru: he retained power, and exerted himself to form a confederation of Peru (already divided by him into two states) and Bolivia, and he governed under the title of "Protector of the Two Republics," declared a confederation of three states by his own decree.

This arrangement, which met with a powerful resistance, both in Peru and Bolivia, also brought him into collision with the Republic of Chilé, which terminated in his overthrow, the 20th January, 1829, and his exile from the country. After this, a Congress was convoked in Peru, which gave a new constitution in November, 1839, and nominated Gen. Gamarra, who already governed provisionally, President of the Republic. By the constitution of 1839, there is no vice-president, but the President of the Council of State is he who must take the place of the President of the Republic, in case of his absence, sickness or death.

In November, 1841, Gen. Gamarra died, and Seignor Menendez, President of the Council of State, entered into power, but he was deposed in the month of August, 1842, by Gen. Forico. A civil war ensued, and the government passed successively into the hands of Gen. Vidal, Seignor Figuerola and Gen. Vivanco. In 1844, the civil war was brought to an end by Gen. Castilla, and Menendez replaced in power: a Congress was called, in accordance with the provisions of the constitution, and the election of a new President took place. Gen. Don Ramon Castilla was elected to that office, and took possession of the government on the 1st of April, 1845. The term signalized by the constitution for the duration of a Presidency, is six years. The President of the Council of State, who is similar to the Vice-President of the Republic, is nominated by Congress every two years: the present President of the Council is Gen. T. Rufino Echenique, who, on the disability or death of the President, would immediately enter into the exercise of power.

During the short period that Peru has existed as a separate independency, it has made five and rejected four several constitutions: those of 1822, '26, '27, '34 and '39. All these constitutions, however, were very similar in their provisions, and differed mainly in their dispositions relating to the executive: to the method of nomination, to duration and attributes. By the last constitution, which is now in use, Congress is composed of two chambers: a Senate and Chamber of Deputies. Congress can only assemble every two years, and at every re-union, the Deputies are renewed by thirds—the outgoing Deputies are designated by lot.

THE REPUBLIC OF CHILE.

The tract of country forming this republic extends along the west coast of South America, from the desert of Atacama, in 25° 20′, to the Gulf of Guayatecas, in 42° south latitude; some geographers, however, contend that the country terminates in 54°, at the Straits of Magellan. Its length, according to the first description, would be about 1,200 miles; the latter about 2,000 miles. The breadth of the country is unequal, being bounded by the summit of the Andes, but, taking the average, it may be about 120 miles from those mountains to the Pacific Ocean. The southern boundary is a matter of indifference as yet, for the whole country south of the Rio Biobio, is still in the hands of the unsubdued Araucanian Indians, who maintain a species of independence, and have never been conquered. The area is about 144,000 square miles.

This country is indifferently called Chili, Chilé or, according to the Indian vocabulary, Tsheelee.

Chilé is a most picturesque country. The lofty chain of the Andes, which traverses the whole continent of South America, separates this fine country from the Argentine Republic, which forms its eastern boundary. The surface below is indented with vallies and beset with spurs from the main Cordilleras. There are generally, however, sufficient openings through these spurs to admit of mule travelling, by which means intercourse can alone be carried on by the inhabitants, from one district to another. To the traveller that wanders over these delightful vallies, the scenery is frequently grand and imposing. Passing from the north to the south, he never loses sight of the towering summits of the Andes, and by ascending to the summit of the cliffs, the expansive Pacific may be viewed in all its majesty. The highest summits in the range of these mountains are Maflos, in latitude 28° 45′; the Tupungato, in latitude 33° 24′; the Deseabecado, in 35°; the Blanquillo, in 35° 4′; the Langavi, in 35° 24′; the Chillan, in 36°; and the Coccabado, in 43°; some of these are about 23,000 feet above the level of the ocean. The general average height of the Andes is 15,000 feet. There are fourteen volcanoes in a constant state of eruption, and a large number which discharge only at intervals. The two principal passes in the Andes, which lie between the Argentine Republic and Chilé, are the Pass of Putamda and that of Palos; the first leads from the city of Mendoza, and is about 200 miles in length; the latter, leads from the city of San Juan, and is considerably longer. To the north, the Andes are broader, but are said to slope gently to the south, and facilitate greatly the construction of means of intercourse. Gen. San Martin, the Liberator of Chilé, crossed over these snow-clad summits with his army, in 1818.

The shores of Chilé are in general high and steep, but the waters are deep almost everywhere. Like Peru, Chilé has an extensive marine border on the Pacific, but is much more convenient for shipping, being indented with bays, which afford safe harbor and anchorage. The most considerable of these is the great Gulf of Guayatecas, in which is situated the Archipelago of Chiloe. Few countries are so well watered as Chilé. The melting of the snow on the Andes causes a perpetual flow of water down their slopes, and forms numerous rivers. They are more than 100 in number, and more than fifty disembogue into the ocean. The principal navigable rivers are the Huasco, Lospentos, Maypu, Maule, Chillan, Ilata, Biobio, Imperial and Valdivia. The greater number of the rivers are, however, very short, but tend to irrigate the land, and render the soil very fertile; and through a large portion of the country there is no valley, nor scarcely a field, which is not so situated that it may be regularly irrigated from some river or stream. There are some small lakes, both in the northern and southern provinces, but of no importance.

The islands of the Archipelago of Chiloe are forty-seven in number; of these, but thirty-two are inhabited, the others are sterile and unfit for cultivation. Chiloe, or El Ancud, as it is sometimes called, is by far the largest, and gives its name to the whole cluster. Chiloe forms one of the provinces of Chilé. The islands of San Juan Fernandez, situated 400 miles west, in the Pacific, are also an appendage to Chilé. Their chief importance is derived from their having been the residence of Alexander Selkirk, the Scottish sailor, from whose adventures the celebrated story of Robinson Crusoe was made up by Daniel De Foe. These are further described in a separate article.

The climate is equable and healthy; diseases of an epidemic nature are scarcely known. On the coast the heat, which is sometimes excessive in the interior, is much modified by the immense bulk of adjacent waters. In the interior the temperature in summer often rises to 90° Fahr., and, occasionally, to 95° and 100° in the shade, while on the coast it seldom attains a greater elevation than 85° in the day time, and sinks in the night to 70° or 75°. At Santiago, the capital, the mean temperature of summer, from December to March, is about 84½° during the day, and 58° at night. Cool and pleasant breezes from the ocean set inland in the evening, and dispel the lassitude of the overheated inhabitants. The winter sets in with the month of June, but, unlike the northern winter, presents none of the horrors of a snow storm, nor the biting energies of a frost; on the upper regions and in the mountains, however, snow falls abundantly, and covers the summits from June to November. The rainy season commences in April and lasts till August, but this is only in the southern provinces. North of Santiago the rainy season is limited to a few occasional showers, and in the arid province of Coquimbo rain never falls, but the heavy dews of the night counterpoise the want of it.

The northern provinces being out of the range of the volcanic region of the Cordilleras—the eruptions of which seem to act as safety-valves—are especially subject to earthquakes. In some parts the earth is in a constant state of agitation, and experiences daily shocks, and the country is frequently desolated for miles in extent. In 1819, the city of Copiapo was totally destroyed; and in 1835, Conception, and other towns on the coast in the middle provinces, were nearly ruined. Talcahuana suffered more than any other place during the earthquake of 1835; but one house was left standing. What added to the devastation, was the inundation of the place by three heavy seas, which swept all before them. The features of the harbor and the bay were materially altered; one cove was filled up, and became high land, and two small islets in the harbor were much increased in size, while a large one at the mouth of the bay sunk in part. Off the coast the effects were equally apparent; a portion of the Island of Juan Fernandez became sunken, and a rock was thrown up near the coast, and in what was heretofore considered a safe track for vessels, on which a short time after, a British sloop-of-war struck, and was foundered. The year 1847 was also a terrible time along the Pacific coast of South America, from the Isthmus of Darien to the southern extremity of the continent; numerous towns were desolated, and great tracts of the country laid waste.

The geological structure of Chilé presents many interesting peculiarities According to Schmidtmeyer, the higher chain of the Andes is chiefly composed of argillaceous schist, while the lower chains are of granite formation. Sienitic, basaltic, and feldspar porphyries; serpentines, of various colors; quartz, hornblende, and other slates; pudding-stone and gypsum—abound in the Cordilleras, and the finest statuary marble is said to be found in the province of Copiapo.

Chilé is extremely rich in metals; silver is found there at a greater elevation than other metals; it is also met with in the vallies and basins of the lower ranges; but, in general, it has been observed to decrease in abundance the further distant we are from the Andes. Gold is most plentiful in the lower bowels of the mountains, and is also found in abundance in the vallies in every part of the country. Most, or perhaps all, of the rivers wash down gold in the form of grains or dust. The useful metals are also found in abundance: copper, lead and iron are especially abundant; but excepting copper, from which great wealth is drawn to the nation, these metals are not much sought after. Zinc, antimony, manganese, arsenic, tin, sulphur, (so pure as to require no refining,) alum, salt and nitre, are very plentiful.

The statistics of the mining operations are little known. The mines are mostly in the province of Coquimbo, department of Copiapo, which contains upwards of 100, in full work. The quantity of gold produced, annually, is from 4,000 to 5,000 marcs. The average product of the silver mines is stated to be 16,000 marcs, and of the copper mines 100 to 120,000 quintals, half of which comes from the mines of Checo, which are worked by an English company. The great increase of mining operations, undertaken by foreign houses, render all existing statistics useless, and no possible calculation can foresee the amount of future products from sources so unlimited as the mines of Chilé. The exports of the precious and useful metals vary considerably in the course of years, but will average the annual value of 350,000 dollars. Mines of quicksilver have been found.

The condition of the actual miners is sad and lamentable: they are virtually the slaves of the proprietors and capitalists, who reap the fruit of their labors, and appropriate to their own use the riches that should, in some manner, indemnify the poor man for his toils.

There are also vast fields of coal in the northern provinces. Several extensive mines are now in operation near Conception, and the trade in this article has become considerable. In Valparaiso it is now the common article of fuel, and large quantities are supplied to steamships visiting the coasts.

The vegetable productions of Chilé are diversified as the latitudes and elevation of the country vary. At Conception, in the south, the eye is delighted with the richest and most luxuriant foliage: at Valparaiso, which is further north, the hills are clad with stunted brush-wood, and the ground looks everywhere naked and starved; and at Coquimbo, somewhat higher up, even this ill-favored appearance degenerates, and nothing is found but the prickly pear and a scanty sprinkling of a wiry grass. The desert of Atacama succeeds, and forms a dreary waste, alike hostile to animal and vegetable life. The southern parts of Chilé, indeed, are the only fruitful portions of these regions. There, everything useful to man, and appropriate for the support of cattle, is produced in abundance: it is a country of corn, wine and oil.

Forests of vast extent cover the southern provinces and country of the Araucanian nations. The flanks of the Andes exhibit profuse vegetation. The *mimosa farnesiana* flourishes over all the country, and the *Algarob* is almost as common. The *Quillai*, the bark of which furnishes a natural soap, is brought to the towns as an article of trade; laurels, cypresses and other evergreens grow to such a size as to be highly useful for their timber Most European fruits flourish, but tropical plants seldom survive transplanting. Chilé produces many hard woods, which are used by the people instead of iron.

Wheat is the staple grain of the country, and is raised extensively for exportation: it succeeds best at an elevation of 3,000 to 5,000 feet above the level of the ocean. The province of Aconcagua, which is the best cultivated of any in the country, sends considerable quantities of grain to Valparaiso. Rye is wholly unknown in Chilé, but barley is grown in the south, and Indian corn, buckwheat and oats are not altogether neglected The potatoe, which, from its being the universal diet of Irishmen, has obtained the soubriquet of "Irish," is a native of, and was originally brought from this country: in this, its natural soil, it grows abundantly and to the greatest perfection. Kidney-beans are raised for exportation, and find a market in Brazil and Peru. Gourds are much cultivated, and are of fine flavor, and are as extensively used by the Chilese as the potatoe by the people in the United States. Watermelons are cultivated in all parts, and prove a grateful means of allaying the effects of heat and thirst. The grape, in great variety, furnishes the wines of the country.

The animals of Chilé are those common to the southern part of the continent: the jaguar, llama, guanaco, numerous monkeys and other wild animals roam through the vast forests. A kind of beaver, the *castor huidibrius,* inhabits the margin of the rivers; and the chinchilla abounds in the desert country of the north: both are highly prized for their furs, which form a rich article for export. The great condor of the Andes, several species of vultures, pelicans and other water fowl, flocks of parrots, paroquets, &c., form a long catalogue of the birds of Chilé, and the whale, dolphin, cod, &c., are inhabitants of the adjacent seas. The skunk, which emits a nauseous odor when pursued, is a native of Chilé: otherwise the country enjoys a pre-eminent freedom from the presence of noxious and venomous animals, serpents, reptiles, insects, &c.

The soil and climate of Chilé are essentially proper for successful agriculture, and the facilities with which lands are irrigated, would argue much in favor of the development of all its agricultural resources. Chilé, however, does not contain a laboring population: ease and plenty are the only ambition of Indo-Spanish races. The implements of husbandry are essentially original and of the most barbarous construction. Iron is scarcely ever used, though in plenty—the harrow consists of a heap of bushes, tied together and pressed by a weight, which is dragged over the ground: the spade and hoe are almost unknown. Lands are cultivated until worn out, with the interval of a fallow every four or five years: no manure is used. The productiveness of the soil of Chilé, however, appears to have been formerly much overrated. Mr. Miers observes, that a piece of ground recently cleared may produce to the extent of from one hundred to two hundred fold during the first year; but such lands are now scarce in the cultivated parts of Chilé, and the average of the wheat fields may be from eight to twelve, or of the best crops twelve to twenty fold. Reaping is performed by means of a rough sickle, and the corn is thrashed out in a hard dry spot of ground, by being galloped over by horses. It is then left in the air for some months, and not housed until the approach of the rainy season.

Few farms are arable: such as are so, are situated in narrow vallies, and are of small extent. Cattle-breeding is the most important branch of rural industry. Farms, of immense size, are appropriated to this purpose, and it is not uncommon to find from 5,000 to 20,000 head of cattle at a single hacienda, and belonging to one proprietor. Black cattle are plentiful, but neither the beef nor milk they produce are of much value. The horses of Chilé are a noble breed, swift, docile, and far superior to those of Buenos Ayres: they are so strong, says Schmidtmeyer, and hardy, as to be able to carry their riders about 80 miles a day, at a gallop, with very little rest, and no other food than lucerne grass. The mules and asses are of a good size, hardy and strong; the former are the general beasts of burden, and are used especially by travellers in crossing the Cordilleras. Goats are plentiful, but the sheep are inferior, both in their mutton and their wool. The hogs of Chilé are small, and not very good: they are little valued, and seldom consumed by the inhabitants. During the dry season, the cattle suffer severely.

The condition of the laborers on the farms is almost that of serfs. The lands are cultivated under a species of feudal tenure, having been originally apportioned, after the Spanish conquest, to 360 proprietors, in an equal number of tracts. On this subject, Miers remarks, "The proprietors of these grazing estates usually reside with their families in the towns, and keep on their farms a *major-domo*, or steward, under whom are a head and subordinate herdsmen, and these are assisted, sometimes, by a few tenants, who hold their dwellings under the proprietor, by a kind of feudal tenure, being obliged to give their services in any kind of labor that is required of them, without pay, or for a very small remuneration. Land is never leased out to the agricultural tenant, but from year to year: the latter having neither oxen for plowing, mares for thrashing, nor capital to get in their crops, and all these and all other kinds of assistance come from the proprietor, who is repaid out of the produce of the land, which he besides generally buys up at two-thirds or half of what the other might sell it for, could he command the necessary funds to harvest it." Again, the same author says, "The tenant is scarcely ever allowed to build his hut on the cultivated grounds, to enclose his rented lands with fences, or to possess any cattle: and the multitude of other arbitrary practises tend to keep the peon in that state of servitude in which it is the object of the proprietor to retain him."

The coasts present good fishing-grounds, and, with good boats, good nets, and good government regulations, the Chilese might be made good fishermen; but owing in part to some ill-advised measures adopted by government, the fishermen have become a reckless and worthless class. They seldom fish more than a mile from shore, using only canoes of the rudest possible construction, or rafts, supported on large seal skin air-bags, both urged on by means of the double-bladed paddle, used first on one side and then on the other.

The manufactures of Chilé are of the rudest kind, and quite in a state of infancy. They are good potters, and make light and strong earthenware jars, that ring like metal. Hempen cloths, indifferent hemp cordage, soap, copper wares, made in a very rough manner; leather, brandy, tallow and charcoal, are among the chief articles of manufacture. The other lighter articles are chiefly made by women, and are entirely of a domestic nature.

Chilé is the only republic, formed from Spanish America, that has retained and increased its valuable commerce, since its separation from the parent country. Its increase has been comparatively rapid of late years. In exchange for the precious metals, furs, and other exports to foreign parts, Chilé receives many articles of luxury, use, and necessity. England supplies her chief wants in cotton and woollen goods, hardware, &c.; Germany, in linen; silks, paper, perfumery, leather, wines, and brandies, are brought from France, and innumerable other articles are obtained from the United States of America, both of domestic and foreign manufactures. A large amount of commerce is also carried on with the states of Central and South America The chief exports of Chilé are bullion, copper, hides, tallow, pulse, wheat, fruits, drugs, &c.

VALPARAISO is the chief commercial seaport of Chilé, and centre of foreign trade. In 1842, the arrivals at this port amounted to 375 vessels, having an aggregate of 101,075 tons burthen, of which about 10,000 tons were British, 7,000 United States, and 28,000 Peruvian. The departures were 311 vessels, of 82,300 tonnage, of which 15,000 were British, 31,000 Peruvian, 10,000 Brazilian, and only 2,000 United States. The annual average export of Chilian products, from 1836 to 1840, has been stated at £1,139,913, or $5,515,179. The trade between the United States and Chilé, in 1844,* designating the principal staples, exhibits the following results:

Exports to Chilé.		*Imports from Chilé.*	
Fish, Oil, and Sperm Candles	$6,953	Bullion and Specie	$185,117
Staves. Shingles, and Planks	7,535	Copper—pigs, bars, &c.	355,842
Masts, Spars, Naval Stores	2,122	Dye-Woods	3,445
Provisions, Beer, Spirits	63,489	Leghorn, straw, &c. hats	18,833
Bread Stuffs	28,462	Wool	19,847
Tobacco	6,411	Cocoa	26,431
Wax	9,258	Hemp	2,234
Sugar	22,550	Manufactures	9,470
Manufactures	703,951	Sundries	127,951
Sundries	5,914	Salt	600
Foreign Goods	248,576		
Total	$1,105,221	Total	$750,370

In favor of the United States, $454,851.

The value of this trade, for a series of years, as exhibited by the United States Treasury Reports, was as annexed:

Years.	IMPORTS INTO UNITED STATES.	EXPORTS FROM UNITED STATES. *Domestic.*	*Foreign.*	*Total.*
1840	$1,616,859	$1,372,254	$356,575	$1,728,829
1841	1,230,980	846,410	256,578	1,102,988
1844	750,370	856,645	248,756	1,105,221
1846	1,275,960	1,539,136	229,434	1,768,670
1847	1,716,703	1,461,347	210,263	1,671,610

The number of vessels, with their aggregate tonnage, employed in the commerce between the two states, amounted, during the year ending 30th June, 1847, to the figures herewith annexed, designating the arrivals and clearances:

	Ships.	*Tonnage.*
Arrivals in United States' Ports	21	8,508
Clearances from do.	23	8,262

* Vide De Bow's Com. Rev., July, 1848.

The republic is divided into eight departments, which are again subdivided into provinces and districts. The departments, according to the partition of 1824, are as follow:

Departments.	*Principal Cities and Towns.*
SANTIAGO	Santiago, *Rosario*, &c.
ACONCAGUA	Aconcagua, *Colorado*, &c.
COQUIMBO	Copiapo, *Coquimbo*, *Guasco*, &c.
CONCHAGUA	Curico, *Lora*, *La Constitution*, &c.
MAULE	Cauquenes, *Negunche*, &c.
CONCEPCION	Concepcion, *Baluco*, &c.
VALDIVIA	Valdivia, *San Fernando*, &c.
CHILOE, IS. OF,	San Carlos, *Castro*, &c.

Beside the above divisions, there is a large tract of country south of the Rio Biobio inhabited by the Araucanian Indians, and which has received the appellation of Araucania. Its limits are indefinite and unsettled.

The population of Chilé has been set down at various amounts, from 1,200,000 to 1,600,000. The only census that has been taken of Chilé was in 1812, previous to the revolution; it then amounted to the first statement. Since that time, however, causes have operated both against and in favor of an increase, but there is no doubt that the natural increase has been more than sufficient to counterbalance the waste of life in the wars that have ravaged the country; and it is not unreasonable to presume that the population at the present day may be 1,500,000 souls. This enumeration is exclusive of the Indian tribes inhabiting Araucania.

The people are mostly of Spanish and Indian descent, but there are some Negroes and Mulattoes. "The Chilians," says Mr. Miers, "though they may be said to possess, in no degree, a single virtue, have the credit of possessing fewer vices than other Creoles; there is a passiveness, an evenness about them, approaching the Chinese, whom they strongly resemble in many respects: even in their physiognomy they have the broad low forehead and contracted eyes; they have the same cunning, the same egotism, and the same disposition to petty theft." This character is too general to apply to a whole population, and must be taken with some qualification. The same authority continues, "They are moderate in their food, but frequently very dissipated in their habits, and in the towns very fond of dress and display. Highway robberies are very rare, and so are murders, in the country, but not in the towns. Education, or any taste for the fine arts, have hitherto made but little progress."

SANTIAGO, the capital of Chilé, and seat of government, is situated in a delightful plain on the south bank of the Mapocho, a branch of the Maypu, 90 miles from the seaboard, and 20 miles from the Andes. The city is built at an elevation of 2,000 feet above the level of the ocean, which renders the climate agreeable and salubrious. Its aspect is irregular and picturesque. The dark tints of the fig and olive, with the lighter hues of the mimosa, mingled with steeples and houses, produce a novel and imposing effect. The city is regularly laid out, the streets intersecting each other at right angles, and inclosing in the middle a spacious open square, on the sides of which are the principal buildings, and in the centre a beautiful fountain. The public buildings are the cathedral, the university, mint, churches, convents, hospitals, &c. These are not only handsome buildings, but large and magnificent. The houses have in general only one floor, and being surrounded by large gardens, the town appears completely overshadowed with foliage, and each house standing by itself, and being strongly barricaded towards the street, forms a little fortress. The streets are well-paved and furnished with side-walks. The Alameda, a mile in length, and planted with a double row of trees, is one of the finest promenades in South America. The vicinity of Santiago presents the most romantic and sublime prospects; the waters of the ocean and the height of the Andes alone intercept the sight. Santiago, however, is not only the metropolis of Chilé, and the residence of its primate, but an emporium of its commerce, which is increased by its vicinity to the richest mines in the country. The population amounts to about 80,000 persons, chiefly of Spanish descent.

VALPARAISO, the principal seaport, is about 60 miles north of Santiago, and is in latitude 33° 11′ 9″ south, and longitude 71° 31′ 8″ west. Population, 40,000. The city is built on a high, rugged promontory, which projects into the ocean, forming, with the shore, a deep crescent, the cavity of which, opening to the north, forms the harbor. The waters of this bay are deep, and sufficiently capacious to ride a large fleet; the anchorage is perfectly safe, and protected from the violence of all winds, except the north, which sometimes dashes the water in great force against the shores. The city itself is inconvenient, and badly built, but its appearance from sea is imposing, the houses being scattered on the beach and at the foot of a precipitous range of hills. There are several fine buildings, however, to redeem the general features of the city, as the custom-house, churches, and convents, &c. The harbor is well defended by the castle and two forts at the north end of the Almendral, and another fort inland. There is no mole, or any facility for landing goods, except by launches, which are moored to the shore, and across these all packages are brought, on men's shoulders or by boats, which, however, can land in all weathers in Fisherman's Bay, between the Castle and Fort San Antonio. The harbor generally presents some British and American flags, and, occasionally, vessels of other foreign nations visit this port; but the greatest amount of the shipping is composed of coasters from Central America, and the neighboring states of Bolivia, Peru, &c. The markets of Valparaiso are well-supplied with all meats and vegetables, and at moderate prices, and its climate is generally agreeable. Mr. Miers, (*Trav. in Chilé,*) a recent visitor to Valparaiso, gives a very poor account of the accommodations of the place. "Independent of the want of society," says he, "there are no public amusements, no theatre, commercial, reading or news room; no parade, not even a single spot to walk upon, nor any retirement or exit from the town, but over the barren hills, which renders the exercise more a toil than a pleasure. In short, in spite of its matchless and beautiful climate, I do not know, in all Chilé, a spot representing a more uncomfortable and cheerless place of residence than Valparaiso."

CONCEPÇION, the second city of Chilé, in point of rank, stands to the north of the Rio Biobio, a league from the sea, and contains 13,000 inhabitants. It was originally built three leagues to the north of its present position, but having been twice destroyed by earthquakes, the inhabitants removed hither. TALCAHUANA, the port of Conception, is six miles distant on the south-west side of the bay of Conception. This bay is one of the largest and safest on the Pacific coast: it is ten miles long from north to south, and nine from east to west. The mouth of the bay opens towards the north, and is divided by the Island of Quiriquina into two channels; the eastern and safest is two miles broad, and the western about a mile and a half: both have sufficient depth for the largest sized vessels, and a safe anchorage is attainable in any part of the bay.

The most important sea-ports not already mentioned, are, 1st. COPIAPO, situated immediately at the mouth of the river of the same name, in lat. 27° 15′ S. The harbor affords good anchorage, is easy of access for vessels of any burden, and as it opens towards the west, is protected from the northerly and southerly winds. 2d. COQUIMBO, or La Serana, in lat. 29° 54′ S., on the south bank of the river Coquimbo, within half a league of the coast. Its harbor is a fine capacious bay, easy of access, and protected from all winds as well as the swell of the sea. It is the chief port of the mining country, and the richest of the copper-mines are in its vicinity. 3d. The PORT OF VALDIVIA, in lat. 39° 50′ S., is one of the safest, strongest and most capacious harbors on the western coast of America: but there is little cultivated territory or civilized population in its vicinity, to make it of much importance at present. The village, which is the chief place of the province of the same name, is about 16 miles from the coast, and consists of a few ill-constructed wooden huts, which were for the most part destroyed by the earthquake of 1837. The whole line of the river is well protected by fortifications, and during the war of independence this valuable station was captured by a very inferior force under Lord Cochrane, on the 3d February, 1820. The depth of water in the bay is from five to seven fathoms, and ships of the line ride in perfect safety on its capacious bosom.

There are several other towns and ports of inferior pretensions to those already noted, but not of sufficient importance to require further notice or comment.

There are few works of public importance in Chilé: Poeppig says, that there are but three or four bridges of any size in the whole country, and these were mostly ruined during the war. The mountain torrents and ravines are crossed in some places by Indian hanging bridges, made of oziers and thongs of raw hides, which sometimes sway from side to side with the weight of the person crossing them, in a terrific manner. The attention of the government, however, has lately been turned to works of internal improvement. Canals and railroads are projected, and roads of every kind will soon embrace every part of the country. There is also an effort being made to open and improve new ports, so as to facilitate the exportation of produce from the interior.

The coins of Spain are still used by the Chilese: their national coinage is limited, but the constant labors of the mints will soon furnish a sufficient currency for the country. The new coinage is of the same standard and denomination as those of the mother country, viz.: doubloons, dollars, half dollars, quarters, eighths and sixteenths. The impresses are, however, altered to a national character.

The weights and measures are exactly in accordance with those of Spain.

The public finances of Chilé have, for a long time, been in the most prosperous condition: the revenue has exceeded the expenses since 1835, and large surplusses have been set aside to be applied to the liquidation of the public debt, incurred in the infancy of the republic. According to the latest accounts, the annual receipts amount to about 3,000,000 dollars, and the expenses of the government consume about 2,000,000 dollars. The best criterion of the prosperity of Chilese finance, is ascertained by a reference to the price of stock in the London market—the Chilian bonds are sold at par, and often command a premium. This, indeed, is the only state of the late Spanish possessions that is able to pay its way, and maintain in the world an independent pecuniary station.

The army and navy of Chilé are on a respectable footing. The navy, which is gradually increasing, consists of several sloops and brigs, and some small steamers. A very handsome and strong steamer was built for this government at New-York, which sailed for its destination in the spring of 1848. It was fitted in the most magnificent style, and fully in order of war. There is every prospect of this country acquiring great political and military power: the abilities of its rulers, while they maintain all peaceful at home, will command, by their energy, the respect of other nations, and prove the best palladium for the liberties of the whole people. The battles fought during the revolution are a sufficient guarantee that the nation is as capable of defending itself from exterior attacks as it was of expelling the proud Spaniard. The army amounts to 2,876 men, and the national guard to 60,000.

The government of Chilé is that of a constitutional integral republic. There were attempts to perfect a constitution immediately after the first revolt, in 1810, but it was many years before a plan, suitable to the condition of the country, could be agreed upon. In 1811, the first project was submitted, which scarcely saw public light: in 1818, the Senate and Executive framed another, with the title of "provisional," which was annulled, in 1822, by a third, which also proved to be an entire failure, and caused the downfall of the Supreme Director, O'Higgins. In 1825, a small party attempted to introduce the federative system, and built a project which never became a law. In 1828, the first suitable constitution was proclaimed, but experience having proved that it limited very much the action of the government, it was reformed in 1833, and since then the operation of the government has been expeditious, civil wars have ceased, the country is flourishing, agriculture and commerce have developed themselves, and the credit of the nation, within the country and abroad, is superior to that of any other South American state.

The general features of the Chilese constitution are:—The legislative body is composed of two Chambers, one of Senators, with 20 members, selected by electoral colleges for nine years, and renewed by third parts every three years;—the other of Deputies, elected directly by the people. Only those can vote who know how to read and write; who have property, industry or income, (the amount of which a special law designates every ten years;) and those who are inscribed in the register of their respective corporations. Besides the common attributions of each Chamber and of the Congress, which are perfectly classified in the constitution, there are some very peculiar, which have produced a salutary effect; as, to grant the President of Chilé extraordinary faculties whenever found convenient, provided they shall be well defined and for a determinate period. Congress meets every year on the 1st of June, and adjourns on the 1st of September, but it can prolong its sessions for 30 days, and be convened at any time by the President. Neither the Senators nor Deputies have any salaries, which keep these employments in the hands of rich and independent people. This is not, however, a constitutional provision. Before the adjournment of Congress, the Senate appoints a *conservative committee* of seven senators, one of the duties of which is to watch over the observance of the constitution and laws, and take proper means to that effect.

The executive power is composed of a President, with all the faculties of a constitutional king, but responsible for his acts. The term for which he is elected is five years, but he may be re-elected once more. He is assisted by four secretaries; one of Home and Foreign Relations; one of Justice, Public Instruction and Worship; one of War and Navy, and the other of the Treasury. The President appoints them and removes them at his pleasure. He is assisted also by a Council of State of his own nomination, generally composed of the most enlightened persons of the different ranks of society. During the recess of Congress, if there should be a foreign invasion, or an internal commotion, the President, with the consent of the Council of State, may declare one or more parts of the republic in *estado de sitio*, i. e. in the district, department or province so declared, the power of the constitution is suspended; but the public authority cannot condemn by itself, nor apply penalties, except those of arrest or removal from one place to another.

The Provinces of Chilé are governed by intendentes or governors, appointed every three years by the President, of whom they are the natural and immediate agents. In the exercise of their duties and faculties, they are subject to a special law.

The judicial power, independent from the legislative and executive in its action, owes its nomination to the President, but no judge can ever be removed from office, but in virtue of a sentence of condemnation of the tribunal established by law.

The rights of the people, their individual security and property, are well provided for in the constitution.

The national religion is Roman Catholic: the clergy are not as numerous, however, as in some portions of Spanish America, and are under the subordination of the Archbishop of Santiago. The wealth of the church is great, and it is said that one-third of all the territory belongs to the institutions. Convents and nunneries abound throughout the republic. All other religions are allowed to be professed, but toleration does not go so far as to allow of the *public* exercise of any other than the holy apostolic. No one, however, is interfered with, whatever his religion, so that he does not disturb the peace of society.

The history of this country is romantic in the extreme. Previous to the Spanish conquest, Chilé belonged to the Incas of Peru. In 1535, Pizarro sent Almagro to invade the territory, and in 1540, Valdivia: the latter of whom conquered all the territory, except Araucania. The country remained in the hands of Spain till the entrance of the French into the Peninsula, in 1809, and the overthrow of the Bourbons. The revolution, which ended in the separation of Chilé from the parent state, commenced at Santiago, the capital, on the 18th September, 1810, by establishing a junta, who apparently governed the country in the name of Ferdinand VII., but afterwards, without disguise, as an independent government. After many contests, the patriot forces were entirely subdued at the battle of Rancagua, fought on the 5th October, 1814, and the Spanish authority became re-established throughout the country. The battle of Chacabuco (17th February, 1817,) reversed the position of affairs: the patriot army gained a great victory, and occupied the capital and most of the provinces. In March, of the year 1818, however, the Spaniards got some advantages at Cancha-rayada, and again dispersed and defeated the people: but on the 5th of the next month, the great battle of Maypu was fought: the patriots were successful in driving away the enemy from all the provinces, except those of Valdivia and Chiloe. The result of this battle was, the independence of Chilé, which was formally proclaimed on the 18th September, 1818. The Spanish forces occupied Valdivia and Chiloe until the 15th January, 1826, when they were finally subdued, and every remnant of their army driven from the country. Chilé since then has been prosperous as a whole—civil wars and differences have occasionally embroiled its peace, but of late the country has been entirely pacified, and in the event of nothing interrupting its present well-being, it will soon be one of the most flourishing nations of the world, and its people, who are beginning to appreciate the value of education, and its alliance with the enjoyment of true liberty, will henceforth hold a high station in the scale of civilization.

In the first years of the republic, the people were governed by juntas, but subsequently a Supreme Directorship was established, and ultimately under the constitution, a President became the arbitrator of the destinies of the nation. The following persons have held these high offices since 1817, the period when the juntas were abolished:

Name	Office		Date
Barnardo O'Higgins,	Sup. Director,		16th Feb., 1817.
Ramon Freire,	" "		31st March, 1823.
Manuel Blanco Encalada,	"	*ad interim*	8th July, 1826.
Augustin Eyzaguirre,	" "		9th Sept., 1826.
Ramon Freire,	" "	*ad interim*	24th Jan., 1827.
Francisco Antonio Pinto,	President		5th May, 1827.
Francisco Ramon Vicuña	"		29th Oct., 1829.
Francisco Ruiz Tagle	"		17th Feb., 1830, (resigned.)
Jose Tomas Ovallé,	"		31st March, 1830, (died.)
Fernando Errazuriz,	"		22d March, 1831.
Joaquin Prieto,	"		18th Sept. 1831, (two terms.)
Manuel Bulnes,	"		18th Sept. 1841, (two terms.)

The independence of Chilé was finally recognized by Spain, in a treaty of peace and friendship, signed at Madrid on the 25th August, 1844, and the ratifications were exchanged on the 28th September, 1845.

JUAN FERNANDEZ,

Consists of a group of islands in the Pacific Ocean, about 400 miles west of the Republic of Chilé: there are two chief islands and several smaller islets. Lat. S. 33° 40'., long. W. 79°. The largest of these islands is called *Mas-a-tierra,* to distinguish it from *Mas-a-fuero,* a volcanic rock, 90 miles west of the group. It is from 10 to 12 miles long, and about 60 miles broad, its area being nearly 70 square miles. The line of the coast is very irregular, presenting a number of bays and head-lands: the chief harbors are Port English, on the south side, visited by Anson, in 1741, Carteret, in 1767, and Vancouver, in 1795; Port Juan, on the west, and Cumberland Bay, on the north.

The northern portion is of a lofty basaltic formation, intersected by narrow but fruitful and well-wooded vallies, while the southerly portion is less elevated, and of a barren nature and rocky. The fig and the vine flourish luxuriantly on the hills, and among the larger trees are sandal, cork, and a species of palm, called *Chuta,* bearing a rich fruit. The wild goat is seen among the rocks, and seals and walrusses beset the shores: fish, especially cod, are plentiful in the surrounding waters.

The islands are very subject to earthquakes, two of which, those of 1751 and 1835, are said to have done immense damage. In the earthquake of

1825, an eruption burst through the sea, about a mile from land, where the depth is from 50 to 80 fathoms; smoke and water were ejected during the day, and flames were seen by night.

Juan Fernandez (the name popularly applied only to the islet of Mas-a-tierra) was discovered by a Spanish navigator, who gave to it his own name and formed an establishment, which, however, was soon abandoned. During the 17th century, it was a resort of the buccaneers, who were in the habit of cruising off the coast of Peru and Chilé to intercept the valuable convoys of Spain. More recently it was the solitary dwelling of Alexander Selkirk, a Scottish seaman, who being shipwrecked, inhabited this island for four years. The adventures of this individual formed a theme for De Foe, and were the basis on which he constructed his inimitable novel of *Robinson Crusoe.*

The Spanish government took possession of the island in 1750, and built a fort: however, all their works were destroyed the following year by the great earthquake which ravaged those parts. The fort and a town were rebuilt somewhat further inland; and were in good order and inhabited when Carteret visited the island in 1767, but soon after this they were finally abandoned by Spain.

The Chilese government attempted to form it into a penal settlement in 1819, but the undertaking was relinquished on account of the expense of sustaining it.

The island is now in the possession of an enterprising American gentleman, who has leased it from the government of Chilé, with the intention of forming a depôt for whalers cruising in the Pacific Ocean. For this purpose, he has brought 150 families of natives from the Sandwich Islands, and will employ them in cultivating the land, rearing cattle, and so improving Cumberland Bay, as to make it a safe harbor for whalers and other vessels in the Pacific and East India trade.

THE ARGENTINE REPUBLIC,

The most extensive of the South American governments, is a confederation of a number of independent states, which formerly constituted the provinces of the Spanish Viceroyalty of Buenos Ayres, and which has since been known under the names of the "United Provinces of La Plata," the "United States of South America," &c. Though shorn of several fine provinces, both at the period of the revolution, and subsequently, it still occupies a vast territory, extending at the present time between the 22d and 41st parallels of south latitude, and the meridians of 54° and 72° west longitude. It is bounded on the north by Bolivia; on the east by Brazil, Paraguay and Uruguay, from all which it is separated by the Paraguay, Parana and Uruguay rivers; on the south by the Atlantic Ocean and Patagonia, the latter of which, indeed, it claims as a part of its territory; and on the west by Chilé, from which it is divided by the chain of the Andes. The length of this country, from north to south, is from 1,300 to 1,400 miles, and its breadth from 300 to 1,100; its area has been estimated at 726,000 square miles.

The territory included within the above-mentioned limits, is mostly comprised within the great valley of La Plata, and its branches: one of the most extraordinary vallies in the world, both as it respects its magnitude and its peculiar soil and surface. The region which is watered by this vast river, and its tributaries, rises towards the west into lofty mountains, whose bases extend into immense plains, which terminate on the margins of the La Plata and the shores of the Atlantic. Perhaps no country in the world presents so level a surface as this; west and south of La Plata, is one extended plain, embracing all the varieties, from the richest alluvial soils, to the high, broken and sterile wastes; and most of this tract is destitute of timber, except on the margins of the rivers. The lower section of this interminable level, extending from the northern part of the province of Cordova, and south on the borders of the River La Plata and the Atlantic, far into Patagonia, and from the river and coast into the interior to the highlands, at the foot of the Andes, is usually called the "*Pampas*," and extends nearly 1,500 miles from north to south, with a breadth, in many parts, of nearly five hundred miles; over all this immense space there is scarcely a tree or shrub, or single perennial plant, to be seen. There are neither hills nor eminences, and the undulations are so gentle, as only to be perceived by taking a long view over its surface. The keen winds, called "*pamperos*," sweep over this unsheltered plain without the least obstruction. The surface of the earth appears to be a soft, black, rich soil, without stone, gravel or sand, but on the banks of some of the rivers, and in some other places, reddish clay seems to form the superficial crust.

The Pampas are principally useful for pasturage; they support numerous herds of horned cattle, horses, mules, and sheep; deer, ostriches, and wild dogs, also abound. Thousands of these are to be seen at one view.

The more elevated plains, to the north and west of the Pampas, are likewise generally destitute of timber, except on their water-courses, but have a soil more dry and sandy. The rivers here are more numerous, and the country is copiously supplied with pure water. The country east of La Plata has generally a waving or undulating surface, and everywhere abundantly irrigated with never-failing springs and streams of the purest water. This tract is found clothed with stately forests, with the exception of some of the lower river districts, and has a rich and fertile soil, producing, in great abundance, all the varied productions of temperate regions.

The River La Plata embodies most of the interior waters of the Argentine Republic. Its principal head-water is the Paraguay, which rises in Brazil, in latitude 13° south, and after a course of 1,250 miles, receiving numerous branches, and passing through the great lake or morass of the Xaraes, it assumes the name of La Plata, at its junction with the River Parana, about 750 miles from the sea; and the latter river is said to afford a boat navigation of 1,500 miles further into the interior. The two great eastern branches of the La Plata and Paraguay are the Parana and Uruguay; the first unites with the Paraguay, after a course of 900 miles—500 of which are navigable; the Uruguay has its source in Brazil, and, after a southerly course of 1,000 miles, discharges its waters into the La Plata, above the city of Buenos Ayres, having, in its course, received the Negro, and a number of other considerable rivers. The principal western branches of the Paraguay and La Plata are the Pilcomayo, which rises in Peru, and, after a course of 1,100 miles, empties, by two mouths, 50 miles apart, into the Paraguay, securing a good navigation to the higher provinces;

the Rio Grande, which unites with the Paraguay 50 miles above the mouth of the Parana, after a course of 800 miles, nearly the whole of which admits of navigation; and the River Salado, which, after a southerly course of 800 miles, enters the La Plata at Santa Fe. The Saladillo, and innumerable smaller streams, also flow from the west into the La Plata. The Colorado and Negro, both vast rivers, flow directly into the Atlantic, after a general course south-east and east. There are few bays or harbors of importance, except the great bay of the La Plata, which is the most extensive in the world, and affords harbors of vast magnitude to the two capitals of Buenos Ayres and Montevideo.

There are several lakes in this country, but all are very diminutive, when compared with those magnificent bodies of fresh water, which give character to the topography of the northern half of the continent.

The geological structure of the Argentine Republic is as peculiar as its surface; the shores of the Rio Plata present the greatest contrast—the north shore is elevated, and, like the islands in the river's bed above Buenos Ayres, composed of granite, gneiss, and clay-slate; while on the south, every trace of rock is lost, and, for hundreds of miles inland, not a pebble is to be met with. The whole Pampas are one immense bed of alluvial sand, quietly deposited during the lapse of ages, in what was anciently a gulf of the Atlantic, and of which the estuary of the La Plata is now the only remaining portion, which of itself is even now rapidly filling up, and it is probable, in future times, that the river will enter the Atlantic like the Amazon, Orinoco, &c., by a delta, instead of one wide mouth, as it now does. In the alluvion of the Pampas, quantities of marine shells, and the Megatherium, Olypoldon, &c., have been found, and its whole wide area is one vast sepulchre of extinct quadrupeds.

The precious metals, with copper, lead, iron, &c., are found in different parts of the country. In the west and north-west, gold and silver have been obtained in considerable quantities. Iron exists in Chaco in extensive veins, intermixed with nickel and cobalt. Salt is the most abundant mineral, and exists in a state of efflorescence over the surface of immense tracts, in a multitude of springs and pools, and in mines of rock salt. Epsom and glauber salts, limestone, gypsum, alum, mineral pitch, and abundance of sulphur, are to be found in the vicinity of the Andes, besides bituminous shale, with appearances of coal in many places; and it is said that there are extensive bodies of coal in the extreme north-west angle of the country.

The vegetable products of the northern parts, include most of those which flourish between the tropics; while in the south they are in general similar to those of Europe. But even as far south as Corrientes, cotton, tobacco, rice, sugar-cane, indigo and many other articles of primary importance in the markets, may be produced to almost any extent; and a large tract of the country is extremely well adapted to the culture of wheat, maize and other grains. The vine flourishes to perfection, and a good full-bodied wine and some brandy is made in the provinces of Rioja and Mendoza. Figs, oranges, peaches, walnuts, apples and other fruit flourish in luxuriance in the central and southern provinces. The sparsity of the population is the only drawback to the full development of the agricultural resources of this highly favored country.

The climate is subject to great extremes of temperature in winter and summer; but the gradations are regular. The winter is about as cold as the month of November in New-York, and the ground is sometimes covered with a white frost, but ice is seldom formed. In summer, the heat is oppressively hot, but both heat and moisture vary considerably on the same parallel: at Buenos Ayres the heat is tempered by the sea breezes and moisture from the Atlantic, but on proceeding inland, these modifying influences are gradually lost, and in the far west the air is extremely dry: no dew falls at night; in the hottest weather there is apparently no perspiration, and the dead animals lie on the plain, dried up in their skins.

The chief source of wealth is the immense herds of horned cattle which wander over the wide-extending Pampas. In the single province of Buenos Ayres there are about three or four millions head of cattle. The horses of the Pampas are similar to the common Spanish breed, and of all colors; they wander wild in immense herds, being caught indiscriminately when wanted. Among the Indians mare's flesh is the common animal food. The sheep are of very inferior quality, and the wool, though improved of late years, is still of the coarsest descriptions, and scarcely worth the cleaning: goats and hogs are also quite of an inferior breed. The singular animal, the *coypou*, which furnishes the skins, known in commerce by the name of *nutria*, is abundant in Buenos Ayres, and the chinchilla abounds in many districts. On the slopes of the Andes are found guanacos, llamas, vicunas, &c. Wild boars, deer, with jaguars, pumas, armadillos, &c., are also met with. Monkies are plentiful. The *biscacha*, a rodent quadruped, which makes travelling over the Pampas dangerous by its burrowing propensities, is very abundant; and condors, vultures, and numerous birds of rich plumage, inhabit the country. Its greatest pests are giant ants, locusts, immense bugs, mosquitos, and other descriptions of the insect tribe.

Sir Woodbine Parish gives the following as the several independent states of the Argentine Confederacy, and their population, &c.

	Provinces.		*Population.*		*Chief Towns.*	*Population.*
1.	BUENOS AYRES	Total superficial area 726,000 sq. m.	180,000 to	200,000	Buenos Ayres	100,000
2.	SANTA FE		15,000	20,000	Santa Fé	5,000
3.	ENTRE RIOS		25,000	30,000	Parana	15,000
4.	CORRIENTES		35,000	40,000	Corrientes	16,000
5.	CORDOVA		80,000	85,000	Cordova	10,000
6.	SANTIAGO		45,000	50,000	Santiago	8,000
7.	TUCUMAN		40,000	45,000	Tucuman	5,000
8.	SALTA		50,000	60,000	Salta	9,000
9.	CATAMARCA		30,000	35,000	Catamarca	2,000
10.	RIOJA		18,000	20,000	Rioja	2,500
11.	SAN LUIS		20,000	25,000	San Luis	3,000
12.	MENDOZA		35,000	40,000	Mendoza	20,000
13.	SAN JUAN		22,000	25,000	San Juan	12,000
	GRAN CHACO,			(the Indian Territory.)		
		Total	600,000	675,000		

The population, however, as given in the above table, must be taken as very imperfect, and as a mere approximation to the reality: it omits altogether the Indians, who form, in fact, the greater portion of the whole. It is probable that the actual population may not fall far short of 1,200,000 to 1,500,000, which are about the extreme estimates of modern writers.

The social condition of man over the whole of Spanish America wears a uniform character. The Creoles, who are now everywhere the governing class, are acute, polite, courteous, indolent, without enterprize, passionately fond of diversion, especially in the forms of dancing and gaming. The general moral attitude of the female portion is debased, and what show of virtue there is among the ladies is the effect of constraint. The men are jealous and revengeful, and intrigue and murder are the two usual consequences of these lawless passions. The lower orders ape the characteristics of the upper class, and are generally immoral and licentious in their lives.

The native whites are generally of Spanish descent, and retain to the present day many of the habits and traits of the old Spaniards, whose language they speak. The country people of the interior, the "*gauchos*," are rude but hospitable, and from infancy the men are almost constantly on horseback, riding over the vast plains in search of cattle and horses; these are taken with the lasso, which, by continued practice, is thrown with wonderful dexterity and precision. The *lasso* is a rope about 40 feet long, made either of hemp or hide, but more generally of the latter: one end is fastened by an iron ring to the saddle-girth, and the other, being rigged in the form of a noose, is coiled up with the whole rope and hung at the saddle-bow. Thus equipped, and with a junk of jerken beef under his saddle for food, the hunter sets out. On perceiving a herd, he approaches it cautiously, marks with his eye the noblest animal as his victim, then taking the lasso from its place, whirls it through the air so that the noose falls about the head of his object, which it has no sooner reached, then putting spurs to his horse, he darts off at a gallop, dragging the captured animal behind him.

The lower limbs of these people grow conformably with their constant habit of riding—in consequence of which, they never appear well, except on horseback. Their food and habits of living are coarse and rude—a bull's hide thrown upon the ground generally furnishes them with a bed, either at home or on the pampas, and although rum and other spirits are manufactured to a considerable extent in the upper provinces, these people are very temperate.

The population is comprised in several distinct tribes, dispersed over the pampas and unsettled territories. The most prominent of these are the *Chiriviones*, the *Pampas*, and the *Mattacas*. The first are a quiet, inoffensive people, residing at the *cinco pueblos itiuri*, or Five Towns, in the northern part of the territory known as the Gran Chaco; they number about 12,000, and live together in a state of almost primitive simplicity. As a means of defence they keep constantly ready for duty five hundred warriors armed with lances, but if unmolested are inoffensive. They are a fine looking race, with complexions of a soft copper color, and their women are exceedingly beautiful. Their towns are built on the borders of the Pilcomayo, in the waters of which it is a custom for the old and young to bathe twice a day. The *Pampas* are a ferocious and brutal race; having no local habitation, but roving in bands over the plains, on horseback, committing depredations and murder upon the whites whenever they are found defenceless, and carrying the young women away into the pampas for wives. The Mattacas are an indolent and filthy race, and being of migratory habits, the camps of their wandering tribes are often met with in the various parts of the country. Their oldest male member is worshipped as their deity, but he is required to live a solitary life, and only presents himself to his people at long stated intervals.

The manufactures, like agriculture, are very little attended to in this country. Pouches, saddle-cloths, blankets, &c., are made by the Indian women, and sold in great numbers to the inhabitants of Tucuman, Salta, &c. CORDOVA is the principal manufacturing town; but the above kind of goods, and morocco leather, with wooden bowls and dishes, comprise the chief articles made there. It is probable that this state of things will continue to exist, as the manufactures of England and America are supplied at cheap rates, in exchange for the raw materials of the country, and, of course, depress all speculative enterprises in this department of industry, and the natural indolence of the people will ever prevent them from excelling in anything.

The external commerce of the country is monopolized by Buenos Ayres. The country is dependent on foreign supplies for almost every article, both of manufactures and tropical produce. These are supplied from England, Spain, and the United States. The imports consist of calico, cottons and woollens; the produce of the West Indies and other countries, &c.; the exports are the hides, tallow, hair and horns of the cattle slaughtered by the *gauchos*, and some few other articles, among which are some mineral substances. The present disturbed state of the country, and the pending blockade, has caused an almost total suspension of commerce, and from a similar reason we are uninformed of the present amounts; the latest information on this subject represents the statistics of 1843, at which date the value of the exports were about $8,000,000. The United States enjoy a considerable portion of the trade of Buenos Ayres; the remainder, with little exception, is carried on by British merchants. There is also a large inland trade carried by means of mules and wagons, which cross the large plains to the city of Mendoza, and the mining districts at the base of the Andes. They carry from the sea-board the foreign imports, and bring back the mineral wealth of those regions, with some few other commodities gathered up on the route.

The annexed table* will exhibit the principal items of export in 1843:

DESCRIPTION OF GOODS.	QUANTITIES.	VALUE. *Piastres.*	VALUE. *Francs.*
Hides	1,459,992	65,000,000	21,024,000
" salted	518,381	26,955,000	8,626,000
" horses	50,238	1,105,000	354,000
Skins, sheep, *doz*	94,921	2,848,000	911,000
" goat "	39,695	1,191,000	381,000
" calf "	6,236	187,000	60,000
" otter, *lbs.*	312,612	1,094,000	350,000
" deer, *doz*	4,658	56,000	18,000
Horse hair, *arrobas*	109,488	4,380,000	1,402,000
Wool, "	468,790	10,313,000	3,300,000
Tallow, "	390,216	9,755,000	3,122,000
Ostrich Feathers, *lbs.*	15,500	233,000	75,000
Salt Meat, *quintals*	162,184	5,676,000	1,816,000
Leather shavings "	9,556	239,000	76,000
Candles, *cases*	2,394	96,000	31,000
Horns, *number*	1,035,325	312,000	100,000
Bones, *lbs*	1,462,500	241,000	77,000

Total Exports, in piastres.............130,381,000
" " francs.................41,723,000
" " £ sterling.............1,649,000
" " dollars, about.........8,000,000

* De Bow's Com. Rev., July, 1848. These statistics are imperfect, but, at the same time, the best to be had.

The commerce between this state and the United States, for the year ending 30th June, 1846, was—Imports into the United States, $799,213; and exports from United States' ports, $185,425. Since this period, the ports of the Argentine have been blockaded, and, of course, no transactions can have taken place directly.

Buenos Ayres, the principal city of the Argentine confederacy, is situated on the south-western shore of the La Plata, in latitude 24° 36′ south. It is regularly built, and the streets, which are well-paved and clean, intersect each other at right angles; but the city contains no public buildings of any importance, except, perhaps, the cathedral, a large and handsome building, the interior of which is profusely decorated with carving and gilding. The population amounts from 70 to 100,000, of whom from 15 to 20,000 are foreign, chiefly English and French. Though close to the river, the city has no harbor, and ships drawing 16 or 17 feet of water anchor in the outer roads, seven or eight miles from the shore, loading and unloading by means of lighters. Between the outer and inner roads there is a dangerous bar, and the water becomes so shallow on the beach, that even boats cannot come close to the shore, but are met in the water by ox-carts, in which the goods are deposited at no little risk, and sometimes with much loss. The climate of this district is in general mild and healthy—in fact, it was for this reason that the Spaniards gave it its present name, which signifies "*good air.*"

The City of Corrientes, founded in 1588, is situated in latitude 27° 27′ south, at the junction of the Parana and Paraguay rivers, which afford every facility for an active commercial intercourse with the remote parts of the confederacy, as well as with the sea; but without steam navigation, which has not yet been introduced to any extent, these cannot be made available.

Cordova is situated in latitude 31° 26′ south, 172 leagues distant, by the post-road, from Buenos Ayres, in a pleasant valley, on the banks of the Rimero River. It contains many churches, and is the seat of a university, once celebrated, but now dwindled down to the dimensions of a provincial school. It was at this university that the celebrated Dr. Francia, late Dictator of Paraguay, was educated. At present Cordova forms a sort of centre between the upper provinces and Buenos Ayres.

The other principal cities are:—Santiago del Estero, a miserable, ill-built place, in latitude 27° 47′ south; and forty leagues beyond Santiago is the City of San Miguel de Tucuman, on an elevated plain, where the climate, though hot, is dry and salubrious; and where nature has been so prodigal of her choicest gifts, that the province of Tucuman well merits its appellation of the "Garden of the Argentine." The city contains from 7 to 8,000 inhabitants. Catamarca, sixty leagues south-west of Tucuman, contains about 4,000 inhabitants; the City of Salta, in latitude 24° 30′ south, and 414 leagues from Buenos Ayres, contains between 8 and 9,000 inhabitants, and is celebrated as a mule market; Mendoza, in 32° 50′ south latitude, and 69° 15′ west longitude, and 4,891 feet above the level of the sea, contains about 10,000 inhabitants. The most southern settlement of the Buenos Ayreans is the little town, Del Carmen, on the Rio Negro.

The government of this country is nominally a representative republic or confederation, each of the provinces being, to a certain degree, independent of the rest, and in the enjoyment of their own executive and legislative authorities. But, in 1835, Gen. Rosas, who was unanimously called to the Presidency, refused to act unless invested for a period with extraordinary powers. These were accordingly granted him, so that at present the government is a nearly absolute dictatorship, presenting, however, a favorable contrast to the dictatorship of the neighboring State of Paraguay, as it was, under the rule of Dr. Francia. There is a junta or parliament of 44 members, half annually renewed by popular election; and a senate of two deputies from each state. The State Governments consist of the popular assemblies and governors, who are elected by the delegates. But though democratic in theory, they are quite otherwise in practice; the lower classes bowing with obsequious deference to the nominees of the upper classes, and if any appeal is ever made by the latter to the people, it is generally from the necessity of supporting by a demonstration of brute force the pretensions of some particular candidate. There is a trite saying in Buenos Ayres, "*Rosas nominates—the people elect;*" meaning, probably, that he is in the habit of so moulding the several legislatures as to secure his own ends by *popular* means.

The powers of the President are constitutionally very extensive: he appoints all civil, military and judicial officers; but he, as well as his ministers, are responsible for their actions, (i. e. *according to the constitution,*) and liable to impeachment.

The military force of the republic is of uncertain amount. The soldiers have generally to be collected to meet an emergency, or are called upon to *undergo* an expedition whenever the caprice of the ruler demands their services. The national militia comprises all males of ripe age, but this body is never called into existence except in case of invasion.

The State of Buenos Ayres alone supports the expenses of the government; the other states contributing nothing *directly* to the general disbursements of the confederation. The annual amount of the public revenue, is from 12 to 15,000,000 dollars, a sum insufficient to meet the ordinary expenses; and there is a public debt of about 40,000,000 dollars, bearing interest at six per centum.

The discovery of the country, now known by the name of the Argentine Republic, took place somewhat later than that of other parts of South America on the Atlantic. The honor of the discovery is claimed by the Spaniards. Juan Diaz de Solis, having sailed from Spain in 1515, to explore Brazil, arrived at the mouth of the Rio de la Plata, and took formal possession of the country; but, deceived by the friendly appearance of the Indians, and being off his guard, he was slain with the few attendants who had landed in company. In 1526, Sebastian Cabot, then in the Spanish service, being also on a voyage to the coast of Brazil, entered the same river, and discovered an island, which he called St. Gabriel. Advancing about 12 leagues, he found a fine river flowing into the great stream: this he named St. Salvador, and, causing his fleet to enter, debarked his men and built a fort, in which he left a garrison, while he proceeded further up and discovered the Paraguay. In consequence of receiving a considerable quantity of silver from the Indians, who procured it from the mines of Peru, he imagined that mines of this precious metal existed in the interior, and accordingly gave to the river the name of Rio de la Plata, or the river of silver. The Spanish government, having conceived a high idea of the value of the country, determined to colonize it; and, to prevent any interference on the part of other nations, Don Pedro de Mendoza was sent out, and founded the city of Buenos Ayres, in 1535. From the earliest period after the colonization, until the establishment of a vice-royalty, the government was dependent upon that of Peru; though the chief of Buenos Ayres had the title of Captain-General. Buenos Ayres continued for a long time almost unknown, all the inhabited parts of the kingdom lying at a considerable distance from the ocean; and in consequence of the restrictions imposed upon its commerce, having no other communication with Europe than by the annual fleet from Spain, it languished in poverty and obscurity. So extensive and fertile a country could not, however, remain forever concealed. As the population increased, though it was but slowly, and the agricultural produce multiplied, the evil consequences of the restrictions were more severely felt. The reiterated remonstrances of the people at last opened the eyes of the Spanish government to the importance of the colony. A relaxation took place in the system of commercial monopoly, which had been rigorously adhered to; and finally, in order to a put a stop to a contraband trade that had been carried to an alarming height, register ships were allowed to sail under a license from the council of the Indies, at any time of the year. The consequence was, that the annual flota was lessened from 15,000 to 2,000 tons of shipping; and, in 1748, it sailed for the last time to Cadiz.

Other amendments of the mercantile system were made soon afterwards. In 1774, a free trade was allowed between several of the American ports; and, in 1778, and the succeeding year, several Spanish sea-ports were allowed an open trade to Buenos Ayres and the ports of the Pacific. Buenos Ayres was now advancing rapidly into political and commercial importance: this was rendered stable by the erection of the government into a vice-royalty in 1778, and since that period its trade progressively increased until the war between Spain and England, when a material interruption was given to it. Nothing of moment appears in the history of Buenos Ayres, until July, 1806, when the capital was taken by surprise by a British army, under Gen. Beresford, which suddenly invaded the country. These troops, proceeding from the Cape of Good Hope, found the country entirely defenceless, there being only a handful of regular troops, and the militia being unarmed and undisciplined. The British enjoyed their triumph only a few weeks, when a small body of the militia, under the command of General Liniers, a French officer, invested the city, and forced them to surrender at discretion on the 12th August. Soon after the surrender of General Beresford's army, another body of troops, in number about 5,000, arrived from the Cape of Good Hope, under Sir Home Popham, who, after taking Fort Maldonado, at the mouth of La Plata, laid siege to Montevideo. The Spanish garrison made a resolute and glorious defence, and finally compelled the besiegers to withdraw disgracefully from the contest. Other troops arrived some time afterwards, under Sir Samuel Auchmuty, and the number of the British bearing a vast superiority over that of the garrison, another attempt was made, and the town was finally carried by storm, after a defence which reflects the highest honor upon its little garrison. It was now determined by the British commanders to proceed against Buenos Ayres, as soon as certain expected reinforcements arrived. In May, 1807, these succours arrived, under General Whitelocke, who assumed the chief command, and was joined on the 15th of June by General Crawford. The invading army now amounted to upwards of 12,000 men, all regular and disciplined soldiers. On the appointed day they embarked in boats, and sailing up the river, debarked below the capital. They were permitted to approach the town without molestation; but no sooner had they entered it, than they were received by the indignant inhabitants with one tremendous and well-directed fire of grape and musketry. Every house was converted into a fortress, from which vengeance was poured out upon the invaders of the soil. The British troops were thrown into confusion, and endeavored to find safety in a disgraceful flight. General Whitelocke, finding that the patriotism of the people was not to be overcome, and having no means of escape, surrendered this formidable army prisoners of war to the militia of Buenos Ayres; and thus ended the second British invasion of this province.

The important services which Liniers had rendered the people at once elevated him to distinction. The viceroy, Sobremonte, was deposed, and the French general placed in his stead. The invasion of Spain, however, and the deposition of Ferdinand VII., produced a counter-revolution in the public opinion. Liniers was desirous of establishing the authority of the Emperor Napoleon in America as well as in Old Spain; but Don Josef de Goyeneche, who had been sent out by the junta of Cadiz, caused the inhabitants of Buenos Ayres to proclaim Ferdinand, advising at the same time that a junta should be immediately formed. So powerful and well-concerted were his measures, that on the 1st of January, 1809, the people rose in all parts of the city, and demanded the establishment of a junta. They were, however, dispersed; and the leaders punished by the troops, who still remained faithful to Liniers. But this temporary triumph was not of long continuance. In August, 1809, Cisneros, the new viceroy, arrived from Spain, and Liniers was deposed by the junta, which now solemnly declared their rights. Liniers was then exiled to Cordova; but the spirit of insurrection had spread itself too widely by this time to admit of the new viceroy continuing long in the exercise of his functions. Commotion succeeded to commotion; and on the 26th of May, 1810, a provisional government assembled itself, deposed the new viceroy, and sent him to Spain. Against this measure the interior provinces and the city of Montevideo protested. Liniers formed an army in the neighborhood of Cordova; and in Potosi another was assembled, under General Nieto. To check these a force marched from Buenos Ayres. Liniers and Nieto were defeated, and themselves and six of their principal officers beheaded.

These decisive measures did not, however, extinguish the spirit of disaffection to the cause of emancipation. A force was put in motion in Paraguay, under the governor, Velasco, who was, however, defeated, taken prisoner, and sent to Buenos Ayres. Montevideo still remained faithful to the mother country; but, in December, 1816, a body of Portuguese troops entered the Banda Oriental, and took possession of the city, and all the principal places on the eastern shore of the Uruguay, and of the country between the Parana and the Uruguay, and the province remained in their possession until 1825, when they were re-annexed to the government of Buenos Ayres. Buenos Ayres, though independent, de facto, after the revolution of 1810, was not so in name. The junta professed to pay allegiance to the government of Spain, and all decrees were issued in the name of Ferdinand VII. At length, on the 9th of July, 1816, the minds of the people being fully prepared for it, a formal declaration of independence was made by the general congress. No opposition was made to the measure in Buenos Ayres, as no Spanish troops had remained there since 1810. An unfortunate dissension, however, broke out between the provinces on the east bank of the La Plata and the general confederation, which arose from a dispute between the government of Buenos Ayres and General Artigas, one of the officers appointed to reduce Montevideo. The contest between them continued for several years, and many engagements took place, in most of which Artigas was successful.

From this period, though the independence of the country was fully established, intestine commotions continually recurring, have completely prostrated the energies of the people, and a state of anarchy has overshadowed the whole land. In 1828, the Banda Oriental was finally separated from the republic, and became an independent state, under guarantee of Brazil, the Argentine Republic, England and France. Nothing, however, of external importance occurred in regard to this nation, until the recent political disturbances in the Banda Oriental. The history of the transactions which occurred in that republic are detailed elsewhere. On this occasion Rosas, the governor of Buenos Ayres, took sides with Oribe, the President *de jure* of that country, and against Rivera, the President *de facto*. The result has been the intervention of the guarantees, England, France, and Brazil, and the blockade by the two latter of the ports of La Plata. The settlement of this question is looked to by mercantile communities with anxiety. Rosas is obstinate—the intervention is resolute; nor is it probable that the opinions of either party can be easily changed. Both countries, in the meanwhile, are suffering from the suppression of com merce, the stagnation of trade, and that want of confidence which alone can give tone to the interests of a civilized community. The honors that England and France have earned for their interference are of a very questionable character, and, even if successful, which is problematical, the only benefit they can expect to reap, is an accumulated debt, wherewith to burden their own people, for years to come.

THE DICTATORSHIP OF PARAGUAY.

The territory of this state lies between the parallels of 20° and 27° south latitude, and between the Rivers Paraguay and Parana. It is about 500 miles long and 200 in width, its area being estimated at 74,000 square miles. On the north and east it is bounded by the empire of Brazil, and on the south and west by the Argentine Republic. It formerly belonged to the Spanish Viceroyalty of Buenos Ayres, but early in the revolution withdrew itself from the conflict, and assumed an independent position, both in regard to Spain and the other colonies, and since that period has maintained an exclusive attitude, and constantly pursued a policy somewhat similar to that of China, of denying to foreigners access to the country. It resembles China, indeed, in many respects; both are tea-producing countries—both are subject to a species of patriarchial rule—the inhabitants, in moral and physical construction, are very similar, and both are actuated in all public affairs by a jealousy of foreigners; the objects of the two in regard to foreigners, however, are different: China excludes them from prejudice, Paraguay from policy; the design of the government being to make the country depend solely on its internal resources.

Paraguay is an inland peninsula, enclosed on all sides, except the north, by immense rivers. A chain of mountains, known as the Sierra Amambahy, which enters Paraguay on the north, and is a continuation of the

Sierra Santa Barbara, of Brazil, runs through its centre to about 26° south latitude. From this chain many rivers flow on each side, to join the Paraguay and Parana; but none of these require special notice, though in the rainy season they are often surcharged by the torrents, and overflowing, spread devastation over extensive tracts. The great rivers, Paraguay and Parana, are fully described in considering the Argentine Republic. The only lake of importance in the whole country is Ypao, but in several parts there are extensive marshes, presenting a succession of lagunes, or small collections of fresh water. The climate is temperate, but damp; resembling, in a great measure, that of Buenos Ayres on the sea-board.

Paraguay, in point of fertility, forms a striking and favorable contrast to the adjacent parts of the Argentine Republic. It is well-wooded, and diversified with undulating hills and verdant vales. "I was glad," says Mr. Robertson, who entered it at Neembucú, "to meet with much more frequent traces of cultivation and industry, than were to be found in the solitary tracts, over which I had heretofore sped my monotonous way. White-washed cottages often peeped from among the trees, and around them were considerable fields of cotton, yucca, and tobacco plants. The Indian corn and sugar cane were also frequently to be seen in the vicinity of the farm-houses, of a better character than cottages; and there was abundance of wood and of prickly pear. With the latter, the cultivated country, as well as the potreros or paddocks, were invariably well-fenced."—(*Letters from Paraguay*, vol. i., 259–'60.) Rice, maize, yucca, and kitchen vegetables, are now cultivated on an extended scale; and the growth of cotton, which had formerly been wholly received from Corrientes, suffices for home consumption. The breeding of horses or horned cattle has been equally encouraged; and, instead of receiving cattle from Entre Rios, the farmers have now a surplus stock. The total prohibition of intercourse between Paraguay and other countries, has contributed much to these results, as the people thus turned to the cultivation of the soil all the industry which, under the old government, had been applied to navigation and the collection of the Yerba maté for foreign markets.

The Yerba maté, or Paraguay tea, is the leaf of the Ilex Paraguayensis, an evergreen about the size of an orange tree, growing wild, and in great abundance, in the dense forests in the north and east provinces, to which the natives resort in great numbers for its collection. It is difficult to penetrate the country where it is found; but the profits derived from the articles are ample, Paraguay tea being in as general demand through the Argentine Republic, Chilé, and many parts of Peru, as the teas of China are in Europe and the United States. Its collection is undertaken by merchants in Asuncion, who each employ a master-workman, or abilitador, and from 20 to 50 peons, the master providing axes, knives, tobacco, mules, bullocks for slaughter, and other provisions, with money advanced to him by the merchant. The boughs of the yerba, with the leaves attached, are first hewn down and scorched; the leaves being then roughly removed, and dried by being placed over a wide arch of wood-work, under which a large fire is kindled; and, together with the small twigs, they are afterward ground to powder by a rude wooden mill. The tea is next weighed and stored, by the overseer, who pays the peons for it at the rate of two reals, or 25 cents, each arroba of 25 pounds. It is next rammed tightly into bags of bull's hide, which are left to dry in the sun, and contain from 200 lbs. to 220 lbs. each; and in this state it goes to market. Mr. Robertson estimates that, for six months' work, the peon may earn about £57, or $274, in wages, but he has run into debt to his master £12, or $58, before entering the woods, and as much more while employed there, for neither of which sums has he got half the value; of the remaining balance, £33, he spends nearly £12 in ornaments for his horse, £5 more in personal decorations, and the rest in gambling, to which all are very much addicted. "In a month the peon re-sells his horse, furniture, and personal apparel; and in a fortnight after that he is left without a cent, and in a week more he is found naked in the *Yerbales*."—(***Robertson.***)

The custom of using an infusion of this herb, is common throughout the most part of Spanish America; it originated among the natives, and has been adopted by the colonists. This is made by infusing a pinch of the yerba in a cup or maté (from which the tea derives its appellative) of hot water, and is imbibed through a tube, pierced with holes at the lower part, which permit only the passage of the fluid and keep back the leaves, which float on the surface. Sugar and a little lemon peel are used to give it a flavor. It is the common beverage, and is used at all meals and repasts. It is customary among the lower classes to pass the same maté from mouth to mouth, but this usage has been discontinued in refined society. Some virtues are ascribed to this plant; it is certainly diuretic and diaphoretic,—on some it acts as a sedative, on others as an excitant. The habit of using when once acquired is not easily relinquished, and when taken to excess it brings on a train of disorders similar, in many respects, to those caused by the abuse of ardent spirits.

Almost half the whole territory is national property. It consists of pasturage lands and forests, which have never been granted to individuals, the estates of Jesuit missionaries, and other religious corporations; and a great number of country-houses and farming establishments confiscated by the former dictator, Dr. Francia. This celebrated man paid great attention to the improvement of agriculture. He has let a great portion of the lands, at a moderate rent, and for an unlimited period, under the single, but indefinite condition, that they shall be cultivated or turned into pasturage. On other parts of the lands he established large farms, where thousands of cattle and horses are bred. These supplied his cavalry with horses and his troops with bread; besides which they furnished great numbers of cattle for the consumption of the capital. The migration of the peons is prohibited, which prevents accumulations of people in particular places, and insures the cultivation of the whole country. The arbitrary measures adopted in this country will not coincide with ideas of republican liberty, as existing in the United States; but there is no doubt but that the policy of Paraguay, however anomalous, has proved salutary, and tended much to civilize the inhabitants.

Manufactures received considerable impulse from the prohibition of foreign commerce. The people had previously imported cotton, woollen, and almost all other manufactured goods, and there used to be no such thing as a good workman in Paraguay. But the exercise of ingenuity was excited, not only by necessity but by terror. Except in special cases, no ingress or egress of individuals or merchandise to and from Paraguay, is permitted; but a large smuggling trade is, nevertheless, carried on with the adjacent republics, especially in the article of Paraguay tea. While Paraguay remained a Spanish province, the annual value of its produce fell little short of $1,500,000; of Paraguay tea, 8,000,000 lbs. were annually sent to Santa Fé and Buenos Ayres, besides 1,000,000 lbs. tobacco, large quantities of timber, cotton, sugar, molasses, spirits, &c. But this trade has been, with little exception, wholly suspended, except when the governor requires a supply of foreign articles, which he obtains readily in exchange for maté.

The government of Paraguay is an anomaly in the present times. It approaches as near to an absolute despotism as can well be conceived; the dictatorship of Sylla, in ancient Rome, being the only model with which it may be compared. The state is nominally republican, having a so styled congress of several hundreds of members; but the entire sovereignty resides in the dictator or governor, who is not only commander-in-chief, but head of the church, the law, and every other branch of the administration. In the time of Francia, (it may be different now,) there was no law save what was dictated by himself, and his rewards and punishments were as tyrannical and barbarous as his policy was generally oppressive. All bowed down at his nod, and the whole country and people seemed to be expressly created and sustained for his especial pleasure.

The population of Paraguay is estimated to be 300,000, (*American Almanac*,) but it has been variously stated at 150,000 and upwards, by different authors. This consists of native Spaniards, (a small moiety,) Indians, (the great bulk,) Negroes, and the mixed races, sprung from the amalgamation of these original stocks. The condition of the people is lamentable, but their position, without any incentives to ambition, is at least nugatorily a happy one: little to do, the necessaries of life abundant, and the state untroubled by foreigners. The people are slothful and live at ease, especially when they are at a distance from the rod of the despot who rules the beautiful land of which they are the unworthy habitants.

The military force comprises about 3,000 men, chiefly cavalry; besides which there is a militia, composed of every *free* male citizen, 17 years of age, and capable of bearing arms. The naval force consists of only a few brigantines and gun-boats to protect the river-coasts from smugglers and foreign invasion.

The amount of revenue is uncertain: it is derived from the state lands, which comprise half the territory, tithes in kind from all species of produce, the right to levy, which is sold to the highest bidder every year, taxes upon shops and storehouses in the capital, the droit d'aubaine or right to the property of foreigners dying in Paraguay, fines, postages, sales, stamps and commercial dues, &c. The principal expenditures are in support of the army and navy, and purchase of war stores. There is no public debt.

The state of education in Paraguay is respectable, and public schools are plentifully distributed throughout: "it is a rare occurrence," says Reugger & Longchaups, "in this country, where no printing-press exists, to find a free man who cannot read and write." Morals are at a low ebb. The religion of the country is that of Rome, but the state has an ultimate authority over the churches and missions, and the governor assumes a guardianship over all religious interests.

The country is divided into 20 sections or *commandancias*, exclusive of a territory in the south-east, called the Missions, occupying 600 square leagues, and governed by a special officer. Beside Asuncion, there are but four towns in Paraguay: the other collections of houses being mere villages. The cabildo, or municipal government of the several towns, is chosen annually by the people. Indians as well as Creoles, and mixed races, are eligible to all town offices. There is, in all parts, perfect security of person and property : each district being made responsible for every murder or theft committed within its limits. Mendicity is unknown, as all persons are obliged to be employed at some calling.

Asuncion, the capital, is finely situated on an eminence, on the left bank of the Paraguay, in south latitude 25° 16′. It is an ill-built town, with unpaved streets and houses little better than huts. The only good buildings are the convents. What has been called its "beautiful cathedral," is a paltry white-washed fabric; and its government-house, styled the national palace, though extensive, is mean. It contains about 10,000 inhabitants, and is the centre of considerable trade in hides, tobacco, timber, yerba maté, wax, &c. ; and the adjacent country is comparatively well cultured and populous.

Paraguay was discovered in 1526, by Sebastian Cabot. The Jesuits, from Brazil, afterwards established several missions in the south part of the country, and were supposed to have effected astonishing improvements in the condition and habits of the natives; but no sooner had they been expelled, in 1768, than the fabric they had so long and industriously been framing, fell straightway to pieces, and the Indians relapsed into their former barbarism. In 1776, Paraguay became a province of the vice-royalty of Buenos Ayres, and as such remained until the breaking out of the revolution, in 1810, when it unostentatiously withdrew from all intercourse with the outer world. In 1813, Fulgentia Yegros was succeeded by José Gaspar Francia as president of the revolutionary junta, and soon after the Congress of Deputies appointed a joint executive, consisting of Dr. Francia as first consul, and Yegros as second consul, but on the following year, Francia ordered the assembling of a Congress of one thousand Deputies, and with great art contrived to have his own partizans elected. This servile congress appointed their Chief "Dictator" for three years. The history of this remarkable man presents many anomalies. He was a native of Paraguay, who had studied law at the University of Cordova, in the Argentine Republic, and conceived the idea of placing himself at the head of affairs in this country through the influence of the superstition of the natives, and so far became successful as to obtain a most unqualified and unbounded dictatorship; nor was his course of policy, when in power, less singular than the means by which he obtained his position. At the end of the three years for which he was appointed, he was chosen "Dictator for life," and thus his power became unchangeable. His first great theory of national polity was, to place his country in a position of actual independence of all other countries, and, to this end, he, after a short time, ceased all intercourse with foreigners, and even prohibited his own people from leaving and strangers from coming into his territory. Some, who chanced to set foot in Paraguay, suddenly found themselves in a vast prison; guards were posted at every outlet to prevent escape from the country, and thus they were held prisoners at large, and, without the assignment of a cause, for years. Bonpland, the celebrated botanist, was so held in durance for nine years; Don Pablo Soria, and his companions, who explored the Rio Vermejo, were takeu on their arrival at the Rio Paraguay, and held five years, with the whole country for a prison. In connection with this course of policy, Francia set into operation a code of stringent laws of his own creation, compelling each man to follow such employment as he should dictate, by which means the country derived at least one advantage, viz. : habits of industry among the people which previously were not known: agriculture flourished *per force*, and manufactures took a start, but in no branch of employment could a person become rich or independent; the proceeds, beyond their actual necessities, went into the dictator's coffers, which greatly aided the revenues of the country.

Thus shut from the world, and under a tyranny more singular and grinding than bloody, the people of Paraguay seem to have been in a fair way to lose what little refinement civilization had before invested them with: the women appeared naked in public, and female house-servants performed their domestic duties, or waited upon company, with no covering, except a cloth about the loins, and all the natural delicacy of the sex was merged in an arbitrary custom.

In 1826, the Argentines having expelled the Spaniards from their territory, Francia declared anew his country's independence, and in the following year its assumed position was formally recognized by the Emperor of Brazil, but has not yet been recognized as independent by Spain. In 1841, Dr. Francia died, at Asuncion, and was succeeded by a junta. The exclusive policy of the government, however, interrupts all further inquiry into its present condition: the best account of this country will be found in the Brothers Robertson's Letters from Paraguay, a work full of highly interesting matter. Some correct ideas of the country may also be gleaned from the very interesting work lately published by Col. King, long a resident of the Argentine Republic, and the narrative of whose adventures are second only in lively incident and spirited description to the world renowned history of Robinson Crusoe. A General Lopez is now the nominal head of the government, but his attributes are little understood.

THE REPUBLIC OF URUGUAY.

This is a very compact territory, extending along the northern shore of the estuary of the Rio de la Plata, and is bounded on the west by the River Uruguay, on the south-east by the Atlantic Ocean, and on the north-east and north by the territory of the Empire of Brazil. It lies between 30° and 35° S. latitude and 52° and 59° W. longitude. It is of nearly a circular form, and is supposed to embrace an area of 120,000 square miles. It was formerly a portion of the vice-royalty of Buenos Ayres; being afterwards subdued by the Portuguese, it became a province of Brazil, but at last, by articles of a treaty between Brazil and Buenos Ayres, it became an independent republic.

This country is little known to foreigners. The coast presents the aspect of a low flat plain, without wood of any kind, and as far as the eye can reach, quite level in appearance with the water, except in the single instance of the highland of Monte Video. Inland, however, and particularly in the north, the country is intersected by hill-ranges, alternating with vallies traversed by considerable affluents of the Uruguay. In this territory, the humidity of the soil, which is washed by numerous rivers, is corrected by the pampero, a remarkably dry wind. The climate of Uruguay is proverbially healthy, and it is evident that the thinness of the population must arise from the mode of life followed by the settlers, or from political causes, and not from any deficient fertility of the soil or other natural or necessary cause.

Uruguay is divided into *nine* departments, and possesses three principal towns, Montevideo, La Colonia and Maldonado; *fifteen* small towns and *eight* hamlets, without including estancias or farms, and ranchos or cottages. The population is variously estimated at from 120,000 to 200,000.

Agriculture has been much interrupted of late years by political causes: the crops are chiefly of cereal grains and the other staples peculiar to the La Plata country. Grazing is the chief employment of the farmer. In manufactures, no progress has been made: not even a tolerable carpenter is to be found in the territory.

The PORT OF MONTEVIDEO, on account of its contiguity to the ocean and its own conformation, is the best on either side of the Rio de la Plata, and has greatly the advantage of Buenos Ayres in a commercial point of view. Its form is that of a large circular basin, exposed only on the south-west; its average depth is about 16 feet, except after a long continuance of the pamperos or south-west winds, which sometimes cause the waters to rise from four to six feet above the ordinary level. The city of Montevideo is the capital of the state, and is well fortified by a citadel. It contains 10,000 inhabitants. The houses are built of stone or brick, but are seldom more than one story high and flat-roofed, and the streets are unpaved, so that they are either clouded with dust or loaded with mud, as the weather happens to be wet or dry. The town is supplied with water, and contains no public buildings of any importance: the cathedral, however, is said to be handsome. On the top of the hill, from which the city derives its name, is a light-house, 475 feet above the level of the sea. The commerce of this city, which includes that of the whole republic, is very considerable. Its exports consist of the animal products natural to the country, as hides, tallow, horns, hair, &c., and its imports are mostly dry-goods and hardware; flour, sugar, wines, tobacco, boots, shoes, salt, &c. The trade is principally with Brazil, Great Britain, the United States, France, Sardinia, Spain and Portugal.

The other ports are Maldonado and Colonia del Sacramento, but are too insignificant to require further notice: the principal commercial transactions are done in Montevideo.

The country, though comparatively small in limit, has, from time to time, and does, at the present period, occupy much of the attention of the world. It was originally a part of Buenos Ayres, but when the latter country threw off the Spanish yoke, Uruguay, by the influence of Artigas, was not included in the confederation. Subsequently, and after the defeat of Artigas, who had fled into Paraguay, and was there imprisoned by Dr. Francia, in a convent, from which he never escaped, it was seized upon by the Emperor of Brazil, and by him held as a province of the empire, under the name of Cisplatina. This connection, however, was not satisfactory to the people of the country. In 1825, they declared their independence, and 1828, by the aid of the armies of the Argentine Republic, under General Albia, the Brazilians were driven out and the independence of the country secured under treaty between the Argentine Republic and Brazil. This independence was acknowledged and guaranteed by France and Great Britain. A constitution was then formed, similar to that of the United States, with the exception that this was an integral instead of a federal republic. This constitution provided for a President, whose term of service should be four years, and a Senate and Legislature, the former for six and the latter for three years. Under this arrangement, the country at once entered upon the enjoyment of a progressive prosperity. The first President was Fructuoso Rivera, who was elected in November, 1830. Under his administration, all the resources of the country were developed and its commerce prospered. Rivera's term ended on the 24th October, 1834, and as specified by the constitution the President of the Senate assumed the Presidency *ad interim,* till the next March election, when Manuel Oribe was chosen to the chief magistracy. The policy pursued by Oribe, rendered him obnoxious to the people, and in 1836, a revolt broke out against him, headed by the Ex-President. The intervention of the French was sought by the Riveristas, and eventually Oribe was obliged to resign. This occurred 23d October, 1838, leaving about one year and a half of his term unexpired. Rivera re-assumed power, and on the 11th November dissolved the constitutional Congress, and proclaimed himself dictator. His first step was to call together a "Council of Notables," and by this power, created by himself, he was elected President *de facto.* The Argentines, jealous of the new republic, and viewing it as a serious competitor in commerce, rendered his administration extremely irksome, and in 1840, openly commenced hostilities by aiding and encouraging the former president to regain the supreme government. Oribe, at the head of a considerable force, entered Uruguay, and proclaimed himself president. His advance was met by Rivera with a small army, and the latter was beaten and compelled to take refuge in the capital, Montevideo, which is a well fortified and walled city. From that place, Rivera called upon England and France to comply with the terms of the guarantee, and aid him in sustaining the independence of the country. The object of Rosas, Governor of Buenos Ayres, seemed evidently to gain possession of the Uruguay, and attach it as a province to his own confederacy, and after considerable delay, the attention of England and France was given to the subject. A small combined fleet was sent to those powers, with a demand upon Oribe to evacuate the country: the demand was not complied with, and as Governor Rosas openly favored the invaders, supplying them with men, arms and munitions, the port of Buenos Ayres was placed under blockade, and early in 1846, a fleet of sail and steam vessels was sent up the Parana, with a view of obtaining horses from Paraguay and the province of Corrientes, the first of which about the same time declared war against Buenos Ayres, and the latter was in a state of revolution. At Vuelta de l'Obligado, a severe battle was fought between the combined fleets and the forces of Rosas, which resulted in the dispersion of the Argentines and the opening of the river to commerce for the time, but the allies eventually relinquished the undertaking, and returned to Montevideo, without effecting the design they had in view when they set out on the expedition. This war is still pending, but England has withdrawn from the contest.

The constitutional term for which Rivera was elected, terminated on the 1st March, 1843, and the legislature resolved not to elect another President, but appointed Don Joaquin Suarez, President, *ad interim.* This man is but a tool in the hands of Rivera, and a fence to cover his constitutional disability to serve another term. It is now the desire of the right thinking of all parties that both Rivera and Oribe shall withdraw from the presidential contest, and leave the people to choose for themselves a chief to rule over their destinies: such a course would be likely to bring about the settlement of all disputes and secure the independence of the country. This, however, can never take place until all foreign intervention ceases.

THE EMPIRE OF BRAZIL.

The vast territories of Brazil, in extent and importance, are second only to the giant empires of Russia and China, in the eastern hemisphere, and the extended limits of the United States of America, in the western world. Brazil stretches along about two-thirds the eastern coast of South America, while its superficial area occupies nearly half its whole extent. It lies between 4° 17′ north, and 33° south latitude; its most easterly point is Cape San Augustin, in 34° 58′ west longitude; its western limit is uncertain—it probably reaches the 75th meridian. The length, from north to south, is 2,500 to 2,600 miles, and its breadth, from east to west, between 2,000 and 2,300 miles. The coast on the Atlantic is more than 4,000 miles long, and its area has been estimated at from 2,300,000 to 2,700,000 square miles. The Atlantic Ocean forms its eastern and southern boundary; Guayana and Venezuela, from which it is separated by a chain of mountains, under the various names of Sierra Tuhuny, Sierra Pecaraima, &c., and the Rio Oyapoco, lie on the north, and its western boundary is formed by the republics of La Plata, Peru, Bolivia and Equador. The country which was originally included under the name of Brazil, is proved, by ancient maps, to have extended only from the sea-coast to the Rio San Pedro; the Portuguese, however, have never ceased adding accessions to the country, and their possession has, from time to time, been acknowledged by Spain.

The form of Brazil may be said to resemble almost that of a heart, of which the greatest diameter, from east to west, in a straight line from Cape San Roque to Peru, approaches an extent of 33 degrees. The east side of Brazil is traversed, from north to south, by a range of mountains, of which the average height is about 3,000 feet; it is known by the name of Sierra do Mars, and its greatest height is 4,100 feet. This range divides the coast land from the campos, or unwooded country, the average elevation of which is about 2,000 feet. It gradually becomes lower on approaching Paraguay, until it is lost on the low and swampy plains inhabited by the Guaycurus Indians. The highest range of the Brazilian mountains is that which traverses the centre of the country, the greatest altitude of which is 6,000 feet. The Brazilian System may be divided into three different ranges:

(1.) The *Cerro do Mars*, or coast range, is by far the most picturesque of the Brazilian chains, and in some parts approaches within a few miles of the sea, while in others it sweeps inland for 120 to 140 miles. The soil near the coast is rich in the extreme, and literally teems with exuberant vegetation. At a distance, and near the mountains, are the ancient forests, whose gigantic trees and countless shrubs attest the excellency of the soil on which they grow. On crossing the Cerro do Mars the barren table-land, (*the Campos Geraes,*) is exhibited in all its native nakedness. Gold and diamonds are frequently found in the vallies. The Cerro do Mars commences in the Campos do Vacaria, sinks abruptly in the direction of the Rio Doce, and loses itself completely at Bahia. The celebrated Monte Pascoal, seen by the early navigators, forms a part of this chain. It is worthy of remark, that the plants growing on the Campos, are altogether distinct from those growing on the Atlantic side of the mountains, and quite a different race of animals inhabit these vast elevated deserts.

(2.) The *Cerro do Mantequeira*, or *Espinacho*, the central chain, is more extensive than the former, and comprises the highest points in Brazil, viz.: the Itacolami, the Cerro do Carassa, and the Itambé. This range traverses the province of Minas Geraes, running, in its northerly course, through Bahia and Pernambuco, and in its southerly course, through San Paulo and Rio Grande.

(3.) The *Cerro dos Vertentes*, or Water-separating Mountain, so called because it divides the eastern tributaries of the rivers Amazon and La Plata from the River San Francisco. This chain is sometimes called the Brazilian Pyrenees. Its loftiest summits are those Cerro do Canastra and Marcella, where, on one side, the Rio San Francisco, and on the other, the most important tributaries of the Rio Grande take their rise; and the Pyreneos, in the Province of Goyaz, where the tributaries of the Parana are found.

Nearly two-thirds of Brazil consist of high land and mountains. Estimates have been given of the comparative quality of the country under tillage, and that still in a wild state, or occupied by rivers, lakes, swamps, &c.; but, from the limited knowledge possessed of this empire, even by the Brazilians themselves, such estimates must be entirely futile. It is, however, abundantly certain that the extent of cultivated land bears but a very small proportion indeed to that of the whole country—perhaps, not more than two or three per centum.

Brazil, above all other countries, has been favored by nature with all the advantages and requisitions for carrying on an extensive commerce; its principal cities are on the coasts; its harbors are the finest in the world, and its large rivers, most of which are navigable to a great distance inland, are connected therewith in such a way as to facilitate the transit of inland products, and ensure their ultimate shipment to foreign countries. The principal rivers are:

1. The *Amazon*, that mighty stream which almost divides the continent, and which is generally considered the longest river in the world. It is formed by the junction of the modern Marañon (Tunguragua) with the Ucayale, or ancient Marañon; it enters Brazil at San Francisco de Tabatinja, and flows from west to east along the immense northern province of Para, discharging itself into the Atlantic in about the meridian of 50° west longitude. Its principal tributaries are—the Madeira, which takes its rise in the Bolivian province of Potosi, and flows a distance of 700 leagues; the Xingu, in the province of Matto Grosso, itself possessing many smaller confluents; the Rio Negro, the recipient of more than 40 tributaries, which rises in New-Grenada, and loses itself in the north of Brazil, after a course of 700 leagues; the Tapajoz, which rises in the Matto Grosso; and, in addition to these, are upwards of sixty others, of less importance and magnitude, which give bulk to the vast volume of water that constitutes the Amazon.

2. The *Rio Pardo*, which traverses a portion of the province of San Paulo, rises in the district of San Joäo del Rey, and empties itself into the Parana.

3. The *Rio Doce*, traversing the province of Espiritu Santo, and serving as a sort of means of uniting the interior of Minas Geraes with the coast.

4. The *Para*, or *Tocantins*, formed by the junction of the Araguay and Tocantins, properly so-called; the former is the principal branch; it traverses the provinces of Goyaz and Para, and empties itself into the Atlantic. At the mouth of the Para, the phenomenon of the *bore*, to which the

Indians have given the name of *pororoca*, manifests itself in a very striking manner. Three days previous to the new or full moon, when the tides are highest, an immense wave, upwards of fifteen feet in perpendicular height, rushes from shore to shore with a tremendous noise, and is succeeded immediately by a second and third, and sometimes by a fourth. The tide, instead of occupying six hours to flow, attains its greatest height in a few minutes. The roaring of the *pororoca* is heard distinctly at the distance of two leagues.

5. The ***Rio San Francisco***, one of the largest of the Brazilian rivers, rises in the vicinity of Parana, in the province of Minas Geraes. It is the only river of importance between Bahia and Pernambuco. Its course is interrupted by the cascade of Paolo Affonso.

6. The ***Rio Grande do Sul***, in the province of San Pedro.

7. The ***Parana***, which separates Brazil from Paraguay and the Argentine Republic, and forms also the boundary line between the provinces of San Paulo, Matto-Grosso and Goyaz; its chief tributaries are the Rio Pardo, the Itahy and the Aguapehy.

In addition to the above, may be mentioned the Parnahyba, in the province of Maranhao; the Oyapoko, dividing French Guayana from Brazil; the Paraguacu, emptying itself into the bay of Bahia de Todos Santos; the Rio Itapecuri, in the province of Maranham; the Rio Grande do Norte; the Jiquihona, so celebrated for its diamonds; the Jaquaribe, &c., &c.

Many of the rivers of Brazil, especially the Amazon, like the Nile, overflow their banks, and subject the country to extensive inundations, attended with an injurious effect upon the health. The navigation of many is interrupted at a distance from the coast by dangerous falls and rapids, and the mouths of many of the smaller rivers are subject to winds and currents, which render them extremely unsafe to the navigator.

The lakes of Brazil are of little account; they are few in number, and small in extent. The principal are the Los Patos and Mirim, the former of which is merely a widening of the Rio Grande de San Pedro. There are also those of Juperanam, Jiguiba, Manguaba, Parapetinga, Jaguarassu, &c. &c.

The soil, in a country so extensive as Brazil, must, of necessity, be very various in character and composition. In the neighborhood of Rio Janeiro it consists, in a great measure, of plains, which bear every indication of former inundations; those which, during the high tides, are covered by the sea, have degenerated into swamps, upon which we find the Rhizophora of Linnæus; those that lie higher consist of quicksands, and seem almost incapable of cultivation. The marshy plains, at a distance from the sea, might, perhaps, by dint of draining, be made available for the purposes of growing rice and the sugar-cane. The soil upon the heights, which surround these plains, consists of a mixture of clay and coarse quartz sand; it retains but little moisture, and in times of drought becomes extremely hard. A few miles from the town, traces of considerable improvement are observed. A pretty deep layer of rich quartz sand rests upon a bottom of granite or decayed feldspar; the soil is much injured, however, by the universal growth of the mandioca. The soil of Brazil is generally well-adapted for the cultivation of this plant; its tendency is, nevertheless, to exhaust it completely in the course of a few years; a plantation never yields more than three crops, after which it is abandoned. In the mountainous districts in the interior, which are still covered by their native woods, the excellence of the soil is amply proved by the size and abundance of the trees. Neglected for centuries, a layer of the richest mould has been formed of their fallen leaves and decayed trunks, which, resting again upon a rich and deep bed of clay, is of a red or yellow color, as it contains more or less of the oxides of iron. Between Rio Janeiro and Villa Rica, the soil is everywhere of hard and excellent white clay; the mountains are of granite, in which the amphibole predominates.

The mineral products of Brazil are chiefly confined to the more rare and valuable descriptions: the most celebrated, though not the most important, are diamonds. These are principally found in the Provinces of Minas Geraes, Minas Novas, Goyaz and Matto Grosso; but it is supposed that they exist in several of the other provinces of the empire. The diamonds found in Minas Geraes are generally the largest, but they are not of the purest water. The most celebrated diamond mines in Brazil are those of Serrado Frio, which are also known by the name of Arrayal Diamantino, or Diamond District. These mines were not actually discovered until the government of Dom. Lorenco d'Almeida, although the diamonds were known to have been in the possession of the Negroes, who met with them accidentally while employed in gold washing, and other persons, ignorant of their value, long before that period. They were first exported from Brazil to Lisbon, in 1726, by Bernardo da Silva Lobo. This district is surrounded by almost inaccessible rocks, and was formerly guarded by so much vigilance, that not even the governor of the province had the liberty of entering it without the special permission of the director of the mines.

The mines are wrought by accumulating the *cascalhao*, a kind of ferrugenous earth, (in which the diamonds are found mixed with flints,) and washing it. The former operation is generally performed during the hot season, at a time when the beds of the rivers and torrents are dry, and the diamond sand can be easily extracted. When the wet season arrives, the washing commences: it is performed in the open air and frequently under sheds. At the bottom of the bed glides a small stream, which occupies one of its sides. Seats raised, and without backs, are arranged along the shed, in such a manner, that the subaltern officers (*feitores*,) are enabled to watch the negroes at work. One feitor superintends eight negroes. Each negro works in a compartment of the shed, separated or walled off, as it were, from the others. The cascalhao to be examined, is placed in troughs close to the stream, and the negroes are introduced entirely naked, excepting in time of extreme cold, when they are allowed a kind of waistcoat, but without either pockets or lining. They are furnished with an alavanca, a kind of handspike, by means of which they separate the earth from the flint, and then taking the largest stones in their hands, they proceed to search for the diamonds. When a negro discovers a diamond, he shows it to the feitor, and then deposits it in a large wooden vessel suspended in the middle of the shed. If any negro is fortunate enough to discover one, weighing seven carats, he is purchased by government, and obtains his liberty: the discovery of a stone of less weight, also confers liberty on the finder, but with some restrictions. Various premiums are distributed according to the value of the stone, even to a quid of tobacco. Formerly there were as many as 30,000 negroes employed in the mines, but according to Freiyreiss, the number employed at the time of his visit to Brazil, (1823,) did not exceed 20,000.

There is great difference in the size of the diamonds found: some are so small, that 16 or 20 would not weigh a carat. It is rarely that in the course of a year, more than two or three were found weighing from 17 to 20 carats, and two years may pass without discovering one of the weight of 30 carats. The mines are under the direction of an imperial board, and the government receives one-fifth of all the products. The value of these mines has been over-estimated; it is an ascertained fact, that less than 3,500,000 carats have been found since the opening of the mines in 1728, to the present time. The actual value of this amount does not reach $30,000,000, a sum about equal to one year's exports of all other productions of Brazil. Figures put visions to flight, and the much talked of riches of Brazil from her diamond mines, become but a small, very small item of the national wealth. The whole value of the amount of diamonds, indeed, seems inadequate to pay, even the bare expenses, of employing 20,000 or 30,000 negroes for a space of 120 years, without calculating on any profits to be derived by the miner, who is mulcted heavily by the government, and has to supply a heavy capital in the prosecution of his searches. It would be interesting to have an exposé of the credit and debit side of this question.

In America, after Mexico and Peru, Brazil has furnished the largest quantity of the precious metals. Gold is supposed to exist in great abundance in San Paulo and the neighborhood of the river Ytènes. The most celebrated mines are those of Congo Soco, about 40 leagues from Villa Rica: they now belong to the "Anglo-Brazilian Mining Company," which purchased them in 1825, for £70,000 sterling. The gold about Villa Rica is found in the form of powder or fine dust, in crystals, and sometimes, though rarely, in whole lumps. A mass, weighing 16 pounds, was once found. The gold formations differ much in various parts of the country. The produce of the mines was most considerable the first half of the century in which they were discovered. Towards the close of the last century, 70 or 80 arrobas were annually smelted at Villa Rica; while previous to the arrival of the English company, it had dwindled down to forty. During the first six months of 1829, the Anglo-Brazilian Company, from their mines at Congo Soco alone, gathered 2,037 lb. 14 oz. 15 grs.; and according to Malte Brun, in the same year, exported from Rio Janeiro to England, gold, in ingots, to the value of 4,166,000 francs. This fact plainly shows, that the gradual falling off in the quantities yielded, was not on account of any growing scarcity, but from a want of care and activity on the part of the miners. The government has one-fifth of all the produce.

Iron abounds in the mountains and in the Province of Minas Geraes: near the village of Ypanema, in the mountain of Araasojava, is a mine of magnetic iron-stone, known to contain from 80 to 90 per cent. of pure iron. San Paula has many rich and extensive mines, which have been worked by a number of Swedes, who were brought over in 1810, by the Conde de Linhares. In the smelting and other operations, the Swedish method is practised.

Among the other mineral productions of Brazil, platina, found in the Province of Minas Geraes, is the most valuable. Copper is also found in the same province. Precious stones abound in Brazil, especially topazes, of which there are a great many varieties, found principally in the district of Capaô. In some parts of Minas Novas, white and blue topazes are found, though the usual color is yellow. The fifth of all these precious minerals and stones goes to the imperial treasury, and it is from this source alone that any estimate of the value of the Brazilian mines can be made up.

But even if facts were furnished from this source, they would be insufficient from which to form an accurate estimate, as it is well known that large and unknown quantities of things of this kind are smuggled from the country unaccounted for. Perhaps one-third of the whole undergoes this process.

For a long period the mining pursuits formed the sole objects of all classes, to the neglect of more worthy and needful sources of industry and support, and threw a most powerful obstacle in the way of improvement in the country; but more latterly the energies of the inhabitants have been turned to the cultivation of the soil, which is so rich and productive as to render the mining operations, even at this period, of very inferior importance; and the traffic in gold and diamonds is now comparatively inconsiderable.

The climate of Brazil is as various as the positions of the several portions of the country, and presents all the transitions of the torrid and temperate zones. Along the coast, the ordinary temperature is from 19° to 20°, (*Reaumer*,) with some modifications, according to localities: thus, while the thermometer seldom rises above 21½° at Bahia, it sometimes stands as high as 25° and 26° at Rio Janeiro. Winter is severe in the southern provinces, and it even freezes at Rio Grande de San Pedro and San Catarina. The climate, in the vicinity of San Paulo, is usually accounted the most agreeable, and the temperature permits the growth of European fruits. The west wind, in the interior of Brazil, is unwholesome, as it passes over vast marshy forests. The sea-coast from Para to Olinda, appears to possess a similar climate to Guayana, and notwithstanding the astronomical position of Brazil, between the equator and the tropics, the atmosphere, owing to the height of the greater portion of the country, is, in general, temperate, rather than hot. Pernambuco and a few of the other provinces suffer occasionally from drought, to which, however, the coast lands are seldom subject.

The following remarks, by Mr. Von Langsdorff, formerly Russian consul at Rio, upon the seasons of Brazil, are in the main true: he says, "Winter, in this country, resembles summer in the north of Europe; while spring and autumn are unconsciously lost in winter and summer." Of Brazil, then, it may be more truly said than of any other country.

"Stern winter smiles on this auspicious clime;
The fields are florid in eternal prime;
From the bleak pole no winds inclement blow,
Mould the round hail, or flake the fleecy snow;
But from the breezy deep the groves inhale
The fragrant murmurs of the eastern gale!"

The seasons may be properly reduced to two—the rainy and the dry season, although some divide them into four, namely: the spring, commencing in September; the summer in December; the autumn in March; and the winter in June. The season of rains usually sets in about October or November, and is preceded in some parts by fogs, thick groups of clouds and sudden gusts of wind, as well as by occasional showers, and the temperature is also extremely variable. This season generally lasts till March. The period of its commencement, however, varies according to the latitude, natural position and other climatic influences of localities.

As the northern parts of Brazil are situated near the middle of the torrid zone, the heat in the lower regions is often sultry and oppressive, but the moisture of the atmosphere keeps vegetation in perpetual vigor. Here there is little difference in the seasons: the days and nights scarcely vary in length; the sun declines only a few degrees from his vertical position; the trees never lose their foliage, nor is the ground ever destitute of flowers. Many of the trees and plants are adorned with blossoms of the most beautiful kinds, which being intermixed with leaves of the brightest green, impart to the forests of these regions a splendor unparalleled in the temperate zones. Near the shores of the Atlantic, where the trade wind constantly blows, its refreshing influence is daily felt. In the more elevated parts, and at a greater distance from the equator, the climate is proportionally mild. In reference to this part of the New World, it has been emphatically observed,—"A finer country than Brazil—one blessed with a more genial climate, or possessing a more fruitful soil; one more happily diversified with wood and water; intersected with navigable rivers; or richer in mineral treasures, is scarcely to be found in the whole compass of the globe."

The vegetable products of Brazil are unrivalled in regard to variety and luxuriance by those of any other nation of the world. Among the most important, are those of sugar, coffee, cotton, gum-elastic, rice, tobacco, maize, wheat, mandioc, beans, cassava-root, bananas, ipecacuanha, ginger, yams, oranges, figs, &c., &c. But first of all rank sugar, coffee, the gum elastic and cotton, which form the staple articles of the country, and the culture of which has, of late years, increased with almost unexampled rapidity. Sugar is principally raised in the Province of Bahia and other provinces on the coast, and the value of the exports of this article alone are estimated at from 10 to 15 millions of dollars annually.

Coffee is even more extensively cultivated than sugar. It is principally produced in Rio, and enjoys celebrity in all parts of the world. Its flavor has been very much improved of late by careful cultivation, and skill in the management of the plant, and is little inferior to the best samples of Mocha.

In consequence of the great and constantly-increasing demand for gum elastic, or "*caoutchouc*," (a corruption of the name given it by the aborigines of Brazil, "cahuchu,") in England and the United States of America, from the almost daily new uses to which it is found applicable, the attention of the Brazilian government and legislature has been called to the expediency, and even necessity, of promoting the propagation of the trees from which it is extracted, (*seringa elastica.*) In the year 1828, the quantity exported did not exceed 4,000 milreis in value, and 20,000 lbs. in weight; whereas, in the financial years 1845–'46, it amounted to upwards of 8,000,000 lbs., besides 415,953 pairs of shoes, the whole valued at 500,000 milreis! It becomes, therefore, a matter of great importance for Brazil, not only to preserve this branch of her trade in its present flourishing state, but likewise to be able to augment its production in proportion to its increased consumption. No other branch of its export trade is so profitable, since nothing but manual labor is required; and one man employed in its collection can obtain extract sufficient in one day to make ten pairs of shoes, the current price of which, being 300 reis, give three milreis per diem, equal to $1 75 a day, which, in this cheap country, may be considered equivalent to $3 in the United States. Unless some means are speedily adopted of planting and cultivating the "seringa elastica," so as to ensure an adequate and constant supply of "caoutchouc" of the first quality, recourse must be had to other trees which produce an inferior article.

Cotton appears to be the next principal product of the fertile soil of Brazil; and is mostly of very superior quality—scarcely inferior to Sea-Island. It is grown in the provinces of Pernambuco, Maranham, and some others, in the north; but its cultivation does not, from some reason, experience the same rapidity of increased amount, as is found to exist in sugar and coffee. The exports of this article are chiefly made to Great Britain.

Tobacco, of an inferior quality, is grown on the islands of the Bay ot Rio Janeiro, and some few other places; it is, however, quite an unimportant article, and by no means can be considered as a Brazilian staple. Rice is largely cultivated; Mandioca, however, is the main dependence of the people.

The tea plant can be cultivated with success, as the soil and climate has been found favorable to its production. But still little attention is paid to its culture or increase, as labor here is neither as abundant or cheap, as in China, which renders all attempts at competition unsuccessful.

The extensive forests of Brazil furnish almost every variety of useful and ornamental woods, in requisition for ship-building, carpenters' work, and dyeing. Drugs of a great variety are procured in Brazil. One of the most celebrated and valuable of its trees is the "Cæsalpina Brazilletto," yielding a beautiful red dye. It was from the abundance of this wood, found by the early navigators, that the country received the name of Brazil. It is found in great abundance and fine quality in Pernambuco; but being a government monopoly, it has been cut down so improvidently, that it is now seldom seen within several leagues of the coast. The carassato, or castor tree, is indigenous, and much cultivated for the sake of the oil extracted from its seeds, in general use for lamps, and other purposes. Rosewood is plentiful, and cocoa is in general use among the people, and forms one of the chief articles of the internal trade. The nuts of Brazil, also, form an article of trade, though not of any great importance.

The Brazilian forests are full of rapacious animals; among which are the tiger-cat; the hyæna; the saratu, an animal about the size of a fox, but far more ferocious; the jaguar, or tiger of South America; the sloth, and the porcupine. The planters are much annoyed by ounces; wild hogs are common, and the singular animal called the anta or tapir: the latter resembles the hog in shape, but is much larger; it is, in fact, the largest of the native quadrupeds, timid and harmless, is amphibious, and capable of remaining for a long time at the bottom of the lakes, without coming up to respire. When killed its flesh is generally eaten, and is said to differ but little from that of the ox.

European domestic animals are abundant; the increase, especially of the ox and horse, has been astonishingly great. Vast herds of wild cattle are met with in all the open parts of the country, especially on the llanos, or plains, in the southern provinces. Sheep have not increased so rapidly.

The "emu," or American ostrich, is found in the plains, and the forests swarm with innumerable varieties of birds, monkeys, &c. In the marshy countries the boa constrictor attains an enormous size, and they are also infested with the coral-snake, and other venomous reptiles. The beauty and variety of the insect tribe is astonishing; the air is actually alive with all the colors of the rainbow, from the prevalence of these beautiful creatures.

The Brazilian birds are distinguished for the variety and splendor of their plumage. Red, blue and green parrots frequent the tops of the trees. The *jaccos*, the *hoccos*, and different kinds of pigeons, fill the woods. The orioles resort to the orange groves, and their sentinels, stationed at a distance, announce with a screaming noise the approach of man. Chattering manakins mislead the hunter, and the metallic tones of the Uraponga resound through the forest, like the strokes of a hammer on an anvil. The toucan (*Anser Americanus*) is prized for its feathers, which are of a lemon and bright red color, with transversal black stripes reaching to the extremities of its wings. The different species of humming-birds are more numerous in Brazil than in any other country of America. One sort of these beautiful little birds is called by the people the *Gnanthê engera*, or winged flower. Naturalists have observed in the woods more than ten species of wild bees; many of which produce honey of an aromatic flavor. If the inhabitants were more industrious, cochineal might be exported with profit, for the *Cactus coccinellifer*, and the insect peculiar to it, are found in the province of San Paulo.

Manufactures, unless we call the preparation of sugar and caoutchouc manufactures, can hardly be said to exist in Brazil; and are restricted to the production of the coarsest cloths, the tanning of leather, and a few of those that are most simple and necessary; but a great number of trades are carried on. "The European stranger at Rio," says Dr. Von Spix, (*Travels*, vol. i., 198,) "is astonished at the number of gold and silver smiths and jewellers, who, like the other tradesmen, live together in one street, which calls to mind the magnificent *Ruas de Ouro* and *de Prata*, of Lisbon. The workmanship of these artizans is, indeed, inferior to that of the European, but is not destitute of taste and solidity. Many trades, which are necessary in Europe, are, at present, almost superfluous in the interior of the country, on account of the circumscribed wants of the inhabitants. In the capital, however, and the other towns on the coast, joiners, whitesmiths, and other artizans, are numerous; but tanners, soap-boilers, and workers in steel, are scarce. There is great demand for mechanics to build sugar and other mills, to construct machines for working the gold mines, &c., and very high wages are paid them. Hitherto no china, glass, cloth, or hat manufactures, have been established in the capital; and their erection would not be advisable in a country which can obtain the productions of European industry on the lowest terms, in exchange for the produce of its rich soil."

The commerce of Brazil is very extensive; her existing commercial system is one of great freedom and liberality, and is well-calculated to accelerate the development of her resources. The duties on exports and imports are moderate, and are imposed for the sake of *revenue alone, and not for prohibition.*

The *imports* comprise all sorts of manufactured goods, suitable for the people and climate, particularly cottons, linens, woollens and hardware, from England; flour, provisions and coarse cottons, from the United States; wines, silk, salt, brandy, &c., from France and Portugal; linens, lace, &c., from Hamburg, &c., &c. But the largest and most valuable of all the articles imported does not appear in the lists of imports. According to a convention entered into between England and Brazil, the import of slaves should have ceased in 1830. Far, however, from this being the case, the importation is carried on with greater safety, and in greater numbers at present than at any former period; it is difficult, however, on such a subject to get at anything like accurate information; but it is ascertained that between 70 and 80,000 negroes are annually brought into the country. Whatever may be the result of this prodigious importation of Africans, there appears but little hope of its reduction. The boundless extent of fertile and uncultivated lands in Brazil, are admirably suited for the growth of the great staples, and the increasing demand for these, and the sparseness of the present population, constitute irresistible temptations to the enterprising planter; while the shortness of the voyage, and the facilities which the coast affords for secure landing, enable them to be introduced with an ease and expedition unknown anywhere else. By making the trade piracy, and ordaining capital punishment to offenders, might check it somewhat, but nothing short of this will ever be found effectual in suppressing this inhuman traffic.

The *exports* have chiefly been enumerated in the account of the productions of the country. Coffee, sugar, cotton and gum elastic, are the principal; hides, and other animal products; gold and diamonds; cabinet and dye woods, drugs, gums, nuts, &c., are those of secondary importance. The export trade is chiefly carried on with the United States, England, Hamburg, &c.

The following is a statement of the commerce between the United States and Brazil, for the years 1830–'47 inclusive—showing the amount of foreign and United States tonnage employed, and the value of the imports and exports, to and from Brazil:

	American Tonnage.		Foreign Tonnage.		*Value of Imports into United States.*	*Value of Exports from United States.*
Years.	*Entered.*	*Cleared.*	*Entered.*	*Cleared.*		
1830	38,005	44,450	248	601	$2,491,460	$1,843,239
1831	29,855	36,892	1,360	203	2,375,829	2,076,095
1832	31,222	30,439	3,314	356	3,890,845	2,054,794
1833	35,024	49,736	208	1,017	5,089,693	3,272,101
1834	34,900	37,092	3,089	1,977	4,729,989	2,059,351
1835	34,720	39,269	753	2,554	5,574,466	2,508,656
1836	39,259	45,533	4,341	3,062	7,210,190	3,094,936
1837	25,122	19,576	5,766	4,107	4,991,983	1,743,209
1838	23,037	30,623	276	1,601	3,191,238	2,657,194
1839	34,457	39,431	2,367	3,183	5,292,955	2,637,485
1840	32,588	34,189	5,578	1,764	4,297,296	2,506,574
1841	41,684	47,604	4,503	3,101	6,302,653	3,517,273
1842	37,058	38,778	5,593	2,643	5,948,814	2,601,502
1843	32,466	32,066	2,179	1,395	3,947,658	1,792,288
1844	48,550	46,250	14,802	1,816	6,883,806	2,818,252
1845	50.230	40,716	2,481	2,077	6,084,599	2,837,950
1846	61,014	48,026	4,952	4,682	7,441,803	3,142,395
1847	—	—	—	—	7,096,160	2,566,938

The weights and measures of Brazil are the same as those in use in Portugal. The currency consists almost entirely of copper, or paper issued by the government. The smallest value is one ree, corresponding to one-half mill of the United States currency, and the smallest coin is of ten rees; the largest, of eighty, or four vintens. One thousand rees make a milree; the smallest paper note, about equal in value to half a dollar There are various issues, from one milree to a thousand. Except at Rio, and upon the remote frontiers, gold and silver will not circulate. The amount of bills in the province of Para, is never adequate to the wants of the people, and their tendency is always to the city. Furthermore, by the operations of the government, even the little currency that is floating is constantly fluctuating in value; and, but a few years since, one milree was nearly or quite equivalent in value to one dollar in silver.

Brazil is divided into 18 provinces, for the purposes of district government, with as many presidents to administer their affairs, and subdivided into comarcas. The following statement of the area, population, and chief town of each province, is taken from the Weimar Almanac, 1839:

Provinces.	Area in Square Miles.	Population.	Chief Towns.
1. Para	530,000	143,073	Para.
2. Rio Negro	424,000	48,237	Barcellos.
3. Maranham	68,073	182,986	San Luis de Maranham.
4. Piauhi	60,547	46,296	Oeiras.
5. Ceara	70,193	272,713	Aracate.
6. Rio Grande do Norte	31,227	68,736	Natal.
7. Parahyba	19,768	246,232	Parahyba.
8. Pernambuco	29,935	602,205	Pernambuco.
9. Alagoas	19,292	256,956	Porto Calvo.
10. Seregippe del Rey	18,147	267,523	Seregippe.
11. Bahia	154,675	559,650	Bahia or San Salvador.
12. Espiritu Santo	37,905	73,996	Vittoria.
13. Rio Janeiro	189,316	589,650	Rio Janeiro.
14. San Paulo	191,012	610,632	San Paulo.
15. Minas Geraes	253,573	928,933	Villa Rica.
16. Goyaz	313,760	150,000	Villa Boa.
17. Matto-Grosso	426,459	82,000	Villa Bella.
18. Fernando	1,060	600	—
Total	2,738,942	5,130,418	

The above table can be but little relied upon, as it presents many blunders, perceptible at once by any one acquainted with the several districts, and it omits altogether the provinces of Porto Seguro, San Catarina, and Rio Grande do Sul; the two latter, however, are subject to Rio Janeiro, and may be included in its estimates. It is, however, the best and only one attainable, and has been re-published in all works treating upon the subject without remark. These provinces may be divided into—1. The provinces on the northern coast: Para, Maranham, Piauhi, Ceara, Rio Grande do Norte, Parahyba, Pernambuco, Seregippe del Rey, and Bahia. 2. The provinces on the southern coast: Porto Seguro, Espiritu Santo, Rio de Janeiro, San Paulo, San Catarina, and Rio Grande do Sul. 3. The provinces of the interior: Minas Geraes, Para (partly,) San Paulo (partly,) Matto-Grosso, and Goyaz.

The actual population of Brazil is not known; it has been variously stated.—Cannabich, upon the authority of documents existing in the empire, stated, in 1830, the amount at 5,735,000; Malte-Brun estimates it, for the same year, at 5,340,000. Balbi computes the total at 5,300,000, subdivided as follows:

Portuguese or Fihlos do Reino, Creoles, &c.	900,000
Mestizos (free) and Mulattoes	600,000
" (slaves)	250,000
Free Negroes	180,000
Negro Slaves	2,926,500
Converted Indians	300,000
Independent Indians, European Settlers, &c.	150,000

But we are satisfied that the highest of these estimates is very decidedly under the mark, especially in regard to the number of negro slaves, and that the population of Brazil may, at present, be safely estimated at 7,000,000.

In Brazil, unlike the Spanish and English colonies, there is hardly any political division of castes, and very few of those galling and degrading distinctions, which have been made by all other nations in the management of their colonies. The mildness of the laws affecting the colored population are remarkable. Amalgamation is permitted, and is not at all unfrequent.

It will be seen, from the previous table, that the number of aborigines is very inconsiderable, and the diseases introduced by Europeans are said to produce a fearful mortality among them. Shortly after the settlements were first made, an epidemic smallpox broke out among them, and swept off two-thirds of the population.

The *Brazileros,* or native Brazilians—those born of Portuguese parents in Brazil—amount to about 600,000; they appear to inherit all the idleness and inactivity of their European ancestors. The *Creoles,* are those born in Brazil, of African mothers; the *Mamlucos,* are the offspring of the Whites and Indians; the *Curibocos,* of Negroes and Indians; and the *Cubros,* of the Mulattoes and Negroes.

Our remarks have hitherto been confined to the European and other settlers in Brazil; but there are besides many indigenous tribes, that have been designated by Portuguese writers under the general name of Anthropophagi. These savages, delighting in cruelty, became, under the government of the Jesuits, social, peaceable, and humane; the indefatigable perseverance of their missionaries surmounted the greatest obstacles. The natives are strong and well made, their complexion is copper-colored, their hair is black and sleek. Mr. Mawe saw a native chief, and fifty of his followers, in Canta Gallo, a district northward of Rio Janeiro; the dress of the men consisted of a waistcoat and pair of drawers, the women wore a shift and petticoat, with a handkerchief tied round the head after the fashion of the Portuguese; the whole party seemed to be in a wretched condition, and depended chiefly for a subsistence on the produce of the chase. Their skill in the use of the bow was much admired: Mr. Mawe placed some oranges at the distance of thirty yards, and they did not miss one; he next showed them a banana tree, about eight inches in circumference, at the distance of forty yards, and every man struck it with his arrow. Astonished by these repeated proofs of their address, he went with some of them to the chase; they observed the birds sooner than he did; they crept with great ease through thickets and brushwood, and never failed to bring down their game. They ate their meat raw, and were not at the trouble of plucking the feathers from their wild fowl. Like most savages, they are very fond of spirituous liquors; if rum be given them, they generally quarrel about it, as each man wishes to have more than his neighbor. Their great aversion to labor prevents them from cultivating the ground, or from working for hire; even the gold and silver, with which their country abounds, are never sought for by the natives. The savages observed by Mr. Mawe belonged probably to the tribe of the Boticudos, who live in the eastern mountains of Minas Geraes. Although they were several times conquered, and very cruelly treated by the Paulistas, the first people that penetrated into their territory, they still maintain their independence and defend their possessions. Being unable to contend openly against the Portuguese, they have recourse to stratagem; they sometimes conceal themselves among the branches of trees, and watch an opportunity of discharging their arrows against a negro or European traveller: at other times they dig pits, fill them with pointed stakes, and cover them with twigs and leaves. After having marked out a house, and ascertained its strength, they set it on fire, and fall upon its unfortunate inhabitants while they are attempting to escape. They bear an implacable hatred against the negroes, and evince much delight in eating them: but they are terrified by fire-arms, and betake themselves to flight on hearing the report of a gun. Such as are taken prisoners cannot be subdued either by stripes or kindness; many, despairing of ever being able to regain their freedom, refuse sustenance, and perish from hunger. Don Pedro, when prince regent, published a proclamation, commanding them to live in villages, and to become Christians; they were offered his protection if they complied, and threatened with a war of extermination in the event of their refusal. It had no effect.

The Puris inhabit a country in the neighborhood of the Boticudos; they still resist the Brazilians, and an eye-witness informs us, that they roast and eat their prisoners. The Tupis, who occupied at one time the whole of San tos and San Paulo, are now reduced to a few wandering bands, that inhabit the confines of the Argentine provinces on the Uruguay. They speak a dialect of the Guarani language, which is widely spread over all the interior and southern districts of Brazil. The Carigais, or southern neighbors of the Tupis, are considered the most peaceable of the native tribes. The country of the Tupinaquis extended from the river Guirican to the river Camama, and the Topinambos inhabited the coast between the Camama and the San Francisco do Norte; but these two tribes, and several others, are now either extinct, or mingled with the Portuguese settlers. Some travellers have confounded with the Topinambos two or three fierce and wandering tribes on the banks of the Tocantins. The Petivares are scattered over the north-eastern districts of Brazil; many among them are partly civilized, and acquainted with agriculture. The Molagagos, a wandering tribe on the banks of the Paraguay, are remarkable for their fair complexion and lofty stature. The tribes on the banks of the Amazon are the Pauxis, the Urubaquis, the Aycuaris, the Yomnais, and many others, whose names need not be enumerated. The Cuiabas and Buiazas occupy the central mountains of Matto-Grosso; and the Parexis have given their name to an extensive district in South America. The Barbados, on the banks of the Sypotuba, are distinguished by their long beards from the other natives of the new continent. Some of the numerous tribes formerly concentrated on the fertile banks of the Paraguay, have been dispersed or destroyed by the Spaniards, the Portuguese, or the Paulistas; others, at the approach of foreign invaders, fled into countries less favored by nature, and several thousand natives were removed by the Jesuits to their settlements on the Uruguay and the Parana. So great a number of them entered into alliances with the Portuguese and Spaniards, that there is hardly a man on the frontiers whose countenance does not indicate the traces of his Indian descent. The Guaycoros, or Indian horsemen, are renowned for their strength and courage among the aborigines, on the banks of the Paraguay. They occupy both sides of the river, from the Taquari and the mountains of Albuquerque to a distance of a hundred leagues. Armed with bows and long lances, they wage war against the Spaniards and Portuguese; and although often defeated in battle, they have never been completely subdued. The Guaycoros make excursions into the neighboring countries for the purpose of procuring horses in exchange for coarse cotton goods, which they themselves manufacture.

The inhabitants of many countries in South America form a remarkable exception to the famous system of the influence of climate on the physical character of man. A feeble and peaceful people dwelt on the cold mountains of Peru; a hardy and warlike race wandered under the burning sun of Brazil. Their enemies, notwithstanding the great advantage which they have derived from the use of fire-arms, cannot boast of having subdued them. They have never been vanquished by raw or undisciplined troops, and the cause of their defeat has been attributed to dissensions amongst themselves, and to their ignorance of European warfare. "The Province St. Vincent," say the Portuguese writers, "was conquered by the famous Tebireza; that of Bahia by the valiant Toebira, and that of Pernambuco by Stagiba, whose name in the Indian language signifies an arm of iron. We have gained Para and Maranham by the efforts of the famous Tomagia and the invincible Camarao, who immortalized himself at the re-taking of Pernambuco, in the war against the Dutch."

The Brazilian Indians are chiefly distinguished for their bravery and bodily strength; when suffering excruciating pain, they brave their tormentors, and boast that they may take away their lives, but that they can never deprive them of their courage. Lery and his companions could not stretch the bows used by the Indians of Tamoy, in the neighborhood of Rio de Janeiro; and the same writer confesses that he was obliged to use all his strength in stretching a bow which belonged to a boy about ten years of age. The inhabitants of Ouctacazes, one of the most fertile districts in the government of Brazil, are so valiant, that, according to the statement of a Portuguese writer, they suffer death rather than endure the disgrace of being vanquished; they have never been defeated by the Brazilians, nor even by the Europeans; they consider slavery an intolerable evil. These savages, at one time formidable enemies of the colonists, have proved themselves of late years faithful allies to the settlers in the *Campos dos Ouctacazes*, in Minas Geraes. The natives have resisted the arms, but submitted to the mild and generous policy of the Portuguese.

The Guarani, or, as many writers term it, the Brazilian language, is the one most generally known by the natives. Its different dialects are spoken by different tribes; and its primitives are unlike any of Asiatic origin. Some have affirmed, that there is a resemblance between it and certain dialects spoken by the South Sea Islanders; but it is agreed on all hands, that no American language has so little analogy with any other known tongue. The syntax of its particles, moods and tenses, is very different from that of European languages. It has two affirmative and two negative conjugations, and its active and neuter verbs are not conjugated in the same manner. A great number of adverbs, or rather syllables placed at the end of words, serve to mark different shades of meaning. Many substantives express the definition or sense attached to them, thus, *Tupa*, or God, signifies literally, Who is he? The word *couna*, or woman, resembles the *kona* of the Scandinavians; but this analogy is of no consequence, for the proper meaning of *couna* is a nimble tongue. However widely diffused this language may be, it does not extend over the whole of Brazil; the learned Hervas has proved, from the manuscripts of the Portuguese Jesuits, that there were fifty-one tribes in the central and northern parts of that country, whose dialects were not formed from the Guarani language; and he has likewise traced a resemblance between some of these dialects, and those spoken by the Caribs.

Rio de Janeiro, or simply Rio, is the capital of the country, and the largest and most important commercial city in South America. It lies on the west side of one of the finest bays in the world, in lat. 22° 54′ 15″ S. and long. 43° 15′ 50″ W. The population is said to be 200,000, one half of which are whites, and the remainder Negro slaves and the mixed races. The city, which is in the shape of a parallelogram, is laid out on level ground, at the foot of hills, and has a handsome appearance from the harbor. The general style of architecture is mean: the streets are, however, well laid out, intersecting each other at right angles, and paved with blocks of granite, with water courses in the centre. The houses, which are of granite and wood, are only two stories high, rough and whitewashed, and covered with red tiles. There are about 40 churches in the city, but in general they are indifferent structures. The Cathedral of Nossa Senhora da Gloria, on a lofty hill, on the south side of the city, is a conspicuous object from a distance, and especially from the bay. There are several convents: a *misericordia*, with a hospital attached; a foundling hospital; and various other religious and charitable institutions.

The royal palace forms two sides of a *largo* or oblong space, opening to the bay, near the principal landing place. It consists, partly, of the old palace of the viceroys and partly of an old Carmelite convent, and is wholly destitute of architectural beauty. Among the other public buildings may be specified, a new and handsome theatre, the exchange, the old Jesuit's college, the Episcopal palace and royal villa of Christovia, in the environs. There are also sundry lyceums and schools, and a great many private and licenced academies. Among the principal educational institutions, are the college of surgery, military and commercial schools, an academy of arts and a national museum. An extensive botanic garden adorns the suburbs, and near the palace is the public library, containing from 50,000 to 70,000 volumes. Several daily and weekly papers are published at Rio, but they are said to be, without exception, the most worthless publications of their class anywhere to be met with.

The police and health of the city have been materially improved during the last twenty years. Water is conveyed into the city by means of a magnificent aqueduct, constructed in 1740, from a neigboring lofty hill, called the Corcovado. Rio is very indifferently lighted, and the accommodations for strangers are inadequate and mostly inferior. The market-place consists of a collection of filthy booths, for the sale of vegetables, which are abundant, excellent and cheap. Butchers' meat is sold in shops, scattered up and down the city.

The harbor of Rio is one of the finest in the world: its entrance is marked by a remarkable hill, in the form of a sugar-loaf, 900 feet in height, close to its west side; while, on the other side of the bay, one mile and a half distant, is the fort of Santa Cruz, on which is a light-house: there is also a light-house on Isla Raza, about ten miles south from the mouth of the harbor. There are about 100 small islets lying on the bosom of the bay, like stars bespangling the blue sky. Ships may enter day or night, as there are no obstructions or dangers to dread. The largest ships may safely ride in this extensive bay, which is capacious enough to accommodate the shipping of all nations. The arsenal, the dock-yard and marine establishments, are on a small island within the harbor.

The commerce of Rio is very extensive, and has increased rapidly during the last few years. It is now by far the greatest mart for the export of coffee. The shipments of this important article, which, in 1830, amounted to only 396,785 bags, have increased with such an unexampled rapidity, that, in 1847 they amounted to 1,626,857 bags, that is (taking the bag at 154 lbs.) to 250,535,978 lbs.; being more than equal to all the exports of coffee from all other ports of the world! Of this amount, the United States received 721,217 bags, and all Europe 897,434 bags. The exports of this article, in 1847, show an increase over those of 1846, of 127,612 bags. Sugar is also an important export from Rio: the other great exports are hides, rice, tobacco, rum, tapioca, ipecacuanha, manioc flour, &c.; the export of cotton has almost entirely ceased; and that of gold and diamonds is almost clandestine. The average aggregate value of the exports of Rio is about 30,000,000 reis yearly.

The currency of Rio and of Brazil generally, is in a very vitiated state, and since the substitution of copper and paper for silver, has declined more than one-half in value.

The other principal towns are San Catarina, in the province of the same name, which has from 5 to 6,000 inhabitants: the principal ports in this district are, Laguna and San Francisco; Portalegre, in Rio Grande do Sul, and its port San Pedro, the population of which is about 1,200; the seaports of Victoria, Espiritu Santo and Puerto Seguro; Bahia, or San Salvador, the harbor of which is magnificent; Pernambuco, which owes its importance to its trade in cotton,—population 70,000, and many others, both on the coast and inland, which the space, allotted to this article, prevents a further mention of.

The greatest want of Brazil, at the present time, appears to be a good system of elementary education. Hitherto, most schools established in the empire, have been under the direction of ecclesiastics, alike bigoted and uninstructed, and the increase of such schools could only be an additional misfortune to the country. Luckily, however, the influence of the clergy is becoming day by day diminished, and several respectable academies have been opened in the large cities, uninfluenced by the church. But, speaking generally, there are as yet no means in Brazil by which even the children of the middle classes can acquire anything like a really good and useful education. Till some efficient measures be really taken to supply this defect, but little improvement need be looked for, either in the morals or literature of the people.

The literature of Brazil, from the foregoing statement, may be said to be as yet in its infancy. Until 1808, there had not been a printing-press in the country, nor a newspaper to record the passing events of its history. It is a curious fact, that forty years ago, not a single paper was published in a country which has now forty, regularly issued. The first work of importanec published in Brazil, however, did not appear until 1817. It was the "Corografia Brazilica, ou Relaçao historico-geographico do Reino do Brazil," by Manoel Ayres de Cazal, printed at Rio, in 2 vols. 4to. The few works written by Brazilians, prior to the introduction of the press, were printed at Lisbon.

Minas Geraes has produced a poet in the person of Gonzaga, whose songs are extremely popular among the people. His poems, chiefly lyrical, under the title of "Marilla de Dirces," por T. A. E.," were published at Bahia, in three parts, and have gone through numerous editions. When Brazil shall one day have a literature of its own, Gonzaga "will have the glory of having attempted the first Anacreontic tones of the lyre on the banks of the pastoral Rio Grande, and of the romantic Jequitinhonho."

Notwithstanding Pedro I. established two universities, literature appears to have made no progress in Brazil. All the literary talent, such as it is, is monopolized by the newspapers, though none of them are conducted with anything of ability approaching those of England or the United States, nor is the circulation sufficient for their support. There are no books issued with advantage to the publishers, but such, as in most countries, would be indicted by a grand jury; while the "Art of being Happy," a translation from a French work, was left to sleep on the shelves of the vender, the "Art of Stealing" was bought up as fast as it could be prepared; and, at the present day, there is scarcely a house in Brazil that does not contain this manual of morals and shadow of Brazilian morality. Such is the literature of Brazil; there Paul de Kock might luxuriate.

The established religion of Brazil is the Roman Catholic; but all other religions are tolerated. The Jews were the first settlers, and are still a numerous body. One of the chief sects at Rio is that known under the name of "Sebastianistas," in honor of the patron saint of the city; their chief point of faith is the re-appearance of King Don Sebastian of Portugal, killed in the disastrous battle of Alcaçarquiver, in 1578, who they suppose did not perish, but are firmly persuaded that he is still alive! This, in fact, was long the popular belief in Portugal.

The affairs of the church are under the superintendence of the Archbishop of Bahia; the bishops of Rio, Pernambuco, Maranham, Para and San Paulo, and two "prelacias" with episcopal powers, at Goyaz and Cuyaba. Monasteries and nunneries are extremely numerous in many parts of Brazil. The Saints' days are celebrated with as much splendor at Rio as at Rome itself; and the "Intrudu," or Carnival, is magnificently kept. Measures, however, have been taken to reduce the number of monastic institutions; the revenues of some revert to the crown at a stated time, and no new establishments are to be founded.

The Army and Navy of the empire are on a respectable footing. The land forces amount to 60,000 or 65,000 men; of which 15,000 are regular troops, the remainder consists of regular and local militia—the first of which may be sent on foreign service, but the latter are constituted to protect the provinces, and put down internal disorders. The navy numbers 1 ship of the line, 5 frigates, 6 corvettes, 13 schooners, 4 war steamers, &c.; but they are said to be in a very inefficient state.

The revenue is chiefly derived from duties on exports and imports; from tenths and duties on sales of lands and houses; the mining duties and the revenue of the diamond districts. The whole amounts to the sum of about 18,000,000 dollars annually. The national debt is near $100,000,000, the interest on which consumes near one-third of the revenue, and the army and navy another third.

Prior to 1808, Brazil was merely a Portuguese colony, but when John IV. came to reside in Rio, it was raised to the dignity of an independent monarchy. In 1822, Don Pedro was declared emperor, and in 1824, the present constitution was promulgated and sworn to. The spirit of this constitution is monarchial. The legislature consists of two chambers; a senate, appointed by the emperor, and a house of representatives, elected by the people. The ministers of the emperor are responsible, and may be impeached. Any elector is eligible to become a representative, provided he has a certain net revenue. The number of senators is 54, and of deputies, 548; they receive salaries. The parliamentary term is quartennial, and each annual sitting lasts four months. The executive power is delegated to six ministers, under whose control are placed all matters connected with the interior, foreign affairs, justice, marine, war, and finance. A respectable diplomatic and consular system has been established. There is also a "nobility" in Brazil, the only artificial manufacture of the kind in America;

in 1837, it was composed of 16 marquises, 6 counts, 19 viscounts, 20 barons, and 13 "*ladies*." The titles are not hereditary.

The judiciary of Brazil is a mere farce, being entangled by a system of delay and expense, that completely abandons the poor to the will and power of the rich. The prosecution of criminals is left entirely to the parties injured, and it is not unfrequent that crimes go unpunished, the parties being unwilling to undergo the trouble and expense of prosecution. In this state of things "Lynch Law" is too often resorted to, and private revenge supplies the place of public justice. The laws are also complex and unsatisfactory; indeed, everything has yet to be done in these matters.

The discovery of Brazil, has, by some, been attributed to Martin Behem, who is said to have visited the coast so early as 1484; but the better opinion has allowed the merit, if it can properly be so called, of having first seen this part of South America, to Pedro Alvarez Cabral. Emanuel, king of Portugal, had equipped a squadron of 13 sail, carrying 1,200 soldiers and sailors, for a voyage to the East Indies, under the command of Cabral. The admiral, quitting Lisbon on the 9th of March, 1500, struck out to sea to avoid the storms of the Cape of Good Hope; and, steering his course southward, fell in, accidentally, on the 24th of April, with the continent of South America, which he at first supposed to be a large island on the coast of Africa. In this conjecture he was soon undeceived, when the natives came in sight. Having discovered a good harbor, he anchored his vessels, and called the bay Puerto Seguro. On the next day he sent a boat on shore, and, having secured two of the natives, treated them so kindly, that when they were set free, their report drew their countrymen to the beach, where they welcomed the Portuguese with shouts and rejoicings. Cabral then landed with a body of troops, and having erected the cross, and celebrated high mass under the spreading branches of a lofty tree, he took possession of the country in the name of his sovereign. In token of the cross which he had thus erected, he called the land Santa Cruz; but the name was afterwards altered by King Emanuel to that of Brazil, after the red wood which the country produces so abundantly.

Having conceived a high idea of the fertility, and other natural advantages of the country, Cabral despatched a ship to Lisbon, with an account of the event. The Portuguese, however, notwithstanding the flattering report of Cabral, entertained for some time no very favorable opinion of the country, having found, by a survey of the coast, and of the rivers and bays, that it afforded neither gold nor silver, the great objects of ambition in those days; and, accordingly, they sent none thither but convicts, and women of abandoned character. Two ships were annually sent from Portugal, to carry to the new world the refuse of the human race, and to receive from thence cargoes of parrots and dye-woods. Ginger was afterwards added, but, in a short time, prohibited, lest the cultivation of it might interfere with the sale of the same article from India. In 1548, the Jews, many of whom had taken refuge in Portugal, were persecuted by the Inquisition, and banished to Brazil. Here they would probably have perished, but for the assistance of some enterprising friends, with whom they had been formerly connected, and who enabled them to procure sugar canes from Madeira, and to begin the cultivation of that article. The court of Lisbon, notwithstanding its prejudices against the settlers of Brazil, began to perceive that a colony might be beneficial to the mother-country, without producing gold or silver; and, like other mother-countries, having left the colony to struggle, unassisted, through the difficulties of the first settlement, sent over a governor to regulate and superintend it, as soon as those difficulties were surmounted. Thomas de Souza, a wise and able man, was the first governor. Notwithstanding the talents he possessed, De Souza found it very difficult to succeed in inducing the natives, who were dispersed through the forests and plains, to associate with each other, to fix on settled habitations, and to submit to the Portuguese government. Dissatisfaction ensued, which at length terminated in war. Souza did not bring with him a sufficient number of men to conclude hostilities speedily. By building St. Salvador, in 1549, at the Bay of All-Saints, he established a central and rallying point for the colony; but the great object of reducing the Indians to submission was effected by the Jesuits, who, insinuating themselves among the savages, and gaining their affections by presents and acts of kindness, brought them to regard the Portuguese as a humane and benevolent people.

The increasing prosperity of Brazil, which became visible to Europe at the beginning of the 17th century, excited the envy of the French, Spaniards, and Dutch, successively. The latter, however, were the principal enemies with whom the Portuguese had to contend, for the dominion of Brazil. Their admiral, Willekins, was, in 1624, detached with a powerful squadron, and a considerable number of soldiers and marines; and, having cast anchor before St. Salvador, he landed his forces, expelled the inhabitants, and took possession of the town, and of the whole country, in the name of the United Provinces. His first act was the publication of a manifesto, in the name of the States, allowing liberty of conscience to all who were willing to take an oath of fidelity to the Republic of Holland. Having plundered the people of St. Salvador of their wealth, he returned to Europe, leaving Colonel Van Dort, as governor, with a strong garrison for his support. The Spaniards next sent a formidable fleet, under Frederic de Toledo, manned with 12,000 soldiers and marines, who, immediately on their arrival, laid siege to San Salvador, and compelled the Dutch to surrender, after an obstinate resistance, and the loss of its governor, Van Dort. When the affairs of the Dutch assumed a more favorable aspect at home, they despatched Admiral Henry Lonk, in the beginning of 1630, with 46 men of war, to attempt the entire conquest of Brazil. After several obstinate engagements, he succeeded in reducing Pernambuco, one of the most considerable and best fortified provinces of the country. Having returned to Europe, he left behind him troops, which reduced, in the years 1633, 1634, and 1635, the three provinces of Temeraca, Paraiba, and Rio Grande. These, as well as Pernambuco, furnished yearly a large quantity of sugar, a great deal of wood for dyeing, and other commodities. The Dutch were so elated with the acquisition of wealth which flowed from the sale of these productions, that they determined to conquer all Brazil, and entrusted Maurice of Nassau, with the direction of the enterprise. This distinguished officer reached the place of his destination in the beginning of 1637. He found his soldiers well disciplined, and their commanders experienced and able men. He was successively opposed by Albuquerque, Banjola, Lewis Rocca de Borgia, and by Cameron, a Brazilian, who was devotedly attached to the Portuguese, and who wanted no qualification necessary to a general, but to have learned the art of war under able officers. These commanders exerted their utmost efforts to defend the possessions under their protection, but their endeavors proved ineffectual. The Dutch seized upon Seara, Seregippe, and the greater part of Bahia. Seven of the 15 provinces which composed the colony, had already submitted to them, and they flattered themselves that one or two campaigns would make them masters of the remainder, when they were suddenly checked by the revolution, which banished Philip IV. from the throne of Portugal, and gave to the Portuguese independence, and a native sovereign. The seven provinces of Brazil, which had remained unsubdued, imitated the example of the mother-country, by throwing off the Spanish yoke. The Dutch, then, as enemies of the Spaniards, became friends to the Portuguese. The two parties soon came to an agreement. The Dutch relinquished that part of Brazil which they had not conquered, to the Portuguese, and the latter, in their turn, confirmed the title of the Dutch to the seven provinces of which they were in actual possession. This division gave rise to the name of the Brazils, in place of the former appellation. The Dutch government soon began to oppress the Portuguese colonists, who took up arms in self-defence; and, after an obstinate contest, and without an open support from the mother-country, drove them out of several of the provinces. Finding they were not able to retain possession of the country, the Dutch entered into a treaty, by which they ceded all their interest to the Portuguese, for a pecuniary compensation. The dominion of Portugal was now extended over all Brazil, which was honored by giving title to the presumptive heir of the crown. During the 18th century, Brazil remained in the peaceful possession of the Portuguese, with no other exception than the transient occupation of the fortress of St. Sacrament, by the Spaniards, which was restored soon afterwards by the treaty of peace.

From that period until the beginning of the present century, no event of importance appears to have occurred in Brazilian history. In the year 1806, Portugal having been invaded by the French, the royal family, to escape the danger of captivity, embarked for Brazil, under convoy of a British squadron, which was at that time blockading the mouth of the Tagus. From the moment of their arrival at Brazil, a revolution took place in the character and situation of the country. From the station of a province, Brazil rose at once to the dignity and importance of an independent nation, and Portugal sunk from her ancient superiority to the appearance of a province. The consequences of this change were in the highest degree favorable to the prosperity of Brazil. Commerce was thrown open with other nations, and a sudden spring was given to improvement, which even the impolitic regulations of the court did not check. The revolutionary ferment which had displayed itself in other parts of South America, extended to Brazil. In 1817, an insurrection broke out in Pernambuco, which it was first supposed would spread over the whole country: but the port of Pernambuco being blockaded, and troops arriving from the surrounding provinces, the insurgents were overpowered, and their leaders executed.

The revolution of Portugal, in 1820, and the adoption of the constitution in 1821, recalled the king again to Lisbon. Soon after these events, a struggle commenced between the Portuguese, who wished to recover their former ascendency over Brazil, and the Brazilians, who were resolved to preserve their newly-acquired liberties, which ended in the complete separation of all connection, other than subsists with independent states, between the two countries. The government of Brazil having been entrusted to the crown prince, Don Pedro, he refused to admit the troops sent out by Portugal to support his authority, or obey the instructions of the king, his father. In the following year, 1822, Brazil was declared to be a free and independent state, and Don Pedro was proclaimed emperor. After many stormy debates, the project of a constitution, submitted by the emperor, was accepted; but the disputes between the emperor and deputies having continued, the former abdicated the throne in 1831, in favor of his infant son, Don Pedro II., and singular as it may appear, the rights of the latter have been scrupulously preserved. Brazil was recognized by Portugal as an independent empire, 7th September, 1825, and subsequently by the other nations of Europe.

Don Pedro II., the present emperor, was born 2d December, 1825, and therefore was not of age to govern the country, until 1842. A provisional government, or "Council of Regency," was formed on the abdication of Pedro I., consisting of three members, named by the Senate. This council was soon succeeded by another, but the power was shortly afterwards vested in an individual. The emperor assumed the powers on his attaining his majority, since which time the prosperity of Brazil has been onwards; its commerce has expanded, and in spite of the nefarious system pursued by those in authority, the resources of the empire have been developed in a most extraordinary degree.

GUAYANA.

This name was formerly applied to all that vast region of country which lies between the rivers Amazon and Orinoco; but since the revolt of the South Americans from colonial dependence, the greater portions (formerly Spanish and Portuguese Guayana) have been attached to the Republic of Venezuela and the Empire of Brazil. At present, the term Guayana, is confined to the colonies of England, France and Holland, which occupy but a small strip of coast, and some inland territory, between lat. 8° 40′ and 4° N., and long. 57° 30′ and 60° W.

BRITISH GUAYANA,

(ESSEQUIBO, DEMERARA AND BERBICE,)

Occupies the most westerly portion of this region, and comprises more than one half of the territory. It is separated from the Dutch colony by the river Corentyn, having Venezuela on the north and west, and Brazil on the south, the exact boundaries of which are not well defined. The whole territory is said to have an area of 76,000 square miles, but the title to a great portion of this is disputed by Venezuela and Brazil.

The physical geography of this country presents an alluvial flat, extending from the coast inland, varying in breadth from 10 to 40 miles, and terminating at the foot of a range of sand hills from 30 to 130 feet high. The inland country is traversed by several ranges of mountains, which frequently rise 1,000 to 5,000 feet above the ocean. These chains form many rapids and cataracts in the greater rivers, and contain the sources of the Berbice and Mazaruni rivers. The highest point is Mount Roraima, lat. 5° 9′ 30″ N. and long. 60° 47′ W., which has an elevation of 7,500 feet. Between the first and second chains of hills are some extensive savannas, which approach the sea-shore, east of the river Berbice. With the exception of these savannas and the swamps of the Berbice, the interior is mostly covered with hill ranges and dense forests.

The principal rivers of the country flow in a northerly direction, following the general slope of the coast. The Essequibo rises in the mountains, 0° 40′ north of the equator, and after a course of about 600 miles, discharges its waters into the Atlantic, by an estuary, nearly 20 miles wide. Its entrance is impeded by shoals, and it is navigable for vessels only 50 miles from its mouth. The Corentyn rises in lat. 1° 30′ N. and long. 57° W., and enters the ocean about latitude 5° 30′. Between these are the rivers Berbice and Demerara; the former may be ascended for 165 miles, by vessels drawing seven feet of water: the latter is navigable 85 miles from its mouth. The Mazaruni, Cuyuni, &c., are affluents of the Essequibo, and of considerable size. All the large rivers bring down great quantities of detritus, which being deposited around their mouths and estuaries, renders the whole coast shoal. For 12 or 15 miles seaward, the mud bottom is covered by only three or four feet of water, in consequence of which, the approach to the coast is difficult, and at times, even to small boats, impracticable.

These deposits around the coasts rest upon deep strata of strong clay of different kinds, alternating with others of sand and beds of small shells; and these again on a granitic formation, which begins to appear on the surface of the second chain of mountains. The granite rocks, in the interior, sometimes assume the most astonishing and imposing shapes: mural precipices, with cascades, 1,400 or 1,500 feet high, descending over them, and granite boulders, of huge size, spread over immense tracts. A natural pyramid, called the Ataraipu, wooded to the height of 350 feet, rises in latitude 2° 55′ N., and from this point ascends in naked grandeur to a further elevation of 900 feet. The other chief rocks are porphyry, and various kinds of trap, gneiss, clay-slate, sandstone, colored ochres, &c.: there is a total absence of limestone and its modifications. Traces of iron are frequent, but none of the precious metals have been discovered. Next to granite, excellent pipe and other clays are the most valuable and useful mineral productions of the country.

Situated but a few degrees north of the equator, Guayana partakes essentially of the characteristics of a tropical climate. The mean temperature at Georgetown is 81° 2′ *Fahr.*, the maximum 90°, and the minimum 74°, on the coast. Two wet and two dry seasons constitute the changes of the year: the great dry season begins at the latter end of August, and continues to the end of November, after which, showers of rain follow till the end of January: the dry season thence commences, and lasts until the middle of August, when the rain comes down in torrents, and the swollen rivers, unable to retain their beds, break over their banks and inundate the country. During the rains, the winds generally blow from the west, and in the dry season mostly from the ocean, particularly in the day time. Hurricanes are unknown, gales unfrequent: thunder and lightning occur at the changes of the seasons, but then only slightly. The settlements on the coast are unhealthy, but the interior, on the contrary, rejoices in perpetual spring, and possesses as fine a climate as any tropical country.

The animals and vegetables of Guayana are chiefly those common to the northern half of South America: among the first are the jaguar, puma, peccari, &c.; and among the latter, many valuable trees and shrubs, yielding timber and other valuable commercial commodities. Arnatto, used extensively for cheese-coloring, grows wild in profusion on the banks of the Upper Corentyn. Sugar-canes, cotton and coffee are staple agricultural products

Large quantities are grown, but the culture has materially diminished since 1837, no doubt owing to the cessation of slave-labor, which had been used previous to that date.

British Guayana consists of three separate colonies. They are as follows:

	White Population.	*Black and Mixed Races.*	*Total.*
Essequibo, Demerara,	3,006	71,986	74,992
Berbice,	570	21,019	21,589
Total	3,576	93,005	96,581

Beside the population above stated, there are 15,000 or 20,000 native Indians in the territory, and, of late, a large number of Coolies have been imported from Asia, to supply the place of the emancipated slaves; together, these will make an aggregate population of about 120,000. The whites are partly Dutch and partly English; but most of them Protestants. The schools of the colonies educate about 11,000 children.

The commerce of Guayana, as well as the amount of products raised, has materially declined; in many cases, indeed, as much as 30 per cent. The property annually created by the products of the soil, trades, manufactures, &c., is about 17½ millions of dollars, and the value of property in the colonies may be set down at 125,000,000 dollars. The staples, at the present time, are sugar, rum, coffee, and cotton; cotton and coffee were formerly almost exclusively grown, but now in a great measure they have been superseded by the culture of sugar.

The Indians have generally some indigenous cotton growing round their huts, and among the *Macusis*, (on the Rupununi,) it is raised to a considerable extent. It comes to perfection in most parts of the country; but it is cultivated by the colonists only on the coasts, and even there it has been almost abandoned, the planters being undersold by those of the United States. There are numerous other products, which, as yet, neither form articles of export nor of internal consumption, for which both the soil and climate are suitable, and which might be raised to advantage, if laborers were attainable. Among these are rice, maize, millet, wheat, cocoa, vanilla, (a native of Guayana,) tobacco, cinnamon, &c. Between the Berbice and Essequibo there is a tract of many thousand acres, possessing the means of constant irrigation, on a small portion of which three crops a year have been repeatedly raised; but, at present, it is all a complete wilderness. The coast region, which is covered with a deep layer of vegetable mould, is capable of raising from 6,000 to 8,000 lbs. of sugar, and from 20,000 to 30,000 lbs. of plantains to the acre; but to cultivate this soil dams and embankments are necessary, and agriculture is conducted at a great outlay, and on vast estates. At present the whole country is lying waste for want of hands to cultivate it.

The government is vested in a governor and court of policy, consisting, beside the governor, of the chief-justice, attorney-general, collector of the customs and government secretary, and an equal number of official persons elected by the colonists, through the college of electors. The laws are chiefly a modification of English common law. The general policy of government does not, however, satisfy the people, and it is probable, since they have joined the "West India League," that before long they will take the management of their affairs into their own hands.

The public revenue is derived from taxes on produce; on incomes of 500 dollars and upwards; on imports not of the growth and manufacture of England, and from assessments on horses, carriages, wine and spirit licenses, &c. In 1846, it amounted to 600,000 dollars, and the expenses to a somewhat larger amount. The portion of the £20,000,000 falling to this country, as compensation for emancipating the slaves, was £4,268,809.

The means of travelling and transportation are ample for so small a colony; four steamers, of 90 horse-power, ply regularly between Georgetown and New-Amsterdam, and a railway has been projected from the capital to Mahaica. There are about 300 miles of public highways in the territory.

The colonists use the English imperial measures in all commercial transactions, but those of Holland in the retail trade. The monies of England, France and Holland: in fact, the monies of all nations, pass current, or are taken as bullion.

The provision for religious purposes is liberal; in 1839, it amounted to £22,942, which sum was distributed among 18 ministers of the English Church, two of the church of Holland, five Roman Catholic, five church of Scotland, and several of dissenting churches.

The military establishment consists of one regiment of the line, and a detachment of another. The colonial militia has been disbanded.

The only towns worthy of note are Georgetown and New-Amsterdam. Georgetown, formerly Stabroëk, is the capital, and seat of government. It lies on the east bank of the Demerara, near its mouth; latitude 6° 49′ 20″, longitude 58° 11′ 30″ west. Population, about 20,000, of which 16,000 are colored. It is said to be a handsome city, adorned with good public buildings, and several charitable institutions; the houses of private citizens are generally built of wood, two stories high, with projecting roofs, having verandahs and porticos, and surrounded by gardens separated by trenches. The streets are wide, regularly laid out, and traversed by canals. Shops and stores are well supplied with European goods; the markets are also well-provided. Fort William Frederic, a small mud erection, about a mile from the city, overlooks the mouth of the river.

New Amsterdam, on the Berbice, in latitude 6° 15′ north, longitude 57° 27′ west, extending about 1½ miles along the river, is intersected by canals, and has about 3,000 inhabitants. It has all the conveniences of a commercial port, and institutions for religious and educational purposes. The wharves and warehouses are commodious. It is less unhealthy than Georgetown.

The coast of Guayana was discovered by Vasco Nunez, in 1504. The Dutch, who were the first European settlers, established some colonies near the Pomeroon, and elsewhere, in its neighborhood, in 1580, and several farther to the east a few years afterwards. The first English settlement was made in 1630. Most of Guayana, however, remained in the hands of the Dutch, until 1796, when Essequibo and Demerara were surrendered to England. They were restored to the Republic in 1802, but re-captured by the British during the subsequent year. The present territory, called "British Guayana," has remained in the hands of the English ever since, but Surinam was relinquished at the general pacification in 1814.

DUTCH GUAYANA.

Surinam lies between the English and French possessions, and extends along the coasts from the Corentyn, which separates it from Berbice, to the Maroni, which divides it from Cayenne: its length being about 250 miles, and its area about 38,500 square miles.

The general physical characteristics of Dutch Guayana are much the same as those of the British possessions, and will not need to be repeated. All the rivers run in a north direction: the principal is the Surinam, which runs through the centre of the colony, and falls into the Atlantic, after a course of 300 miles, but is navigable for ships only about ten or twelve miles from the coast. Paramaraibo is situated near its mouth. The population of this territory, exclusive of Indians and Maroons, is probably 6,500, chiefly Dutch, French and Jews; the remainder Negroes. The maroons are the descendants of runaway negroes, who established a species of independence in the interior, and were very troublesome during the last century; they have now, however, adopted more settled habits, and receive annual presents from the government of weapons, arms, &c., and form a kind of military frontier to the settled parts of the colony.

The commerce of the country is chiefly appropriated by the mother country: about 50 ships are employed in the trade, and annually transport to Europe about 25,000,000 lbs. of sugar and 4,000,000 lbs. of coffee, and to some extent cotton, cocoa and other articles, among which are cabinet woods, gums, balsams and drugs, which are the produce of the interior. The chief imports are arms and manufactured goods from Holland and provisions from the United States, for which they receive syrups and rums. They have some commerce with the West Indies, and smuggling is carried on with the Colombian states and the adjoining colonies to some extent.

The government is vested in a governor-general and privy council: besides this, there is a colonial council, whose functions are not well ascertained. The fort of Zeelandia, a little north of the capital, is the residence of the governor, and seat of most of the government establishments.

Paramaraibo is the capital of the colony, and has a population of 2,000, three-fourths of which are black and of the mixed races. It is neatly laid out in the Dutch style, and is situated on the right bank of the Surinam, 15 miles from its mouth, where the river affords excellent anchorage; has a Roman Catholic, English and Lutheran churches, German and Portuguese Jews' synagogues, an exchange, &c., and is the centre of the trade of the colony. The inhabitants are chiefly engaged in commerce: manufactures may be said not to exist. The colony has repeatedly been in the hands of the British, but was finally relinquished, in 1814, to the Dutch government.

FRENCH GUAYANA.

Cayenne is the most easterly of the three colonies, and extends along the coast from the river Maroni to the Oyapok, which forms the boundary, according to the Brazilian convention of 1817. It lies between the 2° and 6° north latitude, and the meridians of 51° 30′ and 54° west longitude. Its length, from north to south, is 250 miles, and the breadth varies from 100 to 190 miles; comprising an area of about 21,648 square miles. Cayenne, itself, is an island.

The coast is an alluvial flat, of great fertility, and the sea so shallow, that, except at the mouth of the rivers, ships cannot approach the shore: there is only one roadstead in which vessels can ride in safety—that of Cayenne. The highlands of the interior are very fertile, and few countries are better supplied with water. The climate and natural productions are, in every respect, similar to those of the British and Dutch colonies, with the addition of pepper, cloves, cinnamon and nutmegs. The settled or cultivated lands do not extend over more than one-eighth of the whole, the rest being left to the Indians and wild beasts.

French Guayana is divided into two districts: that of Cayenne and that of Sinnamary; and 14 communes, composing six electoral arrondisements, and sending 16 deputies to the colonial council. The government is vested in a governor, assisted by a privy council of seven members and the colonial council, elected by the people, for five years. The revenue is derived from house taxes, export duties, customs, licenses, land sales, &c.: this is the only colony in Guayana that has an income superior to its expenses.

The first French settlement was made in the Island of Cayenne, in 1604, and with but few short interruptions from the English and Dutch, that nation held the station ever since, and the rest of the colony, till 1809, when it was taken by the British and Portuguese, and annexed to the dominions of the latter: but at the peace of Paris, it was again given up to its present owners. Guayana is now, according to French revolutionary principles, an integral portion of the French Republic, and as such, is entitled to representation in the national councils. Slavery is forever abolished.

PATAGONIA.

Patagonia is the name of that extensive tract of land comprising the southern extremity of the South American continent, and lying south of the Argentine Republic, from which it is separated by the Rio Negro, and the Republic of Chilé, which terminates at the Gulf of Guaytecas. That portion of the country, however, which lies west of the Andes has been claimed as an integral part of Chilé, and by some geographers is entitled New Chilé. The Argentine Republic has, in like manner, laid a claim to the country east of the Andes. Little is known of these regions beyond the mere outline of the coast. The Andes in Patagonia appear to consist of but one Cordillera, the mean height of which may be estimated at 3,000 feet above the ocean; but opposite Chiloe there are some mountains of a superior elevation, which may, perhaps, reach to the height of 5,000 or 6,000 feet. The west coast is abrupt, very much broken, and skirted by a great number of irregularly-shaped islands. The east coast has been more explored. The surface of the country appears to rise from the Atlantic to the Andes, in a succession of steppes or terraces, all of which are alike arid and sterile, the upper soil, consisting chiefly of marine gravelly deposits, covered with coarse, wiry grass. No wood is seen larger than a small thorny shrub, fit only for the purposes of fuel, except on the banks of a few of the rivers, subject to inundation, when herbage and some trees are occasionally found. This sterility prevails over the whole extent of the plain country of Patagonia, the complete similarity of which, almost in every part, is one of its most striking characteristics. It is stated, however, by the Indians on the Rio Negro, which forms the northern boundary of Patagonia, that near the Andes, wheat, maize, beans, lentils, pease, &c., are raised. This latter region, however, is not placed under the same circumstances as the country more to the eastward, nor is it subject to the causes which mainly occasion its sterility.

The geological formation of Patagonia is almost unknown. Porphyry; basalt; sandstone, containing numerous organic remains; and a friable rock, greatly resembling, but not identical with chalk, are among the mineral products of the eastern portion of the country. The zoology of Patagonia is as limited as its *flora*. Guanacos are met with sometimes in herds of several hundreds; their enemy, the puma, and a small species of fox, are almost the only other wild quadrupeds at all abundant, except mice. The latter are of many species, and so numerous that, according to Mr. Darwin, Patagonia, poor as she is in some respects, can, perhaps, boast of a greater stock of small *rodentia* than any other country of the world.—(*Voy. of the Beagle and Adventure.*) The condor and the cassawary are included among the few species of birds; the reptile and insect tribes present nothing remarkable.

The principal rivers of Patagonia fall into the Atlantic, having their sources at the eastern foot of the Andes, and generally running in a south-eastern direction. Among these are the Rio Negro, 700 miles long; the Camerones and the Port Desire rivers; on the western coast the rivers are numerous, but have short courses from the Andes to the Pacific Ocean. In the interior there are several lakes of considerable size. Lake Nauclapi, in the north-west part of the eastern division; Tehuel, near the Rio Negro; and Colugnape, the source of Port Desire River, are the principal. Several of the lakes are salt. The Strait of Magellan is a passage from the Atlantic to the Pacific Ocean, between Patagonia and Terra del Fuego; this Strait is 300 miles in length, and, in some parts, not more than two miles wide; but at the eastern entrance the breadth is 24, and at the western 30 miles. This passage was discovered and navigated by Magellan, in 1520, and several navigators have since sailed through it; but, at the present day, it is seldom used, being considered dangerous; and vessels navigating the South Seas usually go round Cape Horn, which was discovered in 1616, by Jacob Le Maire, and was so called by him after the town of Hoern, in Holland. This Cape is on Hermit Island, south of Terra del Fuego, and must not be confounded with that of False Cape Horn, a promontory forming the most southern extremity of Terra del Fuego.

The climate of this country is much colder than in the north, under the same parallels of latitude, which is imputed to the tops of the Andes, which traverse it, being covered with snow. A great deal of rain falls in these mountains. The west wind is the most prevalent, and having been robbed of its moisture in passing the Andes, comes over the eastern slope as a blight; the east wind, which is the only wind that brings any moisture over the sterile steppes, seldom blows.

The exaggerated notions of man, in Patagonia, which were fostered by the marvellous narrations of early navigators, have been fully counteracted by the observations of more modern travellers. The giant portrayed by the imaginative pens of the former, have been reduced within their proper proportions, and the inhabitants of these desert regions are again brought within the pale of humanity. The native Indians are, indeed, a tall and bulky race, and though not absolutely gigantic, they may be said, after rejecting all hyperbolical exaggerations, to be the tallest people of whom we have any accounts, the average height of the men being not less than six feet. Their heads and features are large, but their hands and feet small, and their limbs neither so muscular nor so large-boned as their height and apparent stoutness would induce one to suppose. In color, they are of dark brown copper shade: their hair is black, lank and coarse, and tied above the temples by a fillet of plaited or twisted sinews. A large mantle of guanaco skins loosely gathered about them, and hanging from the shoulders to the ancles, is, with a kind of drawers and buskins, their chief article of dress, and adds much to the bulkiness of their appearance. They neither pierce the nose or ears, nor paint their faces. In their habits, they are essentially nomadic, and live in tents, made of skins hung on poles, and exist on the fruits of the chase and fishing. Both men and women ride on horseback, and are often furnished with accoutrements of great splendor. which they procure from Chilé and Buenos Ayres. Their arms consist of a long tapering lance, a knife, or if it can be procured, a scimitar, and the *balas*, a missile weapon of singular kind, carried in the girdle, and consisting of two round stones, covered with leather, each weighing about a pound. These are fastened to the two ends of a string, about 18 feet in length, and used as a sling, one stone being kept in the hand, and the other whirled round the head till it is supposed to have acquired sufficient force, when they are together discharged at the object. The Patagonians are so expert in the management of this double-headed shot, that they will hit a mark not bigger than a shilling, with both the stones, at the distance of fifty yards. It is not customary with them, however, to strike either the guanaco or ostrich with them; but to discharge them so, that the cord comes against the legs of the ostrich, or the fore-legs of the guanaco, and is twisted round them by the force and swing of the balls, so that the animal being unable to run, falls a sure prey to the hunter. These people, as is usual with all nomadic tribes, live under a number of petty chiefs, who seem to possess but little authority over them. The only change of life they have undergone, from their contact with Europeans, seems to be in the use of horses, with which they were unacquainted previous to the arrival of the Spaniards.

Patagonia was discovered by Magellan, in 1519. The badness of its harbors, which are mostly difficult and dangerous of access, and afford little or no security for vessels above the size of a brig, has hindered the formation of any settlements, except at Port Julian, about lat. 40° 16′ S. and long. 67° 40′ W., where the Spaniards settled in 1774, but speedily abandoned the establishment. Several other attempts have been made, but without success, and it is now thought that this extensive territory must remain forever in the desert state in which it has been found. The officers of the "Adventure" undertook to explore the eastern part of the country, but principally confined their observations to the vicinity of the great rivers. The coasts are rarely visited by any but whale vessels, which call at Port Desire, Santa Cruz, &c., and the nature of the country is not such as to hold out any hope of its ever emerging from its present state of savage barbarism. The Republic of Chilé, however, has of late designed to colonize this country; but the Argentine government, jealous of its more enterprising neighbor, has claimed for itself all the lands situated north of the Straits of Magellan and east of the Andes. At presem, the enterprise is suspended, and may ultimately fall through, on account of this interference, if not from the natural incapacity of the country for colonization.

The rocky coast of Patagonia has, of late years, become celebrated for its depositaries of "guano," and hence has been much resorted to by vessels of all nations, in order to procure this valuable article. Immense quantities are annually carrried off. "Guano" is the excrement of birds, which, through an indefinite series of ages, has accumulated on these sterile shores. It is useful as a manure, and is also highly prized as an agent in several manufacturing processes. As a manure, it is considered more active than any other in use, and truly its effect on vegetation is wonderful. Ammoniacal salts seem to be the pervading and powerful agent in this compost. A short time ago, the government of the Argentine Republic, the nominal claimants of the country, sent to the British government an account, to the amount of $2,000,000, for this substance, *surreptitiously* taken off by British subjects, and appeared actually to expect its unquestioned payment! If there is any justice in this claim, it will be paid, and if paid, it will be a full recognition, by Great Britain, of Argentine sovereignty over these, as yet, unappropriated regions.

The origin of the appellative Patagonia has been disputed. Magellan called the natives Pata-gones, because their shoes resembled the hoofs of the guanaco.* Others insisted that their ordinary stature exceeded seven feet, and for that they were termed πενταγκωνες, or men of five cubits. The latter is the more probable derivation of the name of the country.

SOUTH AMERICAN ISLANDS.

Having reached the extremity of the American continent, we may take an excursion to the neighboring isles; although many of them are not subject to America, still they are less removed from it than from every other country.

THE MAGELLANIC ARCHIPELAGO.

To the south of Patagonia, there are a number of cold, barren, and mountainous islands; volcanoes, which cannot melt, brighten or illumine the perpetual snow in these dismal regions. "Here it was that the sailors observed fires on the southern shores of the Strait of Magellan, for which reason the land on that side was called Terra del Fuego." Narrow channels, strong currents, and boisterous winds, render it dangerous to enter into this desolate labyrinth. The coast, which is composed of granite, lava, and basaltic rocks, is inaccessible in many places. Cataracts interrupt the stillness that reigns there; seals sport in the bays, or repose their unwieldly bodies on the sand. A great many penguins, and other birds of the Antarctic Ocean,

* *Patagon*, in Spanish, signifies one who has large feet.

flock to these shores, and pursue their prey without molestation. Captain Cook discovered Christmas Sound, a good haven for ships that double Cape Horn. Staten Land, a detached island, which may be considered as forming a part of the archipelago, was discovered by Le Maire. The northern and eastern coasts are more favored by nature than the southern and western; towards the Atlantic Ocean, the mountains are not so steep, a rich verdure decks the vallies, and some useful animals are found in the woods and pastures.

"The natives of these islands," says Capt. Wilkes, "are not more than five feet high, of a light copper color, which is much concealed by smut and dirt, particularly on their faces, which they mark vertically with charcoal. They have short faces, narrow foreheads, and high cheek-bones. Their eyes are small, and usually black, the upper lids in the inner corner overlapping the under one, and bear a strong resemblance to those of the Chinese. The nose is broad and flat, with wide-spread nostrils, mouth large, teeth white, large and regular. The hair is long, lank and black, hanging over the face, and is covered with white ashes, which gives them a hideous appearance. The whole face is compressed. Their bodies are remarkable from the great development of the chest, shoulders, and vertebral column; their arms are long, and out of proportion; their legs small, and ill-made. There is, in fact, little difference between the size of the ankle and leg; and, when standing, the skin at the knee hangs in a large, loose fold. In some the muscles of the leg appear almost wanting, and possess very little strength. The want of development of the muscles of the legs is owing to their constant sitting posture, both in their huts and canoes. Their skin is sensibly colder than ours. It is impossible to fancy anything in human nature more filthy. They are an ill-shapen and ugly race." * * * * * "The children were quite small." * * * * "Their canoes are constructed of bark, and sewed with shreds of whalebone, seal-skin and twigs. They are sharp at both ends, and are kept in shape, as well as strengthened, by a number of stretchers lashed to the gunwale." * * * "The Indians seldom venture outside the kelp, by the aid of which they pull themselves along; and their paddles are so small as to be of little use in propelling their canoes, unless it is calm." * * * * Their huts are generally found built close to the shore, at the head of some small bay, in a secluded spot, and sheltered from the prevailing winds. They are built of boughs or small trees, stuck in the earth, and brought together at the top, where they are firmly bound by bark, sedge and twigs; smaller branches are then interlaced, forming a tolerably compact wicker-work, and on this grass, turf and bark, are laid, making the hut quite warm, and impervious to the wind and snow, though not quite so to the rain." These huts are of a circular form, from seven to eight feet in diameter, and four or five feet high, with an oval hole to creep in at. The fire is built in an excavation in the middle of the clay floor. These people almost live on shell-fish, and the usual accompaniment to their hut is a heap of shells. They are armed with slings, and spears of rude construction, with which they strike their fish as well as defend themselves. They are naturally very grave, and seldom express surprise. The facility with which they repeated words was truly wonderful, and their powers of mimicry often became annoying. The women appeared to be modest, but they are extremely ugly, and much begrimmed. The men employ themselves in building huts, obtaining food, and providing for their daily wants. The women are generally seen paddling their canoes. They bury their dead in caves.

FALKLAND ISLANDS.

The Malouine Islands, called formerly by the English geographers, Hawkins' Maidenland, and at present the Falkland Islands, are about seventy-six leagues north-east from Staten Land, and a hundred and ten eastward of the Straits of Magellan. The two largest islands are separated from each other by a broad channel, called by the Spaniards the Straits of San Carlos, but better known by the name of Falkland's Channel. They were first seen by Capt. Davis, who sailed under Sir T. Cavendish, in 1592; and next by Sir Richard Hawkins, who called them Hawkins' Maidenland, in honor of Queen Elizabeth. The mountains in these islands are not very lofty; the soil on the heights adjacent to the sea is composed of a dark vegetable mould; copper pyrites, yellow and red ochre, are found below the surface. Pernetty observed a natural amphitheatre, formed by regular layers of porphyritic sand-stone. No wood grows on these islands; the Spaniards were at the trouble of bringing plants from Buenos-Ayres, but their labor was vain, for every tree perished in a short time. The gladiolus, or sword grass, is very common, and rises to a great height; when seen at a distance, it has the appearance of a verdant thicket. The grass is luxuriant; celery, cresses, and other herbs, have been noticed by travellers. The vegetables are not unlike those of Canada; but the *epipactis*, the *tithymalus resinosus*, and a shrub which resemble the rosemary, are much similar to the plants of Chilé. A great variety of seals, to which the common people have given the name of sea-lions, sea-calves, and sea-wolves, bask in the sword-grass. The Spaniards brought eight hundred head of oxen to these islands in the year 1780, and they increased so rapidly that their number amounted to eight thousand in 1795. These islands are unoccupied, but nominally belong to Great Britain. The Argentine Republic, however, prefers a substantial claim to sovereignty over them.

ISLAND OF GEORGIA.

Although the Island of Georgia does not belong to any nation, we mention it in this place, on account of its vicinity to the Falkland Islands. It was discovered by La Roche in 1675, and afterwards explored by Captain Cook in 1775, who gave it its present name. Georgia, situated about four hundred and twenty leagues east from Cape Horn, consists of horizontal layers of black slate stone. The rocks are generally covered with ice, and no shrub can pierce through the perpetual snow that lies in the valleys; pimpernal, a few lichens, and some tufts of coarse grass, are all the plants that have been observed; and the lark is the only land-bird which has been seen on the island.

SANDWICH LAND, &c.

Captain Cook discovered Sandwich Land, or the Southern Thule, at a hundred and fifty leagues to the south-east of Georgia, and in the 59th degree of south latitude. Other groups extend to the southern pole, and occasion, perhaps, the icebergs and variations in the course of currents, which have too often misled the adventurous navigator.

South Shetland, and several of the groups of islands extending from 60° to 64° south latitude, were discovered in 1820. These contain little worthy of notice. The low grounds are sterile, and the hills and rocks covered with eternal snows. The seas in the vicinity abound with seals and other animals common to the Antarctic regions. Recent observations render it probable that similar islands extend to the southern pole.

INDEX TO VOLUME I.

A.

N.

T.

U.

V.

www.ingramcontent.com/pod-product-compliance
Lightning Source LLC
LaVergne TN
LVHW021059110826
845150LV00001B/125

* 9 7 8 1 4 2 5 5 6 6 2 4 1 *